TENNYSON

Poems and Plays

TENNYSON

Poems and Plays

EDITED BY

T. HERBERT WARREN

REVISED AND ENLARGED BY

FREDERICK PAGE

OXFORD UNIVERSITY PRESS

LONDON   OXFORD   NEW YORK

1971

ALFRED TENNYSON

Born, Somersby, Lincolnshire, 6 August 1809
Died, Aldworth, Haslemere, Surrey, 6 October 1892

Oxford University Press

LONDON OXFORD NEW YORK
GLASGOW TORONTO MELBOURNE WELLINGTON
CAPE TOWN SALISBURY IBADAN NAIROBI DAR ES SALAAM LUSAKA ADDIS ABABA
BOMBAY CALCUTTA MADRAS KARACHI LAHORE DACCA
KUALA LUMPUR SINGAPORE HONG KONG TOKYO

SBN 19 281115 0

This OXFORD STANDARD AUTHORS edition, based on
Sir T. Herbert Warren's *Poems of Tennyson 1830–1870*
(1912), revised and enlarged by Frederick Page to take
in the later poems and the plays, first published by
Oxford University Press, London, 1953, with the title
The Complete Poetical Works of Tennyson; reprinted 1965
with the present title

First issued as an Oxford University Press paperback 1971

PRINTED IN GREAT BRITAIN

CONTENTS

▼

CONTENTS

CONTENTS

vii

CONTENTS

CONTENTS

CONTENTS

x

CONTENTS

CONTENTS

CONTENTS

CONTENTS

CONTENTS

APPENDIX OF POEMS NOT INCLUDED IN THE AUTHOR'S FINAL EDITION

CONTENTS

TO THE QUEEN

Revered, beloved—O you that hold
  A nobler office upon earth
  Than arms, or power of brain, or birth
Could give the warrior kings of old,

Victoria,—since your Royal grace
  To one of less desert allows
  This laurel greener from the brows
Of him that utter'd nothing base;

And should your greatness, and the care
  That yokes with empire, yield you time
  To make demand of modern rhyme
If aught of ancient worth be there;

Then—while a sweeter music wakes,
  And thro' wild March the throstle calls,
  Where all about your palace-walls
The sun-lit almond-blossom shakes—

Take, Madam, this poor book of song;
  For tho' the faults were thick as dust
  In vacant chambers, I could trust
Your kindness. May you rule us long,

And leave us rulers of your blood
  As noble till the latest day!
  May children of our children say,
'She wrought her people lasting good;

'Her court was pure; her life serene;
  God gave her peace; her land reposed;
  A thousand claims to reverence closed
In her as Mother, Wife, and Queen;

'And statesmen at her council met
  Who knew the seasons when to take
  Occasion by the hand, and make
The bounds of freedom wider yet

'By shaping some august decree,
  Which kept her throne unshaken still,
  Broad-based upon her people's will,
And compass'd by the inviolate sea.'

March 1851

1

B

JUVENILIA

CLARIBEL

A MELODY

I

WHERE Claribel low-lieth
  The breezes pause and die,
    Letting the rose-leaves fall:
But the solemn oak-tree sigheth,
    Thick-leaved, ambrosial,
  With an ancient melody
  Of an inward agony,
Where Claribel low-lieth.

II

At eve the beetle boometh
  Athwart the thicket lone:
At noon the wild bee hummeth
  About the moss'd headstone:
At midnight the moon cometh,
  And looketh down alone.
Her song the lintwhite swelleth,
The clear-voiced mavis dwelleth,
  The callow throstle lispeth,
The slumbrous wave outwelleth,
  The babbling runnel crispeth,
The hollow grot replieth
  Where Claribel low-lieth.

NOTHING WILL DIE

WHEN will the stream be aweary of flowing
  Under my eye?
When will the wind be aweary of blowing
  Over the sky?
When will the clouds be aweary of fleeting?
When will the heart be aweary of beating?
  And nature die?
Never, oh! never, nothing will die;
  The stream flows,
  The wind blows,
  The cloud fleets,
  The heart beats,
    Nothing will die.

Nothing will die;
All things will change
Thro' eternity.
'Tis the world's winter;

Autumn and summer
Are gone long ago;
Earth is dry to the centre,
But spring, a new comer,
A spring rich and strange,
Shall make the winds blow
Round and round,
Thro' and thro',
  Here and there,
  Till the air
And the ground
Shall be fill'd with life anew.

The world was never made;
It will change, but it will not fade.
So let the wind range;
For even and morn
  Ever will be
  Thro' eternity.
Nothing was born;
Nothing will die;
All things will change.

ALL THINGS WILL DIE

CLEARLY the blue river chimes in its flowing
  Under my eye;
Warmly and broadly the south winds are
  blowing
    Over the sky.
One after another the white clouds are
  fleeting;
Every heart this May morning in joyance
  is beating
    Full merrily;
  Yet all things must die.
The stream will cease to flow;
The wind will cease to blow;
The clouds will cease to fleet;
The heart will cease to beat;
  For all things must die.
    All things must die.
Spring will come never more.
  Oh! vanity!
Death waits at the door.
See! our friends are all forsaking
The wine and the merrymaking.

We are call'd—we must go.
Laid low, very low,
In the dark we must lie.
The merry glees are still;
The voice of the bird
Shall no more be heard,
Nor the wind on the hill.
    Oh! misery!
Hark, death is calling
While I speak to ye,
The jaw is falling,
The red cheek paling,
The strong limbs failing;
Ice with the warm blood mixing;
The eyeballs fixing.
Nine times goes the passing bell:
Ye merry souls, farewell.
    The old earth
    Had a birth,
    As all men know,
    Long ago.
And the old earth must die.
So let the warm winds range,
And the blue wave beat the shore;
    For even and morn
    Ye will never see
    Thro' eternity.
All things were born.
Ye will come never more,
For all things must die.

LEONINE ELEGIACS

LOW-FLOWING breezes are roaming the
    broad valley dimm'd in the gloaming:
Thoro' the black-stemm'd pines only the
    far river shines.
Creeping thro' blossomy rushes and bowers
    of rose-blowing bushes,
Down by the poplar tall rivulets babble
    and fall.
Barketh the shepherd-dog cheerly; the
    grasshopper carolleth clearly;
Deeply the wood-dove coos; shrilly the
    owlet halloos;
Winds creep; dews fall chilly: in her first
    sleep earth breathes stilly:
Over the pools in the burn water-gnats
    murmur and mourn.
Sadly the far kine loweth: the glimmering
    water outfloweth:

Twin peaks shadow'd with pine slope to
    the dark hyaline.
Low-throned Hesper is stayed between the
    two peaks; but the Naiad
Throbbing in mild unrest holds him be-
    neath in her breast.
The ancient poetess singeth, that Hesperus
    all things bringeth,
Smoothing the wearied mind: bring me
    my love, Rosalind.
Thou comest morning or even; she cometh
    not morning or even.
False-eyed Hesper, unkind, where is my
    sweet Rosalind?

SUPPOSED CONFESSIONS

OF A SECOND-RATE SENSITIVE MIND

O GOD! my God! have mercy now.
I faint, I fall. Men say that Thou
Didst die for me, for such as *me*,
Patient of ill, and death, and scorn,
And that my sin was as a thorn
Among the thorns that girt Thy brow,
Wounding Thy soul.—That even now,
In this extremest misery
Of ignorance, I should require
A sign! and if a bolt of fire
Would rive the slumbrous summer noon
While I do pray to Thee alone,
Think my belief would stronger grow!
Is not my human pride brought low?
The boastings of my spirit still?
The joy I had in my freewill
All cold, and dead, and corpse-like grown?
And what is left to me, but Thou,
And faith in Thee? Men pass me by;
Christians with happy countenances—
And children all seem full of Thee!
And women smile with saint-like glances
Like Thine own mother's when she bow'd
Above Thee, on that happy morn
When angels spake to men aloud,
And Thou and peace to earth were born.
Goodwill to me as well as all—
I one of them: my brothers they:
Brothers in Christ—a world of peace
And confidence, day after day;
And trust and hope till things should cease,
And then one Heaven receive us all.

How sweet to have a common faith!
To hold a common scorn of death!
And at a burial to hear
The creaking cords which wound and eat
Into my human heart, whene'er
Earth goes to earth, with grief, not fear,
With hopeful grief, were passing sweet!

Thrice happy state again to be
The trustful infant on the knee!
Who lets his rosy fingers play
About his mother's neck, and knows
Nothing beyond his mother's eyes.
They comfort him by night and day;
They light his little life alway;
He hath no thought of coming woes;
He hath no care of life or death;
Scarce outward signs of joy arise,
Because the Spirit of happiness
And perfect rest so inward is;
And loveth so his innocent heart,
Her temple and her place of birth,
Where she would ever wish to dwell,
Life of the fountain there, beneath
Its salient springs, and far apart,
Hating to wander out on earth,
Or breathe into the hollow air,
Whose chillness would make visible
Her subtil, warm, and golden breath,
Which mixing with the infant's blood,
Fulfils him with beatitude.
Oh! sure it is a special care
Of God, to fortify from doubt,
To arm in proof, and guard about
With triple-mailèd trust, and clear
Delight, the infant's dawning year.

Would that my gloomed fancy were
As thine, my mother, when with brows
Propt on thy knees, my hands upheld
In thine, I listen'd to thy vows,
For me outpour'd in holiest prayer—
For me unworthy!—and beheld
Thy mild deep eyes upraised, that knew
The beauty and repose of faith,
And the clear spirit shining thro'.
Oh! wherefore do we grow awry
From roots which strike so deep? why
     dare
Paths in the desert? Could not I
Bow myself down, where thou hast knelt,

To the earth—until the ice would melt
Here, and I feel as thou hast felt?
What Devil had the heart to scathe
Flowers thou hadst rear'd—to brush the
     dew
From thine own lily, when thy grave
Was deep, my mother, in the clay?
Myself? Is it thus? Myself? Had I
So little love for thee? But why
Prevail'd not thy pure prayers? Why pray
To one who heeds not, who can save
But will not? Great in faith, and strong
Against the grief of circumstance
Wert thou, and yet unheard. What if
Thou pleadest still, and seest me drive
Thro' utter dark a full-sail'd skiff,
Unpiloted i' the echoing dance
Of reboant whirlwinds, stooping low
Unto the death, not sunk! I know
At matins and at evensong,
That thou, if thou wert yet alive,
In deep and daily prayers would'st strive
To reconcile me with thy God.
Albeit, my hope is gray, and cold
At heart, thou wouldest murmur still—
'Bring this lamb back into Thy fold,
My Lord, if so it be Thy will.'
Would'st tell me I must brook the rod
And chastisement of human pride;
That pride, the sin of devils, stood
Betwixt me and the light of God!
That hitherto I had defied
And had rejected God—that grace
Would drop from his o'er-brimming love,
As manna on my wilderness,
If I would pray—that God would move
And strike the hard, hard rock, and thence,
Sweet in their utmost bitterness,
Would issue tears of penitence
Which would keep green hope's life. Alas!
I think that pride hath now no place
Nor sojourn in me. I am void,
Dark, formless, utterly destroyed.

Why not believe then? Why not yet
Anchor thy frailty there, where man
Hath moor'd and rested? Ask the sea
At midnight, when the crisp slope waves
After a tempest, rib and fret
The broad-imbased beach, why he
Slumbers not like a mountain tarn?

4

Wherefore his ridges are not curls
And ripples of an inland mere?
Wherefore he moaneth thus, nor can
Draw down into his vexed pools
All that blue heaven which hues and paves
The other? I am too forlorn,
Too shaken: my own weakness fools
My judgment, and my spirit whirls,
Moved from beneath with doubt and fear.

'Yet,' said I, in my morn of youth,
The unsunn'd freshness of my strength,
When I went forth in quest of truth,
'It is man's privilege to doubt,
If so be that from doubt at length,
Truth may stand forth unmoved of change,
An image with profulgent brows,
And perfect limbs, as from the storm
Of running fires and fluid range
Of lawless airs, at last stood out
This excellence and solid form
Of constant beauty. For the Ox
Feeds in the herb, and sleeps, or fills
The horned valleys all about,
And hollows of the fringed hills
In summer heats, with placid lows
Unfearing, till his own blood flows
About his hoof. And in the flocks
The lamb rejoiceth in the year,
And raceth freely with his fere,
And answers to his mother's calls
From the flower'd furrow. In a time,
Of which he wots not, run short pains
Thro' his warm heart; and then, from
    whence
He knows not, on his light there falls
A shadow; and his native slope,
Where he was wont to leap and climb,
Floats from his sick and filmed eyes,
And something in the darkness draws
His forehead earthward, and he dies.
Shall man live thus, in joy and hope
As a young lamb, who cannot dream,
Living, but that he shall live on?
Shall we not look into the laws
Of life and death, and things that seem,
And things that be, and analyse
Our double nature, and compare
All creeds till we have found the one,
If one there be?' Ay me! I fear
All may not doubt, but everywhere

Some must clasp Idols. Yet, my God,
Whom call I Idol? Let Thy dove
Shadow me over, and my sins
Be unremember'd, and Thy love
Enlighten me. Oh teach me yet
Somewhat before the heavy clod
Weighs on me, and the busy fret
Of that sharp-headed worm begins
In the gross blackness underneath.

O weary life! O weary death!
O spirit and heart made desolate!
O damned vacillating state!

THE KRAKEN

BELOW the thunders of the upper deep;
Far, far beneath in the abysmal sea,
His ancient, dreamless, uninvaded sleep
The Kraken sleepeth: faintest sunlights
    flee
About his shadowy sides: above him swell
Huge sponges of millennial growth and
    height;
And far away into the sickly light,
From many a wondrous grot and secret
    cell
Unnumber'd and enormous polypi
Winnow with giant arms the slumbering
    green.
There hath he lain for ages and will lie
Battening upon huge seaworms in his
    sleep,
Until the latter fire shall heat the deep;
Then once by man and angels to be seen,
In roaring he shall rise and on the surface
    die.

SONG

THE winds, as at their hour of birth,
    Leaning upon the ridged sea,
Breathed low around the rolling earth
    With mellow preludes, 'We are free.'

The streams through many a lilied row
    Down-carolling to the crisped sea,
Low-tinkled with a bell-like flow
    Atween the blossoms, 'We are free.'

5

LILIAN

I

AIRY, fairy Lilian,
Flitting, fairy Lilian,
When I ask her if she love me,
Claps her tiny hands above me,
Laughing all she can;
She'll not tell me if she love me,
Cruel little Lilian.

II

When my passion seeks
Pleasance in love-sighs,
She, looking thro' and thro' me
Thoroughly to undo me,
Smiling, never speaks:
So innocent-arch, so cunning-simple,
From beneath her gathered wimple
Glancing with black-beaded eyes,
Till the lightning laughters dimple
The baby-roses in her cheeks;
Then away she flies.

III

Prythee weep, May Lilian!
Gaiety without eclipse
Wearieth me, May Lilian;
Thro' my very heart it thrilleth
When from crimson-threaded lips
Silver-treble laughter trilleth:
Prythee weep, May Lilian.

IV

Praying all I can,
If prayers will not hush thee,
Airy Lilian,
Like a rose-leaf I will crush thee,
Fairy Lilian.

ISABEL

I

EYES not down-dropt nor over-bright, but
fed
With the clear-pointed flame of chastity,
Clear, without heat, undying, tended by
Pure vestal thoughts in the translucent
fane
Of her still spirit; locks not wide-dispread,
Madonna-wise on either side her
head;

Sweet lips whereon perpetually did
reign
The summer calm of golden charity,
Were fixed shadows of thy fixed mood,
Revered Isabel, the crown and head,
The stately flower of female fortitude,
Of perfect wifehood and pure lowli-
head.

II

The intuitive decision of a bright
And thorough-edged intellect to part
Error from crime; a prudence to with-
hold;
The laws of marriage character'd in
gold
Upon the blanched tablets of her heart;
A love still burning upward, giving light
To read those laws; an accent very low
In blandishment, but a most silver flow
Of subtle-paced counsel in distress,
Right to the heart and brain, tho' unde-
scried,
Winning its way with extreme gentle-
ness
Thro' all the outworks of suspicious pride;
A courage to endure and to obey;
A hate of gossip parlance, and of sway,
Crown'd Isabel, thro' all her placid life,
The queen of marriage, a most perfect wife.

III

The mellow'd reflex of a winter moon;
A clear stream flowing with a muddy one,
Till in its onward current it absorbs
With swifter movement and in purer
light
The vexed eddies of its wayward
brother:
A leaning and upbearing parasite,
Clothing the stem, which else had
fallen quite
With cluster'd flower-bells and ambro-
sial orbs
Of rich fruit-bunches leaning on each
other—
Shadow forth thee:— the world hath
not another
(Tho' all her fairest forms are types of thee,
And thou of God in thy great charity)
Of such a finish'd chasten'd purity.

MARIANA

'Mariana in the moated grange.'
Measure for Measure

WITH blackest moss the flower-plots
Were thickly crusted, one and all:
The rusted nails fell from the knots
That held the pear to the gable-wall.
The broken sheds look'd sad and strange:
Unlifted was the clinking latch;
Weeded and worn the ancient thatch
Upon the lonely moated grange.
    She only said, 'My life is dreary,
        He cometh not,' she said;
    She said, 'I am aweary, aweary,
        I would that I were dead!'

Her tears fell with the dews at even;
    Her tears fell ere the dews were dried;
She could not look on the sweet heaven,
    Either at morn or eventide.
After the flitting of the bats,
    When thickest dark did trance the sky,
She drew her casement-curtain by,
    And glanced athwart the glooming flats.
    She only said, 'The night is dreary,
        He cometh not,' she said;
    She said, 'I am aweary, aweary,
        I would that I were dead!'

Upon the middle of the night,
    Waking she heard the night-fowl crow;
The cock sung out an hour ere light:
    From the dark fen the oxen's low
Came to her: without hope of change,
    In sleep she seem'd to walk forlorn,
Till cold winds woke the gray-eyed
        morn
About the lonely moated grange.
    She only said, 'The day is dreary,
        He cometh not,' she said;
    She said, 'I am aweary, aweary,
        I would that I were dead!'

About a stone-cast from the wall
    A sluice with blacken'd waters slept,
And o'er it many, round and small,
    The cluster'd marish-mosses crept.
Hard by a poplar shook alway,
    All silver-green with gnarled bark:
For leagues no other tree did mark
The level waste, the rounding gray.

    She only said, 'My life is dreary,
        He cometh not,' she said;
    She said, 'I am aweary, aweary,
        I would that I were dead!'

And ever when the moon was low,
    And the shrill winds were up and away,
In the white curtain, to and fro,
    She saw the gusty shadow sway.
But when the moon was very low,
    And wild winds bound within their cell,
The shadow of the poplar fell
    Upon her bed, across her brow.
    She only said, 'The night is dreary,
        He cometh not,' she said;
    She said, 'I am aweary, aweary,
        I would that I were dead!'

All day within the dreamy house,
    The doors upon their hinges creak'd;
The blue fly sung in the pane; the mouse
    Behind the mouldering wainscot shriek'd,
Or from the crevice peer'd about.
    Old faces glimmer'd thro' the doors,
    Old footsteps trod the upper floors,
Old voices called her from without.
    She only said, 'My life is dreary,
        He cometh not,' she said;
    She said, 'I am aweary, aweary,
        I would that I were dead!'

The sparrow's chirrup on the roof,
    The slow clock ticking, and the sound
Which to the wooing wind aloof
    The poplar made, did all confound
Her sense; but most she loathed the hour
    When the thick-moted sunbeam lay
    Athwart the chambers, and the day
Was sloping toward his western bower.
    Then, said she, 'I am very dreary,
        He will not come,' she said;
    She wept, 'I am aweary, aweary,
        Oh God, that I were dead!'

TO ——

I

CLEAR-HEADED friend, whose joyful scorn,
    Edged with sharp laughter, cuts atwain
    The knots that tangle human creeds,
The wounding cords that bind and strain

The heart until it bleeds,
Ray-fringed eyelids of the morn
  Roof not a glance so keen as thine:
  If aught of prophecy be mine,
Thou wilt not live in vain.

II

Low-cowering shall the Sophist sit;
  Falsehood shall bare her plaited brow:
  Fair-fronted Truth shall droop not now
With shrilling shafts of subtle wit.
Nor martyr-flames, nor trenchant swords
  Can do away that ancient lie;
  A gentler death shall Falsehood die,
Shot thro' and thro' with cunning words.

III

Weak Truth a-leaning on her crutch,
  Wan, wasted Truth in her utmost need,
  Thy kingly intellect shall feed,
  Until she be an athlete bold,
And weary with a finger's touch
  Those writhed limbs of lightning speed;
Like that strange angel which of old,
  Until the breaking of the light,
Wrestled with wandering Israel,
  Past Yabbok brook the livelong night,
And heaven's mazed signs stood still
In the dim tract of Penuel.

MADELINE

I

THOU art not steep'd in golden languors,
  No tranced summer calm is thine,
  Ever varying Madeline.
  Thro' light and shadow thou dost range,
  Sudden glances, sweet and strange,
Delicious spites and darling angers,
  And airy forms of flitting change.

II

Smiling, frowning, evermore,
Thou art perfect in love-lore.
Revealings deep and clear are thine
Of wealthy smiles; but who may know
Whether smile or frown be fleeter?
Whether smile or frown be sweeter,
  Who may know?
Frowns perfect-sweet along the brow
Light-glooming over eyes divine,
Like little clouds sun-fringed, are thine,

  Ever varying Madeline.
Thy smile and frown are not aloof
  From one another,
  Each to each is dearest brother;
Hues of the silken sheeny woof
Momently shot into each other.
  All the mystery is thine;
Smiling, frowning, evermore,
Thou art perfect in love-lore,
  Ever varying Madeline.

III

A subtle, sudden flame,
  By veering passion fann'd,
  About thee breaks and dances:
  When I would kiss thy hand,
The flush of anger'd shame
  O'erflows thy calmer glances,
And o'er black brows drops down
  A sudden-curved frown:
But when I turn away,
Thou, willing me to stay,
  Wooest not, nor vainly wranglest;
  But, looking fixedly the while,
All my bounding heart entanglest
  In a golden-netted smile;
Then in madness and in bliss,
If my lips should dare to kiss
Thy taper fingers amorously,
Again thou blushest angerly;
And o'er black brows drops down
A sudden-curved frown.

SONG—THE OWL

I

WHEN cats run home and light is come,
  And dew is cold upon the ground,
And the far-off stream is dumb,
  And the whirring sail goes round,
  And the whirring sail goes round;
    Alone and warming his five wits,
    The white owl in the belfry sits.

II

When merry milkmaids click the latch,
  And rarely smells the new-mown hay,
And the cock hath sung beneath the thatch
  Twice or thrice his roundelay,
  Twice or thrice his roundelay;
    Alone and warming his five wits,
    The white owl in the belfry sits.

8

SECOND SONG

TO THE SAME

I

THY tuwhits are lull'd, I wot,
Thy tuwhoos of yesternight,
Which upon the dark afloat,
So took echo with delight,
So took echo with delight,
　That her voice untuneful grown,
　Wears all day a fainter tone.

II

I would mock thy chaunt anew;
But I cannot mimick it;
Not a whit of thy tuwhoo,
Thee to woo to thy tuwhit,
Thee to woo to thy tuwhit,
　With a lengthen'd loud halloo,
　Tuwhoo, tuwhit, tuwhit, tuwhoo-o-o.

RECOLLECTIONS OF THE ARABIAN NIGHTS

WHEN the breeze of a joyful dawn blew free
In the silken sail of infancy,
The tide of time flow'd back with me,
　The forward-flowing tide of time;
And many a sheeny summer-morn,
Adown the Tigris I was borne,
By Bagdat's shrines of fretted gold,
High-walled gardens green and old;
True Mussulman was I and sworn,
　For it was in the golden prime
　Of good Haroun Alraschid.

Anight my shallop, rustling thro'
The low and bloomed foliage, drove
The fragrant, glistening deeps, and clove
The citron-shadows in the blue:
By garden porches on the brim,
The costly doors flung open wide,
Gold glittering thro' lamplight dim,
And broider'd sofas on each side:
　In sooth it was a goodly time,
　For it was in the golden prime
　Of good Haroun Alraschid.

Often, where clear-stemm'd platans guard
The outlet, did I turn away

The boat-head down a broad canal
From the main river sluiced, where all
The sloping of the moon-lit sward
Was damask-work, and deep inlay
Of braided blooms unmown, which crept
Adown to where the water slept.
　A goodly place, a goodly time,
　For it was in the golden prime
　Of good Haroun Alraschid.

A motion from the river won
Ridged the smooth level, bearing on
My shallop thro' the star-strown calm,
Until another night in night
I enter'd, from the clearer light,
Imbower'd vaults of pillar'd palm,
Imprisoning sweets, which, as they clomb
Heavenward, were stay'd beneath the dome
　Of hollow boughs,—A goodly time,
　For it was in the golden prime
　Of good Haroun Alraschid.

Still onward; and the clear canal
Is rounded to as clear a lake.
From the green rivage many a fall
Of diamond rillets musical,
Thro' little crystal arches low
Down from the central fountain's flow,
Fall'n silver-chiming, seemed to shake
The sparkling flints beneath the prow.
　A goodly place, a goodly time,
　For it was in the golden prime
　Of good Haroun Alraschid.

Above thro' many a bowery turn
A walk with vary-colour'd shells
Wander'd engrain'd. On either side
All round about the fragrant marge
From fluted vase, and brazen urn
In order, eastern flowers large,
Some dropping low their crimson bells
Half-closed, and others studded wide
　With disks and tiars, fed the time
　With odour in the golden prime
　Of good Haroun Alraschid.

Far off, and where the lemon grove
In closest coverture upsprung,
The living airs of middle night
Died round the bulbul as he sung;
Not he: but something which possess'd
The darkness of the world, delight,

Life, anguish, death, immortal love,
Ceasing not, mingled, unrepress'd,
　Apart from place, withholding time,
　But flattering the golden prime
　　Of good Haroun Alraschid.

Black the garden-bowers and grots
Slumber'd: the solemn palms were ranged
Above, unwoo'd of summer wind:
A sudden splendour from behind
Flush'd all the leaves with rich gold-green,
And, flowing rapidly between
Their interspaces, counterchanged
The level lake with diamond-plots
　Of dark and bright. A lovely time,
　For it was in the golden prime
　　Of good Haroun Alraschid.

Dark-blue the deep sphere overhead,
Distinct with vivid stars inlaid,
Grew darker from that under-flame:
So, leaping lightly from the boat,
With silver anchor left afloat,
In marvel whence that glory came
Upon me, as in sleep I sank
In cool soft turf upon the bank,
　Entranced with that place and time,
　So worthy of the golden prime
　　Of good Haroun Alraschid.

Thence thro' the garden I was drawn—
A realm of pleasance, many a mound,
And many a shadow-chequer'd lawn
Full of the city's stilly sound,
And deep myrrh-thickets blowing round
The stately cedar, tamarisks,
Thick rosaries of scented thorn,
Tall orient shrubs, and obelisks
　Graven with emblems of the time,
　In honour of the golden prime
　　Of good Haroun Alraschid.

With dazed vision unawares
From the long alley's latticed shade
Emerged, I came upon the great
Pavilion of the Caliphat.
Right to the carven cedarn doors,
Flung inward over spangled floors,
Broad-based flights of marble stairs
Ran up with golden balustrade,

After the fashion of the time,
And humour of the golden prime
　　Of good Haroun Alraschid.

The fourscore windows all alight
As with the quintessence of flame,
A million tapers flaring bright
From twisted silvers look'd to shame
The hollow-vaulted dark, and stream'd
Upon the mooned domes aloof
In inmost Bagdat, till there seem'd
Hundreds of crescents on the roof
　Of night new-risen, that marvellous time
　To celebrate the golden prime
　　Of good Haroun Alraschid.

Then stole I up, and trancedly
Gazed on the Persian girl alone,
Serene with argent-lidded eyes
Amorous, and lashes like to rays
Of darkness, and a brow of pearl
Tressed with redolent ebony,
In many a dark delicious curl,
Flowing beneath her rose-hued zone;
　The sweetest lady of the time,
　Well worthy of the golden prime
　　Of good Haroun Alraschid.

Six columns, three on either side,
Pure silver, underpropt a rich
Throne of the massive ore, from which
Down-droop'd, in many a floating fold,
Engarlanded and diaper'd
With inwrought flowers, a cloth of gold.
Thereon, his deep eye laughter-stirr'd
With merriment of kingly pride,
　Sole star of all that place and time,
　I saw him—in his golden prime,
　　THE GOOD HAROUN ALRASCHID.

ODE TO MEMORY

ADDRESSED TO ——

I

Thou who stealest fire,
From the fountains of the past,
To glorify the present; oh, haste,
　Visit my low desire!
Strengthen me, enlighten me!
I faint in this obscurity,
Thou dewy dawn of memory.

II

Come not as thou camest of late,
Flinging the gloom of yesternight
On the white day; but robed in soften'd
light
    Of orient state.
Whilome thou camest with the morning
    mist,
Even as a maid, whose stately brow
The dew-impearled winds of dawn have
    kiss'd,
    When she, as thou,
Stays on her floating locks the lovely freight
Of overflowing blooms, and earliest shoots
Of orient green, giving safe pledge of fruits,
Which in wintertide shall star
The black earth with brilliance rare.

III

Whilome thou camest with the morning
    mist,
And with the evening cloud,
Showering thy gleaned wealth into my
    open breast
(Those peerless flowers which in the rudest
    wind
    Never grow sere,
When rooted in the garden of the mind,
    Because they are the earliest of the year).
    Nor was the night thy shroud.
In sweet dreams softer than unbroken rest
Thou leddest by the hand thine infant
    Hope.
The eddying of her garments caught from
    thee
The light of thy great presence; and the
    cope
Of the half-attain'd futurity,
    Tho' deep not fathomless,
Was cloven with the million stars which
    tremble
O'er the deep mind of dauntless infancy.
Small thought was there of life's distress;
For sure she deem'd no mist of earth could
    dull
Those spirit-thrilling eyes so keen and
    beautiful:
Sure she was nigher to heaven's spheres,
Listening the lordly music flowing from
    The illimitable years.

O strengthen me, enlighten me!
I faint in this obscurity,
Thou dewy dawn of memory.

IV

Come forth, I charge thee, arise,
Thou of the many tongues, the myriad
    eyes!
Thou comest not with shows of flaunting
    vines
    Unto mine inner eye,
    Divinest Memory!
Thou wert not nursed by the waterfall
Which ever sounds and shines
A pillar of white light upon the wall
Of purple cliffs, aloof descried:
Come from the woods that belt the gray
    hill-side,
The seven elms, the poplars four
That stand beside my father's door,
And chiefly from the brook that loves
To purl o'er matted cress and ribbed sand,
Or dimple in the dark of rushy coves,
Drawing into his narrow earthern urn,
    In every elbow and turn,
The filter'd tribute of the rough woodland,
    O! hither lead thy feet!
Pour round mine ears the livelong bleat
Of the thick-fleeced sheep from wattled
    folds,
    Upon the ridged wolds,
When the first matin-song hath waken'd
    loud
Over the dark dewy earth forlorn,
What time the amber morn
Forth gushes from beneath a low-hung
    cloud.

V

Large dowries doth the raptured eye
    To the young spirit present
      When first she is wed;
      And like a bride of old
    In triumph led,
      With music and sweet showers
      Of festal flowers,
Unto the dwelling she must sway.
Well hast thou done, great artist Memory,
    In setting round thy first experiment
    With royal frame-work of wrought
    gold;

Needs must thou dearly love thy first essay,
And foremost in thy various gallery
    Place it, where sweetest sunlight falls
    Upon the storied walls;
        For the discovery
And newness of thine art so pleased thee,
That all which thou hast drawn of fairest
    Or boldest since, but lightly weighs
With thee unto the love thou bearest
The first-born of thy genius. Artist-like,
Ever retiring thou dost gaze
On the prime labour of thine early days:
No matter what the sketch might be;
Whether the high field on the bushless Pike,
    Or even a sand-built ridge
Of heaped hills that mound the sea,
Overblown with murmurs harsh,
Or even a lowly cottage whence we see
Stretch'd wide and wild the waste enor-
    mous marsh,
Where from the frequent bridge,
Like emblems of infinity,
The trenched waters run from sky to sky;
Or a garden bower'd close
With plaited alleys of the trailing rose,
Long alleys falling down to twilight grots,
Or opening upon level plots
Of crowned lilies, standing near
Purple-spiked lavender:
Whither in after life retired
From brawling storms,
From weary wind,
With youthful fancy re-inspired,
    We may hold converse with all forms
Of the many-sided mind,
And those whom passion hath not blinded,
Subtle-thoughted, myriad-minded.

My friend, with you to live alone,
Were how much better than to own
A crown, a sceptre, and a throne!

O strengthen me, enlighten me!
I faint in this obscurity,
Thou dewy dawn of memory.

SONG

I

A SPIRIT haunts the year's last hours
Dwelling amid these yellowing bowers:
    To himself he talks;
For at eventide, listening earnestly,
At his work you may hear him sob and
    sigh
    In the walks;
Earthward he boweth the heavy stalks
Of the mouldering flowers:
    Heavily hangs the broad sunflower
        Over its grave i' the earth so chilly;
    Heavily hangs the hollyhock,
        Heavily hangs the tiger-lily.

II

The air is damp, and hush'd, and close,
As a sick man's room when he taketh
    repose
        An hour before death;
My very heart faints and my whole soul
    grieves
At the moist rich smell of the rotting leaves,
    And the breath
        Of the fading edges of box beneath,
And the year's last rose.
    Heavily hangs the broad sunflower
        Over its grave i' the earth so chilly;
    Heavily hangs the hollyhock,
        Heavily hangs the tiger-lily.

A CHARACTER

WITH a half-glance upon the sky
At night he said, 'The wanderings
Of this most intricate Universe
Teach me the nothingness of things.'
Yet could not all creation pierce
Beyond the bottom of his eye.

He spake of beauty: that the dull
Saw no divinity in grass,
Life in dead stones, or spirit in air;
Then looking as 'twere in a glass,
He smooth'd his chin and sleek'd his hair
And said the earth was beautiful.

He spake of virtue: not the gods
More purely, when they wish to charm
Pallas and Juno sitting by:
And with a sweeping of the arm,
And a lack-lustre dead-blue eye,
Devolved his rounded periods.

Most delicately hour by hour
He canvass'd human mysteries,
And trod on silk, as if the winds
Blew his own praises in his eyes,
And stood aloof from other minds
In impotence of fancied power.

With lips depress'd as he were meek,
Himself unto himself he sold:
Upon himself himself did feed:
Quiet, dispassionate, and cold,
And other than his form of creed,
With chisell'd features clear and sleek.

THE POET

THE poet in a golden clime was born,
  With golden stars above;
Dower'd with the hate of hate, the scorn
    of scorn,
    The love of love.

He saw thro' life and death, thro' good and
    ill,
  He saw thro' his own soul.
The marvel of the everlasting will,
  An open scroll,

Before him lay: with echoing feet he
    threaded
  The secretest walks of fame:
The viewless arrows of his thoughts were
    headed
    And wing'd with flame,

Like Indian reeds blown from his silver
    tongue,
  And of so fierce a flight,
From Calpe unto Caucasus they sung,
    Filling with light

And vagrant melodies the winds which bore
  Them earthward till they lit;
Then, like the arrow-seeds of the field
    flower,
    The fruitful wit

Cleaving, took root, and springing forth
    anew
  Where'er they fell, behold,
Like to the mother plant in semblance,
    grew
    A flower all gold,

And bravely furnish'd all abroad to fling
  The winged shafts of truth,
To throng with stately blooms the breath-
    ing spring
    Of Hope and Youth.

So many minds did gird their orbs with
    beams,
  Tho' one did fling the fire.
Heaven flow'd upon the soul in many
    dreams
    Of high desire.

Thus truth was multiplied on truth, the
    world
  Like one great garden show'd,
And thro' the wreaths of floating dark
    upcurl'd,
    Rare sunrise flow'd.

And Freedom rear'd in that august sunrise
  Her beautiful bold brow,
When rites and forms before his burning
    eyes
    Melted like snow.

There was no blood upon her maiden robes
  Sunn'd by those orient skies;
But round about the circles of the globes
    Of her keen eyes

And in her raiment's hem was traced in
    flame
  WISDOM, a name to shake
All evil dreams of power—a sacred name.
    And when she spake,

Her words did gather thunder as they ran,
  And as the lightning to the thunder
Which follows it, riving the spirit of man,
    Making earth wonder,

So was their meaning to her words. No
    sword
  Of wrath her right arm whirl'd,
But one poor poet's scroll, and with *his*
    word
    She shook the world.

THE POET'S MIND

I

VEX not thou the poet's mind
  With thy shallow wit:
Vex not thou the poet's mind;
  For thou canst not fathom it.

Clear and bright it should be ever,
Flowing like a crystal river;
Bright as light, and clear as wind.

II

Dark-brow'd sophist, come not anear;
    All the place is holy ground;
    Hollow smile and frozen sneer
        Come not here.
    Holy water will I pour
    Into every spicy flower
Of the laurel-shrubs that hedge it around.
The flowers would faint at your cruel
        cheer.
    In your eye there is death,
    There is frost in your breath
    Which would blight the plants.
        Where you stand you cannot hear
            From the groves within
            The wild-bird's din.
In the heart of the garden the merry bird
        chants.
It would fall to the ground if you came
        in.
    In the middle leaps a fountain
        Like sheet lightning,
        Ever brightening
With a low melodious thunder;
All day and all night it is ever drawn
From the brain of the purple mountain
Which stands in the distance yonder:
It springs on a level of bowery lawn,
And the mountain draws it from Heaven
        above,
And it sings a song of undying love;
And yet, tho' its voice be so clear and full,
You never would hear it; your ears are so
        dull;
So keep where you are: you are foul with
        sin;
It would shrink to the earth if you came in.

THE SEA-FAIRIES

Slow sail'd the weary mariners and saw,
Betwixt the green brink and the running
        foam,
Sweet faces, rounded arms, and bosoms
        prest
To little harps of gold; and while they
        mused

Whispering to each other half in fear,
Shrill music reach'd them on the middle
        sea.

Whither away, whither away, whither
        away? fly no more.
Whither away from the high green field,
        and the happy blossoming shore?
Day and night to the billow the fountain
        calls:
Down shower the gambolling waterfalls
From wandering over the lea:
Out of the live-green heart of the dells
They freshen the silvery-crimson shells,
And thick with white bells the clover-hill
        swells
High over the full-toned sea:
O hither, come hither and furl your sails,
Come hither to me and to me:
Hither, come hither and frolic and play;
Here it is only the mew that wails;
We will sing to you all the day:
Mariner, mariner, furl your sails,
For here are the blissful downs and dales,
And merrily, merrily carol the gales,
And the spangle dances in bight and
        bay,
And the rainbow forms and flies on the
        land
Over the islands free;
And the rainbow lives in the curve of the
        sand;
Hither, come hither and see;
And the rainbow hangs on the poising
        wave,
And sweet is the colour of cove and cave,
And sweet shall your welcome be:
O hither, come hither, and be our lords,
For merry brides are we:
We will kiss sweet kisses, and speak sweet
        words:
O listen, listen, your eyes shall glisten
With pleasure and love and jubilee:
O listen, listen, your eyes shall glisten
When the sharp clear twang of the golden
        chords
Runs up the ridged sea.
Who can light on as happy a shore
All the world o'er, all the world o'er?
Whither away? listen and stay: mariner,
        mariner, fly no more.

THE DESERTED HOUSE

I

LIFE and Thought have gone away
        Side by side,
    Leaving door and windows wide:
Careless tenants they!

II

    All within is dark as night:
        In the windows is no light;
    And no murmur at the door,
    So frequent on its hinge before.

III

Close the door, the shutters close,
    Or thro' the windows we shall see
    The nakedness and vacancy
Of the dark deserted house.

IV

Come away: no more of mirth
        Is here or merry-making sound.
    The house was builded of the earth,
    And shall fall again to ground.

V

Come away: for Life and Thought
        Here no longer dwell;
    But in a city glorious—
A great and distant city—have bought
A mansion incorruptible.
Would they could have stayed with us!

THE DYING SWAN

I

THE plain was grassy, wild and bare,
Wide, wild, and open to the air,
Which had built up everywhere
    An under-roof of doleful gray.
With an inner voice the river ran,
Adown it floated a dying swan,
        And loudly did lament.
It was the middle of the day.
Ever the weary wind went on,
        And took the reed-tops as it went.

II

Some blue peaks in the distance rose,
And white against the cold-white sky,
Shone out their crowning snows.
    One willow over the river wept,
And shook the wave as the wind did sigh;
Above in the wind was the swallow,
        Chasing itself at its own wild will,
    And far thro' the marish green and
        still
    The tangled water-courses slept,
Shot over with purple, and green, and
    yellow.

III

The wild swan's death-hymn took the soul
Of that waste place with joy
Hidden in sorrow: at first to the ear
The warble was low, and full and clear;
And floating about the under-sky,
Prevailing in weakness, the coronach
    stole
Sometimes afar, and sometimes anear;
But anon her awful jubilant voice,
With a music strange and manifold,
Flow'd forth on a carol free and bold;
As when a mighty people rejoice
With shawms, and with cymbals, and
    harps of gold,
And the tumult of their acclaim is roll'd
Thro' the open gates of the city afar,
To the shepherd who watcheth the evening
    star.
And the creeping mosses and clambering
    weeds,
And the willow-branches hoar and dank,
And the wavy swell of the soughing reeds,
And the wave-worn horns of the echoing
    bank,
And the silvery marish-flowers that
    throng
The desolate creeks and pools among,
Were flooded over with eddying song.

A DIRGE

I

Now is done thy long day's work;
Fold thy palms across thy breast,
Fold thine arms, turn to thy rest.
        Let them rave.
Shadows of the silver birk
Sweep the green that folds thy grave.
        Let them rave.

II

Thee nor carketh care nor slander;
Nothing but the small cold worm
Fretteth thine enshrouded form.
Let them rave.
Light and shadow ever wander
O'er the green that folds thy grave.
Let them rave.

III

Thou wilt not turn upon thy bed;
Chaunteth not the brooding bee
Sweeter tones than calumny?
Let them rave.
Thou wilt never raise thine head
From the green that folds thy grave.
Let them rave.

IV

Crocodiles wept tears for thee;
The woodbine and eglatere
Drip sweeter dews than traitor's tear.
Let them rave.
Rain makes music in the tree
O'er the green that folds thy grave.
Let them rave.

V

Round thee blow, self-pleached deep,
Bramble roses, faint and pale,
And long purples of the dale.
Let them rave.
These in every shower creep
Thro' the green that folds thy grave.
Let them rave.

VI

The gold-eyed kingcups fine;
The frail bluebell peereth over
Rare broidry of the purple clover.
Let them rave.
Kings have no such couch as thine,
As the green that folds thy grave.
Let them rave.

VII

Wild words wander here and there:
God's great gift of speech abused
Makes thy memory confused:
But let them rave.

The balm-cricket carols clear
In the green that folds thy grave.
Let them rave.

LOVE AND DEATH

WHAT time the mighty moon was gathering light
Love paced the thymy plots of Paradise,
And all about him roll'd his lustrous eyes;
When, turning round a cassia, full in view,
Death, walking all alone beneath a yew,
And talking to himself, first met his sight:
'You must begone,' said Death, 'these walks are mine.'
Love wept and spread his sheeny vans for flight;
Yet ere he parted said, 'This hour is thine:
Thou art the shadow of life, and as the tree
Stands in the sun and shadows all beneath,
So in the light of great eternity
Life eminent creates the shade of death;
The shadow passeth when the tree shall fall,
But I shall reign for ever over all.'

THE BALLAD OF ORIANA

My heart is wasted with my woe,
        Oriana.
There is no rest for me below,
        Oriana.
When the long dun wolds are ribb'd with snow,
And loud the Norland whirlwinds blow,
        Oriana,
Alone I wander to and fro,
        Oriana.

Ere the light on dark was growing,
        Oriana,
At midnight the cock was crowing,
        Oriana:
Winds were blowing, waters flowing,
We heard the steeds to battle going,
        Oriana;
Aloud the hollow bugle blowing,
        Oriana.

In the yew-wood black as night,
        Oriana,
Ere I rode into the fight,
        Oriana,

16

While blissful tears blinded my sight
By star-shine and by moonlight,
  Oriana,
I to thee my troth did plight,
  Oriana.

She stood upon the castle wall,
  Oriana:
She watch'd my crest among them all,
  Oriana:
She saw me fight, she heard me call,
When forth there stept a foeman tall,
  Oriana,
Atween me and the castle wall,
  Oriana.

The bitter arrow went aside,
  Oriana:
The false, false arrow went aside,
  Oriana:
The damned arrow glanced aside,
And pierced thy heart, my love, my bride,
  Oriana!
Thy heart, my life, my love, my bride,
  Oriana!

Oh! narrow, narrow was the space,
  Oriana.
Loud, loud rung out the bugle's brays,
  Oriana.
Oh! deathful stabs were dealt apace,
The battle deepen'd in its place,
  Oriana;
But I was down upon my face,
  Oriana.

They should have stabb'd me where I lay,
  Oriana!
How could I rise and come away,
  Oriana?
How could I look upon the day?
They should have stabb'd me where I lay,
  Oriana—
They should have trod me into clay,
  Oriana.

O breaking heart that will not break,
  Oriana!
O pale, pale face so sweet and meek,
  Oriana!
Thou smilest, but thou dost not speak,

And then the tears run down my cheek,
  Oriana:
What wantest thou? whom dost thou seek,
  Oriana?

I cry aloud: none hear my cries,
  Oriana.
Thou comest atween me and the skies,
  Oriana.
I feel the tears of blood arise
Up from my heart unto my eyes,
  Oriana.
Within thy heart my arrow lies,
  Oriana.

O cursed hand! O cursed blow!
  Oriana!
O happy thou that liest low,
  Oriana!
All night the silence seems to flow
Beside me in my utter woe,
  Oriana.
A weary, weary way I go,
  Oriana.

When Norland winds pipe down the sea,
  Oriana,
I walk, I dare not think of thee,
  Oriana.
Thou liest beneath the greenwood tree,
I dare not die and come to thee,
  Oriana.
I hear the roaring of the sea,
  Oriana.

CIRCUMSTANCE

Two children in two neighbour villages
Playing mad pranks along the heathy leas;
Two strangers meeting at a festival;
Two lovers whispering by an orchard wall;
Two lives bound fast in one with golden
      ease;
Two graves grass-green beside a gray
      church-tower,
Wash'd with still rains and daisy blos-
      somed;
Two children in one hamlet born and
      bred;
So runs the round of life from hour to
      hour.

THE MERMAN

I

WHO would be
A merman bold,
Sitting alone,
Singing alone
Under the sea,
With a crown of gold,
On a throne?

II

I would be a merman bold,
I would sit and sing the whole of the day;
I would fill the sea-halls with a voice of
        power;
But at night I would roam abroad and play
With the mermaids in and out of the rocks,
Dressing their hair with the white sea-
        flower;
And holding them back by their flowing
        locks
I would kiss them often under the sea,
And kiss them again till they kiss'd me
        Laughingly, laughingly;
And then we would wander away, away
To the pale-green sea-groves straight and
        high,
        Chasing each other merrily.

III

There would be neither moon nor star;
But the wave would make music above us
        afar—
Low thunder and light in the magic
        night—
        Neither moon nor star.
We would call aloud in the dreamy dells,
Call to each other and whoop and cry
        All night, merrily, merrily;
They would pelt me with starry spangles
        and shells,
Laughing and clapping their hands be-
        tween,
        All night, merrily, merrily:
But I would throw to them back in mine
Turkis and agate and almondine:
Then leaping out upon them unseen
I would kiss them often under the sea,
And kiss them again till they kiss'd me
        Laughingly, laughingly.

Oh! what a happy life were mine
Under the hollow-hung ocean green!
Soft are the moss-beds under the sea;
We would live merrily, merrily.

THE MERMAID

I

WHO would be
A mermaid fair,
Singing alone,
Combing her hair
Under the sea,
In a golden curl
With a comb of pearl,
On a throne?

II

I would be a mermaid fair;
I would sing to myself the whole of the day;
With a comb of pearl I would comb my
        hair;
And still as I comb'd I would sing and say,
'Who is it loves me? who loves not me?'
I would comb my hair till my ringlets
        would fall
        Low adown, low adown,
From under my starry sea-bud crown
        Low adown and around,
And I should look like a fountain of gold
        Springing alone
        With a shrill inner sound,
        Over the throne
        In the midst of the hall;
Till that great sea-snake under the sea
From his coiled sleeps in the central deeps
Would slowly trail himself sevenfold
Round the hall where I sate, and look in
        at the gate
With his large calm eyes for the love of me.
And all the mermen under the sea
Would feel their immortality
Die in their hearts for the love of me.

III

But at night I would wander away, away,
        I would fling on each side my low-
        flowing locks,
And lightly vault from the throne and play
        With the mermen in and out of the
        rocks;

18

We would run to and fro, and hide and seek,
  On the broad sea-wolds in the crimson
    shells,
  Whose silvery spikes are nighest the sea.
But if any came near I would call, and
    shriek,
And adown the steep like a wave I would
    leap
  From the diamond-ledges that jut from
    the dells;
For I would not be kiss'd by all who would
    list,
Of the bold merry mermen under the sea;
They would sue me, and woo me, and
    flatter me,
In the purple twilights under the sea;
But the king of them all would carry me,
Woo me, and win me, and marry me,
In the branching jaspers under the sea;
Then all the dry pied things that be
In the hueless mosses under the sea
Would curl round my silver feet silently,
All looking up for the love of me.
And if I should carol aloud, from aloft
All things that are forked, and horned,
    and soft
Would lean out from the hollow sphere of
    the sea,
All looking down for the love of me.

ADELINE

I

MYSTERY of mysteries,
  Faintly smiling Adeline,
Scarce of earth nor all divine,
Nor unhappy, nor at rest,
  But beyond expression fair
  With thy floating flaxen hair;
Thy rose-lips and full blue eyes
  Take the heart from out my breast.
Wherefore those dim looks of thine,
Shadowy, dreaming Adeline?

II

Whence that aery bloom of thine,
  Like a lily which the sun
Looks thro' in his sad decline,
  And a rose-bush leans upon,
Thou that faintly smilest still,
  As a Naiad in a well,

Looking at the set of day,
Or a phantom two hours old
Of a maiden past away,
Ere the placid lips be cold?
Wherefore those faint smiles of thine,
  Spiritual Adeline?

III

What hope or fear or joy is thine?
Who talketh with thee, Adeline?
  For sure thou art not all alone.
  Do beating hearts of salient springs
Keep measure with thine own?
    Hast thou heard the butterflies
    What they say betwixt their wings?
    Or in stillest evenings
With what voice the violet woos
To his heart the silver dews?
  Or when little airs arise,
  How the merry bluebell rings
    To the mosses underneath?
    Hast thou look'd upon the breath
Of the lilies at sunrise?
Wherefore that faint smile of thine,
Shadowy, dreaming Adeline?

IV

Some honey-converse feeds thy mind,
  Some spirit of a crimson rose
  In love with thee forgets to close
  His curtains, wasting odorous sighs
All night long on darkness blind.
What aileth thee? whom waitest thou
With thy soften'd, shadow'd brow,
  And those dew-lit eyes of thine,
  Thou faint smiler, Adeline?

V

Lovest thou the doleful wind
  When thou gazest at the skies?
Doth the low-tongued Orient
    Wander from the side of the morn,
    Dripping with Sabæan spice
On thy pillow, lowly bent
  With melodious airs lovelorn,
Breathing Light against thy face,
While his locks a-drooping twined
  Round thy neck in subtle ring
Make a carcanet of rays,
  And ye talk together still,

In the language wherewith Spring
Letters cowslips on the hill?
Hence that look and smile of thine,
Spiritual Adeline.

MARGARET

I

O SWEET pale Margaret,
O rare pale Margaret,
What lit your eyes with tearful power,
Like moonlight on a falling shower?
Who lent you, love, your mortal dower
Of pensive thought and aspect pale,
Your melancholy sweet and frail
As perfume of the cuckoo-flower?
From the westward-winding flood,
From the evening-lighted wood,
From all things outward you have won
A tearful grace, as tho' you stood
Between the rainbow and the sun.
The very smile before you speak,
That dimples your transparent cheek,
Encircles all the heart, and feedeth
The senses with a still delight
Of dainty sorrow without sound,
Like the tender amber round,
Which the moon about her spreadeth,
Moving thro' a fleecy night.

II

You love, remaining peacefully,
To hear the murmur of the strife,
But enter not the toil of life.
Your spirit is the calmed sea,
Laid by the tumult of the fight.
You are the evening star, alway
Remaining betwixt dark and bright:
Lull'd echoes of laborious day
Come to you, gleams of mellow light
Float by you on the verge of night.

III

What can it matter, Margaret,
What songs below the waning stars
The lion-heart, Plantagenet,
Sang looking thro' his prison bars?
Exquisite Margaret, who can tell
The last wild thought of Chatelet,
Just ere the falling axe did part
The burning brain from the true heart,
Even in her sight he loved so well?

IV

A fairy shield your Genius made
And gave you on your natal day.
Your sorrow, only sorrow's shade,
Keeps real sorrow far away.
You move not in such solitudes,
You are not less divine,
But more human in your moods,
Than your twin-sister, Adeline.
Your hair is darker, and your eyes
Touch'd with a somewhat darker hue,
And less aërially blue,
But ever trembling thro' the dew
Of dainty-woeful sympathies.

V

O sweet pale Margaret,
O rare pale Margaret,
Come down, come down, and hear me
speak:
Tie up the ringlets on your cheek:
The sun is just about to set,
The arching limes are tall and shady,
And faint, rainy lights are seen,
Moving in the leavy beech.
Rise from the feast of sorrow, lady,
Where all day long you sit between
Joy and woe, and whisper each.
Or only look across the lawn,
Look out below your bower-eaves,
Look down, and let your blue eyes dawn
Upon me thro' the jasmine-leaves.

ROSALIND

I

My Rosalind, my Rosalind,
My frolic falcon, with bright eyes,
Whose free delight, from any height of
rapid flight,
Stoops at all game that wing the skies,
My Rosalind, my Rosalind,
My bright-eyed, wild-eyed falcon, whither,
Careless both of wind and weather,
Whither fly ye, what game spy ye,
Up or down the streaming wind?

II

The quick lark's closest-caroll'd strains,
The shadow rushing up the sea,
The lightning flash atween the rains,
The sunlight driving down the lea,

The leaping stream, the very wind,
That will not stay, upon his way,
To stoop the cowslip to the plains,
Is not so clear and bold and free
As you, my falcon Rosalind.
You care not for another's pains,
Because you are the soul of joy,
Bright metal all without alloy.
Life shoots and glances thro' your veins,
And flashes off a thousand ways,
Thro' lips and eyes in subtle rays,
Your hawk-eyes are keen and bright,
Keen with triumph, watching still
To pierce me thro' with pointed light;
But oftentimes they flash and glitter
Like sunshine on a dancing rill,
And your words are seeming-bitter,
Sharp and few, but seeming-bitter
From excess of swift delight.

III

Come down, come home, my Rosalind,
My gay young hawk, my Rosalind:
Too long you keep the upper skies;
Too long you roam and wheel at will;
But we must hood your random eyes,
That care not whom they kill,
And your cheek, whose brilliant hue
Is so sparkling-fresh to view,
Some red heath-flower in the dew,
Touch'd with sunrise. We must bind
And keep you fast, my Rosalind,
Fast, fast, my wild-eyed Rosalind,
And clip your wings, and make you love:
When we have lured you from above,
And that delight of frolic flight, by day or
    night,
From North to South,
We'll bind you fast in silken cords,
And kiss away the bitter words
From off your rosy mouth.

ELEÄNORE

I

THY dark eyes open'd not,
    Nor first reveal'd themselves to English
        air,
        For there is nothing here,
Which, from the outward to the inward
    brought,
Moulded thy baby thought.

Far off from human neighbourhood,
    Thou wert born, on a summer morn,
A mile beneath the cedar-wood.
Thy bounteous forehead was not fann'd
    With breezes from our oaken glades,
But thou wert nursed in some delicious land
Of lavish lights, and floating shades:
And flattering thy childish thought
    The oriental fairy brought,
    At the moment of thy birth,
From old well-heads of haunted rills,
And the hearts of purple hills,
    And shadow'd coves on a sunny shore,
    The choicest wealth of all the earth,
    Jewel or shell, or starry ore,
    To deck thy cradle, Eleänore.

II

Or the yellow-banded bees,
Thro' half-open lattices
Coming in the scented breeze,
    Fed thee, a child, lying alone,
        With whitest honey in fairy gardens
            cull'd—
    A glorious child, dreaming alone,
    In silk-soft folds, upon yielding down,
With the hum of swarming bees
        Into dreamful slumber lull'd.

III

Who may minister to thee?
Summer herself should minister
    To thee, with fruitage golden-rinded
    On golden salvers, or it may be,
Youngest Autumn, in a bower
Grape-thicken'd from the light, and
    blinded
        With many a deep-hued bell-like
            flower
Of fragrant trailers, when the air
        Sleepeth over all the heaven,
        And the crag that fronts the Even,
        All along the shadowing shore,
Crimsons over an inland mere,
        Eleänore!

IV

How may full-sail'd verse express,
    How may measured words adore
    The full-flowing harmony
Of thy swan-like stateliness,
        Eleänore?

The luxuriant symmetry
Of thy floating gracefulness,
   Eleänore?
Every turn and glance of thine,
Every lineament divine,
   Eleänore,
And the steady sunset glow,
That stays upon thee? For in thee
Is nothing sudden, nothing single;
Like two streams of incense free
From one censer in one shrine,
Thought and motion mingle,
Mingle ever. Motions flow
To one another, even as tho'
   They were modulated so
   To an unheard melody,
Which lives about thee, and a sweep
Of richest pauses, evermore
Drawn from each other mellow-deep;
Who may express thee, Eleänore?

V

I stand before thee, Eleänore;
   I see thy beauty gradually unfold,
Daily and hourly, more and more.
I muse, as in a trance, the while
   Slowly, as from a cloud of gold,
Comes out thy deep ambrosial smile.
I muse, as in a trance, whene'er
   The languors of thy love-deep eyes
Float on to me. I would I were
   So tranced, so rapt in ecstasies,
To stand apart, and to adore,
Gazing on thee for evermore,
Serene, imperial Eleänore!

VI

Sometimes, with most intensity
Gazing, I seem to see
Thought folded over thought, smiling
   asleep,
Slowly awaken'd, grow so full and deep
In thy large eyes, that, overpower'd quite,
I cannot veil, or droop my sight,
But am as nothing in its light:
As tho' a star, in inmost heaven set,
Ev'n while we gaze on it,
Should slowly round his orb, and slowly
   grow
To a full face, there like a sun remain
Fix'd—then as slowly fade again,

And draw itself to what it was before;
   So full, so deep, so slow,
   Thought seems to come and go
In thy large eyes, imperial Eleänore.

VII

As thunder-clouds that, hung on high,
   Roof'd the world with doubt and fear,
Floating thro' an evening atmosphere,
   Grow golden all about the sky;
In thee all passion becomes passionless,
Touch'd by thy spirit's mellowness,
Losing his fire and active might
   In a silent meditation,
Falling into a still delight,
   And luxury of contemplation:
As waves that up a quiet cove
   Rolling slide, and lying still
   Shadow forth the banks at will:
Or sometimes they swell and move,
   Pressing up against the land,
   With motions of the outer sea:
   And the self-same influence
   Controlleth all the soul and sense
Of Passion gazing upon thee.
His bow-string slacken'd, languid Love,
   Leaning his cheek upon his hand,
Droops both his wings, regarding thee,
   And so would languish evermore,
   Serene, imperial Eleänore.

VIII

But when I see thee roam, with tresses
   unconfined,
While the amorous, odorous wind
Breathes low between the sunset and the
   moon;
   Or, in a shadowy saloon,
On silken cushions half reclined;
   I watch thy grace; and in its place
My heart a charmed slumber keeps,
   While I muse upon thy face;
And a languid fire creeps
   Thro' my veins to all my frame,
Dissolvingly and slowly: soon
   From thy rose-red lips MY name
Floweth; and then, as in a swoon,
   With dinning sound my ears are rife,
   My tremulous tongue faltereth,
   I lose my colour, I lose my breath,
   I drink the cup of a costly death,

Brimm'd with delirious draughts of warm-
    est life.
    I die with my delight, before
      I hear what I would hear from thee;
      Yet tell my name again to me,
I *would* be dying evermore,
    So dying ever, Eleänore.

KATE

I KNOW her by her angry air,
    Her bright black eyes, her bright black
      hair,
    Her rapid laughters wild and shrill,
As laughters of the woodpecker
    From the bosom of a hill.
'Tis Kate—she sayeth what she will:
For Kate hath an unbridled tongue,
    Clear as the twanging of a harp.
    Her heart is like a throbbing star.
Kate hath a spirit ever strung
    Like a new bow, and bright and sharp
    As edges of the scymetar.
Whence shall she take a fitting mate?
    For Kate no common love will feel;
My woman-soldier, gallant Kate,
    As pure and true as blades of steel.

Kate saith 'the world is void of might.'
    Kate saith 'the men are gilded flies.'
    Kate snaps her fingers at my vows;
Kate will not hear of lovers' sighs.
    I would I were an arméd knight,
    Far-famed for well-won enterprise,
      And wearing on my swarthy brows
The garland of new-wreathed emprise:
    For in a moment I would pierce
The blackest files of clanging fight,
    And strongly strike to left and right,
    In dreaming of my lady's eyes.
      Oh! Kate loves well the bold and
      fierce;
    But none are bold enough for Kate,
    She cannot find a fitting mate.

I

MY life is full of weary days,
    But good things have not kept aloof,
Nor wander'd into other ways:
    I have not lack'd thy mild reproof,
Nor golden largess of thy praise.

And now shake hands across the brink
    Of that deep grave to which I go:
Shake hands once more: I cannot sink
    So far—far down, but I shall know
    Thy voice, and answer from below.

II

When in the darkness over me
    The four-handed mole shall scrape,
Plant thou no dusky cypress-tree,
    Nor wreathe thy cap with doleful crape,
    But pledge me in the flowing grape.

And when the sappy field and wood
    Grow green beneath the showery gray,
And rugged barks begin to bud,
    And thro' damp holts new-flush'd with
      may,
    Ring sudden scritches of the jay,

Then let wise Nature work her will,
    And on my clay her darnel grow;
Come only, when the days are still,
    And at my headstone whisper low,
    And tell me if the woodbines blow.

EARLY SONNETS

I

As when with downcast eyes we muse and
    brood,
And ebb into a former life, or seem
To lapse far back in some confused dream
To states of mystical similitude;
If one but speaks or hems or stirs his chair,
Ever the wonder waxeth more and more,
So that we say, 'All this hath been before,
All this hath been, I know not when or
    where.'
So, friend, when first I look'd upon your
    face,
Our thought gave answer each to each, so
    true—
Opposed mirrors each reflecting each—
That tho' I knew not in what time or place,
Methought that I had often met with you,
And either lived in either's heart and
    speech.

II

TO J. M. K.

My hope and heart is with thee—thou
    wilt be
A latter Luther, and a soldier-priest
To scare church-harpies from the master's
    feast;
Our dusted velvets have much need of
    thee:
Thou art no sabbath-drawler of old saws,
Distill'd from some worm-canker'd homily;
But spurr'd at heart with fieriest energy
To embattail and to wall about thy cause
With iron-worded proof, hating to hark
The humming of the drowsy pulpit-drone
Half God's good sabbath, while the worn-
    out clerk
Brow-beats his desk below. Thou from a
    throne
Mounted in heaven wilt shoot into the dark
Arrows of lightnings. I will stand and
    mark.

III

Mine be the strength of spirit, full and free,
Like some broad river rushing down alone,
With the selfsame impulse wherewith he
    was thrown
From his loud fount upon the echoing
    lea:—
Which with increasing might doth forward
    flee
By town, and tower, and hill, and cape,
    and isle,
And in the middle of the green salt sea
Keeps his blue waters fresh for many a mile.
Mine be the power which ever to its sway
Will win the wise at once, and by degrees
May into uncongenial spirits flow;
Ev'n as the warm gulf-stream of Florida
Floats far away into the Northern seas
The lavish growths of southern Mexico.

IV

ALEXANDER

Warrior of God, whose strong right arm
    debased
The throne of Persia, when her Satrap
    bled
At Issus by the Syrian gates, or fled

Beyond the Memmian naphtha-pits, dis-
    graced
For ever—thee (thy pathway sand-erased)
Gliding with equal crowns two serpents led
Joyful to that palm-planted fountain-fed
Ammonian Oasis in the waste.
There in a silent shade of laurel brown
Apart the Chamian Oracle divine
Shelter'd his unapproached mysteries:
High things were spoken there, unhanded
    down;
Only they saw thee from the secret shrine
Returning with hot cheek and kindled eyes.

V

BUONAPARTE

He thought to quell the stubborn hearts
    of oak,
Madman!—to chain with chains, and bind
    with bands
That island queen who sways the floods
    and lands
From Ind to Ind, but in fair daylight woke,
When from her wooden walls,—lit by sure
    hands,—
With thunders, and with lightnings, and
    with smoke,—
Peal after peal, the British battle broke,
Lulling the brine against the Coptic sands.
We taught him lowlier moods, when Elsi-
    nore
Heard the war moan along the distant sea,
Rocking with shatter'd spars, with sudden
    fires
Flamed over: at Trafalgar yet once more
We taught him: late he learned humility
Perforce, like those whom Gideon school'd
    with briers.

VI

POLAND

How long, O God, shall men be ridden
    down,
And trampled under by the last and least
Of men? The heart of Poland hath not
    ceased
To quiver, tho' her sacred blood doth
    drown
The fields, and out of every smouldering
    town

Cries to Thee, lest brute Power be increased,
Till that o'ergrown Barbarian in the East
Transgress his ample bound to some new crown:—
Cries to Thee, 'Lord, how long shall these things be?
How long this icy-hearted Muscovite
Oppress the region?' Us, O Just and Good,
Forgive, who smiled when she was torn in three;
Us, who stand now, when we should aid the right—
A matter to be wept with tears of blood!

VII

CARESS'D or chidden by the slender hand,
And singing airy trifles this or that,
Light Hope at Beauty's call would perch and stand,
And run thro' every change of sharp and flat;
And Fancy came and at her pillow sat,
When Sleep had bound her in his rosy band,
And chased away the still-recurring gnat,
And woke her with a lay from fairy land.
But now they live with Beauty less and less,
For Hope is other Hope and wanders far,
Nor cares to lisp in love's delicious creeds;
And Fancy watches in the wilderness,
Poor Fancy sadder than a single star,
That sets at twilight in a land of reeds.

VIII

THE form, the form alone is eloquent!
A nobler yearning never broke her rest
Than but to dance and sing, be gaily drest,
And win all eyes with all accomplishment:
Yet in the whirling dances as we went,
My fancy made me for a moment blest
To find my heart so near the beauteous breast
That once had power to rob it of content.
A moment came the tenderness of tears,
The phantom of a wish that once could move,
A ghost of passion that no smiles restore—
For ah! the slight coquette, she cannot love,

And if you kiss'd her feet a thousand years,
She still would take the praise, and care no more.

IX

WAN Sculptor, weepest thou to take the cast
Of those dead lineaments that near thee lie?
O sorrowest thou, pale Painter, for the past,
In painting some dead friend from memory?
Weep on: beyond his object Love can last:
His object lives: more cause to weep have I:
My tears, no tears of love, are flowing fast,
No tears of love, but tears that Love can die.
I pledge her not in any cheerful cup,
Nor care to sit beside her where she sits—
Ah pity—hint it not in human tones,
But breathe it into earth and close it up
With secret death for ever, in the pits
Which some green Christmas crams with weary bones.

X

IF I were loved, as I desire to be,
What is there in the great sphere of the earth,
And range of evil between death and birth,
That I should fear,—if I were loved by thee?
All the inner, all the outer world of pain
Clear Love would pierce and cleave, if thou wert mine,
As I have heard that, somewhere in the main,
Fresh-water springs come up through bitter brine.
'Twere joy, not fear, claspt hand-in-hand with thee,
To wait for death—mute—careless of all ills,
Apart upon a mountain, tho' the surge
Of some new deluge from a thousand hills
Flung leagues of roaring foam into the gorge
Below us, as far on as eye could see.

XI
THE BRIDESMAID

O BRIDESMAID, ere the happy knot was tied,
Thine eyes so wept that they could hardly
    see;
Thy sister smiled and said, 'No tears for
    me!
A happy bridesmaid makes a happy bride.'
And then, the couple standing side by
    side,
Love lighted down between them full of
    glee,
And over his left shoulder laugh'd at thee,
'O happy bridesmaid, make a happy bride.'
And all at once a pleasant truth I learn'd,
For while the tender service made thee
    weep,
I loved thee for the tear thou couldst not
    hide,
And prest thy hand, and knew the press
    return'd,
And thought, 'My life is sick of single
    sleep:
O happy bridesmaid, make a happy bride!'

THE LADY OF SHALOTT
AND OTHER POEMS

THE LADY OF SHALOTT

PART I

ON either side the river lie
Long fields of barley and of rye,
That clothe the wold and meet the sky;
And thro' the field the road runs by
    To many-tower'd Camelot;
And up and down the people go,
Gazing where the lilies blow
Round an island there below,
    The island of Shalott.

Willows whiten, aspens quiver,
Little breezes dusk and shiver
Thro' the wave that runs for ever
By the island in the river
    Flowing down to Camelot.
Four gray walls, and four gray towers,
Overlook a space of flowers,
And the silent isle imbowers
    The Lady of Shalott.

By the margin, willow-veil'd,
Slide the heavy barges trail'd
By slow horses; and unhail'd
The shallop flitteth silken-sail'd
    Skimming down to Camelot:
But who hath seen her wave her hand?
Or at the casement seen her stand?
Or is she known in all the land,
    The Lady of Shalott?

Only reapers, reaping early
In among the bearded barley,
Hear a song that echoes cheerly
From the river winding clearly,
    Down to tower'd Camelot:
And by the moon the reaper weary,
Piling sheaves in uplands airy,
Listening, whispers, ''Tis the fairy
    Lady of Shalott.'

PART II

THERE she weaves by night and day
A magic web with colours gay.
She has heard a whisper say,
A curse is on her if she stay
    To look down to Camelot.
She knows not what the curse may be,
And so she weaveth steadily,
And little other care hath she,
    The Lady of Shalott.

And moving thro' a mirror clear
That hangs before her all the year,
Shadows of the world appear.
There she sees the highway near
    Winding down to Camelot:
There the river eddy whirls,
And there the surly village-churls,
And the red cloaks of market girls,
    Pass onward from Shalott.

Sometimes a troop of damsels glad,
An abbot on an ambling pad,
Sometimes a curly shepherd-lad,
Or long-hair'd page in crimson clad,
 Goes by to tower'd Camelot;
And sometimes thro' the mirror blue
The knights come riding two and two:
She hath no loyal knight and true,
 The Lady of Shalott.

But in her web she still delights
To weave the mirror's magic sights,
For often thro' the silent nights
A funeral, with plumes and lights
 And music, went to Camelot:
Or when the moon was overhead,
Came two young lovers lately wed;
'I am half sick of shadows,' said
 The Lady of Shalott.

PART III

A BOW-SHOT from her bower-eaves,
He rode between the barley-sheaves,
The sun came dazzling thro' the leaves,
And flamed upon the brazen greaves
 Of bold Sir Lancelot.
A red-cross knight for ever kneel'd
To a lady in his shield,
That sparkled on the yellow field,
 Beside remote Shalott.

The gemmy bridle glitter'd free,
Like to some branch of stars we see
Hung in the golden Galaxy.
The bridle bells rang merrily
 As he rode down to Camelot:
And from his blazon'd baldric slung
A mighty silver bugle hung,
And as he rode his armour rung,
 Beside remote Shalott.

All in the blue unclouded weather
Thick-jewell'd shone the saddle-leather,
The helmet and the helmet-feather
Burn'd like one burning flame together,
 As he rode down to Camelot.
As often thro' the purple night,
Below the starry clusters bright,
Some bearded meteor, trailing light,
 Moves over still Shalott.

His broad clear brow in sunlight glow'd;
On burnish'd hooves his war-horse trode;
From underneath his helmet flow'd
His coal-black curls as on he rode,
 As he rode down to Camelot.
From the bank and from the river
He flash'd into the crystal mirror,
'Tirra lirra,' by the river
 Sang Sir Lancelot.

She left the web, she left the loom,
She made three paces thro' the room,
She saw the water-lily bloom,
She saw the helmet and the plume,
 She look'd down to Camelot.
Out flew the web and floated wide;
The mirror crack'd from side to side;
'The curse is come upon me,' cried
 The Lady of Shalott.

PART IV

IN the stormy east-wind straining,
The pale yellow woods were waning,
The broad stream in his banks complain-
 ing,
Heavily the low sky raining
 Over tower'd Camelot;
Down she came and found a boat
Beneath a willow left afloat,
And round about the prow she wrote
 The Lady of Shalott.

And down the river's dim expanse
Like some bold seër in a trance,
Seeing all his own mischance—
With a glassy countenance
 Did she look to Camelot.
And at the closing of the day
She loosed the chain, and down she lay;
The broad stream bore her far away,
 The Lady of Shalott.

Lying, robed in snowy white
That loosely flew to left and right—
The leaves upon her falling light—
Thro' the noises of the night
 She floated down to Camelot:
And as the boat-head wound along
The willowy hills and fields among,
They heard her singing her last song,
 The Lady of Shalott.

Heard a carol, mournful, holy,
Chanted loudly, chanted lowly,
Till her blood was frozen slowly,
And her eyes were darken'd wholly,
    Turn'd to tower'd Camelot.
For ere she reach'd upon the tide
The first house by the water-side,
Singing in her song she died,
    The Lady of Shalott.

Under tower and balcony,
By garden-wall and gallery,
A gleaming shape she floated by,
Dead-pale between the houses high,
    Silent into Camelot.
Out upon the wharfs they came,
Knight and burgher, lord and dame,
And round the prow they read her name,
    The Lady of Shalott.

Who is this? and what is here?
And in the lighted palace near
Died the sound of royal cheer;
And they cross'd themselves for fear,
    All the knights at Camelot:
But Lancelot mused a little space;
He said, 'She has a lovely face;
God in his mercy lend her grace,
    The Lady of Shalott.'

MARIANA IN THE SOUTH

WITH one black shadow at its feet,
  The house thro' all the level shines,
Close-latticed to the brooding heat,
  And silent in its dusty vines:
A faint-blue ridge upon the right,
  An empty river-bed before,
  And shallows on a distant shore,
In glaring sand and inlets bright.
    But 'Ave Mary,' made she moan,
    And 'Ave Mary,' night and morn,
    And 'Ah,' she sang, 'to be all alone,
    To live forgotten, and love forlorn.'

She, as her carol sadder grew,
  From brow and bosom slowly down
Thro' rosy taper fingers drew
  Her streaming curls of deepest brown
To left and right, and made appear,
    Still-lighted in a secret shrine,
    Her melancholy eyes divine,

The home of woe without a tear.
    And 'Ave Mary,' was her moan,
    'Madonna, sad is night and morn,'
    And 'Ah,' she sang, 'to be all alone,
    To live forgotten, and love forlorn.'

Till all the crimson changed, and past
  Into deep orange o'er the sea,
Low on her knees herself she cast,
  Before Our Lady murmur'd she;
Complaining, 'Mother, give me grace
  To help me of my weary load.'
And on the liquid mirror glow'd
The clear perfection of her face.
    'Is this the form,' she made her moan,
    'That won his praises night and
      morn?'
    And 'Ah,' she said, 'but I wake alone,
    I sleep forgotten, I wake forlorn.'

Nor bird would sing, nor lamb would bleat,
  Nor any cloud would cross the vault,
But day increased from heat to heat,
  On stony drought and steaming salt;
Till now at noon she slept again,
  And seem'd knee-deep in mountain
    grass,
And heard her native breezes pass,
And runlets babbling down the glen.
    She breathed in sleep a lower moan,
    And murmuring, as at night and
      morn,
    She thought, 'My spirit is here alone,
    Walks forgotten, and is forlorn.'

Dreaming, she knew it was a dream:
  She felt he was and was not there.
She woke: the babble of the stream
  Fell, and, without, the steady glare
Shrank one sick willow sere and small.
  The river-bed was dusty-white;
  And all the furnace of the light
Struck up against the blinding wall.
    She whisper'd, with a stifled moan
    More inward than at night or morn,
    'Sweet Mother, let me not here alone
    Live forgotten and die forlorn.'

And, rising, from her bosom drew
  Old letters, breathing of her worth,
For 'Love,' they said, 'must needs be true,
  To what is loveliest upon earth.'

An image seem'd to pass the door,
  To look at her with slight, and say
  'But now thy beauty flows away,
So be alone for evermore.'
      'O cruel heart,' she changed her tone,
      'And cruel love, whose end is scorn,
  Is this the end, to be left alone,
      To live forgotten, and die forlorn?'

But sometimes in the falling day
  An image seem'd to pass the door,
To look into her eyes and say,
  'But thou shalt be alone no more.'
And flaming downward over all
  From heat to heat the day decreased,
And slowly rounded to the east
      The one black shadow from the wall.
      'The day to night,' she made her
          moan,
      'The day to night, the night to
          morn,
      And day and night I am left alone
      To live forgotten, and love forlorn.'

At eve a dry cicala sung,
  There came a sound as of the sea;
Backward the lattice-blind she flung,
  And lean'd upon the balcony.
There all in spaces rosy-bright
  Large Hesper glitter'd on her tears,
  And deepening thro' the silent spheres
Heaven over Heaven rose the night.
And weeping then she made her moan,
  'The night comes on that knows not
      morn,
When I shall cease to be all alone,
  To live forgotten, and love forlorn.'

THE TWO VOICES

A STILL small voice spake unto me,
'Thou art so full of misery,
Were it not better not to be?'

Then to the still small voice I said;
'Let me not cast in endless shade
What is so wonderfully made.'

To which the voice did urge reply;
'To-day I saw the dragon-fly
Come from the wells where he did lie.

'An inner impulse rent the veil
Of his old husk: from head to tail
Came out clear plates of sapphire mail.

'He dried his wings: like gauze they grew;
Thro' crofts and pastures wet with dew
A living flash of light he flew.'

I said, 'When first the world began,
Young Nature thro' five cycles ran,
And in the sixth she moulded man.

'She gave him mind, the lordliest
Proportion, and, above the rest,
Dominion in the head and breast.'

Thereto the silent voice replied;
'Self-blinded are you by your pride:
Look up thro' night: the world is wide.

'This truth within thy mind rehearse,
That in a boundless universe
Is boundless better, boundless worse.

'Think you this mould of hopes and fears
Could find no statelier than his peers
In yonder hundred million spheres?'

It spake, moreover, in my mind:
'Tho' thou wert scatter'd to the wind,
Yet is there plenty of the kind.'

Then did my response clearer fall:
'No compound of this earthly ball
Is like another, all in all.'

To which he answer'd scoffingly;
'Good soul! suppose I grant it thee,
Who'll weep for thy deficiency?

'Or will one beam be less intense,
When thy peculiar difference
Is cancell'd in the world of sense?'

I would have said, 'Thou canst not know,'
But my full heart, that work'd below,
Rain'd thro' my sight its overflow.

Again the voice spake unto me:
'Thou art so steep'd in misery,
Surely 'twere better not to be.

'Thine anguish will not let thee sleep,
Nor any train of reason keep:
Thou canst not think, but thou wilt weep.'

I said, 'The years with change advance:
If I make dark my countenance,
I shut my life from happier chance.

'Some turn this sickness yet might take,
Ev'n yet.' But he: 'What drug can make
A wither'd palsy cease to shake?'

I wept, 'Tho' I should die, I know
That all about the thorn will blow
In tufts of rosy-tinted snow;

'And men, thro' novel spheres of thought
Still moving after truth long sought,
Will learn new things when I am not.'

'Yet,' said the secret voice, 'some time,
Sooner or later, will gray prime
Make thy grass hoar with early rime.

'Not less swift souls that yearn for light,
Rapt after heaven's starry flight,
Would sweep the tracts of day and night.

'Not less the bee would range her cells,
The furzy prickle fire the dells,
The foxglove cluster dappled bells.'

I said that 'all the years invent;
Each month is various to present
The world with some development.

'Were this not well, to bide mine hour,
Tho' watching from a ruin'd tower
How grows the day of human power?'

'The highest-mounted mind,' he said,
'Still sees the sacred morning spread
The silent summit overhead.

'Will thirty seasons render plain
Those lonely lights that still remain,
Just breaking over land and main?

'Or make that morn, from his cold crown
And crystal silence creeping down,
Flood with full daylight glebe and town?

'Forerun thy peers, thy time, and let
Thy feet, millenniums hence, be set
In midst of knowledge, dream'd not yet.

'Thou hast not gain'd a real height,
Nor art thou nearer to the light,
Because the scale is infinite.

''Twere better not to breathe or speak,
Than cry for strength, remaining weak,
And seem to find, but still to seek.

'Moreover, but to seem to find
Asks what thou lackest, thought resign'd,
A healthy frame, a quiet mind.'

I said, 'When I am gone away,
"He dared not tarry," men will say,
Doing dishonour to my clay.'

'This is more vile,' he made reply,
'To breathe and loathe, to live and sigh,
Than once from dread of pain to die.

'Sick art thou—a divided will
Still heaping on the fear of ill
The fear of men, a coward still.

'Do men love thee? Art thou so bound
To men, that how thy name may sound
Will vex thee lying underground?

'The memory of the wither'd leaf
In endless time is scarce more brief
Than of the garner'd Autumn-sheaf.

'Go, vexed Spirit, sleep in trust;
The right ear, that is fill'd with dust,
Hears little of the false or just.'

'Hard task, to pluck resolve,' I cried,
'From emptiness and the waste wide
Of that abyss, or scornful pride!

'Nay—rather yet that I could raise
One hope that warm'd me in the days
While still I yearn'd for human praise.

'When, wide in soul and bold of tongue,
Among the tents I paused and sung,
The distant battle flash'd and rung.

'I sung the joyful Pæan clear,
And, sitting, burnish'd without fear
The brand, the buckler, and the spear—

'Waiting to strive a happy strife,
To war with falsehood to the knife,
And not to lose the good of life—

'Some hidden principle to move,
To put together, part and prove,
And mete the bounds of hate and love—

'As far as might be, to carve out
Free space for every human doubt,
That the whole mind might orb about—

'To search thro' all I felt or saw,
The springs of life, the depths of awe,
And reach the law within the law:

'At least, not rotting like a weed,
But, having sown some generous seed,
Fruitful of further thought and deed,

'To pass, when Life her light withdraws,
Not void of righteous self-applause,
Nor in a merely selfish cause—

'In some good cause, not in mine own,
To perish, wept for, honour'd, known,
And like a warrior overthrown;

'Whose eyes are dim with glorious tears,
When, soil'd with noble dust, he hears
His country's war-song thrill his ears:

'Then dying of a mortal stroke,
What time the foeman's line is broke,
And all the war is roll'd in smoke.'

'Yea!' said the voice, 'thy dream was good,
While thou abodest in the bud.
It was the stirring of the blood.

'If Nature put not forth her power
About the opening of the flower,
Who is it that could live an hour?

'Then comes the check, the change, the fall,
Pain rises up, old pleasures pall.
There is one remedy for all.

'Yet hadst thou, thro' enduring pain,
Link'd month to month with such a chain
Of knitted purport, all were vain.

'Thou hadst not between death and birth
Dissolved the riddle of the earth.
So were thy labour little-worth.

'That men with knowledge merely play'd,
I told thee—hardly nigher made,
Tho' scaling slow from grade to grade;

'Much less this dreamer, deaf and blind,
Named man, may hope some truth to find,
That bears relation to the mind.

'For every worm beneath the moon
Draws different threads, and late and soon
Spins, toiling out his own cocoon.

'Cry, faint not: either Truth is born
Beyond the polar gleam forlorn,
Or in the gateways of the morn.

'Cry, faint not, climb: the summits slope
Beyond the furthest flights of hope,
Wrapt in dense cloud from base to cope.

'Sometimes a little corner shines,
As over rainy mist inclines
A gleaming crag with belts of pines.

'I will go forward, sayest thou,
I shall not fail to find her now.
Look up, the fold is on her brow.

'If straight thy track, or if oblique,
Thou know'st not. Shadows thou dost strike,
Embracing cloud, Ixion-like;

'And owning but a little more
Than beasts, abidest lame and poor,
Calling thyself a little lower

'Than angels. Cease to wail and brawl!
Why inch by inch to darkness crawl?
There is one remedy for all.'

'O dull, one-sided voice,' said I,
'Wilt thou make everything a lie,
To flatter me that I may die?

'I know that age to age succeeds,
Blowing a noise of tongues and deeds,
A dust of systems and of creeds.

'I cannot hide that some have striven,
Achieving calm, to whom was given
The joy that mixes man with Heaven:

'Who, rowing hard against the stream,
Saw distant gates of Eden gleam,
And did not dream it was a dream;

'But heard, by secret transport led,
Ev'n in the charnels of the dead,
The murmur of the fountain-head—

'Which did accomplish their desire,
Bore and forbore, and did not tire,
Like Stephen, an unquenched fire.

31

'He heeded not reviling tones,
Nor sold his heart to idle moans,
Tho' cursed and scorn'd, and bruised with
   stones:

'But looking upward, full of grace,
He pray'd, and from a happy place
God's glory smote him on the face.'

The sullen answer slid betwixt:
'Not that the grounds of hope were fix'd,
The elements were kindlier mix'd.'

I said, 'I toil beneath the curse,
But, knowing not the universe,
I fear to slide from bad to worse.

'And that, in seeking to undo
One riddle, and to find the true,
I knit a hundred others new:

'Or that this anguish fleeting hence,
Unmanacled from bonds of sense,
Be fix'd and froz'n to permanence:

'For I go, weak from suffering here:
Naked I go, and void of cheer:
What is it that I may not fear?'

'Consider well,' the voice replied,
'His face, that two hours since hath died;
Wilt thou find passion, pain or pride?

'Will he obey when one commands?
Or answer should one press his hands?
He answers not, nor understands.

'His palms are folded on his breast:
There is no other thing express'd
But long disquiet merged in rest.

'His lips are very mild and meek:
Tho' one should smite him on the cheek,
And on the mouth, he will not speak.

'His little daughter, whose sweet face
He kiss'd, taking his last embrace,
Becomes dishonour to her race—

'His sons grow up that bear his name,
Some grow to honour, some to shame,—
But he is chill to praise or blame.

'He will not hear the north-wind rave,
Nor, moaning, household shelter crave
From winter rains that beat his grave.

'High up the vapours fold and swim:
About him broods the twilight dim:
The place he knew forgetteth him.'

'If all be dark, vague voice,' I said,
'These things are wrapt in doubt and
   dread,
Nor canst thou show the dead are dead.

'The sap dries up: the plant declines.
A deeper tale my heart divines.
Know I not Death? the outward signs?

'I found him when my years were few;
A shadow on the graves I knew,
And darkness in the village yew.

'From grave to grave the shadow crept:
In her still place the morning wept:
Touch'd by his feet the daisy slept.

'The simple senses crown'd his head:
"Omega! thou art Lord," they said,
"We find no motion in the dead."

'Why, if man rot in dreamless ease,
Should that plain fact, as taught by these,
Not make him sure that he shall cease?

'Who forged that other influence,
That heat of inward evidence,
By which he doubts against the sense?

'He owns the fatal gift of eyes,
That read his spirit blindly wise,
Not simple as a thing that dies.

'Here sits he shaping wings to fly:
His heart forebodes a mystery:
He names the name Eternity.

'That type of Perfect in his mind
In Nature can he nowhere find.
He sows himself on every wind.

'He seems to hear a Heavenly Friend,
And thro' thick veils to apprehend
A labour working to an end.

'The end and the beginning vex
His reason: many things perplex,
With motions, checks, and counterchecks.

' He knows a baseness in his blood
At such strange war with something good,
He may not do the thing he would.

'Heaven opens inward, chasms yawn,
Vast images in glimmering dawn,
Half shown, are broken and withdrawn.

'Ah! sure within him and without,
Could his dark wisdom find it out,
There must be answer to his doubt,

'But thou canst answer not again.
With thine own weapon art thou slain,
Or thou wilt answer but in vain.

'The doubt would rest, I dare not solve.
In the same circle we revolve.
Assurance only breeds resolve.'

As when a billow, blown against,
Falls back, the voice with which I fenced
A little ceased, but recommenced.

'Where wert thou when thy father play'd
In his free field, and pastime made,
A merry boy in sun and shade?

'A merry boy they call'd him then,
He sat upon the knees of men
In days that never come again.

'Before the little ducts began
To feed thy bones with lime, and ran
Their course, till thou wert also man:

'Who took a wife, who rear'd his race,
Whose wrinkles gather'd on his face,
Whose troubles number with his days:

'A life of nothings, nothing-worth,
From that first nothing ere his birth
To that last nothing under earth!'

'These words,' I said, 'are like the rest;
No certain clearness, but at best
A vague suspicion of the breast:

'But if I grant, thou mightst defend
The thesis which thy words intend—
That to begin implies to end;

'Yet how should I for certain hold,
Because my memory is so cold,
That I first was in human mould?

'I cannot make this matter plain,
But I would shoot, howe'er in vain,
A random arrow from the brain.

'It may be that no life is found,
Which only to one engine bound
Falls off, but cycles always round.

'As old mythologies relate,
Some draught of Lethe might await
The slipping thro' from state to state.

'As here we find in trances, men
Forget the dream that happens then,
Until they fall in trance again.

'So might we, if our state were such
As one before, remember much,
For those two likes might meet and touch.

'But, if I lapsed from nobler place,
Some legend of a fallen race
Alone might hint of my disgrace;

'Some vague emotion of delight
In gazing up an Alpine height,
Some yearning toward the lamps of night;

'Or if thro' lower lives I came—
Tho' all experience past became
Consolidate in mind and frame—

'I might forget my weaker lot;
For is not our first year forgot?
The haunts of memory echo not.

'And men, whose reason long was blind,
From cells of madness unconfined,
Oft lose whole years of darker mind.

'Much more, if first I floated free,
As naked essence, must I be
Incompetent of memory:

'For memory dealing but with time,
And he with matter, could she climb
Beyond her own material prime?

'Moreover, something is or seems,
That touches me with mystic gleams,
Like glimpses of forgotten dreams—

'Of something felt, like something here;
Of something done, I know not where;
Such as no language may declare.'

The still voice laugh'd. 'I talk,' said he
'Not with thy dreams. Suffice it thee
Thy pain is a reality.'

'But thou,' said I, 'hast missed thy mark,
Who sought'st to wreck my mortal ark,
By making all the horizon dark.

'Why not set forth, if I should do
This rashness, that which might ensue
With this old soul in organs new?

'Whatever crazy sorrow saith,
No life that breathes with human breath
Has ever truly long'd for death.

''Tis life, whereof our nerves are scant,
Oh life, not death, for which we pant;
More life, and fuller, that I want.'

I ceased, and sat as one forlorn.
Then said the voice, in quiet scorn,
'Behold, it is the Sabbath morn.'

And I arose, and I released
The casement, and the light increased
With freshness in the dawning east.

Like soften'd airs that blowing steal,
When meres begin to uncongeal,
The sweet church bells began to peal.

On to God's house the people prest:
Passing the place where each must rest,
Each enter'd like a welcome guest.

One walk'd between his wife and child,
With measured footfall firm and mild,
And now and then he gravely smiled.

The prudent partner of his blood
Lean'd on him, faithful, gentle, good,
Wearing the rose of womanhood.

And in their double love secure,
The little maiden walk'd demure,
Pacing with downward eyelids pure.

These three made unity so sweet,
My frozen heart began to beat,
Remembering its ancient heat.

I blest them, and they wander'd on:
I spoke, but answer came there none:
The dull and bitter voice was gone.

A second voice was at mine ear,
A little whisper silver-clear,
A murmur, 'Be of better cheer.'

As from some blissful neighbourhood,
A notice faintly understood,
'I see the end, and know the good.'

A little hint to solace woe,
A hint, a whisper breathing low,
'I may not speak of what I know.'

Like an Æolian harp that wakes
No certain air, but overtakes
Far thought with music that it makes:

Such seem'd the whisper at my side:
'What is it thou knowest, sweet voice?' I
    cried.
'A hidden hope,' the voice replied:

So heavenly-toned, that in that hour
From out my sullen heart a power
Broke, like the rainbow from the shower,

To feel, altho' no tongue can prove,
That every cloud, that spreads above
And veileth love, itself is love.

And forth into the fields I went,
And Nature's living motion lent
The pulse of hope to discontent.

I wonder'd at the bounteous hours,
The slow result of winter showers:
You scarce could see the grass for flowers.

I wonder'd, while I paced along:
The woods were fill'd so full with song,
There seem'd no room for sense of wrong;

And all so variously wrought,
I marvell'd how the mind was brought
To anchor by one gloomy thought;

And wherefore rather I made choice
To commune with that barren voice,
Than him that said, 'Rejoice! Rejoice!'

THE MILLER'S DAUGHTER

I see the wealthy miller yet,
  His double chin, his portly size,
And who that knew him could forget
  The busy wrinkles round his eyes?
The slow wise smile that, round about
  His dusty forehead drily curl'd,
Seem'd half-within and half-without,
  And full of dealings with the world?

In yonder chair I see him sit,
  Three fingers round the old silver cup—
I see his gray eyes twinkle yet
  At his own jest—gray eyes lit up
With summer lightnings of a soul
  So full of summer warmth, so glad,
So healthy, sound, and clear and whole,
  His memory scarce can make me sad.

Yet fill my glass: give me one kiss:
  My own sweet Alice, we must die.
There's somewhat in this world amiss
  Shall be unriddled by and by.
There's somewhat flows to us in life,
  But more is taken quite away.
Pray, Alice, pray, my darling wife,
  That we may die the self-same day.

Have I not found a happy earth?
  I least should breathe a thought of pain.
Would God renew me from my birth
  I'd almost live my life again.
So sweet it seems with thee to walk,
  And once again to woo thee mine—
It seems in after-dinner talk
  Across the walnuts and the wine—

To be the long and listless boy
  Late-left an orphan of the squire,
Where this old mansion mounted high
  Looks down upon the village spire:
For even here, where I and you
  Have lived and loved alone so long,
Each morn my sleep was broken thro'
  By some wild skylark's matin song.

And oft I heard the tender dove
  In firry woodlands making moan;
But ere I saw your eyes, my love,
  I had no motion of my own.
For scarce my life with fancy play'd
  Before I dream'd that pleasant dream—
Still hither thither idly sway'd
  Like those long mosses in the stream.

Or from the bridge I lean'd to hear
  The milldam rushing down with noise,
And see the minnows everywhere
  In crystal eddies glance and poise
The tall flag-flowers when they sprung
  Below the range of stepping-stones,
Or those three chestnuts near, that hung
  In masses thick with milky cones.

But, Alice, what an hour was that,
  When after roving in the woods
('Twas April then), I came and sat
  Below the chestnuts, when their buds
Were glistening to the breezy blue;
  And on the slope, an absent fool,
I cast me down, nor thought of you,
  But angled in the higher pool.

A love-song I had somewhere read,
  An echo from a measured strain,
Beat time to nothing in my head
  From some odd corner of the brain.
It haunted me, the morning long,
  With weary sameness in the rhymes,
The phantom of a silent song,
  That went and came a thousand times.

Then leapt a trout. In lazy mood
  I watch'd the little circles die;
They past into the level flood,
  And there a vision caught my eye;
The reflex of a beauteous form,
  A glowing arm, a gleaming neck,
As when a sunbeam wavers warm
  Within the dark and dimpled beck.

For you remember, you had set,
  That morning, on the casement-edge
A long green box of mignonette,
  And you were leaning from the ledge
And when I raised my eyes, above
  They met with two so full and bright—
Such eyes! I swear to you, my love,
  That these have never lost their light.

I loved, and love dispell'd the fear
  That I should die an early death:
For love possess'd the atmosphere,
  And fill'd the breast with purer breath.
My mother thought, What ails the boy?
  For I was alter'd, and began
To move about the house with joy,
  And with the certain step of man.

I loved the brimming wave that swam
  Thro' quiet meadows round the mill,
The sleepy pool above the dam,
  The pool beneath it never still,
The meal-sacks on the whiten'd floor,
  The dark round of the dripping wheel,
The very air about the door
  Made misty with the floating meal.

And oft in ramblings on the wold,
  When April nights began to blow,
And April's crescent glimmer'd cold,
  I saw the village lights below;
I knew your taper far away,
  And full at heart of trembling hope,
From off the wold I came, and lay
  Upon the freshly-flower'd slope.

The deep brook groan'd beneath the mill;
  And 'by that lamp,' I thought, 'she sits!'
The white chalk-quarry from the hill
  Gleam'd to the flying moon by fits.
'O that I were beside her now!
  O will she answer if I call?
O would she give me vow for vow,
  Sweet Alice, if I told her all?'

Sometimes I saw you sit and spin;
  And, in the pauses of the wind,
Sometimes I heard you sing within;
  Sometimes your shadow cross'd the
    blind.
At last you rose and moved the light,
  And the long shadow of the chair
Flitted across into the night,
  And all the casement darken'd there.

But when at last I dared to speak,
  The lanes, you know, were white with
    may, •
Your ripe lips moved not, but your cheek
  Flush'd like the coming of the day;
And so it was—half-sly, half-shy,
  You would, and would not, little one!
Although I pleaded tenderly,
  And you and I were all alone.

And slowly was my mother brought
  To yield consent to my desire:
She wish'd me happy, but she thought
  I might have look'd a little higher;
And I was young—too young to wed:
  'Yet must I love her for your sake;
Go fetch your Alice here,' she said:
  Her eyelid quiver'd as she spake.

And down I went to fetch my bride:
  But, Alice, you were ill at ease;
This dress and that by turns you tried,
  Too fearful that you should not please.

I loved you better for your fears,
  I knew you could not look but well;
And dews, that would have fall'n in tears,
  I kiss'd away before they fell.

I watch'd the little flutterings,
  The doubt my mother would not see;
She spoke at large of many things,
  And at the last she spoke of me;
And turning look'd upon your face,
  As near this door you sat apart,
And rose, and, with a silent grace
  Approaching, press'd you heart to heart.

Ah, well—but sing the foolish song
  I gave you, Alice, on the day
When, arm in arm, we went along,
  A pensive pair, and you were gay
With bridal flowers—that I may seem,
  As in the nights of old, to lie
Beside the mill-wheel in the stream,
  While those full chestnuts whisper by.

  It is the miller's daughter,
    And she is grown so dear, so dear,
  That I would be the jewel
    That trembles in her ear:
  For hid in ringlets day and night,
  I'd touch her neck so warm and white.

  And I would be the girdle
    About her dainty dainty waist,
  And her heart would beat against me,
    In sorrow and in rest:
  And I should know if it beat right,
  I'd clasp it round so close and tight.

  And I would be the necklace,
    And all day long to fall and rise
  Upon her balmy bosom,
    With her laughter or her sighs,
  And I would lie so light, so light,
  I scarce should be unclasp'd at night.

A trifle, sweet! which true love spells—
  True love interprets—right alone.
His light upon the letter dwells,
  For all the spirit is his own.
So, if I waste words now, in truth
  You must blame Love. His early rage
Had force to make me rhyme in youth,
  And makes me talk too much in age.

And now those vivid hours are gone,
  Like mine own life to me thou art,
Where Past and Present, wound in one,
  Do make a garland for the heart:

So sing that other song I made,
Half-anger'd with my happy lot,
The day, when in the chestnut shade
I found the blue Forget-me-not.

> Love that hath us in the net,
> Can he pass, and we forget?
> Many suns arise and set.
> Many a chance the years beget.
> Love the gift is Love the debt.
> Even so.
> Love is hurt with jar and fret.
> Love is made a vague regret.
> Eyes with idle tears are wet.
> Idle habit links us yet.
> What is love? for we forget:
> Ah, no! no!

Look thro' mine eyes with thine. True
wife,
Round my true heart thine arms entwine
My other dearer life in life,
Look thro' my very soul with thine!
Untouch'd with any shade of years,
May those kind eyes for ever dwell!
They have not shed a many tears,
Dear eyes, since first I knew them well.

Yet tears they shed: they had their part
Of sorrow: for when time was ripe,
The still affection of the heart
Became an outward breathing type,
That into stillness past again,
And left a want unknown before;
Although the loss had brought us pain,
That loss but made us love the more,

With farther lookings on. The kiss,
The woven arms, seem but to be
Weak symbols of the settled bliss,
The comfort, I have found in thee:
But that God bless thee, dear—who
wrought
Two spirits to one equal mind—
With blessings beyond hope or thought,
With blessings which no words can find.

Arise, and let us wander forth,
To yon old mill across the wolds;
For look, the sunset, south and north,
Winds all the vale in rosy folds,
And fires your narrow casement glass,
Touching the sullen pool below:
On the chalk-hill the bearded grass
Is dry and dewless. Let us go.

FATIMA

O Love, Love, Love! O withering might!
O sun, that from thy noonday height
Shudderest when I strain my sight,
Throbbing thro' all thy heat and light,
Lo, falling from my constant mind,
Lo, parch'd and wither'd, deaf and blind,
I whirl like leaves in roaring wind.

Last night I wasted hateful hours
Below the city's eastern towers:
I thirsted for the brooks, the showers:
I roll'd among the tender flowers:
I crush'd them on my breast, my mouth;
I look'd athwart the burning drouth
Of that long desert to the south.

Last night, when some one spoke his
name,
From my swift blood that went and came
A thousand little shafts of flame
Were shiver'd in my narrow frame.
O Love, O fire! once he drew
With one long kiss my whole soul thro'
My lips, as sunlight drinketh dew.

Before he mounts the hill, I know
He cometh quickly: from below
Sweet gales, as from deep gardens, blow
Before him, striking on my brow.
In my dry brain my spirit soon,
Down-deepening from swoon to swoon,
Faints like a dazzled morning moon.

The wind sounds like a silver wire,
And from beyond the noon a fire
Is pour'd upon the hills, and nigher
The skies stoop down in their desire;
And, isled in sudden seas of light,
My heart, pierced thro' with fierce
delight,
Bursts into blossom in his sight.

My whole soul waiting silently,
All naked in a sultry sky,
Droops blinded with his shining eye:
I *will* possess him or will die.
I will grow round him in his place,
Grow, live, die looking on his face,
Die, dying clasp'd in his embrace.

ŒNONE

THERE lies a vale in Ida, lovelier
Than all the valleys of Ionian hills.
The swimming vapour slopes athwart the
glen,
Puts forth an arm, and creeps from pine to
pine,
And loiters, slowly drawn. On either hand
The lawns and meadow-ledges midway
down
Hang rich in flowers, and far below them
roars
The long brook falling thro' the clov'n
ravine
In cataract after cataract to the sea.
Behind the valley topmost Gargarus
Stands up and takes the morning: but in
front
The gorges, opening wide apart, reveal
Troas and Ilion's column'd citadel,
The crown of Troas.
    Hither came at noon
Mournful Œnone, wandering forlorn
Of Paris, once her playmate on the hills.
Her cheek had lost the rose, and round her
neck
Floated her hair or seem'd to float in rest.
She, leaning on a fragment twined with
vine,
Sang to the stillness, till the mountain-
shade
Sloped downward to her seat from the upper
cliff.

'O mother Ida, many-fountain'd Ida,
Dear mother Ida, harken ere I die.
For now the noonday quiet holds the hill:
The grasshopper is silent in the grass:
The lizard, with his shadow on the stone,
Rests like a shadow, and the winds are
dead.
The purple flower droops: the golden bee
Is lily-cradled: I alone awake.
My eyes are full of tears, my heart of love,
My heart is breaking, and my eyes are dim,
And I am all aweary of my life.

'O mother Ida, many-fountain'd Ida,
Dear mother Ida, harken ere I die.
Hear me, O Earth, hear me, O Hills, O
Caves

That house the cold crown'd snake! O
mountain brooks,
I am the daughter of a River-God,
Hear me, for I will speak, and build up all
My sorrow with my song, as yonder walls
Rose slowly to a music slowly breathed,
A cloud that gather'd shape: for it may be
That, while I speak of it, a little while
My heart may wander from its deeper woe.

'O mother Ida, many-fountain'd Ida,
Dear mother Ida, harken ere I die.
I waited underneath the dawning hills,
Aloft the mountain lawn was dewy-dark,
And dewy dark aloft the mountain pine:
Beautiful Paris, evil-hearted Paris,
Leading a jet-black goat white-horn'd,
white-hooved,
Came up from reedy Simois all alone.

'O mother Ida, harken ere I die.
Far-off the torrent call'd me from the cleft:
Far up the solitary morning smote
The streaks of virgin snow. With down-
dropt eyes
I sat alone: white-breasted like a star
Fronting the dawn he moved; a leopard
skin
Droop'd from his shoulder, but his sunny
hair
Cluster'd about his temples like a God's:
And his cheek brighten'd as the foam-bow
brightens
When the wind blows the foam, and all my
heart
Went forth to embrace him coming ere he
came.

'Dear mother Ida, harken ere I die.
He smiled, and opening out his milk-white
palm
Disclosed a fruit of pure Hesperian gold,
That smelt ambrosially, and while I look'd
And listen'd, the full-flowing river of
speech
Came down upon my heart.
    '"My own Œnone,
Beautiful-brow'd Œnone, my own soul,
Behold this fruit, whose gleaming rind in-
grav'n
'For the most fair,' would seem to award it
thine,

38

As lovelier than whatever Oread haunt
The knolls of Ida, loveliest in all grace
Of movement, and the charm of married
　　brows."

'Dear mother Ida, harken ere I die.
He prest the blossom of his lips to mine,
And added "This was cast upon the board,
When all the full-faced presence of the
　　Gods
Ranged in the halls of Peleus; whereupon
Rose feud, with question unto whom 'twere
　　due:
But light-foot Iris brought it yester-eve,
Delivering, that to me, by common voice
Elected umpire, Herè comes to-day,
Pallas and Aphroditè, claiming each
This meed of fairest. Thou, within the
　　cave
Behind yon whispering tuft of oldest pine,
Mayst well behold them unbeheld, unheard
Hear all, and see thy Paris judge of Gods."

'Dear mother Ida, harken ere I die.
It was the deep midnoon: one silvery cloud
Had lost his way between the piney sides
Of this long glen. Then to the bower they
　　came,
Naked they came to that smooth-swarded
　　bower,
And at their feet the crocus brake like fire,
Violet, amaracus, and asphodel,
Lotos and lilies: and a wind arose,
And overhead the wandering ivy and vine,
This way and that, in many a wild festoon
Ran riot, garlanding the gnarled boughs
With bunch and berry and flower thro'
　　and thro'.

'O mother Ida, harken ere I die.
On the tree-tops a crested peacock lit,
And o'er him flow'd a golden cloud, and
　　lean'd
Upon him, slowly dropping fragrant dew.
Then first I heard the voice of her, to
　　whom
Coming thro' Heaven, like a light that
　　grows
Larger and clearer, with one mind the Gods
Rise up for reverence. She to Paris made
Proffer of royal power, ample rule

Unquestion'd, overflowing revenue
Wherewith to embellish state, "from many
　　a vale
And river-sunder'd champaign clothed
　　with corn,
Or labour'd mine undrainable of ore.
Honour," she said, "and homage, tax and
　　toll,
From many an inland town and haven
　　large,
Mast-throng'd beneath her shadowing
　　citadel
In glassy bays among her tallest towers."

'O mother Ida, harken ere I die.
Still she spake on and still she spake of
　　power,
"Which in all action is the end of all;
Power fitted to the season; wisdom-bred
And throned of wisdom—from all neigh-
　　bour crowns
Alliance and allegiance, till thy hand
Fail from the sceptre-staff. Such boon
　　from me,
From me, Heaven's Queen, Paris, to thee
　　king-born,
A shepherd all thy life but yet king-born,
Should come most welcome, seeing men,
　　in power
Only, are likest gods, who have attain'd
Rest in a happy place and quiet seats
Above the thunder, with undying bliss
In knowledge of their own supremacy."

'Dear mother Ida, harken ere I die.
She ceased, and Paris held the costly fruit
Out at arm's-length, so much the thought
　　of power
Flatter'd his spirit; but Pallas where she
　　stood
Somewhat apart, her clear and bared limbs
O'erthwarted with the brazen-headed spear
Upon her pearly shoulder leaning cold,
The while, above, her full and earnest eye
Over her snow-cold breast and angry cheek
Kept watch, waiting decision, made reply.

　　"'Self-reverence, self-knowledge, self-
　　control,
These three alone lead life to sovereign
　　power.

Yet not for power (power of herself
Would come uncall'd for) but to live by
   law,
Acting the law we live by without fear;
And, because right is right, to follow right
Were wisdom in the scorn of consequence."

  'Dear mother Ida, harken ere I die.
Again she said: "I woo thee not with gifts.
Sequel of guerdon could not alter me
To fairer. Judge thou me by what I am,
So shalt thou find me fairest.
              Yet, indeed,
If gazing on divinity disrobed
Thy mortal eyes are frail to judge of fair,
Unbias'd by self-profit, oh! rest thee sure
That I shall love thee well and cleave to
   thee,
So that my vigour, wedded to thy blood,
Shall strike within thy pulses, like a God's,
To push thee forward thro' a life of shocks,
Dangers, and deeds, until endurance grow
Sinew'd with action, and the full-grown
   will,
Circled thro' all experiences, pure law,
Commeasure perfect freedom."
            'Here she ceas'd,
And Paris ponder'd, and I cried, "O Paris,
Give it to Pallas!" but he heard me not,
Or hearing would not hear me, woe is me!

  'O mother Ida, many-fountain'd Ida,
Dear mother Ida, harken ere I die.
Idalian Aphroditè beautiful,
Fresh as the foam, new-bathed in Paphian
   wells,
With rosy slender fingers backward drew
From her warm brows and bosom her deep
   hair
Ambrosial, golden round her lucid throat
And shoulder: from the violets her light foot
Shone rosy-white, and o'er her rounded
   form
Between the shadows of the vine-bunches
Floated the glowing sunlights, as she
   moved.

  'Dear mother Ida, harken ere I die.
She with a subtle smile in her mild eyes,
The herald of her triumph, drawing nigh
Half-whisper'd in his ear, "I promise thee

The fairest and most loving wife in Greece,"
She spoke and laugh'd: I shut my sight for
   fear:
But when I look'd, Paris had raised his arm,
And I beheld great Herè's angry eyes,
As she withdrew into the golden cloud,
And I was left alone within the bower;
And from that time to this I am alone,
And I shall be alone until I die.

  'Yet, mother Ida, harken ere I die.
Fairest—why fairest wife? am I not fair?
My love hath told me so a thousand times.
Methinks I must be fair, for yesterday,
When I past by, a wild and wanton pard,
Eyed like the evening star, with playful tail
Crouch'd fawning in the weed. Most loving
   is she?
Ah me, my mountain shepherd, that my
   arms
Were wound about thee, and my hot lips
   prest
Close, close to thine in that quick-falling
   dew
Of fruitful kisses, thick as Autumn rains
Flash in the pools of whirling Simois.

  'O mother, hear me yet before I die.
They came, they cut away my tallest pines,
My tall dark pines, that plumed the craggy
   ledge
High over the blue gorge, and all between
The snowy peak and snow-white cataract
Foster'd the callow eaglet—from beneath
Whose thick mysterious boughs in the dark
   morn
The panther's roar came muffled, while I
   sat
Low in the valley. Never, never more
Shall lone Œnone see the morning mist
Sweep thro' them; never see them over-
   laid
With narrow moon-lit slips of silver cloud,
Between the loud stream and the trembling
   stars.

  'O mother, hear me yet before I die.
I wish that somewhere in the ruin'd folds,
Among the fragments tumbled from the
   glens,
Or the dry thickets, I could meet with her

The Abominable, that uninvited came
Into the fair Peleïan banquet-hall,
And cast the golden fruit upon the board,
And bred this change; that I might speak
    my mind,
And tell her to her face how much I hate
Her presence, hated both of Gods and men.

'O mother, hear me yet before I die.
Hath he not sworn his love a thousand
    times,
In this green valley, under this green hill,
Ev'n on this hand, and sitting on this stone?
Seal'd it with kisses? water'd it with tears?
O happy tears, and how unlike to these!
O happy Heaven, how canst thou see my
    face?
O happy earth, how canst thou bear my
    weight?
O death, death, death, thou ever-floating
    cloud,
There are enough unhappy on this earth,
Pass by the happy souls, that love to live:
I pray thee, pass before my light of life,
And shadow all my soul, that I may die.
Thou weighest heavy on the heart within,
Weigh heavy on my eyelids: let me die.

'O mother, hear me yet before I die.
I will not die alone, for fiery thoughts
Do shape themselves within me, more and
    more,
Whereof I catch the issue, as I hear
Dead sounds at night come from the in-
    most hills,
Like footsteps upon wool. I dimly see
My far-off doubtful purpose, as a mother
Conjectures of the features of her child
Ere it is born: her child!—a shudder comes
Across me: never child be born of me,
Unblest, to vex me with his father's eyes!

'O mother, hear me yet before I die.
Hear me, O earth. I will not die alone,
Lest their shrill happy laughter come to
    me
Walking the cold and starless road of
    Death
Uncomforted, leaving my ancient love
With the Greek woman. I will rise and go
Down into Troy, and ere the stars come
    forth

Talk with the wild Cassandra, for she says
A fire dances before her, and a sound
Rings ever in her ears of armèd men.
What this may be I know not, but I know
That, wheresoe'er I am by night and day,
All earth and air seem only burning fire.'

THE SISTERS

We were two daughters of one race:
She was the fairest in the face:
    The wind is blowing in turret and tree.
They were together, and she fell;
Therefore revenge became me well.
    O the Earl was fair to see!

She died: she went to burning flame:
She mix'd her ancient blood with shame.
    The wind is howling in turret and tree.
Whole weeks and months, and early and
    late,
To win his love I lay in wait:
    O the Earl was fair to see!

I made a feast; I bad him come;
I won his love, I brought him home.
    The wind is roaring in turret and tree.
And after supper, on a bed,
Upon my lap he laid his head:
    O the Earl was fair to see!

I kiss'd his eyelids into rest:
His ruddy cheek upon my breast.
    The wind is raging in turret and tree.
I hated him with the hate of hell,
But I loved his beauty passing well.
    O the Earl was fair to see!

I rose up in the silent night:
I made my dagger sharp and bright.
    The wind is raving in turret and tree.
As half-asleep his breath he drew,
Three times I stabb'd him thro' and thro'.
    O the Earl was fair to see!

I curl'd and comb'd his comely head,
He look'd so grand when he was dead.
    The wind is blowing in turret and tree.
I wrapt his body in the sheet,
And laid him at his mother's feet.
    O the Earl was fair to see!

TO ——

WITH THE FOLLOWING POEM

I SEND you here a sort of allegory,
(For you will understand it) of a soul,
A sinful soul possess'd of many gifts,
A spacious garden full of flowering weeds,
A glorious Devil, large in heart and brain,
That did love Beauty only, (Beauty seen
In all varieties of mould and mind)
And Knowledge for its beauty; or if Good,
Good only for its beauty, seeing not
That Beauty, Good, and Knowledge, are
    three sisters
That doat upon each other, friends to man,
Living together under the same roof,
And never can be sunder'd without tears.
And he that shuts Love out, in turn shall
    be
Shut out from Love, and on her threshold
    lie
Howling in outer darkness. Not for this
Was common clay ta'en from the common
    earth
Moulded by God, and temper'd with the
    tears
Of angels to the perfect shape of man.

THE PALACE OF ART

I BUILT my soul a lordly pleasure-house,
    Wherein at ease for aye to dwell.
I said, 'O Soul, make merry and carouse,
    Dear soul, for all is well.'

A huge crag-platform, smooth as burnish'd
    brass
I chose. The ranged ramparts bright
From level meadow-bases of deep grass
    Suddenly scaled the light.

Thereon I built it firm. Of ledge or shelf
    The rock rose clear, or winding stair.
My soul would live alone unto herself
    In her high palace there.

And 'while the world runs round and
    round,' I said,
    'Reign thou apart, a quiet king,
Still as, while Saturn whirls, his stedfast
    shade
    Sleeps on his luminous ring.'

To which my soul made answer readily:
    'Trust me, in bliss I shall abide
In this great mansion, that is built for me,
    So royal-rich and wide.'

* * * *
* * * *

Four courts I made, East, West and South
    and North,
    In each a squared lawn, wherefrom
The golden gorge of dragons spouted forth
    A flood of fountain-foam.

And round the cool green courts there ran
    a row
    Of cloisters, branch'd like mighty woods,
Echoing all night to that sonorous flow
    Of spouted fountain-floods.

And round the roofs a gilded gallery
    That lent broad verge to distant lands,
Far as the wild swan wings, to where the
    sky
    Dipt down to sea and sands.

From those four jets four currents in one
    swell
    Across the mountain stream'd below
In misty folds, that floating as they fell
    Lit up a torrent-bow.

And high on every peak a statue seem'd
    To hang on tiptoe, tossing up
A cloud of incense of all odour steam'd
    From out a golden cup.

So that she thought, 'And who shall gaze
    upon
    My palace with unblinded eyes,
While this great bow will waver in the sun,
    And that sweet incense rise?'

For that sweet incense rose and never
    fail'd,
    And, while day sank or mounted higher
The light aërial gallery, golden-rail'd,
    Burnt like a fringe of fire.

Likewise the deep-set windows, stain'd and
    traced,
    Would seem slow-flaming crimson fires
From shadow'd grots of arches interlaced,
    And tipt with frost-like spires.

* * * *

* * * *

Full of long-sounding corridors it was,
  That over-vaulted grateful gloom,
Thro' which the livelong day my soul did
    pass,
    Well-pleased, from room to room.

Full of great rooms and small the palace
    stood,
  All various, each a perfect whole
From living Nature, fit for every mood
  And change of my still soul.

For some were hung with arras green and
    blue,
  Showing a gaudy summer-morn,
Where with puff'd cheek the belted hunter
    blew
    His wreathed bugle-horn.

One seem'd all dark and red—a tract of
    sand,
  And some one pacing there alone,
Who paced for ever in a glimmering land,
  Lit with a low large moon.

One show'd an iron coast and angry waves.
  You seem'd to hear them climb and
    fall
And roar rock-thwarted under bellowing
    caves,
    Beneath the windy wall.

And one, a full-fed river winding slow
  By herds upon an endless plain,
The ragged rims of thunder brooding low,
  With shadow-streaks of rain.

And one, the reapers at their sultry toil.
  In front they bound the sheaves. Behind
Were realms of upland, prodigal in oil,
  And hoary to the wind.

And one a foreground black with stones
    and slags,
  Beyond, a line of heights, and higher
All barr'd with long white cloud the scorn-
    ful crags,
    And highest, snow and fire.

And one, an English home—gray twilight
    pour'd
  On dewy pastures, dewy trees,
Softer than sleep—all things in order
    stored,
    A haunt of ancient Peace.

Nor these alone, but every landscape fair,
  As fit for every mood of mind,
Or gay, or grave, or sweet, or stern, was
    there
    Not less than truth design'd.

* * * *

* * * *

Or the maid-mother by a crucifix,
  In tracts of pasture sunny-warm,
Beneath branch-work of costly sardonyx
  Sat smiling, babe in arm.

Or in a clear-wall'd city on the sea,
  Near gilded organ-pipes, her hair
Wound with white roses, slept St. Cecily;
  An angel look'd at her.

Or thronging all one porch of Paradise
  A group of Houris bow'd to see
The dying Islamite, with hands and eyes
  That said, We wait for thee.

Or mythic Uther's deeply-wounded son
  In some fair space of sloping greens
Lay, dozing in the vale of Avalon
  And watch'd by weeping queens.

Or hollowing one hand against his ear,
  To list a foot-fall, ere he saw
The wood-nymph, stay'd the Ausonian
    king to hear
    Of wisdom and of law.

Or over hills with peaky tops engrail'd,
  And many a tract of palm and rice,
The throne of Indian Cama slowly sail'd
  A summer fann'd with spice.

Or sweet Europa's mantle blew unclasp'd,
  From off her shoulder backward borne:
From one hand droop'd a crocus: one hand
    grasp'd
    The mild bull's golden horn.

Or else flush'd Ganymede, his rosy thigh
   Half-buried in the Eagle's down,
Sole as a flying star shot thro' the sky
   Above the pillar'd town.

Nor these alone: but every legend fair
   Which the supreme Caucasian mind
Carved out of Nature for itself, was there,
   Not less than life, design'd.

      *   *   *   *
      *   *   *   *

Then in the towers I placed great bells
   that swung,
   Moved of themselves, with silver sound;
And with choice paintings of wise men I
   hung
   The royal dais round.

For there was Milton like a seraph strong,
   Beside him Shakespeare bland and mild;
And there the world-worn Dante grasp'd
   his song,
   And somewhat grimly smiled.

And there the Ionian father of the rest;
   A million wrinkles carved his skin;
A hundred winters snow'd upon his breast,
   From cheek and throat and chin.

Above, the fair hall-ceiling stately-set
   Many an arch high up did lift,
And angels rising and descending met
   With interchange of gift.

Below was all mosaic choicely plann'd
   With cycles of the human tale
Of this wide world, the times of every land
   So wrought, they will not fail.

The people here, a beast of burden slow,
   Toil'd onward, prick'd with goads and
   stings;
Here play'd, a tiger, rolling to and fro
   The heads and crowns of kings;

Here rose, an athlete, strong to break or
   bind
All force in bonds that might endure,
And here once more like some sick man
   declined,
   And trusted any cure.

But over these she trod: and those great
   bells
   Began to chime. She took her throne:
She sat betwixt the shining Oriels,
   To sing her songs alone.

And thro' the topmost Oriels' coloured
   flame
   Two godlike faces gazed below;
Plato the wise, and large-brow'd Verulam,
   The first of those who know.

And all those names, that in their motion
   were
   Full-welling fountain-heads of change,
Betwixt the slender shafts were blazon'd
   fair
   In diverse raiment strange:

Thro' which the lights, rose, amber,
   emerald, blue,
   Flush'd in her temples and her eyes,
And from her lips, as morn from Memnon,
   drew
   Rivers of melodies.

No nightingale delighteth to prolong
   Her low preamble all alone,
More than my soul to hear her echo'd
   song
   Throb thro' the ribbed stone;

Singing and murmuring in her feastful
   mirth,
   Joying to feel herself alive,
Lord over Nature, Lord of the visible
   earth,
   Lord of the senses five;

Communing with herself: 'All these are
   mine,
   And let the world have peace or wars,
'Tis one to me.' She—when young night
   divine
   Crown'd dying day with stars,

Making sweet close of his delicious toils—
   Lit light in wreaths and anadems,
And pure quintessences of precious oils
   In hollow'd moons of gems,

To mimic heaven; and clapt her hands
  and cried,
'I marvel if my still delight
In this great house so royal-rich, and wide,
  Be flatter'd to the height.

'O all things fair to sate my various eyes!
  O shapes and hues that please me well!
O silent faces of the Great and Wise,
  My Gods, with whom I dwell!

'O God-like isolation which art mine,
  I can but count thee perfect gain,
What time I watch the darkening droves of
  swine
  That range on yonder plain.

'In filthy sloughs they roll a prurient skin,
  They graze and wallow, breed and sleep;
And oft some brainless devil enters in,
  And drives them to the deep.'

Then of the moral instinct would she prate
  And of the rising from the dead,
As hers by right of full-accomplish'd Fate;
  And at the last she said:

'I take possession of man's mind and deed.
  I care not what the sects may brawl.
I sit as God holding no form of creed,
  But contemplating all.'

  * * * *
  * * * *

Full oft the riddle of the painful earth
  Flash'd thro' her as she sat alone,
Yet not the less held she her solemn mirth,
  And intellectual throne.

And so she throve and prosper'd: so three
  years
  She prosper'd: on the fourth she fell,
Like Herod, when the shout was in his ears,
  Struck thro' with pangs of hell.

Lest she should fail and perish utterly,
  God, before whom ever lie bare
The abysmal deeps of Personality,
  Plagued her with sore despair.

When she would think, where'er she turn'd
  her sight
The airy hand confusion wrought,

Wrote, 'Mene, mene,' and divided quite
  The kingdom of her thought.

Deep dread and loathing of her solitude
  Fell on her, from which mood was born
Scorn of herself; again, from out that
  mood
  Laughter at her self-scorn.

'What! is not this my place of strength,'
  she said,
  'My spacious mansion built for me,
Whereof the strong foundation-stones were
  laid
  Since my first memory?'

But in dark corners of her palace stood
  Uncertain shapes; and unawares
On white-eyed phantasms weeping tears
  of blood,
  And horrible nightmares,

And hollow shades enclosing hearts of
  flame,
  And, with dim fretted foreheads all,
On corpses three-months-old at noon she
  came,
  That stood against the wall.

A spot of dull stagnation, without light
  Or power of movement, seem'd my soul,
'Mid onward-sloping motions infinite
  Making for one sure goal.

A still salt pool, lock'd in with bars of sand,
  Left on the shore; that hears all night
The plunging seas draw backward from
  the land
  Their moon-led waters white.

A star that with the choral starry dance
  Join'd not, but stood, and standing saw
The hollow orb of moving Circumstance
  Roll'd round by one fix'd law.

Back on herself her serpent pride had
  curl'd.
  'No voice,' she shriek'd in that lone hall,
'No voice breaks thro' the stillness of this
  world:
  One deep, deep silence all!'

She, mouldering with the dull earth's
  mouldering sod,
Inwrapt tenfold in slothful shame,
Lay there exiled from eternal God,
  Lost to her place and name;

And death and life she hated equally,
  And nothing saw, for her despair,
But dreadful time, dreadful eternity,
  No comfort anywhere;

Remaining utterly confused with fears,
  And ever worse with growing time,
And ever unrelieved by dismal tears,
  And all alone in crime:

Shut up as in a crumbling tomb, girt round
  With blackness as a solid wall,
Far off she seem'd to hear the dully sound
  Of human footsteps fall.

As in strange lands a traveller walking slow,
  In doubt and great perplexity,
A little before moon-rise hears the low
  Moan of an unknown sea;

And knows not if it be thunder, or a sound
  Of rocks thrown down, or one deep cry
Of great wild beasts; then thinketh, 'I have
  found
  A new land, but I die.'

She howl'd aloud, 'I am on fire within.
  There comes no murmur of reply.
What is it that will take away my sin,
  And save me lest I die?'

So when four years were wholly finished,
  She threw her royal robes away.
'Make me a cottage in the vale,' she said,
  'Where I may mourn and pray.

'Yet pull not down my palace towers, that are
  So lightly, beautifully built:
Perchance I may return with others there
  When I have purged my guilt.'

LADY CLARA VERE DE VERE

Lady Clara Vere de Vere,
  Of me you shall not win renown:
You thought to break a country heart
  For pastime, ere you went to town.

At me you smiled, but unbeguiled
  I saw the snare, and I retired:
The daughter of a hundred Earls,
  You are not one to be desired.

Lady Clara Vere de Vere,
  I know you proud to bear your name,
Your pride is yet no mate for mine,
  Too proud to care from whence I came.
Nor would I break for your sweet sake
  A heart that doats on truer charms.
A simple maiden in her flower
  Is worth a hundred coats-of-arms.

Lady Clara Vere de Vere,
  Some meeker pupil you must find,
For were you queen of all that is,
  I could not stoop to such a mind.
You sought to prove how I could love,
  And my disdain is my reply.
The lion on your old stone gates
  Is not more cold to you than I.

Lady Clara Vere de Vere,
  You put strange memories in my head.
Not thrice your branching limes have
  blown
Since I beheld young Laurence dead.
Oh your sweet eyes, your low replies:
  A great enchantress you may be;
But there was that across his throat
  Which you had hardly cared to see.

Lady Clara Vere de Vere,
  When thus he met his mother's view,
She had the passions of her kind,
  She spake some certain truths of you.
Indeed I heard one bitter word
  That scarce is fit for you to hear;
Her manners had not that repose
  Which stamps the caste of Vere de Vere.

Lady Clara Vere de Vere,
  There stands a spectre in your hall:
The guilt of blood is at your door:
  You changed a wholesome heart to gall.
You held your course without remorse,
  To make him trust his modest worth,
And, last, you fix'd a vacant stare,
  And slew him with your noble birth.

46

Trust me, Clara Vere de Vere,
From yon blue heavens above us bent
The gardener Adam and his wife
Smile at the claims of long descent.
Howe'er it be, it seems to me,
'Tis only noble to be good.
Kind hearts are more than coronets,
And simple faith than Norman blood.

I know you, Clara Vere de Vere,
You pine among your halls and towers:
The languid light of your proud eyes
Is wearied of the rolling hours.

In glowing health, with boundless wealth,
But sickening of a vague disease,
You know so ill to deal with time,
You needs must play such pranks as
these.

Clara, Clara Vere de Vere,
If time be heavy on your hands,
Are there no beggars at your gate,
Nor any poor about your lands?
Oh! teach the orphan-boy to read,
Or teach the orphan-girl to sew,
Pray Heaven for a human heart,
And let the foolish yeoman go.

THE MAY QUEEN

You must wake and call me early, call me early, mother dear;
To-morrow 'ill be the happiest time of all the glad New-year;
Of all the glad New-year, mother, the maddest merriest day;
For I'm to be Queen o' the May, mother, I'm to be Queen o' the May.

There's many a black black eye, they say, but none so bright as mine;
There's Margaret and Mary, there's Kate and Caroline:
But none so fair as little Alice in all the land they say,
So I'm to be Queen o' the May, mother, I'm to be Queen o' the May.

I sleep so sound all night, mother, that I shall never wake,
If you do not call me loud when the day begins to break:
But I must gather knots of flowers, and buds and garlands gay,
For I'm to be Queen o' the May, mother, I'm to be Queen o' the May.

As I came up the valley whom think ye should I see,
But Robin leaning on the bridge beneath the hazel-tree?
He thought of that sharp look, mother, I gave him yesterday,
But I'm to be Queen o' the May, mother, I'm to be Queen o' the May.

He thought I was a ghost, mother, for I was all in white,
And I ran by him without speaking, like a flash of light.
They call me cruel-hearted, but I care not what they say,
For I'm to be Queen o' the May, mother, I'm to be Queen o' the May.

They say he's dying all for love, but that can never be:
They say his heart is breaking, mother—what is that to me?
There's many a bolder lad 'ill woo me any summer day,
And I'm to be Queen o' the May, mother, I'm to be Queen o' the May.

Little Effie shall go with me to-morrow to the green,
And you'll be there, too, mother, to see me made the Queen;
For the shepherd lads on every side 'ill come from far away,
And I'm to be Queen o' the May, mother, I'm to be Queen o' the May.

THE MAY QUEEN

The honeysuckle round the porch has wov'n its wavy bowers,
And by the meadow-trenches blow the faint sweet cuckoo-flowers;
And the wild marsh-marigold shines like fire in swamps and hollows gray,
And I'm to be Queen o' the May, mother, I'm to be Queen o' the May.

The night-winds come and go, mother, upon the meadow-grass,
And the happy stars above them seem to brighten as they pass;
There will not be a drop of rain the whole of the livelong day,
And I'm to be Queen o' the May, mother, I'm to be Queen o' the May.

All the valley, mother, 'ill be fresh and green and still,
And the cowslip and the crowfoot are over all the hill,
And the rivulet in the flowery dale 'ill merrily glance and play,
For I'm to be Queen o' the May, mother, I'm to be Queen o' the May.

So you must wake and call me early, call me early, mother dear,
To-morrow 'ill be the happiest time of all the glad New-year:
To-morrow 'ill be of all the year the maddest merriest day,
For I'm to be Queen o' the May, mother, I'm to be Queen o' the May.

NEW-YEAR'S EVE

IF you're waking call me early, call me early, mother dear,
For I would see the sun rise upon the glad New-year.
It is the last New-year that I shall ever see,
Then you may lay me low i' the mould and think no more of me.

To-night I saw the sun set: he set and left behind
The good old year, the dear old time, and all my peace of mind;
And the New-year's coming up, mother, but I shall never see
The blossom on the blackthorn, the leaf upon the tree.

Last May we made a crown of flowers: we had a merry day;
Beneath the hawthorn on the green they made me Queen of May;
And we danced about the may-pole and in the hazel copse,
Till Charles's Wain came out above the tall white chimney-tops.

There's not a flower on all the hills: the frost is on the pane:
I only wish to live till the snowdrops come again:
I wish the snow would melt and the sun come out on high:
I long to see a flower so before the day I die.

The building rook 'ill caw from the windy tall elm-tree,
And the tufted plover pipe along the fallow lea,
And the swallow 'ill come back again with summer o'er the wave,
But I shall lie alone, mother, within the mouldering grave.

Upon the chancel-casement, and upon that grave of mine,
In the early early morning the summer sun 'ill shine,
Before the red cock crows from the farm upon the hill,
When you are warm-asleep, mother, and all the world is still.

THE MAY QUEEN

When the flowers come again, mother, beneath the waning light
You'll never see me more in the long gray fields at night;
When from the dry dark wold the summer airs blow cool
On the oat-grass and the sword-grass, and the bulrush in the pool.

You'll bury me, my mother, just beneath the hawthorn shade,
And you'll come sometimes and see me where I am lowly laid.
I shall not forget you, mother, I shall hear you when you pass,
With your feet above my head in the long and pleasant grass.

I have been wild and wayward, but you'll forgive me now;
You'll kiss me, my own mother, and forgive me ere I go;
Nay, nay, you must not weep, nor let your grief be wild,
You should not fret for me, mother, you have another child.

If I can I'll come again, mother, from out my resting-place;
Tho' you'll not see me, mother, I shall look upon your face;
Tho' I cannot speak a word, I shall harken what you say,
And be often, often with you when you think I'm far away.

Goodnight, goodnight, when I have said goodnight for evermore,
And you see me carried out from the threshold of the door;
Don't let Effie come to see me till my grave be growing green:
She'll be a better child to you than ever I have been.

She'll find my garden-tools upon the granary floor:
Let her take 'em: they are hers: I shall never garden more:
But tell her, when I'm gone, to train the rosebush that I set
About the parlour-window and the box of mignonette.

Goodnight, sweet mother: call me before the day is born.
All night I lie awake, but I fall asleep at morn;
But I would see the sun rise upon the glad New-year,
So, if you're waking, call me, call me early, mother dear.

CONCLUSION

I THOUGHT to pass away before, and yet alive I am;
And in the fields all round I hear the bleating of the lamb.
How sadly, I remember, rose the morning of the year!
To die before the snowdrop came, and now the violet's here.

O sweet is the new violet, that comes beneath the skies,
And sweeter is the young lamb's voice to me that cannot rise,
And sweet is all the land about, and all the flowers that blow,
And sweeter far is death than life to me that long to go.

It seem'd so hard at first, mother, to leave the blessed sun,
And now it seems as hard to stay, and yet His will be done!
But still I think it can't be long before I find release;
And that good man, the clergyman, has told me words of peace.

O blessings on his kindly voice and on his silver hair!
And blessings on his whole life long, until he meet me there!
O blessings on his kindly heart and on his silver head!
A thousand times I blest him, as he knelt beside my bed.

He taught me all the mercy, for he show'd me all the sin.
Now, tho' my lamp was lighted late, there's One will let me in:
Nor would I now be well, mother, again if that could be,
For my desire is but to pass to Him that died for me.

I did not hear the dog howl, mother, or the death-watch beat,
There came a sweeter token when the night and morning meet:
But sit beside my bed, mother, and put your hand in mine,
And Effie on the other side, and I will tell the sign.

All in the wild March-morning I heard the angels call;
It was when the moon was setting, and the dark was over all;
The trees began to whisper, and the wind began to roll,
And in the wild March-morning I heard them call my soul.

For lying broad awake I thought of you and Effie dear;
I saw you sitting in the house, and I no longer here;
With all my strength I pray'd for both, and so I felt resign'd,
And up the valley came a swell of music on the wind.

I thought that it was fancy, and I listen'd in my bed,
And then did something speak to me—I know not what was said;
For great delight and shuddering took hold of all my mind,
And up the valley came again the music on the wind.

But you were sleeping; and I said, 'It's not for them: it's mine.'
And if it come three times, I thought, I take it for a sign.
And once again it came, and close beside the window-bars,
Then seem'd to go right up to Heaven and die among the stars.

So now I think my time is near. I trust it is. I know
The blessed music went that way my soul will have to go.
And for myself, indeed, I care not if I go to-day.
But, Effie, you must comfort *her* when I am past away.

And say to Robin a kind word, and tell him not to fret;
There's many a worthier than I, would make him happy yet.
If I had lived—I cannot tell—I might have been his wife;
But all these things have ceased to be, with my desire of life.

O look! the sun begins to rise, the heavens are in a glow;
He shines upon a hundred fields, and all of them I know.
And there I move no longer now, and there his light may shine—
Wild flowers in the valley for other hands than mine.

O sweet and strange it seems to me, that ere this day is done
The voice, that now is speaking, may be beyond the sun—
For ever and for ever with those just souls and true—
And what is life, that we should moan? why make we such ado?

For ever and for ever, all in a blessed home—
And there to wait a little while till you and Effie come—
To lie within the light of God, as I lie upon your breast—
And the wicked cease from troubling, and the weary are at rest.

THE LOTOS-EATERS

'COURAGE!' he said, and pointed toward
the land,
'This mounting wave will roll us shore-
ward soon.'
In the afternoon they came unto a land
In which it seemed always afternoon.
All round the coast the languid air did
swoon,
Breathing like one that hath a weary dream.
Full-faced above the valley stood the moon;
And like a downward smoke, the slender
stream
Along the cliff to fall and pause and fall
did seem.

A land of streams! some, like a downward
smoke,
Slow-dropping veils of thinnest lawn, did
go;
And some thro' wavering lights and
shadows broke,
Rolling a slumbrous sheet of foam below.
They saw the gleaming river seaward flow
From the inner land: far off, three
mountain-tops,
Three silent pinnacles of aged snow,
Stood sunset-flush'd: and, dew'd with
showery drops,
Up-clomb the shadowy pine above the
woven copse.

The charmed sunset linger'd low adown
In the red West: thro' mountain clefts the
dale
Was seen far inland, and the yellow down
Border'd with palm, and many a winding
vale
And meadow, set with slender galingale;
A land where all things always seem'd the
same!
And round about the keel with faces pale,
Dark faces pale against that rosy flame,
The mild-eyed melancholy Lotos-eaters
came.

Branches they bore of that enchanted stem,
Laden with flower and fruit, whereof they
gave
To each, but whoso did receive of them,
And taste, to him the gushing of the wave

Far far away did seem to mourn and rave
On alien shores; and if his fellow spake,
His voice was thin, as voices from the
grave;
And deep-asleep he seem'd, yet all awake,
And music in his ears his beating heart did
make.

They sat them down upon the yellow sand,
Between the sun and moon upon the shore;
And sweet it was to dream of Fatherland,
Of child, and wife, and slave; but ever-
more
Most weary seem'd the sea, weary the oar,
Weary the wandering fields of barren foam.
Then some one said, 'We will return no
more;'
And all at once they sang, 'Our island home
Is far beyond the wave; we will no longer
roam.'

CHORIC SONG

I

THERE is sweet music here that softer falls
Than petals from blown roses on the grass,
Or night-dews on still waters between walls
Of shadowy granite, in a gleaming pass;
Music that gentlier on the spirit lies,
Than tir'd eyelids upon tir'd eyes;
Music that brings sweet sleep down from
the blissful skies.
Here are cool mosses deep,
And thro' the moss the ivies creep,
And in the stream the long-leaved flowers
weep,
And from the craggy ledge the poppy
hangs in sleep.

II

Why are we weigh'd upon with heaviness
And utterly consumed with sharp distress,
While all things else have rest from
weariness?
All things have rest: why should we toil
alone,
We only toil, who are the first of things,
And make perpetual moan,
Still from one sorrow to another thrown:
Nor ever fold our wings,
And cease from wanderings,

Nor steep our brows in slumber's holy
    balm;
Nor harken what the inner spirit sings,
'There is no joy but calm!'
Why should we only toil, the roof and
    crown of things?

III

Lo! in the middle of the wood,
The folded leaf is woo'd from out the bud
With winds upon the branch, and there
Grows green and broad, and takes no care,
Sun-steep'd at noon, and in the moon
Nightly dew-fed; and turning yellow
Falls, and floats adown the air.
Lo! sweeten'd with the summer light,
The full-juiced apple, waxing over-mellow,
Drops in a silent autumn night.
All its allotted length of days,
The flower ripens in its place,
Ripens and fades, and falls, and hath no toil,
Fast-rooted in the fruitful soil.

IV

Hateful is the dark-blue sky,
Vaulted o'er the dark-blue sea.
Death is the end of life; ah, why
Should life all labour be?
Let us alone. Time driveth onward fast,
And in a little while our lips are dumb.
Let us alone. What is it that will last?
All things are taken from us, and become
Portions and parcels of the dreadful Past.
Let us alone. What pleasure can we have
To war with evil? Is there any peace
In ever climbing up the climbing wave?
All things have rest, and ripen toward the
    grave
In silence; ripen, fall and cease:
Give us long rest or death, dark death, or
    dreamful ease.

V

How sweet it were, hearing the downward
    stream,
With half-shut eyes ever to seem
Falling asleep in a half-dream!
To dream and dream, like yonder amber
    light,
Which will not leave the myrrh-bush on
    the height;

To hear each other's whisper'd speech;
Eating the Lotos day by day,
To watch the crisping ripples on the beach,
And tender curving lines of creamy spray;
To lend our hearts and spirits wholly
To the influence of mild-minded melan-
    choly;
To muse and brood and live again in
    memory,
With those old faces of our infancy
Heap'd over with a mound of grass,
Two handfuls of white dust, shut in an
    urn of brass!

VI

Dear is the memory of our wedded lives,
And dear the last embraces of our wives
And their warm tears: but all hath suffer'd
    change:
For surely now our household hearths are
    cold:
Our sons inherit us: our looks are strange:
And we should come like ghosts to trouble
    joy.
Or else the island princes over-bold
Have eat our substance, and the minstrel
    sings
Before them of the ten years' war in Troy,
And our great deeds, as half-forgotten
    things.
Is there confusion in the little isle?
Let what is broken so remain.
The Gods are hard to reconcile:
'Tis hard to settle order once again.
There *is* confusion worse than death,
Trouble on trouble, pain on pain,
Long labour unto aged breath,
Sore task to hearts worn out by many wars
And eyes grown dim with gazing on the
    pilot-stars.

VII

But, propt on beds of amaranth and moly,
How sweet (while warm airs lull us, blow-
    ing lowly)
With half-dropt eyelid still,
Beneath a heaven dark and holy,
To watch the long bright river drawing
    slowly
His waters from the purple hill—

52

To hear the dewy echoes calling
From cave to cave thro' the thick-twined
  vine—
To watch the emerald-colour'd water
  falling
Thro' many a wov'n acanthus-wreath
  divine!
Only to hear and see the far-off sparkling
  brine,
Only to hear were sweet, stretch'd out
  beneath the pine.

VIII

The Lotos blooms below the barren peak:
The Lotos blows by every winding creek:
All day the wind breathes low with mel-
  lower tone:
Thro' every hollow cave and alley lone
Round and round the spicy downs the
  yellow Lotos-dust is blown.
We have had enough of action, and of
  motion we,
Roll'd to starboard, roll'd to larboard,
  when the surge was seething free,
Where the wallowing monster spouted his
  foam-fountains in the sea.
Let us swear an oath, and keep it with an
  equal mind,
In the hollow Lotos-land to live and lie
  reclined
On the hills like Gods together, careless of
  mankind.
For they lie beside their nectar, and the
  bolts are hurl'd
Far below them in the valleys, and the
  clouds are lightly curl'd
Round their golden houses, girdled with
  the gleaming world:
Where they smile in secret, looking over
  wasted lands,
Blight and famine, plague and earthquake,
  roaring deeps and fiery sands,
Clanging fights, and flaming towns, and
  sinking ships, and praying hands.
But they smile, they find a music centred
  in a doleful song
Steaming up, a lamentation and an ancient
  tale of wrong,
Like a tale of little meaning tho' the words
  are strong;

Chanted from an ill-used race of men that
  cleave the soil,
Sow the seed, and reap the harvest with
  enduring toil,
Storing yearly little dues of wheat, and
  wine and oil;
Till they perish and they suffer—some, 'tis
  whisper'd—down in hell
Suffer endless anguish, others in Elysian
  valleys dwell,
Resting weary limbs at last on beds of
  asphodel.
Surely, surely, slumber is more sweet than
  toil, the shore
Than labour in the deep mid-ocean, wind
  and wave and oar;
Oh rest ye, brother mariners, we will not
  wander more.

A DREAM OF FAIR WOMEN

I READ, before my eyelids dropt their shade,
  'The Legend of Good Women,' long ago
Sung by the morning star of song, who
  made
  His music heard below;

Dan Chaucer, the first warbler, whose
  sweet breath
Preluded those melodious bursts that fill
The spacious times of great Elizabeth
  With sounds that echo still.

And, for a while, the knowledge of his art
  Held me above the subject, as strong
  gales
Hold swollen clouds from raining, tho' my
  heart,
  Brimful of those wild tales,

Charged both mine eyes with tears. In
  every land
I saw, wherever light illumineth,
Beauty and anguish walking hand in hand
  The downward slope to death.

Those far-renowned brides of ancient song
Peopled the hollow dark, like burning
  stars,
And I heard sounds of insult, shame, and
  wrong,
  And trumpets blown for wars;

53

And clattering flints batter'd with clanging
hoofs;
  And I saw crowds in column'd sanc-
  tuaries;
And forms that pass'd at windows and on
roofs
  Of marble palaces;

Corpses across the threshold; heroes tall
  Dislodging pinnacle and parapet
Upon the tortoise creeping to the wall;
  Lances in ambush set;

And high shrine-doors burst thro' with
heated blasts
  That run before the fluttering tongues
  of fire;
White surf wind-scatter'd over sails and
masts,
  And ever climbing higher;

Squadrons and squares of men in brazen
plates,
  Scaffolds, still sheets of water, divers
  woes,
Ranges of glimmering vaults with iron
grates,
  And hush'd seraglios.

So shape chased shape as swift as, when
to land
  Bluster the winds and tides the self-same
  way,
Crisp foam-flakes scud along the level sand,
  Torn from the fringe of spray.

I started once, or seem'd to start in pain,
  Resolved on noble things, and strove to
  speak,
As when a great thought strikes along the
brain,
  And flushes all the cheek.

And once my arm was lifted to hew down
  A cavalier from off his saddle-bow,
That bore a lady from a leaguer'd town;
  And then, I know not how,

All those sharp fancies, by down-lapsing
thought
  Stream'd onward, lost their edges, and
  did creep

Roll'd on each other, rounded, smooth'd,
and brought
  Into the gulfs of sleep.

At last methought that I had wander'd far
  In an old wood: fresh-wash'd in coolest
  dew
The maiden splendours of the morning star
  Shook in the stedfast blue.

Enormous elm-tree-boles did stoop and lean
  Upon the dusky brushwood underneath
Their broad curved branches, fledged with
clearest green,
  New from its silken sheath.

The dim red morn had died, her journey
done,
  And with dead lips smiled at the twilight
  plain,
Half-fall'n across the threshold of the sun,
  Never to rise again.

There was no motion in the dumb dead air,
  Not any song of bird or sound of rill;
Gross darkness of the inner sepulchre
  Is not so deadly still

As that wide forest. Growths of jasmine
turn'd
  Their humid arms festooning tree to
  tree,
And at the root thro' lush green grasses
burn'd
  The red anemone.

I knew the flowers, I knew the leaves, I
knew
  The tearful glimmer of the languid dawn
On those long, rank, dark wood-walks
drench'd in dew,
  Leading from lawn to lawn.

The smell of violets, hidden in the green,
  Pour'd back into my empty soul and frame
The times when I remember to have been
  Joyful and free from blame.

And from within me a clear under-tone
  Thrill'd thro' mine ears in that unbliss-
  ful clime,
'Pass freely thro': the wood is all thine own,
  Until the end of time.'

At length I saw a lady within call,
  Stiller than chisell'd marble, standing
    there;
A daughter of the gods, divinely tall,
  And most divinely fair.

Her loveliness with shame and with sur-
    prise
  Froze my swift speech: she turning on
    my face
The star-like sorrows of immortal eyes,
  Spoke slowly in her place.

'I had great beauty: ask thou not my
    name:
  No one can be more wise than destiny.
Many drew swords and died. Where'er I
    came
  I brought calamity.'

'No marvel, sovereign lady: in fair field
  Myself for such a face had boldly died,'
I answer'd free; and turning I appeal'd
  To one that stood beside.

But she, with sick and scornful looks averse,
  To her full height her stately stature
    draws;
'My youth,' she said, 'was blasted with a
    curse:
  This woman was the cause.

'I was cut off from hope in that sad place,
  Which men call'd Aulis in those iron
    years:
My father held his hand upon his face;
  I, blinded with my tears,

'Still strove to speak: my voice was thick
    with sighs
  As in a dream. Dimly I could descry
The stern black-bearded kings with wolfish
    eyes,
  Waiting to see me die.

'The high masts flicker'd as they lay afloat;
  The crowds, the temples, waver'd, and
    the shore;
The bright death quiver'd at the victim's
    throat;
  Touch'd; and I knew no more.'

Whereto the other with a downward brow;
  'I would the white cold heavy-plunging
    foam,
Whirl'd by the wind, had roll'd me deep
    below,
  Then when I left my home.'

Her slow full words sank thro' the silence
    drear,
  As thunder-drops fall on a sleeping sea:
Sudden I heard a voice that cried, 'Come
    here,
  That I may look on thee.'

I turning saw, throned on a flowery rise,
  One sitting on a crimson scarf unroll'd;
A queen, with swarthy cheeks and bold
    black eyes,
  Brow-bound with burning gold.

She, flashing forth a haughty smile, began:
  'I govern'd men by change, and so I
    sway'd
All moods. 'Tis long since I have seen a
    man.
  Once, like the moon, I made

'The ever-shifting currents of the blood
  According to my humour ebb and flow.
I have no men to govern in this wood:
  That makes my only woe.

'Nay—yet it chafes me that I could not
    bend
  One will; nor tame and tutor with mine
    eye
That dull cold-blooded Cæsar. Prythee,
    friend,
  Where is Mark Antony?

'The man, my lover, with whom I rode
    sublime
  On Fortune's neck: we sat as God by
    God:
The Nilus would have risen before his time
  And flooded at our nod.

'We drank the Libyan Sun to sleep, and lit
  Lamps which out-burn'd Canopus. O
    my life
In Egypt! O the dalliance and the wit,
  The flattery and the strife,

'And the wild kiss, when fresh from war's
   alarms,
   My Hercules, my Roman Antony,
My mailed Bacchus leapt into my arms,
   Contented there to die!

'And there he died: and when I heard my
   name
   Sigh'd forth with life I would not brook
   my fear
Of the other: with a worm I balk'd his fame.
   What else was left? look here!'

(With that she tore her robe apart, and half
   The polish'd argent of her breast to sight
Laid bare. Thereto she pointed with a
   laugh,
   Showing the aspick's bite.)

'I died a Queen. The Roman soldier found
   Me lying dead, my crown about my brows,
A name for ever!—lying robed and
   crown'd,
   Worthy a Roman spouse.'

Her warbling voice, a lyre of widest range
   Struck by all passion, did fall down and
   glance
From tone to tone, and glided thro' all
   change
   Of liveliest utterance.

When she made pause I knew not for
   delight;
   Because with sudden motion from the
   ground
She raised her piercing orbs, and fill'd
   with light
   The interval of sound.

Still with their fires Love tipt his keenest
   darts;
   As once they drew into two burning
   rings
All beams of Love, melting the mighty
   hearts
   Of captains and of kings.

Slowly my sense undazzled. Then I heard
   A noise of some one coming thro' the
   lawn,
And singing clearer than the crested bird
   That claps his wings at dawn.

'The torrent brooks of hallow'd Israel
   From craggy hollows pouring, late and
   soon,
Sound all night long, in falling thro' the
   dell,
   Far-heard beneath the moon.

'The balmy moon of blessed Israel
   Floods all the deep-blue gloom with
   beams divine:
All night the splinter'd crags that wall the
   dell
   With spires of silver shine.'

As one that museth where broad sunshine
   laves
   The lawn by some cathedral, thro' the
   door
Hearing the holy organ rolling waves
   Of sound on roof and floor

Within, and anthem sung, is charm'd and
   tied
   To where he stands,—so stood I, when
   that flow
Of music left the lips of her that died
   To save her father's vow;

The daughter of the warrior Gileadite,
   A maiden pure; as when she went along
From Mizpeh's tower'd gate with welcome
   light,
   With timbrel and with song.

My words leapt forth: 'Heaven heads the
   count of crimes
   With that wild oath.' She render'd
   answer high:
'Not so, nor once alone; a thousand times
   I would be born and die.

'Single I grew, like some green plant,
   whose root
   Creeps to the garden water-pipes beneath,
Feeding the flower; but ere my flower to
   fruit
   Changed, I was ripe for death.

'My God, my land, my father—these did
   move
   Me from my bliss of life, that Nature
   gave,

Lower'd softly with a threefold cord of
love
    Down to a silent grave.

'And I went mourning, "No fair Hebrew
boy
Shall smile away my maiden blame
among
The Hebrew mothers"—emptied of all
joy,
    Leaving the dance and song,

'Leaving the olive-gardens far below,
Leaving the promise of my bridal bower,
The valleys of grape-loaded vines that glow
    Beneath the battled tower.

'The light white cloud swam over us.
Anon
We heard the lion roaring from his den;
We saw the large white stars rise one by
one,
    Or, from the darken'd glen,

'Saw God divide the night with flying
flame,
And thunder on the everlasting hills.
I heard Him, for He spake, and grief
became
    A solemn scorn of ills.

'When the next moon was roll'd into the
sky,
Strength came to me that equall'd my
desire.
How beautiful a thing it was to die
    For God and for my sire!

'It comforts me in this one thought to
dwell,
That I subdued me to my father's will;
Because the kiss he gave me, ere I fell,
    Sweetens the spirit still.

'Moreover it is written that my race
Hew'd Ammon, hip and thigh, from
Aroer
On Arnon unto Minneth.' Here her face
    Glow'd, as I look'd at her.

She lock'd her lips: she left me where I
stood:
    'Glory to God,' she sang, and past afar,

Thridding the sombre boskage of the
wood,
    Toward the morning-star.

Losing her carol I stood pensively,
As one that from a casement leans his
head,
When midnight bells cease ringing suddenly,
    And the old year is dead.

'Alas! alas!' a low voice, full of care,
Murmur'd beside me: 'Turn and look
on me:
I am that Rosamond, whom men call fair,
    If what I was I be.

'Would I had been some maiden coarse
and poor!
O me, that I should ever see the light!
Those dragon eyes of anger'd Eleanor
    Do hunt me, day and night.'

She ceased in tears, fallen from hope and
trust:
To whom the Egyptian: 'O, you tamely
died!
You should have clung to Fulvia's waist,
and thrust
    The dagger thro' her side.'

With that sharp sound the white dawn's
creeping beams,
Stol'n to my brain, dissolved the mystery
Of folded sleep. The captain of my dreams
    Ruled in the eastern sky.

Morn broaden'd on the borders of the
dark,
Ere I saw her, who clasp'd in her last
trance
Her murder'd father's head, or Joan of
Arc,
    A light of ancient France;

Or her who knew that Love can vanquish
Death,
Who kneeling, with one arm about her
king,
Drew forth the poison with her balmy
breath,
    Sweet as new buds in Spring.

No memory labours longer from the deep
  Gold-mines of thought to lift the hidden
    ore
That glimpses, moving up, than I from
    sleep
  To gather and tell o'er

Each little sound and sight. With what dull
    pain
  Compass'd, how eagerly I sought to
    strike
Into that wondrous track of dreams again!
  But no two dreams are like.

As when a soul laments, which hath been
    blest,
  Desiring what is mingled with past years,
In yearnings that can never be exprest
  By signs or groans or tears;

Because all words, tho' cull'd with choicest
    art,
  Failing to give the bitter of the sweet,
Wither beneath the palate, and the heart
  Faints, faded by its heat.

THE BLACKBIRD

O BLACKBIRD! sing me something well:
  While all the neighbours shoot thee round,
  I keep smooth plats of fruitful ground,
Where thou may'st warble, eat and dwell.

The espaliers and the standards all
  Are thine; the range of lawn and park:
  The unnetted black-hearts ripen dark,
All thine, against the garden wall.

Yet, tho' I spared thee all the spring,
  Thy sole delight is, sitting still,
  With that gold dagger of thy bill
To fret the summer jenneting.

A golden bill! the silver tongue,
  Cold February loved, is dry:
  Plenty corrupts the melody
That made thee famous once, when young:

And in the sultry garden-squares,
  Now thy flute-notes are changed to
    coarse,
  I hear thee not at all, or hoarse
As when a hawker hawks his wares.

Take warning! he that will not sing
  While yon sun prospers in the blue,
  Shall sing for want, ere leaves are new,
Caught in the frozen palms of Spring.

THE DEATH OF THE OLD
YEAR

FULL knee-deep lies the winter snow,
  And the winter winds are wearily sigh-
    ing:
Toll ye the church-bell sad and slow,
And tread softly and speak low,
For the old year lies a-dying.
    Old year, you must not die;
    You came to us so readily,
    You lived with us so steadily,
    Old year, you shall not die.

He lieth still: he doth not move:
He will not see the dawn of day.
He hath no other life above.
He gave me a friend, and a true true-love,
And the New-year will take 'em away.
    Old year, you must not go;
    So long as you have been with us,
    Such joy as you have seen with us,
    Old year, you shall not go.

He froth'd his bumpers to the brim;
A jollier year we shall not see.
But tho' his eyes are waxing dim,
And tho' his foes speak ill of him,
He was a friend to me.
    Old year, you shall not die;
    We did so laugh and cry with you,
    I've half a mind to die with you,
    Old year, if you must die.

He was full of joke and jest,
But all his merry quips are o'er.
To see him die, across the waste
His son and heir doth ride post-haste,
But he'll be dead before.
    Every one for his own.
    The night is starry and cold, my
      friend,
    And the New-year blithe and bold,
      my friend,
    Comes up to take his own.

How hard he breathes! over the snow
I heard just now the crowing cock.
The shadows flicker to and fro:
The cricket chirps: the light burns low:
'Tis nearly twelve o'clock.
 Shake hands, before you die.
 Old year, we'll dearly rue for you:
 What is it we can do for you?
 Speak out before you die.

His face is growing sharp and thin.
Alack! our friend is gone.
Close up his eyes: tie up his chin:
Step from the corpse, and let him in
That standeth there alone,
 And waiteth at the door.
 There's a new foot on the floor, my
  friend,
 And a new face at the door, my friend,
 A new face at the door.

TO J. S.

THE wind, that beats the mountain, blows
More softly round the open wold,
And gently comes the world to those
That are cast in gentle mould.

And me this knowledge bolder made,
Or else I had not dared to flow
In these words toward you, and invade
Even with a verse your holy woe.

'Tis strange that those we lean on most,
 Those in whose laps our limbs are
  nursed,
Fall into shadow, soonest lost:
 Those we love first are taken first.

God gives us love. Something to love
He lends us; but, when love is grown
To ripeness, that on which it throve
Falls off, and love is left alone.

This is the curse of time. Alas!
In grief I am not all unlearn'd;
Once thro' mine own doors Death did pass;
One went, who never hath return'd.

He will not smile—not speak to me
Once more. Two years his chair is seen
Empty before us. That was he
Without whose life I had not been.

Your loss is rarer; for this star
Rose with you thro' a little arc
Of heaven, nor having wander'd far
Shot on the sudden into dark.

I knew your brother: his mute dust
I honour and his living worth:
A man more pure and bold and just
Was never born into the earth.

I have not look'd upon you nigh,
Since that dear soul hath fall'n asleep.
Great Nature is more wise than I:
I will not tell you not to weep.

And tho' mine own eyes fill with dew,
Drawn from the spirit thro' the brain,
I will not even preach to you,
'Weep, weeping dulls the inward pain.'

Let Grief be her own mistress still.
She loveth her own anguish deep
More than much pleasure. Let her will
Be done—to weep or not to weep.

I will not say 'God's ordinance
Of Death is blown in every wind;'
For that is not a common chance
That takes away a noble mind.

His memory long will live alone
In all our hearts, as mournful light
That broods above the fallen sun,
And dwells in heaven half the night.

Vain solace! Memory standing near
Cast down her eyes, and in her throat
Her voice seem'd distant, and a tear
Dropt on the letters as I wrote.

I wrote I know not what. In truth,
How *should* I soothe you anyway,
Who miss the brother of your youth?
Yet something I did wish to say:

For he too was a friend to me:
Both are my friends, and my true breast
Bleedeth for both: yet it may be
That only silence suiteth best.

Words weaker than your grief would make
Grief more. 'Twere better I should cease
Although myself could almost take
The place of him that sleeps in peace.

Sleep sweetly, tender heart, in peace:
  Sleep, holy spirit, blessed soul,
While the stars burn, the moons increase,
  And the great ages onward roll.

Sleep till the end, true soul and sweet.
  Nothing comes to thee new or strange.
Sleep full of rest from head to feet;
` Lie still, dry dust, secure of change.

ON A MOURNER

I

NATURE, so far as in her lies,
  Imitates God, and turns her face
To every land beneath the skies,
  Counts nothing that she meets with base,
  But lives and loves in every place;

II

Fills out the homely quickset-screens,
  And makes the purple lilac ripe,
Steps from her airy hill, and greens
  The swamp, where humm'd the drop-
    ping snipe,
  With moss and braided marish-pipe;

III

And on thy heart a finger lays,
  Saying, 'Beat quicker, for the time
Is pleasant, and the woods and ways
  Are pleasant, and the beech and lime
  Put forth and feel a gladder clime.'

IV

And murmurs of a deeper voice,
  Going before to some far shrine,
Teach that sick heart the stronger choice,
  Till all thy life one way incline
  With one wide Will that closes thine.

V

And when the zoning eve has died
  Where yon dark valleys wind forlorn,
Come Hope and Memory, spouse and
    bride,
  From out the borders of the morn,
  With that fair child betwixt them born.

VI

And when no mortal motion jars
  The blackness round the tombing sod,
Thro' silence and the trembling stars
  Comes Faith from tracts no feet have
    trod,
  And Virtue, like a household god

VII

Promising empire; such as those
  Once heard at dead of night to greet
Troy's wandering prince, so that he rose
  With sacrifice, while all the fleet
  Had rest by stony hills of Crete.

———

You ask me, why, tho' ill at ease,
  Within this region I subsist,
  Whose spirits falter in the mist,
And languish for the purple seas.

It is the land that freemen till,
  That sober-suited Freedom chose,
  The land, where girt with friends or
    foes
A man may speak the thing he will;

A land of settled government,
  A land of just and old renown,
  Where Freedom slowly broadens down
From precedent to precedent:

Where faction seldom gathers head,
  But by degrees to fullness wrought,
  The strength of some diffusive thought
Hath time and space to work and spread.

Should banded unions persecute
  Opinion, and induce a time
  When single thought is civil crime,
And individual freedom mute;

Tho' Power should make from land to land
  The name of Britain trebly great—
  Tho' every channel of the State
Should fill and choke with golden sand—

Yet, waft me from the harbour-mouth,
  Wild wind! I seek a warmer sky,
  And I will see before I die
The palms and temples of the South.

———

Of old sat Freedom on the heights,
  The thunders breaking at her feet:
Above her shook the starry lights:
  She heard the torrents meet.

There in her place she did rejoice,
  Self-gather'd in her prophet-mind,
But fragments of her mighty voice
  Came rolling on the wind.

Then stept she down thro' town and field
  To mingle with the human race,
And part by part to men reveal'd
  The fullness of her face—

Grave mother of majestic works,
  From her isle-altar gazing down,
Who, God-like, grasps the triple forks,
  And, King-like, wears the crown:

Her open eyes desire the truth.
  The wisdom of a thousand years
Is in them. May perpetual youth
  Keep dry their light from tears;

That her fair form may stand and shine,
  Make bright our days and light our
    dreams,
Turning to scorn with lips divine
  The falsehood of extremes!

———

Love thou thy land, with love far-brought
  From out the storied Past, and used
  Within the Present, but transfused
Thro' future time by power of thought.

True love turn'd round on fixed poles,
  Love, that endures not sordid ends,
  For English natures, freemen, friends,
Thy brothers and immortal souls.

But pamper not a hasty time,
  Nor feed with crude imaginings
  The herd, wild hearts and feeble wings
That every sophister can lime.

Deliver not the tasks of might
  To weakness, neither hide the ray
  From those, not blind, who wait for day,
Tho' sitting girt with doubtful light.

Make knowledge circle with the winds;
  But let her herald, Reverence, fly
  Before her to whatever sky
Bear seed of men and growth of minds.

Watch what main-currents draw the years:
  Cut Prejudice against the grain:
  But gentle words are always gain:
Regard the weakness of thy peers:

Nor toil for title, place, or touch
  Of pension, neither count on praise:
  It grows to guerdon after-days:
Nor deal in watch-words overmuch:

Not clinging to some ancient saw;
  Not master'd by some modern term;
  Not swift nor slow to change, but firm:
And in its season bring the law;

That from Discussion's lip may fall
  With Life, that, working strongly,
    binds—
  Set in all lights by many minds,
To close the interests of all.

For Nature also, cold and warm,
  And moist and dry, devising long,
  Thro' many agents making strong,
Matures the individual form.

Meet is it changes should control
  Our being, lest we rust in ease.
  We all are changed by still degrees,
All but the basis of the soul.

So let the change which comes be free
  To ingroove itself with that which flies,
  And work, a joint of state, that plies
Its office, moved with sympathy.

A saying, hard to shape in act;
  For all the past of Time reveals
  A bridal dawn of thunder-peals,
Wherever Thought hath wedded Fact.

Ev'n now we hear with inward strife
  A motion toiling in the gloom—
  The Spirit of the years to come
Yearning to mix himself with Life.

A slow-develop'd strength awaits
  Completion in a painful school;
  Phantoms of other forms of rule,
New Majesties of mighty States—

The warders of the growing hour,
  But vague in vapour, hard to mark;
  And round them sea and air are dark
With great contrivances of Power.

Of many changes, aptly join'd,
  Is bodied forth the second whole.
  Regard gradation, lest the soul
Of Discord race the rising wind;

A wind to puff your idol-fires,
  And heap their ashes on the head;
  To shame the boast so often made,
That we are wiser than our sires.

Oh yet, if Nature's evil star
  Drive men in manhood, as in youth,
  To follow flying steps of Truth
Across the brazen bridge of war—

If New and Old, disastrous feud
  Must ever shock, like armed foes,
  And this be true, till Time shall close,
That Principles are rain'd in blood;

Not yet the wise of heart would cease
  To hold his hope thro' shame and guilt,
  But with his hand against the hilt,
Would pace the troubled land, like Peace;

Not less, tho' dogs of Faction bay,
  Would serve his kind in deed and word,
  Certain, if knowledge bring the sword,
That knowledge takes the sword away—

Would love the gleams of good that broke
  From either side, nor veil his eyes:
  And if some dreadful need should rise
Would strike, and firmly, and one stroke:

To-morrow yet would reap to-day,
  As we bear blossom of the dead;
  Earn well the thrifty months, nor wed
Raw Haste, half-sister to Delay.

ENGLAND AND AMERICA
IN 1782

O THOU, that sendest out the man
  To rule by land and sea,
Strong mother of a Lion-line,
Be proud of those strong sons of thine
  Who wrench'd their rights from thee!

What wonder, if in noble heat
  Those men thine arms withstood,
Retaught the lesson thou hadst taught,
And in thy spirit with thee fought—
  Who sprang from English blood!

But Thou rejoice with liberal joy,
  Lift up thy rocky face,
And shatter, when the storms are black,
In many a streaming torrent back,
  The seas that shock thy base!

Whatever harmonies of law
  The growing world assume,
Thy work is thine—The single note
From that deep chord which Hampden
  smote
Will vibrate to the doom.

THE GOOSE

I KNEW an old wife lean and poor,
  Her rags scarce held together;
There strode a stranger to the door,
  And it was windy weather.

He held a goose upon his arm,
  He utter'd rhyme and reason,
'Here, take the goose, and keep you warm,
  It is a stormy season.'

She caught the white goose by the leg,
  A goose—'twas no great matter.
The goose let fall a golden egg
  With cackle and with clatter.

She dropt the goose, and caught the pelf,
  And ran to tell her neighbours;
And bless'd herself, and cursed herself,
  And rested from her labours.

And feeding high, and living soft,
  Grew plump and able-bodied;
Until the grave churchwarden doff'd,
  The parson smirk'd and nodded.

So sitting, served by man and maid,
  She felt her heart grow prouder:
But ah! the more the white goose laid
  It clack'd and cackled louder.

It clutter'd here, it chuckled there;
   It stirr'd the old wife's mettle:
She shifted in her elbow-chair,
   And hurl'd the pan and kettle.

'A quinsy choke thy cursed note!'
   Then wax'd her anger stronger.
'Go, take the goose, and wring her throat,
   I will not bear it longer.'

Then yelp'd the cur, and yawl'd the cat;
   Ran Gaffer, stumbled Gammer.
The goose flew this way and flew that,
   And fill'd the house with clamour.

As head and heels upon the floor
   They flounder'd all together,
There strode a stranger to the door,
   And it was windy weather:

He took the goose upon his arm,
   He utter'd words of scorning;
'So keep you cold, or keep you warm,
   It is a stormy morning.'

The wild wind rang from park and plain,
   And round the attics rumbled,
Till all the tables danced again,
   And half the chimneys tumbled.

The glass blew in, the fire blew out,
   The blast was hard and harder.
Her cap blew off, her gown blew up,
   And a whirlwind clear'd the larder:

And while on all sides breaking loose
   Her household fled the danger,
Quoth she, 'The Devil take the goose,
   And God forget the stranger!'

ENGLISH IDYLS

AND OTHER POEMS

THE EPIC

AT Francis Allen's on the Christmas-eve,—
The game of forfeits done—the girls all
   kiss'd
Beneath the sacred bush and past away—
The parson Holmes, the poet Everard
   Hall,
The host, and I sat round the wassail-
   bowl,
Then half-way ebb'd: and there we held
   a talk,
How all the old honour had from Christmas
   gone,
Or gone, or dwindled down to some odd
   games
In some odd nooks like this; till I, tired out
With cutting eights that day upon the
   pond,
Where, three times slipping from the outer
   edge,
I bump'd the ice into three several stars,
Fell in a doze; and half-awake I heard
The parson taking wide and wider sweeps,
Now harping on the church-commis-
   sioners,
Now hawking at Geology and schism;

Until I woke, and found him settled down
Upon the general decay of faith
Right thro' the world, 'at home was little
   left,
And none abroad: there was no anchor,
   none,
To hold by.' Francis, laughing, clapt his
   hand
On Everard's shoulder, with 'I hold by
   him.'
'And I,' quoth Everard, 'by the wassail-
   bowl.'
'Why yes,' I said, 'we knew your gift that
   way
At college: but another which you had,
I mean of verse (for so we held it then),
What came of that?' 'You know,' said
   Frank, 'he burnt
His epic, his King Arthur, some twelve
   books'—
And then to me demanding why? 'Oh, sir,
He thought that nothing new was said, or
   else
Something so said 'twas nothing—that a
   truth
Looks freshest in the fashion of the day:
God knows: he has a mint of reasons: ask.

It pleased *me* well enough.' 'Nay, nay,' said Hall,
'Why take the style of those heroic times?
For nature brings not back the Mastodon,
Nor we those times; and why should any man
Remodel models? these twelve books of mine
Were faint Homeric echoes, nothing-worth,
Mere chaff and draff, much better burnt.'
  'But I,'
Said Francis, 'pick'd the eleventh from this hearth
And have it: keep a thing, its use will come.
I hoard it as a sugar-plum for Holmes.'
He laugh'd, and I, tho' sleepy, like a horse
That hears the corn-bin open, prick'd my ears;
For I remember'd Everard's college fame
When we were Freshmen: then at my request
He brought it; and the poet little urged,
But with some prelude of disparagement,
Read, mouthing out his hollow oes and aes,
Deep-chested music, and to this result.

MORTE D'ARTHUR

So all day long the noise of battle roll'd
Among the mountains by the winter sea;
Until King Arthur's table, man by man,
Had fallen in Lyonnesse about their Lord,
King Arthur: then, because his wound was deep,
The bold Sir Bedivere uplifted him,
Sir Bedivere, the last of all his knights,
And bore him to a chapel nigh the field,
A broken chancel with a broken cross,
That stood on a dark strait of barren land.
On one side lay the Ocean, and on one
Lay a great water, and the moon was full.
  Then spake King Arthur to Sir Bedivere:
'The sequel of to-day unsolders all
The goodliest fellowship of famous knights
Whereof this world holds record. Such a sleep
They sleep—the men I loved. I think that we
Shall never more, at any future time,
Delight our souls with talk of knightly deeds,

Walking about the gardens and the halls
Of Camelot, as in the days that were.
I perish by this people which I made,—
Tho' Merlin sware that I should come again
To rule once more—but let what will be, be,
I am so deeply smitten thro' the helm
That without help I cannot last till morn.
Thou therefore take my brand Excalibur,
Which was my pride: for thou rememberest how
In those old days, one summer noon, an arm
Rose up from out the bosom of the lake,
Clothed in white samite, mystic, wonderful,
Holding the sword—and how I row'd across
And took it, and have worn it, like a king:
And, wheresoever I am sung or told
In aftertime, this also shall be known:
But now delay not: take Excalibur,
And fling him far into the middle mere:
Watch what thou seëst, and lightly bring me word.'
  To him replied the bold Sir Bedivere:
'It is not meet, Sir King, to leave thee thus,
Aidless, alone, and smitten thro' the helm.
A little thing may harm a wounded man.
Yet I thy hest will all perform at full,
Watch what I see, and lightly bring thee word.'
  So saying, from the ruin'd shrine he stept
And in the moon athwart the place of tombs,
Where lay the mighty bones of ancient men,
Old knights, and over them the sea-wind sang
Shrill, chill, with flakes of foam. He, stepping down
By zig-zag paths, and juts of pointed rock,
Came on the shining levels of the lake.
  There drew he forth the brand Excalibur,
And o'er him, drawing it, the winter moon,
Brightening the skirts of a long cloud, ran forth
And sparkled keen with frost against the hilt:

64

For all the haft twinkled with diamond
    sparks,
Myriads of topaz-lights, and jacinth-work
Of subtlest jewellery. He gazed so long
That both his eyes were dazzled, as he
    stood,
This way and that dividing the swift mind,
In act to throw: but at the last it seem'd
Better to leave Excalibur conceal'd
There in the many-knotted waterflags,
That whistled stiff and dry about the marge.
So strode he back slow to the wounded
    King.
    Then spake King Arthur to Sir Bedi-
    vere:
'Hast thou perform'd my mission which I
    gave?
What is it thou hast seen? or what hast
    heard?'
    And answer made the bold Sir Bedivere:
'I heard the ripple washing in the reeds,
And the wild water lapping on the crag.'
    To whom replied King Arthur, faint and
    pale:
'Thou hast betray'd thy nature and thy
    name,
Not rendering true answer, as beseem'd
Thy fëalty, nor like a noble knight:
For surer sign had follow'd, either hand,
Or voice, or else a motion of the mere.
This is a shameful thing for men to lie.
Yet now, I charge thee, quickly go again
As thou art lief and dear, and do the thing
I bad thee, watch, and lightly bring me
    word.'
    Then went Sir Bedivere the second time
Across the ridge, and paced beside the
    mere,
Counting the dewy pebbles, fix'd in
    thought;
But when he saw the wonder of the hilt,
How curiously and strangely chased, he
    smote
His palms together, and he cried aloud,
    'And if indeed I cast the brand away,
Surely a precious thing, one worthy note,
Should thus be lost for ever from the earth,
Which might have pleased the eyes of many
    men.
What good should follow this, if this were
    done?

What harm, undone? deep harm to dis-
    obey,
Seeing obedience is the bond of rule.
Were it well to obey then, if a king demand
An act unprofitable, against himself?
The King is sick, and knows not what he
    does.
What record, or what relic of my lord
Should be to aftertime, but empty breath
And rumours of a doubt? but were this
    kept,
Stored in some treasure-house of mighty
    kings,
Some one might show it at a joust of arms,
Saying, "King Arthur's sword, Excalibur,
Wrought by the lonely maiden of the Lake.
Nine years she wrought it, sitting in the
    deeps
Upon the hidden bases of the hills."
So might some old man speak in the after-
    time
To all the people, winning reverence.
But now much honour and much fame
    were lost.'
    So spake he, clouded with his own con-
    ceit,
And hid Excalibur the second time,
And so strode back slow to the wounded
    King.
    Then spoke King Arthur, breathing
    heavily:
'What is it thou hast seen? or what hast
    heard?'
    And answer made the bold Sir Bedivere:
'I heard the water lapping on the crag,
And the long ripple washing in the reeds.'
    To whom replied King Arthur, much in
    wrath:
'Ah, miserable and unkind, untrue,
Unknightly, traitor-hearted! Woe is me!
Authority forgets a dying king,
Laid widow'd of the power in his eye
That bow'd the will. I see thee what thou
    art,
For thou, the latest-left of all my knights,
In whom should meet the offices of all,
Thou wouldst betray me for the precious
    hilt;
Either from lust of gold, or like a girl
Valuing the giddy pleasure of the eyes.
Yet, for a man may fail in duty twice,

And the third time may prosper, get thee
hence:
But, if thou spare to fling Excalibur,
I will arise and slay thee with my hands.'
  Then quickly rose Sir Bedivere, and ran,
And, leaping down the ridges lightly,
plunged
Among the bulrush-beds, and clutch'd the
sword,
And strongly wheel'd and threw it. The
great brand
Made lightnings in the splendour of the
moon,
And flashing round and round, and whirl'd
in an arch,
Shot like a streamer of the northern morn,
Seen where the moving isles of winter
shock
By night, with noises of the northern sea.
So flash'd and fell the brand Excalibur:
But ere he dipt the surface, rose an arm
Clothed in white samite, mystic, wonderful,
And caught him by the hilt, and brandish'd
him
Three times, and drew him under in the
mere.
And lightly went the other to the King.
  Then spoke King Arthur, drawing
thicker breath:
'Now see I by thine eyes that this is done.
Speak out: what is it thou hast heard, or
seen?'
  And answer made the bold Sir Bedivere:
'Sir King, I closed mine eyelids, lest the
gems
Should blind my purpose, for I never saw,
Nor shall see, here or elsewhere, till I die,
Not tho' I live three lives of mortal men,
So great a miracle as yonder hilt.
Then with both hands I flung him, wheel-
ing him;
But when I look'd again, behold an arm,
Clothed in white samite, mystic, wonderful,
That caught him by the hilt, and brandish'd
him
Three times, and drew him under in the
mere.'
  And answer made King Arthur, breath-
ing hard:
'My end draws nigh; 'tis time that I were
gone.

Make broad thy shoulders to receive my
weight,
And bear me to the margin; yet I fear
My wound hath taken cold, and I shall
die.'
  So saying, from the pavement he half
rose,
Slowly, with pain, reclining on his arm,
And looking wistfully with wide blue eyes
As in a picture. Him Sir Bedivere
Remorsefully regarded thro' his tears,
And would have spoken, but he found not
words,
Then took with care, and kneeling on one
knee,
O'er both his shoulders drew the languid
hands,
And rising bore him thro' the place of
tombs.
  But, as he walk'd, King Arthur panted
hard,
Like one that feels a nightmare on his bed
When all the house is mute. So sigh'd the
King,
Muttering and murmuring at his ear,
'Quick, quick!
I fear it is too late, and I shall die.'
But the other swiftly strode from ridge to
ridge,
Clothed with his breath, and looking, as
he walk'd,
Larger than human on the frozen hills.
He heard the deep behind him, and a cry
Before. His own thought drove him, like
a goad.
Dry clash'd his harness in the icy caves
And barren chasms, and all to left and right
The bare black cliff clang'd round him, as
he based
His feet on juts of slippery crag that rang
Sharp-smitten with the dint of armed
heels—
And on a sudden, lo! the level lake,
And the long glories of the winter moon.
  Then saw they how there hove a dusky
barge,
Dark as a funeral scarf from stem to stern,
Beneath them; and descending they were
ware
That all the decks were dense with stately
forms

Black-stoled, black-hooded, like a dream
—by these
Three Queens with crowns of gold—and
from them rose
A cry that shiver'd to the tingling stars,
And, as it were one voice an agony
Of lamentation, like a wind, that shrills
All night in a waste land, where no one
comes,
Or hath come, since the making of the
world.
Then murmur'd Arthur, 'Place me in
the barge,'
And to the barge they came. There those
three Queens
Put forth their hands, and took the King,
and wept.
But she, that rose the tallest of them all
And fairest, laid his head upon her lap,
And loosed the shatter'd casque, and chafed
his hands,
And call'd him by his name, complaining
loud,
And dropping bitter tears against his brow
Striped with dark blood: for all his face
was white
And colourless, and like the wither'd moon
Smote by the fresh beam of the springing
east;
And all his greaves and cuisses dash'd with
drops
Of onset; and the light and lustrous curls—
That made his forehead like a rising sun
High from the dïas-throne—were parch'd
with dust;
Or, clotted into points and hanging loose,
Mix'd with the knightly growth that
fringed his lips.
So like a shatter'd column lay the King;
Not like that Arthur who, with lance in
rest,
From spur to plume a star of tournament,
Shot thro' the lists at Camelot, and charged
Before the eyes of ladies and of kings.
Then loudly cried the bold Sir Bedivere,
'Ah! my Lord Arthur, whither shall I go?
Where shall I hide my forehead and my
eyes?
For now I see the true old times are dead,
When every morning brought a noble
chance,

And every chance brought out a noble
knight.
Such times have been not since the light
that led
The holy Elders with the gift of myrrh.
But now the whole ROUND TABLE is dis-
solved
Which was an image of the mighty world;
And I, the last, go forth companionless,
And the days darken round me, and the
years,
Among new men, strange faces, other
minds.'
    And slowly answered Arthur from the
barge:
'The old order changeth, yielding place to
new,
And God fulfils Himself in many ways,
Lest one good custom should corrupt the
world.
Comfort thyself: what comfort is in me?
I have lived my life, and that which I have
done
May He within Himself make pure! but
thou,
If thou shouldst never see my face again,
Pray for my soul. More things are wrought
by prayer
Than this world dreams of. Wherefore, let
thy voice
Rise like a fountain for me night and day.
For what are men better than sheep or
goats
That nourish a blind life within the brain,
If, knowing God, they lift not hands of
prayer
Both for themselves and those who call
them friend?
For so the whole round earth is every way
Bound by gold chains about the feet of
God.
But now farewell. I am going a long way
With these thou seëst—if indeed I go—
(For all my mind is clouded with a doubt)
To the island-valley of Avilion;
Where falls not hail, or rain, or any snow,
Nor ever wind blows loudly; but it lies
Deep-meadow'd, happy, fair with orchard-
lawns
And bowery hollows crown'd with summer
sea,

Where I will heal me of my grievous
  wound.'
  So said he, and the barge with oar and sail
Moved from the brink, like some full-
  breasted swan
That, fluting a wild carol ere her death,
Ruffles her pure cold plume, and takes the
  flood
With swarthy webs. Long stood Sir Bedi-
  vere
Revolving many memories, till the hull
Look'd one black dot against the verge of
  dawn,
And on the mere the wailing died away.

Here ended Hall, and our last light, that
  long
Had wink'd and threaten'd darkness, flared
  and fell:
At which the Parson, sent to sleep with
  sound,
And waked with silence, grunted 'Good!'
  but we
Sat rapt: it was the tone with which he
  read—
Perhaps some modern touches here and
  there
Redeem'd it from the charge of nothing-
  ness—
Or else we loved the man, and prized his
  work;
I know not: but we sitting, as I said,
The cock crew loud; as at that time of
  year
The lusty bird takes every hour for dawn:
Then Francis, muttering, like a man ill-
  used,
'There now—that's nothing!' drew a little
  back,
And drove his heel into the smoulder'd log,
That sent a blast of sparkles up the flue;
And so to bed; where yet in sleep I seem'd
To sail with Arthur under looming shores,
Point after point; till on to dawn, when
  dreams
Begin to feel the truth and stir of day,
To me, methought, who waited with a
  crowd,
There came a bark that, blowing forward,
  bore

King Arthur, like a modern gentleman
Of stateliest port; and all the people cried,
'Arthur is come again: he cannot die.'
Then those that stood upon the hills behind
Repeated—'Come again, and thrice as
  fair;'
And, further inland, voices echo'd—'Come
With all good things, and war shall be no
  more.'
At this a hundred bells began to peal,
That with the sound I woke, and heard
  indeed
The clear church-bells ring in the Christ-
  mas-morn.

THE GARDENER'S DAUGHTER

OR, THE PICTURES

THIS morning is the morning of the day,
When I and Eustace from the city went
To see the Gardener's Daughter; I and he,
Brothers in Art; a friendship so complete
Portion'd in halves between us, that we
  grew
The fable of the city where we dwelt.
  My Eustace might have sat for Hercules;
So muscular he spread, so broad of breast.
He, by some law that holds in love, and
  draws
The greater to the lesser, long desired
A certain miracle of symmetry,
A miniature of loveliness, all grace
Summ'd up and closed in little;—Juliet,
  she
So light of foot, so light of spirit—oh, she
To me myself, for some three careless
  moons,
The summer pilot of an empty heart
Unto the shores of nothing! Know you not
Such touches are but embassies of love,
To tamper with the feelings, ere he found
Empire for life? but Eustace painted her,
And said to me, she sitting with us then,
'When will *you* paint like this?' and I
  replied,
(My words were half in earnest, half in
  jest,)
''Tis not your work, but Love's. Love,
  unperceived,

A more ideal Artist he than all,
Came, drew your pencil from you, made
   those eyes
Darker than darkest pansies, and that hair
More black than ashbuds in the front of
   March.'
And Juliet answer'd laughing, 'Go and see
The Gardener's daughter: trust me, after
   that,
You scarce can fail to match his master-
   piece.'
And up we rose, and on the spur we went.

   Not wholly in the busy world, nor quite
Beyond it, blooms the garden that I love.
News from the humming city comes to it
In sound of funeral or of marriage bells;
And, sitting muffled in dark leaves, you hear
The windy clanging of the minster clock;
Although between it and the garden lies
A league of grass, wash'd by a slow broad
   stream,
That, stirr'd with languid pulses of the oar,
Waves all its lazy lilies, and creeps on,
Barge-laden, to three arches of a bridge
Crown'd with the minster-towers.
               The fields between
Are dewy-fresh, browsed by deep-udder'd
   kine,
And all about the large lime feathers low,
The lime a summer home of murmurous
   wings.

   In that still place she, hoarded in herself,
Grew, seldom seen; not less among us lived
Her fame from lip to lip. Who had not
   heard
Of Rose, the Gardener's daughter? Where
   was he,
So blunt in memory, so old at heart,
At such a distance from his youth in grief,
That, having seen, forgot? The common
   mouth,
So gross to express delight, in praise of her
Grew oratory. Such a lord is Love,
And Beauty such a mistress of the world.

   And if I said that Fancy, led by Love,
Would play with flying forms and images,
Yet this is also true, that, long before
I look'd upon her, when I heard her name
My heart was like a prophet to my heart,
And told me I should love. A crowd of
   hopes,

That sought to sow themselves like winged
   seeds,
Born out of everything I heard and saw,
Flutter'd about my senses and my soul;
And vague desires, like fitful blasts of balm
To one that travels quickly, made the air
Of Life delicious, and all kinds of thought,
That verged upon them, sweeter than the
   dream
Dream'd by a happy man, when the dark
   East,
Unseen, is brightening to his bridal morn.

   And sure this orbit of the memory folds
For ever in itself the day we went
To see her. All the land in flowery squares,
Beneath a broad and equal-blowing wind,
Smelt of the coming summer, as one large
   cloud
Drew downward: but all else of heaven
   was pure
Up to the Sun, and May from verge to
   verge,
And May with me from head to heel. And
   now,
As tho' 'twere yesterday, as tho' it were
The hour just flown, that morn with all its
   sound,
(For those old Mays had thrice the life of
   these,)
Rings in mine ears. The steer forgot to
   graze,
And, where the hedge-row cuts the path-
   way, stood,
Leaning his horns into the neighbour field,
And lowing to his fellows. From the woods
Came voices of the well-contented doves.
The lark could scarce get out his notes for
   joy,
But shook his song together as he near'd
His happy home, the ground. To left and
   right,
The cuckoo told his name to all the hills;
The mellow ouzel fluted in the elm;
The redcap whistled; and the nightingale
Sang loud, as tho' he were the bird of day.

   And Eustace turn'd, and smiling said to
   me,
'Hear how the bushes echo! by my life,
These birds have joyful thoughts. Think
   you they sing
Like poets, from the vanity of song?

Or have they any sense of why they sing?
And would they praise the heavens for
  what they have?'
And I made answer, 'Were there nothing
  else
For which to praise the heavens but only
  love,
That only love were cause enough for
  praise.'
  Lightly he laugh'd, as one that read my
  thought,
And on we went; but ere an hour had
  pass'd,
We reach'd a meadow slanting to the
  North;
Down which a well-worn pathway courted
  us
To one green wicket in a privet hedge;
This, yielding, gave into a grassy walk
Thro' crowded lilac-ambush trimly pruned;
And one warm gust, full-fed with perfume,
  blew
Beyond us, as we enter'd in the cool.
The garden stretches southward. In the
  midst
A cedar spread his dark-green layers of
  shade.
The garden-glasses glanced, and momently
The twinkling laurel scatter'd silver lights.
'Eustace,' I said, 'this wonder keeps the
  house.'
He nodded, but a moment afterwards
He cried, 'Look! look!' Before he ceased
  I turn'd
And, ere a star can wink, beheld her there.
  For up the porch there grew an Eastern
  rose,
That, flowering high, the last night's gale
  had caught,
And blown across the walk. One arm
  aloft—
Gown'd in pure white, that fitted to the
  shape—
Holding the bush, to fix it back, she stood,
A single stream of all her soft brown hair
Pour'd on one side: the shadow of the
  flowers
Stole all the golden gloss, and, wavering
Lovingly lower, trembled on her waist—
Ah, happy shade—and still went wavering
  down,

But, ere it touch'd a foot, that might have
  danced
The greensward into greener circles, dipt,
And mix'd with shadows of the common
  ground!
But the full day dwelt on her brows, and
  sunn'd
Her violet eyes, and all her Hebe bloom,
And doubled his own warmth against her
  lips,
And on the bounteous wave of such a
  breast
As never pencil drew. Half light, half
  shade,
She stood, a sight to make an old man
  young.
  So rapt, we near'd the house; but she,
  a Rose
In roses, mingled with her fragrant toil,
Nor heard us come, nor from her tendance
  turn'd
Into the world without; till close at hand,
And almost ere I knew mine own intent,
This murmur broke the stillness of that air
Which brooded round about her:
                           'Ah, one rose,
One rose, but one, by those fair fingers
  cull'd,
Were worth a hundred kisses press'd on
  lips
Less exquisite than thine.'
                           She look'd: but all
Suffused with blushes—neither self-pos-
  sess'd
Nor startled, but betwixt this mood and
  that,
Divided in a graceful quiet—paused,
And dropt the branch she held, and turn-
  ing, wound
Her looser hair in braid, and stirr'd her lips
For some sweet answer, tho' no answer
  came,
Nor yet refused the rose, but granted it,
And moved away, and left me, statue-like,
In act to render thanks.
                           I, that whole day,
Saw her no more, altho' I linger'd there
Till every daisy slept, and Love's white
  star
Beam'd thro' the thicken'd cedar in the
  dusk.

So home we went, and all the livelong
way
With solemn gibe did Eustace banter me.
'Now,' said he, 'will you climb the top of
Art.
You cannot fail but work in hues to dim
The Titianic Flora. Will you match
My Juliet? you, not you,—the Master,
Love,
A more ideal Artist he than all.'
    So home I went, but could not sleep for
joy,
Reading her perfect features in the gloom,
Kissing the rose she gave me o'er and o'er,
And shaping faithful record of the glance
That graced the giving—such a noise of
life
Swarm'd in the golden present, such a
voice
Call'd to me from the years to come, and
such
A length of bright horizon rimm'd the
dark.
And all that night I heard the watchman
peal
The sliding season: all that night I heard
The heavy clocks knolling the drowsy
hours.
The drowsy hours, dispensers of all good,
O'er the mute city stole with folded wings,
Distilling odours on me as they went
To greet their fairer sisters of the East.
    Love at first sight, first-born, and heir
to all,
Made this night thus. Henceforward squall
nor storm
Could keep me from that Eden where she
dwelt.
Light pretexts drew me; sometimes a
Dutch love
For tulips; then for roses, moss or musk,
To grace my city rooms; or fruits and
cream
Served in the weeping elm; and more and
more
A word could bring the colour to my
cheek;
A thought would fill my eyes with happy
dew;
Love trebled life within me, and with each
The year increased.

    The daughters of the year,
One after one, thro' that still garden
pass'd;
Each garlanded with her peculiar flower
Danced into light, and died into the shade;
And each in passing touch'd with some
new grace
Or seem'd to touch her, so that day by
day,
Like one that never can be wholly known,
Her beauty grew; till Autumn brought an
hour
For Eustace, when I heard his deep 'I
will,'
Breathed, like the covenant of a God, to
hold
From thence thro' all the worlds: but I
rose up
Full of his bliss, and following her dark
eyes
Felt earth as air beneath me, till I reach'd
The wicket-gate, and found her standing
there.
    There sat we down upon a garden
mound,
Two mutually enfolded; Love, the third,
Between us, in the circle of his arms
Enwound us both; and over many a range
Of waning lime the gray cathedral towers,
Across a hazy glimmer of the west,
Reveal'd their shining windows: from them
clash'd
The bells; we listen'd; with the time we
play'd,
We spoke of other things; we coursed
about
The subject most at heart, more near and
near,
Like doves about a dovecote, wheeling
round
The central wish, until we settled there.
    Then, in that time and place, I spoke to
her,
Requiring, tho' I knew it was mine own,
Yet for the pleasure that I took to hear,
Requiring at her hand the greatest gift,
A woman's heart, the heart of her I loved;
And in that time and place she answer'd
me,
And in the compass of three little words,
More musical than ever came in one,

The silver fragments of a broken voice,
Made me most happy, faltering, 'I am
thine.'
Shall I cease here? Is this enough to say
That my desire, like all strongest hopes,
By its own energy fulfill'd itself,
Merged in completion? Would you learn
at full
How passion rose thro' circumstantial
grades
Beyond all grades develop'd? and indeed
I had not staid so long to tell you all,
But while I mused came Memory with sad
eyes,
Holding the folded annals of my youth;
And while I mused, Love with knit brows
went by,
And with a flying finger swept my lips,
And spake, 'Be wise: not easily forgiven
Are those, who setting wide the doors that
bar
The secret bridal chambers of the heart,
Let in the day.' Here, then, my words have
end.
Yet might I tell of meetings, of fare-
wells—
Of that which came between, more sweet
than each,
In whispers, like the whispers of the leaves
That tremble round a nightingale—in sighs
Which perfect Joy, perplex'd for utterance,
Stole from her sister Sorrow. Might I not
tell
Of difference, reconcilement, pledges
given,
And vows, where there was never need of
vows,
And kisses, where the heart on one wild
leap
Hung tranced from all pulsation, as above
The heavens between their fairy fleeces
pale
Sow'd all their mystic gulfs with fleeting
stars;
Or while the balmy glooming, crescent-lit,
Spread the light haze along the river-
shores,
And in the hollows; or as once we met
Unheedful, tho' beneath a whispering rain
Night slid down one long stream of sighing
wind,

And in her bosom bore the baby, Sleep.
But this whole hour your eyes have been
intent
On that veil'd picture—veil'd, for what it
holds
May not be dwelt on by the common day.
This prelude has prepared thee. Raise thy
soul;
Make thine heart ready with thine eyes:
the time
Is come to raise the veil.
                                    Behold her there,
As I beheld her ere she knew my heart,
My first, last love; the idol of my youth,
The darling of my manhood, and, alas!
Now the most blessed memory of mine
age.

DORA

WITH farmer Allan at the farm abode
William and Dora. William was his son,
And she his niece. He often look'd at them,
And often thought, 'I'll make them man
and wife.'
Now Dora felt her uncle's will in all,
And yearn'd toward William; but the
youth, because
He had been always with her in the house,
Thought not of Dora.
                              Then there came a day
When Allan call'd his son, and said, 'My
son:
I married late, but I would wish to see
My grandchild on my knees before I die:
And I have set my heart upon a match.
Now therefore look to Dora; she is well
To look to; thrifty too beyond her age.
She is my brother's daughter: he and I
Had once hard words, and parted, and he
died
In foreign lands; but for his sake I bred
His daughter Dora: take her for your wife;
For I have wish'd this marriage, night and
day,
For many years.' But William answer'd
short;
'I cannot marry Dora; by my life,
I will not marry Dora.' Then the old man
Was wroth, and doubled up his hands, and
said:

'You will not, boy! you dare to answer thus!
But in my time a father's word was law,
And so it shall be now for me. Look to it;
Consider, William: take a month to think,
And let me have an answer to my wish;
Or, by the Lord that made me, you shall pack,
And never more darken my doors again.'
But William answer'd madly; bit his lips,
And broke away. The more he look'd at her
The less he liked her; and his ways were harsh;
But Dora bore them meekly. Then before
The month was out he left his father's house,
And hired himself to work within the fields;
And half in love, half spite, he woo'd and wed
A labourer's daughter, Mary Morrison.

    Then, when the bells were ringing, Allan call'd
His niece and said: 'My girl, I love you well;
But if you speak with him that was my son,
Or change a word with her he calls his wife,
My home is none of yours. My will is law.'
And Dora promised, being meek. She thought,
'It cannot be: my uncle's mind will change!'

    And days went on, and there was born a boy
To William; then distresses came on him;
And day by day he pass'd his father's gate,
Heart-broken, and his father help'd him not.
But Dora stored what little she could save,
And sent it them by stealth, nor did they know
Who sent it; till at last a fever seized
On William, and in harvest time he died.
    Then Dora went to Mary. Mary sat
And look'd with tears upon her boy, and thought
Hard things of Dora. Dora came and said:
    'I have obey'd my uncle until now,
And I have sinn'd, for it was all thro' me

This evil came on William at the first.
But, Mary, for the sake of him that's gone,
And for your sake, the woman that he chose,
And for this orphan, I am come to you:
You know there has not been for these five years
So full a harvest: let me take the boy,
And I will set him in my uncle's eye
Among the wheat; that when his heart is glad
Of the full harvest, he may see the boy,
And bless him for the sake of him that's gone.'
    And Dora took the child, and went her way
Across the wheat, and sat upon a mound
That was unsown, where many poppies grew.
Far off the farmer came into the field
And spied her not; for none of all his men
Dare tell him Dora waited with the child;
And Dora would have risen and gone to him,
But her heart fail'd her; and the reapers reap'd,
And the sun fell, and all the land was dark.
    But when the morrow came, she rose and took
The child once more, and sat upon the mound;
And made a little wreath of all the flowers
That grew about, and tied it round his hat
To make him pleasing in her uncle's eye.
Then when the farmer pass'd into the field
He spied her, and he left his men at work,
And came and said: 'Where were you yesterday?
Whose child is that? What are you doing here?'
So Dora cast her eyes upon the ground,
And answer'd softly, 'This is William's child!'
'And did I not,' said Allan, 'did I not
Forbid you, Dora?' Dora said again:
'Do with me as you will, but take the child,
And bless him for the sake of him that's gone!'
And Allan said, 'I see it is a trick
Got up betwixt you and the woman there.
I must be taught my duty, and by you!

You knew my word was law, and yet you dared
To slight it. Well—for I will take the boy;
But go you hence, and never see me more.'
So saying, he took the boy that cried aloud
And struggled hard. The wreath of flowers fell
At Dora's feet. She bow'd upon her hands,
And the boy's cry came to her from the field,
More and more distant. She bow'd down her head,
Remembering the day when first she came,
And all the things that had been. She bow'd down
And wept in secret; and the reapers reap'd,
And the sun fell, and all the land was dark.
Then Dora went to Mary's house, and stood
Upon the threshold. Mary saw the boy
Was not with Dora. She broke out in praise
To God, that help'd her in her widowhood.
And Dora said, 'My uncle took the boy;
But, Mary, let me live and work with you:
He says that he will never see me more.'
Then answer'd Mary, 'This shall never be,
That thou shouldst take my trouble on thyself:
And, now I think, he shall not have the boy,
For he will teach him hardness, and to slight
His mother; therefore thou and I will go,
And I will have my boy, and bring him home;
And I will beg of him to take thee back:
But if he will not take thee back again,
Then thou and I will live within one house,
And work for William's child, until he grows
Of age to help us.'
                    So the women kiss'd
Each other, and set out, and reach'd the farm.
The door was off the latch: they peep'd, and saw
The boy set up betwixt his grandsire's knees,
Who thrust him in the hollows of his arm,
And clapt him on the hands and on the cheeks,
Like one that loved him: and the lad stretch'd out

And babbled for the golden seal, that hung
From Allan's watch, and sparkled by the fire.
Then they came in: but when the boy beheld
His mother, he cried out to come to her:
And Allan set him down, and Mary said:
'O Father!—if you let me call you so—
I never came a-begging for myself,
Or William, or this child; but now I come
For Dora: take her back; she loves you well.
O Sir, when William died, he died at peace
With all men; for I ask'd him, and he said,
He could not ever rue his marrying me—
I had been a patient wife: but, Sir, he said
That he was wrong to cross his father thus:
"God bless him!" he said, "and may he never know
The troubles I have gone thro'!" Then he turn'd
His face and pass'd—unhappy that I am!
But now, Sir, let me have my boy, for you
Will make him hard, and he will learn to slight
His father's memory; and take Dora back,
And let all this be as it was before.'
So Mary said, and Dora hid her face
By Mary. There was silence in the room;
And all at once the old man burst in sobs:—
'I have been to blame—to blame. I have kill'd my son.
I have kill'd him—but I loved him—my dear son.
May God forgive me!—I have been to blame.
Kiss me, my children.'
                    Then they clung about
The old man's neck, and kiss'd him many times.
And all the man was broken with remorse;
And all his love came back a hundredfold;
And for three hours he sobb'd o'er William's child
Thinking of William.
                    So those four abode
Within one house together; and as years
Went forward, Mary took another mate;
But Dora lived unmarried till her death.

AUDLEY COURT

'The Bull, the Fleece are cramm'd, and
      not a room
For love or money. Let us picnic there
At Audley Court.'
        I spoke, while Audley feast
Humm'd like a hive all round the narrow
      quay,
To Francis, with a basket on his arm,
To Francis just alighted from the boat,
And breathing of the sea. 'With all my
      heart,'
Said Francis. Then we shoulder'd thro'
      the swarm,
And rounded by the stillness of the beach
To where the bay runs up its latest horn.
  We left the dying ebb that faintly lipp'd
The flat red granite; so by many a sweep
Of meadow smooth from aftermath we
      reach'd
The griffin-guarded gates, and pass'd thro'
      all
The pillar'd dusk of sounding sycamores,
And cross'd the garden to the gardener's
      lodge,
With all its casements bedded, and its walls
And chimneys muffled in the leafy vine.
  There, on a slope of orchard, Francis
      laid
A damask napkin wrought with horse and
      hound,
Brought out a dusky loaf that smelt of
      home,
And, half-cut-down, a pasty costly-made,
Where quail and pigeon, lark and leveret
      lay,
Like fossils of the rock, with golden yolks
Imbedded and injellied; last, with these,
A flask of cider from his father's vats,
Prime, which I knew; and so we sat and eat
And talk'd old matters over; who was dead,
Who married, who was like to be, and how
The races went, and who would rent the
      hall:
Then touch'd upon the game, how scarce
      it was
This season; glancing thence, discuss'd the
      farm,
The four-field system, and the price of
      grain;

And struck upon the corn-laws, where we
      split,
And came again together on the king
With heated faces; till he laugh'd aloud;
And, while the blackbird on the pippin
      hung
To hear him, clapt his hand in mine and
      sang—
  'Oh! who would fight and march and
      countermarch,
Be shot for sixpence in a battle-field,
And shovell'd up into some bloody trench
Where no one knows? but let me live my
      life.
  'Oh! who would cast and balance at a
      desk,
Perch'd like a crow upon a three-legg'd
      stool,
Till all his juice is dried, and all his joints
Are full of chalk? but let me live my life.
  'Who'd serve the state? for if I carved
      my name
Upon the cliffs that guard my native land,
I might as well have traced it in the sands;
The sea wastes all: but let me live my life.
  'Oh! who would love? I woo'd a woman
      once,
But she was sharper than an eastern wind,
And all my heart turn'd from her, as a
      thorn
Turns from the sea; but let me live my
      life.'
  He sang his song, and I replied with
      mine:
I found it in a volume, all of songs,
Knock'd down to me, when old Sir
      Robert's pride,
His books—the more the pity, so I said—
Came to the hammer here in March—and
      this—
I set the words, and added names I knew.
  'Sleep, Ellen Aubrey, sleep, and dream
      of me:
Sleep, Ellen, folded in thy sister's arm,
And sleeping, haply dream her arm is
      mine.
  'Sleep, Ellen, folded in Emilia's arm;
Emilia, fairer than all else but thou,
For thou art fairer than all else that is.
  'Sleep, breathing health and peace upon
      her breast:

Sleep, breathing love and trust against her
    lip:
I go to-night: I come to-morrow morn.
  'I go, but I return: I would I were
The pilot of the darkness and the dream.
Sleep, Ellen Aubrey, love, and dream of
    me.'
  So sang we each to either, Francis Hale,
The farmer's son, who lived across the
    bay,
My friend; and I, that having wherewithal,
And in the fallow leisure of my life
A rolling stone of here and everywhere,
Did what I would; but ere the night we
    rose
And saunter'd home beneath a moon, that,
    just
In crescent, dimly rain'd about the leaf
Twilights of airy silver, till we reach'd
The limit of the hills; and as we sank
From rock to rock upon the glooming
    quay,
The town was hush'd beneath us: lower
    down
The bay was oily calm; the harbour-buoy,
Sole star of phosphorescence in the calm,
With one green sparkle ever and anon
Dipt by itself, and we were glad at heart.

WALKING TO THE MAIL

  John. I'M glad I walk'd. How fresh the
    meadows look
Above the river, and, but a month ago,
The whole hill-side was redder than a fox.
Is yon plantation where this byway joins
The turnpike?
  James.   Yes.
  John.   And when does this come by?
  James. The mail? At one o'clock.
  John.   What is it now?
  James. A quarter to.
  John.   Whose house is that I see?
No, not the County Member's with the
    vane:
Up higher with the yew-tree by it, and
    half
A score of gables.
  James. That? Sir Edward Head's:
But he's abroad: the place is to be sold.
  John. Oh, his. He was not broken.

  James.   No, sir, he,
Vex'd with a morbid devil in his blood
That veil'd the world with jaundice, hid
    his face
From all men, and commercing with him-
    self,
He lost the sense that handles daily life—
That keeps us all in order more or less—
And sick of home went overseas for change.
  John. And whither?
  James. Nay, who knows? he's here and
    there.
But let him go; his devil goes with him,
As well as with his tenant, Jocky Dawes.
  John. What's that?
  James. You saw the man—on Monday,
    was it?—
There by the humpback'd willow; half
    stands up
And bristles; half has fall'n and made a
    bridge;
And there he caught the younker tickling
    trout—
Caught *in flagrante*—what's the Latin
    word?—
Delicto: but his house, for so they say,
Was haunted with a jolly ghost, that shook
The curtains, whined in lobbies, tapt at
    doors,
And rummaged like a rat: no servant
    stay'd:
The farmer vext packs up his beds and
    chairs,
And all his household stuff; and with his
    boy
Betwixt his knees, his wife upon the tilt,
Sets out, and meets a friend who hails him,
    'What!
You're flitting!' 'Yes, we're flitting,' says
    the ghost
(For they had pack'd the thing among the
    beds,)
'Oh well,' says he, 'you flitting with us
    too—
Jack, turn the horses' heads and home
    again.'
  John. He left *his* wife behind; for so I
    heard.
  James. He left her, yes. I met my lady
    once;
A woman like a butt, and harsh as crabs.

John. Oh yet but I remember, ten years
    back—
'Tis now at least ten years—and then she
    was—
You could not light upon a sweeter thing:
A body slight and round, and like a pear
In growing, modest eyes, a hand, a foot
Lessening in perfect cadence, and a skin
As clean and white as privet when it
    flowers.
    James. Ay, ay, the blossom fades, and
    they that loved
At first like dove and dove were cat and
    dog.
She was the daughter of a cottager,
Out of her sphere. What betwixt shame
    and pride,
New things and old, himself and her, she
    sour'd
To what she is: a nature never kind!
Like men, like manners: like breeds like,
    they say:
Kind nature is the best: those manners
    next
That fit us like a nature second-hand;
Which are indeed the manners of the great.
    John. But I had heard it was this bill
    that past,
And fear of change at home, that drove
    him hence.
    James. That was the last drop in the cup
    of gall.
I once was near him, when his bailiff
    brought
A Chartist pike. You should have seen
    him wince
As from a venomous thing: he thought
    himself
A mark for all, and shudder'd, lest a cry
Should break his sleep by night, and his
    nice eyes
Should see the raw mechanic's bloody
    thumbs
Sweat on his blazon'd chairs; but, sir, you
    know
That these two parties still divide the
    world—
Of those that want, and those that have:
    and still
The same old sore breaks out from age to
    age

With much the same result. Now I myself,
A Tory to the quick, was as a boy
Destructive, when I had not what I would.
I was at school—a college in the South:
There lived a flayflint near; we stole his
    fruit,
His hens, his eggs; but there was law for
    us;
We paid in person. He had a sow, sir. She,
With meditative grunts of much content,
Lay great with pig, wallowing in sun and
    mud.
By night we dragg'd her to the college
    tower
From her warm bed, and up the cork-
    screw stair
With hand and rope we haled the groaning
    sow,
And on the leads we kept her till she
    pigg'd.
Large range of prospect had the mother
    sow,
And but for daily loss of one she loved
As one by one we took them—but for
    this—
As never sow was higher in this world—
Might have been happy: but what lot is
    pure?
We took them all, till she was left alone
Upon her tower, the Niobe of swine,
And so return'd unfarrow'd to her sty.
    John. They found you out?
    James.   Not they.
    John.   Well—after all—
What know we of the secret of a man?
His nerves were wrong. What ails us, who
    are sound,
That we should mimic this raw fool the
    world,
Which charts us all in its coarse blacks or
    whites,
As ruthless as a baby with a worm,
As cruel as a schoolboy ere he grows
To Pity—more from ignorance than will.
    But put your best foot forward, or I
    fear
That we shall miss the mail: and here it
    comes
With five at top: as quaint a four-in-hand
As you shall see—three pyebalds and a
    roan.

EDWIN MORRIS

OR, THE LAKE

O ME, my pleasant rambles by the lake,
My sweet, wild, fresh three quarters of a
  year,
My one Oasis in the dust and drouth
Of city life! I was a sketcher then:
See here, my doing: curves of mountain,
  bridge,
Boat, island . ruins of a castle, built
When men knew how to build, upon a rock
With turrets lichen-gilded like a rock:
And here, new-comers in an ancient hold,
New-comers from the Mersey, million-
  aires .
Here lived the Hills—a Tudor-chimnied
  bulk
Of mellow brickwork on an isle of bowers.
O me, my pleasant rambles by the lake
With Edwin Morris and with Edward Bull
The curate; he was fatter than his cure.

But Edwin Morris, he that knew the
  names,
Long learned names of agaric, moss and
  fern,
Who forged a thousand theories of the
  rocks,
Who taught me how to skate, to row, to
  swim,
Who read me rhymes elaborately good,
His own—I call'd him Crichton, for he
  seem'd
All-perfect, finish'd to the finger nail.

And once I ask'd him of his early life,
And his first passion; and he answer'd me;
And well his words became him: was he not
A full-cell'd honeycomb of eloquence
Stored from all flowers? Poet-like he spoke.

'My love for Nature is as old as I;
But thirty moons, one honeymoon to that,
And three rich sennights more, my love
  for her,
My love for Nature and my love for her,
Of different ages, like twin-sisters grew,
Twin-sisters differently beautiful.
To some full music rose and sank the sun,
And some full music seem'd to move and
  change

With all the varied changes of the dark,
And either twilight and the day between;
For daily hope fulfill'd, to rise again
Revolving toward fulfilment, made it sweet
To walk, to sit, to sleep, to wake, to
  breathe.'

Or this or something like to this he spoke.
Then said the fat-faced curate Edward
  Bull,
'I take it, God made the woman for the
  man,
And for the good and increase of the world.
A pretty face is well, and this is well,
To have a dame indoors, that trims us up,
And keeps us tight; but these unreal ways
Seem but the theme of writers, and indeed
Worn threadbare. Man is made of solid
  stuff.
I say, God made the woman for the man,
And for the good and increase of the
  world.'

'Parson,' said I, 'you pitch the pipe too
  low:
But I have sudden touches, and can run
My faith beyond my practice into his:
Tho' if, in dancing after Letty Hill,
I do not hear the bells upon my cap,
I scarce have other music: yet say on.
What should one give to light on such a
  dream?'
I ask'd him half-sardonically.

                              'Give?
Give all thou art,' he answer'd, and a light
Of laughter dimpled in his swarthy cheek;
'I would have hid her needle in my heart,
To save her little finger from a scratch
No deeper than the skin: my ears could
  hear
Her lightest breath; her least remark was
  worth
The experience of the wise. I went and
  came;
Her voice fled always thro' the summer
  land;
I spoke her name alone. Thrice-happy
  days!
The flower of each, those moments when
  we met,
The crown of all, we met to part no more.'

Were not his words delicious, I a beast
To take them as I did? but something
    jarr'd;
Whether he spoke too largely; that there
    seem'd
A touch of something false, some self-
    conceit,
Or over-smoothness: howsoe'er it was,
He scarcely hit my humour, and I said:

'Friend Edwin, do not think yourself
    alone
Of all men happy. Shall not Love to me,
As in the Latin song I learnt at school,
Sneeze out a full God-bless-you right and
    left?
But you can talk: yours is a kindly vein:
I have, I think,—Heaven knows—as much
    within;
Have, or should have, but for a thought or
    two,
That like a purple beech among the greens
Looks out of place: 'tis from no want in
    her:
It is my shyness, or my self-distrust,
Or something of a wayward modern mind
Dissecting passion. Time will set me right.'

So spoke I knowing not the things that
    were.
Then said the fat-faced curate, Edward
    Bull;
'God made the woman for the use of man,
And for the good and increase of the
    world.'
And I and Edwin laughed; and now we
    paused
About the windings of the marge to hear
The soft wind blowing over meadowy
    holms
And alders, garden-isles; and now we left
The clerk behind us, I and he, and ran
By ripply shallows of the lisping lake,
Delighted with the freshness and the
    sound.

But, when the bracken rusted on their
    crags,
My suit had wither'd, nipt to death by
    him
That was a God, and is a lawyer's clerk,
The rentroll Cupid of our rainy isles.

'Tis true, we met; one hour I had, no
    more:
She sent a note, the seal an *Elle vous suit*,
The close, 'Your Letty, only yours;' and
    this
Thrice underscored. The friendly mist of
    morn
Clung to the lake. I boated over, ran
My craft aground, and heard with beating
    heart
The Sweet-Gale rustle round the shelving
    keel;
And out I stept, and up I crept: she moved,
Like Proserpine in Enna, gathering flowers:
Then low and sweet I whistled thrice; and
    she,
She turn'd, we closed, we kiss'd, swore faith,
    I breathed
In some new planet: a silent cousin stole
Upon us and departed: 'Leave,' she cried,
'O leave me!' 'Never, dearest, never: here
I brave the worst:' and while we stood like
    fools
Embracing, all at once a score of pugs
And poodles yell'd within, and out they
    came
Trustees and Aunts and Uncles. 'What,
    with him!
Go' (shrill'd the cotton-spinning chorus);
    'him!'
I choked. Again they shriek'd the burthen
    'Him!'
Again with hands of wild rejection 'Go!—
Girl, get you in!' She went—and in one
    month
They wedded her to sixty thousand pounds,
To lands in Kent and messuages in York,
And slight Sir Robert with his watery smile
And educated whisker. But for me,
They set an ancient creditor to work:
It seems I broke a close with force and
    arms:
There came a mystic token from the king
To greet the sheriff, needless courtesy!
I read, and fled by night, and flying turn'd:
Her taper glimmer'd in the lake below:
I turn'd once more, close-button'd to the
    storm;
So left the place, left Edwin, nor have seen
Him since, nor heard of her, nor cared to
    hear.

Nor cared to hear? perhaps: yet long ago
I have pardon'd little Letty; not indeed,
It may be, for her own dear sake but this,
She seems a part of those fresh days to me;
For in the dust and drouth of London life
She moves among my visions of the lake,
While the prime swallow dips his wing, or
    then
While the gold-lily blows, and overhead
The light cloud smoulders on the summer
    crag.

ST. SIMEON STYLITES

ALTHO' I be the basest of mankind,
From scalp to sole one slough and crust
    of sin,
Unfit for earth, unfit for heaven, scarce
    meet
For troops of devils, mad with blasphemy,
I will not cease to grasp the hope I hold
Of saintdom, and to clamour, mourn and
    sob,
Battering the gates of heaven with storms
    of prayer,
Have mercy, Lord, and take away my sin.
    Let this avail, just, dreadful, mighty
    God,
This not be all in vain, that thrice ten
    years,
Thrice multiplied by superhuman pangs,
In hungers and in thirsts, fevers and cold,
In coughs, aches, stitches, ulcerous throes
    and cramps,
A sign betwixt the meadow and the cloud,
Patient on this tall pillar I have borne
Rain, wind, frost, heat, hail, damp, and
    sleet, and snow;
And I had hoped that ere this period closed
Thou wouldst have caught me up into thy
    rest,
Denying not these weather-beaten limbs
The meed of saints, the white robe and the
    palm.
    O take the meaning, Lord: I do not
    breathe,
Not whisper, any murmur of complaint.
Pain heap'd ten-hundred-fold to this, were
    still
Less burthen, by ten-hundred-fold, to
    bear,

Than were those lead-like tons of sin, that
    crush'd
My spirit flat before thee.
                    O Lord, Lord,
Thou knowest I bore this better at the
    first,
For I was strong and hale of body then;
And tho' my teeth, which now are dropt
    away,
Would chatter with the cold, and all my
    beard
Was tagg'd with icy fringes in the moon,
I drown'd the whoopings of the owl with
    sound
Of pious hymns and psalms, and some-
    times saw
An angel stand and watch me, as I sang.
Now am I feeble grown; my end draws
    nigh;
I hope my end draws nigh: half deaf I am,
So that I scarce can hear the people hum
About the column's base, and almost blind,
And scarce can recognise the fields I know;
And both my thighs are rotted with the
    dew;
Yet cease I not to clamour and to cry,
While my stiff spine can hold my weary
    head,
Till all my limbs drop piecemeal from the
    stone,
Have mercy, mercy: take away my sin.
    O Jesus, if thou wilt not save my soul,
Who may be saved? who is it may be
    saved?
Who may be made a saint, if I fail here?
Show me the man hath suffer'd more
    than I.
For did not all thy martyrs die one death?
For either they were stoned, or crucified,
Or burn'd in fire, or boil'd in oil, or sawn
In twain beneath the ribs; but I die here
To-day, and whole years long, a life of
    death.
Bear witness, if I could have found a way
(And heedfully I sifted all my thought)
More slowly-painful to subdue this home
Of sin, my flesh, which I despise and hate,
I had not stinted practice, O my God.
    For not alone this pillar-punishment,
Not this alone I bore: but while I lived
In the white convent down the valley there,

For many weeks about my loins I wore
The rope that haled the buckets from the
    well,
Twisted as tight as I could knot the noose;
And spake not of it to a single soul,
Until the ulcer, eating thro' my skin,
Betray'd my secret penance, so that all
My brethren marvell'd greatly. More than
    this
I bore, whereof, O God, thou knowest all.
    Three winters, that my soul might grow
    to thee,
I lived up there on yonder mountain
    side.
My right leg chain'd into the crag, I lay
Pent in a roofless close of ragged stones;
Inswathed sometimes in wandering mist,
    and twice
Black'd with thy branding thunder, and
    sometimes
Sucking the damps for drink, and eating
    not,
Except the spare chance-gift of those that
    came
To touch my body and be heal'd, and live:
And they say then that I work'd miracles,
Whereof my fame is loud amongst man-
    kind,
Cured lameness, palsies, cancers. Thou,
    O God,
Knowest alone whether this was or no.
Have mercy, mercy! cover all my sin.
    Then, that I might be more alone with
    thee,
Three years I lived upon a pillar, high
Six cubits, and three years on one of
    twelve;
And twice three years I crouch'd on one
    that rose
Twenty by measure; last of all, I grew
Twice ten long weary weary years to this,
That numbers forty cubits from the soil.
    I think that I have borne as much as
    this—
Or else I dream—and for so long a time,
If I may measure time by yon slow light,
And this high dial, which my sorrow
    crowns—
So much—even so.
                    And yet I know not well,
For that the evil ones come here, and say,

'Fall down, O Simeon: thou hast suffer'd
    long
For ages and for ages!' then they prate
Of penances I cannot have gone thro',
Perplexing me with lies; and oft I fall,
Maybe for months, in such blind lethargies
That Heaven, and Earth, and Time are
    choked.
                                    But yet
Bethink thee, Lord, while thou and all the
    saints
Enjoy themselves in heaven, and men on
    earth
House in the shade of comfortable roofs,
Sit with their wives by fires, eat wholesome
    food,
And wear warm clothes, and even beasts
    have stalls,
I, 'tween the spring and downfall of the
    light,
Bow down one thousand and two hundred
    times,
To Christ, the Virgin Mother, and the
    saints;
Or in the night, after a little sleep,
I wake: the chill stars sparkle; I am wet
With drenching dews, or stiff with crack-
    ling frost.
I wear an undress'd goatskin on my back;
A grazing iron collar grinds my neck;
And in my weak, lean arms I lift the cross,
And strive and wrestle with thee till I die:
O mercy, mercy! wash away my sin.
    O Lord, thou knowest what a man I am;
A sinful man, conceived and born in sin:
'Tis their own doing; this is none of mine;
Lay it not to me. Am I to blame for this,
That here come those that worship me?
    Ha! ha!
They think that I am somewhat. What
    am I?
The silly people take me for a saint,
And bring me offerings of fruit and flowers:
And I, in truth (thou wilt bear witness
    here)
Have all in all endured as much, and more
Than many just and holy men, whose
    names
Are register'd and calendar'd for saints.
    Good people, you do ill to kneel to me.
What is it I can have done to merit this?

I am a sinner viler than you all.
It may be I have wrought some miracles,
And cured some halt and maim'd; but
    what of that?
It may be, no one, even among the saints,
May match his pains with mine; but what
    of that?
Yet do not rise; for you may look on me,
And in your looking you may kneel to God.
Speak! is there any of you halt or maim'd?
I think you know I have some power with
    Heaven
From my long penance: let him speak his
    wish.
    Yes, I can heal him. Power goes forth
    from me.
They say that they are heal'd. Ah, hark!
    they shout
'St. Simeon Stylites.' Why, if so,
God reaps a harvest in me. O my soul,
God reaps a harvest in thee. If this be,
Can I work miracles and not be saved?
This is not told of any. They were saints.
It cannot be but that I shall be saved;
Yea, crown'd a saint. They shout, 'Behold
    a saint!'
And lower voices saint me from above.
Courage, St. Simeon! This dull chrysalis
Cracks into shining wings, and hope ere
    death
Spreads more and more and more, that
    God hath now
Sponged and made blank of crimeful
    record all
My mortal archives.
                    O my sons, my sons,
I, Simeon of the pillar, by surname
Stylites, among men; I, Simeon,
The watcher on the column till the end;
I, Simeon, whose brain the sunshine bakes;
I, whose bald brows in silent hours become
Unnaturally hoar with rime, do now
From my high nest of penance here pro-
    claim
That Pontius and Iscariot by my side
Show'd like fair seraphs. On the coals I
    lay,
A vessel full of sin: all hell beneath
Made me boil over. Devils pluck'd my
    sleeve,
Abaddon and Asmodeus caught at me.

I smote them with the cross; they swarm'd
    again.
In bed like monstrous apes they crush'd
    my chest:
They flapp'd my light out as I read: I saw
Their faces grow between me and my
    book;
With colt-like whinny and with hoggish
    whine
They burst my prayer. Yet this way was
    left,
And by this way I 'scaped them. Mortify
Your flesh, like me, with scourges and with
    thorns;
Smite, shrink not, spare not. If it may be,
    fast
Whole Lents, and pray. I hardly, with
    slow steps,
With slow, faint steps, and much exceed-
    ing pain,
Have scrambled past those pits of fire, that
    still
Sing in mine ears. But yield not me the
    praise:
God only thro' his bounty hath thought fit,
Among the powers and princes of this
    world,
To make me an example to mankind,
Which few can reach to. Yet I do not say
But that a time may come—yea, even now,
Now, now, his footsteps smite the thresh-
    old stairs
Of life—I say, that time is at the doors
When you may worship me without re-
    proach;
For I will leave my relics in your land,
And you may carve a shrine about my dust,
And burn a fragrant lamp before my bones,
When I am gather'd to the glorious saints.
    While I spake then, a sting of shrewd-
    est pain
Ran shrivelling thro' me, and a cloudlike
    change,
In passing, with a grosser film made thick
These heavy, horny eyes. The end! the
    end!
Surely the end! What's here? a shape, a
    shade,
A flash of light. Is that the angel there
That holds a crown? Come, blessed
    brother, come.

I know thy glittering face. I waited long;
My brows are ready. What! deny it now?
Nay, draw, draw, draw nigh. So I clutch
    it. Christ!
'Tis gone: 'tis here again; the crown! the
    crown!
So now 'tis fitted on and grows to me,
And from it melt the dews of Paradise,
Sweet! sweet! spikenard, and balm, and
    frankincense.
Ah! let me not be fool'd, sweet saints: I
    trust
That I am whole, and clean, and meet for
    Heaven.

Speak, if there be a priest, a man of God,
Among you there, and let him presently
Approach, and lean a ladder on the shaft,
And climbing up into my airy home,
Deliver me the blessed sacrament;
For by the warning of the Holy Ghost,
I prophesy that I shall die to-night,
A quarter before twelve.
                But thou, O Lord,
Aid all this foolish people; let them take
Example, pattern: lead them to thy light.

THE TALKING OAK

ONCE more the gate behind me falls;
    Once more before my face
I see the moulder'd Abbey-walls,
    That stand within the chace.

Beyond the lodge the city lies,
    Beneath its drift of smoke;
And ah! with what delighted eyes
    I turn to yonder oak.

For when my passion first began,
    Ere that, which in me burn'd,
The love, that makes me thrice a man,
    Could hope itself return'd;

To yonder oak within the field
    I spoke without restraint,
And with a larger faith appeal'd
    Than Papist unto Saint.

For oft I talk'd with him apart,
    And told him of my choice,
Until he plagiarised a heart,
    And answer'd with a voice.

Tho' what he whisper'd under Heaven
    None else could understand;
I found him garrulously given,
    A babbler in the land.

But since I heard him make reply
    Is many a weary hour;
'Twere well to question him, and try
    If yet he keeps the power.

Hail, hidden to the knees in fern,
    Broad Oak of Sumner-chace,
Whose topmost branches can discern
    The roofs of Sumner-place!

Say thou, whereon I carved her name,
    If ever maid or spouse,
As fair as my Olivia, came
    To rest beneath thy boughs.—

'O Walter, I have shelter'd here
    Whatever maiden grace
The good old Summers, year by year
    Made ripe in Sumner-chace:

'Old Summers, when the monk was fat,
    And, issuing shorn and sleek,
Would twist his girdle tight, and pat
    The girls upon the cheek,

'Ere yet, in scorn of Peter's-pence,
    And number'd bead, and shrift,
Bluff Harry broke into the spence
    And turn'd the cowls adrift:

'And I have seen some score of those
    Fresh faces, that would thrive
When his man-minded offset rose
    To chase the deer at five;

'And all that from the town would stroll,
    Till that wild wind made work
In which the gloomy brewer's soul
    Went by me, like a stork:

'The slight she-slips of loyal blood,
    And others, passing praise,
Strait-laced, but all-too-full in bud
    For puritanic stays:

'And I have shadow'd many a group
    Of beauties, that were born
In teacup-times of hood and hoop,
    Or while the patch was worn;

'And, leg and arm with love-knots gay,
  About me leap'd and laugh'd
The modish Cupid of the day,
  And shrill'd his tinsel shaft.

'I swear (and else may insects prick
  Each leaf into a gall)
This girl, for whom your heart is sick,
  Is three times worth them all;

'For those and theirs, by Nature's law,
  Have faded long ago;
But in these latter springs I saw
  Your own Olivia blow,

'From when she gamboll'd on the greens
  A baby-germ, to when
The maiden blossoms of her teens
  Could number five from ten.

'I swear, by leaf, and wind, and rain,
  (And hear me with thine ears,)
That, tho' I circle in the grain
  Five hundred rings of years—

'Yet, since I first could cast a shade,
  Did never creature pass
So slightly, musically made,
  So light upon the grass:

'For as to fairies, that will flit
  To make the greensward fresh,
I hold them exquisitely knit,
  But far too spare of flesh.'

Oh, hide thy knotted knees in fern,
  And overlook the chace;
And from thy topmost branch discern
  The roofs of Sumner-place.

But thou, whereon I carved her name,
  That oft hast heard my vows,
Declare when last Olivia came
  To sport beneath thy boughs.

'O yesterday, you know, the fair
  Was holden at the town;
Her father left his good arm-chair,
  And rode his hunter down.

'And with him Albert came on his.
  I look'd at him with joy:
As cowslip unto oxlip is,
  So seems she to the boy.

'An hour had past—and, sitting straight
  Within the low-wheel'd chaise,
Her mother trundled to the gate
  Behind the dappled grays.

'But as for her, she stay'd at home,
  And on the roof she went,
And down the way you use to come,
  She look'd with discontent.

'She left the novel half-uncut
  Upon the rosewood shelf;
She left the new piano shut:
  She could not please herself.

'Then ran she, gamesome as the colt,
  And livelier than a lark
She sent her voice thro' all the holt
  Before her, and the park.

'A light wind chased her on the wing,
  And in the chase grew wild,
As close as might be would he cling
  About the darling child:

'But light as any wind that blows
  So fleetly did she stir,
The flower, she touch'd on, dipt and rose,
  And turn'd to look at her.

'And here she came, and round me play'd,
  And sang to me the whole
Of those three stanzas that you made
  About my "giant bole;"

'And in a fit of frolic mirth
  She strove to span my waist:
Alas, I was so broad of girth,
  I could not be embraced.

'I wish'd myself the fair young beech
  That here beside me stands,
That round me, clasping each in each,
  She might have lock'd her hands.

'Yet seem'd the pressure thrice as sweet
  As woodbine's fragile hold,
Or when I feel about my feet
  The berried briony fold.'

O muffle round thy knees with fern,
  And shadow Sumner-chace!
Long may thy topmost branch discern
  The roofs of Sumner-place!

But tell me, did she read the name
  I carved with many vows
When last with throbbing heart I came
  To rest beneath thy boughs?

'O yes, she wander'd round and round
  These knotted knees of mine,
And found, and kiss'd the name she found,
  And sweetly murmur'd thine.

'A teardrop trembled from its source,
  And down my surface crept.
My sense of touch is something coarse,
  But I believe she wept.

'Then flush'd her cheek with rosy light,
  She glanced across the plain;
But not a creature was in sight:
  She kiss'd me once again.

'Her kisses were so close and kind,
  That, trust me on my word,
Hard wood I am, and wrinkled rind,
  But yet my sap was stirr'd:

'And even into my inmost ring
  A pleasure I discern'd,
Like those blind motions of the Spring,
  That show the year is turn'd.

'Thrice-happy he that may caress
  The ringlet's waving balm—
The cushions of whose touch may press
  The maiden's tender palm.

'I, rooted here among the groves
  But languidly adjust
My vapid vegetable loves
  With anthers and with dust:

'For ah! my friend, the days were brief
  Whereof the poets talk,
When that, which breathes within the leaf,
  Could slip its bark and walk.

'But could I, as in times foregone,
  From spray, and branch, and stem,
Have suck'd and gather'd into one
  The life that spreads in them,

'She had not found me so remiss;
  But lightly issuing thro',
I would have paid her kiss for kiss,
  With usury thereto.'

O flourish high, with leafy towers,
  And overlook the lea,
Pursue thy loves among the bowers
  But leave thou mine to me.

O flourish, hidden deep in fern,
  Old oak, I love thee well;
A thousand thanks for what I learn
  And what remains to tell.

''Tis little more: the day was warm;
  At last, tired out with play,
She sank her head upon her arm
  And at my feet she lay.

'Her eyelids dropp'd their silken eaves.
  I breathed upon her eyes
Thro' all the summer of my leaves
  A welcome mix'd with sighs.

'I took the swarming sound of life—
  The music from the town—
The murmurs of the drum and fife
  And lull'd them in my own.

'Sometimes I let a sunbeam slip,
  To light her shaded eye;
A second flutter'd round her lip
  Like a golden butterfly;

'A third would glimmer on her neck
  To make the necklace shine;
Another slid, a sunny fleck,
  From head to ancle fine,

'Then close and dark my arms I spread,
  And shadow'd all her rest—
Dropt dews upon her golden head,
  An acorn in her breast.

'But in a pet she started up,
  And pluck'd it out, and drew
My little oakling from the cup,
  And flung him in the dew.

'And yet it was a graceful gift—
  I felt a pang within
As when I see the woodman lift
  His axe to slay my kin.

'I shook him down because he was
  The finest on the tree.
He lies beside thee on the grass.
  O kiss him once for me.

'O kiss him twice and thrice for me,
   That have no lips to kiss,
For never yet was oak on lea
   Shall grow so fair as this.'

Step deeper yet in herb and fern,
   Look further thro' the chace,
Spread upward till thy boughs discern
   The front of Sumner-place.

This fruit of thine by Love is blest,
   That but a moment lay
Where fairer fruit of Love may rest
   Some happy future day.

I kiss it twice, I kiss it thrice,
   The warmth it thence shall win
To riper life may magnetise
   The baby-oak within.

But thou, while kingdoms overset,
   Or lapse from hand to hand,
Thy leaf shall never fail, nor yet
   Thine acorn in the land.

May never saw dismember thee,
   Nor wielded axe disjoint,
That art the fairest-spoken tree
   From here to Lizard-point.

O rock upon thy towery-top
   All throats that gurgle sweet!
All starry culmination drop
   Balm-dews to bathe thy feet!

All grass of silky feather grow—
   And while he sinks or swells
The full south-breeze around thee blow
   The sound of minster bells.

The fat earth feed thy branchy root,
   That under deeply strikes!
The northern morning o'er thee shoot,
   High up, in silver spikes!

Nor ever lightning char thy grain,
   But, rolling as in sleep,
Low thunders bring the mellow rain,
   That makes thee broad and deep!

And hear me swear a solemn oath,
   That only by thy side
Will I to Olive plight my troth,
   And gain her for my bride.

And when my marriage morn may fall,
   She, Dryad-like, shall wear
Alternate leaf and acorn-ball
   In wreath about her hair.

And I will work in prose and rhyme,
   And praise thee more in both
Than bard has honour'd beech or lime,
   Or that Thessalian growth,

In which the swarthy ringdove sat,
   And mystic sentence spoke;
And more than England honours that,
   Thy famous brother-oak,

Wherein the younger Charles abode
   Till all the paths were dim,
And far below the Roundhead rode,
   And humm'd a surly hymn.

LOVE AND DUTY

Of love that never found his earthly close,
What sequel? Streaming eyes and breaking
   hearts?
Or all the same as if he had not been?
   Not so. Shall Error in the round of time
Still father Truth? O shall the braggart
   shout
For some blind glimpse of freedom work
   itself
Thro' madness, hated by the wise, to law
System and empire? Sin itself be found
The cloudy porch oft opening on the Sun?
And only he, this wonder, dead, become
Mere highway dust? or year by year alone
Sit brooding in the ruins of a life,
Nightmare of youth, the spectre of him-
   self?
   If this were thus, if this, indeed, were all,
Better the narrow brain, the stony heart,
The staring eye glazed o'er with sapless
   days,
The long mechanic pacings to and fro,
The set gray life, and apathetic end.
But am I not the nobler thro' thy love?
O three times less unworthy! likewise thou
Art more thro' Love, and greater than thy
   years.
The Sun will run his orbit, and the Moon
Her circle. Wait, and Love himself will
   bring

The drooping flower of knowledge changed to fruit
Of wisdom. Wait: my faith is large in Time,
And that which shapes it to some perfect end.
Will some one say, Then why not ill for good?
Why took ye not your pastime? To that man
My work shall answer, since I knew the right
And did it; for a man is not as God,
But then most Godlike being most a man.
—So let me think 'tis well for thee and me—
Ill-fated that I am, what lot is mine
Whose foresight preaches peace, my heart so slow
To feel it! For how hard it seem'd to me,
When eyes, love-languid thro' half-tears would dwell
One earnest, earnest moment upon mine,
Then not to dare to see! when thy low voice,
Faltering, would break its syllables, to keep
My own full-tuned,—hold passion in a leash,
And not leap forth and fall about thy neck,
And on thy bosom (deep desired relief!)
Rain out the heavy mist of tears, that weigh'd
Upon my brain, my senses and my soul!
For Love himself took part against himself
To warn us off, and Duty loved of Love—
O this world's curse,—beloved but hated—came
Like Death betwixt thy dear embrace and mine,
And crying, 'Who is this? behold thy bride,'
She push'd me from thee.
                    If the sense is hard
To alien ears, I did not speak to these—
No, not to thee, but to thyself in me:
Hard is my doom and thine: thou knowest it all.
  Could Love part thus? was it not well to speak,

To have spoken once? It could not but be well.
The slow sweet hours that bring us all things good,
The slow sad hours that bring us all things ill,
And all good things from evil, brought the night
In which we sat together and alone,
And to the want, that hollow'd all the heart,
Gave utterance by the yearning of an eye,
That burn'd upon its object thro' such tears
As flow but once a life.
                    The trance gave way
To those caresses, when a hundred times
In that last kiss, which never was the last,
Farewell, like endless welcome, lived and died.
Then follow'd counsel, comfort, and the words
That make a man feel strong in speaking truth;
Till now the dark was worn, and overhead
The lights of sunset and of sunrise mix'd
In that brief night; the summer night, that paused
Among her stars to hear us; stars that hung
Love-charm'd to listen: all the wheels of Time
Spun round in station, but the end had come.
  O then like those, who clench their nerves to rush
Upon their dissolution, we two rose,
There—closing like an individual life—
In one blind cry of passion and of pain,
Like bitter accusation ev'n to death,
Caught up the whole of love and utter'd it,
And bade adieu for ever.
                    Live—yet live—
Shall sharpest pathos blight us, knowing all
Life needs for life is possible to will—
Live happy; tend thy flowers; be tended by
My blessing! Should my Shadow cross thy thoughts
Too sadly for their peace, remand it thou
For calmer hours to Memory's darkest hold,

If not to be forgotten—not at once—
Not all forgotten. Should it cross thy
dreams,
O might it come like one that looks con-
tent,
With quiet eyes unfaithful to the truth,
And point thee forward to a distant light,
Or seem to lift a burthen from thy heart
And leave thee freër, till thou wake re-
fresh'd
Then when the first low matin-chirp hath
grown
Full quire, and morning driv'n her plow
of pearl
Far furrowing into light the mounded rack,
Beyond the fair green field and eastern sea.

THE GOLDEN YEAR

WELL, you shall have that song which
Leonard wrote:
It was last summer on a tour in Wales:
Old James was with me: we that day had
been
Up Snowdon; and I wish'd for Leonard
there,
And found him in Llanberis: then we crost
Between the lakes, and clamber'd half way
up
The counter side; and that same song of his
He told me; for I banter'd him, and swore
They said he lived shut up within himself,
A tongue-tied Poet in the feverous days,
That, setting the *how much* before the *how*,
Cry, like the daughters of the horseleech,
'Give,
Cram us with all,' but count not me the
herd!
To which 'They call me what they will,'
he said:
'But I was born too late: the fair new
forms,
That float about the threshold of an age,
Like truths of Science waiting to be
caught—
Catch me who can, and make the catcher
crown'd—
Are taken by the forelock. Let it be.
But if you care indeed to listen, hear
These measured words, my work of yester-
morn.

'We sleep and wake and sleep, but all
things move;
The Sun flies forward to his brother Sun;
The dark Earth follows wheel'd in her
ellipse;
And human things returning on them-
selves
Move onward, leading up the golden year.
'Ah, tho' the times, when some new
thought can bud,
Are but as poets' seasons when they flower,
Yet oceans daily gaining on the land,
Have ebb and flow conditioning their
march,
And slow and sure comes up the golden
year.
'When wealth no more shall rest in
mounded heaps,
But smit with freër light shall slowly melt
In many streams to fatten lower lands,
And light shall spread, and man be liker
man
Thro' all the season of the golden year.
'Shall eagles not be eagles? wrens be
wrens?
If all the world were falcons, what of that?
The wonder of the eagle were the less,
But he not less the eagle. Happy days
Roll onward, leading up the golden year.
'Fly, happy happy sails, and bear the
Press;
Fly happy with the mission of the Cross;
Knit land to land, and blowing havenward
With silks, and fruits, and spices, clear of
toll,
Enrich the markets of the golden year.
'But we grow old. Ah! when shall all
men's good
Be each man's rule, and universal Peace
Lie like a shaft of light across the land,
And like a lane of beams athwart the sea,
Thro' all the circle of the golden year?'
    Thus far he flow'd, and ended; where-
upon
'Ah, folly!' in mimic cadence answer'd
James—
'Ah, folly! for it lies so far away,
Not in our time, nor in our children's time,
'Tis like the second world to us that live;
'Twere all as one to fix our hopes on
Heaven

As on this vision of the golden year.'
With that he struck his staff against the rocks
And broke it,—James,—you know him,—old, but full
Of force and choler, and firm upon his feet,
And like an oaken stock in winter woods,
O'erflourish'd with the hoary clematis:
Then added, all in heat:
            'What stuff is this!
Old writers push'd the happy season back,—
The more fools they,—we forward: dreamers both:
You most, that in an age, when every hour
Must sweat her sixty minutes to the death,
Live on, God love us, as if the seedsman, rapt
Upon the teeming harvest, should not plunge
His hand into the bag: but well I know
That unto him who works, and feels he works,
This same grand year is ever at the doors.'
  He spoke; and, high above, I heard them blast
The steep slate-quarry, and the great echo flap
And buffet round the hills, from bluff to bluff.

ULYSSES

It little profits that an idle king,
By this still hearth, among these barren crags,
Match'd with an aged wife, I mete and dole
Unequal laws unto a savage race,
That hoard, and sleep, and feed, and know not me.
I cannot rest from travel: I will drink
Life to the lees: all times I have enjoy'd
Greatly, have suffer'd greatly, both with those
That loved me, and alone; on shore, and when
Thro' scudding drifts the rainy Hyades
Vext the dim sea: I am become a name;
For always roaming with a hungry heart
Much have I seen and known; cities of men

And manners, climates, councils, governments,
Myself not least, but honour'd of them all;
And drunk delight of battle with my peers,
Far on the ringing plains of windy Troy.
I am a part of all that I have met;
Yet all experience is an arch wherethro'
Gleams that untravell'd world, whose margin fades
For ever and for ever when I move.
How dull it is to pause, to make an end,
To rust unburnish'd, not to shine in use!
As tho' to breathe were life. Life piled on life
Were all too little, and of one to me
Little remains: but every hour is saved
From that eternal silence, something more,
A bringer of new things; and vile it were
For some three suns to store and hoard myself,
And this gray spirit yearning in desire
To follow knowledge like a sinking star,
Beyond the utmost bound of human thought.
  This is my son, mine own Telemachus,
To whom I leave the sceptre and the isle—
Well-loved of me, discerning to fulfil
This labour, by slow prudence to make mild
A rugged people, and thro' soft degrees
Subdue them to the useful and the good.
Most blameless is he, centred in the sphere
Of common duties, decent not to fail
In offices of tenderness, and pay
Meet adoration to my household gods,
When I am gone. He works his work, I mine.
  There lies the port; the vessel puffs her sail:
There gloom the dark broad seas. My mariners,
Souls that have toil'd, and wrought, and thought with me—
That ever with a frolic welcome took
The thunder and the sunshine, and opposed
Free hearts, free foreheads—you and I are old;
Old age hath yet his honour and his toil;
Death closes all: but something ere the end,
Some work of noble note, may yet be done,

Not unbecoming men that strove with
   Gods.
The lights begin to twinkle from the rocks:
The long day wanes: the slow moon climbs:
   the deep
Moans round with many voices. Come,
   my friends,
'Tis not too late to seek a newer world.
Push off, and sitting well in order smite
The sounding furrows; for my purpose
   holds
To sail beyond the sunset, and the baths
Of all the western stars, until I die.
It may be that the gulfs will wash us down:
It may be we shall touch the Happy Isles,
And see the great Achilles, whom we knew.
Tho' much is taken, much abides; and
   tho'
We are not now that strength which in old
   days
Moved earth and heaven; that which we
   are, we are;
One equal temper of heroic hearts,
Made weak by time and fate, but strong in
   will
To strive, to seek, to find, and not to yield.

TITHONUS

THE woods decay, the woods decay and
   fall,
The vapours weep their burthen to the
   ground,
Man comes and tills the field and lies
   beneath,
And after many a summer dies the swan.
Me only cruel immortality
Consumes: I wither slowly in thine arms,
Here at the quiet limit of the world,
A white-hair'd shadow roaming like a
   dream
The ever-silent spaces of the East,
Far-folded mists, and gleaming halls of
   morn.

Alas! for this gray shadow, once a man—
So glorious in his beauty and thy choice,
Who madest him thy chosen, that he
   seem'd
To his great heart none other than a God!
I ask'd thee, 'Give me immortality.'

Then didst thou grant mine asking with a
   smile,
Like wealthy men who care not how they
   give.
But thy strong Hours indignant work'd
   their wills,
And beat me down and marr'd and wasted
   me,
And tho' they could not end me, left me
   maim'd
To dwell in presence of immortal youth,
Immortal age beside immortal youth,
And all I was, in ashes. Can thy love,
Thy beauty, make amends, tho' even now,
Close over us, the silver star, thy guide,
Shines in those tremulous eyes that fill with
   tears
To hear me? Let me go: take back thy
   gift:
Why should a man desire in any way
To vary from the kindly race of men,
Or pass beyond the goal of ordinance
Where all should pause, as is most meet
   for all?

A soft air fans the cloud apart; there
   comes
A glimpse of that dark world where I was
   born.
Once more the old mysterious glimmer
   steals
From thy pure brows, and from thy
   shoulders pure,
And bosom beating with a heart renew'd.
Thy cheek begins to redden thro' the
   gloom,
Thy sweet eyes brighten slowly close to
   mine,
Ere yet they blind the stars, and the wild
   team
Which love thee, yearning for thy yoke,
   arise,
And shake the darkness from their loosen'd
   manes,
And beat the twilight into flakes of fire.

Lo! ever thus thou growest beautiful
In silence, then before thine answer
   given
Departest, and thy tears are on my cheek.

Why wilt thou ever scare me with thy
  tears,
And make me tremble lest a saying learnt,
In days far-off, on that dark earth, be true?
'The Gods themselves cannot recall their
  gifts.'

Ay me! ay me! with what another heart
In days far-off, and with what other eyes
I used to watch—if I be he that watch'd—
The lucid outline forming round thee; saw
The dim curls kindle into sunny rings;
Changed with thy mystic change, and felt
  my blood
Glow with the glow that slowly crimson'd
  all
Thy presence and thy portals, while I lay,
Mouth, forehead, eyelids, growing dewy-
  warm
With kisses balmier than half-opening buds
Of April, and could hear the lips that
  kiss'd

Whispering I knew not what of wild and
  sweet,
Like that strange song I heard Apollo sing,
While Ilion like a mist rose into towers.

Yet hold me not for ever in thine East:
How can my nature longer mix with thine?
Coldly thy rosy shadows bathe me, cold
Are all thy lights, and cold my wrinkled feet
Upon thy glimmering thresholds, when the
  steam
Floats up from those dim fields about the
  homes
Of happy men that have the power to die,
And grassy barrows of the happier dead.
Release me, and restore me to the ground;
Thou seëst all things, thou wilt see my
  grave:
Thou wilt renew thy beauty morn by
  morn;
I earth in earth forget these empty courts,
And thee returning on thy silver wheels.

LOCKSLEY HALL

COMRADES, leave me here a little, while as yet 'tis early morn:
Leave me here, and when you want me, sound upon the bugle-horn.

'Tis the place, and all around it, as of old, the curlews call,
Dreary gleams about the moorland flying over Locksley Hall;

Locksley Hall, that in the distance overlooks the sandy tracts,
And the hollow ocean-ridges roaring into cataracts.

Many a night from yonder ivied casement, ere I went to rest,
Did I look on great Orion sloping slowly to the West.

Many a night I saw the Pleiads, rising thro' the mellow shade,
Glitter like a swarm of fire-flies tangled in a silver braid.

Here about the beach I wander'd, nourishing a youth sublime
With the fairy tales of science, and the long result of Time;

When the centuries behind me like a fruitful land reposed;
When I clung to all the present for the promise that it closed:

When I dipt into the future far as human eye could see;
Saw the Vision of the world, and all the wonder that would be.——

In the Spring a fuller crimson comes upon the robin's breast;
In the Spring the wanton lapwing gets himself another crest;

In the Spring a livelier iris changes on the burnish'd dove;
In the Spring a young man's fancy lightly turns to thoughts of love.

Then her cheek was pale and thinner than should be for one so young,
And her eyes on all my motions with a mute observance hung.

And I said, 'My cousin Amy, speak, and speak the truth to me,
Trust me, cousin, all the current of my being sets to thee.'

On her pallid cheek and forehead came a colour and a light,
As I have seen the rosy red flushing in the northern night.

And she turn'd—her bosom shaken with a sudden storm of sighs—
All the spirit deeply dawning in the dark of hazel eyes—

Saying, 'I have hid my feelings, fearing they should do me wrong;'
Saying, 'Dost thou love me, cousin?' weeping, 'I have loved thee long.'

Love took up the glass of Time, and turn'd it in his glowing hands;
Every moment, lightly shaken, ran itself in golden sands.

Love took up the harp of Life, and smote on all the chords with might;
Smote the chord of Self, that, trembling, pass'd in music out of sight.

Many a morning on the moorland did we hear the copses ring,
And her whisper throng'd my pulses with the fulness of the Spring.

Many an evening by the waters did we watch the stately ships,
And our spirits rush'd together at the touching of the lips.

O my cousin, shallow-hearted! O my Amy, mine no more!
O the dreary, dreary moorland! O the barren, barren shore!

Falser than all fancy fathoms, falser than all songs have sung,
Puppet to a father's threat, and servile to a shrewish tongue!

Is it well to wish thee happy?—having known me—to decline
On a range of lower feelings and a narrower heart than mine!

Yet it shall be: thou shalt lower to his level day by day,
What is fine within thee growing coarse to sympathise with clay.

As the husband is, the wife is: thou art mated with a clown,
And the grossness of his nature will have weight to drag thee down.

He will hold thee, when his passion shall have spent its novel force,
Something better than his dog, a little dearer than his horse.

What is this? his eyes are heavy: think not they are glazed with wine.
Go to him: it is thy duty: kiss him: take his hand in thine.

It may be my lord is weary, that his brain is overwrought:
Soothe him with thy finer fancies, touch him with thy lighter thought.

He will answer to the purpose, easy things to understand—
Better thou wert dead before me, tho' I slew thee with my hand!

Better thou and I were lying, hidden from the heart's disgrace,
Roll'd in one another's arms, and silent in a last embrace.

Cursed be the social wants that sin against the strength of youth!
Cursed be the social lies that warp us from the living truth!

Cursed be the sickly forms that err from honest Nature's rule!
Cursed be the gold that gilds the straiten'd forehead of the fool!

Well—'tis well that I should bluster!—Hadst thou less unworthy proved—
Would to God—for I had loved thee more than ever wife was loved.

Am I mad, that I should cherish that which bears but bitter fruit?
I will pluck it from my bosom, tho' my heart be at the root.

Never, tho' my mortal summers to such length of years should come
As the many-winter'd crow that leads the clanging rookery home.

Where is comfort? in division of the records of the mind?
Can I part her from herself, and love her, as I knew her, kind?

I remember one that perish'd: sweetly did she speak and move:
Such a one do I remember, whom to look at was to love.

Can I think of her as dead, and love her for the love she bore?
No—she never loved me truly: love is love for evermore.

Comfort? comfort scorn'd of devils! this is truth the poet sings,
That a sorrow's crown of sorrow is remembering happier things.

Drug thy memories, lest thou learn it, lest thy heart be put to proof,
In the dead unhappy night, and when the rain is on the roof.

Like a dog, he hunts in dreams, and thou art staring at the wall,
Where the dying night-lamp flickers, and the shadows rise and fall.

Then a hand shall pass before thee, pointing to his drunken sleep,
To thy widow'd marriage-pillows, to the tears that thou wilt weep.

Thou shalt hear the 'Never, never,' whisper'd by the phantom years,
And a song from out the distance in the ringing of thine ears;

And an eye shall vex thee, looking ancient kindness on thy pain.
Turn thee, turn thee on thy pillow: get thee to thy rest again.

Nay, but Nature brings thee solace; for a tender voice will cry.
'Tis a purer life than thine; a lip to drain thy trouble dry.

Baby lips will laugh me down: my latest rival brings thee rest.
Baby fingers, waxen touches, press me from the mother's breast.

O, the child too clothes the father with a dearness not his due.
Half is thine and half is his: it will be worthy of the two.

O, I see thee old and formal, fitted to thy petty part,
With a little hoard of maxims preaching down a daughter's heart.

'They were dangerous guides the feelings—she herself was not exempt—
Truly, she herself had suffer'd'—Perish in thy self-contempt!

Overlive it—lower yet—be happy! wherefore should I care?
I myself must mix with action, lest I wither by despair.

What is that which I should turn to, lighting upon days like these?
Every door is barr'd with gold, and opens but to golden keys.

Every gate is throng'd with suitors, all the markets overflow.
I have but an angry fancy: what is that which I should do?

I had been content to perish, falling on the foeman's ground,
When the ranks are roll'd in vapour, and the winds are laid with sound.

But the jingling of the guinea helps the hurt that Honour feels,
And the nations do but murmur, snarling at each other's heels.

Can I but relive in sadness? I will turn that earlier page.
Hide me from my deep emotion, O thou wondrous Mother-Age!

Make me feel the wild pulsation that I felt before the strife,
When I heard my days before me, and the tumult of my life;

Yearning for the large excitement that the coming years would yield
Eager-hearted as a boy when first he leaves his father's field,

And at night along the dusky highway near and nearer drawn,
Sees in heaven the light of London flaring like a dreary dawn;

And his spirit leaps within him to be gone before him then,
Underneath the light he looks at, in among the throngs of men:

Men, my brothers, men the workers, ever reaping something new:
That which they have done but earnest of the things that they shall do:

For I dipt into the future, far as human eye could see,
Saw the Vision of the world, and all the wonder that would be;

Saw the heavens fill with commerce, argosies of magic sails,
Pilots of the purple twilight, dropping down with costly bales;

Heard the heavens fill with shouting, and there rain'd a ghastly dew
From the nations' airy navies grappling in the central blue;

Far along the world-wide whisper of the south-wind rushing warm,
With the standards of the peoples plunging thro' the thunder-storm;

Till the war-drum throbb'd no longer, and the battle-flags were furl'd
In the Parliament of man, the Federation of the world.

There the common sense of most shall hold a fretful realm in awe,
And the kindly earth shall slumber, lapt in universal law.

So I triumph'd ere my passion sweeping thro' me left me dry,
Left me with the palsied heart, and left me with the jaundiced eye;

Eye, to which all order festers, all things here are out of joint:
Science moves, but slowly slowly, creeping on from point to point:

Slowly comes a hungry people, as a lion creeping nigher,
Glares at one that nods and winks behind a slowly-dying fire.

Yet I doubt not thro' the ages one increasing purpose runs,
And the thoughts of men are widen'd with the process of the suns.

What is that to him that reaps not harvest of his youthful joys,
Tho' the deep heart of existence beat for ever like a boy's?

Knowledge comes, but wisdom lingers, and I linger on the shore,
And the individual withers, and the world is more and more.

Knowledge comes, but wisdom lingers, and he bears a laden breast,
Full of sad experience, moving toward the stillness of his rest.

Hark, my merry comrades call me, sounding on the bugle-horn,
They to whom my foolish passion were a target for their scorn:

Shall it not be scorn to me to harp on such a moulder'd string?
I am shamed thro' all my nature to have loved so slight a thing.

Weakness to be wroth with weakness! woman's pleasure, woman's pain—
Nature made them blinder motions bounded in a shallower brain:

Woman is the lesser man, and all thy passions, match'd with mine,
Are as moonlight unto sunlight, and as water unto wine—

Here at least, where nature sickens, nothing. Ah, for some retreat
Deep in yonder shining Orient, where my life began to beat;

Where in wild Mahratta-battle fell my father evil-starr'd;—
I was left a trampled orphan, and a selfish uncle's ward.

Or to burst all links of habit—there to wander far away,
On from island unto island at the gateways of the day.

Larger constellations burning, mellow moons and happy skies,
Breadths of tropic shade and palms in cluster, knots of Paradise.

Never comes the trader, never floats an European flag,
Slides the bird o'er lustrous woodland, swings the trailer from the crag;

Droops the heavy-blossom'd bower, hangs the heavy-fruited tree—
Summer isles of Eden lying in dark-purple spheres of sea.

There methinks would be enjoyment more than in this march of mind
In the steamship, in the railway, in the thoughts that shake mankind.

There the passions cramp'd no longer shall have scope and breathing space;
I will take some savage woman, she shall rear my dusky race.

Iron-jointed, supple-sinew'd, they shall dive, and they shall run,
Catch the wild goat by the hair, and hurl their lances in the sun;

Whistle back the parrot's call, and leap the rainbows of the brooks,
Not with blinded eyesight poring over miserable books—

Fool, again the dream, the fancy! but I *know* my words are wild,
But I count the gray barbarian lower than the Christian child.

I, to herd with narrow foreheads, vacant of our glorious gains,
Like a beast with lower pleasures, like a beast with lower pains!

Mated with a squalid savage—what to me were sun or clime?
I the heir of all the ages, in the foremost files of time—

I that rather held it better men should perish one by one,
Than that earth should stand at gaze like Joshua's moon in Ajalon!

Not in vain the distance beacons. Forward, forward let us range,
Let the great world spin for ever down the ringing grooves of change.

Thro' the shadow of the globe we sweep into the younger day:
Better fifty years of Europe than a cycle of Cathay.

Mother-Age (for mine I knew not) help me as when life begun:
Rift the hills, and roll the waters, flash the lightnings, weigh the Sun.

O, I see the crescent promise of my spirit hath not set.
Ancient founts of inspiration well thro' all my fancy yet.

Howsoever these things be, a long farewell to Locksley Hall!
Now for me the woods may wither, now for me the roof-tree fall.

Comes a vapour from the margin, blackening over heath and holt,
Cramming all the blast before it, in its breast a thunderbolt.

Let it fall on Locksley Hall, with rain or hail, or fire or snow;
For the mighty wind arises, roaring seaward, and I go.

GODIVA

I WAITED *for the train at Coventry;*
I hung with grooms and porters on the bridge,
*To watch the three tall spires; and there I
shaped*
The city's ancient legend into this:—
  Not only we, the latest seed of Time,
New men, that in the flying of a wheel
Cry down the past, not only we, that prate
Of rights and wrongs, have loved the
    people well,
And loathed to see them overtax'd; but she
Did more, and underwent, and overcame,
The woman of a thousand summers back,
Godiva, wife to that grim Earl, who ruled
In Coventry: for when he laid a tax
Upon his town, and all the mothers brought
Their children, clamouring, 'If we pay, we
    starve!'

She sought her lord, and found him, where
    he strode
About the hall, among his dogs, alone,
His beard a foot before him, and his hair
A yard behind. She told him of their tears,
And pray'd him, 'If they pay this tax, they
    starve.'
Whereat he stared, replying, half-amazed,
'You would not let your little finger ache
For such as *these?*'—'But I would die,'
    said she.
He laugh'd, and swore by Peter and by
    Paul:
Then fillip'd at the diamond in her ear;
'Oh ay, ay, ay, you talk!'—'Alas!' she said,
'But prove me what it is I would not do.'
And from a heart as rough as Esau's hand,
He answer'd, 'Ride you naked thro' the
    town,
And I repeal it;' and nodding, as in scorn,

He parted, with great strides among his
dogs.
So left alone, the passions of her mind,
As winds from all the compass shift and
blow,
Made war upon each other for an hour,
Till pity won. She sent a herald forth,
And bade him cry, with sound of trumpet,
all
The hard condition; but that she would
loose
The people: therefore, as they loved her
well,
From then till noon no foot should pace
the street,
No eye look down, she passing; but that all
Should keep within, door shut, and win-
dow barr'd.
  Then fled she to her inmost bower, and
there
Unclasp'd the wedded eagles of her belt,
The grim Earl's gift; but ever at a breath
She linger'd, looking like a summer moon
Half-dipt in cloud: anon she shook her
head,
And shower'd the rippled ringlets to her
knee;
Unclad herself in haste; adown the stair
Stole on; and, like a creeping sunbeam, slid
From pillar unto pillar, until she reach'd
The gateway; there she found her palfrey
trapt
In purple blazon'd with armorial gold.
  Then she rode forth, clothed on with
chastity:
The deep air listen'd round her as she rode,
And all the low wind hardly breathed for
fear.
The little wide-mouth'd heads upon the
spout
Had cunning eyes to see: the barking cur
Made her cheek flame: her palfrey's foot-
fall shot
Light horrors thro' her pulses: the blind
walls
Were full of chinks and holes; and over-
head
Fantastic gables, crowding, stared: but she
Not less thro' all bore up, till, last, she saw
The white-flower'd elder-thicket from the
field

Gleam thro' the Gothic archway in the
wall.
  Then she rode back, clothed on with
chastity
And one low churl, compact of thankless
earth,
The fatal byword of all years to come,
Boring a little auger-hole in fear,
Peep'd—but his eyes, before they had their
will,
Were shrivell'd into darkness in his head,
And dropt before him. So the Powers, who
wait
On noble deeds, cancell'd a sense mis-
used;
And she, that knew not, pass'd: and all at
once,
With twelve great shocks of sound, the
shameless noon
Was clash'd and hammer'd from a hundred
towers,
One after one: but even then she gain'd
Her bower; whence reissuing, robed and
crown'd,
To meet her lord, she took the tax away
And built herself an everlasting name.

THE DAY-DREAM

PROLOGUE

O LADY FLORA, let me speak:
  A pleasant hour has passed away
While, dreaming on your damask cheek,
  The dewy sister-eyelids lay.
As by the lattice you reclined,
  I went thro' many wayward moods
To see you dreaming—and, behind,
  A summer crisp with shining woods.
And I too dream'd, until at last
  Across my fancy, brooding warm,
The reflex of a legend past,
  And loosely settled into form.
And would you have the thought I had,
  And see the vision that I saw,
Then take the broidery-frame, and add
  A crimson to the quaint Macaw,
And I will tell it. Turn your face,
  Nor look with that too-earnest eye—
The rhymes are dazzled from their place
  And order'd words asunder fly.

THE DAY-DREAM

THE SLEEPING PALACE

I

THE varying year with blade and sheaf
  Clothes and reclothes the happy plains,
Here rests the sap within the leaf,
  Here stays the blood along the veins.
Faint shadows, vapours lightly curl'd,
  Faint murmurs from the meadows come,
Like hints and echoes of the world
  To spirits folded in the womb.

II

Soft lustre bathes the range of urns
  On every slanting terrace-lawn.
The fountain to his place returns
  Deep in the garden lake withdrawn.
Here droops the banner on the tower,
  On the hall-hearths the festal fires,
The peacock in his laurel bower,
  The parrot in his gilded wires.

III

Roof-haunting martins warm their eggs:
  In these, in those the life is stay'd.
The mantles from the golden pegs
  Droop sleepily: no sound is made,
Not even of a gnat that sings.
  More like a picture seemeth all
Than those old portraits of old kings,
  That watch the sleepers from the wall.

IV

Here sits the Butler with a flask
  Between his knees, half-drain'd; and
    there
The wrinkled steward at his task,
  The maid-of-honour blooming fair;
The page has caught her hand in his:
  Her lips are sever'd as to speak:
His own are pouted to a kiss:
  The blush is fix'd upon her cheek.

V

Till all the hundred summers pass,
  The beams, that thro' the Oriel shine,
Make prisms in every carven glass,
  And beaker brimm'd with noble wine.
Each baron at the banquet sleeps,
  Grave faces gather'd in a ring.
His state the king reposing keeps.
  He must have been a jovial king.

VI

All round a hedge upshoots, and shows
  At distance like a little wood;
Thorns, ivies, woodbine, mistletoes,
  And grapes with bunches red as blood;
All creeping plants, a wall of green
  Close-matted, bur and brake and briar,
And glimpsing over these, just seen,
  High up, the topmost palace spire.

VII

When will the hundred summers die,
  And thought and time be born again,
And newer knowledge, drawing nigh,
  Bring truth that sways the soul of men?
Here all things in their place remain,
  As all were order'd, ages since.
Come, Care and Pleasure, Hope and Pain,
  And bring the fated fairy Prince.

THE SLEEPING BEAUTY

I

YEAR after year unto her feet,
  She lying on her couch alone,
Across the purple coverlet,
  The maiden's jet-black hair has grown,
On either side her tranced form
  Forth streaming from a braid of pearl:
The slumbrous light is rich and warm,
  And moves not on the rounded curl.

II

The silk star-broider'd coverlid
  Unto her limbs itself doth mould
Languidly ever; and, amid
  Her full black ringlets downward roll'd,
Glows forth each softly-shadow'd arm
  With bracelets of the diamond bright:
Her constant beauty doth inform
  Stillness with love, and day with light.

III

She sleeps: her breathings are not heard
  In palace chambers far apart.
The fragrant tresses are not stirr'd
  That lie upon her charmed heart.
She sleeps: on either hand upswells
  The gold-fringed pillow lightly prest:
She sleeps, nor dreams, but ever dwells
  A perfect form in perfect rest.

THE ARRIVAL

I

ALL precious things, discover'd late,
  To those that seek them issue forth;
For love in sequel works with fate,
  And draws the veil from hidden worth.
He travels far from other skies—
  His mantle glitters on the rocks—
A fairy Prince, with joyful eyes,
  And lighter-footed than the fox.

II

The bodies and the bones of those
  That strove in other days to pass,
Are wither'd in the thorny close,
  Or scatter'd blanching on the grass.
He gazes on the silent dead:
  'They perish'd in their daring deeds.'
This proverb flashes thro' his head,
  'The many fail: the one succeeds.'

III

He comes, scarce knowing what he seeks:
  He breaks the hedge: he enters there:
The colour flies into his cheeks:
  He trusts to light on something fair;
For all his life the charm did talk
  About his path, and hover near
With words of promise in his walk,
  And whisper'd voices at his ear.

IV

More close and close his footsteps wind:
  The Magic Music in his heart
Beats quick and quicker, till he find
  The quiet chamber far apart.
His spirit flutters like a lark,
  He stoops—to kiss her—on his knee.
'Love, if thy tresses be so dark,
  How dark those hidden eyes must be!'

THE REVIVAL

I

A TOUCH, a kiss! the charm was snapt.
  There rose a noise of striking clocks,
And feet that ran, and doors that clapt,
  And barking dogs, and crowing cocks;
A fuller light illumined all,
  A breeze thro' all the garden swept,
A sudden hubbub shook the hall,
  And sixty feet the fountain leapt.

II

The hedge broke in, the banner blew,
  The butler drank, the steward scrawl'd,
The fire shot up, the martin flew,
  The parrot scream'd, the peacock
    squall'd,
The maid and page renew'd their strife,
  The palace bang'd, and buzz'd and
    clackt,
And all the long-pent stream of life
  Dash'd downward in a cataract.

III

And last with these the king awoke,
  And in his chair himself uprear'd,
And yawn'd, and rubb'd his face, and
    spoke,
  'By holy rood, a royal beard!
How say you? we have slept, my lords.
  My beard has grown into my lap.'
The barons swore, with many words,
  'Twas but an after-dinner's nap.

IV

'Pardy,' return'd the king, 'but still
  My joints are somewhat stiff or so.
My lord, and shall we pass the bill
  I mention'd half an hour ago?'
The chancellor, sedate and vain,
  In courteous words return'd reply:
But dallied with his golden chain,
  And, smiling, put the question by.

THE DEPARTURE

I

AND on her lover's arm she leant,
  And round her waist she felt it fold,
And far across the hills they went
  In that new world which is the old:
Across the hills, and far away
  Beyond their utmost purple rim,
And deep into the dying day
  The happy princess follow'd him.

II

'I'd sleep another hundred years,
  O love, for such another kiss;'
'O wake for ever, love,' she hears,
  'O love, 'twas such as this and this.'

And o'er them many a sliding star,
And many a merry wind was borne,
And, stream'd thro' many a golden bar,
The twilight melted into morn.

III

'O eyes long laid in happy sleep!'
'O happy sleep, that lightly fled!'
'O happy kiss, that woke thy sleep!'
'O love, thy kiss would wake the dead!'
And o'er them many a flowing range
Of vapour buoy'd the crescent-bark,
And, rapt thro' many a rosy change,
The twilight died into the dark.

IV

'A hundred summers! can it be?
And whither goest thou, tell me where?'
'O seek my father's court with me,
For there are greater wonders there.'
And o'er the hills, and far away
Beyond their utmost purple rim,
Beyond the night, across the day,
Thro' all the world she follow'd him.

MORAL

I

So, Lady Flora, take my lay,
And if you find no moral there,
Go, look in any glass and say,
What moral is in being fair.
Oh, to what uses shall we put
The wildweed-flower that simply blows?
And is there any moral shut
Within the bosom of the rose?

II

But any man that walks the mead,
In bud or blade, or bloom, may find,
According as his humours lead,
A meaning suited to his mind.
And liberal applications lie
In Art like Nature, dearest friend;
So 'twere to cramp its use, if I
Should hook it to some useful end.

L'ENVOI

I

You shake your head. A random string
Your finer female sense offends.
Well—were it not a pleasant thing
To fall asleep with all one's friends;

To pass with all our social ties
To silence from the paths of men;
And every hundred years to rise
And learn the world, and sleep again;
To sleep thro' terms of mighty wars,
And wake on science grown to more,
On secrets of the brain, the stars,
As wild as aught of fairy lore;
And all that else the years will show,
The Poet-forms of stronger hours,
The vast Republics that may grow,
The Federations and the Powers;
Titanic forces taking birth
In divers seasons, divers climes;
For we are Ancients of the earth,
And in the morning of the times.

II

So sleeping, so aroused from sleep
Thro' sunny decads new and strange,
Or gay quinquenniads would we reap
The flower and quintessence of change.

III

Ah, yet would I—and would I might!
So much your eyes my fancy take—
Be still the first to leap to light
That I might kiss those eyes awake!
For, am I right, or am I wrong,
To choose your own you did not care;
You'd have *my* moral from the song,
And I will take my pleasure there:
And, am I right or am I wrong,
My fancy, ranging thro' and thro',
To search a meaning for the song,
Perforce will still revert to you;
Nor finds a closer truth than this
All-graceful head, so richly curl'd,
And evermore a costly kiss
The prelude to some brighter world.

IV

For since the time when Adam first
Embraced his Eve in happy hour,
And every bird of Eden burst
In carol, every bud to flower
What eyes, like thine, have waken'd
  hopes,
What lips, like thine, so sweetly join'd?
Where on the double rosebud droops
The fulness of the pensive mind;

Which all too dearly self-involved,
  Yet sleeps a dreamless sleep to me;
A sleep by kisses undissolved,
  That lets thee neither hear nor see:
But break it. In the name of wife,
  And in the rights that name may give,
Are clasp'd the moral of thy life,
  And that for which I care to live.

EPILOGUE

So, Lady Flora, take my lay,
  And, if you find a meaning there,
O whisper to your glass, and say,
  'What wonder, if he thinks me fair?'
What wonder I was all unwise,
  To shape the song for your delight
Like long-tail'd birds of Paradise
  That float thro' Heaven, and cannot
    light?
Or old-world trains, upheld at court
  By Cupid-boys of blooming hue—
But take it—earnest wed with sport,
  And either sacred unto you.

AMPHION

My father left a park to me,
  But it is wild and barren,
A garden too with scarce a tree,
  And waster than a warren:
Yet say the neighbours when they call,
  It is not bad but good land,
And in it is the germ of all
  That grows within the woodland.

O had I lived when song was great
  In days of old Amphion,
And ta'en my fiddle to the gate,
  Nor cared for seed or scion!
And had I lived when song was great,
  And legs of trees were limber,
And ta'en my fiddle to the gate,
  And fiddled in the timber!

'Tis said he had a tuneful tongue,
  Such happy intonation,
Wherever he sat down and sung
  He left a small plantation;
Wherever in a lonely grove
  He set up his forlorn pipes,
The gouty oak began to move,
  And flounder into hornpipes.

The mountain stirr'd its bushy crown,
  And, as tradition teaches,
Young ashes pirouetted down
  Coquetting with young beeches;
And briony-vine and ivy-wreath
  Ran forward to his rhyming,
And from the valleys underneath
  Came little copses climbing.

The linden broke her ranks and rent
  The woodbine wreaths that bind her,
And down the middle, buzz! she went
  With all her bees behind her:
The poplars, in long order due,
  With cypress promenaded,
The shock-head willows two and two
  By rivers gallopaded.

Came wet-shod alder from the wave,
  Came yews, a dismal coterie;
Each pluck'd his one foot from the grave,
  Poussetting with a sloe-tree:
Old elms came breaking from the vine,
  The vine stream'd out to follow,
And, sweating rosin, plump'd the pine
  From many a cloudy hollow.

And wasn't it a sight to see,
  When, ere his song was ended,
Like some great landslip, tree by tree,
  The country-side descended;
And shepherds from the mountain-eaves
  Look'd down, half-pleased, half-fright-
    en'd,
As dash'd about the drunken leaves
  The random sunshine lighten'd!

Oh, nature first was fresh to men,
  And wanton without measure;
So youthful and so flexile then,
  You moved her at your pleasure.
Twang out, my fiddle! shake the twigs!
  And make her dance attendance;
Blow, flute, and stir the stiff-set sprigs,
  And scirrhous roots and tendons.

'Tis vain! in such a brassy age
  I could not move a thistle;
The very sparrows in the hedge
  Scarce answer to my whistle;

Or at the most, when three-parts-sick
  With strumming and with scraping,
A jackass heehaws from the rick,
  The passive oxen gaping.

But what is that I hear? a sound
  Like sleepy counsel pleading;
O Lord!—'tis in my neighbour's ground,
  The modern Muses reading.
They read Botanic Treatises,
  And Works on Gardening thro' there,
And Methods of transplanting trees
  To look as if they grew there.

The wither'd Misses! how they prose
  O'er books of travell'd seamen,
And show you slips of all that grows
  From England to Van Diemen.
They read in arbours clipt and cut,
  And alleys, faded places,
By squares of tropic summer shut
  And warm'd in crystal cases.

But these, tho' fed with careful dirt,
  Are neither green nor sappy;
Half-conscious of the garden-squirt,
  The spindlings look unhappy.
Better to me the meanest weed
  That blows upon its mountain,
The vilest herb that runs to seed
  Beside its native fountain.

And I must work thro' months of toil,
  And years of cultivation,
Upon my proper patch of soil
  To grow my own plantation.
I'll take the showers as they fall,
  I will not vex my bosom:
Enough if at the end of all
  A little garden blossom.

ST. AGNES' EVE

DEEP on the convent-roof the snows
  Are sparkling to the moon:
My breath to heaven like vapour goes:
  May my soul follow soon!
The shadows of the convent-towers
  Slant down the snowy sward,
Still creeping with the creeping hours
  That lead me to my Lord:

Make Thou my spirit pure and clear
  As are the frosty skies,
Or this first snowdrop of the year
  That in my bosom lies.

As these white robes are soil'd and dark,
  To yonder shining ground;
As this pale taper's earthly spark,
  To yonder argent round;
So shows my soul before the Lamb,
  My spirit before Thee;
So in mine earthly house I am,
  To that I hope to be.
Break up the heavens, O Lord! and far,
  Thro' all yon starlight keen,
Draw me, thy bride, a glittering star,
  In raiment white and clean.

He lifts me to the golden doors;
  The flashes come and go;
All heaven bursts her starry floors,
  And strows her lights below,
And deepens on and up! the gates
  Roll back, and far within
For me the Heavenly Bridegroom waits,
  To make me pure of sin.
The sabbaths of Eternity,
  One sabbath deep and wide—
A light upon the shining sea—
  The Bridegroom with his bride!

SIR GALAHAD

My good blade carves the casques of men,
  My tough lance thrusteth sure,
My strength is as the strength of ten,
  Because my heart is pure.
The shattering trumpet shrilleth high,
  The hard brands shiver on the steel,
The splinter'd spear-shafts crack and fly,
  The horse and rider reel:
They reel, they roll in clanging lists,
  And when the tide of combat stands,
Perfume and flowers fall in showers,
  That lightly rain from ladies' hands.

How sweet are looks that ladies bend
  On whom their favours fall!
For them I battle till the end,
  To save from shame and thrall:
But all my heart is drawn above,
  My knees are bow'd in crypt and shrine:

I never felt the kiss of love,
　　Nor maiden's hand in mine.
More bounteous aspects on me beam,
　　Me mightier transports move and thrill;
So keep I fair thro' faith and prayer
　　A virgin heart in work and will.

When down the stormy crescent goes,
　　A light before me swims,
Between dark stems the forest glows,
　　I hear a noise of hymns:
Then by some secret shrine I ride;
　　I hear a voice but none are there;
The stalls are void, the doors are wide,
　　The tapers burning fair.
Fair gleams the snowy altar-cloth,
　　The silver vessels sparkle clean,
The shrill bell rings, the censer swings,
　　And solemn chaunts resound between.

Sometimes on lonely mountain-meres
　　I find a magic bark;
I leap on board: no helmsman steers:
　　I float till all is dark.
A gentle sound, an awful light!
　　Three angels bear the holy Grail:
With folded feet, in stoles of white,
　　On sleeping wings they sail.
Ah, blessed vision! blood of God!
　　My spirit beats her mortal bars,
As down dark tides the glory slides,
　　And star-like mingles with the stars.

When on my goodly charger borne
　　Thro' dreaming towns I go,
The cock crows ere the Christmas morn,
　　The streets are dumb with snow.
The tempest crackles on the leads,
　　And, ringing, springs from brand and
　　　　mail;
But o'er the dark a glory spreads,
　　And gilds the driving hail.
I leave the plain, I climb the height;
　　No branchy thicket shelter yields;
But blessed forms in whistling storms
　　Fly o'er waste fens and windy fields.

A maiden knight—to me is given
　　Such hope, I know not fear;
I yearn to breathe the airs of heaven
　　That often meet me here.

I muse on joy that will not cease,
　　Pure spaces clothed in living beams,
Pure lilies of eternal peace,
　　Whose odours haunt my dreams;
And, stricken by an angel's hand,
　　This mortal armour that I wear,
This weight and size, this heart and eyes,
　　Are touch'd, are turn'd to finest air.

The clouds are broken in the sky,
　　And thro' the mountain-walls
A rolling organ-harmony
　　Swells up, and shakes and falls.
Then move the trees, the copses nod,
　　Wings flutter, voices hover clear:
'O just and faithful knight of God!
　　Ride on! the prize is near.'
So pass I hostel, hall, and grange;
　　By bridge and ford, by park and pale,
All'-arm'd I ride, whate'er betide,
　　Until I find the holy Grail.

EDWARD GRAY

SWEET Emma Moreland of yonder town
　　Met me walking on yonder way,
'And have you lost your heart?' she said;
　　'And are you married yet, Edward
　　　　Gray?'

Sweet Emma Moreland spoke to me:
　　Bitterly weeping I turn'd away:
'Sweet Emma Moreland, love no more
　　Can touch the heart of Edward Gray.

'Ellen Adair she loved me well,
　　Against her father's and mother's will:
To-day I sat for an hour and wept,
　　By Ellen's grave, on the windy hill.

'Shy she was, and I thought her cold;
　　Thought her proud, and fled over the
　　　　sea;
Fill'd I was with folly and spite,
　　When Ellen Adair was dying for me.

'Cruel, cruel the words I said!
　　Cruelly came they back to-day:
"You're too slight and fickle," I said,
　　"To trouble the heart of Edward Gray."

'There I put my face in the grass—
　　Whisper'd, "Listen to my despair:
I repent me of all I did:
　　Speak a little, Ellen Adair!"

'Then I took a pencil, and wrote
  On the mossy stone, as I lay,
"Here lies the body of Ellen Adair;
  And here the heart of Edward Gray!"

'Love may come, and love may go,
  And fly, like a bird, from tree to tree;
But I will love no more, no more,
  Till Ellen Adair come back to me.

'Bitterly wept I over the stone:
  Bitterly weeping I turn'd away:
There lies the body of Ellen Adair!
  And there the heart of Edward Gray!'

WILL WATERPROOF'S LYRICAL MONOLOGUE

MADE AT THE COCK

O PLUMP head-waiter at The Cock,
  To which I most resort,
How goes the time? 'Tis five o'clock.
  Go fetch a pint of port:
But let it not be such as that
  You set before chance-comers,
But such whose father-grape grew fat
  On Lusitanian summers.

No vain libation to the Muse,
  But may she still be kind,
And whisper lovely words, and use
  Her influence on the mind,
To make me write my random rhymes,
  Ere they be half-forgotten;
Nor add and alter, many times,
  Till all be ripe and rotten.

I pledge her, and she comes and dips
  Her laurel in the wine,
And lays it thrice upon my lips,
  These favour'd lips of mine;
Until the charm have power to make
  New lifeblood warm the bosom,
And barren commonplaces break
  In full and kindly blossom.

I pledge her silent at the board;
  Her gradual fingers steal
And touch upon the master-chord
  Of all I felt and feel.
Old wishes, ghosts of broken plans,
  And phantom hopes assemble;
And that child's heart within the man's
  Begins to move and tremble.

Thro' many an hour of summer suns,
  By many pleasant ways,
Against its fountain upward runs
  The current of my days:
I kiss the lips I once have kiss'd;
  The gas-light wavers dimmer;
And softly, thro' a vinous mist,
  My college friendships glimmer.

I grow in worth, and wit, and sense,
  Unboding critic-pen,
Or that eternal want of pence,
  Which vexes public men,
Who hold their hands to all, and cry
  For that which all deny them—
Who sweep the crossings, wet or dry,
  And all the world go by them.

Ah yet, tho' all the world forsake,
  Tho' fortune clip my wings,
I will not cramp my heart, nor take
  Half-views of men and things.
Let Whig and Tory stir their blood;
  There must be stormy weather;
But for some true result of good
  All parties work together.

Let there be thistles, there are grapes;
  If old things, there are new;
Ten thousand broken lights and shapes,
  Yet glimpses of the true.
Let raffs be rife in prose and rhyme,
  We lack not rhymes and reasons,
As on this whirligig of Time
  We circle with the seasons.

This earth is rich in man and maid;
  With fair horizons bound:
This whole wide earth of light and shade
  Comes out a perfect round.
High over roaring Temple-bar,
  And set in Heaven's third story,
I look at all things as they are,
  But thro' a kind of glory.

Head-waiter, honour'd by the guest
  Half-mused, or reeling ripe,
The pint, you brought me, was the best
  That ever came from pipe.
But tho' the port surpasses praise,
  My nerves have dealt with stiffer.
Is there some magic in the place?
  Or do my peptics differ?

For since I came to live and learn,
  No pint of white or red
Had ever half the power to turn
  This wheel within my head,
Which bears a season'd brain about,
  Unsubject to confusion,
Tho' soak'd and saturate, out and out,
  Thro' every convolution.

For I am of a numerous house,
  With many kinsmen gay,
Where long and largely we carouse
  As who shall say me nay:
Each month, a birth-day coming on,
  We drink defying trouble,
Or sometimes two would meet in one,
  And then we drank it double;

Whether the vintage, yet unkept,
  Had relish fiery-new,
Or elbow-deep in sawdust, slept,
  As old as Waterloo;
Or stow'd, when classic Canning died,
  In musty bins and chambers,
Had cast upon its crusty side
  The gloom of ten Decembers.

The Muse, the jolly Muse, it is!
  She answer'd to my call,
She changes with that mood or this,
  Is all-in-all to all:
She lit the spark within my throat,
  To make my blood run quicker,
Used all her fiery will, and smote
  Her life into the liquor.

And hence this halo lives about
  The waiter's hands, that reach
To each his perfect pint of stout,
  His proper chop to each.
He looks not like the common breed
  That with the napkin dally;
I think he came like Ganymede,
  From some delightful valley.

The Cock was of a larger egg
  Than modern poultry drop,
Stept forward on a firmer leg,
  And cramm'd a plumper crop;
Upon an ampler dunghill trod,
  Crow'd lustier late and early,
Sipt wine from silver, praising God,
  And raked in golden barley.

A private life was all his joy,
  Till in a court he saw
A something-pottle-bodied boy
  That knuckled at the taw:
He stoop'd and clutch'd him, fair and good,
  Flew over roof and casement:
His brothers of the weather stood
  Stock-still for sheer amazement.

But he, by farmstead, thorpe and spire,
  And follow'd with acclaims,
A sign to many a staring shire
  Came crowing over Thames.
Right down by smoky Paul's they bore,
  Till, where the street grows straiter,
One fix'd for ever at the door,
  And one became head-waiter.

———

But whither would my fancy go?
  How out of place she makes
The violet of a legend blow
  Among the chops and steaks!
'Tis but a steward of the can,
  One shade more plump than common;
As just and mere a serving-man
  As any born of woman.

I ranged too high: what draws me down
  Into the common day?
Is it the weight of that half-crown,
  Which I shall have to pay?
For, something duller than at first,
  Nor wholly comfortable,
I sit, my empty glass reversed,
  And thrumming on the table:

Half fearful that, with self at strife,
  I take myself to task;
Lest of the fulness of my life
  I leave an empty flask:
For I had hope, by something rare
  To prove myself a poet:
But, while I plan and plan, my hair
  Is gray before I know it.

So fares it since the years began,
  Till they be gather'd up;
The truth, that flies the flowing can,
  Will haunt the vacant cup:
And others' follies teach us not,
  Nor much their wisdom teaches;
And most, of sterling worth, is what
  Our own experience preaches.

Ah, let the rusty theme alone!
  We know not what we know.
But for my pleasant hour, 'tis gone;
  'Tis gone, and let it go.
'Tis gone: a thousand such have slipt
  Away from my embraces,
And fall'n into the dusty crypt
  Of darken'd forms and faces.

Go, therefore, thou! thy betters went
  Long since, and came no more;
With peals of genial clamour sent
  From many a tavern-door,
With twisted quirks and happy hits,
  From misty men of letters;
The tavern-hours of mighty wits—
  Thine elders and thy betters.

Hours, when the Poet's words and looks
  Had yet their native glow;
Nor yet the fear of little books
  Had made him talk for show;
But, all his vast heart sherris-warm'd,
  He flash'd his random speeches,
Ere days, that deal in ana, swarm'd
  His literary leeches.

So mix for ever with the past,
  Like all good things on earth!
For should I prize thee, couldst thou last
  At half thy real worth?
I hold it good, good things should pass:
  With time I will not quarrel:
It is but yonder empty glass
  That makes me maudlin-moral.

Head-waiter of the chop-house here,
  To which I most resort,
I too must part: I hold thee dear
  For this good pint of port.
For this, thou shalt from all things suck
  Marrow of mirth and laughter;
And wheresoe'er thou move, good luck
  Shall fling her old shoe after.

But thou wilt never move from hence,
  The sphere thy fate allots:
Thy latter days increased with pence
  Go down among the pots:
Thou battenest by the greasy gleam
  In haunts of hungry sinners,
Old boxes, larded with the steam
  Of thirty thousand dinners.

We fret, we fume, would shift our skins,
  Would quarrel with our lot;
Thy care is, under polish'd tins,
  To serve the hot-and-hot;
To come and go, and come again,
  Returning like the pewit,
And watch'd by silent gentlemen,
  That trifle with the cruet.

Live long, ere from thy topmost head
  The thick-set hazel dies;
Long, ere the hateful crow shall tread
  The corners of thine eyes:
Live long, nor feel in head or chest
  Our changeful equinoxes,
Till mellow Death, like some late guest,
  Shall call thee from the boxes.

But when he calls, and thou shalt cease
  To pace the gritted floor,
And, laying down an unctuous lease
  Of life, shalt earn no more;
No carved cross-bones, the types of Death
  Shall show thee past to Heaven:
But carved cross-pipes, and, underneath,
  A pint-pot neatly graven.

LADY CLARE

It was the time when lilies blow,
  And clouds are highest up in air,
Lord Ronald brought a lily-white doe
  To give his cousin, Lady Clare.

I trow they did not part in scorn:
  Lovers long-betroth'd were they:
They two will wed the morrow morn:
  God's blessing on the day!

'He does not love me for my birth,
  Nor for my lands so broad and fair;
He loves me for my own true worth,
  And that is well,' said Lady Clare.

In there came old Alice the nurse,
  Said, 'Who was this that went from
    thee?'
'It was my cousin,' said Lady Clare,
  'To-morrow he weds with me.'

'O God be thank'd!' said Alice the nurse,
  'That all comes round so just and fair:
Lord Ronald is heir of all your lands,
  And you are *not* the Lady Clare.'

'Are ye out of your mind, my nurse, my
  nurse?'
Said Lady Clare, 'that ye speak so wild?'
'As God's above,' said Alice the nurse,
  'I speak the truth: you are my child.

'The old Earl's daughter died at my breast;
  I speak the truth, as I live by bread!
I buried her like my own sweet child,
  And put my child in her stead.'

'Falsely, falsely have ye done,
  O mother,' she said, 'if this be true,
To keep the best man under the sun
  So many years from his due.'

'Nay now, my child,' said Alice the nurse,
  'But keep the secret for your life,
And all you have will be Lord Ronald's,
  When you are man and wife.'

'If I'm a beggar born,' she said,
  'I will speak out, for I dare not lie.
Pull off, pull off, the brooch of gold,
  And fling the diamond necklace by.'

'Nay now, my child,' said Alice the nurse,
  'But keep the secret all ye can.'
She said, 'Not so: but I will know
  If there be any faith in man.'

'Nay now, what faith?' said Alice the nurse,
  'The man will cleave unto his right.'
'And he shall have it,' the lady replied,
  'Tho' I should die to-night.'

'Yet give one kiss to your mother dear!
  Alas, my child, I sinn'd for thee.'
'O mother, mother, mother,' she said,
  'So strange it seems to me.

'Yet here's a kiss for my mother dear,
  My mother dear, if this be so,
And lay your hand upon my head,
  And bless me, mother, ere I go.'

She clad herself in a russet gown,
  She was no longer Lady Clare:
She went by dale, and she went by down,
  With a single rose in her hair.

The lily-white doe Lord Ronald had
  brought
Leapt up from where she lay,

Dropt her head in the maiden's hand,
  And follow'd her all the way.

Down stept Lord Ronald from his tower:
  'O Lady Clare, you shame your worth!
Why come you drest like a village maid
  That are the flower of the earth?'

'If I come drest like a village maid,
  I am but as my fortunes are:
I am a beggar born,' she said,
  'And not the Lady Clare.'

'Play me no tricks,' said Lord Ronald,
  'For I am yours in word and in deed.
Play me no tricks,' said Lord Ronald,
  'Your riddle is hard to read.'

O and proudly stood she up!
  Her heart within her did not fail:
She look'd into Lord Ronald's eyes,
  And told him all her nurse's tale.

He laugh'd a laugh of merry scorn:
  He turn'd and kiss'd her where she
    stood:
'If you are not the heiress born,
  And I,' said he, 'the next in blood—

'If you are not the heiress born,
  And I,' said he, 'the lawful heir,
We two will wed to-morrow morn,
  And you shall still be Lady Clare.'

THE CAPTAIN
A LEGEND OF THE NAVY

HE that only rules by terror
  Doeth grievous wrong.
Deep as Hell I count his error.
  Let him hear my song.
Brave the Captain was: the seamen
  Made a gallant crew,
Gallant sons of English freemen,
  Sailors bold and true.
But they hated his oppression,
  Stern he was and rash;
So for every light transgression
  Doom'd them to the lash.
Day by day more harsh and cruel
  Seem'd the Captain's mood.
Secret wrath like smother'd fuel
  Burnt in each man's blood.

Yet he hoped to purchase glory,
  Hoped to make the name
Of his vessel great in story,
  Wheresoe'er he came.
So they past by capes and islands,
  Many a harbour-mouth,
Sailing under palmy highlands
  Far within the South.
On a day when they were going
  O'er the lone expanse,
In the north, her canvas flowing,
  Rose a ship of France.
Then the Captain's colour heighten'd,
  Joyful came his speech:
But a cloudy gladness lighten'd
  In the eyes of each.
'Chase,' he said: the ship flew forward,
  And the wind did blow;
Stately, lightly, went she Norward,
  Till she near'd the foe.
Then they look'd at him they hated,
  Had what they desired:
Mute with folded arms they waited—
  Not a gun was fired.
But they heard the foeman's thunder
  Roaring out their doom;
All the air was torn in sunder,
  Crashing went the boom,
Spars were splinter'd, decks were shatter'd,
  Bullets fell like rain;
Over mast and deck were scatter'd
  Blood and brains of men.
Spars were splinter'd; decks were broken:
  Every mother's son—
Down they dropt—no word was spoken—
  Each beside his gun.
On the decks as they were lying,
  Were their faces grim.
In their blood, as they lay dying,
  Did they smile on him.
Those, in whom he had reliance
  For his noble name,
With one smile of still defiance
  Sold him unto shame.
Shame and wrath his heart confounded,
  Pale he turn'd and red,
Till himself was deadly wounded
  Falling on the dead.
Dismal error! fearful slaughter!
  Years have wander'd by,
Side by side beneath the water

Crew and Captain lie;
There the sunlit ocean tosses
  O'er them mouldering,
And the lonely seabird crosses
  With one waft of the wing.

THE LORD OF BURLEIGH

IN her ear he whispers gaily,
  'If my heart by signs can tell,
Maiden, I have watch'd thee daily,
  And I think thou lov'st me well.'
She replies, in accents fainter,
  'There is none I love like thee.'
He is but a landscape-painter,
  And a village maiden she.
He to lips, that fondly falter,
  Presses his without reproof:
Leads her to the village altar,
  And they leave her father's roof.
'I can make no marriage present:
  Little can I give my wife.
Love will make our cottage pleasant,
  And I love thee more than life.'
They by parks and lodges going
  See the lordly castles stand:
Summer woods, about them blowing,
  Made a murmur in the land.
From deep thought himself he rouses,
  Says to her that loves him well,
'Let us see these handsome houses
  Where the wealthy nobles dwell.'
So she goes by him attended,
  Hears him lovingly converse,
Sees whatever fair and splendid
  Lay betwixt his home and hers;
Parks with oak and chestnut shady,
  Parks and order'd gardens great,
Ancient homes of lord and lady,
  Built for pleasure and for state.
All he shows her makes him dearer:
  Evermore she seems to gaze
On that cottage growing nearer,
  Where they twain will spend their days
O but she will love him truly!
  He shall have a cheerful home;
She will order all things duly,
  When beneath his roof they come.
Thus her heart rejoices greatly,
  Till a gateway she discerns
With armorial bearings stately,

And beneath the gate she turns;
Sees a mansion more majestic
Than all those she saw before:
Many a gallant gay domestic
Bows before him at the door.
And they speak in gentle murmur,
 When they answer to his call,
While he treads with footstep firmer,
 Leading on from hall to hall.
And, while now she wonders blindly,
 Nor the meaning can divine,
Proudly turns he round and kindly,
 'All of this is mine and thine.'
Here he lives in state and bounty,
 Lord of Burleigh, fair and free,
Not a lord in all the county
 Is so great a lord as he.
All at once the colour flushes
 Her sweet face from brow to chin:
As it were with shame she blushes,
 And her spirit changed within.
Then her countenance all over
 Pale again as death did prove:
But he clasp'd her like a lover,
 And he cheer'd her soul with love.
So she strove against her weakness,
 Tho' at times her spirit sank:
Shaped her heart with woman's meekness
 To all duties of her rank:
And a gentle consort made he,
 And her gentle mind was such
That she grew a noble lady,
 And the people loved her much.
But a trouble weigh'd upon her,
 And perplex'd her, night and morn,
With the burthen of an honour
 Unto which she was not born.
Faint she grew, and ever fainter,
 And she murmur'd, 'Oh, that he
Were once more that landscape-painter
 Which did win my heart from me!'
So she droop'd and droop'd before him,
 Fading slowly from his side:
Three fair children first she bore him,
 Then before her time she died.
Weeping, weeping late and early,
 Walking up and pacing down,
Deeply mourn'd the Lord of Burleigh,
 Burleigh-house by Stamford-town.
And he came to look upon her,
 And he look'd at her and said,

'Bring the dress and put it on her,
 That she wore when she was wed.'
Then her people, softly treading,
 Bore to earth her body, drest
In the dress that she was wed in,
 That her spirit might have rest.

THE VOYAGE

I

WE left behind the painted buoy
 That tosses at the harbour-mouth;
And madly danced our hearts with joy,
 As fast we fleeted to the South:
How fresh was every sight and sound
 On open main or winding shore!
We knew the merry world was round,
 And we might sail for evermore.

II

Warm broke the breeze against the brow,
 Dry sang the tackle, sang the sail:
The Lady's-head upon the prow
 Caught the shrill salt, and sheer'd the
  gale.
The broad seas swell'd to meet the keel,
 And swept behind; so quick the run,
We felt the good ship shake and reel,
 We seem'd to sail into the Sun!

III

How oft we saw the Sun retire,
 And burn the threshold of the night,
Fall from his Ocean-lane of fire,
 And sleep beneath his pillar'd light!
How oft the purple-skirted robe
 Of twilight slowly downward drawn,
As thro' the slumber of the globe
 Again we dash'd into the dawn!

IV

New stars all night above the brim
 Of waters lighten'd into view;
They climb'd as quickly, for the rim
 Changed every moment as we flew.
Far ran the naked moon across
 The houseless ocean's heaving field,
Or flying shone, the silver boss
 Of her own halo's dusky shield;

V

The peaky islet shifted shapes,
  High towns on hills were dimly seen,
We past long lines of Northern capes
  And dewy Northern meadows green.
We came to warmer waves, and deep
  Across the boundless east we drove,
Where those long swells of breaker sweep
  The nutmeg rocks and isles of clove.

VI

By peaks that flamed, or, all in shade,
  Gloom'd the low coast and quivering
    brine
With ashy rains, that spreading made
  Fantastic plume or sable pine;
By sands and steaming flats, and floods
  Of mighty mouth, we scudded fast,
And hills and scarlet-mingled woods
  Glow'd for a moment as we past.

VII

O hundred shores of happy climes,
  How swiftly stream'd ye by the bark!
At times the whole sea burn'd, at times
  With wakes of fire we tore the dark;
At times a carven craft would shoot
  From havens hid in fairy bowers,
With naked limbs and flowers and fruit,
  But we nor paused for fruit nor flowers.

VIII

For one fair Vision ever fled
  Down the waste waters day and night,
And still we follow'd where she led,
  In hope to gain upon her flight.
Her face was evermore unseen,
  And fixt upon the far sea-line;
But each man murmur'd, 'O my Queen,
  I follow till I make thee mine.'

IX

And now we lost her, now she gleam'd
  Like Fancy made of golden air,
Now nearer to the prow she seem'd
  Like Virtue firm, like Knowledge fair,
Now high on waves that idly burst
  Like Heavenly Hope she crown'd the
    sea,
And now, the bloodless point reversed,
  She bore the blade of Liberty.

X

And only one among us—him
  We pleased not—he was seldom pleased:
He saw not far: his eyes were dim:
  But ours he swore were all diseased.
'A ship of fools,' he shriek'd in spite,
  'A ship of fools,' he sneer'd and wept.
And overboard one stormy night
  He cast his body, and on we swept.

XI

And never sail of ours was furl'd,
  Nor anchor dropt at eve or morn;
We lov'd the glories of the world,
  But laws of nature were our scorn.
For blasts would rise and rave and cease,
  But whence were those that drove the
    sail
Across the whirlwind's heart of peace,
  And to and thro' the counter gale?

XII

Again to colder climes we came,
  For still we follow'd where she led:
Now mate is blind and captain lame,
  And half the crew are sick or dead,
But, blind or lame or sick or sound,
  We follow that which flies before:
We know the merry world is round,
  And we may sail for evermore.

SIR LAUNCELOT AND QUEEN GUINEVERE

A FRAGMENT

LIKE souls that balance joy and pain,
With tears and smiles from heaven again
The maiden Spring upon the plain
Came in a sun-lit fall of rain.
  In crystal vapour everywhere
Blue isles of heaven laugh'd between,
And far, in forest-deeps unseen,
The topmost elm-tree gather'd green
  From draughts of balmy air.

Sometimes the linnet piped his song:
Sometimes the throstle whistled strong:
Sometimes the sparhawk, wheel'd along,
Hush'd all the groves from fear of wrong:

By grassy capes with fuller sound
In curves the yellowing river ran,
And drooping chestnut-buds began
To spread into the perfect fan,
  Above the teeming ground.

Then, in the boyhood of the year,
Sir Launcelot and Queen Guinevere
Rode thro' the coverts of the deer,
With blissful treble ringing clear.
  She seem'd a part of joyous Spring
A gown of grass-green silk she wore,
Buckled with golden clasps before;
A light-green tuft of plumes she bore
  Closed in a golden ring.

Now on some twisted ivy-net,
Now by some tinkling rivulet,
In mosses mixt with violet
Her cream-white mule his pastern set:
  And fleeter now she skimm'd the plains
Than she whose elfin prancer springs
By night to eery warblings,
When all the glimmering moorland rings
  With jingling bridle-reins.

As fast she fled thro' sun and shade,
The happy winds upon her play'd,
Blowing the ringlet from the braid:
She look'd so lovely, as she sway'd
  The rein with dainty finger-tips,
A man had given all other bliss,
And all his worldly worth for this,
To waste his whole heart in one kiss
  Upon her perfect lips.

A FAREWELL

FLOW down, cold rivulet, to the sea,
  Thy tribute wave deliver:
No more by thee my steps shall be,
  For ever and for ever.

Flow, softly flow, by lawn and lea,
  A rivulet then a river:
No where by thee my steps shall be,
  For ever and for ever.

But here will sigh thine alder tree,
  And here thine aspen shiver;
And here by thee will hum the bee,
  For ever and for ever.

A thousand suns will stream on thee,
  A thousand moons will quiver;
But not by thee my steps shall be,
  For ever and for ever.

THE BEGGAR MAID

HER arms across her breast she laid;
  She was more fair than words can say:
Bare-footed came the beggar maid
  Before the king Cophetua.
In robe and crown the king stept down,
  To meet and greet her on her way;
'It is no wonder,' said the lords,
  'She is more beautiful than day.'

As shines the moon in clouded skies,
  She in her poor attire was seen:
One praised her ancles, one her eyes,
  One her dark hair and lovesome mien.
So sweet a face, such angel grace,
  In all that land had never been:
Cophetua sware a royal oath:
  'This beggar maid shall be my queen!'

THE EAGLE

FRAGMENT

HE clasps the crag with crooked hands;
Close to the sun in lonely lands,
Ring'd with the azure world, he stands.

The wrinkled sea beneath him crawls;
He watches from his mountain walls,
And like a thunderbolt he falls.

———

MOVE eastward, happy earth, and leave
  Yon orange sunset waning slow:
From fringes of the faded eve,
  O, happy planet, eastward go;
Till over thy dark shoulder glow
  Thy silver sister-world, and rise
To glass herself in dewy eyes
  That watch me from the glen below.

Ah, bear me with thee, smoothly borne,
  Dip forward under starry light,
And move me to my marriage-morn,
  And round again to happy night.

———

'COME NOT, WHEN I AM DEAD'

COME not, when I am dead,
　To drop thy foolish tears upon my grave,
To trample round my fallen head,
　And vex the unhappy dust thou wouldst
　　not save.
There let the wind sweep and the plover
　　cry;
　　But thou, go by.

Child, if it were thine error or thy crime
　I care no longer, being all unblest:
Wed whom thou wilt, but I am sick of
　　Time,
　And I desire to rest.
Pass on, weak heart, and leave me where
　　I lie:
　　Go by, go by.

THE LETTERS

I

STILL on the tower stood the vane,
　A black yew gloom'd the stagnant air,
I peer'd athwart the chancel pane
　And saw the altar cold and bare.
A clog of lead was round my feet,
　A band of pain across my brow;
'Cold altar, Heaven and earth shall meet
　Before you hear my marriage vow.'

II

I turn'd and humm'd a bitter song
　That mock'd the wholesome human
　　heart,
And then we met in wrath and wrong,
　We met, but only meant to part.
Full cold my greeting was and dry;
　She faintly smiled, she hardly moved;
I saw with half-unconscious eye
　She wore the colours I approved.

III

She took the little ivory chest,
　With half a sigh she turn'd the key,
Then raised her head with lips comprest,
　And gave my letters back to me.
And gave the trinkets and the rings,
　My gifts, when gifts of mine could
　　please;
As looks a father on the things
　Of his dead son, I look'd on these.

IV

She told me all her friends had said;
　I raged against the public liar;
She talk'd as if her love were dead,
　But in my words were seeds of fire.
'No more of love; your sex is known:
　I never will be twice deceived.
Henceforth I trust the man alone,
　The woman cannot be believed.

V

'Thro' slander, meanest spawn of Hell—
　And women's slander is the worst,
And you, whom once I lov'd so well,
　Thro' you, my life will be accurst.'
I spoke with heart, and heat and force,
　I shook her breast with vague alarms—
Like torrents from a mountain source
　We rush'd into each other's arms.

VI

We parted: sweetly gleam'd the stars,
　And sweet the vapour-braided blue,
Low breezes fann'd the belfry bars,
　As homeward by the church I drew.
The very graves appear'd to smile,
　So fresh they rose in shadow'd swells
'Dark porch,' I said, 'and silent aisle,
　There comes a sound of marriage bells.'

THE VISION OF SIN

I

I HAD a vision when the night was late:
A youth came riding toward a palace-gate.
He rode a horse with wings, that would
　　have flown,
But that his heavy rider kept him down.
And from the palace came a child of sin,
And took him by the curls, and led him in,
Where sat a company with heated eyes,
Expecting when a fountain should arise:
A sleepy light upon their brows and lips—
As when the sun, a crescent of eclipse,
Dreams over lake and lawn, and isles and
　　capes—
Suffused them, sitting, lying, languid
　　shapes,
By heaps of gourds, and skins of wine, and
　　piles of grapes.

II

Then methought I heard a mellow sound,
Gathering up from all the lower ground;
Narrowing in to where they sat assembled
Low voluptuous music winding trembled,
Wov'n in circles: they that heard it sigh'd,
Panted hand-in-hand with faces pale,
Swung themselves, and in low tones re-
    plied;
Till the fountain spouted, showering wide
Sleet of diamond-drift and pearly hail;
Then the music touch'd the gates and died;
Rose again from where it seem'd to fail,
Storm'd in orbs of song, a growing gale;
Till thronging in and in, to where they
    waited,
As 'twere a hundred-throated nightingale,
The strong tempestuous treble throbb'd
    and palpitated;
Ran into its giddiest whirl of sound,
Caught the sparkles, and in circles,
Purple gauzes, golden hazes, liquid mazes,
Flung the torrent rainbow round:
Then they started from their places,
Moved with violence, changed in hue,
Caught each other with wild grimaces,
Half-invisible to the view,
Wheeling with precipitate paces
To the melody, till they flew,
Hair, and eyes, and limbs, and faces,
Twisted hard in fierce embraces,
Like to Furies, like to Graces,
Dash'd together in blinding dew:
Till, kill'd with some luxurious agony,
The nerve-dissolving melody
Flutter'd headlong from the sky.

III

And then I look'd up toward a mountain-
    tract,
That girt the region with high cliff and
    lawn:
I saw that every morning, far withdrawn
Beyond the darkness and the cataract,
God made Himself an awful rose of dawn,
Unheeded: and detaching, fold by fold,
From those still heights, and, slowly draw-
    ing near,
A vapour heavy, hueless, formless, cold,
Came floating on for many a month and
    year,

Unheeded: and I thought I would have
    spoken,
And warn'd that madman ere it grew too
    late:
But, as in dreams, I could not. Mine was
    broken,
When that cold vapour touch'd the palace
    gate,
And link'd again. I saw within my head
A gray and gap-tooth'd man as lean as
    death,
Who slowly rode across a wither'd heath,
And lighted at a ruin'd inn, and said:

IV

'Wrinkled ostler, grim and thin!
    Here is custom come your way;
Take my brute, and lead him in,
    Stuff his ribs with mouldy hay.

'Bitter barmaid, waning fast!
    See that sheets are on my bed;
What! the flower of life is past:
    It is long before you wed.

'Slip-shod waiter, lank and sour,
    At the Dragon on the heath!
Let us have a quiet hour,
    Let us hob-and-nob with Death.

'I am old, but let me drink;
    Bring me spices, bring me wine;
I remember, when I think,
    That my youth was half divine.

'Wine is good for shrivell'd lips,
    When a blanket wraps the day,
When the rotten woodland drips,
    And the leaf is stamp'd in clay.

'Sit thee down, and have no shame,
    Cheek by jowl, and knee by knee:
What care I for any name?
    What for order or degree?

'Let me screw thee up a peg:
    Let me loose thy tongue with wine:
Callest thou that thing a leg?
    Which is thinnest? thine or mine?

'Thou shalt not be saved by works:
    Thou hast been a sinner too:
Ruin'd trunks on wither'd forks,
    Empty scarecrows, I and you!

113

'Fill the cup, and fill the can:
  Have a rouse before the morn:
Every moment dies a man,
  Every moment one is born.

'We are men of ruin'd blood;
  Therefore comes it we are wise.
Fish are we that love the mud,
  Rising to no fancy-flies.

'Name and fame! to fly sublime
  Thro' the courts, the camps, the schools,
Is to be the ball of Time,
  Bandied by the hands of fools.

'Friendship!—to be two in one—
  Let the canting liar pack!
Well I know, when I am gone,
  How she mouths behind my back.

'Virtue!—to be good and just—
  Every heart, when sifted well,
Is a clot of warmer dust,
  Mix'd with cunning sparks of hell.

'O! we two as well can look
  Whited thought and cleanly life
As the priest, above his book
  Leering at his neighbour's wife.

'Fill the cup, and fill the can:
  Have a rouse before the morn:
Every moment dies a man,
  Every moment one is born.

'Drink, and let the parties rave:
  They are fill'd with idle spleen;
Rising, falling, like a wave,
  For they know not what they mean.

'He that roars for liberty
  Faster binds a tyrant's power;
And the tyrant's cruel glee
  Forces on the freer hour.

'Fill the can, and fill the cup:
  All the windy ways of men
Are but dust that rises up,
  And is lightly laid again.

'Greet her with applausive breath,
  Freedom, gaily doth she tread;
In her right a civic wreath,
  In her left a human head.

'No, I love not what is new;
  She is of an ancient house:
And I think we know the hue
  Of that cap upon her brows.

'Let her go! her thirst she slakes
  Where the bloody conduit runs,
Then her sweetest meal she makes
  On the first-born of her sons.

'Drink to lofty hopes that cool—
  Visions of a perfect State:
Drink we, last, the public fool,
  Frantic love and frantic hate.

'Chant we now some wicked stave,
  Till thy drooping courage rise,
And the glow-worm of the grave
  Glimmer in thy rheumy eyes.

'Fear not thou to loose thy tongue;
  Set thy hoary fancies free;
What is loathsome to the young
  Savours well to thee and me.

'Change, reverting to the years,
  When thy nerves could understand
What there is in loving tears,
  And the warmth of hand in hand.

'Tell me tales of thy first love—
  April hopes, the fools of chance;
Till the graves begin to move,
  And the dead begin to dance.

'Fill the can, and fill the cup:
  All the windy ways of men
Are but dust that rises up,
  And is lightly laid again.

'Trooping from their mouldy dens
  The chap-fallen circle spreads:
Welcome, fellow-citizens,
  Hollow hearts and empty heads!

'You are bones, and what of that?
  Every face, however full,
Padded round with flesh and fat,
  Is but modell'd on a skull.

'Death is king, and Vivat Rex!
  Tread a measure on the stones,
Madam—if I know your sex,
  From the fashion of your bones.

'No, I cannot praise the fire
  In your eye—nor yet your lip:
All the more do I admire
  Joints of cunning workmanship.

'Lo! God's likeness—the ground-plan—
  Neither modell'd, glazed, nor framed:
Buss me, thou rough sketch of man,
  Far too naked to be shamed!

'Drink to Fortune, drink to Chance,
  While we keep a little breath!
Drink to heavy Ignorance!
  Hob-and-nob with brother Death!

'Thou art mazed, the night is long,
  And the longer night is near:
What! I am not all as wrong
  As a bitter jest is dear.

'Youthful hopes, by scores, to all,
  When the locks are crisp and curl'd;
Unto me my maudlin gall
  And my mockeries of the world.

'Fill the cup, and fill the can:
  Mingle madness, mingle scorn!
Dregs of life, and lees of man:
  Yet we will not die forlorn.'

V

The voice grew faint: there came a further
    change:
Once more uprose the mystic mountain-
    range:
Below were men and horses pierced with
    worms,
And slowly quickening into lower forms;
By shards and scurf of salt, and scum of
    dross,
Old plash of rains, and refuse patch'd with
    moss.
Then some one spake: 'Behold! it was a
    crime
Of sense avenged by sense that wore with
    time.'
Another said: 'The crime of sense became
The crime of malice, and is equal blame.'
And one: 'He had not wholly quench'd his
    power;
A little grain of conscience made him sour.'
At last I heard a voice upon the slope
Cry to the summit, 'Is there any hope?'

To which an answer peal'd from that high
    land,
But in a tongue no man could understand;
And on the glimmering limit far with-
    drawn
God made Himself an awful rose of dawn.

TO ——

AFTER READING A LIFE AND LETTERS

'Cursed be he that moves my bones.'
                    Shakespeare's Epitaph

YOU might have won the Poet's name,
  If such be worth the winning now,
  And gain'd a laurel for your brow
Of sounder leaf than I can claim;

But you have made the wiser choice,
  A life that moves to gracious ends
  Thro' troops of unrecording friends,
A deedful life, a silent voice:

And you have miss'd the irreverent doom
  Of those that wear the Poet's crown:
  Hereafter, neither knave nor clown
Shall hold their orgies at your tomb.

For now the Poet cannot die,
  Nor leave his music as of old,
  But round him ere he scarce be cold
Begins the scandal and the cry:

'Proclaim the faults he would not show:
  Break lock and seal: betray the trust:
  Keep nothing sacred: 'tis but just
The many-headed beast should know.'

Ah shameless! for he did but sing
  A song that pleased us from its worth;
  No public life was his on earth,
No blazon'd statesman he, nor king.

He gave the people of his best:
  His worst he kept, his best he gave.
  My Shakespeare's curse on clown and
    knave
Who will not let his ashes rest!

Who make it seem more sweet to be
  The little life of bank and brier,
  The bird that pipes his lone desire
And dies unheard within his tree,

Than he that warbles long and loud
  And drops at Glory's temple-gates,
  For whom the carrion vulture waits
To tear his heart before the crowd!

TO E. L., ON HIS TRAVELS IN GREECE

ILLYRIAN woodlands, echoing falls
  Of water, sheets of summer glass,
  The long divine Peneïan pass,
The vast Akrokeraunian walls,

Tomohrit, Athos, all things fair,
  With such a pencil, such a pen,
  You shadow forth to distant men,
I read and felt that I was there:

And trust me while I turn'd the page,
  And track'd you still on classic ground,
  I grew in gladness till I found
My spirits in the golden age.

For me the torrent ever pour'd
  And glisten'd—here and there alone
  The broad-limb'd Gods at random thrown
By fountain-urns;—and Naiads oar'd

A glimmering shoulder under gloom
  Of cavern pillars; on the swell
  The silver lily heaved and fell;
And many a slope was rich in bloom

From him that on the mountain lea
  By dancing rivulets fed his flocks
  To him who sat upon the rocks,
And fluted to the morning sea.

———

BREAK, break, break,
  On thy cold gray stones, O Sea!
And I would that my tongue could utter
  The thoughts that arise in me.

O well for the fisherman's boy,
  That he shouts with his sister at play!
O well for the sailor lad,
  That he sings in his boat on the bay!

And the stately ships go on
  To their haven under the hill;
But O for the touch of a vanish'd hand,
  And the sound of a voice that is still!

Break, break, break,
  At the foot of thy crags, O sea!
But the tender grace of a day that is dead
  Will never come back to me.

THE POET'S SONG

THE rain had fallen, the Poet arose,
  He pass'd by the town and out of the street,
A light wind blew from the gates of the sun,
  And waves of shadow went over the wheat,
And he sat him down in a lonely place,
  And chanted a melody loud and sweet,
That made the wild-swan pause in her cloud,
  And the lark drop down at his feet.

The swallow stopt as he hunted the fly,
  The snake slipt under a spray,
The wild hawk stood with the down on his beak,
  And stared, with his foot on the prey,
And the nightingale thought, 'I have sung many songs,
  But never a one so gay,
For he sings of what the world will be
  When the years have died away.'

ENOCH ARDEN

AND OTHER POEMS

ENOCH ARDEN

Long lines of cliff breaking have left a
  chasm;
And in the chasm are foam and yellow
  sands;
Beyond, red roofs about a narrow wharf
In cluster; then a moulder'd church; and
  higher
A long street climbs to one tall-tower'd
  mill;
And high in heaven behind it a gray down
With Danish barrows; and a hazelwood,
By autumn nutters haunted, flourishes
Green in a cuplike hollow of the down.

Here on this beach a hundred years ago,
Three children of three houses, Annie Lee,
The prettiest little damsel in the port,
And Philip Ray the miller's only son,
And Enoch Arden, a rough sailor's lad
Made orphan by a winter shipwreck, play'd
Among the waste and lumber of the shore,
Hard coils of cordage, swarthy fishing-nets,
Anchors of rusty fluke, and boats updrawn;
And built their castles of dissolving sand
To watch them overflow'd, or following up
And flying the white breaker, daily left
The little footprint daily wash'd away.

A narrow cave ran in beneath the cliff:
In this the children play'd at keeping
  house.
Enoch was host one day, Philip the next,
While Annie still was mistress; but at
  times
Enoch would hold possession for a week:
'This is my house and this my little wife.'
'Mine too' said Philip 'turn and turn
  about:'
When, if they quarrell'd, Enoch stronger-
  made
Was master: then would Philip, his blue
  eyes
All flooded with the helpless wrath of tears,
Shriek out 'I hate you, Enoch,' and at this
The little wife would weep for company,

And pray them not to quarrel for her sake,
And say she would be little wife to both.

But when the dawn of rosy childhood
  past,
And the new warmth of life's ascending
  sun
Was felt by either, either fixt his heart
On that one girl; and Enoch spoke his love,
But Philip loved in silence; and the girl
Seem'd kinder unto Philip than to him;
But she loved Enoch; tho' she knew it not,
And would if ask'd deny it. Enoch set
A purpose evermore before his eyes,
To hoard all savings to the uttermost,
To purchase his own boat, and make a
  home
For Annie: and so prosper'd that at last
A luckier or a bolder fisherman,
A carefuller in peril, did not breathe
For leagues along that breaker-beaten coast
Than Enoch. Likewise had he served a
  year
On board a merchantman, and made him-
  self
Full sailor; and he thrice had pluck'd a life
From the dread sweep of the down-stream-
  ing seas:
And all men look'd upon him favourably:
And ere he touch'd his one-and-twentieth
  May
He purchased his own boat, and made a
  home
For Annie, neat and nestlike, halfway up
The narrow street that clamber'd toward
  the mill.

Then, on a golden autumn eventide,
The younger people making holiday,
With bag and sack and basket, great and
  small,
Went nutting to the hazels. Philip stay'd
(His father lying sick and needing him)
An hour behind; but as he climb'd the hill,
Just where the prone edge of the wood
  began

117

To feather toward the hollow, saw the pair,
Enoch and Annie, sitting hand-in-hand,
His large gray eyes and weather-beaten
face
All-kindled by a still and sacred fire,
That burn'd as on an altar. Philip look'd,
And in their eyes and faces read his doom;
Then, as their faces drew together, groan'd,
And slipt aside, and like a wounded life
Crept down into the hollows of the wood;
There, while the rest were loud in merry-
making,
Had his dark hour unseen, and rose and
past
Bearing a lifelong hunger in his heart.

So these were wed, and merrily rang the
bells,
And merrily ran the years, seven happy
years,
Seven happy years of health and com-
petence,
And mutual love and honourable toil;
With children; first a daughter. In him
woke,
With his first babe's first cry, the noble
wish
To save all earnings to the uttermost,
And give his child a better bringing-up
Than his had been, or hers; a wish re-
new'd,
When two years after came a boy to be
The rosy idol of her solitudes,
While Enoch was abroad on wrathful seas,
Or often journeying landward; for in truth
Enoch's white horse, and Enoch's ocean-
spoil
In ocean-smelling osier, and his face,
Rough-redden'd with a thousand winter
gales,
Not only to the market-cross were known,
But in the leafy lanes behind the down,
Far as the portal-warding lion-whelp,
And peacock-yewtree of the lonely Hall,
Whose Friday fare was Enoch's minister-
ing.

Then came a change, as all things human
change.
Ten miles to northward of the narrow port
Open'd a larger haven: thither used

Enoch at times to go by land or sea;
And once when there, and clambering on
a mast
In harbour, by mischance he slipt and fell:
A limb was broken when they lifted him;
And while he lay recovering there, his wife
Bore him another son, a sickly one:
Another hand crept too across his trade
Taking her bread and theirs: and on him
fell,
Altho' a grave and staid God-fearing man,
Yet lying thus inactive, doubt and gloom.
He seem'd, as in a nightmare of the night,
To see his children leading evermore
Low miserable lives of hand-to-mouth,
And her, he loved, a beggar: then he pray'd
'Save them from this, whatever comes to
me.'
And while he pray'd, the master of that
ship
Enoch had served in, hearing his mis-
chance,
Came, for he knew the man and valued
him,
Reporting of his vessel China-bound,
And wanting yet a boatswain. Would he go?
There yet were many weeks before she
sail'd,
Sail'd from this port. Would Enoch have
the place?
And Enoch all at once assented to it,
Rejoicing at that answer to his prayer.

So now that shadow of mischance ap-
pear'd
No graver than as when some little cloud
Cuts off the fiery highway of the sun,
And isles a light in the offing: yet the
wife—
When he was gone—the children—what to
do?
Then Enoch lay long-pondering on his
plans;
To sell the boat—and yet he loved her
well—
How many a rough sea had he weather'd
in her!
He knew her, as a horseman knows his
horse—
And yet to sell her—then with what she
brought

Buy goods and stores—set Annie forth in
    trade
With all that seamen needed or their
    wives—
So might she keep the house while he was
    gone.
Should he not trade himself out yonder? go
This voyage more than once? yea twice or
    thrice—
As oft as needed—last, returning rich,
Become the master of a larger craft,
With fuller profits lead an easier life,
Have all his pretty young ones educated,
And pass his days in peace among his own.

Thus Enoch in his heart determined all:
Then moving homeward came on Annie
    pale,
Nursing the sickly babe, her latest-born.
Forward she started with a happy cry,
And laid the feeble infant in his arms;
Whom Enoch took, and handled all his
    limbs,
Appraised his weight and fondled father-
    like,
But had no heart to break his purposes
To Annie, till the morrow, when he spoke.

Then first since Enoch's golden ring
    had girt
Her finger, Annie fought against his will:
Yet not with brawling opposition she,
But manifold entreaties, many a tear,
Many a sad kiss by day by night renew'd
(Sure that all evil would come out of it)
Besought him, supplicating, if he cared
For her or his dear children, not to go.
He not for his own self caring but her,
Her and her children, let her plead in vain;
So grieving held his will, and bore it thro'.

For Enoch parted with his old sea-friend,
Bought Annie goods and stores, and set his
    hand
To fit their little streetward sitting-room
With shelf and corner for the goods and
    stores.
So all day long till Enoch's last at home,
Shaking their pretty cabin, hammer and
    axe,
Auger and saw, while Annie seem'd to hear

Her own death-scaffold raising, shrill'd
    and rang,
Till this was ended, and his careful hand,—
The space was narrow,—having order'd
    all
Almost as neat and close as Nature packs
Her blossom or her seedling, paused; and
    he,
Who needs would work for Annie to the
    last,
Ascending tired, heavily slept till morn.

And Enoch faced this morning of fare-
    well
Brightly and boldly. All his Annie's fears,
Save as his Annie's, were a laughter to
    him.
Yet Enoch as a brave God-fearing man
Bow'd himself down, and in that mystery
Where God-in-man is one with man-in-
    God,
Pray'd for a blessing on his wife and babes
Whatever came to him: and then he said
'Annie, this voyage by the grace of God
Will bring fair weather yet to all of us.
Keep a clean hearth and a clear fire for me,
For I'll be back, my girl, before you know
    it.'
Then lightly rocking baby's cradle 'and he,
This pretty, puny, weakly little one,—
Nay—for I love him all the better for it—
God bless him, he shall sit upon my knees
And I will tell him tales of foreign parts,
And make him merry, when I come home
    again.
Come, Annie, come, cheer up before I go.'

Him running on thus hopefully she
    heard,
And almost hoped herself; but when he
    turn'd
The current of his talk to graver things
In sailor fashion roughly sermonizing
On providence and trust in Heaven, she
    heard,
Heard and not heard him; as the village
    girl,
Who sets her pitcher underneath the
    spring,
Musing on him that used to fill it for her,
Hears and not hears, and lets it overflow.

At length she spoke 'O Enoch, you are
wise;
And yet for all your wisdom well know I
That I shall look upon your face no more.'

'Well then,' said Enoch, 'I shall look on
yours.
Annie, the ship I sail in passes here
(He named the day) get you a seaman's
glass,
Spy out my face, and laugh at all your
fears.'

But when the last of those last moments
came,
'Annie, my girl, cheer up, be comforted,
Look to the babes, and till I come again
Keep everything shipshape, for I must go.
And fear no more for me; or if you fear
Cast all your cares on God; that anchor
holds.
Is He not yonder in those uttermost
Parts of the morning? if I flee to these
Can I go from Him? and the sea is His,
The sea is His: He made it.'

Enoch rose,
Cast his strong arms about his drooping
wife,
And kiss'd his wonder-stricken little ones;
But for the third, the sickly one, who slept
After a night of feverous wakefulness,
When Annie would have raised him Enoch
said
'Wake him not; let him sleep; how should
the child
Remember this?' and kiss'd him in his cot.
But Annie from her baby's forehead clipt
A tiny curl, and gave it: this he kept
Thro' all his future; but now hastily caught
His bundle, waved his hand, and went his
way.

She when the day, that Enoch
mention'd, came,
Borrow'd a glass, but all in vain: perhaps
She could not fix the glass to suit her eye;
Perhaps her eye was dim, hand tremulous;
She saw him not: and while he stood on
deck
Waving, the moment and the vessel past.

Ev'n to the last dip of the vanishing sail
She watch'd it, and departed weeping for
him;
Then, tho' she mourn'd his absence as his
grave,
Set her sad will no less to chime with his,
But throve not in her trade, not being bred
To barter, nor compensating the want
By shrewdness, neither capable of lies,
Nor asking overmuch and taking less,
And still foreboding 'what would Enoch
say?'
For more than once, in days of difficulty
And pressure, had she sold her wares for
less
Than what she gave in buying what she
sold:
She fail'd and sadden'd knowing it; and
thus,
Expectant of that news which never came,
Gain'd for her own a scanty sustenance,
And lived a life of silent melancholy.

Now the third child was sickly-born and
grew
Yet sicklier, tho' the mother cared for it
With all a mother's care: nevertheless,
Whether her business often call'd her from
it,
Or thro' the want of what it needed most,
Or means to pay the voice who best could
tell
What most it needed—howsoe'er it was,
After a lingering,—ere she was aware,—
Like the caged bird escaping suddenly,
The little innocent soul flitted away.

In that same week when Annie buried it,
Philip's true heart, which hunger'd for her
peace
(Since Enoch left he had not look'd upon
her),
Smote him, as having kept aloof so long.
'Surely,' said Philip, 'I may see her now,
May be some little comfort;' therefore
went,
Past thro' the solitary room in front,
Paused for a moment at an inner door,
Then struck it thrice, and, no one opening,
Enter'd; but Annie, seated with her grief,
Fresh from the burial of her little one,

Cared not to look on any human face,
But turn'd her own toward the wall and
  wept.
Then Philip standing up said falteringly
'Annie, I came to ask a favour of you.'

He spoke; the passion in her moan'd
  reply
'Favour from one so sad and so forlorn
As I am!' half abash'd him; yet unask'd,
His bashfulness and tenderness at war,
He set himself beside her, saying to her:

  'I came to speak to you of what he
    wish'd,
Enoch, your husband: I have ever said
You chose the best among us—a strong
  man:
For where he fixt his heart he set his hand
To do the thing he will'd, and bore it thro'.
And wherefore did he go this weary way,
And leave you lonely? not to see the
  world—
For pleasure?—nay, but for the where-
  withal
To give his babes a better bringing-up
Than his had been, or yours: that was his
  wish.
And if he come again, vext will he be
To find the precious morning hours were
  lost.
And it would vex him even in his grave,
If he could know his babes were running
  wild
Like colts about the waste. So, Annie,
  now—
Have we not known each other all our lives?
I do beseech you by the love you bear
Him and his children not to say me nay—
For, if you will, when Enoch comes again
Why then he shall repay me—if you will,
Annie—for I am rich and well-to-do.
Now let me put the boy and girl to school:
This is the favour that I came to ask.'

  Then Annie with her brows against the
    wall
Answer'd 'I cannot look you in the face,
I seem so foolish and so broken down.
When you came in my sorrow broke me
  down;

And now I think your kindness breaks me
  down;
But Enoch lives; that is borne in on me:
He will repay you: money can be repaid;
Not kindness such as yours.'

                          And Philip ask'd
'Then you will let me, Annie?'

                          There she turn'd,
She rose, and fixt her swimming eyes upon
  him,
And dwelt a moment on his kindly face,
Then calling down a blessing on his head
Caught at his hand, and wrung it pas-
  sionately,
And past into the little garth beyond.
So lifted up in spirit he moved away.

  Then Philip put the boy and girl to
    school,
And bought them needful books, and
    everyway,
Like one who does his duty by his own,
Made himself theirs; and tho' for Annie's
    sake,
Fearing the lazy gossip of the port,
He oft denied his heart his dearest wish,
And seldom crost her threshold, yet he
    sent
Gifts by the children, garden-herbs and
    fruit,
The late and early roses from his wall,
Or conies from the down, and now and
    then,
With some pretext of fineness in the meal
To save the offence of charitable, flour
From his tall mill that whistled on the
    waste.

  But Philip did not fathom Annie's mind:
Scarce could the woman when he came
    upon her,
Out of full heart and boundless gratitude
Light on a broken word to thank him with.
But Philip was her children's all-in-all;
From distant corners of the street they ran
To greet his hearty welcome heartily;
Lords of his house and of his mill were
    they;
Worried his passive ear with petty wrongs

ENOCH ARDEN

Or pleasures, hung upon him, play'd with
him
And call'd him Father Philip. Philip gain'd
As Enoch lost; for Enoch seem'd to them
Uncertain as a vision or a dream,
Faint as a figure seen in early dawn
Down at the far end of an avenue,
Going we know not where: and so ten
years,
Since Enoch left his hearth and native land,
Fled forward, and no news of Enoch came.

It chanced one evening Annie's children
long'd
To go with others, nutting to the wood,
And Annie would go with them; then they
begg'd
For Father Philip (as they call'd him) too:
Him, like the working bee in blossom-dust,
Blanch'd with his mill, they found; and
saying to him
'Come with us Father Philip' he denied;
But when the children pluck'd at him to
go,
He laugh'd, and yielded readily to their
wish,
For was not Annie with them? and they
went.

But after scaling half the weary down,
Just where the prone edge of the wood
began
To feather toward the hollow, all her force
Fail'd her; and sighing, 'Let me rest' she
said:
So Philip rested with her well-content;
While all the younger ones with jubilant
cries
Broke from their elders, and tumultuously
Down thro' the whitening hazels made a
plunge
To the bottom, and dispersed, and bent or
broke
The lithe reluctant boughs to tear away
Their tawny clusters, crying to each other
And calling, here and there, about the
wood.

But Philip sitting at her side forgot
Her presence, and remember'd one dark
hour

Here in this wood, when like a wounded
life
He crept into the shadow: at last he said,
Lifting his honest forehead, 'Listen, Annie,
How merry they are down yonder in the
wood.
Tired, Annie?' for she did not speak a
word.
'Tired?' but her face had fall'n upon her
hands;
At which, as with a kind of anger in him,
'The ship was lost,' he said, 'the ship was
lost!
No more of that! why should you kill
yourself
And make them orphans quite?' And
Annie said
'I thought not of it: but—I know not
why—
Their voices make me feel so solitary.'

Then Philip coming somewhat closer
spoke.
'Annie, there is a thing upon my mind,
And it has been upon my mind so long,
That tho' I know not when it first came
there,
I know that it will out at last. O Annie,
It is beyond all hope, against all chance,
That he who left you ten long years ago
Should still be living; well then—let me
speak:
I grieve to see you poor and wanting help:
I cannot help you as I wish to do
Unless—they say that women are so
quick—
Perhaps you know what I would have you
know—
I wish you for my wife. I fain would prove
A father to your children: I do think
They love me as a father: I am sure
That I love them as if they were mine
own;
And I believe, if you were fast my wife,
That after all these sad uncertain years,
We might be still as happy as God grants
To any of his creatures. Think upon it:
For I am well-to-do—no kin, no care,
No burthen, save my care for you and
yours:
And we have known each other all our lives,

122

And I have loved you longer than you
    know.'

    Then answer'd Annie; tenderly she
      spoke:
'You have been as God's good angel in our
    house.
God bless you for it, God reward you for it,
Philip, with something happier than my-
    self.
Can one love twice? can you be ever loved
As Enoch was? what is it that you ask?'
'I am content' he answer'd 'to be loved
A little after Enoch.' 'O' she cried,
Scared as it were, 'dear Philip, wait a
    while:
If Enoch comes—but Enoch will not
    come—
Yet wait a year, a year is not so long:
Surely I shall be wiser in a year:
O wait a little!' Philip sadly said
'Annie, as I have waited all my life
I well may wait a little.' 'Nay' she cried
'I am bound: you have my promise—in a
    year:
Will you not bide your year as I bide
    mine?'
And Philip answer'd 'I will bide my year.'

    Here both were mute, till Philip glancing
    up
Beheld the dead flame of the fallen day
Pass from the Danish barrow overhead;
Then fearing night and chill for Annie,
    rose
And sent his voice beneath him thro' the
    wood.
Up came the children laden with their
    spoil;
Then all descended to the port, and there
At Annie's door he paused and gave his
    hand,
Saying gently 'Annie, when I spoke to you,
That was your hour of weakness. I was
    wrong,
I am always bound to you, but you are free.'
Then Annie weeping answer'd 'I am
    bound.'

    She spoke; and in one moment as it
    were,

While yet she went about her household
    ways,
Ev'n as she dwelt upon his latest words,
That he had loved her longer than she
    knew,
That autumn into autumn flash'd again,
And there he stood once more before her
    face,
Claiming her promise. 'Is it a year?' she
    ask'd.
'Yes, if the nuts' he said 'be ripe again:
Come out and see.' But she—she put him
    off—
So much to look to—such a change—a
    month—
Give her a month—she knew that she was
    bound—
A month—no more. Then Philip with his
    eyes
Full of that lifelong hunger, and his voice
Shaking a little like a drunkard's hand,
'Take your own time, Annie, take your
    own time.'
And Annie could have wept for pity of
    him;
And yet she held him on delayingly
With many a scarce-believable excuse,
Trying his truth and his long-sufferance,
Till half-another year had slipt away.

    By this the lazy gossips of the port,
Abhorrent of a calculation crost,
Began to chafe as at a personal wrong.
Some thought that Philip did but trifle
    with her;
Some that she but held off to draw him on;
And others laugh'd at her and Philip too,
As simple folk that knew not their own
    minds,
And one, in whom all evil fancies clung
Like serpent eggs together, laughingly
Would hint at worse in either. Her own
    son
Was silent, tho' he often look'd his wish;
But evermore the daughter prest upon her
To wed the man so dear to all of them
And lift the household out of poverty;
And Philip's rosy face contracting grew
Careworn and wan; and all these things
    fell on her
Sharp as reproach.

At last one night it chanced
That Annie could not sleep, but earnestly
Pray'd for a sign 'my Enoch is he gone?'
Then compass'd round by the blind wall of
    night
Brook'd not the expectant terror of her
    heart,
Started from bed, and struck herself a light,
Then desperately seized the holy Book,
Suddenly set it wide to find a sign,
Suddenly put her finger on the text,
'Under the palm-tree.' That was nothing
    to her:
No meaning there: she closed the Book
    and slept:
When lo! her Enoch sitting on a height,
Under a palm-tree, over him the Sun:
'He is gone,' she thought, 'he is happy, he
    is singing
Hosanna in the highest: yonder shines
The Sun of Righteousness, and these be
    palms
Whereof the happy people strowing cried
"Hosanna in the highest!"' Here she woke,
Resolved, sent for him and said wildly to
    him
'There is no reason why we should not
    wed.'
'Then for God's sake,' he answer'd, 'both
    our sakes,
So you will wed me, let it be at once.'

So these were wed and merrily rang the
    bells,
Merrily rang the bells and they were wed.
But never merrily beat Annie's heart.
A footstep seem'd to fall beside her path,
She knew not whence; a whisper on her
    ear,
She knew not what; nor loved she to be
    left
Alone at home, nor ventured out alone.
What ail'd her then, that ere she enter'd,
    often
Her hand dwelt lingeringly on the latch,
Fearing to enter: Philip thought he knew:
Such doubts and fears were common to
    her state,
Being with child: but when her child was
    born,
Then her new child was as herself renew'd,

Then the new mother came about her
    heart,
Then her good Philip was her all-in-all,
And that mysterious instinct wholly died.

And where was Enoch? prosperously
    sail'd
The ship 'Good Fortune,' tho' at setting
    forth
The Biscay, roughly ridging eastward,
    shook
And almost overwhelm'd her, yet unvext
She slipt across the summer of the world,
Then after a long tumble about the Cape
And frequent interchange of foul and fair,
She passing thro' the summer world again,
The breath of heaven came continually
And sent her sweetly by the golden isles,
Till silent in her oriental haven.

There Enoch traded for himself, and
    bought
Quaint monsters for the market of those
    times,
A gilded dragon, also, for the babes.

Less lucky her home-voyage: at first
    indeed
Thro' many a fair sea-circle, day by day,
Scarce-rocking, her full-busted figure-head
Stared o'er the ripple feathering from her
    bows:
Then follow'd calms, and then winds
    variable,
Then baffling, a long course of them; and
    last
Storm, such as drove her under moonless
    heavens
Till hard upon the cry of 'breakers' came
The crash of ruin, and the loss of all
But Enoch and two others. Half the night,
Buoy'd upon floating tackle and broken
    spars,
These drifted, stranding on an isle at morn
Rich, but the loneliest in a lonely sea.

No want was there of human sustenance,
Soft fruitage, mighty nuts, and nourishing
    roots;
Nor save for pity was it hard to take
The helpless life so wild that it was tame.
There in a seaward-gazing mountain-gorge

They built, and thatch'd with leaves of
    palm, a hut,
Half hut, half native cavern. So the three,
Set in this Eden of all plenteousness,
Dwelt with eternal summer, ill-content.

For one, the youngest, hardly more than
    boy,
Hurt in that night of sudden ruin and
    wreck,
Lay lingering out a five-years' death-in-
    life.
They could not leave him. After he was
    gone,
The two remaining found a fallen stem;
And Enoch's comrade, careless of himself,
Fire-hollowing this in Indian fashion, fell
Sun-stricken, and that other lived alone.
In those two deaths he read God's warning
    'wait.'

The mountain wooded to the peak, the
    lawns
And winding glades high up like ways to
    Heaven,
The slender coco's drooping crown of
    plumes,
The lightning flash of insect and of bird,
The lustre of the long convolvuluses
That coil'd around the stately stems, and
    ran
Ev'n to the limit of the land, the glows
And glories of the broad belt of the world,
All these he saw: but what he fain had seen
He could not see, the kindly human face,
Nor ever hear a kindly voice, but heard
The myriad shriek of wheeling ocean-fowl,
The league-long roller thundering on the
    reef,
The moving whisper of huge trees that
    branch'd
And blossom'd in the zenith, or the sweep
Of some precipitous rivulet to the wave,
As down the shore he ranged, or all day
    long
Sat often in the seaward-gazing gorge,
A shipwreck'd sailor, waiting for a sail:
No sail from day to day, but every day
The sunrise broken into scarlet shafts
Among the palms and ferns and precipices;
The blaze upon the waters to the east;

The blaze upon his island overhead;
The blaze upon the waters to the west;
Then the great stars that globed themselves
    in Heaven,
The hollower-bellowing ocean, and again
The scarlet shafts of sunrise—but no sail.

There often as he watch'd or seem'd to
    watch,
So still, the golden lizard on him paused,
A phantom made of many phantoms moved
Before him haunting him, or he himself
Moved haunting people, things and places,
    known
Far in a darker isle beyond the line;
The babes, their babble, Annie, the small
    house,
The climbing street, the mill, the leafy
    lanes,
The peacock-yewtree and the lonely Hall,
The horse he drove, the boat he sold, the
    chill
November dawns and dewy-glooming
    downs,
The gentle shower, the smell of dying
    leaves,
And the low moan of leaden-colour'd seas.

Once likewise, in the ringing of his ears,
Tho' faintly, merrily—far and far away—
He heard the pealing of his parish bells;
Then, tho' he knew not wherefore, started
    up
Shuddering, and when the beauteous hate-
    ful isle
Return'd upon him, had not his poor heart
Spoken with That, which being every-
    where
Lets none, who speaks with Him, seem all
    alone,
Surely the man had died of solitude.

Thus over Enoch's early-silvering head
The sunny and rainy seasons came and
    went
Year after year. His hopes to see his own,
And pace the sacred old familiar fields,
Not yet had perish'd, when his lonely
    doom
Came suddenly to an end. Another ship
(She wanted water) blown by baffling
    winds,

Like the 'Good Fortune', from her destined course,
Stay'd by this isle, not knowing where she lay:
For since the mate had seen at early dawn
Across a break on the mist-wreathen isle
The silent water slipping from the hills,
They sent a crew that landing burst away
In search of stream or fount, and fill'd the shores
With clamour. Downward from his mountain gorge
Stept the long-hair'd long-bearded solitary,
Brown, looking hardly human, strangely clad,
Muttering and mumbling, idiotlike it seem'd,
With inarticulate rage, and making signs
They knew not what: and yet he led the way
To where the rivulets of sweet water ran;
And ever as he mingled with the crew,
And heard them talking, his long-bounden tongue
Was loosen'd, till he made them understand;
Whom, when their casks were fill'd, they took aboard:
And there the tale he utter'd brokenly,
Scarce-credited at first but more and more,
Amazed and melted all who listen'd to it:
And clothes they gave him and free passage home;
But oft he work'd among the rest and shook
His isolation from him. None of these
Came from his country, or could answer him,
If question'd, aught of what he cared to know.
And dull the voyage was with long delays,
The vessel scarce sea-worthy; but evermore
His fancy fled before the lazy wind
Returning, till beneath a clouded moon
He like a lover down thro' all his blood
Drew in the dewy meadowy morning-breath
Of England, blown across her ghostly wall:
And that same morning officers and men
Levied a kindly tax upon themselves,
Pitying the lonely man, and gave him it:
Then moving up the coast they landed him,
Ev'n in that harbour whence he sail'd before.

There Enoch spoke no word to any one,
But homeward—home—what home? had he a home?
His home, he walk'd. Bright was that afternoon,
Sunny but chill; till drawn thro' either chasm,
Where either haven open'd on the deeps,
Roll'd a sea-haze and whelm'd the world in gray;
Cut off the length of highway on before,
And left but narrow breadth to left and right
Of wither'd holt or tilth or pasturage.
On the nigh-naked tree the robin piped
Disconsolate, and thro' the dripping haze
The dead weight of the dead leaf bore it down:
Thicker the drizzle grew, deeper the gloom;
Last, as it seem'd, a great mist-blotted light
Flared on him, and he came upon the place.

Then down the long street having slowly stolen,
His heart foreshadowing all calamity,
His eyes upon the stones, he reach'd the home
Where Annie lived and loved him, and his babes
In those far-off seven happy years were born;
But finding neither light nor murmur there
(A bill of sale gleam'd thro' the drizzle) crept
Still downward thinking 'dead or dead to me!'

Down to the pool and narrow wharf he went,
Seeking a tavern which of old he knew,
A front of timber-crost antiquity,
So propt, worm-eaten, ruinously old,
He thought it must have gone; but he was gone
Who kept it; and his widow Miriam Lane,

With daily-dwindling profits held the
house;
A haunt of brawling seamen once, but now
Stiller, with yet a bed for wandering men.
There Enoch rested silent many days.

But Miriam Lane was good and garru-
lous,
Nor let him be, but often breaking in,
Told him, with other annals of the port,
Not knowing—Enoch was so brown, so
bow'd,
So broken—all the story of his house.
His baby's death, her growing poverty,
How Philip put her little ones to school,
And kept them in it, his long wooing her,
Her slow consent, and marriage, and the
birth
Of Philip's child: and o'er his countenance
No shadow past, nor motion: any one,
Regarding, well had deem'd he felt the tale
Less than the teller: only when she closed
'Enoch, poor man, was cast away and lost'
He, shaking his gray head pathetically,
Repeated muttering 'cast away and lost;'
Again in deeper inward whispers 'lost!'

But Enoch yearn'd to see her face again;
'If I might look on her sweet face again
And know that she is happy.' So the
thought
Haunted and harass'd him, and drove him
forth,
At evening when the dull November day
Was growing duller twilight, to the hill.
There he sat down gazing on all below;
There did a thousand memories roll upon
him,
Unspeakable for sadness. By and by
The ruddy square of comfortable light,
Far-blazing from the rear of Philip's house,
Allured him, as the beacon-blaze allures
The bird of passage, till he madly strikes
Against it, and beats out his weary life.

For Philip's dwelling fronted on the
street,
The latest house to landward; but behind,
With one small gate that open'd on the
waste,
Flourish'd a little garden square and
wall'd:

And in it throve an ancient evergreen,
A yewtree, and all round it ran a walk
Of shingle, and a walk divided it:
But Enoch shunn'd the middle walk and
stole
Up by the wall, behind the yew; and
thence
That which he better might have shunn'd,
if griefs
Like his have worse or better, Enoch saw.

For cups and silver on the burnish'd
board
Sparkled and shone; so genial was the
hearth:
And on the right hand of the hearth he saw
Philip, the slighted suitor of old times,
Stout, rosy, with his babe across his knees;
And o'er her second father stoopt a girl,
A later but a loftier Annie Lee,
Fair-hair'd and tall, and from her lifted
hand
Dangled a length of ribbon and a ring
To tempt the babe, who rear'd his creasy
arms,
Caught at and ever miss'd it, and they
laugh'd;
And on the left hand of the hearth he saw
The mother glancing often toward her
babe,
But turning now and then to speak with
him,
Her son, who stood beside her tall and
strong,
And saying that which pleased him, for he
smiled.

Now when the dead man come to life
beheld
His wife his wife no more, and saw the
babe
Hers, yet not his, upon the father's knee,
And all the warmth, the peace, the happi-
ness,
And his own children tall and beautiful,
And him, that other, reigning in his place,
Lord of his rights and of his children's
love,—
Then he, tho' Miriam Lane had told him
all,

Because things seen are mightier than
   things heard,
Stagger'd and shook, holding the branch,
   and fear'd
To send abroad a shrill and terrible cry,
Which in one moment, like the blast of
   doom,
Would shatter all the happiness of the
   hearth.

He therefore turning softly like a thief,
Lest the harsh shingle should grate under-
   foot,
And feeling all along the garden-wall,
Lest he should swoon and tumble and be
   found,
Crept to the gate, and open'd it, and
   closed,
As lightly as a sick man's chamber-door,
Behind him, and came out upon the waste.

And there he would have knelt, but that
   his knees
Were feeble, so that falling prone he dug
His fingers into the wet earth, and pray'd.

'Too hard to bear! why did they take
   me thence?
O God Almighty, blessed Saviour, Thou
That didst uphold me on my lonely isle,
Uphold me, Father, in my loneliness
A little longer! aid me, give me strength
Not to tell her, never to let her know.
Help me not to break in upon her peace.
My children too! must I not speak to
   these?
They know me not. I should betray my-
   self.
Never: No father's kiss for me—the girl
So like her mother, and the boy, my son.'

There speech and thought and nature
   fail'd a little,
And he lay tranced; but when he rose and
   paced
Back toward his solitary home again,
All down the long and narrow street he
   went
Beating it in upon his weary brain,
As tho' it were the burthen of a song,
'Not to tell her, never to let her know.'

He was not all unhappy. His resolve
Upbore him, and firm faith, and evermore
Prayer from a living source within the will,
And beating up thro' all the bitter world,
Like fountains of sweet water in the sea,
Kept him a living soul. 'This miller's wife'
He said to Miriam 'that you spoke about,
Has she no fear that her first husband
   lives?'
'Ay, ay, poor soul' said Miriam, 'fear
   enow!
If you could tell her you had seen him
   dead,
Why, that would be her comfort;' and he
   thought
'After the Lord has call'd me she shall
   know,
I wait His time,' and Enoch set himself,
Scorning an alms, to work whereby to live.
Almost to all things could he turn his hand.
Cooper he was and carpenter, and wrought
To make the boatmen fishing-nets, or
   help'd
At lading and unlading the tall barks,
That brought the stinted commerce of
   those days;
Thus earn'd a scanty living for himself:
Yet since he did but labour for himself,
Work without hope, there was not life in it
Whereby the man could live; and as the
   year
Roll'd itself round again to meet the day
When Enoch had return'd, a languor came
Upon him, gentle sickness, gradually
Weakening the man, till he could do no
   more,
But kept the house, his chair, and last his
   bed.
And Enoch bore his weakness cheerfully.
For sure no gladlier does the stranded
   wreck
See thro' the gray skirts of a lifting squall
The boat that bears the hope of life ap-
   proach
To save the life despair'd of, than he saw
Death dawning on him, and the close of
   all.

For thro' that dawning gleam'd a kindlier hope
On Enoch thinking 'after I am gone,

Then may she learn I lov'd her to the last.'
He call'd aloud for Miriam Lane and said
'Woman, I have a secret—only swear,
Before I tell you—swear upon the book
Not to reveal it, till you see me dead.'
'Dead,' clamour'd the good woman, 'hear
  him talk!
I warrant, man, that we shall bring you
  round.'
'Swear' added Enoch sternly 'on the book.'
And on the book, half-frighted, Miriam
  swore.
Then Enoch rolling his gray eyes upon her,
'Did you know Enoch Arden of this town?'
'Know him?' she said 'I knew him far
  away.
Ay, ay, I mind him coming down the
  street;
Held his head high, and cared for no man,
  he.'
Slowly and sadly Enoch answer'd her;
'His head is low, and no man cares for him.
I think I have not three days more to live;
I am the man.' At which the woman gave
A half-incredulous, half-hysterical cry.
'You Arden, you! nay,—sure he was a foot
Higher than you be.' Enoch said again
'My God has bow'd me down to what I am;
My grief and solitude have broken me;
Nevertheless, know you that I am he
Who married—but that name has twice
  been changed—
I married her who married Philip Ray.
Sit, listen.' Then he told her of his voyage,
His wreck, his lonely life, his coming back,
His gazing in on Annie, his resolve,
And how he kept it. As the woman heard,
Fast flow'd the current of her easy tears,
While in her heart she yearn'd incessantly
To rush abroad all round the little haven,
Proclaiming Enoch Arden and his woes;
But awed and promise-bounden she for-
  bore,
Saying only 'See your bairns before you go!
Eh, let me fetch 'em, Arden,' and arose
Eager to bring them down, for Enoch hung
A moment on her words, but then replied:

'Woman, disturb me not now at the last,
But let me hold my purpose till I die.
Sit down again; mark me and understand,

While I have power to speak. I charge you
  now,
When you shall see her, tell her that I died
Blessing her, praying for her, loving her;
Save for the bar between us, loving her
As when she laid her head beside my own.
And tell my daughter Annie, whom I saw
So like her mother, that my latest breath
Was spent in blessing her and praying for
  her.
And tell my son that I died blessing him.
And say to Philip that I blest him too;
He never meant us any thing but good.
But if my children care to see me dead,
Who hardly knew me living, let them come,
I am their father; but she must not come,
For my dead face would vex her after-life.
And now there is but one of all my blood
Who will embrace me in the world-to-be:
This hair is his: she cut it off and gave it,
And I have borne it with me all these years.
And thought to bear it with me to my
  grave;
But now my mind is changed, for I shall
  see him,
My babe in bliss: wherefore when I am
  gone,
Take, give her this, for it may comfort her:
It will moreover be a token to her,
That I am he.'

            He ceased; and Miriam Lane
Made such a voluble answer promising all,
That once again he roll'd his eyes upon her
Repeating all he wish'd, and once again
She promised.

            Then the third night after this,
While Enoch slumber'd motionless and pale,
And Miriam watch'd and dozed at inter-
  vals,
There came so loud a calling of the sea,
That all the houses in the haven rang.
He woke, he rose, he spread his arms
  abroad
Crying with a loud voice 'A sail! a sail!
I am saved;' and so fell back and spoke no
  more.

So past the strong heroic soul away.
And when they buried him the little port
Had seldom seen a costlier funeral.

THE BROOK

HERE, by this brook, we parted; I to the
    East
And he for Italy—too late—too late:
One whom the strong sons of the world
    despise;
For lucky rhymes to him were scrip and
    share,
And mellow metres more than cent for
    cent;
Nor could he understand how money
    breeds,
Thought it a dead thing; yet himself could
    make
The thing that is not as the thing that is.
O had he lived! In our schoolbooks we say,
Of those that held their heads above the
    crowd,
They flourish'd then or then; but life in
    him
Could scarce be said to flourish, only
    touch'd
On such a time as goes before the leaf,
When all the wood stands in a mist of
    green,
And nothing perfect: yet the brook he
    loved,
For which, in branding summers of Bengal,
Or ev'n the sweet half-English Neilgherry
    air
I panted, seems, as I re-listen to it,
Prattling the primrose fancies of the boy,
To me that loved him; for 'O brook,' he
    says,
'O babbling brook,' says Edmund in his
    rhyme,
'Whence come you?' and the brook, why
    not? replies.

    I come from haunts of coot and hern,
      I make a sudden sally,
    And sparkle out among the fern,
      To bicker down a valley.

    By thirty hills I hurry down,
      Or slip between the ridges,
    By twenty thorps, a little town,
      And half a hundred bridges.

    Till last by Philip's farm I flow
      To join the brimming river,
    For men may come and men may go
      But I go on for ever.

'Poor lad, he died at Florence, quite worn
    out,
Travelling to Naples. There is Darnley
    bridge,
It has more ivy; there the river; and there
Stands Philip's farm where brook and river
    meet.

    I chatter over stony ways,
      In little sharps and trebles,
    I bubble into eddying bays,
      I babble on the pebbles.

    With many a curve my banks I fret
      By many a field and fallow,
    And many a fairy foreland set
      With willow-weed and mallow.

    I chatter, chatter, as I flow
      To join the brimming river,
    For men may come and men may go,
      But I go on for ever.

'But Philip chatter'd more than brook or
    bird;
Old Philip; all about the fields you caught
His weary daylong chirping, like the dry
High-elbow'd grigs that leap in summer
    grass.

    I wind about, and in and out,
      With here a blossom sailing,
    And here and there a lusty trout,
      And here and there a grayling,

    And here and there a foamy flake
      Upon me, as I travel
    With many a silvery waterbreak
      Above the golden gravel,

    And draw them all along, and flow
      To join the brimming river,
    For men may come and men may go,
      But I go on for ever.

'O darling Katie Willows, his one child!
A maiden of our century, yet most meek;
A daughter of our meadows, yet not coarse;
Straight, but as lissome as a hazel wand;
Her eyes a bashful azure, and her hair
In gloss and hue the chestnut, when the
    shell
Divides threefold to show the fruit within.

'Sweet Katie, once I did her a good turn,
Her and her far-off cousin and betrothed,
James Willows, of one name and heart with
    her.

For here I came, twenty years back—the week
Before I parted with poor Edmund; crost
By that old bridge which, half in ruins then,
Still makes a hoary eyebrow for the gleam
Beyond it, where the waters marry—crost,
Whistling a random bar of Bonny Doon,
And push'd at Philip's garden-gate. The gate,
Half-parted from a weak and scolding hinge,
Stuck; and he clamour'd from a casement, "Run"
To Katie somewhere in the walks below,
"Run, Katie!" Katie never ran: she moved
To meet me, winding under woodbine bowers,
A little flutter'd, with her eyelids down,
Fresh apple-blossom, blushing for a boon.

'What was it? less of sentiment than sense
Had Katie; not illiterate; nor of those
Who dabbling in the fount of fictive tears,
And nursed by mealy-mouth'd philanthropies,
Divorce the Feeling from her mate the Deed.

'She told me. She and James had quarrell'd. Why?
What cause of quarrel? None, she said, no cause;
James had no cause: but when I prest the cause,
I learnt that James had flickering jealousies
Which anger'd her. Who anger'd James? I said.
But Katie snatch'd her eyes at once from mine,
And sketching with her slender pointed foot
Some figure like a wizard pentagram
On garden gravel, let my query pass
Unclaim'd, in flushing silence, till I ask'd
If James were coming. "Coming every day,"
She answer'd, "ever longing to explain,
But evermore her father came across
With some long-winded tale, and broke him short;

And James departed vext with him and her."
How could I help her? "Would I—was it wrong?"
(Claspt hands and that petitionary grace
Of sweet seventeen subdued me ere she spoke)
"O would I take her father for one hour,
For one half-hour, and let him talk to me!"
And even while she spoke, I saw where James
Made toward us, like a wader in the surf,
Beyond the brook, waist-deep in meadow-sweet.

'O Katie, what I suffer'd for your sake!
For in I went, and call'd old Philip out
To show the farm: full willingly he rose:
He led me thro' the short sweet-smelling lanes
Of his wheat-suburb, babbling as he went.
He praised his land, his horses, his machines;
He praised his ploughs, his cows, his hogs, his dogs;
He praised his hens, his geese, his guinea-hens;
His pigeons, who in session on their roofs
Approved him, bowing at their own deserts:
Then from the plaintive mother's teat he took
Her blind and shuddering puppies, naming each,
And naming those, his friends, for whom they were:
Then crost the common into Darnley chase
To show Sir Arthur's deer. In copse and fern
Twinkled the innumerable ear and tail.
Then, seated on a serpent-rooted beech,
He pointed out a pasturing colt, and said:
"That was the four-year-old I sold the Squire."
And there he told a long long-winded tale
Of how the Squire had seen the colt at grass,
And how it was the thing his daughter wish'd,
And how he sent the bailiff to the farm

To learn the price, and what the price he
    ask'd,
And how the bailiff swore that he was
    mad,
But he stood firm; and so the matter hung;
He gave them line: and five days after that
He met the bailiff at the Golden Fleece,
Who then and there had offer'd something
    more,
But he stood firm; and so the matter hung;
He knew the man; the colt would fetch its
    price;
He gave them line: and how by chance at
    last
(It might be May or April, he forgot,
The last of April or the first of May)
He found the bailiff riding by the farm,
And, talking from the point, he drew
    him in,
And there he mellow'd all his heart with ale,
Until they closed a bargain, hand in hand.

'Then, while I breathed in sight of
    haven, he,
Poor fellow, could he help it? recom-
    menced,
And ran thro' all the coltish chronicle,
Wild Will, Black Bess, Tantivy, Tallyho,
Reform, White Rose, Bellerophon, the Jilt,
Arbaces, and Phenomenon, and the rest,
Till, not to die a listener, I arose,
And with me Philip, talking still; and so
We turn'd our foreheads from the falling
    sun,
And following our own shadows thrice as
    long
As when they follow'd us from Philip's
    door,
Arrived, and found the sun of sweet con-
    tent
Re-risen in Katie's eyes, and all things
    well.

    I steal by lawns and grassy plots,
      I slide by hazel covers;
    I move the sweet forget-me-nots
      That grow for happy lovers.

    I slip, I slide, I gloom, I glance,
      Among my skimming swallows;
    I make the netted sunbeam dance
      Against my sandy shallows.

    I murmur under moon and stars
      In brambly wildernesses;
    I linger by my shingly bars;
    I loiter round my cresses;

    And out again I curve and flow
      To join the brimming river,
    For men may come and men may go,
      But I go on for ever.

Yes, men may come and go; and these are
    gone,
All gone. My dearest brother, Edmund,
    sleeps,
Not by the well-known stream and rustic
    spire,
But unfamiliar Arno, and the dome
Of Brunelleschi; sleeps in peace: and he,
Poor Philip, of all his lavish waste of words
Remains the lean P. W. on his tomb:
I scraped the lichen from it: Katie walks
By the long wash of Australasian seas
Far off, and holds her head to other stars,
And breathes in April-autumns. All are
    gone.'

So Lawrence Aylmer, seated on a stile
In the long hedge, and rolling in his mind
Old waifs of rhyme, and bowing o'er the
    brook
A tonsured head in middle age forlorn,
Mused, and was mute. On a sudden a low
    breath
Of tender air made tremble in the hedge
The fragile bindweed-bells and briony
    rings;
And he look'd up. There stood a maiden
    near,
Waiting to pass. In much amaze he stared
On eyes a bashful azure, and on hair
In gloss and hue the chestnut, when the
    shell
Divides threefold to show the fruit within:
Then, wondering, ask'd her 'Are you from
    the farm?'
'Yes' answer'd she. 'Pray stay a little: par-
    don me;
What do they call you?' 'Katie.' 'That were
    strange.
What surname?' 'Willows.' 'No!' 'That is
    my name.'
'Indeed!' and here he look'd so self-
    perplext,

That Katie laugh'd, and laughing blush'd,
till he
Laugh'd also, but as one before he wakes,
Who feels a glimmering strangeness in his
dream.
Then looking at her; 'Too happy, fresh
and fair,
Too fresh and fair in our sad world's best
bloom,
To be the ghost of one who bore your
name
About these meadows, twenty years ago.'

'Have you not heard?' said Katie, 'we
came back.
We bought the farm we tenanted before.
Am I so like her? so they said on board.
Sir, if you knew her in her English days,
My mother, as it seems you did, the days
That most she loves to talk of, come with
me.
My brother James is in the harvest-field:
But she—you will be welcome—O, come
in!'

AYLMER'S FIELD
1793

DUST are our frames; and, gilded dust, our
pride
Looks only for a moment whole and sound;
Like that long-buried body of the king,
Found lying with his urns and ornaments,
Which at a touch of light, an air of heaven,
Slipt into ashes, and was found no more.

Here is a story which in rougher shape
Came from a grizzled cripple, whom I saw
Sunning himself in a waste field alone—
Old, and a mine of memories—who had
served,
Long since, a bygone Rector of the place,
And been himself a part of what he told.

SIR AYLMER AYLMER, that almighty man,
The county God—in whose capacious hall,
Hung with a hundred shields, the family
tree
Sprang from the midriff of a prostrate
king—
Whose blazing wyvern weathercock'd the
spire,

Stood from his walls and wing'd his entry-
gates
And swang besides on many a windy sign—
Whose eyes from under a pyramidal head
Saw from his windows nothing save his
own—
What lovelier of his own had he than her,
His only child, his Edith, whom he loved
As heiress and not heir regretfully?
But 'he that marries her marries her name'
This fiat somewhat soothed himself and
wife,
His wife a faded beauty of the Baths,
Insipid as the Queen upon a card;
Her all of thought and bearing hardly more
Than his own shadow in a sickly sun.

A land of hops and poppy-mingled corn,
Little about it stirring save a brook!
A sleepy land, where under the same wheel
The same old rut would deepen year by
year;
Where almost all the village had one name;
Where Aylmer followed Aylmer at the Hall
And Averill Averill at the Rectory
Thrice over; so that Rectory and Hall,
Bound in an immemorial intimacy,
Were open to each other; tho' to dream
That Love could bind them closer well had
made
The hoar hair of the Baronet bristle up
With horror, worse than had he heard his
priest
Preach an inverted scripture, sons of men
Daughters of God; so sleepy was the land.

And might not Averill, had he will'd
it so,
Somewhere beneath his own low range of
roofs,
Have also set his many-shielded tree?
There was an Aylmer-Averill marriage
once.
When the red rose was redder than itself,
And York's white rose as red as Lancas-
ter's,
With wounded peace which each had
prick'd to death.
'Not proven' Averill said, or laughingly
'Some other race of Averills'—prov'n or no,
What cared he? what, if other or the same?

133

He lean'd not on his fathers but himself.
But Leolin, his brother, living oft
With Averill, and a year or two before
Call'd to the bar, but ever call'd away
By one low voice to one dear neighbour-
    hood,
Would often, in his walks with Edith,
    claim
A distant kinship to the gracious blood
That shook the heart of Edith hearing him.

Sanguine he was: a but less vivid hue
Than of that islet in the chestnut-bloom
Flamed in his cheek; and eager eyes, that
    still
Took joyful note of all things joyful,
    beam'd,
Beneath a manelike mass of rolling gold,
Their best and brightest, when they dwelt
    on hers,
Edith, whose pensive beauty, perfect else,
But subject to the season or the mood,
Shone like a mystic star between the less
And greater glory varying to and fro,
We know not wherefore; bounteously
    made,
And yet so finely, that a troublous touch
Thinn'd, or would seem to thin her in a
    day,
A joyous to dilate, as toward the light.
And these had been together from the first.
Leolin's first nurse was, five years after,
    hers:
So much the boy foreran; but when his
    date
Doubled her own, for want of playmates,
    he
(Since Averill was a decad and a half
His elder, and their parents underground)
Had tost his ball and flown his kite, and
    roll'd
His hoop to pleasure Edith, with her dipt
Against the rush of the air in the prone
    swing,
Made blossom-ball or daisy-chain,
    arranged
Her garden, sow'd her name and kept it
    green
In living letters, told her fairy-tales,
Show'd her the fairy footings on the grass,
The little dells of cowslip, fairy palms,

The petty marestail forest, fairy pines,
Or from the tiny pitted target blew
What look'd a flight of fairy arrows aim'd
All at one mark, all hitting: make-believes
For Edith and himself: or else he forged,
But that was later, boyish histories
Of battle, bold adventure, dungeon, wreck,
Flights, terrors, sudden rescues, and true
    love
Crown'd after trial; sketches rude and faint,
But where a passion yet unborn perhaps
Lay hidden as the music of the moon
Sleeps in the plain eggs of the nightingale.
And thus together, save for college-times
Or Temple-eaten terms, a couple, fair
As ever painter painted, poet sang,
Or Heaven in lavish bounty moulded, grew.
And more and more, the maiden woman-
    grown,
He wasted hours with Averill; there, when
    first
The tented winter-field was broken up
Into that phalanx of the summer spears
That soon should wear the garland; there
    again
When burr and bine were gather'd; lastly
    there
At Christmas; ever welcome at the Hall,
On whose dull sameness his full tide of
    youth
Broke with a phosphorescence charming
    even
My lady; and the Baronet yet had laid
No bar between them: dull and self-
    involved,
Tall and erect, but bending from his height
With half-allowing smiles for all the world,
And mighty courteous in the main—his
    pride
Lay deeper than to wear it as his ring—
He, like an Aylmer in his Aylmerism,
Would care no more for Leolin's walking
    with her
Than for his old Newfoundland's, when
    they ran
To loose him at the stables, for he rose
Twofooted at the limit of his chain,
Roaring to make a third: and how should
    Love,
Whom the cross-lightnings of four chance-
    met eyes

Flash into fiery life from nothing, follow
Such dear familiarities of dawn?
Seldom, but when he does, Master of all.

  So these young hearts not knowing that
    they loved,
Not she at least, nor conscious of a bar
Between them, nor by plight or broken ring
Bound, but an immemorial intimacy,
Wander'd at will, and oft accompanied
By Averill: his, a brother's love, that hung
With wings of brooding shelter o'er her
    peace,
Might have been other, save for Leolin's—
Who knows? but so they wander'd, hour
    by hour
Gather'd the blossom that rebloom'd, and
    drank
The magic cup that fill'd itself anew.

  A whisper half reveal'd her to herself.
For out beyond her lodges, where the
    brook
Vocal, with here and there a silence, ran
By sallowy rims, arose the labourers'
    homes,
A frequent haunt of Edith, on low knolls
That dimpling died into each other, huts
At random scatter'd, each a nest in bloom.
Her art, her hand, her counsel all had
    wrought
About them: here was one that, summer-
    blanch'd,
Was parcel-bearded with the traveller's-
    joy
In Autumn, parcel ivy-clad; and here
The warm-blue breathings of a hidden
    hearth
Broke from a bower of vine and honey-
    suckle:
One look'd all rosetree, and another wore
A close-set robe of jasmine sown with stars:
This had a rosy sea of gillyflowers
About it; this, a milky-way on earth,
Like visions in the Northern dreamer's
    heavens,
A lily-avenue climbing to the doors;
One, almost to the martin-haunted eaves
A summer burial deep in hollyhocks;
Each, its own charm; and Edith's every-
    where;

And Edith ever visitant with him,
He but less loved than Edith, of her poor:
For she—so lowly-lovely and so loving,
Queenly responsive when the loyal hand
Rose from the clay it work'd in as she past,
Not sowing hedgerow texts and passing by,
Nor dealing goodly counsel from a height
That makes the lowest hate it, but a voice
Of comfort and an open hand of help,
A splendid presence flattering the poor
    roofs
Revered as theirs, but kindlier than them-
    selves
To ailing wife or wailing infancy
Or old bedridden palsy,—was adored;
He, loved for her and for himself. A grasp
Having the warmth and muscle of the
    heart,
A childly way with children, and a laugh
Ringing like proven golden coinage true,
Were no false passport to that easy realm,
Where once with Leolin at her side the girl,
Nursing a child, and turning to the warmth
The tender pink five-beaded baby-soles,
Heard the good mother softly whisper
    'Bless,
God bless 'em: marriages are made in
    Heaven.'

  A flash of semi-jealousy clear'd it to her.
My lady's Indian kinsman unannounced
With half a score of swarthy faces came.
His own, tho' keen and bold and soldierly
Sear'd by the close ecliptic, was not fair;
Fairer his talk, a tongue that ruled the hour,
Tho' seeming boastful: so when first he
    dash'd
Into the chronicle of a deedful day,
Sir Aylmer half forgot his lazy smile
Of patron 'Good! my lady's kinsman!
    good!'
My lady with her fingers interlock'd,
And rotatory thumbs on silken knees,
Call'd all her vital spirits into each ear
To listen: unawares they flitted off,
Busying themselves about the flowerage
That stood from out a stiff brocade in
    which,
The meteor of a splendid season, she,
Once with this kinsman, ah so long ago,
Stept thro' the stately minuet of those days:

But Edith's eager fancy hurried with him
Snatch'd thro' the perilous passes of his
life:
Till Leolin ever watchful of her eye,
Hated him with a momentary hate.
Wife-hunting, as the rumour ran, was he:
I know not, for he spoke not, only shower'd
His oriental gifts on everyone
And most on Edith: like a storm he came,
And shook the house, and like a storm he
went.

Among the gifts he left her (possibly
He flow'd and ebb'd uncertain, to return
When others had been tested) there was
one,
A dagger, in rich sheath with jewels on it
Sprinkled about in gold that branch'd itself
Fine as ice-ferns on January panes
Made by a breath. I know not whence at
first,
Nor of what race, the work; but as he told
The story, storming a hill-fort of thieves
He got it; for their captain after fight,
His comrades having fought their last
below,
Was climbing up the valley; at whom he
shot:
Down from the beetling crag to which he
clung
Tumbled the tawny rascal at his feet,
This dagger with him, which when now
admired
By Edith whom his pleasure was to please,
At once the costly Sahib yielded to her.

And Leolin, coming after he was gone,
Tost over all her presents petulantly:
And when she show'd the wealthy scab-
bard, saying
'Look what a lovely piece of workmanship!'
Slight was his answer 'Well—I care not
for it:'
Then playing with the blade he prick'd his
hand,
'A gracious gift to give a lady, this!'
'But would it be more gracious' ask'd the
girl
'Were I to give this gift of his to one
That is no lady?' 'Gracious? No' said he.
'Me?—but I cared not for it. O pardon me,

I seem to be ungraciousness itself.'
'Take it' she added sweetly, 'tho' his gift;
For I am more ungracious ev'n than you,
I care not for it either;' and he said
'Why then I love it:' but Sir Aylmer past,
And neither loved nor liked the thing he
heard.

The next day came a neighbour. Blues
and reds
They talk'd of: blues were sure of it, he
thought:
Then of the latest fox—where started—
kill'd
In such a bottom: 'Peter had the brush,
My Peter, first:' and did Sir Aylmer know
That great pock-pitten fellow had been
caught?
Then made his pleasure echo, hand to hand,
And rolling as it were the substance of it
Between his palms a moment up and
down—
'The birds were warm, the birds were
warm upon him;
We have him now:' and had Sir Aylmer
heard—
Nay, but he must—the land was ringing
of it—
This blacksmith border-marriage—one
they knew—
Raw from the nursery—who could trust
a child?
That cursed France with her egalities!
And did Sir Aylmer (deferentially
With nearing chair and lower'd accent)
think—
For people talk'd—that it was wholly wise
To let that handsome fellow Averill walk
So freely with his daughter? people
talk'd—
The boy might get a notion into him;
The girl might be entangled ere she knew.
Sir Aylmer Aylmer slowly stiffening spoke:
'The girl and boy, Sir, know their differ-
ences!'
'Good,' said his friend, 'but watch!' and
he, 'Enough,
More than enough, Sir! I can guard my
own.'
They parted, and Sir Aylmer Aylmer
watch'd.

Pale, for on her the thunders of the house
Had fallen first, was Edith that same night;
Pale as the Jephtha's daughter, a rough piece
Of early rigid colour, under which
Withdrawing by the counter door to that
Which Leolin open'd, she cast back upon him
A piteous glance, and vanish'd. He, as one
Caught in a burst of unexpected storm,
And pelted with outrageous epithets,
Turning beheld the Powers of the House
On either side the hearth, indignant; her,
Cooling her false cheek with a featherfan,
Him, glaring by his own stale devil spurr'd,
And, like a beast hard-ridden, breathing hard.
'Ungenerous, dishonourable, base,
Presumptuous! trusted as he was with her,
The sole succeeder to their wealth, their lands,
The last remaining pillar of their house,
The one transmitter of their ancient name,
Their child.' 'Our child!' 'Our heiress!'
'Ours!' for still,
Like echoes from beyond a hollow, came
Her sicklier iteration. Last he said,
'Boy, mark me! for your fortunes are to make.
I swear you shall not make them out of mine.
Now inasmuch as you have practised on her,
Perplext her, made her half forget herself,
Swerve from her duty to herself and us—
Things in an Aylmer deem'd impossible,
Far as we track ourselves—I say that this—
Else I withdraw favour and countenance
From you and yours for ever—shall you do.
Sir, when you see her—but you shall not see her—
No, you shall write, and not to her, but me:
And you shall say that having spoken with me,
And after look'd into yourself, you find
That you meant nothing—as indeed you know
That you meant nothing. Such a match as this!

Impossible, prodigious!' These were words,
As meted by his measure of himself,
Arguing boundless forbearance: after which,
And Leolin's horror-stricken answer, 'I
So foul a traitor to myself and her,
Never oh never,' for about as long
As the wind-hover hangs in balance, paused
Sir Aylmer reddening from the storm within,
Then broke all bonds of courtesy, and crying
'Boy, should I find you by my doors again,
My men shall lash you from them like a dog;
Hence!' with a sudden execration drove
The footstool from before him, and arose;
So, stammering 'scoundrel' out of teeth that ground
As in a dreadful dream, while Leolin still
Retreated half-aghast, the fierce old man
Follow'd, and under his own lintel stood
Storming with lifted hands, a hoary face
Meet for the reverence of the hearth, but now,
Beneath a pale and unimpassion'd moon,
Vext with unworthy madness, and deform'd.

Slowly and conscious of the rageful eye
That watch'd him, till he heard the ponderous door
Close, crashing with long echoes thro' the land,
Went Leolin; then, his passions all in flood
And masters of his motion, furiously
Down thro' the bright lawns to his brother's ran,
And foam'd away his heart at Averill's ear:
Whom Averill solaced as he might, amazed:
The man was his, had been his father's, friend:
He must have seen, himself had seen it long;
He must have known, himself had known: besides,
He never yet had set his daughter forth
Here in the woman-markets of the west,

Where our Caucasians let themselves be
    sold.
Some one, he thought, had slander'd
    Leolin to him.
'Brother, for I have loved you more as son
Than brother, let me tell you: I myself—
What is their pretty saying? jilted, is it?
Jilted I was: I say it for your peace.
Pain'd, and, as bearing in myself the shame
The woman should have borne, humiliated,
I lived for years a stunted sunless life;
Till after our good parents past away
Watching your growth, I seem'd again to
    grow.
Leolin, I almost sin in envying you:
The very whitest lamb in all my fold
Loves you: I know her: the worst thought
    she has
Is whiter even than her pretty hand:
She must prove true: for, brother, where
    two fight
The strongest wins, and truth and love are
    strength,
And you are happy: let her parents be.'

But Leolin cried out the more upon
    them—
Insolent, brainless, heartless! heiress,
    wealth,
Their wealth, their heiress! wealth enough
    was theirs
For twenty matches. Were he lord of this,
Why twenty boys and girls should marry
    on it,
And forty blest ones bless him, and him-
    self
Be wealthy still, ay wealthier. He believed
This filthy marriage-hindering Mammon
    made
The harlot of the cities: nature crost
Was mother of the foul adulteries
That saturate soul with body. Name, too!
    name,
Their ancient name! they *might* be proud;
    its worth
Was being Edith's. Ah how pale she had
    look'd
Darling, to-night! they must have rated
    her
Beyond all tolerance. These old pheasant-
    lords,

These partridge-breeders of a thousand
    years,
Who had mildew'd in their thousands,
    doing nothing
Since Egbert—why, the greater their dis-
    grace!
Fall back upon a name! rest, rot in that!
Not *keep* it noble, make it nobler? fools,
With such a vantage-ground for nobleness!
He had known a man, a quintessence of
    man,
The life of all—who madly loved—and he,
Thwarted by one of these old father-fools,
Had rioted his life out, and made an end.
He would not do it! her sweet face and
    faith
Held him from that: but he had powers,
    he knew it:
Back would he to his studies, make a name,
Name, fortune too: the world should ring
    of him
To shame these mouldy Aylmers in their
    graves:
Chancellor, or what is greatest would he
    be—
'O brother, I am grieved to learn your
    grief—
Give me my fling, and let me say my say.'

At which, like one that sees his own
    excess,
And easily forgives it as his own,
He laugh'd; and then was mute; but
    presently
Wept like a storm: and honest Averill
    seeing
How low his brother's mood had fallen,
    fetch'd
His richest beeswing from a binn reserved
For banquets, praised the waning red, and
    told
The vintage—when *this* Aylmer came of
    age—
Then drank and past it; till at length the
    two,
Tho' Leolin flamed and fell again, agreed
That much allowance must be made for
    men.
After an angry dream this kindlier glow
Faded with morning, but his purpose
    held.

Yet once by night again the lovers met,
A perilous meeting under the tall pines
That darken'd all the northward of her
Hall.
Him, to her meek and modest bosom prest
In agony, she promised that no force,
Persuasion, no, nor death could alter her:
He, passionately hopefuller, would go,
Labour for his own Edith, and return
In such a sunlight of prosperity
He should not be rejected. 'Write to me!
They loved me, and because I love their
child
They hate me: there is war between us,
dear,
Which breaks all bonds but ours; we must
remain
Sacred to one another.' So they talk'd,
Poor children, for their comfort: the wind
blew;
The rain of heaven, and their own bitter
tears,
Tears, and the careless rain of heaven,
mixt
Upon their faces, as they kiss'd each other
In darkness, and above them roar'd the
pine.

So Leolin went; and as we task ourselves
To learn a language known but smatter-
ingly
In phrases here and there at random, toil'd
Mastering the lawless science of our law,
That codeless myriad of precedent,
That wilderness of single instances,
Thro' which a few, by wit or fortune led,
May beat a pathway out to wealth and
fame.
The jests, that flash'd about the pleader's
room,
Lightning of the hour, the pun, the scurri-
lous tale,—
Old scandals buried now seven decads deep
In other scandals that have lived and died,
And left the living scandal that shall die—
Were dead to him already; bent as he was
To make disproof of scorn, and strong in
hopes,
And prodigal of all brain-labour he,
Charier of sleep, and wine, and exercise,
Except when for a breathing-while at eve,

Some niggard fraction of an hour, he ran
Beside the river-bank: and then indeed
Harder the times were, and the hands of
power
Were bloodier, and the according hearts of
men
Seem'd harder too; but the soft river-
breeze,
Which fann'd the gardens of that rival rose
Yet fragrant in a heart remembering
His former talks with Edith, on him
breathed
Far purelier in his rushings to and fro,
After his books, to flush his blood with air,
Then to his books again. My lady's cousin,
Half-sickening of his pension'd afternoon,
Drove in upon the student once or twice,
Ran a Malayan amuck against the times,
Had golden hopes for France and all man-
kind,
Answer'd all queries touching those at
home
With a heaved shoulder and a saucy smile,
And fain had haled him out into the world,
And air'd him there: his nearer friend
would say
'Screw not the chord too sharply lest it
snap.'
Then left alone he pluck'd her dagger forth
From where his worldless heart had kept
it warm,
Kissing his vows upon it like a knight,
And wrinkled benchers often talk'd of him
Approvingly, and prophesied his rise:
For heart, I think, help'd head: her letters
too,
Tho' far between, and coming fitfully
Like broken music, written as she found
Or made occasion, being strictly watch'd,
Charm'd him thro' every labyrinth till he
saw
An end, a hope, a light breaking upon him.

But they that cast her spirit into flesh,
Her worldly-wise begetters, plagued them-
selves
To sell her, those good parents, for her
good.
Whatever eldest-born of rank or wealth
Might lie within their compass, him they
lured

Into their net made pleasant by the baits
Of gold and beauty, wooing him to woo.
So month by month the noise about their
  doors,
And distant blaze of those dull banquets,
  made
The nightly wirer of their innocent hare
Falter before he took it. All in vain.
Sullen, defiant, pitying, wroth, return'd
Leolin's rejected rivals from their suit
So often, that the folly taking wings
Slipt o'er those lazy limits down the wind
With rumour, and became in other fields
A mockery to the yeomen over ale,
And laughter to their lords: but those at
  home,
As hunters round a hunted creature draw
The cordon close and closer toward the
  death,
Narrow'd her goings out and comings in;
Forbad her first the house of Averill,
Then closed her access to the wealthier
  farms,
Last from her own home-circle of the poor
They barr'd her: yet she bore it: yet her
  cheek
Kept colour: wondrous! but, O mystery!
What amulet drew her down to that old
  oak,
So old, that twenty years before, a part
Falling had let appear the brand of John—
Once grovelike, each huge arm a tree, but
  now
The broken base of a black tower, a cave
Of touchwood, with a single flourishing
  spray.
There the manorial lord too curiously
Raking in that millennial touchwood-dust
Found for himself a bitter treasure-trove;
Burst his own wyvern on the seal, and read
Writhing a letter from his child, for which
Came at the moment Leolin's emissary,
A crippled lad, and coming turn'd to fly,
But scared with threats of jail and halter
  gave
To him that fluster'd his poor parish wits
The letter which he brought, and swore
  besides
To play their go-between as heretofore
Nor let them know themselves betray'd;
  and then,

Soul-stricken at their kindness to him,
  went
Hating his own lean heart and miserable.

Thenceforward oft from out a despot
  dream
The father panting woke, and oft, as dawn
Aroused the black republic on his elms,
Sweeping the frothfly from the fescue
  brush'd
Thro' the dim meadow toward his treasure-
  trove,
Seized it, took home, and to my lady,—
  who made
A downward crescent of her minion mouth,
Listless in all despondence,—read; and
  tore,
As if the living passion symbol'd there
Were living nerves to feel the rent; and
  burnt,
Now chafing at his own great self defied,
Now striking on huge stumbling-blocks of
  scorn
In babyisms, and dear diminutives
Scatter'd all over the vocabulary
Of such a love as like a chidden child,
After much wailing, hush'd itself at last
Hopeless of answer: then tho' Averill wrote
And bad him with good heart sustain him-
  self—
All would be well—the lover heeded not,
But passionately restless came and went,
And rustling once at night about the place,
There by a keeper shot at, slightly hurt,
Raging return'd: nor was it well for her
Kept to the garden now, and grove of pines,
Watch'd even there; and one was set to
  watch
The watcher, and Sir Aylmer watch'd
  them all,
Yet bitterer from his readings: once indeed,
Warm'd with his wines, or taking pride in
  her,
She look'd so sweet, he kiss'd her tenderly
Not knowing what possess'd him: that one
  kiss
Was Leolin's one strong rival upon earth;
Seconded, for my lady follow'd suit,
Seem'd hope's returning rose: and then
  ensued
A Martin's summer of his faded love,

Or ordeal by kindness; after this
He seldom crost his child without a sneer;
The mother flow'd in shallower acrimonies:
Never one kindly smile, one kindly word:
So that the gentle creature shut from all
Her charitable use, and face to face
With twenty months of silence, slowly lost
Nor greatly cared to lose, her hold on life.
Last, some low fever ranging round to spy
The weakness of a people or a house,
Like flies that haunt a wound, or deer, or
men,
Or almost all that is, hurting the hurt—
Save Christ as we believe him—found the
girl
And flung her down upon a couch of fire,
Where careless of the household faces near,
And crying upon the name of Leolin,
She, and with her the race of Aylmer, past.

Star to star vibrates light: may soul to soul
Strike thro' a finer element of her own?
So,—from afar,—touch as at once? or why
That night, that moment, when she named
his name,
Did the keen shriek 'Yes love, yes, Edith,
yes,'
Shrill, till the comrade of his chambers
woke,
And came upon him half-arisen from sleep,
With a weird bright eye, sweating and
trembling,
His hair as it were crackling into flames,
His body half flung forward in pursuit,
And his long arms stretch'd as to grasp a
flyer:
Nor knew he wherefore he had made the
cry;
And being much befool'd and idioted
By the rough amity of the other, sank
As into sleep again. The second day,
My lady's Indian kinsman rushing in,
A breaker of the bitter news from home,
Found a dead man, a letter edged with death
Beside him, and the dagger which himself
Gave Edith, redden'd with no bandit's
blood:
'From Edith' was engraven on the blade.

Then Averill went and gazed upon his
death.

And when he came again, his flock be-
lieved—
Beholding how the years which are not
Time's
Had blasted him—that many thousand
days
Were clipt by horror from his term of life.
Yet the sad mother, for the second death
Scarce touch'd her thro' that nearness of
the first,
And being used to find her pastor texts,
Sent to the harrow'd brother, praying him
To speak before the people of her child,
And fixt the Sabbath. Darkly that day rose:
Autumn's mock sunshine of the faded
woods
Was all the life of it; for hard on these,
A breathless burthen of low-folded heavens
Stifled and chill'd at once; but every roof
Sent out a listener: many too had known
Edith among the hamlets round, and since
The parents' harshness and the hapless
loves
And double death were widely murmur'd,
left
Their own gray tower, or plain-faced
tabernacle,
To hear him; all in mourning these, and
those
With blots of it about them, ribbon, glove
Or kerchief; while the church,—one night,
except
For greenish glimmerings thro' the lancets,
—made
Still paler the pale head of him, who
tower'd
Above them, with his hopes in either grave.

Long o'er his bent brows linger'd Averill,
His face magnetic to the hand from which
Livid he pluck'd it forth, and labour'd thro'
His brief prayer-prelude, gave the verse
'Behold,
Your house is left unto you desolate!'
But lapsed into so long a pause again
As half amazed half frighted all his flock:
Then from his height and loneliness of
grief
Bore down in flood, and dash'd his angry
heart
Against the desolations of the world.

Never since our bad earth became one
  sea,
Which rolling o'er the palaces of the proud,
And all but those who knew the living
  God—
Eight that were left to make a purer
  world—
When since had flood, fire, earthquake,
  thunder, wrought
Such waste and havock as the idolatries,
Which from the low light of mortality
Shot up their shadows to the Heaven of
  Heavens,
And worshipt their own darkness in the
  Highest?
'Gash thyself, priest, and honour thy brute
  Baäl,
And to thy worst self sacrifice thyself,
For with thy worst self hast thou clothed
  thy God.
Then came a Lord in no wise like to Baäl.
The babe shall lead the lion. Surely now
The wilderness shall blossom as the rose.
Crown thyself, worm, and worship thine
  own lusts!
No coarse and blockish God of acreage
Stands at thy gate for thee to grovel to—
Thy God is far diffused in noble groves
And princely halls, and farms, and flowing
  lawns,
And heaps of living gold that daily grow,
And title-scrolls and gorgeous heraldries.
In such a shape dost thou behold thy God.
Thou wilt not gash thy flesh for *him;* for
  thine
Fares richly, in fine linen, not a hair
Ruffled upon the scarfskin, even while
The deathless ruler of thy dying house
Is wounded to the death that cannot die;
And tho' thou numberest with the followers
Of One who cried, "Leave all and follow
  me."
Thee therefore with His light about thy
  feet,
Thee with His message ringing in thine
  ears,
Thee shall thy brother man, the Lord from
  Heaven,
Born of a village girl, carpenter's son,
Wonderful, Prince of peace, the Mighty
  God,

Count the more base idolater of the two;
Crueller: as not passing thro' the fire
Bodies, but souls—thy children's—thro'
  the smoke,
The blight of low desires—darkening thine
  own
To thine own likeness; or if one of these,
Thy better born unhappily from thee,
Should, as by miracle, grow straight and
  fair—
Friends, I was bid to speak of such a one
By those who most have cause to sorrow
  for her—
Fairer than Rachel by the palmy well,
Fairer than Ruth among the fields of corn,
Fair as the Angel that said "Hail!" she
  seem'd,
Who entering fill'd the house with sudden
  light.
For so mine own was brighten'd: where
  indeed
The roof so lowly but that beam of Heaven
Dawn'd sometime thro' the doorway?
  whose the babe
Too ragged to be fondled on her lap,
Warm'd at her bosom? The poor child
  of shame
The common care whom no one cared for,
  leapt
To greet her, wasting his forgotten heart,
As with the mother he had never known,
In gambols; for her fresh and innocent eyes
Had such a star of morning in their blue,
That all neglected places of the field
Broke into nature's music when they saw
  her.
Low was her voice, but won mysterious
  way
Thro' the seal'd ear to which a louder one
Was all but silence—free of alms her
  hand—
The hand that robed your cottage-walls
  with flowers
Has often toil'd to clothe your little ones;
How often placed upon the sick man's
  brow
Cool'd it, or laid his feverous pillow
  smooth!
Had you one sorrow and she shared it not?
One burthen and she would not lighten it?
One spiritual doubt she did not soothe?

Or when some heat of difference sparkled
  out,
How sweetly would she glide between your
  wraths,
And steal you from each other! for she
  walk'd
Wearing the light yoke of that Lord of love,
Who still'd the rolling wave of Galilee!
And one—of him I was not bid to speak—
Was always with her, whom you also knew.
Him too you loved, for he was worthy love.
And these had been together from the
  first;
They might have been together till the last.
Friends, this frail bark of ours, when sorely
  tried,
May wreck itself without the pilot's guilt,
Without the captain's knowledge: hope
  with me.
Whose shame is that, if he went hence with
  shame?
Nor mine the fault, if losing both of these
I cry to vacant chairs and widow'd walls,
"My house is left unto me desolate."'

  While thus he spoke, his hearers wept;
    but some,
Sons of the glebe, with other frowns than
  those
That knit themselves for summer shadow,
  scowl'd
At their great lord. He, when it seem'd he
  saw
No pale sheet-lightnings from afar, but
  fork'd
Of the near storm, and aiming at his head,
Sat anger-charm'd from sorrow, soldier-
  like,
Erect: but when the preacher's cadence
  flow'd
Softening thro' all the gentle attributes
Of his lost child, the wife, who watch'd his
  face,
Paled at a sudden twitch of his iron mouth;
And 'O pray God that he hold up' she
  thought
'Or surely I shall shame myself and him.'

  'Nor yours the blame—for who beside
    your hearths
Can take her place—if echoing me you cry

"Our house is left unto us desolate"?
But thou, O thou that killest, hadst thou
  known,
O thou that stonest, hadst thou understood
The things belonging to thy peace and
  ours!
Is there no prophet but the voice that calls
Doom upon kings, or in the waste "Re-
  pent"?
Is not our own child on the narrow way,
Who down to those that saunter in the
  broad
Cries "Come up hither," as a prophet to
  us?
Is there no stoning save with flint and
  rock?
Yes, as the dead we weep for testify—
No desolation but by sword and fire?
Yes, as your moanings witness, and my-
  self
Am lonelier, darker, earthlier for my loss.
Give me your prayers, for he is past your
  prayers,
Not past the living fount of pity in Heaven.
But I that thought myself long-suffering,
  meek,
Exceeding "poor in spirit"—how the words
Have twisted back upon themselves, and
  mean
Vileness, we are grown so proud—I wish'd
  my voice
A rushing tempest of the wrath of God
To blow these sacrifices thro' the world—
Sent like the twelve-divided concubine
To inflame the tribes: but there—out yon-
  der—earth
Lightens from her own central Hell—O
  there
The red fruit of an old idolatry—
The heads of chiefs and princes fall so
  fast,
They cling together in the ghastly sack—
The land all shambles—naked marriages
Flash from the bridge, and ever-murder'd
  France,
By shores that darken with the gathering
  wolf,
Runs in a river of blood to the sick sea.
Is this a time to madden madness then?
Was this a time for these to flaunt their
  pride?

May Pharaoh's darkness, folds as dense as
    those
Which hid the Holiest from the people's
    eyes
Ere the great death, shroud this great sin
    from all!
Doubtless our narrow world must can-
    vass it:
O rather pray for those and pity them,
Who, thro' their own desire accomplish'd,
    bring
Their own gray hairs with sorrow to the
    grave—
Who broke the bond which they desired to
    break,
Which else had link'd their race with times
    to come—
Who wove coarse webs to snare her purity,
Grossly contriving their dear daughter's
    good—
Poor souls, and knew not what they did,
    but sat
Ignorant, devising their own daughter's
    death!
May not that earthly chastisement suffice?
Have not our love and reverence left them
    bare?
Will not another take their heritage?
Will there be children's laughter in their
    hall
For ever and for ever, or one stone
Left on another, or is it a light thing
That I, their guest, their host, their ancient
    friend,
I made by these the last of all my race,
Must cry to these the last of theirs, as cried
Christ ere His agony to those that swore
Not by the temple but the gold, and made
Their own traditions God, and slew the
    Lord,
And left their memories a world's curse—
    "Behold,
Your house is left unto you desolate"?'

    Ended he had not, but she brook'd no
    more:
Long since her heart had beat remorse-
    lessly,
Her crampt-up sorrow pain'd her, and a
    sense
Of meanness in her unresisting life.

Then their eyes vext her; for on entering
He had cast the curtains of their seat
    aside—
Black velvet of the costliest—she herself
Had seen to that: fain had she closed them
    now,
Yet dared not stir to do it, only near'd
Her husband inch by inch, but when she
    laid,
Wifelike, her hand in one of his, he veil'd
His face with the other, and at once, as falls
A creeper when the prop is broken, fell
The woman shrieking at his feet, and
    swoon'd.
Then her own people bore along the nave
Her pendent hands, and narrow meagre face
Seam'd with the shallow cares of fifty years:
And her the Lord of all the landscape
    round
Ev'n to its last horizon, and of all
Who peer'd at him so keenly, follow'd out
Tall and erect, but in the middle aisle
Reel'd, as a footsore ox in crowded ways
Stumbling across the market to his death,
Unpitied; for he groped as blind, and
    seem'd
Always about to fall, grasping the pews
And oaken finials till he touch'd the door;
Yet to the lychgate, where his chariot stood,
Strode from the porch, tall and erect again.

    But nevermore did either pass the gate
Save under pall with bearers. In one
    month,
Thro' weary and yet ever wearier hours,
The childless mother went to seek her
    child;
And when he felt the silence of his house
About him, and the change and not the
    change,
And those fixt eyes of painted ancestors
Staring for ever from their gilded walls
On him their last descendant, his own head
Began to droop, to fall; the man became
Imbecile; his one word was 'desolate;'
Dead for two years before his death was he;
But when the second Christmas came,
    escaped
His keepers, and the silence which he felt,
To find a deeper in the narrow gloom
By wife and child; nor wanted at his end

The dark retinue reverencing death
At golden thresholds; nor from tender
    hearts,
And those who sorrow'd o'er a vanish'd
    race,
Pity, the violet on the tyrant's grave.
Then the great Hall was wholly broken
    down,
And the broad woodland parcell'd into
    farms;
And where the two contrived their
    daughter's good,
Lies the hawk's cast, the mole has made
    his run,
The hedgehog underneath the plantain
    bores,
The rabbit fondles his own harmless face,
The slow-worm creeps, and the thin
    weasel there
Follows the mouse, and all is open field.

SEA DREAMS

A CITY clerk, but gently born and bred;
His wife, an unknown artist's orphan
    child—
One babe was theirs, a Margaret, three
    years old:
They, thinking that her clear germander
    eye
Droopt in the giant-factoried city-gloom,
Came, with a month's leave given them,
    to the sea:
For which his gains were dock'd, however
    small:
Small were his gains, and hard his work;
    besides,
Their slender household fortunes (for the
    man
Had risk'd his little) like the little thrift,
Trembled in perilous places o'er a deep:
And oft, when sitting all alone, his face
Would darken, as he cursed his credulous-
    ness,
And that one unctuous mouth which lured
    him, rogue,
To buy strange shares in some Peruvian
    mine.
Now seaward-bound for health they gain'd
    a coast,
All sand and cliff and deep-inrunning cave,

At close of day; slept, woke, and went the
    next,
The Sabbath, pious variers from the
    church,
To chapel; where a heated pulpiteer,
Not preaching simple Christ to simple
    men,
Announced the coming doom, and ful-
    minated
Against the scarlet woman and her creed;
For sideways up he swung his arms, and
    shriek'd
'Thus, thus with violence,' ev'n as if he
    held
The Apocalyptic millstone, and himself
Were that great Angel; 'Thus with violence
Shall Babylon be cast into the sea;
Then comes the close.' The gentle-hearted
    wife
Sat shuddering at the ruin of a world;
He at his own: but when the wordy storm
Had ended, forth they came and paced the
    shore,
Ran in and out the long sea-framing caves,
Drank the large air, and saw, but scarce
    believed
(The sootflake of so many a summer still
Clung to their fancies) that they saw, the
    sea.
So now on sand they walk'd, and now on
    cliff,
Lingering about the thymy promontories,
Till all the sails were darken'd in the west,
And rosed in the east: then homeward and
    to bed:
Where she, who kept a tender Christian
    hope,
Haunting a holy text, and still to that
Returning, as the bird returns, at night,
'Let not the sun go down upon your
    wrath,'
Said, 'Love, forgive him:' but he did not
    speak;
And silenced by that silence lay the wife,
Remembering her dear Lord who died for
    all,
And musing on the little lives of men,
And how they mar this little by their feuds.

But while the two were sleeping, a full
    tide

Rose with ground-swell, which, on the foremost rocks
Touching, upjetted in spirts of wild sea-smoke,
And scaled in sheets of wasteful foam, and fell
In vast sea-cataracts—ever and anon
Dead claps of thunder from within the cliffs
Heard thro' the living roar. At this the babe,
Their Margaret cradled near them, wail'd and woke
The mother, and the father suddenly cried,
'A wreck, a wreck!' then turn'd, and groaning said,

　'Forgive! How many will say, "forgive," and find
A sort of absolution in the sound
To hate a little longer! No; the sin
That neither God nor man can well forgive,
Hypocrisy, I saw it in him at once.
Is it so true that second thoughts are best?
Not first, and third, which are a riper first?
Too ripe, too late! they come too late for use.
Ah love, there surely lives in man and beast
Something divine to warn them of their foes:
And such a sense, when first I fronted him,
Said, "Trust him not;" but after, when I came
To know him more, I lost it, knew him less;
Fought with what seem'd my own uncharity;
Sat at his table; drank his costly wines;
Made more and more allowance for his talk;
Went further, fool! and trusted him with all,
All my poor scrapings from a dozen years
Of dust and deskwork: there is no such mine,
None; but a gulf of ruin, swallowing gold,
Not making. Ruin'd! ruin'd! the sea roars
Ruin: a fearful night!'

　　　　　　　'Not fearful; fair,'
Said the good wife, 'if every star in heaven
Can make it fair: you do but hear the tide.
Had you ill dreams?'

　　　　　'O yes,' he said, 'I dream'd
Of such a tide swelling toward the land,
And I from out the boundless outer deep
Swept with it to the shore, and enter'd one
Of those dark caves that run beneath the cliffs.
I thought the motion of the boundless deep
Bore thro' the cave, and I was heaved upon it
In darkness: then I saw one lovely star
Larger and larger. "What a world," I thought,
"To live in!" but in moving on I found
Only the landward exit of the cave,
Bright with the sun upon the stream beyond:
And near the light a giant woman sat,
All over earthy, like a piece of earth,
A pickaxe in her hand: then out I slipt
Into a land all sun and blossom, trees
As high as heaven, and every bird that sings:
And here the night-light flickering in my eyes
Awoke me.'

　　　'That was then your dream,' she said,
'Not sad, but sweet.'

　　　　　　'So sweet, I lay,' said he,
'And mused upon it, drifting up the stream
In fancy, till I slept again, and pieced
The broken vision; for I dream'd that still
The motion of the great deep bore me on,
And that the woman walk'd upon the brink:
I wonder'd at her strength, and ask'd her of it:
"It came," she said, "by working in the mines:"
O then to ask her of my shares, I thought;
And ask'd; but not a word; she shook her head.
And then the motion of the current ceased,
And there was rolling thunder; and we reach'd
A mountain, like a wall of burs and thorns;
But she with her strong feet up the steep hill

SEA DREAMS

Trod out a path: I follow'd; and at top
She pointed seaward: there a fleet of glass,
That seem'd a fleet of jewels under me,
Sailing along before a gloomy cloud
That not one moment ceased to thunder, past
In sunshine: right across its track there lay,
Down in the water, a long reef of gold,
Or what seem'd gold: and I was glad at first
To think that in our often-ransack'd world
Still so much gold was left; and then I fear'd
Lest the gay navy there should splinter on it,
And fearing waved my arm to warn them off;
An idle signal, for the brittle fleet
(I thought I could have died to save it) near'd,
Touch'd, clink'd, and clash'd, and vanish'd, and I woke,
I heard the clash so clearly. Now I see
My dream was Life; the woman honest Work;
And my poor venture but a fleet of glass
Wreck'd on a reef of visionary gold.'

'Nay,' said the kindly wife to comfort him,
'You raised your arm, you tumbled down and broke
The glass with little Margaret's medicine in it;
And, breaking that, you made and broke your dream:
A trifle makes a dream, a trifle breaks.'

'No trifle,' groan'd the husband; 'yesterday
I met him suddenly in the street, and ask'd
That which I ask'd the woman in my dream.
Like her, he shook his head. "Show me the books!"
He dodged me with a long and loose account.
"The books, the books!" but he, he could not wait,
Bound on a matter he of life and death:
When the great Books (see Daniel seven and ten)

Were open'd, I should find he meant me well;
And then began to bloat himself, and ooze
All over with the fat affectionate smile
That makes the widow lean. "My dearest friend,
Have faith, have faith! We live by faith," said he;
"And all things work together for the good
Of those"—it makes me sick to quote him —last
Gript my hand hard, and with God-bless-you went.
I stood like one that had received a blow:
I found a hard friend in his loose accounts,
A loose one in the hard grip of his hand,
A curse in his God-bless-you: then my eyes
Pursued him down the street, and far away,
Among the honest shoulders of the crowd,
Read rascal in the motions of his back,
And scoundrel in the supple-sliding knee.'

'Was he so bound, poor soul?' said the good wife;
'So are we all: but do not call him, love,
Before you prove him, rogue, and proved, forgive.
His gain is loss; for he that wrongs his friend
Wrongs himself more, and ever bears about
A silent court of justice in his breast,
Himself the judge and jury, and himself
The prisoner at the bar, ever condemn'd:
And that drags down his life: then comes what comes
Hereafter: and he meant, he said he meant,
Perhaps he meant, or partly meant, you well.'

' "With all his conscience and one eye askew"—
Love, let me quote these lines, that you may learn
A man is likewise counsel for himself,
Too often, in that silent court of yours—
"With all his conscience and one eye askew,
So false, he partly took himself for true;
Whose pious talk, when most his heart was dry,

147

Made wet the crafty crowsfoot round his
    eye;
Who, never naming God except for gain,
So never took that useful name in vain,
Made Him his catspaw and the Cross his
    tool,
And Christ the bait to trap his dupe and
    fool;
Nor deeds of gift, but gifts of grace he
    forged,
And snake-like slimed his victim ere he
    gorged;
And oft at Bible meetings, o'er the rest
Arising, did his holy oily best,
Dropping the too rough H in Hell and
    Heaven,
To spread the Word by which himself had
    thriven."
How like you this old satire?'

               'Nay,' she said,
'I loathe it: he had never kindly heart,
Nor ever cared to better his own kind,
Who first wrote satire, with no pity in it.
But will you hear *my* dream, for I had one
That altogether went to music? Still
It awed me.'

      Then she told it, having dream'd
Of that same coast.

        —But round the North, a light,
A belt, it seem'd, of luminous vapour, lay,
And ever in it a low musical note
Swell'd up and died; and, as it swell'd, a
    ridge
Of breaker issued from the belt, and still
Grew with the growing note, and when
    the note
Had reach'd a thunderous fulness, on those
    cliffs
Broke, mixt with awful light (the same as
    that
Living within the belt) whereby she saw
That all those lines of cliffs were cliffs no
    more,
But huge cathedral fronts of every age,
Grave, florid, stern, as far as eye could see,
One after one: and then the great ridge
    drew,
Lessening to the lessening music, back,

And past into the belt and swell'd again
Slowly to music: ever when it broke
The statues, king or saint, or founder
    fell;
Then from the gaps and chasms of ruin
    left
Came men and women in dark clusters
    round,
Some crying, 'Set them up! they shall not
    fall!'
And others, 'Let them lie, for they have
    fall'n.'
And still they strove and wrangled: and
    she grieved
In her strange dream, she knew not why,
    to find
Their wildest wailings never out of tune
With that sweet note; and ever as their
    shrieks
Ran highest up the gamut, that great wave
Returning, while none mark'd it, on the
    crowd
Broke, mixt with awful light, and show'd
    their eyes
Glaring, and passionate looks, and swept
    away
The men of flesh and blood, and men of
    stone,
To the waste deeps together.

                'Then I fixt
My wistful eyes on two fair images,
Both crown'd with stars and high among
    the stars,—
The Virgin Mother standing with her child
High up on one of those dark minster-
    fronts—
Till she began to totter, and the child
Clung to the mother, and sent out a cry
Which mixt with little Margaret's, and I
    woke,
And my dream awed me:—well—but what
    are dreams?
Yours came but from the breaking of a
    glass,
And mine but from the crying of a child.'

    'Child? No!' said he, 'but this tide's
    roar, and his,
Our Boanerges with his threats of doom,
And loud-lung'd Antibabylonianisms

(Altho' I grant but little music there)
Went both to make your dream: but if
   there were
A music harmonizing our wild cries,
Sphere-music such as that you dream'd
   about,
Why, that would make our passions far too
   like
The discords dear to the musician. No—
One shriek of hate would jar all the hymns
   of heaven:
True Devils with no ear, they howl in tune
With nothing but the Devil!'

           ' "True" indeed!
One of our town, but later by an hour
Here than ourselves, spoke with me on the
   shore;
While you were running down the sands,
   and made
The dimpled flounce of the sea-furbelow
   flap,
Good man, to please the child. She brought
   strange news.
Why were you silent when I spoke to-
   night?
I had set my heart on your forgiving him
Before you knew. We *must* forgive the
   dead.'

  'Dead! who is dead?'

          'The man your eye pursued.
A little after you had parted with him,
He suddenly dropt dead of heart-disease.'

'Dead? he? of heart-disease? what heart
   had he
To die of? dead!'

        'Ah, dearest, if there be
A devil in man, there is an angel too,
And if he did that wrong you charge him
   with,
His angel broke his heart. But your rough
   voice
(You spoke so loud) has roused the child
   again.
Sleep, little birdie, sleep! will she not sleep

Without her "little birdie"? well then,
   sleep,
And I will sing you "birdie." '

             Saying this,
The woman half turn'd round from him
   she loved,
Left him one hand, and reaching thro' the
   night
Her other, found (for it was close beside)
And half-embraced the basket cradle-head
With one soft arm, which, like the pliant
   bough
That moving moves the nest and nestling,
   sway'd
The cradle, while she sang this baby song.

What does little birdie say
In her nest at peep of day?
Let me fly, says little birdie,
Mother, let me fly away.
Birdie, rest a little longer,
Till the little wings are stronger.
So she rests a little longer,
Then she flies away.

What does little baby say,
In her bed at peep of day?
Baby says, like little birdie,
Let me rise and fly away.
Baby, sleep a little longer,
Till the little limbs are stronger.
If she sleeps a little longer,
Baby too shall fly away.

'She sleeps: let us too, let all evil, sleep.
He also sleeps—another sleep than ours.
He can do no more wrong: forgive him,
   dear,
And I shall sleep the sounder!'

            Then the man,
'His deeds yet live, the worst is yet to come.
Yet let your sleep for this one night be
   sound:
I do forgive him!'

        'Thanks, my love,' she said,
'Your own will be the sweeter,' and they
   slept.

LUCRETIUS

LUCRETIUS

Lucilia, wedded to Lucretius, found
Her master cold; for when the morning
    flush
Of passion and the first embrace had died
Between them, tho' he lov'd her none the
    less,
Yet often when the woman heard his foot
Return from pacings in the field, and ran
To greet him with a kiss, the master took
Small notice, or austerely, for—his mind
Half buried in some weightier argument,
Or fancy-borne perhaps upon the rise
And long roll of the Hexameter—he past
To turn and ponder those three hundred
    scrolls
Left by the Teacher, whom he held divine.
She brook'd it not; but wrathful, petulant,
Dreaming some rival, sought and found a
    witch
Who brew'd the philtre which had power,
    they said,
To lead an errant passion home again.
And this, at times, she mingled with his
    drink,
And this destroy'd him; for the wicked broth
Confused the chemic labour of the blood,
And tickling the brute brain within the
    man's
Made havock among those tender cells, and
    check'd
His power to shape: he loathed himself;
    and once
After a tempest woke upon a morn
That mock'd him with returning calm, and
    cried:

'Storm in the night! for thrice I heard
    the rain
Rushing; and once the flash of a thunder-
    bolt—
Methought I never saw so fierce a fork—
Struck out the streaming mountain-side,
    and show'd
A riotous confluence of watercourses
Blanching and billowing in a hollow of it,
Where all but yester-eve was dusty-dry.

'Storm, and what dreams, ye holy Gods,
    what dreams!

For thrice I waken'd after dreams. Per-
    chance
We do but recollect the dreams that come
Just ere the waking: terrible! for it seem'd
A void was made in Nature; all her bonds
Crack'd; and I saw the flaring atom-
    streams
And torrents of her myriad universe,
Ruining along the illimitable inane,
Fly on to clash together again, and make
Another and another frame of things
For ever: that was mine, my dream, I
    knew it—
Of and belonging to me, as the dog
With inward yelp and restless forefoot
    plies
His function of the woodland: but the next!
I thought that all the blood by Sylla shed
Came driving rainlike down again on earth,
And where it dash'd the reddening
    meadow, sprang
No dragon warriors from Cadmean teeth,
For these I thought my dream would show
    to me,
But girls, Hetairai, curious in their art,
Hired animalisms, vile as those that made
The mulberry-faced Dictator's orgies
    worse
Than aught they fable of the quiet Gods.
And hands they mixt, and yell'd and round
    me drove
In narrowing circles till I yell'd again
Half-suffocated, and sprang up, and saw—
Was it the first beam of my latest day?

'Then, then, from utter gloom stood out
    the breasts,
The breasts of Helen, and hoveringly a
    sword
Now over and now under, now direct,
Pointed itself to pierce, but sank down
    shamed
At all that beauty; and as I stared, a fire,
The fire that left a roofless Ilion,
Shot out of them, and scorch'd me that I
    woke.

'Is this thy vengeance, holy Venus, thine,
Because I would not one of thine own
    doves,
Not ev'n a rose, were offer'd to thee? thine,

150

Forgetful how my rich procemion makes
Thy glory fly along the Italian field,
In lays that will outlast thy Deity?

'Deity? nay, thy worshippers. My tongue
Trips, or I speak profanely. Which of these
Angers thee most, or angers thee at all?
Not if thou be'st of those who, far aloof
From envy, hate and pity, and spite and
  scorn,
Live the great life which all our greatest
  fain
Would follow, center'd in eternal calm.

'Nay, if thou canst, O Goddess, like
  ourselves
Touch, and be touch'd, then would I cry
  to thee
To kiss thy Mavors, roll thy tender arms
Round him, and keep him from the lust of
  blood
That makes a steaming slaughter-house of
  Rome.

'Ay, but I meant not thee; I meant not
  her,
Whom all the pines of Ida shook to see
Slide from that quiet heaven of hers, and
  tempt
The Trojan, while his neat-herds were
  abroad;
Nor her that o'er her wounded hunter wept
Her Deity false in human-amorous tears;
Nor whom her beardless apple-arbiter
Decided fairest. Rather, O ye Gods,
Poet-like, as the great Sicilian called
Calliope to grace his golden verse—
Ay, and this Kypris also—did I take
That popular name of thine to shadow forth
The all-generating powers and genial heat
Of Nature, when she strikes thro' the thick
  blood
Of cattle, and light is large, and lambs are
  glad
Nosing the mother's udder, and the bird
Makes his heart voice amid the blaze of
  flowers:
Which things appear the work of mighty
  Gods.

'The Gods! and if I go *my* work is left
Unfinish'd—*if* I go. The Gods, who haunt

The lucid interspace of world and world,
Where never creeps a cloud, or moves a
  wind,
Nor ever falls the least white star of snow,
Nor ever lowest roll of thunder moans,
Nor sound of human sorrow mounts to mar
Their sacred everlasting calm! and such,
Not all so fine, nor so divine a calm,
Not such, nor all unlike it, man may gain
Letting his own life go. The Gods, the
  Gods!
If all be atoms, how then should the Gods
Being atomic not be dissoluble,
Not follow the great law? My master held
That Gods there are, for all men so believe.
I prest my footsteps into his, and meant
Surely to lead my Memmius in a train
Of flowery clauses onward to the proof
That Gods there are, and deathless.
  Meant? I meant?
I have forgotten what I meant: my mind
Stumbles, and all my faculties are lamed.

'Look where another of our Gods, the
  Sun,
Apollo, Delius, or of older use
All-seeing Hyperion—what you will—
Has mounted yonder; since he never
  sware,
Except his wrath were wreak'd on wretched
  man,
That he would only shine among the dead
Hereafter; tales! for never yet on earth
Could dead flesh creep, or bits of roast-
  ing ox
Moan round the spit—nor knows he what
  he sees;
King of the East altho' he seem, and girt
With song and flame and fragrance, slowly
  lifts
His golden feet on those empurpled stairs
That climb into the windy halls of heaven:
And here he glances on an eye new-born,
And gets for greeting but a wail of pain;
And here he stays upon a freezing orb
That fain would gaze upon him to the last;
And here upon a yellow eyelid fall'n
And closed by those who mourn a friend
  in vain,
Not thankful that his troubles are no more.
And me, altho' his fire is on my face

LUCRETIUS

Blinding, he sees not, nor at all can tell
Whether I mean this day to end myself,
Or lend an ear to Plato where he says,
That men like soldiers may not quit the
post
Allotted by the Gods: but he that holds
The Gods are careless, wherefore need he
care
Greatly for them, nor rather plunge at
once,
Being troubled, wholly out of sight, and
sink
Past earthquake—ay, and gout and stone,
that break
Body toward death, and palsy, death-in-
life,
And wretched age—and worst disease of
all,
These prodigies of myriad nakednesses,
And twisted shapes of lust, unspeakable,
Abominable, strangers at my hearth
Not welcome, harpies miring every dish,
The phantom husks of something foully
done,
And fleeting thro' the boundless uni-
verse,
And blasting the long quiet of my breast
With animal heat and dire insanity?

'How should the mind, except it loved
them, clasp
These idols to herself? or do they fly
Now thinner, and now thicker, like the
flakes
In a fall of snow, and so press in, perforce
Of multitude, as crowds that in an hour
Of civic tumult jam the doors, and bear
The keepers down, and throng, their rags
and they
The basest, far into that council-hall
Where sit the best and stateliest of the
land?

'Can I not fling this horror off me again,
Seeing with how great ease Nature can
smile,
Balmier and nobler from her bath of storm,
At random ravage? and how easily
The mountain there has cast his cloudy
slough,
Now towering o'er him in serenest air,

A mountain o'er a mountain,—ay, and
within
All hollow as the hopes and fears of men?

'But who was he, that in the garden
snared
Picus and Faunus, rustic Gods? a tale
To laugh at—more to laugh at in myself—
For look! what is it? there? yon arbutus
Totters; a noiseless riot underneath
Strikes through the wood, sets all the tops
quivering—
The mountain quickens into Nymph and
Faun;
And here an Oread—how the sun delights
To glance and shift about her slippery
sides,
And rosy knees and supple roundedness,
And budded bosom-peaks—who this way
runs
Before the rest—A satyr, a satyr, see,
Follows; but him I proved impossible;
Twy-natured is no nature: yet he draws
Nearer and nearer, and I scan him now
Beastlier than any phantom of his kind
That ever butted his rough brother-brute
For lust or lusty blood or provender:
I hate, abhor, spit, sicken at him; and she
Loathes him as well; such a precipitate
heel,
Fledged as it were with Mercury's ankle-
wing,
Whirls her to me: but will she fling herself,
Shameless upon me? Catch her, goat-foot:
nay,
Hide, hide them, million-myrtled wilder-
ness,
And cavern-shadowing laurels, hide! do I
wish—
What?—that the bush were leafless? or to
whelm
All of them in one massacre? O ye Gods,
I know you careless, yet, behold, to you
From childly wont and ancient use I call—
I thought I lived securely as yourselves—
No lewdness, narrowing envy, monkey-
spite,
No madness of ambition, avarice, none:
No larger feast than under plane or pine
With neighbours laid along the grass, to
take

152

Only such cups as left us friendly-warm,
Affirming each his own philosophy—
Nothing to mar the sober majesties
Of settled, sweet, Epicurean life.
But now it seems some unseen monster lays
His vast and filthy hands upon my will,
Wrenching it backward into his; and spoils
My bliss in being; and it was not great;
For save when shutting reasons up in
   rhythm,
Or Heliconian honey in living words,
To make a truth less harsh, I often grew
Tired of so much within our little life,
Or of so little in our little life—
Poor little life that toddles half an hour
Crown'd with a flower or two, and there
   an end—
And since the nobler pleasure seems to
   fade,
Why should I, beastlike as I find myself,
Not manlike end myself?—our privilege—
What beast has heart to do it? And what
   man,
What Roman would be dragg'd in triumph
   thus?
Not I; not he, who bears one name with
   her
Whose death-blow struck the dateless
   doom of kings,
When, brooking not the Tarquin in her
   veins,
She made her blood in sight of Collatine
And all his peers, flushing the guiltless air,
Spout from the maiden fountain in her
   heart.
And from it sprang the Commonwealth,
   which breaks
As I am breaking now!

   'And therefore now
Let her, that is the womb and tomb of all,
Great Nature, take, and forcing far apart
Those blind beginnings that have made
   me man,
Dash them anew together at her will
Thro' all her cycles—into man once more,

Or beast or bird or fish, or opulent flower:
But till this cosmic order everywhere
Shatter'd into one earthquake in one day
Cracks all to pieces,—and that hour per-
   haps
Is not so far when momentary man
Shall seem no more a something to himself,
But he, his hopes and hates, his homes and
   fanes,
And even his bones long laid within the
   grave,
The very sides of the grave itself shall pass,
Vanishing, atom and void, atom and void,
Into the unseen for ever,—till that hour,
My golden work in which I told a truth
That stays the rolling Ixionian wheel,
And numbs the Fury's ringlet-snake, and
   plucks
The mortal soul from out immortal hell,
Shall stand: ay, surely: then it fails at last
And perishes as I must; for O Thou,
Passionless bride, divine Tranquillity,
Yearn'd after by the wisest of the wise,
Who fail to find thee, being as thou art
Without one pleasure and without one
   pain,
Howbeit I know thou surely must be mine
Or soon or late, yet out of season, thus
I woo thee roughly, for thou carest not
How roughly men may woo thee so they
   win—
Thus—thus: the soul flies out and dies in
   the air.'

With that he drove the knife into his
   side:
She heard him raging, heard him fall;
   ran in,
Beat breast, tore hair, cried out upon her-
   self
As having fail'd in duty to him, shriek'd
That she but meant to win him back, fell
   on him,
Clasp'd, kiss'd him, wail'd: he answer'd,
   'Care not thou!
Thy duty? What is duty? Fare thee well!'

THE PRINCESS

A MEDLEY

SIR Walter Vivian all a summer's day
Gave his broad lawns until the set of sun
Up to the people: thither flock'd at noon
His tenants, wife and child, and thither
  half
The neighbouring borough with their
  Institute
Of which he was the patron. I was there
From college, visiting the son,—the son
A Walter too,—with others of our set,
Five others: we were seven at Vivian-place.

And me that morning Walter show'd the
  house,
Greek, set with busts: from vases in the
  hall
Flowers of all heavens, and lovelier than
  their names,
Grew side by side; and on the pavement
  lay
Carved stones of the Abbey-ruin in the
  park,
Huge Ammonites, and the first bones of
  Time;
And on the tables every clime and age
Jumbled together; celts and calumets,
Claymore and snowshoe, toys in lava, fans
Of sandal, amber, ancient rosaries,
Laborious orient ivory sphere in sphere,
The cursed Malayan crease, and battle-
  clubs
From the isles of palm: and higher on the
  walls,
Betwixt the monstrous horns of elk and
  deer,
His own forefathers' arms and armour
  hung.

And 'this' he said 'was Hugh's at Agin-
  court;
And that was old Sir Ralph's at Ascalon:
A good knight he! we keep a chronicle
With all about him'—which he brought,
  and I
Dived in a hoard of tales that dealt with
  knights,

Half-legend, half-historic, counts and kings
Who laid about them at their wills and
  died;
And mixt with these, a lady, one that
  arm'd
Her own fair head, and sallying thro' the
  gate,
Had beat her foes with slaughter from her
  walls.

'O miracle of women,' said the book,
'O noble heart who, being strait-besieged
By this wild king to force her to his wish,
Nor bent, nor broke, nor shunn'd a
  soldier's death,
But now when all was lost or seem'd as
  lost—
Her stature more than mortal in the burst
Of sunrise, her arm lifted, eyes on fire—
Brake with a blast of trumpets from the
  gate,
And, falling on them like a thunderbolt,
She trampled some beneath her horses'
  heels,
And some were whelm'd with missiles of
  the wall,
And some were push'd with lances from
  the rock,
And part were drown'd within the whirling
  brook:
O miracle of noble womanhood!'

So sang the gallant glorious chronicle;
And, I all rapt in this, 'Come out,' he said,
'To the Abbey: there is Aunt Elizabeth
And sister Lilia with the rest.' We went
(I kept the book and had my finger in it)
Down thro' the park: strange was the sight
  to me;
For all the sloping pasture murmur'd, sown
With happy faces and with holiday.
There moved the multitude, a thousand
  heads:
The patient leaders of their Institute
Taught them with facts. One rear'd a font
  of stone
And drew, from butts of water on the slope,

154

The fountain of the moment, playing, now
A twisted snake, and now a rain of pearls,
Or steep-up spout whereon the gilded ball
Danced like a wisp: and somewhat lower
    down
A man with knobs and wires and vials fired
A cannon: Echo answer'd in her sleep
From hollow fields: and here were tele-
    scopes
For azure views; and there a group of girls
In circle waited, whom the electric shock
Dislink'd with shrieks and laughter: round
    the lake
A little clock-work steamer paddling plied
And shook the lilies: perch'd about the
    knolls
A dozen angry models jetted steam:
A petty railway ran: a fire-balloon
Rose gem-like up before the dusky groves
And dropt a fairy parachute and past:
And there thro' twenty posts of telegraph
They flash'd a saucy message to and fro
Between the mimic stations; so that sport
Went hand in hand with Science; other-
    where
Pure sport: a herd of boys with clamour
    bowl'd
And stump'd the wicket; babies roll'd
    about
Like tumbled fruit in grass; and men and
    maids
Arranged a country dance, and flew thro'
    light
And shadow, while the twangling violin
Struck up with Soldier-laddie, and over-
    head
The broad ambrosial aisles of lofty lime
Made noise with bees and breeze from end
    to end.

  Strange was the sight and smacking of
    the time;
And long we gazed, but satiated at length
Came to the ruins. High-arch'd and ivy-
    claspt,
Of finest Gothic lighter than a fire,
Thro' one wide chasm of time and frost
    they gave
The park, the crowd, the house; but all
    within
The sward was trim as any garden lawn:

And here we lit on Aunt Elizabeth,
And Lilia with the rest, and lady friends
From neighbour seats: and there was
    Ralph himself,
A broken statue propt against the wall,
As gay as any. Lilia, wild with sport,
Half child half woman as she was, had
    wound
A scarf of orange round the stony helm,
And robed the shoulders in a rosy silk,
That made the old warrior from his ivied
    nook
Glow like a sunbeam: near his tomb a feast
Shone, silver-set; about it lay the guests,
And there we join'd them: then the maiden
    Aunt
Took this fair day for text, and from it
    preach'd
An universal culture for the crowd,
And all things great; but we, unworthier,
    told
Of college: he had climb'd across the
    spikes,
And he had squeezed himself betwixt the
    bars,
And he had breathed the Proctor's dogs;
    and one
Discuss'd his tutor, rough to common men,
But honeying at the whisper of a lord;
And one the Master, as a rogue in grain
Veneer'd with sanctimonious theory.

  But while they talk'd, above their heads
    I saw
The feudal warrior lady-clad; which brought
My book to mind: and opening this I read
Of old Sir Ralph a page or two that rang
With tilt and tourney; then the tale of her
That drove her foes with slaughter from
    her walls,
And much I praised her nobleness, and
    'Where,'
Ask'd Walter, patting Lilia's head (she lay
Beside him) 'lives there such a woman
    now?'

  Quick answer'd Lilia 'There are thou-
    sands now
Such women, but convention beats them
    down:
It is but bringing up; no more than that:

155

You men have done it: how I hate you all!
Ah, were I something great! I wish I were
Some mighty poetess, I would shame you
then,
That love to keep us children! O I wish
That I were some great princess, I would
build
Far off from men a college like a man's,
And I would teach them all that men are
taught;
We are twice as quick!' And here she shook
aside
The hand that play'd the patron with her
curls.

And one said smiling 'Pretty were the
sight
If our old halls could change their sex, and
flaunt
With prudes for proctors, dowagers for
deans,
And sweet girl-graduates in their golden
hair.
I think they should not wear our rusty
gowns,
But move as rich as Emperor-moths, or
Ralph
Who shines so in the corner; yet I fear,
If there were many Lilias in the brood,
However deep you might embower the nest,
Some boy would spy it.'
                              At this upon the sward
She tapt her tiny silken-sandal'd foot:
'That's your light way; but I would make
it death
For any male thing but to peep at us.'

Petulant she spoke, and at her self she
laugh'd;
A rosebud set with little wilful thorns,
And sweet as English air could make her,
she:
But Walter hail'd a score of names upon
her,
And 'petty Ogress,' and 'ungrateful Puss,'
And swore he long'd at college, only long'd,
All else was well, for she-society.
They boated and they cricketed; they talk'd
At wine, in clubs, of art, of politics;
They lost their weeks; they vext the souls
of deans;

They rode; they betted; made a hundred
friends,
And caught the blossom of the flying
terms,
But miss'd the mignonette of Vivian-place,
The little hearth-flower Lilia. Thus he
spoke,
Part banter, part affection.
                              'True,' she said,
'We doubt not that. O yes, you miss'd us
much.
I'll stake my ruby ring upon it you did.'

She held it out; and as a parrot turns
Up thro' gilt wires a crafty loving eye,
And takes a lady's finger with all care,
And bites it for true heart and not for harm,
So he with Lilia's. Daintily she shriek'd
And wrung it. 'Doubt my word again!' he
said.
'Come, listen! here is proof that you were
miss'd:
We seven stay'd at Christmas up to read;
And there we took one tutor as to read:
The hard-grain'd Muses of the cube and
square
Were out of season: never man, I think,
So moulder'd in a sinecure as he:
For while our cloisters echo'd frosty feet,
And our long walks were stript as bare as
brooms,
We did but talk you over, pledge you all
In wassail; often, like as many girls—
Sick for the hollies and the yews of home—
As many little trifling Lilias—play'd
Charades and riddles as at Christmas here,
And what's my thought and when and where
and how,
And often told a tale from mouth to mouth
As here at Christmas.'
                              She remember'd that:
A pleasant game, she thought: she liked it
more
Than magic music, forfeits, all the rest.
But these—what kind of tales did men tell
men,
She wonder'd, by themselves?
                              A half-disdain
Perch'd on the pouted blossom of her lips:
And Walter nodded at me; 'He began,
The rest would follow, each in turn; and so

We forged a sevenfold story. Kind? what
    kind?
Chimeras, crotchets, Christmas solecisms,
Seven-headed monsters only made to kill
Time by the fire in winter.'
               'Kill him now,
The tyrant! kill him in the summer too,'
Said Lilia; 'Why not now?' the maiden
    Aunt.
'Why not a summer's as a winter's tale?
A tale for summer as befits the time,
And something it should be to suit the
    place,
Heroic, for a hero lies beneath,
Grave, solemn!'
        Walter warp'd his mouth at this
To something so mock-solemn, that I
    laugh'd
And Lilia woke with sudden-shrilling
    mirth
An echo like a ghostly woodpecker,
Hid in the ruins; till the maiden Aunt
(A little sense of wrong had touch'd her
    face
With colour) turn'd to me with 'As you
    will;
Heroic if you will, or what you will,
Or be yourself your hero if you will.'

'Take Lilia, then, for heroine,' clamour'd
    he,
'And make her some great Princess, six
    feet high,
Grand, epic, homicidal; and be you
The Prince to win her!'
        'Then follow me, the Prince,'
I answer'd, 'each be hero in his turn!
Seven and yet one, like shadows in a
    dream.—
Heroic seems our Princess as required—
But something made to suit with Time
    and place,
A Gothic ruin and a Grecian house,
A talk of college and of ladies' rights,
A feudal knight in silken masquerade,
And, yonder, shrieks and strange experi-
    ments
For which the good Sir Ralph had burnt
    them all—
This *were* a medley! we should have him
    back

Who told the "Winter's tale" to do it for us.
No matter: we will say whatever comes.
And let the ladies sing us, if they will,
From time to time, some ballad or a song
To give us breathing-space.'
             So I began,
And the rest follow'd: and the women sang
Between the rougher voices of the men,
Like linnets in the pauses of the wind:
And here I give the story and the songs.

I

A prince I was, blue-eyed, and fair in face,
Of temper amorous, as the first of May,
With lengths of yellow ringlet, like a girl,
For on my cradle shone the Northern star.

There lived an ancient legend in our
    house.
Some sorcerer, whom a far-off grandsire
    burnt
Because he cast no shadow, had foretold,
Dying, that none of all our blood should
    know
The shadow from the substance, and that
    one
Should come to fight with shadows and to
    fall.
For so, my mother said, the story ran.
And, truly, waking dreams were, more or
    less,
An old and strange affection of the house.
Myself too had weird seizures, Heaven
    knows what:
On a sudden in the midst of men and day,
And while I walk'd and talk'd as hereto-
    fore,
I seem'd to move among a world of ghosts,
And feel myself the shadow of a dream.
Our great court-Galen poised his gilt-head
    cane,
And paw'd his beard, and mutter'd 'cata-
    lepsy.'
My mother pitying made a thousand
    prayers;
My mother was as mild as any saint,
Half-canonized by all that look'd on her,
So gracious was her tact and tenderness:
But my good father thought a king a king;
He cared not for the affection of the house;
He held his sceptre like a pedant's wand

157

To lash offence, and with long arms and
    hands
Reach'd out, and pick'd offenders from the
    mass
For judgment.
          Now it chanced that I had been,
While life was yet in bud and blade,
    betroth'd
To one, a neighbouring Princess: she to me
Was proxy-wedded with a bootless calf
At eight years old; and still from time to
    time
Came murmurs of her beauty from the
    South,
And of her brethren, youths of puissance;
And still I wore her picture by my heart,
And one dark tress; and all around them
    both
Sweet thoughts would swarm as bees about
    their queen.

    But when the days drew nigh that I
    should wed,
My father sent ambassadors with furs
And jewels, gifts, to fetch her: these
    brought back
A present, a great labour of the loom;
And therewithal an answer vague as wind:
Besides, they saw the king; he took the gifts;
He said there was a compact; that was true:
But then she had a will; was he to blame?
And maiden fancies; loved to live alone
Among her women; certain, would not
    wed.

    That morning in the presence room I
    stood
With Cyril and with Florian, my two
    friends:
The first, a gentleman of broken means
(His father's fault) but given to starts and
    bursts
Of revel; and the last, my other heart,
And almost my half-self, for still we moved
Together, twinn'd as horse's ear and eye.

    Now, while they spake, I saw my father's
    face
Grow long and troubled like a rising moon,
Inflamed with wrath: he started on his feet,
Tore the king's letter, snow'd it down, and
    rent

The wonder of the loom thro' warp and
    woof
From skirt to skirt; and at the last he sware
That he would send a hundred thousand
    men,
And bring her in a whirlwind: then he
    chew'd
The thrice-turn'd cud of wrath, and cook'd
    his spleen,
Communing with his captains of the war.

    At last I spoke. 'My father, let me go.
It cannot be but some gross error lies
In this report, this answer of a king,
Whom all men rate as kind and hospitable:
Or, maybe, I myself, my bride once seen,
Whate'er my grief to find her less than
    fame,
May rue the bargain made.' And Florian
    said:
'I have a sister at the foreign court,
Who moves about the Princess; she, you
    know,
Who wedded with a nobleman from thence:
He, dying lately, left her, as I hear,
The lady of three castles in that land:
Thro' her this matter might be sifted
    clean.'
And Cyril whisper'd: 'Take me with you
    too.'
Then laughing 'what, if these weird
    seizures come
Upon you in those lands, and no one near
To point you out the shadow from the
    truth!
Take me: I'll serve you better in a strait;
I grate on rusty hinges here:' but 'No!'
Roar'd the rough king, 'you shall not; we
    ourself
Will crush her pretty maiden fancies dead
In iron gauntlets: break the council up.'

    But when the council broke, I rose and
    past
Thro' the wild woods that hung about the
    town;
Found a still place, and pluck'd her like-
    ness out;
Laid it on flowers, and watch'd it lying
    bathed
In the green gleam of dewy-tassell'd trees:

What were those fancies? wherefore break
  her troth?
Proud look'd the lips: but while I medi-
  tated
A wind arose and rush'd upon the South,
And shook the songs, the whispers, and
  the shrieks
Of the wild woods together; and a Voice
Went with it, 'Follow, follow, thou shalt
  win.'

Then, ere the silver sickle of that month
Became her golden shield, I stole from
  court
With Cyril and with Florian, unperceived,
Cat-footed thro' the town and half in dread
To hear my father's clamour at our backs
With Ho! from some bay-window shake
  the night;
But all was quiet: from the bastion'd walls
Like threaded spiders, one by one, we
  dropt,
And flying reach'd the frontier: then we
  crost
To a livelier land; and so by tilth and
  grange,
And vines, and blowing bosks of wilder-
  ness,
We gain'd the mother-city thick with
  towers,
And in the imperial palace found the king.

His name was Gama; crack'd and small
  his voice,
But bland the smile that like a wrinkling
  wind
On glassy water drove his cheek in lines;
A little dry old man, without a star,
Not like a king: three days he feasted us,
And on the fourth I spake of why we came,
And my betroth'd. 'You do us, Prince,' he
  said,
Airing a snowy hand and signet gem,
'All honour. We remember love ourselves
In our sweet youth: there did a compact pass
Long summers back, a kind of ceremony—
I think the year in which our olives fail'd.
I would you had her, Prince, with all my
  heart,
With my full heart: but there were widows
  here,

Two widows, Lady Psyche, Lady Blanche;
They fed her theories, in and out of place
Maintaining that with equal husbandry
The woman were an equal to the man.
They harp'd on this; with this our ban-
  quets rang;
Our dances broke and buzz'd in knots of
  talk;
Nothing but this; my very ears were hot
To hear them: knowledge, so my daughter
  held,
Was all in all: they had but been, she
  thought,
As children; they must lose the child,
  assume
The woman: then, Sir, awful odes she
  wrote,
Too awful, sure, for what they treated of,
But all she is and does is awful; odes
About this losing of the child; and rhymes
And dismal lyrics, prophesying change
Beyond all reason: these the women sang;
And they that know such things—I sought
  but peace;
No critic I—would call them masterpieces:
They master'd me. At last she begg'd a
  boon,
A certain summer-palace which I have
Hard by your father's frontier: I said no,
Yet being an easy man, gave it: and there,
All wild to found an University
For maidens, on the spur she fled; and
  more
We know not,—only this: they see no men,
Not ev'n her brother Arac, nor the twins
Her brethren, tho' they love her, look upon
  her
As on a kind of paragon; and I
(Pardon me saying it) were much loth to
  breed
Dispute betwixt myself and mine: but
  since
(And I confess with right) you think me
  bound
In some sort, I can give you letters to her;
And yet, to speak the truth, I rate your
  chance
Almost at naked nothing.'
                        Thus the king;
And I, tho' nettled that he seem'd to slur
With garrulous ease and oily courtesies

Our formal compact, yet, not less (all frets
But chafing me on fire to find my bride)
Went forth again with both my friends.
    We rode
Many a long league back to the North.
    At last
From hills, that look'd across a land of
    hope,
We dropt with evening on a rustic town
Set in a gleaming river's crescent-curve,
Close at the boundary of the liberties;
There, enter'd an old hostel, call'd mine
    host
To council, plied him with his richest
    wines,
And show'd the late-writ letters of the king.

He with a long low sibilation, stared
As blank as death in marble; then ex-
    claim'd
Averring it was clear against all rules
For any man to go: but as his brain
Began to mellow, 'If the king,' he said,
'Had given us letters, was he bound to
    speak?
The king would bear him out;' and at the
    last—
The summer of the vine in all his veins—
'No doubt that we might make it worth his
    while.
She once had past that way; he heard her
    speak;
She scared him; life! he never saw the like;
She look'd as grand as doomsday and as
    grave:
And he, he reverenced his liege-lady there;
He always made a point to post with mares;
His daughter and his housemaid were the
    boys:
The land, he understood, for miles about
Was till'd by women; all the swine were
    sows,
And all the dogs'—
            But while he jested thus,
A thought flash'd thro' me which I clothed
    in act,
Remembering how we three presented
    Maid
Or Nymph, or Goddess, at high tide of
    feast,
In masque or pageant at my father's court.

We sent mine host to purchase female gear;
He brought it, and himself, a sight to shake
The midriff of despair with laughter, holp
To lace us up, till, each, in maiden plumes
We rustled: him we gave a costly bribe
To guerdon silence, mounted our good
    steeds,
And boldly ventured on the liberties.

We follow'd up the river as we rode,
And rode till midnight when the college
    lights
Began to glitter firefly-like in copse
And linden alley: then we past an arch,
Whereon a woman-statue rose with wings
From four wing'd horses dark against the
    stars;
And some inscription ran along the front,
But deep in shadow: further on we gain'd
A little street half garden and half house;
But scarce could hear each other speak for
    noise
Of clocks and chimes, like silver hammers
    falling
On silver anvils, and the splash and stir
Of fountains spouted up and showering
    down
In meshes of the jasmine and the rose:
And all about us peal'd the nightingale,
Rapt in her song, and careless of the snare.

There stood a bust of Pallas for a sign,
By two sphere lamps blazon'd like Heaven
    and Earth
With constellation and with continent,
Above an entry: riding in, we call'd;
A plump-arm'd Ostleress and a stable
    wench
Came running at the call, and help'd us
    down.
Then stept a buxom hostess forth, and
    sail'd,
Full-blown, before us into rooms which
    gave
Upon a pillar'd porch, the bases lost
In laurel: her we ask'd of that and this,
And who were tutors. 'Lady Blanche' she
    said,
'And Lady Psyche.' 'Which was prettiest,
Best-natured?' 'Lady Psyche.' 'Hers are
    we,'

One voice, we cried; and I sat down and
    wrote,
In such a hand as when a field of corn
Bows all its ears before the roaring East;

'Three ladies of the Northern empire pray
Your Highness would enroll them with
    your own,
As Lady Psyche's pupils.'
                This I seal'd:
The seal was Cupid bent above a scroll,
And o'er his head Uranian Venus hung,
And raised the blinding bandage from his
    eyes:
I gave the letter to be sent with dawn;
And then to bed, where half in doze I
    seem'd
To float about a glimmering night, and
    watch
A full sea glazed with muffled moonlight,
    swell
On some dark shore just seen that it was
    rich.

II

As thro' the land at eve we went,
  And pluck'd the ripen'd ears,
We fell out, my wife and I,
O we fell out I know not why,
  And kiss'd again with tears.
And blessings on the falling out
  That all the more endears,
When we fall out with those we love
  And kiss again with tears!
For when we came where lies the child
  We lost in other years,
There above the little grave,
O there above the little grave,
  We kiss'd again with tears.

At break of day the College Portress came:
She brought us Academic silks, in hue
The lilac, with a silken hood to each,
And zoned with gold; and now when these
    were on,
And we as rich as moths from dusk cocoons,
She, curtseying her obeisance, let us know
The Princess Ida waited: out we paced,
I first, and following thro' the porch that
    sang
All round with laurel, issued in a court
Compact of lucid marbles, boss'd with
    lengths
Of classic frieze, with ample awnings gay

Betwixt the pillars, and with great urns of
    flowers.
The Muses and the Graces, group'd in
    threes,
Enring'd a billowing fountain in the midst;
And here and there on lattice edges lay
Or book or lute; but hastily we past,
And up a flight of stairs into the hall.

There at a board by tome and paper sat,
With two tame leopards couch'd beside her
    throne,
All beauty compass'd in a female form,
The Princess; liker to the inhabitant
Of some clear planet close upon the Sun,
Than our man's earth; such eyes were in
    her head,
And so much grace and power, breathing
    down
From over her arch'd brows, with every
    turn
Lived thro' her to the tips of her long
    hands,
And to her feet. She rose her height, and
    said:

'We give you welcome: not without re-
    dound
Of use and glory to yourselves ye come,
The first-fruits of the stranger: aftertime,
And that full voice which circles round the
    grave,
Will rank you nobly, mingled up with me.
What! are the ladies of your land so tall?'
'We of the court' said Cyril. 'From the
    court'
She answer'd, 'then ye know the Prince?'
    and he:
'The climax of his age! as tho' there were
One rose in all the world, your Highness
    that,
He worships your ideal:' she replied:
'We scarcely thought in our own hall to
    hear
This barren verbiage, current among men,
Light coin, the tinsel clink of compliment.
Your flight from out your bookless wilds
    would seem
As arguing love of knowledge and of power;
Your language proves you still the child.
    Indeed,

We dream not of him: when we set our
  hand
To this great work, we purposed with our-
  self
Never to wed. You likewise will do well,
Ladies, in entering here, to cast and fling
The tricks, which make us toys of men,
  that so,
Some future time, if so indeed you will,
You may with those self-styled our lords
  ally
Your fortunes, justlier balanced, scale with
  scale.'

  At those high words, we conscious of
  ourselves,
Perused the matting; then an officer
Rose up, and read the statutes, such as
  these:
Not for three years to correspond with
  home;
Not for three years to cross the liberties;
Not for three years to speak with any men;
And many more, which hastily subscribed,
We enter'd on the boards: and 'Now,' she
  cried,
'Ye are green wood, see ye warp not. Look,
  our hall!
Our statues!—not of those that men desire,
Sleek Odalisques, or oracles of mode,
Nor stunted squaws of West or East; but
  she
That taught the Sabine how to rule, and
  she
The foundress of the Babylonian wall,
The Carian Artemisia strong in war,
The Rhodope, that built the pyramid,
Clelia, Cornelia, with the Palmyrene
That fought Aurelian, and the Roman
  brows
Of Agrippina. Dwell with these, and lose
Convention, since to look on noble forms
Makes noble thro' the sensuous organism
That which is higher. O lift your natures
  up:
Embrace our aims: work out your freedom.
  Girls,
Knowledge is now no more a fountain
  seal'd:
Drink deep, until the habits of the slave,
The sins of emptiness, gossip and spite

And slander, die. Better not be at all
Than not be noble. Leave us: you may go:
To-day the Lady Psyche will harangue
The fresh arrivals of the week before;
For they press in from all the provinces,
And fill the hive.'
           She spoke, and bowing waved
Dismissal: back again we crost the court
To Lady Psyche's: as we enter'd in,
There sat along the forms, like morning
  doves
That sun their milky bosoms on the thatch,
A patient range of pupils; she herself
Erect behind a desk of satin-wood,
A quick brunette, well-moulded, falcon-
  eyed,
And on the hither side, or so she look'd,
Of twenty summers. At her left, a child,
In shining draperies, headed like a star,
Her maiden babe, a double April old,
Aglaïa slept. We sat: the Lady glanced:
Then Florian, but no livelier than the dame
That whisper'd 'Asses' ears,' among the
  sedge,
'My sister.' 'Comely, too, by all that's fair,'
Said Cyril. 'O hush, hush!' and she began.

'This world was once a fluid haze of
  light,
Till toward the centre set the starry tides,
And eddied into suns, that wheeling cast
The planets: then the monster, then the
  man;
Tattoo'd or woaded, winter-clad in skins,
Raw from the prime, and crushing down
  his mate;
As yet we find in barbarous isles, and here
Among the lowest.'
           Thereupon she took
A bird's-eye-view of all the ungracious
  past;
Glanced at the legendary Amazon
As emblematic of a nobler age;
Appraised the Lycian custom, spoke of
  those
That lay at wine with Lar and Lucumo;
Ran down the Persian, Grecian, Roman
  lines
Of empire, and the woman's state in each,
How far from just; till warming with her
  theme

She fulmined out her scorn of laws Salique
And little-footed China, touch'd on
Mahomet
With much contempt, and came to
chivalry:
When some respect, however slight, was
paid
To woman, superstition all awry:
However then commenced the dawn: a
beam
Had slanted forward, falling in a land
Of promise; fruit would follow. Deep,
indeed,
Their debt of thanks to her who first had
dared
To leap the rotten pales of prejudice,
Disyoke their necks from custom, and assert
None lordlier than themselves but that
which made
Woman and man. She had founded; they
must build.
Here might they learn whatever men were
taught:
Let them not fear: some said their heads
were less:
Some men's were small; not they the least
of men;
For often fineness compensated size;
Besides the brain was like the hand, and
grew
With using; thence the man's, if more was
more;
He took advantage of his strength to be
First in the field: some ages had been lost;
But woman ripen'd earlier, and her life
Was longer; and albeit their glorious names
Were fewer, scatter'd stars, yet since in
truth
The highest is the measure of the man,
And not the Kaffir, Hottentot, Malay,
Nor those horn-handed breakers of the
glebe,
But Homer, Plato, Verulam; even so
With woman: and in arts of government
Elizabeth and others; arts of war
The peasant Joan and others; arts of grace
Sappho and others vied with any man:
And, last not least, she who had left her
place,
And bow'd her state to them, that they
might grow

To use and power on this Oasis, lapt
In the arms of leisure, sacred from the
blight
Of ancient influence and scorn.

At last
She rose upon a wind of prophecy
Dilating on the future; 'everywhere
Two heads in council, two beside the
hearth,
Two in the tangled business of the world,
Two in the liberal offices of life,
Two plummets dropt for one to sound the
abyss
Of science, and the secrets of the mind:
Musician, painter, sculptor, critic, more:
And everywhere the broad and bounteous
Earth
Should bear a double growth of those rare
souls,
Poets, whose thoughts enrich the blood of
the world.'

She ended here, and beckon'd us: the
rest
Parted; and, glowing full-faced welcome,
she
Began to address us, and was moving on
In gratulation, till as when a boat
Tacks, and the slacken'd sail flaps, all her
voice
Faltering and fluttering in her throat, she
cried
'My brother!' 'Well, my sister.' 'O,' she
said,
'What do you here? and in this dress? and
these?
Why who are these? a wolf within the fold!
A pack of wolves! the Lord be gracious
to me!
A plot, a plot, a plot, to ruin all!'
'No plot, no plot,' he answer'd. 'Wretched
boy,
How saw you not the inscription on the
gate,
LET NO MAN ENTER IN ON PAIN OF DEATH?'
'And if I had,' he answer'd, 'who could
think
The softer Adams of your Academe,
O sister, Sirens tho' they be, were such
As chanted on the blanching bones of
men?'

'But you will find it otherwise' she said.
'You jest: ill jesting with edge-tools! my vow
Binds me to speak, and O that iron will,
That axelike edge unturnable, our Head,
The Princess.' 'Well then, Psyche, take my life,
And nail me like a weasel on a grange
For warning: bury me beside the gate,
And cut this epitaph above my bones;
Here lies a brother by a sister slain,
All for the common good of womankind.'
'Let me die too,' said Cyril, 'having seen
And heard the Lady Psyche.'
          I struck in:
'Albeit so mask'd, Madam, I love the truth;
Receive it; and in me behold the Prince
Your countryman, affianced years ago
To the Lady Ida: here, for here she was,
And thus (what other way was left) I came.'
'O Sir, O Prince, I have no country, none;
If any, this; but none. Whate'er I was
Disrooted, what I am is grafted here.
Affianced, Sir? love-whispers may not breathe
Within this vestal limit, and how should I,
Who am not mine, say, live: the thunderbolt
Hangs silent; but prepare: I speak; it falls.'
'Yet pause,' I said: 'for that inscription there,
I think no more of deadly lurks therein,
Than in a clapper clapping in a garth,
To scare the fowl from fruit: if more there be,
If more and acted on, what follows? war;
Your own work marr'd: for this your Academe,
Whichever side be Victor, in the halloo
Will topple to the trumpet down, and pass
With all fair theories only made to gild
A stormless summer.' 'Let the Princess judge
Of that' she said: 'farewell, Sir—and to you.
I shudder at the sequel, but I go.'

'Are you that Lady Psyche,' I rejoin'd,
'The fifth in line from that old Florian,
Yet hangs his portrait in my father's hall

(The gaunt old Baron with his beetle brow
Sun-shaded in the heat of dusty fights)
As he bestrode my Grandsire, when he fell,
And all else fled? we point to it, and we say,
The loyal warmth of Florian is not cold,
But branches current yet in kindred veins.'
'Are you that Psyche,' Florian added; 'she
With whom I sang about the morning hills,
Flung ball, flew kite, and raced the purple fly,
And snared the squirrel of the glen? are you
That Psyche, wont to bind my throbbing brow,
To smoothe my pillow, mix the foaming draught
Of fever, tell me pleasant tales, and read
My sickness down to happy dreams? are you
That brother-sister Psyche, both in one?
You were that Psyche, but what are you now?'
'You are that Psyche,' Cyril said, 'for whom
I would be that for ever which I seem,
Woman, if I might sit beside your feet,
And glean your scatter'd sapience.'
          Then once more,
'Are you that Lady Psyche,' I began,
'That on her bridal morn before she past
From all her old companions, when the king
Kiss'd her pale cheek, declared that ancient ties
Would still be dear beyond the southern hills;
That were there any of our people there
In want or peril, there was one to hear
And help them? look! for such are these and I.'
'Are you that Psyche,' Florian ask'd, 'to whom,
In gentler days, your arrow-wounded fawn
Came flying while you sat beside the well?
The creature laid his muzzle on your lap,
And sobb'd, and you sobb'd with it, and the blood
Was sprinkled on your kirtle, and you wept.
That was fawn's blood, not brother's, yet you wept.
O by the bright head of my little niece,

You were that Psyche, and what are you
    now?'
'You are that Psyche,' Cyril said again,
'The mother of the sweetest little maid,
That ever crow'd for kisses.'
              'Out upon it!'
She answer'd, 'peace! and why should I
    not play
The Spartan Mother with emotion, be
The Lucius Junius Brutus of my kind?
Him you call great: he for the common
    weal,
The fading politics of mortal Rome,
As I might slay this child, if good need
    were,
Slew both his sons: and I, shall I, on whom
The secular emancipation turns
Of half this world, be swerved from right
    to save
A prince, a brother? a little will I yield.
Best so, perchance, for us, and well for you.
O hard, when love and duty clash! I fear
My conscience will not count me fleckless;
    yet—
Hear my conditions: promise (otherwise
You perish) as you came, to slip away
To-day, to-morrow, soon: it shall be said,
These women were too barbarous, would
    not learn;
They fled, who might have shamed us:
    promise, all.'

    What could we else, we promised each;
      and she,
Like some wild creature newly-caged,
    commenced
A to-and-fro, so pacing till she paused
By Florian; holding out her lily arms
Took both his hands, and smiling faintly
    said:
'I knew you at the first: tho' you have
    grown
You scarce have alter'd: I am sad and glad
To see you, Florian. *I* give thee to death
My brother! it was duty spoke, not I.
My needful seeming harshness, pardon it.
Our mother, is she well?'
              With that she kiss'd
His forehead, then, a moment after, clung
About him, and betwixt them blossom'd up
From out a common vein of memory

Sweet household talk, and phrases of the
    hearth,
And far allusion, till the gracious dews
Began to glisten and to fall: and while
They stood, so rapt, we gazing, came a
    voice,
'I brought a message here from Lady
    Blanche.'
Back started she, and turning round we
    saw
The Lady Blanche's daughter where she
    stood,
Melissa, with her hand upon the lock,
A rosy blonde, and in a college gown,
That clad her like an April daffodilly
(Her mother's colour) with her lips apart,
And all her thoughts as fair within her eyes,
As bottom agates seen to wave and float
In crystal currents of clear morning seas.

    So stood that same fair creature at the
    door.
Then Lady Psyche, 'Ah—Melissa—you!
You heard us?' and Melissa, 'O pardon me
I heard, I could not help it, did not wish:
But, dearest Lady, pray you fear me not,
Nor think I bear that heart within my
    breast,
To give three gallant gentlemen to death.'
'I trust you,' said the other, 'for we two
Were always friends, none closer, elm and
    vine:
But yet your mother's jealous tempera-
    ment—
Let not your prudence, dearest, drowse, or
    prove
The Danaïd of a leaky vase, for fear
This whole foundation ruin, and I lose
My honour, these their lives.' 'Ah, fear
    me not'
Replied Melissa; 'no—I would not tell,
No, not for all Aspasia's cleverness,
No, not to answer, Madam, all those hard
    things
That Sheba came to ask of Solomon.'
'Be it so' the other, 'that we still may lead
The new light up, and culminate in peace,
For Solomon may come to Sheba yet.'
Said Cyril, 'Madam, he the wisest man
Feasted the woman wisest then, in halls
Of Lebanonian cedar: nor should you

(Tho', Madam, *you* should answer, *we*
    would ask)
Less welcome find among us, if you came
Among us, debtors for our lives to you,
Myself for something more.' He said not
    what,
But 'Thanks,' she answer'd 'Go: we have
    been too long
Together: keep your hoods about the face;
They do so that affect abstraction here.
Speak little; mix not with the rest; and
    hold
Your promise: all, I trust, may yet be well.'

We turn'd to go, but Cyril took the child,
And held her round the knees against his
    waist,
And blew the swoll'n cheek of a trumpeter,
While Psyche watch'd them, smiling, and
    the child
Push'd her flat hand against his face and
    laugh'd;
And thus our conference closed.
               And then we stroll'd
For half the day thro' stately theatres
Bench'd crescent-wise. In each we sat, we
    heard
The grave Professor. On the lecture slate
The circle rounded under female hands
With flawless demonstration: follow'd then
A classic lecture, rich in sentiment,
With scraps of thundrous Epic lilted out
By violet-hooded Doctors, elegies
And quoted odes, and jewels five-words
    long
That on the stretch'd forefinger of all Time
Sparkle for ever: then we dipt in all
That treats of whatsoever is, the state,
The total chronicles of man, the mind,
The morals, something of the frame, the
    rock,
The star, the bird, the fish, the shell, the
    flower,
Electric, chemic laws, and all the rest,
And whatsoever can be taught and known;
Till like three horses that have broken
    fence,
And glutted all night long breast-deep in
    corn,
We issued gorged with knowledge, and I
    spoke:

'Why, Sirs, they do all this as well as we.'
'They hunt old trails' said Cyril 'very well;
But when did woman ever yet invent?'
'Ungracious!' answer'd Florian; 'have you
    learnt
No more from Psyche's lecture, you that
    talk'd
The trash that made me sick, and almost
    sad?'
'O trash' he said, 'but with a kernel in it.
Should I not call her wise, who made me
    wise?
And learnt? I learnt more from her in a
    flash,
Than if my brainpan were an empty hull,
And every Muse tumbled a science in.
A thousand hearts lie fallow in these halls,
And round these halls a thousand baby
    loves
Fly twanging headless arrows at the hearts,
Whence follows many a vacant pang; but O
With me, Sir, enter'd in the bigger boy,
The Head of all the golden-shafted firm,
The long-limb'd lad that had a Psyche too;
He cleft me thro' the stomacher; and now
What think you of it, Florian? do I chase
The substance or the shadow? will it hold?
I have no sorcerer's malison on me,
No ghostly hauntings like his Highness. I
Flatter myself that always everywhere
I know the substance when I see it. Well,
Are castles shadows? Three of them? Is
    she
The sweet proprietress a shadow? If not,
Shall those three castles patch my tatter'd
    coat?
For dear are those three castles to my wants,
And dear is sister Psyche to my heart,
And two dear things are one of double
    worth,
And much I might have said, but that my
    zone
Unmann'd me: then the Doctors! O to hear
The Doctors! O to watch the thirsty plants
Imbibing! once or twice I thought to roar,
To break my chain, to shake my mane:
    but thou,
Modulate me, Soul of mincing mimicry!
Make liquid treble of that bassoon, my
    throat;
Abase those eyes that ever loved to meet

Star-sisters answering under crescent
  brows;
Abate the stride, which speaks of man, and
  loose
A flying charm of blushes o'er this cheek,
Where they like swallows coming out of
  time
Will wonder why they came: but hark the
  bell
For dinner, let us go!'
             And in we stream'd
Among the columns, pacing staid and still
By twos and threes, till all from end to end
With beauties every shade of brown and fair
In colours gayer than the morning mist,
The long hall glitter'd like a bed of flowers.
How might a man not wander from his wits
Pierced thro' with eyes, but that I kept
  mine own
Intent on her, who rapt in glorious dreams,
The second-sight of some Astræan age,
Sat compass'd with professors: they, the
  while,
Discuss'd a doubt and tost it to and fro:
A clamour thicken'd, mixt with inmost
  terms
Of art and science: Lady Blanche alone
Of faded form and haughtiest lineaments,
With all her autumn tresses falsely brown,
Shot sidelong daggers at us, a tiger-cat
In act to spring.
         At last a solemn grace
Concluded, and we sought the gardens:
  there
One walk'd reciting by herself, and one
In this hand held a volume as to read,
And smoothed a petted peacock down with
  that:
Some to a low song oar'd a shallop by,
Or under arches of the marble bridge
Hung, shadow'd from the heat: some hid
  and sought
In the orange thickets: others tost a ball
Above the fountain-jets, and back again
With laughter: others lay about the lawns,
Of the older sort, and murmur'd that their
  May
Was passing: what was learning unto
  them?
They wish'd to marry; they could rule a
  house;

Men hated learned women: but we three
Sat muffled like the Fates; and often came
Melissa hitting all we saw with shafts
Of gentle satire, kin to charity,
That harm'd not: then day droopt; the
  chapel bells
Call'd us: we left the walks; we mixt with
  those
Six hundred maidens clad in purest white,
Before two streams of light from wall to
  wall,
While the great organ almost burst his
  pipes,
Groaning for power, and rolling thro' the
  court
A long melodious thunder to the sound
Of solemn psalms, and silver litanies,
The work of Ida, to call down from Heaven
A blessing on her labours for the world.

III

Sweet and low, sweet and low,
  Wind of the western sea,
Low, low, breathe and blow,
  Wind of the western sea!
Over the rolling waters go,
Come from the dying moon, and blow,
  Blow him again to me;
While my little one, while my pretty one, sleeps.

Sleep and rest, sleep and rest,
  Father will come to thee soon;
Rest, rest, on mother's breast,
  Father will come to thee soon;
Father will come to his babe in the nest,
Silver sails all out of the west
  Under the silver moon:
Sleep, my little one, sleep, my pretty one, sleep.

Morn in the white wake of the morning star
Came furrowing all the orient into gold.
We rose, and each by other drest with care
Descended to the court that lay three parts
In shadow, but the Muses' heads were
  touch'd
Above the darkness from their native East.

There while we stood beside the fount,
  and watch'd
Or seem'd to watch the dancing bubble,
  approach'd
Melissa, tinged with wan from lack of
  sleep,
Or grief, and glowing round her dewy eyes

The circled Iris of a night of tears;
'And fly,' she cried, 'O fly, while yet you
    may!
My mother knows:' and when I ask'd her
    'how,'
'My fault' she wept 'my fault! and yet not
    mine;
Yet mine in part. O hear me, pardon me.
My mother, 'tis her wont from night to
    night
To rail at Lady Psyche and her side.
She says the Princess should have been the
    Head,
Herself and Lady Psyche the two arms;
And so it was agreed when first they came;
But Lady Psyche was the right hand now,
And she the left, or not, or seldom used;
Hers more than half the students, all the
    love.
And so last night she fell to canvass you:
Her countrywomen! she did not envy her.
"Who ever saw such wild barbarians?
Girls?—more like men!" and at these
    words the snake,
My secret, seem'd to stir within my breast;
And oh, Sirs, could I help it, but my cheek
Began to burn and burn, and her lynx eye
To fix and make me hotter, till she laugh'd:
"O marvellously modest maiden, you!
Men! girls, like men! why, if they had been
    men
You need not set your thoughts in rubric
    thus
For wholesale comment." Pardon, I am
    shamed
That I must needs repeat for my excuse
What looks so little graceful: "men" (for
    still
My mother went revolving on the word)
"And so they are,—very like men indeed—
And with that woman closeted for hours!"
Then came these dreadful words out one
    by one,
"Why—these—*are*—men:" I shudder'd:
    "and you know it."
"O ask me nothing," I said: "And she
    knows too,
And she conceals it." So my mother
    clutch'd
The truth at once, but with no word from
    me;

And now thus early risen she goes to inform
The Princess: Lady Psyche will be crush'd;
But you may yet be saved, and therefore
    fly:
But heal me with your pardon ere you go.'

'What pardon, sweet Melissa, for a
    blush?'
Said Cyril: 'Pale one, blush again: than
    wear
Those lilies, better blush our lives away.
Yet let us breathe for one hour more in
    Heaven'
He added, 'lest some classic Angel speak
In scorn of us, "They mounted, Gany-
    medes,
To tumble, Vulcans, on the second morn."
But I will melt this marble into wax
To yield us farther furlough:' and he went.

Melissa shook her doubtful curls, and
    thought
He scarce would prosper. 'Tell us,' Florian
    ask'd,
'How grew this feud betwixt the right and
    left.'
'O long ago,' she said, 'betwixt these two
Division smoulders hidden; 'tis my mother,
Too jealous, often fretful as the wind
Pent in a crevice: much I bear with her:
I never knew my father, but she says
(God help her) she was wedded to a fool;
And still she rail'd against the state of
    things.
She had the care of Lady Ida's youth,
And from the Queen's decease she brought
    her up.
But when your sister came she won the
    heart
Of Ida: they were still together, grew
(For so they said themselves) inosculated;
Consonant chords that shiver to one note;
One mind in all things: yet my mother still
Affirms your Psyche thieved her theories,
And angled with them for her pupil's love:
She calls her plagiarist; I know not what:
But I must go: I dare not tarry,' and, light,
As flies the shadow of a bird, she fled.

Then murmur'd Florian gazing after her,
'An open-hearted maiden, true and pure.

If I could love, why this were she: how
    pretty
Her blushing was, and how she blush'd
    again,
As if to close with Cyril's random wish:
Not like your Princess cramm'd with erring
    pride,
Nor like poor Psyche whom she drags in
    tow.'

  'The crane,' I said, 'may chatter of the
    crane,
The dove may murmur of the dove, but I
An eagle clang an eagle to the sphere.
My princess, O my princess! true she errs,
But in her own grand way: being herself
Three times more noble than three score
    of men,
She sees herself in every woman else,
And so she wears her error like a crown
To blind the truth and me: for her, and
    her,
Hebes are they to hand ambrosia, mix
The nectar; but—ah she—whene'er she
    moves
The Samian Herè rises and she speaks
A Memnon smitten with the morning
    Sun.'

  So saying from the court we paced, and
    gain'd
The terrace ranged along the Northern
    front,
And leaning there on those balusters, high
Above the empurpled champaign, drank
    the gale
That blown about the foliage underneath,
And sated with the innumerable rose,
Beat balm upon our eyelids. Hither came
Cyril, and yawning 'O hard task,' he cried;
'No fighting shadows here! I forced a way
Thro' solid opposition crabb'd and gnarl'd.
Better to clear prime forests, heave and
    thump
A league of street in summer solstice down,
Than hammer at this reverend gentle-
    woman.
I knock'd and, bidden, enter'd; found her
    there
At point to move, and settled in her eyes
The green malignant light of coming storm.

Sir, I was courteous, every phrase well-
    oil'd,
As man's could be; yet maiden-meek I
    pray'd
Concealment: she demanded who we
    were,
And why we came? I fabled nothing fair,
But, your example pilot, told her all.
Up went the hush'd amaze of hand and eye.
But when I dwelt upon your old affiance,
She answer'd sharply that I talk'd astray.
I urged the fierce inscription on the gate,
And our three lives. True—we had limed
    ourselves
With open eyes, and we must take the
    chance.
But such extremes, I told her, well might
    harm
The woman's cause. "Not more than
    now," she said,
"So puddled as it is with favouritism."
I tried the mother's heart. Shame might
    befall
Melissa, knowing, saying not she knew:
Her answer was "Leave me to deal with
    that."
I spoke of war to come and many deaths,
And she replied, her duty was to speak,
And duty duty, clear of consequences.
I grew discouraged, Sir; but since I knew
No rock so hard but that a little wave
May beat admission in a thousand years,
I recommenced; "Decide not ere you
    pause.
I find you here but in the second place,
Some say the third—the authentic found-
    ress you.
I offer boldly: we will seat you highest:
Wink at our advent: help my prince to
    gain
His rightful bride, and here I promise you
Some palace in our land, where you shall
    reign
The head and heart of all our fair she-
    world,
And your great name flow on with broaden-
    ing time
For ever." Well, she balanced this a little,
And told me she would answer us to-day,
Meantime be mute: thus much, nor more
    I gain'd.'

He ceasing, came a message from the
    Head.
'That afternoon the Princess rode to take
The dip of certain strata to the North.
Would we go with her? we should find the
    land
Worth seeing; and the river made a fall
Out yonder:' then she pointed on to where
A double hill ran up his furrowy forks
Beyond the thick-leaved platans of the vale.

Agreed to, this, the day fled on thro' all
Its range of duties to the appointed hour.
Then summon'd to the porch we went.
    She stood
Among her maidens, higher by the head,
Her back against a pillar, her foot on one
Of those tame leopards. Kittenlike he roll'd
And paw'd about her sandal. I drew near;
I gazed. On a sudden my strange seizure
    came
Upon me, the weird vision of our house:
The Princess Ida seem'd a hollow show,
Her gay-furr'd cats a painted fantasy,
Her college and her maidens, empty masks,
And I myself the shadow of a dream,
For all things were and were not. Yet I felt
My heart beat thick with passion and with
    awe;
Then from my breast the involuntary sigh
Brake, as she smote me with the light of
    eyes
That lent my knee desire to kneel, and
    shook
My pulses, till to horse we got, and so
Went forth in long retinue following up
The river as it narrow'd to the hills.

I rode beside her and to me she said:
'O friend, we trust that you esteem'd us not
Too harsh to your companion yestermorn;
Unwillingly we spake.' 'No—not to her,'
I answer'd, 'but to one of whom we spake
Your Highness might have seem'd the
    thing you say.'
'Again?' she cried, 'are you ambassadresses
From him to me? we give you, being
    strange,
A license: speak, and let the topic die.'

    I stammer'd that I knew him—could
    have wish'd—

'Our king expects—was there no pre-
    contract?
There is no truer-hearted—ah, you seem
All he prefigured, and he could not see
The bird of passage flying south but long'd
To follow: surely, if your Highness keep
Your purport, you will shock him ev'n to
    death,
Or baser courses, children of despair.'

'Poor boy,' she said, 'can he not read—
    no books?
Quoit, tennis, ball—no games? nor deals
    in that
Which men delight in, martial exercise?
To nurse a blind ideal like a girl,
Methinks he seems no better than a girl;
As girls were once, as we ourself have been:
We had our dreams; perhaps he mixt with
    them:
We touch on our dead self, nor shun to
    do it,
Being other—since we learnt our meaning
    here,
To lift the woman's fall'n divinity
Upon an even pedestal with man.'

She paused, and added with a haughtier
    smile
'And as to precontracts, we move, my
    friend,
At no man's beck, but know ourself and
    thee,
O Vashti, noble Vashti! Summon'd out
She kept her state, and left the drunken
    king
To brawl at Shushan underneath the
    palms.'

'Alas your Highness breathes full East,'
    I said,
'On that which leans to you. I know the
    Prince,
I prize his truth: and then how vast a work
To assail this gray preëminence of man!
You grant me license; might I use it?
    think;
Ere half be done perchance your life may
    fail;
Then comes the feebler heiress of your
    plan,

And takes and ruins all; and thus your pains
May only make that footprint upon sand
Which old-recurring waves of prejudice
Resmooth to nothing: might I dread that you,
With only Fame for spouse and your great deeds
For issue, yet may live in vain, and miss,
Meanwhile, what every woman counts her due,
Love, children, happiness?'
                    And she exclaim'd,
'Peace, you young savage of the Northern wild!
What! tho' your Prince's love were like a God's,
Have we not made ourself the sacrifice?
You are bold indeed: we are not talk'd to thus:
Yet will we say for children, would they grew
Like field-flowers everywhere! we like them well:
But children die; and let me tell you, girl,
Howe'er you babble, great deeds cannot die;
They with the sun and moon renew their light
For ever, blessing those that look on them.
Children—that men may pluck them from our hearts,
Kill us with pity, break us with ourselves—
O—children—there is nothing upon earth
More miserable than she that has a son
And sees him err: nor would we work for fame;
Tho' she perhaps might reap the applause of Great,
Who learns the one POU STO whence after-hands
May move the world, tho' she herself effect
But little: wherefore up and act, nor shrink
For fear our solid aim be dissipated
By frail successors. Would, indeed, we had been,
In lieu of many mortal flies, a race
Of giants living, each, a thousand years,
That we might see our own work out, and watch
The sandy footprint harden into stone.'

I answer'd nothing, doubtful in myself
If that strange Poet-princess with her grand
Imaginations might at all be won.
And she broke out interpreting my thoughts:

'No doubt we seem a kind of monster to you;
We are used to that: for women, up till this
Cramp'd under worse than South-sea-isle taboo,
Dwarfs of the gynæceum, fail so far
In high desire, they know not, cannot guess
How much their welfare is a passion to us.
If we could give them surer, quicker proof—
Oh if our end were less achievable
By slow approaches, than by single act
Of immolation, any phase of death,
We were as prompt to spring against the pikes,
Or down the fiery gulf as talk of it,
To compass our dear sisters' liberties.'

She bow'd as if to veil a noble tear;
And up we came to where the river sloped
To plunge in cataract, shattering on black blocks
A breadth of thunder. O'er it shook the woods,
And danced the colour, and, below, stuck out
The bones of some vast bulk that lived and roar'd
Before man was. She gazed awhile and said,
'As these rude bones to us, are we to her
That will be.' 'Dare we dream of that,' I ask'd,
'Which wrought us, as the workman and his work,
That practice betters?' 'How,' she cried, 'you love
The metaphysics! read and earn our prize,
A golden brooch: beneath an emerald plane
Sits Diotima, teaching him that died
Of hemlock; our device; wrought to the life;
She rapt upon her subject, he on her:

171

For there are schools for all.' 'And yet' I
    said
'Methinks I have not found among them all
One anatomic.' 'Nay, we thought of that,'
She answer'd, 'but it pleased us not: in
    truth
We shudder but to dream our maids should
    ape
Those monstrous males that carve the
    living hound,
And cram him with the fragments of the
    grave,
Or in the dark dissolving human heart,
And holy secrets of this microcosm,
Dabbling a shameless hand with shameful
    jest,
Encarnalize their spirits: yet we know
Knowledge is knowledge, and this matter
    hangs:
Howbeit ourself, foreseeing casualty,
Nor willing men should come among us,
    learnt,
For many weary moons before we came,
This craft of healing. Were you sick, our-
    self
Would tend upon you. To your question
    now,
Which touches on the workman and his
    work.
Let there be light and there was light:
    'tis so:
For was, and is, and will be, are but is;
And all creation is one act at once,
The birth of light: but we that are not all,
As parts, can see but parts, now this, now
    that,
And live, perforce, from thought to
    thought, and make
One act a phantom of succession: thus
Our weakness somehow shapes the shadow,
    Time;
But in the shadow will we work, and mould
The woman to the fuller day.'
                                    She spake
With kindled eyes: we rode a league
    beyond,
And, o'er a bridge of pinewood crossing,
    came
On flowery levels underneath the crag,
Full of all beauty. 'O how sweet' I said
(For I was half-oblivious of my mask)

'To linger here with one that loved us.'
'Yea,'
She answer'd, 'or with fair philosophies
That lift the fancy; for indeed these fields
Are lovely, lovelier not the Elysian lawns,
Where paced the Demigods of old, and
    saw
The soft white vapour streak the crowned
    towers
Built to the Sun:' then, turning to her
    maids,
'Pitch our pavilion here upon the sward;
Lay out the viands.' At the word, they
    raised
A tent of satin, elaborately wrought
With fair Corinna's triumph; here she
    stood,
Engirt with many a florid maiden-cheek,
The woman-conqueror; woman-conquer'd
    there
The bearded Victor of ten-thousand
    hymns,
And all the men mourn'd at his side: but
    we
Set forth to climb; then, climbing, Cyril
    kept
With Psyche, with Melissa Florian, I
With mine affianced. Many a little hand
Glanced like a touch of sunshine on the
    rocks,
Many a light foot shone like a jewel set
In the dark crag: and then we turn'd, we
    wound
About the cliffs, the copses, out and in,
Hammering and clinking, chattering stony
    names
Of shale and hornblende, rag and trap and
    tuff,
Amygdaloid and trachyte, till the Sun
Grew broader toward his death and fell,
    and all
The rosy heights came out above the lawns.

IV

The splendour falls on castle walls
    And snowy summits old in story:
The long light shakes across the lakes,
    And the wild cataract leaps in glory.
Blow, bugle, blow, set the wild echoes flying,
Blow, bugle; answer, echoes, dying, dying,
    dying.

O hark, O hear! how thin and clear,
  And thinner, clearer, farther going!
O sweet and far from cliff and scar
  The horns of Elfland faintly blowing!
Blow, let us hear the purple glens replying:
Blow, bugle; answer, echoes, dying, dying,
  dying.

O love, they die in yon rich sky,
  They faint on hill or field or river:
Our echoes roll from soul to soul,
  And grow for ever and for ever.
Blow, bugle, blow, set the wild echoes flying,
And answer, echoes, answer, dying, dying,
  dying.

'There sinks the nebulous star we call the
  Sun,
If that hypothesis of theirs be sound'
Said Ida; 'let us down and rest;' and we
Down from the lean and wrinkled preci-
  pices,
By every coppice-feather'd chasm and
  cleft,
Dropt thro' the ambrosial gloom to where
  below
No bigger than a glow-worm shone the tent
Lamp-lit from the inner. Once she lean'd
  on me,
Descending; once or twice she lent her
  hand,
And blissful palpitations in the blood,
Stirring a sudden transport rose and fell.

But when we planted level feet, and dipt
Beneath the satin dome and enter'd in,
There leaning deep in broider'd down we
  sank
Our elbows: on a tripod in the midst
A fragrant flame rose, and before us glow'd
Fruit, blossom, viand, amber wine, and
  gold.

Then she, 'Let some one sing to us:
  lightlier move
The minutes fledged with music:' and a
  maid,
Of those beside her, smote her harp, and
  sang.

'Tears, idle tears, I know not what they
  mean,
Tears from the depth of some divine despair
Rise in the heart, and gather to the eyes,
In looking on the happy Autumn-fields,
And thinking of the days that are no more.

'Fresh as the first beam glittering on a sail,
That brings our friends up from the under-
  world,
Sad as the last which reddens over one
That sinks with all we love below the verge;
So sad, so fresh, the days that are no more.

'Ah, sad and strange as in dark summer
  dawns
The earliest pipe of half-awaken'd birds
To dying ears, when unto dying eyes
The casement slowly grows a glimmering
  square;
So sad, so strange, the days that are no more.

'Dear as remember'd kisses after death,
And sweet as those by hopeless fancy feign'd
On lips that are for others; deep as love,
Deep as first love, and wild with all regret;
O Death in Life, the days that are no more.'

She ended with such passion that the
  tear,
She sang of, shook and fell, an erring pearl
Lost in her bosom: but with some dis-
  dain
Answer'd the Princess, 'If indeed there
  haunt
About the moulder'd lodges of the Past
So sweet a voice and vague, fatal to men,
Well needs it we should cram our ears with
  wool
And so pace by: but thine are fancies
  hatch'd
In silken-folded idleness; nor is it
Wiser to weep a true occasion lost,
But trim our sails, and let old bygones be,
While down the streams that float us each
  and all
To the issue, goes, like glittering bergs of
  ice,
Throne after throne, and molten on the
  waste
Becomes a cloud: for all things serve their
  time
Toward that great year of equal mights
  and rights,
Nor would I fight with iron laws, in the
  end
Found golden: let the past be past; let be
Their cancell'd Babels: tho' the rough kex
  break
The starr'd mosaic, and the beard-blown
  goat
Hang on the shaft, and the wild figtree split

Their monstrous idols, care not while we
    hear
A trumpet in the distance pealing news
Of better, and Hope, a poising eagle, burns
Above the unrisen morrow:' then to me;
'Know you no song of your own land,' she
    said,
'Not such as moans about the retrospect,
But deals with the other distance and the
    hues
Of promise; not a death's-head at the
    wine.'

Then I remember'd one myself had
    made,
What time I watch'd the swallow winging
    south
From mine own land, part made long since,
    and part
Now while I sang, and maidenlike as far
As I could ape their treble, did I sing.

'O Swallow, Swallow, flying, flying South,
Fly to her, and fall upon her gilded eaves,
And tell her, tell her, what I tell to thee.

'O tell her, Swallow, thou that knowest each,
That bright and fierce and fickle is the South,
And dark and true and tender is the North.

'O Swallow, Swallow, if I could follow, and
    light
Upon her lattice, I would pipe and trill,
And cheep and twitter twenty million loves.

'O were I thou that she might take me in,
And lay me on her bosom, and her heart
Would rock the snowy cradle till I died.

'Why lingereth she to clothe her heart with
    love,
Delaying as the tender ash delays
To clothe herself, when all the woods are green?

'O tell her, Swallow, that thy brood is flown:
Say to her, I do but wanton in the South,
But in the North long since my nest is made.

'O tell her, brief is life but love is long,
And brief the sun of summer in the North,
And brief the moon of beauty in the South.

'O Swallow, flying from the golden woods,
Fly to her, and pipe and woo her, and make her
    mine,
And tell her, tell her, that I follow thee.'

I ceased, and all the ladies, each at each,
Like the Ithacensian suitors in old time,

Stared with great eyes, and laugh'd with
    alien lips,
And knew not what they meant; for still
    my voice
Rang false: but smiling 'Not for thee,' she
    said,
'O Bulbul, any rose of Gulistan
Shall burst her veil: marsh-divers, rather,
    maid,
Shall croak thee sister, or the meadow-
    crake
Grate her harsh kindred in the grass: and
    this
A mere love-poem! O for such, my friend,
We hold them slight: they mind us of the
    time
When we made bricks in Egypt. Knaves
    are men,
That lute and flute fantastic tenderness,
And dress the victim to the offering up,
And paint the gates of Hell with Paradise,
And play the slave to gain the tyranny.
Poor soul! I had a maid of honour once;
She wept her true eyes blind for such a one,
A rogue of canzonets and serenades.
I loved her. Peace be with her. She is dead.
So they blaspheme the muse! But great is
    song
Used to great ends: ourself have often tried
Valkyrian hymns, or into rhythm have
    dash'd
The passion of the prophetess; for song
Is duer unto freedom, force and growth
Of spirit than to junketing and love.
Love is it? Would this same mock-love,
    and this
Mock-Hymen were laid up like winter bats,
Till all men grew to rate us at our worth,
Not vassals to be beat, nor pretty babes
To be dandled, no, but living wills, and
    sphered
Whole in ourselves and owed to none.
    Enough!
But now to leaven play with profit you,
Know you no song, the true growth of
    your soil,
That gives the manners of your country-
    women?'

She spoke and turn'd her sumptuous
    head with eyes

Of shining expectation fixt on mine.
Then while I dragg'd my brains for such a
    song,
Cyril, with whom the bell-mouth'd glass
    had wrought,
Or master'd by the sense of sport, began
To troll a careless, careless tavern-catch
Of Moll and Meg, and strange experiences
Unmeet for ladies. Florian nodded at him,
I frowning; Psyche flush'd and wann'd and
    shook;
The lilylike Melissa droop'd her brows;
'Forbear,' the Princess cried; 'Forbear,
    Sir' I;
And heated thro' and thro' with wrath
    and love,
I smote him on the breast; he started up;
There rose a shriek as of a city sack'd;
Melissa clamour'd 'Flee the death;' 'To
    horse'
Said Ida; 'home! to horse!' and fled, as
    flies
A troop of snowy doves athwart the dusk,
When some one batters at the dovecote-
    doors,
Disorderly the women. Alone I stood
With Florian, cursing Cyril, vext at heart,
In the pavilion: there like parting hopes
I heard them passing from me: hoof by
    hoof,
And every hoof a knell to my desires,
Clang'd on the bridge; and then another
    shriek,
'The Head, the Head, the Princess, O the
    Head!'
For blind with rage she miss'd the plank,
    and roll'd
In the river. Out I sprang from glow to
    gloom:
There whirl'd her white robe like a blos-
    som'd branch
Rapt to the horrible fall: a glance I gave,
No more; but woman-vested as I was
Plunged; and the flood drew; yet I caught
    her; then
Oaring one arm, and bearing in my left
The weight of all the hopes of half the
    world,
Strove to buffet to land in vain. A tree
Was half-disrooted from his place and
    stoop'd

To drench his dark locks in the gurgling
    wave
Mid-channel. Right on this we drove and
    caught,
And grasping down the boughs I gain'd
    the shore.

There stood her maidens glimmeringly
    group'd
In the hollow bank. One reaching forward
    drew
My burthen from mine arms; they cried
    'she lives:'
They bore her back into the tent: but I,
So much a kind of shame within me
    wrought,
Not yet endured to meet her opening eyes,
Nor found my friends; but push'd alone
    on foot
(For since her horse was lost I left her
    mine)
Across the woods, and less from Indian
    craft
Than beelike instinct hiveward, found at
    length
The garden portals. Two great statues, Art
And Science, Caryatids, lifted up
A weight of emblem, and betwixt were
    valves
Of open-work in which the hunter rued
His rash intrusion, manlike, but his brows
Had sprouted, and the branches thereupon
Spread out at top, and grimly spiked the
    gates.

    A little space was left between the horns,
Thro' which I clamber'd o'er at top with
    pain,
Dropt on the sward, and up the linden
    walks,
And, tost on thoughts that changed from
    hue to hue,
Now poring on the glowworm, now the
    star,
I paced the terrace, till the Bear had
    wheel'd
Thro' a great arc his seven slow suns.
                                    A step
Of lightest echo, then a loftier form
Than female, moving thro' the uncertain
    gloom,

Disturb'd me with the doubt 'if this were
    she,'
But it was Florian. 'Hist O Hist,' he said,
'They seek us: out so late is out of rules.
Moreover "seize the strangers" is the cry.
How came you here?' I told him: 'I'
    said he,
'Last of the train, a moral leper, I,
To whom none spake, half-sick at heart,
    return'd.
Arriving all confused among the rest
With hooded brows I crept into the hall,
And, couch'd behind a Judith, underneath
The head of Holofernes peep'd and saw.
Girl after girl was call'd to trial: each
Disclaim'd all knowledge of us: last of all,
Melissa: trust me, Sir, I pitied her.
She, question'd if she knew us men, at first
Was silent; closer prest, denied it not:
And then, demanded if her mother knew,
Or Psyche, she affirm'd not, or denied:
From whence the Royal mind, familiar
    with her,
Easily gather'd either guilt. She sent
For Psyche, but she was not there; she
    call'd
For Psyche's child to cast it from the doors;
She sent for Blanche to accuse her face to
    face;
And I slipt out: but whither will you now?
And where are Psyche, Cyril? both are
    fled:
What, if together? that were not so well.
Would rather we had never come! I dread
His wildness, and the chances of the dark.'

'And yet,' I said, 'you wrong him more
    than I
That struck him: this is proper to the
    clown,
Tho' smock'd, or furr'd and purpled, still
    the clown,
To harm the thing that trusts him, and to
    shame
That which he says he loves: for Cyril,
    howe'er
He deal in frolic, as to-night—the song
Might have been worse and sinn'd in
    grosser lips
Beyond all pardon—as it is, I hold
These flashes on the surface are not he.

He has a solid base of temperament:
But as the waterlily starts and slides
Upon the level in little puffs of wind,
Tho' anchor'd to the bottom, such is he.'

Scarce had I ceased when from a
    tamarisk near
Two Proctors leapt upon us, crying,
    'Names:'
He, standing still, was clutch'd; but I
    began
To thrid the musky-circled mazes, wind
And double in and out the boles, and race
By all the fountains: fleet I was of foot:
Before me shower'd the rose in flakes;
    behind
I heard the puff'd pursuer; at mine ear
Bubbled the nightingale and heeded not,
And secret laughter tickled all my soul.
At last I hook'd my ankle in a vine,
That claspt the feet of a Mnemosyne,
And falling on my face was caught and
    known.

They haled us to the Princess where she
    sat
High in the hall: above her droop'd a lamp,
And made the single jewel on her brow
Burn like the mystic fire on a mast-head,
Prophet of storm: a handmaid on each side
Bow'd toward her, combing out her long
    black hair
Damp from the river; and close behind her
    stood
Eight daughters of the plough, stronger
    than men,
Huge women blowzed with health, and
    wind, and rain,
And labour. Each was like a Druid rock;
Or like a spire of land that stands apart
Cleft from the main, and wail'd about with
    mews.

Then, as we came, the crowd dividing
    clove
An advent to the throne: and there beside,
Half-naked as if caught at once from bed
And tumbled on the purple footcloth, lay
The lily-shining child; and on the left,
Bow'd on her palms and folded up from
    wrong,

Her round white shoulder shaken with her
    sobs,
Melissa knelt; but Lady Blanche erect
Stood up and spake, an affluent orator.

'It was not thus, O Princess, in old days:
You prized my counsel, lived upon my lips:
I led you then to all the Castalies;
I fed you with the milk of every Muse;
I loved you like this kneeler, and you me
Your second mother: those were gracious
    times.
Then came your new friend: you began to
    change—
I saw it and grieved—to slacken and to cool;
Till taken with her seeming openness
You turn'd your warmer currents all to her,
To me you froze: this was my meed for all.
Yet I bore up in part from ancient love,
And partly that I hoped to win you back,
And partly conscious of my own deserts,
And partly that you were my civil head,
And chiefly you were born for something
    great,
In which I might your fellow-worker be,
When time should serve; and thus a noble
    scheme
Grew up from seed we two long since had
    sown;
In us true growth, in her a Jonah's gourd,
Up in one night and due to sudden sun:
We took this palace; but even from the first
You stood in your own light and darken'd
    mine.
What student came but that you planed
    her path
To Lady Psyche, younger, not so wise,
A foreigner, and I your countrywoman,
I your old friend and tried, she new in all?
But still her lists were swell'd and mine
    were lean;
Yet I bore up in hope she would be known:
Then came these wolves: *they* knew her:
    they endured,
Long-closeted with her the yestermorn,
To tell her what they were, and she to hear:
And me none told: not less to an eye like
    mine
A lidless watcher of the public weal,
Last night, their mask was patent, and my
    foot

Was to you: but I thought again: I fear'd
To meet a cold "We thank you, we shall
    hear of it
From Lady Psyche:" you had gone to her,
She told, perforce; and winning easy grace,
No doubt, for slight delay, remain'd among us
In our young nursery still unknown, the
    stem
Less grain than touchwood, while my
    honest heat
Were all miscounted as malignant haste
To push my rival out of place and power.
But public use required she should be
    known;
And since my oath was ta'en for public use,
I broke the letter of it to keep the sense.
I spoke not then at first, but watch'd them
    well,
Saw that they kept apart, no mischief done;
And yet this day (tho' you should hate me
    for it)
I came to tell you; found that you had gone,
Ridd'n to the hills, she likewise: now, I
    thought,
That surely she will speak; if not, then I:
Did she? These monsters blazon'd what
    they were,
According to the coarseness of their kind,
For thus I hear; and known at last (my
    work)
And full of cowardice and guilty shame,
I grant in her some sense of shame, she
    flies;
And I remain on whom to wreak your rage,
I, that have lent my life to build up yours,
I that have wasted here health, wealth, and
    time,
And talent, I—you know it—I will not
    boast:
Dismiss me, and I prophesy your plan,
Divorced from my experience, will be chaff
For every gust of chance, and men will say
We did not know the real light, but chased
The wisp that flickers where no foot can
    tread.'

She ceased: the Princess answer'd
    coldly, 'Good:
Your oath is broken: we dismiss you: go.
For this lost lamb (she pointed to the child)
Our mind is changed: we take it to ourself.'

Thereat the Lady stretch'd a vulture
  throat,
And shot from crooked lips a haggard
  smile.
'The plan was mine. I built the nest' she
  said
'To hatch the cuckoo. Rise!' and stoop'd
  to updrag
Melissa: she, half on her mother propt,
Half-drooping from her, turn'd her face,
  and cast
A liquid look on Ida, full of prayer,
Which melted Florian's fancy as she hung,
A Niobëan daughter, one arm out,
Appealing to the bolts of Heaven; and
  while
We gazed upon her came a little stir
About the doors, and on a sudden rush'd
Among us, out of breath, as one pursued,
A woman-post in flying raiment. Fear
Stared in her eyes, and chalk'd her face,
  and wing'd
Her transit to the throne, whereby she fell
Delivering seal'd dispatches which the
  Head
Took half-amazed, and in her lion's mood
Tore open, silent we with blind surmise
Regarding, while she read, till over brow
And cheek and bosom brake the wrathful
  bloom
As of some fire against a stormy cloud,
When the wild peasant rights himself, the
  rick
Flames, and his anger reddens in the
  heavens;
For anger most it seem'd, while now her
  breast,
Beaten with some great passion at her
  heart,
Palpitated, her hand shook, and we heard
In the dead hush the papers that she held
Rustle: at once the lost lamb at her feet
Sent out a bitter bleating for its dam;
The plaintive cry jarr'd on her ire; she
  crush'd
The scrolls together, made a sudden turn
As if to speak, but, utterance failing her,
She whirl'd them on to me, as who should
  say
'Read,' and I read—two letters—one her
  sire's.

'Fair daughter, when we sent the Prince
  your way
We knew not your ungracious laws, which
  learnt,
We, conscious of what temper you are
  built,
Came all in haste to hinder wrong, but fell
Into his father's hands, who has this night,
You lying close upon his territory,
Slipt round and in the dark invested you,
And here he keeps me hostage for his son.'

The second was my father's running
  thus:
'You have our son: touch not a hair of his
  head:
Render him up unscathed: give him your
  hand:
Cleave to your contract: tho' indeed we hear
You hold the woman is the better man;
A rampant heresy, such as if it spread
Would make all women kick against their
  Lords
Thro' all the world, and which might well
  deserve
That we this night should pluck your
  palace down;
And we will do it, unless you send us back
Our son, on the instant, whole.'
              So far I read;
And then stood up and spoke impetuously.

'O not to pry and peer on your reserve,
But led by golden wishes, and a hope
The child of regal compact, did I break
Your precinct; not a scorner of your sex
But venerator, zealous it should be
All that it might be: hear me, for I bear,
Tho' man, yet human, whatsoe'er your
  wrongs,
From the flaxen curl to the gray lock a life
Less mine than yours: my nurse would tell
  me of you;
I babbled for you, as babies for the moon,
Vague brightness; when a boy, you stoop'd
  to me
From all high places, lived in all fair lights,
Came in long breezes rapt from inmost
  south
And blown to inmost north; at eve and
  dawn

178

With Ida, Ida, Ida, rang the woods;
The leader wildswan in among the stars
Would clang it, and lapt in wreaths of
    glowworm light
The mellow breaker murmur'd Ida. Now,
Because I would have reach'd you, had
    you been
Sphered up with Cassiopëia, or the en-
    throned
Persephonè in Hades, now at length,
Those winters of abeyance all worn out,
A man I came to see you: but, indeed,
Not in this frequence can I lend full tongue,
O noble Ida, to those thoughts that wait
On you, their centre: let me say but this,
That many a famous man and woman,
    town
And landskip, have I heard of, after seen
The dwarfs of presage: tho' when known,
    there grew
Another kind of beauty in detail
Made them worth knowing; but in you I
    found
My boyish dream involved and dazzled
    down
And master'd, while that after-beauty
    makes
Such head from act to act, from hour to
    hour,
Within me, that except you slay me here,
According to your bitter statute-book,
I cannot cease to follow you, as they say
The seal does music; who desire you more
Than growing boys their manhood; dying
    lips,
With many thousand matters left to do,
The breath of life; O more than poor men
    wealth,
Than sick men health—yours, yours, not
    mine—but half
Without you; with you, whole; and of
    those halves
You worthiest; and howe'er you block and
    bar
Your heart with system out from mine, I
    hold
That it becomes no man to nurse despair,
But in the teeth of clench'd antagonisms
To follow up the worthiest till he die:
Yet that I came not all unauthorized
Behold your father's letter.'

On one knee
Kneeling, I gave it, which she caught, and
    dash'd
Unopen'd at her feet: a tide of fierce
Invective seem'd to wait behind her lips,
As waits a river level with the dam
Ready to burst and flood the world with
    foam:
And so she would have spoken, but there
    rose
A hubbub in the court of half the maids
Gather'd together: from the illumined hall
Long lanes of splendour slanted o'er a
    press
Of snowy shoulders, thick as herded ewes,
And rainbow robes, and gems and gem-
    like eyes,
And gold and golden heads; they to and fro
Fluctuated, as flowers in storm, some red,
    some pale,
All open-mouth'd, all gazing to the light,
Some crying there was an army in the land,
And some that men were in the very walls,
And some they cared not; till a clamour
    grew
As of a new-world Babel, woman-built,
And worse-confounded: high above them
    stood
The placid marble Muses, looking peace.

Not peace she look'd, the Head: but
    rising up
Robed in the long night of her deep hair, so
To the open window moved, remaining
    there
Fixt like a beacon-tower above the waves
Of tempest, when the crimson-rolling eye
Glares ruin, and the wild birds on the
    light
Dash themselves dead. She stretch'd her
    arms and call'd
Across the tumult and the tumult fell.

'What fear ye, brawlers? am not I your
    Head?
On me, me, me, the storm first breaks:
    I dare
All these male thunderbolts: what is it ye
    fear?
Peace! there are those to avenge us and
    they come:

If not,—myself were like enough, O girls,
To unfurl the maiden banner of our rights,
And clad in iron burst the ranks of war,
Or, falling, protomartyr of our cause,
Die: yet I blame you not so much for fear;
Six thousand years of fear have made you
    that
From which I would redeem you: but for
    those
That stir this hubbub—you and you—I
    know
Your faces there in the crowd—to-morrow
    morn
We hold a great convention: then shall
    they
That love their voices more than duty,
    learn
With whom they deal, dismiss'd in shame
    to live
No wiser than their mothers, household
    stuff,
Live chattels, mincers of each other's fame,
Full of weak poison, turnspits for the
    clown,
The drunkard's football, laughing-stocks
    of Time,
Whose brains are in their hands and in
    their heels,
But fit to flaunt, to dress, to dance, to
    thrum,
To tramp, to scream, to burnish, and to
    scour,
For ever slaves at home and fools abroad.'

She, ending, waved her hands: thereat
    the crowd
Muttering, dissolved: then with a smile,
    that look'd
A stroke of cruel sunshine on the cliff,
When all the glens are drown'd in azure
    gloom
Of thunder-shower, she floated to us and
    said:

'You have done well and like a gentle-
    man,
And like a prince: you have our thanks for
    all:
And you look well too in your woman's
    dress:
Well have you done and like a gentleman.

You saved our life: we owe you bitter
    thanks:
Better have died and spilt our bones in the
    flood—
Then men had said—but now—What
    hinders me
To take such bloody vengeance on you
    both?—
Yet since our father—Wasps in our good
    hive,
You would-be quenchers of the light to be,
Barbarians, grosser than your native
    bears—
O would I had his sceptre for one hour!
You that have dared to break our bound,
    and gull'd
Our servants, wrong'd and lied and
    thwarted us—
I wed with thee! *I* bound by precontract
Your bride, your bondslave! not tho' all
    the gold
That veins the world were pack'd to make
    your crown,
And every spoken tongue should lord you.
    Sir,
Your falsehood and yourself are hateful
    to us:
I trample on your offers and on you:
Begone: we will not look upon you more.
Here, push them out at gates.'
                    In wrath she spake.
Then those eight mighty daughters of the
    plough
Bent their broad faces toward us and
    address'd
Their motion: twice I sought to plead my
    cause,
But on my shoulder hung their heavy
    hands,
The weight of destiny: so from her face
They push'd us, down the steps, and thro'
    the court,
And with grim laughter thrust us out at
    gates.

We cross'd the street and gain'd a petty
    mound
Beyond it, whence we saw the lights and
    heard
The voices murmuring. While I listen'd,
    came

On a sudden the weird seizure and the doubt:
I seem'd to move among a world of ghosts;
The Princess with her monstrous woman-guard,
The jest and earnest working side by side,
The cataract and the tumult and the kings
Were shadows; and the long fantastic night
With all its doings had and had not been,
And all things were and were not.
        This went by
As strangely as it came, and on my spirits
Settled a gentle cloud of melancholy;
Not long; I shook it off; for spite of doubts
And sudden ghostly shadowings I was one
To whom the touch of all mischance but came
As night to him that sitting on a hill
Sees the midsummer, midnight, Norway sun
Set into sunrise; then we moved away.

    Thy voice is heard thro' rolling drums,
      That beat to battle where he stands;
    Thy face across his fancy comes,
      And gives the battle to his hands:
    A moment, while the trumpets blow,
      He sees his brood about thy knee;
    The next, like fire he meets the foe,
      And strikes him dead for thine and thee.

So Lilia sang: we thought her half-possess'd,
She struck such warbling fury thro' the words;
And, after, feigning pique at what she call'd
The raillery, or grotesque, or false sub-lime—
Like one that wishes at a dance to change
The music—clapt her hands and cried for war,
Or some grand fight to kill and make an end:
And he that next inherited the tale
Half turning to the broken statue, said,
'Sir Ralph has got your colours: if I prove
Your knight, and fight your battle, what for me?'
It chanced, her empty glove upon the tomb
Lay by her like a model of her hand.
She took it and she flung it. 'Fight' she said,

'And make us all we would be, great and good.'
He knightlike in his cap instead of casque,
A cap of Tyrol borrow'd from the hall,
Arranged the favour, and assumed the Prince.

V

Now, scarce three paces measured from the mound,
We stumbled on a stationary voice,
And 'Stand, who goes?' 'Two from the palace' I.
'The second two: they wait,' he said, 'pass on;
His Highness wakes:' and one, that clash'd in arms,
By glimmering lanes and walls of canvas led
Threading the soldier-city, till we heard
The drowsy folds of our great ensign shake
From blazon'd lions o'er the imperial tent
Whispers of war.
        Entering, the sudden light
Dazed me half-blind: I stood and seem'd to hear,
As in a poplar grove when a light wind wakes
A lisping of the innumerous leaf and dies,
Each hissing in his neighbour's ear; and then
A strangled titter, out of which there brake
On all sides, clamouring etiquette to death,
Unmeasured mirth; while now the two old kings
Began to wag their baldness up and down,
The fresh young captains flash'd their glittering teeth,
The huge bush-bearded Barons heaved and blew,
And slain with laughter roll'd the gilded Squire.

    At length my Sire, his rough cheek wet with tears,
Panted from weary sides 'King, you are free!
We did but keep you surety for our son,
If this be he,—or a draggled mawkin, thou,
That tends her bristled grunters in the sludge:'
For I was drench'd with ooze, and torn with briers,

More crumpled than a poppy from the sheath,
And all one rag, disprinced from head to heel.
Then some one sent beneath his vaulted palm
A whisper'd jest to some one near him, 'Look,
He has been among his shadows.' 'Satan take
The old women and their shadows! (thus the King
Roar'd) make yourself a man to fight with men.
Go: Cyril told us all.'
            As boys that slink
From ferule and the trespass-chiding eye,
Away we stole, and transient in a trice
From what was left of faded woman-slough
To sheathing splendours and the golden scale
Of harness, issued in the sun, that now
Leapt from the dewy shoulders of the Earth,
And hit the Northern hills. Here Cyril met us.
A little shy at first, but by and by
We twain, with mutual pardon ask'd and given
For stroke and song, resolder'd peace, whereon
Follow'd his tale. Amazed he fled away
Thro' the dark land, and later in the night
Had come on Psyche weeping: 'then we fell
Into your father's hand, and there she lies,
But will not speak, nor stir.'
            He show'd a tent
A stone-shot off: we enter'd in, and there
Among piled arms and rough accoutrements,
Pitiful sight, wrapp'd in a soldier's cloak,
Like some sweet sculpture draped from head to foot,
And push'd by rude hands from its pedestal,
All her fair length upon the ground she lay:
And at her head a follower of the camp,
A charr'd and wrinkled piece of womanhood,
Sat watching like a watcher by the dead.

Then Florian knelt, and 'Come' he whisper'd to her,
'Lift up your head, sweet sister: lie not thus.
What have you done but right? you could not slay
Me, nor your prince: look up: be comforted:
Sweet is it to have done the thing one ought,
When fall'n in darker ways.' And likewise I:
'Be comforted: have I not lost her too,
In whose least act abides the nameless charm
That none has else for me?' She heard, she moved,
She moan'd, a folded voice; and up she sat,
And raised the cloak from brows as pale and smooth
As those that mourn half-shrouded over death
In deathless marble. 'Her,' she said, 'my friend—
Parted from her—betray'd her cause and mine—
Where shall I breathe? why kept ye not your faith?
O base and bad! what comfort? none for me!'
To whom remorseful Cyril, 'Yet I pray
Take comfort: live, dear lady, for your child!'
At which she lifted up her voice and cried.

'Ah me, my babe, my blossom, ah, my child,
My one sweet child, whom I shall see no more!
For now will cruel Ida keep her back;
And either she will die from want of care,
Or sicken with ill-usage, when they say
The child is hers—for every little fault,
The child is hers; and they will beat my girl
Remembering her mother: O my flower!
Or they will take her, they will make her hard,
And she will pass me by in after-life
With some cold reverence worse than were she dead.

Ill mother that I was to leave her there,
To lag behind, scared by the cry they
made,
The horror of the shame among them all:
But I will go and sit beside the doors,
And make a wild petition night and day,
Until they hate to hear me like a wind
Wailing for ever, till they open to me,
And lay my little blossom at my feet,
My babe, my sweet Aglaïa, my one child:
And I will take her up and go my way,
And satisfy my soul with kissing her:
Ah! what might that man not deserve of
me
Who gave me back my child?' 'Be com-
forted,'
Said Cyril, 'you shall have it:' but again
She veil'd her brows, and prone she sank,
and so
Like tender things that being caught feign
death,
Spoke not, nor stirr'd.
                    By this a murmur ran
Thro' all the camp and inward raced the
scouts
With rumour of Prince Arac hard at hand.
We left her by the woman, and without
Found the gray kings at parle: and 'Look
you' cried
My father 'that our compact be fulfill'd:
You have spoilt this child; she laughs at
you and man:
She wrongs herself, her sex, and me, and
him;
But red-faced war has rods of steel and
fire;
She yields, or war.'
                    Then Gama turn'd to me:
'We fear, indeed, you spent a stormy time
With our strange girl: and yet they say
that still
You love her. Give us, then, your mind at
large:
How say you, war or not?'
                    'Not war, if possible,
O king,' I said, 'lest from the abuse of war,
The desecrated shrine, the trampled year,
The smouldering homestead, and the
household flower
Torn from the lintel—all the common
wrong—

A smoke go up thro' which I loom to her
Three times a monster: now she lightens
scorn
At him that mars her plan, but then would
hate
(And every voice she talk'd with ratify it,
And every face she look'd on justify it)
The general foe. More soluble is this knot,
By gentleness than war. I want her love.
What were I nigher this altho' we dash'd
Your cities into shards with catapults,
She would not love;—or brought her
chain'd, a slave,
The lifting of whose eyelash is my lord,
Not ever would she love; but brooding
turn
The book of scorn, till all my flitting chance
Were caught within the record of her
wrongs,
And crush'd to death: and rather, Sire,
than this
I would the old God of war himself were
dead,
Forgotten, rusting on his iron hills,
Rotting on some wild shore with ribs of
wreck,
Or like an old-world mammoth bulk'd in
ice,
Not to be molten out.'
                    And roughly spake
My father, 'Tut, you know them not, the
girls.
Boy, when I hear you prate I almost think
That idiot legend credible. Look you, Sir!
Man is the hunter; woman is his game:
The sleek and shining creatures of the
chase,
We hunt them for the beauty of their skins;
They love us for it, and we ride them down.
Wheedling and siding with them! Out! for
shame!
Boy, there's no rose that's half so dear to
them
As he that does the thing they dare not
do,
Breathing and sounding beauteous battle,
comes
With the air of the trumpet round him, and
leaps in
Among the women, snares them by the
score

Flatter'd and fluster'd, wins, tho' dash'd
  with death
He reddens what he kisses: thus I won
Your mother, a good mother, a good wife,
Worth winning; but this firebrand—
  gentleness
To such as her! if Cyril spake her true,
To catch a dragon in a cherry net,
To trip a tigress with a gossamer,
Were wisdom to it.'
                   'Yea but Sire,' I cried,
'Wild natures need wise curbs. The
  soldier? No:
What dares not Ida do that she should
  prize
The soldier? I beheld her, when she rose
The yesternight, and storming in extremes,
Stood for her cause, and flung defiance
  down
Gagelike to man, and had not shunn'd the
  death,
No, not the soldier's: yet I hold her, king,
True woman: but you clash them all in one,
That have as many differences as we.
The violet varies from the lily as far
As oak from elm: one loves the soldier, one
The silken priest of peace, one this, one
  that,
And some unworthily; their sinless faith,
A maiden moon that sparkles on a sty,
Glorifying clown and satyr; whence they
  need
More breadth of culture: is not Ida right?
They worth it? truer to the law within?
Severer in the logic of a life?
Twice as magnetic to sweet influences
Of earth and heaven? and she of whom
  you speak,
My mother, looks as whole as some serene
Creation minted in the golden moods
Of sovereign artists; not a thought, a
  touch,
But pure as lines of green that streak the
  white
Of the first snowdrop's inner leaves; I say,
Not like the piebald miscellany, man,
Bursts of great heart and slips in sensual
  mire,
But whole and one: and take them all-in-all,
Were we ourselves but half as good, as
  kind,

As truthful, much that Ida claims as right
Had ne'er been mooted, but as frankly
  theirs
As dues of Nature. To our point: not war:
Lest I lose all.'
                 'Nay, nay, you spake but sense'
Said Gama. 'We remember love ourself
In our sweet youth; we did not rate him
  then
This red-hot iron to be shaped with blows.
You talk almost like Ida: *she* can talk;
And there is something in it as you say:
But you talk kindlier: we esteem you for
  it.—
He seems a gracious and a gallant Prince,
I would he had our daughter: for the rest,
Our own detention, why, the causes
  weigh'd,
Fatherly fears—you used us courteously—
We would do much to gratify your Prince—
We pardon it; and for your ingress here
Upon the skirt and fringe of our fair land,
You did but come as goblins in the night,
Nor in the furrow broke the ploughman's
  head,
Nor burnt the grange, nor buss'd the
  milking-maid,
Nor robb'd the farmer of his bowl of
  cream:
But let your Prince (our royal word upon it,
He comes back safe) ride with us to our
  lines,
And speak with Arac: Arac's word is thrice
As ours with Ida: something may be
  done—
I know not what—and ours shall see us
  friends.
You, likewise, our late guests, if so you
  will,
Follow us: who knows? we four may build
  some plan
Foursquare to opposition.'
                          Here he reach'd
White hands of farewell to my sire, who
  growl'd
An answer which, half-muffled in his
  beard,
Let so much out as gave us leave to go.

Then rode we with the old king across
  the lawns

Beneath huge trees, a thousand rings of Spring
In every bole, a song on every spray
Of birds that piped their Valentines, and woke
Desire in me to infuse my tale of love
In the old king's ears, who promised help, and oozed
All o'er with honey'd answer as we rode
And blossom-fragrant slipt the heavy dews
Gather'd by night and peace, with each light air
On our mail'd heads: but other thoughts than Peace
Burnt in us, when we saw the embattled squares,
And squadrons of the Prince, trampling the flowers
With clamour: for among them rose a cry
As if to greet the king; they made a halt;
The horses yell'd; they clash'd their arms; the drum
Beat; merrily-blowing shrill'd the martial fife;
And in the blast and bray of the long horn
And serpent-throated bugle, undulated
The banner: anon to meet us lightly pranced
Three captains out; nor ever had I seen
Such thews of men: the midmost and the highest
Was Arac: all about his motion clung
The shadow of his sister, as the beam
Of the East, that play'd upon them, made them glance
Like those three stars of the airy Giant's zone,
That glitter burnish'd by the frosty dark;
And as the fiery Sirius alters hue,
And bickers into red and emerald, shone
Their morions, wash'd with morning, as they came.

And I that prated peace, when first I heard
War-music, felt the blind wildbeast of force,
Whose home is in the sinews of a man,
Stir in me as to strike: then took the king
His three broad sons; with now a wandering hand

And now a pointed finger, told them all:
A common light of smiles at our disguise
Broke from their lips, and, ere the windy jest
Had labour'd down within his ample lungs,
The genial giant, Arac, roll'd himself
Thrice in the saddle, then burst out in words.

'Our land invaded, 'sdeath! and he himself
Your captive, yet my father wills not war:
And, 'sdeath! myself, what care I, war or no?
But then this question of your troth remains:
And there's a downright honest meaning in her;
She flies too high, she flies too high! and yet
She ask'd but space and fairplay for her scheme;
She prest and prest it on me—I myself,
What know I of these things? but, life and soul!
I thought her half-right talking of her wrongs;
I say she flies too high, 'sdeath! what of that?
I take her for the flower of womankind,
And so I often told her, right or wrong,
And, Prince, she can be sweet to those she loves,
And, right or wrong, I care not: this is all,
I stand upon her side: she made me swear it—
'Sdeath—and with solemn rites by candle-light—
Swear by St. something—I forget her name—
Her that talk'd down the fifty wisest men;
She was a princess too; and so I swore.
Come, this is all; she will not: waive your claim:
If not, the foughten field, what else, at once
Decides it, 'sdeath! against my father's will.'

I lagg'd in answer loth to render up
My precontract, and loth by brainless war
To cleave the rift of difference deeper yet;

Till one of those two brothers, half aside
And fingering at the hair about his lip,
To prick us on to combat 'Like to like!
The woman's garment hid the woman's
    heart.'
A taunt that clench'd his purpose like a
    blow!
For fiery-short was Cyril's counter-scoff,
And sharp I answer'd, touch'd upon the
    point
Where idle boys are cowards to their
    shame,
'Decide it here: why not? we are three to
    three.'

Then spake the third 'But three to
    three? no more?
No more, and in our noble sister's cause?
More, more, for honour: every captain
    waits
Hungry for honour, angry for his king.
More, more, some fifty on a side, that each
May breathe himself, and quick! by over-
    throw
Of these or those, the question settled die.'

'Yea,' answer'd I, 'for this wild wreath
    of air,
This flake of rainbow flying on the highest
Foam of men's deeds—this honour, if ye
    will.
It needs must be for honour if at all:
Since, what decision? if we fail, we fail,
And if we win, we fail: she would not keep
Her compact.' ''Sdeath! but we will send
    to her,'
Said Arac, 'worthy reasons why she should
Bide by this issue: let our missive thro',
And you shall have her answer by the
    word.'

'Boys!' shriek'd the old king, but vain-
    lier than a hen
To her false daughters in the pool; for none
Regarded; neither seem'd there more to
    say:
Back rode we to my father's camp, and
    found
He thrice had sent a herald to the gates,
To learn if Ida yet would cede our claim,
Or by denial flush her babbling wells

With her own people's life: three times he
    went:
The first, he blew and blew, but none
    appear'd:
He batter'd at the doors; none came: the
    next,
An awful voice within had warn'd him
    thence:
The third, and those eight daughters of the
    plough
Came sallying thro' the gates, and caught
    his hair,
And so belabour'd him on rib and cheek
They made him wild: not less one glance
    he caught
Thro' open doors of Ida station'd there
Unshaken, clinging to her purpose, firm
Tho' compass'd by two armies and the
    noise
Of arms; and standing like a stately Pine
Set in a cataract on an island-crag,
When storm is on the heights, and right
    and left
Suck'd from the dark heart of the long
    hills roll
The torrents, dash'd to the vale: and yet
    her will
Bred will in me to overcome it or fall.

But when I told the king that I was
    pledged
To fight in tourney for my bride, he clash'd
His iron palms together with a cry;
Himself would tilt it out among the lads:
But overborne by all his bearded lords
With reasons drawn from age and state,
    perforce
He yielded, wroth and red, with fierce
    demur:
And many a bold knight started up in heat,
And sware to combat for my claim till
    death.

All on this side the palace ran the field
Flat to the garden-wall: and likewise here,
Above the garden's glowing blossom-belts,
A column'd entry shone and marble stairs,
And great bronze valves, emboss'd with
    Tomyris
And what she did to Cyrus after fight,
But now fast barr'd: so here upon the flat

THE PRINCESS; A MEDLEY

All that long morn the lists were hammer'd
up,
And all that morn the heralds to and fro,
With message and defiance, went and
came;
Last, Ida's answer, in a royal hand,
But shaken here and there, and rolling
words
Oration-like. I kiss'd it and I read.

  'O brother, you have known the pangs
we felt,
What heats of indignation when we heard
Of those that iron-cramp'd their women's
feet;
Of lands in which at the altar the poor
bride
Gives her harsh groom for bridal-gift a
scourge;
Of living hearts that crack within the fire
Where smoulder their dead despots; and
of those,—
Mothers,—that, all prophetic pity, fling
Their pretty maids in the running flood,
and swoops
The vulture, beak and talon, at the heart
Made for all noble motion: and I saw
That equal baseness lived in sleeker times
With smoother men: the old leaven
leaven'd all:
Millions of throats would bawl for civil
rights,
No woman named: therefore I set my
face
Against all men, and lived but for mine
own.
Far off from men I built a fold for them:
I stored it full of rich memorial:
I fenced it round with gallant institutes,
And biting laws to scare the beasts of prey
And prosper'd; till a rout of saucy boys
Brake on us at our books, and marr'd our
peace,
Mask'd like our maids, blustering I know
not what
Of insolence and love, some pretext held
Of baby troth, invalid, since my will
Seal'd not the bond—the striplings!—for
their sport!—
I tamed my leopards: shall I not tame
these?

Or you? or I? for since you think me
touch'd
In honour—what, I would not aught of
false—
Is not our cause pure? and whereas I know
Your prowess, Arac, and what mother's
blood
You draw from, fight; you failing, I abide
What end soever: fail you will not. Still
Take not his life: he risk'd it for my own;
His mother lives: yet whatsoe'er you do,
Fight and fight well; strike and strike
home. O dear
Brothers, the woman's Angel guards you,
you
The sole men to be mingled with our cause,
The sole men we shall prize in the after-
time,
Your very armour hallow'd, and your
statues
Rear'd, sung to, when, this gad-fly brush'd
aside,
We plant a solid foot into the Time,
And mould a generation strong to move
With claim on claim from right to right,
till she
Whose name is yoked with children's,
know herself;
And Knowledge in our own land make her
free,
And, ever following those two crowned
twins,
Commerce and conquest, shower the fiery
grain
Of freedom broadcast over all that orbs
Between the Northern and the Southern
morn.'

  Then came a postscript dash'd across
the rest.
'See that there be no traitors in your camp:
We seem a nest of traitors—none to trust
Since our arms fail'd—this Egypt-plague
of men!
Almost our maids were better at their
homes,
Than thus man-girdled here: indeed I think
Our chiefest comfort is the little child
Of one unworthy mother; which she left:
She shall not have it back: the child shall
grow

187

To prize the authentic mother of her mind.
I took it for an hour in mine own bed
This morning: there the tender orphan
    hands
Felt at my heart, and seem'd to charm
    from thence
The wrath I nursed against the world:
    farewell.'

    I ceased; he said, 'Stubborn, but she
    may sit
Upon a king's right hand in thunder-
    storms,
And breed up warriors! See now, tho'
    yourself
Be dazzled by the wildfire Love to sloughs
That swallow common sense, the spindling
    king,
This Gama swamp'd in lazy tolerance.
When the man wants weight, the woman
    takes it up,
And topples down the scales; but this is
    fixt
As are the roots of earth and base of all;
Man for the field and woman for the
    hearth:
Man for the sword and for the needle she:
Man with the head and woman with the
    heart:
Man to command and woman to obey;
All else confusion. Look you! the gray
    mare
Is ill to live with, when her whinny shrills
From tile to scullery, and her small good-
    man
Shrinks in his arm-chair while the fires of
    Hell
Mix with his hearth: but you—she's yet a
    colt—
Take, break her: strongly groom'd and
    straitly curb'd
She might not rank with those detestable
That let the bantling scald at home, and
    brawl
Their rights or wrongs like potherbs in the
    street.
They say she's comely; there's the fairer
    chance:
I like her none the less for rating at her!
Besides, the woman wed is not as we,
But suffers change of frame. A lusty brace

Of twins may weed her of her folly. Boy,
The bearing and the training of a child
Is woman's wisdom.'
              Thus the hard old king:
I took my leave, for it was nearly noon:
I pored upon her letter which I held,
And on the little clause 'take not his life:'
I mused on that wild morning in the
    woods,
And on the 'Follow, follow, thou shalt win:'
I thought on all the wrathful king had said,
And how the strange betrothment was to
    end:
Then I remember'd that burnt sorcerer's
    curse
That one should fight with shadows and
    should fall;
And like a flash the weird affection came:
King, camp and college turn'd to hollow
    shows;
I seem'd to move in old memorial tilts,
And doing battle with forgotten ghosts,
To dream myself the shadow of a dream:
And ere I woke it was the point of noon,
The lists were ready. Empanoplied and
    plumed
We enter'd in, and waited, fifty there
Opposed to fifty, till the trumpet blared
At the barrier like a wild horn in a land
Of echoes, and a moment, and once more
The trumpet, and again: at which the
    storm
Of galloping hoofs bare on the ridge of
    spears
And riders front to front, until they closed
In conflict with the crash of shivering
    points,
And thunder. Yet it seem'd a dream, I
    dream'd
Of fighting. On his haunches rose the steed,
And into fiery splinters leapt the lance,
And out of stricken helmets sprang the fire.
Part sat like rocks: part reel'd but kept
    their seats:
Part roll'd on the earth and rose again and
    drew:
Part stumbled mixt with floundering
    horses. Down
From those two bulks at Arac's side, and
    down
From Arac's arm, as from a giant's flail,

The large blows rain'd, as here and every-
   where
He rode the mellay, lord of the ringing
   lists,
And all the plain,—brand, mace, and shaft,
   and shield—
Shock'd, like an iron-clanging anvil bang'd
With hammers; till I thought, can this be
   he
From Gama's dwarfish loins? if this be so,
The mother makes us most—and in my
   dream
I glanced aside, and saw the palace-front
Alive with fluttering scarfs and ladies' eyes,
And highest, among the statues, statue-like,
Between a cymbal'd Miriam and a Jael,
With Psyche's babe, was Ida watching us,
A single band of gold about her hair,
Like a Saint's glory up in heaven: but she
No saint—inexorable—no tenderness—
Too hard, too cruel: yet she sees me fight,
Yea, let her see me fall! with that I drave
Among the thickest and bore down a
   Prince,
And Cyril, one. Yea, let me make my
   dream
All that I would. But that large-moulded
   man,
His visage all agrin as at a wake,
Made at me thro' the press, and, stagger-
   ing back
With stroke on stroke the horse and horse-
   man, came
As comes a pillar of electric cloud,
Flaying the roofs and sucking up the
   drains,
And shadowing down the champaign till
   it strikes
On a wood, and takes, and breaks, and
   cracks, and splits,
And twists the grain with such a roar that
   Earth
Reels, and the herdsmen cry; for every-
   thing
Gave way before him: only Florian, he
That loved me closer than his own right
   eye,
Thrust in between; but Arac rode him
   down:
And Cyril seeing it, push'd against the
   Prince,

With Psyche's colour round his helmet,
   tough,
Strong, supple, sinew-corded, apt at arms;
But tougher, heavier, stronger, he that
   smote
And threw him: last I spurr'd; I felt my
   veins
Stretch with fierce heat; a moment hand
   to hand,
And sword to sword, and horse to horse
   we hung,
Till I struck out and shouted; the blade
   glanced,
I did but shear a feather, and dream and
   truth
Flow'd from me; darkness closed me; and
   I fell.

VI

Home they brought her warrior dead:
   She nor swoon'd, nor utter'd cry:
All her maidens, watching, said,
   'She must weep or she will die.'

Then they praised him, soft and low,
   Call'd him worthy to be loved,
Truest friend and noblest foe;
   Yet she neither spoke nor moved.

Stole a maiden from her place,
   Lightly to the warrior stept,
Took the face-cloth from the face;
   Yet she neither moved nor wept.

Rose a nurse of ninety years,
   Set his child upon her knee—
Like summer tempest came her tears—
   'Sweet my child, I live for thee.'

My dream had never died or lived again.
As in some mystic middle state I lay;
Seeing I saw not, hearing not I heard:
Tho', if I saw not, yet they told me all
So often that I speak as having seen.

   For so it seem'd, or so they said to me,
That all things grew more tragic and more
   strange;
That when our side was vanquish'd and
   my cause
For ever lost, there went up a great cry,
The Prince is slain. My father heard and
   ran
In on the lists, and there unlaced my
   casque

And grovell'd on my body, and after him
Came Psyche, sorrowing for Aglaïa.

But high upon the palace Ida stood
With Psyche's babe in arm: there on the
    roofs
Like that great dame of Lapidoth she sang.

    'Our enemies have fall'n, have fall'n: the
      seed,
The little seed they laugh'd at in the dark,
Has risen and cleft the soil, and grown a bulk
Of spanless girth, that lays on every side
A thousand arms and rushes to the Sun

    'Our enemies have fall'n, have fall'n: they
      came;
The leaves were wet with women's tears: they
    heard
A noise of songs they would not understand:
They mark'd it with the red cross to the fall,
And would have strown it, and are fall'n them-
    selves.

    'Our enemies have fall'n, have fall'n: they
      came,
The woodmen with their axes: lo the tree!
But we will make it faggots for the hearth,
And shape it plank and beam for roof and floor,
And boats and bridges for the use of men.

    'Our enemies have fall'n, have fall'n: they
      struck;
With their own blows they hurt themselves,
    nor knew
There dwelt an iron nature in the grain:
The glittering axe was broken in their arms,
Their arms were shatter'd to the shoulder blade.

    'Our enemies have fall'n, but this shall grow
A night of Summer from the heat, a breadth
Of Autumn, dropping fruits of power: and
    roll'd
With music in the growing breeze of Time,
The tops shall strike from star to star, the fangs
Shall move the stony bases of the world.

    'And now, O maids, behold our sanc-
      tuary
Is violate, our laws broken: fear we not
To break them more in their behoof, whose
    arms
Champion'd our cause and won it with a
    day
Blanch'd in our annals, and perpetual feast,
When dames and heroines of the golden
    year
Shall strip a hundred hollows bare of
    Spring,
To rain an April of ovation round

Their statues, borne aloft, the three: but
    come,
We will be liberal, since our rights are won.
Let them not lie in the tents with coarse
    mankind,
Ill nurses; but descend, and proffer these
The brethren of our blood and cause, that
    there
Lie bruised and maim'd, the tender minis-
    tries
Of female hands and hospitality.'

She spoke, and with the babe yet in her
    arms,
Descending, burst the great bronze valves,
    and led
A hundred maids in train across the Park.
Some cowl'd, and some bare-headed, on
    they came,
Their feet in flowers, her loveliest: by them
    went
The enamour'd air sighing, and on their
    curls
From the high tree the blossom wavering
    fell,
And over them the tremulous isles of light
Slided, they moving under shade: but
    Blanche
At distance follow'd: so they came: anon
Thro' open field into the lists they wound
Timorously; and as the leader of the herd
That holds a stately fretwork to the Sun,
And follow'd up by a hundred airy does,
Steps with a tender foot, light as on air,
The lovely, lordly creature floated on
To where her wounded brethren lay; there
    stay'd;
Knelt on one knee,—the child on one,—
    and prest
Their hands, and call'd them dear de-
    liverers,
And happy warriors, and immortal names,
And said 'You shall not lie in the tents but
    here,
And nursed by those for whom you fought,
    and served
With female hands and hospitality.'

Then, whether moved by this, or was it
    chance,
She past my way. Up started from my side

The old lion, glaring with his whelpless
    eye,
Silent; but when she saw me lying stark,
Dishelm'd and mute, and motionlessly
    pale,
Cold ev'n to her, she sigh'd; and when she
    saw
The haggard father's face and reverend
    beard
Of grisly twine, all dabbled with the blood
Of his own son, shudder'd, a twitch of pain
Tortured her mouth, and o'er her forehead
    past
A shadow, and her hue changed, and she
    said:
'He saved my life: my brother slew him
    for it.'
No more: at which the king in bitter scorn
Drew from my neck the painting and the
    tress,
And held them up: she saw them, and a
    day
Rose from the distance on her memory,
When the good Queen, her mother, shore
    the tress
With kisses, ere the days of Lady Blanche:
And then once more she look'd at my pale
    face:
Till understanding all the foolish work
Of Fancy, and the bitter close of all,
Her iron will was broken in her mind;
Her noble heart was molten in her breast;
She bow'd, she set the child on the earth;
    she laid
A feeling finger on my brows, and presently
'O Sire,' she said, 'he lives: he is not dead:
O let me have him with my brethren here
In our own palace: we will tend on him
Like one of these; if so, by any means,
To lighten this great clog of thanks, that
    make
Our progress falter to the woman's goal.'

She said: but at the happy word 'he lives'
My father stoop'd, re-father'd o'er my
    wounds.
So those two foes above my fallen life,
With brow to brow like night and evening
    mixt
Their dark and gray, while Psyche ever
    stole

A little nearer, till the babe that by us,
Half-lapt in glowing gauze and golden
    brede,
Lay like a new-fall'n meteor on the grass,
Uncared for, spied its mother and began
A blind and babbling laughter, and to
    dance
Its body, and reach its fatling innocent
    arms
And lazy lingering fingers. She the appeal
Brook'd not, but clamouring out 'Mine—
    mine—not yours,
It is not yours, but mine: give me the
    child'
Ceased all on tremble: piteous was the cry:
So stood the unhappy mother open-
    mouth'd,
And turn'd each face her way: wan was her
    cheek
With hollow watch, her blooming mantle
    torn,
Red grief and mother's hunger in her eye,
And down dead-heavy sank her curls, and
    half
The sacred mother's bosom, panting, burst
The laces toward her babe; but she nor
    cared
Nor knew it, clamouring on, till Ida heard,
Look'd up, and rising slowly from me,
    stood
Erect and silent, striking with her glance
The mother, me, the child; but he that lay
Beside us, Cyril, batter'd as he was,
Trail'd himself up on one knee: then he
    drew
Her robe to meet his lips, and down she
    look'd
At the arm'd man sideways, pitying as it
    seem'd,
Or self-involved; but when she learnt his
    face,
Remembering his ill-omen'd song, arose
Once more thro' all her height, and o'er
    him grew
Tall as a figure lengthen'd on the sand
When the tide ebbs in sunshine, and he
    said:

'O fair and strong and terrible! Lioness
That with your long locks play the Lion's
    mane!

But Love and Nature, these are two more
terrible
And stronger. See, your foot is on our
necks,
We vanquish'd, you the Victor of your will.
What would you more? give her the child!
remain
Orb'd in your isolation: he is dead,
Or all as dead: henceforth we let you be:
Win you the hearts of women; and beware
Lest, where you seek the common love of
these,
The common hate with the revolving wheel
Should drag you down, and some great
Nemesis
Break from a darken'd future, crown'd
with fire,
And tread you out for ever: but howsoe'er
Fix'd in yourself, never in your own arms
To hold your own, deny not hers to her.
Give her the child! O if, I say, you keep
One pulse that beats true woman, if you
loved
The breast that fed or arm that dandled
you,
Or own one port of sense not flint to prayer,
Give her the child! or if you scorn to lay it,
Yourself, in hands so lately claspt with
yours,
Or speak to her, your dearest, her one
fault
The tenderness, not yours, that could not
kill,
Give *me* it: *I* will give it her.'
                                        He said:
At first her eye with slow dilation roll'd
Dry flame, she listening; after sank and
sank
And, into mournful twilight mellowing,
dwelt
Full on the child; she took it: 'Pretty bud!
Lily of the vale! half open'd bell of the
woods!
Sole comfort of my dark hour, when a
world
Of traitorous friend and broken system
made
No purple in the distance, mystery,
Pledge of a love not to be mine, farewell;
These men are hard upon us as of old,
We two must part: and yet how fain was I

To dream thy cause embraced in mine, to
think
I might be something to thee, when I felt
Thy helpless warmth about my barren
breast
In the dead prime: but may thy mother
prove
As true to thee as false, false, false to me!
And, if thou needs must bear the yoke, I
wish it
Gentle as freedom'—here she kiss'd it:
then—
'All good go with thee! take it Sir,' and so
Laid the soft babe in his hard-mailed
hands,
Who turn'd half-round to Psyche as she
sprang
To meet it, with an eye that swum in
thanks;
Then felt it sound and whole from head to
foot,
And hugg'd and never hugg'd it close
enough,
And in her hunger mouth'd and mumbled
it,
And hid her bosom with it; after that
Put on more calm and added suppliantly:

'We two were friends: I go to mine own
land
For ever: find some other: as for me
I scarce am fit for your great plans: yet
speak to me,
Say one soft word and let me part forgiven.'

But Ida spoke not, rapt upon the child.
Then Arac. 'Ida—'sdeath! you blame the
man;
You wrong yourselves—the woman is so
hard
Upon the woman. Come, a grace to me!
I am your warrior: I and mine have fought
Your battle: kiss her; take her hand, she
weeps:
'Sdeath! I would sooner fight thrice o'er
than see it.'

But Ida spoke not, gazing on the ground,
And reddening in the furrows of his chin,
And moved beyond his custom, Gama
said:

'I've heard that there is iron in the blood,
And I believe it. Not one word? not one?
Whence drew you this steel temper? not
  from me,
Not from your mother, now a saint with
  saints.
She said you had a heart—I heard her say
  it—
"Our Ida has a heart"—just ere she died—
"But see that some one with authority
Be near her still" and I—I sought for one—
All people said she had authority—
The Lady Blanche: much profit! Not one
  word;
No! tho' your father sues: see how you
  stand
Stiff as Lot's wife, and all the good knights
  maim'd,
I trust that there is no one hurt to death,
For your wild whim: and was it then for
  this,
Was it for this we gave our palace up,
Where we withdrew from summer heats
  and state,
And had our wine and chess beneath the
  planes,
And many a pleasant hour with her that's
  gone,
Ere you were born to vex us? Is it kind?
Speak to her I say: is this not she of whom,
When first she came, all flush'd you said
  to me
Now had you got a friend of your own age,
Now could you share your thought; now
  should men see
Two women faster welded in one love
Than pairs of wedlock; she you walk'd
  with, she
You talk'd with, whole nights long, up in
  the tower,
Of sine and arc, spheroid and azimuth,
And right ascension, Heaven knows what;
  and now
A word, but one, one little kindly word,
Not one to spare her: out upon you, flint!
You love nor her, nor me, nor any; nay,
You shame your mother's judgment too.
  Not one?
You will not? well—no heart have you, or
  such
As fancies like the vermin in a nut

Have fretted all to dust and bitterness.'
So said the small king moved beyond his
  wont.

But Ida stood nor spoke, drain'd of her
  force
By many a varying influence and so long.
Down thro' her limbs a drooping languor
  wept:
Her head a little bent; and on her mouth
A doubtful smile dwelt like a clouded moon
In a still water: then brake out my sire,
Lifting his grim head from my wounds.
                              'O you,
Woman, whom we thought woman even
  now,
And were half fool'd to let you tend our
  son,
Because he might have wish'd it—but we see
The accomplice of your madness unfor-
  given,
And think that you might mix his draught
  with death,
When your skies change again: the rougher
  hand
Is safer: on to the tents: take up the Prince.'

He rose, and while each ear was prick'd
  to attend
A tempest, thro' the cloud that dimm'd
  her broke
A genial warmth and light once more, and
  shone
Thro' glittering drops on her sad friend.
                              'Come hither.
O Psyche,' she cried out, 'embrace me,
  come,
Quick while I melt; make reconcilement
  sure
With one that cannot keep her mind an
  hour:
Come to the hollow heart they slander so!
Kiss and be friends, like children being
  chid!
I seem no more: *I* want forgiveness too:
I should have had to do with none but
  maids,
That have no links with men. Ah false but
  dear,
Dear traitor, too much loved, why?—
  why?—Yet see,

Before these kings we embrace you yet
    once more
With all forgiveness, all oblivion,
And trust, not love, you less.
               And now, O sire,
Grant me your son, to nurse, to wait upon
    him,
Like mine own brother. For my debt to
    him,
This nightmare weight of gratitude, I
    know it;
Taunt me no more: yourself and yours
    shall have
Free adit; we will scatter all our maids
Till happier times each to her proper
    hearth:
What use to keep them here—now? grant
    my prayer.
Help, father, brother, help; speak to the
    king:
Thaw this male nature to some touch of
    that
Which kills me with myself, and drags me
    down
From my fixt height to mob me up with all
The soft and milky rabble of womankind,
Poor weakling ev'n as they are.'
               Passionate tears
Follow'd: the king replied not: Cyril said:
'Your brother, Lady,—Florian,—ask for
    him
Of your great head—for he is wounded
    too—
That you may tend upon him with the
    prince.'
'Ay so,' said Ida with a bitter smile,
'Our laws are broken: let him enter too.'
Then Violet, she that sang the mournful
    song,
And had a cousin tumbled on the plain,
Petition'd too for him. 'Ay so,' she said,
'I stagger in the stream: I cannot keep
My heart an eddy from the brawling hour:
We break our laws with ease, but let it be.'
'Ay so?' said Blanche: 'Amazed am I to
    hear
Your Highness: but your Highness breaks
    with ease
The law your Highness did not make:
    'twas I.
I had been wedded wife, I knew mankind,

And block'd them out; but these men came
    to woo
Your Highness—verily I think to win.'

So she, and turn'd askance a wintry eye:
But Ida with a voice, that like a bell
Toll'd by an earthquake in a trembling
    tower,
Rang ruin, answer'd full of grief and scorn.

'Fling our doors wide! all, all, not one,
    but all,
Not only he, but by my mother's soul,
Whatever man lies wounded, friend or foe,
Shall enter, if he will. Let our girls flit,
Till the storm die! but had you stood by us,
The roar that breaks the Pharos from his
    base
Had left us rock. She fain would sting us too,
But shall not. Pass, and mingle with your
    likes.
We brook no further insult but are gone.'

She turn'd; the very nape of her white
    neck
Was rosed with indignation: but the Prince
Her brother came; the king her father
    charm'd
Her wounded soul with words: nor did
    mine own
Refuse her proffer, lastly gave his hand.

Then us they lifted up, dead weights,
    and bare
Straight to the doors: to them the doors
    gave way
Groaning, and in the Vestal entry shriek'd
The virgin marble under iron heels:
And on they moved and gain'd the hall,
    and there
Rested: but great the crush was, and each
    base,
To left and right, of those tall columns
    drown'd
In silken fluctuation and the swarm
Of female whisperers: at the further end
Was Ida by the throne, the two great cats
Close by her, like supporters on a shield,
Bow-back'd with fear: but in the centre
    stood
The common men with rolling eyes;
    amazed

They glared upon the women, and aghast
The women stared at these, all silent, save
When armour clash'd or jingled, while the
      day,
Descending, struck athwart the hall, and
      shot
A flying splendour out of brass and steel,
That o'er the statues leapt from head to
      head,
Now fired an angry Pallas on the helm,
Now set a wrathful Dian's moon on flame,
And now and then an echo started up,
And shuddering fled from room to room,
      and died
Of fright in far apartments.
                              Then the voice
Of Ida sounded, issuing ordinance:
And me they bore up the broad stairs, and
      thro'
The long-laid galleries past a hundred
      doors
To one deep chamber shut from sound,
      and due
To languid limbs and sickness; left me
      in it;
And others otherwhere they laid; and all
That afternoon a sound arose of hoof
And chariot, many a maiden passing home
Till happier times; but some were left of
      those
Held sagest, and the great lords out and in,
From those two hosts that lay beside the
      walls,
Walk'd at their will, and everything was
      changed.

VII

Ask me no more: the moon may draw the sea;
   The cloud may stoop from heaven and take
      the shape
   With fold to fold, of mountain or of cape;
But O too fond, when have I answer'd thee?
      Ask me no more.

Ask me no more: what answer should I give?
   I love not hollow cheek or faded eye:
   Yet, O my friend, I will not have thee die!
Ask me no more, lest I should bid thee live;
      Ask me no more.

Ask me no more: thy fate and mine are seal'd:
   I strove against the stream and all in vain:
   Let the great river take me to the main:
No more, dear love, for at a touch I yield;
      Ask me no more.

So was their sanctuary violated,
So their fair college turn'd to hospital;
At first with all confusion: by and by
Sweet order lived again with other laws:
A kindlier influence reign'd; and every-
      where
Low voices with the ministering hand
Hung round the sick: the maidens came,
      they talk'd,
They sang, they read: till she not fair began
To gather light, and she that was, became
Her former beauty treble; and to and fro
With books, with flowers, with Angel
      offices,
Like creatures native unto gracious act,
And in their own clear element, they
      moved.

But sadness on the soul of Ida fell,
And hatred of her weakness, blent with
      shame.
Old studies fail'd; seldom she spoke: but
      oft
Clomb to the roofs, and gazed alone for
      hours
On that disastrous leaguer, swarms of men
Darkening her female field: void was her
      use,
And she as one that climbs a peak to gaze
O'er land and main, and sees a great black
      cloud
Drag inward from the deeps, a wall of
      night,
Blot out the slope of sea from verge to
      shore,
And suck the blinding splendour from the
      sand,
And quenching lake by lake and tarn by
      tarn
Expunge the world: so fared she gazing
      there;
So blacken'd all her world in secret, blank
And waste it seem'd and vain; till down
      she came,
And found fair peace once more among the
      sick.

And twilight dawn'd; and morn by morn
      the lark
Shot up and shrill'd in flickering gyres,
      but I

Lay silent in the muffled cage of life:
And twilight gloom'd; and broader-grown
    the bowers
Drew the great night into themselves, and
    Heaven,
Star after star, arose and fell; but I,
Deeper than those weird doubts could
    reach me, lay
Quite sunder'd from the moving Universe,
Nor knew what eye was on me, nor the
    hand
That nursed me, more than infants in their
    sleep.

But Psyche tended Florian: with her oft,
Melissa came; for Blanche had gone, but
    left
Her child among us, willing she should
    keep
Court-favour: here and there the small
    bright head,
A light of healing, glanced about the couch,
Or thro' the parted silks the tender face
Peep'd, shining in upon the wounded man
With blush and smile, a medicine in them-
    selves
To wile the length from languorous hours,
    and draw
The sting from pain; nor seem'd it strange
    that soon
He rose up whole, and those fair charities
Join'd at her side; nor stranger seem'd that
    hearts
So gentle, so employ'd, should close in
    love,
Than when two dewdrops on the petal
    shake
To the same sweet air, and tremble deeper
    down,
And slip at once all-fragrant into one.

Less prosperously the second suit ob-
    tain'd
At first with Psyche. Not tho' Blanche had
    sworn
That after that dark night among the fields
She needs must wed him for her own good
    name;
Not tho' he built upon the babe restored;
Nor tho' she liked him, yielded she, but
    fear'd

To incense the Head once more; till on a day
When Cyril pleaded, Ida came behind
Seen but of Psyche: on her foot she hung
A moment, and she heard, at which her face
A little flush'd, and she past on; but each
Assumed from thence a half-consent in-
    volved
In stillness, plighted troth, and were at
    peace.

Nor only these: Love in the sacred halls
Held carnival at will, and flying struck
With showers of random sweet on maid
    and man.
Nor did her father cease to press my claim,
Nor did mine own, now reconciled; nor yet
Did those twin brothers, risen again and
    whole;
Nor Arac, satiate with his victory.

But I lay still, and with me oft she sat:
Then came a change; for sometimes I
    would catch
Her hand in wild delirium, gripe it hard,
And fling it like a viper off, and shriek
'You are not Ida;' clasp it once again,
And call her Ida, tho' I knew her not,
And call her sweet, as if in irony,
And call her hard and cold which seem'd
    a truth:
And still she fear'd that I should lose my
    mind,
And often she believed that I should die:
Till out of long frustration of her care,
And pensive tendance in the all-weary
    noons,
And watches in the dead, the dark, when
    clocks
Throbb'd thunder thro' the palace floors,
    or call'd
On flying Time from all their silver
    tongues—
And out of memories of her kindlier days,
And sidelong glances at my father's grief,
And at the happy lovers heart in heart—
And out of hauntings of my spoken love,
And lonely listenings to my mutter'd
    dream,
And often feeling of the helpless hands,
And wordless broodings on the wasted
    cheek—

From all a closer interest flourish'd up,
Tenderness touch by touch, and last, to
these,
Love, like an Alpine harebell hung with
tears
By some cold morning glacier; frail at first
And feeble, all unconscious of itself,
But such as gather'd colour day by day.

Last I woke sane, but well-nigh close to
death
For weakness: it was evening: silent light
Slept on the painted walls, wherein were
wrought
Two grand designs; for on one side arose
The women up in wild revolt, and storm'd
At the Oppian law. Titanic shapes, they
cramm'd
The forum, and half-crush'd among the
rest
A dwarf-like Cato cower'd. On the other
side
Hortensia spoke against the tax; behind,
A train of dames: by axe and eagle sat,
With all their foreheads drawn in Roman
scowls,
And half the wolf's-milk curdled in their
veins,
The fierce triumvirs; and before them
paused
Hortensia pleading: angry was her face.

I saw the forms: I knew not where I was:
They did but look like hollow shows; nor
more
Sweet Ida: palm to palm she sat: the dew
Dwelt in her eyes, and softer all her shape
And rounder seem'd: I moved: I sigh'd: a
touch
Came round my wrist, and tears upon my
hand:
Then all for languor and self-pity ran
Mine down my face, and with what life I
had,
And like a flower that cannot all unfold,
So drench'd it is with tempest, to the sun,
Yet, as it may, turns toward him, I on her
Fixt my faint eyes, and utter'd whisper-
ingly:

'If you be, what I think you, some sweet
dream,

I would but ask you to fulfil yourself:
But if you be that Ida whom I knew,
I ask you nothing: only, if a dream,
Sweet dream, be perfect. I shall die
to-night.
Stoop down and seem to kiss me ere I die.'

I could no more, but lay like one in
trance,
That hears his burial talk'd of by his
friends,
And cannot speak, nor move, nor make one
sign,
But lies and dreads his doom. She turn'd;
she paused;
She stoop'd; and out of languor leapt a cry;
Leapt fiery Passion from the brinks of
death;
And I believed that in the living world
My spirit closed with Ida's at the lips;
Till back I fell, and from mine arms she
rose
Glowing all over noble shame; and all
Her falser self slipt from her like a robe,
And left her woman, lovelier in her mood
Than in her mould that other, when she
came
From barren deeps to conquer all with
love;
And down the streaming crystal dropt; and
she
Far-fleeted by the purple island-sides,
Naked, a double light in air and wave,
To meet her Graces, where they deck'd
her out
For worship without end; nor end of mine,
Stateliest, for thee! but mute she glided
forth,
Nor glanced behind her, and I sank and
slept,
Fill'd thro' and thro' with Love, a happy
sleep.

Deep in the night I woke: she, near me,
held
A volume of the Poets of her land:
There to herself, all in low tones, she read.

'Now sleeps the crimson petal, now the white;
Nor waves the cypress in the palace walk;
Nor winks the gold fin in the porphyry font:
The fire-fly wakens: waken thou with me.

Now droops the milkwhite peacock like a ghost,
And like a ghost she glimmers on to me.

Now lies the Earth all Danaë to the stars,
And all thy heart lies open unto me.

Now slides the silent meteor on, and leaves
A shining furrow, as thy thoughts in me.

Now folds the lily all her sweetness up,
And slips into the bosom of the lake:
So fold thyself, my dearest, thou, and slip
Into my bosom and be lost in me.'

I heard her turn the page; she found a small
Sweet Idyl, and once more, as low, she read:

'Come down, O maid, from yonder mountain height:
What pleasure lives in height (the shepherd sang)
In height and cold, the splendour of the hills?
But cease to move so near the Heavens, and cease
To glide a sunbeam by the blasted Pine,
To sit a star upon the sparkling spire;
And come, for Love is of the valley, come,
For Love is of the valley, come thou down
And find him; by the happy threshold, he,
Or hand in hand with Plenty in the maize,
Or red with spirted purple of the vats,
Or foxlike in the vine; nor cares to walk
With Death and Morning on the silver horns,
Nor wilt thou snare him in the white ravine,
Nor find him dropt upon the firths of ice,
That huddling slant in furrow-cloven falls
To roll the torrent out of dusky doors:
But follow; let the torrent dance thee down
To find him in the valley; let the wild
Lean-headed Eagles yelp alone, and leave
The monstrous ledges there to slope, and spill
Their thousand wreaths of dangling water-smoke,
That like a broken purpose waste in air:
So waste not thou; but come; for all the vales
Await thee; azure pillars of the hearth
Arise to thee: the children call, and I
Thy shepherd pipe, and sweet is every sound,
Sweeter thy voice, but every sound is sweet;
Myriads of rivulets hurrying thro' the lawn,
The moan of doves in immemorial elms,
And murmuring of innumerable bees.'

So she low-toned; while with shut eyes I lay
Listening; then look'd. Pale was the perfect face;
The bosom with long sighs labour'd; and meek

Seem'd the full lips, and mild the luminous eyes,
And the voice trembled and the hand. She said
Brokenly, that she knew it, she had fail'd
In sweet humility; had fail'd in all;
That all her labour was but as a block
Left in the quarry; but she still were loth,
She still were loth to yield herself to one
That wholly scorn'd to help their equal rights
Against the sons of men, and barbarous laws.
She pray'd me not to judge their cause from her
That wrong'd it, sought far less for truth than power
In knowledge: something wild within her breast,
A greater than all knowledge, beat her down.
And she had nursed me there from week to week:
Much had she learnt in little time. In part
It was ill counsel had misled the girl
To vex true hearts: yet was she but a girl—
'Ah fool, and made myself a Queen of farce!
When comes another such? never, I think,
Till the Sun drop, dead, from the signs.'
Her voice
Choked, and her forehead sank upon her hands,
And her great heart thro' all the faultful Past
Went sorrowing in a pause I dared not break;
Till notice of a change in the dark world
Was lispt about the acacias, and a bird,
That early woke to feed her little ones,
Sent from a dewy breast a cry for light:
She moved, and at her feet the volume fell.

'Blame not thyself too much,' I said, 'nor blame
Too much the sons of men and barbarous laws;
These were the rough ways of the world till now.
Henceforth thou hast a helper, me, that know

The woman's cause is man's: they rise or
    sink
Together, dwarf'd or godlike, bond or free:
For she that out of Lethe scales with man
The shining steps of Nature, shares with
    man
His nights, his days, moves with him to
    one goal,
Stays all the fair young planet in her
    hands—
If she be small, slight-natured, miserable,
How shall men grow? but work no more
    alone!
Our place is much: as far as in us lies
We two will serve them both in aiding
    her—
Will clear away the parasitic forms
That seem to keep her up but drag her
    down—
Will leave her space to burgeon out of all
Within her—let her make herself her own
To give or keep, to live and learn and be
All that not harms distinctive womanhood.
For woman is not undevelopt man,
But diverse: could we make her as the man,
Sweet Love were slain: his dearest bond
    is this,
Not like to like, but like in difference.
Yet in the long years liker must they grow;
The man be more of woman, she of man;
He gain in sweetness and in moral height,
Nor lose the wrestling thews that throw
    the world;
She mental breadth, nor fail in childward
    care,
Nor lose the childlike in the larger mind;
Till at the last she set herself to man,
Like perfect music unto noble words;
And so these twain, upon the skirts of
    Time,
Sit side by side, full-summ'd in all their
    powers,
Dispensing harvest, sowing the To-be,
Self-reverent each and reverencing each,
Distinct in individualities,
But like each other ev'n as those who love.
Then comes the statelier Eden back to men:
Then reign the world's great bridals, chaste
    and calm:
Then springs the crowning race of human-
    kind.

May these things be!'
                Sighing she spoke 'I fear
They will not.'
      'Dear, but let us type them now
In our own lives, and this proud watch-
    word rest
Of equal; seeing either sex alone
Is half itself, and in true marriage lies
Nor equal, nor unequal: each fulfils
Defect in each, and always thought in
    thought,
Purpose in purpose, will in will, they grow,
The single pure and perfect animal,
The two-cell'd heart beating, with one full
    stroke,
Life.'

    And again sighing she spoke: 'A dream
That once was mine! what woman taught
    you this?'

    'Alone,' I said, 'from earlier than I
    know,
Immersed in rich foreshadowings of the
    world,
I loved the woman: he, that doth not, lives
A drowning life, besotted in sweet self,
Or pines in sad experience worse than
    death,
Or keeps his wing'd affections clipt with
    crime:
Yet was there one thro' whom I loved her,
    one
Not learned, save in gracious household
    ways,
Not perfect, nay, but full of tender wants,
No Angel, but a dearer being, all dipt
In Angel instincts, breathing Paradise,
Interpreter between the Gods and men,
Who look'd all native to her place, and yet
On tiptoe seem'd to touch upon a sphere
Too gross to tread, and all male minds
    perforce
Sway'd to her from their orbits as they
    moved,
And girdled her with music. Happy he
With such a mother! faith in womankind
Beats with his blood, and trust in all things
    high
Comes easy to him, and tho' he trip and
    fall
He shall not blind his soul with clay.'

'But I,'
Said Ida, tremulously, 'so all unlike—
It seems you love to cheat yourself with
    words:
This mother is your model. I have heard
Of your strange doubts: they well might
    be: I seem
A mockery to my own self. Never, Prince;
You cannot love me.'
                    'Nay but thee' I said
'From yearlong poring on thy pictured
    eyes,
Ere seen I loved, and loved thee seen, and
    saw
Thee woman thro' the crust of iron moods
That mask'd thee from men's reverence
    up, and forced
Sweet love on pranks of saucy boyhood:
    now,
Giv'n back to life, to life indeed, thro' thee,
Indeed I love: the new day comes, the
    light
Dearer for night, as dearer thou for faults
Lived over: lift thine eyes; my doubts are
    dead,
My haunting sense of hollow shows: the
    change,
This truthful change in thee has kill'd it.
    Dear,
Look up, and let thy nature strike on mine,
Like yonder morning on the blind half-
    world;
Approach and fear not; breathe upon my
    brows;
In that fine air I tremble, all the past
Melts mist-like into this bright hour, and
    this
Is morn to more, and all the rich to-come
Reels, as the golden Autumn woodland
    reels
Athwart the smoke of burning weeds. For-
    give me,
I waste my heart in signs: let be. My bride,
My wife, my life. O we will walk this world,
Yoked in all exercise of noble end,
And so thro' those dark gates across the
    wild
That no man knows. Indeed I love thee:
    come,
Yield thyself up: my hopes and thine are
    one:

Accomplish thou my manhood and thy-
    self;
Lay thy sweet hands in mine and trust
    to me.'

CONCLUSION

So closed our tale, of which I give you all
The random scheme as wildly as it rose:
The words are mostly mine; for when we
    ceased
There came a minute's pause, and Walter
    said,
'I wish she had not yielded!' then to me,
'What, if you drest it up poetically!'
So pray'd the men, the women: I gave
    assent:
Yet how to bind the scatter'd scheme of
    seven
Together in one sheaf? What style could
    suit?
The men required that I should give
    throughout
The sort of mock-heroic gigantesque,
With which we banter'd little Lilia first:
The women—and perhaps they felt their
    power,
For something in the ballads which they
    sang,
Or in their silent influence as they sat,
Had ever seem'd to wrestle with burlesque,
And drove us, last, to quite a solemn
    close—
They hated banter, wish'd for something
    real,
A gallant fight, a noble princess—why
Not make her true-heroic—true-sublime?
Or all, they said, as earnest as the close?
Which yet with such a framework scarce
    could be.
Then rose a little feud betwixt the two,
Betwixt the mockers and the realists:
And I, betwixt them both, to please them
    both,
And yet to give the story as it rose,
I moved as in a strange diagonal,
And maybe neither pleased myself nor
    them.

But Lilia pleased me, for she took no
    part
In our dispute: the sequel of the tale

Had touch'd her; and she sat, she pluck'd
the grass,
She flung it from her, thinking: last, she
fixt
A showery glance upon her aunt, and said,
'You—tell us what we are' who might have
told,
For she was cramm'd with theories out of
books,
But that there rose a shout: the gates were
closed
At sunset, and the crowd were swarming
now,
To take their leave, about the garden rails.

So I and some went out to these: we
climb'd
The slope to Vivian-place, and turning saw
The happy valleys, half in light, and half
Far-shadowing from the west, a land of
peace;
Gray halls alone among their massive
groves;
Trim hamlets; here and there a rustic tower
Half-lost in belts of hop and breadths of
wheat;
The shimmering glimpses of a stream; the
seas;
A red sail, or a white; and far beyond,
Imagined more than seen, the skirts of
France.

'Look there, a garden!' said my college
friend,
The Tory member's elder son, 'and there!
God bless the narrow sea which keeps her
off,
And keep our Britain, whole within herself,
A nation yet, the rulers and the ruled—
Some sense of duty, something of a faith,
Some reverence for the laws ourselves have
made,
Some patient force to change them when
we will,
Some civic manhood firm against the
crowd—
But yonder, whiff! there comes a sudden
heat,
The gravest citizen seems to lose his head,
The king is scared, the soldier will not
fight,

The little boys begin to shoot and stab,
A kingdom topples over with a shriek
Like an old woman, and down rolls the
world
In mock heroics stranger than our own;
Revolts, republics, revolutions, most
No graver than a schoolboys' barring out;
Too comic for the solemn things they are,
Too solemn for the comic touches in them,
Like our wild Princess with as wise a dream
As some of theirs—God bless the narrow
seas!
I wish they were a whole Atlantic broad.'

'Have patience,' I replied, 'ourselves are
full
Of social wrong; and maybe wildest dreams
Are but the needful preludes of the truth:
For me, the genial day, the happy crowd,
The sport half-science, fill me with a faith.
This fine old world of ours is but a
child
Yet in the go-cart. Patience! Give it time
To learn its limbs: there is a hand that
guides.'

In such discourse we gain'd the garden
rails,
And there we saw Sir Walter where he
stood,
Before a tower of crimson holly-hoaks,
Among six boys, head under head, and
look'd
No little lily-handed Baronet he,
A great broad-shoulder'd genial English-
man,
A lord of fat prize-oxen and of sheep,
A raiser of huge melons and of pine,
A patron of some thirty charities,
A pamphleteer on guano and on grain,
A quarter-sessions chairman, abler none;
Fair-hair'd and redder than a windy morn;
Now shaking hands with him, now him, of
those
That stood the nearest—now address'd to
speech—
Who spoke few words and pithy, such as
closed
Welcome, farewell, and welcome for the
year
To follow: a shout rose again, and made

The long line of the approaching rookery
    swerve
From the elms, and shook the branches of
    the deer
From slope to slope thro' distant ferns,
    and rang
Beyond the bourn of sunset; O, a shout
More joyful than the city-roar that hails
Premier or king! Why should not these
    great Sirs
Give up their parks some dozen times a
    year
To let the people breathe? So thrice they
    cried,
I likewise, and in groups they stream'd
    away.

But we went back to the Abbey, and
    sat on,
So much the gathering darkness charm'd:
    we sat
But spoke not, rapt in nameless reverie,
Perchance upon the future man: the
    walls
Blacken'd about us, bats wheel'd, and owls
    whoop'd,
And gradually the powers of the night,
That range above the region of the wind,
Deepening the courts of twilight broke
    them up
Thro' all the silent spaces of the worlds,
Beyond all thought into the Heaven of
    Heavens.

Last little Lilia, rising quietly,
Disrobed the glimmering statue of Sir
    Ralph
From those rich silks, and home well-
    pleased we went.

ODE ON THE DEATH OF THE DUKE OF WELLINGTON

PUBLISHED IN 1852

I

Bury the Great Duke
    With an empire's lamentation,
Let us bury the Great Duke
    To the noise of the mourning of a mighty
        nation,
Mourning when their leaders fall,
Warriors carry the warrior's pall,
And sorrow darkens hamlet and hall.

II

Where shall we lay the man whom we
    deplore?
Here, in streaming London's central roar.
Let the sound of those he wrought for,
And the feet of those he fought for,
Echo round his bones for evermore.

III

Lead out the pageant: sad and slow,
As fits an universal woe,
Let the long procession go,
And let the sorrowing crowd about it grow
And let the mournful martial music blow;
The last great Englishman is low.

IV

Mourn, for to us he seems the last,
Remembering all his greatness in the Past.
No more in soldier fashion will he greet
With lifted hand the gazer in the street.
O friends, our chief state-oracle is mute:
Mourn for the man of long-enduring
    blood,
The statesman-warrior, moderate, reso-
    lute,
Whole in himself, a common good.
Mourn for the man of amplest influence,
Yet clearest of ambitious crime,
Our greatest yet with least pretence,
Great in council and great in war,
Foremost captain of his time,
Rich in saving common-sense,
And, as the greatest only are,
In his simplicity sublime.
O good gray head which all men knew,
O voice from which their omens all men
    drew,
O iron nerve to true occasion true,
O fall'n at length that tower of strength
    Which stood four-square to all the winds
        that blew!
Such was he whom we deplore.
The long self-sacrifice of life is o'er.
The great World-victor's victor will be
    seen no more.

V

All is over and done:
Render thanks to the Giver,
England, for thy son.
Let the bell be toll'd.
Render thanks to the Giver,
And render him to the mould.
Under the cross of gold
That shines over city and river,
There he shall rest for ever
Among the wise and the bold.
Let the bell be toll'd:
And a reverent people behold
The towering car, the sable steeds:
Bright let it be with its blazon'd deeds,
Dark in its funeral fold.
Let the bell be toll'd:
And a deeper knell in the heart be knoll'd;
And the sound of the sorrowing anthem
    roll'd
Thro' the dome of the golden cross;
And the volleying cannon thunder his loss;
He knew their voices of old.
For many a time in many a clime
His captain's-ear has heard them boom
Bellowing victory, bellowing doom:
When he with those deep voices wrought,
Guarding realms and kings from shame;
With those deep voices our dead captain
    taught
The tyrant, and assert his claim
In that dread sound to the great name,
Which he has worn so pure of blame,
In praise and in dispraise the same,
A man of well-attemper'd frame.
O civic muse, to such a name,
To such a name for ages long,
To such a name,
Preserve a broad approach of fame,
And ever-echoing avenues of song.

VI

Who is he that cometh, like an honour'd
    guest,
With banner and with music, with soldier
    and with priest,
With a nation weeping, and breaking on
    my rest?
Mighty Seaman, this is he
Was great by land as thou by sea.

Thine island loves thee well, thou famous
    man,
The greatest sailor since our world began.
Now, to the roll of muffled drums,
To thee the greatest soldier comes;
For this is he
Was great by land as thou by sea;
His foes were thine; he kept us free;
O give him welcome, this is he
Worthy of our gorgeous rites,
And worthy to be laid by thee;
For this is England's greatest son,
He that gain'd a hundred fights,
Nor ever lost an English gun;
This is he that far away
Against the myriads of Assaye
Clash'd with his fiery few and won;
And underneath another sun,
Warring on a later day,
Round affrighted Lisbon drew
The treble works, the vast designs
Of his labour'd rampart-lines,
Where he greatly stood at bay,
Whence he issued forth anew,
And ever great and greater grew,
Beating from the wasted vines
Back to France her banded swarms,
Back to France with countless blows,
Till o'er the hills her eagles flew
Beyond the Pyrenean pines,
Follow'd up in valley and glen
With blare of bugle, clamour of men,
Roll of cannon and clash of arms,
And England pouring on her foes.
Such a war had such a close.
Again their ravening eagle rose
In anger, wheel'd on Europe-shadowing
    wings,
And barking for the thrones of kings;
Till one that sought but Duty's iron crown
On that loud sabbath shook the spoiler
    down;
A day of onsets of despair!
Dash'd on every rocky square
Their surging charges foam'd themselves
    away;
Last, the Prussian trumpet blew;
Thro' the long-tormented air
Heaven flash'd a sudden jubilant ray,
And down we swept and charged and
    overthrew.

So great a soldier taught us there,
What long-enduring hearts could do
In that world-earthquake, Waterloo!
Mighty Seaman, tender and true,
And pure as he from taint of craven guile,
O saviour of the silver-coasted isle,
O shaker of the Baltic and the Nile,
If aught of things that here befall
Touch a spirit among things divine,
If love of country move thee there at all,
Be glad, because his bones are laid by thine!
And thro' the centuries let a people's voice
In full acclaim,
A people's voice,
The proof and echo of all human fame,
A people's voice, when they rejoice
At civic revel and pomp and game,
Attest their great commander's claim
With honour, honour, honour, honour to
him,
Eternal honour to his name.

VII

A people's voice! we are a people yet.
Tho' all men else their nobler dreams
forget,
Confused by brainless mobs and lawless
Powers;
Thank Him who isled us here, and roughly
set
His Briton in blown seas and storming
showers,
We have a voice, with which to pay the debt
Of boundless love and reverence and regret
To those great men who fought, and kept it
ours.
And keep it ours, O God, from brute
control;
O Statesmen, guard us, guard the eye, the
soul
Of Europe, keep our noble England whole,
And save the one true seed of freedom
sown
Betwixt a people and their ancient throne,
That sober freedom out of which there
springs
Our loyal passion for our temperate kings;
For, saving that, ye help to save mankind
Till public wrong be crumbled into dust,
And drill the raw world for the march of
mind,

Till crowds at length be sane and crowns
be just.
But wink no more in slothful overtrust.
Remember him who led your hosts;
He bad you guard the sacred coasts.
Your cannons moulder on the seaward
wall;
His voice is silent in your council-hall
For ever; and whatever tempests lour
For ever silent; even if they broke
In thunder, silent; yet remember all
He spoke among you, and the Man who
spoke;
Who never sold the truth to serve the hour,
Nor palter'd with Eternal God for power;
Who let the turbid streams of rumour
flow
Thro' either babbling world of high and
low;
Whose life was work, whose language rife
With rugged maxims hewn from life;
Who never spoke against a foe;
Whose eighty winters freeze with one
rebuke
All great self-seekers trampling on the
right:
Truth-teller was our England's Alfred
named;
Truth-lover was our English Duke;
Whatever record leap to light
He never shall be shamed.

VIII

Lo, the leader in these glorious wars
Now to glorious burial slowly borne,
Follow'd by the brave of other lands,
He, on whom from both her open hands
Lavish Honour shower'd all her stars,
And affluent Fortune emptied all her horn.
Yea, let all good things await
Him who cares not to be great,
But as he saves or serves the state.
Not once or twice in our rough island-
story,
The path of duty was the way to glory:
He that walks it, only thirsting
For the right, and learns to deaden
Love of self, before his journey closes,
He shall find the stubborn thistle bursting
Into glossy purples, which outredden
All voluptuous garden-roses.

Not once or twice in our fair island-story,
The path of duty was the way to glory:
He, that ever following her commands,
On with toil of heart and knees and hands,
Thro' the long gorge to the far light has
    won
His path upward, and prevail'd,
Shall find the toppling crags of Duty
    scaled
Are close upon the shining table-lands
To which our God Himself is moon and
    sun.
Such was he: his work is done.
But while the races of mankind endure,
Let his great example stand
Colossal, seen of every land,
And keep the soldier firm, the statesman
    pure:
Till in all lands and thro' all human story
The path of duty be the way to glory:
And let the land whose hearths he saved
    from shame
For many and many an age proclaim
At civic revel and pomp and game,
And when the long-illumined cities flame,
Their ever-loyal iron leader's fame,
With honour, honour, honour, honour to
    him,
Eternal honour to his name.

IX

Peace, his triumph will be sung
By some yet unmoulded tongue
Far on in summers that we shall not see:
Peace, it is a day of pain
For one about whose patriarchal knee
Late the little children clung:
O peace, it is a day of pain
For one, upon whose hand and heart and
    brain
Once the weight and fate of Europe hung.
Ours the pain, be his the gain!
More than is of man's degree
Must be with us, watching here
At this, our great solemnity.
Whom we see not we revere;
We revere, and we refrain
From talk of battles loud and vain,
And brawling memories all too free
For such a wise humility
As befits a solemn fane:

We revere, and while we hear
The tides of Music's golden sea
Setting toward eternity,
Uplifted high in heart and hope are we,
Until we doubt not that for one so true
There must be other nobler work to do
Than when he fought at Waterloo,
And Victor he must ever be.
For tho' the Giant Ages heave the hill
And break the shore, and evermore
Make and break, and work their will;
Tho' world on world in myriad myriads
    roll
Round us, each with different powers,
And other forms of life than ours,
What know we greater than the soul?
On God and Godlike men we build our
    trust.
Hush, the Dead March wails in the people's
    ears:
The dark crowd moves, and there are sobs
    and tears:
The black earth yawns: the mortal dis-
    appears;
Ashes to ashes, dust to dust;
He is gone who seem'd so great.—
Gone; but nothing can bereave him
Of the force he made his own
Being here, and we believe him
Something far advanced in State,
And that he wears a truer crown
Than any wreath that man can weave him.
Speak no more of his renown,
Lay your earthly fancies down,
And in the vast cathedral leave him,
God accept him, Christ receive him.

1852.

THE THIRD OF FEBRUARY
1852

My Lords, we heard you speak: you told
    us all
    That England's honest censure went too
    far;
That our free press should cease to brawl,
    Not sting the fiery Frenchman into war.
It was our ancient privilege, my Lords,
To fling whate'er we felt, not fearing, into
    words.

We love not this French God, the child of
   Hell,
   Wild War, who breaks the converse of
      the wise;
But though we love kind Peace so well,
   We dare not ev'n by silence sanction lies.
It might be safe our censures to withdraw;
And yet, my Lords, not well: there is a
   higher law.

As long as we remain, we must speak free,
   Tho' all the storm of Europe on us break;
No little German state are we,
   But the one voice in Europe: we *must*
      speak;
That if to-night our greatness were struck
   dead,
There might be left some record of the
   things we said.

If you be fearful, then must we be bold.
   Our Britain cannot salve a tyrant o'er.
Better the waste Atlantic roll'd
   On her and us and ours for evermore.
What! have we fought for Freedom from
   our prime,
At last to dodge and palter with a public
   crime?

Shall we fear *him?* our own we never fear'd.
   From our first Charles by force we
      wrung our claims.
Prick'd by the Papal spur, we rear'd,
   We flung the burthen of the second
      James.
I say, we *never* feared! and as for these,
We broke them on the land, we drove
   them on the seas.

And you, my Lords, you make the people
   muse
   In doubt if you be of our Barons' breed—
Were those your sires who fought at Lewes?
   Is this the manly strain of Runnymede?
O fall'n nobility, that, overawed,
Would lisp in honey'd whispers of this
   monstrous fraud!

We feel, at least, that silence here were sin,
   Not ours the fault if we have feeble
      hosts—
If easy patrons of their kin

Have left the last free race with naked
   coasts!
They knew the precious things they had to
   guard:
For us, we will not spare the tyrant one
   hard word.

Tho' niggard throats of Manchester may
   bawl,
   What England was, shall her true sons
      forget?
We are not cotton-spinners all,
   But some love England and her honour
      yet.
And these in our Thermopylæ shall stand,
And hold against the world this honour of
   the land.

THE CHARGE OF THE LIGHT BRIGADE

I

HALF a league, half a league,
   Half a league onward,
All in the valley of Death
   Rode the six hundred .
'Forward, the Light Brigade!
Charge for the guns!' he said:
Into the valley of Death
   Rode the six hundred.

II

'Forward, the Light Brigade!'
Was there a man dismay'd?
Not tho' the soldier knew
   Some one had blunder'd:
Their's not to make reply,
Their's not to reason why,
Their's but to do and die:
Into the valley of Death
   Rode the six hundred.

III

Cannon to right of them,
Cannon to left of them,
Cannon in front of them
   Volley'd and thunder'd;
Storm'd at with shot and shell,
Boldly they rode and well,
Into the jaws of Death,
Into the mouth of Hell
   Rode the six hundred.

IV

Flash'd all their sabres bare,
Flash'd as they turn'd in air
Sabring the gunners there,
Charging an army, while
All the world wonder'd:
Plunged in the battery-smoke
Right thro' the line they broke;
Cossack and Russian
Reel'd from the sabre-stroke
Shatter'd and sunder'd.
Then they rode back, but not,
Not the six hundred.

V

Cannon to right of them,
Cannon to left of them,
Cannon behind them
Volley'd and thunder'd;
Storm'd at with shot and shell,
While horse and hero fell,
They that had fought so well
Came thro' the jaws of Death,
Back from the mouth of Hell,
All that was left of them,
Left of six hundred.

VI

When can their glory fade?
O the wild charge they made!
All the world wonder'd.
Honour the charge they made!
Honour the Light Brigade,
Noble six hundred!

ODE SUNG AT THE OPENING
OF THE INTERNATIONAL
EXHIBITION

I

Uplift a thousand voices full and sweet,
In this wide hall with earth's invention
  stored,
And praise the invisible universal Lord,
Who lets once more in peace the nations
  meet,
Where Science, Art, and Labour have
  outpour'd
Their myriad horns of plenty at our feet.

II

O silent father of our Kings to be
Mourn'd in this golden hour of jubilee,
For this, for all, we weep our thanks to
  thee!

III

The world-compelling plan was thine,—
And, lo! the long laborious miles
Of Palace; lo! the giant aisles,
Rich in model and design;
Harvest-tool and husbandry,
Loom and wheel and enginery,
Secrets of the sullen mine,
Steel and gold, and corn and wine,
Fabric rough, or fairy-fine,
Sunny tokens of the Line,
Polar marvels, and a feast
Of wonder, out of West and East,
And shapes and hues of Art divine!
All of beauty, all of use,
That one fair planet can produce,
  Brought from under every star,
Blown from over every main,
And mixt, as life is mixt with pain,
  The works of peace with works of war.

IV

Is the goal so far away?
Far, how far no tongue can say,
Let us dream our dream to-day.

V

O ye, the wise who think, the wise who
  reign,
From growing commerce loose her latest
  chain,
And let the fair white-wing'd peacemaker
  fly
To happy havens under all the sky,
And mix the seasons and the golden hours;
Till each man find his own in all men's
  good,
And all men work in noble brotherhood,
Breaking their mailed fleets and armed
  towers,
And ruling by obeying Nature's powers,
And gathering all the fruits of earth and
  crown'd with all her flowers.

A WELCOME TO ALEXANDRA

MARCH 7, 1863

SEA-KINGS' daughter from over the sea,
Alexandra!
Saxon and Norman and Dane are we,
But all of us Danes in our welcome of thee,
Alexandra!
Welcome her, thunders of fort and of fleet!
Welcome her, thundering cheer of the
street!
Welcome her, all things youthful and sweet,
Scatter the blossom under her feet!
Break, happy land, into earlier flowers!
Make music, O bird, in the new-budded
bowers!
Blazon your mottoes of blessing and
prayer!
Welcome her, welcome her, all that is ours!
Warble, O bugle, and trumpet, blare!
Flags, flutter out upon turrets and towers!
Flames, on the windy headland flare!
Utter your jubilee, steeple and spire!
Clash, ye bells, in the merry March air!
Flash, ye cities, in rivers of fire!
Rush to the roof, sudden rocket, and higher
Melt into stars for the land's desire!
Roll and rejoice, jubilant voice,
Roll as a ground-swell dash'd on the strand,
Roar as the sea when he welcomes the land,
And welcome her, welcome the land's
desire,
The sea-kings' daughter as happy as fair,
Blissful bride of a blissful heir,
Bride of the heir of the kings of the sea—
O joy to the people and joy to the throne,
Come to us, love us and make us your own:
For Saxon or Dane or Norman we,
Teuton or Celt, or whatever we be,
We are each all Dane in our welcome of
thee,
Alexandra!

A WELCOME TO HER
ROYAL HIGHNESS
MARIE ALEXANDROVNA
DUCHESS OF EDINBURGH

MARCH 7, 1874

I

THE Son of him with whom we strove for
power—

Whose will is lord thro' all his world-
domain—
Who made the serf a man, and burst his
chain—
Has given our Prince his own imperial
Flower,
Alexandrovna.
And welcome, Russian flower, a people's
pride,
To Britain, when her flowers begin to
blow!
From love to love, from home to home
you go,
From mother unto mother, stately bride,
Marie Alexandrovna!

II

The golden news along the steppes is
blown,
And at thy name the Tartar tents are
stirr'd;
Elburz and all the Caucasus have heard;
And all the sultry palms of India known,
Alexandrovna.
The voices of our universal sea
On capes of Afric as on cliffs of Kent,
The Maoris and that Isle of Continent,
And loyal pines of Canada murmur thee,
Marie Alexandrovna!

III

Fair empires branching, both, in lusty
life!—
Yet Harold's England fell to Norman
swords;
Yet thine own land has bow'd to Tartar
hordes
Since English Harold gave its throne a
wife,
Alexandrovna!
For thrones and peoples are as waifs that
swing,
And float or fall, in endless ebb and flow;
But who love best have best the grace to
know
That Love by right divine is deathless king,
Marie Alexandrovna!

IV

And Love has led thee to the stranger land,
  Where men are bold and strongly say
    their say;—
See, empire upon empire smiles to-day,
As thou with thy young lover hand in
    hand,
            Alexandrovna!
So now thy fuller life is in the west,
  Whose hand at home was gracious to thy
    poor:
  Thy name was blest within the narrow
    door;
Here also, Marie, shall thy name be blest,
        Marie Alexandrovna!

V

Shall fears and jealous hatreds flame again?
  Or at thy coming, Princess, everywhere,
    The blue heaven break, and some
      diviner air
Breathe thro' the world and change the
      hearts of men,
            Alexandrovna?
But hearts that change not, love that can-
    not cease,
And peace be yours, the peace of soul in
    soul!
And howsoever this wild world may roll,
Between your peoples truth and manful
    peace,
        Alfred—Alexandrovna!

THE GRANDMOTHER

I

AND Willy, my eldest-born, is gone, you say, little Anne?
Ruddy and white, and strong on his legs, he looks like a man.
And Willy's wife has written: she never was over-wise,
Never the wife for Willy: he wouldn't take my advice.

II

For, Annie, you see, her father was not the man to save,
Hadn't a head to manage, and drank himself into his grave.
Pretty enough, very pretty! but I was against it for one.
Eh!—but he wouldn't hear me—and Willy, you say, is gone.

III

Willy, my beauty, my eldest-born, the flower of the flock;
Never a man could fling him: for Willy stood like a rock.
'Here's a leg for a babe of a week!' says doctor; and he would be bound,
There was not his like that year in twenty parishes round.

IV

Strong of his hands, and strong on his legs, but still of his tongue!
I ought to have gone before him: I wonder he went so young.
I cannot cry for him, Annie: I have not long to stay;
Perhaps I shall see him the sooner, for he lived far away.

V

Why do you look at me, Annie? you think I am hard and cold;
But all my children have gone before me, I am so old:
I cannot weep for Willy, nor can I weep for the rest;
Only at your age, Annie, I could have wept with the best.

VI

For I remember a quarrel I had with your father, my dear,
All for a slanderous story, that cost me many a tear.
I mean your grandfather, Annie: it cost me a world of woe,
Seventy years ago, my darling, seventy years ago.

VII

For Jenny, my cousin, had come to the place, and I knew right well
That Jenny had tript in her time: I knew, but I would not tell.
And she to be coming and slandering me, the base little liar!
But the tongue is a fire as you know, my dear, the tongue is a fire.

VIII

And the parson made it his text that week, and he said likewise,
That a lie which is half a truth is ever the blackest of lies,
That a lie which is all a lie may be met and fought with outright,
But a lie which is part a truth is a harder matter to fight.

IX

And Willy had not been down to the farm for a week and a day;
And all things look'd half-dead, tho' it was the middle of May.
Jenny, to slander me, who knew what Jenny had been!
But soiling another, Annie, will never make oneself clean.

X

And I cried myself well-nigh blind, and all of an evening late
I climb'd to the top of the garth, and stood by the road at the gate.
The moon like a rick on fire was rising over the dale,
And whit, whit, whit, in the bush beside me chirrupt the nightingale.

XI

All of a sudden he stopt: there past by the gate of the farm,
Willy,—he didn't see me,—and Jenny hung on his arm.
Out into the road I started, and spoke I scarce knew how;
Ah, there's no fool like the old one—it makes me angry now.

XII

Willy stood up like a man, and look'd the thing that he meant;
Jenny, the viper, made me a mocking curtsey and went.
And I said, 'Let us part: in a hundred years it'll all be the same,
You cannot love me at all, if you love not my good name.'

XIII

And he turn'd, and I saw his eyes all wet, in the sweet moonshine:
'Sweetheart, I love you so well that your good name is mine.
And what do I care for Jane, let her speak of you well or ill;
But marry me out of hand: we two shall be happy still.'

XIV

'Marry you, Willy!' said I, 'but I needs must speak my mind,
And I fear you'll listen to tales, be jealous and hard and unkind.'
But he turn'd and claspt me in his arms, and answer'd, 'No, love, no;'
Seventy years ago, my darling, seventy years ago.

XV

So Willy and I were wedded: I wore a lilac gown;
And the ringers rang with a will, and he gave the ringers a crown.
But the first that ever I bare was dead before he was born,
Shadow and shine is life, little Annie, flower and thorn.

XVI

That was the first time, too, that ever I thought of death.
There lay the sweet little body that never had drawn a breath.
I had not wept, little Anne, not since I had been a wife;
But I wept like a child that day, for the babe had fought for his life.

XVII

His dear little face was troubled, as if with anger or pain:
I look'd at the still little body—his trouble had all been in vain.
For Willy I cannot weep, I shall see him another morn:
But I wept like a child for the child that was dead before he was born.

XVIII

But he cheer'd me, my good man, for he seldom said me nay:
Kind, like a man, was he; like a man, too, would have his way:
Never jealous—not he: we had many a happy year;
And he died, and I could not weep—my own time seem'd so near.

XIX

But I wish'd it had been God's will that I, too, then could have died:
I began to be tired a little, and fain had slept at his side.
And that was ten years back, or more, if I don't forget:
But as to the children, Annie, they're all about me yet.

XX

Pattering over the boards, my Annie who left me at two,
Patter she goes, my own little Annie, an Annie like you:
Pattering over the boards, she comes and goes at her will,
While Harry is in the five-acre and Charlie ploughing the hill.

XXI

And Harry and Charlie, I hear them too—they sing to their team:
Often they come to the door in a pleasant kind of a dream.
They come and sit by my chair, they hover about my bed—
I am not always certain if they be alive or dead.

THE GRANDMOTHER

XXII

And yet I know for a truth, there's none of them left alive;
For Harry went at sixty, your father at sixty-five:
And Willy, my eldest-born, at nigh threescore and ten;
I knew them all as babies, and now they're elderly men.

XXIII

For mine is a time of peace, it is not often I grieve;
I am oftener sitting at home in my father's farm at eve:
And the neighbours come and laugh and gossip, and so do I;
I find myself often laughing at things that have long gone by.

XXIV

To be sure the preacher says, our sins should make us sad:
But mine is a time of peace, and there is Grace to be had;
And God, not man, is the Judge of us all when life shall cease;
And in this Book, little Annie, the message is one of Peace.

XXV

And age is a time of peace, so it be free from pain,
And happy has been my life; but I would not live it again.
I seem to be tired a little, that's all, and long for rest;
Only at your age, Annie, I could have wept with the best.

XXVI

So Willy has gone, my beauty, my eldest-born, my flower;
But how can I weep for Willy, he has but gone for an hour,—
Gone for a minute, my son, from this room into the next;
I, too, shall go in a minute. What time have I to be vext?

XXVII

And Willy's wife has written, she never was over-wise.
Get me my glasses, Annie: thank God that I keep my eyes.
There is but a trifle left you, when I shall have past away.
But stay with the old woman now: you cannot have long to stay.

NORTHERN FARMER

OLD STYLE

I

Wheer 'asta beän saw long and meä liggin' 'ere aloän?
Noorse? thourt nowt o' a noorse: whoy, Doctor's abeän an' agoän:
Says that I moänt 'a naw moor aäle: but I beänt a fool:
Git ma my aäle, fur I beänt a-gawin' to breäk my rule.

II

Doctors, they knaws nowt, fur a says what's nawways true:
Naw soort o' koind o' use to saäy the things that a do.
I've 'ed my point o' aäle ivry noight sin' I beän 'ere.
An' I've 'ed my quart ivry market-noight for foorty year.

III

Parson's a beän loikewoise, an' a sittin' 'ere o' my bed.
'The amoighty's a taäkin o' you[1] to 'issén, my friend,' a said,
An' a towd ma my sins, an's toithe were due, an' I gied it in hond;
I done moy duty boy 'um, as I 'a done boy the lond.

IV

Larn'd a ma' beä. I reckons I 'annot sa mooch to larn.
But a cast oop, thot a did, 'bout Bessy Marris's barne.
Thaw a knaws I hallus voäted wi' Squoire an' choorch an' staäte,
An' i' the woost o' toimes I wur niver agin the raäte.

V

An' I hallus coom'd to 's chooch afoor moy Sally wur deäd,
An' 'eärd 'um a bummin' awaäy loike a buzzard-clock[2] ower my 'eäd,
An' I niver knaw'd whot a meän'd but I thowt a 'ad summut to saäy,
An' I thowt a said whot a owt to 'a said an' I coom'd awaäy.

VI

Bessy Marris's barne! tha knaws she laäid it to meä.
Mowt a beän, mayhap, for she wur a bad un, sheä.
'Siver, I kep 'um, I kep 'um, my lass, tha mun understond;
I done moy duty boy 'um as I 'a done boy the lond.

VII

But Parson a cooms an' a goäs, an' a says it eäsy an' freeä
'The amoighty's a taäkin o' you to 'issén, my friend,' says 'eä.
I weänt saäy men be loiars, thaw summun said it in 'aäste:
But 'e reäds wonn sarmin a weeäk, an' I 'a stubb'd Thurnaby waäste.

VIII

D'ya moind the waäste, my lass? naw, naw, tha was not born then;
Theer wur a boggle in it, I often 'eärd 'um mysen;
Moäst loike a butter-bump,[3] fur I 'eärd 'um about an' about,
But I stubb'd 'um oop wi' the lot, an' raäved an' rembled 'um out.

IX

Keäper's it wur; fo' they fun 'um theer a-laäid of 'is faäce
Down i' the woild 'enemies[4] afoor I coom'd to the plaäce.
Noäks or Thimbleby—toäner[5] 'ed shot 'um as deäd as a naäil.
Noäks wur 'ang'd for it oop at 'soize—but git ma my aäle.

X

Dubbut looök at the waäste: theer warn't not feeäd for a cow;
Nowt at all but bracken an' fuzz, an' looök at it now—
Warnt worth nowt a haäcre, an' now theer's lots o' feeäd,
Fourscoor[1] yows upon it an' some on it down i' seeäd.[6]

---

[1] ou as in hour.   [2] Cockchafer.   [3] Bittern.   [4] Anemones.   [5] One or other.   [6] Clover.

NORTHERN FARMER. OLD STYLE

XI

Nobbut a bit on it's left, an' I meän'd to 'a stubb'd it at fall,
Done it ta-year I meän'd, an' runn'd plow thruff it an' all,
If godamoighty an' parson 'ud nobbut let ma aloän,
Meä, wi' haäte hoonderd haäcre o' Squoire's, an' lond o' my oän.

XII

Do godamoighty knaw what a's doing a-taäkin' o' meä?
I beänt wonn as saws 'ere a beän an' yonder a peä;
An' Squoire 'ull be sa mad an' all—a' dear a' dear!
And I 'a managed for Squoire coom Michaelmas thutty year.

XIII

A mowt 'a taäen owd Joänes, as 'ant not a aäpoth o' sense,
Or a mowt 'a taäen young Robins—a niver mended a fence:
But goadamoighty a moost taäke meä an' taäke ma now
Wi' aäf the cows to cauve an' Thurnaby hoälms to plow!

XIV

Loook 'ow quoloty smoiles when they seeäs ma a passin' boy,
Says to thessén naw doubt 'what a man a beä sewer-loy!'
Fur they knaws what I beän to Squoire sin fust a coom'd to the 'All;
I done moy duty by Squoire an' I done moy duty boy hall.

XV

Squoire's i' Lunnon, an' summun I reckons 'ull 'a to wroite,
For whoä's to howd the lond ater meä thot muddles ma quoit;
Sartin-sewer I beä, thot a weänt niver give it to Joänes,
Naw, nor a moänt to Robins—a niver rembles the stoäns.

XVI

But summun 'ull come ater meä mayhap wi' 'is kittle o' steäm
Huzzin' an' maäzin' the blessed feälds wi' the Divil's oän teäm.
Sin' I mun doy I mun doy, thaw loife they says is sweet,
But sin' I mun doy I mun doy, for I couldn abeär to see it.

XVII

What atta stannin' theer fur, an' doesn bring ma the aäle?
Doctor's a 'toättler, lass, an a's halus i' the owd taäle;
I weänt breäk rules fur Doctor, a knaws naw moor nor a floy;
Git ma my aäle I tell tha, an' if I mun doy I mun doy.

NORTHERN FARMER

NEW STYLE

I

Dosn't thou 'ear my 'erse's legs, as they canters awaäy?
Proputty, proputty, proputty—that's what I 'ears 'em saäy.
Proputty, proputty, proputty—Sam, thou's an ass for thy paaïns:
Theer's moor sense i' one o' 'is legs nor in all thy braaïns.

II

Woä—theer's a craw to pluck wi' tha, Sam: yon's parson's 'ouse—
Dosn't thou knaw that a man mun be eäther a man or a mouse?
Time to think on it then; for thou'll be twenty to weeäk.[1]
Proputty, proputty—woä then woä—let ma 'ear mysén speäk.

III

Me an' thy muther, Sammy, 'as beän a-talkin' o' thee;
Thou's beän talkin' to muther, an' she beän a tellin' it me.
Thou'll not marry for munny—thou's sweet upo' parson's lass—
Noä—thou'll marry for luvv—an' we boäth on us thinks tha an ass.

IV

Seeä'd her todaäy goä by—Saäint's-daäy—they was ringing the bells.
She's a beauty thou thinks—an' soä is scoors o' gells,
Them as 'as munny an' all—wot's a beauty?—the flower as blaws.
But proputty, proputty sticks, an' proputty, proputty graws.

V

Do'ant be stunt:[2] taäke time: I knaws what maäkes tha sa mad.
Warn't I craäzed fur the lasses mysén when I wur a lad?
But I knaw'd a Quaäker feller as often 'as towd ma this:
'Doänt thou marry for munny, but goä wheer munny is!'

VI

An' I went wheer munny war: an' thy muther coom to 'and,
Wi' lots o' munny laaïd by, an' a nicetish bit o' land.
Maäybe she warn't a beauty:—I niver giv it a thowt—
But warn't she as good to cuddle an' kiss as a lass as 'ant nowt?

VII

Parson's lass 'ant nowt, an' she weänt 'a nowt when 'e's deäd,
Mun be a guvness, lad, or summut, and addle[3] her breäd:
Why? fur 'e's nobbut a curate, an' weänt niver git hissen clear,
An' 'e maäde the bed as 'e ligs on afoor 'e coom'd to the shere.

VIII

'An thin 'e coom'd to the parish wi' lots o' Varsity debt,
Stook to his taaïl they did, an' 'e 'ant got shut on 'em yet.
An' 'e ligs on 'is back i' the grip, wi' noän to lend 'im a shuvv,
Woorse nor a far-welter'd[4] yowe: fur, Sammy, 'e married fur luvv.

IX

Luvv? what's luvv? thou can luvv thy lass an' 'er munny too,
Maäkin' 'em goä togither as they've good right to do.
Could'n I luvv thy muther by cause o' 'er munny laaïd by?
Naäy—fur I luvv'd 'er a vast sight moor fur it: reäson why.

---

[1] This week.   [2] Obstinate.   [3] Earn.
[4] Or fow-welter'd,—said of a sheep lying on its back.

X

Ay an' thy muther says thou wants to marry the lass,
Cooms of a gentleman burn: an' we boäth on us thinks tha an ass.
Woä then, proputty, wiltha?—an ass as near as mays nowt[1]—
Woä then, wiltha? dangtha!—the bees is as fell as owt.[2]

XI

Breäk me a bit o' the esh for his 'eäd, lad, out o' the fence!
Gentleman burn! what's gentleman burn? is it shillins an' pence?
Proputty, proputty's ivrything 'ere, an', Sammy, I'm blest
If it isn't the saäme opp yonder, fur them as 'as it's the best.

XII

Tis'n them as 'as munny as breäks into 'ouses an' steäls,
Them as 'as coäts to their backs an' taäkes their regular meäls.
Noä, but it's them as niver knaws wheer a meäl's to be 'ad.
Taäke my word for it, Sammy, the poor in a loomp is bad.

XIII

Them or thir feythers, tha sees, mun 'a beän a laäzy lot,
Fur work mun 'a gone to the gittin' whiniver munny was got.
Feyther 'ad ammost nowt; leästways 'is munny was 'id.
But 'e tued an' moil'd 'issén deäd, an 'e died a good un, 'e did.

XIV

Loook thou theer wheer Wrigglesby beck cooms out by the 'ill!
Feyther run oop to the farm, an' I runs oop to the mill;
An' I'll run oop to the brig, an' that thou'll live to see;
And if thou marries a good un I'll leäve the land to thee.

XV

Thim's my noätions, Sammy, wheerby I means to stick;
But if thou marries a bad un, I'll leäve the land to Dick.—
Coom oop, proputty, proputty—that's what I 'ears 'im saäy—
Proputty, proputty, proputty—canter an' canter awaäy.

[1] Makes nothing.   [2] The flies are as fierce as anything.

THE DAISY
WRITTEN AT EDINBURGH

O LOVE, what hours were thine and mine,
In lands of palm and southern pine;
  In lands of palm, of orange-blossom,
Of olive, aloe, and maize and vine.

What Roman strength Turbia show'd
In ruin, by the mountain road;
  How like a gem, beneath, the city
Of little Monaco, basking, glow'd.

How richly down the rocky dell
The torrent vineyard streaming fell

To meet the sun and sunny waters,
That only heaved with a summer swell.

What slender campanili grew
By bays, the peacock's neck in hue;
  Where, here and there, on sandy beaches
A milky-bell'd amaryllis blew.

How young Columbus seem'd to rove,
Yet present in his natal grove,

Now watching high on mountain cornice,
And steering, now, from a purple cove,

Now pacing mute by ocean's rim;
Till, in a narrow street and dim,
    I stay'd the wheels at Cogoletto,
And drank, and loyally drank to him.

Nor knew we well what pleased us most,
Not the clipt palm of which they boast;
    But distant colour, happy hamlet,
A moulder'd citadel on the coast,

Or tower, or high hill-convent, seen
A light amid its olives green;
    Or olive-hoary cape in ocean;
Or rosy blossom in hot ravine,

Where oleanders flush'd the bed
Of silent torrents, gravel-spread;
    And, crossing, oft we saw the glisten
Of ice, far up on a mountain head.

We loved that hall, tho' white and cold,
Those niched shapes of noble mould,
    A princely people's awful princes,
The grave, severe Genovese of old.

At Florence too what golden hours,
In those long galleries, were ours;
    What drives about the fresh Cascinè,
Or walks in Boboli's ducal bowers.

In bright vignettes, and each complete,
Of tower or duomo, sunny-sweet,
    Or palace, how the city glitter'd,
Thro' cypress avenues, at our feet.

But when we crost the Lombard plain
Remember what a plague of rain;
    Of rain at Reggio, rain at Parma;
At Lodi, rain, Piacenza, rain.

And stern and sad (so rare the smiles
Of sunlight) look'd the Lombard piles;
    Porch-pillars on the lion resting,
And sombre, old, colonnaded aisles.

O Milan, O the chanting quires,
The giant windows' blazon'd fires,
    The height, the space, the gloom, the
    glory!
A mount of marble, a hundred spires!

I climb'd the roofs at break of day;
Sun-smitten Alps before me lay.
    I stood among the silent statues,
And statued pinnacles, mute as they.

How faintly-flush'd, how phantom-fair,
Was Monte Rosa, hanging there
    A thousand shadowy-pencill'd valleys
And snowy dells in a golden air.

Remember how we came at last
To Como; shower and storm and blast
    Had blown the lake beyond his limit,
And all was flooded; and how we past

From Como, when the light was gray,
And in my head, for half the day,
    The rich Virgilian rustic measure
Of Lari Maxume, all the way,

Like ballad-burthen music, kept,
As on The Lariano crept
    To that fair port below the castle
Of Queen Theodolind, where we slept;

Or hardly slept, but watch'd awake
A cypress in the moonlight shake,
    The moonlight touching o'er a terrace
One tall Agavè above the lake.

What more? we took our last adieu,
And up the snowy Splugen drew,
    But ere we reach'd the highest summit
I pluck'd a daisy, I gave it you.

It told of England then to me,
And now it tells of Italy.
    O love, we two shall go no longer
To lands of summer across the sea;

So dear a life your arms enfold
Whose crying is a cry for gold:
    Yet here to-night in this dark city,
When ill and weary, alone and cold,

I found, tho' crush'd to hard and dry,
This nurseling of another sky
    Still in the little book you lent me,
And where you tenderly laid it by:

And I forgot the clouded Forth,
The gloom that saddens Heaven and Earth
    The bitter east, the misty summer
And gray metropolis of the North.

Perchance, to lull the throbs of pain,
Perchance, to charm a vacant brain,
  Perchance, to dream you still beside me,
My fancy fled to the South again.

TO THE REV. F. D. MAURICE

COME, when no graver cares employ,
Godfather, come and see your boy:
  Your presence will be sun in winter,
Making the little one leap for joy.

For, being of that honest few,
Who give the Fiend himself his due,
  Should eighty-thousand college-councils
Thunder 'Anathema,' friend, at you;

Should all our churchmen foam in spite
At you, so careful of the right,
  Yet one lay-hearth would give you wel-
    come
(Take it and come) to the Isle of Wight;

Where, far from noise and smoke of town,
I watch the twilight falling brown
  All round a careless-order'd garden
Close to the ridge of a noble down.

You'll have no scandal while you dine,
But honest talk and wholesome wine,
  And only hear the magpie gossip
Garrulous under a roof of pine:

For groves of pine on either hand,
To break the blast of winter, stand;
  And further on, the hoary Channel
Tumbles a billow on chalk and sand;

Where, if below the milky steep
Some ship of battle slowly creep,
  And on thro' zones of light and shadow
Glimmer away to the lonely deep,

We might discuss the Northern sin
Which made a selfish war begin;
  Dispute the claims, arrange the chances;
Emperor, Ottoman, which shall win:

Or whether war's avenging rod
Shall lash all Europe into blood;
  Till you should turn to dearer matters,
Dear to the man that is dear to God;

How best to help the slender store,
How mend the dwellings, of the poor;

How gain in life, as life advances,
Valour and charity more and more.

Come, Maurice, come: the lawn as yet
Is hoar with rime, or spongy-wet;
  But when the wreath of March has
    blossom'd,
Crocus, anemone, violet,

Or later, pay one visit here,
For those are few we hold as dear;
  Nor pay but one, but come for many,
Many and many a happy year.

January, 1854.

WILL

I

O WELL for him whose will is strong!
He suffers, but he will not suffer long;
He suffers, but he cannot suffer wrong:
For him nor moves the loud world's ran-
    dom mock,
Nor all Calamity's hugest waves confound,
Who seems a promontory of rock,
That, compass'd round with turbulent
    sound,
In middle ocean meets the surging shock,
Tempest-buffeted, citadel-crown'd.

II

But ill for him who, bettering not with time,
Corrupts the strength of heaven-descended
    Will,
And ever weaker grows thro' acted crime,
Or seeming-genial venial fault,
Recurring and suggesting still!
He seems as one whose footsteps halt,
Toiling in immeasurable sand,
And o'er a weary sultry land,
Far beneath a blazing vault,
Sown in a wrinkle of the monstrous hill,
The city sparkles like a grain of salt.

IN THE VALLEY OF
CAUTERETZ

ALL along the valley, stream that flashest
    white,
Deepening thy voice with the deepening
    of the night,

All along the valley, where thy waters flow,
I walk'd with one I loved two and thirty
    years ago.
All along the valley, while I walk'd to-day,
The two and thirty years were a mist that
    rolls away;
For all along the valley, down thy rocky
    bed,
Thy living voice to me was as the voice of
    the dead,
And all along the valley, by rock and cave
    and tree,
The voice of the dead was a living voice
    to me.

IN THE GARDEN AT
SWAINSTON

NIGHTINGALES warbled without,
  Within was weeping for thee:
Shadows of three dead men
  Walk'd in the walks with me,
Shadows of three dead men and thou
  wast one of the three.

Nightingales sang in his woods:
  The Master was far away:
Nightingales warbled and sang
  Of a passion that lasts but a day;
Still in the house in his coffin the Prince
  of courtesy lay.

Two dead men have I known
  In courtesy like to thee:
Two dead men have I loved
  With a love that ever will be:
Three dead men have I loved and thou
  art last of the three.

THE FLOWER

ONCE in a golden hour
  I cast to earth a seed.
Up there came a flower,
  The people said, a weed.

To and fro they went
  Thro' my garden-bower,
And muttering discontent
  Cursed me and my flower.

Then it grew so tall
  It wore a crown of light,
But thieves from o'er the wall
  Stole the seed by night.

Sow'd it far and wide
  By every town and tower,
Till all the people cried,
  'Splendid is the flower.'

Read my little fable:
  He that runs may read.
Most can raise the flowers now,
  For all have got the seed.

And some are pretty enough,
  And some are poor indeed;
And now again the people
  Call it but a weed.

REQUIESCAT

FAIR is her cottage in its place,
  Where yon broad water sweetly slowly
    glides.
It sees itself from thatch to base
  Dream in the sliding tides.

And fairer she, but ah how soon to die!
  Her quiet dream of life this hour may
    cease.
Her peaceful being slowly passes by
  To some more perfect peace.

THE SAILOR BOY

HE rose at dawn and, fired with hope,
  Shot o'er the seething harbour-bar,
And reach'd the ship and caught the rope,
  And whistled to the morning star.

And while he whistled long and loud
  He heard a fierce mermaiden cry,
'O boy, tho' thou art young and proud,
  I see the place where thou wilt lie.

'The sands and yeasty surges mix
  In caves about the dreary bay,
And on thy ribs the limpet sticks,
  And in thy heart the scrawl shall play.'

'Fool,' he answer'd, 'death is sure
  To those that stay and those that roam,
But I will nevermore endure
  To sit with empty hands at home.

'My mother clings about my neck,
  My sisters crying, "Stay for shame;"
My father raves of death and wreck,
  They are all to blame, they are all to blame.

'God help me! save I take my part
  Of danger on the roaring sea,
A devil rises in my heart,
  Far worse than any death to me.'

THE ISLET

'WHITHER, O whither, love, shall we go,
For a score of sweet little summers or so?'
The sweet little wife of the singer said,
On the day that follow'd the day she was wed,
'Whither, O whither, love, shall we go?
And the singer shaking his curly head
Turn'd as he sat, and struck the keys
There at his right with a sudden crash,
Singing, 'And shall it be over the seas
With a crew that is neither rude nor rash,
But a bevy of Eroses apple-cheek'd,
In a shallop of crystal ivory-beak'd,
With a satin sail of a ruby glow,
To a sweet little Eden on earth that I know,
A mountain islet pointed and peak'd;
Waves on a diamond shingle dash,
Cataract brooks to the ocean run,
Fairily-delicate palaces shine
Mixt with myrtle and clad with vine,
And overstream'd and silvery-streak'd
With many a rivulet high against the Sun
The facets of the glorious mountain flash
Above the valleys of palm and pine.'

'Thither, O thither, love, let us go.'

'No, no, no!
For in all that exquisite isle, my dear,
There is but one bird with a musical throat,
And his compass is but of a single note,
That it makes one weary to hear.'

'Mock me not! mock me not! love, let us go.'

'No, love, no.
For the bud ever breaks into bloom on the tree,
And a storm never wakes on the lonely sea,
And a worm is there in the lonely wood,
That pierces the liver and blackens the blood;
And makes it a sorrow to be.'

CHILD-SONGS

I

THE CITY CHILD

DAINTY little maiden, whither would you wander?
  Whither from this pretty home, the home where mother dwells?
'Far and far away,' said the dainty little maiden,
'All among the gardens, auriculas, anemones,
  Roses and lilies and Canterbury-bells.'

Dainty little maiden, whither would you wander?
  Whither from this pretty house, this city-house of ours?
'Far and far away,' said the dainty little maiden,
'All among the meadows, the clover and the clematis,
  Daisies and kingcups and honeysuckle-flowers.'

II

MINNIE AND WINNIE

MINNIE and Winnie
  Slept in a shell.
Sleep, little ladies!
  And they slept well.

Pink was the shell within,
  Silver without;
Sounds of the great sea
  Wander'd about.

Sleep, little ladies!
  Wake not soon!
Echo on echo
  Dies to the moon.

Two bright stars
  Peep'd into the shell.
'What are they dreaming of?
  Who can tell?'

Started a green linnet
  Out of the croft;
Wake, little ladies,
  The sun is aloft!

THE SPITEFUL LETTER

HERE, it is here, the close of the year,
  And with it a spiteful letter.
My name in song has done him much
    wrong,
  For himself has done much better.

O little bard, is your lot so hard,
  If men neglect your pages?
I think not much of yours or of mine.
  I hear the roll of the ages.

Rhymes and rhymes in the range of the
    times!
  Are mine for the moment stronger?
Yet hate me not, but abide your lot,
  I last but a moment longer.

This faded leaf, our names are as brief;
  What room is left for a hater?
Yet the yellow leaf hates the greener leaf,
  For it hangs one moment later.

Greater than I—is that your cry?
  And men will live to see it.
Well—if it be so—so it is, you know;
  And if it be so, so be it.

Brief, brief is a summer leaf,
  But this is the time of hollies.
O hollies and ivies and evergreens,
  How I hate the spites and the follies!

LITERARY SQUABBLES

AH God! the petty fools of rhyme
  That shriek and sweat in pigmy wars
Before the stony face of Time,
  And look'd at by the silent stars:

Who hate each other for a song,
  And do their little best to bite
And pinch their brethren in the throng,
  And scratch the very dead for spite:

And strain to make an inch of room
  For their sweet selves, and cannot hear
The sullen Lethe rolling doom
  On them and theirs and all things here:

When one small touch of Charity
  Could lift them nearer God-like state
Than if the crowded Orb should cry
  Like those who cried Diana great:

And I too, talk, and lose the touch
  I talk of. Surely, after all,
The noblest answer unto such
  Is perfect stillness when they brawl.

THE VICTIM

I

A PLAGUE upon the people fell,
  A famine after laid them low,
Then thorpe and byre arose in fire,
  For on them brake the sudden foe;
So thick they died the people cried,
  'The Gods are moved against the land.'
The Priest in horror about his altar
  To Thor and Odin lifted a hand:
    'Help us from famine
    And plague and strife!
    What would you have of us?
    Human life?
    Were it our nearest,
    Were it our dearest,
    (Answer, O answer)
    We give you his life.'

II

But still the foeman spoil'd and burn'd,
  And cattle died, and deer in wood,
And bird in air, and fishes turn'd
  And whiten'd all the rolling flood;
And dead men lay all over the way,
  Or down in a furrow scathed with flame:
And ever and aye the Priesthood moan'd,
  Till at last it seem'd that an answer came.
    'The King is happy
    In child and wife;
    Take you his dearest,
    Give us a life.'

III

The Priest went out by heath and hill;
  The King was hunting in the wild;
They found the mother sitting still;
  She cast her arms about the child.
The child was only eight summers old,
  His beauty still with his years increased,
His face was ruddy, his hair was gold,
  He seem'd a victim due to the priest.
    The Priest beheld him,
    And cried with joy,
    'The Gods have answer'd:
    We give them the boy.'

IV

The King return'd from out the wild,
  He bore but little game in hand;
The mother said, 'They have taken the
      child
  To spill his blood and heal the land:
The land is sick, the people diseased,
  And blight and famine on all the lea:
The holy Gods, they must be appeased,
  So I pray you tell the truth to me.
    They have taken our son,
    They will have his life.
    Is *he* your dearest?
    Or I, the wife?'

V

The King bent low, with hand on brow,
  He stay'd his arms upon his knee:
'O wife, what use to answer now?
  For now the Priest has judged for me.'
The King was shaken with holy fear;
  'The Gods,' he said, 'would have chosen
      well;
Yet both are near, and both are dear,
  And which the dearest I cannot tell!'
    But the Priest was happy,
    His victim won:
    'We have his dearest,
    His only son!'

VI

The rites prepared, the victim bared,
  The knife uprising toward the blow
To the altar-stone she sprang alone,
  'Me, not my darling, no!'
He caught her away with a sudden cry;
  Suddenly from him brake his wife,
And shrieking '*I* am his dearest, I—
  I am his dearest!' rush'd on the knife.
    And the Priest was happy,
    'O, Father Odin,
    We give you a life.
    Which was his nearest?
    Who was his dearest?
    The Gods have answer'd;
    We give them the wife!'

WAGES

GLORY of warrior, glory of orator, glory of song,
  Paid with a voice flying by to be lost on an endless sea—
Glory of Virtue, to fight, to struggle, to right the wrong—
  Nay, but she aim'd not at glory, no lover of glory she:
Give her the glory of going on, and still to be.

The wages of sin is death: if the wages of Virtue be dust,
  Would she have heart to endure for the life of the worm and the fly?
She desires no isles of the blest, no quiet seats of the just,
  To rest in a golden grove, or to bask in a summer sky:
Give her the wages of going on, and not to die.

THE HIGHER PANTHEISM

THE sun, the moon, the stars, the seas, the hills and the plains—
Are not these, O Soul, the Vision of Him who reigns?

Is not the Vision He? tho' He be not that which He seems?
Dreams are true while they last, and do we not live in dreams?

THE HIGHER PANTHEISM

Earth, these solid stars, this weight of body and limb,
Are they not sign and symbol of thy division from Him?

Dark is the world to thee: thyself art the reason why;
For is He not all but that which has power to feel 'I am I'?

Glory about thee, without thee; and thou fulfillest thy doom
Making Him broken gleams, and a stifled splendour and gloom.

Speak to Him thou for He hears, and Spirit with Spirit can meet—
Closer is He than breathing, and nearer than hands and feet.

God is law, say the wise; O Soul, and let us rejoice,
For if He thunder by law the thunder is yet His voice.

Law is God, say some: no God at all, says the fool;
For all we have power to see is a straight staff bent in a pool;

And the ear of man cannot hear, and the eye of man cannot see;
But if we could see and hear, this Vision—were it not He?

THE VOICE AND THE PEAK

I

THE voice and the Peak
    Far over summit and lawn,
The lone glow and long roar
    Green-rushing from the rosy thrones of
        dawn!

II

All night have I heard the voice
    Rave over the rocky bar,
But thou wert silent in heaven,
    Above thee glided the star.

III

Hast thou no voice, O Peak,
    That standest high above all?
'I am the voice of the Peak,
    I roar and rave for I fall.

IV

'A thousand voices go
    To North, South, East, and West;
They leave the heights and are troubled,
    And moan and sink to their rest.

V

'The fields are fair beside them,
    The chestnut towers in his bloom;
But they—they feel the desire of the
        deep—
    Fall, and follow their doom.

VI

'The deep has power on the height,
    And the height has power on the deep;
They are raised for ever and ever,
    And sink again into sleep.'

VII

Not raised for ever and ever,
    But when their cycle is o'er,
The valley, the voice, the peak, the star
    Pass, and are found no more.

VIII

The Peak is high and flush'd
    At his highest with sunrise fire;
The Peak is high, and the stars are high,
    And the thought of a man is higher.

IX

A deep below the deep,
    And a height beyond the height!
Our hearing is not hearing,
    And our seeing is not sight.

X

The voice and the Peak
    Far into heaven withdrawn,
The lone glow and long roar
    Green-rushing from the rosy thrones of
        dawn!

'FLOWER IN THE CRANNIED WALL'

FLOWER in the crannied wall,
I pluck you out of the crannies,
I hold you here, root and all, in my hand,
Little flower—but *if* I could understand
What you are, root and all, and all in all,
I should know what God and man is.

A DEDICATION

DEAR, near and true—no truer Time himself
Can prove you, tho' he make you evermore
Dearer and nearer, as the rapid of life
Shoots to the fall—take this and pray
  that he

Who wrote it, honouring your sweet faith
  in him,
May trust himself; and after praise and
  scorn,
As one who feels the immeasurable
  world,
Attain the wise indifference of the wise;
And after Autumn past—if left to pass
His autumn into seeming-leafless days—
Draw toward the long frost and longest
  night,
Wearing his wisdom lightly, like the fruit
Which in our winter woodland looks a
  flower.[1]

[1] The fruit of the Spindle-tree (*Euonymus
Europæus*).

EXPERIMENTS

BOÄDICEA

WHILE about the shore of Mona those Neronian legionaries
Burnt and broke the grove and altar of the Druid and Druidess,
Far in the East Boädicéa, standing loftily charioted,
Mad and maddening all that heard her in her fierce volubility,
Girt by half the tribes of Britain, near the colony Cámulodúne,
Yell'd and skriek'd between her daughters o'er a wild confederacy.

'They that scorn the tribes and call us Britain's barbarous populaces,
Did they hear me, would they listen, did they pity me supplicating?
Shall I heed them in their anguish? shall I brook to be supplicated?
Hear Icenian, Catieuchlanian, hear Coritanian, Trinobant!
Must their ever-ravening eagle's beak and talon annihilate us?
Tear the noble heart of Britain, leave it gorily quivering?
Bark an answer, Britain's raven! bark and blacken innumerable,
Blacken round the Roman carrion, make the carcase a skeletor,
Kite and kestrel, wolf and wolfkin, from the wilderness, wallow in it,
Till the face of Bel be brighten'd, Taranis be propitiated.
Lo their colony half-defended! lo their colony, Cámulodúne!
There the horde of Roman robbers mock at a barbarous adversary.
There the hive of Roman liars worship an emperor-idiot.
Such is Rome, and this her deity: hear it, Spirit of Cássivëlaún!

'Hear it, Gods! the Gods have heard it, O Icenian, O Coritanian!
Doubt not ye the Gods have answer'd, Catieuchlanian, Trinobant.
These have told us all their anger in miraculous utterances,
Thunder, a flying fire in heaven, a murmur heard aërially,
Phantom sound of blows descending, moan of an enemy massacred.
Phantom wail of women and children, multitudinous agonies.
Bloodily flow'd the Tamesa rolling phantom bodies of horses and men;

224

Then a phantom colony smoulder'd on the refluent estuary;
Lastly yonder yester-even, suddenly giddily tottering—
There was one who watch'd and told me—down their statue of Victory fell.
Lo their precious Roman bantling, lo the colony Cámulodúne,
Shall we teach it a Roman lesson? shall we care to be pitiful?
Shall we deal with it as an infant? shall we dandle it amorously?

'Hear Icenian, Catieuchlanian, hear Coritanian, Trinobant!
While I roved about the forest, long and bitterly meditating,
There I heard them in the darkness, at the mystical ceremony,
Loosely robed in flying raiment, sang the terrible prophetesses,
"Fear not, isle of blowing woodland, isle of silvery parapets!
Tho' the Roman eagle shadow thee, tho' the gathering enemy narrow thee,
Thou shalt wax and he shall dwindle, thou shalt be the mighty one yet!
Thine the liberty, thine the glory, thine the deeds to be celebrated,
Thine the myriad-rolling ocean, light and shadow illimitable,
Thine the lands of lasting summer, many-blossoming Paradises,
Thine the North and thine the South and thine the battle-thunder of God,"
So they chanted: how shall Britain light upon auguries happier?
So they chanted in the darkness, and there cometh a victory now.

'Hear Icenian, Catieuchlanian, hear Coritanian, Trinobant!
Me the wife of rich Prasútagus, me the lover of liberty,
Me they seized and me they tortured, me they lash'd and humiliated,
Me the sport of ribald Veterans, mine of ruffian violators!
See they sit, they hide their faces, miserable in ignominy!
Wherefore in me burns an anger, not by blood to be satiated.
Lo the palaces and the temple, lo the colony Cámulodúne!
There they ruled, and thence they wasted all the flourishing territory,
Thither at their will they haled the yellow-ringleted Britoness—
Bloodily, bloodily fall the battle-axe, unexhausted, inexorable.
Shout Icenian, Catieuchlanian, shout Coritanian, Trinobant,
Till the victim hear within and yearn to hurry precipitously
Like the leaf in a roaring whirlwind, like the smoke in a hurricane whirl'd.
Lo the colony, there they rioted in the city of Cúnobelíne!
There they drank in cups of emerald, there at tables of ebony lay,
Rolling on their purple couches in their tender effeminacy.
There they dwelt and there they rioted; there—there—they dwell no more.
Burst the gates, and burn the palaces, break the works of the statuary,
Take the hoary Roman head and shatter it, hold it abominable,
Cut the Roman boy to pieces in his lust and voluptuousness,
Lash the maiden into swooning, me they lash'd and humiliated,
Chop the breasts from off the mother, dash the brains of the little one out,
Up my Britons, on my chariot, on my chargers, trample them under us.'

So the Queen Boädicéa, standing loftily charioted,
Brandishing in her hand a dart and rolling glances lioness-like,
Yell'd and shriek'd between her daughters in her fierce volubility.
Till her people all around the royal chariot agitated,
Madly dash'd the darts together, writhing barbarous lineäments,
Made the noise of frosty woodlands, when they shiver in January,

I

BOÄDICEA

Roar'd as when the roaring breakers boom and blanch on the precipices,
Yell'd as when the winds of winter tear an oak on a promontory.
So the silent colony hearing her tumultuous adversaries
Clash the darts and on the buckler beat with rapid unanimous hand,
Thought on all her evil tyrannies, all her pitiless avarice,
Till she felt the heart within her fall and flutter tremulously,
Then her pulses at the clamouring of her enemy fainted away.
Out of evil evil flourishes, out of tyranny tyranny buds.
Ran the land with Roman slaughter, multitudinous agonies.
Perish'd many a maid and matron, many a valorous legionary,
Fell the colony, city, and citadel, London, Verulam, Cámulodúne.

IN QUANTITY

ON TRANSLATIONS OF HOMER

Hexameters and Pentameters

THESE lame hexameters the strong-wing'd music of Homer!
No—but a most burlesque barbarous experiment.
When was a harsher sound ever heard, ye Muses, in England?
When did a frog coarser croak upon our Helicon?
Hexameters no worse than daring Germany gave us,
Barbarous experiment, barbarous hexameters.

MILTON

Alcaics

O MIGHTY-MOUTH'D inventor of harmonies,
O skill'd to sing of Time or Eternity,
God-gifted organ-voice of England,
Milton, a name to resound for ages;
Whose Titan angels, Gabriel, Abdiel,
Starr'd from Jehovah's gorgeous armouries,
Tower, as the deep-domed empyrëan
Rings to the roar of an angel onset—
Me rather all that bowery loneliness,
The brooks of Eden mazily murmuring,
And bloom profuse and cedar arches
Charm, as a wanderer out in ocean,
Where some refulgent sunset of India
Streams o'er a rich ambrosial ocean isle,
And crimson-hued the stately palm-
woods
Whisper in odorous heights of even.

Hendecasyllabics

O YOU chorus of indolent reviewers,
Irresponsible, indolent reviewers,
Look, I come to the test, a tiny poem
All composed in a metre of Catullus,
All in quantity, careful of my motion,
Like the skater on ice that hardly bears him,
Lest I fall unawares before the people,
Waking laughter in indolent reviewers.
Should I flounder awhile without a tumble
Thro' this metrification of Catullus,
They should speak to me not without a
welcome,
All that chorus of indolent reviewers.
Hard, hard, hard is it, only not to tumble,
So fantastical is the dainty metre.
Wherefore slight me not wholly, nor be-
lieve me
Too presumptuous, indolent reviewers.
O blatant Magazines, regard me rather—
Since I blush to belaud myself a moment—
As some rare little rose, a piece of inmost
Horticultural art, or half coquette-like
Maiden, not to be greeted unbenignly.

SPECIMEN OF A TRANSLATION OF THE ILIAD IN BLANK VERSE

So Hector spake; the Trojans roar'd
applause;
Then loosed their sweating horses from
the yoke,
And each beside his chariot bound his own;
And oxen from the city, and goodly sheep

SPECIMEN OF A TRANSLATION OF THE ILIAD

In haste they drove, and honey-hearted wine
And bread from out the houses brought, and heap'd
Their firewood, and the winds from off the plain
Roll'd the rich vapour far into the heaven.
And these all night upon the bridge[1] of war
Sat glorying; many a fire before them blazed:
As when in heaven the stars about the moon
Look beautiful, when all the winds are laid,

And every height comes out, and jutting peak
And valley, and the immeasurable heavens
Break open to their highest, and all the stars
Shine, and the Shepherd gladdens in his heart:
So many a fire between the ships and stream
Of Xanthus blazed before the towers of Troy,
A thousand on the plain; and close by each
Sat fifty in the blaze of burning fire;
And eating hoary grain and pulse the steeds,
Fixt by their cars, waited the golden dawn.

[1] Or, ridge.

Iliad VIII. 542–561.

THE WINDOW

OR, THE SONG OF THE WRENS

FOUR years ago Mr. Sullivan requested me to write a little song-cycle, German fashion, for him to exercise his art upon. He had been very successful in setting such old songs as 'Orpheus with his lute,' and I drest up for him, partly in the old style, a puppet, whose almost only merit is, perhaps, that it can dance to Mr. Sullivan's instrument. I am sorry that my four-year-old puppet should have to dance at all in the dark shadow of these days; but the music is now completed, and I am bound by my promise.

December, 1870.

A. TENNYSON.

THE WINDOW

ON THE HILL

THE lights and shadows fly!
Yonder it brightens and darkens down on the plain.
A jewel, a jewel dear to a lover's eye!
Oh is it the brook, or a pool, or her window pane,
    When the winds are up in the morning?

Clouds that are racing above,
And winds and lights and shadows that cannot be still,
All running on one way to the home of my love,
You are all running on, and I stand on the slope of the hill,
    And the winds are up in the morning!

Follow, follow the chase!
And my thoughts are as quick and as quick, ever on, on, on.

O lights, are you flying over her sweet little face?
And my heart is there before you are come, and gone,
    When the winds are up in the morning!

Follow them down the slope!
And I follow them down to the window-pane of my dear,
    And it brightens and darkens and brightens like my hope,
    And it darkens and brightens and darkens like my fear,
    And the winds are up in the morning.

AT THE WINDOW

Vine, vine and eglantine,
Clasp her window, trail and twine!
Rose, rose and clematis,
Trail and twine and clasp and kiss,

227

Kiss, kiss; and make her a bower
All of flowers, and drop me a flower,
Drop me a flower.

Vine, vine and eglantine,
Cannot a flower, a flower, be mine?
Rose, rose and clematis,
Drop me a flower, a flower, to kiss,
Kiss, kiss—and out of her bower
All of flowers, a flower, a flower,
Dropt, a flower.

GONE

Gone!
Gone, till the end of the year,
Gone, and the light gone with her, and
left me in shadow here!
Gone—flitted away,
Taken the stars from the night and the sun
from the day!
Gone, and a cloud in my heart, and a storm
in the air!
Flown to the east or the west, flitted I
know not where!
Down in the south is a flash and a groan:
she is there! she is there!

WINTER

The frost is here,
And fuel is dear,
And woods are sear,
And fires burn clear,
And frost is here
And has bitten the heel of the going year.

Bite, frost, bite!
You roll up away from the light
The blue wood-louse, and the plump
dormouse,
And the bees are still'd, and the flies are
kill'd,
And you bite far into the heart of the
house,
But not into mine.

Bite, frost, bite!
The woods are all the searer,
The fuel is all the dearer,
The fires are all the clearer,
My spring is all the nearer,
You have bitten into the heart of the earth,
But not into mine.

SPRING

Birds' love and birds' song
Flying here and there,
Birds' song and birds' love,
And you with gold for hair!
Birds' song and birds' love,
Passing with the weather,
Men's song and men's love,
To love once and for ever.

Men's love and birds' love,
And women's love and men's!
And you my wren with a crown of gold,
You my queen of the wrens!
You the queen of the wrens—
We'll be birds of a feather,
I'll be King of the Queen of the wrens,
And all in a nest together.

THE LETTER

Where is another sweet as my sweet,
Fine of the fine, and shy of the shy?
Fine little hands, fine little feet—
Dewy blue eye.
Shall I write to her? shall I go?
Ask her to marry me by and by?
Somebody said that she'd say no;
Somebody knows that she'll say ay!

Ay or no, if ask'd to her face?
Ay or no, from shy of the shy?
Go, little letter, apace, apace,
Fly;
Fly to the light in the valley below—
Tell my wish to her dewy blue eye:
Somebody said that she'd say no;
Somebody knows that she'll say ay!

NO ANSWER

The mist and the rain, the mist and the
rain!
Is it ay or no? is it ay or no?
And never a glimpse of her window pane!
And I may die but the grass will grow,
And the grass will grow when I am gone,
And the wet west wind and the world will
go on.

Ay is the song of the wedded spheres,
No is trouble and cloud and storm,
Ay is life for a hundred years,

No will push me down to the worm,
And when I am there and dead and gone,
The wet west wind and the world will
    go on.

The wind and the wet, the wind and the
    wet!
Wet west wind how you blow, you blow!
And never a line from my lady yet!
Is it ay or no? is it ay or no?
Blow then, blow, and when I am gone,
The wet west wind and the world may
    go on.

NO ANSWER

Winds are loud and you are dumb,
Take my love, for love will come,
    Love will come but once a life.
Winds are loud and winds will pass!
Spring is here with leaf and grass:
    Take my love and be my wife.
After-loves of maids and men
Are but dainties drest again:
Love me now, you'll love me then:
    Love can love but once a life.

THE ANSWER

Two little hands that meet,
Claspt on her seal, my sweet!
Must I take you and break you,
Two little hands that meet?
I must take you, and break you,
And loving hands must part—
Take, take—break, break—
Break—you may break my heart.
    Faint heart never won—
    Break, break, and all's done.

AY

Be merry, all birds, to-day,
    Be merry on earth as you never were
        merry before,
Be merry in heaven, O larks, and far away,
    And merry for ever and ever, and one
        day more.
            Why?
    For it's easy to find a rhyme.
Look, look, how he flits,
    The fire-crown'd king of the wrens,
        from out of the pine!

Look how they tumble the blossom, the
    mad little tits!
'Cuck-oo! Cuck-oo!' was ever a May so
    fine?
            Why?
    For it's easy to find a rhyme.
O merry the linnet and dove,
    And swallow and sparrow and throstle,
        and have your desire!
O merry my heart, you have gotten the
        wings of love,
    And flit like the king of the wrens with
        a crown of fire.
            Why?
    For it's ay ay, ay ay.

WHEN

Sun comes, moon comes,
    Time slips away.
Sun sets, moon sets,
    Love, fix a day.

'A year hence, a year hence.'
    'We shall both be gray.'
'A month hence, a month hence.
    'Far, far away.'

'A week hence, a week hence.'
    'Ah, the long delay.'
'Wait a little, wait a little,
    You shall fix a day.'

'To-morrow, love, to-morrow,
    And that's an age away.'
Blaze upon her window, sun,
    And honour all the day.

MARRIAGE MORNING

Light, so low upon earth,
    You send a flash to the sun.
Here is the golden close of love,
    All my wooing is done.
Oh, the woods and the meadows,
    Woods where we hid from the wet,
Stiles where we stay'd to be kind,
    Meadows in which we met!

Light, so low in the vale
    You flash and lighten afar,
For this is the golden morning of love,
    And you are his morning star.

Flash, I am coming, I come,
  By meadow and stile and wood,
Oh, lighten into my eyes and my heart,
  Into my heart and my blood!

Heart, are you great enough
  For a love that never tires?

O heart, are you great enough for
  love?
I have heard of thorns and briers.
Over the thorns and briers,
  Over the meadows and stiles,
Over the world to the end of it
  Flash for a million miles.

IN MEMORIAM A. H. H.

OBIIT MDCCCXXXIII

STRONG Son of God, immortal Love,
  Whom we, that have not seen thy face,
  By faith, and faith alone, embrace,
Believing where we cannot prove;

Thine are these orbs of light and shade;
  Thou madest Life in man and brute;
  Thou madest Death; and lo, thy foot
Is on the skull which thou hast made.

Thou wilt not leave us in the dust:
  Thou madest man, he knows not why,
  He thinks he was not made to die;
And thou hast made him: thou art just.

Thou seemest human and divine,
  The highest, holiest manhood, thou:
  Our wills are ours, we know not how;
Our wills are ours, to make them thine.

Our little systems have their day;
  They have their day and cease to be:
  They are but broken lights of thee,
And thou, O Lord, art more than they.

We have but faith: we cannot know;
  For knowledge is of things we see;
  And yet we trust it comes from thee,
A beam in darkness: let it grow.

Let knowledge grow from more to more,
  But more of reverence in us dwell;
  That mind and soul, according well,
May make one music as before,

But vaster. We are fools and slight;
  We mock thee when we do not fear:
  But help thy foolish ones to bear;
Help thy vain worlds to bear thy light.

Forgive what seem'd my sin in me;
  What seem'd my worth since I began;
  For merit lives from man to man,
And not from man, O Lord, to thee.

Forgive my grief for one removed,
  Thy creature, whom I found so fair.
  I trust he lives in thee, and there
I find him worthier to be loved.

Forgive these wild and wandering cries,
  Confusions of a wasted youth;
  Forgive them where thy fail in truth,
And in thy wisdom make me wise.

                 1849.

I

I HELD it truth, with him who sings
  To one clear harp in divers tones,
  That men may rise on stepping-stones
Of their dead selves to higher things.

But who shall so forecast the years
  And find in loss a gain to match?
  Or reach a hand thro' time to catch
The far-off interest of tears?

Let Love clasp Grief lest both be drown'd,
  Let darkness keep her raven gloss:
  Ah, sweeter to be drunk with loss,
To dance with death, to beat the ground,

Than that the victor Hours should scorn
  The long result of love, and boast,
  'Behold the man that loved and lost,
But all he was is overworn.'

II

Old Yew, which graspest at the stones
  That name the under-lying dead,
  Thy fibres net the dreamless head,
Thy roots are wrapt about the bones.

The seasons bring the flower again,
　And bring the firstling to the flock;
　And in the dusk of thee, the clock
Beats out the little lives of men.

O not for thee the glow, the bloom,
　Who changest not in any gale,
　Nor branding summer suns avail
To touch thy thousand years of gloom:

And gazing on thee, sullen tree,
　Sick for thy stubborn hardihood,
　I seem to fail from out my blood
And grow incorporate into thee.

III

O Sorrow, cruel fellowship,
　O Priestess in the vaults of Death,
　O sweet and bitter in a breath,
What whispers from thy lying lip?

'The stars,' she whispers, 'blindly run;
　A web is wov'n across the sky;
　From out waste places comes a cry,
And murmurs from the dying sun:

'And all the phantom, Nature, stands—
　With all the music in her tone,
　A hollow echo of my own,—
A hollow form with empty hands.'

And shall I take a thing so blind,
　Embrace her as my natural good;
　Or crush her, like a vice of blood,
Upon the threshold of the mind?

IV

To Sleep I give my powers away;
　My will is bondsman to the dark;
　I sit within a helmless bark,
And with my heart I muse and say:

O heart, how fares it with thee now,
　That thou should'st fail from thy desire,
　Who scarcely darest to inquire,
'What is it makes me beat so low?'

Something it is which thou hast lost,
　Some pleasure from thine early years.
　Break, thou deep vase of chilling tears,
That grief hath shaken into frost!

Such clouds of nameless trouble cross
　All night below the darken'd eyes;
　With morning wakes the will, and cries,
'Thou shalt not be the fool of loss.'

V

I sometimes hold it half a sin
　To put in words the grief I feel;
　For words, like Nature, half reveal
And half conceal the Soul within.

But, for the unquiet heart and brain,
　A use in measured language lies;
　The sad mechanic exercise,
Like dull narcotics, numbing pain.

In words, like weeds, I'll wrap me o'er,
　Like coarsest clothes against the cold:
　But that large grief which these enfold
Is given in outline and no more.

VI

One writes, that 'Other friends remain,'
　That 'Loss is common to the race'—
　And common is the commonplace,
And vacant chaff well meant for grain.

That loss is common would not make
　My own less bitter, rather more:
　Too common! Never morning wore
To evening, but some heart did break.

O father, wheresoe'er thou be,
　Who pledgest now thy gallant son;
　A shot, ere half thy draught be done,
Hath still'd the life that beat from thee.

O mother, praying God will save
　Thy sailor,—while thy head is bow'd,
　His heavy-shotted hammock-shroud
Drops in his vast and wandering grave.

Ye know no more than I who wrought
　At that last hour to please him well;
　Who mused on all I had to tell,
And something written, something
　　thought;

Expecting still his advent home;
　And ever met him on his way
　With wishes, thinking, 'here to-day,'
Or 'here to-morrow will he come.'

O somewhere, meek, unconscious dove,
   That sittest ranging golden hair;
   And glad to find thyself so fair,
Poor child, that waitest for thy love!

For now her father's chimney glows
   In expectation of a guest;
   And thinking 'this will please him best,'
She takes a riband or a rose;

For he will see them on to-night;
   And with the thought her colour burns;
   And, having left the glass, she turns
Once more to set a ringlet right;

And, even when she turn'd, the curse
   Had fallen, and her future Lord
   Was drown'd in passing thro' the ford,
Or kill'd in falling from his horse.

O what to her shall be the end?
   And what to me remains of good?
   To her, perpetual maidenhood,
And unto me no second friend.

VII

Dark house, by which once more I stand
   Here in the long unlovely street,
   Doors, where my heart was used to beat
So quickly, waiting for a hand,

A hand that can be clasp'd no more—
   Behold me, for I cannot sleep,
   And like a guilty thing I creep
At earliest morning to the door.

He is not here; but far away
   The noise of life begins again,
   And ghastly thro' the drizzling rain
On the bald street breaks the blank day.

VIII

A happy lover who has come
   To look on her that loves him well,
   Who 'lights and rings the gateway bell,
And learns her gone and far from home;

He saddens, all the magic light
   Dies off at once from bower and hall,
   And all the place is dark, and all
The chambers emptied of delight:

So find I every pleasant spot
   In which we two were wont to meet,
   The field, the chamber and the street,
For all is dark where thou art not.

Yet as that other, wandering there
   In those deserted walks, may find
   A flower beat with rain and wind,
Which once she foster'd up with care;

So seems it in my deep regret,
   O my forsaken heart, with thee
   And this poor flower of poesy
Which little cared for fades not yet.

But since it pleased a vanish'd eye,
   I go to plant it on his tomb,
   That if it can it there may bloom,
Or dying, there at least may die.

IX

Fair ship, that from the Italian shore
   Sailest the placid ocean-plains
   With my lost Arthur's loved remains,
Spread thy full wings, and waft him o'er.

So draw him home to those that mourn
   In vain; a favourable speed
   Ruffle thy mirror'd mast, and lead
Thro' prosperous floods his holy urn.

All night no ruder air perplex
   Thy sliding keel, till Phosphor, bright
   As our pure love, thro' early light
Shall glimmer on the dewy decks.

Sphere all your lights around, above;
   Sleep, gentle heavens, before the prow;
   Sleep, gentle winds, as he sleeps now,
My friend, the brother of my love;

My Arthur, whom I shall not see
   Till all my widow'd race be run;
   Dear as the mother to the son,
More than my brothers are to me.

X

I hear the noise about thy keel;
   I hear the bell struck in the night:
   I see the cabin-window bright;
I see the sailor at the wheel.

Thou bring'st the sailor to his wife,
　And travell'd men from foreign lands;
　And letters unto trembling hands;
And, thy dark freight, a vanish'd life.

So bring him: we have idle dreams:
　This look of quiet flatters thus
　Our home-bred fancies: O to us,
The fools of habit, sweeter seems

To rest beneath the clover sod,
　That takes the sunshine and the rains,
　Or where the kneeling hamlet drains
The chalice of the grapes of God;

Than if with thee the roaring wells
　Should gulf him fathom-deep in brine;
　And hands so often clasp'd in mine,
Should toss with tangle and with shells.

XI

Calm is the morn without a sound,
　Calm as to suit a calmer grief,
　And only thro' the faded leaf
The chestnut pattering to the ground:

Calm and deep peace on this high wold,
　And on these dews that drench the furze,
　And all the silvery gossamers
That twinkle into green and gold:

Calm and still light on yon great plain
　That sweeps with all its autumn bowers,
　And crowded farms and lessening towers,
To mingle with the bounding main:

Calm and deep peace in this wide air,
　These leaves that redden to the fall;
　And in my heart, if calm at all,
If any calm, a calm despair:

Calm on the seas, and silver sleep,
　And waves that sway themselves in rest,
　And dead calm in that noble breast
Which heaves but with the heaving deep.

XII

Lo, as a dove when up she springs
　To bear thro' Heaven a tale of woe,
　Some dolorous message knit below
The wild pulsation of her wings;

Like her I go; I cannot stay;
　I leave this mortal ark behind,
　A weight of nerves without a mind,
And leave the cliffs, and haste away

O'er ocean-mirrors rounded large,
　And reach the glow of southern skies,
　And see the sails at distance rise,
And linger weeping on the marge,

And saying; 'Comes he thus, my friend?
　Is this the end of all my care?'
　And circle moaning in the air:
'Is this the end? Is this the end?'

And forward dart again, and play
　About the prow, and back return
　To where the body sits, and learn
That I have been an hour away.

XIII

Tears of the widower, when he sees
　A late-lost form that sleep reveals,
　And moves his doubtful arms, and feels
Her place is empty, fall like these;

Which weep a loss for ever new,
　A void where heart on heart reposed;
　And, where warm hands have prest and
　　closed,
Silence, till I be silent too.

Which weep the comrade of my choice,
　An awful thought, a life removed,
　The human-hearted man I loved,
A Spirit, not a breathing voice.

Come Time, and teach me, many years,
　I do not suffer in a dream;
　For now so strange do these things seem,
Mine eyes have leisure for their tears;

My fancies time to rise on wing,
　And glance about the approaching sails,
　As tho' they brought but merchants'
　　bales,
And not the burthen that they bring.

XIV

If one should bring me this report,
　That thou hadst touch'd the land to-day,
　And I went down unto the quay,
And found thee lying in the port;

And standing, muffled round with woe,
  Should see thy passengers in rank
  Come stepping lightly down the plank,
And beckoning unto those they know;

And if along with these should come
  The man I held as half-divine;
  Should strike a sudden hand in mine,
And ask a thousand things of home;

And I should tell him all my pain,
  And how my life had droop'd of late,
  And he should sorrow o'er my state
And marvel what possess'd my brain;

And I perceived no touch of change,
  No hint of death in all his frame,
  But found him all in all the same,
I should not feel it to be strange.

XV

To-night the winds begin to rise
  And roar from yonder dropping day:
  The last red leaf is whirl'd away,
The rooks are blown about the skies;

The forest crack'd, the waters curl'd,
  The cattle huddled on the lea;
  And wildly dash'd on tower and tree
The sunbeam strikes along the world:

And but for fancies, which aver
  That all thy motions gently pass
  Athwart a plane of molten glass,
I scarce could brook the strain and stir

That makes the barren branches loud;
  And but for fear it is not so,
  The wild unrest that lives in woe
Would dote and pore on yonder cloud

That rises upward always higher,
  And onward drags a labouring breast,
  And topples round the dreary west,
A looming bastion fringed with fire.

XVI

What words are these have fall'n from me?
  Can calm despair and wild unrest
  Be tenants of a single breast,
Or sorrow such a changeling be?

Or doth she only seem to take
  The touch of change in calm or storm;
  But knows no more of transient form
In her deep self, than some dead lake

That holds the shadow of a lark
  Hung in the shadow of a heaven?
  Or has the shock, so harshly given,
Confused me like the unhappy bark

That strikes by night a craggy shelf,
  And staggers blindly ere she sink?
  And stunn'd me from my power to think
And all my knowledge of myself;

And made me that delirious man
  Whose fancy fuses old and new,
  And flashes into false and true,
And mingles all without a plan?

XVII

Thou comest, much wept for: such a breeze
  Compell'd thy canvas, and my prayer
  Was as the whisper of an air
To breathe thee over lonely seas.

For I in spirit saw thee move
  Thro' circles of the bounding sky,
  Week after week: the days go by:
Come quick, thou bringest all I love.

Henceforth, wherever thou may'st roam,
  My blessing, like a line of light,
  Is on the waters day and night,
And like a beacon guards thee home.

So may whatever tempest mars
  Mid-ocean, spare thee, sacred bark;
  And balmy drops in summer dark
Slide from the bosom of the stars.

So kind an office hath been done,
  Such precious relics brought by thee;
  The dust of him I shall not see
Till all my widow'd race be run.

XVIII

'Tis well; 'tis something; we may stand
  Where he in English earth is laid,
  And from his ashes may be made
The violet of his native land.

'Tis little; but it looks in truth
  As if the quiet bones were blest
  Among familiar names to rest
And in the places of his youth.

Come then, pure hands, and bear the head
  That sleeps or wears the mask of sleep,
  And come, whatever loves to weep,
And hear the ritual of the dead.

Ah yet, ev'n yet, if this might be,
  I, falling on his faithful heart,
  Would breathing thro' his lips impart
The life that almost dies in me;

That dies not, but endures with pain,
  And slowly forms the firmer mind,
  Treasuring the look it cannot find,
The words that are not heard again.

XIX

The Danube to the Severn gave
  The darken'd heart that beat no more;
  They laid him by the pleasant shore,
And in the hearing of the wave.

There twice a day the Severn fills;
  The salt sea-water passes by,
  And hushes half the babbling Wye,
And makes a silence in the hills.

The Wye is hush'd nor moved along,
  And hush'd my deepest grief of all,
  When fill'd with tears that cannot fall,
I brim with sorrow drowning song.

The tide flows down, the wave again
  Is vocal in its wooded walls;
  My deeper anguish also falls,
And I can speak a little then.

XX

The lesser griefs that may be said,
  That breathe a thousand tender vows,
  Are but as servants in a house
Where lies the master newly dead;

Who speak their feeling as it is,
  And weep the fulness from the mind:
  'It will be hard,' they say, 'to find
Another service such as this.'

My lighter moods are like to these,
  That out of words a comfort win;
  But there are other griefs within,
And tears that at their fountain freeze;

For by the hearth the children sit
  Cold in that atmosphere of Death,
  And scarce endure to draw the breath,
Or like to noiseless phantoms flit:

But open converse is there none,
  So much the vital spirits sink
  To see the vacant chair, and think,
'How good! how kind! and he is gone.'

XXI

I sing to him that rests below,
  And, since the grasses round me wave,
  I take the grasses of the grave,
And make them pipes whereon to blow.

The traveller hears me now and then,
  And sometimes harshly will he speak:
  'This fellow would make weakness weak,
And melt the waxen hearts of men.'

Another answers, 'Let him be,
  He loves to make parade of pain,
  That with his piping he may gain
The praise that comes to constancy.'

A third is wroth: 'Is this an hour
  For private sorrow's barren song,
  When more and more the people throng
The chairs and thrones of civil power?

'A time to sicken and to swoon,
  When Science reaches forth her arms
  To feel from world to world, and charms
Her secret from the latest moon?'

Behold, ye speak an idle thing:
  Ye never knew the sacred dust:
  I do but sing because I must,
And pipe but as the linnets sing:

And one is glad; her note is gay,
  For now her little ones have ranged;
  And one is sad; her note is changed,
Because her brood is stol'n away.

XXII

The path by which we twain did go,
  Which led by tracts that pleased us well,
  Thro' four sweet years arose and fell,
From flower to flower, from snow to snow:

And we with singing cheer'd the way,
  And, crown'd with all the season lent,
  From April on to April went,
And glad at heart from May to May:

But where the path we walk'd began
  To slant the fifth autumnal slope,
  As we descended following Hope,
There sat the Shadow fear'd of man;

Who broke our fair companionship,
  And spread his mantle dark and cold,
  And wrapt thee formless in the fold,
And dull'd the murmur on thy lip,

And bore thee where I could not see
  Nor follow, tho' I walk in haste,
  And think, that somewhere in the waste
The Shadow sits and waits for me.

XXIII

Now, sometimes in my sorrow shut,
  Or breaking into song by fits,
  Alone, alone, to where he sits,
The Shadow cloak'd from head to foot,

Who keeps the keys of all the creeds,
  I wander, often falling lame,
  And looking back to whence I came,
Or on to where the pathway leads;

And crying, How changed from where it
      ran
  Thro' lands where not a leaf was dumb;
  But all the lavish hills would hum
The murmur of a happy Pan:

When each by turns was guide to each,
  And Fancy light from Fancy caught,
  And Thought leapt out to wed with
      Thought
Ere Thought could wed itself with Speech;

And all we met was fair and good,
  And all was good that Time could bring,
  And all the secret of the Spring
Moved in the chambers of the blood;

And many an old philosophy
  On Argive heights divinely sang,
  And round us all the thicket rang
To many a flute of Arcady.

XXIV

And was the day of my delight
  As pure and perfect as I say?
  The very source and fount of Day
Is dash'd with wandering isles of night.

If all was good and fair we met,
  This earth had been the Paradise
  It never look'd to human eyes
Since our first Sun arose and set.

And is it that the haze of grief
  Makes former gladness loom so great?
  The lowness of the present state,
That sets the past in this relief?

Or that the past will always win
  A glory from its being far;
  And orb into the perfect star
We saw not, when we moved therein?

XXV

I know that this was Life,—the track
  Whereon with equal feet we fared;
  And then, as now, the day prepared
The daily burden for the back.

But this it was that made me move
  As light as carrier-birds in air;
  I loved the weight I had to bear,
Because it needed help of Love:

Nor could I weary, heart or limb,
  When mighty Love would cleave in
      twain
  The lading of a single pain,
And part it, giving half to him.

XXVI

Still onward winds the dreary way;
  I with it; for I long to prove
  No lapse of moons can canker Love,
Whatever fickle tongues may say.

And if that eye which watches guilt
  And goodness, and hath power to see
  Within the green the moulder'd tree,
And towers fall'n as soon as built—

Oh, if indeed that eye foresee
  Or see (in Him is no before)
  In more of life true life no more
And Love the indifference to be,

Then might I find, ere yet the morn
  Breaks hither over Indian seas,
  That Shadow waiting with the keys,
To shroud me from my proper scorn.

XXVII

I envy not in any moods
  The captive void of noble rage,
  The linnet born within the cage,
That never knew the summer woods:

I envy not the beast that takes
  His license in the field of time,
  Unfetter'd by the sense of crime,
To whom a conscience never wakes;

Nor, what may count itself as blest,
  The heart that never plighted troth
  But stagnates in the weeds of sloth;
Nor any want-begotten rest.

I hold it true, whate'er befall;
  I feel it, when I sorrow most;
  'Tis better to have loved and lost
Than never to have loved at all.

XXVIII

The time draws near the birth of Christ:
  The moon is hid; the night is still;
  The Christmas bells from hill to hill
Answer each other in the mist.

Four voices of four hamlets round,
  From far and near, on mead and moor,
  Swell out and fail, as if a door
Were shut between me and the sound:

Each voice four changes on the wind,
  That now dilate, and now decrease,
  Peace and goodwill, goodwill and peace,
Peace and goodwill, to all mankind.

This year I slept and woke with pain,
  I almost wish'd no more to wake,
  And that my hold on life would break
Before I heard those bells again:

But they my troubled spirit rule,
  For they controll'd me when a boy;
  They bring me sorrow touch'd with joy,
The merry merry bells of Yule.

XXIX

With such compelling cause to grieve
  As daily vexes household peace,
  And chains regret to his decease,
How dare we keep our Christmas-eve;

Which brings no more a welcome guest
  To enrich the threshold of the night
  With shower'd largess of delight
In dance and song and games and jest?

Yet go, and while the holly boughs
  Entwine the cold baptismal font,
  Make one wreath more for Use and Wont,
That guard the portals of the house;

Old sisters of a day gone by,
  Gray nurses, loving nothing new;
  Why should they miss their yearly due
Before their time? They too will die.

XXX

With trembling fingers did we weave
  The holly round the Christmas hearth;
  A rainy cloud possess'd the earth,
And sadly fell our Christmas-eve.

At our old pastimes in the hall
  We gambol'd, making vain pretence
  Of gladness, with an awful sense
Of one mute Shadow watching all.

We paused: the winds were in the beech:
  We heard them sweep the winter land;
  And in a circle hand-in-hand
Sat silent, looking each at each.

Then echo-like our voices rang;
  We sung, tho' every eye was dim,
  A merry song we sang with him
Last year: impetuously we sang:

We ceased: a gentler feeling crept
  Upon us: surely rest is meet:
  'They rest,' we said, 'their sleep is sweet,'
And silence follow'd, and we wept.

Our voices took a higher range;
    Once more we sang: 'They do not die
    Nor lose their mortal sympathy,
Nor change to us, although they change;

'Rapt from the fickle and the frail
    With gather'd power, yet the same,
    Pierces the keen seraphic flame
From orb to orb, from veil to veil.'

Rise, happy morn, rise, holy morn,
    Draw forth the cheerful day from night:
    O Father, touch the east, and light
The light that shone when Hope was born.

XXXI

When Lazarus left his charnel-cave,
    And home to Mary's house return'd,
    Was this demanded—if he yearn'd
To hear her weeping by his grave?

'Where wert thou, brother, those four
        days?'
    There lives no record of reply,
    Which telling what it is to die
Had surely added praise to praise.

From every house the neighbours met,
    The streets were fill'd with joyful sound,
    A solemn gladness even crown'd
The purple brows of Olivet.

Behold a man raised up by Christ!
    The rest remaineth unreveal'd;
    He told it not; or something seal'd
The lips of that Evangelist.

XXXII

Her eyes are homes of silent prayer,
    Nor other thought her mind admits
    But, he was dead, and there he sits,
And he that brought him back is there.

Then one deep love doth supersede
    All other, when her ardent gaze
    Roves from the living brother's face,
And rests upon the Life indeed.

All subtle thought, all curious fears,
    Borne down by gladness so complete,
    She bows, she bathes the Saviour's feet
With costly spikenard and with tears.

Thrice blest whose lives are faithful
        prayers,
    Whose loves in higher love endure;
    What souls possess themselves so pure,
Or is there blessedness like theirs?

XXXIII

O thou that after toil and storm
    Mayst seem to have reach'd a purer air,
    Whose faith has centre everywhere,
Nor cares to fix itself to form,

Leave thou thy sister when she prays,
    Her early Heaven, her happy views;
    Nor thou with shadow'd hint confuse
A life that leads melodious days.

Her faith thro' form is pure as thine,
    Her hands are quicker unto good:
    Oh, sacred be the flesh and blood
To which she links a truth divine!

See thou, that countest reason ripe
    In holding by the law within,
    Thou fail not in a world of sin,
And ev'n for want of such a type.

XXXIV

My own dim life should teach me this,
    That life shall live for evermore,
    Else earth is darkness at the core,
And dust and ashes all that is;

This round of green, this orb of flame,
    Fantastic beauty; such as lurks
    In some wild Poet, when he works
Without a conscience or an aim.

What then were God to such as I?
    'Twere hardly worth my while to choose
    Of things all mortal, or to use
A little patience ere I die;

'Twere best at once to sink to peace,
    Like birds the charming serpent draws,
    To drop head-foremost in the jaws
Of vacant darkness and to cease.

XXXV

Yet if some voice that man could trust
    Should murmur from the narrow house,
    'The cheeks drop in; the body bows;
Man dies: nor is there hope in dust:'

Might I not say? 'Yet even here,
　But for one hour, O Love, I strive
　To keep so sweet a thing alive:'
But I should turn mine ears and hear

The moanings of the homeless sea,
　The sound of streams that swift or slow
　Draw down Æonian hills, and sow
The dust of continents to be;

And Love would answer with a sigh,
　'The sound of that forgetful shore
　Will change my sweetness more and
　　more,
Half-dead to know that I shall die.'

O me, what profits it to put
　An idle case? If Death were seen
　At first as Death, Love had not been,
Or been in narrowest working shut,

Mere fellowship of sluggish moods,
　Or in his coarsest Satyr-shape
　Had bruised the herb and crush'd the
　　grape,
And bask'd and batten'd in the woods.

XXXVI

Tho' truths in manhood darkly join,
　Deep-seated in our mystic frame,
　We yield all blessing to the name
Of Him that made them current coin;

For Wisdom dealt with mortal powers,
　Where truth in closest words shall fail,
　When truth embodied in a tale
Shall enter in at lowly doors.

And so the Word had breath, and wrought
　With human hands the creed of creeds
　In loveliness of perfect deeds,
More strong than all poetic thought;

Which he may read that binds the sheaf,
　Or builds the house, or digs the grave,
　And those wild eyes that watch the wave
In roarings round the coral reef.

XXXVII

Urania speaks with darken'd brow:
　'Thou pratest here where thou art least;
　This faith has many a purer priest,
And many an abler voice than thou.

'Go down beside thy native rill,
　On thy Parnassus set thy feet,
　And hear thy laurel whisper sweet
About the ledges of the hill.'

And my Melpomene replies,
　A touch of shame upon her cheek:
　'I am not worthy ev'n to speak
Of thy prevailing mysteries;

'For I am but an earthly Muse,
　And owning but a little art
　To lull with song an aching heart,
And render human love his dues;

'But brooding on the dear one dead,
　And all he said of things divine,
　(And dear to me as sacred wine
To dying lips is all he said),

'I murmur'd, as I came along,
　Of comfort clasp'd in truth reveal'd;
　And loiter'd in the master's field,
And darken'd sanctities with song.'

XXXVIII

With weary steps I loiter on,
　Tho' always under alter'd skies
　The purple from the distance dies,
My prospect and horizon gone.

No joy the blowing season gives,
　The herald melodies of spring,
　But in the songs I love to sing
A doubtful gleam of solace lives.

If any care for what is here
　Survive in spirits render'd free,
　Then are these songs I sing of thee
Not all ungrateful to thine ear.

XXXIX

Old warder of these buried bones,
　And answering now my random stroke
　With fruitful cloud and living smoke,
Dark yew, that graspest at the stones

And dippest toward the dreamless head,
　To thee too comes the golden hour
　When flower is feeling after flower;
But Sorrow—fixt upon the dead,

And darkening the dark graves of men,—
  What whisper'd from her lying lips?
  Thy gloom is kindled at the tips,
And passes into gloom again.

XL

Could we forget the widow'd hour
  And look on Spirits breathed away,
  As on a maiden in the day
When first she wears her orange-flower!

When crown'd with blessing she doth rise
  To take her latest leave of home,
  And hopes and light regrets that come
Make April of her tender eyes;

And doubtful joys the father move,
  And tears are on the mother's face,
  As parting with a long embrace
She enters other realms of love;

Her office there to rear, to teach,
  Becoming as is meet and fit
  A link among the days, to knit
The generations each with each;

And, doubtless, unto thee is given
  A life that bears immortal fruit
  In those great offices that suit
The full-grown energies of heaven.

Ay me, the difference I discern!
  How often shall her old fireside
  Be cheer'd with tidings of the bride,
How often she herself return,

And tell them all they would have told,
  And bring her babe, and make her boast,
  Till even those that miss'd her most
Shall count new things as dear as old:

But thou and I have shaken hands,
  Till growing winters lay me low;
  My paths are in the fields I know,
And thine in undiscover'd lands.

XLI

Thy spirit ere our fatal loss
  Did ever rise from high to higher;
  As mounts the heavenward altar-fire,
As flies the lighter thro' the gross.

But thou art turn'd to something strange,
  And I have lost the links that bound
  Thy changes; here upon the ground,
No more partaker of thy change.

Deep folly! yet that this could be—
  That I could wing my will with might
  To leap the grades of life and light,
And flash at once, my friend, to thee.

For tho' my nature rarely yields
  To that vague fear implied in death;
  Nor shudders at the gulfs beneath,
The howlings from forgotten fields;

Yet oft when sundown skirts the moor
  An inner trouble I behold,
  A spectral doubt which makes me cold,
That I shall be thy mate no more,

Tho' following with an upward mind
  The wonders that have come to thee,
  Thro' all the secular to-be,
But evermore a life behind.

XLII

I vex my heart with fancies dim:
  He still outstript me in the race;
  It was but unity of place
That made me dream I rank'd with him.

And so may Place retain us still,
  And he the much-beloved again,
  A lord of large experience, train
To riper growth the mind and will:

And what delights can equal those
  That stir the spirit's inner deeps,
  When one that loves but knows not, reaps
A truth from one that loves and knows?

XLIII

If Sleep and Death be truly one,
  And every spirit's folded bloom
  Thro' all its intervital gloom
In some long trance should slumber on;

Unconscious of the sliding hour,
  Bare of the body, might it last,
  And silent traces of the past
Be all the colour of the flower:

So then were nothing lost to man;
  So that still garden of the souls
  In many a figured leaf enrolls
The total world since life began;

And love will last as pure and whole
  As when he loved me here in Time,
  And at the spiritual prime
Rewaken with the dawning soul.

XLIV

How fares it with the happy dead?
  For here the man is more and more;
  But he forgets the days before
God shut the doorways of his head.

The days have vanish'd, tone and tint,
  And yet perhaps the hoarding sense
  Gives out at times (he knows not whence)
A little flash, a mystic hint;

And in the long harmonious years
  (If Death so taste Lethean springs),
  May some dim touch of earthly things
Surprise thee ranging with thy peers.

If such a dreamy touch should fall,
  O turn thee round, resolve the doubt;
  My guardian angel will speak out
In that high place, and tell thee all.

XLV

The baby new to earth and sky,
  What time his tender palm is prest
  Against the circle of the breast,
Has never thought that 'this is I:'

But as he grows he gathers much,
  And learns the use of 'I,' and 'me,'
  And finds 'I am not what I see,
And other than the things I touch.'

So rounds he to a separate mind
  From whence clear memory may begin,
  As thro' the frame that binds him in
His isolation grows defined.

This use may lie in blood and breath,
  Which else were fruitless of their due,
  Had man to learn himself anew
Beyond the second birth of Death.

XLVI

We ranging down this lower track,
  The path we came by, thorn and flower,
  Is shadow'd by the growing hour,
Lest life should fail in looking back.

So be it: there no shade can last
  In that deep dawn behind the tomb,
  But clear from marge to marge shall bloom
The eternal landscape of the past;

A lifelong tract of time reveal'd;
  The fruitful hours of still increase;
  Days order'd in a wealthy peace,
And those five years its richest field.

O Love, thy province were not large,
  A bounded field, nor stretching far;
  Look also, Love, a brooding star,
A rosy warmth from marge to marge.

XLVII

That each, who seems a separate whole,
  Should move his rounds, and fusing all
  The skirts of self again, should fall
Remerging in the general Soul,

Is faith as vague as all unsweet:
  Eternal form shall still divide
  The eternal soul from all beside;
And I shall know him when we meet:

And we shall sit at endless feast,
  Enjoying each the other's good:
  What vaster dream can hit the mood
Of Love on earth? He seeks at least

Upon the last and sharpest height,
  Before the spirits fade away,
  Some landing-place, to clasp and say,
'Farewell! We lose ourselves in light.'

XLVIII

If these brief lays, of Sorrow born,
  Were taken to be such as closed
  Grave doubts and answers here proposed,
Then these were such as men might scorn:

Her care is not to part and prove;
  She takes, when harsher moods remit,
  What slender shade of doubt may flit,
And makes it vassal unto love:

And hence, indeed, she sports with words,
  But better serves a wholesome law,
  And holds it sin and shame to draw
The deepest measure from the chords:

Nor dare she trust a larger lay,
  But rather loosens from the lip
  Short swallow-flights of song, that dip
Their wings in tears, and skim away.

XLIX

From art, from nature, from the schools,
  Let random influences glance,
  Like light in many a shiver'd lance
That breaks about the dappled pools:

The lightest wave of thought shall lisp,
  The fancy's tenderest eddy wreathe,
  The slightest air of song shall breathe
To make the sullen surface crisp.

And look thy look, and go thy way,
  But blame not thou the winds that make
  The seeming-wanton ripple break,
The tender-pencil'd shadow play.

Beneath all fancied hopes and fears
  Ay me, the sorrow deepens down,
  Whose muffled motions blindly drown
The bases of my life in tears.

L

Be near me when my light is low,
  When the blood creeps, and the nerves
    prick
  And tingle; and the heart is sick,
And all the wheels of Being slow.

Be near me when the sensuous frame
  Is rack'd with pangs that conquer trust;
  And Time, a maniac scattering dust,
And Life, a Fury slinging flame.

Be near me when my faith is dry,
  And men the flies of latter spring,
  That lay their eggs, and sting and sing
And weave their petty cells and die.

Be near me when I fade away,
  To point the term of human strife,
  And on the low dark verge of life
The twilight of eternal day.

LI

Do we indeed desire the dead
  Should still be near us at our side?
  Is there no baseness we would hide?
No inner vileness that we dread?

Shall he for whose applause I strove,
  I had such reverence for his blame,
  See with clear eye some hidden shame
And I be lessen'd in his love?

I wrong the grave with fears untrue:
  Shall love be blamed for want of faith?
  There must be wisdom with great Death:
The dead shall look me thro' and thro'.

Be near us when we climb or fall:
  Ye watch, like God, the rolling hours
  With larger other eyes than ours,
To make allowance for us all.

LII

I cannot love thee as I ought,
  For love reflects the thing beloved;
  My words are only words, and moved
Upon the topmost froth of thought.

'Yet blame not thou thy plaintive song,'
  The Spirit of true love replied;
  'Thou canst not move me from thy side,
Nor human frailty do me wrong.

'What keeps a spirit wholly true
  To that ideal which he bears?
  What record? not the sinless years
That breathed beneath the Syrian blue:

'So fret not, like an idle girl,
  That life is dash'd with flecks of sin.
  Abide: thy wealth is gather'd in,
When Time hath sunder'd shell from pearl.'

LIII

How many a father have I seen,
  A sober man, among his boys,
  Whose youth was full of foolish noise,
Who wears his manhood hale and green:

And dare we to this fancy give,
  That had the wild oat not been sown,
  The soil, left barren, scarce had grown
The grain by which a man may live?

Or, if we held the doctrine sound
  For life outliving heats of youth,
  Yet who would preach it as a truth
To those that eddy round and round?

Hold thou the good: define it well:
  For fear divine Philosophy
  Should push beyond her mark, and be
Procuress to the Lords of Hell.

LIV

Oh yet we trust that somehow good
  Will be the final goal of ill,
  To pangs of nature, sins of will,
Defects of doubt, and taints of blood;

That nothing walks with aimless feet;
  That not one life shall be destroy'd,
  Or cast as rubbish to the void,
When God hath made the pile complete;

That not a worm is cloven in vain;
  That not a moth with vain desire
  Is shrivell'd in a fruitless fire,
Or but subserves another's gain.

Behold, we know not anything;
  I can but trust that good shall fall
  At last—far off—at last, to all,
And every winter change to spring.

So runs my dream: but what am I?
  An infant crying in the night:
  An infant crying for the light:
And with no language but a cry.

LV

The wish, that of the living whole
  No life may fail beyond the grave,
  Derives it not from what we have
The likest God within the soul?

Are God and Nature then at strife,
  That Nature lends such evil dreams?
  So careful of the type she seems,
So careless of the single life;

That I, considering everywhere
  Her secret meaning in her deeds,
  And finding that of fifty seeds,
She often brings but one to bear,

I falter where I firmly trod,
  And falling with my weight of cares
  Upon the great world's altar-stairs
That slope thro' darkness up to God,

I stretch lame hands of faith, and grope,
  And gather dust and chaff, and call
  To what I feel is Lord of all,
And faintly trust the larger hope.

LVI

'So careful of the type'? but no.
  From scarped cliff and quarried stone
  She cries, 'A thousand types are gone:
I care for nothing, all shall go.

'Thou makest thine appeal to me:
  I bring to life, I bring to death:
  The spirit does but mean the breath:
I know no more.' And he, shall he,

Man, her last work, who seem'd so fair,
  Such splendid purpose in his eyes,
  Who roll'd the psalm to wintry skies,
Who built him fanes of fruitless prayer,

Who trusted God was love indeed
  And love Creation's final law—
  Tho' Nature, red in tooth and claw
With ravine, shriek'd against his creed—

Who loved, who suffer'd countless ills,
  Who battled for the True, the Just,
  Be blown about the desert dust,
Or seal'd within the iron hills?

No more? A monster then, a dream,
  A discord. Dragons of the prime,
  That tare each other in their slime,
Were mellow music match'd with him.

O life as futile, then, as frail!
  O for thy voice to soothe and bless!
  What hope of answer, or redress?
Behind the veil, behind the veil.

LVII

Peace; come away: the song of woe
  Is after all an earthly song:
  Peace; come away: we do him wrong
To sing so wildly: let us go.

Come; let us go: your cheeks are pale;
  But half my life I leave behind:
  Methinks my friend is richly shrined;
But I shall pass; my work will fail.

Yet in these ears, till hearing dies,
  One set slow bell will seem to toll
  The passing of the sweetest soul
That ever look'd with human eyes.

I hear it now, and o'er and o'er,
  Eternal greetings to the dead;
  And 'Ave, Ave, Ave,' said,
'Adieu, adieu' for evermore.

LVIII

In those sad words I took farewell:
  Like echoes in sepulchral halls,
  As drop by drop the water falls
In vaults and catacombs, they fell;

And, falling, idly broke the peace
  Of hearts that beat from day to day,
  Half-conscious of their dying clay,
And those cold crypts where they shall cease.

The high Muse answer'd: 'Wherefore grieve
  Thy brethren with a fruitless tear?
  Abide a little longer here,
And thou shalt take a nobler leave.'

LIX

O Sorrow, wilt thou live with me
  No casual mistress, but a wife,
  My bosom-friend and half of life;
As I confess it needs must be;

O Sorrow, wilt thou rule my blood,
  Be sometimes lovely like a bride,
  And put thy harsher moods aside,
If thou wilt have me wise and good.

My centred passion cannot move.
  Nor will it lessen from to-day;
  But I'll have leave at times to play
As with the creature of my love;

And set thee forth, for thou art mine,
  With so much hope for years to come,
  That, howsoe'er I know thee, some
Could hardly tell what name were thine.

LX

He past; a soul of nobler tone:
  My spirit loved and loves him yet,
  Like some poor girl whose heart is set
On one whose rank exceeds her own.

He mixing with his proper sphere,
  She finds the baseness of her lot,
  Half jealous of she knows not what,
And envying all that meet him there.

The little village looks forlorn;
  She sighs amid her narrow days,
  Moving about the household ways,
In that dark house where she was born.

The foolish neighbours come and go,
  And tease her till the day draws by:
  At night she weeps, 'How vain am I!
How should he love a thing so low?'

LXI

If, in thy second state sublime,
  Thy ransom'd reason change replies
  With all the circle of the wise,
The perfect flower of human time;

And if thou cast thine eyes below,
  How dimly character'd and slight,
  How dwarf'd a growth of cold and night,
How blanch'd with darkness must I grow!

Yet turn thee to the doubtful shore,
  Where thy first form was made a man;
  I loved thee, Spirit, and love, nor can
The soul of Shakspeare love thee more.

LXII

Tho' if an eye that's downward cast
  Could make thee somewhat blench or fail,
  Then be my love an idle tale,
And fading legend of the past;

And thou, as one that once declined,
  When he was little more than boy,
  On some unworthy heart with joy,
But lives to wed an equal mind;

And breathes a novel world, the while
  His other passion wholly dies,
  Or in the light of deeper eyes
Is matter for a flying smile.

LXIII

Yet pity for a horse o'er-driven,
   And love in which my hound has part,
   Can hang no weight upon my heart
In its assumptions up to heaven;

And I am so much more than these,
   As thou, perchance, art more than I,
   And yet I spare them sympathy,
And I would set their pains at ease.

So mayst thou watch me where I weep,
   As, unto vaster motions bound,
   The circuits of thine orbit round
A higher height, a deeper deep.

LXIV

Dost thou look back on what hath been,
   As some divinely gifted man,
   Whose life in low estate began
And on a simple village green;

Who breaks his birth's invidious bar,
   And grasps the skirts of happy chance,
   And breasts the blows of circumstance,
And grapples with his evil star;

Who makes by force his merit known
   And lives to clutch the golden keys,
   To mould a mighty state's decrees,
And shape the whisper of the throne;

And moving up from high to higher,
   Becomes on Fortune's crowning slope
   The pillar of a people's hope,
The centre of a world's desire;

Yet feels, as in a pensive dream,
   When all his active powers are still,
   A distant dearness in the hill,
A secret sweetness in the stream,

The limit of his narrower fate,
   While yet beside its vocal springs
   He play'd at counsellors and kings,
With one that was his earliest mate;

Who ploughs with pain his native lea
   And reaps the labour of his hands,
   Or in the furrow musing stands;
'Does my old friend remember me?'

LXV

Sweet soul, do with me as thou wilt;
   I lull a fancy trouble-tost
   With 'Love's too precious to be lost,
A little grain shall not be spilt.'

And in that solace can I sing,
   Till out of painful phases wrought
   There flutters up a happy thought,
Self-balanced on a lightsome wing:

Since we deserved the name of friends,
   And thine effect so lives in me,
   A part of mine may live in thee
And move thee on to noble ends.

LXVI

You thought my heart too far diseased;
   You wonder when my fancies play
   To find me gay among the gay,
Like one with any trifle pleased.

The shade by which my life was crost,
   Which makes a desert in the mind,
   Has made me kindly with my kind,
And like to him whose sight is lost;

Whose feet are guided thro' the land,
   Whose jest among his friends is free,
   Who takes the children on his knee,
And winds their curls about his hand:

He plays with threads, he beats his chair
   For pastime, dreaming of the sky;
   His inner day can never die,
His night of loss is always there.

LXVII

When on my bed the moonlight falls,
   I know that in thy place of rest
   By that broad water of the west,
There comes a glory on the walls:

Thy marble bright in dark appears,
   As slowly steals a silver flame
   Along the letters of thy name,
And o'er the number of thy years.

The mystic glory swims away;
   From off my bed the moonlight dies;
   And closing eaves of wearied eyes
I sleep till dusk is dipt in gray:

And then I know the mist is drawn
A lucid veil from coast to coast,
And in the dark church like a ghost
Thy tablet glimmers to the dawn.

LXVIII

When in the down I sink my head,
Sleep, Death's twin-brother, times my
breath;
Sleep, Death's twin-brother, knows not
Death,
Nor can I dream of thee as dead:

I walk as ere I walk'd forlorn,
When all our path was fresh with dew,
And all the bugle breezes blew
Reveillée to the breaking morn.

But what is this? I turn about,
I find a trouble in thine eye,
Which makes me sad I know not why,
Nor can my dream resolve the doubt:

But ere the lark hath left the lea
I wake, and I discern the truth;
It is the trouble of my youth
That foolish sleep transfers to thee.

LXIX

I dream'd there would be Spring no more,
That Nature's ancient power was lost:
The streets were black with smoke and
frost,
They chatter'd trifles at the door:

I wander'd from the noisy town,
I found a wood with thorny boughs:
I took the thorns to bind my brows,
I wore them like a civic crown:

I met with scoffs, I met with scorns
From youth and babe and hoary hairs:
They call'd me in the public squares
The fool that wears a crown of thorns:

They call'd me fool, they call'd me child:
I found an angel of the night;
The voice was low, the look was bright;
He look'd upon my crown and smiled:

He reach'd the glory of a hand,
That seem'd to touch it into leaf:
The voice was not the voice of grief,
The words were hard to understand.

LXX

I cannot see the features right,
When on the gloom I strive to paint
The face I know; the hues are faint
And mix with hollow masks of night;

Cloud-towers by ghostly masons wrought,
A gulf that ever shuts and gapes,
A hand that points, and palled shapes
In shadowy thoroughfares of thought;

And crowds that stream from yawning
doors,
And shoals of pucker'd faces drive;
Dark bulks that tumble half alive,
And lazy lengths on boundless shores;

Till all at once beyond the will
I hear a wizard music roll,
And thro' a lattice on the soul
Looks thy fair face and makes it still.

LXXI

Sleep, kinsman thou to death and trance
And madness, thou hast forged at last
A night-long Present of the Past
In which we went thro' summer France.

Hadst thou such credit with the soul?
Then bring an opiate trebly strong,
Drug down the blindfold sense of wrong
That so my pleasure may be whole;

While now we talk as once we talk'd
Of men and minds, the dust of change,
The days that grow to something strange,
In walking as of old we walk'd

Beside the river's wooded reach,
The fortress, and the mountain ridge,
The cataract flashing from the bridge,
The breaker breaking on the beach.

LXXII

Risest thou thus, dim dawn, again,
And howlest, issuing out of night,
With blasts that blow the poplar white,
And lash with storm the streaming pane?

Day, when my crown'd estate begun
To pine in that reverse of doom,
Which sicken'd every living bloom,
And blurr'd the splendour of the sun;

Who usherest in the dolorous hour
  With thy quick tears that make the rose
  Pull sideways, and the daisy close
Her crimson fringes to the shower;

Who might'st have heaved a windless flame
  Up the deep East, or, whispering, play'd
  A chequer-work of beam and shade
Along the hills, yet look'd the same.

As wan, as chill, as wild as now;
  Day, mark'd as with some hideous crime,
  When the dark hand struck down thro'
      time,
And cancell'd nature's best: but thou,

Lift as thou may'st thy burthen'd brows
  Thro' clouds that drench the morning
      star,
  And whirl the ungarner'd sheaf afar,
And sow the sky with flying boughs,

And up thy vault with roaring sound
  Climb thy thick noon, disastrous day;
  Touch thy dull goal of joyless gray,
And hide thy shame beneath the ground.

LXXIII

So many worlds, so much to do,
  So little done, such things to be,
  How know I what had need of thee,
For thou wert strong as thou wert true?

The fame is quench'd that I foresaw,
  The head hath miss'd an earthly wreath:
  I curse not nature, no, nor death;
For nothing is that errs from law.

We pass; the path that each man trod
  Is dim, or will be dim, with weeds:
  What fame is left for human deeds
In endless age? It rests with God.

O hollow wraith of dying fame,
  Fade wholly, while the soul exults,
  And self-infolds the large results
Of force that would have forged a name.

LXXIV

As sometimes in a dead man's face,
  To those that watch it more and more,
  A likeness, hardly seen before,
Comes out—to some one of his race:

So, dearest, now thy brows are cold,
  I see thee what thou art, and know
  Thy likeness to the wise below,
Thy kindred with the great of old.

But there is more than I can see,
  And what I see I leave unsaid,
  Nor speak it, knowing Death has made
His darkness beautiful with thee.

LXXV

I leave thy praises unexpress'd
  In verse that brings myself relief,
  And by the measure of my grief
I leave thy greatness to be guess'd;

What practice howsoe'er expert
  In fitting aptest words to things,
  Or voice the richest-toned that sings,
Hath power to give thee as thou wert?

I care not in these fading days
  To raise a cry that lasts not long,
  And round thee with the breeze of song
To stir a little dust of praise.

Thy leaf has perish'd in the green,
  And, while we breathe beneath the sun,
  The world which credits what is done
Is cold to all that might have been.

So here shall silence guard thy fame;
  But somewhere, out of human view,
  Whate'er thy hands are set to do
Is wrought with tumult of acclaim.

LXXVI

Take wings of fancy, and ascend,
  And in a moment set thy face
  Where all the starry heavens of space
Are sharpen'd to a needle's end;

Take wings of foresight; lighten thro'
  The secular abyss to come,
  And lo, thy deepest lays are dumb
Before the mouldering of a yew;

And if the matin songs, that woke
  The darkness of our planet, last,
  Thine own shall wither in the vast,
Ere half the lifetime of an oak.

Ere these have clothed their branchy
    bowers
  With fifty Mays, thy songs are vain;
  And what are they when these remain
The ruin'd shells of hollow towers?

LXXVII

What hope is here for modern rhyme
  To him, who turns a musing eye
  On songs, and deeds, and lives, that lie
Foreshorten'd in the tract of time?

These mortal lullabies of pain
  May bind a book, may line a box,
  May serve to curl a maiden's locks;
Or when a thousand moons shall wane

A man upon a stall may find,
  And, passing, turn the page that tells
  A grief, then changed to something else,
Sung by a long-forgotten mind.

But what of that? My darken'd ways
  Shall ring with music all the same;
  To breathe my loss is more than fame,
To utter love more sweet than praise.

LXXVIII

Again at Christmas did we weave
  The holly round the Christmas hearth;
  The silent snow possess'd the earth,
And calmly fell our Christmas-eve:

The yule-clog sparkled keen with frost,
  No wing of wind the region swept,
  But over all things brooding slept
The quiet sense of something lost.

As in the winters left behind,
  Again our ancient games had place,
  The mimic picture's breathing grace,
And dance and song and hoodman-blind.

Who show'd a token of distress?
  No single tear, no mark of pain:
  O sorrow, then can sorrow wane?
O grief, can grief be changed to less?

O last regret, regret can die!
  No—mixt with all this mystic frame,
  Her deep relations are the same,
But with long use her tears are dry.

LXXIX

'More than my brothers are to me,'—
  Let this not vex thee, noble heart!
  I know thee of what force thou art
To hold the costliest love in fee.

But thou and I are one in kind,
  As moulded like in Nature's mint;
  And hill and wood and field did print
The same sweet forms in either mind.

For us the same cold streamlet curl'd
  Thro' all his eddying coves; the same
  All winds that roam the twilight came
In whispers of the beauteous world.

At one dear knee we proffer'd vows,
  One lesson from one book we learn'd,
  Ere childhood's flaxen ringlet turn'd
To black and brown on kindred brows.

And so my wealth resembles thine,
  But he was rich where I was poor,
  And he supplied my want the more
As his unlikeness fitted mine.

LXXX

If any vague desire should rise,
  That holy Death ere Arthur died
  Had moved me kindly from his side,
And dropt the dust on tearless eyes;

Then fancy shapes, as fancy can,
  The grief my loss in him had wrought,
  A grief as deep as life or thought,
But stay'd in peace with God and man.

I make a picture in the brain;
  I hear the sentence that he speaks;
  He bears the burthen of the weeks
But turns his burthen into gain.

His credit thus shall set me free;
  And, influence-rich to soothe and save,
  Unused example from the grave
Reach out dead hands to comfort me.

LXXXI

Could I have said while he was here,
  'My love shall now no further range;
  There cannot come a mellower change,
For now is love mature in ear.'

Love, then, had hope of richer store:
  What end is here to my complaint?
  This haunting whisper makes me faint,
'More years had made me love thee more.'

But Death returns an answer sweet:
  'My sudden frost was sudden gain,
  And gave all ripeness to the grain,
It might have drawn from after-heat.'

LXXXII

I wage not any feud with Death
  For changes wrought on form and face;
  No lower life that earth's embrace
May breed with him, can fright my faith.

Eternal process moving on,
  From state to state the spirit walks;
  And these are but the shatter'd stalks,
Or ruin'd chrysalis of one.

Nor blame I Death, because he bare
  The use of virtue out of earth:
  I know transplanted human worth
Will bloom to profit, otherwhere.

For this alone on Death I wreak
  The wrath that garners in my heart;
  He put our lives so far apart
We cannot hear each other speak.

LXXXIII

Dip down upon the northern shore,
  O sweet new-year delaying long;
  Thou doest expectant nature wrong;
Delaying long, delay no more.

What stays thee from the clouded noons,
  Thy sweetness from its proper place?
  Can trouble live with April days,
Or sadness in the summer moons?

Bring orchis, bring the foxglove spire,
  The little speedwell's darling blue,
  Deep tulips dash'd with fiery dew,
Laburnums, dropping-wells of fire.

O thou, new-year, delaying long,
  Delayest the sorrow in my blood,
  That longs to burst a frozen bud
And flood a fresher throat with song.

LXXXIV

When I contemplate all alone
  The life that had been thine below,
  And fix my thoughts on all the glow
To which thy crescent would have grown;

I see thee sitting crown'd with good,
  A central warmth diffusing bliss
  In glance and smile, and clasp and kiss,
On all the branches of thy blood;

Thy blood, my friend, and partly mine;
  For now the day was drawing on,
  When thou should'st link thy life with
    one
Of mine own house, and boys of thine

Had babbled 'Uncle' on my knee;
  But that remorseless iron hour
  Made cypress of her orange flower,
Despair of Hope, and earth of thee.

I seem to meet their least desire,
  To clap their cheeks, to call them mine.
  I see their unborn faces shine
Beside the never-lighted fire.

I see myself an honour'd guest,
  Thy partner in the flowery walk
  Of letters, genial table-talk,
Or deep dispute, and graceful jest;

While now thy prosperous labour fills
  The lips of men with honest praise,
  And sun by sun the happy days
Descend below the golden hills

With promise of a morn as fair;
  And all the train of bounteous hours
  Conduct by paths of growing powers,
To reverence and the silver hair;

Till slowly worn her earthly robe,
  Her lavish mission richly wrought,
  Leaving great legacies of thought,
Thy spirit should fail from off the globe;

What time mine own might also flee,
  As link'd with thine in love and fate,
  And, hovering o'er the dolorous strait
To the other shore, involved in thee,

Arrive at last the blessed goal,
  And He that died in Holy Land
  Would reach us out the shining hand,
And take us as a single soul.

What reed was that on which I leant?
  Ah, backward fancy, wherefore wake
  The old bitterness again, and break
The low beginnings of content.

LXXXV

This truth came borne with bier and pall,
  I felt it, when I sorrow'd most,
  'Tis better to have loved and lost,
Than never to have loved at all——

O true in word, and tried in deed,
  Demanding, so to bring relief
  To this which is our common grief,
What kind of life is that I lead;

And whether trust in things above
  Be dimm'd of sorrow, or sustain'd;
  And whether love for him have drain'd
My capabilities of love;

Your words have virtue such as draws
  A faithful answer from the breast,
  Thro' light reproaches, half exprest
And loyal unto kindly laws.

My blood an even tenor kept,
  Till on mine ear this message falls,
  That in Vienna's fatal walls
God's finger touch'd him, and he slept.

The great Intelligences fair
  That range above our mortal state,
  In circle round the blessed gate,
Received and gave him welcome there;

And led him thro' the blissful climes,
  And show'd him in the fountain fresh
  All knowledge that the sons of flesh
Shall gather in the cycled times.

But I remain'd, whose hopes were dim,
  Whose life, whose thoughts were little
    worth,
  To wander on a darken'd earth,
Where all things round me breathed of
    him.

O friendship, equal-poised control,
  O heart, with kindliest motion warm,
  O sacred essence, other form,
O solemn ghost, O crowned soul!

Yet none could better know than I,
  How much of act at human hands
  The sense of human will demands
By which we dare to live or die.

Whatever way my days decline,
  I felt and feel, tho' left alone,
  His being working in mine own,
The footsteps of his life in mine;

A life that all the Muses deck'd
  With gifts of grace, that might express
  All-comprehensive tenderness,
All-subtilising intellect:

And so my passion hath not swerved
  To works of weakness, but I find
  An image comforting the mind,
And in my grief a strength reserved.

Likewise the imaginative woe,
  That loved to handle spiritual strife,
  Diffused the shock thro' all my life,
But in the present broke the blow.

My pulses therefore beat again
  For other friends that once I met;
  Nor can it suit me to forget
The mighty hopes that make us men.

I woo your love: I count it crime
  To mourn for any overmuch;
  I, the divided half of such
A friendship as had master'd Time;

Which masters Time indeed, and is
  Eternal, separate from fears:
  The all-assuming months and years
Can take no part away from this:

But Summer on the steaming floods,
  And Spring that swells the narrow
    brooks,
  And Autumn, with a noise of rooks,
That gather in the waning woods,

And every pulse of wind and wave
  Recalls, in change of light or gloom,
  My old affection of the tomb,
And my prime passion in the grave:

My old affection of the tomb,
   A part of stillness, yearns to speak:
   'Arise, and get thee forth and seek
A friendship for the years to come.

'I watch thee from the quiet shore;
   Thy spirit up to mine can reach;
   But in dear words of human speech
We two communicate no more.'

And I, 'Can clouds of nature stain
   The starry clearness of the free?
   How is it? Canst thou feel for me
Some painless sympathy with pain?'

And lightly does the whisper fall;
   ''Tis hard for thee to fathom this;
   I triumph in conclusive bliss,
And that serene result of all.'

So hold I commerce with the dead;
   Or so methinks the dead would say;
   Or so shall grief with symbols play
And pining life be fancy-fed.

Now looking to some settled end,
   That these things pass, and I shall prove
   A meeting somewhere, love with love,
I crave your pardon, O my friend;

If not so fresh, with love as true,
   I, clasping brother-hands, aver
   I could not, if I would, transfer
The whole I felt for him to you.

For which be they that hold apart
   The promise of the golden hours?
   First love, first friendship, equal powers,
That marry with the virgin heart.

Still mine, that cannot but deplore,
   That beats within a lonely place,
   That yet remembers his embrace,
But at his footstep leaps no more,

My heart, tho' widow'd, may not rest
   Quite in the love of what is gone,
   But seeks to beat in time with one
That warms another living breast.

Ah, take the imperfect gift I bring,
   Knowing the primrose yet is dear,
   The primrose of the later year,
As not unlike to that of Spring.

LXXXVI

Sweet after showers, ambrosial air,
   That rollest from the gorgeous gloom
   Of evening over brake and bloom
And meadow, slowly breathing bare

The round of space, and rapt below
   Thro' all the dewy-tassel'd wood,
   And shadowing down the horned flood
In ripples, fan my brows and blow

The fever from my cheek, and sigh
   The full new life that feeds thy breath
   Throughout my frame, till Doubt and Death,
Ill brethren, let the fancy fly

From belt to belt of crimson seas
   On leagues of odour streaming far,
   To where in yonder orient star
A hundred spirits whisper 'Peace.'

LXXXVII

I past beside the reverend walls
   In which of old I wore the gown;
   I roved at random thro' the town,
And saw the tumult of the halls;

And heard once more in college fanes
   The storm their high-built organs make,
   And thunder-music, rolling, shake
The prophet blazon'd on the panes;

And caught once more the distant shout,
   The measured pulse of racing oars
   Among the willows; paced the shores
And many a bridge, and all about

The same gray flats again, and felt
   The same, but not the same; and last
   Up that long walk of limes I past
To see the rooms in which he dwelt.

Another name was on the door:
   I linger'd; all within was noise
   Of songs, and clapping hands, and boys
That crash'd the glass and beat the floor;

Where once we held debate, a band
   Of youthful friends, on mind and art,
   And labour, and the changing mart,
And all the framework of the land;

When one would aim an arrow fair,
  But send it slackly from the string;
  And one would pierce an outer ring,
And one an inner, here and there;

And last the master-bowman, he,
  Would cleave the mark. A willing ear
  We lent him. Who, but hung to hear
The rapt oration flowing free

From point to point, with power and grace
  And music in the bounds of law,
  To those conclusions when we saw
The God within him light his face,

And seem to lift the form, and glow
  In azure orbits heavenly-wise;
  And over those ethereal eyes
The bar of Michael Angelo.

LXXXVIII

Wild bird, whose warble, liquid sweet,
  Rings Eden thro' the budded quicks,
  O tell me where the senses mix,
O tell me where the passions meet,

Whence radiate: fierce extremes employ
  Thy spirits in the darkening leaf,
  And in the midmost heart of grief
Thy passion clasps a secret joy:

And I—my harp would prelude woe—
  I cannot all command the strings;
  The glory of the sum of things
Will flash along the chords and go.

LXXXIX

Witch-elms that counterchange the floor
  Of this flat lawn with dusk and bright;
  And thou, with all thy breadth and
    height
Of foliage, towering sycamore;

How often, hither wandering down,
  My Arthur found your shadows fair,
  And shook to all the liberal air
The dust and din and steam of town:

He brought an eye for all he saw;
  He mixt in all our simple sports;
  They pleased him, fresh from brawling
    courts
And dusty purlieus of the law.

O joy to him in this retreat,
  Immantled in ambrosial dark,
  To drink the cooler air, and mark
The landscape winking thro' the heat:

O sound to rout the brood of cares,
  The sweep of scythe in morning dew,
  The gust that round the garden flew,
And tumbled half the mellowing pears!

O bliss, when all in circle drawn
  About him, heart and ear were fed
  To hear him, as he lay and read
The Tuscan poets on the lawn:

Or in the all-golden afternoon
  A guest, or happy sister, sung,
  Or here she brought the harp and
    flung
A ballad to the brightening moon:

Nor less it pleased in livelier moods,
  Beyond the bounding hill to stray,
  And break the livelong summer day
With banquet in the distant woods;

Whereat we glanced from theme to theme,
  Discuss'd the books to love or hate,
  Or touch'd the changes of the state,
Or threaded some Socratic dream;

But if I praised the busy town,
  He loved to rail against it still,
  For 'ground in yonder social mill
We rub each other's angles down,

'And merge' he said 'in form and gloss
  The picturesque of man and man.'
  We talk'd: the stream beneath us ran,
The wine-flask lying couch'd in moss,

Or cool'd within the glooming wave;
  And last, returning from afar,
  Before the crimson-circled star
Had fall'n into her father's grave,

And brushing ankle-deep in flowers,
  We heard behind the woodbine veil
  The milk that bubbled in the pail,
And buzzings of the honied hours.

XC

He tasted love with half his mind,
　Nor ever drank the inviolate spring
　Where nighest heaven, who first could
　　fling
This bitter seed among mankind;

That could the dead, whose dying eyes
　Were closed with wail, resume their life,
　They would but find in child and wife
An iron welcome when they rise:

'Twas well, indeed, when warm with wine,
　To pledge them with a kindly tear,
　To talk them o'er, to wish them here,
To count their memories half divine;

But if they came who past away,
　Behold their brides in other hands;
　The hard heir strides about their lands,
And will not yield them for a day.

Yea, tho' their sons were none of these,
　Not less the yet-loved sire would make
　Confusion worse than death, and shake
The pillars of domestic peace.

Ah dear, but come thou back to me:
　Whatever change the years have wrought,
　I find not yet one lonely thought
That cries against my wish for thee.

XCI

When rosy plumelets tuft the larch,
　And rarely pipes the mounted thrush;
　Or underneath the barren bush
Flits by the sea-blue bird of March;

Come, wear the form by which I know
　Thy spirit in time among thy peers;
　The hope of unaccomplish'd years
Be large and lucid round thy brow.

When summer's hourly-mellowing change
　May breathe, with many roses sweet,
　Upon the thousand waves of wheat,
That ripple round the lonely grange;

Come: not in watches of the night,
　But where the sunbeam broodeth warm,
　Come, beauteous in thine after form,
And like a finer light in light.

XCII

If any vision should reveal
　Thy likeness, I might count it vain
　As but the canker of the brain;
Yea, tho' it spake and made appeal

To chances where our lots were cast
　Together in the days behind,
　I might but say, I hear a wind
Of memory murmuring the past.

Yea, tho' it spake and bared to view
　A fact within the coming year;
　And tho' the months, revolving near,
Should prove the phantom-warning true,

They might not seem thy prophecies,
　But spiritual presentiments,
　And such refraction of events
As often rises ere they rise.

XCIII

I shall not see thee. Dare I say
　No spirit ever brake the band
　That stays him from the native land
Where first he walk'd when claspt in clay?

No visual shade of some one lost,
　But he, the Spirit himself, may come
　Where all the nerve of sense is numb;
Spirit to Spirit, Ghost to Ghost.

O, therefore from thy sightless range
　With gods in unconjectured bliss,
　O, from the distance of the abyss
Of tenfold-complicated change,

Descend, and touch, and enter; hear
　The wish too strong for words to name;
　That in this blindness of the frame
My Ghost may feel that thine is near.

XCIV

How pure at heart and sound in head,
　With what divine affections bold
　Should be the man whose thought
　　would hold
An hour's communion with the dead.

In vain shalt thou, or any, call
　The spirits from their golden day,
　Except, like them, thou too canst say,
My spirit is at peace with all.

They haunt the silence of the breast,
  Imaginations calm and fair,
  The memory like a cloudless air,
The conscience as a sea at rest:

But when the heart is full of din,
  And doubt beside the portal waits,
  They can but listen at the gates,
And hear the household jar within.

XCV

By night we linger'd on the lawn,
  For underfoot the herb was dry;
  And genial warmth; and o'er the sky
The silvery haze of summer drawn;

And calm that let the tapers burn
  Unwavering: not a cricket chirr'd:
  The brook alone far-off was heard,
And on the board the fluttering urn:

And bats went round in fragrant skies,
  And wheel'd or lit the filmy shapes
  That haunt the dusk, with ermine capes
And woolly breasts and beaded eyes;

While now we sang old songs that peal'd
  From knoll to knoll, where, couch'd at
    ease,
  The white kine glimmer'd, and the trees
Laid their dark arms about the field.

But when those others, one by one,
  Withdrew themselves from me and
    night,
  And in the house light after light
Went out, and I was all alone,

A hunger seized my heart; I read
  Of that glad year which once had been,
  In those fall'n leaves which kept their
    green,
The noble letters of the dead:

And strangely on the silence broke
  The silent-speaking words, and strange
  Was love's dumb cry defying change
To test his worth; and strangely spoke

The faith, the vigour, bold to dwell
  On doubts that drive the coward back,
  And keen thro' wordy snares to track
Suggestion to her inmost cell.

So word by word, and line by line,
  The dead man touch'd me from the past,
  And all at once it seem'd at last
The living soul was flash'd on mine,

And mine in this was wound, and whirl'd
  About empyreal heights of thought,
  And came on that which is, and caught
The deep pulsations of the world,

Æonian music measuring out
  The steps of Time—the shocks of
    Chance—
  The blows of Death. At length my
    trance
Was cancell'd, stricken thro' with doubt.

Vague words! but ah, how hard to frame
  In matter-moulded forms of speech,
  Or ev'n for intellect to reach
Thro' memory that which I became:

Till now the doubtful dusk reveal'd
  The knolls once more where, couch'd at
    ease,
  The white kine glimmer'd, and the trees
Laid their dark arms about the field:

And suck'd from out the distant gloom
  A breeze began to tremble o'er
  The large leaves of the sycamore,
And fluctuate all the still perfume,

And gathering freshlier overhead,
  Rock'd the full-foliaged elms, and swung
  The heavy-folded rose, and flung
The lilies to and fro, and said

'The dawn, the dawn,' and died away;
  And East and West, without a breath,
  Mixt their dim lights, like life and death,
To broaden into boundless day.

XCVI

You say, but with no touch of scorn,
  Sweet-hearted, you, whose light-blue
    eyes
  Are tender over drowning flies,
You tell me, doubt is Devil-born.

I know not: one indeed I knew
  In many a subtle question versed,
  Who touch'd a jarring lyre at first,
But ever strove to make it true:

Perplext in faith, but pure in deeds,
　At last he beat his music out.
　There lives more faith in honest doubt,
Believe me, than in half the creeds.

He fought his doubts and gather'd strength,
　He would not make his judgement blind,
　He faced the spectres of the mind
And laid them: thus he came at length

To find a stronger faith his own;
　And Power was with him in the night,
　Which makes the darkness and the light,
And dwells not in the light alone,

But in the darkness and the cloud,
　As over Sinai's peaks of old,
　While Israel made their gods of gold,
Altho' the trumpet blew so loud.

XCVII

My love has talk'd with rocks and trees;
　He finds on misty mountain-ground
　His own vast shadow glory-crown'd;
He sees himself in all he sees.

Two partners of a married life—
　I look'd on these and thought of thee
　In vastness and in mystery,
And of my spirit as of a wife.

These two—they dwelt with eye on eye,
　Their hearts of old have beat in tune,
　Their meetings made December June,
Their every parting was to die.

Their love has never past away;
　The days she never can forget
　Are earnest that he loves her yet,
Whate'er the faithless people say.

Her life is lone, he sits apart,
　He loves her yet, she will not weep,
　Tho' rapt in matters dark and deep
He seems to slight her simple heart.

He thrids the labyrinth of the mind,
　He reads the secret of the star,
　He seems so near and yet so far,
He looks so cold: she thinks him kind.

She keeps the gift of years before,
　A wither'd violet is her bliss:
　She knows not what his greatness is,
For that, for all, she loves him more.

For him she plays, to him she sings
　Of early faith and plighted vows;
　She knows but matters of the house,
And he, he knows a thousand things.

Her faith is fixt and cannot move,
　She darkly feels him great and wise,
　She dwells on him with faithful eyes,
'I cannot understand: I love.'

XCVIII

You leave us: you will see the Rhine,
　And those fair hills I sail'd below,
　When I was there with him; and go
By summer belts of wheat and vine

To where he breathed his latest breath,
　That City. All her splendour seems
　No livelier than the wisp that gleams
On Lethe in the eyes of Death.

Let her great Danube rolling fair
　Enwind her isles, unmark'd of me:
　I have not seen, I will not see
Vienna; rather dream that there,

A treble darkness, Evil haunts
　The birth, the bridal; friend from friend
　Is oftener parted, fathers bend
Above more graves, a thousand wants

Gnarr at the heels of men, and prey
　By each cold hearth, and sadness flings
　Her shadow on the blaze of kings:
And yet myself have heard him say,

That not in any mother town
　With statelier progress to and fro
　The double tides of chariots flow
By park and suburb under brown

Of lustier leaves; nor more content,
　He told me, lives in any crowd,
　When all is gay with lamps, and loud
With sport and song, in booth and tent,

255

Imperial halls, or open plain;
  And wheels the circled dance, and breaks
  The rocket molten into flakes
Of crimson or in emerald rain.

XCIX

Risest thou thus, dim dawn, again,
  So loud with voices of the birds,
  So thick with lowings of the herds,
Day, when I lost the flower of men;

Who tremblest thro' thy darkling red
  On yon swoll'n brook that bubbles fast
  By meadows breathing of the past,
And woodlands holy to the dead;

Who murmurest in the foliaged eaves
  A song that slights the coming care,
  And Autumn laying here and there
A fiery finger on the leaves;

Who wakenest with thy balmy breath
  To myriads on the genial earth,
  Memories of bridal, or of birth,
And unto myriads more, of death.

O wheresoever those may be,
  Betwixt the slumber of the poles,
  To-day they count as kindred souls;
They know me not, but mourn with me.

C

I climb the hill: from end to end
  Of all the landscape underneath,
  I find no place that does not breathe
Some gracious memory of my friend;

No gray old grange, or lonely fold,
  Or low morass and whispering reed,
  Or simple stile from mead to mead,
Or sheepwalk up the windy wold;

Nor hoary knoll of ash and haw
  That hears the latest linnet trill,
  Nor quarry trench'd along the hill
And haunted by the wrangling daw;

Nor runlet tinkling from the rock;
  Nor pastoral rivulet that swerves
  To left and right thro' meadowy curves,
That feed the mothers of the flock;

But each has pleased a kindred eve,
  And each reflects a kindlier day;
  And, leaving these, to pass away,
I think once more he seems to die.

CI

Unwatch'd, the garden bough shall sway,
  The tender blossom flutter down,
  Unloved, that beech will gather brown,
This maple burn itself away;

Unloved, the sun-flower, shining fair,
  Ray round with flames her disk of seed,
  And many a rose-carnation feed
With summer spice the humming air;

Unloved, by many a sandy bar,
  The brook shall babble down the plain,
  At noon or when the lesser wain
Is twisting round the polar star;

Uncared for, gird the windy grove,
  And flood the haunts of hern and crake;
  Or into silver arrows break
The sailing moon in creek and cove;

Till from the garden and the wild
  A fresh association blow,
  And year by year the landscape grow
Familiar to the stranger's child;

As year by year the labourer tills
  His wonted glebe, or lops the glades;
  And year by year our memory fades
From all the circle of the hills.

CII

We leave the well-beloved place
  Where first we gazed upon the sky;
  The roofs, that heard our earliest cry,
Will shelter one of stranger race.

We go, but ere we go from home,
  As down the garden-walks I move,
  Two spirits of a diverse love
Contend for loving masterdom.

One whispers, 'Here thy boyhood sung
  Long since its matin song, and heard
  The low love-language of the bird
In native hazels tassel-hung.'

The other answers, 'Yea, but here
  Thy feet have stray'd in after hours
  With thy lost friend among the bowers,
And this hath made them trebly dear.'

These two have striven half the day,
  And each prefers his separate claim,
  Poor rivals in a losing game,
That will not yield each other way.

I turn to go: my feet are set
  To leave the pleasant fields and farms;
  They mix in one another's arms
To one pure image of regret.

CIII

On that last night before we went
  From out the doors where I was bred,
  I dream'd a vision of the dead,
Which left my after-morn content.

Methought I dwelt within a hall,
  And maidens with me: distant hills
  From hidden summits fed with rills
A river sliding by the wall.

The hall with harp and carol rang.
  They sang of what is wise and good
  And graceful. In the centre stood
A statue veil'd, to which they sang;

And which, tho' veil'd, was known to me,
  The shape of him I loved, and love
  For ever: then flew in a dove
And brought a summons from the sea:

And when they learnt that I must go
  They wept and wail'd, but led the way
  To where a little shallop lay
At anchor in the flood below;

And on by many a level mead,
  And shadowing bluff that made the
      banks,
  We glided winding under ranks
Of iris, and the golden reed;

And still as vaster grew the shore
  And roll'd the floods in grander space,
  The maidens gather'd strength and
      grace
And presence, lordlier than before;

And I myself, who sat apart
  And watch'd them, wax'd in every limb;
  I felt the thews of Anakim,
The pulses of a Titan's heart;

As one would sing the death of war,
  And one would chant the history
  Of that great race, which is to be,
And one the shaping of a star;

Until the forward-creeping tides
  Began to foam, and we to draw
  From deep to deep, to where we saw
A great ship lift her shining sides.

The man we loved was there on deck,
  But thrice as large as man he bent
  To greet us. Up the side I went,
And fell in silence on his neck:

Whereat those maidens with one mind
  Bewail'd their lot; I did them wrong:
  'We served thee here,' they said, 'so
      long,
And wilt thou leave us now behind?'

So rapt I was, they could not win
  An answer from my lips, but he
  Replying, 'Enter likewise ye
And go with us:' they enter'd in.

And while the wind began to sweep
  A music out of sheet and shroud,
  We steer'd her toward a crimson cloud
That landlike slept along the deep.

CIV

The time draws near the birth of Christ;
  The moon is hid, the night is still;
  A single church below the hill
Is pealing, folded in the mist.

A single peal of bells below,
  That wakens at this hour of rest
  A single murmur in the breast,
That these are not the bells I know.

Like strangers' voices here they sound,
  In lands where not a memory strays,
  Nor landmark breathes of other days,
But all is new unhallow'd ground.

CV

To-night ungather'd let us leave
This laurel, let this holly stand:
We live within the stranger's land,
And strangely falls our Christmas-eve.

Our father's dust is left alone
And silent under other snows:
There in due time the woodbine blows,
The violet comes, but we are gone.

No more shall wayward grief abuse
The genial hour with mask and mime;
For change of place, like growth of time,
Has broke the bond of dying use.

Let cares that petty shadows cast,
By which our lives are chiefly proved,
A little spare the night I loved,
And hold it solemn to the past.

But let no footstep beat the floor,
Nor bowl of wassail mantle warm;
For who would keep an ancient form
Thro' which the spirit breathes no more?

Be neither song, nor game, nor feast;
Nor harp be touch'd, nor flute be blown;
No dance, no motion, save alone
What lightens in the lucid east

Of rising worlds by yonder wood.
Long sleeps the summer in the seed;
Run out your measured arcs, and lead
The closing cycle rich in good.

CVI

Ring out, wild bells, to the wild sky,
The flying cloud, the frosty light:
The year is dying in the night;
Ring out, wild bells, and let him die.

Ring out the old, ring in the new,
Ring, happy bells, across the snow:
The year is going, let him go;
Ring out the false, ring in the true.

Ring out the grief that saps the mind,
For those that here we see no more;
Ring out the feud of rich and poor,
Ring in redress to all mankind.

Ring out a slowly dying cause,
And ancient forms of party strife;
Ring in the nobler modes of life,
With sweeter manners, purer laws.

Ring out the want, the care, the sin,
The faithless coldness of the times;
Ring out, ring out thy mournful rhymes,
But ring the fuller minstrel in.

Ring out false pride in place and blood,
The civic slander and the spite;
Ring in the love of truth and right,
Ring in the common love of good.

Ring out old shapes of foul disease;
Ring out the narrowing lust of gold;
Ring out the thousand wars of old,
Ring in the thousand years of peace.

Ring in the valiant man and free,
The larger heart, the kindlier hand;
Ring out the darkness of the land,
Ring in the Christ that is to be.

CVII

It is the day when he was born,
A bitter day that early sank
Behind a purple-frosty bank
Of vapour, leaving night forlorn.

The time admits not flowers or leaves
To deck the banquet. Fiercely flies
The blast of North and East, and ice
Makes daggers at the sharpen'd eaves,

And bristles all the brakes and thorns
To yon hard crescent, as she hangs
Above the wood which grides and clangs
Its leafless ribs and iron horns

Together, in the drifts that pass
To darken on the rolling brine
That breaks the coast. But fetch the
wine,
Arrange the board and brim the glass;

Bring in great logs and let them lie,
To make a solid core of heat;
Be cheerful-minded, talk and treat
Of all things ev'n as he were by;

We keep the day. With festal cheer,
   With books and music, surely we
   Will drink to him, whate'er he be,
And sing the songs he loved to hear.

All these have been, and thee mine eyes
   Have look'd on: if they look'd in vain,
   My shame is greater who remain,
Nor let thy wisdom make me wise.

CVIII

I will not shut me from my kind,
   And, lest I stiffen into stone,
   I will not eat my heart alone,
Nor feed with sighs a passing wind:

What profit lies in barren faith,
   And vacant yearning, tho' with might
   To scale the heaven's highest height,
Or dive below the wells of Death?

What find I in the highest place,
   But mine own phantom chanting
      hymns?
And on the depths of death there swims
The reflex of a human face.

I'll rather take what fruit may be
   Of sorrow under human skies:
   'Tis held that sorrow makes us wise,
Whatever wisdom sleep with thee.

CIX

Heart-affluence in discursive talk
   From household fountains never dry;
   The critic clearness of an eye,
That saw thro' all the Muses' walk;

Seraphic intellect and force
   To seize and throw the doubts of man;
   Impassion'd logic, which outran
The hearer in its fiery course;

High nature amorous of the good,
   But touch'd with no ascetic gloom;
   And passion pure in snowy bloom
Thro' all the years of April blood;

A love of freedom rarely felt,
   Of freedom in her regal seat
   Of England; not the schoolboy heat,
The blind hysterics of the Celt;

And manhood fused with female grace
   In such a sort, the child would twine
   A trustful hand, unask'd, in thine,
And find his comfort in thy face;

CX

Thy converse drew us with delight,
   The men of rathe and riper years:
   The feeble soul, a haunt of fears,
Forgot his weakness in thy sight.

On thee the loyal-hearted hung,
   The proud was half disarm'd of pride,
   Nor cared the serpent at thy side
To flicker with his double tongue.

The stern were mild when thou wert by,
   The flippant put himself to school
   And heard thee, and the brazen fool
Was soften'd, and he knew not why;

While I, thy nearest, sat apart,
   And felt thy triumph was as mine;
   And loved them more, that they were
      thine,
The graceful tact, the Christian art;

Nor mine the sweetness or the skill,
   But mine the love that will not tire,
   And, born of love, the vague desire
That spurs an imitative will.

CXI

The churl in spirit, up or down
   Along the scale of ranks, thro' all,
   To him who grasps a golden ball,
By blood a king, at heart a clown;

The churl in spirit, howe'er he veil
   His want in forms for fashion's sake,
   Will let his coltish nature break
At seasons thro' the gilded pale:

For who can always act? but he,
   To whom a thousand memories call,
   Not being less but more than all
The gentleness he seem'd to be,

Best seem'd the thing he was, and join'd
   Each office of the social hour
   To noble manners, as the flower
And native growth of noble mind;

Nor ever narrowness or spite,
　Or villain fancy fleeting by,
　Drew in the expression of an eye,
Where God and Nature met in light;

And thus he bore without abuse
　The grand old name of gentleman,
　Defamed by every charlatan,
And soil'd with all ignoble use.

CXII

High wisdom holds my wisdom less,
　That I, who gaze with temperate eyes
　On glorious insufficiencies,
Set light by narrower perfectness.

But thou, that fillest all the room
　Of all my love, art reason why
　I seem to cast a careless eye
On souls, the lesser lords of doom.

For what wert thou? some novel power
　Sprang up for ever at a touch,
　And hope could never hope too much,
In watching thee from hour to hour,

Large elements in order brought,
　And tracts of calm from tempest made,
　And world-wide fluctuation sway'd
In vassal tides that follow'd thought.

CXIII

'Tis held that sorrow makes us wise;
　Yet how much wisdom sleeps with thee
　Which not alone had guided me,
But served the seasons that may rise;

For can I doubt, who knew thee keen
　In intellect, with force and skill
　To strive, to fashion, to fulfil—
I doubt not what thou wouldst have been:

A life in civic action warm,
　A soul on highest mission sent,
　A potent voice of Parliament,
A pillar steadfast in the storm,

Should licensed boldness gather force,
　Becoming, when the time has birth,
　A lever to uplift the earth
And roll it in another course,

With thousand shocks that come and go,
　With agonies, with energies,
　With overthrowings, and with cries,
And undulations to and fro.

CXIV

Who loves not Knowledge? Who shall rail
　Against her beauty? May she mix
　With men and prosper! Who shall fix
Her pillars? Let her work prevail.

But on her forehead sits a fire:
　She sets her forward countenance
　And leaps into the future chance,
Submitting all things to desire.

Half-grown as yet, a child, and vain—
　She cannot fight the fear of death.
　What is she, cut from love and faith,
But some wild Pallas from the brain

Of Demons? fiery-hot to burst
　All barriers in her onward race
　For power. Let her know her place;
She is the second, not the first.

A higher hand must make her mild,
　If all be not in vain; and guide
　Her footsteps, moving side by side
With wisdom, like the younger child:

For she is earthly of the mind,
　But Wisdom heavenly of the soul.
　O, friend, who camest to thy goal
So early, leaving me behind,

I would the great world grew like thee,
　Who grewest not alone in power
　And knowledge, but by year and hour
In reverence and in charity.

CXV

Now fades the last long streak of snow,
　Now burgeons every maze of quick
　About the flowering squares, and thick
By ashen roots the violets blow.

Now rings the woodland loud and long,
　The distance takes a lovelier hue,
　And drown'd in yonder living blue
The lark becomes a sightless song.

Now dance the lights on lawn and lea,
  The flocks are whiter down the vale,
  And milkier every milky sail
On winding stream or distant sea;

Where now the seamew pipes, or dives
  In yonder greening gleam, and fly
  The happy birds, that change their sky
To build and brood; that live their lives

From land to land; and in my breast
  Spring wakens too; and my regret
  Becomes an April violet,
And buds and blossoms like the rest.

CXVI

Is it, then, regret for buried time
  That keenlier in sweet April wakes,
  And meets the year, and gives and takes
The colours of the crescent prime?

Not all: the songs, the stirring air,
  The life re-orient out of dust,
  Cry thro' the sense to hearten trust
In that which made the world so fair.

Not all regret: the face will shine
  Upon me, while I muse alone;
  And that dear voice, I once have known,
Still speak to me of me and mine:

Yet less of sorrow lives in me
  For days of happy commune dead;
  Less yearning for the friendship fled,
Than some strong bond which is to be.

CXVII

O days and hours, your work is this
  To hold me from my proper place,
  A little while from his embrace,
For fuller gain of after bliss:

That out of distance might ensue
  Desire of nearness doubly sweet;
  And unto meeting when we meet,
Delight a hundredfold accrue,

For every grain of sand that runs,
  And every span of shade that steals,
  And every kiss of toothed wheels,
And all the courses of the suns.

CXVIII

Contemplate all this work of Time,
  The giant labouring in his youth;
  Nor dream of human love and truth,
As dying Nature's earth and lime;

But trust that those we call the dead
  Are breathers of an ampler day
  For ever nobler ends. They say
The solid earth whereon we tread

In tracts of fluent heat began,
  And grew to seeming-random forms,
  The seeming prey of cyclic storms,
Till at the last arose the man;

Who throve and branch'd from clime to
    clime,
  The herald of a higher race,
  And of himself in higher place,
If so he type this work of time

Within himself, from more to more;
  Or, crown'd with attributes of woe
  Like glories, move his course, and show
That life is not as idle ore,

But iron dug from central gloom,
  And heated hot with burning fears,
  And dipt in baths of hissing tears,
And batter'd with the shocks of doom

To shape and use. Arise and fly
  The reeling Faun, the sensual feast;
  Move upward, working out the beast,
And let the ape and tiger die.

CXIX

Doors, where my heart was used to beat
  So quickly, not as one that weeps
  I come once more; the city sleeps;
I smell the meadow in the street;

I hear a chirp of birds; I see
  Betwixt the black fronts long-withdrawn
  A light-blue lane of early dawn,
And think of early days and thee,

And bless thee, for thy lips are bland,
  And bright the friendship of thine eye;
  And in my thoughts with scarce a sigh
I take the pressure of thine hand.

CXX

I trust I have not wasted breath:
　　I think we are not wholly brain,
　　Magnetic mockeries; not in vain,
Like Paul with beasts, I fought with
　　Death;

Not only cunning casts in clay:
　　Let Science prove we are, and then
　　What matters Science unto men,
At least to me? I would not stay.

Let him, the wiser man who springs
　　Hereafter, up from childhood shape
　　His action like the greater ape,
But I was *born* to other things.

CXXI

Sad Hesper o'er the buried sun
　　And ready, thou, to die with him,
　　Thou watchest all things ever dim
And dimmer, and a glory done:

The team is loosen'd from the wain,
　　The boat is drawn upon the shore;
　　Thou listenest to the closing door,
And life is darken'd in the brain.

Bright Phosphor, fresher for the night,
　　By thee the world's great work is heard
　　Beginning, and the wakeful bird;
Behind thee comes the greater light:

The market boat is on the stream,
　　And voices hail it from the brink;
　　Thou hear'st the village hammer clink,
And see'st the moving of the team.

Sweet Hesper-Phosphor, double name
　　For what is one, the first, the last,
　　Thou, like my present and my past,
Thy place is changed; thou art the same.

CXXII

Oh, wast thou with me, dearest, then,
　　While I rose up against my doom,
　　And yearn'd to burst the folded gloom,
To bare the eternal Heavens again,

To feel once more, in placid awe,
　　The strong imagination roll
　　A sphere of stars about my soul,
In all her motion one with law;

If thou wert with me, and the grave
　　Divide us not, be with me now,
　　And enter in at breast and brow,
Till all my blood, a fuller wave,

Be quicken'd with a livelier breath,
　　And like an inconsiderate boy,
　　As in the former flash of joy,
I slip the thoughts of life and death;

And all the breeze of Fancy blows,
　　And every dew-drop paints a bow,
　　The wizard lightnings deeply glow,
And every thought breaks out a rose.

CXXIII

There rolls the deep where grew the tree.
　　O earth, what changes hast thou seen!
　　There where the long street roars, hath
　　　been
The stillness of the central sea.

The hills are shadows, and they flow
　　From form to form, and nothing stands;
　　They melt like mist, the solid lands,
Like clouds they shape themselves and go.

But in my spirit will I dwell,
　　And dream my dream, and hold it true;
　　For tho' my lips may breathe adieu,
I cannot think the thing farewell.

CXXIV

That which we dare invoke to bless;
　　Our dearest faith; our ghastliest doubt;
　　He, They, One, All; within, without;
The Power in darkness whom we guess;

I found Him not in world or sun,
　　Or eagle's wing, or insect's eye;
　　Nor thro' the questions men may try,
The petty cobwebs we have spun:

If e'er when faith had fall'n asleep,
　　I heard a voice 'believe no more'
　　And heard an ever-breaking shore
That tumbled in the Godless deep;

A warmth within the breast would melt
　　The freezing reason's colder part,
　　And like a man in wrath the heart
Stood up and answer'd 'I have felt.'

No, like a child in doubt and fear:
  But that blind clamour made me wise;
  Then was I as a child that cries,
But, crying, knows his father near;

And what I am beheld again
  What is, and no man understands;
  And out of darkness came the hands
That reach thro' nature, moulding men.

CXXV

Whatever I have said or sung,
  Some bitter notes my harp would give,
  Yea, tho' there often seem'd to live
A contradiction on the tongue,

Yet Hope had never lost her youth;
  She did but look through dimmer eyes;
  Or Love but play'd with gracious lies,
Because he felt so fix'd in truth:

And if the song were full of care,
  He breathed the spirit of the song;
  And if the words were sweet and strong
He set his royal signet there;

Abiding with me till I sail
  To seek thee on the mystic deeps,
  And this electric force, that keeps
A thousand pulses dancing, fail.

CXXVI

Love is and was my Lord and King,
  And in his presence I attend
  To hear the tidings of my friend,
Which every hour his couriers bring.

Love is and was my King and Lord,
  And will be, tho' as yet I keep
  Within his court on earth, and sleep
Encompass'd by his faithful guard,

And hear at times a sentinel
  Who moves about from place to place,
  And whispers to the worlds of space,
In the deep night, that all is well.

CXXVII

And all is well, tho' faith and form
  Be sunder'd in the night of fear;
  Well roars the storm to those that hear
A deeper voice across the storm,

Proclaiming social truth shall spread,
  And justice, ev'n tho' thrice again
  The red fool-fury of the Seine
Should pile her barricades with dead.

But ill for him that wears a crown,
  And him, the lazar, in his rags:
  They tremble, the sustaining crags;
The spires of ice are toppled down,

And molten up, and roar in flood;
  The fortress crashes from on high,
  The brute earth lightens to the sky,
And the great Æon sinks in blood,

And compass'd by the fires of Hell;
  While thou, dear spirit, happy star,
  O'erlook'st the tumult from afar,
And smilest, knowing all is well.

CXXVIII

The love that rose on stronger wings,
  Unpalsied when he met with Death,
  Is comrade of the lesser faith
That sees the course of human things.

No doubt vast eddies in the flood
  Of onward time shall yet be made,
  And throned races may degrade;
Yet O ye mysteries of good,

Wild Hours that fly with Hope and Fear,
  If all your office had to do
  With old results that look like new;
If this were all your mission here,

To draw, to sheathe a useless sword,
  To fool the crowd with glorious lies,
  To cleave a creed in sects and cries,
To change the bearing of a word,

To shift an arbitrary power,
  To cramp the student at his desk,
  To make old bareness picturesque
And tuft with grass a feudal tower;

Why then my scorn might well descend
  On you and yours. I see in part
  That all, as in some piece of art,
Is toil coöperant to an end.

CXXIX

Dear friend, far off, my lost desire,
So far, so near in woe and weal;
O loved the most, when most I feel
There is a lower and a higher;

Known and unknown; human, divine;
Sweet human hand and lips and eye;
Dear heavenly friend that canst not die,
Mine, mine, for ever, ever mine;

Strange friend, past, present, and to be;
Loved deeplier, darklier understood;
Behold, I dream a dream of good,
And mingle all the world with thee.

CXXX

Thy voice is on the rolling air;
I hear thee where the waters run;
Thou standest in the rising sun,
And in the setting thou art fair.

What art thou then? I cannot guess;
But tho' I seem in star and flower
To feel thee some diffusive power,
I do not therefore love thee less:

My love involves the love before;
My love is vaster passion now;
Tho' mix'd with God and Nature thou,
I seem to love thee more and more.

Far off thou art, but ever nigh;
I have thee still, and I rejoice;
I prosper, circled with thy voice;
I shall not lose thee tho' I die.

CXXXI

O living will that shalt endure
When all that seems shall suffer shock,
Rise in the spiritual rock,
Flow thro' our deeds and make them pure,

That we may lift from out of dust
A voice as unto him that hears,
A cry above the conquer'd years
To one that with us works, and trust,

With faith that comes of self-control,
The truths that never can be proved
Until we close with all we loved,
And all we flow from, soul in soul.

O true and tried, so well and long,
Demand not thou a marriage lay;
In that it is thy marriage day
Is music more than any song.

Nor have I felt so much of bliss
Since first he told me that he loved
A daughter of our house; nor proved
Since that dark day a day like this;

Tho' I since then have number'd o'er
Some thrice three years: they went and
came,
Remade the blood and changed the
frame,
And yet is love not less, but more;

No longer caring to embalm
In dying songs a dead regret,
But like a statue solid-set,
And moulded in colossal calm.

Regret is dead, but love is more
Than in the summers that are flown,
For I myself with these have grown
To something greater than before;

Which makes appear the songs I made
As echoes out of weaker times,
As half but idle brawling rhymes,
The sport of random sun and shade.

But where is she, the bridal flower,
That must be made a wife ere noon?
She enters, glowing like the moon
Of Eden on its bridal bower:

On me she bends her blissful eyes
And then on thee; they meet thy look
And brighten like the star that shook
Betwixt the palms of paradise.

O when her life was yet in bud,
He too foretold the perfect rose.
For thee she grew, for thee she grows
For ever, and as fair as good.

And thou art worthy; full of power;
As gentle; liberal-minded, great,
Consistent; wearing all that weight
Of learning lightly like a flower.

IN MEMORIAM A. H. H.

But now set out: the noon is near,
　And I must give away the bride;
　She fears not, or with thee beside
And me behind her, will not fear.

For I that danced her on my knee,
　That watch'd her on her nurse's arm,
　That shielded all her life from harm
At last must part with her to thee;

Now waiting to be made a wife,
　Her feet, my darling, on the dead;
　Their pensive tablets round her head,
And the most living words of life

Breathed in her ear. The ring is on,
　The 'wilt thou' answer'd, and again
　The 'wilt thou' ask'd, till out of twain
Her sweet 'I will' has made you one.

Now sign your names, which shall be read,
　Mute symbols of a joyful morn,
　By village eyes as yet unborn;
The names are sign'd, and overhead

Begins the clash and clang that tells
　The joy to every wandering breeze;
　The blind wall rocks, and on the trees
The dead leaf trembles to the bells.

O happy hour, and happier hours
　Await them. Many a merry face
　Salutes them—maidens of the place,
That pelt us in the porch with flowers.

O happy hour, behold the bride
　With him to whom her hand I gave.
　They leave the porch, they pass the
　　　grave
That has to-day its sunny side.

To-day the grave is bright for me,
　For them the light of life increased,
　Who stay to share the morning feast,
Who rest to-night beside the sea.

Let all my genial spirits advance
　To meet and greet a whiter sun;
　My drooping memory will not shun
The foaming grape of eastern France.

It circles round, and fancy plays,
　And hearts are warm'd and faces bloom,
　As drinking health to bride and groom
We wish them store of happy days.

Nor count me all to blame if I
　Conjecture of a stiller guest,
　Perchance, perchance, among the rest,
And, tho' in silence, wishing joy.

But they must go, the time draws on,
　And those white-favour'd horses wait;
　They rise, but linger; it is late;
Farewell, we kiss, and they are gone.

A shade falls on us like the dark
　From little cloudlets on the grass,
　But sweeps away as out we pass
To range the woods, to roam the park,

Discussing how their courtship grew,
　And talk of others that are wed,
　And how she look'd, and what he said,
And back we come at fall of dew.

Again the feast, the speech, the glee,
　The shade of passing thought, the wealth
　Of words and wit, the double health,
The crowning cup, the three-times-three,

And last the dance;—till I retire:
　Dumb is that tower which spake so loud,
　And high in heaven the streaming cloud,
And on the downs a rising fire:

And rise, O moon, from yonder down,
　Till over down and over dale
　All night the shining vapour sail
And pass the silent-lighted town,

The white-faced halls, the glancing rills,
　And catch at every mountain head,
　And o'er the friths that branch and
　　　spread
Their sleeping silver thro' the hills;

And touch with shade the bridal doors,
　With tender gloom the roof, the wall;
　And breaking let the splendour fall
To spangle all the happy shores

By which they rest, and ocean sounds,
　And, star and system rolling past,
　A soul shall draw from out the vast
And strike his being into bounds,

And, moved thro' life of lower phase,
　Result in man, be born and think,
　And act and love, a closer link
Betwixt us and the crowning race

Of those that, eye to eye, shall look
  On knowledge; under whose command
  Is Earth and Earth's, and in their hand
Is Nature like an open book;

No longer half-akin to brute,
  For all we thought and loved and did,
  And hoped, and suffer'd, is but seed
Of what in them is flower and fruit;

Whereof the man, that with me trod
  This planet, was a noble type
  Appearing ere the times were ripe,
That friend of mine who lives in God,

That God, which ever lives and loves,
  One God, one law, one element,
  And one far-off divine event,
To which the whole creation moves.

MAUD; A MONODRAMA

PART I

I

I

I HATE the dreadful hollow behind the little wood,
Its lips in the field above are dabbled with blood-red heath,
The red-ribb'd ledges drip with a silent horror of blood,
And Echo there, whatever is ask'd her, answers 'Death.'

II

For there in the ghastly pit long since a body was found,
His who had given me life—O father! O God! was it well?—
Mangled, and flatten'd, and crush'd, and dinted into the ground:
There yet lies the rock that fell with him when he fell.

III

Did he fling himself down? who knows? for a vast speculation had fail'd,
And ever he mutter'd and madden'd, and ever wann'd with despair,
And out he walk'd when the wind like a broken worldling wail'd,
And the flying gold of the ruin'd woodlands drove thro' the air.

IV

I remember the time, for the roots of my hair were stirr'd
By a shuffled step, by a dead weight trail'd, by a whisper'd fright,
And my pulses closed their gates with a shock on my heart as I heard
The shrill-edged shriek of a mother divide the shuddering night.

V

Villainy somewhere! whose? One says, we are villains all.
Not he: his honest fame should at least by me be maintained:
But that old man, now lord of the broad estate and the Hall,
Dropt off gorged from a scheme that had left us flaccid and drain'd.

VI

Why do they prate of the blessings of Peace? we have made them a curse,
Pickpockets, each hand lusting for all that is not its own;
And lust of gain, in the spirit of Cain, is it better or worse
Than the heart of the citizen hissing in war on his own hearthstone?

VII

But these are the days of advance, the works of the men of mind,
When who but a fool would have faith in a tradesman's ware or his word?
Is it peace or war? Civil war, as I think, and that of a kind
The viler, as underhand, not openly bearing the sword.

VIII

Sooner or later I too may passively take the print
Of the golden age—why not? I have neither hope nor trust;
May make my heart as a millstone, set my face as a flint,
Cheat and be cheated, and die: who knows? we are ashes and dust.

IX

Peace sitting under her olive, and slurring the days gone by,
When the poor are hovell'd and hustled together, each sex, like swine,
When only the ledger lives, and when only not all men lie;
Peace in her vineyard—yes!—but a company forges the wine.

X

And the vitriol madness flushes up in the ruffian's head,
Till the filthy by-lane rings to the yell of the trampled wife,
And chalk and alum and plaster are sold to the poor for bread,
And the spirit of murder works in the very means of life,

XI

And Sleep must lie down arm'd, for the villainous centre-bits
Grind on the wakeful ear in the hush of the moonless nights,
While another is cheating the sick of a few last gasps, as he sits
To pestle a poison'd poison behind his crimson lights.

XII

When a Mammonite mother kills her babe for a burial fee,
And Timour-Mammon grins on a pile of children's bones,
Is it peace or war? better, war! loud war by land and by sea,
War with a thousand battles, and shaking a hundred thrones.

XIII

For I trust if an enemy's fleet came yonder round by the hill,
And the rushing battle-bolt sang from the three-decker out of the foam,
That the smooth-faced snubnosed rogue would leap from his counter and till,
And strike, if he could, were it but with his cheating yardwand, home.——

XIV

What! am I raging alone as my father raged in his mood?
Must *I* too creep to the hollow and dash myself down and die
Rather than hold by the law that I made, nevermore to brood
On a horror of shatter'd limbs and a wretched swindler's lie?

XV

Would there be sorrow for *me*? there was *love* in the passionate shriek,
Love for the silent thing that had made false haste to the grave—
Wrapt in a cloak, as I saw him, and thought he would rise and speak
And rave at the lie and the liar, ah God, as he used to rave.

XVI

I am sick of the Hall and the hill, I am sick of the moor and the main.
Why should I stay? can a sweeter chance ever come to me here?
O, having the nerves of motion as well as the nerves of pain,
Were it not wise if I fled from the place and the pit and the fear?

XVII

Workmen up at the Hall!—they are coming back from abroad;
The dark old place will be gilt by the touch of a millionaire:
I have heard, I know not whence, of the singular beauty of Maud;
I play'd with the girl when a child; she promised then to be fair,

XVIII

Maud with her venturous climbings and tumbles and childish escapes,
Maud the delight of the village, the ringing joy of the Hall,
Maud with her sweet purse-mouth when my father dangled the grapes,
Maud the beloved of my mother, the moon-faced darling of all,—

XIX

What is she now? My dreams are bad. She may bring me a curse.
No, there is fatter game on the moor; she will let me alone.
Thanks, for the fiend best knows whether woman or man be the worse.
I will bury myself in myself, and the Devil may pipe to his own.

II

Long have I sigh'd for a calm: God grant I may find it at last!
It will never be broken by Maud, she has neither savour nor salt,
But a cold and clear-cut face, as I found when her carriage past,
Perfectly beautiful: let it be granted her: where is the fault?
All that I saw (for her eyes were downcast, not to be seen)
Faultily faultless, icily regular, splendidly null,
Dead perfection, no more; nothing more, if it had not been
For a chance of travel, a paleness, an hour's defect of the rose,
Or an underlip, you may call it a little too ripe, too full,
Or the least little delicate aquiline curve in a sensitive nose,
From which I escaped heart-free, with the least little touch of spleen.

III

Cold and clear-cut face, why come you so cruelly meek,
Breaking a slumber in which all spleenful folly was drown'd,
Pale with the golden beam of an eyelash dead on the cheek,
Passionless, pale, cold face, star-sweet on a gloom profound;

Womanlike, taking revenge too deep for a transient wrong
Done but in thought to your beauty, and ever as pale as before
Growing and fading and growing upon me without a sound,
Luminous, gemlike, ghostlike, deathlike, half the night long
Growing and fading and growing, till I could bear it no more,
But arose, and all by myself in my own dark garden ground,
Listening now to the tide in its broad-flung shipwrecking roar,
Now to the scream of a madden'd beach dragg'd down by the wave,
Walk'd in a wintry wind by a ghastly glimmer, and found
The shining daffodil dead, and Orion low in his grave.

IV

I

A million emeralds break from the ruby-budded lime
In the little grove where I sit—ah, wherefore cannot I be
Like things of the season gay, like the bountiful season bland,
When the far-off sail is blown by the breeze of a softer clime,
Half-lost in the liquid azure bloom of a crescent of sea,
The silent sapphire-spangled marriage ring of the land?

II

Below me, there, is the village, and looks how quiet and small!
And yet bubbles o'er like a city, with gossip, scandal, and spite;
And Jack on his ale-house bench has as many lies as a Czar;
And here on the landward side, by a red rock, glimmers the Hall;
And up in the high Hall-garden I see her pass like a light;
But sorrow seize me if ever that light be my leading star!

III

When have I bow'd to her father, the wrinkled head of the race?
I met her to-day with her brother, but not to her brother I bow'd:
I bow'd to his lady-sister as she rode by on the moor;
But the fire of a foolish pride flash'd over her beautiful face.
O child, you wrong your beauty, believe it, in being so proud;
Your father has wealth well-gotten, and I am nameless and poor.

IV

I keep but a man and a maid, ever ready to slander and steal;
I know it, and smile a hard-set smile, like a stoic, or like
A wiser epicurean, and let the world have its way:
For nature is one with rapine, a harm no preacher can heal;
The Mayfly is torn by the swallow, the sparrow spear'd by the shrike,
And the whole little wood where I sit is a world of plunder and prey.

V

We are puppets, Man in his pride, and Beauty fair in her flower;
Do we move ourselves, or are moved by an unseen hand at a game
That pushes us off from the board, and others ever succeed?
Ah yet, we cannot be kind to each other here for an hour;
We whisper, and hint, and chuckle, and grin at a brother's shame;
However we brave it out, we men are a little breed.

VI

A monstrous eft was of old the Lord and Master of Earth,
For him did his high sun flame, and his river billowing ran,
And he felt himself in his force to be Nature's crowning race.
As nine months go to the shaping an infant ripe for his birth,
So many a million of ages have gone to the making of man:
He now is first, but is he the last? is he not too base?

VII

The man of science himself is fonder of glory, and vain,
An eye well-practised in nature, a spirit bounded and poor;
The passionate heart of the poet is whirl'd into folly and vice.
I would not marvel at either, but keep a temperate brain;
For not to desire or admire, if a man could learn it, were more
Than to walk all day like the sultan of old in a garden of spice.

VIII

For the drift of the Maker is dark, an Isis hid by the veil.
Who knows the ways of the world, how God will bring them about?
Our planet is one, the suns are many, the world is wide.
Shall I weep if a Poland fall? shall I shriek if a Hungary fail?
Or an infant civilisation be ruled with rod or with knout?
I have not made the world, and He that made it will guide.

IX

Be mine a philosopher's life in the quiet woodland ways,
Where if I cannot be gay let a passionless peace be my lot,
Far-off from the clamour of liars belied in the hubbub of lies;
From the long-neck'd geese of the world that are ever hissing dispraise
Because their natures are little, and, whether he heed it or not,
Where each man walks with his head in a cloud of poisonous flies.

X

And most of all would I flee from the cruel madness of love,
The honey of poison-flowers and all the measureless ill.
Ah Maud, you milkwhite fawn, you are all unmeet for a wife.
Your mother is mute in her grave as her image in marble above;
Your father is ever in London, you wander about at your will;
You have but fed on the roses and lain in the lilies of life.

V

I

A voice by the cedar tree
In the meadow under the Hall!
She is singing an air that is known to me,
A passionate ballad gallant and gay,

A martial song like a trumpet's call!
Singing alone in the morning of life,
In the happy morning of life and of May,
Singing of men that in battle array,
Ready in heart and ready in hand,
March with banner and bugle and fife
To the death, for their native land.

II

Maud with her exquisite face,
And wild voice pealing up to the sunny sky,
And feet like sunny gems on an English
    green,
Maud in the light of her youth and her
    grace,
Singing of Death, and of Honour that
    cannot die,
Till I well could weep for a time so sordid
    and mean,
And myself so languid and base.

III

Silence, beautiful voice!
Be still, for you only trouble the mind
With a joy in which I cannot rejoice,
A glory I shall not find.
Still! I will hear you no more,
For your sweetness hardly leaves me a
    choice,
But to move to the meadow and fall before
Her feet on the meadow grass, and adore,
Not her, who is neither courtly nor kind,
Not her, not her, but a voice.

VI

I

Morning arises stormy and pale,
No sun, but a wannish glare
In fold upon fold of hueless cloud,
And the budded peaks of the wood are
    bow'd
Caught and cuff'd by the gale:
I had fancied it would be fair.

II

Whom but Maud should I meet
Last night, when the sunset burn'd
On the blossom'd gable-ends
At the head of the village street,
Whom but Maud should I meet?
And she touch'd my hand with a smile so
    sweet,
She made me divine amends
For a courtesy not return'd.

III

And thus a delicate spark
Of glowing and growing light

Thro' the livelong hours of the dark
Kept itself warm in the heart of my dreams,
Ready to burst in a colour'd flame;
Till at last when the morning came
In a cloud, it faded, and seems
But an ashen-gray delight.

IV

What if with her sunny hair,
And smile as sunny as cold,
She meant to weave me a snare
Of some coquettish deceit,
Cleopatra-like as of old
To entangle me when we met,
To have her lion roll in a silken net
And fawn at a victor's feet.

V

Ah, what shall I be at fifty
Should Nature keep me alive,
If I find the world so bitter
When I am but twenty-five?
Yet, if she were not a cheat,
If Maud were all that she seem'd,
And her smile were all that I dream'd,
Then the world were not so bitter
But a smile could make it sweet.

VI

What if tho' her eye seem'd full
Of a kind intent to me,
What if that dandy-despot, he,
That jewell'd mass of millinery,
That oil'd and curl'd Assyrian Bull
Smelling of musk and of insolence,
Her brother, from whom I keep aloof,
Who wants the finer politic sense
To mask, tho' but in his own behoof,
With a glassy smile his brutal scorn—
What if he had told her yestermorn
How prettily for his own sweet sake
A face of tenderness might be feign'd,
And a moist mirage in desert eyes,
That so, when the rotten hustings shake
In another month to his brazen lies,
A wretched vote may be gain'd.

VII

For a raven ever croaks, at my side,
Keep watch and ward, keep watch and
    ward,

Or thou wilt prove their tool.
Yea, too, myself from myself I guard,
For often a man's own angry pride
Is cap and bells for a fool.

VIII

Perhaps the smile and tender tone
Came out of her pitying womanhood,
For am I not, am I not, here alone
So many a summer since she died,
My mother, who was so gentle and good?
Living alone in an empty house,
Here half-hid in the gleaming wood,
Where I hear the dead at midday moan,
And the shrieking rush of the wainscot
    mouse,
And my own sad name in corners cried,
When the shiver of dancing leaves is
    thrown
About its echoing chambers wide,
Till a morbid hate and horror have grown
Of a world in which I have hardly mixt,
And a morbid eating lichen fixt
On a heart half-turn'd to stone.

IX

O heart of stone, are you flesh, and caught
By that you swore to withstand?
For what was it else within me wrought
But, I fear, the new strong wine of love,
That made my tongue so stammer and trip
When I saw the treasured splendour, her
    hand,
Come sliding out of her sacred glove,
And the sunlight broke from her lip?

X

I have play'd with her when a child;
She remembers it now we meet.
Ah well, well, well, I *may* be beguiled
By some coquettish deceit.
Yet, if she were not a cheat,
If Maud were all that she seem'd,
And her smile had all that I dream'd,
Then the world were not so bitter
But a smile could make it sweet.

VII

I

Did I hear it half in a doze
    Long since, I know not where?

Did I dream it an hour ago,
    When asleep in this arm-chair?

II

Men were drinking together,
    Drinking and talking of me;
'Well, if it prove a girl, the boy
    Will have plenty: so let it be.'

III

Is it an echo of something
    Read with a boy's delight,
Viziers nodding together
    In some Arabian night?

IV

Strange, that I hear two men,
    Somewhere, talking of me;
'Well, if it prove a girl, my boy
    Will have plenty: so let it be.'

VIII

She came to the village church,
And sat by a pillar alone;
An angel watching an urn
Wept over her, carved in stone;
And once, but once, she lifted her eyes,
And suddenly, sweetly, strangely blush'd
To find they were met by my own;
And suddenly, sweetly, my heart beat
    stronger
And thicker, until I heard no longer
The snowy-banded, dilettante,
Delicate-handed priest intone;
And thought, is it pride, and mused and
    sigh'd
'No surely, now it cannot be pride.'

IX

I was walking a mile,
More than a mile from the shore,
The sun look'd out with a smile
Betwixt the cloud and the moor
And riding at set of day
Over the dark moor land,
Rapidly riding far away,
She waved to me with her hand.
There were two at her side,
Something flash'd in the sun,
Down by the hill I saw them ride,

In a moment they were gone:
Like a sudden spark
Struck vainly in the night,
Then returns the dark
With no more hope of light.

X

I

Sick, am I sick of a jealous dread?
Was not one of the two at her side
This new-made lord, whose splendour plucks
The slavish hat from the villager's head?
Whose old grandfather has lately died,
Gone to a blacker pit, for whom
Grimy nakedness dragging his trucks
And laying his trams in a poison'd gloom
Wrought, till he crept from a gutted mine
Master of half a servile shire,
And left his coal all turn'd into gold
To a grandson, first of his noble line,
Rich in the grace all women desire,
Strong in the power that all men adore,
And simper and set their voices lower,
And soften as if to a girl, and hold
Awe-stricken breaths at a work divine,
Seeing his gewgaw castle shine,
New as his title, built last year,
There amid perky larches and pine,
And over the sullen-purple moor
(Look at it) pricking a cockney ear.

II

What, has he found my jewel out?
For one of the two that rode at her side
Bound for the Hall, I am sure was he:
Bound for the Hall, and I think for a bride,
Blithe would her brother's acceptance be.
Maud could be gracious too, no doubt
To a lord, a captain, a padded shape,
A bought commission, a waxen face,
A rabbit mouth that is ever agape—
Bought? what is it he cannot buy?
And therefore splenetic, personal, base,
A wounded thing with a rancorous cry,
At war with myself and a wretched race,
Sick, sick to the heart of life, am I.

III

Last week came one to the county town,
To preach our poor little army down,

And play the game of the despot kings,
Tho' the state has done it and thrice as well:
This broad-brimm'd hawker of holy things,
Whose ear is cramm'd with his cotton, and rings
Even in dreams to the chink of his pence,
This huckster put down war! can he tell
Whether war be a cause or a consequence?
Put down the passions that make earth Hell!
Down with ambition, avarice, pride,
Jealousy, down! cut off from the mind
The bitter springs of anger and fear;
Down too, down at your own fireside,
With the evil tongue and the evil ear,
For each is at war with mankind.

IV

I wish I could hear again
The chivalrous battle-song
That she warbled alone in her joy!
I might persuade myself then
She would not do herself this great wrong,
To take a wanton dissolute boy
For a man and leader of men.

V

Ah God, for a man with heart, head, hand,
Like some of the simple great ones gone
For ever and ever by,
One still strong man in a blatant land,
Whatever they call him, what care I,
Aristocrat, democrat, autocrat—one
Who can rule and dare not lie.

VI

And ah for a man to arise in me,
That the man I am may cease to be!

XI

I

O let the solid ground
    Not fail beneath my feet
Before my life has found
    What some have found so sweet;
Then let come what come may,
What matter if I go mad,
I shall have had my day.

II

Let the sweet heavens endure,
  Not close and darken above me
Before I am quite quite sure
  That there is one to love me;
Then let come what come may
To a life that has been so sad,
I shall have had my day.

XII

I

Birds in the high Hall-garden
  When twilight was falling,
Maud, Maud, Maud, Maud,
  They were crying and calling.

II

Where was Maud? in our wood;
  And I, who else, was with her.
Gathering woodland lilies,
  Myriads blow together.

III

Birds in our wood sang
  Ringing thro' the valleys,
Maud is here, here, here
  In among the lilies.

IV

I kiss'd her slender hand,
  She took the kiss sedately;
Maud is not seventeen,
  But she is tall and stately.

V

I to cry out on pride
  Who have won her favour!
O Maud were sure of Heaven
  If lowliness could save her.

VI

I know the way she went
  Home with her maiden posy,
For her feet have touch'd the meadows
  And left the daisies rosy.

VII

Birds in the high Hall-garden
  Were crying and calling to her,
Where is Maud, Maud, Maud?
  One is come to woo her.

VIII

Look, a horse at the door,
  And little King Charley snarling,
Go back, my lord, across the moor,
  You are not her darling.

XIII

I

Scorn'd, to be scorn'd by one that I scorn,
Is that a matter to make me fret?
That a calamity hard to be borne?
Well, he may live to hate me yet.
Fool that I am to be vext with his pride!
I past him, I was crossing his lands;
He stood on the path a little aside;
His face, as I grant, in spite of spite,
Has a broad-blown comeliness, red and
  white,
And six feet two, as I think, he stands;
But his essences turn'd the live air sick,
And barbarous opulence jewel-thick
Sunn'd itself on his breast and his hands.

II

Who shall call me ungentle, unfair,
I long'd so heartily then and there
To give him the grasp of fellowship;
But while I past he was humming an air,
Stopt, and then with a riding whip
Leisurely tapping a glossy boot,
And curving a contumelious lip,
Gorgonised me from head to foot
With a stony British stare.

III

Why sits he here in his father's chair?
That old man never comes to his place:
Shall I believe him ashamed to be seen?
For only once, in the village street,
Last year, I caught a glimpse of his face,
A gray old wolf and a lean.
Scarcely, now, would I call him a cheat;
For then, perhaps, as a child of deceit,
She might by a true descent be untrue;
And Maud is as true as Maud is sweet:
Tho' I fancy her sweetness only due
To the sweeter blood by the other side;
Her mother has been a thing complete,
However she came to be so allied.
And fair without, faithful within,

Maud to him is nothing akin:
Some peculiar mystic grace
Made her only the child of her mother,
And heap'd the whole inherited sin
On that huge scapegoat of the race,
All, all upon the brother.

IV

Peace, angry spirit, and let him be!
Has not his sister smiled on me?

XIV

I

Maud has a garden of roses
And lilies fair on a lawn;
There she walks in her state
And tends upon bed and bower,
And thither I climb'd at dawn
And stood by her garden-gate;
A lion ramps at the top,
He is claspt by a passion-flower.

II

Maud's own little oak-room
(Which Maud, like a precious stone
Set in the heart of the carven gloom,
Lights with herself, when alone
She sits by her music and books
And her brother lingers late
With a roystering company) looks
Upon Maud's own garden-gate:
And I thought as I stood, if a hand, as white
As ocean-foam in the moon, were laid
On the hasp of the window, and my Delight
Had a sudden desire, like a glorious ghost,
to glide,
Like a beam of the seventh Heaven, down
to my side,
There were but a step to be made.

III

The fancy flatter'd my mind,
And again seem'd overbold;
Now I thought that she cared for me,
Now I thought she was kind
Only because she was cold.

IV

I heard no sound where I stood
But the rivulet on from the lawn
Running down to my own dark wood;

Or the voice of the long sea-wave as it
swell'd
Now and then in the dim-gray dawn;
But I look'd, and round, all round the
house I beheld
The death-white curtain drawn;
Felt a horror over me creep,
Prickle my skin and catch my breath,
Knew that the death-white curtain meant
but sleep,
Yet I shudder'd and thought like a fool of
the sleep of death.

XV

So dark a mind within me dwells,
And I make myself such evil cheer,
That if *I* be dear to some one else,
Then some one else may have much to
fear;
But if *I* be dear to some one else,
Then I should be to myself more dear.
Shall I not take care of all that I think,
Yea ev'n of wretched meat and drink,
If I be dear,
If I be dear to some one else.

XVI

I

This lump of earth has left his estate
The lighter by the loss of his weight;
And so that he find what he went to seek,
And fulsome Pleasure clog him, and drown
His heart in the gross mud-honey of town,
He may stay for a year who has gone for a
week:
But this is the day when I must speak,
And I see my Oread coming down,
O this is the day!
O beautiful creature, what am I
That I dare to look her way;
Think I may hold dominion sweet,
Lord of the pulse that is lord of her breast,
And dream of her beauty with tender
dread,
From the delicate Arab arch of her feet
To the grace that, bright and light as the
crest
Of a peacock, sits on her shining head,
And she knows it not: O, if she knew it,
To know her beauty might half undo it.

I know it the one bright thing to save
My yet young life in the wilds of Time,
Perhaps from madness, perhaps from
    crime,
Perhaps from a selfish grave.

II

What, if she be fasten'd to this fool lord,
Dare I bid her abide by her word?
Should I love her so well if she
Had given her word to a thing so low?
Shall I love her as well if she
Can break her word were it even for me?
I trust that it is not so.

III

Catch not my breath, O clamorous heart,
Let not my tongue be a thrall to my eye,
For I must tell her before we part,
I must tell her, or die.

XVII

Go not, happy day,
    From the shining fields,
Go not, happy day,
    Till the maiden yields.
Rosy is the West,
    Rosy is the South,
Roses are her cheeks,
    And a rose her mouth
When the happy Yes
    Falters from her lips,
Pass and blush the news
    Over glowing ships;
Over blowing seas,
    Over seas at rest,
Pass the happy news,
    Blush it thro' the West;
Till the red man dance
    By his red cedar-tree,
And the red man's babe
    Leap, beyond the sea.
Blush from West to East,
    Blush from East to West,
Till the West is East,
    Blush it thro' the West.
Rosy is the West,
    Rosy is the South,
Roses are her cheeks,
    And a rose her mouth.

XVIII

I

I have led her home, my love, my only
    friend.
There is none like her, none.
And never yet so warmly ran my blood
And sweetly, on and on
Calming itself to the long-wish'd-for end,
Full to the banks, close on the promised
    good.

II

None like her, none.
Just now the dry-tongued laurels' pattering
    talk
Seem'd her light foot along the garden walk,
And shook my heart to think she comes
    once more;
But even then I heard her close the door,
The gates of Heaven are closed, and she is
    gone.

III

There is none like her, none.
Nor will be when our summers have
    deceased.
O, art thou sighing for Lebanon
In the long breeze that streams to thy
    delicious East,
Sighing for Lebanon,
Dark cedar, tho' thy limbs have here
    increased,
Upon a pastoral slope as fair,
And looking to the South, and fed
With honey'd rain and delicate air,
And haunted by the starry head
Of her whose gentle will has changed my
    fate,
And made my life a perfumed altar-flame;
And over whom thy darkness must have
    spread
With such delight as theirs of old, thy great
Forefathers of the thornless garden, there
Shadowing the snow-limb'd Eve from
    whom she came.

IV

Here will I lie, while these long branches
    sway,
And you fair stars that crown a happy day
Go in and out as if at merry play,

Who am no more so all forlorn,
As when it seem'd far better to be born
To labour and the mattock-harden'd hand,
Than nursed at ease and brought to under-
    stand
A sad astrology, the boundless plan
That makes you tyrants in your iron skies,
Innumerable, pitiless, passionless eyes,
Cold fires, yet with power to burn and
    brand
His nothingness into man.

V

But now shine on, and what care I,
Who in this stormy gulf have found a pearl
The countercharm of space and hollow sky,
And do accept my madness, and would die
To save from some slight shame one simple
    girl.

VI

Would die; for sullen-seeming Death may
    give
More life to Love than is or ever was
In our low world, where yet 'tis sweet to
    live.
Let no one ask me how it came to pass;
It seems that I am happy, that to me
A livelier emerald twinkles in the grass,
A purer sapphire melts into the sea.

VII

Not die; but live a life of truest breath,
And teach true life to fight with mortal
    wrongs.
O, why should Love, like men in drinking-
    songs,
Spice his fair banquet with the dust of
    death?
Make answer, Maud my bliss,
Maud made my Maud by that long loving
    kiss,
Life of my life, wilt thou not answer this?
'The dusky strand of Death inwoven here
With dear Love's tie, makes Love himself
    more dear.'

VIII

Is that enchanted moan only the swell
Of the long waves that roll in yonder bay?
And hark the clock within, the silver knell

Of twelve sweet hours that past in bridal
    white,
And died to live, long as my pulses play;
But now by this my love has closed her
    sight
And given false death her hand, and stol'n
    away
To dreamful wastes where footless fancies
    dwell
Among the fragments of the golden day.
May nothing there her maiden grace
    affright!
Dear heart, I feel with thee the drowsy spell.
My bride to be, my evermore delight,
My own heart's heart, my ownest own,
    farewell;
It is but for a little space I go:
And ye meanwhile far over moor and fell
Beat to the noiseless music of the night!
Has our whole earth gone nearer to the
    glow
Of your soft splendours that you look so
    bright?
_I_ have climb'd nearer out of lonely Hell.
Beat, happy stars, timing with things below,
Beat with my heart more blest than heart
    can tell,
Blest, but for some dark undercurrent woe
That seems to draw—but it shall not be so:
Let all be well, be well.

XIX

I

Her brother is coming back to-night,
Breaking up my dream of delight.

II

My dream? do I dream of bliss?
I have walk'd awake with Truth.
O when did a morning shine
So rich in atonement as this
For my dark-dawning youth,
Darken'd watching a mother decline
And that dead man at her heart and mine:
For who was left to watch her but I?
Yet so did I let my freshness die.

III

I trust that I did not talk
To gentle Maud in our walk

MAUD

(For often in lonely wanderings
I have cursed him even to lifeless things)
But I trust that I did not talk,
Not touch on her father's sin:
I am sure I did but speak
Of my mother's faded cheek
When it slowly grew so thin,
That I felt she was slowly dying
Vext with lawyers and harass'd with debt:
For how often I caught her with eyes all
  wet,
Shaking her head at her son and sighing
A world of trouble within!

IV

And Maud too, Maud was moved
To speak of the mother she loved
As one scarce less forlorn,
Dying abroad and it seems apart
From him who had ceased to share her
  heart,
And ever mourning over the feud,
The household Fury sprinkled with blood
By which our houses are torn:
How strange was what she said,
When only Maud and the brother
Hung over her dying bed—
That Maud's dark father and mine
Had bound us one to the other,
Betrothed us over their wine,
On the day when Maud was born;
Seal'd her mine from her first sweet breath.
Mine, mine by a right, from birth till
  death.
Mine, mine—our fathers have sworn.

V

But the true blood spilt had in it a heat
To dissolve the precious seal on a bond,
That, if left uncancell'd, had been so
  sweet:
And none of us thought of a something
  beyond,
A desire that awoke in the heart of the
  child,
As it were a duty done to the tomb,
To be friends for her sake, to be recon-
  ciled;
And I was cursing them and my doom,
And letting a dangerous thought run wild
While often abroad in the fragrant gloom

Of foreign churches—I see her there,
Bright English lily, breathing a prayer
To be friends, to be reconciled!

VI

But then what a flint is he!
Abroad, at Florence, at Rome,
I find whenever she touch'd on me
This brother had laugh'd her down,
And at last, when each came home,
He had darken'd into a frown,
Chid her, and forbid her to speak
To me, her friend of the years before;
And this was what had redden'd her cheek
When I bow'd to her on the moor.

VII

Yet Maud, altho' not blind
To the faults of his heart and mind,
I see she cannot but love him,
And says he is rough but kind,
And wishes me to approve him,
And tells me, when she lay
Sick once, with a fear of worse,
That he left his wine and horses and play,
Sat with her, read to her, night and day,
And tended her like a nurse.

VIII

Kind? but the deathbed desire
Spurn'd by this heir of the liar—
Rough but kind? yet I know
He has plotted against me in this,
That he plots against me still.
Kind to Maud? that were not amiss.
Well, rough but kind; why let it be so:
For shall not Maud have her will?

IX

For, Maud, so tender and true,
As long as my life endures
I feel I shall owe you a debt,
That I never can hope to pay;
And if ever I should forget
That I owe this debt to you
And for your sweet sake to yours;
O then, what then shall I say?—
If ever I *should* forget,
May God make me more wretched
Than ever I have been yet!

278

X

So now I have sworn to bury
All this dead body of hate,
I feel so free and so clear
By the loss of that dead weight,
That I should grow light-headed, I fear,
Fantastically merry;
But that her brother comes, like a blight
On my fresh hope, to the Hall to-night.

XX

I

Strange, that I felt so gay,
Strange, that I tried to-day
To beguile her melancholy;
The Sultan, as we name him,—
She did not wish to blame him—
But he vext her and perplext her
With his worldly talk and folly:
Was it gentle to reprove her
For stealing out of view
From a little lazy lover
Who but claims her as his due?
Or for chilling his caresses
By the coldness of her manners,
Nay, the plainness of her dresses?
Now I know her but in two,
Nor can pronounce upon it
If one should ask me whether
The habit, hat, and feather,
Or the frock and gipsy bonnet
Be the neater and completer;
For nothing can be sweeter
Than maiden Maud in either.

II

But to-morrow, if we live,
Our ponderous squire will give
A grand political dinner
To half the squirelings near;
And Maud will wear her jewels,
And the bird of prey will hover,
And the titmouse hope to win her
With his chirrup at her ear.

III

A grand political dinner
To the men of many acres,
A gathering of the Tory,
A dinner and then a dance

For the maids and marriage-makers,
And every eye but mine will glance
At Maud in all her glory.

IV

For I am not invited,
But, with the Sultan's pardon,
I am all as well delighted,
For I know her own rose-garden,
And mean to linger in it
Till the dancing will be over;
And then, oh then, come out to me
For a minute, but for a minute,
Come out to your own true lover,
That your true lover may see
Your glory also, and render
All homage to his own darling,
Queen Maud in all her splendour.

XXI

Rivulet crossing my ground,
And bringing me down from the Hall
This garden-rose that I found,
Forgetful of Maud and me,
And lost in trouble and moving round
Here at the head of a tinkling fall,
And trying to pass to the sea;
O Rivulet, born at the Hall,
My Maud has sent it by thee
(If I read her sweet will right)
On a blushing mission to me,
Saying in odour and colour, 'Ah, be
Among the roses to-night.'

XXII

I

Come into the garden, Maud,
  For the black bat, night, has flown,
Come into the garden, Maud,
  I am here at the gate alone;
And the woodbine spices are wafted abroad,
  And the musk of the rose is blown.

II

For a breeze of morning moves,
  And the planet of Love is on high,
Beginning to faint in the light that she loves
  On a bed of daffodil sky,
To faint in the light of the sun she loves,
  To faint in his light, and to die.

III

All night have the roses heard
  The flute, violin, bassoon;
All night has the casement jessamine
    stirr'd
  To the dancers dancing in tune;
Till a silence fell with the waking bird,
  And a hush with the setting moon.

IV

I said to the lily, 'There is but one
  With whom she has heart to be gay.
When will the dancers leave her alone?
  She is weary of dance and play.'
Now half to the setting moon are gone,
  And half to the rising day;
Low on the sand and loud on the stone
  The last wheel echoes away.

V

I said to the rose, 'The brief night goes
  In babble and revel and wine.
O young lord-lover, what sighs are those,
  For one that will never be thine?
But mine, but mine,' so I sware to the rose,
  'For ever and ever, mine.'

VI

And the soul of the rose went into my
    blood,
  As the music clash'd in the hall;
And long by the garden lake I stood,
  For I heard your rivulet fall
From the lake to the meadow and on to the
    wood,
  Our wood, that is dearer than all;

VII

From the meadow your walks have left so
    sweet
  That whenever a March-wind sighs
He sets the jewel-print of your feet
  In violets blue as your eyes,
To the woody hollows in which we meet
  And the valleys of Paradise.

VIII

The slender acacia would not shake
  One long milk-bloom on the tree;
The white lake-blossom fell into the lake
  As the pimpernel dozed on the lea;

But the rose was awake all night for your
    sake,
  Knowing your promise to me;
The lilies and roses were all awake,
  They sigh'd for the dawn and thee.

IX

Queen rose of the rosebud garden of girls,
  Come hither, the dances are done,
In gloss of satin and glimmer of pearls,
  Queen lily and rose in one;
Shine out, little head, sunning over with
    curls,
  To the flowers, and be their sun.

X

There has fallen a splendid tear
  From the passion-flower at the gate.
She is coming, my dove, my dear;
  She is coming, my life, my fate;
The red rose cries, 'She is near, she is
    near;'
  And the white rose weeps, 'She is late;'
The larkspur listens, 'I hear, I hear;'
  And the lily whispers, 'I wait.'

XI

She is coming, my own, my sweet;
  Were it ever so airy a tread,
My heart would hear her and beat,
  Were it earth in an earthy bed;
My dust would hear her and beat,
  Had I lain for a century dead;
Would start and tremble under her feet,
  And blossom in purple and red.

PART II

I

I

'THE fault was mine, the fault was mine'—
Why am I sitting here so stunn'd and still,
Plucking the harmless wild-flower on the
    hill?—
It is this guilty hand!—
And there rises ever a passionate cry
From underneath in the darkening land—
What is it, that has been done?
O dawn of Eden bright over earth and sky,
The fires of Hell brake out of thy rising
    sun,

The fires of Hell and of Hate;
For she, sweet soul, had hardly spoken a
    word,
When her brother ran in his rage to the
    gate,
He came with the babe-faced lord;
Heap'd on her terms of disgrace,
And while she wept, and I strove to be
    cool,
He fiercely gave me the lie,
Till I with as fierce an anger spoke,
And he struck me, madman, over the face,
Struck me before the languid fool,
Who was gaping and grinning by:
Struck for himself an evil stroke;
Wrought for his house an irredeemable
    woe;
For front to front in an hour we stood,
And a million horrible bellowing echoes
    broke
From the red-ribb'd hollow behind the
    wood,
And thunder'd up into Heaven the Christ-
    less code,
That must have life for a blow.
Ever and ever afresh they seem'd to
    grow.
Was it he lay there with a fading eye?
'The fault was mine,' he whisper'd, 'fly!'
Then glided out of the joyous wood
The ghastly Wraith of one that I know;
And there rang on a sudden a passionate
    cry,
A cry for a brother's blood:
It will ring in my heart and my ears, till I
    die, till I die.

II

Is it gone? my pulses beat—
What was it? a lying trick of the brain?
Yet I thought I saw her stand,
A shadow there at my feet,
High over the shadowy land.
It is gone; and the heavens fall in a gentle
    rain,
When they should burst and drown with
    deluging storms
The feeble vassals of wine and anger and
    lust,
The little hearts that know not how to
    forgive:

Arise, my God, and strike, for we hold
    Thee just,
Strike dead the whole weak race of veno-
    mous worms,
That sting each other here in the dust;
We are not worthy to live.

II

I

See what a lovely shell,
Small and pure as a pearl,
Lying close to my foot,
Frail, but a work divine,
Made so fairily well
With delicate spire and whorl,
How exquisitely minute,
A miracle of design!

II

What is it? a learned man
Could give it a clumsy name.
Let him name it who can,
The beauty would be the same.

III

The tiny cell is forlorn,
Void of the little living will
That made it stir on the shore.
Did he stand at the diamond door
Of his house in a rainbow frill?
Did he push, when he was uncurl'd,
A golden foot or a fairy horn
Thro' his dim water-world?

IV

Slight, to be crush'd with a tap
Of my finger-nail on the sand,
Small, but a work divine,
Frail, but of force to withstand,
Year upon year, the shock
Of cataract seas that snap
The three decker's oaken spine
Athwart the ledges of rock,
Here on the Breton strand!

V

Breton, not Briton; here
Like a shipwreck'd man on a coast
Of ancient fable and fear—
Plagued with a flitting to and fro,

A disease, a hard mechanic ghost
That never came from on high
Nor ever arose from below,
But only moves with the moving eye,
Flying along the land and the main—
Why should it look like Maud?
Am I to be overawed
By what I cannot but know
Is a juggle born of the brain?

VI

Back from the Breton coast,
Sick of a nameless fear,
Back to the dark sea-line
Looking, thinking of all I have lost;
An old song vexes my ear;
But that of Lamech is mine.

VII

For years, a measureless ill,
For years, for ever, to part—
But she, she would love me still;
And as long, O God, as she
Have a grain of love for me,
So long, no doubt, no doubt,
Shall I nurse in my dark heart,
However weary, a spark of will
Not to be trampled out.

VIII

Strange, that the mind, when fraught
With a passion so intense
One would think that it well
Might drown all life in the eye,—
That it should, by being so overwrought,
Suddenly strike on a sharper sense
For a shell, or a flower, little things
Which else would have been past by!
And now I remember, I,
When he lay dying there,
I noticed one of his many rings
(For he had many, poor worm) and thought
It is his mother's hair.

IX

Who knows if he be dead?
Whether I need have fled?
Am I guilty of blood?
However this may be,
Comfort her, comfort her, all things good,
While I am over the sea!

Let me and my passionate love go by,
But speak to her all things holy and high,
Whatever happen to me!
Me and my harmful love go by;
But come to her waking, find her asleep,
Powers of the height, Powers of the deep,
And comfort her tho' I die.

III

Courage, poor heart of stone!
I will not ask thee why
Thou canst not understand
That thou art left for ever alone:
Courage, poor stupid heart of stone.—
Or if I ask thee why,
Care not thou to reply:
She is but dead, and the time is at hand
When thou shalt more than die.

IV

I

O that 'twere possible
After long grief and pain
To find the arms of my true love
Round me once again!

II

When I was wont to meet her
In the silent woody places
By the home that gave me birth,
We stood tranced in long embraces
Mixt with kisses sweeter sweeter
Than anything on earth.

III

A shadow flits before me,
Not thou, but like to thee:
Ah Christ, that it were possible
For one short hour to see
The souls we loved, that they might tell us
What and where they be.

IV

It leads me forth at evening,
It lightly winds and steals
In a cold white robe before me,
When all my spirit reels
At the shouts, the leagues of lights,
And the roaring of the wheels.

V

Half the night I waste in sighs,
Half in dreams I sorrow after
The delight of early skies;
In a wakeful doze I sorrow
For the hand, the lips, the eyes,
For the meeting of the morrow,
The delight of happy laughter,
The delight of low replies.

VI

'Tis a morning pure and sweet,
And a dewy splendour falls
On the little flower that clings
To the turrets and the walls;
'Tis a morning pure and sweet,
And the light and shadow fleet;
She is walking in the meadow,
And the woodland echo rings;
In a moment we shall meet;
She is singing in the meadow
And the rivulet at her feet
Ripples on in light and shadow
To the ballad that she sings.

VII

Do I hear her sing as of old,
My bird with the shining head,
My own dove with the tender eye?
But there rings on a sudden a passionate
    cry,
There is some one dying or dead,
And a sullen thunder is roll'd;
For a tumult shakes the city,
And I wake, my dream is fled;
In the shuddering dawn, behold,
Without knowledge, without pity,
By the curtains of my bed
That abiding phantom cold.

VIII

Get thee hence, nor come again,
Mix not memory with doubt,
Pass, thou deathlike type of pain,
Pass and cease to move about!
'Tis the blot upon the brain
That *will* show itself without.

IX

Then I rise, the eavedrops fall,
And the yellow vapours choke

The great city sounding wide;
The day comes, a dull red ball
Wrapt in drifts of lurid smoke
On the misty river-tide.

X

Thro' the hubbub of the market
I steal, a wasted frame,
It crosses here, it crosses there,
Thro' all that crowd confused and loud,
The shadow still the same;
And on my heavy eyelids
My anguish hangs like shame.

XI

Alas for her that met me,
That heard me softly call,
Came glimmering thro' the laurels
At the quiet evenfall,
In the garden by the turrets
Of the old manorial hall.

XII

Would the happy spirit descend,
From the realms of light and song,
In the chamber or the street,
As she looks among the blest,
Should I fear to greet my friend
Or to say 'Forgive the wrong,'
Or to ask her, 'Take me, sweet,
To the regions of thy rest'?

XIII

But the broad light glares and beats,
And the shadow flits and fleets
And will not let me be;
And I loathe the squares and streets,
And the faces that one meets,
Hearts with no love for me:
Always I long to creep
Into some still cavern deep,
There to weep, and weep, and weep
My whole soul out to thee.

V

I

Dead, long dead,
Long dead!
And my heart is a handful of dust,
And the wheels go over my head,
And my bones are shaken with pain,

For into a shallow grave they are thrust,
Only a yard beneath the street,
And the hoofs of the horses beat, beat,
The hoofs of the horses beat,
Beat into my scalp and my brain,
With never an end to the stream of passing
    feet,
Driving, hurrying, marrying, burying,
Clamour and rumble, and ringing and
    clatter,
And here beneath it is all as bad,
For I thought the dead had peace, but it is
    not so;
To have no peace in the grave, is that not
    sad?
But up and down and to and fro,
Ever about me the dead men go;
And then to hear a dead man chatter
Is enough to drive one mad.

II

Wretchedest age, since Time began,
They cannot even bury a man;
And tho' we paid our tithes in the days
    that are gone,
Not a bell was rung, not a prayer was read;
It is that which makes us loud in the world
    of the dead;
There is none that does his work, not one;
A touch of their office might have sufficed,
But the churchmen fain would kill their
    church,
As the churches have kill'd their Christ.

III

See, there is one of us sobbing,
No limit to his distress;
And another, a lord of all things, praying
To his own great self, as I guess;
And another, a statesman there, betraying
His party-secret, fool, to the press;
And yonder a vile physician, blabbing
The case of his patient—all for what?
To tickle the maggot born in an empty
    head,
And wheedle a world that loves him not,
For it is but a world of the dead.

IV

Nothing but idiot gabble!
For the prophecy given of old

And then not understood,
Has come to pass as foretold;
Not let any man think for the public good,
But babble, merely for babble.
For I never whisper'd a private affair
Within the hearing of cat or mouse,
No, not to myself in the closet alone,
But I heard it shouted at once from the top
    of the house;
Everything came to be known.
Who told *him* we were there?

V

Not that gray old wolf, for he came not
    back
From the wilderness, full of wolves, where
    he used to lie;
He has gather'd the bones for his o'er-
    grown whelp to crack;
Crack them now for yourself, and howl,
    and die.

VI

Prophet, curse me the blabbing lip,
And curse me the British vermin, the rat;
I know not whether he came in the
    Hanover ship,
But I know that he lies and listens mute
In an ancient mansion's crannies and holes:
Arsenic, arsenic, sure, would do it,
Except that now we poison our babes,
    poor souls!
It is all used up for that.

VII

Tell him now: she is standing here at my
    head;
Not beautiful now, not even kind;
He may take her now; for she never speaks
    her mind,
But is ever the one thing silent here.
She is not *of* us, as I divine;
She comes from another stiller world of
    the dead,
Stiller, not fairer than mine.

VIII

But I know where a garden grows,
Fairer than aught in the world beside,
All made up of the lily and rose
That blow by night, when the season is
    good,

To the sound of dancing music and flutes:
It is only flowers, they had no fruits,
And I almost fear they are not roses, but
    blood;
For the keeper was one, so full of pride,
He linkt a dead man there to a spectral
    bride;
For he, if he had not been a Sultan of
    brutes,
Would he have that hole in his side?

IX

But what will the old man say?
He laid a cruel snare in a pit
To catch a friend of mine one stormy
    day;
Yet now I could even weep to think
    of it;
For what will the old man say
When he comes to the second corpse in
    the pit?

X

Friend, to be struck by the public foe,
Then to strike him and lay him low,
That were a public merit, far,
Whatever the Quaker holds, from sin;
But the red life spilt for a private blow—
I swear to you, lawful and lawless war
Are scarcely even akin.

XI

O me, why have they not buried me deep
    enough?
Is it kind to have made me a grave so
    rough,
Me, that was never a quiet sleeper?
Maybe still I am but half-dead;
Then I cannot be wholly dumb;
I will cry to the steps above my head
And somebody, surely, some kind heart
    will come
To bury me, bury me
Deeper, ever so little deeper.

PART III

VI

I

My life has crept so long on a broken wing
Thro' cells of madness, haunts of horror and fear,
That I come to be grateful at last for a little thing:
My mood is changed, for it fell at a time of year
When the face of night is fair on the dewy downs,
And the shining daffodil dies, and the Charioteer
And starry Gemini hang like glorious crowns
Over Orion's grave low down in the west,
That like a silent lightning under the stars
She seem'd to divide in a dream from a band of the blest,
And spoke of a hope for the world in the coming wars—
'And in that hope, dear soul, let trouble have rest,
Knowing I tarry for thee,' and pointed to Mars
As he glow'd like a ruddy shield on the Lion's breast.

II

And it was but a dream, yet it yielded a dear delight
To have look'd, tho' but in a dream, upon eyes so fair,
That had been in a weary world my one thing bright;
And it was but a dream, yet it lighten'd my despair
When I thought that a war would arise in defence of the right,
That an iron tyranny now should bend or cease,

The glory of manhood stand on his ancient height,
Nor Britain's one sole God be the millionaire:
No more shall commerce be all in all, and Peace
Pipe on her pastoral hillock a languid note,
And watch her harvest ripen, her herd increase,
Nor the cannon-bullet rust on a slothful shore,
And the cobweb woven across the cannon's throat
Shall shake its threaded tears in the wind no more.

III

And as months ran on and rumour of battle grew,
'It is time, it is time, O passionate heart,' said I
(For I cleaved to a cause that I felt to be pure and true),
'It is time, O passionate heart and morbid eye,
That old hysterical mock-disease should die.'
And I stood on a giant deck and mix'd my breath
With a loyal people shouting a battle cry,
Till I saw the dreary phantom arise and fly
Far into the North, and battle, and seas of death.

IV

Let it go or stay, so I wake to the higher aims
Of a land that has lost for a little her lust of gold,
And love of a peace that was full of wrongs and shames,
Horrible, hateful, monstrous, not to be told;
And hail once more to the banner of battle unroll'd!
Tho' many a light shall darken, and many shall weep
For those that are crush'd in the clash of jarring claims,
Yet God's just wrath shall be wreak'd on a giant liar;
And many a darkness into the light shall leap,
And shine in the sudden making of splendid names,
And noble thought be freër under the sun,
And the heart of a people beat with one desire;
For the peace, that I deem'd no peace, is over and done,
And now by the side of the Black and the Baltic deep,
And deathful-grinning mouths of the fortress, flames
The blood-red blossom of war with a heart of fire.

V

Let it flame or fade, and the war roll down like a wind,
We have proved we have hearts in a cause, we are noble still,
And myself have awaked, as it seems, to the better mind;
It is better to fight for the good than to rail at the ill;
I have felt with my native land, I am one with my kind,
I embrace the purpose of God, and the doom assign'd.

IDYLLS OF THE KING

IN TWELVE BOOKS

'Flos Regum Arthurus.'—JOSEPH OF EXETER

DEDICATION

THESE to His Memory—since he held
    them dear,
Perchance as finding there unconsciously
Some image of himself—I dedicate,
I dedicate, I consecrate with tears—
These Idylls.

        And indeed He seems to me
Scarce other than my king's ideal knight,
'Who reverenced his conscience as his king;
Whose glory was, redressing human wrong;
Who spake no slander, no, nor listen'd to it;
Who loved one only and who clave to
    her—'
Her—over all whose realms to their last
    isle,
Commingled with the gloom of imminent
    war,
The shadow of His loss drew like eclipse,
Darkening the world. We have lost him:
    he is gone:
We know him now: all narrow jealousies
Are silent; and we see him as he moved,
How modest, kindly, all-accomplish'd,
    wise,
With what sublime repression of himself,
And in what limits, and how tenderly;
Not swaying to this faction or to that;
Not making his high place the lawless
    perch
Of wing'd ambitions, nor a vantage-ground
For pleasure; but thro' all this tract of
    years
Wearing the white flower of a blameless
    life,
Before a thousand peering littlenesses,

In that fierce light which beats upon a
    throne,
And blackens every blot: for where is he,
Who dares foreshadow for an only son
A lovelier life, a more unstain'd, than his?
Or how should England dreaming of *his*
    sons
Hope more for these than some inheritance
Of such a life, a heart, a mind as thine,
Thou noble Father of her Kings to be,
Laborious for her people and her poor—
Voice in the rich dawn of an ampler day—
Far-sighted summoner of War and Waste
To fruitful strifes and rivalries of peace—
Sweet nature gilded by the gracious gleam
Of letters, dear to Science, dear to Art,
Dear to thy land and ours, a Prince indeed,
Beyond all titles, and a household name,
Hereafter, thro' all times, Albert the Good.

    Break not, O woman's-heart, but still
    endure;
Break not, for thou art Royal, but endure,
Remembering all the beauty of that star
Which shone so close beside Thee that ye
    made
One light together, but has past and leaves
The Crown a lonely splendour.

               May all love,
His love, unseen but felt, o'ershadow Thee,
The love of all Thy sons encompass Thee,
The love of all Thy daughters cherish
    Thee,
The love of all Thy people comfort Thee,
Till God's love set Thee at his side again!

THE COMING OF ARTHUR

LEODOGRAN, the King of Cameliard,
Had one fair daughter, and none other
    child;
And she was fairest of all flesh on earth,
Guinevere, and in her his one delight.

For many a petty king ere Arthur came
Ruled in this isle, and ever waging war
Each upon other, wasted all the land;
And still from time to time the heathen
    host

Swarm'd overseas, and harried what was
    left.
And so there grew great tracts of wilder-
    ness,
Wherein the beast was ever more and more,
But man was less and less, till Arthur came.
For first Aurelius lived and fought and
    died,
And after him King Uther fought and
    died,
But either fail'd to make the kingdom one.
And after these King Arthur for a space,
And thro' the puissance of his Table
    Round,
Drew all their petty princedoms under
    him,
Their king and head, and made a realm,
    and reign'd.

And thus the land of Cameliard was
    waste,
Thick with wet woods, and many a beast
    therein,
And none or few to scare or chase the
    beast;
So that wild dog, and wolf and boar and
    bear
Came night and day, and rooted in the
    fields,
And wallow'd in the gardens of the King.
And ever and anon the wolf would steal
The children and devour, but now and
    then,
Her own brood lost or dead, lent her fierce
    teat
To human sucklings; and the children,
    housed
In her foul den, there at their meat would
    growl,
And mock their foster-mother on four feet,
Till, straighten'd, they grew up to wolf-like
    men,
Worse than the wolves. And King Leodo-
    gran
Groan'd for the Roman legions here again,
And Cæsar's eagle: then his brother king,
Urien, assail'd him: last a heathen horde,
Reddening the sun with smoke and earth
    with blood,
And on the spike that split the mother's
    heart

Spitting the child, brake on him, till,
    amazed,
He knew not whither he should turn for
    aid.

But—for he heard of Arthur newly
    crown'd,
Tho' not without an uproar made by those
Who cried, 'He is not Uther's son'—the
    King
Sent to him, saying, 'Arise, and help us
    thou!
For here between the man and beast we
    die.'

And Arthur yet had done no deed of
    arms,
But heard the call, and came: and
    Guinevere
Stood by the castle walls to watch him
    pass;
But since he neither wore on helm or
    shield
The golden symbol of his kinglihood,
But rode a simple knight among his
    knights,
And many of these in richer arms than he,
She saw him not, or mark'd not, if she saw,
One among many, tho' his face was bare.
But Arthur, looking downward as he past,
Felt the light of her eyes into his life
Smite on the sudden, yet rode on, and
    pitch'd
His tents beside the forest. Then he drave
The heathen; after, slew the beast, and
    fell'd
The forest, letting in the sun, and made
Broad pathways for the hunter and the
    knight
And so return'd.

                    For while he linger'd there,
A doubt that ever smoulder'd in the hearts
Of those great Lords and Barons of his
    realm
Flash'd forth and into war: for most of
    these,
Colleaguing with a score of petty kings,
Made head against him, crying, 'Who is he
That he should rule us? who hath proven
    him
King Uther's son? for lo! we look at him,

And find nor face nor bearing, limbs nor
   voice,
Are like to those of Uther whom we knew.
This is the son of Gorloïs, not the King;
This is the son of Anton, not the King.'

And Arthur, passing thence to battle,
   felt
Travail, and throes and agonies of the life,
Desiring to be join'd with Guinevere;
And thinking as he rode, 'Her father said
That there between the man and beast they
   die.
Shall I not lift her from this land of beasts
Up to my throne, and side by side with me?
What happiness to reign a lonely king,
Vext—O ye stars that shudder over me,
O earth that soundest hollow under me,
Vext with waste dreams? for saving I be
   join'd
To her that is the fairest under heaven,
I seem as nothing in the mighty world,
And cannot will my will, nor work my
   work
Wholly, nor make myself in mine own
   realm
Victor and lord. But were I join'd with
   her,
Then might we live together as one life,
And reigning with one will in everything
Have power on this dark land to lighten it,
And power on this dead world to make it
   live.'

Thereafter—as he speaks who tells the
   tale—
When Arthur reach'd a field-of-battle
   bright
With pitch'd pavilions of his foe, the world
Was all so clear about him, that he saw
The smallest rock far on the faintest hill,
And even in high day the morning star.
So when the King had set his banner
   broad,
At once from either side, with trumpet-
   blast,
And shouts, and clarions shrilling unto
   blood,
The long-lanced battle let their horses run.
And now the Barons and the kings pre-
   vail'd,

And now the King, as here and there that
   war
Went swaying; but the Powers who walk
   the world
Made lightnings and great thunders over
   him,
And dazed all eyes, till Arthur by main
   might,
And mightier of his hands with every blow,
And leading all his knighthood threw the
   kings
Carádos, Urien, Cradlemont of Wales,
Claudias, and Clariance of Northumber-
   land,
The King Brandagoras of Latangor,
With Anguisant of Erin, Morganore,
And Lot of Orkney. Then, before a voice
As dreadful as the shout of one who sees
To one who sins, and deems himself alone
And all the world asleep, they swerved and
   brake
Flying, and Arthur call'd to stay the brands
That hack'd among the flyers, 'Ho! they
   yield!'
So like a painted battle the war stood
Silenced, the living quiet as the dead,
And in the heart of Arthur joy was lord.
He laugh'd upon his warrior whom he
   loved
And honour'd most. 'Thou dost not doubt
   me King,
So well thine arm hath wrought for me
   to-day.'
'Sir and my liege,' he cried, 'the fire of God
Descends upon thee in the battle-field:
I know thee for my King!' Whereat the
   two,
For each had warded either in the fight,
Sware on the field of death a deathless love.
And Arthur said, 'Man's word is God in
   man:
Let chance what will, I trust thee to the
   death.'

Then quickly from the foughten field he
   sent
Ulfius, and Brastias, and Bedivere,
His new-made knights, to King Leodo-
   gran,
Saying, 'If I in aught have served thee well,
Give me thy daughter Guinevere to wife.'

Whom when he heard, Leodogran in
   heart
Debating—'How should I that am a king,
However much he holp me at my need,
Give my one daughter saving to a king,
And a king's son?'—lifted his voice, and
   call'd
A hoary man, his chamberlain, to whom
He trusted all things, and of him required
His counsel: 'Knowest thou aught of
   Arthur's birth?'

   Then spake the hoary chamberlain and
   said,
'Sir King, there be but two old men that
   know:
And each is twice as old as I; and one
Is Merlin, the wise man that ever served
King Uther thro' his magic art; and one
Is Merlin's master (so they call him) Bleys,
Who taught him magic; but the scholar
   ran
Before the master, and so far, that Bleys
Laid magic by, and sat him down, and
   wrote
All things and whatsoever Merlin did
In one great annal-book, where after-years
Will learn the secret of our Arthur's birth.'

   To whom the King Leodogran replied,
'O friend, had I been holpen half as well
By this King Arthur as by thee to-day,
Then beast and man had had their share
   of me:
But summon here before us yet once more
Ulfius, and Brastias, and Bedivere.'

   Then, when they came before him, the
   King said,
'I have seen the cuckoo chased by lesser
   fowl,
And reason in the chase: but wherefore
   now
Do these your lords stir up the heat of war,
Some calling Arthur born of Gorloïs,
Others of Anton? Tell me, ye yourselves,
Hold ye this Arthur for King Uther's son?'

   And Ulfius and Brastias answer'd, 'Ay.'
Then Bedivere, the first of all his knights
Knighted by Arthur at his crowning,
   spake—

For bold in heart and act and word was he,
Whenever slander breathed against the
   King—

   'Sir, there be many rumours on this
   head:
For there be those who hate him in their
   hearts,
Call him baseborn, and since his ways are
   sweet,
And theirs are bestial, hold him less than
   man:
And there be those who deem him more
   than man,
And dream he dropt from heaven: but my
   belief
In all this matter—so ye care to learn—
Sir, for ye know that in King Uther's time
The prince and warrior Gorloïs, he that
   held
Tintagil castle by the Cornish sea,
Was wedded with a winsome wife, Ygerne:
And daughters had she borne him,—one
   whereof,
Lot's wife, the Queen of Orkney, Bellicent,
Hath ever like a loyal sister cleaved
To Arthur,—but a son she had not borne.
And Uther cast upon her eyes of love:
But she, a stainless wife to Gorloïs,
So loathed the bright dishonour of his love,
That Gorloïs and King Uther went to war:
And overthrown was Gorloïs and slain.
Then Uther in his wrath and heat besieged
Ygerne within Tintagil, where her men,
Seeing the mighty swarm about their walls,
Left her and fled, and Uther enter'd in,
And there was none to call to but himself.
So, compass'd by the power of the King,
Enforced she was to wed him in her tears,
And with a shameful swiftness: afterward,
Not many moons, King Uther died him-
   self,
Moaning and wailing for an heir to rule
After him, lest the realm should go to
   wrack.
And that same night, the night of the new
   year,
By reason of the bitterness and grief
That vext his mother, all before his time
Was Arthur born, and all as soon as born
Deliver'd at a secret postern-gate

To Merlin, to be holden far apart
Until his hour should come; because the
lords
Of that fierce day were as the lords of this,
Wild beasts, and surely would have torn
the child
Piecemeal among them, had they known;
for each
But sought to rule for his own self and
hand,
And many hated Uther for the sake
Of Gorloïs. Wherefore Merlin took the
child,
And gave him to Sir Anton, an old knight
And ancient friend of Uther; and his wife
Nursed the young prince, and rear'd him
with her own;
And no man knew. And ever since the
lords
Have foughten like wild beasts among
themselves,
So that the realm has gone to wrack: but
now,
This year, when Merlin (for his hour had
come)
Brought Arthur forth, and set him in the
hall,
Proclaiming, "Here is Uther's heir, your
king,"
A hundred voices cried, "Away with him!
No king of ours! a son of Gorloïs he,
Or else the child of Anton, and no king,
Or else baseborn." Yet Merlin thro' his
craft,
And while the people clamour'd for a king,
Had Arthur crown'd; but after, the great
lords
Banded, and so brake out in open war.'

Then while the King debated with him-
self
If Arthur were the child of shamefulness,
Or born the son of Gorloïs, after death,
Or Uther's son, and born before his
time,
Or whether there were truth in anything
Said by these three, there came to Came-
liard,
With Gawain and young Modred, her two
sons,
Lot's wife, the Queen of Orkney, Bellicent;

Whom as he could, not as he would, the
King
Made feast for, saying, as they sat at meat,

'A doubtful throne is ice on summer seas.
Ye come from Arthur's court. Victor his
men
Report him! Yea, but ye—think ye this
king—
So many those that hate him, and so strong,
So few his knights, however brave they
be—
Hath body enow to hold his foemen down?'

'O King,' she cried, 'and I will tell thee:
few,
Few, but all brave, all of one mind with
him;
For I was near him when the savage yells
Of Uther's peerage died, and Arthur sat
Crown'd on the daïs, and his warriors cried,
"Be thou the king, and we will work thy
will
Who love Thee." Then the King in low
deep tones,
And simple words of great authority,
Bound them by so strait vows to his own
self,
That when they rose, knighted from kneel-
ing, some
Were pale as at the passing of a ghost,
Some flush'd, and others dazed, as one
who wakes
Half-blinded at the coming of a light.

'But when he spake and cheer'd his
Table Round
With large, divine, and comfortable words,
Beyond my tongue to tell thee—I beheld
From eye to eye thro' all their Order flash
A momentary likeness of the King:
And ere it left their faces, thro' the cross
And those around it and the Crucified,
Down from the casement over Arthur,
smote
Flame-colour, vert and azure, in three
rays,
One falling upon each of three fair queens,
Who stood in silence near his throne, the
friends
Of Arthur, gazing on him, tall, with bright
Sweet faces, who will help him at his need.

'And there I saw mage Merlin, whose vast wit
And hundred winters are but as the hands
Of loyal vassals toiling for their liege.

'And near him stood the Lady of the Lake,
Who knows a subtler magic than his own—
Clothed in white samite, mystic, wonderful.
She gave the King his huge cross-hilted sword,
Whereby to drive the heathen out: a mist
Of incense curl'd about her, and her face
Wellnigh was hidden in the minster gloom;
But there was heard among the holy hymns
A voice as of the waters, for she dwells
Down in a deep; calm, whatsoever storms
May shake the world, and when the surface rolls,
Hath power to walk the waters like our Lord.

'There likewise I beheld Excalibur
Before him at his crowning borne, the sword
That rose from out the bosom of the lake,
And Arthur row'd across and took it—rich
With jewels, elfin Urim, on the hilt,
Bewildering heart and eye—the blade so bright
That men are blinded by it—on one side,
Graven in the oldest tongue of all this world,
"Take me," but turn the blade and ye shall see,
And written in the speech ye speak yourself,
"Cast me away!" And sad was Arthur's face
Taking it, but old Merlin counsell'd him,
"Take thou and strike! the time to cast away
Is yet far-off." So this great brand the king
Took, and by this will beat his foemen down.'

Thereat Leodogran rejoiced, but thought
To sift his doubtings to the last, and ask'd,
Fixing full eyes of question on her face,
'The swallow and the swift are near akin,
But thou art closer to this noble prince,
Being his own dear sister;' and she said,
'Daughter of Gorloïs and Ygerne am I;'
'And therefore Arthur's sister?' ask'd the King.
She answer'd, 'These be secret things,' and sign'd
To those two sons to pass, and let them be.
And Gawain went, and breaking into song
Sprang out, and follow'd by his flying hair
Ran like a colt, and leapt at all he saw:
But Modred laid his ear beside the doors,
And there half-heard; the same that afterward
Struck for the throne, and striking found his doom.

And then the Queen made answer, 'What know I?
For dark my mother was in eyes and hair,
And dark in hair and eyes am I; and dark
Was Gorloïs, yea and dark was Uther too,
Wellnigh to blackness; but this King is fair
Beyond the race of Britons and of men.
Moreover, always in my mind I hear
A cry from out the dawning of my life,
A mother weeping, and I hear her say,
"O that ye had some brother, pretty one,
To guard thee on the rough ways of the world."'

'Ay,' said the King, 'and hear ye such a cry?
But when did Arthur chance upon thee first?'

'O King!' she cried, 'and I will tell thee true:
He found me first when yet a little maid:
Beaten I had been for a little fault
Whereof I was not guilty; and out I ran
And flung myself down on a bank of heath,
And hated this fair world and all therein,
And wept, and wish'd that I were dead; and he—
I know not whether of himself he came,
Or brought by Merlin, who, they say, can walk
Unseen at pleasure—he was at my side,
And spake sweet words, and comforted my heart,
And dried my tears, being a child with me.

And many a time he came, and evermore
As I grew greater grew with me; and sad
At times he seem'd, and sad with him
    was I,
Stern too at times, and then I loved him
    not,
But sweet again, and then I loved him well.
And now of late I see him less and less,
But those first days had golden hours for
    me,
For then I surely thought he would be
    king.

'But let me tell thee now another tale:
For Bleys, our Merlin's master, as they say,
Died but of late, and sent his cry to me,
To hear him speak before he left his life.
Shrunk like a fairy changeling lay the
    mage;
And when I enter'd told me that himself
And Merlin ever served about the King,
Uther, before he died; and on the night
When Uther in Tintagil past away
Moaning and wailing for an heir, the two
Left the still King, and passing forth to
    breathe,
Then from the castle gateway by the
    chasm
Descending thro' the dismal night—a night
In which the bounds of heaven and earth
    were lost—
Beheld, so high upon the dreary deeps
It seem'd in heaven, a ship, the shape
    thereof
A dragon wing'd, and all from stem to stern
Bright with a shining people on the decks,
And gone as soon as seen. And then the
    two
Dropt to the cove, and watch'd the great
    sea fall,
Wave after wave, each mightier than the
    last,
Till last, a ninth one, gathering half the
    deep
And full of voices, slowly rose and plunged
Roaring, and all the wave was in a flame:
And down the wave and in the flame was
    borne
A naked babe, and rode to Merlin's feet,
Who stoopt and caught the babe, and cried
    "The King!

Here is an heir for Uther!" And the fringe,
Of that great breaker, sweeping up the
    strand,
Lash'd at the wizard as he spake the word,
And all at once all round him rose in fire,
So that the child and he were clothed in
    fire.
And presently thereafter follow'd calm,
Free sky and stars: "And this same child,"
    he said,
"Is he who reigns; nor could I part in
    peace
Till this were told." And saying this the
    seer
Went thro' the strait and dreadful pass of
    death,
Not ever to be question'd any more
Save on the further side; but when I met
Merlin, and ask'd him if these things were
    truth—
The shining dragon and the naked child
Descending in the glory of the seas—
He laugh'd as is his wont, and answer'd me
In riddling triplets of old time, and said:

' "Rain, rain, and sun! a rainbow in the
    sky!
A young man will be wiser by and by;
An old man's wit may wander ere he die.
  Rain, rain, and sun! a rainbow on the
    lea!
And truth is this to me, and that to thee;
And truth or clothed or naked let it be.
  Rain, sun, and rain! and the free blossom
    blows:
Sun, rain, and sun! and where is he who
    knows?
From the great deep to the great deep he
    goes."

'So Merlin riddling anger'd me; but
    thou
Fear not to give this King thine only child,
Guinevere: so great bards of him will sing
Hereafter; and dark sayings from of old
Ranging and ringing thro' the minds of
    men,
And echo'd by old folk beside their fires
For comfort after their wage-work is done,
Speak of the King; and Merlin in our time
Hath spoken also, not in jest, and sworn

Tho' men may wound him that he will
    not die,
But pass, again to come; and then or now
Utterly smite the heathen underfoot,
Till these and all men hail him for their
    king.'

She spake and King Leodogran rejoiced,
But musing 'Shall I answer yea or nay?'
Doubted, and drowsed, nodded and slept,
    and saw,
Dreaming, a slope of land that ever grew,
Field after field, up to a height, the peak
Haze-hidden, and thereon a phantom king,
Now looming, and now lost; and on the
    slope
The sword rose, the hind fell, the herd was
    driven,
Fire glimpsed; and all the land from roof
    and rick,
In drifts of smoke before a rolling wind,
Stream'd to the peak, and mingled with
    the haze
And made it thicker; while the phantom
    king
Sent out at times a voice; and here or
    there
Stood one who pointed toward the voice,
    the rest
Slew on and burnt, crying, 'No king of
    ours,
No son of Uther, and no king of ours;'
Till with a wink his dream was changed,
    the haze
Descended, and the solid earth became
As nothing, but the King stood out in
    heaven,
Crown'd. And Leodogran awoke, and sent
Ulfius, and Brastias and Bedivere,
Back to the court of Arthur answering yea.

Then Arthur charged his warrior whom
    he loved
And honour'd most, Sir Lancelot, to ride
    forth
And bring the Queen;—and watch'd him
    from the gates:
And Lancelot past away among the flowers,
(For then was latter April) and return'd
Among the flowers, in May, with Guine-
    vere.

To whom arrived, by Dubric the high
    saint,
Chief of the church in Britain, and before
The stateliest of her altar-shrines, the
    King
That morn was married, while in stainless
    white,
The fair beginners of a nobler time,
And glorying in their vows and him, his
    knights
Stood round him, and rejoicing in his joy.
Far shone the fields of May thro' open
    door,
The sacred altar blossom'd white with
    May,
The Sun of May descended on their King,
They gazed on all earth's beauty in their
    Queen,
Roll'd incense, and there past along the
    hymns
A voice as of the waters, while the two
Sware at the shrine of Christ a deathless
    love:
And Arthur said, 'Behold, thy doom is
    mine.
Let chance what will, I love thee to the
    death!'
To whom the Queen replied with drooping
    eyes,
'King and my lord, I love thee to the
    death!'
And holy Dubric spread his hands and
    spake,
'Reign ye, and live and love, and make the
    world
Other, and may thy Queen be one with
    thee,
And all this Order of thy Table Round
Fulfil the boundless purpose of their
    King!'

So Dubric said; but when they left the
    shrine
Great Lords from Rome before the portal
    stood,
In scornful stillness gazing as they past;
Then while they paced a city all on fire
With sun and cloth of gold, the trumpets
    blew,
And Arthur's knighthood sang before the
    King:—

'Blow trumpet, for the world is white
with May;
Blow trumpet, the long night hath roll'd
away!
Blow thro' the living world—"Let the
King reign."

'Shall Rome or Heathen rule in Arthur's
realm?
Flash brand and lance, fall battleaxe upon
helm,
Fall battleaxe, and flash brand! Let the
King reign.

'Strike for the King and live! his knights
have heard
That God hath told the King a secret word.
Fall battleaxe, and flash brand! Let the
King reign.

'Blow trumpet! he will lift us from the
dust.
Blow trumpet! live the strength and die
the lust!
Clang battleaxe, and clash brand! Let the
King reign.

'Strike for the King and die! and if thou
diest,
The King is King, and ever wills the
highest.
Clang battleaxe, and clash brand! Let the
King reign.

'Blow, for our Sun is mighty in his May!
Blow, for our Sun is mightier day by day!
Clang battleaxe, and clash brand! Let the
King reign.

'The King will follow Christ, and we
the King
In whom high God hath breathed a secret
thing.
Fall battleaxe, and flash brand! Let the
King reign.'

So sang the knighthood, moving to their
hall.
There at the banquet those great Lords
from Rome,
The slowly-fading mistress of the world,
Strode in, and claim'd their tribute as of
yore.
But Arthur spake, 'Behold, for these have
sworn
To wage my wars, and worship me their
King;
The old order changeth, yielding place to
new;
And we that fight for our fair father Christ,
Seeing that ye be grown too weak and old
To drive the heathen from your Roman
wall,
No tribute will we pay:' so those great
lords
Drew back in wrath, and Arthur strove
with Rome.

And Arthur and his knighthood for a
space
Were all one will, and thro' that strength
the King
Drew in the petty princedoms under him,
Fought, and in twelve great battles overcame
The heathen hordes, and made a realm and
reign'd.

THE ROUND TABLE

GARETH AND LYNETTE

THE last tall son of Lot and Bellicent,
And tallest, Gareth, in a showerful spring
Stared at the spate. A slender-shafted Pine

Lost footing, fell, and so was whirl'd away.
'How he went down,' said Gareth, 'as a
false knight
Or evil king before my lance if lance
Were mine to use—O senseless cataract,

Bearing all down in thy precipitancy—
And yet thou art but swollen with cold
    snows
And mine is living blood: thou dost His
    will,
The Maker's, and not knowest, and I that
    know,
Have strength and wit, in my good mother's
    hall
Linger with vacillating obedience,
Prison'd, and kept and coax'd and whistled
    to—
Since the good mother holds me still a
    child!
Good mother is bad mother unto me!
A worse were better; yet no worse would I.
Heaven yield her for it, but in me put force
To weary her ears with one continuous
    prayer,
Until she let me fly discaged to sweep
In ever-highering eagle-circles up
To the great Sun of Glory, and thence
    swoop
Down upon all things base, and dash them
    dead,
A knight of Arthur, working out his will,
To cleanse the world. Why, Gawain, when
    he came
With Modred hither in the summertime,
Ask'd me to tilt with him, the proven
    knight.
Modred for want of worthier was the
    judge.
Then I so shook him in the saddle, he said,
"Thou hast half prevail'd against me,"
    said so—he—
Tho' Modred biting his thin lips was mute,
For he is alway sullen: what care I?'

    And Gareth went, and hovering round
    her chair
Ask'd, 'Mother, tho' ye count me still the
    child,
Sweet mother, do ye love the child?' She
    laugh'd,
'Thou art but a wild-goose to question it.'
'Then, mother, an ye love the child,' he
    said,
'Being a goose and rather tame than wild,
Hear the child's story.' 'Yea, my well-
    beloved,

An 'twere but of the goose and golden
    eggs.'

    And Gareth answer'd her with kindling
    eyes,
'Nay, nay, good mother, but this egg of
    mine
Was finer gold than any goose can lay;
For this an Eagle, a royal Eagle, laid
Almost beyond eye-reach, on such a palm
As glitters gilded in thy Book of Hours.
And there was ever haunting round the
    palm
A lusty youth, but poor, who often saw
The splendour sparkling from aloft, and
    thought
"An I could climb and lay my hand upon it,
Then were I wealthier than a leash of
    kings."
But ever when he reach'd a hand to climb,
One, that had loved him from his child-
    hood, caught
And stay'd him, "Climb not lest thou
    break thy neck,
I charge thee by my love," and so the boy,
Sweet mother, neither clomb, nor brake
    his neck,
But brake his very heart in pining for it,
And past away.'

    To whom the mother said,
'True love, sweet son, had risk'd himself
    and climb'd,
And handed down the golden treasure to
    him.'

    And Gareth answer'd her with kindling
    eyes,
'Gold? said I gold?—ay then, why he, or
    she,
Or whosoe'er it was, or half the world
Had ventured—had the thing I spake of
    been
Mere gold—but this was all of that true
    steel,
Whereof they forged the brand Excalibur,
And lightnings play'd about it in the storm,
And all the little fowl were flurried at it,
And there were cries and clashings in the
    nest,
That sent him from his senses: let me go.'

Then Bellicent bemoan'd herself and
  said,
'Hast thou no pity upon my loneliness?
Lo, where thy father Lot beside the hearth
Lies like a log, and all but smoulder'd out!
For ever since when traitor to the King
He fought against him in the Baron's war,
And Arthur gave him back his territory,
His age hath slowly droopt, and now lies
  there
A yet-warm corpse, and yet unburiable,
No more; nor sees, nor hears, nor speaks,
  nor knows.
And both thy brethren are in Arthur's hall,
Albeit neither loved with that full love
I feel for thee, nor worthy such a love:
Stay therefore thou; red berries charm the
  bird,
And thee, mine innocent, the jousts, the
  wars,
Who never knewest finger-ache, nor pang
Of wrench'd or broken limb—an often
  chance
In those brain-stunning shocks, and
  tourney-falls,
Frights to my heart; but stay: follow the
  deer
By these tall firs and our fast-falling burns;
So make thy manhood mightier day by
  day;
Sweet is the chase: and I will seek thee
  out
Some comfortable bride and fair, to grace
Thy climbing life, and cherish my prone
  year,
Till falling into Lot's forgetfulness
I know not thee, myself, nor anything.
Stay, my best son! ye are yet more boy
  than man.'

Then Gareth, 'An ye hold me yet for
  child,
Hear yet once more the story of the child.
For, mother, there was once a King, like
  ours.
The prince his heir, when tall and mar-
  riageable,
Ask'd for a bride; and thereupon the King
Set two before him. One was fair, strong,
  arm'd—
But to be won by force—and many men

Desired her; one, good lack, no man
  desired.
And these were the conditions of the King:
That save he won the first by force, he
  needs
Must wed that other, whom no man
  desired,
A red-faced bride who knew herself so
  vile,
That evermore she long'd to hide herself,
Nor fronted man or woman, eye to eye—
Yea—some she cleaved to, but they died
  of her.
And one—they call'd her Fame; and one,
  —O Mother,
How can ye keep me tether'd to you—
  Shame.
Man am I grown, a man's work must I do.
Follow the deer? follow the Christ, the
  King,
Live pure, speak true, right wrong, follow
  the King—
Else, wherefore born?'

         To whom the mother said,
'Sweet son, for there be many who deem
  him not,
Or will not deem him, wholly proven
  King—
Albeit in mine own heart I knew him King,
When I was frequent with him in my
  youth,
And heard him Kingly speak, and doubted
  him
No more than he, himself; but felt him
  mine,
Of closest kin to me: yet—wilt thou leave
Thine easeful biding here, and risk thine
  all,
Life, limbs, for one that is not proven
  King?
Stay, till the cloud that settles round his
  birth
Hath lifted but a little. Stay, sweet son.'

And Gareth answer'd quickly, 'Not an
  hour,
So that ye yield me—I will walk thro' fire,
Mother, to gain it—your full leave to go.
Not proven, who swept the dust of ruin'd
  Rome

From off the threshold of the realm, and crush'd
The Idolaters, and made the people free?
Who should be King save him who makes us free?'

So when the Queen, who long had sought in vain
To break him from the intent to which he grew,
Found her son's will unwaveringly one,
She answer'd craftily, 'Will ye walk thro' fire?
Who walks thro' fire will hardly heed the smoke.
Ay, go then, an ye must: only one proof,
Before thou ask the King to make thee knight,
Of thine obedience and thy love to me,
Thy mother,—I demand.'

And Gareth cried,
'A hard one, or a hundred, so I go.
Nay—quick! the proof to prove me to the quick!'

But slowly spake the mother looking at him,
'Prince, thou shalt go disguised to Arthur's hall,
And hire thyself to serve for meats and drinks
Among the scullions and the kitchen-knaves,
And those that hand the dish across the bar.
Nor shalt thou tell thy name to anyone.
And thou shalt serve a twelvemonth and a day.'

For so the Queen believed that when her son
Beheld his only way to glory lead
Low down thro' villain kitchen-vassalage,
Her own true Gareth was too princely-proud
To pass thereby; so should he rest with her,
Closed in her castle from the sound of arms.

Silent awhile was Gareth, then replied,
'The thrall in person may be free in soul,
And I shall see the jousts. Thy son am I,
And since thou art my mother, must obey.
I therefore yield me freely to thy will;
For hence will I, disguised, and hire myself
To serve with scullions and with kitchen-knaves;
Nor tell my name to any—no, not the King.'

Gareth awhile linger'd. The mother's eye
Full of the wistful fear that he would go,
And turning toward him wheresoe'er he turn'd,
Perplext his outward purpose, till an hour,
When waken'd by the wind which with full voice
Swept bellowing thro' the darkness on to dawn,
He rose, and out of slumber calling two
That still had tended on him from his birth,
Before the wakeful mother heard him, went.

The three were clad like tillers of the soil.
Southward they set their faces. The birds made
Melody on branch, and melody in mid air.
The damp hill-slopes were quicken'd into green,
And the live green had kindled into flowers,
For it was past the time of Easterday.

So, when their feet were planted on the plain
That broaden'd toward the base of Camelot,
Far off they saw the silver-misty morn
Rolling her smoke about the Royal mount,
That rose between the forest and the field.
At times the summit of the high city flash'd;
At times the spires and turrets half-way down
Prick'd thro' the mist; at times the great gate shone
Only, that open'd on the field below:
Anon, the whole fair city had disappear'd.

Then those who went with Gareth were
    amazed,
One crying, 'Let us go no further, lord.
Here is a city of Enchanters, built
By fairy Kings.' The second echo'd him,
'Lord, we have heard from our wise man
    at home
To Northward, that this King is not the
    King,
But only changeling out of Fairyland,
Who drave the heathen hence by
    sorcery
And Merlin's glamour.' Then the first
    again,
'Lord, there is no such city anywhere,
But all a vision.'

                 Gareth answer'd them
With laughter, swearing he had glamour
    enow
In his own blood, his princedom, youth
    and hopes,
To plunge old Merlin in the Arabian sea;
So push'd them all unwilling toward the
    gate.
And there was no gate like it under heaven.
For barefoot on the keystone, which was
    lined
And rippled like an ever-fleeting wave,
The Lady of the Lake stood: all her dress
Wept from her sides as water flowing away;
But like the cross her great and goodly
    arms
Stretch'd under all the cornice and upheld:
And drops of water fell from either hand;
And down from one a sword was hung,
    from one
A censer, either worn with wind and storm;
And o'er her breast floated the sacred fish;
And in the space to left of her, and right,
Were Arthur's wars in weird devices done,
New things and old co-twisted, as if Time
Were nothing, so inveterately, that men
Were giddy gazing there; and over all
High on the top were those three Queens,
    the friends
Of Arthur, who should help him at his
    need.

Then those with Gareth for so long a
    space

Stared at the figures, that at last it seem'd
The dragon-boughts and elvish emblem-
    ings
Began to move, seethe, twine and curl:
    they call'd
To Gareth, 'Lord, the gateway is alive.'

    And Gareth likewise on them fixt his
    eyes
So long, that ev'n to him they seem'd to
    move.
Out of the city a blast of music peal'd.
Back from the gate started the three, to
    whom
From out thereunder came an ancient man,
Long-bearded, saying, 'Who be ye, my
    sons?'

    Then Gareth, 'We be tillers of the soil,
Who leaving share in furrow come to see
The glories of our King: but these, my
    men,
(Your city moved so weirdly in the mist)
Doubt if the King be King at all, or come
From Fairyland; and whether this be built
By magic, and by fairy Kings and Queens;
Or whether there be any city at all,
Or all a vision: and this music now
Hath scared them both, but tell thou these
    the truth.'

    Then that old Seer made answer playing
    on him
And saying, 'Son, I have seen the good
    ship sail
Keel upward, and mast downward, in the
    heavens,
And solid turrets topsy-turvy in air:
And here is truth; but an it please thee not,
Take thou the truth as thou hast told it me.
For truly as thou sayest, a Fairy King
And Fairy Queens have built the city, son;
They came from out a sacred mountain-
    cleft
Toward the sunrise, each with harp in
    hand,
And built it to the music of their harps.
And, as thou sayest, it is enchanted, son,
For there is nothing in it as it seems
Saving the King; tho' some there be that
    hold

The King a shadow, and the city real:
Yet take thou heed of him, for, so thou pass
Beneath this archway, then wilt thou
    become
A thrall to his enchantments, for the King
Will bind thee by such vows, as is a shame
A man should not be bound by, yet the
    which
No man can keep; but, so thou dread to
    swear,
Pass not beneath this gateway, but abide
Without, among the cattle of the field.
For an ye heard a music, like enow
They are building still, seeing the city is
    built
To music, therefore never built at all,
And therefore built for ever.'

                        Gareth spake
Anger'd, 'Old Master, reverence thine own
    beard
That looks as white as utter truth, and
    seems
Wellnigh as long as thou art statured tall!
Why mockest thou the stranger that hath
    been
To thee fair-spoken?'

                    But the Seer replied,
'Know ye not then the Riddling of the
    Bards?
"Confusion, and illusion, and relation,
Elusion, and occasion, and evasion"?
I mock thee not but as thou mockest me,
And all that see thee, for thou art not who
Thou seemest, but I know thee who thou
    art.
And now thou goest up to mock the King,
Who cannot brook the shadow of any lie.'

Unmockingly the mocker ending here
Turn'd to the right, and past along the
    plain;
Whom Gareth looking after said, 'My men,
Our one white lie sits like a little ghost
Here on the threshold of our enterprise.
Let love be blamed for it, not she, nor I:
Well, we will make amends.'

                    With all good cheer
He spake and laugh'd, then enter'd with
    his twain

Camelot, a city of shadowy palaces
And stately, rich in emblem and the work
Of ancient kings who did their days in
    stone;
Which Merlin's hand, the Mage at Arthur's
    court,
Knowing all arts, had touch'd, and every-
    where
At Arthur's ordinance, tipt with lessening
    peak
And pinnacle, and had made it spire to
    heaven.
And ever and anon a knight would pass
Outward, or inward to the hall: his arms
Clash'd; and the sound was good to
    Gareth's ear.
And out of bower and casement shyly
    glanced
Eyes of pure women, wholesome stars of
    love;
And all about a healthful people stept
As in the presence of a gracious king.

Then into hall Gareth ascending heard
A voice, the voice of Arthur, and beheld
Far over heads in that long-vaulted hall
The splendour of the presence of the King
Throned, and delivering doom—and look'd
    no more—
But felt his young heart hammering in his
    ears,
And thought, 'For this half-shadow of a lie
The truthful King will doom me when I
    speak.'
Yet pressing on, tho' all in fear to find
Sir Gawain or Sir Modred, saw nor one
Nor other, but in all the listening eyes
Of those tall knights, that ranged about the
    throne,
Clear honour shining like the dewy star
Of dawn, and faith in their great King,
    with pure
Affection, and the light of victory,
And glory gain'd, and evermore to gain.

Then came a widow crying to the King,
'A boon, Sir King! Thy father, Uther, reft
From my dead lord a field with violence:
For howsoe'er at first he proffer'd gold,
Yet, for the field was pleasant in our eyes,
We yielded not; and then he reft us of it
Perforce, and left us neither gold nor field.'

Said Arthur, 'Whether would ye? gold
or field?'
To whom the woman weeping, 'Nay, my
lord,
The field was pleasant in my husband's
eye.'

And Arthur, 'Have thy pleasant field
again,
And thrice the gold for Uther's use thereof,
According to the years. No boon is here,
But justice, so thy say be proven true.
Accursed, who from the wrongs his father
did
Would shape himself a right!'

     And while she past,
Came yet another widow crying to him,
'A boon, Sir King! Thine enemy, King,
am I.
With thine own hand thou slewest my dear
lord,
A knight of Uther in the Barons' war,
When Lot and many another rose and
fought
Against thee, saying thou wert basely born.
I held with these, and loathe to ask thee
aught.
Yet lo! my husband's brother had my son
Thrall'd in his castle, and hath starved him
dead;
And standeth seized of that inheritance
Which thou that slewest the sire hast left
the son.
So tho' I scarce can ask it thee for hate,
Grant me some knight to do the battle
for me,
Kill the foul thief, and wreak me for my
son.'

Then strode a good knight forward,
crying to him,
'A boon, Sir King! I am her kinsman, I.
Give me to right her wrong, and slay the
man.'

Then came Sir Kay, the seneschal, and
cried,
'A boon, Sir King! ev'n that thou grant
her none,
This railer, that hath mock'd thee in full
hall—

None; or the wholesome boon of gyve and
gag.'

But Arthur, 'We sit King, to help the
wrong'd
Thro' all our realm. The woman loves her
lord.
Peace to thee, woman, with thy loves and
hates!
The kings of old had doom'd thee to the
flames,
Aurelius Emrys would have scourged thee
dead,
And Uther slit thy tongue: but get thee
hence—
Lest that rough humour of the kings of old
Return upon me! Thou that art her kin,
Go likewise; lay him low and slay him not,
But bring him here, that I may judge the
right,
According to the justice of the King:
Then, be he guilty, by that deathless King
Who lived and died for men, the man shall
die.'

Then came in hall the messenger of
Mark,
A name of evil savour in the land,
The Cornish king. In either hand he bore
What dazzled all, and shone far-off as
shines
A field of charlock in the sudden sun
Between two showers, a cloth of palest
gold,
Which down he laid before the throne, and
knelt,
Delivering, that his lord, the vassal king,
Was ev'n upon his way to Camelot;
For having heard that Arthur of his grace
Had made his goodly cousin, Tristram,
knight,
And, for himself was of the greater state,
Being a king, he trusted his liege-lord
Would yield him this large honour all the
more;
So pray'd him well to accept this cloth of
gold,
In token of true heart and feälty.

Then Arthur cried to rend the cloth, to
rend
In pieces, and so cast it on the hearth.

An oak-tree smoulder'd there. 'The goodly knight!
What! shall the shield of Mark stand among these?'
For, midway down the side of that long hall
A stately pile,—whereof along the front,
Some blazon'd, some but carven, and some blank,
There ran a treble range of stony shields,—
Rose, and high-arching overbrow'd the hearth.
And under every shield a knight was named:
For this was Arthur's custom in his hall;
When some good knight had done one noble deed,
His arms were carven only; but if twain
His arms were blazon'd also; but if none,
The shield was blank and bare without a sign
Saving the name beneath; and Gareth saw
The shield of Gawain blazon'd rich and bright,
And Modred's blank as death; and Arthur cried
To rend the cloth and cast it on the hearth.

'More like are we to reave him of his crown
Than make him knight because men call him king.
The kings we found, ye know we stay'd their hands
From war among themselves, but left them kings;
Of whom were any bounteous, merciful,
Truth-speaking, brave, good livers, them we enroll'd
Among us, and they sit within our hall.
But Mark hath tarnish'd the great name of king,
As Mark would sully the low state of churl:
And, seeing he hath sent us cloth of gold,
Return, and meet, and hold him from our eyes,
Lest we should lap him up in cloth of lead,
Silenced for ever—craven—a man of plots,
Craft, poisonous counsels, wayside ambushings—
No fault of thine: let Kay the seneschal

Look to thy wants, and send thee satisfied—
Accursed, who strikes nor lets the hand be seen!'

And many another suppliant crying came
With noise of ravage wrought by beast and man,
And evermore a knight would ride away.

Last, Gareth leaning both hands heavily
Down on the shoulders of the twain, his men,
Approach'd between them toward the King, and ask'd,
'A boon, Sir King (his voice was all ashamed),
For see ye not how weak and hungerworn
I seem—leaning on these? grant me to serve
For meat and drink among thy kitchenknaves
A twelvemonth and a day, nor seek my name.
Hereafter I will fight.'

　　　　　　To him the King,
'A goodly youth and worth a goodlier boon!
But so thou wilt no goodlier, then must Kay,
The master of the meats and drinks, be thine.'

He rose and past; then Kay, a man of mien
Wan-sallow as the plant that feels itself
Root-bitten by white lichen,

　　　　　　'Lo ye now!
This fellow hath broken from some Abbey, where,
God wot, he had not beef and brewis enow,
However that might chance! but an he work,
Like any pigeon will I cram his crop,
And sleeker shall he shine than any hog.'

Then Lancelot standing near, 'Sir Seneschal,
Sleuth-hound thou knowest, and gray, and all the hounds;

A horse thou knowest, a man thou dost not
  know:
Broad brows and fair, a fluent hair and
  fine,
High nose, a nostril large and fine, and
  hands
Large, fair and fine!—Some young lad's
  mystery—
But, or from sheepcot or king's hall, the
  boy
Is noble-natured. Treat him with all grace,
Lest he should come to shame thy judging
  of him.'

Then Kay, 'What murmurest thou of
  mystery?
Think ye this fellow will poison the King's
  dish?
Nay, for he spake too fool-like: mystery!
Tut, an the lad were noble, he had ask'd
For horse and armour: fair and fine, for-
  sooth!
Sir Fine-face, Sir Fair-hands? but see thou
  to it
That thine own fineness, Lancelot, some
  fine day
Undo thee not—and leave my man to me.'

So Gareth all for glory underwent
The sooty yoke of kitchen-vassalage;
Ate with young lads his portion by the
  door,
And couch'd at night with grimy kitchen-
  knaves.
And Lancelot ever spake him pleasantly,
But Kay the seneschal, who loved him not,
Would hustle and harry him, and labour
  him
Beyond his comrade of the hearth, and set
To turn the broach, draw water, or hew
  wood,
Or grosser tasks; and Gareth bow'd him-
  self
With all obedience to the King, and
  wrought
All kind of service with a noble ease
That graced the lowliest act in doing it.
And when the thralls had talk among
  themselves,
And one would praise the love that linkt
  the King

And Lancelot—how the King had saved
  his life
In battle twice, and Lancelot once the
  King's—
For Lancelot was the first in Tournament,
But Arthur mightiest on the battle-field—
Gareth was glad. Or if some other told,
How once the wandering forester at dawn,
Far over the blue tarns and hazy seas,
On Caer-Eryri's highest found the King,
A naked babe, of whom the Prophet spake,
'He passes to the Isle Avilion,
He passes and is heal'd and cannot die'—
Gareth was glad. But if their talk were foul,
Then would he whistle rapid as any lark,
Or carol some old roundelay, and so loud
That first they mock'd, but, after, rever-
  enced him.
Or Gareth telling some prodigious tale
Of knights, who sliced a red life-bubbling
  way
Thro' twenty folds of twisted dragon, held
All in a gap-mouth'd circle his good mates
Lying or sitting round him, idle hands,
Charm'd; till Sir Kay, the seneschal, would
  come
Blustering upon them, like a sudden wind
Among dead leaves, and drive them all
  apart.
Or when the thralls had sport among them-
  selves,
So there were any trial of mastery,
He, by two yards in casting bar or stone
Was counted best; and if there chanced a
  joust,
So that Sir Kay nodded him leave to go,
Would hurry thither, and when he saw the
  knights
Clash like the coming and retiring wave,
And the spear spring, and good horse reel,
  the boy
Was half beyond himself for ecstasy.

So for a month he wrought among the
  thralls;
But in the weeks that follow'd, the good
  Queen,
Repentant of the word she made him swear,
And saddening in her childless castle, sent,
Between the in-crescent and de-crescent
  moon,

Arms for her son, and loosed him from his
vow.

This, Gareth hearing from a squire of
Lot
With whom he used to play at tourney
once,
When both were children, and in lonely
haunts
Would scratch a ragged oval on the sand,
And each at either dash from either end—
Shame never made girl redder than Gareth
joy.
He laugh'd; he sprang. 'Out of the smoke,
at once
I leap from Satan's foot to Peter's knee—
These news be mine, none other's—nay,
the King's—
Descend into the city:' whereon he sought
The King alone, and found, and told him
all.

'I have stagger'd thy strong Gawain in
a tilt
For pastime; yea, he said it: joust can I.
Make me thy knight—in secret! let my
name
Be hidd'n, and give me the first quest, I
spring
Like flame from ashes.'

Here the King's calm eye
Fell on, and check'd, and made him flush,
and bow
Lowly, to kiss his hand, who answer'd him,
'Son, the good mother let me know thee
here,
And sent her wish that I would yield thee
thine.
Make thee my knight? my knights are
sworn to vows
Of utter hardihood, utter gentleness,
And, loving, utter faithfulness in love,
And uttermost obedience to the King.'

Then Gareth, lightly springing from his
knees,
'My King, for hardihood I can promise
thee.
For uttermost obedience make demand
Of whom ye gave me to, the Seneschal,
No mellow master of the meats and drinks!

And as for love, God wot, I love not yet,
But love I shall, God willing.'

And the King—
'Make thee my knight in secret? yea,
but he,
Our noblest brother, and our truest man,
And one with me in all, he needs must
know.'

'Let Lancelot know, my King, let
Lancelot know,
Thy noblest and thy truest!'

And the King—
'But wherefore would ye men should won-
der at you?
Nay, rather for the sake of me, their King,
And the deed's sake my knighthood do the
deed,
Than to be noised of.'

Merrily Gareth ask'd,
'Have I not earn'd my cake in baking of it?
Let be my name until I make my name!
My deeds will speak: it is but for a day.'
So with a kindly hand on Gareth's arm
Smiled the great King, and half-unwillingly
Loving his lusty youthhood yielded to him.
Then, after summoning Lancelot privily,
'I have given him the first quest: he is not
proven.
Look therefore when he calls for this in
hall,
Thou get to horse and follow him far away,
Cover the lions on thy shield, and see
Far as thou mayest, he be nor ta'en nor
slain.'

Then that same day there past into the
hall
A damsel of high lineage, and a brow
May-blossom, and a cheek of apple-
blossom,
Hawk-eyes; and lightly was her slender
nose
Tip-tilted like the petal of a flower;
She into hall past with her page and cried,

'O King, for thou hast driven the foe
without,
See to the foe within! bridge, ford, beset

By bandits, everyone that owns a tower
The Lord for half a league. Why sit ye
    there?
Rest would I not, Sir King, an I were king,
Till ev'n the lonest hold were all as free
From cursed bloodshed, as thine altar-
    cloth
From that best blood it is a sin to spill.'

'Comfort thyself,' said Arthur, 'I nor
    mine
Rest: so my knighthood keep the vows
    they swore,
The wastest moorland of our realm shall be
Safe, damsel, as the centre of this hall.
What is thy name? thy need?'

                'My name?' she said—
'Lynette my name; noble; my need, a
    knight
To combat for my sister, Lyonors,
A lady of high lineage, of great lands,
And comely, yea, and comelier than myself.
She lives in Castle Perilous: a river
Runs in three loops about her living-place;
And o'er it are three passings, and three
    knights
Defend the passings, brethren, and a
    fourth
And of that four the mightiest, holds her
    stay'd
In her own castle, and so besieges her
To break her will, and make her wed with
    him:
And but delays his purport till thou send
To do the battle with him, thy chief man
Sir Lancelot whom he trusts to overthrow,
Then wed, with glory: but she will not wed
Save whom she loveth, or a holy life.
Now therefore have I come for Lancelot.'

Then Arthur mindful of Sir Gareth
    ask'd,
'Damsel, ye know this Order lives to crush
All wrongers of the Realm. But say, these
    four,
Who be they? What the fashion of the
    men?'

'They be of foolish fashion, O Sir King,
The fashion of that old knight-errantry

Who ride abroad, and do but what they
    will;
Courteous or bestial from the moment,
    such
As have nor law nor king; and three of
    these
Proud in their fantasy call themselves the
    Day,
Morning-Star, and Noon-Sun, and Even-
    ing-Star,
Being strong fools; and never a whit more
    wise
The fourth, who alway rideth arm'd in
    black,
A huge man-beast of boundless savagery.
He names himself the Night and oftener
    Death,
And wears a helmet mounted with a skull,
And bears a skeleton figured on his arms,
To show that who may slay or scape the
    three,
Slain by himself, shall enter endless night.
And all these four be fools, but mighty
    men,
And therefore am I come for Lancelot.'

Hereat Sir Gareth call'd from where he
    rose,
A head with kindling eyes above the throng,
'A boon, Sir King—this quest!' then—
    for he mark'd
Kay near him groaning like a wounded
    bull—
'Yea, King, thou knowest thy kitchen-
    knave am I,
And mighty thro' thy meats and drinks
    am I,
And I can topple over a hundred such.
Thy promise, King,' and Arthur glancing
    at him,
Brought down a momentary brow. 'Rough,
    sudden,
And pardonable, worthy to be knight—
Go therefore,' and all hearers were
    amazed.

But on the damsel's forehead shame,
    pride, wrath
Slew the May-white: she lifted either arm,
'Fie on thee, King! I ask'd for thy chief
    knight,

And thou hast given me but a kitchen-
  knave.'
Then ere a man in hall could stay her,
  turn'd,
Fled down the lane of access to the King,
Took horse, descended the slope street,
  and past
The weird white gate, and paused without,
  beside
The field of tourney, murmuring 'kitchen-
  knave.'

Now two great entries open'd from the
  hall,
At one end one, that gave upon a range
Of level pavement where the King would
  pace
At sunrise, gazing over plain and wood;
And down from this a lordly stairway
  sloped
Till lost in blowing trees and tops of
  towers;
And out by this main doorway past the
  King.
But one was counter to the hearth, and
  rose
High that the highest-crested helm could
  ride
Therethro' nor graze: and by this entry
  fled
The damsel in her wrath, and on to this
Sir Gareth strode, and saw without the
  door
King Arthur's gift, the worth of half a
  town,
A warhorse of the best, and near it stood
The two that out of north had follow'd
  him:
This bare a maiden shield, a casque; that
  held
The horse, the spear; whereat Sir Gareth
  loosed
A cloak that dropt from collar-bone to heel,
A cloth of roughest web, and cast it down,
And from it like a fuel-smother'd fire,
That lookt half-dead, brake bright, and
  flash'd as those
Dull-coated things, that making slide apart
Their dusk wing-cases, all beneath there
  burns
A jewell'd harness, ere they pass and fly.

So Gareth ere he parted flash'd in arms.
Then as he donn'd the helm, and took the
  shield
And mounted horse and graspt a spear, of
  grain
Storm-strengthen'd on a windy site, and
  tipt
With trenchant steel, around him slowly
  prest
The people, while from out of kitchen
  came
The thralls in throng, and seeing who had
  work'd
Lustier than any, and whom they could
  but love,
Mounted in arms, threw up their caps and
  cried,
'God bless the King, and all his fellowship!'
And on thro' lanes of shouting Gareth rode
Down the slope street, and past without
  the gate.

So Gareth past with joy; but as the cur
Pluckt from the cur he fights with, ere his
  cause
Be cool'd by fighting, follows, being named,
His owner, but remembers all, and growls
Remembering, so Sir Kay beside the door
Mutter'd in scorn of Gareth whom he used
To harry and hustle.

                    'Bound upon a quest
With horse and arms—the King hath past
  his time—
My scullion knave! Thralls to your work
  again,
For an your fire be low ye kindle mine!
Will there be dawn in West and eve in
  East?
Begone!—my knave!—belike and like
  enow
Some old head-blow not heeded in his
  youth
So shook his wits they wander in his
  prime—
Crazed! How the villain lifted up his voice,
Nor shamed to bawl himself a kitchen-
  knave.
Tut: he was tame and meek enow with me,
Till peacock'd up with Lancelot's noticing.
Well—I will after my loud knave, and learn

Whether he know me for his master yet.
Out of the smoke he came, and so my lance
Hold, by God's grace, he shall into the mire—
Thence, if the King awaken from his craze,
Into the smoke again.'

But Lancelot said,
'Kay, wherefore wilt thou go against the King,
For that did never he whereon ye rail,
But ever meekly served the King in thee?
Abide: take counsel; for this lad is great
And lusty, and knowing both of lance and sword.'

'Tut, tell not me,' said Kay, 'ye are over-fine
To mar stout knaves with foolish courtesies:'
Then mounted, on thro' silent faces rode
Down the slope city, and out beyond the gate.

But by the field of tourney lingering yet
Mutter'd the damsel, 'Wherefore did the King
Scorn me? for, were Sir Lancelot lackt, at least
He might have yielded to me one of those
Who tilt for lady's love and glory here,
Rather than—O sweet heaven! O fie upon him—
His kitchen-knave.'

To whom Sir Gareth drew
(And there were none but few goodlier than he)
Shining in arms, 'Damsel, the quest is mine.
Lead, and I follow.' She thereat, as one
That smells a foul-flesh'd agaric in the holt,
And deems it carrion of some woodland thing,
Or shrew, or weasel, nipt her slender nose
With petulant thumb and finger, shrilling, 'Hence!
Avoid, thou smellest all of kitchen-grease.
And look who comes behind,' for there was Kay.
'Knowest thou not me? thy master? I am Kay.
We lack thee by the hearth.'

And Gareth to him,
'Master no more! too well I know thee, ay—
The most ungentle knight in Arthur's hall.'
'Have at thee then,' said Kay: they shock'd, and Kay
Fell shoulder-slipt, and Gareth cried again,
'Lead, and I follow,' and fast away she fled.

But after sod and shingle ceased to fly
Behind her, and the heart of her good horse
Was nigh to burst with violence of the beat,
Perforce she stay'd, and overtaken spoke.

'What doest thou, scullion, in my fellowship?
Deem'st thou that I accept thee aught the more
Or love thee better, that by some device
Full cowardly, or by mere unhappiness,
Thou hast overthrown and slain thy master—thou!—
Dish-washer and broach-turner, loon!—to me
Thou smellest all of kitchen as before.'

'Damsel,' Sir Gareth answer'd gently, 'say
Whate'er ye will, but whatsoe'er ye say,
I leave not till I finish this fair quest,
Or die therefore.'

'Ay, wilt thou finish it?
Sweet lord, how like a noble knight he talks!
The listening rogue hath caught the manner of it.
But, knave, anon thou shalt be met with, knave,
And then by such a one that thou for all
The kitchen brewis that was ever supt
Shalt not once dare to look him in the face.'

'I shall assay,' said Gareth with a smile
That madden'd her, and away she flash'd again
Down the long avenues of a boundless wood,
And Gareth following was again beknaved.

'Sir Kitchen-knave, I have miss'd the only way

Where Arthur's men are set along the
  wood;
The wood is nigh as full of thieves as
  leaves:
If both be slain, I am rid of thee; but yet,
Sir Scullion, canst thou use that spit of
  thine?
Fight, an thou canst: I have miss'd the
  only way.'

So till the dusk that follow'd evensong
Rode on the two, reviler and reviled;
Then after one long slope was mounted,
  saw,
Bowl-shaped, thro' tops of many thousand
  pines
A gloomy-gladed hollow slowly sink
To westward—in the deeps whereof a
  mere,
Round as the red eye of an Eagle-owl,
Under the half-dead sunset glared; and
  shouts
Ascended, and there brake a servingman
Flying from out of the black wood, and
  crying,
'They have bound my lord to cast him in
  the mere.'
Then Gareth, 'Bound am I to right the
  wrong'd,
But straitlier bound am I to bide with thee.'
And when the damsel spake contempt-
  uously,
'Lead, and I follow,' Gareth cried again,
'Follow, I lead!' so down among the pines
He plunged; and there, blackshadow'd
  nigh the mere,
And mid-thigh-deep in bulrushes and reed,
Saw six tall men haling a seventh along,
A stone about his neck to drown him in it.
Three with good blows he quieted, but
  three
Fled thro' the pines; and Gareth loosed
  the stone
From off his neck, then in the mere beside
Tumbled it; oilily bubbled up the mere.
Last, Gareth loosed his bonds and on free
  feet
Set him, a stalwart Baron, Arthur's friend.

'Well that ye came, or else these caitiff
  rogues

Had wreak'd themselves on me; good
  cause is theirs
To hate me, for my wont hath ever been
To catch my thief, and then like vermin
  here
Drown him, and with a stone about his
  neck;
And under this wan water many of them
Lie rotting, but at night let go the stone,
And rise, and flickering in a grimly light
Dance on the mere. Good now, ye have
  saved a life
Worth somewhat as the cleanser of this
  wood.
And fain would I reward thee worship-
  fully.
What guerdon will ye?'

                    Gareth sharply spake,
'None! for the deed's sake have I done the
  deed,
In uttermost obedience to the King.
But wilt thou yield this damsel harbour-
  age?'

    Whereat the Baron saying, 'I well
      believe
You be of Arthur's Table,' a light laugh
Broke from Lynette, 'Ay, truly of a truth,
And in a sort, being Arthur's kitchen-
  knave!—
But deem not I accept thee aught the
  more,
Scullion, for running sharply with thy spit
Down on a rout of craven foresters.
A thresher with his flail had scatter'd them.
Nay—for thou smellest of the kitchen
  still.
But an this lord will yield us harbourage,
  Well.'

    So she spake. A league beyond the
      wood,
All in a full-fair manor and a rich,
His towers where that day a feast had been
Held in high hall, and many a viand left,
And many a costly cate, received the three.
And there they placed a peacock in his
  pride
Before the damsel, and the Baron set
Gareth beside her, but at once she rose.

'Meseems, that here is much discourtesy,
Setting this knave, Lord Baron, at my side.
Hear me—this morn I stood in Arthur's
   hall,
And pray'd the King would grant me
   Lancelot
To fight the brotherhood of Day and
   Night—
The last a monster unsubduable
Of any save of him for whom I call'd—
Suddenly bawls this frontless kitchen-
   knave,
"The quest is mine; thy kitchen-knave
   am I,
And mighty thro' thy meats and drinks
   am I."
Then Arthur all at once gone mad replies,
"Go therefore," and so gives the quest to
   him—
Him—here—a villain fitter to stick swine
Than ride abroad redressing women's
   wrong,
Or sit beside a noble gentlewoman.'

   Then half-ashamed and part-amazed,
    the lord
Now look'd at one and now at other, left
The damsel by the peacock in his pride,
And, seating Gareth at another board,
Sat down beside him, ate and then began.

   'Friend, whether thou be kitchen-knave,
    or not,
Or whether it be the maiden's fantasy,
And whether she be mad, or else the King,
Or both or neither, or thyself be mad,
I ask not: but thou strikest a strong stroke,
For strong thou art and goodly therewithal,
And saver of my life; and therefore now,
For here be mighty men to joust with,
   weigh
Whether thou wilt not with thy damsel
   back
To crave again Sir Lancelot of the King.
Thy pardon; I but speak for thine avail,
The saver of my life.'

           And Gareth said,
'Full pardon, but I follow up the quest,
Despite of Day and Night and Death and
   Hell.'

So when, next morn, the lord whose life
   he saved
Had, some brief space, convey'd them on
   their way
And left them with God-speed, Sir Gareth
   spake,
'Lead, and I follow.' Haughtily she replied,

   'I fly no more: I allow thee for an hour.
Lion and stoat have isled together, knave,
In time of flood. Nay, furthermore,
   methinks
Some ruth is mine for thee. Back wilt
   thou, fool?
For hard by here is one will overthrow
And slay thee: then will I to court again,
And shame the King for only yielding me
My champion from the ashes of his hearth.'

   To whom Sir Gareth answer'd cour-
    teously,
'Say thou they say, and I will do my deed.
Allow me for mine hour, and thou wilt find
My fortunes all as fair as hers who lay
Among the ashes and wedded the King's
   son.'

   Then to the shore of one of those long
    loops
Wherethro' the serpent river coil'd, they
   came.
Rough-thicketed were the banks and steep;
   the stream
Full, narrow; this a bridge of single arc
Took at a leap; and on the further side
Arose a silk pavilion, gay with gold
In streaks and rays, and all Lent-lily in hue,
Save that the dome was purple, and above,
Crimson, a slender banneret fluttering.
And therebefore the lawless warrior paced
Unarm'd, and calling, 'Damsel, is this he,
The champion thou hast brought from
   Arthur's hall?
For whom we let thee pass.' 'Nay, nay,'
   she said,
'Sir Morning-Star. The King in utter
   scorn
Of thee and thy much folly hath sent thee
   here
His kitchen-knave: and look thou to thy-
   self:

See that he fall not on thee suddenly,
And slay thee unarm'd: he is not knight
  but knave.'

  Then at his call, 'O daughters of the
  Dawn,
And servants of the Morning-Star, ap-
  proach,
Arm me,' from out the silken curtain-folds
Bare-footed and bare-headed three fair
  girls
In gilt and rosy raiment came: their feet
In dewy grasses glisten'd; and the hair
All over glanced with dewdrop or with
  gem
Like sparkles in the stone Avanturine.
These arm'd him in blue arms, and gave a
  shield
Blue also, and thereon the morning star.
And Gareth silent gazed upon the knight,
Who stood a moment, ere his horse was
  brought,
Glorying; and in the stream beneath him,
  shone
Immingled with Heaven's azure waver-
  ingly,
The gay pavilion and the naked feet,
His arms, the rosy raiment, and the star.

  Then she that watch'd him, 'Wherefore
  stare ye so?
Thou shakest in thy fear: there yet is time:
Flee down the valley before he get to
  horse.
Who will cry shame? Thou art not knight
  but knave.'

  Said Gareth, 'Damsel, whether knave or
  knight,
Far liefer had I fight a score of times
Than hear thee so missay me and revile.
Fair words were best for him who fights
  for thee;
But truly foul are better, for they send
That strength of anger thro' mine arms, I
  know
That I shall overthrow him.'

              And he that bore
The star, when mounted, cried from o'er
  the bridge,
'A kitchen-knave, and sent in scorn of me!

Such fight not I, but answer scorn with
  scorn.
For this were shame to do him further
  wrong
Than set him on his feet, and take his horse
And arms, and so return him to the King.
Come, therefore, leave thy lady lightly,
  knave.
Avoid: for it beseemeth not a knave
To ride with such a lady.'

               'Dog, thou liest.
I spring from loftier lineage than thine
  own.'
He spake; and all at fiery speed the two
Shock'd on the central bridge, and either
  spear
Bent but not brake, and either knight at
  once,
Hurl'd as a stone from out of a catapult
Beyond his horse's crupper and the bridge,
Fell, as if dead; but quickly rose and drew,
And Gareth lash'd so fiercely with his
  brand
He drave his enemy backward down the
  bridge,
The damsel crying, 'Well-stricken, kitchen-
  knave!'
Till Gareth's shield was cloven; but one
  stroke
Laid him that clove it grovelling on the
  ground.

  Then cried the fall'n, 'Take not my life:
  I yield.'
And Gareth, 'So this damsel ask it of me
Good—I accord it easily as a grace.'
She reddening, 'Insolent scullion: I of
  thee?
I bound to thee for any favour ask'd!'
'Then shall he die.' And Gareth there
  unlaced
His helmet as to slay him, but she shriek'd,
'Be not so hardy, scullion, as to slay
One nobler than thyself.' 'Damsel, thy
  charge
Is an abounding pleasure to me. Knight,
Thy life is thine at her command. Arise
And quickly pass to Arthur's hall, and say
His kitchen-knave hath sent thee. See thou
  crave

His pardon for thy breaking of his laws.
Myself, when I return, will plead for thee,
Thy shield is mine—farewell; and, damsel,
    thou,
Lead, and I follow.'

               And fast away she fled.
Then when he came upon her, spake,
    'Methought,
Knave, when I watch'd thee striking on
    the bridge
The savour of thy kitchen came upon me
A little faintlier: but the wind hath
    changed:
I scent it twenty-fold.' And then she sang,
'"O morning star" (not that tall felon
    there
Whom thou by sorcery or unhappiness
Or some device, hast foully overthrown),
"O morning star that smilest in the blue,
O star, my morning dream hath proven
    true,
Smile sweetly, thou! my love hath smiled
    on me."

    'But thou begone, take counsel, and
    away,
For hard by here is one that guards a
    ford—
The second brother in their fool's parable—
Will pay thee all thy wages, and to boot.
Care not for shame: thou art not knight
    but knave.'

    To whom Sir Gareth answer'd, laugh-
    ingly,
'Parables? Hear a parable of the knave.
When I was kitchen-knave among the rest
Fierce was the hearth, and one of my co-
    mates
Own'd a rough dog, to whom he cast his
    coat,
"Guard it," and there was none to meddle
    with it.
And such a coat art thou, and thee the
    King
Gave me to guard, and such a dog am I,
To worry, and not to flee—and—knight
    or knave—
The knave that doth thee service as full
    knight

Is all as good, meseems, as any knight
Toward thy sister's freeing.'

              'Ay, Sir Knave!
Ay, knave, because thou strikest as a
    knight,
Being but knave, I hate thee all the more.'

    'Fair damsel, you should worship me
    the more,
That, being but knave, I throw thine
    enemies.'

    'Ay, ay,' she said, 'but thou shalt meet
    thy match.'

So when they touch'd the second river-
    loop,
Huge on a huge red horse, and all in mail
Burnish'd to blinding, shone the Noonday
    Sun
Beyond a ranging shallow. As if the flower,
That blows a globe of after arrowlets,
Ten thousand-fold had grown, flash'd the
    fierce shield,
All sun; and Gareth's eyes had flying blots
Before them when he turn'd from watch-
    ing him.
He from beyond the roaring shallow roar'd,
'What doest thou, brother, in my marches
    here?'
And she athwart the shallow shrill'd again,
'Here is a kitchen-knave from Arthur's
    hall
Hath overthrown thy brother, and hath
    his arms.'
'Ugh!' cried the Sun, and vizoring up a
    red
And cipher face of rounded foolishness,
Push'd horse across the foamings of the
    ford,
Whom Gareth met midstream: no room
    was there
For lance or tourney-skill: four strokes
    they struck
With sword, and these were mighty; the
    new knight
Had fear he might be shamed; but as the
    Sun
Heaved up a ponderous arm to strike the
    fifth,

The hoof of his horse slipt in the stream,
    the stream
Descended, and the Sun was wash'd away.

Then Gareth laid his lance athwart the
    ford;
So drew him home; but he that fought no
    more,
As being all bone-batter'd on the rock,
Yielded; and Gareth sent him to the King.
'Myself when I return will plead for thee.'
'Lead, and I follow.' Quietly she led.
'Hath not the good wind, damsel, changed
    again?'
'Nay, not a point: nor art thou victor here.
There lies a ridge of slate across the ford;
His horse thereon stumbled—ay, for I
    saw it.

'"O Sun" (not this strong fool whom
    thou, Sir Knave,
Hast overthrown thro' mere unhappiness),
"O Sun, that wakenest all to bliss or pain,
O moon, that layest all to sleep again,
Shine sweetly: twice my love hath smiled
    on me."

'What knowest thou of lovesong or of
    love?
Nay, nay, God wot, so thou wert nobly
    born,
Thou hast a pleasant presence. Yea, per-
    chance,—

'"O dewy flowers that open to the sun,
O dewy flowers that close when day is
    done,
Blow sweetly: twice my love hath smiled
    on me."

'What knowest thou of flowers, except,
    belike,
To garnish meats with? hath not our good
    King
Who lent me thee, the flower of kitchen-
    dom,
A foolish love for flowers? what stick ye
    round
The pasty? wherewithal deck the boar's
    head?
Flowers? nay, the boar hath rosemaries
    and bay.

'"O birds, that warble to the morning
    sky,
O birds that warble as the day goes by,
Sing sweetly: twice my love hath smiled
    on me."

'What knowest thou of birds, lark, mavis,
    merle,
Linnet? what dream ye when they utter
    forth
May-music growing with the growing
    light,
Their sweet sun-worship? these be for the
    snare
(So runs thy fancy) these be for the spit,
Larding and basting. See thou have not
    now
Larded thy last, except thou turn and fly.
There stands the third fool of their
    allegory.'

For there beyond a bridge of treble bow,
All in a rose-red from the west, and all
Naked it seem'd, and glowing in the broad
Deep-dimpled current underneath, the
    knight,
That named himself the Star of Evening,
    stood.

And Gareth, 'Wherefore waits the mad-
    man there
Naked in open dayshine?' 'Nay,' she cried,
'Not naked, only wrapt in harden'd skins
That fit him like his own; and so ye cleave
His armour off him, these will turn the
    blade.'

Then the third brother shouted o'er the
    bridge,
'O brother-star, why shine ye here so low?
Thy ward is higher up: but have ye slain
The damsel's champion?' and the damsel
    cried,

'No star of thine, but shot from Arthur's
    heaven
With all disaster unto thine and thee!
For both thy younger brethren have gone
    down
Before this youth; and so wilt thou, Sir
    Star;
Art thou not old?'

'Old, damsel, old and hard,
Old, with the might and breath of twenty
    boys.'
Said Gareth, 'Old, and over-bold in brag!
But that same strength which threw the
    Morning Star
Can throw the Evening.'

                    Then that other blew
A hard and deadly note upon the horn.
'Approach and arm me!' With slow steps
    from out
An old storm-beaten, russet, many-stain'd
Pavilion, forth a grizzled damsel came,
And arm'd him in old arms, and brought
    a helm
With but a drying evergreen for crest,
And gave a shield whereon the Star of
    Even
Half-tarnish'd and half-bright, his emblem,
    shone.
But when it glitter'd o'er the saddle-bow,
They madly hurl'd together on the bridge;
And Gareth overthrew him, lighted, drew,
There met him drawn, and overthrew him
    again,
But up like fire he started: and as oft
As Gareth brought him grovelling on his
    knees,
So many a time he vaulted up again;
Till Gareth panted hard, and his great
    heart,
Foredooming all his trouble was in vain,
Labour'd within him, for he seem'd as one
That all in later, sadder age begins
To war against ill uses of a life,
But these from all his life arise, and cry,
'Thou hast made us lords, and canst not
    put us down!'
He half despairs; so Gareth seem'd to strike
Vainly, the damsel clamouring all the
    while,
'Well done, knave-knight, well stricken, O
    good knight-knave—
O knave, as noble as any of all the knights—
Shame me not, shame me not. I have
    prophesied—
Strike, thou art worthy of the Table
    Round—
His arms are old, he trusts the harden'd
    skin—

Strike—strike—the wind will never change
    again.'
And Gareth hearing ever stronglier smote,
And hew'd great pieces of his armour off
    him,
But lash'd in vain against the harden'd
    skin,
And could not wholly bring him under,
    more
Than loud Southwesterns, rolling ridge on
    ridge,
The buoy that rides at sea, and dips and
    springs
For ever; till at length Sir Gareth's brand
Clash'd his, and brake it utterly to the hilt.
'I have thee now;' but forth that other
    sprang,
And, all unknightlike, writhed his wiry
    arms
Around him, till he felt, despite his mail,
Strangled, but straining ev'n his uttermost
Cast, and so hurl'd him headlong o'er the
    bridge
Down to the river, sink or swim, and cried,
'Lead, and I follow.'

                    But the damsel said,
'I lead no longer; ride thou at my side;
Thou art the kingliest of all kitchen-
    knaves.

'"O trefoil, sparkling on the rainy plain,
O rainbow with three colours after rain,
Shine sweetly: thrice my love hath smiled
    on me."

'Sir,—and, good faith, I fain had added
    —Knight,
But that I heard thee call thyself a knave,—
Shamed am I that I so rebuked, reviled,
Missaid thee; noble I am; and thought the
    King
Scorn'd me and mine; and now thy par-
    don, friend,
For thou hast ever answer'd courteously,
And wholly bold thou art, and meek withal
As any of Arthur's best, but, being knave,
Hast mazed my wit: I marvel what thou art.'

'Damsel,' he said, 'you be not all to
    blame,
Saving that you mistrusted our good King

313

Would handle scorn, or yield you, asking,
    one
Not fit to cope your quest. You said your
    say;
Mine answer was my deed. Good sooth!
    I hold
He scarce is knight, yea but half-man, nor
    meet
To fight for gentle damsel, he, who lets
His heart be stirr'd with any foolish heat
At any gentle damsel's waywardness.
Shamed? care not! thy foul sayings fought
    for me:
And seeing now thy words are fair,
    methinks
There rides no knight, not Lancelot, his
    great self,
Hath force to quell me.'

           Nigh upon that hour
When the lone hern forgets his melancholy,
Lets down his other leg, and stretching,
    dreams
Of goodly supper in the distant pool,
Then turn'd the noble damsel smiling at
    him,
And told him of a cavern hard at hand,
Where bread and baken meats and good
    red wine
Of Southland, which the Lady Lyonors
Had sent her coming champion, waited
    him.

Anon they past a narrow comb wherein
Were slabs of rock with figures, knights on
    horse
Sculptured, and deckt in slowly-waning
    hues.
'Sir Knave, my knight, a hermit once was
    here,
Whose holy hand hath fashion'd on the
    rock
The war of Time against the soul of
    man.
And yon four fools have suck'd their
    allegory
From these damp walls, and taken but the
    form.
Know ye not these?' and Gareth lookt and
    read—
In letters like to those the vexillary

Hath left crag-carven o'er the streaming
    Gelt—
'PHOSPHORUS,' then 'MERIDIES'—'HES-
    PERUS'—
'NOX'—'MORS,' beneath five figures,
    armed men,
Slab after slab, their faces forward all,
And running down the Soul, a Shape that
    fled
With broken wings, torn raiment and loose
    hair,
For help and shelter to the hermit's cave.
'Follow the faces, and we find it. Look,
Who comes behind?'

          For one—delay'd at first
Thro' helping back the dislocated Kay
To Camelot, then by what thereafter
    chanced,
The damsel's headlong error thro' the
    wood—
Sir Lancelot, having swum the river-
    loops—
His blue shield-lions cover'd—softly drew
Behind the twain, and when he saw the
    star
Gleam, on Sir Gareth's turning to him,
    cried,
'Stay, felon knight, I avenge me for my
    friend.'
And Gareth crying prick'd against the cry;
But when they closed—in a moment—at
    one touch
Of that skill'd spear, the wonder of the
    world—
Went sliding down so easily, and fell,
That when he found the grass within his
    hands
He laugh'd; the laughter jarr'd upon
    Lynette:
Harshly she ask'd him, 'Shamed and over-
    thrown,
And tumbled back into the kitchen-knave,
Why laugh ye? that ye blew your boast in
    vain?'
'Nay, noble damsel, but that I, the son
Of old King Lot and good Queen Bellicent,
And victor of the bridges and the ford,
And knight of Arthur, here lie thrown by
    whom
I know not, all thro' mere unhappiness—

Device and sorcery and unhappiness—
Out, sword; we are thrown!' And Lancelot
    answer'd, 'Prince,
O Gareth—thro' the mere unhappiness
Of one who came to help thee, not to harm,
Lancelot, and all as glad to find thee whole,
As on the day when Arthur knighted him.'

    Then Gareth, 'Thou—Lancelot!—thine
    the hand
That threw me? An some chance to mar
    the boast
Thy brethren of thee make—which could
    not chance—
Had sent thee down before a lesser spear,
Shamed had I been, and sad—O Lancelot
    —thou!'

    Whereat the maiden, petulant, 'Lance-
    lot,
Why came ye not, when call'd? and where-
    fore now
Come ye, not call'd? I gloried in my knave,
Who being still rebuked, would answer
    still
Courteous as any knight—but now, if
    knight,
The marvel dies, and leaves me fool'd and
    trick'd,
And only wondering wherefore play'd
    upon:
And doubtful whether I and mine be
    scorn'd.
Where should be truth if not in Arthur's
    hall,
In Arthur's presence? Knight, knave,
    prince and fool,
I hate thee and for ever.'

                    And Lancelot said,
'Blessed be thou, Sir Gareth! knight art
    thou
To the King's best wish. O damsel, be you
    wise
To call him shamed, who is but over-
    thrown?
Thrown have I been, nor once, but many
    a time.
Victor from vanquish'd issues at the last,
And overthrower from being overthrown.
With sword we have not striven; and thy
    good horse

And thou are weary; yet not less I felt
Thy manhood thro' that wearied lance of
    thine.
Well hast thou done; for all the stream is
    freed,
And thou hast wreak'd his justice on his
    foes,
And when reviled, hast answer'd graciously,
And makest merry when overthrown.
    Prince, Knight,
Hail, Knight and Prince, and of our Table
    Round!'

    And then when turning to Lynette he
    told
The tale of Gareth, petulantly she said,
'Ay well—ay well—for worse than being
    fool'd
Of others, is to fool one's self. A cave,
Sir Lancelot, is hard by, with meats and
    drinks
And forage for the horse, and flint for fire.
But all about it flies a honeysuckle.
Seek, till we find.' And when they sought
    and found,
Sir Gareth drank and ate, and all his life
Past into sleep; on whom the maiden
    gazed.
'Sound sleep be thine! sound cause to sleep
    hast thou.
Wake lusty! Seem I not as tender to him
As any mother? Ay, but such a one
As all day long hath rated at her child,
And vext his day, but blesses him asleep—
Good lord, how sweetly smells the honey-
    suckle
In the hush'd night, as if the world were
    one
Of utter peace, and love, and gentleness!
O Lancelot, Lancelot'—and she clapt her
    hands—
'Full merry am I to find my goodly knave
Is knight and noble. See now, sworn have I,
Else yon black felon had not let me pass,
To bring thee back to do the battle with
    him.
Thus an thou goest, he will fight thee first;
Who doubts thee victor? so will my knight-
    knave
Miss the full flower of this accomplish-
    ment.'

Said Lancelot, 'Peradventure he, you name,
May know my shield. Let Gareth, an he will,
Change his for mine, and take my charger, fresh,
Not to be spurr'd, loving the battle as well
As he that rides him.' 'Lancelot-like,' she said,
'Courteous in this, Lord Lancelot, as in all.'

And Gareth, wakening, fiercely clutch'd the shield;
'Ramp ye lance-splintering lions, on whom all spears
Are rotten sticks! ye seem agape to roar!
Yea, ramp and roar at leaving of your lord!—
Care not, good beasts, so well I care for you.
O noble Lancelot, from my hold on these
Streams virtue—fire—thro' one that will not shame
Even the shadow of Lancelot under shield.
Hence: let us go.'

                              Silent the silent field
They traversed. Arthur's harp tho' summer-wan,
In counter motion to the clouds, allured
The glance of Gareth dreaming on his
  ͵ liege.
A star shot: 'Lo,' said Gareth, 'the foe
  ͵ falls!'
An owl whoopt: 'Hark the victor pealing there!'
Suddenly she that rode upon his left
Clung to the shield that Lancelot lent him, crying,
'Yield, yield him this again: 'tis he must fight:
I curse the tongue that all thro yesterday
Reviled thee, and hath wrought on Lancelot now
To lend thee horse and shield: wonders ye have done;
Miracles ye cannot: here is glory enow
In having flung the three: I see thee maim'd,
Mangled: I swear thou canst not fling the fourth.'

'And wherefore, damsel? tell me all ye know.
You cannot scare me; nor rough face, or voice,
Brute bulk of limb, or boundless savagery
Appal me from the quest.'

                              'Nay, Prince,' she cried,
'God wot, I never look'd upon the face,
Seeing he never rides abroad by day;
But watch'd him have I like a phantom pass
Chilling the night: nor have I heard the voice.
Always he made his mouthpiece of a page
Who came and went, and still reported him
As closing in himself the strength of ten,
And when his anger tare him, massacring
Man, woman, lad and girl—yea, the soft babe!
Some hold that he hath swallow'd infant flesh,
Monster! O Prince, I went for Lancelot first,
The quest is Lancelot's: give him back the shield.'

Said Gareth laughing, 'An he fight for this,
Belike he wins it as the better man:
Thus—and not else!'

                              But Lancelot on him urged
All the devisings of their chivalry
When one might meet a mightier than himself;
How best to manage horse, lance, sword and shield,
And so fill up the gap where force might fail
With skill and fineness. Instant were his words.

Then Gareth, 'Here be rules. I know but one—
To dash against mine enemy and to win.
Yet have I watch'd thee victor in the joust,
And seen thy way.' 'Heaven help thee,' sigh'd Lynette.

Then for a space, and under cloud that grew

To thunder-gloom palling all stars, they
   rode
In converse till she made her palfrey halt,
Lifted an arm, and softly whisper'd
   'There.'
And all the three were silent seeing, pitch'd
Beside the Castle Perilous on flat field,
A huge pavilion like a mountain peak
Sunder the glooming crimson on the
   marge,
Black, with black banner, and a long black
   horn
Beside it hanging; which Sir Gareth graspt,
And so, before the two could hinder him,
Sent all his heart and breath thro' all the
   horn.
Echo'd the walls; a light twinkled; anon
Came lights and lights, and once again he
   blew;
Whereon were hollow tramplings up and
   down
And muffled voices heard, and shadows
   past;
Till high above him, circled with her maids,
The Lady Lyonors at a window stood,
Beautiful among lights, and waving to him
White hands, and courtesy; but when the
   Prince
Three times had blown—after long hush—
   at last—
The huge pavilion slowly yielded up,
Thro' those black foldings, that which
   housed therein.
High on a nightblack horse, in nightblack
   arms,
With white breast-bone, and barren ribs of
   Death,
And crown'd with fleshless laughter—
   some ten steps—
In the half-light—thro' the dim dawn—
   advanced
The monster, and then paused, and spake
   no word.

But Gareth spake and all indignantly,
'Fool, for thou hast, men say, the strength
   of ten,
Canst thou not trust the limbs thy God
   hath given,
But must, to make the terror of thee more,
Trick thyself out in ghastly imageries

Of that which Life hath done with, and the
   clod,
Less dull than thou, will hide with mantling
   flowers
As if for pity?' But he spake no word;
Which set the horror higher: a maiden
   swoon'd;
The Lady Lyonors wrung her hands and
   wept,
As doom'd to be the bride of Night and
   Death;
Sir Gareth's head prickled beneath his
   helm;
And ev'n Sir Lancelot thro' his warm
   blood felt
Ice strike, and all that mark'd him were
   aghast.

At once Sir Lancelot's charger fiercely
   neigh'd,
And Death's dark war-horse bounded for-
   ward with him.
Then those that did not blink the terror,
   saw
That Death was cast to ground, and slowly
   rose.
But with one stroke Sir Gareth split the
   skull.
Half fell to right and half to left and lay.
Then with a stronger buffet he clove the
   helm
As throughly as the skull; and out from
   this
Issued the bright face of a blooming boy
Fresh as a flower new-born, and crying,
   'Knight,
Slay me not: my three brethren bad me
   do it,
To make a horror all about the house,
And stay the world from Lady Lyonors.
They never dream'd the passes would be
   past.'
Answer'd Sir Gareth graciously to one
Not many a moon his younger, 'My fair
   child,
What madness made thee challenge the
   chief knight
Of Arthur's hall?' 'Fair Sir, they bad me
   do it.
They hate the King, and Lancelot, the
   King's friend,

They hoped to slay him somewhere on the stream,
They never dream'd the passes could be past.'

Then sprang the happier day from underground;
And Lady Lyonors and her house, with dance
And revel and song, made merry over Death,
As being after all their foolish fears
And horrors only proven a blooming boy.
So large mirth lived and Gareth won the quest.

And he that told the tale in older times
Says that Sir Gareth wedded Lyonors,
But he, that told it later, says Lynette.

THE MARRIAGE OF GERAINT

THE brave Geraint, a knight of Arthur's court,
A tributary prince of Devon, one
Of that great Order of the Table Round,
Had married Enid, Yniol's only child,
And loved her, as he loved the light of Heaven.
And as the light of Heaven varies, now
At sunrise, now at sunset, now by night
With moon and trembling stars, so loved Geraint
To make her beauty vary day by day,
In crimsons and in purples and in gems.
And Enid, but to please her husband's eye,
Who first had found and loved her in a state
Of broken fortunes, daily fronted him
In some fresh splendour; and the Queen herself,
Grateful to Prince Geraint for service done,
Loved her, and often with her own white hands
Array'd and deck'd her, as the loveliest,
Next after her own self, in all the court.
And Enid loved the Queen, and with true heart
Adored her, as the stateliest and the best
And loveliest of all women upon earth.
And seeing them so tender and so close,

Long in their common love rejoiced Geraint.
But when a rumour rose about the Queen,
Touching her guilty love for Lancelot,
Tho' yet there lived no proof, nor yet was heard
The world's loud whisper breaking into storm,
Not less Geraint believed it; and there fell
A horror on him, lest his gentle wife,
Thro' that great tenderness for Guinevere,
Had suffer'd, or should suffer any taint
In nature: wherefore going to the King,
He made this pretext, that his princedom lay
Close on the borders of a territory,
Wherein were bandit earls, and caitiff knights,
Assassins, and all flyers from the hand
Of Justice, and whatever loathes a law:
And therefore, till the King himself should please
To cleanse this common sewer of all his realm,
He craved a fair permission to depart,
And there defend his marches; and the King
Mused for a little on his plea, but, last,
Allowing it, the Prince and Enid rode,
And fifty knights rode with them, to the shores
Of Severn, and they past to their own land;
Where, thinking, that if ever yet was wife
True to her lord, mine shall be so to me,
He compass'd her with sweet observances
And worship, never leaving her, and grew
Forgetful of his promise to the King,
Forgetful of the falcon and the hunt,
Forgetful of the tilt and tournament,
Forgetful of his glory and his name,
Forgetful of his princedom and its cares.
And this forgetfulness was hateful to her.
And by and by the people, when they met
In twos and threes, or fuller companies,
Began to scoff and jeer and babble of him
As of a prince whose manhood was all gone,
And molten down in mere uxoriousness.
And this she gather'd from the people's eyes:
This too the women who attired her head,

To please her, dwelling on his boundless
love,
Told Enid, and they sadden'd her the
more:
And day by day she thought to tell Geraint,
But could not out of bashful delicacy;
While he that watch'd her sadden, was the
more
Suspicious that her nature had a taint.

At last, it chanced that on a summer
morn
(They sleeping each by either) the new sun
Beat thro' the blindless casement of the
room,
And heated the strong warrior in his
dreams;
Who, moving, cast the coverlet aside,
And bared the knotted column of his
throat,
The massive square of his heroic breast,
And arms on which the standing muscle
sloped,
As slopes a wild brook o'er a little stone,
Running too vehemently to break upon it.
And Enid woke and sat beside the couch,
Admiring him, and thought within herself,
Was ever man so grandly made as he?
Then, like a shadow, past the people's
talk
And accusation of uxoriousness
Across her mind, and bowing over him,
Low to her own heart piteously she said:

'O noble breast and all-puissant arms,
Am I the cause, I the poor cause that men
Reproach you, saying all your force is
gone?
I *am* the cause, because I dare not speak
And tell him what I think and what they
say.
And yet I hate that he should linger here;
I cannot love my lord and not his name.
Far liefer had I gird his harness on him,
And ride with him to battle and stand by,
And watch his mightful hand striking great
blows
At caitiffs and at wrongers of the world.
Far better were I laid in the dark earth,
Not hearing any more his noble voice,
Not to be folded more in these dear arms,

And darken'd from the high light in his
eyes,
Than that my lord thro' me should suffer
shame.
Am I so bold, and could I so stand by,
And see my dear lord wounded in the strife,
Or maybe pierced to death before mine
eyes,
And yet not dare to tell him what I think,
And how men slur him, saying all his force
Is melted into mere effeminacy?
O me, I fear that I am no true wife.'

Half inwardly, half audibly she spoke,
And the strong passion in her made her
weep
True tears upon his broad and naked
breast,
And these awoke him, and by great mis-
chance
He heard but fragments of her later words,
And that she fear'd she was not a true wife.
And then he thought, 'In spite of all my
care,
For all my pains, poor man, for all my
pains,
She is not faithful to me, and I see her
Weeping for some gay knight in Arthur's
hall.'
Then tho' he loved and reverenced her too
much
To dream she could be guilty of foul act,
Right thro' his manful breast darted the
pang
That makes a man, in the sweet face of her
Whom he loves most, lonely and miserable.
At this he hurl'd his huge limbs out of bed,
And shook his drowsy squire awake and
cried,
'My charger and her palfrey;' then to her,
'I will ride forth into the wilderness;
For tho' it seems my spurs are yet to win,
I have not fall'n so low as some would wish.
And thou, put on thy worst and meanest
dress
And ride with me.' And Enid ask'd,
amazed,
'If Enid errs, let Enid learn her fault.'
But he, 'I charge thee, ask not, but obey.'
Then she bethought her of a faded silk,
A faded mantle and a faded veil,

And moving toward a cedarn cabinet,
Wherein she kept them folded reverently
With sprigs of summer laid between the
    folds,
She took them, and array'd herself therein,
Remembering when first he came on her
Drest in that dress, and how he loved her
    in it,
And all her foolish fears about the dress,
And all his journey to her, as himself
Had told her, and their coming to the
    court.

For Arthur on the Whitsuntide before
Held court at old Caerleon upon Usk.
There on a day, he sitting high in hall,
Before him came a forester of Dean,
Wet from the woods, with notice of a hart
Taller than all his fellows, milky-white,
First seen that day: these things he told the
    King.
Then the good King gave order to let blow
His horns for hunting on the morrow morn.
And when the Queen petition'd for his
    leave
To see the hunt, allow'd it easily.
So with the morning all the court were
    gone.
But Guinevere lay late into the morn,
Lost in sweet dreams, and dreaming of her
    love
For Lancelot, and forgetful of the hunt;
But rose at last, a single maiden with her,
Took horse, and forded Usk, and gain'd
    the wood;
There, on a little knoll beside it, stay'd
Waiting to hear the hounds; but heard
    instead
A sudden sound of hoofs, for Prince
    Geraint,
Late also, wearing neither hunting-dress
Nor weapon, save a golden-hilted brand,
Came quickly flashing thro' the shallow
    ford
Behind them, and so gallop'd up the knoll.
A purple scarf, at either end whereof
There swung an apple of the purest gold,
Sway'd round about him, as he gallop'd up
To join them, glancing like a dragon-fly
In summer suit and silks of holiday.
Low bow'd the tributary Prince, and she

Sweetly and statelily, and with all grace
Of womanhood and queenhood, answer'd
    him:
'Late, late, Sir Prince,' she said, 'later
    than we!'
'Yea, noble Queen,' he answer'd, 'and so
    late
That I but come like you to see the hunt,
Not join it.' 'Therefore wait with me,' she
    said;
'For on this little knoll, if anywhere,
There is good chance that we shall hear the
    hounds:
Here often they break covert at our feet.'

And while they listen'd for the distant
    hunt,
And chiefly for the baying of Cavall,
King Arthur's hound of deepest mouth,
    there rode
Full slowly by a knight, lady, and dwarf;
Whereof the dwarf lagg'd latest, and the
    knight
Had vizor up, and show'd a youthful face,
Imperious, and of haughtiest lineaments.
And Guinevere, not mindful of his face
In the King's hall, desired his name, and
    sent
Her maiden to demand it of the dwarf;
Who being vicious, old and irritable,
And doubling all his master's vice of pride,
Made answer sharply that she should not
    know.
'Then will I ask it of himself,' she said.
'Nay, by my faith, thou shalt not,' cried
    the dwarf;
'Thou art not worthy ev'n to speak of him;'
And when she put her horse toward the
    knight,
Struck at her with his whip, and she
    return'd
Indignant to the Queen; whereat Geraint
Exclaiming, 'Surely I will learn the name,'
Made sharply to the dwarf, and ask'd it of
    him,
Who answer'd as before; and when the
    Prince
Had put his horse in motion toward the
    knight,
Struck at him with his whip, and cut his
    cheek.

The Prince's blood spirted upon the scarf,
Dyeing it; and his quick, instinctive hand
Caught at the hilt, as to abolish him:
But he, from his exceeding manfulness
And pure nobility of temperament,
Wroth to be wroth at such a worm,
  refrain'd
From ev'n a word, and so returning said:

'I will avenge this insult, noble Queen,
Done in your maiden's person to yourself:
And I will track this vermin to their
  earths:
For tho' I ride unarm'd, I do not doubt
To find, at some place I shall come at, arms
On loan, or else for pledge; and, being
  found,
Then will I fight him, and will break his
  pride
And on the third day will again be here,
So that I be not fall'n in fight. Farewell.'

'Farewell, fair Prince,' answer'd the
  stately Queen.
'Be prosperous in this journey, as in all;
And may you light on all things that you
  love,
And live to wed with her whom first you
  love:
But ere you wed with any, bring your
  bride,
And I, were she the daughter of a king,
Yea, tho' she were a beggar from the hedge,
Will clothe her for her bridals like the sun.'

And Prince Geraint, now thinking that
  he heard
The noble hart at bay, now the far horn,
A little vext at losing of the hunt,
A little at the vile occasion, rode,
By ups and downs, thro' many a grassy
  glade
And valley, with fixt eye following the
  three.
At last they issued from the world of wood,
And climb'd upon a fair and even ridge,
And show'd themselves against the sky,
  and sank.
And thither came Geraint, and underneath
Beheld the long street of a little town
In a long valley, on one side whereof,

White from the mason's hand, a fortress
  rose;
And on one side a castle in decay,
Beyond a bridge that spann'd a dry ravine:
And out of town and valley came a noise
As of a broad brook o'er a shingly bed
Brawling, or like a clamour of the rooks
At distance, ere they settle for the night.

And onward to the fortress rode the
  three,
And enter'd, and were lost behind the
  walls.
'So,' thought Geraint, 'I have track'd him
  to his earth.'
And down the long street riding wearily,
Found every hostel full, and everywhere
Was hammer laid to hoof, and the hot hiss
And bustling whistle of the youth who
  scour'd
His master's armour; and of such a one
He ask'd, 'What means the tumult in the
  town?'
Who told him, scouring still, 'The sparrow-
  hawk!'
Then riding close behind an ancient churl,
Who, smitten by the dusty sloping beam,
Went sweating underneath a sack of corn,
Ask'd yet once more what meant the hub-
  bub here?
Who answer'd gruffly, 'Ugh! the sparrow-
  hawk.'
Then riding further past an armourer's,
Who, with back turn'd, and bow'd above
  his work,
Sat riveting a helmet on his knee,
He put the self-same query, but the man
Not turning round, nor looking at him,
  said:
'Friend, he that labours for the sparrow-
  hawk
Has little time for idle questioners.'
Whereat Geraint flash'd into sudden
  spleen:
'A thousand pips eat up your sparrow-
  hawk!
Tits, wrens, and all wing'd nothings peck
  him dead!
Ye think the rustic cackle of your bourg
The murmur of the world! What is it
  to me?

O wretched set of sparrows, one and all,
Who pipe of nothing but of sparrow-
hawks!
Speak, if ye be not like the rest, hawk-mad,
Where can I get me harbourage for the
night?
And arms, arms, arms to fight my enemy?
Speak!'
Whereat the armourer turning all amazed
And seeing one so gay in purple silks,
Came forward with the helmet yet in hand
And answer'd, 'Pardon me, O stranger
knight;
We hold a tourney here to-morrow morn,
And there is scantly time for half the work.
Arms? truth! I know not: all are wanted
here.
Harbourage? truth, good truth, I know
not, save,
It may be, at Earl Yniol's, o'er the bridge
Yonder.' He spoke and fell to work again.

Then rode Geraint, a little spleenful yet,
Across the bridge that spann'd the dry
ravine.
There musing sat the hoary-headed Earl,
(His dress a suit of fray'd magnificence,
Once fit for feasts of ceremony) and said:
'Whither, fair son?' to whom Geraint
replied,
'O friend, I seek a harbourage for the
night.'
Then Yniol, 'Enter therefore and partake
The slender entertainment of a house
Once rich, now poor, but ever open-
door'd.'
'Thanks, venerable friend,' replied Geraint;
'So that ye do not serve me sparrow-hawks
For supper, I will enter, I will eat
With all the passion of a twelve hours' fast.'
Then sigh'd and smiled the hoary-headed
Earl,
And answer'd, 'Graver cause than yours is
mine
To curse this hedgerow thief, the sparrow-
hawk:
But in, go in; for save yourself desire it,
We will not touch upon him ev'n in jest.'

Then rode Geraint into the castle court,
His charger trampling many a prickly star

Of sprouted thistle on the broken stones.
He look'd and saw that all was ruinous.
Here stood a shatter'd archway plumed
with fern;
And here had fall'n a great part of a tower,
Whole, like a crag that tumbles from the
cliff,
And like a crag was gay with wilding
flowers:
And high above a piece of turret stair,
Worn by the feet that now were silent,
wound
Bare to the sun, and monstrous ivy-stems
Claspt the gray walls with hairy-fibred
arms,
And suck'd the joining of the stones, and
look'd
A knot, beneath, of snakes, aloft, a grove.

And while he waited in the castle court,
The voice of Enid, Yniol's daughter, rang
Clear thro' the open casement of the hall,
Singing; and as the sweet voice of a bird,
Heard by the lander in a lonely isle,
Moves him to think what kind of bird it is
That sings so delicately clear, and make
Conjecture of the plumage and the form;
So the sweet voice of Enid moved Geraint;
And made him like a man abroad at morn
When first the liquid note beloved of men
Comes flying over many a windy wave
To Britain, and in April suddenly
Breaks from a coppice gemm'd with green
and red,
And he suspends his converse with a friend,
Or it may be the labour of his hands,
To think or say, 'There is the nightingale;'
So fared it with Geraint, who thought and
said,
'Here, by God's grace, is the one voice
for me.'

It chanced the song that Enid sang was
one
Of Fortune and her wheel, and Enid sang:

'Turn, Fortune, turn thy wheel and
lower the proud;
Turn thy wild wheel thro' sunshine, storm,
and cloud;
Thy wheel and thee we neither love nor hate.

'Turn, Fortune, turn thy wheel with
      smile or frown;
With that wild wheel we go not up or
      down;
Our hoard is little, but our hearts are great.

  'Smile and we smile, the lords of many
      lands;
Frown and we smile, the lords of our own
      hands;
For man is man and master of his fate.

  'Turn, turn thy wheel above the staring
      crowd;
Thy wheel and thou are shadows in the
      cloud;
Thy wheel and thee we neither love nor
      hate.'

  'Hark, by the bird's song ye may learn
      the nest,'
Said Yniol; 'enter quickly.' Entering then,
Right o'er a mount of newly-fallen stones,
The dusky-rafter'd many-cobweb'd hall,
He found an ancient dame in dim brocade;
And near her, like a blossom vermeil-
      white,
That lightly breaks a faded flower-sheath,
Moved the fair Enid, all in faded silk,
Her daughter. In a moment thought
      Geraint,
'Here by God's rood is the one maid for me.'
But none spake word except the hoary
      Earl:
'Enid, the good knight's horse stands in
      the court;
Take him to stall, and give him corn, and
      then
Go to the town and buy us flesh and wine;
And we will make us merry as we may.
Our hoard is little, but our hearts are
      great.'

  He spake: the Prince, as Enid past him,
      fain
To follow, strode a stride, but Yniol caught
His purple scarf, and held, and said, 'For-
      bear!
Rest! the good house, tho' ruin'd, O my son,
Endures not that her guest should serve
      himself.'

And reverencing the custom of the house
Geraint, from utter courtesy, forbore.

  So Enid took his charger to the stall;
And after went her way across the bridge,
And reach'd the town, and while the
      Prince and Earl
Yet spoke together, came again with one,
A youth, that following with a costrel bore
The means of goodly welcome, flesh and
      wine.
And Enid brought sweet cakes to make
      them cheer,
And in her veil enfolded, manchet bread.
And then, because their hall must also
      serve
For kitchen, boil'd the flesh, and spread
      the board,
And stood behind, and waited on the three.
And seeing her so sweet and serviceable,
Geraint had longing in him evermore
To stoop and kiss the tender little thumb,
That crost the trencher as she laid it down:
But after all had eaten, then Geraint,
For now the wine made summer in his
      veins,
Let his eye rove in following, or rest
On Enid at her lowly handmaid-work,
Now here, now there, about the dusky
      hall;
Then suddenly addrest the hoary Earl:

  'Fair Host and Earl, I pray your
      courtesy;
This sparrow-hawk, what is he? tell me of
      him.
His name? but no, good faith, I will not
      have it:
For if he be the knight whom late I saw
Ride into that new fortress by your town,
White from the mason's hand, then have I
      sworn
From his own lips to have it—I am Geraint
Of Devon—for this morning when the
      Queen
Sent her own maiden to demand the name,
His dwarf, a vicious under-shapen thing,
Struck at her with his whip, and she
      return'd
Indignant to the Queen; and then I swore
That I would track this caitiff to his hold,

And fight and break his pride, and have it
of him.
And all unarm'd I rode, and thought to
find
Arms in your town, where all the men are
mad;
They take the rustic murmur of their bourg
For the great wave that echoes round the
world;
They would not hear me speak: but if ye
know
Where I can light on arms, or if yourself
Should have them, tell me, seeing I have
sworn
That I will break his pride and learn his
name,
Avenging this great insult done the Queen.'

Then cried Earl Yniol, 'Art thou he
indeed,
Geraint, a name far-sounded among men
For noble deeds? and truly I, when first
I saw you moving by me on the bridge,
Felt ye were somewhat, yea, and by your
state
And presence might have guess'd you one
of those
That eat in Arthur's hall at Camelot.
Nor speak I now from foolish flattery;
For this dear child hath often heard me
praise
Your feats of arms, and often when I
paused
Hath ask'd again, and ever loved to hear;
So grateful is the noise of noble deeds
To noble hearts who see but acts of wrong:
O never yet had woman such a pair
Of suitors as this maiden; first Limours,
A creature wholly given to brawls and wine,
Drunk even when he woo'd; and be he
dead
I know not, but he past to the wild land.
The second was your foe, the sparrow-
hawk,
My curse, my nephew—I will not let his
name
Slip from my lips if I can help it—he,
When I that knew him fierce and turbulent
Refused her to him, then his pride awoke;
And since the proud man often is the mean,
He sow'd a slander in the common ear,

Affirming that his father left him gold,
And in my charge, which was not ren-
der'd to him;
Bribed with large promises the men who
served
About my person, the more easily
Because my means were somewhat broken
into
Thro' open doors and hospitality;
Raised my own town against me in the
night
Before my Enid's birthday, sack'd my
house;
From mine own earldom foully ousted me;
Built that new fort to overawe my friends,
For truly there are those who love me yet;
And keeps me in this ruinous castle here,
Where doubtless he would put me soon to
death,
But that his pride too much despises me:
And I myself sometimes despise myself;
For I have let men be, and have their way;
Am much too gentle, have not used my
power:
Nor know I whether I be very base
Or very manful, whether very wise
Or very foolish; only this I know,
That whatsoever evil happen to me,
I seem to suffer nothing heart or limb,
But can endure it all most patiently.'

'Well said, true heart,' replied Geraint,
'but arms,
That if the sparrow-hawk, this nephew,
fight
In next day's tourney I may break his pride.'

And Yniol answer'd, 'Arms, indeed, but
old
And rusty, old and rusty, Prince Geraint,
Are mine, and therefore at thine asking,
thine.
But in this tournament can no man tilt,
Except the lady he loves best be there.
Two forks are fixt into the meadow ground,
And over these is placed a silver wand,
And over that a golden sparrow-hawk,
The prize of beauty for the fairest there.
And this, what knight soever be in field
Lays claim to for the lady at his side,
And tilts with my good nephew thereupon,

Who being apt at arms and big of bone
Has ever won it for the lady with him,
And toppling over all antagonism
Has earn'd himself the name of sparrow-
hawk.
But thou, that hast no lady, canst not fight.'

To whom Geraint with eyes all bright
replied,
Leaning a little toward him, 'Thy leave!
Let *me* lay lance in rest, O noble host,
For this dear child, because I never saw,
Tho' having seen all beauties of our time,
Nor can see elsewhere, anything so fair.
And if I fall her name will yet remain
Untarnish'd as before; but if I live,
So aid me Heaven when at mine utter-
most,
As I will make her truly my true wife.'

Then, howsoever patient, Yniol's heart
Danced in his bosom, seeing better days.
And looking round he saw not Enid there,
(Who hearing her own name had stol'n
away)
But that old dame, to whom full tenderly
And fondling all her hand in his he said,
'Mother, a maiden is a tender thing,
And best by her that bore her understood.
Go thou to rest, but ere thou go to rest
Tell her, and prove her heart toward the
Prince.'

So spake the kindly-hearted Earl, and
she
With frequent smile and nod departing
found,
Half disarray'd as to her rest, the girl;
Whom first she kiss'd on either cheek, and
then
On either shining shoulder laid a hand,
And kept her off and gazed upon her face,
And told her all their converse in the hall,
Proving her heart: but never light and
shade
Coursed one another more on open ground
Beneath a troubled heaven, than red and
pale
Across the face of Enid hearing her;
While slowly falling as a scale that falls,
When weight is added only grain by grain,

Sank her sweet head upon her gentle
breast;
Nor did she lift an eye nor speak a word,
Rapt in the fear and in the wonder of it;
So moving without answer to her rest
She found no rest, and ever fail'd to draw
The quiet night into her blood, but lay
Contemplating her own unworthiness;
And when the pale and bloodless east
began
To quicken to the sun, arose, and raised
Her mother too, and hand in hand they
moved
Down to the meadow where the jousts were
held,
And waited there for Yniol and Geraint.

And thither came the twain, and when
Geraint
Beheld her first in field, awaiting him,
He felt, were she the prize of bodily force,
Himself beyond the rest pushing could
move
The chair of Idris. Yniol's rusted arms
Were on his princely person, but thro'
these
Princelike his bearing shone; and errant
knights
And ladies came, and by and by the town
Flow'd in, and settling circled all the lists.
And there they fixt the forks into the
ground,
And over these they placed the silver wand,
And over that the golden sparrow-hawk.
Then Yniol's nephew, after trumpet blown,
Spake to the lady with him and pro-
claim'd,
'Advance and take, as fairest of the fair,
What I these two years past have won for
thee,
The prize of beauty.' Loudly spake the
Prince,
'Forbear: there is a worthier,' and the
knight
With some surprise and thrice as much
disdain
Turn'd, and beheld the four, and all his
face
Glow'd like the heart of a great fire at Yule,
So burnt he was with passion, crying out,
'Do battle for it then,' no more; and thrice

They clash'd together, and thrice they
    brake their spears.
Then each, dishorsed and drawing, lash'd
    at each
So often and with such blows, that all the
    crowd
Wonder'd, and now and then from distant
    walls
There came a clapping as of phantom hands.
So twice they fought, and twice they
    breathed, and still
The dew of their great labour, and the
    blood
Of their strong bodies, flowing, drain'd
    their force.
But either's force was match'd till Yniol's
    cry,
'Remember that great insult done the
    Queen,'
Increased Geraint's, who heaved his blade
    aloft,
And crack'd the helmet thro', and bit the
    bone,
And fell'd him, and set foot upon his breast,
And said, 'Thy name?' To whom the
    fallen man
Made answer, groaning, 'Edyrn, son of
    Nudd!
Ashamed am I that I should tell it thee.
My pride is broken: men have seen my
    fall.'
'Then, Edyrn, son of Nudd,' replied
    Geraint,
'These two things shalt thou do, or else
    thou diest.
First, thou thyself, with damsel and with
    dwarf,
Shalt ride to Arthur's court, and coming
    there,
Crave pardon for that insult done the
    Queen,
And shalt abide her judgment on it; next,
Thou shalt give back their earldom to thy
    kin.
These two things shalt thou do, or thou
    shalt die.'
And Edyrn answer'd, 'These things will
    I do,
For I have never yet been overthrown,
And thou hast overthrown me, and my
    pride

Is broken down, for Enid sees my fall!'
And rising up, he rode to Arthur's court,
And there the Queen forgave him easily.
And being young, he changed and came to
    loathe
His crime of traitor, slowly drew himself
Bright from his old dark life, and fell at last
In the great battle fighting for the King.

But when the third day from the hunting-
    morn
Made a low splendour in the world, and
    wings
Moved in her ivy, Enid, for she lay
With her fair head in the dim-yellow light,
Among the dancing shadows of the birds,
Woke and bethought her of her promise
    given
No later than last eve to Prince Geraint—
So bent he seem'd on going the third day,
He would not leave her, till her promise
    given—
To ride with him this morning to the court,
And there be made known to the stately
    Queen,
And there be wedded with all ceremony.
At this she cast her eyes upon her dress,
And thought it never yet had look'd so
    mean.
For as a leaf in mid-November is
To what it was in mid-October, seem'd
The dress that now she look'd on to the
    dress
She look'd on ere the coming of Geraint.
And still she look'd, and still the terror
    grew
Of that strange bright and dreadful thing,
    a court,
All staring at her in her faded silk:
And softly to her own sweet heart she said:

'This noble prince who won our earldom
    back,
So splendid in his acts and his attire,
Sweet heaven, how much I shall discredit
    him!
Would he could tarry with us here awhile
But being so beholden to the Prince,
It were but little grace in any of us,
Bent as he seem'd on going this third day,
To seek a second favour at his hands.

Yet if he could but tarry a day or two,
Myself would work eye dim, and finger lame,
Far liefer than so much discredit him.'

And Enid fell in longing for a dress
All branch'd and flower'd with gold, a costly gift
Of her good mother, given her on the night
Before her birthday, three sad years ago,
That night of fire, when Edyrn sack'd their house,
And scatter'd all they had to all the winds:
For while the mother show'd it, and the two
Were turning and admiring it, the work
To both appear'd so costly, rose a cry
That Edyrn's men were on them, and they fled
With little save the jewels they had on,
Which being sold and sold had bought them bread:
And Edyrn's men had caught them in their flight,
And placed them in this ruin; and she wish'd
The Prince had found her in her ancient home;
Then let her fancy flit across the past,
And roam the goodly places that she knew;
And last bethought her how she used to watch,
Near that old home, a pool of golden carp;
And one was patch'd and blurr'd and lustreless
Among his burnish'd brethren of the pool;
And half asleep she made comparison
Of that and these to her own faded self
And the gay court, and fell asleep again;
And dreamt herself was such a faded form
Among her burnish'd sisters of the pool;
But this was in the garden of a king;
And tho' she lay dark in the pool, she knew
That all was bright; that all about were birds
Of sunny plume in gilded trellis-work;
That all the turf was rich in plots that look'd
Each like a garnet or a turkis in it;
And lords and ladies of the high court went
In silver tissue talking things of state;

And children of the King in cloth of gold
Glanced at the doors or gambol'd down the walks;
And while she thought 'They will not see me,' came
A stately queen whose name was Guinevere,
And all the children in their cloth of gold
Ran to her, crying, 'If we have fish at all
Let them be gold; and charge the gardeners now
To pick the faded creature from the pool,
And cast it on the mixen that it die.'
And therewithal one came and seized on her,
And Enid started waking, with her heart
All overshadow'd by the foolish dream,
And lo! it was her mother grasping her
To get her well awake; and in her hand
A suit of bright apparel, which she laid
Flat on the couch, and spoke exultingly:

'See here, my child, how fresh the colours look,
How fast they hold like colours of a shell
That keeps the wear and polish of the wave.
Why not? It never yet was worn, I trow:
Look on it, child, and tell me if ye know it.'

And Enid look'd, but all confused at first,
Could scarce divide it from her foolish dream:
Then suddenly she knew it and rejoiced,
And answer'd, 'Yea, I know it; your good gift,
So sadly lost on that unhappy night;
Your own good gift!' 'Yea, surely,' said the dame,
'And gladly given again this happy morn.
For when the jousts were ended yesterday,
Went Yniol thro' the town, and everywhere
He found the sack and plunder of our house
All scatter'd thro' the houses of the town;
And gave command that all which once was ours
Should now be ours again: and yester-eve,
While ye were talking sweetly with your Prince,

Came one with this and laid it in my hand,
For love or fear, or seeking favour of us,
Because we have our earldom back again.
And yester-eve I would not tell you of it,
But kept it for a sweet surprise at morn.
Yea, truly is it not a sweet surprise?
For I myself unwillingly have worn
My faded suit, as you, my child, have
    yours,
And howsoever patient, Yniol his.
Ah, dear, he took me from a goodly house,
With store of rich apparel, sumptuous fare,
And page, and maid, and squire, and
    seneschal,
And pastime both of hawk and hound, and
    all
That appertains to noble maintenance.
Yea, and he brought me to a goodly house;
But since our fortune swerved from sun to
    shade,
And all thro' that young traitor, cruel need
Constrain'd us, but a better time has
    come;
So clothe yourself in this, that better fits
Our mended fortunes and a Prince's bride:
For tho' ye won the prize of fairest fair,
And tho' I heard him call you fairest fair,
Let never maiden think, however fair,
She is not fairer in new clothes than old.
And should some great court-lady say, the
    Prince
Hath pick'd a ragged-robin from the hedge,
And like a madman brought her to the
    court,
Then were ye shamed, and, and, worse, might
    shame the Prince
To whom we are beholden; but I know,
When my dear child is set forth at her best,
That neither court nor country, tho' they
    sought
Thro' all the provinces like those of old
That lighted on Queen Esther, has her
    match.'

    Here ceased the kindly mother out of
        breath;
And Enid listen'd brightening as she lay;
Then, as the white and glittering star of
    morn
Parts from a bank of snow, and by and by
Slips into golden cloud, the maiden rose,

And left her maiden couch,
    self,
Help'd by the mother's care
    eye,
Without a mirror, in the g
Who, after, turn'd her daugh
    said,
She never yet had seen her
And call'd her like that mai
Whom Gwydion made by
    flowers,
And sweeter than the bride .
Flur, for whose love the
    first
Invaded Britain, 'But we
As this great Prince invad
Not beat him back, but
    with joy.
And I can scarcely ride wi
For old am I, and rough the
But Yniol goes, and I full
I see my princess as I se
Clothed with my gift, an
    gay.'

    But while the wome
        Geraint
Woke where he slept in t
    call'd
For Enid, and when Yni
Of that good mother ma
In such apparel as migh
His princess, or indeed
He answer'd: 'Earl, entr
Albeit I give no reason
That she ride with me i
Yniol with that hard m
Like flaws in summer la
For Enid, all abash'd s
Dared not to glance at
    face,
But silently, in all obe
Her mother silent too,
Laid from her limbs
    gift,
And robed them in he
And so descended. N
More than Geraint
    attired;
And glancing all at o
As careful robins eye

Made her cheek burn and either eyelid fell,
But rested with her sweet face satisfied;
Then seeing cloud upon the mother's brow,
Her by both hands he caught, and sweetly
    said,

'O my new mother, be not wroth or
        grieved
At thy new son, for my petition to her.
When late I left Caerleon, our great Queen,
In words whose echo lasts, they were so
    sweet,
Made promise, that whatever bride I
    brought,
Herself would clothe her like the sun in
    Heaven.
Thereafter, when I reach'd this ruin'd hall,
Beholding one so bright in dark estate,
I vow'd that could I gain her, our fair
    Queen,
No hand but hers, should make your Enid
    burst
Sunlike from cloud—and likewise thought
    perhaps,
That service done so graciously would bind
The two together; fain I would the two
Should love each other: how can Enid find
A nobler friend? Another thought was
    mine;
I came among you here so suddenly,
That tho' her gentle presence at the lists
Might well have served for proof that I
    was loved,
I doubted whether daughter's tenderness,
Or easy nature, might not let itself
Be moulded by your wishes for her weal;
Or whether some false sense in her own self
Of my contrasting brightness, overbore
Her fancy dwelling in this dusky hall;
And such a sense might make her long for
    court
And all its perilous glories: and I thought,
That could I someway prove such force in
    her
Link'd with such love for me, that at a
    word
(No reason given her) she could cast aside
A splendour dear to women, new to her,
And therefore dearer; or if not so new,
Yet therefore tenfold dearer by the power
Of intermitted usage; then I felt

That I could rest, a rock in ebbs and flows,
Fixt on her faith. Now, therefore, I do rest,
A prophet certain of my prophecy,
That never shadow of mistrust can cross
Between us. Grant me pardon for my
    thoughts:
And for my strange petition I will make
Amends hereafter by some gaudy-day,
When your fair child shall wear your costly
    gift
Beside your own warm hearth, with, on her
    knees,
Who knows? another gift of the high God,
Which, maybe, shall have learn'd to lisp you
    thanks.'

He spoke: the mother smiled, but half in
    tears,
Then brought a mantle down and wrapt
    her in it,
And claspt and kiss'd her, and they rode
    away.

Now thrice that morning Guinevere had
    climb'd
The giant tower, from whose high crest,
    they say,
Men saw the goodly hills of Somerset,
And white sails flying on the yellow sea;
But not to goodly hill or yellow sea
Look'd the fair Queen, but up the vale of
    Usk,
By the flat meadow, till she saw them
    come;
And then descending met them at the
    gates,
Embraced her with all welcome as a friend,
And did her honour as the Prince's bride,
And clothed her for her bridals like the
    sun;
And all that week was old Caerleon gay.
For by the hands of Dubric, the high saint,
They twain were wedded with all cere-
    mony.

And this was on the last year's Whitsun-
    tide.
But Enid ever kept the faded silk,
Remembering how first he came on her,
Drest in that dress, and how he loved her
    in it,

329

And all her foolish fears about the dress,
And all his journey toward her, as himself
Had told her, and their coming to the court.

And now this morning when he said to her,
'Put on your worst and meanest dress,' she found
And took it, and array'd herself therein.

GERAINT AND ENID

O PURBLIND race of miserable men,
How many among us at this very hour
Do forge a life-long trouble for ourselves,
By taking true for false, or false for true;
Here, thro' the feeble twilight of this world
Groping, how many, until we pass and reach
That other, where we see as we are seen!

So fared it with Geraint, who issuing forth
That morning, when they both had got to horse,
Perhaps because he loved her passionately,
And felt that tempest brooding round his heart,
Which, if he spoke at all, would break perforce
Upon a head so dear in thunder, said:
'Not at my side. I charge thee ride before,
Ever a good way on before; and this
I charge thee, on thy duty as a wife,
Whatever happens, not to speak to me,
No, not a word!' and Enid was aghast;
And forth they rode, but scarce three paces on,
When crying out, 'Effeminate as I am,
I will not fight my way with gilded arms,
All shall be iron;' he loosed a mighty purse,
Hung at his belt, and hurl'd it toward the squire.
So the last sight that Enid had of home
Was all the marble threshold flashing, strown
With gold and scatter'd coinage, and the squire
Chafing his shoulder: then he cried again,

'To the wilds!' and Enid leading down the tracks
Thro' which he bad her lead him on, they past
The marches, and by bandit-haunted holds,
Gray swamps and pools, waste places of the hern,
And wildernesses, perilous paths, they rode:
Round was their pace at first, but slacken'd soon:
A stranger meeting them had surely thought
They rode so slowly and they look'd so pale,
That each had suffer'd some exceeding wrong.
For he was ever saying to himself,
'O I that wasted time to tend upon her,
To compass her with sweet observances,
To dress her beautifully and keep her true'—
And there he broke the sentence in his heart
Abruptly, as a man upon his tongue
May break it, when his passion masters him.
And she was ever praying the sweet heavens
To save her dear lord whole from any wound.
And ever in her mind she cast about
For that unnoticed failing in herself,
Which made him look so cloudy and so cold;
Till the great plover's human whistle amazed
Her heart, and glancing round the waste she fear'd
In every wavering brake an ambuscade.
Then thought again, 'If there be such in me,
I might amend it by the grace of Heaven,
If he would only speak and tell me of it.'

But when the fourth part of the day was gone,
Then Enid was aware of three tall knights
On horseback, wholly arm'd, behind a rock
In shadow, waiting for them, caitiffs all;
And heard one crying to his fellow, 'Look,

Here comes a laggard hanging down his
head,
Who seems no bolder than a beaten hound;
Come, we will slay him and will have his
horse
And armour, and his damsel shall be ours.'

Then Enid ponder'd in her heart, and
said:
'I will go back a little to my lord,
And I will tell him all their caitiff talk;
For, be he wroth even to slaying me,
Far liefer by his dear hand had I die,
Than that my lord should suffer loss or
shame.'

Then she went back some paces of
return,
Met his full frown timidly firm, and said;
'My lord, I saw three bandits by the rock
Waiting to fall on you, and heard them
boast
That they would slay you, and possess your
horse
And armour, and your damsel should be
theirs.'

He made a wrathful answer: 'Did I wish
Your warning or your silence? one com-
mand
I laid upon you, not to speak to me,
And thus ye keep it! Well then, look—for
now,
Whether ye wish me victory or defeat,
Long for my life, or hunger for my death,
Yourself shall see my vigour is not lost.'

Then Enid waited pale and sorrowful,
And down upon him bare the bandit three.
And at the midmost charging, Prince
Geraint
Drave the long spear a cubit thro' his
breast
And out beyond; and then against his brace
Of comrades, each of whom had broken on
him
A lance that splinter'd like an icicle,
Swung from his brand a windy buffet out
Once, twice, to right, to left, and stunn'd
the twain
Or slew them, and dismounting like a man
That skins the wild beast after slaying him,

Stript from the three dead wolves of
woman born
The three gay suits of armour which they
wore,
And let the bodies lie, but bound the suits
Of armour on their horses, each on each,
And tied the bridle-reins of all the three
Together, and said to her, 'Drive them on
Before you;' and she drove them thro' the
waste.

He follow'd nearer: ruth began to work
Against his anger in him, while he watch'd
The being he loved best in all the world,
With difficulty in mild obedience
Driving them on: he fain had spoken to
her,
And loosed in words of sudden fire the
wrath
And smoulder'd wrong that burnt him all
within;
But evermore it seem'd an easier thing
At once without remorse to strike her dead,
Than to cry 'Halt,' and to her own bright
face
Accuse her of the least immodesty:
And thus tongue-tied, it made him wroth
the more
That she *could* speak whom his own ear
had heard
Call herself false: and suffering thus he
made
Minutes an age: but in scarce longer time
Than at Caerleon the full-tided Usk,
Before he turn to fall seaward again,
Pauses, did Enid, keeping watch, behold
In the first shallow shade of a deep wood,
Before a gloom of stubborn-shafted oaks,
Three other horsemen waiting, wholly
arm'd,
Whereof one seem'd far larger than her
lord,
And shook her pulses, crying, 'Look, a
prize!
Three horses and three goodly suits of
arms,
And all in charge of whom? a girl: set on.'
'Nay,' said the second, 'yonder comes a
knight.'
The third, 'A craven; how he hangs his
head.'

The giant answer'd merrily, 'Yea, but one?
Wait here, and when he passes fall upon
    him.'

  And Enid ponder'd in her heart and said,
'I will abide the coming of my lord,
And I will tell him all their villainy.
My lord is weary with the fight before,
And they will fall upon him unawares.
I needs must disobey him for his good;
How should I dare obey him to his harm?
Needs must I speak, and tho' he kill me
    for it,
I save a life dearer to me than mine.'

  And she abode his coming, and said to
    him
With timid firmness, 'Have I leave to speak?'
He said, 'Ye take it, speaking,' and she
    spoke.

  'There lurk three villains yonder in the
    wood,
And each of them is wholly arm'd, and one
Is larger-limb'd than you are, and they say
That they will fall upon you while ye pass.'

  To which he flung a wrathful answer
    back:
'And if there were an hundred in the wood,
And every man were larger-limb'd than I,
And all at once should sally out upon me,
I swear it would not ruffle me so much
As you that not obey me. Stand aside,
And if I fall, cleave to the better man.'

  And Enid stood aside to wait the event,
Not dare to watch the combat, only breathe
Short fits of prayer, at every stroke a breath.
And he, she dreaded most, bare down
    upon him.
Aim'd at the helm, his lance err'd; but
    Geraint's,
A little in the late encounter strain'd,
Struck thro' the bulky bandit's corselet
    home,
And then brake short, and down his enemy
    roll'd,
And there lay still; as he that tells the tale
Saw once a great piece of a promontory,
That had a sapling growing on it, slide

From the long shore-cliff's windy walls to
    the beach,
And there lie still, and yet the sapling grew:
So lay the man transfixt. His craven pair
Of comrades making slowlier at the Prince,
When now they saw their bulwark fallen,
    stood;
On whom the victor, to confound them
    more,
Spurr'd with his terrible war-cry; for as
    one,
That listens near a torrent mountain-brook,
All thro' the crash of the near cataract hears
The drumming thunder of the huger fall
At distance, were the soldiers wont to hear
His voice in battle, and be kindled by it,
And foemen scared, like that false pair who
    turn'd
Flying, but, overtaken, died the death
Themselves had wrought on many an
    innocent.

  Thereon Geraint, dismounting, pick'd
    the lance
That pleased him best, and drew from
    those dead wolves
Their three gay suits of armour, each from
    each,
And bound them on their horses, each on
    each,
And tied the bridle-reins of all the three
Together, and said to her, 'Drive them on
Before you,' and she drove them thro' the
    wood.

  He follow'd nearer still: the pain she had
To keep them in the wild ways of the wood,
Two sets of three laden with jingling arms,
Together, served a little to disedge
The sharpness of that pain about her heart:
And they themselves, like creatures gently
    born
But into bad hands fall'n, and now so long
By bandits groom'd, prick'd their light
    ears, and felt
Her low firm voice and tender government.

  So thro' the green gloom of the wood
    they past,
And issuing under open heavens beheld
A little town with towers, upon a rock,

And close beneath, a meadow gemlike
    chased
In the brown wild, and mowers mowing
    in it:
And down a rocky pathway from the place
There came a fair-hair'd youth, that in his
    hand
Bare victual for the mowers: and Geraint
Had ruth again on Enid looking pale:
Then, moving downward to the meadow
    ground,
He, when the fair-hair'd youth came by
    him, said,
'Friend, let her eat; the damsel is so faint.'
'Yea, willingly,' replied the youth; 'and
    thou,
My lord, eat also, tho' the fare is coarse,
And only meet for mowers;' then set down
His basket, and dismounting on the sward
They let the horses graze, and ate them-
    selves.
And Enid took a little delicately,
Less having stomach for it than desire
To close with her lord's pleasure; but
    Geraint
Ate all the mowers' victual unawares,
And when he found all empty, was amazed;
And 'Boy,' said he, 'I have eaten all, but
    take
A horse and arms for guerdon; choose the
    best.'
He, reddening in extremity of delight,
'My lord, you overpay me fifty-fold.'
'Ye will be all the wealthier,' cried the
    Prince.
'I take it as free gift, then,' said the boy,
'Not guerdon; for myself can easily,
While your good damsel rests, return, and
    fetch
Fresh victual for these mowers of our Earl;
For these are his, and all the field is his,
And I myself am his; and I will tell him
How great a man thou art: he loves to know
When men of mark are in his territory:
And he will have thee to his palace here,
And serve thee costlier than with mowers'
    fare.'

Then said Geraint, 'I wish no better
    fare:
I never ate with angrier appetite

Than when I left your mowers dinnerless.
And into no Earl's palace will I go.
I know, God knows, too much of palaces!
And if he want me, let him come to me.
But hire us some fair chamber for the
    night,
And stalling for the horses, and return
With victual for these men, and let us
    know.'

'Yea, my kind lord,' said the glad youth,
    and went,
Held his head high, and thought himself a
    knight,
And up the rocky pathway disappear'd,
Leading the horse, and they were left alone.

But when the Prince had brought his
    errant eyes
Home from the rock, sideways he let them
    glance
At Enid, where she droopt: his own false
    doom,
That shadow of mistrust should never cross
Betwixt them, came upon him, and he
    sigh'd;
Then with another humorous ruth re-
    mark'd
The lusty mowers labouring dinnerless,
And watch'd the sun blaze on the turning
    scythe,
And after nodded sleepily in the heat.
But she, remembering her old ruin'd hall,
And all the windy clamour of the daws
About her hollow turret, pluck'd the grass
There growing longest by the meadow's
    edge,
And into many a listless annulet,
Now over, now beneath her marriage
    ring,
Wove and unwove it, till the boy return'd
And told them of a chamber, and they
    went;
Where, after saying to her, 'If ye will,
Call for the woman of the house,' to which
She answer'd, 'Thanks, my lord;' the two
    remain'd
Apart by all the chamber's width, and mute
As creatures voiceless thro' the fault of
    birth,
Or two wild men supporters of a shield,

Painted, who stare at open space, nor
    glance
The one at other, parted by the shield.

  On a sudden, many a voice along the
    street,
And heel against the pavement echoing,
    burst
Their drowse; and either started while the
    door,
Push'd from without, drave backward to
    the wall,
And midmost of a rout of roisterers,
Femininely fair and dissolutely pale,
Her suitor in old years before Geraint,
Enter'd, the wild lord of the place,
    Limours.
He moving up with pliant courtliness,
Greeted Geraint full face, but stealthily,
In the mid-warmth of welcome and graspt
    hand,
Found Enid with the corner of his eye,
And knew her sitting sad and solitary.
Then cried Geraint for wine and goodly
    cheer
To feed the sudden guest, and sump-
    tuously
According to his fashion, bad the host
Call in what men soever were his friends,
And feast with these in honour of their
    Earl;
'And care not for the cost; the cost is mine.'

  And wine and food were brought, and
    Earl Limours
Drank till he jested with all ease, and told
Free tales, and took the word and play'd
    upon it,
And made it of two colours; for his talk,
When wine and free companions kindled
    him,
Was wont to glance and sparkle like a gem
Of fifty facets; thus he moved the Prince
To laughter and his comrades to applause.
Then, when the Prince was merry, ask'd
    Limours,
'Your leave, my lord, to cross the room,
    and speak
To your good damsel there who sits apart,
And seems so lonely?' 'My free leave,' he
    said;

'Get her to speak: she doth not speak to
    me.'
Then rose Limours, and looking at his
    feet,
Like him who tries the bridge he fears may
    fail,
Crost and came near, lifted adoring eyes,
Bow'd at her side and utter'd whisperingly:

  'Enid, the pilot star of my lone life,
Enid, my early and my only love,
Enid, the loss of whom hath turn'd me
    wild—
What chance is this? how is it I see you
    here?
Ye are in my power at last, are in my
    power.
Yet fear me not: I call mine own self wild,
But keep a touch of sweet civility
Here in the heart of waste and wilderness.
I thought, but that your father came be-
    tween,
In former days you saw me favourably.
And if it were so do not keep it back:
Make me a little happier: let me know it:
Owe you me nothing for a life half-lost?
Yea, yea, the whole dear debt of all you are.
And, Enid, you and he, I see with joy,
Ye sit apart, you do not speak to him,
You come with no attendance, page or maid,
To serve you—doth he love you as of old?
For, call it lovers' quarrels, yet I know
Tho' men may bicker with the things they
    love,
They would not make them laughable in
    all eyes,
Not while they loved them; and your
    wretched dress,
A wretched insult on you, dumbly speaks
Your story, that this man loves you no
    more.
Your beauty is no beauty to him now:
A common chance—right well I know it—
    pall'd—
For I know men: nor will ye win him back,
For the man's love once gone never returns.
But here is one who loves you as of old;
With more exceeding passion than of old:
Good, speak the word: my followers ring
    him round:
He sits unarm'd; I hold a finger up;

They understand: nay; I do not mean
    blood:
Nor need ye look so scared at what I say:
My malice is no deeper than a moat,
No stronger than a wall: there is the keep;
He shall not cross us more; speak but the
    word:
Or speak it not; but then by Him that
    made me
The one true lover whom you ever own'd,
I will make use of all the power I have.
O pardon me! the madness of that hour,
When first I parted from thee, moves me
    yet.'

    At this the tender sound of his own
    voice
And sweet self-pity, or the fancy of it,
Made his eye moist; but Enid fear'd his
    eyes,
Moist as they were, wine-heated from the
    feast;
And answer'd with such craft as women
    use,
Guilty or guiltless, to stave off a chance
That breaks upon them perilously, and
    said:

    'Earl, if you love me as in former years,
And do not practise on me, come with
    morn,
And snatch me from him as by violence;
Leave me to-night: I am weary to the
    death.'

    Low at leave-taking, with his brandish'd
    plume
Brushing his instep, bow'd the all-amorous
    Earl,
And the stout Prince bad him a loud good-
    night.
He moving homeward babbled to his men,
How Enid never loved a man but him,
Nor cared a broken egg-shell for her lord.

    But Enid left alone with Prince Geraint,
Debating his command of silence given,
And that she now perforce must violate it,
Held commune with herself, and while she
    held
He fell asleep, and Enid had no heart

To wake him, but hung o'er him, wholly
    pleased
To find him yet unwounded after fight,
And hear him breathing low and equally.
Anon she rose, and stepping lightly, heap'd
The pieces of his armour in one place,
All to be there against a sudden need;
Then dozed awhile herself, but overtoil'd
By that day's grief and travel, evermore
Seem'd catching at a rootless thorn, and
    then
Went slipping down horrible precipices,
And strongly striking out her limbs awoke;
Then thought she heard the wild Earl at
    the door,
With all his rout of random followers,
Sound on a dreadful trumpet, summoning
    her;
Which was the red cock shouting to the
    light,
As the gray dawn stole o'er the dewy world,
And glimmer'd on his armour in the room.
And once again she rose to look at it,
But touch'd it unawares: jangling, the
    casque
Fell, and he started up and stared at her.
Then breaking his command of silence
    given,
She told him all that Earl Limours had
    said,
Except the passage that he loved her not;
Nor left untold the craft herself had used;
But ended with apology so sweet,
Low-spoken, and of so few words, and
    seem'd
So justified by that necessity,
That tho' he thought 'was it for him she
    wept
In Devon?' he but gave a wrathful groan,
Saying, 'Your sweet faces make good
    fellows fools
And traitors. Call the host and bid him
    bring
Charger and palfrey.' So she glided out
Among the heavy breathings of the house,
And like a household Spirit at the walls
Beat, till she woke the sleepers, and
    return'd:
Then tending her rough lord, tho' all
    unask'd,
In silence, did him service as a squire;

Till issuing arm'd he found the host and
    cried,
'Thy reckoning, friend?' and ere he learnt
    it, 'Take
Five horses and their armours;' and the
    host
Suddenly honest, answer'd in amaze,
'My lord, I scarce have spent the worth of
    one!'
'Ye will be all the wealthier,' said the
    Prince,
And then to Enid, 'Forward! and to-day
I charge you, Enid, more especially,
What thing soever ye may hear, or see,
Or fancy (tho' I count it of small use
To charge you) that ye speak not but obey.'

    And Enid answer'd, 'Yea, my lord, I
    know
Your wish, and would obey; but riding
    first,
I hear the violent threats you do not hear,
I see the danger which you cannot see:
Then not to give you warning, that seems
    hard;
Almost beyond me: yet I would obey.'

    'Yea so,' said he, 'do it: be not too wise;
Seeing that ye are wedded to a man,
Not all mismated with a yawning clown,
But one with arms to guard his head and
    yours,
With eyes to find you out however far,
And ears to hear you even in his dreams.'

    With that he turn'd and look'd as keenly
    at her
As careful robins eye the delver's toil;
And that within her, which a wanton fool,
Or hasty judger would have call'd her
    guilt,
Made her cheek burn and either eyelid fall.
And Geraint look'd and was not satisfied.

    Then forward by a way which, beaten
    broad,
Led from the territory of false Limours
To the waste earldom of another earl,
Doorm, whom his shaking vassals call'd
    the Bull,
Went Ènid with her sullen follower on.

Once she look'd back, and when she saw
    him ride
More near by many a rood than yester-
    morn,
It wellnigh made her cheerful; till Geraint
Waving an angry hand as who should say
'Ye watch me,' sadden'd all her heart
    again.

But while the sun yet beat a dewy blade,
The sound of many a heavily-galloping
    hoof
Smote on her ear, and turning round she
    saw
Dust, and the points of lances bicker in it.
Then not to disobey her lord's behest,
And yet to give him warning, for he rode
As if he heard not, moving back she held
Her finger up, and pointed to the dust.
At which the warrior in his obstinacy,
Because she kept the letter of his word,
Was in a manner pleased, and turning,
    stood.

And in the moment after, wild Limours,
Borne on a black horse, like a thunder-
    cloud
Whose skirts are loosen'd by the breaking
    storm,
Half ridden off with by the thing he rode,
And all in passion uttering a dry shriek,
Dash'd on Geraint, who closed with him,
    and bore
Down by the length of lance and arm
    beyond
The crupper, and so left him stunn'd or
    dead,
And overthrew the next that follow'd him,
And blindly rush'd on all the rout behind.
But at the flash and motion of the man
They vanish'd panic-stricken, like a shoal
Of darting fish, that on a summer morn
Adown the crystal dykes at Camelot
Come slipping o'er their shadows on the
    sand,
But if a man who stands upon the brink
But lift a shining hand against the sun,
There is not left the twinkle of a fin
Betwixt the cressy islets white in flower;
So, scared but at the motion of the man,
Fled all the boon companions of the Earl,
And left him lying in the public way;
So vanish friendships only made in wine.

Then like a stormy sunlight smiled Geraint,
Who saw the chargers of the two that fell
Start from their fallen lords, and wildly fly,
Mixt with the flyers. 'Horse and man,' he said,
'All of one mind and all right-honest friends!
Not a hoof left: and I methinks till now
Was honest—paid with horses and with arms;
I cannot steal or plunder, no nor beg:
And so what say ye, shall we strip him there
Your lover? has your palfrey heart enough
To bear his armour? shall we fast, or dine?
No?—then do thou, being right honest, pray
That we may meet the horsemen of Earl Doorm,
I too would still be honest.' Thus he said:
And sadly gazing on her bridle-reins,
And answering not one word, she led the way.

But as a man to whom a dreadful loss
Falls in a far land and he knows it not,
But coming back he learns it, and the loss
So pains him that he sickens nigh to death;
So fared it with Geraint, who being prick'd
In combat with the follower of Limours,
Bled underneath his armour secretly,
And so rode on, nor told his gentle wife
What ail'd him, hardly knowing it himself,
Till his eye darken'd and his helmet wagg'd;
And at a sudden swerving of the road,
Tho' happily down on a bank of grass,
The Prince, without a word, from his horse fell.

And Enid heard the clashing of his fall,
Suddenly came, and at his side all pale
Dismounting, loosed the fastenings of his arms,
Nor let her true hand falter, nor blue eye
Moisten, till she had lighted on his wound,
And tearing off her veil of faded silk
Had bared her forehead to the blistering sun,
And swathed the hurt that drain'd her dear lord's life.

Then after all was done that hand could do,
She rested, and her desolation came
Upon her, and she wept beside the way.

And many past, but none regarded her,
For in that realm of lawless turbulence,
A woman weeping for her murder'd mate
Was cared as much for as a summer shower:
One took him for a victim of Earl Doorm,
Nor dared to waste a perilous pity on him:
Another hurrying past, a man-at-arms,
Rode on a mission to the bandit Earl;
Half whistling and half singing a coarse song,
He drove the dust against her veilless eyes:
Another, flying from the wrath of Doorm
Before an ever-fancied arrow, made
The long way smoke beneath him in his fear;
At which her palfrey whinnying lifted heel,
And scour'd into the coppices and was lost,
While the great charger stood, grieved like a man.

But at the point of noon the huge Earl Doorm,
Broad-faced with under-fringe of russet beard,
Bound on a foray, rolling eyes of prey,
Came riding with a hundred lances up;
But ere he came, like one that hails a ship,
Cried out with a big voice, 'What, is he dead?'
'No, no, not dead!' she answer'd in all haste.
'Would some of your kind people take him up,
And bear him hence out of this cruel sun?
Most sure am I, quite sure, he is not dead.'

Then said Earl Doorm: 'Well, if he be not dead,
Why wail ye for him thus? ye seem a child.
And be he dead, I count you for a fool;
Your wailing will not quicken him: dead or not,
Ye mar a comely face with idiot tears.
Yet, since the face *is* comely—some of you,
Here, take him up, and bear him to our hall:

337

An if he live, we will have him of our band;
And if he die, why earth has earth enough
To hide him. See ye take the charger too,
A noble one.'
                        He spake, and past away,
But left two brawny spearmen, who advanced,
Each growling like a dog, when his good bone
Seems to be pluck'd at by the village boys
Who love to vex him eating, and he fears
To lose his bone, and lays his foot upon it,
Gnawing and growling: so the ruffians growl'd,
Fearing to lose, and all for a dead man,
Their chance of booty from the morning's raid,
Yet raised and laid him on a litter-bier,
Such as they brought upon their forays out
For those that might be wounded; laid him on it
All in the hollow of his shield, and took
And bore him to the naked hall of Doorm,
(His gentle charger following him unled)
And cast him and the bier in which he lay
Down on an oaken settle in the hall,
And then departed, hot in haste to join
Their luckier mates, but growling as before,
And cursing their lost time, and the dead man,
And their own Earl, and their own souls, and her.
They might as well have blest her: she was deaf
To blessing or to cursing save from one.

  So for long hours sat Enid by her lord,
There in the naked hall, propping his head,
And chafing his pale hands, and calling to him.
Till at the last he waken'd from his swoon,
And found his own dear bride propping his head,
And chafing his faint hands, and calling to him;
And felt the warm tears falling on his face;
And said to his own heart, 'She weeps for me:'
And yet lay still, and feign'd himself as dead,
That he might prove her to the uttermost,

And say to his own heart, 'She weeps for me.'

  But in the falling afternoon return'd
The huge Earl Doorm with plunder to the hall.
His lusty spearmen follow'd him with noise:
Each hurling down a heap of things that rang
Against the pavement, cast his lance aside,
And doff'd his helm: and then there flutter'd in,
Half-bold, half-frighted, with dilated eyes,
A tribe of women, dress'd in many hues,
And mingled with the spearmen: and Earl Doorm
Struck with a knife's haft hard against the board,
And call'd for flesh and wine to feed his spears.
And men brought in whole hogs and quarter beeves,
And all the hall was dim with steam of flesh:
And none spake word, but all sat down at once,
And ate with tumult in the naked hall,
Feeding like horses when you hear them feed;
Till Enid shrank far back into herself,
To shun the wild ways of the lawless tribe.
But when Earl Doorm had eaten all he would,
He roll'd his eyes about the hall, and found
A damsel drooping in a corner of it.
Then he remember'd her, and how she wept;
And out of her there came a power upon him;
And rising on the sudden he said, 'Eat!
I never yet beheld a thing so pale.
God's curse, it makes me mad to see you weep.
Eat! Look yourself. Good luck had your good man,
For were I dead who is it would weep for me?
Sweet lady, never since I first drew breath
Have I beheld a lily like yourself.

338

And so there lived some colour in your
    cheek,
There is not one among my gentlewomen
Were fit to wear your slipper for a glove.
But listen to me, and by me be ruled,
And I will do the thing I have not done,
For ye shall share my earldom with me,
    girl,
And we will live like two birds in one nest,
And I will fetch you forage from all fields,
For I compel all creatures to my will.'

He spoke: the brawny spearman let his
    cheek
Bulge with the unswallow'd piece, and
    turning stared;
While some, whose souls the old serpent
    long had drawn
Down, as the worm draws in the wither'd
    leaf
And makes it earth, hiss'd each at other's
    ear
What shall not be recorded—women they,
Women, or what had been those gracious
    things,
But now desired the humbling of their
    best,
Yea, would have help'd him to it: and all
    at once
They hated her, who took no thought of
    them,
But answer'd in low voice, her meek head
    yet
Drooping, 'I pray you of your courtesy,
He being as he is, to let me be.'

She spake so low he hardly heard her
    speak,
But like a mighty patron, satisfied
With what himself had done so graciously,
Assumed that she had thank'd him, adding,
    'Yea,
Eat and be glad, for I account you mine.'

She answer'd meekly, 'How should I be
    glad
Henceforth in all the world at anything,
Until my lord arise and look upon me?'

Here the huge Earl cried out upon her
    talk,
As all but empty heart and weariness

And sickly nothing; suddenly seized on
    her,
And bare her by main violence to the
    board,
And thrust the dish before her, crying,
    'Eat.'

'No, no,' said Enid, vext, 'I will not eat
Till yonder man upon the bier arise,
And eat with me.' 'Drink, then,' he
    answer'd. 'Here!'
(And fill'd a horn with wine and held it to
    her,)
'Lo! I, myself, when flush'd with fight, or
    hot,
God's curse, with anger—often I myself,
Before I well have drunken, scarce can eat:
Drink therefore and the wine will change
    your will.'

'Not so,' she cried, 'by Heaven, I will
    not drink
Till my dear lord arise and bid me do it,
And drink with me; and if he rise no more,
I will not look at wine until I die.'

At this he turn'd all red and paced his
    hall,
Now gnaw'd his under, now his upper lip,
And coming up close to her, said at last:
'Girl, for I see ye scorn my courtesies,
Take warning: yonder man is surely dead;
And I compel all creatures to my will.
Not eat nor drink? And wherefore wail for
    one,
Who put your beauty to this flout and
    scorn
By dressing it in rags? Amazed am I,
Beholding how ye butt against my wish,
That I forbear you thus: cross me no more.
At least put off to please me this poor gown,
This silken rag, this beggar-woman's weed:
I love that beauty should go beautifully:
For see ye not my gentlewomen here,
How gay, how suited to the house of one
Who loves that beauty should go beauti-
    fully?
Rise therefore; robe yourself in this: obey.'

He spoke, and one among his gentle-
    women
Display'd a splendid silk of foreign loom,

Where like a shoaling sea the lovely blue
Play'd into green, and thicker down the
    front
With jewels than the sward with drops of
    dew,
When all night long a cloud clings to the
    hill,
And with the dawn ascending lets the day
Strike where it clung: so thickly shone the
    gems.

But Enid answer'd, harder to be moved
Than hardest tyrants in their day of power,
With life-long injuries burning unavenged,
And now their hour has come; and Enid
    said:

'In this poor gown my dear lord found
    me first,
And loved me serving in my father's hall:
In this poor gown I rode with him to court,
And there the Queen array'd me like the
    sun:
In this poor gown he bad me clothe myself,
When now we rode upon this fatal quest
Of honour, where no honour can be gain'd:
And this poor gown I will not cast aside
Until himself arise a living man,
And bid me cast it. I have griefs enough:
Pray you be gentle, pray you let me be:
I never loved, can never love but him:
Yea, God, I pray you of your gentleness,
He being as he is, to let me be.'

Then strode the brute Earl up and down
    his hall,
And took his russet beard between his
    teeth;
Last, coming up quite close, and in his
    mood
Crying, 'I count it of no more avail,
Dame, to be gentle than ungentle with you;
Take my salute,' unknightly with flat hand,
However lightly, smote her on the cheek.

Then Enid, in her utter helplessness,
And since she thought, 'He had not dared
    to do it,
Except he surely knew my lord was dead,'
Sent forth a sudden sharp and bitter cry,
As of a wild thing taken in the trap,

Which sees the trapper coming thro' the
    wood.

This heard Geraint, and grasping at his
    sword,
(It lay beside him in the hollow shield),
Made but a single bound, and with a sweep
    of it
Shore thro' the swarthy neck, and like a
    ball
The russet-bearded head roll'd on the
    floor.
So died Earl Doorm by him he counted
    dead.
And all the men and women in the hall
Rose when they saw the dead man rise, and
    fled
Yelling as from a spectre, and the two
Were left alone together, and he said:

'Enid, I have used you worse than that
    dead man;
Done you more wrong: we both have
    undergone
That trouble which has left me thrice your
    own:
Henceforward I will rather die than doubt.
And here I lay this penance on myself,
Not, tho' mine own ears heard you yester-
    morn—
You thought me sleeping, but I heard you
    say,
I heard you say, that you were no true wife:
I swear I will not ask your meaning in it:
I do believe yourself against yourself,
And will henceforward rather die than
    doubt.'

And Enid could not say one tender word,
She felt so blunt and stupid at the heart:
She only pray'd him, 'Fly, they will return
And slay you; fly, your charger is without,
My palfrey lost.' 'Then, Enid, shall you
    ride
Behind me.' 'Yea,' said Enid, 'let us go.'
And moving out they found the stately
    horse,
Who now no more a vassal to the thief,
But free to stretch his limbs in lawful fight,
Neigh'd with all gladness as they came,
    and stoop'd

340

With a low whinny toward the pair: and
    she
Kiss'd the white star upon his noble front,
Glad also; then Geraint upon the horse
Mounted, and reach'd a hand, and on his
    foot
She set her own and climb'd; he turn'd his
    face
And kiss'd her climbing, and she cast her
    arms
About him, and at once they rode away.

And never yet, since high in Paradise
O'er the four rivers the first roses blew,
Came purer pleasure unto mortal kind
Than lived thro' her, who in that perilous
    hour
Put hand to hand beneath her husband's
    heart,
And felt him hers again: she did not weep,
But o'er her meek eyes came a happy mist
Like that which kept the heart of Eden
    green
Before the useful trouble of the rain:
Yet not so misty were her meek blue eyes
As not to see before them on the path,
Right in the gateway of the bandit hold,
A knight of Arthur's court, who laid his
    lance
In rest, and made as if to fall upon him,
Then, fearing for his hurt and loss of blood,
She, with her mind all full of what had
    chanced,
Shriek'd to the stranger 'Slay not a dead
    man!'
'The voice of Enid,' said the knight; but
    she,
Beholding it was Edyrn son of Nudd,
Was moved so much the more, and
    shriek'd again,
'O cousin, slay not him who gave you life.'
And Edyrn moving frankly forward spake:
'My lord Geraint, I greet you with all love;
I took you for a bandit knight of Doorm;
And fear not, Enid, I should fall upon him,
Who love you, Prince, with something of
    the love
Wherewith we love the Heaven that
    chastens us.
For once, when I was up so high in pride
That I was halfway down the slope to Hell,

By overthrowing me you threw me higher.
Now, made a knight of Arthur's Table
    Round,
And since I knew this Earl, when I myself
Was half a bandit in my lawless hour,
I come the mouthpiece of our King to
    Doorm
(The King is close behind me) bidding him
Disband himself, and scatter all his powers,
Submit, and hear the judgment of the
    King.'

'He hears the judgment of the King of
    kings,'
Cried the wan Prince; 'and lo, the powers
    of Doorm
Are scatter'd,' and he pointed to the field,
Where, huddled here and there on mound
    and knoll,
Were men and women staring and aghast,
While some yet fled; and then he plainlier
    told
How the huge Earl lay slain within his hall.
But when the knight besought him,
    'Follow me,
Prince, to the camp, and in the King's own
    ear
Speak what has chanced; ye surely have
    endured
Strange chances here alone;' that other
    flush'd,
And hung his head, and halted in reply,
Fearing the mild face of the blameless
    King,
And after madness acted question ask'd:
Till Edyrn crying, 'If ye will not go
To Arthur, then will Arthur come to you,'
'Enough,' he said, 'I follow,' and they
    went.
But Enid in their going had two fears,
One from the bandit scatter'd in the field,
And one from Edyrn. Every now and then,
When Edyrn rein'd his charger at her side,
She shrank a little. In a hollow land,
From which old fires have broken, men
    may fear
Fresh fire and ruin. He, perceiving, said:

'Fair and dear cousin, you that most had
    cause
To fear me, fear no longer, I am changed.

GERAINT AND ENID

Yourself were first the blameless cause to
    make
My nature's prideful sparkle in the blood
Break into furious flame; being repulsed
By Yniol and yourself, I schemed and
    wrought
Until I overturn'd him; then set up
(With one main purpose ever at my heart)
My haughty jousts, and took a paramour;
Did her mock-honour as the fairest fair,
And, toppling over all antagonism,
So wax'd in pride, that I believed myself
Unconquerable, for I was wellnigh mad:
And, but for my main purpose in these
    jousts,
I should have slain your father, seized
    yourself.
I lived in hope that sometime you would
    come
To these my lists with him whom best you
    loved;
And there, poor cousin, with your meek
    blue eyes,
The truest eyes that ever answer'd Heaven,
Behold me overturn and trample on him.
Then, had you cried, or knelt, or pray'd
    to me,
I should not less have kill'd him. And you
    came,—
But once you came,—and with your own
    true eyes
Beheld the man you loved (I speak as one
Speaks of a service done him) overthrow
My proud self, and my purpose three years
    old,
And set his foot upon me, and give me life.
There was I broken down; there was I
    saved:
Tho' thence I rode all-shamed, hating the
    life
He gave me, meaning to be rid of it.
And all the penance the Queen laid upon
    me
Was but to rest awhile within her court;
Where first as sullen as a beast new-caged,
And waiting to be treated like a wolf,
Because I knew my deeds were known, I
    found,
Instead of scornful pity or pure scorn,
Such fine reserve and noble reticence,
Manners so kind, yet stately, such a grace

Of tenderest courtesy, that I began
To glance behind me at my former life,
And find that it had been the wolf's indeed:
And oft I talk'd with Dubric, the high
    saint,
Who, with mild heat of holy oratory,
Subdued me somewhat to that gentleness,
Which, when it weds with manhood, makes
    a man.
And you were often there about the Queen,
But saw me not, or mark'd not if you saw;
Nor did I care or dare to speak with you,
But kept myself aloof till I was changed;
And fear not, cousin; I am changed in-
    deed.'

He spoke, and Enid easily believed,
Like simple noble natures, credulous
Of what they long for, good in friend or foe,
There most in those who most have done
    them ill.
And when they reach'd the camp the King
    himself
Advanced to greet them, and beholding
    her
Tho' pale, yet happy, ask'd her not a word,
But went apart with Edyrn, whom he held
In converse for a little, and return'd,
And, gravely smiling, lifted her from horse,
And kiss'd her with all pureness, brother-
    like,
And show'd an empty tent allotted her,
And glancing for a minute, till he saw her
Pass into it, turn'd to the Prince, and said:

'Prince, when of late ye pray'd me for
    my leave
To move to your own land, and there
    defend
Your marches, I was prick'd with some
    reproof,
As one that let foul wrong stagnate and be,
By having look'd too much thro' alien eyes,
And wrought too long with delegated
    hands,
Not used mine own: but now behold me
    come
To cleanse this common sewer of all my
    realm,
With Edyrn and with others: have ye
    look'd

342

At Edyrn? have ye seen how nobly
    changed?
This work of his is great and wonderful.
His very face with change of heart is
    changed.
The world will not believe a man repents:
And this wise world of ours is mainly right.
Full seldom doth a man repent, or use
Both grace and will to pick the vicious
    quitch
Of blood and custom wholly out of him,
And make all clean, and plant himself
    afresh.
Edyrn has done it, weeding all his heart
As I will weed this land before I go.
I, therefore, made him of our Table Round,
Not rashly, but have proved him every-
    way
One of our noblest, our most valorous,
Sanest and most obedient: and indeed
This work of Edyrn wrought upon him-
    self
After a life of violence, seems to me
A thousand-fold more great and wonderful
Than if some knight of mine, risking his
    life,
My subject with my subjects under him,
Should make an onslaught single on a
    realm
Of robbers, tho' he slew them one by one,
And were himself nigh wounded to the
    death.'

    So spake the King; low bow'd the
    Prince, and felt
His work was neither great nor wonderful,
And past to Enid's tent; and thither came
The King's own leech to look into his hurt;
And Enid tended on him there; and there
Her constant motion round him, and the
    breath
Of her sweet tendance hovering over him,
Fill'd all the genial courses of his blood
With deeper and with ever deeper love,
As the south-west that blowing Bala lake
Fills all the sacred Dee. So past the days.

    But while Geraint lay healing of his hurt,
The blameless King went forth and cast
    his eyes
On each of all whom Uther left in charge

Long since, to guard the justice of the
    King:
He look'd and found them wanting; and as
    now
Men weed the white horse on the Berk-
    shire hills
To keep him bright and clean as heretofore,
He rooted out the slothful officer
Or guilty, which for bribe had wink'd at
    wrong,
And in their chairs set up a stronger race
With hearts and hands, and sent a thou-
    sand men
To till the wastes, and moving everywhere
Clear'd the dark places and let in the law,
And broke the bandit holds and cleansed
    the land.

    Then, when Geraint was whole again,
    they past
With Arthur to Caerleon upon Usk.
There the great Queen once more em-
    braced her friend,
And clothed her in apparel like the day.
And tho' Geraint could never take again
That comfort from their converse which
    he took
Before the Queen's fair name was breathed
    upon,
He rested well content that all was well.
Thence after tarrying for a space they rode,
And fifty knights rode with them to the
    shores
Of Severn, and they past to their own
    land.
And there he kept the justice of the King
So vigorously yet mildly, that all hearts
Applauded, and the spiteful whisper died:
And being ever foremost in the chase,
And victor at the tilt and tournament,
They call'd him the great Prince and man
    of men.
But Enid, whom her ladies loved to call
Enid the Fair, a grateful people named
Enid the Good; and in their halls arose
The cry of children, Enids and Geraints
Of times to be; nor did he doubt her more,
But rested in her fealty, till he crown'd
A happy life with a fair death, and fell
Against the heathen of the Northern Sea
In battle, fighting for the blameless King.

BALIN AND BALAN

PELLAM the King, who held and lost with
   Lot
In that first war, and had his realm restored
But render'd tributary, fail'd of late
To send his tribute; wherefore Arthur
   call'd
His treasurer, one of many years, and
   spake,
'Go thou with him and him and bring it
   to us,
Lest we should set one truer on his throne.
Man's word is God in man.'

               His Baron said
'We go but harken: there be two strange
   knights
Who sit near Camelot at a fountain-side,
A mile beneath the forest, challenging
And overthrowing every knight who comes.
Wilt thou I undertake them as we pass,
And send them to thee?'

          Arthur laugh'd upon him.
'Old friend, too old to be so young, depart,
Delay not thou for ought, but let them sit,
Until they find a lustier than themselves.'

So these departed. Early, one fair dawn,
The light-wing'd spirit of his youth
   return'd
On Arthur's heart; he arm'd himself and
   went,
So coming to the fountain-side beheld
Balin and Balan sitting statuelike,
Brethren, to right and left the spring, that
   down,
From underneath a plume of lady-fern,
Sang, and the sand danced at the bottom
   of it.
And on the right of Balin Balin's horse
Was fast beside an alder, on the left
Of Balan Balan's near a poplartree.
'Fair Sirs,' said Arthur, 'wherefore sit ye
   here?'
Balin and Balan answer'd 'For the sake
Of glory; we be mightier men than all
In Arthur's court; that also have we
   proved;
For whatsoever knight against us came
Or I or he have easily overthrown.'

'I too,' said Arthur, 'am of Arthur's hall,
But rather proven in his Paynim wars
Than famous jousts; but see, or proven or
   not,
Whether me likewise ye can overthrow.'
And Arthur lightly smote the brethren
   down,
And lightly so return'd, and no man knew.

Then Balin rose, and Balan, and beside
The carolling water set themselves again,
And spake no word until the shadow
   turn'd;
When from the fringe of coppice round
   them burst
A spangled pursuivant, and crying 'Sirs,
Rise, follow! ye be sent for by the King,'
They follow'd; whom when Arthur seeing
   ask'd
'Tell me your names; why sat ye by the
   well?'
Balin the stillness of a minute broke
Saying 'An unmelodious name to thee,
Balin, "the Savage"—that addition thine—
My brother and my better, this man here,
Balan. I smote upon the naked skull
A thrall of thine in open hall, my hand
Was gauntleted, half slew him; for I heard
He had spoken evil of me; thy just wrath
Sent me a three-years' exile from thine
   eyes.
I have not lived my life delightsomely:
For I that did that violence to thy thrall,
Had often wrought some fury on myself,
Saving for Balan: those three kingless
   years
Have past—were wormwood-bitter to me.
   King,
Methought that if we sat beside the well,
And hurl'd to ground what knight soever
   spurr'd
Against us, thou would'st take me gladlier
   back,
And make, as ten-times worthier to be
   thine
Than twenty Balins, Balan knight. I have
   said.
Not so—not all. A man of thine to-day
Abash'd us both, and brake my boast. Thy
   will?'
Said Arthur 'Thou hast ever spoken truth;

Thy too fierce manhood would not let thee
  lie.
Rise, my true knight. As children learn, be
  thou
Wiser for falling! walk with me, and move
To music with thine Order and the King.
Thy chair, a grief to all the brethren, stands
Vacant, but thou retake it, mine again!'

Thereafter, when Sir Balin enter'd hall,
The Lost one Found was greeted as in
  Heaven
With joy that blazed itself in woodland
  wealth
Of leaf, and gayest garlandage of flowers,
Along the walls and down the board; they
  sat,
And cup clash'd cup; they drank and some
  one sang,
Sweet-voiced, a song of welcome, where-
  upon
Their common shout in chorus, mounting,
  made
Those banners of twelve battles overhead
Stir, as they stirr'd of old, when Arthur's
  host
Proclaim'd him Victor, and the day was
  won.

Then Balan added to their Order lived
A wealthier life than heretofore with these
And Balin, till their embassage return'd.

'Sir King' they brought report 'we
  hardly found,
So bush'd about it is with gloom, the hall
Of him to whom ye sent us, Pellam, once
A Christless foe of thine as ever dash'd
Horse against horse; but seeing that thy
  realm
Hath prosper'd in the name of Christ, the
  King
Took, as in rival heat, to holy things;
And finds himself descended from the
  Saint
Arimathæan Joseph; him who first
Brought the great faith to Britain over seas;
He boasts his life as purer than thine own;
Eats scarce enow to keep his pulse abeat;
Hath push'd aside his faithful wife, nor
  lets

Or dame or damsel enter at his gates
Lest he should be polluted. This gray King
Show'd us a shrine wherein were wonders
  —yea—
Rich arks with priceless bones of martyr-
  dom,
Thorns of the crown and shivers of the
  cross,
And therewithal (for thus he told us)
  brought
By holy Joseph hither, that same spear
Wherewith the Roman pierced the side of
  Christ.
He much amazed us; after, when we
  sought
The tribute, answer'd "I have quite fore-
  gone
All matters of this world: Garlon, mine
  heir,
Of him demand it," which this Garlon
  gave
With much ado, railing at thine and thee.

'But when we left, in those deep woods
  we found
A knight of thine spear-stricken from
  behind,
Dead, whom we buried; more than one
  of us
Cried out on Garlon, but a woodman there
Reported of some demon in the woods
Was once a man, who driven by evil
  tongues
From all his fellows, lived alone, and came
To learn black magic, and to hate his kind
With such a hate, that when he died, his
  soul
Became a Fiend, which, as the man in life
Was wounded by blind tongues he saw not
  whence,
Strikes from behind. This woodman
  show'd the cave
From which he sallies, and wherein he
  dwelt.
We saw the hoof-print of a horse, no more.'

Then Arthur, 'Let who goes before me,
  see
He do not fall behind me: foully slain
And villainously! who will hunt for me
This demon of the woods?' Said Balan, 'I'!

So claim'd the quest and rode away, but
    first,
Embracing Balin, 'Good my brother, hear!
Let not thy moods prevail, when I am gone
Who used to lay them! hold them outer
    fiends,
Who leap at thee to tear thee; shake them
    aside,
Dreams ruling when wit sleeps! yea, but
    to dream
That any of these would wrong thee,
    wrongs thyself.
Witness their flowery welcome. Bound are
    they
To speak no evil. Truly save for fears,
My fears for thee, so rich a fellowship
Would make me wholly blest: thou one of
    them,
Be one indeed: consider them, and all
Their bearing in their common bond of
    love,
No more of hatred than in Heaven itself,
No more of jealousy than in Paradise.'

So Balan warn'd, and went; Balin re-
    main'd:
Who—for but three brief moons had
    glanced away
From being knighted till he smote the
    thrall,
And faded from the presence into years
Of exile—now would strictlier set himself
To learn what Arthur meant by courtesy,
Manhood, and knighthood; wherefore
    hover'd round
Lancelot, but when he mark'd his high
    sweet smile
In passing, and a transitory word
Make knight or churl or child or damsel
    seem
From being smiled at happier in them-
    selves—
Sigh'd, as a boy lame-born beneath a
    height,
That glooms his valley, sighs to see the
    peak
Sun-flush'd, or touch at night the northern
    star;
For one from out his village lately climb'd
And brought report of azure lands and
    fair,

Far seen to left and right; and he himself
Hath hardly scaled with help a hundred
    feet
Up from the base: so Balin marvelling oft
How far beyond him Lancelot seem'd to
    move,
Groan'd, and at times would mutter,
    'These be gifts,
Born with the blood, not learnable, divine,
Beyond *my* reach. Well had I foughten—
    well—
In those fierce wars, struck hard—and had
    I crown'd
With my slain self the heaps of whom I
    slew—
So—better!—But this worship of the
    Queen,
That honour too wherein she holds him—
    this,
This was the sunshine that hath given the
    man
A growth, a name that branches o'er the
    rest,
And strength against all odds, and what the
    King
So prizes—overprizes—gentleness.
Her likewise would I worship an I might.
I never can be close with her, as he
That brought her hither. Shall I pray the
    King
To let me bear some token of his Queen
Whereon to gaze, remembering her—
    forget
My heats and violences? live afresh?
What, if the Queen disdain'd to grant it!
    nay
Being so stately-gentle, would she make
My darkness blackness? and with how
    sweet grace
She greeted my return! Bold will I be—
Some goodly cognizance of Guinevere,
In lieu of this rough beast upon my
    shield,
Langued gules, and tooth'd with grinning
    savagery.'

And Arthur, when Sir Balin sought him,
    said
'What wilt thou bear?' Balin was bold, and
    ask'd
To bear her own crown-royal upon shield,

Whereat she smiled and turn'd her to the
    King,
Who answer'd 'Thou shalt put the crown
    to use.
The crown is but the shadow of the King,
And this a shadow's shadow, let him have it,
So this will help him of his violences!'
'No shadow' said Sir Balin 'O my Queen,
But light to me! no shadow, O my King,
But golden earnest of a gentler life!'

So Balin bare the crown, and all the
    knights
Approved him, and the Queen, and all the
    world
Made music, and he felt his being move
In music with his Order, and the King.

The nightingale, full-toned in middle
    May,
Hath ever and anon a note so thin
It seems another voice in other groves;
Thus, after some quick burst of sudden
    wrath,
The music in him seem'd to change, and
    grow
Faint and far-off.

            And once he saw the thrall
His passion half had gauntleted to death,
That causer of his banishment and shame,
Smile at him, as he deem'd, presump-
    tuously:
His arm half rose to strike again, but fell:
The memory of that cognizance on shield
Weighted it down, but in himself he
    moan'd:

'Too high this mount of Camelot for me:
These high-set courtesies are not for me.
Shall I not rather prove the worse for these?
Fierier and stormier from restraining,
    break
Into some madness ev'n before the Queen?'

Thus, as a hearth lit in a mountain home,
And glancing on the window, when the
    gloom
Of twilight deepens round it, seems a flame
That rages in the woodland far below,
So when his moods were darken'd, court
    and King

And all the kindly warmth of Arthur's hall
Shadow'd an angry distance: yet he strove
To learn the graces of their Table, fought
Hard with himself, and seem'd at length in
    peace.

Then chanced, one morning, that Sir
    Balin sat
Close-bower'd in that garden nigh the
    hall.
A walk of roses ran from door to door;
A walk of lilies crost it to the bower:
And down that range of roses the great
    Queen
Came with slow steps, the morning on her
    face;
And all in shadow from the counter door
Sir Lancelot as to meet her, then at once,
As if he saw not, glanced aside, and paced
The long white walk of lilies toward the
    bower.
Follow'd the Queen; Sir Balin heard her
    'Prince,
Art thou so little loyal to thy Queen,
As pass without good morrow to thy
    Queen?'
To whom Sir Lancelot with his eyes on
    earth,
'Fain would I still be loyal to the Queen.'
'Yea so' she said 'but so to pass me by—
So loyal scarce is loyal to thyself,
Whom all men rate the king of courtesy.
Let be: ye stand, fair lord, as in a dream.'

Then Lancelot with his hand among the
    flowers
'Yea—for a dream. Last night methought
    I saw
That maiden Saint who stands with lily in
    hand
In yonder shrine. All round her prest the
    dark,
And all the light upon her silver face
Flow'd from the spiritual lily that she
    held.
Lo! these her emblems drew mine eyes—
    away:
For see, how perfect-pure! As light a flush
As hardly tints the blossom of the quince
Would mar their charm of stainless maiden-
    hood.'

'Sweeter to me' she said 'this garden rose
Deep-hued and many-folded! sweeter still
The wild-wood hyacinth and the bloom of
     May.
Prince, we have ridd'n before among the
     flowers
In those fair days—not all as cool as these,
Tho' season-earlier. Art thou sad? or sick?
Our noble King will send thee his own
     leech—
Sick? or for any matter anger'd at me?'

     Then Lancelot lifted his large eyes; they
          dwelt
Deep-tranced on hers, and could not fall:
     her hue
Changed at his gaze: so turning side by
     side
They past, and Balin started from his
     bower.

'Queen? subject? but I see not what I
     see.
Damsel and lover? hear not what I hear.
My father hath begotten me in his wrath.
I suffer from the things before me, know,
Learn nothing; am not worthy to be
     knight;
A churl, a clown!' and in him gloom on
     gloom
Deepen'd: he sharply caught his lance and
     shield,
Nor stay'd to crave permission of the King,
But, mad for strange adventure, dash'd
     away.

He took the selfsame track as Balan, saw
The fountain where they sat together, sigh'd
'Was I not better there with him?' and
     rode
The skyless woods, but under open blue
Came on the hoarhead woodman at a bough
Wearily hewing. 'Churl, thine axe!' he
     cried,
Descended, and disjointed it at a blow:
To whom the woodman utter'd wonder-
     ingly
'Lord, thou couldst lay the Devil of these
     woods
If arm of flesh could lay him.' Balin cried

'Him, or the viler devil who plays his part,
To lay that devil would lay the Devil in
     me.'
'Nay' said the churl, 'our devil is a truth,
I saw the flash of him but yestereven.
And some *do* say that our Sir Garlon too
Hath learn'd black magic, and to ride
     unseen.
Look to the cave.' But Balin answer'd him
'Old fabler, these be fancies of the churl,
Look to thy woodcraft,' and so leaving
     him,
Now with slack rein and careless of him-
     self,
Now with dug spur and raving at himself,
Now with droopt brow down the long
     glades he rode;
So mark'd not on his right a cavern-chasm
Yawn over darkness, where, nor far within,
The whole day died, but, dying, gleam'd
     on rocks
Roof-pendent, sharp; and others from the
     floor,
Tusklike, arising, made that mouth of night
Whereout the Demon issued up from Hell.
He mark'd not this, but blind and deaf to
     all
Save that chain'd rage, which ever yelpt
     within,
Past eastward from the falling sun. At once
He felt the hollow-beaten mosses thud
And tremble, and then the shadow of a
     spear,
Shot from behind him, ran along the
     ground.
Sideways he started from the path, and
     saw,
With pointed lance as if to pierce, a shape,
A light of armour by him flash, and pass
And vanish in the woods; and follow'd
     this,
But all so blind in rage that unawares
He burst his lance against a forest bough,
Dishorsed himself, and rose again, and fled
Far, till the castle of a King, the hall
Of Pellam, lichen-bearded, grayly draped
With streaming grass, appear'd, low-built
     but strong;
The ruinous donjon as a knoll of moss,
The battlement overtopt with ivytods,
A home of bats, in every tower an owl.

Then spake the men of Pellam crying 'Lord,
Why wear ye this crown-royal upon shield?'
Said Balin 'For the fairest and the best
Of ladies living gave me this to bear.'
So stall'd his horse, and strode across the court,
But found the greetings both of knight and King
Faint in the low dark hall of banquet: leaves
Laid their green faces flat against the panes,
Sprays grated, and the canker'd boughs without
Whined in the wood; for all was hush'd within,
Till when at feast Sir Garlon likewise ask'd
'Why wear ye that crown-royal?' Balin said
'The Queen we worship, Lancelot, I, and all,
As fairest, best and purest, granted me
To bear it!' Such a sound (for Arthur's knights
Were hated strangers in the hall) as makes
The white swan-mother, sitting, when she hears
A strange knee rustle thro' her secret reeds,
Made Garlon, hissing; then he sourly smiled.
'Fairest I grant her: I have seen; but best,
Best, purest? *thou* from Arthur's hall, and yet
So simple! hast thou eyes, or if, are these
So far besotted that they fail to see
This fair wife-worship cloaks a secret shame?
Truly, ye men of Arthur be but babes.'

A goblet on the board by Balin, boss'd
With holy Joseph's legend, on his right
Stood, all of massiest bronze: one side had sea
And ship and sail and angels blowing on it:
And one was rough with wattling, and the walls
Of that low church he built at Glastonbury.
This Balin graspt, but while in act to hurl,
Thro' memory of that token on the shield
Relax'd his hold: 'I will be gentle' he thought

'And passing gentle' caught his hand away
Then fiercely to Sir Garlon 'Eyes have I
That saw to-day the shadow of a spear,
Shot from behind me, run along the ground;
Eyes too that long have watch'd how Lancelot draws
From homage to the best and purest, might,
Name, manhood, and a grace, but scantly thine,
Who, sitting in thine own hall, canst endure
To mouth so huge a foulness—to thy guest,
Me, me of Arthur's Table. Felon talk!
Let be! no more!'

But not the less by night
The scorn of Garlon, poisoning all his rest,
Stung him in dreams. At length, and dim thro' leaves
Blinkt the white morn, sprays grated, and old boughs
Whined in the wood. He rose, descended, met
The scorner in the castle court, and fain,
For hate and loathing, would have past him by;
But when Sir Garlon utter'd mocking-wise;
'What, wear ye still that same crown-scandalous?'
His countenance blacken'd, and his forehead veins
Bloated, and branch'd; and tearing out of sheath
The brand, Sir Balin with a fiery 'Ha!
So thou be shadow, here I make thee ghost,'
Hard upon helm smote him, and the blade flew
Splintering in six, and clinkt upon the stones.
Then Garlon, reeling slowly backward, fell,
And Balin by the banneret of his helm
Dragg'd him, and struck, but from the castle a cry
Sounded across the court, and—men-at-arms,

A score with pointed lances, making at
   him—
He dash'd the pummel at the foremost face,
Beneath a low door dipt, and made his feet
Wings thro' a glimmering gallery, till he
   mark'd
The portal of King Pellam's chapel wide
And inward to the wall; he stept behind;
Thence in a moment heard them pass like
   wolves
Howling; but while he stared about the
   shrine,
In which he scarce could spy the Christ for
   Saints,
Beheld before a golden altar lie
The longest lance his eyes had ever seen,
Point-painted red; and seizing thereupon
Push'd thro' an open casement down,
   lean'd on it,
Leapt in a semicircle, and lit on earth;
Then hand at ear, and harkening from
   what side
The blindfold rummage buried in the walls
Might echo, ran the counter path, and
   found
His charger, mounted on him and away.
An arrow whizz'd to the right, one to the
   left,
One overhead; and Pellam's feeble cry
'Stay, stay him! he defileth heavenly things
With earthly uses'—made him quickly dive
Beneath the boughs, and race thro' many
   a mile
Of dense and open, till his goodly horse,
Arising wearily at a fallen oak,
Stumbled headlong, and cast him face to
   ground.

   Half-wroth he had not ended, but all
   glad,
Knightlike, to find his charger yet unlamed,
Sir Balin drew the shield from off his neck,
Stared at the priceless cognizance, and
   thought
'I have shamed thee so that now thou
   shamest me,
Thee will I bear no more,' high on a
   branch
Hung it, and turn'd aside into the woods,
And there in gloom cast himself all along,
Moaning 'My violences, my violences!'

But now the wholesome music of the
   wood
Was dumb'd by one from out the hall of
   Mark
A damsel-errant, warbling, as she rode
The woodland alleys, Vivien, with her
   Squire.

'The fire of Heaven has kill'd the barren
   cold,
And kindled all the plain and all the wold.
The new leaf ever pushes off the old.
The fire of Heaven is not the flame of Hell.

'Old priest, who mumble worship in your
   quire—
Old monk and nun, ye scorn the world's
   desire,
Yet in your frosty cells ye feel the fire!
The fire of Heaven is not the flame of Hell.

'The fire of Heaven is on the dusty ways.
The wayside blossoms open to the blaze.
The whole wood-world is one full peal of
   praise.
The fire of Heaven is not the flame of Hell.

'The fire of Heaven is lord of all things
   good,
And starve not thou this fire within thy
   blood,
But follow Vivien thro' the fiery flood!
The fire of Heaven is not the flame of Hell!'

   Then turning to her Squire 'This fire of
   Heaven,
This old sun-worship, boy, will rise again,
And beat the cross to earth, and break the
   King
And all his Table.'

             Then they reach'd a glade,
Where under one long lane of cloudless air
Before another wood, the royal crown
Sparkled, and swaying upon a restless elm
Drew the vague glance of Vivien, and her
   Squire;
Amazed were these; 'Lo there' she cried—
   'a crown—
Borne by some high lord-prince of Arthur's
   hall,

And there a horse! the rider? where is he?
See, yonder lies one dead within the wood.
Not dead; he stirs!—but sleeping. I will
 speak.
Hail, royal knight, we break on thy sweet
 rest,
Not, doubtless, all unearn'd by noble
 deeds.
But bounden art thou, if from Arthur's hall,
To help the weak. Behold, I fly from
 shame,
A lustful King, who sought to win my love
Thro' evil ways: the knight, with whom I
 rode,
Hath suffer'd misadventure, and my squire
Hath in him small defence; but thou, Sir
 Prince,
Wilt surely guide me to the warrior King,
Arthur the blameless, pure as any maid,
To get me shelter for my maidenhood.
I charge thee by that crown upon thy
 shield,
And by the great Queen's name, arise and
 hence.'

And Balin rose, 'Thither no more! nor
 Prince
Nor knight am I, but one that hath de-
 famed
The cognizance she gave me: here I dwell
Savage among the savage woods, here
 die—
Die: let the wolves' black maws en-
 sepulchre
Their brother beast, whose anger was his
 lord.
O me, that such a name as Guinevere's,
Which our high Lancelot hath so lifted up,
And been thereby uplifted, should thro'
 me,
My violence, and my villainy, come to
 shame.'

Thereat she suddenly laugh'd and shrill,
 anon.
Sigh'd all as suddenly. Said Balin to her
'Is this thy courtesy—to mock me, ha?
Hence, for I will not with thee.' Again she
 sigh'd
'Pardon, sweet lord! we maidens often
 laugh

When sick at heart, when rather we should
 weep.
I knew thee wrong'd. I brake upon thy
 rest,
And now full loth am I to break thy dream,
But thou art man, and canst abide a
 truth,
Tho' bitter. Hither, boy—and mark me
 well.
Dost thou remember at Caerleon once—
A year ago—nay, then I love thee not—
Ay, thou rememberest well—one summer
 dawn—
By the great tower—Caerleon upon Usk—
Nay, truly we were hidden: this fair lord,
The flower of all their vestal knighthood,
 knelt
In amorous homage—knelt—what else?—
 O ay
Knelt, and drew down from out his night-
 black hair
And mumbled that white hand whose
 ring'd caress
Had wander'd from her own King's golden
 head,
And lost itself in darkness, till she cried—
I thought the great tower would crash
 down on both—
"Rise, my sweet King, and kiss me on the
 lips,
Thou art my King." This lad, whose
 lightest word
Is mere white truth in simple nakedness,
Saw them embrace: he reddens, cannot
 speak,
So bashful, he! but all the maiden Saints,
The deathless mother-maidenhood of
 Heaven,
Cry out upon her. Up then, ride with me!
Talk not of shame! thou canst not, an thou
 would'st,
Do these more shame than these have done
 themselves.'

She lied with ease; but horror-stricken
 he,
Remembering that dark bower at Camelot,
Breathed in a dismal whisper 'It is truth.'
Sunnily she smiled 'And even in this lone
 wood,
Sweet lord, ye do right well to whisper this.

Fools prate, and perish traitors. Woods
    have tongues,
As walls have ears: but thou shalt go
    with me,
And we will speak at first exceeding low.
Meet is it the good King be not deceived.
See now, I set thee high on vantage ground,
From whence to watch the time, and
    eagle-like
Stoop at thy will on Lancelot and the
    Queen.'

    She ceased; his evil spirit upon him
    leapt,
He ground his teeth together, sprang with
    a yell,
Tore from the branch, and cast on earth,
    the shield,
Drove his mail'd heel athwart the royal
    crown,
Stampt all into defacement, hurl'd it from
    him
Among the forest weeds, and cursed the
    tale,
The told-of, and the teller.

                That weird yell,
Unearthlier than all shriek of bird or beast,
Thrill'd thro' the woods; and Balan lurking
    there
(His quest was unaccomplish'd) heard and
    thought
'The scream of that Wood-devil I came to
    quell!'
Then nearing 'Lo! he hath slain some
    brother-knight,
And tramples on the goodly shield to show
His loathing of our Order and the Queen.
My quest, meseems, is here. Or devil or
    man
Guard thou thine head.' Sir Balin spake
    not word,
But snatch'd a sudden buckler from the
    Squire,
And vaulted on his horse, and so they
    crash'd
In onset, and King Pellam's holy spear,
Reputed to be red with sinless blood,
Redden'd at once with sinful, for the point
Across the maiden shield of Balan prick'd
The hauberk to the flesh; and Balin's horse

Was wearied to the death, and, when they
    clash'd,
Rolling back upon Balin, crush'd the man
Inward, and either fell, and swoon'd away.

    Then to her Squire mutter'd the damsel
    'Fools!
This fellow hath wrought some foulness
    with his Queen:
Else never had he borne her crown, nor
    raved
And thus foam'd over at a rival name:
But thou, Sir Chick, that scarce hast broken
    shell,
Art yet half-yolk, not even come to down—
Who never sawest Caerleon upon Usk—
And yet hast often pleaded for my love—
See what I see, be thou where I have been,
Or else Sir Chick—dismount and loose
    their casques
I fain would know what manner of men
    they be.'
And when the Squire had loosed them,
    'Goodly!—look!
They might have cropt the myriad flower
    of May,
And butt each other here, like brainless
    bulls,
Dead for one heifer!'

             Then the gentle Squire
'I hold them happy, so they died for love:
And, Vivien, tho' ye beat me like your dog,
I too could die, as now I live, for thee.'

    'Live on, Sir Boy,' she cried. 'I better
    prize
The living dog than the dead lion: away!
I cannot brook to gaze upon the dead.'
Then leapt her palfrey o'er the fallen oak,
And bounding forward 'Leave them to the
    wolves.'

    But when their foreheads felt the cooling
    air,
Balin first woke, and seeing that true face,
Familiar up from cradle-time, so wan,
Crawl'd slowly with low moans to where
    he lay,
And on his dying brother cast himself
Dying; and *he* lifted faint eyes; he felt

One near him; all at once they found the world,
Staring wild-wide; then with a childlike wail,
And drawing down the dim disastrous brow
That o'er him hung, he kiss'd it, moan'd and spake;

'O Balin, Balin, I that fain had died
To save thy life, have brought thee to thy death.
Why had ye not the shield I knew? and why
Trampled ye thus on that which bare the Crown?'

Then Balin told him brokenly, and in gasps,
All that had chanced, and Balan moan'd again.

'Brother, I dwelt a day in Pellam's hall:
This Garlon mock'd me, but I heeded not.
And one said "Eat in peace! a liar is he,
And hates thee for the tribute!" this good knight
Told me, that twice a wanton damsel came,
And sought for Garlon at the castle-gates,
Whom Pellam drove away with holy heat.
I well believe this damsel, and the one
Who stood beside thee even now, the same.
"She dwells among the woods" he said "and meets
And dallies with him in the Mouth of Hell."
Foul are their lives; foul are their lips; they lied.
Pure as our own true Mother is our Queen.'

'O brother' answer'd Balin 'woe is me!
My madness all thy life has been thy doom,
Thy curse, and darken'd all thy day; and now
The night has come. I scarce can see thee now.
Goodnight! for we shall never bid again
Goodmorrow—Dark my doom was here, and dark
It will be there. I see thee now no more.

I would not mine again should darken thine,
Goodnight, true brother.'

Balan answer'd low
'Goodnight, true brother here! goodmorrow there!
We two were born together, and we die
Together by one doom:' and while he spoke
Closed his death-drowsing eyes, and slept the sleep
With Balin, either lock'd in either's arm.

MERLIN AND VIVIEN

A STORM was coming, but the winds were still,
And in the wild woods of Broceliande,
Before an oak, so hollow, huge and old
It look'd a tower of ivied masonwork,
At Merlin's feet the wily Vivien lay.

For he that always bare in bitter grudge
The slights of Arthur and his Table, Mark
The Cornish King, had heard a wandering voice,
A minstrel of Caerleon by strong storm
Blown into shelter at Tintagil, say
That out of naked knightlike purity
Sir Lancelot worshipt no unmarried girl
But the great Queen herself, fought in her name,
Sware by her—vows like theirs, that high in heaven
Love most, but neither marry, nor are given
In marriage, angels of our Lord's report.

He ceased, and then—for Vivien sweetly said
(She sat beside the banquet nearest Mark),
'And is the fair example follow'd, Sir,
In Arthur's household?'—answer'd innocently:

'Ay, by some few—ay, truly—youths that hold
It more beseems the perfect virgin knight
To worship woman as true wife beyond
All hopes of gaining, than as maiden girl.
They place their pride in Lancelot and the Queen.

N

So passionate for an utter purity
Beyond the limit of their bond, are these,
For Arthur bound them not to singleness.
Brave hearts and clean! and yet—God guide
  them—young.'

  Then Mark was half in heart to hurl his
    cup
Straight at the speaker, but forbore: he
  rose
To leave the hall, and, Vivien following
  him,
Turn'd to her: 'Here are snakes within the
  grass;
And you methinks, O Vivien, save ye fear
The monkish manhood, and the mask of
  pure
Worn by this court, can stir them till they
  sting.'

  And Vivien answer'd, smiling scorn-
    fully,
'Why fear? because that foster'd at *thy*
  court
I savour of thy—virtues? fear them? no.
As Love, if Love be perfect, casts out fear,
So Hate, if Hate be perfect, casts out fear.
My father died in battle against the King,
My mother on his corpse in open field;
She bore me there, for born from death
  was I
Among the dead and sown upon the
  wind—
And then on thee! and shown the truth
  betimes,
That old true filth, and bottom of the well,
Where Truth is hidden. Gracious lessons
  thine
And maxims of the mud! "This Arthur
  pure!
Great Nature thro' the flesh herself hath
  made
Gives him the lie! There is no being pure,
My cherub; saith not Holy Writ the
  same?"—
If I were Arthur, I would have thy blood.
Thy blessing, stainless King! I bring thee
  back,
When I have ferreted out their burrowings,
The hearts of all this Order in mine hand—
Ay—so that fate and craft and folly close,

Perchance, one curl of Arthur's golden
  beard.
To me this narrow grizzled fork of thine
Is cleaner-fashion'd—Well, I loved thee
  first,
That warps the wit.'

          Loud laugh'd the graceless Mark.
But Vivien, into Camelot stealing, lodged
Low in the city, and on a festal day
When Guinevere was crossing the great
  hall
Cast herself down, knelt to the Queen, and
  wail'd.

  'Why kneel ye there? What evil have ye
    wrought?
Rise!' and the damsel bidden rise arose
And stood with folded hands and down-
  ward eyes
Of glancing corner, and all meekly said,
'None wrought, but suffer'd much, an
  orphan maid!
My father died in battle for thy King,
My mother on his corpse—in open field,
The sad sea-sounding wastes of Lyonesse—
Poor wretch—no friend!—and now by
  Mark the King
For that small charm of feature mine, pur-
  sued—
If any such be mine—I fly to thee.
Save, save me thou—Woman of women—
  thine
The wreath of beauty, thine the crown of
  power,
Be thine the balm of pity, O Heaven's own
  white
Earth-angel, stainless bride of stainless
  King—
Help, for he follows! take me to thyself!
O yield me shelter for mine innocency
Among thy maidens!'

          Here her slow sweet eyes
Fear-tremulous, but humbly hopeful, rose
Fixt on her hearer's, while the Queen who
  stood
All glittering like May sunshine on May
  leaves
In green and gold, and plumed with green
  replied,

'Peace, child! of overpraise and overblame
We choose the last. Our noble Arthur, him
Ye scarce can overpraise, will hear and know.
Nay—we believe all evil of thy Mark—
Well, we shall test thee farther; but this
    hour
We ride a-hawking with Sir Lancelot.
He hath given us a fair falcon which he
    train'd;
We go to prove it. Bide ye here the while.'

    She past; and Vivien murmur'd after
    'Go!
I bide the while.' Then thro' the portal-
    arch
Peering askance, and muttering broken-
    wise,
As one that labours with an evil dream,
Beheld the Queen and Lancelot get to
    horse.

    'Is that the Lancelot? goodly—ay, but
    gaunt:
Courteous—amends for gauntness—takes
    her hand—
That glance of theirs, but for the street,
    had been
A clinging kiss—how hand lingers in hand!
Let go at last!—thy ride away—to hawk
For waterfowl. Royaller game is mine.
For such a supersensual sensual bond
As that gray cricket chirpt of at our
    hearth—
Touch flax with flame—a glance will serve
    —the liars!
Ah little rat that borest in the dyke
Thy hole by night to let the boundless deep
Down upon far-off cities while they
    dance—
Or dream—of thee they dream'd not—nor
    of me
These—ay, but each of either: ride, and
    dream
The mortal dream that never yet was
    mine—
Ride, ride and dream until ye wake—to me!
Then, narrow court and lubber King, fare-
    well!
For Lancelot will be gracious to the rat,
And our wise Queen, if knowing that I
    know,

Will hate, loathe, fear—but honour me the
    more.'

    Yet while they rode together down the
    plain,
Their talk was all of training, terms of art,
Diet and seeling, jesses, leash and lure.
'She is too noble' he said 'to check at pies,
Nor will she rake: there is no baseness in
    her.'
Here when the Queen demanded as by
    chance
'Know ye the stranger woman?' 'Let her
    be,'
Said Lancelot and unhooded casting off
The goodly falcon free; she tower'd; her
    bells,
Tone under tone, shrill'd; and they lifted
    up
Their eager faces, wondering at the
    strength,
Boldness and royal knighthood of the bird
Who pounced her quarry and slew it. Many
    a time
As once—of old—among the flowers—
    they rode.

    But Vivien half-forgotten of the Queen
Among her damsels broidering sat, heard,
    watch'd
And whisper'd: thro' the peaceful court
    she crept
And whisper'd: then as Arthur in the
    highest
Leaven'd the world, so Vivien in the
    lowest,
Arriving at a time of golden rest,
And sowing one ill hint from ear to ear,
While all the heathen lay at Arthur's feet,
And no quest came, but all was joust and
    play,
Leaven'd his hall. They heard and let
    her be.

    Thereafter as an enemy that has left
Death in the living waters, and withdrawn,
The wily Vivien stole from Arthur's court.

    She hated all the knights, and heard in
    thought
Their lavish comment when her name was
    named.

For once, when Arthur walking all alone,
Vext at a rumour issued from herself
Of some corruption crept among his
    knights,
Had met her, Vivien, being greeted fair,
Would fain have wrought upon his cloudy
    mood
With reverent eyes mock-loyal, shaken
    voice,
And flutter'd adoration, and at last
With dark sweet hints of some who prized
    him more
Than who should prize him most; at which
    the King
Had gazed upon her blankly and gone by:
But one had watch'd, and had not held his
    peace:
It made the laughter of an afternoon
That Vivien should attempt the blameless
    King.
And after that, she set herself to gain
Him, the most famous man of all those
    times,
Merlin, who knew the range of all their
    arts,
Had built the King his havens, ships, and
    halls,
Was also Bard, and knew the starry
    heavens;
The people call'd him Wizard; whom at
    first
She play'd about with slight and sprightly
    talk,
And vivid smiles, and faintly-venom'd
    points
Of slander, glancing here and grazing
    there;
And yielding to his kindlier moods, the
    Seer
Would watch her at her petulance, and
    play,
Ev'n when they seem'd unloveable, and
    laugh
As those that watch a kitten; thus he grew
Tolerant of what he half disdain'd, and she,
Perceiving that she was but half disdain'd,
Began to break her sports with graver fits,
Turn red or pale, would often when they
    met
Sigh fully, or all-silent gaze upon him
With such a fixt devotion, that the old man,

Tho' doubtful, felt the flattery, and at
    times
Would flatter his own wish in age for love,
And half believe her true: for thus at times
He waver'd; but that other clung to him,
Fixt in her will, and so the seasons went.

Then fell on Merlin a great melancholy;
He walk'd with dreams and darkness, and
    he found
A doom that ever poised itself to fall,
An ever-moaning battle in the mist,
World-war of dying flesh against the life,
Death in all life and lying in all love,
The meanest having power upon the
    highest,
And the high purpose broken by the worm.

So leaving Arthur's court he gain'd the
    beach;
There found a little boat, and stept into it;
And Vivien follow'd, but he mark'd her
    not.
She took the helm and he the sail; the boat
Drave with a sudden wind across the deeps,
And touching Breton sands, they dis-
    embark'd.
And then she follow'd Merlin all the way,
Ev'n to the wild woods of Broceliande.
For Merlin once had told her of a charm,
The which if any wrought on anyone
With woven paces and with waving arms,
The man so wrought on ever seem'd to lie
Closed in the four walls of a hollow tower,
From which was no escape for evermore;
And none could find that man for ever-
    more,
Nor could he see but him who wrought
    the charm
Coming and going, and he lay as dead
And lost to life and use and name and
    fame.
And Vivien ever sought to work the charm
Upon the great Enchanter of the Time,
As fancying that her glory would be great
According to his greatness whom she
    quench'd.

There lay she all her length and kiss'd
    his feet,
As if in deepest reverence and in love.

A twist of gold was round her hair; a robe
Of samite without price, that more exprest
Than hid her, clung about her lissome
limbs,
In colour like the satin-shining palm
On sallows in the windy gleams of March:
And while she kiss'd them, crying,
'Trample me,
Dear feet, that I have follow'd thro' the
world,
And I will pay you worship; tread me
down
And I will kiss you for it;' he was mute:
So dark a forethought roll'd about his
brain,
As on a dull day in an Ocean cave
The blind wave feeling round his long sea-
hall
In silence: wherefore, when she lifted up
A face of sad appeal, and spake and said,
'O Merlin, do ye love me?' and again,
'O Merlin, do ye love me?' and once more,
'Great Master, do ye love me?' he was
mute.
And lissome Vivien, holding by his heel,
Writhed toward him, slided up his knee
and sat,
Behind his ankle twined her hollow feet
Together, curved an arm about his neck,
Clung like a snake; and letting her left
hand
Droop from his mighty shoulder, as a leaf,
Made with her right a comb of pearl to
part
The lists of such a beard as youth gone out
Had left in ashes: then he spoke and said,
Not looking at her, 'Who are wise in love
Love most, say least,' and Vivien answer'd
quick,
'I saw the little elf-god eyeless once
In Arthur's arras hall at Camelot:
But neither eyes nor tongue—O stupid
child!
Yet you are wise who say it; let me think
Silence is wisdom: I am silent then,
And ask no kiss;' then adding all at once,
'And lo, I clothe myself with wisdom,'
drew
The vast and shaggy mantle of his beard
Across her neck and bosom to her knee,
And call'd herself a gilded summer fly

Caught in a great old tyrant spider's web,
Who meant to eat her up in that wild wood
Without one word. So Vivien call'd herself,
But rather seem'd a lovely baleful star
Veil'd in gray vapour; till he sadly smiled:
'To what request for what strange boon,'
he said,
'Are these your pretty tricks and fooleries,
O Vivien, the preamble? yet my thanks,
For these have broken up my melancholy.'

And Vivien answer'd smiling saucily,
'What, O my Master, have ye found your
voice?
I bid the stranger welcome. Thanks at last!
But yesterday you never open'd lip,
Except indeed to drink: no cup had we:
In mine own lady palms I cull'd the spring
That gather'd trickling dropwise from the
cleft,
And made a pretty cup of both my hands
And offer'd you it kneeling: then you drank
And knew no more, nor gave me one poor
word;
O no more thanks than might a goat have
given
With no more sign of reverence than a
beard.
And when we halted at that other well,
And I was faint to swooning, and you lay
Foot-gilt with all the blossom-dust of those
Deep meadows we had traversed, did you
know
That Vivien bathed your feet before her
own?
And yet no thanks: and all thro' this wild
wood
And all this morning when I fondled you:
Boon, ay, there was a boon, one not so
strange—
How had I wrong'd you? surely ye are
wise,
But such a silence is more wise than kind.'

And Merlin lock'd his hand in hers and
said:
'O did ye never lie upon the shore,
And watch the curl'd white of the coming
wave
Glass'd in the slippery sand before it
breaks?

357

Ev'n such a wave, but not so pleasurable,
Dark in the glass of some presageful mood,
Had I for three days seen, ready to fall.
And then I rose and fled from Arthur's
    court
To break the mood. You follow'd me un-
    ask'd;
And when I look'd, and saw you following
    still,
My mind involved yourself the nearest
    thing
In that mind-mist: for shall I tell you
    truth?
You seem'd that wave about to break upon
    me
And sweep me from my hold upon the
    world,
My use and name and fame. Your pardon ,
    child.
Your pretty sports have brighten'd all
    again.
And ask your boon, for boon I owe you
    thrice,
Once for wrong done you by confusion,
    next
For thanks it seems till now neglected, last
For these your dainty gambols: wherefore
    ask;
And take this boon so strange and not so
    strange.'

    And Vivien answer'd smiling mourn-
        fully:
'O not so strange as my long asking it,
Not yet so strange as you yourself are
    strange,
Nor half so strange as that dark mood of
    yours.
I ever fear'd ye were not wholly mine;
And see, yourself have own'd ye did me
    wrong.
The people call you prophet: let it be:
Be not of those that can expound them-
    selves.
Take Vivien for expounder; she will call
That three-days-long presageful gloom of
    yours
No presage, but the same mistrustful mood
That makes you seem less noble than your-
    self,
Whenever I have ask'd this very boon,

Now ask'd again: for see you not, dear love,
That such a mood as that, which lately
    gloom'd
Your fancy when ye saw me following you,
Must make me fear still more you are not
    mine,
Must make me yearn still more to prove
    you mine,
And make me wish still more to learn this
    charm
Of woven paces and of waving hands,
As proof of trust. O Merlin, teach it me.
The charm so taught will charm us both
    to rest.
For, grant me some slight power upon
    your fate,
I, feeling that you felt me worthy trust,
Should rest and let you rest, knowing you
    mine.
And therefore be as great as ye are named,
Not muffled round with selfish reticence.
How hard you look and how denyingly!
O, if you think this wickedness in me,
That I should prove it on you unawares,
That makes me passing wrathful; then our
    bond
Had best be loosed for ever: but think or
    not,
By Heaven that hears I tell you the clean
    truth,
As clean as blood of babes, as white as
    milk:
O Merlin, may this earth, if ever I,
If these unwitty wandering wits of mine,
Ev'n in the jumbled rubbish of a dream,
Have tript on such conjectural treachery—
May this hard earth cleave to the Nadir
    hell
Down, down, and close again, and nip me
    flat,
If I be such a traitress. Yield my boon,
Till which I scarce can yield you all I am;
And grant my re-reiterated wish,
The great proof of your love: because I
    think,
However wise, ye hardly know me yet.'

    And Merlin loosed his hand from hers
        and said,
'I never was less wise, however wise,
Too curious Vivien, tho' you talk of trust,

Than when I told you first of such a charm.
Yea, if ye talk of trust I tell you this,
Too much I trusted when I told you that,
And stirr'd this vice in you which ruin'd man
Thro' woman the first hour; for howsoe'er
In children a great curiousness be well,
Who have to learn themselves and all the world,
In you, that are no child, for still I find
Your face is practised when I spell the lines,
I call it,—well I will not call it vice:
But since you name yourself the summer fly,
I well could wish a cobweb for the gnat,
That settles, beaten back, and beaten back
Settles, till one could yield for weariness:
But since I will not yield to give you power
Upon my life and use and name and fame,
Why will ye never ask some other boon?
Yea, by God's rood, I trusted you too much.'

And Vivien, like the tenderest-hearted maid
That ever bided tryst at village stile,
Made answer, either eyelid wet with tears:
'Nay, Master, be not wrathful with your maid;
Caress her: let her feel herself forgiven
Who feels no heart to ask another boon.
I think ye hardly know the tender rhyme
Of "trust me not at all or all in all."
I heard the great Sir Lancelot sing it once,
And it shall answer for me. Listen to it.

'"In Love, if Love be Love, if Love be ours,
Faith and unfaith can ne'er be equal powers:
Unfaith in aught is want of faith in all.

'"It is the little rift within the lute,
That by and by will make the music mute,
And ever widening slowly silence all.

'"The little rift within the lover's lute
Or little pitted speck in garner'd fruit,
That rotting inward slowly moulders all.

'"It is not worth the keeping: let it go:
But shall it? answer, darling, answer, no.
And trust me not at all or all in all."

O Master, do ye love my tender rhyme?'

And Merlin look'd and half believed her true,
So tender was her voice, so fair her face,
So sweetly gleam'd her eyes behind her tears
Like sunlight on the plain behind a shower:
And yet he answer'd half indignantly:

'Far other was the song that once I heard
By this huge oak, sung nearly where we sit:
For here we met, some ten or twelve of us,
To chase a creature that was current then
In these wild woods, the hart with golden horns.
It was the time when first the question rose
About the founding of a Table Round,
That was to be, for love of God and men
And noble deeds, the flower of all the world.
And each incited each to noble deeds.
And while we waited, one, the youngest of us,
We could not keep him silent, out he flash'd,
And into such a song, such fire for fame,
Such trumpet-blowings in it, coming down
To such a stern and iron-clashing close,
That when he stopt we long'd to hurl together,
And should have done it; but the beauteous beast
Scared by the noise upstarted at our feet,
And like a silver shadow slipt away
Thro' the dim land; and all day long we rode
Thro' the dim land against a rushing wind,
That glorious rounded echoing in our ears,
And chased the flashes of his golden horns
Until they vanish'd by the fairy well
That laughs at iron—as our warriors did—
Where children cast their pins and nails, and cry,
"Laugh, little well!" but touch it with a sword,

It buzzes fiercely round the point; and there
We lost him: such a noble song was that.
But, Vivien, when you sang me that sweet rhyme,
I felt as tho' you knew this cursed charm,
Were proving it on me, and that I lay
And felt them slowly ebbing, name and fame.'

And Vivien answer'd smiling mournfully:
'O mine have ebb'd away for evermore,
And all thro' following you to this wild wood,
Because I saw you sad, to comfort you.
Lo now, what hearts have men! they never mount
As high as woman in her selfless mood.
And touching fame, howe'er ye scorn my song,
Take one verse more—the lady speaks it—this:

'"My name, once mine, now thine, is closelier mine,
For fame, could fame be mine, that fame were thine,
And shame, could shame be thine, that shame were mine.
So trust me not at all or all in all."

'Says she not well? and there is more—this rhyme
Is like the fair pearl-necklace of the Queen,
That burst in dancing, and the pearls were spilt;
Some lost, some stolen, some as relics kept.
But nevermore the same two sister pearls
Ran down the silken thread to kiss each other
On her white neck—so is it with this rhyme:
It lives dispersedly in many hands,
And every minstrel sings it differently;
Yet is there one true line, the pearl of pearls:
"Man dreams of Fame while woman wakes to love."
Yea! Love, tho' Love were of the grossest, carves

A portion from the solid present, eats
And uses, careless of the rest; but Fame,
The Fame that follows death is nothing to us;
And what is Fame in life but half-disfame,
And counterchanged with darkness? ye yourself
Know well that Envy calls you Devil's son,
And since ye seem the Master of all Art,
They fain would make you Master of all vice.'

And Merlin lock'd his hand in hers and said,
'I once was looking for a magic weed,
And found a fair young squire who sat alone,
Had carved himself a knightly shield of wood,
And then was painting on it fancied arms,
Azure, an Eagle rising or, the Sun
In dexter chief; the scroll "I follow fame."
And speaking not, but leaning over him,
I took his brush and blotted out the bird,
And made a Gardener putting in a graff,
With this for motto, "Rather use than fame."
You should have seen him blush; but afterwards
He made a stalwart knight. O Vivien,
For you, methinks you think you love me well;
For me, I love you somewhat; rest: and Love
Should have some rest and pleasure in himself,
Not ever be too curious for a boon,
Too prurient for a proof against the grain
Of him ye say ye love: but Fame with men,
Being but ampler means to serve mankind,
Should have small rest or pleasure in herself,
But work as vassal to the larger love,
That dwarfs the petty love of one to one.
Use gave me Fame at first, and Fame again
Increasing gave me use. Lo, there my boon!
What other? for men sought to prove me vile,
Because I fain had given them greater wits:
And then did Envy call me Devil's son:

The sick weak beast seeking to help herself
By striking at her better, miss'd, and brought
Her own claw back, and wounded her own heart.
Sweet were the days when I was all unknown,
But when my name was lifted up, the storm
Brake on the mountain and I cared not for it.
Right well know I that Fame is half-disfame,
Yet needs must work my work. That other fame,
To one at least, who hath not children, vague,
The cackle of the unborn about the grave,
I cared not for it: a single misty star,
Which is the second in a line of stars
That seem a sword beneath a belt of three,
I never gazed upon it but I dreamt
Of some vast charm concluded in that star
To make fame nothing. Wherefore, if I fear,
Giving you power upon me thro' this charm,
That you might play me falsely, having power,
However well ye think ye love me now
(As sons of kings loving in pupilage
Have turn'd to tyrants when they came to power)
I rather dread the loss of use than fame;
If you—and not so much from wickedness,
As some wild turn of anger, or a mood
Of overstrain'd affection, it may be,
To keep me all to your own self,—or else
A sudden spurt of woman's jealousy,—
Should try this charm on whom ye say ye love.'

And Vivien answer'd smiling as in wrath:
'Have I not sworn? I am not trusted. Good!
Well, hide it, hide it; I shall find it out;
And being found take heed of Vivien.
A woman and not trusted, doubtless I
Might feel some sudden turn of anger born
Of your misfaith; and your fine epithet
Is accurate too, for this full love of mine

Without the full heart back may merit well
Your term of overstrain'd. So used as I,
My daily wonder is, I love at all.
And as to woman's jealousy, O why not?
O to what end, except a jealous one,
And one to make me jealous if I love,
Was this fair charm invented by yourself?
I well believe that all about this world
Ye cage a buxom captive here and there,
Closed in the four walls of a hollow tower
From which is no escape for evermore.'

Then the great Master merrily answer'd her:
'Full many a love in loving youth was mine;
I needed then no charm to keep them mine
But youth and love; and that full heart of yours
Whereof ye prattle, may now assure you mine;
So live uncharm'd. For those who wrought it first,
The wrist is parted from the hand that waved,
The feet unmortised from their ankle-bones
Who paced it, ages back: but will ye hear
The legend as in guerdon for your rhyme?

'There lived a king in the most Eastern East,
Less old than I, yet older, for my blood
Hath earnest in it of far springs to be.
A tawny pirate anchor'd in his port,
Whose bark had plunder'd twenty nameless isles;
And passing one, at the high peep of dawn,
He saw two cities in a thousand boats
All fighting for a woman on the sea.
And pushing his black craft among them all,
He lightly scatter'd theirs and brought her off,
With loss of half his people arrow-slain;
A maid so smooth, so white, so wonderful,
They said a light came from her when she moved:
And since the pirate would not yield her up,
The King impaled him for his piracy;

Then made her Queen: but those isle-
nurtured eyes
Waged such unwilling tho' successful war
On all the youth, they sicken'd; councils
thinn'd,
And armies waned, for magnet-like she
drew
The rustiest iron of old fighters' hearts;
And beasts themselves would worship;
camels knelt
Unbidden, and the brutes of mountain back
That carry kings in castles, bow'd black
knees
Of homage, ringing with their serpent
hands,
To make her smile, her golden ankle-bells.
What wonder, being jealous, that he sent
His horns of proclamation out thro' all
The hundred under-kingdoms that he
sway'd
To find a wizard who might teach the King
Some charm, which being wrought upon
the Queen
Might keep her all his own: to such a one
He promised more than ever king has
given,
A league of mountain full of golden mines,
A province with a hundred miles of coast,
A palace and a princess, all for him:
But on all those who tried and fail'd, the
King
Pronounced a dismal sentence, meaning
by it
To keep the list low and pretenders back,
Or like a king, not to be trifled with—
Their heads should moulder on the city
gates.
And many tried and fail'd, because the
charm
Of nature in her overbore their own:
And many a wizard brow bleach'd on the
walls:
And many weeks a troop of carrion crows
Hung like a cloud above the gateway
towers.'

And Vivien breaking in upon him, said:
'I sit and gather honey; yet, methinks
Thy tongue has tript a little: ask thy-
self,
The lady never made *unwilling* war

With those fine eyes: she had her pleasure
in it,
And made her good man jealous with good
cause.
And lived there neither dame not damsel
then
Wroth at a lover's loss? were all as tame,
I mean, as noble, as their Queen was fair?
Not one to flirt a venom at her eyes,
Or pinch a murderous dust into her drink,
Or make her paler with a poison'd rose?
Well, those were not our days: but did
they find
A wizard? Tell me, was he like to thee?'

She ceased, and made her lithe arm
round his neck
Tighten, and then drew back, and let her
eyes
Speak for her, glowing on him, like a bride's
On her new lord, her own, the first of men.

He answer'd laughing, 'Nay, not like
to me.
At last they found—his foragers for
charms—
A little glassy-headed hairless man,
Who lived alone in a great wild on grass;
Read but one book, and ever reading grew
So grated down and filed away with
thought,
So lean his eyes were monstrous; while
the skin
Clung but to crate and basket, ribs and
spine.
And since he kept his mind on one sole
aim,
Nor ever touch'd fierce wine, nor tasted
flesh,
Nor own'd a sensual wish, to him the wall
That sunders ghosts and shadow-casting
men
Became a crystal, and he saw them thro' it,
And heard their voices talk behind the
wall,
And learnt their elemental secrets, powers
And forces; often o'er the sun's bright eye
Drew the vast eyelid of an inky cloud,
And lash'd it at the base with slanting
storm;
Or in the noon of mist and driving rain,

When the lake whiten'd and the pinewood
    roar'd,
And the cairn'd mountain was a shadow,
    sunn'd
The world to peace again: here was the
    man.
And so by force they dragg'd him to the
    King.
And then he taught the King to charm the
    Queen
In such-wise, that no man could see her
    more,
Nor saw she save the King, who wrought
    the charm,
Coming and going, and she lay as dead,
And lost all use of life: but when the King
Made proffer of the league of golden mines,
The province with a hundred miles of coast,
The palace and the princess, that old man
Went back to his old wild, and lived on
    grass,
And vanish'd, and his book came down
    to me.'

And Vivien answer'd smiling saucily:
'Ye have the book: the charm is written
    in it:
Good: take my counsel: let me know it at
    once:
For keep it like a puzzle chest in chest,
With each chest lock'd and padlock'd
    thirty-fold,
And whelm all this beneath as vast a
    mound
As after furious battle turfs the slain
On some wild down above the windy deep,
I yet should strike upon a sudden means
To dig, pick, open, find and read the
    charm:
Then, if I tried it, who should blame me
    then?'

And smiling as a master smiles at one
That is not of his school, nor any school
But that where blind and naked Ignorance
Delivers brawling judgments, unashamed,
On all things all day long, he answer'd her:

'Thou read the book, my pretty Vivien!
O ay, it is but twenty pages long,
But every page having an ample marge,

And every marge enclosing in the midst
A square of text that looks a little blot,
The text no larger than the limbs of fleas;
And every square of text an awful charm,
Writ in a language that has long gone by.
So long, that mountains have arisen since
With cities on their flanks—thou read the
    book!
And every margin scribbled, crost, and
    cramm'd
With comment, densest condensation, hard
To mind and eye; but the long sleepless
    nights
Of my long life have made it easy to me.
And none can read the text, not even I;
And none can read the comment but
    myself;
And in the comment did I find the charm.
O, the results are simple; a mere child
Might use it to the harm of anyone,
And never could undo it: ask no more:
For tho' you should not prove it upon me,
But keep that oath ye sware, ye might,
    perchance,
Assay it on some one of the Table Round,
And all because ye dream they babble of
    you.'

And Vivien, frowning in true anger,
    said:
'What dare the full-fed liars say of me?
They ride abroad redressing human
    wrongs!
They sit with knife in meat and wine in
    horn!
They bound to holy vows of chastity!
Were I not woman, I could tell a tale.
But you are man, you well can under-
    stand
The shame that cannot be explain'd for
    shame.
Not one of all the drove should touch me:
    swine!'

Then answer'd Merlin careless of her
    words:
'You breathe but accusation vast and
    vague,
Spleen-born, I think, and proofless. If ye
    know,
Set up the charge ye know, to stand or fall!'

And Vivien answer'd frowning wrath-
fully:
'O ay, what say ye to Sir Valence, him
Whose kinsman left him watcher o'er his
wife
And two fair babes, and went to distant
lands;
Was one year gone, and on returning found
Not two but three? there lay the reckling,
one
But one hour old! What said the happy
sire?
A seven-months' babe had been a truer
gift.
Those twelve sweet moons confused his
fatherhood.'

Then answer'd Merlin, 'Nay, I know
the tale.
Sir Valence wedded with an outland dame:
Some cause had kept him sunder'd from
his wife:
One child they had: it lived with her: she
died:
His kinsman travelling on his own affair
Was charged by Valence to bring home
the child.
He brought, not found it therefore: take
the truth.'

'O ay,' said Vivien, 'overtrue a tale.
What say ye then to sweet Sir Sagramore,
That ardent man? "to pluck the flower in
season,"
So says the song, "I trow it is no treason."
O Master, shall we call him overquick
To crop his own sweet rose before the
hour?'

And Merlin answer'd, 'Overquick art
thou
To catch a loathly plume fall'n from the
wing
Of that foul bird of rapine whose whole
prey
Is man's good name: he never wrong'd his
bride.
I know the tale. An angry gust of wind
Puff'd out his torch among the myriad-
room'd
And many-corridor'd complexities

Of Arthur's palace: then he found a door,
And darkling felt the sculptured ornament
That wreathen round it made it seem his
own;
And wearied out made for the couch and
slept,
A stainless man beside a stainless maid;
And either slept, nor knew of other there;
Till the high dawn piercing the royal rose
In Arthur's casement glimmer'd chastely
down,
Blushing upon them blushing, and at once
He rose without a word and parted from
her:
But when the thing was blazed about the
court,
The brute world howling forced them into
bonds,
And as it chanced they are happy, being
pure.'

'O ay,' said Vivien, 'that were likely too.
What say ye then to fair Sir Percivale
And of the horrid foulness that he wrought,
The saintly youth, the spotless lamb of
Christ,
Or some black wether of St. Satan's fold.
What, in the precincts of the chapel-yard,
Among the knightly brasses of the graves,
And by the cold Hic Jacets of the dead!'

And Merlin answer'd careless of her
charge,
'A sober man is Percivale and pure;
But once in life was fluster'd with new
wine,
Then paced for coolness in the chapel-
yard;
Where one of Satan's shepherdesses caught
And meant to stamp him with her master's
mark;
And that he sinn'd is not believable;
For, look upon his face!—but if he sinn'd,
The sin that practice burns into the blood,
And not the one dark hour which brings
remorse,
Will brand us, after, of whose fold we be:
Or else were he, the holy king, whose hymns
Are chanted in the minster, worse than all.
But is your spleen froth'd out, or have ye
more?'

And Vivien answer'd frowning yet in wrath:
'O ay; what say ye to Sir Lancelot, friend
Traitor or true? that commerce with the Queen,
I ask you, is it clamour'd by the child,
Or whisper'd in the corner? do ye know it?'

To which he answer'd sadly, 'Yea, I know it.
Sir Lancelot went ambassador, at first,
To fetch her, and she watch'd him from her walls.
A rumour runs, she took him for the King,
So fixt her fancy on him: let them be.
But have ye no one word of loyal praise
For Arthur, blameless King and stainless man?'

She answer'd with a low and chuckling laugh:
'Man! is he man at all, who knows and winks?
Sees what his fair bride is and does, and winks?
By which the good King means to blind himself,
And blinds himself and all the Table Round
To all the foulness that they work. Myself
Could call him (were it not for womanhood)
The pretty, popular name such manhood earns,
Could call him the main cause of all their crime;
Yea, were he not crown'd King, coward, and fool.'

Then Merlin to his own heart, loathing, said:
'O true and tender! O my liege and King!
O selfless man and stainless gentleman,
Who wouldst against thine own eye-witness fain
Have all men true and leal, all women pure;
How, in the mouths of base interpreters,
From over-fineness not intelligible
To things with every sense as false and foul
As the poach'd filth that floods the middle street,
Is thy white blamelessness accounted blame!'

But Vivien, deeming Merlin overborne
By instance, recommenced, and let her tongue
Rage like a fire among the noblest names,
Polluting, and imputing her whole self,
Defaming and defacing, till she left
Not even Lancelot brave, nor Galahad clean.

Her words had issue other than she will'd.
He dragg'd his eyebrow bushes down, and made
A snowy penthouse for his hollow eyes,
And mutter'd in himself, 'Tell *her* the charm!
So, if she had it, would she rail on me
To snare the next, and if she have it not
So will she rail. What did the wanton say?
"Not mount as high;" we scarce can sink as low:
For men at most differ as Heaven and earth,
But women, worst and best, as Heaven and Hell.
I know the Table Round, my friends of old;
All brave, and many generous, and some chaste.
She cloaks the scar of some repulse with lies;
I well believe she tempted them and fail'd,
Being so bitter: for fine plots may fail,
Tho' harlots paint their talk as well as face
With colours of the heart that are not theirs.
I will not let her know: nine tithes of times
Face-flatterer and backbiter are the same.
And they, sweet soul, that most impute a crime
Are pronest to it, and impute themselves,
Wanting the mental range; or low desire
Not to feel lowest makes them level all;
Yea, they would pare the mountain to the plain,
To leave an equal baseness; and in this

365

Are harlots like the crowd, that if they find
Some stain or blemish in a name of note,
Not grieving that their greatest are so
small,
Inflate themselves with some insane delight,
And judge all nature from her feet of clay,
Without the will to lift their eyes, and see
Her godlike head crown'd with spiritual
fire,
And touching other worlds. I am weary of
her.'

He spoke in words part heard, in
whispers part,
Half-suffocated in the hoary fell
And many-winter'd fleece of throat and
chin.
But Vivien, gathering somewhat of his
mood,
And hearing 'harlot' mutter'd twice or
thrice,
Leapt from her session on his lap, and
stood
Stiff as a viper frozen; loathesome sight,
How from the rosy lips of life and love,
Flash'd the bare-grinning skeleton of
death!
White was her cheek; sharp breaths of
anger puff'd
Her fairy nostril out; her hand half-
clench'd
Went faltering sideways downward to her
belt,
And feeling; had she found a dagger there
(For in a wink the false love turns to hate)
She would have stabb'd him; but she
found it not:
His eye was calm, and suddenly she took
To bitter weeping like a beaten child,
A long, long weeping, not consolable.
Then her false voice made way, broken
with sobs:

'O crueller than was ever told in tale,
Or sung in song! O vainly lavish'd love!
O cruel, there was nothing wild or strange,
Or seeming shameful—for what shame in
love,
So love be true, and not as yours is—
nothing
Poor Vivien had not done to win his trust

Who call'd her what he call'd her—all her
crime,
All—all—the wish to prove him wholly
hers.'

She mused a little, and then clapt her
hands
Together with a wailing shriek, and said:
'Stabb'd through the heart's affections to
the heart!
Seethed like the kid in its own mother's
milk!
Kill'd with a word worse than a life of
blows!
I thought that he was gentle, being great:
O God, that I had loved a smaller man!
I should have found in him a greater heart.
O, I, that flattering my true passion, saw
The knights, the court, the King, dark in
your light,
Who loved to make men darker than they
are,
Because of that high pleasure which I had
To seat you sole upon my pedestal
Of worship—I am answer'd, and hence-
forth
The course of life that seem'd so flowery
to me
With you for guide and master, only you,
Becomes the sea-cliff pathway broken
short,
And ending in a ruin—nothing left,
But into some low cave to crawl, and there,
If the wolf spare me, weep my life away,
Kill'd with inutterable unkindliness.'

She paused, she turn'd away, she hung
her head,
The snake of gold slid from her hair, the
braid
Slipt and uncoil'd itself, she wept afresh,
And the dark wood grew darker toward the
storm
In silence, while his anger slowly died
Within him, till he let his wisdom go
For ease of heart, and half believed her
true:
Call'd her to shelter in the hollow oak,
'Come from the storm,' and having no
reply,
Gazed at the heaving shoulder, and the face

Hand-hidden, as for utmost grief or shame;
Then thrice essay'd, by tenderest-touching
    terms,
To sleek her ruffled peace of mind, in vain.
At last she let herself be conquer'd by him,
And as the cageling newly flown returns,
The seeming-injured simple-hearted thing
Came to her old perch back, and settled
    there.
There while she sat, half-falling from his
    knees,
Half-nestled at his heart, and since he saw
The slow tear creep from her closed eye-
    lid yet,
About her, more in kindness than in love,
The gentle wizard cast a shielding arm.
But she dislink'd herself at once and rose,
Her arms upon her breast across, and
    stood,
A virtuous gentlewoman deeply wrong'd,
Upright and flush'd before him: then she
    said:

'There must be now no passages of love
Betwixt us twain henceforward evermore;
Since, if I be what I am grossly call'd,
What should be granted which your own
    gross heart
Would reckon worth the taking? I will go.
In truth, but one thing now—better have
    died
Thrice than have ask'd it once—could
    make me stay—
That proof of trust—so often ask'd in vain!
How justly, after that vile term of yours,
I find with grief! I might believe you then,
Who knows? once more. Lo! what was
    once to me
Mere matter of the fancy, now hath grown
The vast necessity of heart and life.
Farewell; think gently of me, for I fear
My fate or folly, passing gayer youth
For one so old, must be to love thee still.
But ere I leave thee let me swear once more
That if I schemed against thy peace in
    this,
May yon just heaven, that darkens o'er me,
    send
One flash, that, missing all things else, may
    make
My scheming brain a cinder, if I lie.'

Scarce had she ceased, when out of
    heaven a bolt
(For now the storm was close above them)
    struck,
Furrowing a giant oak, and javelining
With darted spikes and splinters of the
    wood
The dark earth round. He raised his eyes
    and saw
The tree that shone white-listed thro' the
    gloom.
But Vivien, fearing heaven had heard her
    oath,
And dazzled by the livid-flickering fork,
And deafen'd with the stammering cracks
    and claps
That follow'd, flying back and crying out,
'O Merlin, tho' you do not love me, save,
Yet save me!' clung to him and hugg'd
    him close;
And call'd him dear protector in her fright,
Nor yet forgot her practice in her fright,
But wrought upon his mood and hugg'd
    him close.
The pale blood of the wizard at her touch
Took gayer colours, like an opal warm'd.
She blamed herself for telling hearsay tales:
She shook from fear, and for her fault she
    wept
Of petulancy; she call'd him lord and liege,
Her seer, her bard, her silver star of eve,
Her God, her Merlin, the one passionate
    love
Of her whole life; and ever overhead
Bellow'd the tempest, and the rotten
    branch
Snapt in the rushing of the river-rain
Above them; and in change of glare and
    gloom
Her eyes and neck glittering went and
    came;
Till now the storm, its burst of passion
    spent,
Moaning and calling out of other lands,
Had left the ravaged woodland yet once
    more
To peace; and what should not have been
    had been,
For Merlin, overtalk'd and overworn,
Had yielded, told her all the charm, and
    slept.

Then, in one moment, she put forth the
    charm
Of woven paces and of waving hands,
And in the hollow oak he lay as dead,
And lost to life and use and name and fame.

Then crying 'I have made his glory
    mine,'
And shrieking out 'O fool!' the harlot leapt
Adown the forest, and the thicket closed
Behind her, and the forest echo'd 'fool.'

LANCELOT AND ELAINE

ELAINE the fair, Elaine the loveable,
Elaine, the lily maid of Astolat,
High in her chamber up a tower to the east
Guarded the sacred shield of Lancelot;
Which first she placed where morning's
    earliest ray
Might strike it, and awake her with the
    gleam;
Then fearing rust or soilure fashion'd for it
A case of silk, and braided thereupon
All the devices blazon'd on the shield
In their own tinct, and added, of her wit,
A border fantasy of branch and flower,
And yellow-throated nestling in the nest.
Nor rested thus content, but day by day,
Leaving her household and good father,
    climb'd
That eastern tower, and entering barr'd
    her door,
Stript off the case, and read the naked
    shield,
Now guess'd a hidden meaning in his arms,
Now made a pretty history to herself
Of every dint a sword had beaten in it,
And every scratch a lance had made upon it,
Conjecturing when and where: this cut is
    fresh;
That ten years back; this dealt him at
    Caerlyle;
That at Caerleon; this at Camelot:
And ah God's mercy, what a stroke was
    there!
And here a thrust that might have kill'd,
    but God
Broke the strong lance, and roll'd his
    enemy down,
And saved him: so she lived in fantasy.

How came the lily maid by that good
    shield
Of Lancelot, she that knew not ev'n his
    name?
He left it with her, when he rode to tilt
For the great diamond in the diamond
    jousts,
Which Arthur had ordain'd, and by that
    name
Had named them, since a diamond was the
    prize.

For Arthur, long before they crown'd
    him King,
Roving the trackless realms of Lyonnesse,
Had found a glen, gray boulder and black
    tarn.
A horror lived about the tarn, and clave
Like its own mists to all the mountain side:
For here two brothers, one a king, had met
And fought together; but their names were
    lost;
And each had slain his brother at a blow;
And down they fell and made the glen
    abhorr'd:
And there they lay till all their bones were
    bleach'd,
And lichen'd into colour with the crags:
And he, that once was king, had on a crown
Of diamonds, one in front, and four aside.
And Arthur came, and labouring up the
    pass,
All in a misty moonshine, unawares
Had trodden that crown'd skeleton, and
    the skull
Brake from the nape, and from the skull
    the crown
Roll'd into light, and turning on its rims
Fled like a glittering rivulet to the tarn:
And down the shingly scaur he plunged,
    and caught,
And set it on his head, and in his heart
Heard murmurs, 'Lo, thou likewise shalt
    be King.'

Thereafter, when a King, he had the
    gems
Pluck'd from the crown, and show'd them
    to his knights,
Saying, 'These jewels, whereupon I
    chanced

Divinely, are the kingdom's, not the King's—
For public use: henceforward let there be,
Once every year, a joust for one of these:
For so by nine years' proof we needs must learn
Which is our mightiest, and ourselves shall grow
In use of arms and manhood, till we drive
The heathen, who, some say, shall rule the land
Hereafter, which God hinder.' Thus he spoke:
And eight years past, eight jousts had been, and still
Had Lancelot won the diamond of the year,
With purpose to present them to the Queen,
When all were won; but meaning all at once
To snare her royal fancy with a boon
Worth half her realm, had never spoken word.

Now for the central diamond and the last
And largest, Arthur, holding then his court
Hard on the river nigh the place which now
Is this world's hugest, let proclaim a joust
At Camelot, and when the time drew nigh
Spake (for she had been sick) to Guinevere,
'Are you so sick, my Queen, you cannot move
To these fair jousts?' 'Yea, lord,' she said, 'ye know it.'
'Then will ye miss,' he answer'd, 'the great deeds
Of Lancelot, and his prowess in the lists,
A sight ye love to look on.' And the Queen
Lifted her eyes, and they dwelt languidly
On Lancelot, where he stood beside the King.
He thinking that he read her meaning there,
'Stay with me, I am sick; my love is more
Than many diamonds,' yielded; and a heart
Love-loyal to the least wish of the Queen

(However much he yearn'd to make complete
The tale of diamonds for his destined boon)
Urged him to speak against the truth, and say,
'Sir King, mine ancient wound is hardly whole,
And lets me from the saddle;' and the King
Glanced first at him, then her, and went his way.
No sooner gone than suddenly she began:

'To blame, my lord Sir Lancelot, much to blame!
Why go ye not to these fair jousts? the knights
Are half of them our enemies, and the crowd
Will murmur, "Lo the shameless ones, who take
Their pastime now the trustful King is gone!"'
Then Lancelot vext at having lied in vain:
'Are ye so wise? ye were not once so wise,
My Queen, that summer, when ye loved me first.
Then of the crowd ye took no more account
Than of the myriad cricket of the mead,
When its own voice clings to each blade of grass,
And every voice is nothing. As to knights,
Them surely can I silence with all ease.
But now my loyal worship is allow'd
Of all men: many a bard, without offence,
Has link'd our names together in his lay,
Lancelot, the flower of bravery, Guinevere,
The pearl of beauty: and our knights at feast
Have pledged us in this union, while the King
Would listen smiling. How then? is there more?
Has Arthur spoken aught? or would yourself,
Now weary of my service and devoir,
Henceforth be truer to your faultless lord?'

She broke into a little scornful laugh:
'Arthur, my lord, Arthur, the faultless King,
That passionate perfection, my good lord—

369

But who can gaze upon the Sun in heaven?
He never spake word of reproach to me,
He never had a glimpse of mine untruth,
He cares not for me: only here to-day
There gleam'd a vague suspicion in his
    eyes:
Some meddling rogue has tamper'd with
    him—else
Rapt in this fancy of his Table Round,
And swearing men to vows impossible,
To make them like himself: but, friend,
    to me
He is all fault who hath no fault at all:
For who loves me must have a touch of
    earth;
The low sun makes the colour: I am yours,
Not Arthur's, as ye know, save by the
    bond.
And therefore hear my words: go to the
    jousts:
The tiny-trumpeting gnat can break our
    dream
When sweetest; and the vermin voices here
May buzz so loud—we scorn them, but
    they sting.'

Then answer'd Lancelot, the chief of
    knights:
'And with what face, after my pretext
    made,
Shall I appear, O Queen, at Camelot, I
Before a King who honours his own word,
As if it were his God's?'

                'Yea,' said the Queen,
'A moral child without the craft to rule,
Else had he not lost me: but listen to me,
If I must find you wit: we hear it said
That men go down before your spear at a
    touch,
But knowing you are Lancelot; your great
    name,
This conquers: hide it therefore; go un-
    known:
Win! by this kiss you will: and our true
    King
Will then allow your pretext, O my knight,
As all for glory; for to speak him true,
Ye know right well, how meek soe'er he
    seem,
No keener hunter after glory breathes.

He loves it in his knights more than him-
    self:
They prove to him his work: win and
    return.'

Then got Sir Lancelot suddenly to horse,
Wroth at himself. Not willing to be known,
He left the barren-beaten thoroughfare,
Chose the green path that show'd the rarer
    foot,
And there among the solitary downs,
Full often lost in fancy, lost his way;
Till as he traced a faintly-shadow'd track,
That all in loops and links among the dales
Ran to the Castle of Astolat, he saw
Fired from the west, far on a hill, the
    towers.
Thither he made, and blew the gateway
    horn.
Then came an old, dumb, myriad-wrinkled
    man,
Who let him into lodging and disarm'd.
And Lancelot marvell'd at the wordless
    man;
And issuing found the Lord of Astolat
With two strong sons, Sir Torre and Sir
    Lavaine,
Moving to meet him in the castle court;
And close behind them stept the lily maid
Elaine, his daughter: mother of the house
There was not: some light jest among
    them rose
With laughter dying down as the great
    knight
Approach'd them: then the Lord of
    Astolat:
'Whence comest thou, my guest, and by
    what name
Livest between the lips? for by thy state
And presence I might guess thee chief of
    those,
After the King, who eat in Arthur's halls.
Him have I seen: the rest, his Table
    Round,
Known as they are, to me they are un-
    known.'

Then answer'd Lancelot, the chief of
    knights:
'Known am I, and of Arthur's hall, and
    known,

What I by mere mischance have brought,
my shield.
But since I go to joust as one unknown
At Camelot for the diamond, ask me not,
Hereafter ye shall know me—and the
shield—
I pray you lend me one, if such you have,
Blank, or at least with some device not
mine.'

Then said the Lord of Astolat, 'Here is
Torre's:
Hurt in his first tilt was my son, Sir Torre,
And so, God wot, his shield is blank
enough.
His ye can have.' Then added plain Sir
Torre,
'Yea, since I cannot use it, ye may have it.'
Here laugh'd the father saying, 'Fie, Sir
Churl,
Is that an answer for a noble knight?
Allow him! but Lavaine, my younger here,
He is so full of lustihood, he will ride,
Joust for it, and win, and bring it in an
hour,
And set it in this damsel's golden hair,
To make her thrice as wilful as before.'

'Nay, father, nay good father, shame
me not
Before this noble knight,' said young
Lavaine,
'For nothing. Surely I but play'd on Torre:
He seem'd so sullen, vext he could not go:
A jest, no more! for, knight, the maiden
dreamt
That some one put this diamond in her
hand,
And that it was too slippery to be held,
And slipt and fell into some pool or stream,
The castle-well, belike; and then I said
That if I went and if I fought and won it
(But all was jest and joke among ourselves)
Then must she keep it safelier. All was jest.
But, father, give me leave, an if he will,
To ride to Camelot with this noble knight:
Win shall I not, but do my best to win:
Young as I am, yet would I do my best.'

'So ye will grace me,' answer'd Lancelot,
Smiling a moment, 'with your fellowship

O'er these waste downs whereon I lost
myself,
Then were I glad of you as guide and
friend:
And you shall win this diamond,—as I
hear
It is a fair large diamond,—if ye may,
And yield it to this maiden, if ye will.'
'A fair large diamond,' added plain Sir
Torre,
'Such be for queens, and not for simple
maids.'
Then she, who held her eyes upon the
ground,
Elaine, and heard her name so tost about,
Flush'd slightly at the slight disparagement
Before the stranger knight, who, looking
at her,
Full courtly, yet not falsely, thus return'd:
'If what is fair be but for what is fair,
And only queens are to be counted so,
Rash were my judgment then, who deem
this maid
Might wear as fair a jewel as is on earth,
Not violating the bond of like to like.'

He spoke and ceased: the lily maid
Elaine,
Won by the mellow voice before she look'd,
Lifted her eyes, and read his lineaments.
The great and guilty love he bare the
Queen,
In battle with the love he bare his lord,
Had marr'd his face, and mark'd it ere his
time.
Another sinning on such heights with one,
The flower of all the west and all the world,
Had been the sleeker for it: but in him
His mood was often like a fiend, and rose
And drove him into wastes and solitudes
For agony, who was yet a living soul.
Marr'd as he was, he seem'd the goodliest
man
That ever among ladies ate in hall,
And noblest, when she lifted up her eyes.
However marr'd, of more than twice her
years,
Seam'd with an ancient swordcut on the
cheek,
And bruised and bronzed, she lifted up her
eyes

And loved him, with that love which was
    her doom.

Then the great knight, the darling of the
    court,
Loved of the loveliest, into that rude hall
Stept with all grace, and not with half dis-
    dain
Hid under grace, as in a smaller time,
But kindly man moving among his kind:
Whom they with meats and vintage of
    their best
And talk and minstrel melody entertain'd.
And much they ask'd of court and Table
    Round,
And ever well and readily answer'd he:
But Lancelot, when they glanced at Guine-
    vere,
Suddenly speaking of the wordless man,
Heard from the Baron that, ten years
    before,
The heathen caught and reft him of his
    tongue.
'He learnt and warn'd me of their fierce
    design
Against my house, and him they caught
    and maim'd;
But I, my sons, and little daughter fled
From bonds or death, and dwelt among the
    woods
By the great river in a boatman's hut.
Dull days were those, till our good Arthur
    broke
The Pagan yet once more on Badon hill.'

'O there, great lord, doubtless,' Lavaine
    said, rapt
By all the sweet and sudden passion of
    youth
Toward greatness in its elder, 'you have
    fought.
O tell us—for we live apart—you know
Of Arthur's glorious wars.' And Lancelot
    spoke
And answer'd him at full, as having been
With Arthur in the fight which all day
    long
Rang by the white mouth of the violent
    Glem;
And in the four loud battles by the shore
Of Duglas; that on Bassa; then the war

That thunder'd in and out the gloomy
    skirts
Of Celidon the forest; and again
By castle Gurnion, where the glorious
    King
Had on his cuirass worn our Lady's Head,
Carved of one emerald center'd in a sun
Of silver rays, that lighten'd as he breathed;
And at Caerleon had he help'd his lord,
When the strong neighings of the wild
    white Horse
Set every gilded parapet shuddering;
And up in Agned-Cathregonion too,
And down the waste sand-shores of Trath
    Treroit,
Where many a heathen fell; 'and on the
    mount
Of Badon I myself beheld the King
Charge at the head of all his Table Round,
And all his legions crying Christ and him,
And break them; and I saw him, after,
    stand
High on a heap of slain, from spur to plume
Red as the rising sun with heathen blood,
And seeing me, with a great voice he cried,
"They are broken, they are broken!" for
    the King,
However mild he seems at home, nor cares
For triumph in our mimic wars, the
    jousts—
For if his own knight cast him down, he
    laughs
Saying, his knights are better men than
    he—
Yet in this heathen war the fire of God
Fills him: I never saw his like: there lives
No greater leader.'

                    While he utter'd this,
Low to her own heart said the lily maid,
'Save your great self, fair lord;' and when
    he fell
From talk of war to traits of pleasantry—
Being mirthful he, but in a stately kind—
She still took note that when the living
    smile
Died from his lips, across him came a cloud
Of melancholy severe, from which again,
Whenever in her hovering to and fro
The lily maid had striven to make him
    cheer,

There brake a sudden-beaming tenderness
Of manners and of nature: and she thought
That all was nature, all, perchance, for her.
And all night long his face before her lived,
As when a painter, poring on a face,
Divinely thro' all hindrance finds the man
Behind it, and so paints him that his face,
The shape and colour of a mind and life,
Lives for his children, ever at its best
And fullest; so the face before her lived,
Dark-splendid, speaking in the silence, full
Of noble things, and held her from her
    sleep.
Till rathe she rose, half-cheated in the
    thought
She needs must bid farewell to sweet
    Lavaine.
First as in fear, step after step, she stole
Down the long tower-stairs, hesitating:
Anon, she heard Sir Lancelot cry in the
    court,
'This shield, my friend, where is it?' and
    Lavaine
Past inward, as she came from out the
    tower.
There to his proud horse Lancelot turn'd,
    and smooth'd
The glossy shoulder, humming to himself.
Half-envious of the flattering hand, she
    drew
Nearer and stood. He look'd, and more
    amazed
Than if seven men had set upon him, saw
The maiden standing in the dewy light.
He had not dream'd she was so beautiful.
Then came on him a sort of sacred fear,
For silent, tho' he greeted her, she stood
Rapt on his face as if it were a God's.
Suddenly flash'd on her a wild desire,
That he should wear her favour at the tilt.
She braved a riotous heart in asking for it.
'Fair lord, whose name I know not—noble
    it is,
I well believe, the noblest—will you wear
My favour at this tourney?' 'Nay,' said he,
'Fair lady, since I never yet have worn
Favour of any lady in the lists.
Such is my wont, as those, who know me,
    know.'
'Yea, so,' she answer'd; 'then in wearing
    mine

Needs must be lesser likelihood, noble lord,
That those who know should know you.'
    And he turn'd
Her counsel up and down within his mind,
And found it true, and answer'd, 'True,
    my child.
Well, I will wear it: fetch it out to me:
What is it?' and she told him 'A red sleeve
Broider'd with pearls,' and brought it:
    then he bound
Her token on his helmet, with a smile
Saying, 'I never yet have done so much
For any maiden living,' and the blood
Sprang to her face and fill'd her with
    delight;
But left her all the paler, when Lavaine
Returning brought the yet-unblazon'd
    shield,
His brother's; which he gave to Lancelot,
Who parted with his own to fair Elaine:
'Do me this grace, my child, to have my
    shield
In keeping till I come.' 'A grace to me,'
She answer'd, 'twice to-day. I am your
    squire!'
Whereat Lavaine said, laughing, 'Lily
    maid,
For fear our people call you lily maid
In earnest, let me bring your colour back;
Once, twice, and thrice: now get you hence
    to bed:'
So kiss'd her, and Sir Lancelot his own
    hand,
And thus they moved away: she stay'd a
    minute,
Then made a sudden step to the gate, and
    there—
Her bright hair blown about the serious
    face
Yet rosy-kindled with her brother's kiss—
Paused by the gateway, standing near the
    shield
In silence, while she watch'd their arms
    far-off
Sparkle, until they dipt below the downs.
Then to her tower she climb'd, and took
    the shield,
There kept it, and so lived in fantasy.

Meanwhile the new companions past
    away

Far o'er the long backs of the bushless
downs,
To where Sir Lancelot knew there lived a
knight
Not far from Camelot, now for forty years
A hermit, who had pray'd, labour'd and
pray'd,
And ever labouring had scoop'd himself
In the white rock a chapel and a hall
On massive columns, like a shorecliff cave,
And cells and chambers: all were fair and
dry;
The green light from the meadows under-
neath
Struck up and lived along the milky roofs;
And in the meadows tremulous aspen-trees
And poplars made a noise of falling
showers.
And thither wending there that night they
bode.

But when the next day broke from
underground,
And shot red fire and shadows thro' the
cave,
They rose, heard mass, broke fast, and
rode away:
Then Lancelot saying, 'Hear, but hold my
name
Hidden, you ride with Lancelot of the
Lake,'
Abash'd Lavaine, whose instant reverence,
Dearer to true young hearts than their own
praise,
But left him leave to stammer, 'Is it
indeed?'
And after muttering 'The great Lancelot,'
At last he got his breath and answer'd,
'One,
One have I seen—that other, our liege lord,
The dread Pendragon, Britain's King of
kings,
Of whom the people talk mysteriously,
He will be there—then were I stricken blind
That minute, I might say that I had seen.'

So spake Lavaine, and when they reach'd
the lists
By Camelot in the meadow, let his eyes
Run thro' the peopled gallery which half
round

Lay like a rainbow fall'n upon the grass,
Until they found the clear-faced King, who
sat
Robed in red samite, easily to be known,
Since to his crown the golden dragon clung,
And down his robe the dragon writhed in
gold,
And from the carven-work behind him
crept
Two dragons gilded, sloping down to make
Arms for his chair, while all the rest of
them
Thro' knots and loops and folds innumer-
able
Fled ever thro' the woodwork, till they
found
The new design wherein they lost them-
selves,
Yet with all ease, so tender was the work:
And, in the costly canopy o'er him set,
Blazed the last diamond of the nameless
king.

Then Lancelot answer'd young Lavaine
and said,
'Me you call great: mine is the firmer seat,
The truer lance: but there is many a youth
Now crescent, who will come to all I am
And overcome it; and in me there dwells
No greatness, save it be some far-off touch
Of greatness to know well I am not great:
There is the man.' And Lavaine gaped
upon him
As on a thing miraculous, and anon
The trumpets blew; and then did either
side,
They that assail'd, and they that held the
lists,
Set lance in rest, strike spur, suddenly
move,
Meet in the midst, and there so furiously
Shock, that a man far-off might well per-
ceive,
If any man that day were left afield,
The hard earth shake, and a low thunder of
arms.
And Lancelot bode a little, till he saw
Which were the weaker; then he hurl'd
into it
Against the stronger: little need to speak
Of Lancelot in his glory! King, duke, earl,

374

Count, baron—whom he smote, he overthrew.

But in the field were Lancelot's kith and
kin,
Ranged with the Table Round that held
the lists,
Strong men, and wrathful that a stranger
knight
Should do and almost overdo the deeds
Of Lancelot; and one said to the other, 'Lo!
What is he? I do not mean the force
alone—
The grace and versatility of the man!
Is it not Lancelot?' 'When has Lancelot
worn
Favour of any lady in the lists?
Not such his wont, as we, that know him,
know.'
'How then? who then?' a fury seized them
all,
A fiery family passion for the name
Of Lancelot, and a glory one with theirs.
They couch'd their spears and prick'd
their steeds, and thus,
Their plumes driv'n backward by the wind
they made
In moving, all together down upon him
Bare, as a wild wave in the wide North-sea,
Green-glimmering toward the summit,
bears, with all
Its stormy crests that smoke against the
skies,
Down on a bark, and overbears the bark,
And him that helms it, so they overbore
Sir Lancelot and his charger, and a spear
Down-glancing lamed the charger, and a
spear
Prick'd sharply his own cuirass, and the
head
Pierced thro' his side, and there snapt, and
remain'd.

Then Sir Lavaine did well and worship-
fully;
He bore a knight of old repute to the earth,
And brought his horse to Lancelot where
he lay.
He up the side, sweating with agony, got,
But thought to do while he might yet
endure,

And being lustily holpen by the rest,
His party,—tho' it seem'd half-miracle
To those he fought with,—drave his kith
and kin,
And all the Table Round that held the lists,
Back to the barrier; then the trumpets blew
Proclaiming his the prize, who wore the
sleeve
Of scarlet, and the pearls; and all the
knights,
His party, cried 'Advance and take thy prize
The diamond;' but he answer'd, 'Diamond
me
No diamonds! for God's love, a little air!
Prize me no prizes, for my prize is death!
Hence will I, and I charge you, follow me
not.'

He spoke, and vanish'd suddenly from
the field
With young Lavaine into the poplar grove.
There from his charger down he slid, and
sat,
Gasping to Sir Lavaine, 'Draw the lance-
head:'
'Ah my sweet lord Sir Lancelot,' said
Lavaine,
'I dread me, if I draw it, you will die.'
But he, 'I die already with it: draw—
Draw,'—and Lavaine drew, and Sir Lance-
lot gave
A marvellous great shriek and ghastly
groan,
And half his blood burst forth, and down
he sank
For the pure pain, and wholly swoon'd
away.
Then came the hermit out and bare him in,
There stanch'd his wound; and there, in
daily doubt
Whether to live or die, for many a week
Hid from the wide world's rumour by the
grove
Of poplars with their noise of falling
showers,
And ever-tremulous aspen-trees, he lay.

But on that day when Lancelot fled the
lists,
His party, knights of utmost North and
West,

Lords of waste marches, kings of desolate isles,
Came round their great Pendragon, saying to him,
'Lo, Sire, our knight, thro' whom we won the day,
Hath gone sore wounded, and hath left his prize
Untaken, crying that his prize is death.'
'Heaven hinder,' said the King, 'that such an one,
So great a knight as we have seen to-day—
He seem'd to me another Lancelot—
Yea, twenty times I thought him Lance-lot—
He must not pass uncared for. Wherefore, rise,
O Gawain, and ride forth and find the knight.
Wounded and wearied needs must he be near.
I charge you that you get at once to horse.
And, knights and kings, there breathes not one of you
Will deem this prize of ours is rashly given:
His prowess was too wondrous. We will do him
No customary honour: since the knight
Came not to us, of us to claim the prize,
Ourselves will send it after. Rise and take
This diamond, and deliver it, and return,
And bring us where he is, and how he fares,
And cease not from your quest until ye find.'

So saying, from the carven flower above,
To which it made a restless heart, he took,
And gave, the diamond: then from where he sat
At Arthur's right, with smiling face arose,
With smiling face and frowning heart, a Prince
In the mid might and flourish of his May,
Gawain, surnamed The Courteous, fair and strong,
And after Lancelot, Tristram, and Geraint
And Gareth, a good knight, but there-withal
Sir Modred's brother, and the child of Lot,
Nor often loyal to his word, and now

Wroth that the King's command to sally forth
In quest of whom he knew not, made him leave
The banquet, and concourse of knights and kings.

So all in wrath he got to horse and went;
While Arthur to the banquet, dark in mood,
Past, thinking 'Is it Lancelot who hath come
Despite the wound he spake of, all for gain
Of glory, and hath added wound to wound,
And ridd'n away to die?' So fear'd the King,
And, after two days' tarriance there, return'd.
Then when he saw the Queen, embracing ask'd,
'Love, are you yet so sick?' 'Nay, lord,' she said.
'And where is Lancelot?' Then the Queen amazed,
'Was he not with you? won he not your prize?'
'Nay, but one like him.' 'Why that like was he.'
And when the King demanded how she knew,
Said, 'Lord, no sooner had ye parted from us,
Than Lancelot told me of a common talk
That men went down before his spear at a touch,
But knowing he was Lancelot; his great name
Conquer'd; and therefore would he hide his name
From all men, ev'n the King, and to this end
Had made the pretext of a hindering wound,
That he might joust unknown of all, and learn
If his old prowess were in aught decay'd;
And added, "Our true Arthur, when he learns,
Will well allow my pretext, as for gain
Of purer glory."'

Then replied the King:
'Far lovelier in our Lancelot had it been,
In lieu of idly dallying with the truth,
To have trusted me as he hath trusted thee.
Surely his King and most familiar friend
Might well have kept his secret. True,
indeed,
Albeit I know my knights fantastical,
So fine a fear in our large Lancelot
Must needs have moved my laughter: now
remains
But little cause for laughter: his own kin—
Ill news, my Queen, for all who love him,
this!—
His kith and kin, not knowing, set upon
him;
So that he went sore wounded from the
field:
Yet good news too: for goodly hopes are
mine
That Lancelot is no more a lonely heart.
He wore, against his wont, upon his helm
A sleeve of scarlet, broider'd with great
pearls,
Some gentle maiden's gift.'

'Yea, lord,' she said,
'Thy hopes are mine,' and saying that, she
choked,
And sharply turn'd about to hide her face,
Past to her chamber, and there flung her-
self
Down on the great King's couch, and
writhed upon it,
And clench'd her fingers till they bit the
palm,
And shriek'd out 'Traitor' to the unhearing
wall,
Then flash'd into wild tears, and rose again,
And moved about her palace, proud and
pale.

Gawain the while thro' all the region
round
Rode with his diamond, wearied of the
quest,
Touch'd at all points, except the poplar
grove,
And came at last, tho' late, to Astolat:
Whom glittering in enamell'd arms the
maid

Glanced at, and cried, 'What news from
Camelot, lord?
What of the knight with the red sleeve?'
'He won.'
'I knew it,' she said. 'But parted from the
jousts
Hurt in the side,' whereat she caught her
breath;
Thro' her own side she felt the sharp lance
go;
Thereon she smote her hand: wellnigh she
swoon'd:
And, while he gazed wonderingly at her,
came
The Lord of Astolat out, to whom the
Prince
Reported who he was, and on what quest
Sent, that he bore the prize and could not
find
The victor, but had ridd'n a random round
To seek him, and had wearied of the search.
To whom the Lord of Astolat, 'Bide with
us,
And ride no more at random, noble Prince!
Here was the knight, and here he left a
shield;
This will he send or come for: furthermore
Our son is with him; we shall hear anon,
Needs must we hear.' To this the cour-
teous Prince
Accorded with his wonted courtesy,
Courtesy with a touch of traitor in it,
And stay'd; and cast his eyes on fair
Elaine:
Where could be found face daintier? then
her shape
From forehead down to foot, perfect—
again
From foot to forehead exquisitely turn'd:
'Well—if I bide, lo! this wild flower for
me!'
And oft they met among the garden yews,
And there he set himself to play upon her
With sallying wit, free flashes from a height
Above her, graces of the court, and songs,
Sighs, and slow smiles, and golden elo-
quence
And amorous adulation, till the maid
Rebell'd against it, saying to him, 'Prince,
O loyal nephew of our noble King,
Why ask you not to see the shield he left,

Whence you might learn his name? Why
    slight your King,
And lose the quest he sent you on, and
    prove
No surer than our falcon yesterday,
Who lost the hern we slipt her at, and went
To all the winds?' 'Nay, by mine head,'
    said he
'I lose it, as we lose the lark in heaven,
O damsel, in the light of your blue eyes;
But an ye will it let me see the shield.'
And when the shield was brought, and
    Gawain saw
Sir Lancelot's azure lions, crown'd with
    gold,
Ramp in the field, he smote his thigh, and
    mock'd:
'Right was the King! our Lancelot! that
    true man!'
'And right was I,' she answer'd merrily, 'I,
Who dream'd my knight the greatest
    knight of all.'
'And if *I* dream'd,' said Gawain, 'that you
    love
This greatest knight, your pardon! lo, ye
    know it!
Speak therefore: shall I waste myself in
    vain?'
Full simple was her answer, 'What know
    I?
My brethren have been all my fellowship;
And I, when often they have talk'd of love,
Wish'd it had been my mother, for they
    talk'd,
Meseem'd, of what they knew not; so
    myself—
I know not if I know what true love is,
But if I know, then, if I love not him,
I know there is none other I can love.'
'Yea, by God's death,' said he, 'ye love
    him well,
But would not, knew ye what all others
    know,
And whom he loves.' 'So be it,' cried
    Elaine,
And lifted her fair face and moved away:
But he pursued her, calling, 'Stay a little!
One golden minute's grace! he wore your
    sleeve:
Would he break faith with one I may not
    name?

Must our true man change like a leaf at
    last?
Nay—like enow: why then, far be it from
    me
To cross our mighty Lancelot in his loves!
And, damsel, for I deem you know full well
Where your great knight is hidden, let me
    leave
My quest with you; the diamond also: here!
For if you love, it will be sweet to give it;
And if he love, it will be sweet to have it
From your own hand; and whether he love
    or not,
A diamond is a diamond. Fare you well
A thousand times!—a thousand times fare-
    well!
Yet, if he love, and his love hold, we two
May meet at court hereafter: there, I think,
So ye will learn the courtesies of the court,
We two shall know each other.'

                Then he gave,
And slightly kiss'd the hand to which he
    gave,
The diamond, and all wearied of the quest
Leapt on his horse, and carolling as he went
A true-love ballad, lightly rode away.

Thence to the court he past; there told
    the King
What the King knew, 'Sir Lancelot is the
    knight.'
And added, 'Sire, my liege, so much I
    learnt;
But fail'd to find him, tho' I rode all round
The region: but I lighted on the maid
Whose sleeve he wore; she loves him; and
    to her,
Deeming our courtesy is the truest law,
I gave the diamond: she will render it;
For by mine head she knows his hiding-
    place.'

The seldom-frowning King frown'd, and
    replied,
'Too courteous truly! ye shall go no more
On quest of mine, seeing that ye forget
Obedience is the courtesy due to kings.'

He spake and parted. Wroth, but all in
    awe,

378

For twenty strokes of the blood, without a
    word,
Linger'd that other, staring after him:
Then shook his hair, strode off, and buzz'd
    abroad
About the maid of Astolat, and her love.
All ears were prick'd at once, all tongues
    were loosed:
'The maid of Astolat loves Sir Lancelot,
Sir Lancelot loves the maid of Astolat.'
Some read the King's face, some the
    Queen's, and all
Had marvel what the maid might be, but
    most
Predoom'd her as unworthy. One old dame
Came suddenly on the Queen with the
    sharp news.
She, that had heard the noise of it before,
But sorrowing Lancelot should have
    stoop'd so low,
Marr'd her friend's aim with pale tran-
    quillity.
So ran the tale like fire about the court,
Fire in dry stubble a nine-days' wonder
    flared:
Till ev'n the knights at banquet twice or
    thrice
Forgot to drink to Lancelot and the Queen,
And pledging Lancelot and the lily maid
Smiled at each other, while the Queen,
    who sat
With lips severely placid, felt the knot
Climb in her throat, and with her feet
    unseen
Crush'd the wild passion out against the
    floor
Beneath the banquet, where the meats
    became
As wormwood, and she hated all who
    pledged.

But far away the maid in Astolat,
Her guiltless rival, she that ever kept
The one-day-seen Sir Lancelot in her
    heart,
Crept to her father, while he mused alone,
Sat on his knee, stroked his gray face and
    said,
'Father, you call me wilful, and the fault
Is yours who let me have my will, and now,
Sweet father, will you let me lose my wits?'

'Nay,' said he, 'surely.' 'Wherefore, let me
    hence,'
She answer'd, 'and find out our dear
    Lavaine.'
'Ye will not lose your wits for dear Lavaine:
Bide,' answer'd he: 'we needs must hear
    anon
Of him, and of that other.' 'Ay,' she said,
'And of that other, for I needs must hence
And find that other, wheresoe'er he be,
And with mine own hand give his diamond
    to him,
Lest I be found as faithless in the quest
As yon proud Prince who left the quest
    to me.
Sweet father, I behold him in my dreams
Gaunt as it were the skeleton of himself,
Death-pale, for lack of gentle maiden's aid.
The gentler-born the maiden, the more
    bound,
My father, to be sweet and serviceable
To noble knights in sickness, as ye know
When these have worn their tokens: let me
    hence
I pray you.' Then her father nodding said,
'Ay, ay, the diamond: wit ye well, my child,
Right fain were I to learn this knight were
    whole,
Being our greatest: yea, and you must
    give it—
And sure I think this fruit is hung too high
For any mouth to gape for save a queen's—
Nay, I mean nothing: so then, get you
    gone,
Being so very wilful you must go.'

Lightly, her suit allow'd, she slipt away,
And while she made her ready for her ride,
Her father's latest word humm'd in her ear,
'Being so very wilful you must go,'
And changed itself and echo'd in her heart,
'Being so very wilful you must die.'
But she was happy enough and shook it off,
As we shake off the bee that buzzes at us;
And in her heart she answer'd it and said,
'What matter, so I help him back to life?'
Then far away with good Sir Torre for
    guide
Rode o'er the long backs of the bushless
    downs
To Camelot, and before the city-gates

Came on her brother with a happy face
Making a roan horse caper and curvet
For pleasure all about a field of flowers:
Whom when she saw, 'Lavaine,' she cried,
'Lavaine,
How fares my lord Sir Lancelot?' He
amazed,
'Torre and Elaine! why here? Sir Lancelot!
How know ye my lord's name is Lancelot?'
But when the maid had told him all her
tale,
Then turn'd Sir Torre, and being in his
moods
Left them, and under the strange-statued
gate,
Where Arthur's wars were render'd mystic-
ally,
Past up the still rich city to his kin,
His own far blood, which dwelt at Camelot;
And her, Lavaine across the poplar grove
Led to the caves: there first she saw the
casque
Of Lancelot on the wall: her scarlet sleeve,
Tho' carved and cut, and half the pearls
away,
Stream'd from it still; and in her heart she
laugh'd,
Because he had not loosed it from his helm,
But meant once more perchance to tourney
in it.
And when they gain'd the cell wherein he
slept,
His battle-writhen arms and mighty hands
Lay naked on the wolfskin, and a dream
Of dragging down his enemy made them
move.
Then she that saw him lying unsleek, un-
shorn,
Gaunt as it were the skeleton of himself,
Utter'd a little tender dolorous cry.
The sound not wonted in a place so still
Woke the sick knight, and while he roll'd
his eyes
Yet blank from sleep, she started to him,
saying,
'Your prize the diamond sent you by the
King:'
His eyes glisten'd: she fancied 'Is it for
me?'
And when the maid had told him all the
tale

Of King and Prince, the diamond sent, the
quest
Assign'd to her not worthy of it, she knelt
Full lowly by the corners of his bed,
And laid the diamond in his open hand.
Her face was near, and as we kiss the child
That does the task assign'd, he kiss'd her
face.
At once she slipt like water to the floor.
'Alas,' he said, 'your ride hath wearied
you.
Rest must you have.' 'No rest for me,' she
said;
'Nay, for near you, fair lord, I am at rest.'
What might she mean by that? his large
black eyes,
Yet larger thro' his leanness, dwelt upon
her,
Till all her heart's sad secret blazed itself
In the heart's colours on her simple face;
And Lancelot look'd and was perplext in
mind,
And being weak in body said no more;
But did not love the colour; woman's love,
Save one, he not regarded, and so turn'd
Sighing, and feign'd a sleep until he slept.

Then rose Elaine and glided thro' the
fields,
And past beneath the weirdly-sculptured
gates
Far up the dim rich city to her kin;
There bode the night: but woke with dawn,
and past
Down thro' the dim rich city to the fields,
Thence to the cave: so day by day she past
In either twilight ghost-like to and fro
Gliding, and every day she tended him,
And likewise many a night: and Lancelot
Would, tho' he call'd his wound a little
hurt
Whereof he should be quickly whole, at
times
Brain-feverous in his heat and agony, seem
Uncourteous, even he: but the meek maid
Sweetly forbore him ever, being to him
Meeker than any child to a rough nurse,
Milder than any mother to a sick child,
And never woman yet, since man's first
fall,
Did kindlier unto man, but her deep love

Upbore her; till the hermit, skill'd in all
The simples and the science of that time,
Told him that her fine care had saved his
life.
And the sick man forgot her simple blush,
Would call her friend and sister, sweet
Elaine,
Would listen for her coming and regret
Her parting step, and held her tenderly,
And loved her with all love except the love
Of man and woman when they love their
best,
Closest and sweetest, and had died the
death
In any knightly fashion for her sake.
And peradventure had he seen her first
She might have made this and that other
world
Another world for the sick man; but now
The shackles of an old love straiten'd him,
His honour rooted in dishonour stood,
And faith unfaithful kept him falsely true.

Yet the great knight in his mid-sickness
made
Full many a holy vow and pure resolve.
These, as but born of sickness, could not
live:
For when the blood ran lustier in him
again,
Full often the bright image of one face,
Making a treacherous quiet in his heart,
Dispersed his resolution like a cloud.
Then if the maiden, while that ghostly
grace
Beam'd on his fancy, spoke, he answer'd
not,
Or short and coldly, and she knew right
well
What the rough sickness meant, but what
this meant
She knew not, and the sorrow dimm'd her
sight,
And drave her ere her time across the fields
Far into the rich city, where alone
She murmur'd, 'Vain, in vain: it cannot be.
He will not love me: how then? must I
die?'
Then as a little helpless innocent bird,
That has but one plain passage of few
notes,

Will sing the simple passage o'er and o'er
For all an April morning, till the ear
Wearies to hear it, so the simple maid
Went half the night repeating, 'Must I
die?'
And now to right she turn'd, and now to
left,
And found no ease in turning or in rest;
And 'Him or death,' she mutter'd, 'death
or him,'
Again and like a burthen, 'Him or death.'

But when Sir Lancelot's deadly hurt was
whole,
To Astolat returning rode the three.
There morn by morn, arraying her sweet
self
In that wherein she deem'd she look'd her
best,
She came before Sir Lancelot, for she
thought
'If I be loved, these are my festal robes,
If not, the victim's flowers before he fall.'
And Lancelot ever prest upon the maid
That she should ask some goodly gift of
him
For her own self or hers; 'and do not shun
To speak the wish most near to your true
heart;
Such service have ye done me, that I make
My will of yours, and Prince and Lord
am I
In mine own land, and what I will I can.'
Then like a ghost she lifted up her face,
But like a ghost without the power to speak.
And Lancelot saw that she withheld her
wish,
And bode among them yet a little space
Till he should learn it; and one morn it
chanced
He found her in among the garden yews,
And said, 'Delay no longer, speak your wish,
Seeing I go to-day:' then out she brake:
'Going? and we shall never see you more.
And I must die for want of one bold word.'
'Speak: that I live to hear,' he said, 'is
yours.'
Then suddenly and passionately she spoke:
'I have gone mad. I love you: let me die.'
'Ah, sister,' answer'd Lancelot, 'what is
this?'

And innocently extending her white arms,
'Your love,' she said, 'your love—to be
your wife.'
And Lancelot answer'd, 'Had I chosen to
wed,
I had been wedded earlier, sweet Elaine:
But now there never will be wife of mine.'
'No, no,' she cried, 'I care not to be wife,
But to be with you still, to see your face,
To serve you, and to follow you thro' the
world.'
And Lancelot answer'd, 'Nay, the world,
the world,
All ear and eye, with such a stupid heart
To interpret ear and eye, and such a tongue
To blare its own interpretation—nay,
Full ill then should I quit your brother's
love,
And your good father's kindness.' And she
said,
'Not to be with you, not to see your face—
Alas for me then, my good days are done.'
'Nay, noble maid,' he answer'd, 'ten times
nay!
This is not love: but love's first flash in
youth,
Most common: yea, I know it of mine own
self:
And you yourself will smile at your own
self
Hereafter, when you yield your flower of
life
To one more fitly yours, not thrice your
age:
And then will I, for true you are and sweet
Beyond mine old belief in womanhood,
More specially should your good knight be
poor,
Endow you with broad land and territory
Even to the half my realm beyond the seas,
So that would make you happy: further-
more,
Ev'n to the death, as tho' ye were my
blood,
In all your quarrels will I be your knight.
This will I do, dear damsel, for your sake,
And more than this I cannot.'

                              While he spoke
She neither blush'd nor shook, but deathly-
pale

Stood grasping what was nearest, then
replied:
'Of all this will I nothing;' and so fell,
And thus they bore her swooning to her
tower.

Then spake, to whom thro' those black
walls of yew
Their talk had pierced, her father: 'Ay, a
flash,
I fear me, that will strike my blossom dead.
Too courteous are ye, fair Lord Lancelot.
I pray you, use some rough discourtesy
To blunt or break her passion.'

                              Lancelot said,
'That were against me: what I can I will;'
And there that day remain'd, and toward
even
Sent for his shield: full meekly rose the
maid,
Stript off the case, and gave the naked
shield;
Then, when she heard his horse upon the
stones,
Unclasping flung the casement back, and
look'd
Down on his helm, from which her sleeve
had gone.
And Lancelot knew the little clinking sound
And she by tact of love was well aware
That Lancelot knew that she was looking
at him.
And yet he glanced not up, nor waved his
hand,
Nor bad farewell, but sadly rode away.
This was the one discourtesy that he used.

So in her tower alone the maiden sat:
His very shield was gone; only the case,
Her own poor work, her empty labour, left.
But still she heard him, still his picture
form'd
And grew between her and the pictured
wall.
Then came her father, saying in low tones,
'Have comfort,' whom she greeted quietly.
Then came her brethren saying, 'Peace to
thee,
Sweet sister,' whom she answer'd with all
calm.

But when they left her to herself again,
Death, like a friend's voice from a distant
    field
Approaching thro' the darkness, call'd; the
    owls
Wailing had power upon her, and she mixt
Her fancies with the sallow-rifted glooms
Of evening, and the moanings of the wind.

And in those days she made a little song,
And call'd her song 'The Song of Love and
    Death,'
And sang it: sweetly could she make and
    sing.

    'Sweet is true love tho' given in vain, in
        vain;
And sweet is death who puts an end to
    pain:
I know not which is sweeter, no, not I.

    'Love, art thou sweet? then bitter death
        must be:
Love, thou art bitter; sweet is death to me.
O Love, if death be sweeter, let me die.

    'Sweet love, that seems not made to fade
        away,
Sweet death, that seems to make us love-
    less clay,
I know not which is sweeter, no, not I.

    'I fain would follow love, if that could be;
I needs must follow death, who calls for
    me;
Call and I follow, I follow! let me die.'

    High with the last line scaled her voice,
        and this,
All in a fiery dawning wild with wind
That shook her tower, the brothers heard,
    and thought
With shuddering, 'Hark the Phantom of
    the house
That ever shrieks before a death,' and
    call'd
The father, and all three in hurry and fear
Ran to her, and lo! the blood-red light of
    dawn
Flared on her face, she shrilling, 'Let me
    die!'

As when we dwell upon a word we know,
Repeating, till the word we know so well
Becomes a wonder, and we know not why,
So dwelt the father on her face, and thought
'Is this Elaine?' till back the maiden fell,
Then gave a languid hand to each, and lay,
Speaking a still good-morrow with her
    eyes.
At last she said, 'Sweet brothers, yester-
    night
I seem'd a curious little maid again,
As happy as when we dwelt among the
    woods,
And when ye used to take me with the
    flood
Up the great river in the boatman's boat.
Only ye would not pass beyond the cape
That has the poplar on it: there ye fixt
Your limit, oft returning with the tide.
And yet I cried because ye would not pass
Beyond it, and far up the shining flood
Until we found the palace of the King.
And yet ye would not; but this night I
    dream'd
That I was all alone upon the flood,
And then I said, "Now shall I have my
    will:"
And there I woke, but still the wish re-
    main'd.
So let me hence that I may pass at last
Beyond the poplar and far up the flood,
Until I find the palace of the King.
There will I enter in among them all,
And no man there will dare to mock at me;
But there the fine Gawain will wonder at
    me,
And there the great Sir Lancelot muse at
    me;
Gawain, who bad a thousand farewells to
    me,
Lancelot, who coldly went, nor bad me
    one:
And there the King will know me and my
    love,
And there the Queen herself will pity me,
And all the gentle court will welcome me,
And after my long voyage I shall rest!'

    'Peace,' said her father, 'O my child, ye
        seem
Light-headed, for what force is yours to go

So far, being sick? and wherefore would
      ye look
On this proud fellow again, who scorns
      us all?'

Then the rough Torre began to heave
      and move,
And bluster into stormy sobs and say,
'I never loved him: an I meet with him,
I care not howsoever great he be,
Then will I strike at him and strike him
      down,
Give me good fortune, I will strike him
      dead,
For this discomfort he hath done the
      house.'

To whom the gentle sister made reply,
'Fret not yourself, dear brother, nor be
      wroth,
Seeing it is no more Sir Lancelot's fault
Not to love me, than it is mine to love
Him of all men who seems to me the
      highest.'

'Highest?' the father answer'd, echoing
      'highest?'
(He meant to break the passion in her)
      'nay,
Daughter, I know not what you call the
      highest;
But this I know, for all the people know it,
He loves the Queen, and in an open shame:
And she returns his love in open shame;
If this be high, what is it to be low?'

Then spake the lily maid of Astolat:
'Sweet father, all too faint and sick am I
For anger: these are slanders: never yet
Was noble man but made ignoble talk.
He makes no friend who never made a foe.
But now it is my glory to have loved
One peerless, without stain: so let me pass,
My father, howsoe'er I seem to you,
Not all unhappy, having loved God's best
And greatest, tho' my love had no return:
Yet, seeing you desire your child to live,
Thanks, but you work against your own
      desire;
For if I could believe the things you say
I should but die the sooner; wherefore
      cease,

Sweet father, and bid call the ghostly man
Hither, and let me shrive me clean, and
      die.'

So when the ghostly man had come and
      gone,
She with a face, bright as for sin forgiven,
Besought Lavaine to write as she devised
A letter, word for word; and when he
      ask'd
'Is it for Lancelot, is it for my dear lord?
Then will I bear it gladly;' she replied,
'For Lancelot and the Queen and all the
      world,
But I myself must bear it.' Then he wrote
The letter she devised; which being writ
And folded, 'O sweet father, tender and
      true,
Deny me not,' she said—'ye never yet
Denied my fancies—this, however strange,
My latest: lay the letter in my hand
A little ere I die, and close the hand
Upon it; I shall guard it even in death.
And when the heat is gone from out my
      heart,
Then take the little bed on which I died
For Lancelot's love, and deck it like the
      Queen's
For richness, and me also like the Queen
In all I have of rich, and lay me on it.
And let there be prepared a chariot-bier
To take me to the river, and a barge
Be ready on the river, clothed in black.
I go in state to court, to meet the Queen.
There surely I shall speak for mine own
      self,
And none of you can speak for me so well.
And therefore let our dumb old man alone
Go with me, he can steer and row, and he
Will guide me to that palace, to the doors.'

She ceased: her father promised; where-
      upon
She grew so cheerful that they deem'd her
      death
Was rather in the fantasy than the blood.
But ten slow mornings past, and on the
      eleventh
Her father laid the letter in her hand,
And closed the hand upon it, and she died.
So that day there was dole in Astolat.

But when the next sun brake from under-
ground,
Then, those two brethren slowly with bent
brows
Accompanying, the sad chariot-bier
Past like a shadow thro' the field, that
shone
Full-summer, to that stream whereon the
barge,
Pall'd all its length in blackest samite, lay.
There sat the lifelong creature of the house,
Loyal, the dumb old servitor, on deck,
Winking his eyes, and twisted all his face.
So those two brethren from the chariot
took
And on the black decks laid her in her bed,
Set in her hand a lily, o'er her hung
The silken case with braided blazonings,
And kiss'd her quiet brows, and saying to
her
'Sister, farewell for ever,' and again
'Farewell, sweet sister,' parted all in tears.
Then rose the dumb old servitor, and the
dead,
Oar'd by the dumb, went upward with the
flood—
In her right hand the lily, in her left
The letter—all her bright hair streaming
down—
And all the coverlid was cloth of gold
Drawn to her waist, and she herself in
white
All but her face, and that clear-featured
face
Was lovely, for she did not seem as dead,
But fast asleep, and lay as tho' she smiled.

That day Sir Lancelot at the palace
craved
Audience of Guinevere, to give at last
The price of half a realm, his costly gift,
Hard-won and hardly won with bruise and
blow,
With deaths of others, and almost his own,
The nine-years-fought-for diamonds: for
he saw
One of her house, and sent him to the
Queen
Bearing his wish, whereto the Queen
agreed
With such and so unmoved a majesty

She might have seem'd her statue, but
that he,
Low-drooping till he wellnigh kiss'd her
feet
For loyal awe, saw with a sidelong eye
The shadow of some piece of pointed lace,
In the Queen's shadow, vibrate on the
walls,
And parted, laughing in his courtly heart.

All in an oriel on the summer side,
Vine-clad, of Arthur's palace toward the
stream,
They met, and Lancelot kneeling utter'd,
'Queen,
Lady, my liege, in whom I have my joy,
Take, what I had not won except for you,
These jewels, and make me happy, making
them
An armlet for the roundest arm on earth,
Or necklace for a neck to which the swan's
Is tawnier than her cygnet's: these are
words:
Your beauty is your beauty, and I sin
In speaking, yet O grant my worship of it
Words, as we grant grief tears. Such sin in
words
Perchance, we both can pardon: but, my
Queen,
I hear of rumours flying thro' your court.
Our bond, as not the bond of man and wife,
Should have in it an absoluter trust
To make up the defect: let rumours be:
When did not rumours fly? these, as I trust
That you trust me in your own nobleness,
I may not well believe that you believe.'

While thus he spoke, half turn'd away,
the Queen
Brake from the vast oriel-embowering vine
Leaf after leaf, and tore, and cast them off,
Till all the place whereon she stood was
green;
Then, when he ceased, in one cold passive
hand
Received at once and laid aside the gems
There on a table near her, and replied:

'It may be, I am quicker of belief
Than you believe me, Lancelot of the
Lake.

O

Our bond is not the bond of man and wife.
This good is in it, whatsoe'er of ill,
It can be broken easier. I for you
This many a year have done despite and
    wrong
To one whom ever in my heart of hearts
I did acknowledge nobler. What are these?
Diamonds for me! they had been thrice
    their worth
Being your gift, had you not lost your own.
To loyal hearts the value of all gifts
Must vary as the giver's. Not for me!
For her! for your new fancy. Only this
Grant me, I pray you: have your joys
    apart,
I doubt not that however changed, you
    keep
So much of what is graceful: and myself
Would shun to break those bounds of
    courtesy
In which as Arthur's Queen I move and
    rule:
So cannot speak my mind. An end to this!
A strange one! yet I take it with Amen.
So pray you, add my diamonds to her
    pearls;
Deck her with these; tell her, she shines
    me down:
An armlet for an arm to which the Queen's
Is haggard, or a necklace for a neck
O as much fairer—as a faith once fair
Was richer than these diamonds—hers not
    mine—
Nay, by the mother of our Lord himself,
Or hers or mine, mine now to work my
    will—
She shall not have them.'

                    Saying which she seized,
And, thro' the casement standing wide for
    heat,
Flung them, and down they flash'd, and
    smote the stream.
Then from the smitten surface flash'd, as it
    were,
Diamonds to meet them, and they past
    away.
Then while Sir Lancelot leant, in half dis-
    dain
At love, life, all things, on the window
    ledge,

Close underneath his eyes, and right across
Where these had fallen, slowly past the
    barge
Whereon the lily maid of Astolat
Lay smiling, like a star in blackest night.

But the wild Queen, who saw not, burst
    away
To weep and wail in secret; and the barge,
On to the palace-doorway sliding, paused,
There two stood arm'd, and kept the door;
    to whom,
All up the marble stair, tier over tier,
Were added mouths that gaped, and eyes
    that ask'd
'What is it?' but that oarsman's haggard
    face,
As hard and still as is the face that men
Shape to their fancy's eye from broken
    rocks
On some cliff-side, appall'd them, and they
    said,
'He is enchanted, cannot speak—and she,
Look how she sleeps—the Fairy Queen,
    so fair!
Yea, but how pale! what are they? flesh
    and blood?
Or come to take the King to Fairyland?
For some do hold our Arthur cannot die,
But that he passes into Fairyland.'

    While thus they babbled of the King,
        the King
Came girt with knights: then turn'd the
    tongueless man
From the half-face to the full eye, and rose
And pointed to the damsel, and the doors.
So Arthur bad the meek Sir Percivale
And pure Sir Galahad to uplift the maid;
And reverently they bore her into hall.
Then came the fine Gawain and wonder'd
    at her,
And Lancelot later came and mused at her,
And last the Queen herself, and pitied her:
But Arthur spied the letter in her hand,
Stoopt, took, brake seal, and read it; this
    was all:

    'Most noble lord, Sir Lancelot of the
        Lake,
    I, sometime call'd the maid of Astolat,

Come, for you left me taking no farewell,
Hither, to take my last farewell of you.
I loved you, and my love had no return,
And therefore my true love has been my
    death.
And therefore to our Lady Guinevere,
And to all other ladies, I make moan:
Pray for my soul, and yield me burial.
Pray for my soul thou too, Sir Lancelot,
As thou art a knight peerless.'

                        Thus he read;
And ever in the reading, lords and dames
Wept, looking often from his face who read
To hers which lay so silent, and at times,
So touch'd were they, half-thinking that
    her lips,
Who had devised the letter, moved again.

    Then freely spoke Sir Lancelot to them
    all:
'My lord liege Arthur, and all ye that hear,
Know that for this most gentle maiden's
    death
Right heavy am I; for good she was and
    true,
But loved me with a love beyond all love
In women, whomsoever I have known.
Yet to be loved makes not to love again;
Not at my years, however it hold in youth.
I swear by truth and knighthood that I gave
No cause, not willingly, for such a love:
To this I call my friends in testimony,
Her brethren, and her father, who himself
Besought me to be plain and blunt, and use,
To break her passion, some discourtesy
Against my nature: what I could, I did.
I left her and I bad her no farewell;
Tho', had I dreamt the damsel would have
    died,
I might have put my wits to some rough
    use,
And help'd her from herself.'

                    Then said the Queen
(Sea was her wrath, yet working after
    storm)
'Ye might at least have done her so much
    grace,
Fair lord, as would have help'd her from
    her death.'

He raised his head, their eyes met and hers
    fell,
He adding,
            'Queen, she would not be content
Save that I wedded her, which could not be.
Then might she follow me thro' the world,
    she ask'd;
It could not be. I told her that her love
Was but the flash of youth, would darken
    down
To rise hereafter in a stiller flame
Toward one more worthy of her—then
    would I,
More specially were he, she wedded, poor,
Estate them with large land and territory
In mine own realm beyond the narrow
    seas,
To keep them in all joyance: more than
    this
I could not; this she would not, and she
    died.'

    He pausing, Arthur answer'd, 'O my
    knight,
It will be to thy worship, as my knight,
And mine, as head of all our Table Round,
To see that she be buried worshipfully.'

    So toward that shrine which then in all
    the realm
Was richest, Arthur leading, slowly went
The marshall'd Order of their Table
    Round,
And Lancelot sad beyond his wont, to see
The maiden buried, not as one unknown,
Nor meanly, but with gorgeous obsequies,
And mass, and rolling music, like a queen.
And when the knights had laid her comely
    head
Low in the dust of half-forgotten kings,
Then Arthur spake among them, 'Let her
    tomb
Be costly, and her image thereupon,
And let the shield of Lancelot at her feet
Be carven, and her lily in her hand.
And let the story of her dolorous voyage
For all true hearts be blazon'd on her tomb
In letters gold and azure!' which was
    wrought
Thereafter; but when now the lords and
    dames

And people, from the high door streaming,
brake
Disorderly, as homeward each, the Queen,
Who mark'd Sir Lancelot where he moved
apart,
Drew near, and sigh'd in passing, 'Lancelot,
Forgive me; mine was jealousy in love.'
He answer'd with his eyes upon the ground,
'That is love's curse; pass on, my Queen,
forgiven.'
But Arthur, who beheld his cloudy brows,
Approach'd him, and with full affection
said,

'Lancelot, my Lancelot, thou in whom
I have
Most joy and most affiance, for I know
What thou hast been in battle by my side,
And many a time have watch'd thee at the
tilt
Strike down the lusty and long-practised
knight,
And let the younger and unskill'd go by
To win his honour and to make his name,
And loved thy courtesies and thee, a man
Made to be loved; but now I would to
God,
Seeing the homeless trouble in thine eyes,
Thou couldst have loved this maiden,
shaped, it seems,
By God for thee alone, and from her face,
If one may judge the living by the dead,
Delicately pure and marvellously fair,
Who might have brought thee, now a
lonely man
Wifeless and heirless, noble issue, sons
Born to the glory of thy name and fame,
My knight, the great Sir Lancelot of the
Lake.'

Then answer'd Lancelot, 'Fair she was,
my King,
Pure, as you ever wish your knights to be.
To doubt her fairness were to want an eye,
To doubt her pureness were to want a
heart—
Yea, to be loved, if what is worthy love
Could bind him, but free love will not be
bound.'

'Free love, so bound, were freëst,' said
the King.

'Let love be free; free love is for the best:
And, after heaven, on our dull side of
death,
What should be best, if not so pure a love
Clothed in so pure a loveliness? yet thee
She fail'd to bind, tho' being, as I think,
Unbound as yet, and gentle, as I know.'

And Lancelot answer'd nothing, but he
went,
And at the inrunning of a little brook
Sat by the river in a cove, and watch'd
The high reed wave, and lifted up his eyes
And saw the barge that brought her moving
down,
Far-off, a blot upon the stream, and said
Low in himself, 'Ah simple heart and
sweet,
Ye loved me, damsel, surely with a love
Far tenderer than my Queen's. Pray for
thy soul?
Ay, that will I. Farewell too—now at last—
Farewell, fair lily. "Jealousy in love"?
Not rather dead love's harsh heir, jealous
pride?
Queen, if I grant the jealousy as of love,
May not your crescent fear for name and
fame
Speak, as it waxes, of a love that wanes?
Why did the King dwell on my name to
me?
Mine own name shames me, seeming a
reproach,
Lancelot, whom the Lady of the Lake
Caught from his mother's arms—the won-
drous one
Who passes thro' the vision of the night—
She chanted snatches of mysterious hymns
Heard on the winding waters, eve and morn
She kiss'd me saying, "Thou art fair, my
child,
As a king's son," and often in her arms
She bare me, pacing on the dusky mere.
Would she had drown'd me in it, where'er
it be!
For what am I? what profits me my name
Of greatest knight? I fought for it, and
have it:
Pleasure to have it, none; to lose it, pain;
Now grown a part of me: but what use
in it?

To make men worse by making my sin
 known?
Or sin seem less, the sinner seeming great?
Alas for Arthur's greatest knight, a man
Not after Arthur's heart! I needs must
 break
These bonds that so defame me: not with-
 out
She wills it: would I, if she will'd it? nay,
Who knows? but if I would not, then may
 God,
O pray him, send a sudden Angel down
To seize me by the hair and bear me far,
And fling me deep in that forgotten mere,
Among the tumbled fragments of the
 hills.'

So groan'd Sir Lancelot in remorseful
 pain,
Not knowing he should die a holy man.

THE HOLY GRAIL

FROM noiseful arms, and acts of prowess
 done
In tournament or tilt, Sir Percivale,
Whom Arthur and his knighthood call'd
 The Pure,
Had pass'd into the silent life of prayer,
Praise, fast, and alms; and leaving for the
 cowl
The helmet in an abbey far away
From Camelot, there, and not long after,
 died.

And one, a fellow-monk among the rest,
Ambrosius, loved him much beyond the
 rest,
And honour'd him, and wrought into his
 heart
A way by love that waken'd love within,
To answer that which came: and as they
 sat
Beneath a world-old yew-tree, darkening
 half
The cloisters, on a gustful April morn
That puff'd the swaying branches into
 smoke
Above them, ere the summer when he died,
The monk Ambrosius question'd Per-
 civale:

'O brother, I have seen this yew-tree
 smoke,
Spring after spring, for half a hundred
 years:
For never have I known the world without,
Nor ever stray'd beyond the pale: but thee,
When first thou camest—such a courtesy
Spake thro' the limbs and in the voice—I
 knew
For one of those who eat in Arthur's hall;
For good ye are and bad, and like to coins,
Some true, some light, but every one of you
Stamp'd with the image of the King; and
 now
Tell me, what drove thee from the Table
 Round,
My brother? was it earthly passion crost?'

'Nay,' said the knight; 'for no such pas-
 sion mine.
But the sweet vision of the Holy Grail
Drove me from all vainglories, rivalries,
And earthly heats that spring and sparkle
 out
Among us in the jousts, while women
 watch
Who wins, who falls; and waste the
 spiritual strength
Within us, better offer'd up to Heaven.'

To whom the monk: 'The Holy Grail!—
 I trust
We are green in Heaven's eyes; but here
 too much
We moulder—as to things without I
 mean—
Yet one of your own knights, a guest of
 ours,
Told us of this in our refectory,
But spake with such a sadness and so low
We heard not half of what he said. What
 is it?
The phantom of a cup that comes and
 goes?'

'Nay, monk! what phantom?' answer'd
 Percivale.
'The cup, the cup itself, from which our
 Lord
Drank at the last sad supper with his own.
This, from the blessed land of Aromat—

After the day of darkness, when the dead
Went wandering o'er Moriah—the good
  saint
Arimathæan Joseph, journeying brought
To Glastonbury, where the winter thorn
Blossoms at Christmas, mindful of our
  Lord.
And there awhile it bode; and if a man
Could touch or see it, he was heal'd at
  once,
By faith, of all his ills. But then the times
Grew to such evil that the holy cup
Was caught away to Heaven, and dis-
  appear'd.'

  To whom the monk: 'From our old
  books I know
That Joseph came of old to Glastonbury,
And there the heathen Prince, Arviragus,
Gave him an isle of marsh whereon to
  build;
And there he built with wattles from the
  marsh
A little lonely church in days of yore,
For so they say, these books of ours, but
  seem
Mute of this miracle, far as I have read.
But who first saw the holy thing to-day?'

  'A woman,' answer'd Percivale, 'a nun,
And one no further off in blood from me
Than sister; and if ever holy maid
With knees of adoration wore the stone,
A holy maid; tho' never maiden glow'd,
But that was in her earlier maidenhood,
With such a fervent flame of human love,
Which being rudely blunted, glanced and
  shot
Only to holy things; to prayer and praise
She gave herself, to fast and alms. And yet,
Nun as she was, the scandal of the Court,
Sin against Arthur and the Table Round,
And the strange sound of an adulterous
  race,
Across the iron grating of her cell
Beat, and she pray'd and fasted all the
  more.

  'And he to whom she told her sins, or
  what
Her all but utter whiteness held for sin,

A man wellnigh a hundred winters old,
Spake often with her of the Holy Grail,
A legend handed down thro' five or six,
And each of these a hundred winters old,
From our Lord's time. And when King
  Arthur made
His Table Round, and all men's hearts
  became
Clean for a season, surely he had thought
That now the Holy Grail would come
  again;
But sin broke out. Ah, Christ, that it would
  come,
And heal the world of all their wickedness!
"O Father!" ask'd the maiden, "might it
  come
To me by prayer and fasting?" "Nay,"
  said he,
"I know not, for thy heart is pure as snow."
And so she pray'd and fasted, till the sun
Shone, and the wind blew, thro' her, and
  I thought
She might have risen and floated when I
  saw her.

  'For on a day she sent to speak with me.
And when she came to speak, behold her
  eyes
Beyond my knowing of them, beautiful,
Beyond all knowing of them, wonderful,
Beautiful in the light of holiness.
And "O my brother Percivale," she said,
"Sweet brother, I have seen the Holy
  Grail:
For, waked at dead of night, I heard a
  sound
As of a silver horn from o'er the hills
Blown, and I thought, 'It is not Arthur's
  use
To hunt by moonlight;' and the slender
  sound
As from a distance beyond distance grew
Coming upon me—O never harp nor horn,
Nor aught we blow with breath, or touch
  with hand,
Was like that music as it came; and then
Stream'd thro' my cell a cold and silver
  beam,
And down the long beam stole the Holy
  Grail,
Rose-red with beatings in it, as if alive,

Till all the white walls of my cell were
    dyed
With rosy colours leaping on the wall;
And then the music faded, and the Grail
Past, and the beam decay'd, and from the
    walls
The rosy quiverings died into the night.
So now the Holy Thing is here again
Among us, brother, fast thou too and pray,
And tell thy brother knights to fast and
    pray,
That so perchance the vision may be seen
By thee and those, and all the world be
    heal'd."

'Then leaving the pale nun, I spake of
    this
To all men; and myself fasted and pray'd
Always, and many among us many a week
Fasted and pray'd even to the uttermost,
Expectant of the wonder that would be.

'And one there was among us, ever moved
Among us in white armour, Galahad.
"God make thee good as thou art beauti-
    ful,"
Said Arthur, when he dubb'd him knight;
    and none
In so young youth, was ever made a knight
Till Galahad; and this Galahad, when he
    heard
My sister's vision, fill'd me with amaze;
His eyes became so like her own, they
    seem'd
Hers, and himself her brother more than I.

'Sister or brother none had he; but some
Call'd him a son of Lancelot, and some
    said
Begotten by enchantment—chatterers they
Like birds of passage piping up and down,
That gape for flies—we know not whence
    they come;
For when was Lancelot wanderingly lewd?

'But she, the wan sweet maiden, shore
    away
Clean from her forehead all that wealth of
    hair
Which made a silken mat-work for her
    feet;

And out of this she plaited broad and long
A strong sword-belt, and wove with silver
    thread
And crimson in the belt a strange device,
A crimson grail within a silver beam;
And saw the bright boy-knight, and bound
    it on him,
Saying, "My knight, my love, my knight
    of heaven,
O thou, my love, whose love is one with
    mine,
I, maiden, round thee, maiden, bind my
    belt.
Go forth, for thou shalt see what I have
    seen,
And break thro' all, till one will crown thee
    king
Far in the spiritual city:" and as she spake
She sent the deathless passion in her eyes
Thro' him, and made him hers, and laid
    her mind
On him, and he believed in her belief.

'Then came a year of miracle: O brother,
In our great hall there stood a vacant chair,
Fashion'd by Merlin ere he past away,
And carven with strange figures; and in
    and out
The figures, like a serpent, ran a scroll
Of letters in a tongue no man could read.
And Merlin call'd it "The Siege perilous,"
Perilous for good and ill; "for there," he
    said,
"No man could sit but he should lose him-
    self:"
And once by misadvertence Merlin sat
In his own chair, and so was lost; but he,
Galahad, when he heard of Merlin's doom,
Cried, "If I lose myself, I save myself!"

'Then on a summer night it came to pass,
While the great banquet lay along the hall,
That Galahad would sit down in Merlin's
    chair.

'And all at once, as there we sat, we
    heard
A cracking and a riving of the roofs,
And rending, and a blast, and overhead
Thunder, and in the thunder was a cry.
And in the blast there smote along the hall

A beam of light seven times more clear
  than day:
And down the long beam stole the Holy
  Grail
All over cover'd with a luminous cloud,
And none might see who bare it, and it
  past.
But every knight beheld his fellow's face
As in a glory, and all the knights arose,
And staring each at other like dumb men
Stood, till I found a voice and sware a vow.

  'I sware a vow before them all, that I,
Because I had not seen the Grail, would
  ride
A twelvemonth and a day in quest of it,
Until I found and saw it, as the nun
My sister saw it; and Galahad sware the
  vow,
And good Sir Bors, our Lancelot's cousin,
  sware,
And Lancelot sware, and many among the
  knights,
And Gawain sware, and louder than the
  rest.'

  Then spake the monk Ambrosius, asking
  him,
'What said the King? Did Arthur take the
  vow?'

  'Nay, for my lord,' said Percivale, 'the
  King,
Was not in hall: for early that same day,
Scaped thro' a cavern from a bandit hold,
An outraged maiden sprang into the hall
Crying on help: for all her shining hair
Was smear'd with earth, and either milky
  arm
Red-rent with hooks of bramble, and all
  she wore
Torn as a sail that leaves the rope is torn
In tempest: so the King arose and went
To smoke the scandalous hive of those wild
  bees
That made such honey in his realm. How-
  beit
Some little of this marvel he too saw,
Returning o'er the plain that then began
To darken under Camelot; whence the
  King

Look'd up, calling aloud, "Lo, there! the
  roofs
Of our great hall are roll'd in thunder-
  smoke!
Pray Heaven, they be not smitten by the
  bolt."
For dear to Arthur was that hall of ours,
As having there so oft with all his knights
Feasted, and as the stateliest under heaven.

  'O brother, had you known our mighty
  hall,
Which Merlin built for Arthur long ago!
For all the sacred mount of Camelot,
And all the dim rich city, roof by roof,
Tower after tower, spire beyond spire,
By grove, and garden-lawn, and rushing
  brook,
Climbs to the mighty hall that Merlin built.
And four great zones of sculpture, set
  betwixt
With many a mystic symbol, gird the hall:
And in the lowest beasts are slaying men,
And in the second men are slaying beasts,
And on the third are warriors, perfect men,
And on the fourth are men with growing
  wings,
And over all one statue in the mould
Of Arthur, made by Merlin, with a crown,
And peak'd wings pointed to the Northern
  Star.
And eastward fronts the statue, and the
  crown
And both the wings are made of gold, and
  flame
At sunrise till the people in far fields,
Wasted so often by the heathen hordes,
Behold it, crying, "We have still a King."

  'And, brother, had you known our hall
  within,
Broader and higher than any in all the
  lands!
Where twelve great windows blazon
  Arthur's wars,
And all the light that falls upon the board
Streams thro' the twelve great battles of
  our King.
Nay, one there is, and at the eastern end,
Wealthy with wandering lines of mount
  and mere,

Where Arthur finds the brand Excalibur.
And also one to the west, and counter to it,
And blank: and who shall blazon it?
    when and how?—
O there, perchance, when all our wars are
    done,
The brand Excalibur will be cast away.

'So to this hall full quickly rode the
    King,
In horror lest the work by Merlin wrought,
Dreamlike, should on the sudden vanish,
    wrapt
In unremorseful folds of rolling fire.
And in he rode, and up I glanced, and saw
The golden dragon sparkling over all:
And many of those who burnt the hold,
    their arms
Hack'd, and their foreheads grimed with
    smoke, and sear'd,
Follow'd, and in among bright faces, ours,
Full of the vision, prest: and then the King
Spake to me, being nearest, "Percivale,"
(Because the hall was all in tumult—some
Vowing, and some protesting), "what is
    this?"

'O brother, when I told him what had
    chanced,
My sister's vision, and the rest, his face
Darken'd, as I have seen it more than once,
When some brave deed seem'd to be done
    in vain,
Darken; and "Woe is me, my knights," he
    cried,
"Had I been here, ye had not sworn the
    vow."
Bold was mine answer, "Had thyself been
    here,
My King, thou wouldst have sworn."
"Yea, yea," said he,
"Art thou so bold and hast not seen the
    Grail?"

'"Nay, lord, I heard the sound, I saw
    the light,
But since I did not see the Holy Thing,
I sware a vow to follow it till I saw."

'Then when he ask'd us, knight by
    knight, if any

Had seen it, all their answers were as one:
"Nay, lord, and therefore have we sworn
    our vows."

'"Lo now," said Arthur, "have ye seen
    a cloud?
What go ye into the wilderness to see?"

'Then Galahad on the sudden, and in a
    voice
Shrilling along the hall to Arthur, call'd
"But I, Sir Arthur, saw the Holy Grail,
I saw the Holy Grail and heard a cry—
'O Galahad, and O Galahad, follow me.'"

' "Ah, Galahad, Galahad," said the
    King, "for such
As thou art is the vision, not for these.
Thy holy nun and thou have seen a sign—
Holier is none, my Percivale, than she—
A sign to maim this Order which I made.
But ye, that follow but the leader's bell"
(Brother, the King was hard upon his
    knights)
"Taliessin is our fullest throat of song,
And one hath sung and all the dumb will
    sing.
Lancelot is Lancelot, and hath overborne
Five knights at once, and every younger
    knight,
Unproven, holds himself as Lancelot,
Till overborne by one, he learns—and ye,
What are ye? Galahads?—no, nor Per-
    civales"
(For thus it pleased the King to range me
    close
After Sir Galahad); "nay," said he, "but
    men
With strength and will to right the
    wrong'd, of power
To lay the sudden heads of violence flat,
Knights that in twelve great battles
    splash'd and dyed
The strong White Horse in his own
    heathen blood—
But one hath seen, and all the blind will see.
Go, since your vows are sacred, being
    made:
Yet—for ye know the cries of all my realm
Pass thro' this hall—how often, O my
    knights,

Your places being vacant at my side,
This chance of noble deeds will come
    and go
Unchallenged, while ye follow wandering
    fires
Lost in the quagmire! Many of you, yea
    most,
Return no more: ye think I show myself
Too dark a prophet: come now, let us meet
The morrow morn once more in one full
    field
Of gracious pastime, that once more the
    King,
Before ye leave him for this Quest, may
    count
The yet-unbroken strength of all his
    knights,
Rejoicing in that Order which he made."

'So when the sun broke next from under
    ground,
All the great table of our Arthur closed
And clash'd in such a tourney and so full,
So many lances broken—never yet
Had Camelot seen the like, since Arthur
    came;
And I myself and Galahad, for a strength
Was in us from the vision, overthrew
So many knights that all the people cried,
And almost burst the barriers in their heat,
Shouting, "Sir Galahad and Sir Percivale!"

'But when the next day brake from under
    ground—
O brother, had you known our Camelot,
Built by old kings, age after age, so old
The King himself had fears that it would
    fall,
So strange, and rich, and dim; for where
    the roofs
Totter'd toward each other in the sky,
Met foreheads all along the street of those
Who watch'd us pass; and lower, and
    where the long
Rich galleries, lady-laden, weigh'd the
    necks
Of dragons clinging to the crazy walls,
Thicker than drops from thunder, showers
    of flowers
Fell as we past; and men and boys astride
On wyvern, lion, dragon, griffin, swan,

At all the corners, named us each by name,
Calling "God speed!" but in the ways
    below
The knights and ladies wept, and rich and
    poor
Wept, and the King himself could hardly
    speak
For grief, and all in middle street the
    Queen,
Who rode by Lancelot, wail'd and shriek'd
    aloud,
"This madness has come on us for our
    sins."
So to the Gate of the three Queens we
    came,
Where Arthur's wars are render'd mysti-
    cally,
And thence departed every one his way.

'And I was lifted up in heart, and thought
Of all my late-shown prowess in the lists,
How my strong lance had beaten down the
    knights,
So many and famous names; and never
    yet
Had heaven appear'd so blue, nor earth so
    green,
For all my blood danced in me, and I knew
That I should light upon the Holy Grail.

'Thereafter, the dark warning of our
    King,
That most of us would follow wandering
    fires,
Came like a driving gloom across my mind.
Then every evil word I had spoken once,
And every evil thought I had thought of
    old,
And every evil deed I ever did,
Awoke and cried, "This Quest is not for
    thee."
And lifting up mine eyes, I found myself
Alone, and in a land of sand and thorns,
And I was thirsty even unto death;
And I, too, cried, "This Quest is not for
    thee."

'And on I rode, and when I thought my
    thirst
Would slay me, saw deep lawns, and then a
    brook.

With one sharp rapid, where the crisping
    white
Play'd ever back upon the sloping wave,
And took both ear and eye; and o'er the
    brook
Were apple-trees, and apples by the brook
Fallen, and on the lawns. "I will rest here,"
I said, "I am not worthy of the Quest;"
But even while I drank the brook, and ate
The goodly apples, all these things at once
Fell into dust, and I was left alone,
And thirsting, in a land of sand and thorns.

    'And then behold a woman at a door
Spinning; and fair the house whereby she
    sat,
And kind the woman's eyes and innocent,
And all her bearing gracious; and she rose
Opening her arms to meet me, as who
    should say,
"Rest here;" but when I touch'd her, lo!
    she, too,
Fell into dust and nothing, and the house
Became no better than a broken shed,
And in it a dead babe; and also this
Fell into dust, and I was left alone.

    'And on I rode, and greater was my
    thirst.
Then flash'd a yellow gleam across the
    world,
And where it smote the plowshare in the
    field,
The plowman left his plowing, and fell
    down
Before it; where it glitter'd on her pail,
The milkmaid left her milking, and fell
    down
Before it, and I knew not why, but thought
"The sun is rising," tho' the sun had risen.
Then was I ware of one that on me moved
In golden armour with a crown of gold
About a casque all jewels; and his horse
In golden armour jewell'd everywhere:
And on the splendour came, flashing me
    blind;
And seem'd to me the Lord of all the
    world,
Being so huge. But when I thought he
    meant
To crush me, moving on me, lo! he, too,

Open'd his arms to embrace me as he came,
And up I went and touch'd him, and he,
    too,
Fell into dust, and I was left alone
And wearying in a land of sand and thorns.

    'And I rode on and found a mighty hill,
And on the top, a city wall'd: the spires
Prick'd with incredible pinnacles into
    heaven.
And by the gateway stirr'd a crowd; and
    these
Cried to me climbing, "Welcome, Perci-
    vale!
Thou mightiest and thou purest among
    men!"
And glad was I and clomb, but found at top
No man, nor any voice. And thence I past
Far thro' a ruinous city, and I saw
That man had once dwelt there; but there
    I found
Only one man of an exceeding age.
"Where is that goodly company," said I,
"That so cried out upon me?" and he had
Scarce any voice to answer, and yet gasp'd,
"Whence and what art thou?" and even as
    he spoke
Fell into dust, and disappear'd, and I
Was left alone once more, and cried in
    grief,
"Lo, if I find the Holy Grail itself
And touch it, it will crumble into dust."

    'And thence I dropt into a lowly vale,
Low as the hill was high, and where the
    vale
Was lowest, found a chapel, and thereby
A holy hermit in a hermitage,
To whom I told my phantoms, and he
    said:

    ' "O son, thou hast not true humility,
The highest virtue, mother of them all;
For when the Lord of all things made
    Himself
Naked of glory for His mortal change,
'Take thou my robe,' she said, 'for all is
    thine,'
And all her form shone forth with sudden
    light
So that the angels were amazed, and she
Follow'd Him down, and like a flying star

Led on the gray-hair'd wisdom of the east;
But her thou hast not known: for what is
    this
Thou thoughtest of thy prowess and thy
    sins?
Thou hast not lost thyself to save thyself
As Galahad." When the hermit made an
    end,
In silver armour suddenly Galahad shone
Before us, and against the chapel door
Laid lance, and enter'd, and we knelt in
    prayer.
And there the hermit slaked my burning
    thirst,
And at the sacring of the mass I saw
The holy elements alone; but he,
"Saw ye no more? I, Galahad, saw the
    Grail,
The Holy Grail, descend upon the shrine:
I saw the fiery face as of a child
That smote itself into the bread, and went;
And hither am I come; and never yet
Hath what thy sister taught me first to see,
This Holy Thing, fail'd from my side, nor
    come
Cover'd, but moving with me night and
    day,
Fainter by day, but always in the night
Blood-red, and sliding down the blacken'd
    marsh
Blood-red, and on the naked mountain top
Blood-red, and in the sleeping mere below
Blood-red. And in the strength of this I
    rode,
Shattering all evil customs everywhere,
And past thro' Pagan realms, and made
    them mine,
And clash'd with Pagan hordes, and bore
    them down,
And broke thro' all, and in the strength of
    this
Come victor. But my time is hard at hand,
And hence I go; and one will crown me
    king
Far in the spiritual city; and come thou,
    too,
For thou shalt see the vision when I go."

  'While thus he spake, his eye, dwelling
    on mine,
Drew me, with power upon me, till I grew

One with him, to believe as he believed.
Then, when the day began to wane, we
    went.

  'There rose a hill that none but man
    could climb,
Scarr'd with a hundred wintry water-
    courses—
Storm at the top, and when we gain'd it,
    storm
Round us and death; for every moment
    glanced
His silver arms and gloom'd: so quick and
    thick
The lightnings here and there to left and
    right
Struck, till the dry old trunks about us,
    dead,
Yea, rotten with a hundred years of death,
Sprang into fire: and at the base we found
On either hand, as far as eye could see,
A great black swamp and of an evil smell,
Part black, part whiten'd with the bones
    of men,
Not to be crost, save that some ancient
    king
Had built a way, where, link'd with many
    a bridge,
A thousand piers ran into the great Sea.
And Galahad fled along them bridge by
    bridge,
And every bridge as quickly as he crost
Sprang into fire and vanish'd, tho' I
    yearn'd
To follow; and thrice above him all the
    heavens
Open'd and blazed with thunder such as
    seem'd
Shoutings of all the sons of God: and first
At once I saw him far on the great Sea,
In silver-shining armour starry-clear;
And o'er his head the Holy Vessel hung
Clothed in white samite or a luminous
    cloud.
And with exceeding swiftness ran the boat,
If boat it were—I saw not whence it came.
And when the heavens open'd and blazed
    again
Roaring, I saw him like a silver star—
And had he set the sail, or had the boat
Become a living creature clad with wings?

And o'er his head the Holy Vessel hung
Redder than any rose, a joy to me,
For now I knew the veil had been with-
    drawn.
Then in a moment when they blazed again
Opening, I saw the least of little stars
Down on the waste, and straight beyond
    the star
I saw the spiritual city and all her spires
And gateways in a glory like one pearl—
No larger, tho' the goal of all the saints—
Strike from the sea; and from the star
    there shot
A rose-red sparkle to the city, and there
Dwelt, and I knew it was the Holy Grail,
Which never eyes on earth again shall see.
Then fell the floods of heaven drowning
    the deep.
And how my feet recrost the deathful ridge
No memory in me lives; but that I touch'd
The chapel-doors at dawn I know; and
    thence
Taking my war-horse from the holy man,
Glad that no phantom vext me more,
    return'd
To whence I came, the gate of Arthur's
    wars.'

'O brother,' ask'd Ambrosius,—'for in
    sooth
These ancient books—and they would win
    thee—teem,
Only I find not there this Holy Grail,
With miracles and marvels like to these,
Not all unlike; which oftentime I read,
Who read but on my breviary with ease,
Till my head swims; and then go forth and
    pass
Down to the little thorpe that lies so close,
And almost plaster'd like a martin's nest
To these old walls—and mingle with our
    folk;
And knowing every honest face of theirs
As well as ever shepherd knew his sheep,
And every homely secret in their hearts,
Delight myself with gossip and old wives,
And ills and aches, and teethings, lyings-in,
And mirthful sayings, children of the place,
That have no meaning half a league away:
Or lulling random squabbles when they
    rise,

Chafferings and chatterings at the market-
    cross,
Rejoice, small man, in this small world of
    mine,
Yea, even in their hens and in their eggs—
O brother, saving this Sir Galahad,
Came ye on none but phantoms in your
    quest,
No man, no woman?'

        Then Sir Percivale:
'All men, to one so bound by such a vow,
And women were as phantoms. O, my
    brother,
Why wilt thou shame me to confess to thee
How far I falter'd from my quest and vow?
For after I had lain so many nights,
A bedmate of the snail and eft and snake,
In grass and burdock, I was changed to wan
And meagre, and the vision had not come:
And then I chanced upon a goodly town
With one great dwelling in the middle
    of it;
Thither I made, and there was I disarm'd
By maidens each as fair as any flower:
But when they led me into hall, behold,
The Princess of that castle was the one,
Brother, and that one only, who had ever
Made my heart leap; for when I moved of
    old
A slender page about her father's hall,
And she a slender maiden, all my heart
Went after her with longing: yet we twain
Had never kiss'd a kiss, or vow'd a vow.
And now I came upon her once again,
And one had wedded her, and he was dead,
And all his land and wealth and state were
    hers.
And while I tarried, every day she set
A banquet richer than the day before
By me; for all her longing and her will
Was toward me as of old; till one fair morn
I walking to and fro beside a stream
That flash'd across her orchard underneath
Her castle-walls, she stole upon my walk,
And calling me the greatest of all knights,
Embraced me, and so kiss'd me the first
    time,
And gave herself and all her wealth to me.
Then I remember'd Arthur's warning
    word,

That most of us would follow wandering
fires,
And the Quest faded in my heart. Anon,
The heads of all her people drew to me,
With supplication both of knees and
tongue:
"We have heard of thee: thou art our
greatest knight,
Our Lady says it, and we well believe:
Wed thou our Lady, and rule over us,
And thou shalt be as Arthur in our land."
O me, my brother! but one night my vow
Burnt me within, so that I rose and fled,
But wail'd and wept, and hated mine own
self,
And ev'n the Holy Quest, and all but her;
Then after I was join'd with Galahad
Cared not for her, nor anything upon
earth.'

Then said the monk, 'Poor men, when
yule is cold,
Must be content to sit by little fires.
And this am I, so that ye care for me
Ever so little; yea, and blest be Heaven
That brought thee here to this poor house
of ours
Where all the brethren are so hard, to
warm
My cold heart with a friend: but O the pity
To find thine own first love once more—to
hold,
Hold her a wealthy bride within thine arms,
Or all but hold, and then—cast her aside,
Foregoing all her sweetness, like a weed.
For we that want the warmth of double life,
We that are plagued with dreams of some-
thing sweet
Beyond all sweetness in a life so rich,—
Ah, blessed Lord, I speak too earthlywise,
Seeing I never stray'd beyond the cell,
But live like an old badger in his earth,
With earth about him everywhere, despite
All fast and penance. Saw ye none beside,
None of your knights?'

'Yea so,' said Percivale:
'One night my pathway swerving east, I
saw
The pelican on the casque of our Sir Bors
All in the middle of the rising moon:

And toward him spurr'd, and hail'd him,
and he me,
And each made joy of either; then he ask'd,
"Where is he? hast thou seen him—
Lancelot?—Once,"
Said good Sir Bors, "he dash'd across me
—mad,
And maddening what he rode: and when
I cried,
'Ridest thou then so hotly on a quest
So holy,' Lancelot shouted, 'Stay me not!
I have been the sluggard, and I ride apace,
For now there is a lion in the way.'
So vanish'd."

'Then Sir Bors had ridden on
Softly, and sorrowing for our Lancelot,
Because his former madness, once the talk
And scandal of our table, had return'd;
For Lancelot's kith and kin so worship him
That ill to him is ill to them; to Bors
Beyond the rest: he well had been content
Not to have seen, so Lancelot might have
seen,
The Holy Cup of healing; and, indeed,
Being so clouded with his grief and love,
Small heart was his after the Holy Quest:
If God would send the vision, well: if not,
The Quest and he were in the hands of
Heaven.

'And then, with small adventure met,
Sir Bors
Rode to the lonest tract of all the realm,
And found a people there among their
crags,
Our race and blood, a remnant that were
left
Paynim amid their circles, and the stones
They pitch up straight to heaven: and their
wise men
Were strong in that old magic which can
trace
The wandering of the stars, and scoff'd at
him
And this high Quest as at a simple thing:
Told him he follow'd—almost Arthur's
words—
A mocking fire: "what other fire than he,
Whereby the blood beats, and the blossom
blows,

And the sea rolls, and all the world is
warm'd?"
And when his answer chafed them, the
rough crowd,
Hearing he had a difference with their
priests,
Seized him, and bound and plunged him
into a cell
Of great piled stones; and lying bounden
there
In darkness thro' innumerable hours
He heard the hollow-ringing heavens sweep
Over him till by miracle—what else?—
Heavy as it was, a great stone slipt and fell,
Such as no wind could move: and thro'
the gap
Glimmer'd the streaming scud: then came
a night
Still as the day was loud; and thro' the gap
The seven clear stars of Arthur's Table
Round—
For, brother, so one night, because they roll
Thro' such a round in heaven, we named
the stars,
Rejoicing in ourselves and in our King—
And these, like bright eyes of familiar
friends,
In on him shone: "And then to me, to me,"
Said good Sir Bors, "beyond all hopes of
mine,
Who scarce had pray'd or ask'd it for
myself—
Across the seven clear stars—O grace to
me—
In colour like the fingers of a hand
Before a burning taper, the sweet Grail
Glided and past, and close upon it peal'd
A sharp quick thunder." Afterwards, a
maid,
Who kept our holy faith among her kin
In secret, entering, loosed and let him go.'

To whom the monk: 'And I remember
now
That pelican on the casque: Sir Bors it was
Who spake so low and sadly at our board;
And mighty reverent at our grace was he:
A square-set man and honest; and his eyes,
An out-door sign of all the warmth within,
Smiled with his lips—a smile beneath a
cloud,

But heaven had meant it for a sunny one:
Ay, ay, Sir Bors, who else? But when ye
reach'd
The city, found ye all your knights return'd,
Or was there sooth in Arthur's prophecy,
Tell me, and what said each, and what the
King?'

Then answer'd Percivale: 'And that
can I,
Brother, and truly; since the living words
Of so great men as Lancelot and our King
Pass not from door to door and out again,
But sit within the house. O, when we
reach'd
The city, our horses stumbling as they
trode
On heaps of ruin, hornless unicorns,
Crack'd basilisks, and splinter'd cocka-
trices,
And shatter'd talbots, which had left the
stones
Raw, that they fell from, brought us to the
hall.

'And there sat Arthur on the daïs-throne,
And those that had gone out upon the
Quest,
Wasted and worn, and but a tithe of them,
And those that had not, stood before the
King,
Who, when he saw me, rose, and bad me
hail,
Saying, "A welfare in thine eye reproves
Our fear of some disastrous chance for thee
On hill, or plain, at sea, or flooding ford.
So fierce a gale made havoc here of late
Among the strange devices of our kings;
Yea, shook this newer, stronger hall of
ours,
And from the statue Merlin moulded for us
Half-wrench'd a golden wing; but now—
the Quest,
This vision—hast thou seen the Holy Cup,
That Joseph brought of old to Glaston-
bury?"

'So when I told him all thyself hast
heard,
Ambrosius, and my fresh but fixt resolve
To pass away into the quiet life,

He answer'd not, but, sharply turning, ask'd
Of Gawain, "Gawain, was this Quest for thee?"

' "Nay, lord," said Gawain, "not for such as I.
Therefore I communed with a saintly man,
Who made me sure the Quest was not for me;
For I was much awearied of the Quest:
But found a silk pavilion in a field,
And merry maidens in it; and then this gale
Tore my pavilion from the tenting-pin,
And blew my merry maidens all about
With all discomfort; yea, and but for this,
My twelvemonth and a day were pleasant to me."

'He ceased; and Arthur turn'd to whom at first
He saw not, for Sir Bors, on entering, push'd
Athwart the throng to Lancelot, caught his hand,
Held it, and there, half-hidden by him, stood,
Until the King espied him, saying to him,
"Hail, Bors! if ever loyal man and true
Could see it, thou hast seen the Grail;" and Bors,
"Ask me not, for I may not speak of it:
I saw it;" and the tears were in his eyes.

'Then there remain'd but Lancelot, for the rest
Spake but of sundry perils in the storm;
Perhaps, like him of Cana in Holy Writ,
Our Arthur kept his best until the last;
"Thou, too, my Lancelot," ask'd the King, "my friend,
Our mightiest, hath this Quest avail'd for thee?"

' "Our mightiest!" answer'd Lancelot, with a groan;
"O King!"—and when he paused, me-thought I spied
A dying fire of madness in his eyes—
"O King, my friend, if friend of thine I be,
Happier are those that welter in their sin,

Swine in the mud, that cannot see for slime,
Slime of the ditch: but in me lived a sin
So strange, of such a kind, that all of pure,
Noble, and knightly in me twined and clung
Round that one sin, until the wholesome flower
And poisonous grew together, each as each,
Not to be pluck'd asunder; and when thy knights
Sware, I sware with them only in the hope
That could I touch or see the Holy Grail
They might be pluck'd asunder. Then I spake
To one most holy saint, who wept and said,
That save they could be pluck'd asunder, all
My quest were but in vain; to whom I vow'd
That I would work according as he will'd.
And forth I went, and while I yearn'd and strove
To tear the twain asunder in my heart,
My madness came upon me as of old,
And whipt me into waste fields far away;
There was I beaten down by little men,
Mean knights, to whom the moving of my sword
And shadow of my spear had been enow
To scare them from me once; and then I came
All in my folly to the naked shore,
Wide flats, where nothing but coarse grasses grew;
But such a blast, my King, began to blow,
So loud a blast along the shore and sea,
Ye could not hear the waters for the blast,
Tho' heapt in mounds and ridges all the sea
Drove like a cataract, and all the sand
Swept like a river, and the clouded heavens
Were shaken with the motion and the sound.
And blackening in the sea-foam sway'd a boat,
Half-swallow'd in it, anchor'd with a chain;
And in my madness to myself I said,
'I will embark and I will lose myself,
And in the great sea wash away my sin.'
I burst the chain, I sprang into the boat.

Seven days I drove along the dreary deep,
And with me drove the moon and all the
    stars;
And the wind fell, and on the seventh night
I heard the shingle grinding in the surge,
And felt the boat shock earth, and looking
    up,
Behold, the enchanted towers of Carbonek,
A castle like a rock upon a rock,
With chasm-like portals open to the sea,
And steps that met the breaker! there was
    none
Stood near it but a lion on each side
That kept the entry, and the moon was full.
Then from the boat I leapt, and up the
    stairs.
There drew my sword. With sudden-
    flaring manes
Those two great beasts rose upright like a
    man,
Each gript a shoulder, and I stood between;
And, when I would have smitten them,
    heard a voice,
'Doubt not, go forward; if thou doubt, the
    beasts
Will tear thee piecemeal.' Then with
    violence
The sword was dash'd from out my hand,
    and fell.
And up into the sounding hall I past;
But nothing in the sounding hall I saw,
No bench nor table, painting on the wall
Or shield of knight; only the rounded moon
Thro' the tall oriel on the rolling sea.
But always in the quiet house I heard,
Clear as a lark, high o'er me as a lark,
A sweet voice singing in the topmost tower
To the eastward: up I climb'd a thousand
    steps
With pain: as in a dream I seem'd to climb
For ever: at the last I reach'd a door,
A light was in the crannies, and I heard,
'Glory and joy and honour to our Lord
And to the Holy Vessel of the Grail.'
Then in my madness I essay'd the door;
It gave; and thro' a stormy glare, a heat
As from a seventimes-heated furnace, I,
Blasted and burnt, and blinded as I was,
With such a fierceness that I swoon'd
    away—
O, yet methought I saw the Holy Grail,

All pall'd in crimson samite, and around
Great angels, awful shapes, and wings and
    eyes.
And but for all my madness and my sin,
And then my swooning, I had sworn I saw
That which I saw; but what I saw was
    veil'd
And cover'd; and this Quest was not for
    me."

'So speaking, and here ceasing, Lancelot
    left
The hall long silent, till Sir Gawain—nay,
Brother, I need not tell thee foolish
    words,—
A reckless and irreverent knight was he,
Now bolden'd by the silence of his King,—
Well, I will tell thee: "O King, my liege,"
    he said,
"Hath Gawain fail'd in any quest of thine?
When have I stinted stroke in foughten
    field?
But as for thine, my good friend Percivale,
Thy holy nun and thou have driven men
    mad,
Yea, made our mightiest madder than our
    least.
But by mine eyes and by mine ears I swear,
I will be deafer than the blue-eyed cat,
And thrice as blind as any noonday owl,
To holy virgins in their ecstasies,
Henceforward."

    ' "Deafer," said the blameless King,
"Gawain, and blinder unto holy things
Hope not to make thyself by idle vows,
Being too blind to have desire to see.
But if indeed there came a sign from
    heaven,
Blessed are Bors, Lancelot and Percivale,
For these have seen according to their
    sight.
For every fiery prophet in old times,
And all the sacred madness of the bard,
When God made music thro' them, could
    but speak
His music by the framework and the chord;
And as ye saw it ye have spoken truth.

    ' "Nay—but thou errest, Lancelot: never
    yet

Could all of true and noble in knight and
    man
Twine round one sin, whatever it might be,
With such a closeness, but apart there
    grew,
Save that he were the swine thou spakest of,
Some root of knighthood and pure noble-
    ness;
Whereto see thou, that it may bear its
    flower.

  ' "And spake I not too truly, O my
    knights?
Was I too dark a prophet when I said
To those who went upon the Holy Quest,
That most of them would follow wandering
    fires,
Lost in the quagmire?—lost to me and
    gone,
And left me gazing at a barren board,
And a lean Order—scarce return'd a
    tithe—
And out of those to whom the vision came
My greatest hardly will believe he saw;
Another hath beheld it afar off,
And leaving human wrongs to right them-
    selves,
Cares but to pass into the silent life.
And one hath had the vision face to face,
And now his chair desires him here in vain,
However they may crown him otherwhere.

  ' "And some among you held, that if the
    King
Had seen the sight he would have sworn
    the vow:
Not easily, seeing that the King must
    guard
That which he rules, and is but as the hind
To whom a space of land is given to plow.
Who may not wander from the allotted
    field
Before his work be done; but, being done,
Let visions of the night or of the day
Come, as they will; and many a time they
    come,
Until this earth he walks on seems not
    earth,
This light that strikes his eyeball is not
    light,
This air that smites his forehead is not air

But vision—yea, his very hand and foot—
In moments when he feels he cannot die,
And knows himself no vision to himself,
Nor the high God a vision, nor that One
Who rose again: ye have seen what ye
    have seen."

  'So spake the King: I knew not all he
    meant.'

PELLEAS AND ETTARRE

KING ARTHUR made new knights to fill the
    gap
Left by the Holy Quest; and as he sat
In hall at old Caerleon, the high doors
Were softly sunder'd, and thro' these a
    youth,
Pelleas, and the sweet smell of the fields
Past, and the sunshine came along with
    him.

  'Make me thy knight, because I know,
    Sir King,
All that belongs to knighthood, and I love.'
Such was his cry: for having heard the
    King
Had let proclaim a tournament—the prize
A golden circlet and a knightly sword,
Full fain had Pelleas for his lady won
The golden circlet, for himself the sword:
And there were those who knew him near
    the King,
And promised for him: and Arthur made
    him knight.

  And this new knight, Sir Pelleas of the
    isles—
But lately come to his inheritance,
And lord of many a barren isle was he—
Riding at noon, a day or twain before,
Across the forest call'd of Dean, to find
Caerleon and the King, had felt the sun
Beat like a strong knight on his helm, and
    reel'd
Almost to falling from his horse; but saw
Near him a mound of even-sloping side,
Whereon a hundred stately beeches grew,
And here and there great hollies under
    them;
But for a mile all round was open space,

And fern and heath: and slowly Pelleas
    drew
To that dim day, then binding his good
    horse
To a tree, cast himself down; and as he lay
At random looking over the brown earth
Thro' that green-glooming twilight of the
    grove,
It seem'd to Pelleas that the fern without
Burnt as a living fire of emeralds,
So that his eyes were dazzled looking at it.
Then o'er it crost the dimness of a cloud
Floating, and once the shadow of a bird
Flying, and then a fawn; and his eyes
    closed.
And since he loved all maidens, but no
    maid
In special, half-awake he whisper'd,
    'Where?
O where? I love thee, tho' I know thee not.
For fair thou art and pure as Guinevere,
And I will make thee with my spear and
    sword
As famous—O my Queen, my Guinevere,
For I will be thine Arthur when we meet.'

Suddenly waken'd with a sound of talk
And laughter at the limit of the wood,
And glancing thro' the hoary boles, he saw,
Strange as to some old prophet might have
    seem'd
A vision hovering on a sea of fire,
Damsels in divers colours like the cloud
Of sunset and sunrise, and all of them
On horses, and the horses richly trapt
Breast-high in that bright line of bracken
    stood:
And all the damsels talk'd confusedly,
And one was pointing this way, and one
    that,
Because the way was lost.

              And Pelleas rose,
And loosed his horse, and led him to the
    light.
There she that seem'd the chief among
    them said,
'In happy time behold our pilot-star!
Youth, we are damsels-errant, and we ride,
Arm'd as ye see, to tilt against the knights
There at Caerleon, but have lost our way:

To right? to left? straight forward? back
    again?
Which? tell us quickly.'

             Pelleas gazing thought,
'Is Guinevere herself so beautiful?'
For large her violet eyes look'd, and her
    bloom
A rosy dawn kindled in stainless heavens,
And round her limbs, mature in woman-
    hood;
And slender was her hand and small her
    shape;
And but for those large eyes, the haunts of
    scorn,
She might have seem'd a toy to trifle
    with,
And pass and care no more. But while he
    gazed
The beauty of her flesh abash'd the boy,
As tho' it were the beauty of her soul:
For as the base man, judging of the good,
Puts his own baseness in him by default
Of will and nature, so did Pelleas lend
All the young beauty of his own soul to
    hers,
Believing her; and when she spake to him,
Stammer'd, and could not make her a
    reply.
For out of the waste islands had he come,
Where saving his own sisters he had known
Scarce any but the women of his isles,
Rough wives, that laugh'd and scream'd
    against the gulls,
Makers of nets, and living from the sea.

Then with a slow smile turn'd the lady
    round
And look'd upon her people; and as when
A stone is flung into some sleeping tarn,
The circle widens till it lip the marge,
Spread the slow smile thro' all her com-
    pany.
Three knights were thereamong; and they
    too smiled,
Scorning him; for the lady was Ettarre,
And she was a great lady in her land.

Again she said, 'O wild and of the woods,
Knowest thou not the fashion of our
    speech?

Or have the Heavens but given thee a fair face,
Lacking a tongue?'

          'O damsel,' answer'd he,
'I woke from dreams; and coming out of gloom
Was dazzled by the sudden light, and crave
Pardon: but will ye to Caerleon? I
Go likewise: shall I lead you to the King?'

  'Lead then,' she said; and thro' the woods they went.
And while they rode, the meaning in his eyes,
His tenderness of manner, and chaste awe,
His broken utterances and bashfulness,
Were all a burthen to her, and in her heart
She mutter'd, 'I have lighted on a fool,
Raw, yet so stale!' But since her mind was bent
On hearing, after trumpet blown, her name
And title, 'Queen of Beauty,' in the lists
Cried—and beholding him so strong, she thought
That peradventure he will fight for me,
And win the circlet: therefore flatter'd him,
Being so gracious, that he wellnigh deem'd
His wish by hers was echo'd; and her knights
And all her damsels too were gracious to him,
For she was a great lady.

          And when they reach'd
Caerleon, ere they past to lodging, she,
Taking his hand, 'O the strong hand,' she said,
'See! look at mine! but wilt thou fight for me,
And win me this fine circlet, Pelleas,
That I may love thee?'

          Then his helpless heart
Leapt, and he cried, 'Ay! wilt thou if I win?'
'Ay, that will I,' she answer'd, and she laugh'd,
And straitly nipt the hand, and flung it from her;

Then glanced askew at those three knights of hers,
Till all her ladies laugh'd along with her.

  'O happy world,' thought Pelleas, 'all, meseems,
Are happy; I the happiest of them all.'
Nor slept that night for pleasure in his blood,
And green wood-ways, and eyes among the leaves;
Then being on the morrow knighted, sware
To love one only. And as he came away,
The men who met him rounded on their heels
And wonder'd after him, because his face
Shone like the countenance of a priest of old
Against the flame about a sacrifice
Kindled by fire from heaven: so glad was he.

  Then Arthur made vast banquets, and strange knights
From the four winds came in: and each one sat,
Tho' served with choice from air, land, stream, and sea,
Oft in mid-banquet measuring with his eyes
His neighbour's make and might: and Pelleas look'd
Noble among the noble, for he dream'd
His lady loved him, and he knew himself
Loved of the King: and him his new-made knight
Worship, whose lightest whisper moved him more
Than all the ranged reasons of the world.

  Then blush'd and brake the morning of the jousts,
And this was call'd 'The Tournament of Youth:'
For Arthur, loving his young knight, withheld
His older and his mightier from the lists,
That Pelleas might obtain his lady's love,
According to her promise, and remain
Lord of the tourney. And Arthur had the jousts

Down in the flat field by the shore of Usk
Holden: the gilded parapets were crown'd
With faces, and the great tower fill'd with
    eyes
Up to the summit, and the trumpets blew.
There all day long Sir Pelleas kept the field
With honour: so by that strong hand of his
The sword and golden circlet were
    achieved.

Then rang the shout his lady loved: the
    heat
Of pride and glory fired her face; her eye
Sparkled; she caught the circlet from his
    lance,
And there before the people crown'd her-
    self:
So for the last time she was gracious to
    him.

Then at Caerleon for a space—her look
Bright for all others, cloudier on her
    knight—
Linger'd Ettarre: and seeing Pelleas droop,
Said Guinevere, 'We marvel at thee much,
O damsel, wearing this unsunny face
To him who won thee glory!' And she
    said,
'Had ye not held your Lancelot in your
    bower,
My Queen, he had not won.' Whereat the
    Queen,
As one whose foot is bitten by an ant,
Glanced down upon her, turn'd and went
    her way.

But after, when her damsels, and herself,
And those three knights all set their faces
    home,
Sir Pelleas follow'd. She that saw him
    cried,
'Damsels—and yet I should be shamed to
    say it—
I cannot bide Sir Baby. Keep him back
Among yourselves. Would rather that we
    had
Some rough old knight who knew the
    worldly way,
Albeit grizzlier than a bear, to ride
And jest with: take him to you, keep him
    off,

And pamper him with papmeat, if ye will,
Old milky fables of the wolf and sheep,
Such as the wholesome mothers tell their
    boys.
Nay, should ye try him with a merry one
To find his mettle, good: and if he fly us,
Small matter! let him.' This her damsels
    heard,
And mindful of her small and cruel hand,
They, closing round him thro' the journey
    home,
Acted her hest, and always from her side
Restrain'd him with all manner of device,
So that he could not come to speech with
    her.
And when she gain'd her castle, upsprang
    the bridge,
Down rang the grate of iron thro' the
    groove,
And he was left alone in open field.

'These be the ways of ladies,' Pelleas
    thought,
'To those who love them, trials of our faith.
Yea, let her prove me to the uttermost,
For loyal to the uttermost am I.'
So made his moan; and, darkness falling,
    sought
A priory not far off, there lodged, but rose
With morning every day, and, moist or dry,
Full-arm'd upon his charger all day long
Sat by the walls, and no one open'd to him.

And this persistence turn'd her scorn to
    wrath.
Then calling her three knights, she charged
    them, 'Out!
And drive him from the walls.' And out
    they came,
But Pelleas overthrew them as they dash'd
Against him one by one; and these re-
    turn'd,
But still he kept his watch beneath the wall.

Thereon her wrath became a hate; and
    once,
A week beyond, while walking on the walls
With her three knights, she pointed down-
    ward, 'Look,
He haunts me—I cannot breathe—besieges
    me;

Down! strike him! put my hate into your
  strokes,
And drive him from my walls.' And down
  they went,
And Pelleas overthrew them one by one;
And from the tower above him cried
  Ettarre,
'Bind him, and bring him in.'

            He heard her voice;
Then let the strong hand, which had over-
  thrown
Her minion-knights, by those he overthrew
Be bounden straight, and so they brought
  him in.

  Then when he came before Ettarre, the
  sight
Of her rich beauty made him at one glance
More bondsman in his heart than in his
  bonds.
Yet with good cheer he spake, 'Behold me,
  Lady,
A prisoner, and the vassal of thy will;
And if thou keep me in thy donjon here,
Content am I so that I see thy face
But once a day: for I have sworn my vows,
And thou hast given thy promise, and I
  know
That all these pains are trials of my faith,
And that thyself, when thou hast seen me
  strain'd
And sifted to the utmost, wilt at length
Yield me thy love and know me for thy
  knight.'

  Then she began to rail so bitterly,
With all her damsels, he was stricken mute;
But when she mock'd his vows and the
  great King,
Lighted on words: 'For pity of thine own
  self,
Peace, Lady, peace: is he not thine and
  mine?'
'Thou fool,' she said, 'I never heard his
  voice
But long'd to break away. Unbind him now,
And thrust him out of doors; for save he be
Fool to the midmost marrow of his bones,
He will return no more.' And those, her
  three,

Laugh'd, and unbound, and thrust him
  from the gate.

  And after this, a week beyond, again
She call'd them, saying, 'There he watches
  yet,
There like a dog before his master's door!
Kick'd, he returns: do ye not hate him, ye?
Ye know yourselves: how can ye bide at
  peace,
Affronted with his fulsome innocence?
Are ye but creatures of the board and bed,
No men to strike? Fall on him all at once,
And if ye slay him I reck not: if ye fail,
Give ye the slave mine order to be bound,
Bind him as heretofore, and bring him in:
It may be ye shall slay him in his bonds.'

  She spake; and at her will they couch'd
  their spears,
Three against one: and Gawain passing by,
Bound upon solitary adventure, saw
Low down beneath the shadow of those
  towers
A villainy, three to one: and thro' his heart
The fire of honour and all noble deeds
Flash'd, and he call'd, 'I strike upon thy
  side—
The caitiffs!' 'Nay,' said Pelleas, 'but for-
  bear;
He needs no aid who doth his lady's will.'

  So Gawain, looking at the villainy done,
Forbore, but in his heat and eagerness
Trembled and quiver'd, as the dog, with-
  held
A moment from the vermin that he sees
Before him, shivers, ere he springs and
  kills.

  And Pelleas overthrew them, one to
  three;
And they rose up, and bound, and brought
  him in.
Then first her anger, leaving Pelleas,
  burn'd
Full on her knights in many an evil name
Of craven, weakling, and thrice-beaten
  hound:
'Yet, take him, ye that scarce are fit to
  touch,

Far less to bind, your victor, and thrust
    him out,
And let who will release him from his
    bonds.
And if he comes again'—there she brake
    short;
And Pelleas answer'd, 'Lady, for indeed
I loved you and I deem'd you beautiful,
I cannot brook to see your beauty marr'd
Thro' evil spite: and if ye love me not,
I cannot bear to dream you so forsworn:
I had liefer ye were worthy of my love,
Than to be loved again of you—farewell;
And tho' ye kill my hope, not yet my love,
Vex not yourself: ye will not see me more.'

While thus he spake, she gazed upon the
    man
Of princely bearing, tho' in bonds, and
    thought,
'Why have I push'd him from me? this
    man loves,
If love there be: yet him I loved not. Why?
I deem'd him fool? yea, so? or that in him
A something—was it nobler than myself?—
Seem'd my reproach? He is not of my kind.
He could not love me, did he know me well.
Nay, let him go—and quickly.' And her
    knights
Laugh'd not, but thrust him bounden out
    of door.

Forth sprang Gawain, and loosed him
    from his bonds,
And flung them o'er the walls; and after-
    ward,
Shaking his hands, as from a lazar's rag,
'Faith of my body,' he said, 'and art thou
    not—
Yea thou art he, whom late our Arthur
    made
Knight of his table; yea and he that won
The circlet? wherefore hast thou so de-
    famed
Thy brotherhood in me and all the rest,
As let these caitiffs on thee work their will?'

And Pelleas answer'd, 'O, their wills are
    hers
For whom I won the circlet; and mine,
    hers,

Thus to be bounden, so to see her face,
Marr'd tho' it be with spite and mockery
    now,
Other than when I found her in the woods;
And tho' she hath me bounden but in spite,
And all to flout me, when they bring me in,
Let me be bounden, I shall see her face;
Else must I die thro' mine unhappiness.'

And Gawain answer'd kindly tho' in
    scorn,
'Why, let my lady bind me if she will,
And let my lady beat me if she will:
But an she send her delegate to thrall
These fighting hands of mine—Christ kill
    me then
But I will slice him handless by the wrist,
And let my lady sear the stump for him,
Howl as he may. But hold me for your
    friend:
Come, ye know nothing: here I pledge my
    troth,
Yea, by the honour of the Table Round,
I will be leal to thee and work thy work,
And tame thy jailing princess to thine
    hand.
Lend me thine horse and arms, and I will
    say
That I have slain thee. She will let me in
To hear the manner of thy fight and fall;
Then, when I come within her counsels,
    then
From prime to vespers will I chant thy
    praise
As prowest knight and truest lover, more
Than any have sung thee living, till she long
To have thee back in lusty life again,
Not to be bound, save by white bonds and
    warm,
Dearer than freedom. Wherefore now thy
    horse
And armour: let me go: be comforted:
Give me three days to melt her fancy, and
    hope
The third night hence will bring thee news
    of gold.'

Then Pelleas lent his horse and all his
    arms,
Saving the goodly sword, his prize, and
    took

Gawain's, and said, 'Betray me not, but
help—
Art thou not he whom men call light-of-
love?'

'Ay,' said Gawain, 'for women be so
light.'
Then bounded forward to the castle walls,
And raised a bugle hanging from his neck,
And winded it, and that so musically
That all the old echoes hidden in the wall
Rang out like hollow woods at hunting-
tide.

Up ran a score of damsels to the tower;
'Avaunt,' they cried, 'our lady loves thee
not.'
But Gawain lifting up his vizor said,
'Gawain am I, Gawain of Arthur's court,
And I have slain this Pelleas whom ye hate:
Behold his horse and armour. Open gates,
And I will make you merry.'

And down they ran,
Her damsels, crying to their lady, 'Lo!
Pelleas is dead—he told us—he that hath
His horse and armour: will ye let him in?
He slew him! Gawain, Gawain of the court,
Sir Gawain—there he waits below the wall,
Blowing his bugle as who should say him
nay.'

And so, leave given, straight on thro'
open door
Rode Gawain, whom she greeted cour-
teously.
'Dead, is it so?' she ask'd. 'Ay, ay,' said he,
'And oft in dying cried upon your name.'
'Pity on him,' she answer'd, 'a good knight,
But never let me bide one hour at peace.'
'Ay,' thought Gawain, 'and you be fair
enow:
But I to your dead man have given my
troth,
That whom ye loathe, him will I make you
love.'

So those three days, aimless about the
land,
Lost in a doubt, Pelleas wandering
Waited, until the third night brought a
moon

With promise of large light on woods and
ways.

Hot was the night and silent; but a
sound
Of Gawain ever coming, and this lay—
Which Pelleas had heard sung before the
Queen,
And seen her sadden listening—vext his
heart,
And marr'd his rest—'A worm within the
rose.'

'A rose, but one, none other rose had I,
A rose, one rose, and this was wondrous
fair,
One rose, a rose that gladden'd earth and
sky,
One rose, my rose, that sweeten'd all mine
air—
I cared not for the thorns; the thorns were
there.

'One rose, a rose to gather by and by,
One rose, a rose, to gather and to wear,
No rose but one—what other rose had I?
One rose, my rose; a rose that will not
die,—
He dies who loves it,—if the worm be
there.'

This tender rhyme, and evermore the
doubt,
'Why lingers Gawain with his golden
news?'
So shook him that he could not rest, but
rode
Ere midnight to her walls, and bound his
horse
Hard by the gates. Wide open were the
gates,
And no watch kept; and in thro' these he
past,
And heard but his own steps, and his own
heart
Beating, for nothing moved but his own
self,
And his own shadow. Then he crost the
court,
And spied not any light in hall or bower,
But saw the postern portal also wide

Yawning; and up a slope of garden, all
Of roses white and red, and brambles mixt
And overgrowing them, went on, and
found,
Here too, all hush'd below the mellow
moon,
Save that one rivulet from a tiny cave
Came lightening downward, and so spilt
itself
Among the roses, and was lost again.

Then was he ware of three pavilions
rear'd
Above the bushes, gilden-peakt: in one,
Red after revel, droned her lurdane knights
Slumbering, and their three squires across
their feet:
In one, their malice on the placid lip
Froz'n by sweet sleep, four of her damsels
lay:
And in the third, the circlet of the jousts
Bound on her brow, were Gawain and
Ettarre.

Back, as a hand that pushes thro' the leaf
To find a nest and feels a snake, he drew:
Back, as a coward slinks from what he fears
To cope with, or a traitor proven, or hound
Beaten, did Pelleas in an utter shame
Creep with his shadow thro' the court
again,
Fingering at his sword-handle until he
stood
There on the castle-bridge once more, and
thought,
'I will go back, and slay them where they
lie.'

And so went back, and seeing them yet
in sleep
Said, 'Ye, that so dishallow the holy sleep,
Your sleep is death,' and drew the sword,
and thought,
'What! slay a sleeping knight? the King
hath bound
And sworn me to this brotherhood;' again,
'Alas that ever a knight should be so false.'
Then turn'd, and so return'd, and groaning
laid
The naked sword athwart their naked
throats,

There left it, and them sleeping; and she
lay,
The circlet of the tourney round her brows,
And the sword of the tourney across her
throat.

And forth he past, and mounting on his
horse
Stared at her towers that, larger than themselves
In their own darkness, throng'd into the
moon.
Then crush'd the saddle with his thighs,
and clench'd
His hands, and madden'd with himself and
moan'd:

'Would they have risen against me in
their blood
At the last day? I might have answer'd
them
Even before high God. O towers so strong,
Huge, solid, would that even while I gaze
The crack of earthquake shivering to your
base
Split you, and Hell burst up your harlot
roofs
Bellowing, and charr'd you thro' and thro'
within,
Black as the harlot's heart—hollow as a
skull!
Let the fierce east scream thro' your eyelet-
holes,
And whirl the dust of harlots round and
round
In dung and nettles! hiss, snake—I saw
him there—
Let the fox bark, let the wolf yell. Who
yells
Here in the still sweet summer night,
but I—
I, the poor Pelleas whom she call'd her
fool?
Fool, beast—he, she, or I? myself most
fool;
Beast too, as lacking human wit—dis-
graced,
Dishonour'd all for trial of true love—
Love?—we be all alike: only the King
Hath made us fools and liars. O noble vows!
O great and sane and simple race of brutes

That own no lust because they have no
    law!
For why should I have loved her to my
    shame?
I loathe her, as I loved her to my shame.
I never loved her, I but lusted for her—
Away—'

    He dash'd the rowel into his horse,
And bounded forth and vanish'd thro' the
    night.

    Then she, that felt the cold touch on her
    throat,
Awaking knew the sword, and turn'd her-
    self
To Gawain: 'Liar, for thou hast not slain
This Pelleas! here he stood, and might
    have slain
Me and thyself.' And he that tells the tale
Says that her ever-veering fancy turn'd
To Pelleas, as the one true knight on earth,
And only lover; and thro' her love her life
Wasted and pined, desiring him in vain.

    But he by wild and way, for half the
    night,
And over hard and soft, striking the sod
From out the soft, the spark from off the
    hard,
Rode till the star above the wakening sun,
Beside that tower where Percivale was
    cowl'd,
Glanced from the rosy forehead of the
    dawn.
For so the words were flash'd into his heart
He knew not whence or wherefore: 'O
    sweet star,
Pure on the virgin forehead of the dawn!'
And there he would have wept, but felt his
    eyes
Harder and drier than a fountain bed
In summer: thither came the village girls
And linger'd talking, and they come no
    more
Till the sweet heavens have fill'd it from
    the heights
Again with living waters in the change
Of seasons: hard his eyes; harder his heart
Seem'd; but so weary were his limbs,
    that he,

Gasping, 'Of Arthur's hall am I, but here,
Here let me rest and die,' cast himself
    down,
And gulf'd his griefs in inmost sleep; so
    lay,
Till shaken by a dream, that Gawain fired
The hall of Merlin, and the morning star
Reel'd in the smoke, brake into flame, and
    fell.

    He woke, and being ware of some one
    nigh,
Sent hands upon him, as to tear him,
    crying,
'False! and I held thee pure as Guinevere.'

    But Percivale stood near him and replied,
'Am I but false as Guinevere is pure?
Or art thou mazed with dreams? or being
    one
Of our free-spoken Table hast not heard
That Lancelot'—there he check'd himself
    and paused.

    Then fared it with Sir Pelleas as with one
Who gets a wound in battle, and the sword
That made it plunges thro' the wound
    again,
And pricks it deeper: and he shrank and
    wail'd,
'Is the Queen false?' and Percivale was
    mute.
'Have any of our Round Table held their
    vows?'
And Percivale made answer not a word.
'Is the King true?' 'The King!' said Per-
    civale.
'Why then let men couple at once with
    wolves.
What! art thou mad?'

             But Pelleas, leaping up,
Ran thro' the doors and vaulted on his
    horse
And fled: small pity upon his horse had he,
Or on himself, or any, and when he met
A cripple, one that held a hand for alms—
Hunch'd as he was, and like an old dwarf-
    elm
That turns its back on the salt blast, the
    boy

Paused not, but overrode him, shouting,
'False,
And false with Gawain!' and so left him
bruised
And batter'd, and fled on, and hill and
wood
Went ever streaming by him till the
gloom,
That follows on the turning of the world,
Darken'd the common path: he twitch'd
the reins,
And made his beast that better knew it,
swerve
Now off it and now on; but when he saw
High up in heaven the hall that Merlin
built,
Blackening against the dead-green stripes
of even,
'Black nest of rats,' he groan'd, 'ye build
too high.'

Not long thereafter from the city gates
Issued Sir Lancelot riding airily,
Warm with a gracious parting from the
Queen,
Peace at his heart, and gazing at a star
And marvelling what it was: on whom the
boy,
Across the silent seeded meadow-grass
Borne, clash'd: and Lancelot, saying,
'What name hast thou
That ridest here so blindly and so hard?'
'No name, no name,' he shouted, 'a scourge
am I
To lash the treasons of the Table Round.'
'Yea, but thy name?' 'I have many names,'
he cried:
'I am wrath and shame and hate and evil
fame,
And like a poisonous wind I pass to blast
And blaze the crime of Lancelot and the
Queen.'
'First over me,' said Lancelot, 'shalt thou
pass.'
'Fight therefore,' yell'd the youth, and
either knight
Drew back a space, and when they closed,
at once
The weary steed of Pelleas floundering flung
His rider, who call'd out from the dark
field,

'Thou art false as Hell: slay me: I have no
sword.'
Then Lancelot, 'Yea, between thy lips—
and sharp;
But here will I disedge it by thy death.'
'Slay then,' he shriek'd, 'my will is to be
slain,'
And Lancelot, with his heel upon the
fall'n,
Rolling his eyes, a moment stood, then
spake:
'Rise, weakling; I am Lancelot; say thy
say.'

And Lancelot slowly rode his warhorse
back
To Camelot, and Sir Pelleas in brief while
Caught his unbroken limbs from the dark
field,
And follow'd to the city. It chanced that
both
Brake into hall together, worn and pale.
There with her knights and dames was
Guinevere.
Full wonderingly she gazed on Lancelot
So soon return'd, and then on Pelleas, him
Who had not greeted her, but cast himself
Down on a bench, hard-breathing. 'Have
ye fought?'
She ask'd of Lancelot. 'Ay, my Queen,' he
said.
'And thou hast overthrown him?' 'Ay, my
Queen.'
Then she, turning to Pelleas, 'O young
knight,
Hath the great heart of knighthood in thee
fail'd
So far thou canst not bide, unfrowardly,
A fall from *him?*' Then, for he answer'd
not,
'Or hast thou other griefs? If I, the Queen,
May help them, loose thy tongue, and let
me know.'
But Pelleas lifted up an eye so fierce
She quail'd; and he, hissing 'I have no
sword,'
Sprang from the door into the dark. The
Queen
Look'd hard upon her lover, he on her;
And each foresaw the dolorous day to be:
And all talk died, as in a grove all song

Beneath the shadow of some bird of prey;
Then a long silence came upon the hall,
And Modred thought, 'The time is hard at hand.'

THE LAST TOURNAMENT

DAGONET, the fool, whom Gawain in his mood
Had made mock-knight of Arthur's Table Round,
At Camelot, high above the yellowing woods,
Danced like a wither'd leaf before the hall.
And toward him from the hall, with harp in hand,
And from the crown thereof a carcanet
Of ruby swaying to and fro, the prize
Of Tristram in the jousts of yesterday,
Came Tristram, saying, 'Why skip ye so, Sir Fool?'

For Arthur and Sir Lancelot riding once
Far down beneath a winding wall of rock
Heard a child wail. A stump of oak half-dead,
From roots like some black coil of carven snakes,
Clutch'd at the crag, and started thro' mid air
Bearing an eagle's nest: and thro' the tree
Rush'd ever a rainy wind, and thro' the wind
Pierced ever a child's cry: and crag and tree
Scaling, Sir Lancelot from the perilous nest,
This ruby necklace thrice around her neck,
And all unscarr'd from beak or talon, brought
A maiden babe; which Arthur pitying took,
Then gave it to his Queen to rear: the Queen
But coldly acquiescing, in her white arms
Received, and after loved it tenderly,
And named it Nestling; so forgot herself
A moment, and her cares; till that young life
Being smitten in mid heaven with mortal cold
Past from her; and in time the carcanet

Vext her with plaintive memories of the child:
So she, delivering it to Arthur, said,
'Take thou the jewels of this dead innocence,
And make them, an thou wilt, a tourney-prize.'

To whom the King, 'Peace to thine eagle-borne
Dead nestling, and this honour after death,
Following thy will! but, O my Queen, I muse
Why ye not wear on arm, or neck, or zone
Those diamonds that I rescued from the tarn,
And Lancelot won, methought, for thee to wear.'

'Would rather you had let them fall,' she cried,
'Plunge and be lost—ill-fated as they were,
A bitterness to me!—ye look amazed,
Not knowing they were lost as soon as given—
Slid from my hands, when I was leaning out
Above the river—that unhappy child
Past in her barge: but rosier luck will go
With these rich jewels, seeing that they came
Not from the skeleton of a brother-slayer,
But the sweet body of a maiden babe.
Perchance—who knows?—the purest of thy knights
May win them for the purest of my maids.'

She ended, and the cry of a great joust
With trumpet-blowings ran on all the ways
From Camelot in among the faded fields
To furthest towers; and everywhere the knights
Arm'd for a day of glory before the King.

But on the hither side of that loud morn
Into the hall stagger'd, his visage ribb'd
From ear to ear with dogwhip-weals, his nose
Bridge-broken, one eye out, and one hand off,
And one with shatter'd fingers dangling lame,
A churl, to whom indignantly the King,

412

'My churl, for whom Christ died, what
    evil beast
Hath drawn his claws athwart thy face? or
    fiend?
Man was it who marr'd heaven's image in
    thee thus?'

Then, sputtering thro' the hedge of
    splinter'd teeth,
Yet strangers to the tongue, and with
    blunt stump
Pitch-blacken'd sawing the air, said the
    maim'd churl,

'He took them and he drave them to his
    tower—
Some hold he was a table-knight of thine—
A hundred goodly ones—the Red Knight,
    he—
Lord, I was tending swine, and the Red
    Knight
Brake in upon me and drave them to his
    tower;
And when I call'd upon thy name as one
That doest right by gentle and by churl,
Maim'd me and maul'd, and would out-
    right have slain,
Save that he sware me to a message, saying,
"Tell thou the King and all his liars, that I
Have founded my Round Table in the
    North,
And whatsoever his own knights have
    sworn
My knights have sworn the counter to it—
    and say
My tower is full of harlots, like his court,
But mine are worthier, seeing they profess
To be none other than themselves—and say
My knights are all adulterers like his own,
But mine are truer, seeing they profess
To be none other; and say his hour is come,
The heathen are upon him, his long lance
Broken, and his Excalibur a straw." '

Then Arthur turn'd to Kay the sene-
    schal,
'Take thou my churl, and tend him
    curiously
Like a king's heir, till all his hurts be whole.
The heathen—but that ever-climbing
    wave,

Hurl'd back again so often in empty foam,
Hath lain for years at rest—and renegades,
Thieves, bandits, leavings of confusion,
    whom
The wholesome realm is purged of other-
    where,
Friends, thro' your manhood and your
    fealty,—now
Make their last head like Satan in the
    North.
My younger knights, new-made, in whom
    your flower
Waits to be solid fruit of golden deeds,
Move with me toward their quelling, which
    achieved,
The loneliest ways are safe from shore to
    shore.
But thou, Sir Lancelot, sitting in my place
Enchair'd to-morrow, arbitrate the field;
For wherefore shouldst thou care to mingle
    with it,
Only to yield my Queen her own again?
Speak, Lancelot, thou art silent: is it well?'

Thereto Sir Lancelot answer'd, 'It is
    well:
Yet better if the King abide, and leave
The leading of his younger knights to me.
Else, for the King has will'd it, it is well.'

Then Arthur rose and Lancelot follow'd
    him,
And while they stood without the doors,
    the King
Turn'd to him saying, 'Is it then so well?
Or mine the blame that oft I seem as he
Of whom was written, "A sound is in his
    ears"?
The foot that loiters, bidden go,—the
    glance
That only seems half-loyal to command,—
A manner somewhat fall'n from rever-
    ence—
Or have I dream'd the bearing of our
    knights
Tells of a manhood ever less and lower?
Or whence the fear lest this my realm,
    uprear'd,
By noble deeds at one with noble vows,
From flat confusion and brute violences,
Reel back into the beast, and be no more?'

He spoke, and taking all his younger knights,
Down the slope city rode, and sharply turn'd
North by the gate. In her high bower the Queen,
Working a tapestry, lifted up her head,
Watch'd her lord pass, and knew not that she sigh'd.
Then ran across her memory the strange rhyme
Of bygone Merlin, 'Where is he who knows?
From the great deep to the great deep he goes.'

But when the morning of a tournament,
By these in earnest those in mockery call'd
The Tournament of the Dead Innocence,
Brake with a wet wind blowing, Lancelot,
Round whose sick head all night, like birds of prey,
The words of Arthur flying shriek'd, arose,
And down a streetway hung with folds of pure
White samite, and by fountains running wine,
Where children sat in white with cups of gold,
Moved to the lists, and there, with slow sad steps
Ascending, fill'd his double-dragon'd chair.

He glanced and saw the stately galleries,
Dame, damsel, each thro' worship of their Queen
White-robed in honour of the stainless child,
And some with scatter'd jewels, like a bank
Of maiden snow mingled with sparks of fire.
He look'd but once, and vail'd his eyes again.

The sudden trumpet sounded as in a dream
To ears but half-awaked, then one low roll
Of Autumn thunder, and the jousts began:
And ever the wind blew, and yellowing leaf
And gloom and gleam, and shower and shorn plume

Went down it. Sighing weariedly, as one
Who sits and gazes on a faded fire,
When all the goodlier guests are past away,
Sat their great umpire, looking o'er the lists.
He saw the laws that ruled the tournament
Broken, but spake not; once, a knight cast down
Before his throne of arbitration cursed
The dead babe and the follies of the King;
And once the laces of a helmet crack'd,
And show'd him, like a vermin in its hole,
Modred, a narrow face: anon he heard
The voice that billow'd round the barriers roar
An ocean-sounding welcome to one knight,
But newly-enter'd, taller than the rest,
And armour'd all in forest green, whereon
There tript a hundred tiny silver deer,
And wearing but a holly-spray for crest,
With ever-scattering berries, and on shield
A spear, a harp, a bugle—Tristram—late
From overseas in Brittany return'd,
And marriage with a princess of that realm,
Isolt the White—Sir Tristram of the Woods—
Whom Lancelot knew, had held sometime with pain
His own against him, and now yearn'd to shake
The burthen off his heart in one full shock
With Tristram ev'n to death: his strong hands gript
And dinted the gilt dragons right and left,
Until he groan'd for wrath—so many of those,
That ware their ladies' colours on the casque,
Drew from before Sir Tristram to the bounds,
And there with gibes and flickering mockeries
Stood, while he mutter'd, 'Craven crests! O shame!
What faith have these in whom they sware to love?
The glory of our Round Table is no more.'

So Tristram won, and Lancelot gave, the gems,
Not speaking other word than 'Hast thou won?

Art thou the purest, brother? See, the hand
Wherewith thou takest this, is red!' to
   whom
Tristram, half plagued by Lancelot's lan-
   guorous mood,
Made answer, 'Ay, but wherefore toss me
   this
Like a dry bone cast to some hungry
   hound?
Let be thy fair Queen's fantasy. Strength
   of heart
And might of limb, but mainly use and
   skill,
Are winners in this pastime of our King.
My hand—belike the lance hath dript
   upon it—
No blood of mine, I trow; but O chief
   knight,
Right arm of Arthur in the battlefield,
Great brother, thou nor I have made the
   world;
Be happy in thy fair Queen as I in mine.'

And Tristram round the gallery made
   his horse
Caracole; then bow'd his homage, bluntly
   saying,
'Fair damsels, each to him who worships
   each
Sole Queen of Beauty and of love, behold
This day my Queen of Beauty is not here.'
And most of these were mute, some
   anger'd, one
Murmuring, 'All courtesy is dead,' and
   one,
'The glory of our Round Table is no more.'

Then fell thick rain, plume droopt and
   mantle clung,
And pettish cries awoke, and the wan day
Went glooming down in wet and weariness:
But under her black brows a swarthy one
Laugh'd shrilly, crying, 'Praise the patient
   saints,
Our one white day of Innocence hath past,
Tho' somewhat draggled at the skirt. So
   be it.
The snowdrop only, flowering thro' the
   year,
Would make the world as blank as Winter-
   tide.

Come—let us gladden their sad eyes, our
   Queen's
And Lancelot's, at this night's solemnity
With all the kindlier colours of the field.'

So dame and damsel glitter'd at the feast
Variously gay: for he that tells the tale
Liken'd them, saying, as when an hour of
   cold
Falls on the mountain in midsummer snows,
And all the purple slopes of mountain
   flowers
Pass under white, till the warm hour
   returns
With veer of wind, and all are flowers
   again;
So dame and damsel cast the simple white,
And glowing in all colours, the live grass,
Rose-campion, bluebell, kingcup, poppy,
   glanced
About the revels, and with mirth so loud
Beyond all use, that, half-amazed, the
   Queen,
And wroth at Tristram and the lawless
   jousts,
Brake up their sports, then slowly to her
   bower
Parted, and in her bosom pain was lord.

And little Dagonet on the morrow morn,
High over all the yellowing Autumn-tide,
Danced like a wither'd leaf before the hall.
Then Tristram saying, 'Why skip ye so,
   Sir Fool?'
Wheel'd round on either heel, Dagonet
   replied,
'Belike for lack of wiser company;
Or being fool, and seeing too much wit
Makes the world rotten, why, belike I skip
To know myself the wisest knight of all.'
'Ay, fool,' said Tristram, 'but 'tis eating
   dry
To dance without a catch, a roundelay
To dance to.' Then he twangled on his
   harp,
And while he twangled little Dagonet stood
Quiet as any water-sodden log
Stay'd in the wandering warble of a brook;
But when the twangling ended, skipt again;
And being ask'd, 'Why skipt ye not, Sir
   Fool?'

Made answer, 'I had liefer twenty years
Skip to the broken music of my brains
Than any broken music thou canst make.'
Then Tristram, waiting for the quip to
come,
'Good now, what music have I broken,
fool?'
And little Dagonet, skipping, 'Arthur, the
King's;
For when thou playest that air with Queen
Isolt,
Thou makest broken music with thy bride,
Her daintier namesake down in Brittany—
And so thou breakest Arthur's music too.'
'Save for that broken music in thy brains,
Sir Fool,' said Tristram, 'I would break thy
head.
Fool, I came late, the heathen wars were
o'er,
The life had flown, we sware but by the
shell—
I am but a fool to reason with a fool—
Come, thou art crabb'd and sour: but lean
me down,
Sir Dagonet, one of thy long asses' ears,
And harken if my music be not true.

'"Free love—free field—we love but
while we may:
The woods are hush'd, their music is no
more:
The leaf is dead, the yearning past away:
New leaf, new life—the days of frost are
o'er:
New life, new love, to suit the newer day:
New loves are sweet as those that went
before:
Free love—free field—we love but while
we may."

'Ye might have moved slow-measure to
my tune,
Not stood stockstill. I made it in the woods,
And heard it ring as true as tested gold.'

But Dagonet with one foot poised in his
hand,
'Friend, did ye mark that fountain yesterday
Made to run wine?—but this had run
itself

All out like a long life to a sour end—
And them that round it sat with golden
cups
To hand the wine to whosoever came—
The twelve small damosels white as Inno-
cence,
In honour of poor Innocence the babe,
Who left the gems which Innocence the
Queen
Lent to the King, and Innocence the King
Gave for a prize—and one of those white
slips
Handed her cup and piped, the pretty one,
"Drink, drink, Sir Fool," and thereupon
I drank,
Spat—pish—the cup was gold, the draught
was mud.'

And Tristram, 'Was it muddier than thy
gibes?
Is all the laughter gone dead out of thee?—
Not marking how the knighthood mock
thee, fool—
"Fear God: honour the King—his one true
knight—
Sole follower of the vows"—for here be
they
Who knew thee swine enow before I came,
Smuttier than blasted grain: but when the
King
Had made the fool, thy vanity so shot up
It frighted all free fool from out thy heart;
Which left thee less than fool, and less than
swine,
A naked aught—yet swine I hold thee still,
For I have flung thee pearls and find thee
swine.'

And little Dagonet mincing with his feet,
'Knight, an ye fling those rubies round my
neck
In lieu of hers, I'll hold thou hast some
touch
Of music, since I care not for thy pearls.
Swine? I have wallow'd, I have wash'd—
the world
Is flesh and shadow—I have had my day.
The dirty nurse, Experience, in her kind
Hath foul'd me—an I wallow'd, then I
wash'd—
I have had my day and my philosophies—

And thank the Lord I am King Arthur's
    fool.
Swine, say ye? swine, goats, asses, rams
    and geese
Troop'd round a Paynim harper once, who
    thrumm'd
On such a wire as musically as thou
Some such fine song—but never a king's
    fool.'

And Tristram, 'Then were swine, goats,
    asses, geese
The wiser fools, seeing thy Paynim bard
Had such a mastery of his mystery
That he could harp his wife up out of hell.'

Then Dagonet, turning on the ball of
    his foot,
'And whither harp'st thou thine? down!
    and thyself
Down! and two more: a helpful harper
    thou,
That harpest downward! Dost thou know
    the star
We call the harp of Arthur up in heaven?'

And Tristram, 'Ay, Sir Fool, for when
    our King
Was victor wellnigh day by day, the
    knights,
Glorying in each new glory, set his name
High on all hills, and in the signs of
    heaven.'

And Dagonet answer'd, 'Ay, and when
    the land
Was freed, and the Queen false, ye set
    yourself
To babble about him, all to show your
    wit—
And whether he were King by courtesy,
Or King by right—and so went harping
    down
The black king's highway, got so far, and
    grew
So witty that ye play'd at ducks and drakes
With Arthur's vows on the great lake of fire.
Tuwhoo! do ye see it? do ye see the star?'

'Nay, fool,' said Tristram, 'not in open
    day.'

And Dagonet, 'Nay, nor will: I see it and
    hear.
It makes a silent music up in heaven,
And I, and Arthur and the angels hear,
And then we skip.' 'Lo, fool,' he said, 'ye
    talk
Fool's treason: is the King thy brother
    fool?'
Then little Dagonet clapt his hands and
    shrill'd,
'Ay, ay, my brother fool, the king of fools!
Conceits himself as God that he can make
Figs out of thistles, silk from bristles, milk
From burning spurge, honey from hornet-
    combs,
And men from beasts—Long live the king
    of fools!'

And down the city Dagonet danced
    away;
But thro' the slowly-mellowing avenues
And solitary passes of the wood
Rode Tristram toward Lyonnesse and the
    west.
Before him fled the face of Queen Isolt
With ruby-circled neck, but evermore
Past, as a rustle or twitter in the wood
Made dull his inner, keen his outer eye
For all that walk'd, or crept, or perch'd, or
    flew.
Anon the face, as, when a gust hath blown,
Unruffling waters re-collect the shape
Of one that in them sees himself, return'd;
But at the slot or fewmets of a deer,
Or ev'n a fall'n feather, vanish'd again.

So on for all that day from lawn to lawn
Thro' many a league-long bower he rode.
    At length
A lodge of intertwisted beechen-boughs
Furze-cramm'd, and bracken-rooft, the
    which himself
Built for a summer day with Queen Isolt
Against a shower, dark in the golden grove
Appearing, sent his fancy back to where
She lived a moon in that low lodge with
    him:
Till Mark her lord had past, the Cornish
    King,
With six or seven, when Tristram was
    away,

And snatch'd her thence; yet dreading worse than shame
Her warrior Tristram, spake not any word,
But bode his hour, devising wretchedness.

And now that desert lodge to Tristram lookt
So sweet, that halting, in he past, and sank
Down on a drift of foliage random-blown;
But could not rest for musing how to smoothe
And sleek his marriage over to the Queen.
Perchance in lone Tintagil far from all
The tonguesters of the court she had not heard.
But then what folly had sent him overseas
After she left him lonely here? a name?
Was it the name of one in Brittany,
Isolt, the daughter of the King? 'Isolt
Of the white hands' they call'd her: the sweet name
Allured him first, and then the maid herself,
Who served him well with those white hands of hers,
And loved him well, until himself had thought
He loved her also, wedded easily,
But left her all as easily, and return'd.
The black-blue Irish hair and Irish eyes
Had drawn him home—what marvel? then he laid
His brows upon the drifted leaf and dream'd.

He seem'd to pace the strand of Brittany
Between Isolt of Britain and his bride,
And show'd them both the ruby-chain, and both
Began to struggle for it, till his Queen
Graspt it so hard, that all her hand was red.
Then cried the Breton, 'Look, her hand is red!
These be no rubies, this is frozen blood,
And melts within her hand—her hand is hot
With ill desires, but this I gave thee, look,
Is all as cool and white as any flower.'
Follow'd a rush of eagle's wings, and then
A whimpering of the spirit of the child,
Because the twain had spoil'd her carcanet.

He dream'd; but Arthur with a hundred spears
Rode far, till o'er the illimitable reed,
And many a glancing plash and sallowy isle,
The wide-wing'd sunset of the misty marsh
Glared on a huge machicolated tower
That stood with open doors, whereout was roll'd
A roar of riot, as from men secure
Amid their marshes, ruffians at their ease
Among their harlot-brides, an evil song.
'Lo there,' said one of Arthur's youth, for there,
High on a grim dead tree before the tower,
A goodly brother of the Table Round
Swung by the neck: and on the boughs a shield
Showing a shower of blood in a field noir,
And therebeside a horn, inflamed the knights
At that dishonour done the gilded spur,
Till each would clash the shield, and blow the horn.
But Arthur waved them back. Alone he rode.
Then at the dry harsh roar of the great horn,
That sent the face of all the marsh aloft
An ever upward-rushing storm and cloud
Of shriek and plume, the Red Knight heard, and all,
Even to tipmost lance and topmost helm,
In blood-red armour sallying, howl'd to the King,

'The teeth of Hell flay bare and gnash thee flat!—
Lo! art thou not that eunuch-hearted King
Who fain had clipt free manhood from the world—
The woman-worshipper? Yea, God's curse, and I!
Slain was the brother of my paramour
By a knight of thine, and I that heard her whine
And snivel, being eunuch-hearted too,
Sware by the scorpion-worm that twists in hell,
And stings itself to everlasting death,
To hang whatever knight of thine I fought

And tumbled. Art thou King?—Look to
thy life!'

He ended: Arthur knew the voice; the
face
Wellnigh was helmet-hidden, and the name
Went wandering somewhere darkling in
his mind.
And Arthur deign'd not use of word or
sword,
But let the drunkard, as he stretch'd from
horse
To strike him, overbalancing his bulk,
Down from the causeway heavily to the
swamp
Fall, as the crest of some slow-arching
wave,
Heard in dead night along that table-shore,
Drops flat, and after the great waters break
Whitening for half a league, and thin them-
selves,
Far over sands marbled with moon and
cloud,
From less and less to nothing; thus he fell
Head-heavy; then the knights, who watch'd
him, roar'd
And shouted and leapt down upon the
fall'n;
There trampled out his face from being
known,
And sank his head in mire, and slimed
themselves:
Nor heard the King for their own cries,
but sprang
Thro' open doors, and swording right and
left
Men, women, on their sodden faces, hurl'd
The tables over and the wines, and slew
Till all the rafters rang with woman-yells,
And all the pavement stream'd with mas-
sacre:
Then, echoing yell with yell, they fired the
tower,
Which half that autumn night, like the live
North,
Red-pulsing up thro' Alioth and Alcor,
Made all above it, and a hundred meres
About it, as the water Moab saw
Come round by the East, and out beyond
them flush'd
The long low dune, and lazy-plunging sea.

So all the ways were safe from shore to
shore,
But in the heart of Arthur pain was lord.

Then, out of Tristram waking, the red
dream
Fled with a shout, and that low lodge
return'd,
Mid-forest, and the wind among the
boughs.
He whistled his good warhorse left to graze
Among the forest greens, vaulted upon him,
And rode beneath an ever-showering leaf,
Till one lone woman, weeping near a cross,
Stay'd him. 'Why weep ye?' 'Lord,' she
said, 'my man
Hath left me or is dead;' whereon he
thought—
'What, if she hate me now? I would not
this.
What, if she love me still? I would not
that.
I know not what I would'—but said to her,
'Yet weep not thou, lest, if thy mate return,
He find thy favour changed and love thee
not'—
Then pressing day by day thro' Lyonnesse
Last in a roky hollow, belling, heard
The hounds of Mark, and felt the goodly
hounds
Yelp at his heart, but turning, past and
gain'd
Tintagil, half in sea, and high on land,
A crown of towers.

                    Down in a casement sat,
A low sea-sunset glorying round her hair
And glossy-throated grace, Isolt the Queen.
And when she heard the feet of Tristram
grind
The spiring stone that scaled about her
tower,
Flush'd, started, met him at the doors, and
there
Belted his body with her white embrace,
Crying aloud, 'Not Mark—not Mark, my
soul!
The footstep flutter'd me at first: not he:
Catlike thro' his own castle steals my Mark,
But warrior-wise thou stridest thro' his
halls

Who hates thee, as I him—ev'n to the
death.
My soul, I felt my hatred for my Mark
Quicken within me, and knew that thou
wert nigh.'
To whom Sir Tristram smiling, 'I am here.
Let be thy Mark, seeing he is not thine.'

And drawing somewhat backward she
replied,
'Can he be wrong'd who is not ev'n his
own,
But save for dread of thee had beaten me,
Scratch'd, bitten, blinded, marr'd me
somehow—Mark?
What rights are his that dare not strike for
them?
Not lift a hand—not, tho' he found me
thus!
But harken! have ye met him? hence he
went
To-day for three days' hunting—as he
said—
And so returns belike within an hour.
Mark's way, my soul!—but eat not thou
with Mark,
Because he hates thee even more than
fears;
Nor drink: and when thou passest any
wood
Close vizor, lest an arrow from the bush
Should leave me all alone with Mark and
hell.
My God, the measure of my hate for Mark
Is as the measure of my love for thee.'

So, pluck'd one way by hate and one by
love,
Drain'd of her force, again she sat, and
spake
To Tristram, as he knelt before her, say-
ing,
'O hunter, and O blower of the horn,
Harper, and thou hast been a rover too,
For, ere I mated with my shambling king,
Ye twain had fallen out about the bride
Of one—his name is out of me—the prize,
If prize she were—(what marvel—she
could see)—
Thine, friend; and ever since my craven
seeks

To wreck thee villainously: but, O Sir
Knight,
What dame or damsel have ye kneel'd to
last?'

And Tristram, 'Last to my Queen Para-
mount,
Here now to my Queen Paramount of love
And loveliness—ay, lovelier than when
first
Her light feet fell on our rough Lyonnesse,
Sailing from Ireland.'

Softly laugh'd Isolt;
'Flatter me not, for hath not our great
Queen
My dole of beauty trebled?' and he said,
'Her beauty is her beauty, and thine thine,
And thine is more to me—soft, gracious,
kind—
Save when thy Mark is kindled on thy lips
Most gracious; but she, haughty, ev'n to
him,
Lancelot; for I have seen him wan enow
To make one doubt if ever the great Queen
Have yielded him her love.'

To whom Isolt,
'Ah then, false hunter and false harper,
thou
Who brakest thro' the scruple of my bond,
Calling me thy white hind, and saying to
me
That Guinevere had sinn'd against the
highest,
And I—misyoked with such a want of
man—
That I could hardly sin against the lowest.'

He answer'd, 'O my soul, be comforted!
If this be sweet, to sin in leading-strings,
If here be comfort, and if ours be sin,
Crown'd warrant had we for the crowning
sin
That made us happy: but how ye greet me
—fear
And fault and doubt—no word of that fond
tale—
Thy deep heart-yearnings, thy sweet
memories
Of Tristram in that year he was away.'

And, saddening on the sudden, spake
    Isolt,
'I had forgotten all in my strong joy
To see thee—yearnings?—ay! for, hour
    by hour,
Here in the never-ended afternoon,
O sweeter than all memories of thee,
Deeper than any yearnings after thee
Seem'd those far-rolling, westward-smiling
    seas,
Watch'd from this tower. Isolt of Britain
    dash'd
Before Isolt of Brittany on the strand,
Would that have chill'd her bride-kiss?
    Wedded her?
Fought in her father's battles? wounded
    there?
The King was all fulfill'd with grateful-
    ness,
And she, my namesake of the hands, that
    heal'd
Thy hurt and heart with unguent and
    caress—
Well—can I wish her any huger wrong
Than having known thee? her too hast
    thou left
To pine and waste in those sweet memories.
O were I not my Mark's, by whom all men
Are noble, I should hate thee more than
    love.'

And Tristram, fondling her light hands,
    replied,
'Grace, Queen, for being loved: she loved
    me well.
Did I love her? the name at least I loved.
Isolt?—I fought his battles, for Isolt!
The night was dark; the true star set. Isolt!
The name was ruler of the dark——Isolt?
Care not for her! patient, and prayerful,
    meek,
Pale-blooded, she will yield herself to God.'

And Isolt answer'd, 'Yea, and why not I?
Mine is the larger need, who am not meek,
Pale-blooded, prayerful. Let me tell thee
    now.
Here one black, mute midsummer night
    I sat,
Lonely, but musing on thee, wondering
    where,

Murmuring a light song I had heard thee
    sing,
And once or twice I spake thy name aloud.
Then flash'd a levin-brand; and near me
    stood,
In fuming sulphur blue and green, a
    fiend—
Mark's way to steal behind one in the
    dark—
For there was Mark: "He has wedded
    her," he said,
Not said, but hiss'd it: then this crown of
    towers
So shook to such a roar of all the sky,
That here in utter dark I swoon'd away,
And woke again in utter dark, and cried,
"I will flee hence and give myself to
    God"—
And thou wert lying in thy new leman's
    arms.'

Then Tristram, ever dallying with her
    hand,
'May God be with thee, sweet, when old
    and gray,
And past desire!' a saying that anger'd her.
' "May God be with thee, sweet, when
    thou art old,
And sweet no more to me!" I need Him
    now.
For when had Lancelot utter'd aught so
    gross
Ev'n to the swineherd's malkin in the
    mast?
The greater man, the greater courtesy.
Far other were the Tristram, Arthur's
    knight!
But thou, thro' ever harrying thy wild
    beasts—
Save that to touch a harp, tilt with a lance
Becomes thee well—art grown wild beast
    thyself.
How darest thou, if lover, push me even
In fancy from thy side, and set me far
In the gray distance, half a life away,
Her to be loved no more? Unsay it, un-
    swear!
Flatter me rather, seeing me so weak,
Broken with Mark and hate and solitude,
Thy marriage and mine own, that I should
    suck

Lies like sweet wines: lie to me: I believe.
Will ye not lie? not swear, as there ye kneel,
And solemnly as when ye sware to him,
The man of men, our King—My God, the
　　power
Was once in vows when men believed the
　　King!
They lied not then, who sware, and thro'
　　their vows
The King prevailing made his realm:—I
　　say,
Swear to me thou wilt love me ev'n when
　　old,
Gray-hair'd, and past desire, and in
　　despair.'

Then Tristram, pacing moodily up and
　　down,
'Vows! did you keep the vow you made to
　　Mark
More than I mine? Lied, say ye? Nay, but
　　learnt,
The vow that binds too strictly snaps
　　itself—
My knighthood taught me this—ay, being
　　snapt—
We run more counter to the soul thereof
Than had we never sworn. I swear no
　　more.
I swore to the great King, and am for-
　　sworn.
For once—ev'n to the height—I honour'd
　　him.
"Man, is he man at all?" methought, when
　　first
I rode from our rough Lyonnesse, and
　　beheld
That victor of the Pagan throned in hall—
His hair, a sun that ray'd from off a brow
Like hillsnow high in heaven, the steel-
　　blue eyes,
The golden beard that clothed his lips
　　with light—
Moreover, that weird legend of his birth,
With Merlin's mystic babble about his end
Amazed me; then, his foot was on a stool
Shaped as a dragon; he seem'd to me no
　　man,
But Michaël trampling Satan; so I sware,
Being amazed: but this went by—The
　　vows!

O ay—the wholesome madness of an
　　hour—
They served their use, their time; for
　　every knight
Believed himself a greater than himself,
And every follower eyed him as a God;
Till he, being lifted up beyond himself,
Did mightier deeds than elsewise he had
　　done,
And so the realm was made; but then their
　　vows—
First mainly thro' that sullying of our
　　Queen—
Began to gall the knighthood, asking
　　whence
Had Arthur right to bind them to himself?
Dropt down from heaven? wash'd up from
　　out the deep?
They fail'd to trace him thro' the flesh and
　　blood
Of our old kings: whence then? a doubtful
　　lord
To bind them by inviolable vows,
Which flesh and blood perforce would
　　violate:
For feel this arm of mine—the tide within
Red with free chase and heather-scented
　　air,
Pulsing full man; can Arthur make me
　　pure
As any maiden child? lock up my tongue
From uttering freely what I freely hear?
Bind me to one? The wide world laughs
　　at it.
And worldling of the world am I, and know
The ptarmigan that whitens ere his hour
Woos his own end; we are not angels here
Nor shall be: vows—I am woodman of the
　　woods,
And hear the garnet-headed yaffingale
Mock them: my soul, we love but while we
　　may;
And therefore is my love so large for thee,
Seeing it is not bounded save by love.

Here ending, he moved toward her, and
　　she said,
'Good: an I turn'd away my love for thee
To some one thrice as courteous as thy-
　　self—
For courtesy wins woman all as well

As valour may, but he that closes both
Is perfect, he is Lancelot—taller indeed,
Rosier and comelier, thou—but say I loved
This knightliest of all knights, and cast
    thee back
Thine own small saw, "We love but while
    we may,"
Well then, what answer?'

             He that while she spake,
Mindful of what he brought to adorn her
    with,
The jewels, had let one finger lightly touch
The warm white apple of her throat,
    replied,
'Press this a little closer, sweet, until—
Come, I am hunger'd and half-anger'd—
    meat,
Wine, wine—and I will love thee to the
    death,
And out beyond into the dream to come.'

So then, when both were brought to full
    accord,
She rose, and set before him all he will'd;
And after these had comforted the blood
With meats and wines, and satiated their
    hearts—
Now talking of their woodland paradise,
The deer, the dews, the fern, the founts,
    the lawns;
Now mocking at the much ungainliness,
And craven shifts, and long crane legs of
    Mark—
Then Tristram laughing caught the harp,
    and sang:

'Ay, ay, O ay—the winds that bend the
    brier!
A star in heaven, a star within the mere!
Ay, ay, O ay—a star was my desire,
And one was far apart, and one was near:
Ay, ay, O ay—the winds that bow the
    grass!
And one was water and one star was fire,
And one will ever shine and one will pass.
Ay, ay, O ay—the winds that move the
    mere.'

Then in the light's last glimmer Tris-
    tram show'd
And swung the ruby carcanet. She cried,

'The collar of some Order, which our King
Hath newly founded, all for thee, my soul,
For thee, to yield thee grace beyond thy
    peers.'

'Not so, my Queen,' he said, 'but the
    red fruit
Grown on a magic oak-tree in mid-heaven,
And won by Tristram as a tourney-prize,
And hither brought by Tristram for his last
Love-offering and peace-offering unto
    thee.'

He spoke, he turn'd, then, flinging round
    her neck,
Claspt it, and cried 'Thine Order, O my
    Queen!'
But, while he bow'd to kiss the jewell'd
    throat,
Out of the dark, just as the lips had touch'd,
Behind him rose a shadow and a shriek—
'Mark's way,' said Mark, and clove him
    thro' the brain.

That night came Arthur home, and
    while he climb'd,
All in a death-dumb autumn-dripping
    gloom,
The stairway to the hall, and look'd and
    saw
The great Queen's bower was dark,—
    about his feet
A voice clung sobbing till he question'd it,
'What art thou?' and the voice about his
    feet
Sent up an answer, sobbing, 'I am thy fool,
And I shall never make thee smile again.'

GUINEVERE

QUEEN GUINEVERE had fled the court, and
    sat
There in the holy house at Almesbury
Weeping, none with her save a little maid,
A novice: one low light betwixt them
    burn'd
Blurr'd by the creeping mist, for all abroad,
Beneath a moon unseen albeit at full,
The white mist, like a face-cloth to the face,
Clung to the dead earth, and the land was
    still.

For hither had she fled, her cause of
    flight
Sir Modred; he that like a subtle beast
Lay couchant with his eyes upon the
    throne,
Ready to spring, waiting a chance: for this
He chill'd the popular praises of the King
With silent smiles of slow disparagement;
And tamper'd with the Lords of the White
    Horse,
Heathen, the brood by Hengist left; and
    sought
To make disruption in the Table Round
Of Arthur, and to splinter it into feuds
Serving his traitorous end; and all his aims
Were sharpen'd by strong hate for Lance-
    lot.

For thus it chanced one morn when all
    the court,
Green-suited, but with plumes that mock'd
    the may,
Had been, their wont, a-maying and re-
    turn'd,
That Modred still in green, all ear and
    eye,
Climb'd to the high top of the garden-wall
To spy some secret scandal if he might,
And saw the Queen who sat betwixt her
    best
Enid, and lissome Vivien, of her court
The wiliest and the worst; and more than
    this
He saw not, for Sir Lancelot passing by
Spied where he couch'd, and as the gar-
    dener's hand
Picks from the colewort a green caterpillar,
So from the high wall and the flowering
    grove
Of grasses Lancelot pluck'd him by the
    heel,
And cast him as a worm upon the way;
But when he knew the Prince tho' marr'd
    with dust,
He, reverencing king's blood in a bad man,
Made such excuses as he might, and these
Full knightly without scorn; for in those
    days
No knight of Arthur's noblest dealt in
    scorn;
But, if a man were halt or hunch'd, in him

By those whom God had made full-limb'd
    and tall,
Scorn was allow'd as part of his defect,
And he was answer'd softly by the King
And all his Table. So Sir Lancelot holp
To raise the Prince, who rising twice or
    thrice
Full sharply smote his knees, and smiled,
    and went:
But, ever after, the small violence done
Rankled in him and ruffled all his heart,
As the sharp wind that ruffles all day long
A little bitter pool about a stone
On the bare coast.

          But when Sir Lancelot told
This matter to the Queen, at first she
    laugh'd
Lightly, to think of Modred's dusty fall,
Then shudder'd, as the village wife who
    cries
'I shudder, some one steps across my
    grave;'
Then laugh'd again, but faintlier, for
    indeed
She half-foresaw that he, the subtle beast,
Would track her guilt until he found, and
    hers
Would be for evermore a name of scorn.
Henceforward rarely could she front in
    hall,
Or elsewhere, Modred's narrow foxy face,
Heart-hiding smile, and gray persistent
    eye:
Henceforward too, the Powers that tend
    the soul,
To help it from the death that cannot die,
And save it even in extremes, began
To vex and plague her. Many a time for
    hours,
Beside the placid breathings of the King,
In the dead night, grim faces came and
    went
Before her, or a vague spiritual fear—
Like to some doubtful noise of creaking
    doors,
Heard by the watcher in a haunted house,
That keeps the rust of murder on the
    walls—
Held her awake: or if she slept, she
    dream'd

An awful dream; for then she seem'd to
stand
On some vast plain before a setting sun,
And from the sun there swiftly made at her
A ghastly something, and its shadow flew
Before it, till it touch'd her, and she turn'd—
When lo! her own, that broadening from
her feet,
And blackening, swallow'd all the land,
and in it
Far cities burnt, and with a cry she woke.
And all this trouble did not pass but grew;
Till ev'n the clear face of the guileless King,
And trustful courtesies of household life,
Became her bane; and at the last she said,
'O Lancelot, get thee hence to thine own
land,
For if thou tarry we shall meet again,
And if we meet again, some evil chance
Will make the smouldering scandal break
and blaze
Before the people, and our lord the King.'
And Lancelot ever promised, but re-
main'd,
And still they met and met. Again she said,
'O Lancelot, if thou love me get thee
hence.'
And then they were agreed upon a night
(When the good King should not be there)
to meet
And part for ever. Vivien, lurking, heard.
She told Sir Modred. Passion-pale they
met
And greeted. Hands in hands, and eye to
eye,
Low on the border of her couch they sat
Stammering and staring. It was their last
hour,
A madness of farewells. And Modred
brought
His creatures to the basement of the tower
For testimony; and crying with full voice
'Traitor, come out, ye are trapt at last,'
aroused
Lancelot, who rushing outward lionlike
Leapt on him, and hurl'd him headlong,
and he fell
Stunn'd, and his creatures took and bare
him off,
And all was still: then she, 'The end is
come,

And I am shamed for ever;' and he said,
'Mine be the shame; mine was the sin: but
rise,
And fly to my strong castle overseas:
There will I hide thee, till my life shall end,
There hold thee with my life against the
world.'
She answer'd, 'Lancelot, wilt thou hold
me so?
Nay, friend, for we have taken our fare-
wells.
Would God that thou couldst hide me
from myself!
Mine is the shame, for I was wife, and
thou
Unwedded: yet rise now, and let us fly,
For I will draw me into sanctuary,
And bide my doom.' So Lancelot got her
horse,
Set her thereon, and mounted on his own,
And then they rode to the divided way,
There kiss'd, and parted weeping: for he
past,
Love-loyal to the least wish of the Queen,
Back to his land; but she to Almesbury
Fled all night long by glimmering waste
and weald,
And heard the Spirits of the waste and
weald
Moan as she fled, or thought she heard
them moan:
And in herself she moan'd 'Too late, too
late!'
Till in the cold wind that foreruns the
morn,
A blot in heaven, the Raven, flying high,
Croak'd, and she thought, 'He spies a field
of death;
For now the Heathen of the Northern Sea,
Lured by the crimes and frailties of the
court,
Begin to slay the folk, and spoil the land.'

And when she came to Almesbury she
spake
There to the nuns, and said, 'Mine enemies
Pursue me, but, O peaceful Sisterhood,
Receive, and yield me sanctuary, nor ask
Her name to whom ye yield it, till her time
To tell you:' and her beauty, grace and
power,

Wrought as a charm upon them, and they
    spared
To ask it.
                 So the stately Queen abode
For many a week, unknown, among the
    nuns;
Nor with them mix'd, nor told her name,
    nor sought,
Wrapt in her grief, for housel or for shrift,
But communed only with the little maid,
Who pleased her with a babbling heedless-
    ness
Which often lured her from herself; but now,
This night, a rumour wildly blown about
Came, that Sir Modred had usurp'd the
    realm,
And leagued him with the heathen, while
    the King
Was waging war on Lancelot: then she
    thought,
'With what a hate the people and the King
Must hate me,' and bow'd down upon her
    hands
Silent, until the little maid, who brook'd
No silence, brake it, uttering 'Late! so late!
What hour, I wonder, now?' and when she
    drew
No answer, by and by began to hum
An air the nuns had taught her; 'Late, so
    late!'
Which when she heard, the Queen look'd
    up, and said,
'O maiden, if indeed ye list to sing,
Sing, and unbind my heart that I may
    weep.'
Whereat full willingly sang the little maid.

'Late, late, so late! and dark the night
    and chill!
Late, late, so late! but we can enter still.
Too late, too late! ye cannot enter now.

'No light had we: for that we do repent;
And learning this, the bridegroom will
    relent.
Too late, too late! ye cannot enter now.

'No light: so late! and dark and chill the
    night!
O let us in, that we may find the light!
Too late, too late: ye cannot enter now.

'Have we not heard the bridegroom is so
    sweet?
O let us in, tho' late, to kiss his feet!
No, no, too late! ye cannot enter now.'

So sang the novice, while full passion-
    ately,
Her head upon her hands, remembering
Her thought when first she came, wept the
    sad Queen.
Then said the little novice prattling to her,

'O pray you, noble lady, weep no more;
But let my words, the words of one so
    small,
Who knowing nothing knows but to obey,
And if I do not there is penance given—
Comfort your sorrows; for they do not
    flow
From evil done; right sure am I of that,
Who see your tender grace and stateliness.
But weigh your sorrows with our lord the
    King's,
And weighing find them less; for gone
    is he
To wage grim war against Sir Lancelot
    there,
Round that strong castle where he holds
    the Queen;
And Modred whom he left in charge of all,
The traitor—Ah sweet lady, the King's
    grief
For his own self, and his own Queen, and
    realm,
Must needs be thrice as great as any of ours.
For me, I thank the saints, I am not great.
For if there ever come a grief to me
I cry my cry in silence, and have done.
None knows it, and my tears have brought
    me good:
But even were the griefs of little ones
As great as those of great ones, yet this
    grief
Is added to the griefs the great must bear,
That howsoever much they may desire
Silence, they cannot weep behind a cloud:
As even here they talk at Almesbury
About the good King and his wicked
    Queen,
And were I such a King with such a Queen,
Well might I wish to veil her wickedness,
But were I such a King, it could not be.'

Then to her own sad heart mutter'd the
  Queen,
'Will the child kill me with her innocent
  talk?'
But openly she answer'd, 'Must not I,
If this false traitor have displaced his lord,
Grieve with the common grief of all the
  realm?'

'Yea,' said the maid, 'this is all woman's
  grief,
That *she* is woman, whose disloyal life
Hath wrought confusion in the Table
  Round
Which good King Arthur founded, years
  ago,
With signs and miracles and wonders,
  there
At Camelot, ere the coming of the Queen.'

Then thought the Queen within herself
  again,
'Will the child kill me with her foolish
  prate?'
But openly she spake and said to her,
'O little maid, shut in by nunnery walls,
What canst thou know of Kings and Tables
  Round,
Or what of signs and wonders, but the
  signs
And simple miracles of thy nunnery?'

To whom the little novice garrulously,
'Yea, but I know: the land was full of signs
And wonders ere the coming of the Queen.
So said my father, and himself was knight
Of the great Table—at the founding of it;
And rode thereto from Lyonnesse, and he
  said
That as he rode, an hour or maybe twain
After the sunset, down the coast, he heard
Strange music, and he paused, and turning
  —there,
All down the lonely coast of Lyonnesse,
Each with a beacon-star upon his head,
And with a wild sea-light about his feet,
He saw them—headland after headland
  flame
Far on into the rich heart of the west:
And in the light the white mermaiden
  swam,

And strong man-breasted things stood
  from the sea,
And sent a deep sea-voice thro' all the
  land,
To which the little elves of chasm and cleft
Made answer, sounding like a distant horn.
So said my father—yea, and furthermore,
Next morning, while he past the dim-lit
  woods,
Himself beheld three spirits mad with joy
Come dashing down on a tall wayside
  flower,
That shook beneath them, as the thistle
  shakes
When three gray linnets wrangle for the
  seed:
And still at evenings on before his horse
The flickering fairy-circle wheel'd and
  broke
Flying, and link'd again, and wheel'd and
  broke
Flying, for all the land was full of life.
And when at last he came to Camelot,
A wreath of airy dancers hand-in-hand
Swung round the lighted lantern of the
  hall;
And in the hall itself was such a feast
As never man had dream'd; for every
  knight
Had whatsoever meat he long'd for served
By hands unseen; and even as he said
Down in the cellars merry bloated things
Shoulder'd the spigot, straddling on the
  butts
While the wine ran: so glad were spirits
  and men
Before the coming of the sinful Queen.'

Then spake the Queen and somewhat
  bitterly,
'Were they so glad? ill prophets were they
  all,
Spirits and men: could none of them
  foresee,
Not even thy wise father with his signs
And wonders, what has fall'n upon the
  realm?'

To whom the novice garrulously again,
'Yea, one, a bard; of whom my father said,
Full many a noble war-song had he sung,

Ev'n in the presence of an enemy's fleet,
Between the steep cliff and the coming
   wave;
And many a mystic lay of life and death
Had chanted on the smoky mountain-tops,
When round him bent the spirits of the
   hills
With all their dewy hair blown back like
   flame:
So said my father—and that night the bard
Sang Arthur's glorious wars, and sang the
   King
As wellnigh more than man, and rail'd at
   those
Who call'd him the false son of Gorloïs:
For there was no man knew from whence
   he came;
But after tempest, when the long wave
   broke
All down the thundering shores of Bude
   and Bos,
There came a day as still as heaven, and
   then
They found a naked child upon the sands
Of dark Tintagil by the Cornish sea;
And that was Arthur; and they foster'd him
Till he by miracle was approven King:
And that his grave should be a mystery
From all men, like his birth; and could he
   find
A woman in her womanhood as great
As he was in his manhood, then, he sang,
The twain together well might change the
   world.
But even in the middle of his song
He falter'd, and his hand fell from the
   harp,
And pale he turn'd, and reel'd, and would
   have fall'n,
But that they stay'd him up; nor would he
   tell
His vision; but what doubt that he foresaw
This evil work of Lancelot and the Queen?'

Then thought the Queen, 'Lo! they have
   set her on,
Our simple-seeming Abbess and her nuns,
To play upon me,' and bow'd her head nor
   spake.
Whereat the novice crying, with clasp'd
   hands,

Shame on her own garrulity garrulously,
Said the good nuns would check her gad-
   ding tongue
Full often, 'and, sweet lady, if I seem
To vex an ear too sad to listen to me,
Unmannerly, with prattling and the tales
Which my good father told me, check me
   too
Nor let me shame my father's memory, one
Of noblest manners, tho' himself would say
Sir Lancelot had the noblest; and he died,
Kill'd in a tilt, come next, five summers
   back,
And left me; but of others who remain,
And of the two first-famed for courtesy—
And pray you check me if I ask amiss—
But pray you, which had noblest, while
   you moved
Among them, Lancelot or our lord the
   King?'

Then the pale Queen look'd up and
   answer'd her,
'Sir Lancelot, as became a noble knight,
Was gracious to all ladies, and the same
In open battle or the tilting-field
Forbore his own advantage, and the King
In open battle or the tilting-field
Forbore his own advantage, and these two
Were the most nobly-manner'd men of all;
For manners are not idle, but the fruit
Of loyal nature, and of noble mind.'

'Yea,' said the maid, 'be manners such
   fair fruit?
Then Lancelot's needs must be a thousand-
   fold
Less noble, being, as all rumour runs,
The most disloyal friend in all the world.'

To which a mournful answer made the
   Queen:
'O closed about by narrowing nunnery-
   walls,
What knowest thou of the world, and all
   its lights
And shadows, all the wealth and all the
   woe?
If ever Lancelot, that most noble knight,
Were for one hour less noble than himself,
Pray for him that he scape the doom of fire,

And weep for her who drew him to his
   doom.'

'Yea,' said the little novice, 'I pray for
   both;
But I should all as soon believe that his,
Sir Lancelot's, were as noble as the King's,
As I could think, sweet lady, yours would be
Such as they are, were you the sinful
   Queen.'

So she, like many another babbler, hurt
Whom she would soothe, and harm'd
   where she would heal;
For here a sudden flush of wrathful heat
Fired all the pale face of the Queen, who
   cried,
'Such as thou art be never maiden more
For ever! thou their tool, set on to plague
And play upon, and harry me, petty spy
And traitress.' When that storm of anger
   brake
From Guinevere, aghast the maiden rose,
White as her veil, and stood before the
   Queen
As tremulously as foam upon the beach
Stands in a wind, ready to break and fly,
And when the Queen had added 'Get thee
   hence,'
Fled frighted. Then that other left alone
Sigh'd, and began to gather heart again,
Saying in herself, 'The simple, fearful child
Meant nothing, but my own too-fearful
   guilt,
Simpler than any child, betrays itself.
But help me, heaven, for surely I repent.
For what is true repentance but in
   thought—
Not ev'n in inmost thought to think again
The sins that made the past so pleasant
   to us:
And I have sworn never to see him more,
To see him more.'

            And ev'n in saying this,
Her memory from old habit of the mind
Went slipping back upon the golden days
In which she saw him first, when Lancelot
   came,
Reputed the best knight and goodliest
   man,

Ambassador, to lead her to his lord
Arthur, and led her forth, and far ahead
Of his and her retinue moving, they,
Rapt in sweet talk or lively, all on love
And sport and tilts and pleasure, (for the
   time
Was maytime, and as yet no sin was
   dream'd,)
Rode under groves that look'd a paradise
Of blossom, over sheets of hyacinth
That seem'd the heavens upbreaking thro'
   the earth,
And on from hill to hill, and every day
Beheld at noon in some delicious dale
The silk pavilions of King Arthur raised
For brief repast or afternoon repose
By couriers gone before; and on again,
Till yet once more ere set of sun they saw
The Dragon of the great Pendragonship,
That crown'd the state pavilion of the
   King,
Blaze by the rushing brook or silent well.

   But when the Queen immersed in such
   a trance,
And moving thro' the past unconsciously,
Came to that point where first she saw the
   King
Ride toward her from the city, sigh'd to
   find
Her journey done, glanced at him, thought
   him cold,
High, self-contain'd, and passionless, not
   like him,
'Not like my Lancelot'—while she brooded
   thus
And grew half-guilty in her thoughts again,
There rode an armed warrior to the doors.
A murmuring whisper thro' the nunnery
   ran,
Then on a sudden a cry, 'The King.' She
   sat
Stiff-stricken, listening; but when armed
   feet
Thro' the long gallery from the outer doors
Rang coming, prone from off her seat she
   fell,
And grovell'd with her face against the
   floor:
There with her milkwhite arms and
   shadowy hair

She made her face a darkness from the
King:
And in the darkness heard his armed feet
Pause by her; then came silence, then a
voice,
Monotonous and hollow like a Ghost's
Denouncing judgment, but tho' changed,
the King's:

'Liest thou here so low, the child of one
I honour'd, happy, dead before thy shame?
Well is it that no child is born of thee.
The children born of thee are sword and
fire,
Red ruin, and the breaking up of laws,
The craft of kindred and the Godless hosts
Of heathen swarming o'er the Northern
Sea;
Whom I, while yet Sir Lancelot, my right
arm,
The mightiest of my knights, abode with
me,
Have everywhere about this land of Christ
In twelve great battles ruining overthrown.
And knowest thou now from whence I
come—from him,
From waging bitter war with him: and he,
That did not shun to smite me in worse
way,
Had yet that grace of courtesy in him left,
He spared to lift his hand against the King
Who made him knight: but many a knight
was slain;
And many more, and all his kith and kin
Clave to him, and abode in his own land.
And many more when Modred raised
revolt,
Forgetful of their troth and fealty, clave
To Modred, and a remnant stays with me.
And of this remnant will I leave a part,
True men who love me still, for whom I
live,
To guard thee in the wild hour coming on,
Lest but a hair of this low head be harm'd.
Fear not: thou shalt be guarded till my
death.
Howbeit I know, if ancient prophecies
Have err'd not, that I march to meet my
doom.
Thou hast not made my life so sweet to me,
That I the King should greatly care to live;

For thou hast spoilt the purpose of my life.
Bear with me for the last time while I show,
Ev'n for thy sake, the sin which thou hast
sinn'd.
For when the Roman left us, and their law
Relax'd its hold upon us, and the ways
Were fill'd with rapine, here and there a
deed
Of prowess done redress'd a random
wrong.
But I was first of all the kings who drew
The knighthood-errant of this realm and
all
The realms together under me, their Head,
In that fair Order of my Table Round,
A glorious company, the flower of men,
To serve as model for the mighty world,
And be the fair beginning of a time.
I made them lay their hands in mine and
swear
To reverence the King, as if he were
Their conscience, and their conscience as
their King,
To break the heathen and uphold the
Christ,
To ride abroad redressing human wrongs,
To speak no slander, no, nor listen to it,
To honour his own word as if his God's,
To lead sweet lives in purest chastity,
To love one maiden only, cleave to her,
And worship her by years of noble deeds,
Until they won her; for indeed I knew
Of no more subtle master under heaven
Than is the maiden passion for a maid,
Not only to keep down the base in man,
But teach high thought, and amiable words
And courtliness, and the desire of fame,
And love of truth, and all that makes a man.
And all this throve before I wedded thee,
Believing, "lo mine helpmate, one to feel
My purpose and rejoicing in my joy."
Then came thy shameful sin with Lance-
lot;
Then came the sin of Tristram and Isolt;
Then others, following these my mightiest
knights,
And drawing foul ensample from fair
names,
Sinn'd also, till the loathsome opposite
Of all my heart had destined did obtain,
And all thro' thee! so that this life of mine

I guard as God's high gift from scathe and
    wrong,
Not greatly care to lose; but rather think
How sad it were for Arthur, should he live,
To sit once more within his lonely hall,
And miss the wonted number of my
    knights,
And miss to hear high talk of noble deeds
As in the golden days before thy sin.
For which of us, who might be left, could
    speak
Of the pure heart, nor seem to glance at
    thee?
And in thy bowers of Camelot or of Usk
Thy shadow still would glide from room to
    room,
And I should evermore be vext with thee
In hanging robe or vacant ornament,
Or ghostly footfall echoing on the stair.
For think not, tho' thou wouldst not love
    thy lord,
Thy lord has wholly lost his love for thee.
I am not made of so slight elements.
Yet must I leave thee, woman, to thy
    shame.
I hold that man the worst of public foes
Who either for his own or children's sake,
To save his blood from scandal, lets the
    wife
Whom he knows false, abide and rule the
    house:
For being thro' his cowardice allow'd
Her station, taken everywhere for pure,
She like a new disease, unknown to men,
Creeps, no precaution used, among the
    crowd,
Makes wicked lightnings of her eyes, and
    saps
The fealty of our friends, and stirs the
    pulse
With devil's leaps, and poisons half the
    young.
Worst of the worst were that man he that
    reigns!
Better the King's waste hearth and aching
    heart
Than thou reseated in thy place of light,
The mockery of my people, and their bane.'

He paused, and in the pause she crept
    an inch

Nearer, and laid her hands about his feet.
Far off a solitary trumpet blew.
Then waiting by the doors the warhorse
    neigh'd
As at a friend's voice, and he spake again:

'Yet think not that I come to urge thy
    crimes,
I did not come to curse thee, Guinevere,
I, whose vast pity almost makes me die
To see thee, laying there thy golden head,
My pride in happier summers, at my feet.
The wrath which forced my thoughts on
    that fierce law,
The doom of treason and the flaming death,
(When first I learnt thee hidden here) is
    past.
The pang—which while I weigh'd thy
    heart with one
Too wholly true to dream untruth in thee,
Made my tears burn—is also past—in part.
And all is past, the sin is sinn'd, and I,
Lo! I forgive thee, as Eternal God
Forgives: do thou for thine own soul the
    rest.
But how to take last leave of all I loved?
O golden hair, with which I used to play
Not knowing! O imperial-moulded form,
And beauty such as never woman wore,
Until it came a kingdom's curse with
    thee—
I cannot touch thy lips, they are not mine,
But Lancelot's: nay, they never were the
    King's.
I cannot take thy hand; that too is flesh,
And in the flesh thou hast sinn'd; and
    mine own flesh,
Here looking down on thine polluted, cries
"I loathe thee:" yet not less, O Guinevere,
For I was ever virgin save for thee,
My love thro' flesh hath wrought into my
    life
So far, that my doom is, I love thee still.
Let no man dream but that I love thee still.
Perchance, and so thou purify thy soul,
And so thou lean on our fair father Christ,
Hereafter in that world where all are pure
We two may meet before high God, and
    thou
Wilt spring to me, and claim me thine, and
    know

I am thine husband—not a smaller soul,
Nor Lancelot, nor another. Leave me that,
I charge thee, my last hope. Now must I
   hence.
Thro' the thick night I hear the trumpet
   blow:
They summon me their King to lead mine
   hosts
Far down to that great battle in the west,
Where I must strike against the man they
   call
My sister's son—no kin of mine, who
   leagues
With Lords of the White Horse, heathen,
   and knights,
Traitors—and strike him dead, and meet
   myself
Death, or I know not what mysterious
   doom.
And thou remaining here wilt learn the
   event;
But hither shall I never come again,
Never lie by thy side; see thee no more—
Farewell!'

     And while she grovell'd at his feet,
She felt the King's breath wander o'er her
   neck,
And in the darkness o'er her fallen head,
Perceived the waving of his hands that
   blest.

   Then, listening till those armed steps
   were gone,
Rose the pale Queen, and in her anguish
   found
The casement: 'peradventure,' so she
   thought,
'If I might see his face, and not be seen.'
And lo, he sat on horseback at the door!
And near him the sad nuns with each a light
Stood, and he gave them charge about the
   Queen,
To guard and foster her for evermore.
And while he spake to these his helm was
   lower'd,
To which for crest the golden dragon clung
Of Britain; so she did not see the face,
Which then was as an angel's, but she saw,
Wet with the mists and smitten by the
   lights,

The Dragon of the great Pendragonship
Blaze, making all the night a steam of fire.
And even then he turn'd; and more and
   more
The moony vapour rolling round the King,
Who seem'd the phantom of a Giant in it,
Enwound him fold by fold, and made him
   gray
And grayer, till himself became as mist
Before her, moving ghostlike to his doom.

   Then she stretch'd out her arms and
   cried aloud
'Oh Arthur!' there her voice brake sud-
   denly,
Then—as a stream that spouting from a
   cliff
Fails in mid air, but gathering at the base
Re-makes itself, and flashes down the
   vale—
Went on in passionate utterance:

              'Gone—my lord!
Gone thro' my sin to slay and to be slain!
And he forgave me, and I could not speak.
Farewell? I should have answer'd his fare-
   well.
His mercy choked me. Gone, my lord the
   King,
My own true lord! how dare I call him
   mine?
The shadow of another cleaves to me,
And makes me one pollution: he, the King,
Call'd me polluted: shall I kill myself?
What help in that? I cannot kill my sin,
If soul be soul; nor can I kill my shame;
No, nor by living can I live it down.
The days will grow to weeks, the weeks to
   months,
The months will add themselves and make
   the years,
The years will roll into the centuries,
And mine will ever be a name of scorn.
I must not dwell on that defeat of fame.
Let the world be; that is but of the world.
What else? what hope? I think there was a
   hope,
Except he mock'd me when he spake of
   hope;
His hope he call'd it; but he never mocks,
For mockery is the fume of little hearts.

And blessed be the King, who hath for-
    given
My wickedness to him, and left me hope
That in mine own heart I can live down sin
And be his mate hereafter in the heavens
Before high God. Ah great and gentle lord,
Who wast, as is the conscience of a saint
Among his warring senses, to thy knights—
To whom my false voluptuous pride, that
    took
Full easily all impressions from below,
Would not look up, or half-despised the
    height
To which I would not or I could not
    climb—
I thought I could not breathe in that fine air
That pure severity of perfect light—
I yearn'd for warmth and colour which I
    found
In Lancelot—now I see thee what thou art,
Thou art the highest and most human too,
Not Lancelot, nor another. Is there none
Will tell the King I love him tho' so late?
Now—ere he goes to the great Battle? none:
Myself must tell him in that purer life,
But now it were too daring. Ah my God,
What might I not have made of thy fair
    world,
Had I but loved thy highest creature here?
It was my duty to have loved the highest:
It surely was my profit had I known:
It would have been my pleasure had I seen.
We needs must love the highest when we
    see it,
Not Lancelot, nor another.'

                        Here her hand
Grasp'd, made her vail her eyes: she look'd
    and saw
The novice, weeping, suppliant, and said
    to her,
'Yea, little maid, for am *I* not forgiven?'
Then glancing up beheld the holy nuns
All round her, weeping; and her heart was
    loosed
Within her, and she wept with these and
    said,

'Ye know me then, that wicked one, who
    broke
The vast design and purpose of the King.
O shut me round with narrowing nunnery-
    walls,
Meek maidens, from the voices crying
    "shame."
I must not scorn myself: he loves me still.
Let no one dream but that he loves me still.
So let me, if you do not shudder at me,
Nor shun to call me sister, dwell with you;
Wear black and white, and be a nun like
    you,
Fast with your fasts, not feasting with your
    feasts;
Grieve with your griefs, not grieving at your
    joys,
But not rejoicing; mingle with your rites;
Pray and be pray'd for; lie before your
    shrines;
Do each low office of your holy house;
Walk your dim cloister, and distribute dole
To poor sick people, richer in His eyes
Who ransom'd us, and haler too than I;
And treat their loathsome hurts and heal
    mine own;
And so wear out in almsdeed and in prayer
The sombre close of that voluptuous day,
Which wrought the ruin of my lord the
    King.'

She said: they took her to themselves;
    and she
Still hoping, fearing 'is it yet too late?'
Dwelt with them, till in time their Abbess
    died.
Then she, for her good deeds and her pure
    life,
And for the power of ministration in her,
And likewise for the high rank she had
    borne,
Was chosen Abbess, there, an Abbess,
    lived
For three brief years, and there, an Abbess,
    past
To where beyond these voices there is
    peace.

End of 'The Round Table'

433

THAT story which the bold Sir Bedivere,
First made and latest left of all the knights,
Told, when the man was no more than a
    voice
In the white winter of his age, to those
With whom he dwelt, new faces, other
    minds.

For on their march to westward, Bedi-
    vere,
Who slowly paced among the slumbering
    host,
Heard in his tent the moanings of the King:

'I found Him in the shining of the stars,
I mark'd Him in the flowering of His fields,
But in His ways with men I find Him not.
I waged His wars, and now I pass and die.
O me! for why is all around us here
As if some lesser god had made the world,
But had not force to shape it as he would,
Till the High God behold it from beyond,
And enter it, and make it beautiful?
Or else as if the world were wholly fair,
But that these eyes of men are dense and
    dim,
And have not power to see it as it is:
Perchance, because we see not to the
    close;—
For I, being simple, thought to work His
    will,
And have but stricken with the sword in
    vain;
And all whereon I lean'd in wife and friend
Is traitor to my peace, and all my realm
Reels back into the beast, and is no more.
My God, thou hast forgotten me in my
    death:
Nay—God my Christ—I pass but shall not
    die.'

Then, ere that last weird battle in the
    west,
There came on Arthur sleeping, Gawain
    kill'd
In Lancelot's war, the ghost of Gawain
    blown
Along a wandering wind, and past his ear
Went shrilling, 'Hollow, hollow all delight!

Hail, King! to-morrow thou shalt pass
    away.
Farewell! there is an isle of rest for thee.
And I am blown along a wandering wind,
And hollow, hollow, hollow all delight.'
And fainter onward, like wild birds that
    change
Their season in the night and wail their
    way
From cloud to cloud, down the long wind
    the dream
Shrill'd; but in going mingled with dim
    cries
Far in the moonlight haze among the hills,
As of some lonely city sack'd by night,
When all is lost, and wife and child with
    wail
Pass to new lords; and Arthur woke and
    call'd,
'Who spake? A dream. O light upon the
    wind,
Thine, Gawain, was the voice—are these
    dim cries
Thine? or doth all that haunts the waste
    and wild
Mourn, knowing it will go along with me?'

This heard the bold Sir Bedivere and
    spake:
'O me, my King, let pass whatever will,
Elves, and the harmless glamour of the
    field;
But in their stead thy name and glory cling
To all high places like a golden cloud
For ever: but as yet thou shalt not pass.
Light was Gawain in life, and light in death
Is Gawain, for the ghost is as the man;
And care not thou for dreams from him,
    but rise—
I hear the steps of Modred in the west,
And with him many of thy people, and
    knights
Once thine, whom thou hast loved, but
    grosser grown
Than heathen, spitting at their vows and
    thee.
Right well in heart they know thee for the
    King.
Arise, go forth and conquer as of old.'

Then spake King Arthur to Sir Bedivere:
'Far other is this battle in the west
Whereto we move, than when we strove in youth,
And brake the petty kings, and fought with Rome,
Or thrust the heathen from the Roman wall,
And shook him thro' the north. Ill doom is mine
To war against my people and my knights.
The king who fights his people fights himself.
And they my knights, who loved me once, the stroke
That strikes them dead is as my death to me.
Yet let us hence, and find or feel a way
Thro' this blind haze, which ever since I saw
One lying in the dust at Almesbury,
Hath folded in the passes of the world.'

Then rose the King and moved his host by night,
And ever push'd Sir Modred, league by league,
Back to the sunset bound of Lyonnesse—
A land of old upheaven from the abyss
By fire, to sink into the abyss again;
Where fragments of forgotten peoples dwelt,
And the long mountains ended in a coast
Of ever-shifting sand, and far away
The phantom circle of a moaning sea.
There the pursuer could pursue no more,
And he that fled no further fly the King;
And there, that day when the great light of heaven
Burn'd at his lowest in the rolling year,
On the waste sand by the waste sea they closed.
Nor ever yet had Arthur fought a fight
Like this last, dim, weird battle of the west.
A deathwhite mist slept over sand and sea:
Whereof the chill, to him who breathed it, drew
Down with his blood, till all his heart was cold
With formless fear; and ev'n on Arthur fell

Confusion, since he saw not whom he fought.
For friend and foe were shadows in the mist,
And friend slew friend not knowing whom he slew;
And some had visions out of golden youth,
And some beheld the faces of old ghosts
Look in upon the battle; and in the mist
Was many a noble deed, many a base,
And chance and craft and strength in single fights,
And ever and anon with host to host
Shocks, and the splintering spear, the hard mail hewn,
Shield-breakings, and the clash of brands, the crash
Of battleaxes on shatter'd helms, and shrieks
After the Christ, of those who falling down
Look'd up for heaven, and only saw the mist;
And shouts of heathen and the traitor knights,
Oaths, insult, filth, and monstrous blasphemies,
Sweat, writhings, anguish, labouring of the lungs
In that close mist, and cryings for the light,
Moans of the dying, and voices of the dead.

Last, as by some one deathbed after wail
Of suffering, silence follows, or thro' death
Or deathlike swoon, thus over all that shore,
Save for some whisper of the seething seas,
A dead hush fell; but when the dolorous day
Grew drearier toward twilight falling, came
A bitter wind, clear from the North, and blew
The mist aside, and with that wind the tide
Rose, and the pale King glanced across the field
Of battle: but no man was moving there;
Nor any cry of Christian heard thereon,
Nor yet of heathen; only the wan wave
Brake in among dead faces, to and fro
Swaying the helpless hands, and up and down
Tumbling the hollow helmets of the fallen,

And shiver'd brands that once had fought
with Rome,
And rolling far along the gloomy shores
The voice of days of old and days to be.

Then spake King Arthur to Sir Bedivere,
And whiter than the mist that all day long
Had held the field of battle was the King:

'Hearest thou this great voice that shakes
the world,
And wastes the narrow realm whereon we
move,
And beats upon the faces of the dead,
My dead, as tho' they had not died for
me?—
O Bedivere, for on my heart hath fall'n
Confusion, till I know not what I am,
Nor whence I am, nor whether I be King.
Behold, I seem but King among the dead.'

Then spake the bold Sir Bedivere: 'My
King,
King everywhere! and so the dead have
kings,
There also will I worship thee as King.
Yet still thy life is whole, and still I live
Who love thee; but who hates thee, he
that brought
The heathen back among us, yonder stands,
Modred, unharm'd, the traitor of thine
house.'

Then spake the King: 'My house hath
been my doom.
But call not thou this traitor of my house
Who hath but dwelt beneath one roof with
me.
My house are rather they who sware my
vows,
Yea, even while they brake them, own'd
me King.
And well for thee, saying in my dark hour,
When all the purport of my throne hath
fail'd,
That quick or dead thou holdest me for
King.
King am I, whatsoever be their cry;
And one last act of kinghood shalt thou see
Yet, ere I pass.' And uttering this the King
Made at the man: then Modred smote his
liege

Hard on that helm which many a heathen
sword
Had beaten thin; while Arthur at one blow,
Striking the last stroke with Excalibur,
Slew him, and all but slain himself, he fell.

So all day long the noise of battle roll'd
Among the mountains by the winter sea;
Until King Arthur's Table, man by man,
Had fall'n in Lyonnesse about their lord,
King Arthur. Then, because his wound
was deep,
The bold Sir Bedivere uplifted him,
And bore him to a chapel nigh the field,
A broken chancel with a broken cross,
That stood on a dark strait of barren land:
On one side lay the Ocean, and on one
Lay a great water, and the moon was full.

Then spake King Arthur to Sir Bedi-
vere:
'The sequel of to-day unsolders all
The goodliest fellowship of famous knights
Whereof this world holds record. Such a
sleep
They sleep—the men I loved. I think
that we
Shall never more, at any future time,
Delight our souls with talk of knightly
deeds,
Walking about the gardens and the halls
Of Camelot, as in the days that were.
I perish by this people which I made,—
Tho' Merlin sware that I should come
again
To rule once more; but, let what will be,
be,
I am so deeply smitten thro' the helm
That without help I cannot last till morn.
Thou therefore take my brand Excalibur,
Which was my pride:for thou rememberest
how
In those old days, one summer noon, an
arm
Rose up from out the bosom of the lake,
Clothed in white samite, mystic, wonderful,
Holding the sword—and how I row'd
across
And took it, and have worn it, like a king;
And, wheresoever I am sung or told
In aftertime, this also shall be known:

But now delay not: take Excalibur,
And fling him far into the middle mere:
Watch what thou seëst, and lightly bring
me word.'

To him replied the bold Sir Bedivere:
'It is not meet, Sir King, to leave thee thus,
Aidless, alone, and smitten thro' the
helm—
A little thing may harm a wounded man;
Yet I thy hest will all perform at full,
Watch what I see, and lightly bring thee
word.'

So saying, from the ruin'd shrine he
stept,
And in the moon athwart the place of
tombs,
Where lay the mighty bones of ancient
men,
Old knights, and over them the sea-wind
sang
Shrill, chill, with flakes of foam. He,
stepping down
By zigzag paths and juts of pointed rock,
Came on the shining levels of the lake.

There drew he forth the brand Excali-
bur,
And o'er him, drawing it, the winter moon,
Brightening the skirts of a long cloud, ran
forth
And sparkled keen with frost against the
hilt:
For all the haft twinkled with diamond
sparks,
Myriads of topaz-lights, and jacinth-work
Of subtlest jewellery. He gazed so long
That both his eyes were dazzled as he
stood,
This way and that dividing the swift mind,
In act to throw: but at the last it seem'd
Better to leave Excalibur conceal'd
There in the many-knotted waterflags,
That whistled stiff and dry about the
marge.
So strode he back slow to the wounded
King.

Then spake King Arthur to Sir Bedivere:

'Hast thou perform'd my mission which
I gave?
What is it thou hast seen? or what hast
heard?'

And answer made the bold Sir Bedivere:
'I heard the ripple washing in the reeds,
And the wild water lapping on the crag.'

To whom replied King Arthur, faint
and pale:
'Thou hast betray'd thy nature and thy
name,
Not rendering true answer, as beseem'd
Thy fëalty, nor like a noble knight:
For surer sign had follow'd, either hand,
Or voice, or else a motion of the mere.
This is a shameful thing for men to lie.
Yet now, I charge thee, quickly go again,
As thou art lief and dear, and do the thing
I bade thee, watch, and lightly bring me
word.'

Then went Sir Bedivere the second time
Across the ridge, and paced beside the
mere,
Counting the dewy pebbles, fix'd in
thought;
But when he saw the wonder of the hilt,
How curiously and strangely chased, he
smote
His palms together, and he cried aloud:

'And if indeed I cast the brand away,
Surely a precious thing, one worthy note,
Should thus be lost for ever from the earth,
Which might have pleased the eyes of
many men.
What good should follow this, if this were
done?
What harm, undone? Deep harm to dis-
obey,
Seeing obedience is the bond of rule.
Were it well to obey then, if a king demand
An act unprofitable, against himself?
The King is sick, and knows not what he
does.
What record, or what relic of my lord
Should be to aftertime, but empty breath
And rumours of a doubt? But were this
kept,

Stored in some treasure-house of mighty
  kings,
Some one might show it at a joust of arms,
Saying, "King Arthur's sword, Excalibur,
Wrought by the lonely maiden of the Lake.
Nine years she wrought it, sitting in the
  deeps
Upon the hidden bases of the hills."
So might some old man speak in the after-
  time
To all the people, winning reverence.
But now much honour and much fame
  were lost.'

So spake he, clouded with his own con-
  ceit,
And hid Excalibur the second time,
And so strode back slow to the wounded
  King.

Then spoke King Arthur, breathing
  heavily:
'What is it thou hast seen? or what hast
  heard?'

And answer made the bold Sir Bedivere:
'I heard the water lapping on the crag,
And the long ripple washing in the reeds.'

To whom replied King Arthur, much in
  wrath:
'Ah, miserable and unkind, untrue,
Unknightly, traitor-hearted! Woe is me!
Authority forgets a dying king,
Laid widow'd of the power in his eye
That bow'd the will. I see thee what thou
  art,
For thou, the latest-left of all my knights,
In whom should meet the offices of all,
Thou wouldst betray me for the precious
  hilt;
Either from lust of gold, or like a girl
Valuing the giddy pleasure of the eyes.
Yet, for a man may fail in duty twice,
And the third time may prosper, get thee
  hence:
But, if thou spare to fling Excalibur,
I will arise and slay thee with my hands.'

Then quickly rose Sir Bedivere, and ran,
And, leaping down the ridges lightly,
  plunged

Among the bulrush beds, and clutch'd the
  sword,
And strongly wheel'd and threw it. The
  great brand
Made lightnings in the splendour of the
  moon,
And flashing round and round, and whirl'd
  in an arch,
Shot like a streamer of the northern morn,
Seen where the moving isles of winter
  shock
By night, with noises of the Northern Sea.
So flash'd and fell the brand Excalibur:
But ere he dipt the surface, rose an arm
Clothed in white samite, mystic, wonder-
  ful,
And caught him by the hilt, and brandish'd
  him
Three times, and drew him under in the
  mere.
And lightly went the other to the King.

Then spoke King Arthur, drawing
  thicker breath:
'Now see I by thine eyes that this is done.
Speak out: what is it thou hast heard, or
  seen?'

And answer made the bold Sir Bedivere:
'Sir King, I closed mine eyelids, lest the
  gems
Should blind my purpose, for I never saw,
Nor shall see, here or elsewhere, till I die,
Not tho' I live three lives of mortal men,
So great a miracle as yonder hilt.
Then with both hands I flung him, wheel-
  ing him;
But when I look'd again, behold an arm,
Clothed in white samite, mystic, wonder-
  ful,
That caught him by the hilt, and brandish'd
  him
Three times, and drew him under in the
  mere.'

And answer made King Arthur, breathing hard:
'My end draws nigh; 'tis time that I were
  gone.
Make broad thy shoulders to receive my
  weight,

438

And bear me to the margin; yet I fear
My wound hath taken cold, and I shall die.'

So saying, from the pavement he half
rose,
Slowly, with pain, reclining on his arm,
And looking wistfully with wide blue eyes
As in a picture. Him Sir Bedivere
Remorsefully regarded thro' his tears,
And would have spoken, but he found not
words;
Then took with care, and kneeling on one
knee,
O'er both his shoulders drew the languid
hands,
And rising bore him thro' the place of
tombs.

But, as he walk'd, King Arthur panted
hard,
Like one that feels a nightmare on his
bed
When all the house is mute. So sigh'd the
King,
Muttering and murmuring at his ear,
'Quick, quick!
I fear it is too late, and I shall die.'
But the other swiftly strode from ridge to
ridge,
Clothed with his breath, and looking, as
he walk'd,
Larger than human on the frozen hills.
He heard the deep behind him, and a cry
Before. His own thought drove him like a
goad.
Dry clash'd his harness in the icy caves
And barren chasms, and all to left and
right
The bare black cliff clang'd round him, as
he based
His feet on juts of slippery crag that rang
Sharp-smitten with the dint of armed
heels—
And on a sudden, lo! the level lake,
And the long glories of the winter moon.

Then saw they how there hove a dusky
barge,
Dark as a funeral scarf from stem to stern,
Beneath them; and descending they were
ware

That all the decks were dense with stately
forms,
Black-stoled, black-hooded, like a dream—
by these
Three Queens with crowns of gold: and
from them rose
A cry that shiver'd to the tingling stars,
And, as it were one voice, an agony
Of lamentation, like a wind that shrills
All night in a waste land, where no one
comes,
Or hath come, since the making of the
world.

Then murmur'd Arthur, 'Place me in
the barge.'
So to the barge they came. There those
three Queens
Put forth their hands, and took the King,
and wept.
But she, that rose the tallest of them all
And fairest, laid his head upon her lap,
And loosed the shatter'd casque, and
chafed his hands,
And call'd him by his name, complaining
loud,
And dropping bitter tears against a brow
Striped with dark blood: for all his face
was white
And colourless, and like the wither'd moon
Smote by the fresh beam of the springing
east;
And all his greaves and cuisses dash'd with
drops
Of onset; and the light and lustrous curls—
That made his forehead like a rising sun
High from the daïs-throne—were parch'd
with dust;
Or, clotted into points and hanging loose,
Mix'd with the knightly growth that
fringed his lips.
So like a shatter'd column lay the King;
Not like that Arthur who, with lance in rest,
From spur to plume a star of tournament,
Shot thro' the lists at Camelot, and charged
Before the eyes of ladies and of kings.

Then loudly cried the bold Sir Bedivere:
'Ah! my Lord Arthur, whither shall I go?
Where shall I hide my forehead and my
eyes?

439

For now I see the true old times are dead,
When every morning brought a noble
chance,
And every chance brought out a noble
knight.
Such times have been not since the light
that led
The holy Elders with the gift of myrrh.
But now the whole Round Table is dis-
solved
Which was an image of the mighty world,
And I, the last, go forth companionless,
And the days darken round me, and the
years,
Among new men, strange faces, other
minds.'

And slowly answer'd Arthur from the
barge:
'The old order changeth, yielding place to
new,
And God fulfils himself in many ways,
Lest one good custom should corrupt the
world.
Comfort thyself: what comfort is in me?
I have lived my life, and that which I have
done
May He within himself make pure! but
thou,
If thou shouldst never see my face again,
Pray for my soul. More things are wrought
by prayer
Than this world dreams of. Wherefore, let
thy voice
Rise like a fountain for me night and day.
For what are men better than sheep or
goats
That nourish a blind life within the brain,
If, knowing God, they lift not hands of
prayer
Both for themselves and those who call
them friend?
For so the whole round earth is every way
Bound by gold chains about the feet of
God.
But now farewell. I am going a long way
With these thou seest—if indeed I go
(For all my mind is clouded with a
doubt)—
To the island-valley of Avilion;
Where falls not hail, or rain, or any snow,

Nor ever wind blows loudly; but it lies
Deep-meadow'd, happy, fair with orchard
lawns
And bowery hollows crown'd with summer
sea,
Where I will heal me of my grievous
wound.'

So said he, and the barge with oar and sail
Moved from the brink, like some full-
breasted swan
That, fluting a wild carol ere her death,
Ruffles her pure cold plume, and takes the
flood
With swarthy webs. Long stood Sir Bedi-
vere
Revolving many memories, till the hull
Look'd one black dot against the verge of
dawn,
And on the mere the wailing died away.

But when that moan had past for evermore,
The stillness of the dead world's winter
dawn
Amazed him, and he groan'd, 'The King
is gone.'
And therewithal came on him the weird
rhyme,
'From the great deep to the great deep he
goes.'

Whereat he slowly turn'd and slowly
clomb
The last hard footstep of that iron crag;
Thence mark'd the black hull moving yet,
and cried,
'He passes to be King among the dead,
And after healing of his grievous wound
He comes again; but—if he come no
more—
O me, be yon dark Queens in yon black
boat,
Who shriek'd and wail'd, the three whereat
we gazed
On that high day, when, clothed with living
light,
They stood before his throne in silence,
friends
Of Arthur, who should help him at his
need?'

Then from the dawn it seem'd there came, but faint
As from beyond the limit of the world,
Like the last echo born of a great cry,
Sounds, as if some fair city were one voice
Around a king returning from his wars.

Thereat once more he moved about, and clomb

Ev'n to the highest he could climb, and saw,
Straining his eyes beneath an arch of hand,
Or thought he saw, the speck that bare the King,
Down that long water opening on the deep
Somewhere far off, pass on and on, and go
From less to less and vanish into light.
And the new sun rose bringing the new year.

TO THE QUEEN

O LOYAL to the royal in thyself,
And loyal to thy land, as this to thee——
Bear witness, that rememberable day,
When, pale as yet, and fever-worn, the Prince
Who scarce had pluck'd his flickering life again
From halfway down the shadow of the grave,
Past with thee thro' thy people and their love,
And London roll'd one tide of joy thro' all
Her trebled millions, and loud leagues of man
And welcome! witness, too, the silent cry,
The prayer of many a race and creed, and clime—
Thunderless lightnings striking under sea
From sunset and sunrise of all thy realm,
And that true North, whereof we lately heard
A strain to shame us 'keep you to yourselves;
So loyal is too costly! friends—your love
Is but a burthen: loose the bond, and go.'
Is this the tone of empire? here the faith
That made us rulers? this, indeed, her voice
And meaning, whom the roar of Hougoumont
Left mightiest of all peoples under heaven?
What shock has fool'd her since, that she should speak
So feebly? wealthier—wealthier—hour by hour!
The voice of Britain, or a sinking land,
Some third-rate isle half-lost among her seas?

There rang her voice, when the full city peal'd
Thee and thy Prince! The loyal to their crown
Are loyal to their own far sons, who love
Our ocean-empire with her boundless homes
For ever-broadening England, and her throne
In our vast Orient, and one isle, one isle,
That knows not her own greatness: if she knows
And dreads it we are fall'n.——But thou, my Queen,
Not for itself, but thro' thy living love
For one to whom I made it o'er his grave
Sacred, accept this old imperfect tale,
New-old, and shadowing Sense at war with Soul
Rather than that gray king, whose name, a ghost,
Streams like a cloud, man-shaped, from mountain peak,
And cleaves to cairn and cromlech still; or him
Of Geoffrey's book, or him of Malleor's, one
Touch'd by the adulterous finger of a time
That hover'd between war and wantonness,
And crownings and dethronements: take withal
Thy poet's blessing, and his trust that Heaven
Will blow the tempest in the distance back
From thine and ours: for some are scared, who mark,
Or wisely or unwisely, signs of storm,

Waverings of every vane with every wind,
And wordy trucklings to the transient
    hour,
And fierce or careless looseners of the faith,
And Softness breeding scorn of simple
    life,
Or Cowardice, the child of lust for gold,
Or Labour, with a groan and not a voice,
Or Art with poisonous honey stol'n from
    France,
And that which knows, but careful for
    itself,
And that which knows not, ruling that
    which knows

To its own harm: the goal of this great
    world
Lies beyond sight: yet—if our slowly-
    grown
And crown'd Republic's crowning com-
    mon-sense,
That saved her many times, not fail—their
    fears
Are morning shadows huger than the
    shapes
That cast them, not those gloomier which
    forego
The darkness of that battle in the West,
Where all of high and holy dies away.

THE LOVER'S TALE

THE original Preface to 'The Lover's Tale' states that it was composed in my nineteenth year. Two only of the three parts then written were printed, when, feeling the imperfection of the poem, I withdrew it from the press. One of my friends however who, boylike, admired the boy's work, distributed among our common associates of that hour some copies of these two parts, without my knowledge, without the omissions and amendments which I had in contemplation, and marred by the many misprints of the compositor. Seeing that these two parts have of late been mercilessly pirated, and that what I had deemed scarce worthy to live is not allowed to die, may I not be pardoned if I suffer the whole poem at last to come into the light—accompanied with a reprint of the sequel—a work of my mature life—'The Golden Supper'?
    May 1879.

ARGUMENT

JULIAN, whose cousin and foster-sister, Camilla, has been wedded to his friend and rival, Lionel, endeavours to narrate the story of his own love for her, and the strange sequel. He speaks (in Parts II and III) of having been haunted by visions and the sound of bells, tolling for a funeral, and at last ringing for a marriage; but he breaks away, overcome, as he approaches the Event, and a witness to it completes the tale.

I

HERE far away, seen from the topmost cliff,
Filling with purple gloom the vacancies
Between the tufted hills, the sloping seas
Hung in mid-heaven, and half-way down
    rare sails,
White as white clouds, floated from sky to
    sky.
Oh! pleasant breast of waters, quiet bay,
Like to a quiet mind in the loud world,
Where the chafed breakers of the outer sea
Sank powerless, as anger falls aside
And withers on the breast of peaceful love;
Thou didst receive the growth of pines
    that fledged
The hills that watch'd thee, as Love
    watcheth Love,
In thine own essence, and delight thyself

To make it wholly thine on sunny days.
Keep thou thy name of 'Lover's Bay.' See,
    sirs,
Even now the Goddess of the Past, that
    takes
The heart, and sometimes touches but one
    string
That quivers, and is silent, and sometimes
Sweeps suddenly all its half-moulder'd
    chords
To some old melody, begins to play
That air which pleased her first. I feel thy
    breath;
I come, great Mistress of the ear and eye:
Thy breath is of the pinewood; and tho'
    years
Have hollow'd out a deep and stormy strait
Betwixt the native land of Love and me,

Breathe but a little on me, and the sail
Will draw me to the rising of the sun,
The lucid chambers of the morning star,
And East of Life.

        Permit me, friend, I prythee,
To pass my hand across my brows, and
    muse
On those dear hills, that never more will
    meet
The sight that throbs and aches beneath
    my touch,
As tho' there beat a heart in either eye;
For when the outer lights are darken'd
    thus,
The memory's vision hath a keener edge.
It grows upon me now—the semicircle
Of dark-blue waters and the narrow fringe
Of curving beach—its wreaths of dripping
    green—
Its pale pink shells—the summerhouse
    aloft
That open'd on the pines with doors of
    glass,
A mountain nest—the pleasure-boat that
    rock'd,
Light-green with its own shadow, keel to
    keel,
Upon the dappled dimplings of the wave,
That blanch'd upon its side.

             O Love, O Hope!
They come, they crowd upon me all at
    once—
Moved from the cloud of unforgotten
    things,
That sometimes on the horizon of the mind
Lies folded, often sweeps athwart in
    storm—
Flash upon flash they lighten thro' me—
    days
Of dewy dawning and the amber eves
When thou and I, Camilla, thou and I
Were borne about the bay or safely moor'd
Beneath a low-brow'd cavern, where the
    tide
Plash'd, sapping its worn ribs; and all
    without
The slowly-ridging rollers on the cliffs
Clash'd, calling to each other, and thro'
    the arch

Down those loud waters, like a setting star,
Mixt with the gorgeous west the light-
    house shone,
And silver-smiling Venus ere she fell
Would often loiter in her balmy blue,
To crown it with herself.

             Here, too, my love
Waver'd at anchor with me, when day
    hung
From his mid-dome in Heaven's airy halls;
Gleams of the water-circles as they broke,
Flicker'd like doubtful smiles about her
    lips,
Quiver'd a flying glory on her hair,
Leapt like a passing thought across her
    eyes;
And mine with one that will not pass, till
    earth
And heaven pass too, dwelt on my heaven,
    a face
Most starry-fair, but kindled from within
As 'twere with dawn. She was dark-hair'd,
    dark-eyed:
Oh, such dark eyes! a single glance of them
Will govern a whole life from birth to death,
Careless of all things else, led on with light
In trances and in visions: look at them,
You lose yourself in utter ignorance;
You cannot find their depth; for they go
    back,
And farther back, and still withdraw them-
    selves
Quite into the deep soul, that evermore
Fresh springing from her fountains in the
    brain,
Still pouring thro', floods with redundant
    life
Her narrow portals.

             Trust me, long ago
I should have died, if it were possible
To die in gazing on that perfectness
Which I do bear within me: I had died,
But from my farthest lapse, my latest ebb,
Thine image, like a charm of light and
    strength
Upon the waters, push'd me back again
On these deserted sands of barren life.
Tho' from the deep vault where the heart
    of Hope

Fell into dust, and crumbled in the dark—
Forgetting how to render beautiful
Her countenance with quick and healthful
    blood—
Thou didst not sway me upward; could I
    perish
While thou, a meteor of the sepulchre,
Didst swathe thyself all round Hope's quiet
    urn
For ever? He, that saith it, hath o'erstept
The slippery footing of his narrow wit,
And fall'n away from judgment. Thou art
    light,
To which my spirit leaneth all her flowers,
And length of days, and immortality
Of thought, and freshness ever self-
    renew'd.
For Time and Grief abode too long with
    Life,
And, like all other friends i' the world, at
    last
They grew aweary of her fellowship:
So Time and Grief did beckon unto
    Death,
And Death drew nigh and beat the doors
    of Life;
But thou didst sit alone in the inner house,
A wakeful portress, and didst parle with
    Death,—
'This is a charmed dwelling which I hold;'
So Death gave back, and would no further
    come.
Yet is my life nor in the present time,
Nor in the present place. To me alone,
Push'd from his chair of regal heritage,
The Present is the vassal of the Past:
So that, in that I *have* lived, do I live,
And cannot die, and am, in having been—
A portion of the pleasant yesterday,
Thrust forward on to-day and out of place;
A body journeying onward, sick with toil,
The weight as if of age upon my limbs,
The grasp of hopeless grief about my heart,
And all the senses weaken'd, save in that,
Which long ago they had glean'd and
    garner'd up
Into the granaries of memory—
The clear brow, bulwark of the precious
    brain,
Chink'd as you see, and seam'd—and all
    the while

The light soul twines and mingles with the
    growths
Of vigorous early days, attracted, won,
Married, made one with, molten into all
The beautiful in Past of act or place,
And like the all-enduring camel, driven
Far from the diamond fountain by the
    palms,
Who toils across the middle moonlit nights,
Or when the white heats of the blinding
    noons
Beat from the concave sand; yet in him
    keeps
A draught of that sweet fountain that he
    loves,
To stay his feet from falling, and his spirit
From bitterness of death.

                  Ye ask me, friends,
When I began to love. How should I tell
    you?
Or from the after-fulness of my heart,
Flow back again unto my slender spring
And first of love, tho' every turn and depth
Between is clearer in my life than all
Its present flow. Ye know not what ye ask.
How should the broad and open flower tell
What sort of bud it was, when, prest
    together
In its green sheath, close-lapt in silken
    folds,
It seem'd to keep its sweetness to itself,
Yet was not the less sweet for that it
    seem'd?
For young Life knows not when young
    Life was born,
But takes it all for granted: neither Love,
Warm in the heart, his cradle, can remember
Love in the womb, but resteth satisfied,
Looking on her that brought him to the
    light:
Or as men know not when they fall asleep
Into delicious dreams, our other life,
So know I not when I began to love.
This is my sum of knowledge—that my
    love
Grew with myself—say rather, was my
    growth,
My inward sap, the hold I have on earth,
My outward circling air wherewith I
    breathe,

Which yet upholds my life, and evermore
Is to me daily life and daily death:
For how should I have lived and not have
  loved?
Can ye take off the sweetness from the
  flower,
The colour and the sweetness from the
  rose,
And place them by themselves; or set apart
Their motions and their brightness from
  the stars,
And then point out the flower or the star?
Or build a wall betwixt my life and love,
And tell me where I am? 'Tis even thus:
In that I live I love; because I love
I live: whate'er is fountain to the one
Is fountain to the other; and whene'er
Our God unknits the riddle of the one,
There is no shade or fold of mystery
Swathing the other.

                          Many, many years,
(For they seem many and my most of life,
And well I could have linger'd in that
  porch,
So unproportion'd to the dwelling-place,)
In the Maydews of childhood, opposite
The flush and dawn of youth, we lived
  together,
Apart, alone together on those hills.

  Before he saw my day my father died,
And he was happy that he saw it not;
But I and the first daisy on his grave
From the same clay came into light at once.
As Love and I do number equal years,
So she, my love, is of an age with me.
How like each other was the birth of each!
On the same morning, almost the same
  hour,
Under the selfsame aspect of the stars,
(Oh falsehood of all starcraft!) we were
  born.
How like each other was the birth of each!
The sister of my mother—she that bore
Camilla close beneath her beating heart,
Which to the imprison'd spirit of the child,
With its true-touchéd pulses in the flow
And hourly visitation of the blood,
Sent notes of preparation manifold,
And mellow'd echoes of the outer world—

My mother's sister, mother of my love,
Who had a twofold claim upon my heart,
One twofold mightier than the other was,
In giving so much beauty to the world,
And so much wealth as God had charged
  her with—
Loathing to put it from herself for ever,
Left her own life with it; and dying thus,
Crown'd with her highest act the placid
  face
And breathless body of her good deeds
  past.

  So were we born, so orphan'd. She was
  motherless
And I without a father. So from each
Of those two pillars which from earth
  uphold
Our childhood, one had fallen away, and all
The careful burthen of our tender years
Trembled upon the other. He that gave
Her life, to me delightedly fulfill'd
All lovingkindnesses, all offices
Of watchful care and trembling tenderness.
He waked for both: he pray'd for both: he
  slept
Dreaming of both: nor was his love the less
Because it was divided, and shot forth
Boughs on each side, laden with whole-
  some shade,
Wherein we nested sleeping or awake,
And sang aloud the matin-song of life.

  She was my foster-sister: on one arm
The flaxen ringlets of our infancies
Wander'd, the while we rested: one soft lap
Pillow'd us both: a common light of eyes
Was on us as we lay: our baby lips,
Kissing one bosom, ever drew from thence
The stream of life, one stream, one life, one
  blood,
One sustenance, which, still as thought
  grew large,
Still larger moulding all the house of
  thought,
Made all our tastes and fancies like, per-
  haps—
All—all but one; and strange to me, and
  sweet,
Sweet thro' strange years to know that
  whatsoe'er

Our general mother meant for me alone,
Our mutual mother dealt to both of us:
So what was earliest mine in earliest life,
I shared with her in whom myself remains.

As was our childhood, so our infancy,
They tell me, was a very miracle
Of fellow-feeling and communion.
They tell me that we would not be alone,—
We cried when we were parted; when I
    wept,
Her smile lit up the rainbow on my tears,
Stay'd on the cloud of sorrow; that we
    loved
The sound of one-another's voices more
Than the gray cuckoo loves his name, and
    learn'd
To lisp in tune together; that we slept
In the same cradle always, face to face,
Heart beating time to heart, lip pressing lip,
Folding each other, breathing on each
    other,
Dreaming together (dreaming of each other
They should have added), till the morning
    light
Sloped thro' the pines, upon the dewy pane
Falling, unseal'd our eyelids, and we woke
To gaze upon each other. If this be true,
At thought of which my whole soul lan-
    guishes
And faints, and hath no pulse, no breath—
    as tho'
A man in some still garden should infuse
Rich atar in the bosom of the rose,
Till, drunk with its own wine, and overfull
Of sweetness, and in smelling of itself,
It fall on its own thorns—if this be true—
And that way my wish leads me evermore
Still to believe it—'tis so sweet a thought,
Why in the utter stillness of the soul
Doth question'd memory answer not, nor
    tell
Of this our earliest, our closest-drawn,
Most loveliest, earthly-heavenliest har-
    mony?

O blossom'd portal of the lonely house,
Green prelude, April promise, glad new-
    year
Of Being, which with earliest violets
And lavish carol of clear-throated larks

Fill'd all the March of life!—I will not
    speak of thee,
These have not seen thee, these can never
    know thee,
They cannot understand me. Pass we then
A term of eighteen years. Ye would but
    laugh,
If I should tell you how I hoard in thought
The faded rhymes and scraps of ancient
    crones,
Gray relics of the nurseries of the world,
Which are as gems set in my memory,
Because she learnt them with me; or what
    use
To know her father left us just before
The daffodil was blown? or how we found
The dead man cast upon the shore? All this
Seems to the quiet daylight of your minds
But cloud and smoke, and in the dark of
    mine
Is traced with flame. Move with me to the
    event.

There came a glorious morning, such a
    one
As dawns but once a season. Mercury
On such a morning would have flung him-
    self
From cloud to cloud, and swum with
    balanced wings
To some tall mountain: when I said to her,
'A day for Gods to stoop,' she answered,
    'Ay,
And men to soar:' for as that other gazed,
Shading his eyes till all the fiery cloud,
The prophet and the chariot and the steeds,
Suck'd into oneness like a little star
Were drunk into the inmost blue, we stood,
When first we came from out the pines at
    noon,
With hands for eaves, uplooking and almost
Waiting to see some blessed shape in
    heaven,
So bathed we were in brilliance. Never yet
Before or after have I known the spring
Pour with such sudden deluges of light
Into the middle summer; for that day
Love, rising, shook his wings, and charged
    the winds
With spiced May-sweets from bound to
    bound, and blew

Fresh fire into the sun, and from within
Burst thro' the heated buds, and sent his
  soul
Into the songs of birds, and touch'd far-off
His mountain-altars, his high hills, with
  flame
Milder and purer.

    Thro' the rocks we wound:
The great pine shook with lonely sounds
  of joy
That came on the sea-wind. As mountain
  streams
Our bloods ran free: the sunshine seem'd
  to brood
More warmly on the heart than on the
  brow.
We often paused, and, looking back, we
  saw
The clefts and openings in the mountains
  fill'd
With the blue valley and the glistening
  brooks,
And all the low dark groves, a land of love!
A land of promise, a land of memory,
A land of promise flowing with the milk
And honey of delicious memories!
And down to sea, and far as eye could ken,
Each way from verge to verge a Holy Land,
Still growing holier as you near'd the bay,
For there the Temple stood.

    When we had reach'd
The grassy platform on some hill, I stoop'd,
I gather'd the wild herbs, and for her
  brows
And mine made garlands of the selfsame
  flower,
Which she took smiling, and with my work
  thus
Crown'd her clear forehead. Once or twice
  she told me
(For I remember all things) to let grow
The flowers that run poison in their veins,
She said, 'The evil flourish in the world.'
Then playfully she gave herself the lie—
'Nothing in nature is unbeautiful;
So, brother, pluck and spare not.' So I
  wove
Ev'n the dull-blooded poppy-stem, 'whose
  flower,

Hued with the scarlet of a fierce sunrise,
Like to the wild youth of an evil prince,
Is without sweetness, but who crowns him-
  self
Above the naked poisons of his heart
In his old age.' A graceful thought of hers
Grav'n on my fancy! And oh, how like a
  nymph,
A stately mountain nymph she look'd! how
  native
Unto the hills she trod on! While I gazed
My coronal slowly disentwined itself
And fell between us both; tho' while I gazed
My spirit leap'd as with those thrills of
  bliss
That strike across the soul in prayer, and
  show us
That we are surely heard. Methought a
  light
Burst from the garland I had wov'n, and
  stood
A solid glory on her bright black hair;
A light methought broke from her dark,
  dark eyes,
And shot itself into the singing winds;
A mystic light flash'd ev'n from her white
  robe
As from a glass in the sun, and fell about
My footsteps on the mountains.

    Last we came
To what our people call 'The Hill of Woe.'
A bridge is there, that, look'd at from
  beneath
Seems but a cobweb filament to link
The yawning of an earthquake-cloven
  chasm.
And thence one night, when all the winds
  were loud,
A woful man (for so the story went)
Had thrust his wife and child and dash'd
  himself
Into the dizzy depth below. Below,
Fierce in the strength of far descent, a
  stream
Flies with a shatter'd foam along the
  chasm.

The path was perilous, loosely strown
  with crags:
We mounted slowly; yet to both there came

The joy of life in steepness overcome,
And victories of ascent, and looking down
On all that had look'd down on us; and joy
In breathing nearer heaven; and joy to me,
High over all the azure-circled earth,
To breathe with her as if in heaven itself;
And more than joy that I to her became
Her guardian and her angel, raising her
Still higher, past all peril, until she saw
Beneath her feet the region far away,
Beyond the nearest mountain's bosky
    brows,
Arise in open prospect—heath and hill,
And hollow lined and wooded to the lips,
And steep-down walls of battlemented
    rock
Gilded with broom, or shatter'd into spires,
And glory of broad waters interfused,
Whence rose as it were breath and steam
    of gold,
And over all the great wood rioting
And climbing, streak'd or starr'd at
    intervals
With falling brook or blossom'd bush—
    and last,
Framing the mighty landscape to the west,
A purple range of mountain-cones, between
Whose interspaces gush'd in blinding
    bursts
The incorporate blaze of sun and sea.

                                At length
Descending from the point and standing
    both,
There on the tremulous bridge, that from
    beneath
Had seem'd a gossamer filament up in air,
We paused amid the splendour. All the
    west
And ev'n unto the middle south was ribb'd
And barr'd with bloom on bloom. The sun
    below,
Held for a space 'twixt cloud and wave,
    shower'd down
Rays of a mighty circle, weaving over
That various wilderness a tissue of light
Unparallel'd. On the other side, the moon,
Half-melted into thin blue air, stood still,
And pale and fibrous as a wither'd leaf,
Nor yet endured in presence of His eyes
To indue his lustre; most unloverlike,

Since in his absence full of light and joy,
And giving light to others. But this most,
Next to her presence whom I loved so well,
Spoke loudly even into my inmost heart
As to my outward hearing: the loud stream,
Forth issuing from his portals in the crag
(A visible link unto the home of my heart),
Ran amber toward the west, and nigh the
    sea
Parting my own loved mountains was re-
    ceived,
Shorn of its strength, into the sympathy
Of that small bay, which out to open main
Glow'd intermingling close beneath the sun.
Spirit of Love! that little hour was bound
Shut in from Time, and dedicate to thee:
Thy fires from heaven had touch'd it, and
    the earth
They fell on became hallow'd evermore.

    We turn'd: our eyes met: hers were
        bright, and mine
Were dim with floating tears, that shot the
    sunset
In lightnings round me; and my name was
    borne
Upon her breath. Henceforth my name
    has been
A hallow'd memory like the names of old,
A center'd, glory-circled memory,
And a peculiar treasure, brooking not
Exchange or currency: and in that hour
A hope flow'd round me, like a golden mist
Charm'd amid eddies of melodious airs,
A moment, ere the onward whirlwind
    shatter it,
Waver'd and floated—which was less than
    Hope,
Because it lack'd the power of perfect
    Hope;
But which was more and higher than all
    Hope,
Because all other Hope had lower aim;
Even that this name to which her gracious
    lips
Did lend such gentle utterance, this one
    name,
In some obscure hereafter, might in-
    wreathe
(How lovelier, nobler then!) her life, her
    love,

With my life, love, soul, spirit, and heart
   and strength.

'Brother,' she said, 'let this be call'd
   henceforth
The Hill of Hope;' and I replied, 'O sister,
My will is one with thine; the Hill of
   Hope.'
Nevertheless, we did not change the name.

I did not speak: I could not speak my
   love.
Love lieth deep: Love dwells not in lip-
   depths.
Love wraps his wings on either side the
   heart,
Constraining it with kisses close and warm,
Absorbing all the incense of sweet thoughts
So that they pass not to the shrine of sound.
Else had the life of that delighted hour
Drunk in the largeness of the utterance
Of Love; but how should Earthly measure
   mete
The Heavenly-unmeasured or unlimited
   Love,
Who scarce can tune his high majestic
   sense
Unto the thundersong that wheels the
   spheres,
Scarce living in the Æolian harmony,
And flowing odour of the spacious air,
Scarce housed within the circle of this
   Earth,
Be cabin'd up in words and syllables,
Which pass with that which breathes
   them? Sooner Earth
Might go round Heaven, and the strait
   girth of Time
Inswathe the fulness of Eternity,
Than language grasp the infinite of Love.

O day which did enwomb that happy
   hour,
Thou art blessed in the years, divinest day!
O Genius of that hour which dost uphold
Thy coronal of glory like a God,
Amid thy melancholy mates far-seen,
Who walk before thee, ever turning round
To gaze upon thee till their eyes are dim
With dwelling on the light and depth of
   thine,

Thy name is ever worshipp'd among hours!
Had I died then, I had not seem'd to die,
For bliss stood round me like the light of
   Heaven,—
Had I died then, I had not known the
   death;
Yea had the Power from whose right hand
   the light
Of Life issueth, and from whose left hand
   floweth
The Shadow of Death, perennial effluences,
Whereof to all that draw the wholesome
   air,
Somewhile the one must overflow the
   other;
Then had he stemm'd my day with night,
   and driven
My current to the fountain whence it
   sprang,—
Even his own abiding excellence—
On me, methinks, that shock of gloom had
   fall'n
Unfelt, and in this glory I had merged
The other, like the sun I gazed upon,
Which seeming for the moment due to
   death,
And dipping his head low beneath the
   verge,
Yet bearing round about him his own day,
In confidence of unabated strength,
Steppeth from Heaven to Heaven, from
   light to light,
And holdeth his undimmed forehead far
Into a clearer zenith, pure of cloud.

We trod the shadow of the downward
   hill;
We past from light to dark. On the other
   side
Is scoop'd a cavern and a mountain hall,
Which none have fathom'd. If you go
   far in
(The country people rumour) you may
   hear
The moaning of the woman and the child,
Shut in the secret chambers of the rock.
I too have heard a sound—perchance of
   streams
Running far on within its inmost halls,
The home of darkness; but the cavern-
   mouth,

Q

Half overtrailed with a wanton weed,
Gives birth to a brawling brook, that pass-
    ing lightly
Adown a natural stair of tangled roots,
Is presently received in a sweet grave
Of eglantines, a place of burial
Far lovelier than its cradle; for unseen,
But taken with the sweetness of the place,
It makes a constant bubbling melody
That drowns the nearer echoes. Lower
    down
Spreads out a little lake, that, flooding,
    leaves
Low banks of yellow sand; and from the
    woods
That belt it rise three dark, tall cypresses,—
Three cypresses, symbols of mortal woe,
That men plant over graves.

                              Hither we came,
And sitting down upon the golden moss,
Held converse sweet and low—low con-
    verse sweet,
In which our voices bore least part. The
    wind
Told a lovetale beside us, how he woo'd
The waters, and the waters answering
    lisp'd
To kisses of the wind, that, sick with love,
Fainted at intervals, and grew again
To utterance of passion. Ye cannot shape
Fancy so fair as is this memory.
Methought all excellence that ever was
Had drawn herself from many thousand
    years,
And all the separate Edens of this earth,
To centre in this place and time. I listen'd,
And her words stole with most prevailing
    sweetness
Into my heart, as thronging fancies come
To boys and girls when summer days are
    new,
And soul and heart and body are all at ease:
What marvel my Camilla told me all?
It was so happy an hour, so sweet a place,
And I was as the brother of her blood,
And by that name I moved upon her
    breath;
Dear name, which had too much of near-
    ness in it
And heralded the distance of this time!

At first her voice was very sweet and low,
As if she were afraid of utterance;
But in the onward current of her speech,
(As echoes of the hollow-banked brooks
Are fashion'd by the channel which they
    keep),
Her words did of their meaning borrow
    sound,
Her cheek did catch the colour of her
    words.
I heard and trembled, yet I could but hear;
My heart paused—my raised eyelids would
    not fall,
But still I kept my eyes upon the sky.
I seem'd the only part of Time stood still,
And saw the motion of all other things;
While her words, syllable by syllable,
Like water, drop by drop, upon my ear
Fell; and I wish'd, yet wish'd her not to
    speak;
But she spake on, for I did name no wish.
What marvel my Camilla told me all
Her maiden dignities of Hope and Love—
'Perchance,' she said, 'return'd.' Even then
    the stars
Did tremble in their stations as I gazed;
But she spake on, for I did name no wish,
No wish—no hope. Hope was not wholly
    dead,
But breathing hard at the approach of
    Death,—
Camilla, my Camilla, who was mine
No longer in the dearest sense of mine—
For all the secret of her inmost heart,
And all the maiden empire of her mind,
Lay like a map before me, and I saw
There, where I hoped myself to reign as
    king,
There, where that day I crown'd myself as
    king,
There in my realm and even on my throne,
Another! then it seem'd as tho' a link
Of some tight chain within my inmost
    frame
Was riven in twain: that life I heeded not
Flow'd from me, and the darkness of the
    grave,
The darkness of the grave and utter night,
Did swallow up my vision; at her feet,
Even the feet of her I loved, I fell,
Smit with exceeding sorrow unto Death.

Then had the earth beneath me yawning
    cloven
With such a sound as when an iceberg splits
From cope to base—had Heaven from all
    her doors,
With all her golden thresholds clashing,
    roll'd
Her heaviest thunder—I had lain as dead,
Mute, blind and motionless as then I lay;
Dead, for henceforth there was no life
    for me!
Mute, for henceforth what use were words
    to me!
Blind, for the day was as the night to me!
The night to me was kinder than the day;
The night in pity took away my day,
Because my grief as yet was newly born
Of eyes too weak to look upon the light;
And thro' the hasty notice of the ear
Frail Life was startled from the tender love
Of him she brooded over. Would I had lain
Until the plaited ivy-trees had wound
Round my worn limbs, and the wild brier
    had driven
Its knotted thorns thro' my unpaining
    brows,
Leaning its roses on my faded eyes.
The wind had blown above me, and the
    rain
Had fall'n upon me, and the gilded snake
Had nestled in this bosom-throne of Love,
But I had been at rest for evermore.

    Long time entrancement held me. All
        too soon
Life (like a wanton too-officious friend,
Who will not *hear* denial, vain and rude
With proffer of unwish'd-for services)
Entering all the avenues of sense
Past thro' into its citadel, the brain,
With hated warmth of apprehensiveness.
And first the chillness of the sprinkled
    brook
Smote on my brows, and then I seem'd to
    hear
Its murmur, as the drowning seaman hears,
Who with his head below the surface dropt
Listens the muffled booming indistinct
Of the confused floods, and dimly knows
His head shall rise no more: and then
    came in

The white light of the weary moon above,
Diffused and molten into flaky cloud.
Was my sight drunk that it did shape to me
Him who should own that name? Were it
    not well
If so be that the echo of that name
Ringing within the fancy had updrawn
A fashion and a phantasm of the form
It should attach to? Phantom!—had the
    ghastliest
That ever lusted for a body, sucking
The foul steam of the grave to thicken by it,
There in the shuddering moonlight brought
    its face
And what it has for eyes as close to mine
As he did—better that than his, than he
The friend, the neighbour, Lionel, the
    beloved,
The loved, the lover, the happy Lionel,
The low-voiced, tender-spirited Lionel,
All joy, to whom my agony was a joy.
O how her choice did leap forth from his
    eyes!
O how her love did clothe itself in smiles
About his lips! and—not one moment's
    grace—
Then when the effect weigh'd seas upon
    my head
To come my way! to twit me with the
    cause!

    Was not the land as free thro' all her
        ways
To him as me? Was not his wont to walk
Between the going light and growing
    night?
Had I not learnt my loss before he came?
Could that be more because he came my
    way?
Why should he not come my way if he
    would?
And yet to-night, to-night—when all my
    wealth
Flash'd from me in a moment and I fell
Beggar'd for ever—why *should* he come
    my way
Robed in those robes of light I must not
    wear,
With that great crown of beams about his
    brows—
Come like an angel to a damned soul,

To tell him of the bliss he had with God—
Come like a careless and a greedy heir
That scarce can wait the reading of the will
Before he takes possession? Was mine a
      mood
To be invaded rudely, and not rather
A sacred, secret, unapproached woe,
Unspeakable? I was shut up with Grief;
She took the body of my past delight,
Narded and swathed and balm'd it for
      herself,
And laid it in a sepulchre of rock
Never to rise again. I was led mute
Into her temple like a sacrifice;
I was the High Priest in her holiest place,
Not to be loudly broken in upon.

    Oh friend, thoughts deep and heavy as
these well-nigh
O'erbore the limits of my brain: but he
Bent o'er me, and my neck his arm up-
      stay'd.
I thought it was an adder's fold, and once
I strove to disengage myself, but fail'd,
Being so feeble: she bent above me, too;
Wan was her cheek; for whatsoe'er of blight
Lives in the dewy touch of pity had made
The red rose there a pale one—and her
      eyes—
I saw the moonlight glitter on their tears—
And some few drops of that distressful rain
Fell on my face, and her long ringlets
      moved,
Drooping and beaten by the breeze, and
      brush'd
My fallen forehead in their to and fro,
For in the sudden anguish of her heart
Loosed from their simple thrall they had
      flow'd abroad,
And floated on and parted round her neck,
Mantling her form halfway. She, when I
      woke,
Something she ask'd, I know not what, and
      ask'd,
Unanswer'd, since I spake not; for the
      sound
Of that dear voice so musically low,
And now first heard with any sense of pain,
As it had taken life away before,
Choked all the syllables, that strove to rise
From my full heart.

                    The blissful lover, too,
From his great hoard of happiness distill'd
Some drops of solace; like a vain rich man,
That, having always prosper'd in the
      world,
Folding his hands, deals comfortable words
To hearts wounded for ever; yet, in truth,
Fair speech was his and delicate of phrase,
Falling in whispers on the sense, address'd
More to the inward than the outward ear,
As rain of the midsummer midnight soft,
Scarce-heard, recalling fragrance and the
      green
Of the dead spring: but mine was wholly
      dead,
No bud, no leaf, no flower, no fruit for me.
Yet who had done, or who had suffer'd
      wrong?
And why was I to darken their pure love,
If, as I found, they two did love each other,
Because my own was darken'd? Why was I
To cross between their happy star and
      them?
To stand a shadow by their shining doors,
And vex them with my darkness? Did I
      love her?
Ye know that I did love her; to this present
My full-orb'd love has waned not. Did I
      love her,
And could I look upon her tearful eyes?
What had she done to weep? Why should
      she weep?
O innocent of spirit—let my heart
Break rather—whom the gentlest airs of
      Heaven
Should kiss with an unwonted gentleness.
Her love did murder mine? What then?
      She deem'd
I wore a brother's mind: she call'd me
      brother:
She told me all her love: she shall not weep.

    The brightness of a burning thought,
      awhile
In battle with the glooms of my dark will,
Moonlike emerged, and to itself lit up
There on the depth of an unfathom'd woe
Reflex of action. Starting up at once,
As from a dismal dream of my own death,
I, for I loved her, lost my love in Love;
I, for I loved her, graspt the hand she lov'd,

And laid it in her own, and sent my cry
Thro' the blank night to Him who loving
    made
The happy and the unhappy love, that He
Would hold the hand of blessing over
    them,
Lionel, the happy, and her, and her, his
    bride!
Let them so love that men and boys may
    say,
'Lo! how they love each other!' till their
    love
Shall ripen to a proverb, unto all
Known, when their faces are forgot in the
    land—
One golden dream of love, from which may
    death
Awake them with heaven's music in a life
More living to some happier happiness,
Swallowing its precedent in victory.
And as for me, Camilla, as for me,—
The dew of tears is an unwholesome dew,
They will but sicken the sick plant the
    more.
Deem that I love thee but as brothers do,
So shalt thou love me still as sisters do;
Or if thou dream aught farther, dream but
    how
I could have loved thee, had there been
    none else
To love as lovers, loved again by thee.

Or this, or somewhat like to this, I spake,
When I beheld her weep so ruefully;
For sure my love should ne'er indue the
    front
And mask of Hate, who lives on others'
    moans.
Shall Love pledge Hatred in her bitter
    draughts,
And batten on her poisons? Love forbid!
Love passeth not the threshold of cold
    Hate,
And Hate is strange beneath the roof of
    Love.
O Love, if thou be'st Love, dry up these
    tears
Shed for the love of Love; for tho' mine
    image,
The subject of thy power, be cold in her,
Yet, like cold snow, it melteth in the source

Of these sad tears, and feeds their down-
    ward flow.
So Love, arraign'd to judgment and to
    death,
Received unto himself a part of blame,
Being guiltless, as an innocent prisoner,
Who, when the woful sentence hath been
    past,
And all the clearness of his fame hath gone
Beneath the shadow of the curse of man,
First falls asleep in swoon, wherefrom
    awaked,
And looking round upon his tearful friends,
Forthwith and in his agony conceives
A shameful sense as of a cleaving crime—
For whence without some guilt should
    such grief be?

So died that hour, and fell into the
    abysm
Of forms outworn, but not to me outworn,
Who never hail'd another—was there one?
There might be one—one other, worth the
    life
That made it sensible. So that hour died
Like odour rapt into the winged wind
Borne into alien lands and far away.

There be some hearts so airily built, that
    they,
They—when their love is wreck'd—if
    Love can wreck—
On that sharp ridge of utmost doom ride
    highly
Above the perilous seas of Change and
    Chance;
Nay, more, hold out the lights of cheerful-
    ness;
As the tall ship, that many a dreary year
Knit to some dismal sandbank far at sea,
All thro' the livelong hours of utter dark,
Showers slanting light upon the dolorous
    wave.
For me—what light, what gleam on those
    black ways
Where Love could walk with banish'd
    Hope no more?

It was ill-done to part you, Sisters fair;
Love's arms were wreath'd about the neck
    of Hope,

453

And Hope kiss'd Love, and Love drew in
  her breath
In that close kiss, and drank her whisper'd
  tales.
They said that Love would die when Hope
  was gone,
And Love mourn'd long, and sorrow'd
  after Hope;
At last she sought out Memory, and they
  trod
The same old paths where Love had walk'd
  with Hope,
And Memory fed the soul of Love with
  tears.

II

FROM that time forth I would not see her
  more;
But many weary moons I lived alone—
Alone, and in the heart of the great forest.
Sometimes upon the hills beside the sea
All day I watch'd the floating isles of shade,
And sometimes on the shore, upon the
  sands
Insensibly I drew her name, until
The meaning of the letters shot into
My brain; anon the wanton billow wash'd
Them over, till they faded like my love.
The hollow caverns heard me—the black
  brooks
Of the midforest heard me—the soft winds,
Laden with thistledown and seeds of
  flowers,
Paused in their course to hear me, for my
  voice
Was all of thee: the merry linnet knew me,
The squirrel knew me, and the dragonfly
Shot by me like a flash of purple fire.
The rough brier tore my bleeding palms;
  the hemlock,
Brow-high, did strike my forehead as I
  past;
Yet trod I not the wildflower in my path,
Nor bruised the wildbird's egg.

                          Was this the end?
Why grew we then together in one plot?
Why fed we from one fountain? drew one
  sun?
Why were our mothers' branches of one
  stem?

Why were we one in all things, save in that
Where to have been one had been the cope
  and crown
Of all I hoped and fear'd?—if that same
  nearness
Were father to this distance, and that *one*
Vauntcourier to this *double?* if Affection
Living slew Love, and Sympathy hew'd
  out
The bosom-sepulchre of Sympathy?

Chiefly I sought the cavern and the hill
Where last we roam'd together, for the
  sound
Of the loud stream was pleasant, and the
  wind
Came wooingly with woodbine smells.
  Sometimes
All day I sat within the cavern-mouth,
Fixing my eyes on those three cypress-
  cones
That spired above the wood; and with mad
  hand
Tearing the bright leaves of the ivy-screen,
I cast them in the noisy brook beneath,
And watch'd them till they vanish'd from
  my sight
Beneath the bower of wreathed eglantines:
And all the fragments of the living rock
(Huge blocks, which some old trembling of
  the world
Had loosen'd from the mountain, till they
  fell
Half-digging their own graves) these in my
  agony
Did I make bare of all the golden moss,
Wherewith the dashing runnel in the spring
Had liveried them all over. In my brain
The spirit seem'd to flag from thought to
  thought,
As moonlight wandering thro' a mist: my
  blood
Crept like marsh drains thro' all my lan-
  guid limbs;
The motions of my heart seem'd far
  within me,
Unfrequent, low, as tho' it told its pulses;
And yet it shook me, that my frame would
  shudder,
As if 'twere drawn asunder by the rack.
But over the deep graves of Hope and Fear,

454

And all the broken palaces of the Past,
Brooded one master-passion evermore,
Like to a low-hung and a fiery sky
Above some fair metropolis, earth-
    shock'd,—
Hung round with ragged rims and burning
    folds,—
Embathing all with wild and woful hues,
Great hills of ruins, and collapsed masses
Of thundershaken columns indistinct,
And fused together in the tyrannous light—
Ruins, the ruin of all my life and me!

Sometimes I thought Camilla was no
    more,
Some one had told me she was dead, and
    ask'd
If I would see her burial: then I seem'd
To rise, and through the forest-shadow
    borne
With more than mortal swiftness, I ran
    down
The steepy sea-bank, till I came upon
The rear of a procession, curving round
The silver-sheeted bay: in front of which
Six stately virgins, all in white, upbare
A broad earth-sweeping pall of whitest
    lawn,
Wreathed round the bier with garlands: in
    the distance,
From out the yellow woods upon the hill
Look'd forth the summit and the pinnacles
Of a gray steeple—thence at intervals
A low bell tolling. All the pageantry,
Save those six virgins which upheld the
    bier,
Were stoled from head to foot in flowing
    black;
One walk'd abreast with me, and veil'd his
    brow,
And he was loud in weeping and in praise
Of her, we follow'd: a strong sympathy
Shook all my soul: I flung myself upon
    him
In tears and cries: I told him all my love,
How I had loved her from the first; whereat
He shrank and howl'd, and from his brow
    drew back
His hand to push me from him; and the
    face,
The very face and form of Lionel

Flash'd thro' my eyes into my innermost
    brain,
And at his feet I seem'd to faint and fall,
To fall and die away. I could not rise
Albeit I strove to follow. They past on,
The lordly Phantasms! in their floating
    folds
They past and were no more: but I had
    fallen
Prone by the dashing runnel on the grass.

Alway the inaudible invisible thought,
Artificer and subject, lord and slave,
Shaped by the audible and visible,
Moulded the audible and visible;
All crisped sounds of wave and leaf and
    wind,
Flatter'd the fancy of my fading brain;
The cloud-pavilion'd element, the wood,
The mountain, the three cypresses, the cave,
Storm, sunset, glows and glories of the
    moon
Below black firs, when silent-creeping
    winds
Laid the long night in silver streaks and
    bars,
Were wrought into the tissue of my dream:
The moanings in the forest, the loud brook,
Cries of the partridge like a rusty key
Turn'd in a lock, owl-whoop and dorhawk-
    whirr
Awoke me not, but were a part of sleep,
And voices in the distance calling to me
And in my vision bidding me dream on,
Like sounds without the twilight realm of
    dreams,
Which wander round the bases of the hills,
And murmur at the low-dropt eaves of
    sleep,
Half-entering the portals. Oftentimes
The vision had fair prelude, in the end
Opening on darkness, stately vestibules
To caves and shows of Death: whether the
    mind,
With some revenge—even to itself un-
    known,—
Made strange division of its suffering
With her, whom to have suffering view'
    had been
Extremest pain; or that the clear-eye
    Spirit,

Being blunted in the Present, grew at
    length
Prophetical and prescient of whate'er
The Future had in store: or that which
    most
Enchains belief, the sorrow of my spirit
Was of so wide a compass it took in
All I had loved, and my dull agony,
Ideally to her transferr'd, became
Anguish intolerable.

            The day waned;
Alone I sat with her: about my brow
Her warm breath floated in the utterance
Of silver-chorded tones: her lips were
    sunder'd
With smiles of tranquil bliss, which broke
    in light
Like morning from her eyes—her eloquent
    eyes,
(As I have seen them many a hundred
    times)
Fill'd all with pure clear fire, thro' mine
    down rain'd
Their spirit-searching splendours. As a
    vision
Unto a haggard prisoner, iron-stay'd
In damp and dismal dungeons under-
    ground,
Confined on points of faith, when strength
    is shock'd
With torment, and expectancy of worse
Upon the morrow, thro' the ragged walls,
All unawares before his half-shut eyes,
Comes in upon him in the dead of night,
And with the excess of sweetness and of
    awe,
Makes the heart tremble, and the sight run
    over
Upon his steely gyves; so those fair eyes
Shone on my darkness, forms which ever
    stood
Within the magic cirque of memory,
Invisible but deathless, waiting still
The edict of the will to reassume
The semblance of those rare realities
Of which they were the mirrors. Now the
    light
Which was their life, burst through the
    cloud of thought
Keen, irrepressible.

            It was a room
Within the summer-house of which I
    spake,
Hung round with paintings of the sea, and
    one
A vessel in mid-ocean, her heaved prow
Clambering, the mast bent and the ravin
    wind
In her sail roaring. From the outer day,
Betwixt the close-set ivies came a broad
And solid beam of isolated light,
Crowded with driving atomies, and fell
Slanting upon that picture, from prime
    youth
Well-known well-loved. She drew it long
    ago
Forthgazing on the waste and open sea,
One morning when the upblown billow
    ran
Shoreward beneath red clouds, and I had
    pour'd
Into the shadowing pencil's naked forms
Colour and life: it was a bond and seal
Of friendship, spoken of with tearful
    smiles;
A monument of childhood and of love;
The poesy of childhood; my lost love
Symbol'd in storm. We gazed on it
    together
In mute and glad remembrance, and each
    heart
Grew closer to the other, and the eye
Was riveted and charm-bound, gazing like
The Indian on a still-eyed snake, low-
    couch'd—
A beauty which is death; when all at
    once
That painted vessel, as with inner life,
Began to heave upon that painted sea;
An earthquake, my loud heart-beats, made
    the ground
Reel under us, and all at once, soul, life
And breath and motion, past and flow'd
    away
To those unreal billows: round and round
A whirlwind caught and bore us; mighty
    gyres
Rapid and vast, of hissing spray wind-
    driven
Far thro' the dizzy dark. Aloud she
    shriek'd;

My heart was cloven with pain; I wound
    my arms
About her: we whirl'd giddily; the wind
Sung; but I clasp'd her without fear: her
    weight
Shrank in my grasp, and over my dim eyes,
And parted lips which drank her breath,
    down-hung
The jaws of Death: I, groaning, from me
    flung
Her empty phantom: all the sway and
    whirl
Of the storm dropt to windless calm, and I
Down welter'd thro' the dark ever and
    ever.

III

I CAME one day and sat among the stones
Strewn in the entry of the moaning cave;
A morning air, sweet after rain, ran over
The rippling levels of the lake, and blew
Coolness and moisture and all smells of bud
And foliage from the dark and dripping
    woods
Upon my fever'd brows that shook and
    throbb'd
From temple unto temple. To what height
The day had grown I know not. Then
    came on me
The hollow tolling of the bell, and all
The vision of the bier. As heretofore
I walk'd behind with one who veil'd his
    brow.
Methought by slow degrees the sullen bell
Toll'd quicker, and the breakers on the
    shore
Sloped into louder surf: those that went
    with me,
And those that held the bier before my
    face,
Moved with one spirit round about the bay,
Trod swifter steps; and while I walk'd
    with these
In marvel at that gradual change, I thought
Four bells instead of one began to ring,
Four merry bells, four merry marriage-
    bells,
In clanging cadence jangling peal on peal—
A long loud clash of rapid marriage-bells.
Then those who led the van, and those in
    rear,
Rush'd into dance, and like wild Bacchanals

Fled onward to the steeple in the woods:
I, too, was borne along and felt the blast
Beat on my heated eyelids: all at once
The front rank made a sudden halt; the
    bells
Lapsed into frightful stillness; the surge
    fell
From thunder into whispers; those six
    maids
With shrieks and ringing laughter on the
    sand
Threw down the bier; the woods upon the
    hill
Waved with a sudden gust that sweeping
    down
Took the edges of the pall, and blew it far
Until it hung, a little silver cloud
Over the sounding seas: I turn'd: my heart
Shrank in me, like a snowflake in the hand,
Waiting to see the settled countenance
Of her I loved, adorn'd with fading flowers.
But she from out her death-like chrysalis,
She from her bier, as into fresher life,
My sister, and my cousin, and my love,
Leapt lightly clad in bridal white—her hair
Studded with one rich Provence rose—a
    light
Of smiling welcome round her lips—her
    eyes
And cheeks as bright as when she climb'd
    the hill.
One hand she reach'd to those that came
    behind,
And while I mused nor yet endured to take
So rich a prize, the man who stood with
    me
Stept gaily forward, throwing down his
    robes,
And claspt her hand in his: again the bells
Jangled and clang'd: again the stormy surf
Crash'd in the shingle: and the whirling
    rout
Led by those two rush'd into dance, and
    fled
Wind-footed to the steeple in the woods,
Till they were swallow'd in the leafy
    bowers,
And I stood sole beside the vacant bier.

There, there, my latest vision—then the
    event!

IV

THE GOLDEN SUPPER

(*Another speaks*)

He flies the event: he leaves the event to
me:
Poor Julian—how he rush'd away; the
bells,
Those marriage-bells, echoing in ear and
heart—
But cast a parting glance at me, you saw,
As who should say 'Continue.' Well he had
One golden hour—of triumph shall I say?
Solace at least—before he left his home.

Would you had seen him in that hour of
his!
He moved thro' all of it majestically—
Restrain'd himself quite to the close—but
now—

Whether they *were* his lady's marriage-
bells,
Or prophets of them in his fantasy,
I never ask'd: but Lionel and the girl
Were wedded, and our Julian came again
Back to his mother's house among the
pines.
But these, their gloom, the mountains and
the Bay,
The whole land weigh'd him down as Ætna
does
The Giant of Mythology: he would go,
Would leave the land for ever, and had
gone
Surely, but for a whisper, 'Go not yet,'
Some warning—sent divinely—as it seem'd
By that which follow'd—but of this I deem
As of the visions that he told—the event
Glanced back upon them in his after life,
And partly made them—tho' he knew it
not.

And thus he stay'd and would not look
at her—
No not for months: but, when the eleventh
moon
After their marriage lit the lover's Bay,
Heard yet once more the tolling bell, and
said,

Would you could toll me out of life, but
found—
All softly as his mother broke it to him—
A crueller reason than a crazy ear,
For that low knell tolling his lady dead—
Dead—and had lain three days without a
pulse:
All that look'd on her had pronounced her
dead.
And so they bore her (for in Julian's land
They never nail a dumb head up in elm),
Bore her free-faced to the free airs of
heaven,
And laid her in the vault of her own kin.

What did he then? not die: he is here
and hale—
Not plunge headforemost from the moun-
tain there,
And leave the name of Lover's Leap:
not he:
He knew the meaning of the whisper now,
Thought that he knew it. 'This, I stay'd
for this;
O love, I have not seen you for so long.
Now, now, will I go down into the grave,
I will be all alone with all I love,
And kiss her on the lips. She is his no more:
The dead returns to me, and I go down
To kiss the dead.'

The fancy stirr'd him so
He rose and went, and entering the dim
vault,
And, making there a sudden light, beheld
All round about him that which all will be.
The light was but a flash, and went again.
Then at the far end of the vault he saw
His lady with the moonlight on her face;
Her breast as in a shadow-prison, bars
Of black and bands of silver, which the
moon
Struck from an open grating overhead
High in the wall, and all the rest of her
Drown'd in the gloom and horror of the
vault.

'It was my wish,' he said, 'to pass, to
sleep,
To rest, to be with her—till the great
day

Peal'd on us with that music which rights
all,
And raised us hand in hand.' And kneeling
there
Down in the dreadful dust that once was
man,
Dust, as he said, that once was loving
hearts,
Hearts that had beat with such a love as
mine—
Not such as mine, no, nor for such as her—
He softly put his arm about her neck
And kiss'd her more than once, till helpless
death
And silence made him bold—nay, but I
wrong him,
He reverenced his dear lady even in death;
But, placing his true hand upon her heart,
'O, you warm heart,' he moan'd, 'not even
death
Can chill you all at once:' then starting,
thought
His dreams had come again. 'Do I wake or
sleep?
Or am I made immortal, or my love
Mortal once more?' It beat—the heart—
it beat:
Faint—but it beat: at which his own began
To pulse with such a vehemence that it
drown'd
The feebler motion underneath his hand.
But when at last his doubts were satisfied,
He raised her softly from the sepulchre,
And, wrapping her all over with the cloak
He came in, and now striding fast, and now
Sitting awhile to rest, but evermore
Holding his golden burthen in his arms,
So bore her thro' the solitary land
Back to the mother's house where she was
born.

There the good mother's kindly minis-
tering,
With half a night's appliances, recall'd
Her fluttering life: she rais'd an eye that
ask'd
'Where?' till the things familiar to her
youth
Had made a silent answer: then she spoke
'Here! and how came I here?' and learn-
ing it

(They told her somewhat rashly as I think)
At once began to wander and to wail,
'Ay, but you know that you must give me
back:
Send! bid him come;' but Lionel was away—
Stung by his loss had vanish'd, none knew
where.
'He casts me out,' she wept, 'and goes'—a
wail
That seeming something, yet was nothing,
born
Not from believing mind, but shatter'd
nerve,
Yet haunting Julian, as her own reproof
At some precipitance in her burial.
Then, when her own true spirit had
return'd,
'Oh yes, and you,' she said, 'and none but
you?
For you have given me life and love again,
And none but you yourself shall tell him
of it,
And you shall give me back when he
returns.'
'Stay then a little,' answer'd Julian, 'here,
And keep yourself, none knowing, to your-
self;
And I will do your will. I may not stay,
No, not an hour; but send me notice of
him
When he returns, and then will I return,
And I will make a solemn offering of you
To him you love.' And faintly she replied,
'And I will do *your* will, and none shall
know.'

Not know? with such a secret to be
known.
But all their house was old and loved them
both,
And all the house had known the loves of
both;
Had died almost to serve them any way,
And all the land was waste and solitary:
And then he rode away; but after this,
An hour or two, Camilla's travail came
Upon her, and that day a boy was born,
Heir of his face and land, to Lionel.

And thus our lonely lover rode away,
And pausing at a hostel in a marsh,

There fever seized upon him: myself was
then
Travelling that land, and meant to rest an
hour;
And sitting down to such a base repast,
It makes me angry yet to speak of it—
I heard a groaning overhead, and climb'd
The moulder'd stairs (for everything was
vile)
And in a loft, with none to wait on him,
Found, as it seem'd, a skeleton alone,
Raving of dead men's dust and beating
hearts.

A dismal hostel in a dismal land,
A flat malarian world of reed and rush!
But there from fever and my care of him
Sprang up a friendship that may help us
yet.
For while we roam'd along the dreary coast,
And waited for her message, piece by piece
I learnt the drearier story of his life;
And, tho' he loved and honour'd Lionel,
Found that the sudden wail his lady made
Dwelt in his fancy: did he know her worth,
Her beauty even? should he not be taught,
Ev'n by the price that others set upon it,
The value of that jewel he had to guard?

Suddenly came her notice and we past,
I with our lover to his native Bay.

This love is of the brain, the mind, the
soul:
That makes the sequel pure; tho' some
of us
Beginning at the sequel know no more.
Not such am I: and yet I say the bird
That will not hear my call, however sweet,
But if my neighbour whistle answers him—
What matter? there are others in the wood.
Yet when I saw her (and I thought him
crazed,
Tho' not with such a craziness as needs
A cell and keeper), those dark eyes of
hers—
Oh! such dark eyes! and not her eyes alone,
But all from these to where she touch'd on
earth,
For such a craziness as Julian's look'd
No less than one divine apology.

So sweetly and so modestly she came
To greet us, her young hero in her arms!
'Kiss him,' she said. 'You gave me life again.
He, but for you, had never seen it once.
His other father you! Kiss him, and then
Forgive him, if his name be Julian too.'

Talk of lost hopes and broken heart! his
own
Sent such a flame into his face, I knew
Some sudden vivid pleasure hit him there.

But he was all the more resolved to go,
And sent at once to Lionel, praying him
By that great love they both had borne the
dead,
To come and revel for one hour with him
Before he left the land for evermore;
And then to friends—they were not many
—who lived
Scatteringly about that lonely land of his,
And bad them to a banquet of farewells.

And Julian made a solemn feast: I never
Sat at a costlier; for all round his hall
From column on to column, as in a wood,
Not such as here—an equatorial one,
Great garlands swung and blossom'd; and
beneath,
Heirlooms, and ancient miracles of Art,
Chalice and salver, wines that, Heaven
knows when,
Had suck'd the fire of some forgotten sun,
And kept it thro' a hundred years of gloom,
Yet glowing in a heart of ruby—cups
Where nymph and god ran ever round in
gold—
Others of glass as costly—some with gems
Moveable and resettable at will,
And trebling all the rest in value—Ah
heavens!
Why need I tell you all?—suffice to say
That whatsoever such a house as his,
And his was old, has in it rare or fair
Was brought before the guest: and they,
the guests,
Wonder'd at some strange light in Julian's
eyes
(I told you that he had his golden hour),
And such a feast, ill-suited as it seem'd
To such a time, to Lionel's loss and his

And that resolved self-exile from a land
He never would revisit, such a feast
So rich, so strange, and stranger ev'n than
    rich,
But rich as for the nuptials of a king.

And stranger yet, at one end of the hall
Two great funereal curtains, looping down,
Parted a little ere they met the floor,
About a picture of his lady, taken
Some years before, and falling hid the
    frame.
And just above the parting was a lamp:
So the sweet figure folded round with night
Seem'd stepping out of darkness with a
    smile.

Well then—our solemn feast—we ate
    and drank,
And might—the wines being of such
    nobleness—
Have jested also, but for Julian's eyes,
And something weird and wild about it all:
What was it? for our lover seldom spoke,
Scarce touch'd the meats; but ever and
    anon
A priceless goblet with a priceless wine
Arising, show'd he drank beyond his use;
And when the feast was near an end, he
    said:

'There is a custom in the Orient,
    friends—
I read of it in Persia—when a man
Will honour those who feast with him, he
    brings
And shows them whatsoever he accounts
Of all his treasures the most beautiful,
Gold, jewels, arms, whatever it may be.
This custom——'

            Pausing here a moment, all
The guests broke in upon him with meet-
    ing hands
And cries about the banquet—'Beautiful!
Who could desire more beauty at a feast?'

The lover answer'd, 'There is more than
    one
Here sitting who desires it. Laud me not
Before my time, but hear me to the close.

This custom steps yet further when the
    guest
Is loved and honour'd to the uttermost.
For after he hath shown him gems or gold,
He brings and sets before him in rich guise
That which is thrice as beautiful as these,
The beauty that is dearest to his heart—
"O my heart's lord, would I could show
    you," he says,
"Ev'n my heart too." And I propose
    to-night
To show you what is dearest to my heart,
And my heart too.

            'But solve me first a doubt.
I knew a man, nor many years ago;
He had a faithful servant, one who loved
His master more than all on earth beside.
He falling sick, and seeming close on death,
His master would not wait until he died,
But bad his menial bear him from the
    door,
And leave him in the public way to die.
I knew another, not so long ago,
Who found the dying servant, took him
    home,
And fed, and cherish'd him, and saved his
    life.
I ask you now, should this first master
    claim
His service, whom does it belong to? him
Who thrust him out, or him who saved his
    life?'

This question, so flung down before the
    guests,
And balanced either way by each, at length
When some were doubtful how the law
    would hold,
Was handed over by consent of all
To one who had not spoken, Lionel.

Fair speech was his, and delicate of
    phrase.
And he beginning languidly—his loss
Weigh'd on him yet—but warming as he
    went,
Glanced at the point of law, to pass it by,
Affirming that as long as either lived,
By all the laws of love and gratefulness,
The service of the one so saved was due

461

All to the saver—adding, with a smile,
The first for many weeks—a semi-smile
As at a strong conclusion—'body and soul
And life and limbs, all his to work his will.'

Then Julian made a secret sign to me
To bring Camilla down before them all.
And crossing her own picture as she came,
And looking as much lovelier as herself
Is lovelier than all others—on her head
A diamond circlet, and from under this
A veil, that seemed no more than gilded air,
Flying by each fine ear, an Eastern gauze
With seeds of gold—so, with that grace of hers,
Slow-moving as a wave against the wind,
That flings a mist behind it in the sun—
And bearing high in arms the mighty babe,
The younger Julian, who himself was crown'd
With roses, none so rosy as himself—
And over all her babe and her the jewels
Of many generations of his house
Sparkled and flash'd, for he had decked them out
As for a solemn sacrifice of love—
So she came in:—I am long in telling it,
I never yet beheld a thing so strange,
Sad, sweet, and strange together—floated in—
While all the guests in mute amazement rose—
And slowly pacing to the middle hall,
Before the board, there paused and stood, her breast
Hard-heaving, and her eyes upon her feet,
Not daring yet to glance at Lionel.
But him she carried, him nor lights nor feast
Dazed or amazed, nor eyes of men; who cared
Only to use his own, and staring wide
And hungering for the gilt and jewell'd world
About him, look'd, as he is like to prove,
When Julian goes, the lord of all he saw.

'My guests,' said Julian: 'you are honour'd now
Ev'n to the uttermost: in her behold

Of all my treasures the most beautiful,
Of all things upon earth the dearest to me.'
Then waving us a sign to seat ourselves,
Led his dear lady to a chair of state.
And I, by Lionel sitting, saw his face
Fire, and dead ashes and all fire again
Thrice in a second, felt him tremble too,
And heard him muttering, 'So like, so like;
She never had a sister. I knew none.
Some cousin of his and hers—O God, so like!'
And then he suddenly ask'd her if she were.
She shook, and cast her eyes down, and was dumb.
And then some other question'd if she came
From foreign lands, and still she did not speak.
Another, if the boy were hers: but she
To all their queries answer'd not a word,
Which made the amazement more, till one of them
Said, shuddering, 'Her spectre!' But his friend
Replied, in half a whisper, 'Not at least
The spectre that will speak if spoken to.
Terrible pity, if one so beautiful
Prove, as I almost dread to find her, dumb!'

But Julian, sitting by her, answer'd all:
'She is but dumb, because in her you see
That faithful servant whom we spoke about,
Obedient to her second master now;
Which will not last. I have here to-night a guest
So bound to me by common love and loss—
What! shall I bind him more? in his behalf,
Shall I exceed the Persian, giving him
That which of all things is the dearest to me,
Not only showing? and he himself pronounced
That my rich gift is wholly mine to give.

'Now all be dumb, and promise all of you
Not to break in on what I say by word

462

Or whisper, while I show you all my heart.'
And then began the story of his love
As here to-day, but not so wordily—
The passionate moment would not suffer
    that—
Past thro' his visions to the burial; thence
Down to this last strange hour in his own
    hall;
And then rose up, and with him all his
    guests
Once more as by enchantment; all but he,
Lionel, who fain had risen, but fell again,
And sat as if in chains—to whom he said:

'Take my free gift, my cousin, for your
    wife;
And were it only for the giver's sake,
And tho' she seem so like the one you lost,
Yet cast her not away so suddenly,
Lest there be none left here to bring her
    back:
I leave this land for ever.' Here he ceased.

Then taking his dear lady by one hand,
And bearing on one arm the noble babe,
He slowly brought them both to Lionel.
And there the widower husband and dead
    wife
Rush'd each at each with a cry, that rather
    seem'd
For some new death than for a life renew'd;
Whereat the very babe began to wail;
At once they turn'd, and caught and
    brought him in
To their charm'd circle, and, half killing
    him
With kisses, round him closed and claspt
    again.
But Lionel, when at last he freed himself
From wife and child, and lifted up a face
All over glowing with the sun of life,
And love, and boundless thanks—the sight
    of this
So frighted our good friend, that turning
    to me
And saying, 'It is over: let us go'—
There were our horses ready at the doors—
We bad them no farewell, but mounting
    these
He past for ever from his native land;
And I with him, my Julian, back to mine.

TO ALFRED TENNYSON

MY GRANDSON

GOLDEN-HAIR'D Ally whose name is one with
    mine,
Crazy with laughter and babble and earth's
    new wine,
Now that the flower of a year and a half is thine,
O little blossom, O mine, and mine of mine,
Glorious poet who never hast written a line,
Laugh, for the name at the head of my verse is
    thine.
May'st thou never be wrong'd by the name that
    is mine!

THE FIRST QUARREL

(IN THE ISLE OF WIGHT)

I

'WAIT a little,' you say, 'you are sure it 'll
    all come right,'
But the boy was born i' trouble, an' looks
    so wan an' so white:
Wait! an' once I ha' waited—I hadn't to
    wait for long.
Now I wait, wait, wait for Harry.—No, no,
    you are doing me wrong!
Harry and I were married: the boy can
    hold up his head,
The boy was born in wedlock, but after
    my man was dead;
I ha' work'd for him fifteen years, an' I
    work an' I wait to the end.
I am all alone in the world, an' you are my
    only friend.

II

Doctor, if *you* can wait, I'll tell you the
    tale o' my life.
When Harry an' I were children, he call'd
    me his own little wife;
I was happy when I was with him, an'
    sorry when he was away,
An' when we play'd together, I loved him
    better than play;
He workt me the daisy chain—he made me
    the cowslip ball,
He fought the boys that were rude, an' I
    loved him better than all.
Passionate girl tho' I was, an' often at home
    in disgrace,
I never could quarrel with Harry—I had
    but to look in his face.

463

III

There was a farmer in Dorset of Harry's
   kin, that had need
Of a good stout lad at his farm; he sent,
   an' the father agreed;
So Harry was bound to the Dorsetshire
   farm for years an' for years;
I walked with him down to the quay, poor
   lad, an' we parted in tears.
The boat was beginning to move, we heard
   them a-ringing the bell,
'I'll never love any but you, God bless you,
   my own little Nell.'

IV

I was a child, an' he was a child, an' he
   came to harm;
There was a girl, a hussy, that workt with
   him up at the farm,
One had deceived her an' left her alone
   with her sin an' her shame,
And so she was wicked with Harry; the
   girl was the most to blame.

V

And years went over till I that was little
   had grown so tall,
The men would say of the maids, 'Our
   Nelly's the flower of 'em all.'
I didn't take heed o' *them*, but I taught
   myself all I could
To make a good wife for Harry, when
   Harry came home for good.

VI

Often I seem'd unhappy, and often as
   happy too,
For I heard it abroad in the fields 'I'll
   never love any but you;'
'I'll never love any but you' the morning
   song of the lark,
'I'll never love any but you' the nightingale's hymn in the dark.

VII

And Harry came home at last, but he
   look'd at me sidelong and shy,
Vext me a bit, till he told me that so many
   years had gone by,

I had grown so handsome and tall—that
   I might h' forgot him somehow—
For he thought—there were other lads—
   he was fear'd to look at me now.

VIII

Hard was the frost in the field, we were
   married o' Christmas day,
Married among the red berries, an' all as
   merry as May—
Those were the pleasant times, my house
   an' my man were my pride,
We seem'd like ships i' the Channel a
   sailing with wind an' tide.

IX

But work was scant in the Isle, tho' he
   tried the villages round,
So Harry went over the Solent to see if
   work could be found;
An' he wrote 'I ha' six weeks' work, little
   wife, so far as I know;
I'll come for an hour to-morrow, an' kiss
   you before I go.'

X

So I set to righting the house, for wasn't
   he coming that day?
An' I hit on an old deal-box that was
   push'd in a corner away,
It was full of old odds an' ends, an' a letter
   along wi' the rest,
I had better ha' put my naked hand in a
   hornets' nest.

XI

'Sweetheart'—this was the letter—this was
   the letter I read—
'You promised to find me work near you,
   an' I wish I was dead—
Didn't you kiss me an' promise? you
   haven't done it, my lad,
An' I almost died o' your going away, an'
   I wish that I had.'

XII

I too wish that I had—in the pleasant times
   that had past,
Before I quarrell'd with Harry—*my* quarrel
   —the first an' the last.

XIII

For Harry came in, an' I flung him the
    letter that drove me wild,
An' he told it me all at once, as simple as
    any child,
'What can it matter, my lass, what I did
    wi' my single life?
I ha' been as true to you as ever a man to
    his wife;
An' *she* wasn't one o' the worst.' 'Then,' I
    said, 'I'm none o' the best.'
An' he smiled at me, 'Ain't you, my love?
    Come, come, little wife, let it rest!
The man isn't like the woman, no need to
    make such a stir.'
But he anger'd me all the more, an' I said
    'You were keeping with her,
When I was a-loving you all along an' the
    same as before.'
An' he didn't speak for a while, an' he
    anger'd me more and more.
Then he patted my hand in his gentle way,
    'Let bygones be!'
'Bygones! you kept yours hush'd,' I said,
    'when you married me!
By-gones ma' be come-agains; an' *she*—in
    her shame an' her sin—
You'll have her to nurse my child, if I die
    o' my lying in!
You'll make her its second mother! I hate
    her—an' I hate you!'
Ah, Harry, my man, you had better ha'
    beaten me black an' blue
Than ha' spoken as kind as you did, when
    I were so crazy wi' spite,
'Wait a little, my lass, I am sure it 'ill all
    come right.'

XIV

An' he took three turns in the rain, an' I
    watch'd him, an' when he came in
I felt that my heart was hard, he was all
    wet thro' to the skin,
An' I never said 'off wi' the wet,' I never
    said 'on wi' the dry,'
So I knew my heart was hard, when he
    came to bid me goodbye.
'You said that you hated me, Ellen, but
    that isn't true, you know,
I am going to leave you a bit—you'll kiss
    me before I go?'

XV

'Going! you're going to her—kiss her—if
    you will,' I said—
I was near my time wi' the boy, I must ha'
    been light i' my head—
'I had sooner be cursed than kiss'd!'—I
    didn't know well what I meant,
But I turn'd my face from *him*, an' he
    turn'd *his* face an' he went.

XVI

And then he sent me a letter, 'I've gotten
    my work to do;
You wouldn't kiss me, my lass, an' I never
    loved any but you;
I am sorry for all the quarrel an' sorry for
    what she wrote,
I ha' six weeks' work in Jersey an' go to-
    night by the boat.'

XVII

An' the wind began to rise, an' I thought
    of him out at sea,
An' I felt I had been to blame; he was
    always kind to me.
'Wait a little, my lass, I am sure it 'ill all
    come right'—
An' the boat went down that night—the
    boat went down that night.

RIZPAH

17—

I

WAILING, wailing, wailing, the wind over
    land and sea—
And Willy's voice in the wind, 'O mother,
    come out to me.'
Why should he call me to-night, when he
    knows that I cannot go?
For the downs are as bright as day, and the
    full moon stares at the snow.

II

We should be seen, my dear; they would
    spy us out of the town.
The loud black nights for us, and the
    storm rushing over the down,

465

When I cannot see my own hand, but am
    led by the creak of the chain,
And grovel and grope for my son till I find
    myself drenched with the rain.

III

Anything fallen again? nay—what was
    there left to fall?
I have taken them home, I have number'd
    the bones, I have hidden them all.
What am I saying? and what are *you*? do
    you come as a spy?
Falls? what falls? who knows? As the tree
    falls so must it lie.

IV

Who let her in? how long has she been?
    you—what have you heard?
Why did you sit so quiet? you never have
    spoken a word.
O—to pray with me—yes—a lady—none
    of their spies—
But the night has crept into my heart, and
    begun to darken my eyes.

V

Ah—you, that have lived so soft, what
    should *you* know of the night,
The blast and the burning shame and the
    bitter frost and the fright?
I have done it, while you were asleep—
    you were only made for the day.
I have gather'd my baby together—and
    now you may go your way.

VI

Nay—for it's kind of you, Madam, to sit
    by an old dying wife.
But say nothing hard of my boy, I have
    only an hour of life.
I kiss'd my boy in the prison, before he
    went out to die.
'They dared me to do it,' he said, and he
    never has told me a lie.
I whipt him for robbing an orchard once
    when he was but a child—
'The farmer dared me to do it,' he said;
    he was always so wild—
And idle—and couldn't be idle—my Willy
    —he never could rest.
The King should have made him a soldier,
    he would have been one of his best.

VII

But he lived with a lot of wild mates, and
    they never would let him be good;
They swore that he dare not rob the mail,
    and he swore that he would;
And he took no life, but he took one purse,
    and when all was done
He flung it among his fellows—I'll none
    of it, said my son.

VIII

I came into court to the Judge and the
    lawyers. I told them my tale,
God's own truth—but they kill'd him, they
    kill'd him for robbing the mail.
They hang'd him in chains for a show—
    we had always borne a good name—
To be hang'd for a thief—and then put
    away—isn't that enough shame?
Dust to dust—low down—let us hide! but
    they set him so high
That all the ships of the world could stare
    at him, passing by.
God 'ill pardon the hell-black raven and
    horrible fowls of the air,
But not the black heart of the lawyer who
    kill'd him and hang'd him there.

IX

And the jailer forced me away. I had bid
    him my last goodbye;
They had fasten'd the door of his cell.
    'O mother!' I heard him cry.
I couldn't get back tho' I tried, he had
    something further to say,
And now I never shall know it. The jailer
    forced me away.

X

Then since I couldn't but hear that cry of
    my boy that was dead,
They seized me and shut me up: they
    fasten'd me down on my bed.
'Mother, O mother!'—he call'd in the dark
    to me year after year—
They beat me for that, they beat me—you
    know that I couldn't but hear;
And then at the last they found I had
    grown so stupid and still
They let me abroad again—but the
    creatures had worked their will.

XI

Flesh of my flesh was gone, but bone of my
bone was left—
I stole them all from the lawyers—and you,
will you call it a theft?—
My baby, the bones that had suck'd me,
the bones that had laughed and had
cried—
Theirs? O no! they are mine—not theirs—
they had moved in my side.

XII

Do you think I was scared by the bones?
I kiss'd 'em, I buried 'em all—
I can't dig deep, I am old—in the night by
the churchyard wall.
My Willy 'ill rise up whole when the
trumpet of judgment 'ill sound,
But I charge you never to say that I laid
him in holy ground.

XIII

They would scratch him up—they would
hang him again on the cursed tree.
Sin? O yes—we are sinners, I know—let
all that be,
And read me a Bible verse of the Lord's
good will toward me—
'Full of compassion and mercy, the Lord'
—let me hear it again;
'Full of compassion and mercy—long-
suffering.' Yes, O yes!
For the lawyer is born but to murder—the
Saviour lives but to bless.
He'll never put on the black cap except for
the worst of the worst,
And the first may be last—I have heard it
in church—and the last may be first.
Suffering—O long-suffering—yes, as the
Lord must know,
Year after year in the mist and the wind
and the shower and the snow.

XIV

Heard, have you? what? they have told
you he never repented his sin.
How do they know it? are they his mother?
are you of his kin?
Heard! have you ever heard, when the
storm on the downs began,
The wind that 'ill wail like a child and the
sea that 'ill moan like a man?

XV

Election, Election and Reprobation—it's
all very well.
But I go to-night to my boy, and I shall
not find him in Hell.
For I cared so much for my boy that the
Lord has look'd into my care,
And He means me I'm sure to be happy
with Willy, I know not where.

XVI

And if he be lost—but to save my soul, that
is all your desire:
Do you think that I care for my soul if my
boy be gone to the fire?
I have been with God in the dark—go, go,
you may leave me alone—
You never have borne a child—you are
just as hard as a stone.

XVII

Madam, I beg your pardon! I think that
you mean to be kind,
But I cannot hear what you say for my
Willy's voice in the wind—
The snow and the sky so bright—he used
but to call in the dark,
And he calls to me now from the church
and not from the gibbet—for hark!
Nay—you can hear it yourself—it is
coming—shaking the walls—
Willy—the moon's in a cloud——Good-
night. I am going. He calls.

THE NORTHERN COBBLER

I

Waäit till our Sally cooms in, fur thou
mun a' sights[1] to tell.
Eh, but I be maäin glad to seeä tha sa 'arty
an' well.

[1] The vowels ai, pronounced separately
though in the closest conjunction, best render
the sound of the long i and y in this dialect.
But since such words as craïin', daïin', whaï,
aï (I), etc., look awkward except in a page of
express phonetics, I have thought it better to
leave the simple i and y, and to trust that my
readers will give them the broader pronuncia-
tion.

'Cast awaäy on a disolut land wi' a vartical
    soon!'[1]
Strange fur to goä fur to think what saäilors
    a' seëan an' a' doon;
'Summat to drink—sa' 'ot?' I 'a nowt but
    Adam's wine:
What's the 'eät o' this little 'ill-side to the
    'eät o' the line?

II

'What's i' tha bottle a-stanning theer?'
    I'll tell tha. Gin.
But if thou wants thy grog, tha mun goä
    fur it down to the inn.
Naay—fur I be maäin-glad, but thaw tha
    was iver sa dry,
Thou gits naw gin fro' the bottle theer, an'
    I'll tell tha why.

III

Meä an' thy sister was married, when wur
    it? back-end o' June,
Ten year sin', and wa 'greed as well as a
    fiddle i' tune:
I could fettle and clump owd booöts and
    shoes wi' the best on 'em all,
As fer as fro' Thursby thurn hup to
    Harmsby and Hutterby Hall.
We was busy as beeäs i' the bloom an' as
    'appy as 'art could think,
An' then the babby wur burn, and then I
    taäkes to the drink.

IV

An' I weänt gaäinsaäy it, my lad, thaw I be
    hafe shaämed on it now,
We could sing a good song at the Plow, we
    could sing a good song at the Plow;
Thaw once of a frosty night I slither'd an'
    hurted my huck,[2]
An' I coom'd neck-an-crop soomtimes
    slaäpe down i' the squad an' the muck:
An' once I fowt wi' the Taäilor—not hafe
    ov a man, my lad—
Fur he scrawm'd an' scratted my faäce like
    a cat, an' it maäde 'er sa mad
That Sally she turn'd a tongue-banger,[3]
    an' raäted ma, 'Sottin' thy braäins

Guzzlin' an' soäkin' an' smoäkin' an'
    hawmin'[4] about i' the laänes,
Soä sow-droonk that tha doesn not touch
    thy 'at to the Squire;'
An' I looök'd cock-eyed at my noäse an' I
    seeäd 'im a-gittin' o' fire;
But sin' I wur hallus i' liquor an' hallus as
    droonk as a king,
Foälks' coostom flitted awaäy like a kite
    wi' a brokken string.

V

An' Sally she wesh'd foälks' cloäths to keep
    the wolf fro' the door,
Eh but the moor she riled me, she druv me
    to drink the moor,
Fur I fun', when 'er back wur turn'd,
    wheer Sally's owd stockin' wur 'id,
An' I grabb'd the munny she maäde, and
    I weär'd it o' liquor, I did.

VI

An' one night I cooms 'oäm like a bull
    gotten loose at a faäir,
An' she wur a-waäitin' fo'mma, an' cryin'
    and teärin' 'er 'aäir,
An' I tummled athurt the craädle an'
    sweär'd as I'd breäk ivry stick
O' furnitur 'ere i' the 'ouse, an' I gied our
    Sally a kick,
An' I mash'd the taäbles an' chairs, an' she
    an' the babby beäl'd,[5]
Fur I knaw'd naw moor what I did nor a
    mortal beäst o' the feäld.

VII

An' when I waäked i' the murnin' I seeäd
    that our Sally went laämed
Cos' o' the kick as I gied 'er, an' I wur
    dreädful ashaämed;
An' Sally wur sloomy[6] an' draggle taäil'd
    in an owd turn gown,
An' the babby's faäce wurn't wesh'd an'
    the 'ole 'ouse hupside down.

VIII

An' then I minded our Sally sa pratty an'
    neät an' sweeät,
Straät as a pole an' cleän as a flower fro'
    'eäd to feeät:

---

[1] The *oo* short, as in 'wood'.
[2] Hip.   [3] Scold.

[4] Lounging.   [5] Bellowed, cried out.
[6] Sluggish, out of spirits.

An' then I minded the fust kiss I gied 'er
  by Thursby thurn;
Theer wur a lark a-singin' 'is best of a
  Sunday at murn,
Couldn't see 'im, we 'eärd 'im a-mountin'
  oop 'igher an' 'igher,
An' then 'e turn'd to the sun, an' 'e shined
  like a sparkle o' fire.
'Doesn't tha see 'im,' she axes, 'fur I can
  see 'im?' an' I
Seeäd nobbut the smile o' the sun as
  danced in 'er pratty blue eye;
An' I says 'I mun gie tha a kiss,' an' Sally
  says 'Noä, thou moänt,'
But I gied 'er a kiss, an' then anoother, an'
  Sally says 'doänt!'

IX

An' when we coom'd into Meeätin', at fust
  she wur all in a tew,
But, arter, we sing'd the 'ymn togither like
  birds on a beugh;
An' Muggins 'e preäch'd o' Hell-fire an'
  the loov o' God fur men,
An' then upo' coomin' awaäy Sally gied
  me a kiss ov 'ersen.

X

Heer wur a fall fro' a kiss to a kick like
  Saätan as fell
Down out o' heaven i' Hell-fire—thaw
  theer's naw drinkin' i' Hell;
Meä fur to kick our Sally as kep the wolf
  fro' the door,
All along o' the drink, fur I loov'd 'er as
  well as afoor.

XI

Sa like a greät num-cumpus I blubber'd
  awaäy o' the bed—
'Weänt niver do it naw moor;' an' Sally
  loökt up an' she said,
'I'll upowd it[1] tha weänt; thou'rt like the
  rest o' the men,
Thou'll goä sniffin' about the tap till tha
  does it ageän.
Theer's thy hennemy, man, an' I knaws,
  as knaws tha sa well,
That, if tha seeäs 'im an' smells 'im tha'll
  foller 'im slick into Hell.'

          [1] I'll uphold it.

XII

'Naäy,' says I, 'fur I weänt goä sniffin'
  about the tap.'
'Weänt tha?' she says, an' mysen I thowt
  i' mysen 'mayhap.'
'Noä:' an' I started awaäy like a shot, an'
  down to the Hinn,
An' I browt what tha seeäs stannin' theer,
  yon big black bottle o' gin.

XIII

'That caps owt,'[2] says Sally, an' saw she
  begins to cry,
But I puts it inter 'er 'ands an' I says to 'er,
  'Sally,' says I,
'Stan' 'im theer i' the naäme o' the Lord
  an' the power ov 'is Graäce,
Stan' 'im theer, fur I'll looök my hennemy
  straït i' the faäce,
Stan' 'im theer i' the winder, an' let ma
  loook at 'im then,
'E seeäms naw moor nor watter, an' 'e's
  the Divil's oän sen.'

XIV

An' I wur down i' tha mouth, couldn't do
  naw work an' all,
Nasty an' snaggy an' shaäky, an' poonch'd
  my 'and wi' the hawl,
But she wur a power o' coomfut, an'
  sattled 'ersen o' my knee,
An' coäxd an' coodled me oop till ageän
  I feel'd mysen free.

XV

An' Sally she tell'd it about, an' foälk stood
  a-gawmin'[3] in,
As thaw it wur summat bewitch'd istead
  of a quart o' gin;
An' some on 'em said it wur watter—an'
  I wur chousin' the wife,
Fur I couldn't 'owd 'ands off gin, wur it
  nobbut to saäve my life;
An' blacksmith 'e strips me the thick ov 'is
  airm' an' 'e shaws it to me,
'Feëal thou this! thou can't graw this upo'
  watter!' says he.

          [2] That's beyond everything.
          [3] Staring vacantly.

An' Doctor 'e calls o' Sunday an' just as
  candles was lit,
'Thou moänt do it,' he says, 'tha mun
  breäk 'im off bit by bit.'
'Thou'rt but a Methody-man,' says Parson, and laäys down 'is 'at,
An' 'e points to the bottle o' gin, 'but I
  respecks tha fur that;'
An' Squire, his oän very sen, walks down
  fro' the 'All to see,
An' 'e spanks 'is 'and into mine, 'fur I
  respecks tha,' says 'e;
An' coostom ageän draw'd in like a wind
  fro' far an' wide,
And browt me the booöts to be cobbled
  fro' hafe the coontryside.

XVI

An' theer 'e stans an' theer 'e shall stan to
  my dying daäy;
I 'a gotten to loov 'im ageän in anoother
  kind of a waäy,
Proud on 'im, like, my lad, an' I keeäps 'im
  cleän an' bright,
Loovs 'im, an' roobs 'im, an' doosts 'im,
  an' puts 'im back i' the light.

XVII

Wouldn't a pint a' sarved as well as a
  quart? Naw doubt:
But I liked a bigger feller to fight wi' an'
  fowt it out.
Fine an' meller 'e mun be by this, if I cared
  to taäste,
But I moänt, my lad, and I weänt, fur I'd
  feäl mysen cleän disgraäced.

XVIII

An' once I said to the Missis, 'My lass,
  when I cooms to die,
Smash the bottle to smithers, the Divil's in
  'im,' said I.
But arter I chaänged my mind, an' if Sally
  be left aloän,
I'll hev 'im a-buried wi'mma an' taäke 'im
  afoor the Throän.

XIX

Coom thou 'eer—yon laädy a-steppin'
  along the streeät,
Doesn't tha knaw 'er—sa pratty, an' feät,
  an' neät, an' sweeät?

Look at the cloäths on 'er back, thebbe
  ammost spick-span-new,
An' Tommy's faäce be as fresh as a codlin
  wesh'd i' the dew.

XX

'Ere be our Sally an' Tommy, an' we be
  a-goin to dine,
Baäcon an' taätes, an' a beslings puddin'[1]
  an' Adam's wine;
But if tha wants ony grog tha mun goä fur
  it down to the Hinn,
Fur I weänt shed a drop on 'is blood, noä,
  not fur Sally's oän kin.

THE REVENGE

A BALLAD OF THE FLEET

I

At Flores in the Azores Sir Richard
  Grenville lay,
And a pinnace, like a flutter'd bird, came
  flying from far away:
'Spanish ships of war at sea! we have
  sighted fifty-three!'
Then sware Lord Thomas Howard: ''Fore
  God I am no coward;
But I cannot meet them here, for my ships
  are out of gear,
And the half my men are sick. I must fly,
  but follow quick.
We are six ships of the line; can we fight
  with fifty-three?'

II

Then spake Sir Richard Grenville: 'I know
  you are no coward;
You fly them for a moment to fight with
  them again.
But I've ninety men and more that are
  lying sick ashore.
I should count myself the coward if I left
  them, my Lord Howard,
To these Inquisition dogs and the devil-
  doms of Spain.'

III

So Lord Howard past away with five ships
  of war that day,

[1] A pudding made with the first milk of the
cow after calving.

Till he melted like a cloud in the silent
   summer heaven;
But Sir Richard bore in hand all his sick
   men from the land
Very carefully and slow,
Men of Bideford in Devon,
And we laid them on the ballast down
   below;
For we brought them all aboard,
And they blest him in their pain, that they
   were not left to Spain,
To the thumbscrew and the stake, for the
   glory of the Lord.

IV

He had only a hundred seamen to work the
   ship and to fight,
And he sailed away from Flores till the
   Spaniard came in sight,
With his huge sea-castles heaving upon the
   weather bow.
'Shall we fight or shall we fly?
Good Sir Richard, tell us now,
For to fight is but to die!
There'll be little of us left by the time this
   sun be set.'
And Sir Richard said again: 'We be all
   good English men.
Let us bang these dogs of Seville, the
   children of the devil,
For I never turn'd my back upon Don or
   devil yet.'

V

Sir Richard spoke and he laugh'd, and we
   roar'd a hurrah, and so
The little Revenge ran on sheer into the
   heart of the foe,
With her hundred fighters on deck, and
   her ninety sick below;
For half of their fleet to the right and half
   to the left were seen,
And the little Revenge ran on thro' the
   long sea-lane between.

VI

Thousands of their soldiers look'd down
   from their decks and laugh'd,
Thousands of their seamen made mock at
   the mad little craft

Running on and on, till delay'd
By their mountain-like San Philip that, of
   fifteen hundred tons,
And up-shadowing high above us with her
   yawning tiers of guns,
Took the breath from our sails, and we
   stay'd.

VII

And while now the great San Philip hung
   above us like a cloud
Whence the thunderbolt will fall
Long and loud,
Four galleons drew away
From the Spanish fleet that day,
And two upon the larboard and two upon
   the starboard lay,
And the battle-thunder broke from them all.

VIII

But anon the great San Philip, she bethought herself and went
Having that within her womb that had left
   her ill content;
And the rest they came aboard us, and they
   fought us hand to hand,
For a dozen times they came with their
   pikes and musqueteers,
And a dozen times we shook 'em off as a
   dog that shakes his ears
When he leaps from the water to the land.

IX

And the sun went down, and the stars
   came out far over the summer sea,
But never a moment ceased the fight of the
   one and the fifty-three.
Ship after ship, the whole night long, their
   high-built galleons came,
Ship after ship, the whole night long, with
   her battle-thunder and flame;
Ship after ship, the whole night long, drew
   back with her dead and her shame.
For some were sunk and many were shatter'd, and so could fight us no more—
God of battles, was ever a battle like this in
   the world before?

X

For he said 'Fight on! fight on!'
Tho' his vessel was all but a wreck;

And it chanced that, when half of the short
    summer night was gone,
With a grisly wound to be drest he had left
    the deck,
But a bullet struck him that was dressing
    it suddenly dead,
And himself he was wounded again in the
    side and the head,
And he said 'Fight on! fight on!'

XI

And the night went down, and the sun
    smiled out far over the summer sea,
And the Spanish fleet with broken sides
    lay round us all in a ring;
But they dared not touch us again, for they
    fear'd that we still could sting,
So they watch'd what the end would be.
And we had not fought them in vain,
But in perilous plight were we,
Seeing forty of our poor hundred were
    slain,
And half of the rest of us maim'd for life
In the crash of the cannonades and the
    desperate strife;
And the sick men down in the hold were
    most of them stark and cold,
And the pikes were all broken or bent, and
    the powder was all of it spent;
And the masts and the rigging were lying
    over the side;
But Sir Richard cried in his English pride,
'We have fought such a fight for a day and
    a night
As may never be fought again!
We have won great glory, my men!
And a day less or more
At sea or ashore,
We die—does it matter when?
Sink me the ship, Master Gunner—sink
    her, split her in twain!
Fall into the hands of God, not into the
    hands of Spain!'

XII

And the gunner said 'Ay, ay,' but the sea-
    men made reply:
'We have children, we have wives,
And the Lord hath spared our lives.
We will make the Spaniard promise, if we
    yield, to let us go;

We shall live to fight again and to strike
    another blow.'
And the lion there lay dying, and they
    yielded to the foe.

XIII

And the stately Spanish men to their flag-
    ship bore him then,
Where they laid him by the mast, old Sir
    Richard caught at last,
And they praised him to his face with their
    courtly foreign grace;
But he rose upon their decks, and he cried:
'I have fought for Queen and Faith like a
    valiant man and true;
I have only done my duty as a man is
    bound to do:
With a joyful spirit I Sir Richard Grenville
    die!'
And he fell upon their decks, and he died.

XIV

And they stared at the dead that had been
    so valiant and true,
And had holden the power and glory of
    Spain so cheap
That he dared her with one little ship and
    his English few;
Was he devil or man? He was devil for
    aught they knew,
But they sank his body with honour down
    into the deep,
And they mann'd the Revenge with a
    swarthier alien crew,
And away she sail'd with her loss and
    long'd for her own;
When a wind from the lands they had
    ruin'd awoke from sleep,
And the water began to heave and the
    weather to moan,
And or ever that evening ended a great gale
    blew,
And a wave like the wave that is raised by
    an earthquake grew,
Till it smote on their hulls and their sails
    and their masts and their flags,
And the whole sea plunged and fell on the
    shot-shatter'd navy of Spain,
And the little Revenge herself went down
    by the island crags
To be lost evermore in the main.

THE SISTERS

THEY have left the doors ajar; and by their
    clash,
And prelude on the keys, I know the song,
Their favourite—which I call 'The Tables
    Turned.'
Evelyn begins it 'O diviner Air.'

EVELYN

O diviner Air,
Thro' the heat, the drowth, the dust, the
    glare,
Far from out the west in shadowing
    showers,
Over all the meadow baked and bare,
Making fresh and fair
All the bowers and the flowers,
Fainting flowers, faded bowers,
Over all this weary world of ours,
Breathe, diviner Air!

A sweet voice that—you scarce could better
    that.
Now follows Edith echoing Evelyn.

EDITH

O diviner light,
Thro' the cloud that roofs our noon with
    night,
Thro' the blotting mist, the blinding
    showers,
Far from out a sky for ever bright,
Over all the woodland's flooded bowers,
Over all the meadow's drowning flowers,
Over all this ruin'd world of ours,
Break, diviner light!

Marvellously like, their voices—and them-
    selves!
Tho' one is somewhat deeper than the
    other,
As one is somewhat graver than the other—
Edith than Evelyn. Your good Uncle,
    whom
You count the father of your fortune, longs
For this alliance: let me ask you then,
Which voice most takes you? for I do not
    doubt
Being a watchful parent, you are taken
With one or other: tho' sometimes I fear
You may be flickering, fluttering in a doubt

Between the two—which must not be—
    which might
Be death to one: they both are beautiful:
Evelyn is gayer, wittier, prettier, says
The common voice, if one may trust it: she?
No! but the paler and the graver, Edith.
Woo her and gain her then: no wavering,
    boy!
The graver is perhaps the one for you
Who jest and laugh so easily and so well.
For love will go by contrast, as by likes.

No sisters ever prized each other more.
Not so: their mother and her sister loved
More passionately still.
                    But that my best
And oldest friend, your Uncle, wishes it,
And that I know you worthy everyway
To be my son, I might, perchance, be loath
To part them, or part from them: and yet
    one
Should marry, or all the broad lands in
    your view
From this bay window—which our house
    has held
Three hundred years—will pass collater-
    ally.

My father with a child on either knee,
A hand upon the head of either child,
Smoothing their locks, as golden as his own
Were silver, 'get them wedded' would he
    say.
And once my prattling Edith ask'd him
    'why?'
Ay, why? said he, 'for why should I go
    lame?'
Then told them of his wars, and of his
    wound.
For see—this wine—the grape from
    whence it flow'd
Was blackening on the slopes of Portugal,
When that brave soldier, down the terrible
    ridge
Plunged in the last fierce charge at
    Waterloo,
And caught the laming bullet. He left me
    this,
Which yet retains a memory of its youth,
As I of mine, and my first passion. Come!
Here's to your happy union with my child!

473

Yet must you change your name: no
fault of mine!
You say that you can do it as willingly
As birds make ready for their bridal-time
By change of feather: for all that, my boy,
Some birds are sick and sullen when they
moult.
An old and worthy name! but mine that
stirr'd
Among our civil wars and earlier too
Among the Roses, the more venerable.
I care not for a name—no fault of mine.
Once more—a happier marriage than my
own!

You see yon Lombard poplar on the
plain.
The highway running by it leaves a breadth
Of sward to left and right, where, long ago,
One bright May morning in a world of
song,
I lay at leisure, watching overhead
The aërial poplar wave, an amber spire.

I dozed; I woke. An open landaulet
Whirl'd by, which, after it had past me,
show'd
Turning my way, the loveliest face on earth.
The face of one there sitting opposite,
On whom I brought a strange unhappiness,
That time I did not see.

                    Love at first sight
May seem—with goodly rhyme and reason
for it—
Possible—at first glimpse, and for a face
Gone in a moment—strange. Yet once,
when first
I came on lake Llanberris in the dark,
A moonless night with storm—one light-
ning-fork
Flash'd out the lake; and tho' I loiter'd
there
The full day after, yet in retrospect
That less than momentary thunder-sketch
Of lake and mountain conquers all the day.

The Sun himself has limn'd the face
for me.
Not quite so quickly, no, nor half as well.
For look you here—the shadows are too
deep,
And like the critic's blurring comment
make
The veriest beauties of the work appear
The darkest faults: the sweet eyes frown:
the lips
Seem but a gash. My sole memorial
Of Edith—no, the other,—both indeed.

So that bright face was flash'd thro'
sense and soul
And by the poplar vanish'd—to be found
Long after, as it seem'd, beneath the tall
Tree-bowers, and those long-sweeping
beechen boughs
Of our New Forest. I was there alone:
The phantom of the whirling landaulet
For ever past me by: when one quick peal
Of laughter drew me thro' the glimmering
glades
Down to the snowlike sparkle of a cloth
On fern and foxglove. Lo, the face again,
My Rosalind in this Arden—Edith—all
One bloom of youth, health, beauty, happi-
ness,
And moved to merriment at a passing jest.

There one of those about her knowing
me
Call'd me to join them; so with these I
spent
What seem'd my crowning hour, my day
of days.

I woo'd her then, nor unsuccessfully,
The worse for her, for me! was I content?
Ay—no, not quite; for now and then I
thought
Laziness, vague love-longings, the bright
May,
Had made a heated haze to magnify
The charm of Edith—that a man's ideal
Is high in Heaven, and lodged with Plato's
God,
Not findable here—content, and not con-
tent,
In some such fashion as a man may be
That having had the portrait of his friend
Drawn by an artist, looks at it, and says,
'Good! very like! not altogether he.'

As yet I had not bound myself by words,
Only, believing I loved Edith, made

Edith love *me*. Then came the day when I,
Flattering myself that all my doubts were
    fools
Born of the fool this Age that doubts of
    all—
Not I that day of Edith's love or mine—
Had braced my purpose to declare myself:
I stood upon the stairs of Paradise.
The golden gates would open at a word.
I spoke it—told her of my passion, seen
And lost and found again, had got so far,
Had caught her hand, her eyelids fell—I
    heard
Wheels, and a noise of welcome at the
    doors—
On a sudden after two Italian years
Had set the blossom of her health again,
The younger sister, Evelyn, enter'd—
    there,
There was the face, and altogether she.
The mother fell about the daughter's neck,
The sisters closed in one another's arms,
Their people throng'd about them from
    the hall,
And in the thick of question and reply
I fled the house, driven by one angel face,
And all the Furies.

           I was bound to her;
I could not free myself in honour—bound
Not by the sounded letter of the word,
But counterpressures of the yielded hand
That timorously and faintly echoed mine,
Quick blushes, the sweet dwelling of her
    eyes
Upon me when she thought I did not see—
Were these not bonds? nay, nay, but could
    I wed her
Loving the other? do her that great wrong?
Had I not dream'd I loved her yester-
    morn?
Had I not known where Love, at first a fear,
Grew after marriage to full height and
    form?
Yet after marriage, that mock-sister there—
Brother-in-law—the fiery nearness of it—
Unlawful and disloyal brotherhood—
What end but darkness could ensue from
    this
For all the three? So Love and Honour
    jarr'd

Tho' Love and Honour join'd to raise the
    full
High-tide of doubt that sway'd me up and
    down
Advancing nor retreating.

               Edith wrote:
'My mother bids me ask' (I did not tell
    you—
A widow with less guile than many a child.
God help the wrinkled children that are
    Christ's
As well as the plump cheek—she wrought
    us harm,
Poor soul, not knowing) 'are you ill?' (so
    ran
The letter) 'you have not been here of
    late.
You will not find me here. At last I go
On that long-promised visit to the North.
I told your wayside story to my mother
And Evelyn. She remembers you. Farewell.
Pray come and see my mother. Almost
    blind
With ever-growing cataract, yet she thinks
She sees you when she hears. Again fare-
    well.'

Cold words from one I had hoped to
    warm so far
That I could stamp my image on her heart!
'Pray come and see my mother, and fare-
    well.'
Cold, but as welcome as free airs of heaven
After a dungeon's closeness. Selfish,
    strange!
What dwarfs are men! my strangled vanity
Utter'd a stifled cry—to have vext myself
And all in vain for her—cold heart or none—
No bride for me. Yet so my path was clear
To win the sister.

           Whom I woo'd and won.

For Evelyn knew not of my former suit,
Because the simple mother work'd upon
By Edith pray'd me not to whisper of it.
And Edith would be bridesmaid on the day.

But on that day, not being all at ease,
I from the altar glancing back upon her,
Before the first 'I will' was utter'd, saw

The bridesmaid pale, statuelike, passionless—
'No harm, no harm' I turn'd again, and
placed
My ring upon the finger of my bride.

So, when we parted, Edith spoke no
word,
She wept no tear, but round my Evelyn
clung
In utter silence for so long, I thought
'What, will she never set her sister free?'

We left her, happy each in each, and
then,
As tho' the happiness of each in each
Were not enough, must fain have torrents,
lakes,
Hills, the great things of Nature and the
fair,
To lift us as it were from commonplace,
And help us to our joy. Better have sent
Our Edith thro' the glories of the earth,
To change with her horizon, if true Love
Were not his own imperial all-in-all.

Far off we went. My God, I would not
live
Save that I think this gross hard-seeming
world
Is our misshaping vision of the Powers
Behind the world, that make our griefs our
gains.

For on the dark night of our marriage-
day
The great Tragedian, that had quench'd
herself
In that assumption of the bridesmaid—she
That loved me—our true Edith—her brain
broke
With over-acting, till she rose and fled
Beneath a pitiless rush of Autumn rain
To the deaf church—to be let in—to pray
Before that altar—so I think; and there
They found her beating the hard Protest-
ant doors.
She died and she was buried ere we knew.

I learnt it first. I had to speak. At once
The bright quick smile of Evelyn, that had
sunn'd

The morning of our marriage, past away:
And on our home-return the daily want
Of Edith in the house, the garden, still
Haunted us like her ghost; and by and by,
Either from that necessity for talk
Which lives with blindness, or plain
innocence
Of nature, or desire that her lost child
Should earn from both the praise of
heroism,
The mother broke her promise to the dead,
And told the living daughter with what
love
Edith had welcomed my brief wooing of
her,
And all her sweet self-sacrifice and death.

Henceforth that mystic bond betwixt
the twins—
Did I not tell you they were twins?—
prevail'd
So far that no caress could win my wife
Back to that passionate answer of full heart
I had from her at first. Not that her love,
Tho' scarce as great as Edith's power of
love,
Had lessen'd, but the mother's garrulous
wail
For ever woke the unhappy Past again,
Till that dead bridesmaid, meant to be my
bride,
Put forth cold hands between us, and I
fear'd
The very fountains of her life were chill'd;
So took her thence, and brought her here,
and here
She bore a child, whom reverently we call'd
Edith; and in the second year was born
A second—this I named from her own self,
Evelyn; then two weeks—no more—she
joined,
In and beyond the grave, that one she
loved.

Now in this quiet of declining life,
Thro' dreams by night and trances of the
day,
The sisters glide about me hand in hand,
Both beautiful alike, nor can I tell
One from the other, no, nor care to tell
One from the other, only know they come,

They smile upon me, till, remembering
  all
The love they both have borne me, and the
  love
I bore them both—divided as I am
From either by the stillness of the grave—
I know not which of these I love the best.

But *you* love Edith; and her own true
  eyes
Are traitors to her; our quick Evelyn—
The merrier, prettier, wittier, as they talk,
And not without good reason, my good
  son—
Is yet untouch'd: and I that hold them
  both
Dearest of all things—well, I am not sure—
But if there lie a preference eitherway,
And in the rich vocabulary of Love
'Most dearest' be a true superlative—
I think *I* likewise love your Edith most.

THE VILLAGE WIFE; OR, THE ENTAIL[1]

I

'OUSE-KEEPER sent tha my lass, fur New
  Squire coom'd last night.
Butter an' heggs—yis—yis. I'll goä wi' tha
  back: all right;
Butter I warrants be prime, an' I warrants
  the heggs be as well,
Hafe a pint o' milk runs out when ya
  breäks the shell.

II

Sit thysen down fur a bit: hev a glass o'
  cowslip wine!
I liked the owd Squire an' 'is gells as thaw
  they was gells o' mine,
Fur then we was all es one, the Squire an'
  'is darters an' me,
Hall but Miss Annie, the heldest, I niver
  not took to she:
But Nelly, the last of the cletch,[2] I liked
  'er the fust on 'em all,
Fur hoffens we talkt o' my darter es died
  o' the fever at fall:

[1] See note to 'Northern Cobbler.'
[2] A brood of chickens.

An' I thowt 'twur the will o' the Lord, but
  Miss Annie she said it wur draäins,
Fur she hedn't naw coomfut in 'er, an'
  arn'd naw thanks fur 'er paäins.
Eh! thebbe all wi' the Lord my childer,
  I han't gotten none!
Sa new Squire's coom'd wi' 'is taäil in 'is
  'and, an' owd Squire's gone.

III

Fur 'staäte be i' taäil, my lass: tha dosn'
  knaw what that be?
But I knaws the law, I does, for the lawyer
  ha towd it me.
'When theer's naw 'eäd to a 'Ouse by the
  fault o' that ere maäle—
The gells they counts fur nowt, and the
  next un he taäkes the taäil.'

IV

What be the next un like? can tha tell ony
  harm on 'im, lass?—
Naay sit down—naw 'urry—sa cowd!—
  hev another glass!
Straänge an' cowd fur the time! we may
  happen a fall o' snaw—
Not es I cares fur to hear ony harm, but
  I likes to knaw.
An' I 'oäps es 'e beänt boooklarn'd: but 'e
  dosn' not coom fro' the shere;
We'd anew o' that wi' the Squire, an' we
  haätes boooklarnin' ere.

V

Fur Squire wur a Varsity scholard, an'
  niver lookt arter the land—
Whoäts or tonups or taätes—'e 'ed hallus
  a boook 'i 'is 'and,
Hallus aloän wi' 'is boooks, thaw nigh upo'
  seventy year.
An' boooks, what's boooks? thou knaws
  thebbe naither 'ere nor theer.

VI

An' the gells, they hedn't naw taäils, an'
  the lawyer he towd it me
That 'is taäil were soä tied up es he
  couldn't cut down a tree!
'Drat the trees,' says I, to be sewer I
  haätes 'em, my lass,
Fur we puts the muck o' the land an' they
  sucks the muck fro' the grass.

477

VII

An' Squire wur hallus a-smilin', an' gied
  to the tramps goin' by—
An' all o' the wust i' the parish—wi'
  hoffens a drop in 'is eye.
An' ivry darter o' Squire's hed her awn
  ridin-erse to 'ersen,
An' they rampaged about wi' their grooms,
  an' was 'untin' arter the men,
An' hallus a-dallackt[1] an' dizen'd out, an'
  a-buyin' new cloäthes,
While 'e sit like a greät glimmer-gowk[2] wi'
  'is glasses athurt 'is noäse,
An' 'is noäse sa grufted wi' snuff es it
  couldn't be scroob'd awaäy,
Fur atween 'is reädin' an' writing' 'e snifft
  up a box in a daäy,
An' 'e niver runn'd arter the fox, nor arter
  the birds wi' 'is gun,
An' 'e niver not shot one 'are, but 'e leäved
  it to Charlie 'is son,
An' 'e niver not fish'd 'is awn ponds, but
  Charlie 'e cotch'd the pike,
For 'e warn't not burn to the land, an' 'e
  didn't take kind to it like;
But I eärs es 'e'd gie fur a howry[3] owd book
  thutty pound an' moor,
An' 'e'd wrote an owd book, his awn sen,
  sa I knaw'd es'e'd coom to be poor;
An' 'e gied—I be fear'd fur to tell tha 'ow
  much—fur an owd scratted stoän,
An' 'e digg'd up a loomp i' the land an' 'e
  got a brown pot an' a boän,
An' e' bowt owd money, es wouldn't goä,
  wi' good gowd o' the Queen,
An' 'e bowt little statutes all-naäkt an'
  which was a shaame to be seen;
But 'e niver looökt ower a bill, nor 'e niver
  not seed to owt,
An' 'e niver knawd nowt but boooks, an'
  boooks, as thou knaws, beänt nowt.

VIII

But owd Squire's laädy es long es she lived
  she kep 'em all clear,
Thaw es long es she lived I niver hed none
  of 'er darters 'ere;

---

[1] Overdrest in gay colours.
[2] Owl.   [3] Filthy.

But arter she died we was all es one, the
  childer an' me,
An' sarvints runn'd in an' out, an' offens
  we hed 'em to tea.
Lawk! 'ow I laugh'd when the lasses 'ud
  talk o' their Missis's waäys,
An' the Missisis talk'd o' the lasses.—I'll
  tell tha some o' these daäys.
Hoänly Miss Annie were saw stuck oop,
  like 'er mother afoor—
'Er an' 'er blessed darter—they niver
  derken'd my door.

IX

An' Squire 'e smiled an' 'e smiled till 'e'd
  gotten a fright at last,
An' 'e calls fur 'is son, fur the 'turney's
  letters they foller'd sa fast;
But Squire wur afear'd o' 'is son, an' 'e
  says to 'im, meek as a mouse,
'Lad, thou mun cut off thy taäil, or the
  gells 'ull goä to the 'Ouse,
Fur I finds es I be that i' debt, es I 'oäps
  es thou'll 'elp me a bit,
An' if thou'll 'gree to cut off thy taäil I may
  saäve mysen yit.'

X

But Charlie 'e sets back 'is ears, an' 'e
  sweärs, an' 'e says to 'im 'Noa.
I've gotten the 'staäte by the taäil an' be
  dang'd if I iver let goa!
Coom! coom! feyther,' 'e says, 'why
  shouldn't thy boooks be sowd?
I hears es soom o' thy boooks mebbe worth
  their weight i' gowd.'

XI

Heäps an' heäps o' boooks, I ha' see'd 'em,
  belong'd to the Squire,
But the lasses 'ed teärd out leäves i' the
  middle to kindle the fire,
Sa moäst on 'is owd big boooks fetch'd
  nigh to nowt at the saäle,
And Squire were at Charlie ageän to git
  'im to cut off 'is taäil.

XII

Ya wouldn't find Charlie's likes—'e were
  that outdacious at 'oäm,
Not thaw ya went fur to raäke out Hell wi'
  a small-tooth coämb—

Droonk wi' the Quoloty's wine, an' droonk
    wi' the farmer's aäle,
Mad wi' the lasses an' all—an' 'e wouldn't
    cut off the taäil.

XIII

Thou's coom'd oop by the beck; and a
    thurn be a-grawin' theer,
I niver ha seed it sa white wi' the Maäy es
    I see'd it to-year—
Theerabouts Charlie joompt—and it gied
    me a scare tother night,
Fur I thowt it wur Charlie's ghoäst i' the
    derk, fur it looökt sa white.
'Billy,' says 'e, 'hev a joomp!'—thaw the
    banks o' the beck be sa high,
Fur he ca'd 'is 'erse Billy-rough-un, thaw
    niver a hair wur awry;
But Billy fell bakkuds o' Charlie, an'
    Charlie 'e brok 'is neck,
Sa theer wur a hend o' the taäil, fur 'e lost
    'is taäil i' the beck.

XIV

Sa 'is taäil wur lost an' 'is booöks wur gone
    an' 'is boy wur deäd,
An' Squire 'e smiled an' 'e smiled, but 'e
    niver not lift oop 'is 'eäd:
Hallus a soft un Squire! an' 'e smiled, fur
    'e hedn't naw friend,
Sa feyther an' son was buried togither, an'
    this wur the hend.

XV

An' Parson as hesn't the call, nor the
    mooney, but hes the pride,
'E reäds of a sewer an' sartan 'oäp o' the
    tother side;
But I beänt that sewer es the Lord, how-
    siver they praäy'd an' praäy'd,
Lets them inter 'eaven eäsy es leäves their
    debts to be paäid.
Siver the mou'ds rattled down upo' poor
    owd Squire i' the wood,
An' I cried along wi' the gells, fur they
    weänt niver coom to naw good.

XVI

Fur Molly the long un she walkt awaäy wi'
    a hofficer lad,
An' nawbody 'eärd on 'er sin, sa o' coorse
    she be gone to the bad!

An' Lucy wur laäme o' one leg, sweet'arts
    she niver 'ed none—
Straänge an' unheppen[1] Miss Lucy! we
    naämed her 'Dot an' gaw one!'
An' Hetty wur weak i' the hattics, wi'out
    ony harm i' the legs,
An' the fever 'ed baäked Jinny's 'eäd as
    bald as one o' them heggs,
An' Nelly wur up fro' the craädle as big i'
    the mouth as a cow,
An' saw she mun hammergrate,[2] lass, or
    she weänt git a maäte onyhow!
An' es for Miss Annie es call'd me afoor
    my awn foälks to my faäce
'A hignorant village wife as 'ud heve to be
    larn'd her awn plaäce,'
Hes fur Miss Hannie the heldest hes now
    be a-grawin' sa howd,
I knaws that mooch o' sheä, es it beänt not
    fit to be towd!

XVII

Sa I didn't not taäke it kindly ov owd Miss
    Annie to saäy
Es I should be talkin ageän 'em, es soon es
    they went awaäy,
Fur, lawks! 'ow I cried when they went,
    an' our Nelly she gied me 'er 'and,
Fur I'd ha done owt for the Squire an' 'is
    gells es belong'd to the land;
Booöks, es I said afoor, thebbe neyther 'ere
    nor theer!
But I sarved 'em wi' butter an' heggs fur
    huppuds o' twenty year.

XVIII

An' they hallus paäid what I hax'd, sa I
    hallus deal'd wi' the Hall,
An' they knaw'd what butter wur, an' they
    knaw'd what a hegg wur an' all;
Hugger-mugger they lived, but they wasn't
    that eäsy to pleäse,
Till I gied 'em Hinjian curn, an' they laäid
    big heggs es tha seeas;
An' I niver puts saäme[3] i' my butter, they
    does it at Willis's farm,
Taäste another drop o' the wine—tweänt
    do tha naw harm.

[1] Ungainly, awkward.
[2] Emigrate.   [3] Lard.

XIX

Sa new Squire's coom'd wi' 'is taäil in 'is
  'and, an' owd Squire's gone;
I heard 'im a roomlin' by, but arter my
  nightcap wur on;
Sa I hadn't clapt eyes on 'im yit, fur he
  coom'd last night sa laäte—
Pluksh! ! !¹ the hens i' the peäs! why
  didn't tha hesp the gaäte?

IN THE CHILDREN'S
HOSPITAL

EMMIE

I

Our doctor had call'd in another, I never
  had seen him before,
But he sent a chill to my heart when I saw
  him come in at the door,
Fresh from the surgery-schools of France
  and of other lands—
Harsh red hair, big voice, big chest, big
  merciless hands!
Wonderful cures he had done, O yes, but
  they said too of him
He was happier using the knife than in
  trying to save the limb,
And that I can well believe, for he look'd
  so coarse and so red,
I could think he was one of those who
  would break their jests on the dead,
And mangle the living dog that had loved
  him and fawn'd at his knee—
Drench'd with the hellish oorali—that ever
  such things should be!

II

Here was a boy—I am sure that some of
  our children would die
But for the voice of Love, and the smile,
  and the comforting eye—
Here was a boy in the ward, every bone
  seem'd out of its place—
Caught in a mill and crush'd—it was all
  but a hopeless case:
And he handled him gently enough; but
  his voice and his face were not kind,
And it was but a hopeless case, he had seen
  it and made up his mind,

¹ A cry accompanied by a clapping of hands
to scare trespassing fowl.

And he said to me roughly 'The lad will
  need little more of your care.'
'All the more need,' I told him, 'to seek
  the Lord Jesus in prayer;
They are all his children here, and I pray
  for them all as my own:'
But he turn'd to me, 'Ay, good woman, can
  prayer set a broken bone?'
Then he mutter'd half to himself, but I
  know that I heard him say
'All very well—but the good Lord Jesus
  has had his day.'

III

Had? has it come? It has only dawn'd. It
  will come by and by.
O how could I serve in the wards if the
  hope of the world were a lie?
How could I bear with the sights and the
  loathsome smells of disease
But that He said 'Ye do it to me, when ye
  do it to these'?

IV

So he went. And we past to this ward where
  the younger children are laid:
Here is the cot of our orphan, our darling,
  our meek little maid;
Empty you see just now! We have lost her
  who loved her so much—
Patient of pain tho' as quick as a sensitive
  plant to the touch;
Hers was the prettiest prattle, it often
  moved me to tears,
Hers was the gratefullest heart I have found
  in a child of her years—
Nay you remember our Emmie; you used
  to send her the flowers;
How she would smile at 'em, play with
  'em, talk to 'em hours after hours!
They that can wander at will where the
  works of the Lord are reveal'd
Little guess what joy can be got from a
  cowslip out of the field;
Flowers to these 'spirits in prison' are all
  they can know of the spring,
They freshen and sweeten the wards like
  the waft of an Angel's wing;
And she lay with a flower in one hand and
  her thin hands crost on her breast—
Wan, but as pretty as heart can desire, and
  we thought her at rest,

Quietly sleeping—so quiet, our doctor said
  'Poor little dear,
Nurse, I must do it to-morrow; she'll never
  live thro' it, I fear.'

V

I walk'd with our kindly old doctor as far
  as the head of the stair,
Then I return'd to the ward; the child
  didn't see I was there.

VI

Never since I was nurse, had I been so
  grieved and so vext!
Emmie had heard him. Softly she call'd
  from her cot to the next,
'He says I shall never live thro' it, O Annie,
  what shall I do?'
Annie consider'd. 'If I,' said the wise little
  Annie, 'was you,
I should cry to the dear Lord Jesus to help
  me, for, Emmie, you see,
It's all in the picture there: "Little children
  should come to me."'
(Meaning the print that you gave us, I find
  that it always can please
Our children, the dear Lord Jesus with
  children about his knees.)
'Yes, and I will,' said Emmie, 'but then if
  I call to the Lord,
How should he know that it's me? such a
  lot of beds in the ward!'
That was a puzzle for Annie. Again she
  consider'd and said:
'Emmie, you put out your arms, and you
  leave 'em outside on the bed—
The Lord has so *much* to see to! but,
  Emmie, you tell it him plain,
It's the little girl with her arms lying out
  on the counterpane.'

VII

I had sat three nights by the child—I could
  not watch her for four—
My brain had begun to reel—I felt I could
  do it no more.
That was my sleeping-night, but I thought
  that it never would pass.
There was a thunderclap once, and a clatter
  of hail on the glass,

And there was a phantom cry that I heard
  as I tost about,
The motherless bleat of a lamb in the
  storm and the darkness without;
My sleep was broken besides with dreams
  of the dreadful knife
And fears for our delicate Emmie who
  scarce would escape with her life;
Then in the gray of the morning it seem'd
  she stood by me and smiled,
And the doctor came at his hour, and we
  went to see to the child.

VIII

He had brought his ghastly tools: we believed her asleep again—
Her dear, long, lean, little arms lying out
  on the counterpane;
Say that His day is done! Ah why should
  we care what they say?
The Lord of the children had heard her,
  and Emmie had past away.

DEDICATORY POEM TO THE PRINCESS ALICE

DEAD PRINCESS, living Power, if that, which
  lived
True life, live on—and if the fatal kiss,
Born of true life and love, divorce thee not
From earthly love and life—if what we call
The spirit flash not all at once from out
This shadow into Substance—then perhaps
The mellow'd murmur of the people's
  praise
From thine own State, and all our breadth
  of realm,
Where Love and Longing dress thy deeds
  in light,
Ascends to thee; and this March morn that
  sees
Thy Soldier-brother's bridal orange-bloom
Break thro' the yews and cypress of thy
  grave,
And thine Imperial mother smile again.
May send one ray to thee! and who can
  tell—
Thou—England's England-loving daugh-
  ter—thou
Dying so English thou wouldst have her
  flag

Borne on thy coffin—where is he can swear
But that some broken gleam from our poor
   earth
May touch thee, while remembering thee,
   I lay
At thy pale feet this ballad of the deeds
Of England, and her banner in the East?

THE DEFENCE OF LUCKNOW

I

BANNER of England, not for a season, O
   banner of Britain, hast thou
Floated in conquering battle or flapt to the
   battle-cry!
Never with mightier glory than when we
   had rear'd thee on high
Flying at top of the roofs in the ghastly
   siege of Lucknow—
Shot thro' the staff or the halyard, but ever
   we raised thee anew,
And ever upon the topmost roof our banner
   of England blew.

II

Frail were the works that defended the
   hold that we held with our lives—
Women and children among us, God help
   them, our children and wives!
Hold it we might—and for fifteen days or
   for twenty at most.
'Never surrender, I charge you, but every
   man die at his post!'
Voice of the dead whom we loved, our
   Lawrence the best of the brave:
Cold were his brows when we kiss'd him—
   we laid him that night in his grave.
'Every man die at his post!' and there
   hail'd on our houses and halls
Death from their rifle-bullets, and death
   from their cannon-balls,
Death in our innermost chamber, and
   death at our slight barricade,
Death while we stood with the musket, and
   death while we stoopt to the spade,
Death to the dying, and wounds to the
   wounded, for often there fell,
Striking the hospital wall, crashing thro' it,
   their shot and their shell,

Death—for their spies were among us, their
   marksmen were told of our best,
So that the brute bullet broke thro' the
   brain that could think for the rest;
Bullets would sing by our foreheads, and
   bullets would rain at our feet—
Fire from ten thousand at once of the
   rebels that girdled us round—
Death at the glimpse of a finger from over
   the breadth of a street,
Death from the heights of the mosque and
   the palace, and death in the ground!
Mine? yes, a mine! Countermine! down,
   down! and creep thro' the hole!
Keep the revolver in hand! you can hear
   him—the murderous mole!
Quiet, ah! quiet—wait till the point of the
   pickaxe be thro'!
Click with the pick, coming nearer and
   nearer again than before—
Now let it speak, and you fire, and the dark
   pioneer is no more;
And ever upon the topmost roof our banner
   of England blew!

III

Ay, but the foe sprung his mine many
   times, and it chanced on a day
Soon as the blast of that underground
   thunderclap echo'd away,
Dark thro' the smoke and the sulphur like
   so many fiends in their hell—
Cannon-shot, musket-shot, volley on
   volley, and yell upon yell—
Fiercely on all the defences our myriad
   enemy fell.
What have they done? where is it? Out
   yonder. Guard the Redan!
Storm at the Water-gate! storm at the
   Bailey-gate! storm, and it ran
Surging and swaying all round us, as ocean
   on every side
Plunges and heaves at a bank that is daily
   devour'd by the tide—
So many thousands that if they be bold
   enough, who shall escape?
Kill or be kill'd, live or die, they shall know
   we are soldiers and men!
Ready! take aim at their leaders—their
   masses are gapp'd with our grape—

Backward they reel like the wave, like the wave flinging forward again,
Flying and foil'd at the last by the handful they could not subdue;
And ever upon the topmost roof our banner of England blew.

IV

Handful of men as we were, we were English in heart and in limb,
Strong with the strength of the race to command, to obey, to endure,
Each of us fought as if hope for the garrison hung but on him;
Still—could we watch at all points? we were every day fewer and fewer.
There was a whisper among us, but only a whisper that past:
'Children and wives—if the tigers leap into the fold unawares—
Every man die at his post—and the foe may outlive us at last—
Better to fall by the hands that they love, than to fall into theirs!'
Roar upon roar in a moment two mines by the enemy sprung
Clove into perilous chasms our walls and our poor palisades.
Rifleman, true is your heart, but be sure that your hand be as true!
Sharp is the fire of assault, better aimed are your flank fusillades—
Twice do we hurl them to earth from the ladders to which they had clung,
Twice from the ditch where they shelter we drive them with hand-grenades;
And ever upon the topmost roof our banner of England blew.

V

Then on another wild morning another wild earthquake out-tore
Clean from our lines of defence ten or twelve good paces or more.
Rifleman, high on the roof, hidden there from the light of the sun—
One has leapt up on the breach, crying out: 'Follow me, follow me!'—
Mark him—he falls! then another, and *him* too, and down goes he.

Had they been bold enough then, who can tell but the traitors had won?
Boardings and rafters and doors—an embrasure! make way for the gun!
Now double-charge it with grape! It is charged and we fire, and they run.
Praise to our Indian brothers, and let the dark face have his due!
Thanks to the kindly dark faces who fought with us, faithful and few,
Fought with the bravest among us, and drove them, and smote them, and slew,
That ever upon the topmost roof our banner in India blew.

VI

Men will forget what we suffer and not what we do. We can fight!
But to be soldier all day and be sentinel all thro' the night—
Ever the mine and assault, our sallies, their lying alarms,
Bugles and drums in the darkness, and shoutings and soundings to arms,
Ever the labour of fifty that had to be done by five,
Ever the marvel among us that one should be left alive,
Ever the day with its traitorous death from the loopholes around,
Ever the night with its coffinless corpse to be laid in the ground,
Heat like the mouth of a hell, or a deluge of cataract skies,
Stench of old offal decaying, and infinite torment of flies,
Thoughts of the breezes of May blowing over an English field,
Cholera, scurvy, and fever, the wound that *would* not be heal'd,
Lopping away of the limb by the pitiful-pitiless knife,—
Torture and trouble in vain,—for it never could save us a life.
Valour of delicate women who tended the hospital bed,
Horror of women in travail among the dying and dead,
Grief for our perishing children, and never a moment for grief,

Toil and ineffable weariness, faltering
hopes of relief,
Havelock baffled, or beaten, or butcher'd
for all that we knew—
Then day and night, day and night, coming
down on the still-shatter'd walls
Millions of musket-bullets, and thousands
of cannon-balls—
But ever upon the topmost roof our banner
of England blew.

VII

Hark cannonade, fusillade! is it true what
was told by the scout,
Outram and Havelock breaking their way
through the fell mutineers?
Surely the pibroch of Europe is ringing
again in our ears!
All on a sudden the garrison utter a jubilant
shout,
Havelock's glorious Highlanders answer
with conquering cheers,
Sick from the hospital echo them, women
and children come out,
Blessing the wholesome white faces of
Havelock's good fusileers,
Kissing the war-harden'd hand of the
Highlander wet with their tears!
Dance to the pibroch!—saved! we are
saved!—is it you? is it you?
Saved by the valour of Havelock, saved by
the blessing of Heaven!
'Hold it for fifteen days!' we have held it
for eighty-seven!
And ever aloft on the palace roof the old
banner of England blew.

SIR JOHN OLDCASTLE, LORD COBHAM

(IN WALES)

My friend should meet me somewhere
hereabout
To take me to that hiding in the hills.

I have broke their cage, no gilded one,
I trow—
I read no more the prisoner's mute wail
Scribbled or carved upon the pitiless stone;
I find hard rocks, hard life, hard cheer, or
none,

For I am emptier than a friar's brains;
But God is with me in this wilderness,
These wet black passes and foam-churning
chasms—
And God's free air, and hope of better
things.

I would I knew their speech; not now
to glean,
Not now—I hope to do it—some scatter'd
ears,
Some ears for Christ in this wild field of
Wales—
But, bread, merely for bread. This tongue
that wagg'd
They said with such heretical arrogance
Against the proud archbishop Arundel—
So much God's cause was fluent in it—is
here
But as a Latin Bible to the crowd;
'Bara!'—what use? The Shepherd, when
I speak,
Vailing a sudden eyelid with his hard
'Dim Saesneg' passes, wroth at things of
old—
No fault of mine. Had he God's word in
Welsh
He might be kindlier: happily come the
day!

Not least art thou, thou little Bethlehem
In Judah, for in thee the Lord was born;
Nor thou in Britain, little Lutterworth,
Least, for in thee the word was born again.

Heaven-sweet Evangel, ever-living word,
Who whilome spakest to the South in Greek
About the soft Mediterranean shores,
And then in Latin to the Latin crowd,
As good need was—thou hast come to talk
our isle.
Hereafter thou, fulfilling Pentecost,
Must learn to use the tongues of all the
world.
Yet art thou thine own witness that thou
bringest
Not peace, a sword, a fire.
                    What did he say,
My frighted Wiclif-preacher whom I crost
In flying hither? that one night a crowd
Throng'd the waste field about the city
gates:

The king was on them suddenly with a
host.
Why there? they came to hear their
preacher. Then
Some cried on Cobham, on the good Lord
Cobham;
Ay, for they love me! but the king—nor
voice
Nor finger raised against him—took and
hang'd,
Took, hang'd and burnt—how many—
thirty-nine—
Call'd it rebellion—hang'd, poor friends,
as rebels
And burn'd alive as heretics! for your
Priest
Labels—to take the king along with him—
All heresy, treason: but to call men
traitors
May make men traitors.
　　　　　　　　Rose of Lancaster,
Red in thy birth, redder with household
war,
Now reddest with the blood of holy men,
Redder to be, red rose of Lancaster—
If somewhere in the North, as Rumour
sang
Fluttering the hawks of this crown-lusting
line—
By firth and loch thy silver sister grow,[1]
That were my rose, there my allegiance
due.
Self-starved, they say—nay, murder'd,
doubtless dead.
So to this king I cleaved: my friend was he,
Once my fast friend: I would have given
my life
To help his own from scathe, a thousand
lives
To save his soul. He might have come to
learn
Our Wiclif's learning: but the worldly
Priests
Who fear the king's hard common-sense
should find
What rotten piles uphold their mason-
work,
Urge him to foreign war. O had he will'd
I might have stricken a lusty stroke for him,

But he would not; far liever led my
friend
Back to the pure and universal church,
But he would not: whether that heirless
flaw
In his throne's title make him feel so frail,
He leans on Antichrist; or that his mind,
So quick, so capable in soldiership,
In matters of the faith, alas the while!
More worth than all the kingdoms of this
world,
Runs in the rut, a coward to the Priest.

Burnt—good Sir Roger Acton, my dear
friend!
Burnt too, my faithful preacher, Beverley!
Lord give thou power to thy two witnesses!
Lest the false faith make merry over them!
Two—nay but thirty-nine have risen and
stand,
Dark with the smoke of human sacrifice,
Before thy light, and cry continually—
Cry—against whom?

　　　　　　Him, who should bear the sword
Of Justice—what! the kingly, kindly boy;
Who took the world so easily heretofore,
My boon companion, tavern-fellow—him
Who gibed and japed—in many a merry tale
That shook our sides—at Pardoners, Sum-
moners,
Friars, absolution-sellers, monkeries
And nunneries, when the wild hour and
the wine
Had set the wits aflame.
　　　　　　　　　　Harry of Monmouth,
Or Amurath of the East?
　　　　　　　　　　　　Better to sink
Thy fleurs-de-lys in slime again, and fling
Thy royalty back into the riotous fits
Of wine and harlotry—thy shame, and
mine,
Thy comrade—than to persecute the Lord,
And play the Saul that never will be Paul.

Burnt, burnt! and while this mitred
Arundel
Dooms our unlicensed preacher to the
flame,
The mitre-sanction'd harlot draws his
clerks

Into the suburb—their hard celibacy,
Sworn to be veriest ice of pureness, molten
Into adulterous living, or such crimes
As holy Paul—a shame to speak of them—
Among the heathen—
            Sanctuary granted
To bandit, thief, assassin—yea to him
Who hacks his mother's throat—denied to
   him,
Who finds the Saviour in his mother
   tongue.
The Gospel, the Priest's pearl, flung down
   to swine—
The swine, lay-men, lay-women, who will
   come,
God willing, to outlearn the filthy friar.
Ah rather, Lord, than that thy Gospel,
   meant
To course and range thro' all the world,
   should be
Tether'd to these dead pillars of the
   Church—
Rather than so, if thou wilt have it so,
Burst vein, snap sinew, and crack heart,
   and life
Pass in the fire of Babylon! but how long,
O Lord, how long!
        My friend should meet me here,
Here is the copse, the fountain and—a
   Cross!
To thee, dead wood, I bow not head nor
   knees.
Rather to thee, green boscage, work of
   God,
Black holly, and white-flower'd wayfaring-
   tree!
Rather to thee, thou living water, drawn
By this good Wiclif mountain down from
   heaven,
And speaking clearly in thy native tongue—
No Latin—He that thirsteth, come and
   drink!

Eh! how I anger'd Arundel asking me
To worship Holy Cross! I spread mine
   arms,
God's work, I said, a cross of flesh and
   blood
And holier. That was heresy. (My good
   friend
By this time should be with me.) 'Images?'

'Bury them as God's truer images
Are daily buried.' 'Heresy.—Penance?'
'Fast,
Hairshirt and scourge—nay, let a man
   repent,
Do penance in his heart, God hears him.'
'Heresy—
Not shriven, not saved?' 'What profits an
   ill Priest
Between me and my God? I would not
   spurn
Good counsel of good friends, but shrive
   myself
No, not to an Apostle.' 'Heresy.'
(My friend is long in coming.) 'Pil-
   grimages?'
'Drink, bagpipes, revelling, devil's-dances,
   vice.
The poor man's money gone to fat the
   friar.
Who reads of begging saints in Scripture?'
   —'Heresy'—
(Hath he been here—not found me—gone
   again?
Have I mislearnt our place of meeting?)
'Bread—
Bread left after the blessing?' how they
   stared,
That was their main test-question—glared
   at me!
'He veil'd Himself in flesh, and now He
   veils
His flesh in bread, body and bread to-
   gether.'
Then rose the howl of all the cassock'd
   wolves,
'No bread, no bread. God's body!' Arch-
   bishop, Bishop,
Priors, Canons, Friars, bellringers, Parish-
   clerks—
'No bread, no bread!'—'Authority of the
   Church,
Power of the keys!'—Then I, God help
   me, I
So mock'd, so spurn'd, so baited two whole
   days—
I lost myself and fell from evenness,
And rail'd at all the Popes, that ever since
Sylvester shed the venom of world-wealth
Into the church, had only prov'n them-
   selves

Poisoners, murderers. Well—God pardon
all—
Me, them, and all the world—yea, that
proud Priest,
That mock-meek mouth of utter Anti-
christ,
That traitor to King Richard and the truth,
Who rose and doom'd me to the fire.
                                        Amen!
Nay, I can burn, so that the Lord of life
Be by me in my death.
                    Those three! the fourth
Was like the Son of God! Not burnt were
they.
On *them* the smell of burning had not past.
That was a miracle to convert the king.
These Pharisees, this Caiaphas-Arundel
What miracle could turn? *He* here again,
He thwarting their traditions of Himself,
He would be found a heretic to Himself,
And doom'd to burn alive.
                    So, caught, I burn.
Burn? heathen men have borne as much
as this,
For freedom, or the sake of those they
loved,
Or some less cause, some cause far less
than mine;
For every other cause is less than mine.
The moth will singe her wings, and singed
return,
Her love of light quenching her fear of
pain—
How now, my soul, we do not heed the
fire?
Faint-hearted? tut!—faint-stomach'd!
faint as I am,
God willing, I will burn for Him.
                                Who comes?
A thousand marks are set upon my head.
Friend?—foe perhaps—a tussle for it then!
Nay, but my friend. Thou art so well
disguised,
I knew thee not. Hast thou brought bread
with thee?
I have not broken bread for fifty hours.
None? I am damn'd already by the Priest
For holding there was bread where bread
was none—
No bread. My friends await me yonder?
Yes.

Lead on then. *Up* the mountain? Is it far?
Not far. Climb first and reach me down
thy hand.
I am not like to die for lack of bread,
For I must live to testify by fire.[1]

COLUMBUS

CHAINS, my good lord: in your raised
brows I read
Some wonder at our chamber ornaments.
We brought this iron from our isles of gold.

Does the king know you deign to visit
him
Whom once he rose from off his throne to
greet
Before his people, like his brother king?
I saw your face that morning in the crowd.

At Barcelona—tho' you were not then
So bearded. Yes. The city deck'd herself
To meet me, roar'd my name; the king,
the queen
Bad me be seated, speak, and tell them all
The story of my voyage, and while I spoke
The crowd's roar fell as at the 'Peace, be
still!'
And when I ceased to speak, the king, the
queen,
Sank from their thrones, and melted into
tears,
And knelt, and lifted hand and heart and
voice
In praise to God who led me thro' the
waste.
And then the great 'Laudamus' rose to
heaven.

Chains for the Admiral of the Ocean!
chains
For him who gave a new heaven, a new
earth,
As holy John had prophesied of me,
Gave glory and more empire to the kings
Of Spain than all their battles! chains for
him
Who push'd his prows into the setting sun,
And made West East, and sail'd the
Dragon's mouth,

[1] He was burnt on Christmas Day, 1417

And came upon the Mountain of the World,
And saw the rivers roll from Paradise!

Chains! we are Admirals of the Ocean, we,
We and our sons for ever. Ferdinand
Hath sign'd it and our Holy Catholic queen—
Of the Ocean—of the Indies—Admirals we—
Our title, which we never mean to yield,
Our guerdon not alone for what we did,
But our amends for all we might have done—
The vast occasion of our stronger life—
Eighteen long years of waste, seven in your Spain,
Lost, showing courts and kings a truth the babe
Will suck in with his milk hereafter—
earth
A sphere.

Were *you* at Salamanca? No.
We fronted there the learning of all Spain,
All their cosmogonies, their astronomies:
Guess-work *they* guess'd it, but the golden guess
Is morning-star to the full round of truth.
No guess-work! I was certain of my goal;
Some thought it heresy, but that would not hold.
King David call'd the heavens a hide, a tent
Spread over earth, and so this earth was flat:
Some cited old Lactantius: could it be
That trees grew downward, rain fell upward, men
Walk'd like the fly on ceilings? and besides,
The great Augustine wrote that none could breathe
Within the zone of heat; so might there be
Two Adams, two mankinds, and that was clean
Against God's word: thus was I beaten back,
And chiefly to my sorrow by the Church,
And thought to turn my face from Spain, appeal

Once more to France or England; but our Queen
Recall'd me, for at last their Highnesses
Were half-assured this earth might be a sphere.

All glory to the all-blessed Trinity,
All glory to the mother of our Lord,
And Holy Church, from whom I never swerved
Not even by one hair's-breadth of heresy,
I have accomplish'd what I came to do.

Not yet—not all—last night a dream—I sail'd
On my first voyage, harass'd by the frights
Of my first crew, their curses and their groans.
The great flame-banner borne by Teneriffe,
The compass, like an old friend false at last
In our most need, appall'd them, and the wind
Still westward, and the weedy seas—at length
The landbird, and the branch with berries on it,
The carven staff—and last the light, the light
On Guanahani! but I changed the name;
San Salvador I call'd it; and the light
Grew as I gazed, and brought out a broad sky
Of dawning over—not those alien palms,
The marvel of that fair new nature—not
That Indian isle, but our most ancient East
Moriah with Jerusalem; and I saw
The glory of the Lord flash up, and beat
Thro' all the homely town from jasper, sapphire,
Chalcedony, emerald, sardonyx, sardius,
Chrysolite, beryl, topaz, chrysoprase,
Jacynth, and amethyst—and those twelve gates,
Pearl—and I woke, and thought—death—I shall die—
I am written in the Lamb's own Book of Life
To walk within the glory of the Lord
Sunless and moonless, utter light—but no!

The Lord had sent this bright, strange dream to me
To mind me of the secret vow I made
When Spain was waging war against the Moor—
I strove myself with Spain against the Moor.
There came two voices from the Sepulchre,
Two friars crying that if Spain should oust
The Moslem from her limit, he, the fierce
Soldan of Egypt, would break down and raze
The blessed tomb of Christ; whereon I vow'd
That, if our Princes harken'd to my prayer,
Whatever wealth I brought from that new world
Should, in this old, be consecrate to lead
A new crusade against the Saracen,
And free the Holy Sepulchre from thrall.

Gold? I had brought your Princes gold enough
If left alone! Being but a Genovese,
I am handled worse than had I been a Moor,
And breach'd the belting wall of Cambalu,
And given the Great Khan's palaces to the Moor,
Or clutch'd the sacred crown of Prester John,
And cast it to the Moor: but had I brought
From Solomon's now-recover'd Ophir all
The gold that Solomon's navies carried home,
Would that have gilded me? Blue blood of Spain,
Tho' quartering your own royal arms of Spain,
I have not: blue blood and black blood of Spain,
The noble and the convict of Castile,
Howl'd me from Hispaniola; for you know
The flies at home, that ever swarm about
And cloud the highest heads, and murmur down
Truth in the distance—these outbuzz'd me so
That even our prudent king, our righteous queen—
I pray'd them being so calumniated

They would commission one of weight and worth
To judge between my slander'd self and me—
Fonseca my main enemy at their court,
They sent me out his tool, Bovadilla, one
As ignorant and impolitic as a beast—
Blockish irreverence, brainless greed—who sack'd
My dwelling, seized upon my papers, loosed
My captives, feed the rebels of the crown,
Sold the crown-farms for all but nothing, gave
All but free leave for all to work the mines,
Drove me and my good brothers home in chains,
And gathering ruthless gold—a single piece
Weigh'd nigh four thousand Castillanos—so
They tell me—weigh'd him down into the abysm—
The hurricane of the latitude on him fell,
The seas of our discovering over-roll
Him and his gold; the frailer caravel,
With what was mine, came happily to the shore.
There was a glimmering of God's hand.

                                    And God
Hath more than glimmer'd on me. O my lord,
I swear to you I heard his voice between
The thunders in the black Veragua nights,
'O soul of little faith, slow to believe!
Have I not been about thee from thy birth?
Given thee the keys of the great Ocean-sea?
Set thee in light till time shall be no more?
Is it I who have deceived thee or the world?
Endure! thou hast done so well for men, that men
Cry out against thee: was it otherwise
With mine own Son?'

                    And more than once in days
Of doubt and cloud and storm, when drowning hope
Sank all but out of sight, I heard his voice,
'Be not cast down. I lead thee by the hand,

Fear not.' And I shall hear his voice
again—
I know that he has led me all my life,
I am not yet too old to work his will—
His voice again.

          Still for all that, my lord,
I lying here bedridden and alone,
Cast off, put by, scouted by court and
king—
The first discoverer starves—his followers,
all
Flower into fortune—our world's way—
and I,
Without a roof that I can call mine own,
With scarce a coin to buy a meal withal,
And seeing what a door for scoundrel
scum
I open'd to the West, thro' which the lust,
Villany, violence, avarice, of your Spain
Pour'd in on all those happy naked isles—
Their kindly native princes slain or slaved,
Their wives and children Spanish concu-
bines,
Their innocent hospitalities quench'd in
blood,
Some dead of hunger, some beneath the
scourge,
Some over-labour'd, some by their own
hands,—
Yea, the dear mothers, crazing Nature,
kill
Their babies at the breast for hate of
Spain—
Ah God, the harmless people whom we
found
In Hispaniola's island-Paradise!
Who took us for the very Gods from
Heaven,
And we have sent them very fiends from
Hell;
And I myself, myself not blameless, I
Could sometimes wish I had never led the
way.

    Only the ghost of our great Catholic
Queen
Smiles on me, saying, 'Be thou comforted!
This creedless people will be brought to
Christ
And own the holy governance of Rome.'

But who could dream that we, who bore
the Cross
Thither, were excommunicated there,
For curbing crimes that scandalised the
Cross,
By him, the Catalonian Minorite,
Rome's Vicar in our Indies? who believe
These hard memorials of our truth to
Spain
Clung closer to us for a longer term
Than any friend of ours at Court? and yet
Pardon—too harsh, unjust. I am rack'd
with pains.

You see that I have hung them by my
bed,
And I will have them buried in my grave.

Sir, in that flight of ages which are God's
Own voice to justify the dead—perchance
Spain once the most chivalric race on earth,
Spain then the mightiest, wealthiest realm
on earth,
So made by me, may seek to unbury me,
To lay me in some shrine of this old Spain,
Or in that vaster Spain I leave to Spain.
Then some one standing by my grave will
say,
'Behold the bones of Christopher Colòn'—
'Ay, but the chains, what do *they* mean—
the chains?'—
I sorrow for that kindly child of Spain
Who then will have to answer, 'These same
chains
Bound these same bones back thro' the
Atlantic sea,
Which he unchain'd for all the world to
come.'

O Queen of Heaven who seest the souls
in Hell
And purgatory, I suffer all as much
As they do—for the moment. Stay, my son
Is here anon: my son will speak for me
Ablier than I can in these spasms that grind
Bone against bone. You will not. One last
word.

You move about the Court, I pray you
tell
King Ferdinand who plays with me, that
one,

Whose life has been no play with him and
  his
Hidalgos—shipwrecks, famines, fevers,
  fights,
Mutinies, treacheries—wink'd at, and con-
  doned—
That I am loyal to him till the death,
And ready—tho' our Holy Catholic Queen,
Who fain had pledged her jewels on my
  first voyage,
Whose hope was mine to spread the
  Catholic faith,
Who wept with me when I return'd in
  chains,
Who sits beside the blessed Virgin now,
To whom I send my prayer by night and
  day—
She is gone—but you will tell the King,
  that I,
Rack'd as I am with gout, and wrench'd
  with pains
Gain'd in the service of His Highness, yet
Am ready to sail forth on one last voyage,
And readier, if the King would hear, to
  lead
One last crusade against the Saracen,
And save the Holy Sepulchre from thrall.

Going? I am old and slighted: you have
  dared
Somewhat perhaps in coming? my poor
  thanks!
I am but an alien and a Genovese.

THE VOYAGE OF MAELDUNE

(FOUNDED ON AN IRISH LEGEND.
A.D. 700)

I

I WAS the chief of the race—he had stricken
  my father dead—
But I gather'd my fellows together, I swore
  I would strike off his head.
Each of them look'd like a king, and was
  noble in birth as in worth,
And each of them boasted he sprang from
  the oldest race upon earth.
Each was as brave in the fight as the bravest
  hero of song,
And each of them liefer had died than
  have done one another a wrong.

He lived on an isle in the ocean—we sail'd,
  on a Friday morn—
He that had slain my father the day before
  I was born.

II

And we came to the isle in the ocean, and
  there on the shore was he.
But a sudden blast blew us out and away
  thro' a boundless sea.

III

And we came to the Silent Isle that we
  never had touch'd at before,
Where a silent ocean always broke on a
  silent shore,
And the brooks glitter'd on in the light
  without sound, and the long waterfalls
Pour'd in a thunderless plunge to the base
  of the mountain walls,
And the poplar and cypress unshaken by
  storm flourish'd up beyond sight,
And the pine shot aloft from the crag to an
  unbelievable height,
And high in the heaven above it there
  flicker'd a songless lark,
And the cock couldn't crow, and the bull
  couldn't low, and the dog couldn't
  bark.
And round it we went, and thro' it, but
  never a murmur, a breath—
It was all of it fair as life, it was all of it
  quiet as death,
And we hated the beautiful Isle, for whenever we strove to speak
Our voices were thinner and fainter than
  any flittermouse-shriek;
And the men that were mighty of tongue
  and could raise such a battle-cry
That a hundred who heard it would rush
  on a thousand lances and die—
O they to be dumb'd by the charm!—so
  fluster'd with anger were they
They almost fell on each other; but after
  we sail'd away.

IV

And we came to the Isle of Shouting, we
  landed, a score of wild birds
Cried from the topmost summit with
  human voices and words;

491

Once in an hour they cried, and whenever
    their voices peal'd
The steer fell down at the plow and the
    harvest died from the field,
And the men dropt dead in the valleys and
    half of the cattle went lame,
And the roof sank in on the hearth, and
    the dwelling broke into flame;
And the shouting of these wild birds ran
    into the hearts of my crew,
Till they shouted along with the shouting
    and seized one another and slew;
But I drew them the one from the other;
    I saw that we could not stay,
And we left the dead to the birds and we
    sail'd with our wounded away.

V

And we came to the Isle of Flowers: their
    breath met us out on the seas,
For the Spring and the middle Summer
    sat each on the lap of the breeze;
And the red passion-flower to the cliffs,
    and the dark-blue clematis, clung,
And starr'd with a myriad blossom the long
    convolvulus hung;
And the topmost spire of the mountain was
    lilies in lieu of snow,
And the lilies like glaciers winded down,
    running out below
Thro' the fire of the tulip and poppy, the
    blaze of gorse, and the blush
Of millions of roses that sprang without
    leaf or a thorn from the bush;
And the whole isle-side flashing down
    from the peak without ever a tree
Swept like a torrent of gems from the sky
    to the blue of the sea;
And we roll'd upon capes of crocus and
    vaunted our kith and our kin,
And we wallow'd in beds of lilies, and
    chanted the triumph of Finn,
Till each like a golden image was pollen'd
    from head to feet
And each was as dry as a cricket, with thirst
    in the middle-day heat.
Blossom and blossom, and promise of
    blossom, but never a fruit!
And we hated the Flowering Isle, as we
    hated the isle that was mute,

And we tore up the flowers by the million
    and flung them in bight and bay,
And we left but a naked rock, and in anger
    we sail'd away.

VI

And we came to the Isle of Fruits: all
    round from the cliffs and the capes,
Purple or amber, dangled a hundred
    fathom of grapes,
And the warm melon lay like a little sun on
    the tawny sand,
And the fig ran up from the beach and
    rioted over the land,
And the mountain arose like a jewell'd
    throne thro' the fragrant air,
Glowing with all-colour'd plums and with
    golden masses of pear,
And crimson and scarlet of berries that
    flamed upon bine and vine,
But in every berry and fruit was the
    poisonous pleasure of wine;
And the peak of the mountain was apples,
    the hugest that ever were seen,
And they prest, as they grew, on each
    other, with hardly a leaflet between,
And all of them redder than rosiest health
    or than utterest shame,
And setting, when Even descended, the
    very sunset aflame;
And we stay'd three days, and we gorged
    and we madden'd, till every one drew
His sword on his fellow to slay him, and
    ever they struck and they slew;
And myself, I had eaten but sparely, and
    fought till I sunder'd the fray,
Then I bad them remember my father's
    death, and we sail'd away.

VII

And we came to the Isle of Fire: we were
    lured by the light from afar,
For the peak sent up one league of fire to
    the Northern Star;
Lured by the glare and the blare, but
    scarcely could stand upright,
For the whole isle shudder'd and shook
    like a man in a mortal affright;
We were giddy besides with the fruits we
    had gorged, and so crazed that at last

There were some leap'd into the fire; and
    away we sail'd, and we past
Over that undersea isle, where the water is
    clearer than air:
Down we look'd: what a garden! O bliss,
    what a Paradise there!
Towers of a happier time, low down in a
    rainbow deep
Silent palaces, quiet fields of eternal sleep!
And three of the gentlest and best of my
    people, whate'er I could say,
Plunged head down in the sea, and the
    Paradise trembled away.

VIII

And we came to the Bounteous Isle, where
    the heavens lean low on the land,
And ever at dawn from the cloud glitter'd
    o'er us a sunbright hand,
Then it open'd and dropt at the side of
    each man, as he rose from his rest,
Bread enough for his need till the labour-
    less day dipt under the West;
And we wander'd about it and thro' it. O
    never was time so good!
And we sang of the triumphs of Finn, and
    the boast of our ancient blood,
And we gazed at the wandering wave as
    we sat by the gurgle of springs,
And we chanted the songs of the Bards
    and the glories of fairy kings;
But at length we began to be weary, to
    sigh, and to stretch and yawn,
Till we hated the Bounteous Isle and the
    sunbright hand of the dawn,
For there was not an enemy near, but the
    whole green Isle was our own,
And we took to playing at ball, and we
    took to throwing the stone,
And we took to playing at battle, but that
    was a perilous play,
For the passion of battle was in us, we
    slew and we sail'd away.

IX

And we past to the Isle of Witches and
    heard their musical cry—
'Come to us, O come, come' in the stormy
    red of a sky
Dashing the fires and the shadows of dawn
    on the beautiful shapes,

For a wild witch naked as heaven stood on
    each of the loftiest capes,
And a hundred ranged on the rock like
    white sea-birds in a row,
And a hundred gamboll'd and pranced on
    the wrecks in the sand below,
And a hundred splash'd from the ledges,
    and bosom'd the burst of the spray,
But I knew we should fall on each other,
    and hastily sail'd away.

X

And we came in an evil time to the Isle of
    the Double Towers,
One was of smooth-cut stone, one carved
    all over with flowers,
But an earthquake always moved in the
    hollows under the dells,
And they shock'd on each other and butted
    each other with clashing of bells,
And the daws flew out of the Towers and
    jangled and wrangled in vain,
And the clash and boom of the bells rang
    into the heart and the brain,
Till the passion of battle was on us, and
    all took sides with the Towers,
There were some for the clean-cut stone,
    there were more for the carven flowers,
And the wrathful thunder of God peal'd
    over us all the day,
For the one half slew the other, and after
    we sail'd away.

XI

And we came to the Isle of a Saint who
    had sail'd with St. Brendan of yore,
He had lived ever since on the Isle and his
    winters were fifteen score,
And his voice was low as from other worlds,
    and his eyes were sweet,
And his white hair sank to his heels and
    his white beard fell to his feet,
And he spake to me, 'O Maeldune, let be
    this purpose of thine!
Remember the words of the Lord when
    he told us "Vengeance is mine!"
His fathers have slain thy fathers in war or
    in single strife,
Thy fathers have slain his fathers, each
    taken a life for a life,

Thy father had slain his father, how long
    shall the murder last?
Go back to the Isle of Finn and suffer the
    Past to be Past.'
And we kiss'd the fringe of his beard and
    we pray'd as we heard him pray,
And the Holy man he assoil'd us, and sadly
    we sail'd away.

XII

And we came to the Isle we were blown
    from, and there on the shore was he,
The man that had slain my father. I saw
    him and let him be.
O weary was I of the travel, the trouble,
    the strife and the sin,
When I landed again, with a tithe of my
    men, on the Isle of Finn.

DE PROFUNDIS

THE TWO GREETINGS

TO H. T. AUGUST 11, 1852

I

OUT of the deep, my child, out of the deep,
Where all that was to be, in all that was,
Whirl'd for a million æons thro' the vast
Waste dawn of multitudinous-eddying
    light—
Out of the deep, my child, out of the deep,
Thro' all this changing world of changeless
    law,
And every phase of ever-heightening life,
And nine long months of antenatal gloom,
With this last moon, this crescent—her
    dark orb
Touch'd with earth's light—thou comest,
    darling boy;
Our own; a babe in lineament and limb
Perfect, and prophet of the perfect man;
Whose face and form are hers and mine
    in one,
Indissolubly married like our love;
Live, and be happy in thyself, and serve
This mortal race thy kin so well, that men
May bless thee as we bless thee, O young
    life
Breaking with laughter from the dark; and
    may
The fated channel where thy motion lives

Be prosperously shaped, and sway thy
    course
Along the years of haste and random youth
Unshatter'd; then full-current thro' full
    man;
And last in kindly curves, with gentlest fall,
By quiet fields, a slowly-dying power,
To that last deep where we and thou are
    still.

II

I

OUT of the deep, my child, out of the deep,
From that great deep, before our world
    begins,
Whereon the Spirit of God moves as he
    will—
Out of the deep, my child, out of the deep,
From that true world within the world we
    see,
Whereof our world is but the bounding
    shore—
Out of the deep, Spirit, out of the deep,
With this ninth moon, that sends the
    hidden sun
Down yon dark sea, thou comest, darling
    boy.

II

For in the world, which is not ours, They
    said
'Let us make man' and that which should
    be man,
From that one light no man can look upon,
Drew to this shore lit by the suns and
    moons
And all the shadows. O dear Spirit half-lost
In thine own shadow and this fleshly sign
That thou art thou—who wailest being
    born
And banish'd into mystery, and the pain
Of this divisible-indivisible world
Among the numerable-innumerable
Sun, sun, and sun, thro' finite-infinite
    space
In finite-infinite Time—our mortal veil
And shatter'd phantom of that infinite One,
Who made thee unconceivably Thyself
Out of His whole World-self and all in all—
Live thou! and of the grain and husk, the
    grape

And ivyberry, choose; and still depart
From death to death thro' life and life, and
find
Nearer and ever nearer Him, who wrought
Not Matter, nor the finite-infinite,
But this main-miracle, that thou art thou,
With power on thine own act and on the
world.

THE HUMAN CRY

I

HALLOWED be Thy name—Halleluiah!—
Infinite Ideality!
Immeasurable Reality!
Infinite Personality!
Hallowed be Thy name—Halleluiah!

II

We feel we are nothing—for all is Thou
and in Thee;
We feel we are something—*that* also has
come from Thee;
We know we are nothing—but Thou wilt
help us to be.
Hallowed be Thy name—Halleluiah!

PREFATORY SONNET

TO THE 'NINETEENTH CENTURY'

THOSE that of late had fleeted far and fast
To touch all shores, now leaving to the
skill
Of others their old craft seaworthy still,
Have charter'd this; where, mindful of the
past,
Our true co-mates regather round the
mast;
Of diverse tongue, but with a common will
Here, in this roaring moon of daffodil
And crocus, to put forth and brave the
blast;
For some, descending from the sacred
peak
Of hoar high-templed Faith, have leagued
again
Their lot with ours to rove the world about;
And some are wilder comrades, sworn to
seek
If any golden harbour be for men
In seas of Death and sunless gulfs of
Doubt.

TO THE
REV. W. H. BROOKFIELD

BROOKS, for they call'd you so that knew
you best,
Old Brooks, who loved so well to mouth
my rhymes,
How oft we two have heard St. Mary's
chimes!
How oft the Cantab supper, host and guest,
Would echo helpless laughter to your jest!
How oft with him we paced that walk of
limes,
Him, the lost light of those dawn-golden
times,
Who loved you well! Now both are gone
to rest.
You man of humorous-melancholy mark,
Dead of some inward agony—is it so?
Our kindlier, trustier Jaques, past away!
I cannot laud this life, it looks so dark:
Σκιᾶς ὄναρ—dream of a shadow, go—
God bless you. I shall join you in a day.

MONTENEGRO

THEY rose to where their sovran eagle sails,
They kept their faith, their freedom, on
the height,
Chaste, frugal, savage, arm'd by day and
night
Against the Turk; whose inroad nowhere
scales
Their headlong passes, but his footstep
fails,
And red with blood the Crescent reels
from fight
Before their dauntless hundreds, in prone
flight
By thousands down the crags and thro' the
vales.
O smallest among peoples! rough rock-
throne
Of Freedom! warriors beating back the
swarm
Of Turkish Islam for five hundred years,
Great Tsernogora! never since thine own
Black ridges drew the cloud and brake the
storm
Has breathed a race of mightier moun-
taineers.

TO VICTOR HUGO

VICTOR in Drama, Victor in Romance,
Cloud-weaver of phantasmal hopes and
        fears,
French of the French, and Lord of human
        tears;
Child-lover; Bard whose fame-lit laurels
        glance
Darkening the wreaths of all that would
        advance,
Beyond our strait, their claim to be thy
        peers;
Weird Titan by thy winter weight of years
As yet unbroken, Stormy voice of France!
Who dost not love our England—so they
        say;
I know not—England, France, all man to be
Will make one people ere man's race be
        run:
And I, desiring that diviner day,
Yield thee full thanks for thy full courtesy
To younger England in the boy my son.

TRANSLATIONS, ETC.

BATTLE OF BRUNANBURH

Constantinus, King of the Scots, after having
sworn allegiance to Athelstan, allied himself
with the Danes of Ireland under Anlaf, and
invading England, was defeated by Athelstan
and his brother Edmund with great slaughter
at Brunanburh in the year 937.

I

[1]ATHELSTAN King,
Lord among Earls,
Bracelet-bestower and
Baron of Barons,
He with his brother,
Edmund Atheling,
Gaining a lifelong
Glory in battle,
Slew with the sword-edge
There by Brunanburh,
Brake the shield-wall,
Hew'd the lindenwood,[2]
Hack'd the battleshield,
Sons of Edward with hammer'd brands.

II

Theirs was a greatness
Got from their Grandsires—
Theirs that so often in
Strife with their enemies
Struck for their hoards and their hearths
        and their homes.

III

Bow'd the spoiler,
Bent the Scotsman,
Fell the shipcrews
Doom'd to the death.
All the field with blood of the fighters
Flow'd, from when first the great
Sun-star of morningtide,
Lamp of the Lord God
Lord everlasting,
Glode over earth till the glorious creature
Sank to his setting.

IV

There lay many a man
Marr'd by the javelin,
Men of the Northland
Shot over shield.
There was the Scotsman
Weary of war.

V

We the West-Saxons,
Long as the daylight
Lasted, in companies
Troubled the track of the host that we
        hated,
Grimly with swords that were sharp from
        the grindstone,
Fiercely we hack'd at the flyers before us.

VI

Mighty the Mercian,
Hard was his hand-play,

[1] I have more or less availed myself of my
son's prose translation of this poem in the *Con-*
temporary Review (November 1876).
[2] Shields of lindenwood.

496

Sparing not any of
Those that with Anlaf,
Warriors over the
Weltering waters
Borne in the bark's-bosom,
Drew to this island:
Doom'd to the death.

VII

Five young kings put asleep by the sword-
stroke,
Seven strong Earls of the army of Anlaf
Fell on the war-field, numberless numbers,
Shipmen and Scotsmen.

VIII

Then the Norse leader,
Dire was his need of it,
Few were his following,
Fled to his warship:
Fleeted his vessel to sea with the king in it,
Saving his life on the fallow flood.

IX

Also the crafty one,
Constantinus,
Crept to his North again,
Hoar-headed hero!

X

Slender warrant had
He to be proud of
The welcome of war-knives—
He that was reft of his
Folk and his friends that had
Fallen in conflict,
Leaving his son too
Lost in the carnage,
Mangled to morsels,
A youngster in war!

XI

Slender reason had
He to be glad of
The clash of the war-glaive—
Traitor and trickster
And spurner of treaties—
He nor had Anlaf
With armies so broken
A reason for bragging
That they had the better

In perils of battle
On places of slaughter—
The struggle of standards,
The rush of the javelins,
The crash of the charges,[1]
The wielding of weapons—
The play that they play'd with
The children of Edward.

XII

Then with their nail'd prows
Parted the Norsemen, a
Blood-redden'd relic of
Javelins over
The jarring breaker, the deep-sea
billow,
Shaping their way toward Dyflen[2]
again,
Shamed in their souls.

XIII

Also the brethren,
King and Atheling,
Each in his glory,
Went to his own in his own West-Saxon-
land,
Glad of the war.

XIV

Many a carcase they left to be carrion,
Many a livid one, many a sallow-skin—
Left for the white-tail'd eagle to tear it, and
Left for the horny-nibb'd raven to rend it,
and
Gave to the garbaging war-hawk to gorge
it, and
That gray beast, the wolf of the weald.

XV

Never had huger
Slaughter of heroes
Slain by the sword-edge—
Such as old writers
Have writ of in histories—
Hapt in this isle, since
Up from the East hither
Saxon and Angle from
Over the broad billow
Broke into Britain with
Haughty war-workers who

---

[1] Lit. 'the gathering of men.'   [2] Dublin.

Harried the Welshman, when
Earls that were lured by the
Hunger of glory gat
Hold of the land.

ACHILLES OVER THE TRENCH

Iliad, xviii. 202

So saying, light-foot Iris pass'd away.
Then rose Achilles dear to Zeus; and round
The warrior's puissant shoulders Pallas
    flung
Her fringed ægis, and around his head
The glorious goddess wreath'd a golden
    cloud,
And from it lighted an all-shining flame.
As when a smoke from a city goes to
    heaven
Far off from out an island girt by foes,
All day the men contend in grievous war
From their own city, but with set of sun
Their fires flame thickly, and aloft the glare
Flies streaming, if perchance the neigh-
    bours round
May see, and sail to help them in the war;
So from his head the splendour went to
    heaven.
From wall to dyke he stept, he stood, nor
    join'd
The Achæans—honouring his wise
    mother's word—
There standing, shouted, and Pallas far
    away
Call'd; and a boundless panic shook the
    foe.
For like the clear voice when a trumpet
    shrills,
Blown by the fierce beleaguerers of a town,
So rang the clear voice of Æakidês;
And when the brazen cry of Æakidês
Was heard among the Trojans, all their
    hearts
Were troubled, and the full-maned horses
    whirl'd
The chariots backward, knowing griefs at
    hand;

And sheer-astounded were the charioteers
To see the dread, unweariable fire
That always o'er the great Peleion's head
Burn'd, for the bright-eyed goddess made
    it burn.
Thrice from the dyke he sent his mighty
    shout,
Thrice backward reel'd the Trojans and
    allies;
And there and then twelve of their noblest
    died
Among their spears and chariots.

TO PRINCESS FREDERICA ON HER MARRIAGE

O YOU that were eyes and light to the King
    till he past away
From the darkness of life—
He saw not his daughter—he blest her:
    the blind King sees you to-day,
He blesses the wife.

SIR JOHN FRANKLIN

ON THE CENOTAPH IN WESTMINSTER ABBEY

NOT here! the white North has thy bones;
    and thou,
    Heroic sailor-soul,
Art passing on thine happier voyage now
Toward no earthly pole.

TO DANTE

(WRITTEN AT REQUEST OF THE FLORENTINES)

KING, that hast reign'd six hundred years,
    and grown
In power, and ever growest, since thine
    own
Fair Florence honouring thy nativity,
Thy Florence now the crown of Italy,
Hath sought the tribute of a verse from me,
I, wearing but the garland of a day,
Cast at thy feet one flower that fades away.

TIRESIAS

AND OTHER POEMS

TO E. FITZGERALD

OLD FITZ, who from your suburb grange,
  Where once I tarried for a while,
Glance at the wheeling Orb of change,
  And greet it with a kindly smile;
Whom yet I see as there you sit
  Beneath your sheltering garden-tree,
And while your doves about you flit,
  And plant on shoulder, hand and knee,
Or on your head their rosy feet,
  As if they knew your diet spares
Whatever moved in that full sheet
  Let down to Peter at his prayers;
Who live on milk and meal and grass;
  And once for ten long weeks I tried
Your table of Pythagoras,
  And seem'd at first 'a thing enskied'
(As Shakespeare has it) airy-light
  To float above the ways of men,
Then fell from that half-spiritual height
  Chill'd, till I tasted flesh again
One night when earth was winter-black,
  And all the heavens flash'd in frost;
And on me, half-asleep, came back
  That wholesome heat the blood had lost,
And set me climbing icy capes
  And glaciers, over which there roll'd
To meet me long-arm'd vines with grapes
  Of Eshcol hugeness; for the cold
Without, and warmth within me, wrought
  To mould the dream; but none can say
That Lenten fare makes Lenten thought,
  Who reads your golden Eastern lay,
Than which I know no version done
  In English more divinely well;
A planet equal to the sun
  Which cast it, that large infidel
Your Omar; and your Omar drew
  Full-handed plaudits from our best

In modern letters, and from two,
  Old friends outvaluing all the rest,
Two voices heard on earth no more;
  But we old friends are still alive,
And I am nearing seventy-four,
  While you have touch'd at seventy-five,
And so I send a birthday line
  Of greeting; and my son, who dipt
In some forgotten book of mine
  With sallow scraps of manuscript,
And dating many a year ago,
  Has hit on this, which you will take
My Fitz, and welcome, as I know
  Less for its own than for the sake
Of one recalling gracious times,
  When, in our younger London days,
You found some merit in my rhymes,
  And I more pleasure in your praise.

TIRESIAS

I WISH I were as in the years of old,
While yet the blessed daylight made itself
Ruddy thro' both the roofs of sight, and woke
These eyes, now dull, but then so keen to
  seek
The meanings ambush'd under all they
  saw,
The flight of birds, the flame of sacrifice,
What omens may foreshadow fate to man
And woman, and the secret of the Gods.
  My son, the Gods, despite of human
  prayer,
Are slower to forgive than human kings.
The great God, Arês, burns in anger still
Against the guiltless heirs of him from
  Tyre,
Our Cadmus, out of whom thou art, who
  found

Beside the springs of Dircê, smote, and
  still'd
Thro' all its folds the multitudinous beast,
The dragon, which our trembling fathers
  call'd
The God's own son.
        A tale, that told to me,
When but thine age, by age as winter-
  white
As mine is now, amazed, but made me
  yearn
For larger glimpses of that more than man
Which rolls the heavens, and lifts, and lays
  the deep,
Yet loves and hates with mortal hates and
  loves,
And moves unseen among the ways of
  men.
    Then, in my wanderings all the lands
  that lie
Subjected to the Heliconian ridge
Have heard this footstep fall, altho' my
  wont
Was more to scale the highest of the
  heights
With some strange hope to see the nearer
  God.
One naked peak—the sister of the sun
Would climb from out the dark, and linger
  there
To silver all the valleys with her shafts—
There once, but long ago, five-fold thy
  term
Of years, I lay; the winds were dead for
  heat;
The noonday crag made the hand burn;
  and sick
For shadow—not one bush was near—I
  rose
Following a torrent till its myriad falls
Found silence in the hollows underneath.
    There in a secret olive-glade I saw
Pallas Athene climbing from the bath
In anger; yet one glittering foot disturb'd
The lucid well; one snowy knee was prest
Against the margin flowers; a dreadful
  light
Came from her golden hair, her golden
  helm
And all her golden armour on the grass,
And from her virgin breast, and virgin eyes

Remaining fixt on mine, till mine grew
  dark
For ever, and I heard a voice that said
'Henceforth be blind, for thou hast seen
  too much,
And speak the truth that no man may
  believe.'
    Son, in the hidden world of sight, that
  lives
Behind this darkness, I behold her still,
Beyond all work of those who carve the
  stone,
Beyond all dreams of Godlike woman-
  hood,
Ineffable beauty, out of whom, at a glance,
And as it were, perforce, upon me flash'd
The power of prophesying—but to me
No power—so chain'd and coupled with
  the curse
Of blindness and their unbelief, who heard
And heard not, when I spake of famine,
  plague,
Shrine-shattering earthquake, fire, flood,
  thunderbolt,
And angers of the Gods for evil done
And expiation lack'd—no power on Fate,
Theirs, or mine own! for when the crowd
  would roar
For blood, for war, whose issue was their
  doom,
To cast wise words among the multitude
Was flinging fruit to lions; nor, in hours
Of civil outbreak, when I knew the twain
Would each waste each, and bring on both
  the yoke
Of stronger states, was mine the voice to
  curb
The madness of our cities and their kings.
Who ever turn'd upon his heel to hear
My warning that the tyranny of one
Was prelude to the tyranny of all?
My counsel that the tyranny of all
Led backward to the tyranny of one?
    This power hath work'd no good to
  aught that lives,
And these blind hands were useless in their
  wars.
O therefore that the unfulfill'd desire,
The grief for ever born from griefs to be,
The boundless yearning of the Prophet's
  heart—

Could *that* stand forth, and like a statue,
    rear'd
To some great citizen, win all praise from
    all
Who past it, saying, 'That was he!'
                In vain!
Virtue must shape itself in deed, and those
Whom weakness or necessity have cramp'd
Within themselves, immerging, each, his
    urn
In his own well, draw solace as he may.
  Menœceus, thou hast eyes, and I can
    hear
Too plainly what full tides of onset sap
Our seven high gates, and what a weight
    of war
Rides on those ringing axles! jingle of bits,
Shouts, arrows, tramp of the hornfooted
    horse
That grind the glebe to powder! Stony
    showers
Of that ear-stunning hail of Arês crash
Along the sounding walls. Above, below,
Shock after shock, the song-built towers
    and gates
Reel, bruised and butted with the shudder-
    ing
War-thunder of iron rams; and from
    within
The city comes a murmur void of joy,
Lest she be taken captive—maidens, wives,
And mothers with their babblers of the
    dawn,
And oldest age in shadow from the night,
Falling about their shrines before their
    Gods,
And wailing 'Save us.'
            And they wail to thee!
These eyeless eyes, that cannot see thine
    own,
See this, that only in thy virtue lies
The saving of our Thebes; for, yester-
    night,
To me, the great God Arês, whose one
    bliss
Is war, and human sacrifice—himself
Blood-red from battle, spear and helmet
    tipt
With stormy light as on a mast at sea,
Stood out before a darkness, crying
    'Thebes,

Thy Thebes shall fall and perish, for I
    loathe
The seed of Cadmus—yet if one of these
By his own hand—if one of these——'
                 My son,
No sound is breathed so potent to coerce,
And to conciliate, as their names who dare
For that sweet mother land which gave
    them birth
Nobly to do, nobly to die. Their names,
Graven on memorial columns, are a song
Heard in the future; few, but more than
    wall
And rampart, their examples reach a hand
Far thro' all years, and everywhere they
    meet
And kindle generous purpose, and the
    strength
To mould it into action pure as theirs.
  Fairer thy fate than mine, if life's best end
Be to end well! and thou refusing this,
Unvenerable will thy memory be
While men shall move the lips: but if thou
    dare—
Thou, one of these, the race of Cadmus—
    then
No stone is fitted in yon marble girth
Whose echo shall not tongue thy glorious
    doom,
Nor in this pavement but shall ring thy
    name
To every hoof that clangs it, and the
    springs
Of Dircê laving yonder battle-plain,
Heard from the roofs by night, will mur-
    mur thee
To thine own Thebes, while Thebes thro'
    thee shall stand
Firm-based with all her Gods.
                    The Dragon's cave
Half hid, they tell me, now in flowing
    vines—
Where once he dwelt and whence he roll'd
    himself
At dead of night—thou knowest, and that
    smooth rock
Before it, altar-fashion'd, where of late
The woman-breasted Sphinx, with wings
    drawn back,
Folded her lion paws, and look'd to
    Thebes.

There blanch the bones of whom she slew,
and these
Mixt with her own, because the fierce
beast found
A wiser than herself, and dash'd herself
Dead in her rage: but thou art wise enough,
Tho' young, to love thy wiser, blunt the
curse
Of Pallas, hear, and tho' I speak the truth
Believe I speak it, let thine own hand strike
Thy youthful pulses into rest and quench
The red God's anger, fearing not to plunge
Thy torch of life in darkness, rather—thou
Rejoicing that the sun, the moon, the stars
Send no such light upon the ways of men
As one great deed.
　　　　Thither, my son, and there
Thou, that hast never known the embrace
of love,
Offer thy maiden life.
　　　　　This useless hand!
I felt one warm tear fall upon it. Gone!
He will achieve his greatness.
　　　　　But for me,
I would that I were gather'd to my rest,
And mingled with the famous kings of old,
On whom about their ocean-islets flash
The faces of the Gods—the wise man's
word,
Here trampled by the populace underfoot,
There crown'd with worship—and these
eyes will find
The men I knew, and watch the chariot whirl
About the goal again, and hunters race
The shadowy lion, and the warrior-kings,
In height and prowess more than human,
strive
Again for glory, while the golden lyre
Is ever sounding in heroic ears
Heroic hymns, and every way the vales
Wind, clouded with the grateful incense-
fume
Of those who mix all odour to the Gods
On one far height in one far-shining fire.

———

'One height and one far-shining fire'
　And while I fancied that my friend
For this brief idyll would require
　A less diffuse and opulent end,
And would defend his judgment well,

If I should deem it over nice—
The tolling of his funeral bell
　Broke on my Pagan Paradise,
And mixt the dream of classic times
And all the phantoms of the dream,
With present grief, and made the rhymes,
　That miss'd his living welcome, seem
Like would-be guests an hour too late,
Who down the highway moving on
With easy laughter find the gate
　Is bolted, and the master gone.
Gone into darkness, that full light
　Of friendship! past, in sleep, away
By night, into the deeper night!
　The deeper night? A clearer day
Than our poor twilight dawn on earth—
If night, what barren toil to be!
What life, so maim'd by night, were worth
　Our living out? Not mine to me
Remembering all the golden hours
　Now silent, and so many dead,
And him the last; and laying flowers,
　This wreath, above his honour'd head,
And praying that, when I from hence
Shall fade with him into the unknown,
My close of earth's experience
　May prove as peaceful as his own.

THE WRECK

I

HIDE me, Mother! my Fathers belong'd to
the church of old,
I am driven by storm and sin and death to
the ancient fold,
I cling to the Catholic Cross once more, to
the Faith that saves,
My brain is full of the crash of wrecks, and
the roar of waves,
My life itself is a wreck, I have sullied a
noble name,
I am flung from the rushing tide of the
world as a waif of shame,
I am roused by the wail of a child, and
awake to a livid light,
And a ghastlier face than ever has haunted
a grave by night,
I would hide from the storm without, I
would flee from the storm within,
I would make my life one prayer for a soul
that died in his sin,

I was the tempter, Mother, and mine was
    the deeper fall;
I will sit at your feet, I will hide my face,
    I will tell you all.

II

He that they gave me to, Mother, a heed-
    less and innocent bride—
I never have wrong'd his heart, I have only
    wounded his pride—
Spain in his blood and the Jew——dark-
    visaged, stately and tall—
A princelier-looking man never stept thro'
    a Prince's hall.
And who, when his anger was kindled,
    would venture to give him the nay?
And a man men fear is a man to be loved
    by the women they say.
And I could have loved him too, if the
    blossom can doat on the blight,
Or the young green leaf rejoice in the frost
    that sears it at night;
He would open the books that I prized,
    and toss them away with a yawn,
Repell'd by the magnet of Art to the which
    my nature was drawn,
The word of the Poet by whom the deeps
    of the world are stirr'd,
The music that robes it in language be-
    neath and beyond the word!
My Shelley would fall from my hands
    when he cast a contemptuous glance
From where he was poring over his Tables
    of Trade and Finance;
My hands, when I heard him coming
    would drop from the chords or the
    keys,
But ever I fail'd to please him, however I
    strove to please—
All day long far-off in the cloud of the city,
    and there
Lost, head and heart, in the chances of
    dividend, consol, and share—
And at home if I sought for a kindly caress,
    being woman and weak,
His formal kiss fell chill as a flake of snow
    on the cheek:
And so, when I bore him a girl, when I
    held it aloft in my joy,
He look'd at it coldly, and said to me 'Pity
    it isn't a boy.'

The one thing given me, to love and to
    live for, glanced at in scorn!
The child that I felt I could die for—as if
    she were basely born!
I had lived a wild-flower life, I was planted
    now in a tomb;
The daisy will shut to the shadow, I closed
    my heart to the gloom;
I threw myself all abroad—I would play
    my part with the young
By the low foot-lights of the world—and
    I caught the wreath that was flung.

III

Mother, I have not—however their tongues
    may have babbled of me—
Sinn'd thro' an animal vileness, for all but
    a dwarf was he,
And all but a hunchback too; and I look'd
    at him, first, askance,
With pity—not he the knight for an
    amorous girl's romance!
Tho' wealthy enough to have bask'd in the
    light of a dowerless smile,
Having lands at home and abroad in a rich
    West-Indian isle;
But I came on him once at a ball, the heart
    of a listening crowd—
Why, what a brow was there! he was
    seated—speaking aloud
To women, the flower of the time, and
    men at the helm of state—
Flowing with easy greatness and touching
    on all things great,
Science, philosophy, song—till I felt my-
    self ready to weep
For I knew not what, when I heard that
    voice,—as mellow and deep
As a psalm by a mighty master and peal'd
    from an organ,—roll
Rising and falling—for, Mother, the voice
    was the voice of the soul;
And the sun of the soul made day in the
    dark of his wonderful eyes.
Here was the hand that would help me,
    would heal me—the heart that was
    wise!
And he, poor man, when he learnt that I
    hated the ring I wore,
He helpt me with death, and he heal'd me
    with sorrow for evermore.

IV

For I broke the bond. That day my nurse
  had brought me the child.
The small sweet face was flush'd, but it
  coo'd to the Mother and smiled.
'Anything ailing,' I ask'd her, 'with baby?'
  She shook her head,
And the Motherless Mother kiss'd it, and
  turn'd in her haste and fled.

V

Low warm winds had gently breathed us
  away from the land—
Ten long sweet summer days upon deck,
  sitting hand in hand—
When he clothed a naked mind with the
  wisdom and wealth of his own,
And I bow'd myself down as a slave to his
  intellectual throne,
When he coin'd into English gold some
  treasure of classical song,
When he flouted a statesman's error, or
  flamed at a public wrong,
When he rose as it were on the wings of an
  eagle beyond me, and past
Over the range and the change of the world
  from the first to the last,
When he spoke of his tropical home in the
  canes by the purple tide,
And the high star-crowns of his palms on
  the deep-wooded mountain-side,
And cliffs all robed in lianas that dropt to
  the brink of his bay,
And trees like the towers of a minster, the
  sons of a winterless day.
'Paradise there!' so he said, but I seem'd
  in Paradise then
With the first great love I had felt for the
  first and greatest of men;
Ten long days of summer and sin—if it
  must be so—
But days of a larger light than I ever again
  shall know—
Days that will glimmer, I fear, thro' life to
  my latest breath;
'No frost there,' so he said, 'as in truest
  Love no Death.'

VI

Mother, one morning a bird with a warble
  plaintively sweet

Perch'd on the shrouds, and then fell
  fluttering down at my feet;
I took it, he made it a cage, we fondled it,
  Stephen and I,
But it died, and I thought of the child for
  a moment, I scarce know why.

VII

But if sin be sin, not inherited fate, as many
  will say,
My sin to my desolate little one found me
  at sea on a day,
When her orphan wail came borne in the
  shriek of a growing wind,
And a voice rang out in the thunders of
  Ocean and Heaven 'Thou hast sinn'd.'
And down in the cabin were we, for the
  towering crest of the tides
Plunged on the vessel and swept in a
  cataract off from her sides,
And ever the great storm grew with a howl
  and a hoot of the blast
In the rigging, voices of hell—then came
  the crash of the mast.
'The wages of sin is death,' and there I
  began to weep,
'I am the Jonah, the crew should cast me
  into the deep,
For ah God, what a heart was mine to
  forsake her even for you.'
'Never the heart among women,' he said,
  'more tender and true.'
'The heart! not a mother's heart, when I
  left my darling alone.'
'Comfort yourself, for the heart of the
  father will care for his own.'
'The heart of the father will spurn her,' I
  cried, 'for the sin of the wife,
The cloud of the mother's shame will
  enfold her and darken her life.'
Then his pale face twitch'd; 'O Stephen,
  I love you, I love you, and yet'—
As I lean'd away from his arms—'would
  God, we had never met!'
And he spoke not—only the storm; till
  after a little, I yearn'd
For his voice again, and he call'd to me
  'Kiss me!' and there—as I turn'd—
'The heart, the heart!' I kiss'd him, I clung
  to the sinking form,

And the storm went roaring above us, and
he—was out of the storm.

VIII

And then, then, Mother, the ship stagger'd
under a thunderous shock,
That shook us asunder, as if she had struck
and crash'd on a rock;
For a huge sea smote every soul from the
decks of The Falcon but one;
All of them, all but the man that was lash'd
to the helm had gone;
And I fell—and the storm and the days
went by, but I knew no more—
Lost myself—lay like the dead by the dead
on the cabin floor,
Dead to the death beside me, and lost to
the loss that was mine,
With a dim dream, now and then, of a
hand giving bread and wine,
Till I woke from the trance, and the ship
stood still, and the skies were blue,
But the face I had known, O Mother, was
not the face that I knew.

IX

The strange misfeaturing mask that I saw
so amazed me, that I
Stumbled on deck, half mad. I would fling
myself over and die!
But one—he was waving a flag—the one
man left on the wreck—
'Woman'—he graspt at my arm—'stay
there'—I crouch'd upon deck—
'We are sinking, and yet there's hope:
look yonder,' he cried, 'a sail'
In a tone so rough that I broke into passionate tears, and the wail
Of a beaten babe, till I saw that a boat was
nearing us—then
All on a sudden I thought, I shall look on
the child again.

X

They lower'd me down the side, and there
in the boat I lay
With sad eyes fixt on the lost sea-home, as
we glided away,
And I sigh'd, as the low dark hull dipt
under the smiling main,
'Had I stay'd with *him*, I had now—with
him—been out of my pain.'

XI

They took us aboard: the crew were gentle,
the captain kind;
But *I* was the lonely slave of an often-
wandering mind;
For whenever a rougher gust might tumble
a stormier wave,
'O Stephen,' I moan'd, 'I am coming to
thee in thine Ocean-grave.'
And again, when a balmier breeze curl'd
over a peacefuller sea,
I found myself moaning again 'O child, I
am coming to thee.'

XII

The broad white brow of the Isle—that
bay with the colour'd sand—
Rich was the rose of sunset there, as we
drew to the land;
All so quiet the ripple would hardly blanch
into spray
At the feet of the cliff; and I pray'd—'my
child'—for I still could pray—
May her life be as blissfully calm, be never
gloom'd by the curse
Of a sin, not hers!'
                    Was it well with the child?
                    I wrote to the nurse
Who had borne my flower on her hireling
heart; and an answer came
Not from the nurse—nor yet to the wife—
to her maiden name!
I shook as I open'd the letter—I knew that
hand too well—
And from it a scrap, clipt out of the
'deaths' in a paper, fell.
'Ten long sweet summer days' of fever,
and want of care!
And gone—that day of the storm—O
Mother, she came to me there.

DESPAIR

A man and his wife having lost faith in a God,
and hope of a life to come, and being utterly
miserable in this, resolve to end themselves by
drowning. The woman is drowned, but the man
rescued by a minister of the sect he had aban-
doned.

I

Is it you, that preach'd in the chapel there
looking over the sand?

Follow'd us too that night, and dogg'd us, and drew me to land?

II

What did I feel that night? You are curious. How should I tell?

Does it matter so much what I felt? You rescued me—yet—was it well

That you came unwish'd for, uncall'd, between me and the deep and my doom,

Three days since, three more dark days of the Godless gloom

Of a life without sun, without health, without hope, without any delight

In anything here upon earth? but ah God, that night, that night

When the rolling eyes of the lighthouse there on the fatal neck

Of land running out into rock—they had saved many hundreds from wreck—

Glared on our way toward death, I remember I thought, as we past,

Does it matter how many they saved? we are all of us wreck'd at last—

'Do you fear?' and there came thro' the roar of the breaker a whisper, a breath,

'Fear? am I not with you? I am frighted at life not death.'

III

And the suns of the limitless Universe sparkled and shone in the sky,

Flashing with fires as of God, but we knew that their light was a lie—

Bright as with deathless hope—but, however they sparkled and shone,

The dark little worlds running round them were worlds of woe like our own—

No soul in the heaven above, no soul on the earth below,

A fiery scroll written over with lamentation and woe.

IV

See, we were nursed in the drear nightfold of your fatalist creed,

And we turn'd to the growing dawn, we had hoped for a dawn indeed,

When the light of a Sun that was coming would scatter the ghosts of the Past,

And the cramping creeds that had madden'd the peoples would vanish at last,

And we broke away from the Christ, our human brother and friend,

For He spoke, or it seem'd that He spoke, of a Hell without help, without end.

V

Hoped for a dawn and it came, but the promise had faded away;

We had past from a cheerless night to the glare of a drearier day;

He is only a cloud and a smoke who was once a pillar of fire,

The guess of a worm in the dust and the shadow of its desire—

Of a worm as it writhes in a world of the weak trodden down by the strong,

Of a dying worm in a world, all massacre, murder, and wrong.

VI

O we poor orphans of nothing—alone on that lonely shore—

Born of the brainless Nature who knew not that which she bore!

Trusting no longer that earthly flower would be heavenly fruit—

Come from the brute, poor souls—no souls —and to die with the brute——

VII

Nay, but I am not claiming your pity: I know you of old—

Small pity for those that have ranged from the narrow warmth of your fold,

Where you bawl'd the dark side of your faith and a God of eternal rage,

Till you flung us back on ourselves, and the human heart, and the Age.

VIII

But pity—the Pagan held it a vice—was in her and in me,

Helpless, taking the place of the pitying God that should be!

Pity for all that aches in the grasp of an idiot power,

And pity for our own selves on an earth that bore not a flower;

Pity for all that suffers on land or in air or
the deep,
And pity for our own selves till we long'd
for eternal sleep.

IX

'Lightly step over the sands! the waters—
you hear them call!
Life with its anguish, and horrors, and
errors—away with it all!'
And she laid her hand in my own—she
was always loyal and sweet—
Till the points of the foam in the dusk
came playing about our feet.
There was a strong sea-current would
sweep us out to the main.
'Ah God' tho' I felt as I spoke I was taking
the name in vain—
'Ah God' and we turn'd to each other, we
kiss'd, we embraced, she and I,
Knowing the Love we were used to believe
everlasting would die:
We had read their know-nothing books
and we lean'd to the darker side—
Ah God, should we find Him, perhaps,
perhaps, if we died, if we died;
We never had found Him on earth, this
earth is a fatherless Hell—
'Dear Love, for ever and ever, for ever and
ever farewell,'
Never a cry so desolate, not since the
world began,
Never a kiss so sad, no, not since the
coming of man!

X

But the blind wave cast me ashore, and
you saved me, a valueless life.
Not a grain of gratitude mine! You have
parted the man from the wife.
I am left alone on the land, she is all alone
in the sea;
If a curse meant ought, I would curse you
for not having let me be.

XI

Visions of youth—for my brain was drunk
with the water, it seems;
I had past into perfect quiet at length out
of pleasant dreams,

And the transient trouble of drowning—
what was it when match'd with the
pains
Of the hellish heat of a wretched life rushing back thro' the veins?

XII

Why should I live? one son had forged on
his father and fled,
And if I believed in a God, I would thank
him, the other is dead,
And there was a baby-girl, that had never
look'd on the light:
Happiest she of us all, for she past from
the night to the night.

XIII

But the crime, if a crime, of her eldest-
born, her glory, her boast,
Struck hard at the tender heart of the
mother, and broke it almost;
Tho', glory and shame dying out for ever
in endless time,
Does it matter so much whether crown'd
for a virtue, or hang'd for a crime?

XIV

And ruin'd by *him*, by *him*, I stood there,
naked, amazed
In a world of arrogant opulence, fear'd
myself turning crazed,
And I would not be mock'd in a mad-
house! and she, the delicate wife,
With a grief that could only be cured, if
cured, by the surgeon's knife,—

XV

Why should we bear with an hour of torture, a moment of pain,
If every man die for ever, if all his griefs
are in vain,
And the homeless planet at length will be
wheel'd thro' the silence of space,
Motherless evermore of an ever-vanishing
race,
When the worm shall have writhed its last,
and its last brother-worm will have
fled
From the dead fossil skull that is left in
the rocks of an earth that is dead?

XVI

Have I crazed myself over their horrible
infidel writings? O yes,
For these are the new dark ages, you see,
of the popular press,
When the bat comes out of his cave, and
the owls are whooping at noon,
And Doubt is the lord of this dunghill and
crows to the sun and the moon,
Till the Sun and the Moon of our science
are both of them turn'd into blood,
And Hope will have broken her heart,
running after a shadow of good;
For their knowing and know-nothing books
are scatter'd from hand to hand—
We have knelt in your know-all chapel too
looking over the sand.

XVII

What! I should call on that Infinite Love
that has served us so well?
Infinite cruelty rather that made everlasting
Hell,
Made us, foreknew us, foredoom'd us, and
does what he will with his own;
Better our dead brute mother who never
has heard us groan!

XVIII

Hell? if the souls of men were immortal,
as men have been told,
The lecher would cleave to his lusts, and
the miser would yearn for his gold,
And so there were Hell for ever! but were
there a God as you say,
His Love would have power over Hell till
it utterly vanish'd away.

XIX

Ah yet—I have had some glimmer, at
times, in my gloomiest woe,
Of a God behind all—after all—the great
God for aught that I know;
But the God of Love and of Hell together
—they cannot be thought,
If there be such a God, may the Great
God curse him and bring him to
nought!

XX

Blasphemy! whose is the fault? is it mine?
for why would you save
A madman to vex you with wretched
words, who is best in his grave?
Blasphemy! ay, why not, being damn'd
beyond hope of grace?
O would I were yonder with her, and away
from your faith and your face!
Blasphemy! true! I have scared you pale
with my scandalous talk,
But the blasphemy to *my* mind lies all in
the way that you walk.

XXI

Hence! she is gone! can I stay? can I
breathe divorced from the Past?
You needs must have good lynx-eyes if I
do not escape you at last.
Our orthodox coroner doubtless will find
it a felo-de-se,
And the stake and the cross-road, fool, if
you will, does it matter to me?

THE ANCIENT SAGE

A THOUSAND summers ere the time of
Christ
From out his ancient city came a Seer
Whom one that loved, and honour'd him,
and yet
Was no disciple, richly garb'd, but worn
From wasteful living, follow'd—in his
hand
A scroll of verse—till that old man before
A cavern whence an affluent fountain
pour'd
From darkness into daylight, turn'd and
spoke.

This wealth of waters might but seem to
draw
From yon dark cave, but, son, the source
is higher,
Yon summit half-a-league in air—and
higher,
The cloud that hides it—higher still, the
heavens
Whereby the cloud was moulded, and
whereout

The cloud descended. Force is from the heights.
I am wearied of our city, son, and go
To spend my one last year among the hills.
What hast thou there? Some deathsong
 for the Ghouls
To make their banquet relish? let me read.

"How far thro' all the bloom and brake
 That nightingale is heard!
What power but the bird's could make
 This music in the bird?
How summer-bright are yonder skies,
 And earth as fair in hue!
And yet what sign of aught that lies
 Behind the green and blue?
But man to-day is fancy's fool
 As man hath ever been.
The nameless Power, or Powers, that rule
 Were never heard or seen."

If thou would'st hear the Nameless, and
 wilt dive
Into the Temple-cave of thine own self,
There, brooding by the central altar, thou
May'st haply learn the Nameless hath a
 voice,
By which thou wilt abide, if thou be wise,
As if thou knewest, tho' thou canst not
 know;
For Knowledge is the swallow on the lake
That sees and stirs the surface-shadow
 there
But never yet hath dipt into the abysm,
The Abysm of all Abysms, beneath, within
The blue of sky and sea, the green of earth,
And in the million-millionth of a grain
Which cleft and cleft again for evermore,
And ever vanishing, never vanishes,
To me, my son, more mystic than myself,
Or even than the Nameless is to me.
 And when thou sendest thy free soul
 thro' heaven,
Nor understandest bound nor boundless-
 ness,
Thou seest the Nameless of the hundred
 names.
 And if the Nameless should withdraw
 from all
Thy frailty counts most real, all thy world
Might vanish like thy shadow in the dark.

"And since—from when this earth began—
 The Nameless never came
Among us, never spake with man,
 And never named the Name"—

Thou canst not prove the Nameless, O my
 son,
Nor canst thou prove the world thou
 movest in,
Thou canst not prove that thou art body
 alone,
Nor canst thou prove that thou art spirit
 alone,
Nor canst thou prove that thou art both in
 one:
Thou canst not prove thou art immortal, no
Nor yet that thou art mortal—nay my son,
Thou canst not prove that I, who speak
 with thee,
Am not thyself in converse with thyself,
For nothing worthy proving can be proven,
Nor yet disproven: wherefore thou be
 wise,
Cleave ever to the sunnier side of doubt,
And cling to Faith beyond the forms of
 Faith!
She reels not in the storm of warring words,
She brightens at the clash of 'Yes' and
 'No,'
She sees the Best that glimmers thro' the
 Worst,
She feels the Sun is hid but for a night,
She spies the summer thro' the winter bud,
She tastes the fruit before the blossom falls,
She hears the lark within the songless egg,
She finds the fountain where they wail'd
 'Mirage'!

"What Power? aught akin to Mind,
 The mind in me and you?
Or power as of the Gods gone blind
 Who see not what they do?"

But some in yonder city hold, my son,
That none but Gods could build this house
 of ours,
So beautiful, vast, various, so beyond
All work of man, yet, like all work of man,
A beauty with defect——till That which
 knows,
And is not known, but felt thro' what we
 feel

Within ourselves is highest, shall descend
On this half-deed, and shape it at the last
According to the Highest in the Highest.

"What Power but the Years that make
   And break the vase of clay,
And stir the sleeping earth, and wake
   The bloom that fades away?
What rulers but the Days and Hours
   That cancel weal with woe,
And wind the front of youth with flowers,
   And cap our age with snow?"

   The days and hours are ever glancing by,
And seem to flicker past thro' sun and
      shade,
Or short, or long, as Pleasure leads, or
      Pain;
But with the Nameless is nor Day nor
      Hour;
Tho' we, thin minds, who creep from
      thought to thought,
Break into 'Thens' and 'Whens' the Eternal
      Now:
This double seeming of the single world!—
My words are like the babblings in a dream
Of nightmare, when the babblings break
      the dream.
But thou be wise in this dream-world of
      ours,
Nor take thy dial for thy deity,
But make the passing shadow serve thy
      will.

"The years that made the stripling wise
   Undo their work again,
And leave him, blind of heart and eyes,
   The last and least of men;
Who clings to earth, and once would dare
   Hell-heat or Arctic cold,
And now one breath of cooler air
   Would loose him from his hold;
His winter chills him to the root,
   He withers marrow and mind;
The kernel of the shrivell'd fruit
   Is jutting thro' the rind;
The tiger spasms tear his chest,
   The palsy wags his head;
The wife, the sons, who love him best
   Would fain that he were dead;
The griefs by which he once was wrung
   Were never worth the while"—

Who knows? or whether this earth-narrow
      life
Be yet but yolk, and forming in the shell?

"The shaft of scorn that once had stung
   But wakes a dotard smile."

The placid gleam of sunset after storm!

"The stateman's brain that sway'd the past
   Is feebler than his knees;
The passive sailor wrecks at last
   In ever-silent seas;
The warrior hath forgot his arms,
   The Learned all his lore;
The changing market frets or charms
   The merchant's hope no more;
The prophet's beacon burn'd in vain,
   And now is lost in cloud;
The plowman passes, bent with pain,
   To mix with what he plow'd;
The poet whom his Age would quote
   As heir of endless fame—
He knows not ev'n the book he wrote,
   Not even his own name.
For man has overlived his day,
   And, darkening in the light,
Scarce feels the senses break away
   To mix with ancient Night."

The shell must break before the bird can
      fly.

"The years that when my Youth began
   Had set the lily and rose
By all my ways where'er they ran,
   Have ended mortal foes;
My rose of love for ever gone,
   My lily of truth and trust—
They made her lily and rose in one,
   And changed her into dust.
O rosetree planted in my grief,
   And growing, on her tomb,
Her dust is greening in your leaf,
   Her blood is in your bloom.
O slender lily waving there,
   And laughing back the light,
In vain you tell me 'Earth is fair'
   When all is dark as night."

My son, the world is dark with griefs and
      graves,

So dark that men cry out against the Heavens.
Who knows but that the darkness is in man?
The doors of Night may be the gates of Light;
For wert thou born or blind or deaf, and then
Suddenly heal'd, how would'st thou glory in all
The splendours and the voices of the world!
And we, the poor earth's dying race, and yet
No phantoms, watching from a phantom shore
Await the last and largest sense to make
The phantom walls of this illusion fade,
And show us that the world is wholly fair.

"But vain the tears for darken'd years
    As laughter over wine,
And vain the laughter as the tears,
    O brother, mine or thine,

For all that laugh, and all that weep
    And all that breathe are one
Slight ripple on the boundless deep
    That moves, and all is gone."

But that one ripple on the boundless deep
Feels that the deep is boundless, and itself
For ever changing form, but evermore
One with the boundless motion of the deep.

"Yet wine and laughter friends! and set
    The lamps alight, and call
For golden music, and forget
    The darkness of the pall."

If utter darkness closed the day, my son——
But earth's dark forehead flings athwart the heavens
Her shadow crown'd with stars—and yonder—out
To northward—some that never set, but pass
From sight and night to lose themselves in day.
I hate the black negation of the bier,

And wish the dead, as happier than ourselves
And higher, having climb'd one step beyond
Our village miseries, might be borne in white
To burial or to burning, hymn'd from hence
With songs in praise of death, and crown'd with flowers!

"O worms and maggots of to-day
Without their hope of wings!"

But louder than thy rhyme the silent Word
Of that world-prophet in the heart of man.

"Tho' some have gleams or so they say
Of more than mortal things."

To-day? but what of yesterday? for oft
On me, when boy, there came what then I call'd,
Who knew no books and no philosophies,
In my boy-phrase 'The Passion of the Past.'
The first gray streak of earliest summer-dawn,
The last long stripe of waning crimson gloom,
As if the late and early were but one—
A height, a broken grange, a grove, a flower
Had murmurs 'Lost and gone and lost and gone!'
A breath, a whisper—some divine farewell—
Desolate sweetness—far and far away—
What had he loved, what had he lost, the boy?
I know not and I speak of what has been.
    And more, my son! for more than once when I
Sat all alone, revolving in myself
The word that is the symbol of myself,
The mortal limit of the Self was loosed,
And past into the Nameless, as a cloud
Melts into Heaven. I touch'd my limbs, the limbs
Were strange not mine—and yet no shade of doubt,
But utter clearness, and thro' loss of Self

The gain of such large life as match'd with
ours
Were Sun to spark—unshadowable in
words,
Themselves but shadows of a shadow-
world.

"And idle gleams will come and go
But still the clouds remain;"

The clouds themselves are children of the
Sun.

"And Night and Shadow rule below
When only Day should reign."

And Day and Night are children of the
Sun,
And idle gleams to thee are light to me.
Some say, the Light was father of the
Night,
And some, the Night was father of the
Light,
No night no day!—I touch thy world
again—
No ill no good! such counter-terms, my
son,
Are border-races, holding, each its own
By endless war: but night enough is there
In yon dark city: get thee back: and since
The key to that weird casket, which for
thee
But holds a skull, is neither thine nor mine,
But in the hand of what is more than man,
Or in man's hand when man is more than
man,
Let be thy wail and help thy fellow men,
And make thy gold thy vassal not thy king,
And fling free alms into the beggar's bowl,
And send the day into the darken'd heart;
Nor list for guerdon in the voice of men,
A dying echo from a falling wall;
Nor care—for Hunger hath the Evil eye—
To vex the noon with fiery gems, or fold
Thy presence in the silk of sumptuous
looms;
Nor roll thy viands on a luscious tongue,
Nor drown thyself with flies in honied
wine;
Nor thou be rageful, like a handled bee,
And lose thy life by usage of thy sting;
Nor harm an adder thro' the lust for harm,

Nor make a snail's horn shrink for wanton-
ness;
And more—think well! Do-well will follow
thought,
And in the fatal sequence of this world
An evil thought may soil thy children's
blood;
But curb the beast would cast thee in the
mire,
And leave the hot swamp of voluptuous-
ness
A cloud between the Nameless and thyself,
And lay thine uphill shoulder to the wheel,
And climb the Mount of Blessing, whence,
if thou
Look higher, then—perchance—thou
mayest—beyond
A hundred ever-rising mountain lines,
And past the range of Night and Shadow—
see
The high-heaven dawn of more than
mortal day
Strike on the Mount of Vision!
So, farewell.

THE FLIGHT

I

ARE you sleeping? have you forgotten? do
not sleep, my sister dear!
How *can* you sleep? the morning brings
the day I hate and fear;
The cock has crow'd already once, he
crows before his time;
Awake! the creeping glimmer steals, the
hills are white with rime.

II

Ah, clasp me in your arms, sister, ah, fold
me to your breast!
Ah, let me weep my fill once more, and cry
myself to rest!
To rest? to rest and wake no more were
better rest for me,
Than to waken every morning to that face
I loathe to see:

III

I envied your sweet slumber, all night so
calm you lay,
The night was calm, the morn is calm, and
like another day;

But I could wish yon moaning sea would
  rise and burst the shore,
And such a whirlwind blow these woods,
  as never blew before.

IV

For, one by one, the stars went down across
  the gleaming pane,
And project after project rose, and all of
  them were vain;
The blackthorn-blossom fades and falls
  and leaves the bitter sloe,
The hope I catch at vanishes and youth is
  turn'd to woe.

V

Come, speak a little comfort! all night I
  pray'd with tears,
And yet no comfort came to me, and now
  the morn appears,
When he will tear me from your side, who
  bought me for his slave:
This father pays his debt with me, and
  weds me to my grave.

VI

What father, this or mine, was he, who, on
  that summer day
When I had fall'n from off the crag we
  clamber'd up in play,
Found, fear'd me dead, and groan'd, and
  took and kiss'd me, and again
He kiss'd me; and I loved him then; he
  was my father then.

VII

No father now, the tyrant vassal of a tyrant
  vice!
The Godless Jephtha vows his child . . .
  to one cast of the dice.
These ancient woods, this Hall at last will
  go—perhaps have gone,
Except his own meek daughter yield her
  life, heart, soul to one—

VIII

To one who knows I scorn him. O the
  formal mocking bow,
The cruel smile, the courtly phrase that
  masks his malice now—

But often in the sidelong eyes a gleam of
  all things ill—
It is not Love but Hate that weds a bride
  against her will;

IX

Hate, that would pluck from this true
  breast the locket that I wear,
The precious crystal into which I braided
  Edwin's hair!
The love that keeps this heart alive beats
  on it night and day—
One golden curl, his golden gift, before he
  past away.

X

He left us weeping in the woods; his boat
  was on the sand;
How slowly down the rocks he went, how
  loth to quit the land!
And all my life was darken'd, as I saw the
  white sail run,
And darken, up that lane of light into the
  setting sun.

XI

How often have we watch'd the sun fade
  from us thro' the West,
And follow Edwin to those isles, those
  islands of the Blest!
Is *he* not there? would I were there, the
  friend, the bride, the wife,
With him, where summer never dies, with
  Love, the Sun of life!

XII

O would I were in Edwin's arms—once
  more—to feel his breath
Upon my cheek—on Edwin's ship, with
  Edwin, ev'n in death,
Tho' all about the shuddering wreck the
  death-white sea should rave,
Or if lip were laid to lip on the pillows of
  the wave.

XIII

Shall I take *him?* I kneel with *him?* I swear
  and swear forsworn
To love him most, whom most I loathe, to
  honour whom I scorn?

The Fiend would yell, the grave would
    yawn, my mother's ghost would
    rise—
To lie, to lie—in God's own house—the
    blackest of all lies!

XIV

Why—rather than that hand in mine, tho'
    every pulse would freeze,
I'd sooner fold an icy corpse dead of some
    foul disease:
Wed him? I will not wed him, let them
    spurn me from the doors,
And I will wander till I die about the
    barren moors.

XV

The dear, mad bride who stabb'd her
    bridegroom on her bridal night—
If mad, then I am mad, but sane, if she
    were in the right.
My father's madness makes me mad—but
    words are only words!
I am not mad, not yet, not quite—There!
    listen how the birds

XVI

Begin to warble yonder in the budding
    orchard trees!
The lark has past from earth to Heaven
    upon the morning breeze!
How gladly, were I one of those, how early
    would I wake!
And yet the sorrow that I bear is sorrow
    for *his* sake.

XVII

They love their mates, to whom they sing;
    or else their songs, that meet
The morning with such music, would
    never be so sweet!
And tho' these fathers will not hear, the
    blessed Heavens are just,
And Love is fire, and burns the feet would
    trample it to dust.

XVIII

A door was open'd in the house—who?
    who? my father sleeps!
A stealthy foot upon the stair! he—some
    one—this way creeps!

If he? yes, he . . . lurks, listens, fears his
    victim may have fled—
He! where is some sharp-pointed thing?
    he comes, and finds me dead.

XIX

Not he, not yet! and time to act—but how
    my temples burn!
And idle fancies flutter me, I know not
    where to turn;
Speak to me, sister; counsel me; this mar-
    riage must not be.
You only know the love that makes the
    world a world to me!

XX

Our gentle mother, had *she* lived—but we
    were left alone:
That other left us to ourselves; he cared
    not for his own;
So all the summer long we roam'd in these
    wild woods of ours,
My Edwin loved to call us then 'His two
    wild woodland flowers.'

XXI

Wild flowers blowing side by side in God's
    free light and air,
Wild flowers of the secret woods, when
    Edwin found us there,
Wild woods in which we roved with him,
    and heard his passionate vow,
Wild woods in which we rove no more, if
    we be parted now!

XXII

You will not leave me thus in grief to
    wander forth forlorn;
We never changed a bitter word, not once
    since we were born;
Our dying mother join'd our hands; she
    knew this father well;
She bad us love, like souls in Heaven, and
    now I fly from Hell,

XXIII

And you with me; and we shall light upon
    some lonely shore,
Some lodge within the waste sea-dunes,
    and hear the waters roar,

And see the ships from out the West go
    dipping thro' the foam,
And sunshine on that sail at last which
    brings our Edwin home.

XXIV

But look, the morning grows apace, and
    lights the old church-tower,
And lights the clock! the hand points five
    —O me—it strikes the hour—
I bide no more, I meet my fate, whatever
    ills betide!
Arise, my own true sister, come forth! the
    world is wide.

XXV

And yet my heart is ill at ease, my eyes are
    dim with dew,
I seem to see a new-dug grave up yonder
    by the yew!
If we should never more return, but
    wander hand in hand
With breaking hearts, without a friend,
    and in a distant land.

XXVI

O sweet, they tell me that the world is hard,
    and harsh of mind,
But can it be so hard, so harsh, as those
    that should be kind?
That matters not: let come what will; at
    last the end is sure,
And every heart that loves with truth is
    equal to endure.

TOMORROW

I

HER, that yer Honour was spakin' to?
    Whin, yer Honour? last year—
Standin' here be the bridge, when last yer
    Honour was here?
An' yer Honour ye gev her the top of the
    mornin', 'Tomorra' says she.
What did they call her, yer Honour? They
    call'd her Molly Magee.
An' yer Honour's the thrue ould blood
    that always manes to be kind,
But there's rason in all things, yer Honour,
    for Molly was out of her mind.

II

Shure, an' meself remimbers wan night
    comin' down be the sthrame,
An' it seems to me now like a bit of yisther-
    day in a dhrame—
Here where yer Honour seen her—there
    was but a slip of a moon,
But I hard thim—Molly Magee wid her
    batchelor, Danny O'Roon—
'You've been takin' a dhrop o' the crathur'
    an' Danny says 'Troth, an' I been
Dhrinkin' yer health wid Shamus O'Shea
    at Katty's shebeen;[1]
But I must be lavin' ye soon.' 'Ochone are
    ye goin' away?'
'Goin' to cut the Sassenach whate' he says
    'over the say'—
'An' whin will ye meet me agin?' an' I
    hard him 'Molly asthore,
I'll meet you agin tomorra,' says he, 'be
    the chapel-door.'
'An' whin are ye goin' to lave me?' 'O'
    Monday mornin'' says he;
'An' shure thin ye'll meet me tomorra?'
    'Tomorra, tomorra, Machree!'
Thin Molly's ould mother, yer Honour,
    that had no likin' for Dan,
Call'd from her cabin an' tould her to come
    away from the man,
An' Molly Magee kem flyin' acrass me, as
    light as a lark,
An' Dan stood there for a minute, an' thin
    wint into the dark.
But wirrah! the storm that night—the
    tundher, an' rain that fell,
An' the sthrames runnin' down at the
    back o' the glin 'ud 'a dhrownded
    Hell.

III

But airth was at pace nixt mornin', an'
    Hiven in its glory smiled,
As the Holy Mother o' Glory that smiles
    at her sleepin' child—
Ethen—she stept an the chapel-green, an'
    she turn'd herself roun'
Wid a diamond dhrop in her eye, for
    Danny was not to be foun',

[1] Grog-shop.

An' many's the time that I watch'd her at
    mass lettin' down the tear,
For the Divil a Danny was there, yer
    Honour, for forty year.

IV

Och, Molly Magee, wid the red o' the rose
    an' the white o' the May,
An' yer hair as black as the night, an' yer
    eyes as bright as the day!
Achora, yer laste little whishper was sweet
    as the lilt of a bird!
Acushla, ye set me heart batin' to music
    wid ivery word!
An' sorra the Queen wid her sceptre in sich
    an illigant han',
An' the fall of yer foot in the dance was as
    light as snow an the lan',
An' the sun kem out of a cloud whiniver
    ye walkt in the shtreet,
An' Shamus O'Shea was yer shadda, an'
    laid himself undher yer feet,
An' I loved ye meself wid a heart and a
    half, me darlin', and he
'Ud 'a shot his own sowl dead for a kiss of
    ye, Molly Magee.

V

But shure we wor betther frinds whin I
    crack'd his skull for her sake,
An' he ped me back wid the best he could
    give at ould Donovan's wake—
For the boys wor about her agin whin Dan
    didn't come to the fore,
An' Shamus along wid the rest, but she
    put thim all to the door.
An', afther, I thried her meself av the bird
    'ud come to me call,
But Molly, begorrah, 'ud listhen to naither
    at all, at all.

VI

An' her nabours an frinds 'ud consowl an'
    condowl wid her, airly and late,
'Your Danny,' they says, 'niver crasst over
    say to the Sassenach whate;
He's gone to the States, aroon, an' he's
    married another wife,
An' ye'll niver set eyes an the face of the
    thraithur agin in life!

An' to dhrame of a married man, death
    alive, is a mortial sin.'
But Molly says 'I'd his hand-promise, an'
    shure he'll meet me agin.'

VII

An' afther her paärints had inter'd glory,
    an' both in wan day,
She began to spake to herself, the crathur,
    an' whishper, an' say
'Tomorra, Tomorra!' an' Father Molowny
    he tuk her in han',
'Molly, you're manin',' he says, 'me dear,
    av I undherstan',
That ye'll meet your paärints agin an' yer
    Danny O'Roon afore God
Wid his blessed Marthyrs an' Saints;' an'
    she gev him a frindly nod,
'Tomorra, Tomorra,' she says, an' she
    didn't intind to desave,
But her wits wor dead, an' her hair was as
    white as the snow an a grave.

VIII

Arrah now, here last month they wor
    diggin' the bog, an' they foun'
Dhrownded in black bog-wather a corp
    lyin' undher groun'.

IX

Yer Honour's own agint, he says to me
    wanst, at Katty's shebeen,
'The Divil take all the black lan', for a
    blessin' 'ud come wid the green!'
An' where 'ud the poor man, thin, cut his
    bit o' turf for the fire?
But och! bad scran to the bogs whin they
    swallies the man intire!
An' sorra the bog that's in Hiven wid all
    the light an' the glow,
An' there's hate enough, shure, widout
    thim in the Divil's kitchen below.

X

Thim ould blind nagers in Agypt, I hard
    his Riverence say,
Could keep their haithen kings in the flesh
    for the Jidgemint day,

An', faix, be the piper o' Moses, they kep
    the cat an' the dog,
But it 'ud 'a been aisier work av they lived
    be an Irish bog.

XI

How-an-iver they laid this body they foun'
    an the grass
Be the chapel-door, an' the people 'ud see
    it that wint in to mass—
But a frish gineration had riz, an' most of
    the ould was few,
An' I didn't know him meself, an' nōne of
    the parish knew.

XII

But Molly kem limpin' up wid her stick,
    she was lamed iv a knee,
Thin a slip of a gossoon call'd, 'Div ye
    know him, Molly Magee?'
An' she stood up strait as the Queen of the
    world—she lifted her head—
'He said he would meet me tomorra!' an'
    dhropt down dead an the dead.

XIII

Och, Molly, we thought, machree, ye
    would start back agin into life,
Whin we laid yez, aich be aich, at yer wake
    like husban' an' wife.
Sorra the dhry eye thin but was wet for the
    frinds that was gone!
Sorra the silent throat but we hard it cryin'
    'Ochone!'
An' Shamus O'Shea that has now ten
    childer, hansome an' tall,
Him an' his childer wor keenin' as if he
    had lost thim all.

XIV

Thin his Riverence buried thim both in
    wan grave be the dead boor-tree,[1]
The young man Danny O'Roon wid his
    ould woman, Molly Magee.

XV

May all the flowers o' Jeroosilim blossom
    an' spring from the grass,
Imbrashin' an' kissin' aich other—as ye
    did—over yer Crass!

        [1] Elder-tree.

An' the lark fly out o' the flowers wid his
    song to the Sun an' the Moon,
An' tell thim in Hiven about Molly Magee
    an' her Danny O'Roon,
Till Holy St. Pether gets up wid his kays
    an' opens the gate!
An' shure, be the Crass, that's betther nor
    cuttin' the Sassenach whate
To be there wid the Blessed Mother, an'
    Saints an' Marthyrs galore,
An' singin' yer 'Aves' an' 'Pathers' for iver
    an' ivermore.

XVI

An' now that I tould yer Honour whativer
    I hard an' seen,
Yer Honour 'ill give me a thrifle to dhrink
    yer health in potheen.

THE SPINSTER'S
SWEET-ARTS

I

MILK for my sweet-arts, Bess! fur it mun
    be the time about now
When Molly cooms in fro' the far-end close
    wi' her paäils fro' the cow.
Eh! tha be new to the plaäce—thou'rt
    gaäpin'—doesn't tha see
I calls 'em arter the fellers es once was
    sweet upo' me?

II

Naäy to be sewer it be past 'er time. What
    maäkes 'er sa laäte?
Goä to the laäne at the back, an' looök
    thruf Maddison's gaäte!

III

Sweet-arts! Molly belike may 'a lighted
    to-night upo' one.
Sweet-arts! thanks to the Lord that I niver
    not listen'd to noän!
So I sits i' my oän armchair wi' my oän
    kettle theere o' the hob,
An' Tommy the fust, an' Tommy the
    second, an' Steevie an' Rob.

IV

Rob, coom oop 'ere o' my knee. Thou
    that i' spite o' the men
I 'a kep' thruf thick an' thin my two
    'oonderd a-year to mysen;

Yis! thaw tha call'd me es pretty es ony
lass i' the Shere;
An' thou be es pretty a Tabby, but Robby
I seed thruf ya theere.

V

Feyther 'ud saäy I wur ugly es sin, an' I
beänt not vaäin,
But I niver wur downright hugly, thaw
soom 'ud 'a thowt ma plaäin,
An' I wasn't sa plaäin i' pink ribbons, ye
said I wur pretty i' pinks,
An' I liked to 'ear it I did, but I beänt sich
a fool as ye thinks;
Ye was stroäkin ma down wi' the 'air, as
I be a-stroäkin o' you,
But whiniver I lŏŏked i' the glass I wur
sewer that it couldn't be true;
Niver wur pretty, not I, but ye knaw'd it
wur pleasant to 'ear,
Thaw it warn't not me es wur pretty, but
my two 'oonderd a-year.

VI

D'ya mind the murnin' when we was a-
walkin' togither, an' stood
By the claäy'd-oop pond, that the foälk be
sa scared at, i' Gigglesby wood,
Wheer the poor wench drowndid hersen,
black Sal, es 'ed been disgraäced?
An' I feel'd thy arm es I stood wur a-
creeäpin about my waäist;
An' me es wur allus afear'd of a man's
gittin' ower fond,
I sidled awaäy an' awaäy till I plumpt foot
fust i' the pond;
And, Robby, I niver 'a liked tha sa well, as
I did that daäy,
Fur tha joompt in thysen, an' tha hoickt
my feet wi' a flop fro' the claäy.
Ay, stick oop thy back, an' set oop thy
taäil, tha may gie ma a kiss,
Fur I walk'd wi' tha all the way hoam an'
wur niver sa nigh saäyin' Yis.
But wa boäth was i' sich a clat we was
shaämed to cross Gigglesby Greeän,
Fur a cat may lŏŏk at a king thou knaws
but the cat mun be cleän.
Sa we boäth on us kep out o' sight o' the
winders o' Gigglesby Hinn—

Naäy, but the claws o' tha! quiet! they
pricks cleän thruf to the skin—
An' wa boäth slinkt 'oäm by the brokken
shed i' the laäne at the back,
Wheer the poodle runn'd at tha once, an'
thou runn'd oop o' the thack;
An' tha squeedg'd my 'and i' the shed, fur
theere we was forced to 'ide,
Fur I seed that Steevie wur coomin', and
one o' the Tommies beside.

VII

Theere now, what art'a mewin at, Steevie?
for owt I can tell—
Robby wur fust to be sewer, or I mowt 'a
liked tha as well.

VIII

But, Robby, I thowt o' tha all the while I
wur chaängin' my gown,
An' I thowt shall I chaänge my staäte? but,
O Lord, upo' coomin' down—
My bran-new carpet es fresh es a midder
o' flowers i' Maäy—
Why 'edn't tha wiped thy shoes? it wur
clatted all ower wi' claäy.
An' I could 'a cried ammost, fur I seed
that it couldn't be,
An' Robby I gied tha a raätin that sattled
thy coortin o' me.
An' Molly an' me was agreed, as we was
a-cleänin' the floor,
That a man be a durty thing an' a trouble
an' plague wi' indoor.
But I rued it arter a bit, fur I stuck to tha
moor na the rest,
But I couldn't 'a lived wi' a man an' I
knaws it be all fur the best.

IX

Naäy—let ma stroäk tha down till I maäkes
tha es smooth es silk,
But if I 'ed married tha, Robby, thou'd
not 'a been worth thy milk,
Thou'd niver 'a cotch'd ony mice but 'a
left me the work to do,
And 'a taäen to the bottle beside, so es all
that I 'ears be true;
But I loovs tha to maäke thysen 'appy, an'
soa purr awaäy, my dear,
Thou 'ed wellnigh purr'd ma awaäy fro'
my oän two 'oonderd a-year.

x

Sweärin agean, you Toms, as ye used to do
  twelve year sin'!
Ye niver 'eärd Steevie sweär 'cep' it wur
  at a dog coomin' in,
An' boath o' ye mun be fools to be hallus
  a-shawin' your claws,
Fur I niver cared nothink for neither—an'
  one o' ye deäd ye knaws!
Coom give hoäver then, weant ye? I warrant ye soom fine daäy—
Theere, lig down—I shall hev to gie one
  or tother awaäy.
Can't ye taäke pattern by Steevie? ye shant
  hev a drop fro' the paäil.
Steevie be right good manners bang thruf
  to the tip o' the taäil.

XI

Robby, git down wi'tha, wilt tha? let
  Steevie coom oop o' my knee.
Steevie, my lad, thou 'ed very nigh been
  the Steevie fur me!
Robby wur fust to be sewer, 'e wur burn
  an' bred i' the 'ouse,
But thou be es 'ansom a tabby es iver
  patted a mouse.

XII

An' I beänt not vaäin, but I knaws I 'ed
  led tha a quieter life
Nor her wi' the hepitaph yonder! "A
  faäithful an' loovin' wife!"
An' 'cos o' thy farm by the beck, an' thy
  windmill oop o' the croft,
Tha thowt tha would marry ma, did tha?
  but that wur a bit ower soft,
Thaw thou was es soäber es daäy, wi' a
  niced red faäce, an' es cleän
Es a shillin' fresh fro' the mint wi' a bran-
  new 'eäd o' the Queeän,
An' thy farmin' es cleän es thysen', fur,
  Steevie, tha kep' it sa neät
That I niver not spied sa much es a poppy
  along wi' the wheät,
An' the wool of a thistle a-flyin' an' seeädin'
  tha haäted to see;
'Twur es bad es a battle-twig[1] 'ere 'i my
  oän blue chaumber to me.

[1] Earwig.

Ay, roob thy whiskers ageän ma, fur I
  could 'a taäen to tha well,
But fur thy bairns, poor Steevie, a bouncin'
  boy an' a gell.

XIII

An' thou was es fond o' thy bairns es I be
  mysen o' my cats,
But I niver not wish'd fur childer, I hevn't
  naw likin' fur brats;
Pretty anew when ya dresses 'em oop, an'
  they goäs fur a walk,
Or sits wi' their 'ands afoor 'em, an' doesn't
  not 'inder the talk!
But their bottles o' pap, an' their mucky
  bibs, an' the clats an' the clouts,
An' their mashin' their toys to pieäces an'
  maäkin' ma deäf wi' their shouts,
An' hallus a-joompin' about ma as if they
  was set upo' springs,
An' a haxin' ma hawkard questions, an'
  saäyin' ondecent things,
An' a-callin' ma 'hugly' mayhap to my
  faäce, or a teärin' my gown—
Dear! dear! dear! I mun part them
  Tommies—Steevie git down.

XIV

Ye be wuss nor the men-tommies, you.
  I tell'd ya, na moor o' that!
Tom, lig theere o' the cushion, an' tother
  Tom 'ere o' the mat.

XV

Theere! I ha' master'd *them!* Hed I mar-
  ried the Tommies—O Lord,
To loove an' obaäy the Tommies! I
  couldn't 'a stuck by my word.
To be horder'd about, an' waäked, when
  Molly 'd put out the light,
By a man coomin' in wi' a hiccup at ony
  hour o' the night!
An' the taäble staäin'd wi' 'is aäle, an' the
  mud o' 'is boots o' the stairs,
An' the stink o' 'is pipe i' the 'ouse, an' the
  mark o' 'is 'eäd o' the chairs!
An' noän o' my four sweet-arts 'ud 'a let
  me 'a hed my oän waäy,
Sa I likes 'em best wi' taäils when they
  'evn't a word to saäy.

XVI

An' I sits i' my oän little parlour, an'
   sarved by my oän little lass,
Wi' my oän little garden outside, an' my
   oän bed o' sparrow-grass,
An' my oän door-poorch wi' the woodbine
   an' jessmine a-dressin' it greeän,
An' my oän fine Jackman i' purple a roäbin'
   the 'ouse like a Queeän.

XVII

An' the little gells bobs to ma hoffens es
   I be abroad i' the laänes,
When I goäs fur to coomfut the poor es
   be down wi' their haäches an' their
   paäins:
An' a haäf-pot o' jam, or a mossel o' meät
   when it beänt too dear,
They maäkes ma a graäter Laädy nor 'er
   i' the mansion theer,

Hes 'es hallus to hax of a man how much
   to spare or to spend;
An' a spinster I be an' I will be, if soä
   pleäse God, to the hend.

XVIII

Mew! mew!—Bess wi' the milk! what ha
   maäde our Molly sa laäte?
It should 'a been 'ere by seven, an' theere
   —it be strikin' height—
'Cushie wur craäzed fur 'er cauf' well—I
   'eärd 'er a maäkin' 'er moän,
An' I thowt to mysen 'thank God that I
   hevn't naw cauf o' my oän.'
   Theere!
     Set it down!
       Now Robby!
     You Tommies shall waäit to-night
Till Robby an' Steevie 'es 'ed their lap—
   an' it sarves ye right.

LOCKSLEY HALL SIXTY YEARS AFTER

LATE, my grandson! half the morning have I paced these sandy tracts,
Watch'd again the hollow ridges roaring into cataracts,

Wander'd back to living boyhood while I heard the curlews call,
I myself so close on death, and death itself in Locksley Hall.

So—your happy suit was blasted—she the faultless, the divine;
And you liken—boyish babble—this boy-love of yours with mine.

I myself have often babbled doubtless of a foolish past;
Babble, babble; our old England may go down in babble at last.

'Curse him!' curse your fellow-victim? call him dotard in your rage?
Eyes that lured a doting boyhood well might fool a dotard's age.

Jilted for a wealthier! wealthier? yet perhaps she was not wise;
I remember how you kiss'd the miniature with those sweet eyes.

In the hall there hangs a painting—Amy's arms about my neck—
Happy children in a sunbeam sitting on the ribs of wreck.

In my life there was a picture, she that clasp'd my neck had flown;
I was left within the shadow sitting on the wreck alone.

Yours has been a slighter ailment, will you sicken for her sake?
You, not you! your modern amourist is of easier, earthlier make.

Amy loved me, Amy fail'd me, Amy was a timid child;
But your Judith—but your worldling—*she* had never driven me wild.

LOCKSLEY HALL SIXTY YEARS AFTER

She that holds the diamond necklace dearer than the golden ring,
She that finds a winter sunset fairer than a morn of Spring.

She that in her heart is brooding on his briefer lease of life,
While she vows 'till death shall part us,' she the would-be-widow wife.

She the worldling born of worldlings—father, mother—be content,
Ev'n the homely farm can teach us there is something in descent.

Yonder in that chapel, slowly sinking now into the ground,
Lies the warrior, my forefather, with his feet upon the hound.

Cross'd! for once he sail'd the sea to crush the Moslem in his pride;
Dead the warrior, dead his glory, dead the cause in which he died.

Yet how often I and Amy in the mouldering aisle have stood,
Gazing for one pensive moment on that founder of our blood.

There again I stood to-day, and where of old we knelt in prayer,
Close beneath the casement crimson with the shield of Locksley—there,

All in white Italian marble, looking still as if she smiled,
Lies my Amy dead in child-birth, dead the mother, dead the child.

Dead—and sixty years ago, and dead her aged husband now—
I this old white-headed dreamer stoopt and kiss'd her marble brow.

Gone the fires of youth, the follies, furies, curses, passionate tears,
Gone like fires and floods and earthquakes of the planet's dawning years.

Fires that shook me once, but now to silent ashes fall'n away.
Cold upon the dead volcano sleeps the gleam of dying day.

Gone the tyrant of my youth, and mute below the chancel stones,
All his virtues—I forgive them—black in white above his bones.

Gone the comrades of my bivouac, some in fight against the foe,
Some thro' age and slow diseases, gone as all on earth will go.

Gone with whom for forty years my life in golden sequence ran,
She with all the charm of woman, she with all the breadth of man,

Strong in will and rich in wisdom, Edith, yet so lowly-sweet,
Woman to her inmost heart, and woman to her tender feet,

Very woman of very woman, nurse of ailing body and mind,
She that link'd again the broken chain that bound me to my kind.

Here to-day was Amy with me, while I wander'd down the coast,
Near us Edith's holy shadow, smiling at the slighter ghost.

Gone our sailor son thy father, Leonard early lost at sea;
Thou alone, my boy, of Amy's kin and mine art left to me.

Gone thy tender-natured mother, wearying to be left alone,
Pining for the stronger heart that once had beat beside her own.

Truth, for Truth is Truth, he worshipt, being true as he was brave;
Good, for Good is Good, he follow'd, yet he look'd beyond the grave,

Wiser there than you, that crowning barren Death as lord of all,
Deem this over-tragic drama's closing curtain is the pall!

Beautiful was death in him, who saw the death, but kept the deck,
Saving women and their babes, and sinking with the sinking wreck,

Gone for ever! Ever? no—for since our dying race began,
Ever, ever, and for ever was the leading light of man.

Those that in barbarian burials kill'd the slave, and slew the wife
Felt within themselves the sacred passion of the second life.

Indian warriors dream of ampler hunting grounds beyond the night;
Ev'n the black Australian dying hopes he shall return, a white.

Truth for truth, and good for good! The Good, the True, the Pure, the Just
Take the charm 'For ever' from them, and they crumble into dust.

Gone the cry of 'Forward, Forward,' lost within a growing gloom;
Lost, or only heard in silence from the silence of a tomb.

Half the marvels of my morning, triumphs over time and space,
Staled by frequence, shrunk by usage into commonest commonplace!

'Forward' rang the voices then, and of the many mine was one.
Let us hush this cry of 'Forward' till ten thousand years have gone.

Far among the vanish'd races, old Assyrian kings would flay
Captives whom they caught in battle—iron-hearted victors they.

Ages after, while in Asia, he that led the wild Moguls,
Timur built his ghastly tower of eighty thousand human skulls,

Then, and here in Edward's time, an age of noblest English names,
Christian conquerors took and flung the conquer'd Christian into flames.

Love your enemy, bless your haters, said the Greatest of the great;
Christian love among the Churches look'd the twin of heathen hate.

From the golden alms of Blessing man had coin'd himself a curse:
Rome of Cæsar, Rome of Peter, which was crueller? which was worse?

France had shown a light to all men, preach'd a Gospel, all men's good;
Celtic Demos rose a Demon, shriek'd and slaked the light with blood.

Hope was ever on her mountain, watching till the day begun—
Crown'd with sunlight—over darkness—from the still unrisen sun.

Have we grown at last beyond the passions of the primal clan?
'Kill your enemy, for you hate him,' still, 'your enemy' was a man.

Have we sunk below them? peasants maim the helpless horse, and drive
Innocent cattle under thatch, and burn the kindlier brutes alive.

Brutes, the brutes are not your wrongers—burnt at midnight, found at morn,
Twisted hard in mortal agony with their offspring, born-unborn,

Clinging to the silent mother! Are we devils? are we men?
Sweet St. Francis of Assisi, would that he were here again,

He that in his Catholic wholeness used to call the very flowers
Sisters, brothers—and the beasts—whose pains are hardly less than ours!

Chaos, Cosmos! Cosmos, Chaos! who can tell how all will end?
Read the wide world's annals, you, and take their wisdom for your friend.

Hopes the best, but hold the Present fatal daughter of the Past,
Shape your heart to front the hour, but dream not that the hour will last.

Ay, if dynamite and revolver leave you courage to be wise:
When was age so cramm'd with menace? madness? written, spoken lies?

Envy wears the mask of Love, and, laughing sober fact to scorn,
Cries to Weakest as to Strongest, 'Ye are equals, equal-born.'

Equal-born? O yes, if yonder hill be level with the flat.
Charm us, Orator, till the Lion look no larger than the Cat,

Till the Cat thro' that mirage of overheated language loom
Larger than the Lion,—Demos end in working its own doom.

Russia bursts our Indian barrier, shall we fight her? shall we yield?
Pause! before you sound the trumpet, hear the voices from the field.

Those three hundred millions under one Imperial sceptre now,
Shall we hold them? shall we loose them? take the suffrage of the plow.

Nay, but these would feel and follow Truth if only you and you,
Rivals of realm-ruining party, when you speak were wholly true.

Plowmen, Shepherds, have I found, and more than once, and still could find,
Sons of God, and kings of men in utter nobleness of mind,

Truthful, trustful, looking upward to the practised hustings-liar;
So the Higher wields the Lower, while the Lower is the Higher.

Here and there a cotter's babe is royal-born by right divine;
Here and there my lord is lower than his oxen or his swine.

Chaos, Cosmos! Cosmos, Chaos! once again the sickening game;
Freedom, free to slay herself, and dying while they shout her name.

Step by step we gain'd a freedom known to Europe, known to all;
Step by step we rose to greatness,—thro' the tonguesters we may fall.

You that woo the Voices—tell them 'old experience is a fool,'
Teach your flatter'd kings that only those who cannot read can rule.

Pluck the mighty from their seat, but set no meek ones in their place;
Pillory Wisdom in your markets, pelt your offal at her face.

Tumble Nature heel o'er head, and, yelling with the yelling street,
Set the feet above the brain and swear the brain is in the feet.

Bring the old dark ages back without the faith, without the hope,
Break the State, the Church, the Throne, and roll their ruins down the slope.

Authors—essayist, atheist, novelist, realist, rhymester, play your part,
Paint the mortal shame of nature with the living hues of Art.

Rip your brothers' vices open, strip your own foul passions bare;
Down with Reticence, down with Reverence—forward—naked—let them stare.

Feed the budding rose of boyhood with the drainage of your sewer;
Send the drain into the fountain, lest the stream should issue pure.

Set the maiden fancies wallowing in the troughs of Zolaism,—
Forward, forward, ay and backward, downward too into the abysm.

Do your best to charm the worst, to lower the rising race of men;
Have we risen from out the beast, then back into the beast again?

Only 'dust to dust' for me that sicken at your lawless din,
Dust in wholesome old-world dust before the newer world begin.

Heated am I? you—you wonder—well, it scarce becomes mine age—
Patience! let the dying actor mouth his last upon the stage.

Cries of unprogressive dotage ere the dotard fall asleep?
Noises of a current narrowing, not the music of a deep?

Ay, for doubtless I am old, and think gray thoughts, for I am gray:
After all the stormy changes shall we find a changeless May?

After madness, after massacre, Jacobinism and Jacquerie,
Some diviner force to guide us thro' the days I shall not see?

When the schemes and all the systems, Kingdoms and Republics fall,
Something kindlier, higher, holier—all for each and each for all?

All the full-brain, half-brain races, led by Justice, Love, and Truth;
All the millions one at length with all the visions of my youth?

All diseases quench'd by Science, no man halt, or deaf or blind;
Stronger ever born of weaker, lustier body, larger mind?

Earth at last a warless world, a single race, a single tongue—
I have seen her far away—for is not Earth as yet so young?—

Every tiger madness muzzled, every serpent passion kill'd,
Every grim ravine a garden, every blazing desert till'd,

Robed in universal harvest up to either pole she smiles,
Universal ocean softly washing all her warless Isles.

Warless? when her tens are thousands, and her thousands millions, then—
All her harvest all too narrow—who can fancy warless men?

Warless? war will die out late then. Will it ever? late or soon?
Can it, till this outworn earth be dead as yon dead world the moon?

Dead the new astronomy calls her. . . . On this day and at this hour,
In this gap between the sandhills, whence you see the Locksley tower,

Here we met, our latest meeting—Amy—sixty years ago—
She and I—the moon was falling greenish thro' a rosy glow,

Just above the gateway tower, and even where you see her now—
Here we stood and claspt each other, swore the seeming-deathless vow. . . .

Dead, but how her living glory lights the hall, the dune, the grass!
Yet the moonlight is the sunlight, and the sun himself will pass.

Venus near her! smiling downward at this earthlier earth of ours,
Closer on the Sun, perhaps a world of never fading flowers.

Hesper, whom the poet call'd the Bringer home of all good things.
All good things may move in Hesper, perfect peoples, perfect kings.

Hesper—Venus—were we native to that splendour or in Mars,
We should see the Globe we groan in, fairest of their evening stars.

Could we dream of wars and carnage, craft and madness, lust and spite,
Roaring London, raving Paris, in that point of peaceful light?

Might we not in glancing heavenward on a star so silver-fair,
Yearn, and clasp the hands and murmur, 'Would to God that we were there'?

Forward, backward, backward, forward, in the immeasurable sea,
Sway'd by vaster ebbs and flows than can be known to you or me.

All the suns—are these but symbols of innumerable man,
Man or Mind that sees a shadow of the planner or the plan?

Is there evil but on earth? or pain in every peopled sphere?
Well be grateful for the sounding watchword 'Evolution' here.

Evolution ever climbing after some ideal good,
And Reversion ever dragging Evolution in the mud.

What are men that He should heed us? cried the king of sacred song;
Insects of an hour, that hourly work their brother insect wrong,

While the silent Heavens roll, and Suns along their fiery way,
All their planets whirling round them, flash a million miles a day.

Many an Æon moulded earth before her highest, man, was born,
Many an Æon too may pass when earth is manless and forlorn,

Earth so huge, and yet so bounded—pools of salt, and plots of land—
Shallow skin of green and azure—chains of mountain, grains of sand!

Only That which made us, meant us to be mightier by and by,
Set the sphere of all the boundless Heavens within the human eye,

LOCKSLEY HALL SIXTY YEARS AFTER

Sent the shadow of Himself, the boundless, thro' the human soul;
Boundless inward, in the atom, boundless outward, in the Whole.

*   *   *   *   *   *   *   *

Here is Locksley Hall, my grandson, here the lion-guarded gate.
Not to-night in Locksley Hall—to-morrow—you, you come so late.

Wreck'd—your train—or all but wreck'd? a shatter'd wheel? a vicious boy!
Good, this forward, you that preach it, is it well to wish you joy?

Is it well that while we range with Science, glorying in the Time,
City children soak and blacken soul and sense in city slime?

There among the glooming alleys Progress halts on palsied feet,
Crime and hunger cast our maidens by the thousand on the street.

There the Master scrimps his haggard sempstress of her daily bread,
There a single sordid attic holds the living and the dead.

There the smouldering fire of fever creeps across the rotted floor,
And the crowded couch of incest in the warrens of the poor.

Nay, your pardon, cry your 'forward,' yours are hope and youth, but I
Eighty winters leave the dog too lame to follow with the cry,

Lame and old, and past his time, and passing now into the night;
Yet I would the rising race were half as eager for the light.

Light the fading gleam of Even? light the glimmer of the dawn?
Aged eyes may take the growing glimmer for the gleam withdrawn.

Far away beyond her myraid coming changes earth will be
Something other than the wildest modern guess of you and me.

Earth may reach her earthly-worst, or if she gain her earthly-best,
Would she find her human offspring this ideal man at rest?

Forward then, but still remember how the course of Time will swerve,
Crook and turn upon itself in many a backward streaming curve.

Not the Hall to-night, my grandson! Death and Silence hold their own.
Leave the Master in the first dark hour of his last sleep alone.

Worthier soul was he than I am, sound and honest, rustic Squire,
Kindly landlord, boon companion—youthful jealousy is a liar.

Cast the poison from your bosom, oust the madness from your brain.
Let the trampled serpent show you that you have not lived in vain.

Youthful! youth and age are scholars yet but in the lower school,
Nor is he the wisest man who never proved himself a fool.

Yonder lies our young sea-village—Art and Grace are less and less:
Science grows and Beauty dwindles—roofs of slated hideousness!

LOCKSLEY HALL SIXTY YEARS AFTER

There is one old Hostel left us where they swing the Locksley shield,
Till the peasant cow shall butt the 'Lion passant' from his field.

Poor old Heraldry, poor old History, poor old Poetry, passing hence,
In the common deluge drowning old political common-sense!

Poor old voice of eighty crying after voices that have fled!
All I loved are vanish'd voices, all my steps are on the dead.

All the world is ghost to me, and as the phantom disappears,
Forward far and far from here is all the hope of eighty years.

   *   *   *   *   *   *   *

In this Hostel—I remember—I repent it o'er his grave—
Like a clown—by chance he met me—I refused the hand he gave.

From that casement where the trailer mantles all the mouldering bricks—
I was then in early boyhood, Edith but a child of six—

While I shelter'd in this archway from a day of driving showers—
Peept the winsome face of Edith like a flower among the flowers.

Here to-night! the Hall to-morrow, when they toll the Chapel bell!
Shall I hear in one dark room a wailing, 'I have loved thee well.'

Then a peal that shakes the portal—one has come to claim his bride,
Her that shrank, and put me from her, shriek'd, and started from my side—

Silent echoes! You, my Leonard, use and not abuse your day,
Move among your people, know them, follow him who led the way,

Strove for sixty widow'd years to help his homelier brother men,
Served the poor, and built the cottage, raised the school, and drain'd the fen.

Hears he now the Voice that wrong'd him? who shall swear it cannot be?
Earth would never touch her worst, were one in fifty such as he.

Ere she gain her Heavenly-best, a God must mingle with the game:
Nay, there may be those about us whom we neither see nor name,

Felt within us as ourselves, the Powers of Good, the Powers of Ill,
Strowing balm, or shedding poison in the fountains of the Will.

Follow you the Star that lights a desert pathway, yours or mine.
Forward, till you see the highest Human Nature is divine.

Follow Light, and do the Right—for man can half-control his doom—
Till you find the deathless Angel seated in the vacant tomb.

Forward, let the stormy moment fly and mingle with the Past.
I that loathed, have come to love him. Love will conquer at the last.

Gone at eighty, mine own age, and I and you will bear the pall;
Then I leave thee Lord and Master, latest Lord of Locksley Hall.

PROLOGUE
TO GENERAL HAMLEY

OUR birches yellowing and from each
 The light leaf falling fast,
While squirrels from our fiery beech
 Were bearing off the mast,
You came, and look'd and loved the view
 Long-known and loved by me,
Green Sussex fading into blue
 With one gray glimpse of sea;
And, gazing from this height alone,
 We spoke of what had been
Most marvellous in the wars your own
 Crimean eyes had seen;
And now—like old-world inns that take
 Some warrior for a sign
That therewithin a guest may make
 True cheer with honest wine—
Because you heard the lines I read
 Nor utter'd word of blame,
I dare without your leave to head
 These rhymings with your name,
Who know you but as one of those
 I fain would meet again,
Yet know you, as your England knows
 That you and all your men
Were soldiers to her heart's desire,
 When, in the vanish'd year,
You saw the league-long rampart-fire
 Flare from Tel-el-Kebir
Thro' darkness, and the foe was driven,
 And Wolseley overthrew
Arâbi, and the stars in heaven
 Paled, and the glory grew.

THE CHARGE OF THE HEAVY
BRIGADE AT BALACLAVA

OCTOBER 25, 1854

I

THE charge of the gallant three hundred,
 the Heavy Brigade!
Down the hill, down the hill, thousands of
 Russians,
Thousands of horsemen, drew to the
 valley—and stay'd;
For Scarlett and Scarlett's three hundred
 were riding by

When the points of the Russian lances
 arose in the sky;
And he call'd 'Left wheel into line!' and
 they wheel'd and obey'd.
Then he look'd at the host that had halted
 he knew not why,
And he turn'd half round, and he bad his
 trumpeter sound
To the charge, and he rode on ahead, as he
 waved his blade
To the gallant three hundred whose glory
 will never die—
'Follow,' and up the hill, up the hill, up
 the hill,
Follow'd the Heavy Brigade.

II

The trumpet, the gallop, the charge, and
 the might of the fight!
Thousands of horsemen had gather'd there
 on the height,
With a wing push'd out to the left and a
 wing to the right,
And who shall escape if they close? but he
 dash'd up alone
Thro' the great gray slope of men,
Sway'd his sabre, and held his own
Like an Englishman there and then;
All in a moment follow'd with force
Three that were next in their fiery course,
Wedged themselves in between horse and
 horse,
Fought for their lives in the narrow gap
 they had made—
Four amid thousands! and up the hill, up
 the hill,
Gallopt the gallant three hundred, the
 Heavy Brigade.

III

Fell like a cannonshot,
Burst like a thunderbolt,
Crash'd like a hurricane,
Broke thro' the mass from below,
Drove thro' the midst of the foe,
Plunged up and down, to and fro,
Rode flashing blow upon blow,
Brave Inniskillens and Greys
Whirling their sabres in circles of light!
And some of us, all in amaze,
Who were held for a while from the fight,

THE CHARGE OF THE HEAVY BRIGADE

And were only standing at gaze,
When the dark-muffled Russian crowd
Folded its wings from the left and the right,
And roll'd them around like a cloud,—
O mad for the charge and the battle
    were we,
When our own good redcoats sank from
    sight,
Like drops of blood in a dark-gray sea,
And we turn'd to each other, whispering,
    all dismay'd,
'Lost are the gallant three hundred of
    Scarlett's Brigade!'

IV

'Lost one and all' were the words
Mutter'd in our dismay;
But they rode like Victors and Lords
Thro' the forest of lances and swords
In the heart of the Russian hordes,
They rode, or they stood at bay—
Struck with the sword-hand and slew,
Down with the bridle-hand drew
The foe from the saddle and threw
Underfoot there in the fray—
Ranged like a storm or stood like a rock
In the wave of a stormy day;
Till suddenly shock upon shock
Stagger'd the mass from without,
Drove it in wild disarray,
For our men gallopt up with a cheer and a
    shout,
And the foeman surged, and waver'd, and
    reel'd
Up the hill, up the hill, up the hill, out of
    the field,
And over the brow and away.

V

Glory to each and to all, and the charge
    that they made!
Glory to all the three hundred, and all the
    Brigade!

NOTE.—The 'three hundred' of the 'Heavy
Brigade' who made this famous charge were
the Scots Greys and the 2nd squadron of
Inniskillings; the remainder of the 'Heavy
Brigade' subsequently dashing up to their sup-
port.
    The 'three' were Scarlett's aide-de-camp,
Elliot, and the trumpeter and Shegog the
orderly, who had been close behind him.

EPILOGUE

IRENE

NOT this way will you set your name
A star among the stars.

POET

What way?

IRENE

You praise when you should blame
The barbarism of wars.
A juster epoch has begun.

POET

Yet tho' this cheek be gray,
And that bright hair the modern sun,
Those eyes the blue to-day,
You wrong me, passionate little friend.
I would that wars should cease,
I would the globe from end to end
Might sow and reap in peace,
And some new Spirit o'erbear the old,
Or Trade re-frain the Powers
From war with kindly links of gold,
Or Love with wreaths of flowers.
Slav, Teuton, Kelt, I count them all
My friends and brother souls,
With all the peoples, great and small,
That wheel between the poles.
But since, our mortal shadow, Ill
To waste this earth began—
Perchance from some abuse of Will
In worlds before the man
Involving ours—he needs must fight
To make true peace his own,
He needs must combat might with might,
Or Might would rule alone;
And who loves War for War's own sake
Is fool, or crazed, or worse;
But let the patriot-soldier take
His meed of fame in verse;
Nay—tho' that realm were in the wrong
For which her warriors bleed,
It still were right to crown with song
The warrior's noble deed—
A crown the Singer hopes may last,
For so the deed endures;
But Song will vanish in the Vast;
And that large phrase of yours
'A Star among the stars,' my dear,
Is girlish talk at best;

529

For dare we dally with the sphere
  As he did half in jest,
Old Horace? 'I will strike' said he
  'The stars with head sublime,'
But scarce could see, as now we see,
  The man in Space and Time,
So drew perchance a happier lot
  Than ours, who rhyme to-day.
The fires that arch this dusky dot—
  Yon myriad-worlded way—
The vast sun-clusters' gather'd blaze,
  World-isles in lonely skies,
Whole heavens within themselves, amaze
  Our brief humanities;
And so does Earth; for Homer's fame,
  Tho' carved in harder stone—
The falling drop will make his name
  As mortal as my own.

IRENE

No!

POET

  Let it live then—ay, till when?
  Earth passes, all is lost
In what they prophesy, our wise men,
  Sun-flame or sunless frost,
And deed and song alike are swept
  Away, and all in vain
As far as man can see, except
  The man himself remain;
And tho', in this lean age forlorn,
  Too many a voice may cry
That man can have no after-morn,
  Not yet of these am I.
The man remains, and whatsoe'er
  He wrought of good or brave
Will mould him thro' the cycle-year
  That dawns behind the grave.

And here the Singer for his Art
  Not all in vain may plead
'The song that nerves a nation's heart,
  Is in itself a deed.'

TO VIRGIL

WRITTEN AT THE REQUEST OF THE
MANTUANS FOR THE NINETEENTH
CENTENARY OF VIRGIL'S DEATH

I

ROMAN VIRGIL, thou that singest
  Ilion's lofty temples robed in fire,

Ilion falling, Rome arising,
  wars, and filial faith, and Dido's pyre;

II

Landscape-lover, lord of language
  more than he that sang the Works
    and Days,
All the chosen coin of fancy
  flashing out from many a golden
    phrase;

III

Thou that singest wheat and woodland,
  tilth and vineyard, hive and horse and
    herd;
All the charm of all the Muses
  often flowering in a lonely word;

IV

Poet of the happy Tityrus
  piping underneath his beechen
    bowers;
Poet of the poet-satyr
  whom the laughing shepherd bound
    with flowers;

V

Chanter of the Pollio, glorying
  in the blissful years again to be,
Summers of the snakeless meadow,
  unlaborious earth and oarless sea;

VI

Thou that seëst Universal
  Nature moved by Universal Mind;
Thou majestic in thy sadness
  at the doubtful doom of human kind;

VII

Light among the vanish'd ages;
  star that gildest yet this phantom
    shore;
Golden branch amid the shadows,
  kings and realms that pass to rise no
    more;

VIII

Now thy Forum roars no longer,
  fallen every purple Cæsar's dome—
Tho' thine ocean-roll of rhythm
  sound for ever of Imperial Rome—

IX

Now the Rome of slaves hath perish'd,
   and the Rome of freemen holds her
     place,
I, from out the Northern Island
   sunder'd once from all the human
     race,

X

I salute thee, Mantovano,
   I that loved thee since my day began,
Wielder of the stateliest measure
   ever moulded by the lips of man.

THE DEAD PROPHET

182–

I

DEAD!
   And the Muses cried with a stormy cry
'Send them no more, for evermore.
   Let the people die.'

II

Dead!
   'Is it *he* then brought so low?'
And a careless people flock'd from the
     fields
   With a purse to pay for the show.

III

Dead, who had served his time,
   Was one of the people's kings,
Had labour'd in lifting them out of slime,
   And showing them, souls have wings!

IV

Dumb on the winter heath he lay.
   His friends had stript him bare,
And roll'd his nakedness everyway
   That all the crowd might stare.

V

A storm-worn signpost not to be read,
   And a tree with a moulder'd nest
On its barkless bones, stood stark by the
     dead;
   And behind him, low in the West,

VI

With shifting ladders of shadow and light,
   And blurr'd in colour and form,
The sun hung over the gates of Night,
   And glared at a coming storm.

VII

Then glided a vulturous Beldam forth,
   That on dumb death had thriven;
They call'd her 'Reverence' here upon
     earth,
   And 'The Curse of the Prophet' in
     Heaven.

VIII

She knelt—'We worship him'—all but
     wept—
   'So great so noble was he!'
She clear'd her sight, she arose, she swept
   The dust of earth from her knee.

IX

'Great! for he spoke and the people heard,
   And his eloquence caught like a flame
From zone to zone of the world, till his
     Word
   Had won him a noble name.

X

'Noble! he sung, and the sweet sound ran
   Thro' palace and cottage door,
For he touch'd on the whole sad planet of
     man,
   The kings and the rich and the poor;

XI

'And he sung not alone of an old sun set,
   But a sun coming up in his youth!
Great and noble—O yes—but yet—
   For man is a lover of Truth,

XII

'And bound to follow, wherever she go
   Stark-naked, and up or down,
Thro' her high hill-passes of stainless snow,
   Or the foulest sewer of the town—

XIII

'Noble and great—O ay—but then,
   Tho' a prophet should have his due,
Was he noblier-fashion'd than other men?
   Shall we see to it, I and you?

XIV

'For since he would sit on a Prophet's seat,
   As lord of the Human soul,
We needs must scan him from head to feet
   Were it but for a wart or a mole?'

XV

His wife and his child stood by him in tears,
   But she—she push'd them aside.
'Tho' a name may last for a thousand years,
   Yet a truth is a truth,' she cried.

XVI

And she that had haunted his pathway still,
   Had often truckled and cower'd
When he rose in his wrath, and had yielded
     her will
   To the master, as overpower'd,

XVII

She tumbled his helpless corpse about.
   'Small blemish upon the skin!
But I think we know what is fair without
   Is often as foul within.'

XVIII

She crouch'd, she tore him part from part,
   And out of his body she drew
The red 'Blood-eagle'[1] of liver and heart;
   She held them up to the view;

XIX

She gabbled, as she groped in the dead,
   And all the people were pleased;
'See, what a little heart,' she said,
   'And the liver is half-diseased!'

XX

She tore the Prophet after death,
   And the people paid her well.
Lightnings flicker'd along the heath;
   One shriek'd 'The fires of Hell!'

EARLY SPRING

I

ONCE more the Heavenly Power
   Makes all things new,

[1] Old Viking term for lungs, liver, etc., when torn by the conqueror out of the body of the conquered.

And domes the red-plow'd hills
   With loving blue;
The blackbirds have their wills,
   The throstles too.

II

Opens a door in Heaven;
   From skies of glass
A Jacob's ladder falls
   On greening grass,
And o'er the mountain-walls
   Young angels pass.

III

Before them fleets the shower,
   And burst the buds,
And shine the level lands,
   And flash the floods;
The stars are from their hands
   Flung thro' the woods,

IV

The woods with living airs
   How softly fann'd,
Light airs from where the deep,
   All down the sand,
Is breathing in his sleep,
   Heard by the land.

V

O follow, leaping blood,
   The season's lure!
O heart, look down and up
   Serene, secure,
Warm as the crocus cup,
   Like snowdrops, pure!

VI

Past, Future glimpse and fade
   Thro' some slight spell,
A gleam from yonder vale,
   Some far blue fell,
And sympathies, how frail,
   In sound and smell!

VII

Till at thy chuckled note,
   Thou twinkling bird,
The fairy fancies range,
   And, lightly stirr'd,
Ring little bells of change
   From word to word.

VIII

For now the Heavenly Power
Makes all things new,
And thaws the cold, and fills
The flower with dew;
The blackbirds have their wills,
The poets too.

PREFATORY POEM TO MY BROTHER'S SONNETS

MIDNIGHT, JUNE 30, 1879

I

MIDNIGHT—in no midsummer tune
The breakers lash the shores:
The cuckoo of a joyless June
Is calling out of doors:

And thou hast vanish'd from thine own
To that which looks like rest,
True brother, only to be known
By those who love thee best.

II

Midnight—and joyless June gone by,
And from the deluged park
The cuckoo of a worse July
Is calling thro' the dark:

But thou art silent underground,
And o'er thee streams the rain,
True poet, surely to be found
When Truth is found again.

III

And, now to these unsummer'd skies
The summer bird is still,
Far off a phantom cuckoo cries
From out a phantom hill;

And thro' this midnight breaks the sun
Of sixty years away,
The light of days when life begun,
The days that seem to-day,

When all my griefs were shared with thee,
As all my hopes were thine—
As all thou wert was one with me,
May all thou art be mine!

'FRATER AVE ATQUE VALE'

Row us out from Desenzano, to your
Sirmione row!
So they row'd, and there we landed—'O
venusta Sirmio!'
There to me thro' all the groves of olive in
the summer glow,
There beneath the Roman ruin where the
purple flowers grow,
Came that 'Ave atque Vale' of the Poet's
hopeless woe,
Tenderest of Roman poets nineteen-
hundred years ago,
'Frater Ave atque Vale'—as we wander'd
to and fro
Gazing at the Lydian laughter of the Garda
Lake below
Sweet Catullus's all-but-island, olive-
silvery Sirmio!

HELEN'S TOWER[1]

HELEN'S TOWER, here I stand,
Dominant over sea and land.
Son's love built me, and I hold
Mother's love in letter'd gold.
Love is in and out of time,
I am mortal stone and lime.
Would my granite girth were strong
As either love, to last as long!
I should wear my crown entire
To and thro' the Doomsday fire,
And be found of angel eyes
In earth's recurring Paradise.

EPITAPH ON LORD STRAT-FORD DE REDCLIFFE

IN WESTMINSTER ABBEY

THOU third great Canning, stand among
our best
And noblest, now thy long day's work
hath ceased,
Here silent in our Minster of the West
Who wert the voice of England in the
East.

[1] Written at the request of my friend, Lord
Dufferin.

EPITAPH
ON GENERAL GORDON

IN THE GORDON BOYS' NATIONAL
MEMORIAL HOME NEAR WOKING

WARRIOR of God, man's friend, and
tyrant's foe,
Now somewhere dead far in the waste
Soudan,
Thou livest in all hearts, for all men know
This earth has never borne a nobler man.

EPITAPH ON CAXTON

IN ST. MARGARET'S, WESTMINSTER

FIAT LUX (his motto)

THY prayer was 'Light—more Light—
while Time shall last!'
Thou sawest a glory growing on the night,
But not the shadows which that light
would cast,
Till shadows vanish in the Light of Light.

TO THE DUKE OF ARGYLL

O PATRIOT Statesman, be thou wise to
know
The limits of resistance, and the bounds
Determining concession; still be bold
Not only to slight praise but suffer scorn;
And be thy heart a fortress to maintain
The day against the moment, and the
year
Against the day; thy voice, a music heard
Thro' all the yells and counter-yells of
feud
And faction, and thy will, a power to
make
This ever-changing world of circumstance,
In changing, chime with never-changing
Law.

HANDS ALL ROUND

FIRST pledge our Queen this solemn night,
Then drink to England, every guest;
That man 's the best Cosmopolite
Who loves his native country best.
May freedom's oak for ever live
With stronger life from day to day;

That man 's the true Conservative
Who lops the moulder'd branch away.
Hands all round!
God the traitor's hope confound!
To this great cause of Freedom drink, my
friends,
And the great name of England, round
and round.

To all the loyal hearts who long
To keep our English Empire whole!
To all our noble sons, the strong
New England of the Southern Pole!
To England under Indian skies,
To those dark millions of her realm!
To Canada whom we love and prize,
Whatever statesman hold the helm.
Hands all round!
God the traitor's hope confound!
To this great name of England drink, my
friends,
And all her glorious empire, round and
round.

To all our statesmen so they be
True leaders of the land's desire!
To both our Houses, may they see
Beyond the borough and the shire!
We sail'd wherever ship could sail,
We founded many a mighty state;
Pray God our greatness may not fail
Thro' craven fears of being great.
Hands all round!
God the traitor's hope confound!
To this great cause of Freedom drink, my
friends,
And the great name of England, round
and round.

FREEDOM

I

O THOU so fair in summers gone,
While yet thy fresh and virgin soul
Inform'd the pillar'd Parthenon,
The glittering Capitol;

II

So fair in southern sunshine bathed,
But scarce of such majestic mien
As here with forehead vapour-swathed
In meadows ever green;

III

For thou—when Athens reign'd and Rome,
　Thy glorious eyes were dimm'd with
　　pain
To mark in many a freeman's home
　The slave, the scourge, the chain;

IV

O follower of the Vision, still
　In motion to the distant gleam,
Howe'er blind force and brainless will
　May jar thy golden dream

V

Of Knowledge fusing class with class,
Of civic Hate no more to be,
Of Love to leaven all the mass,
　Till every Soul be free;

VI

Who yet, like Nature, wouldst not mar
　By changes all too fierce and fast
This order of Her Human Star,
　This heritage of the past;

VII

O scorner of the party cry
　That wanders from the public good,
Thou—when the nations rear on high
　Their idol smear'd with blood,

VIII

And when they roll their idol down—
　Of saner worship sanely proud;
Thou loather of the lawless crown
　As of the lawless crowd;

IX

How long thine ever-growing mind
　Hath still'd the blast and strown the
　　wave,
Tho' some of late would raise a wind
　To sing thee to thy grave,

X

Men loud against all forms of power—
　Unfurnish'd brows, tempestuous
　　tongues—
Expecting all things in an hour—
　Brass mouths and iron lungs!

TO H.R.H. PRINCESS BEATRICE

Two Suns of Love make day of human life,
Which else with all its pains, and griefs,
　and deaths,
Were utter darkness—one, the Sun of dawn
That brightens thro' the Mother's tender
　eyes,
And warms the child's awakening world—
　and one
The later-rising Sun of spousal Love,
Which from her household orbit draws the
　child
To move in other spheres. The Mother
　weeps
At that white funeral of the single life,
Her maiden daughter's marriage; and her
　tears
Are half of pleasure, half of pain—the child
Is happy—ev'n in leaving *her!* but Thou,
True daughter, whose all-faithful, filial
　eyes
Have seen the loneliness of earthly thrones,
Wilt neither quit the widow'd Crown nor
　let
This later light of Love have risen in vain,
But moving thro' the Mother's home,
　between
The two that love thee, lead a summer life,
Sway'd by each Love, and swaying to each
　Love,
Like some conjectured planet in mid
　heaven
Between two Suns, and drawing down
　from both
The lighted and genial warmth of double
　day.

THE FLEET[1]

I

You, you, *if* you shall fail to understand
　What England is, and what her all-in-
　　all,
On you will come the curse of all the land,
　Should this old England fall
　　Which Nelson left so great.

[1] The speaker said that 'he should like to be
assured that other outlying portions of the
Empire, the Crown colonies, and important
coaling stations were being as promptly and as

II

His isle, the mightiest Ocean-power on
 earth,
 Our own fair isle, the lord of every sea—
Her fuller franchise—what would that be
 worth—
 Her ancient fame of Free—
 Were she . . . a fallen state?

III

Her dauntless army scatter'd, and so
 small,
 Her island-myriads fed from alien
 lands—
The fleet of England is her all-in-all;
 Her fleet is in your hands,
 And in her fleet her Fate.

thoroughly fortified as the various capitals of
the self-governing colonies. He was credibly
informed this was not so. It was impossible,
also, not to feel some degree of anxiety about
the efficacy of present provision to defend and
protect, by means of swift well-armed cruisers,
the immense mercantile fleet of the Empire. A
third source of anxiety, so far as the colonies
were concerned, was the apparently insufficient
provision for the rapid manufacture of arma-
ments and their prompt despatch when ordered
to their colonial destination. Hence the necessity for manufacturing appliances equal to the
requirements, not of Great Britain alone, but
of the whole Empire. But the keystone of the
whole was the necessity for an overwhelmingly
powerful fleet and efficient defence for all neces-
sary coaling stations. This was as essential for
the colonies as for Great Britain. It was the one
condition for the continuance of the Empire.
All that Continental Powers did with respect to
armies England should effect with her navy. It
was essentially a defensive force, and could be
moved rapidly from point to point, but it should
be equal to all that was expected from it. It was
to strengthen the fleet that colonists would first
readily tax themselves, because they realised
how essential a powerful fleet was to the safety,
not only of that extensive commerce sailing in
every sea, but ultimately to the security of the
distant portions of the Empire. Who could
estimate the loss involved in even a brief period
of disaster to the Imperial Navy? Any amount
of money timely expended in preparation would
be quite insignificant when compared with the
possible calamity he had referred to.'—*Extract
from Sir Graham Berry's Speech at the Colonial
Institute, 9th November 1886.*

IV

You, you, that have the ordering of her
 fleet,
 If you should only compass her disgrace,
When all men starve, the wild mob's mil-
 lion feet
 Will kick you from your place,
 But then too late, too late.

OPENING OF THE INDIAN
AND COLONIAL EXHIBITION
BY THE QUEEN

WRITTEN AT THE REQUEST OF THE
PRINCE OF WALES

I

Welcome, welcome with one voice!
In your welfare we rejoice,
Sons and brothers that have sent,
From isle and cape and continent,
Produce of your field and flood,
Mount and mine, and primal wood;
Works of subtle brain and hand,
And splendours of the morning land,
Gifts from every British zone;
 Britons, hold your own!

II

May we find, as ages run,
The mother featured in the son;
And may yours for ever be
That old strength and constancy
Which has made your fathers great
In our ancient island State,
And wherever her flag fly,
Glorying between sea and sky,
Makes the might of Britain known;
 Britons, hold your own!

III

Britain fought her sons of yore—
Britain fail'd; and never more,
Careless of our growing kin,
Shall we sin our fathers' sin,
Men that in a narrower day—
Unprophetic rulers they—
Drove from out the mother's nest
That young eagle of the West
To forage for herself alone;
 Britons, hold your own!

IV

Sharers of our glorious past,
Brothers, must we part at last?
Shall we not thro' good and ill
Cleave to one another still?
Britain's myriad voices call,
'Sons, be welded each and all,
Into one imperial whole,
One with Britain, heart and soul!
One life, one flag, one fleet, one Throne!
Britons, hold your own!

POETS AND THEIR BIBLIOGRAPHIES

OLD poets foster'd under friendlier skies,
    Old Virgil who would write ten lines,
        they say,
    At dawn, and lavish all the golden day
To make them wealthier in his readers'
        eyes;
And you, old popular Horace, you the wise
    Adviser of the nine-years-ponder'd lay,
    And you, that wear a wreath of sweeter
        bay,
Catullus, whose dead songster never dies;
If, glancing downward on the kindly
        sphere
    That once had roll'd you round and
        round the Sun,
    You see your Art still shrined in human
        shelves,
You should be jubilant that you flourish'd
        here
Before the Love of Letters, overdone,
Had swampt the sacred poets with them-
    selves.

TO W. C. MACREADY

1851

FAREWELL, Macready, since to-night we
        part;
Full-handed thunders often have con-
        fessed
    Thy power, well-used to move the
        public breast.
We thank thee with our voice, and from
        the heart.

Farewell, Macready, since this night we
        part,
Go, take thine honours home; rank with
        the best,
Garrick and statelier Kemble, and the
        rest
Who made a nation purer through their
        art.

Thine is it that our drama did not die,
    Nor flicker down to brainless panto-
        mime,
    And those gilt gauds men-children
        swarm to see.

Farewell, Macready; moral, grave, sub-
        lime;
Our Shakespeare's bland and universal
        eye
Dwells pleased, through twice a hundred
        years, on thee.

QUEEN MARY

A DRAMA

DRAMATIS PERSONÆ

QUEEN MARY.
PHILIP, *King of Naples and Sicily, afterwards King of Spain.*
THE PRINCESS ELIZABETH.
REGINALD POLE, *Cardinal and Papal Legate.*
SIMON RENARD, *Spanish Ambassador.*
LE SIEUR DE NOAILLES, *French Ambassador.*
THOMAS CRANMER, *Archbishop of Canterbury.*
SIR NICHOLAS HEATH, *Archbishop of York; Lord Chancellor after Gardiner.*
EDWARD COURTENAY, *Earl of Devon.*
LORD WILLIAM HOWARD, *afterwards Lord Howard, and Lord High Admiral.*
LORD WILLIAMS OF THAME.　　　LORD PAGET.　　　LORD PETRE.
STEPHEN GARDINER, *Bishop of Winchester and Lord Chancellor.*
EDMUND BONNER, *Bishop of London.*　　　THOMAS THIRLBY, *Bishop of Ely.*
SIR THOMAS WYATT ⎱ *Insurrectionary Leaders.*
SIR THOMAS STAFFORD ⎰
SIR RALPH BAGENHALL.　　　　　SIR ROBERT SOUTHWELL.
SIR HENRY BEDINGFIELD.　　　　SIR WILLIAM CECIL.
SIR THOMAS WHITE, *Lord Mayor of London.*
THE DUKE OF ALVA ⎱ *attending on Philip.*
THE COUNT DE FERIA ⎰
PETER MARTYR.　　　FATHER COLE.　　　FATHER BOURNE.
VILLA GARCIA.　　　SOTO.
CAPTAIN BRETT ⎱ *Adherents of Wyatt.*
ANTHONY KNYVETT ⎰
PETERS, *Gentleman of Lord Howard.*
ROGER, *Servant to Noailles.*　　　WILLIAM, *Servant to Wyatt.*
STEWARD OF HOUSEHOLD *to the Princess Elizabeth.*
OLD NOKES *and* NOKES.
MARCHIONESS OF EXETER, *Mother of Courtenay.*
LADY CLARENCE
LADY MAGDALEN DACRES ⎱ *Ladies in Waiting to the Queen.*
ALICE
MAID OF HONOUR *to the Princess Elizabeth.*
JOAN ⎱ *two Country Wives.*
TIB ⎰

Lords *and other* Attendants, Members *of the* Privy Council, Members *of* Parliament, two Gentlemen, Aldermen, Citizens, Peasants, Ushers, Messengers, Guards, Pages, Gospellers, Marshalmen, *etc.*

ACT I

SCENE I

Aldgate richly decorated

CROWD. MARSHALMEN

Marshalman. Stand back, keep a clear lane! When will her Majesty pass, sayst thou? why now, even now; wherefore draw back your heads and your horns before I break them, and make what noise you will with your tongues, so it be not treason. Long live Queen Mary, the lawful and legitimate daughter of Harry the Eighth! Shout, knaves!

Citizens. Long live Queen Mary!

First Citizen. That's a hard word, legitimate; what does it mean?

Second Citizen. It means a bastard.

Third Citizen. Nay, it means true-born.

First Citizen. Why, didn't the Parliament make her a bastard?

Second Citizen. No; it was the Lady Elizabeth.

538

Third Citizen. That was after, man; that was after.

First Citizen. Then which is the bastard?

Second Citizen. Troth, they be both bastards by Act of Parliament and Council.

Third Citizen. Ay, the Parliament can make every true-born man of us a bastard. Old Nokes, can't it make thee a bastard? thou shouldst know, for thou art as white as three Christmasses.

Old Nokes (dreamily). Who's a-passing? King Edward or King Richard?

Third Citizen. No, old Nokes.

Old Nokes. It's Harry!

Third Citizen. It's Queen Mary.

Old Nokes. The blessed Mary's a-passing! [*Falls on his knees.*

Nokes. Let father alone, my masters! he's past your questioning.

Third Citizen. Answer thou for him, then! thou'rt no such cockerel thyself, for thou was born i' the tail end of old Harry the Seventh.

Nokes. Eh! that was afore bastard-making began. I was born true man at five in the forenoon i' the tail of old Harry, and so they can't make me a bastard.

Third Citizen. But if Parliament can make the Queen a bastard, why, it follows all the more that they can make thee one, who art fray'd i' the knees, and out at elbow, and bald o' the back, and bursten at the toes, and down at heels.

Nokes. I was born of a true man and a ring'd wife, and I can't argue upon it; but I and my old woman 'ud burn upon it, that would we.

Marshalman. What are you cackling of bastardy under the Queen's own nose? I'll have you flogg'd and burnt too, by the Rood I will.

First Citizen. He swears by the Rood. Whew!

Second Citizen. Hark! the trumpets.

[*The Procession passes,* MARY *and* ELIZABETH *riding side by side, and disappears under the gate.*

Citizens. Long live Queen Mary! down with all traitors! God save her Grace; and death to Northumberland!

[*Exeunt.*

Manent TWO GENTLEMEN

First Gentleman. By God's light a noble creature, right royal!

Second Gentleman. She looks comelier than ordinary to-day; but to my mind the Lady Elizabeth is the more noble and royal.

First Gentleman. I mean the Lady Elizabeth. Did you hear (I have a daughter in her service who reported it) that she met the Queen at Wanstead with five hundred horse, and the Queen (tho' some say they be much divided) took her hand, call'd her sweet sister, and kiss'd not her alone, but all the ladies of her following.

Second Gentleman. Ay, that was in her hour of joy; there will be plenty to sunder and unsister them again: this Gardiner for one, who is to be made Lord Chancellor, and will pounce like a wild beast out of his cage to worry Cranmer.

First Gentleman. And furthermore, my daughter said that when there rose a talk of the late rebellion, she spoke even of Northumberland pitifully, and of the good Lady Jane as a poor innocent child who had but obeyed her father; and furthermore, she said that no one in her time should be burnt for heresy.

Second Gentleman. Well, sir, I look for happy times.

First Gentleman. There is but one thing against them. I know not if you know.

Second Gentleman. I suppose you touch upon the rumour that Charles, the master of the world, has offer'd her his son Philip, the Pope and the Devil. I trust it is but a rumour.

First Gentleman. She is going now to the Tower to loose the prisoners there, and among them Courtenay, to be made Earl of Devon, of royal blood, of splendid feature, whom the council and all her people wish her to marry. May it be so, for we are many of us Catholics, but few Papists, and the Hot Gospellers will go mad upon it.

Second Gentleman. Was she not betroth'd in her babyhood to the Great Emperor himself?

First Gentleman. Ay, but he's too old.

Second Gentleman. And again to her cousin Reginald Pole, now Cardinal; but I hear that he too is full of aches and broken before his day.

First Gentleman. O, the Pope could dispense with his Cardinalate, and his achage, and his breakage, if that were all: will you not follow the procession?

Second Gentleman. No; I have seen enough for this day.

First Gentleman. Well, I shall follow; if I can get near enough I shall judge with my own eyes whether her Grace incline to this splendid scion of Plantagenet.

[Exeunt.

Scene II

A Room in Lambeth Palace

Cranmer. To Strasburg, Antwerp, Frankfort, Zurich, Worms,

Geneva, Basle—our Bishops from their sees

Or fled, they say, or flying—Poinet, Barlow,

Bale, Scory, Coverdale; besides the Deans

Of Christchurch, Durham, Exeter, and Wells—

Ailmer and Bullingham, and hundreds more;

So they report: I shall be left alone.

No: Hooper, Ridley, Latimer will not fly.

Enter PETER MARTYR

Peter Martyr. Fly, Cranmer! were there nothing else, your name

Stands first of those who sign'd the Letters Patent

That gave her royal crown to Lady Jane.

Cranmer. Stand first it may, but it was written last:

Those that are now her Privy Council, sign'd

Before me: nay, the Judges had pronounced

That our young Edward might bequeath the crown

Of England, putting by his father's will.

Yet I stood out, till Edward sent for me.

The wan boy-king, with his fast-fading eyes

Fixt hard on mine, his frail transparent hand,

Damp with the sweat of death, and griping mine,

Whisper'd me, if I loved him, not to yield

His Church of England to the Papal wolf

And Mary; then I could no more—I sign'd.

Nay, for bare shame of inconsistency,

She cannot pass her traitor council by,

To make me headless.

Peter Martyr. That might be forgiven.

I tell you, fly, my Lord. You do not own

The bodily presence in the Eucharist,

Their wafer and perpetual sacrifice:

Your creed will be your death.

Cranmer. Step after step,

Thro' many voices crying right and left,

Have I climb'd back into the primal church,

And stand within the porch, and Christ with me:

My flight were such a scandal to the faith,

The downfall of so many simple souls,

I dare not leave my post.

Peter Martyr. But you divorced

Queen Catharine and her father; hence, her hate

Will burn till you are burn'd.

Cranmer. I cannot help it.

The Canonists and Schoolmen were with me.

'Thou shalt not wed thy brother's wife.'
—'Tis written,

'They shall be childless.' True, Mary was born,

But France would not accept her for a bride

As being born from incest; and this wrought

Upon the king; and child by child, you know,

Were momentary sparkles out as quick

Almost as kindled; and he brought his doubts

And fears to me. Peter, I'll swear for him

He *did* believe the bond incestuous.

But wherefore am I trenching on the time

That should already have seen your steps a mile

From me and Lambeth? God be with you! Go.

Peter Martyr. Ah, but how fierce a letter
    you wrote against
Their superstition when they slander'd you
For setting up a mass at Canterbury
To please the Queen.
    Cranmer. It was a wheedling monk
Set up the mass.
    Peter Martyr. I know it, my good Lord.
But you so bubbled over with hot terms
Of Satan, liars, blasphemy, Antichrist,
She never will forgive you. Fly, my Lord,
    fly!
    Cranmer. I wrote it, and God grant me
    power to burn!
    Peter Martyr. They have given me a
    safe conduct: for all that
I dare not stay. I fear, I fear, I see you,
Dear friend, for the last time; farewell, and
    fly.
    Cranmer. Fly and farewell, and let me
    die the death.
                    [*Exit* PETER MARTYR.

            Enter OLD SERVANT

O, kind and gentle master, the Queen's
    Officers
Are here in force to take you to the Tower.
    Cranmer. Ay, gentle friend, admit them.
    I will go.
I thank my God it is too late to fly.
                            [*Exeunt.*

            SCENE III

            St. Paul's Cross

FATHER BOURNE *in the pulpit. A crowd.*
MARCHIONESS OF EXETER, COURTENAY.
The SIEUR DE NOAILLES *and his man*
ROGER *in front of the stage. Hubbub.*

    Noailles. Hast thou let fall those papers
in the palace?
    Roger. Ay, sir.
    Noailles. 'There will be no peace for
Mary till Elizabeth lose her head.'
    Roger. Ay, sir.
    Noailles. And the other, 'Long live Eliza-
beth the Queen!'
    Roger. Ay, sir; she needs must tread
    upon them.
    Noailles.   Well.

These beastly swine make such a grunting
    here,
I cannot catch what Father Bourne is
    saying.
    Roger. Quiet a moment, my masters;
hear what the shaveling has to say for
himself.
    Crowd. Hush—hear!
    Bourne. —and so this unhappy land,
long divided in itself, and sever'd from the
faith, will return into the one true fold,
seeing that our gracious Virgin Queen
hath——
    Crowd. No pope! no pope!
    Roger (*to those about him, mimicking*
BOURNE). —hath sent for the holy legate of
the holy father the Pope, Cardinal Pole, to
give us all that holy absolution which——
    First Citizen. Old Bourne to the life!
    Second Citizen. Holy absolution! holy
    Inquisition!
    Third Citizen. Down with the Papist!
                            [*Hubbub.*
    Bourne. —and now that your good
bishop, Bonner, who hath lain so long
under bonds for the faith—   [*Hubbub.*
    Noailles. Friend Roger, steal thou in
    among the crowd,
And get the swine to shout Elizabeth.
Yon gray old Gospeller, sour as midwinter,
Begin with him.
    Roger (*goes*). By the mass, old friend,
we'll have no pope here while the Lady
Elizabeth lives.
    Gospeller. Art thou of the true faith,
fellow, that swearest by the mass?
    Roger. Ay, that am I, new converted,
but the old leaven sticks to my tongue
yet.
    First Citizen. He says right; by the mass
we'll have no mass here.
    Voices of the crowd. Peace! hear him; let
his own words damn the Papist. From
thine own mouth I judge thee—tear him
down!
    Bourne. —and since our Gracious Queen,
let me call her our second Virgin Mary,
hath begun to re-edify the true temple——
    First Citizen. Virgin Mary! we'll have
no virgins here—we'll have the Lady
Elizabeth!

[*Swords are drawn, a knife is hurled
and sticks in the pulpit. The mob
throng to the pulpit stairs.*

Marchioness of Exeter. Son Courtenay,
wilt thou see the holy father
Murdered before thy face? up, son, and
save him!
They love thee, and thou canst not come
to harm.

Courtenay (in the pulpit). Shame, shame,
my masters! are you English-born,
And set yourselves by hundreds against
one?

Crowd. A Courtenay! a Courtenay!

[*A train of Spanish servants crosses
at the back of the stage.*

Noailles. These birds of passage come
before their time:
Stave off the crowd upon the Spaniard
there.

Roger. My masters, yonder's fatter game
for you
Than this old gaping gurgoyle: look you
there—
The Prince of Spain coming to wed our
Queen!
After him, boys! and pelt him from the
city.

[*They seize stones and follow the
Spaniards. Exeunt on the other
side* MARCHIONESS OF EXETER *and*
ATTENDANTS.

Noailles (to ROGER). Stand from me. If
Elizabeth lose her head—
That makes for France.
And if her people, anger'd thereupon,
Arise against her and dethrone the Queen—
That makes for France.
And if I breed confusion anyway—
That makes for France.
                Good-day, my Lord of Devon;
A bold heart yours to beard that raging
mob!

Courtenay. My mother said, Go up; and
up I went.
I knew they would not do me any wrong,
For I am mighty popular with them,
Noailles.

Noailles. You look'd a king.

Courtenay.   Why not? I am
king's blood.

Noailles. And in the whirl of change
may come to be one.

Courtenay. Ah!

Noailles. But does your gracious Queen
entreat you kinglike?

Courtenay. 'Fore God, I think she
entreats me like a child.

Noailles. You've but a dull life in this
maiden court,
I fear, my Lord?

Courtenay. A life of nods and yawns.

Noailles. So you would honour my poor
house to-night,
We might enliven you. Divers honest
fellows,
The Duke of Suffolk lately freed from
prison,
Sir Peter Carew and Sir Thomas Wyatt,
Sir Thomas Stafford, and some more—
we play.

Courtenay. At what?

Noailles.   The Game of Chess.

Courtenay.   The Game of Chess!
I can play well, and I shall beat you there.

Noailles. Ay, but we play with Henry,
King of France,
And certain of his court.
His Highness makes his moves across the
Channel,
We answer him with ours, and there are
messengers
That go between us.

Courtenay. Why, such a game, sir, were
whole years a playing.

Noailles. Nay; not so long I trust. That
all depends
Upon the skill and swiftness of the players.

Courtenay. The King is skilful at it?

Noailles.   Very, my Lord.

Courtenay. And the stakes high?

Noailles.   But not beyond your means.

Courtenay. Well, I'm the first of players.
I shall win.

Noailles. With our advice and in our
company,
And so you well attend to the king's moves,
I think you may.

Courtenay.   When do you meet?

Noailles.   To-night.

Courtenay (aside). I will be there; the
fellow's at his tricks—

Deep—I shall fathom him.   (*Aloud.*)
Good morning, Noailles.
              [*Exit* COURTENAY.
Noailles. Good-day, my Lord. Strange
game of chess! a King
That with her own pawns plays against a
    Queen,
Whose play is all to find herself a King.
Ay; but this fine blue-blooded Courtenay
    seems
Too princely for a pawn. Call him a
    Knight,
That, with an ass's, not a horse's head,
Skips every way, from levity or from fear.
Well, we shall use him somehow, so that
    Gardiner
And Simon Renard spy not out our game
Too early. Roger, thinkest thou that any-
    one
Suspected thee to be my man?
    Roger.   Not one, sir.
Noailles. No! the disguise was perfect.
Let's away.   [*Exeunt.*

SCENE IV

London. A Room in the Palace

ELIZABETH. *Enter* COURTENAY

Courtenay. So yet am I,
Unless my friends and mirrors lie to me,
A goodlier-looking fellow than this Philip.
Pah!
The Queen is ill advised: shall I turn
    traitor?
They've almost talked me into it: yet the
    word
Affrights me somewhat: to be such a one
As Harry Bolingbroke hath a lure in it.
Good now, my Lady Queen, tho' by your
    age,
And by your looks you are not worth the
    having,
Yet by your crown you are.
            [*Seeing* ELIZABETH.
            The Princess there?
If I tried her and la—she's amorous.
Have we not heard of her in Edward's
    time,
Her freaks and frolics with the late Lord
    Admiral?

I do believe she'd yield. I should be still
A party in the state; and then, who
    knows—
    Elizabeth. What are you musing on, my
    Lord of Devon?
    Courtenay. Has not the Queen—
    Elizabeth.   Done what, Sir?
    Courtenay.   —made you follow
The Lady Suffolk and the Lady Len-
    nox?—
You,
The heir presumptive.
    Elizabeth. Why do you ask? you know it.
    Courtenay. You needs must bear it
    hardly.
    Elizabeth.   No, indeed!
I am utterly submissive to the Queen.
    Courtenay. Well, I was musing upon
    that; the Queen
Is both my foe and yours: we should be
    friends.
    Elizabeth. My Lord, the hatred of
    another to us
Is not true bond of friendship.
    Courtenay.   Might it not
Be the rough preface of some closer bond?
    Elizabeth. My Lord, you late were loosed
    from out the Tower,
Where, like a butterfly in a chrysalis,
You spent your life; that broken, out you
    flutter
Thro' the new world, go zigzag, now
    would settle
Upon this flower, now that; but all things
    here
At court are known; you have solicited
The Queen, and been rejected.
    Courtenay.   Flower, she!
Half faded! but you, cousin, are fresh and
    sweet
As the first flower no bee has ever tried.
    Elizabeth. Are you the bee to try me?
    why, but now
I called you butterfly.
    Courtenay.   You did me wrong,
I love not to be called a butterfly:
Why do you call me butterfly?
    Elizabeth. Why do you go so gay then?
    Courtenay.   Velvet and gold.
This dress was made me as the Earl of
    Devon

To take my seat in; looks it not right royal?

Elizabeth. So royal that the Queen forbad you wearing it.

Courtenay. I wear it then to spite her.

Elizabeth. My Lord, my Lord;
I see you in the Tower again. Her Majesty
Hears you affect the Prince—prelates
kneel to you.—

Courtenay. I am the noblest blood in Europe, Madam,
A Courtenay of Devon, and her cousin.

Elizabeth. She hears you make your boast that after all
She means to wed you. Folly, my good Lord.

Courtenay. How folly? a great party in the state
Wills me to wed her.

Elizabeth. Failing her, my Lord,
Doth not as great a party in the state
Will you to wed me?

Courtenay. Even so, fair lady.

Elizabeth. You know to flatter ladies.

Courtenay. Nay, I meant
True matters of the heart.

Elizabeth. My heart, my Lord,
Is no great party in the state as yet.

Courtenay. Great, said you? nay, you shall be great. I love you,
Lay my life in your hands. Can you be close?

Elizabeth. Can you, my Lord?

Courtenay. Close as a miser's casket.
Listen:
The King of France, Noailles the Ambassador,
The Duke of Suffolk and Sir Peter Carew,
Sir Thomas Wyatt, I myself, some others,
Have sworn this Spanish marriage shall not be.
If Mary will not hear us—well—conjecture—
Were I in Devon with my wedded bride,
The people there so worship me—Your ear;
You shall be Queen.

Elizabeth. You speak too low, my Lord;
I cannot hear you.

Courtenay. I'll repeat it.

Elizabeth. No!

Stand further off, or you may lose your head.

Courtenay. I have a head to lose for your sweet sake.

Elizabeth. Have you, my Lord? Best keep it for your own.
Nay, pout not, cousin.
Not many friends are mine, except indeed
Among the many. I believe you mine;
And so you may continue mine, farewell,
And that at once.

Enter MARY, *behind*

Mary. Whispering—leagued together
To bar me from my Philip.

Courtenay. Pray—consider—

Elizabeth (*seeing the* QUEEN). Well, that's
a noble horse of yours, my Lord.
I trust that he will carry you well to-day,
And heal your headache.

Courtenay. You are wild; what headache?
Heartache, perchance; not headache.

Elizabeth (*aside to* COURTENAY). Are you blind?

[COURTENAY *sees the* QUEEN *and exit.*
Exit MARY.

Enter LORD WILLIAM HOWARD

Howard. Was that my Lord of Devon? do not you
Be seen in corners with my Lord of Devon.
He hath fallen out of favour with the Queen.
She fears the Lords may side with you and him
Against her marriage; therefore is he dangerous.
And if this Prince of fluff and feather come
To woo you, niece, he is dangerous everyway.

Elizabeth. Not very dangerous that way, my good uncle.

Howard. But your own state is full of danger here.
The disaffected, heretics, reformers,
Look to you as the one to crown their ends.
Mix not yourself with any plot I pray you;
Nay, if by chance you hear of any such,
Speak not thereof—no, not to your best friend,

Lest you should be confounded with it.
Still—
Perinde ac cadaver—as the priest says,
You know your Latin—quiet as a dead
body.
What was my Lord of Devon telling you?
  Elizabeth. Whether he told me anything
or not,
I follow your good counsel, gracious uncle.
Quiet as a dead body.
  Howard.   You do right well.
I do not care to know; but this I charge
you,
Tell Courtenay nothing. The Lord Chan-
cellor
(I count it as a kind of virtue in him,
He hath not many), as a mastiff dog
May love a puppy cur for no more reason
Than that the twain have been tied up
together,
Thus Gardiner—for the two were fellow-
prisoners
So many years in yon accursed Tower—
Hath taken to this Courtenay. Look to it,
niece,
He hath no fence when Gardiner questions
him;
All oozes out; yet him—because they
know him
The last White Rose, the last Plantagenet
(Nay, there is Cardinal Pole, too), the
people
Claim as their natural leader—ay, some
say,
That you shall marry him, make him King
belike.
  Elizabeth. Do they say so, good uncle?
  Howard.   Ay, good niece!
You should be plain and open with me,
niece.
You should not play upon me.
  Elizabeth.   No, good uncle.

Enter GARDINER

  Gardiner. The Queen would see your
Grace upon the moment.
  Elizabeth. Why, my lord Bishop?
  Gardiner. I think she means to counsel
your withdrawing
To Ashridge, or some other country house.
  Elizabeth. Why, my lord Bishop?

  Gardiner. I do but bring the message,
know no more.
Your Grace will hear her reasons from
herself.
  Elizabeth. 'Tis mine own wish fulfill'd
before the word
Was spoken, for in truth I had meant to
crave
Permission of her Highness to retire
To Ashridge, and pursue my studies there.
  Gardiner. Madam, to have the wish
before the word
Is man's good Fairy—and the Queen is
yours.
I left her with rich jewels in her hand,
Whereof 'tis like enough she means to
make
A farewell present to your Grace.
  Elizabeth.   My Lord,
I have the jewel of a loyal heart.
  Gardiner. I doubt it not, Madam, most
loyal.   [*Bows low and exit.*
  Howard.   See,
This comes of parleying with my Lord of
Devon.
Well, well, you must obey; and I myself
Believe it will be better for your welfare.
Your time will come.
  Elizabeth. I think my time will come.
Uncle,
I am of sovereign nature, that I know,
Not to be quell'd; and I have felt within me
Stirrings of some great doom when God's
just hour
Peals—but this fierce old Gardiner—his
big baldness,
That irritable forelock which he rubs,
His buzzard beak and deep-incavern'd eyes
Half fright me.
  Howard. You've a bold heart; keep it so.
He cannot touch you save that you turn
traitor;
And so take heed I pray you—you are one
Who love that men should smile upon you,
niece.
They'd smile you into treason—some of
them.
  Elizabeth. I spy the rock beneath the
smiling sea.
But if this Philip, the proud Catholic
prince,

And this bald priest, and she that hates me,
    seek
In that lone house, to practise on my life,
By poison, fire, shot, stab—
    Howard.   They will not, niece.
Mine is the fleet and all the power at sea—
Or will be in a moment. If they dared
To harm you, I would blow this Philip
    and all
Your trouble to the dogstar and the devil.
    Elizabeth. To the Pleiads, uncle; they
    have lost a sister.
    Howard. But why say that? what have
    you done to lose her?
Come, come, I will go with you to the
    Queen.   [*Exeunt.*

SCENE V

A Room in the Palace

MARY *with* PHILIP'S *miniature.* ALICE

Mary (*kissing the miniature*). Most
    goodly, Kinglike and an Emperor's
    son,—
A king to be,—is he not noble, girl?
    Alice. Goodly enough, your Grace, and
    yet, methinks,
I have seen goodlier.
    Mary.   Ay; some waxen doll
Thy baby eyes have rested on, belike;
All red and white, the fashion of our land.
But my good mother came (God rest her
    soul)
Of Spain, and I am Spanish in myself,
And in my likings.
    Alice.   By your Grace's leave
Your royal mother came of Spain, but took
To the English red and white. Your royal
    father
(For so they say) was all pure lily and rose
In his youth, and like a lady.
    Mary.   O, just God!
Sweet mother, you had time and cause
    enough
To sicken of his lilies and his roses.
Cast off, betray'd, defamed, divorced, for-
    lorn!
And then the King—that traitor past
    forgiveness,
The false archbishop fawning on him,
    married

The mother of Elizabeth—a heretic
Ev'n as *she* is; but God hath sent me
    here
To take such order with all heretics
That it shall be, before I die, as tho'
My father and my brother had not lived.
What wast thou saying of this Lady Jane,
Now in the Tower?
    Alice. Why, Madam, she was passing
Some chapel down in Essex, and with her
Lady Anne Wharton, and the Lady Anne
Bow'd to the Pyx; but Lady Jane stood up
Stiff as the very backbone of heresy.
And wherefore bow ye not, says Lady
    Anne,
To him within there who made Heaven
    and Earth?
I cannot, and I dare not, tell your Grace
What Lady Jane replied.
    Mary.   But I will have it.
    Alice. She said—pray pardon me, and
    pity her—
She hath harken'd evil counsel—ah! she
    said,
The baker made him.
    Mary.   Monstrous! blasphemous!
She ought to burn. Hence, thou (*Exit*
    ALICE). No—being traitor
Her head will fall: shall it? she is but a
    child.
We do not kill the child for doing that
His father whipt him into doing—a head
So full of grace and beauty! would that
    mine
Were half as gracious! O, my lord to be,
My love, for thy sake only.
I am eleven years older than he is.
But will he care for that?
No, by the holy Virgin, being noble,
But love me only: then the bastard sprout,
My sister, is far fairer than myself.
Will he be drawn to her?
No, being of the true faith with myself.
Paget is for him—for to wed with Spain
Would treble England—Gardiner is against
    him;
The Council, people, Parliament against
    him;
But I will have him! My hard father hated
    me;
My brother rather hated me than loved;

546

My sister cowers and hates me. Holy
  Virgin,
Plead with thy blessed Son; grant me my
  prayer:
Give me my Philip; and we two will lead
The living waters of the Faith again
Back thro' their widow'd channel here,
  and watch
The parch'd banks rolling incense, as of
  old,
To heaven, and kindled with the palms of
  Christ!

Enter USHER

Who waits, sir?
  Usher. Madam, the Lord Chancellor.
  Mary. Bid him come in. (*Enter* GAR-
  DINER.) Good morning, my good
  Lord.   [*Exit* USHER.
  Gardiner. That every morning of your
  Majesty
May be most good, is every morning's
  prayer
Of your most loyal subject, Stephen
  Gardiner.
  Mary. Come you to tell me this, my
  Lord?
  Gardiner. And more.
Your people have begun to learn your
  worth.
Your pious wish to pay King Edward's
  debts,
Your lavish household curb'd, and the
  remission
Of half that subsidy levied on the people,
Make all tongues praise and all hearts beat
  for you.
I'd have you yet more loved: the realm is
  poor,
The exchequer at neap-tide: we might
  withdraw
Part of our garrison at Calais.
  Mary.   Calais!
Our one point on the main, the gate of
  France!
I am Queen of England; take mine eyes,
  mine heart,
But do not lose me Calais.
  Gardiner.   Do not fear it.
Of that hereafter. I say your Grace is
  loved.

That I may keep you thus, who am your
  friend
And ever faithful counsellor, might I
  speak?
  Mary. I can forespeak your speaking.
  Would I marry
Prince Philip, if all England hate him?
  That is
Your question, and I front it with another:
Is it England, or a party? Now, your
  answer.
  Gardiner. My answer is, I wear beneath
  my dress
A shirt of mail: my house hath been
  assaulted,
And when I walk abroad, the populace,
With fingers pointed like so many daggers,
Stab me in fancy, hissing Spain and Philip;
And when I sleep, a hundred men-at-
  arms
Guard my poor dreams for England. Men
  would murder me,
Because they think me favourer of this mar-
  riage.
  Mary. And that were hard upon you,
  my Lord Chancellor.
  Gardiner. But our young Earl of
  Devon—
  Mary.   Earl of Devon?
I freed him from the Tower, placed him
  at Court;
I made him Earl of Devon, and—the fool—
He wrecks his health and wealth on
  courtesans,
And rolls himself in carrion like a dog.
  Gardiner. More like a school-boy that
  hath broken bounds,
Sickening himself with sweets.
  Mary.   I will not hear of him.
Good, then, they will revolt: but I am
  Tudor,
And shall control them.
  Gardiner.   I will help you, Madam,
Even to the utmost. All the church is
  grateful.
You have ousted the mock priest, repul-
  pited
The shepherd of St. Peter, raised the rood
  again,
And brought us back the mass. I am all
  thanks

To God and to your Grace: yet I know
    well,
Your people, and I go with them so far,
Will brook nor Pope nor Spaniard here to
    play
The tyrant, or in commonwealth or
    church.
  Mary (showing the picture). Is this the
    face of one who plays the tyrant?
Peruse it; is it not goodly, ay, and gentle?
  Gardiner. Madam, methinks a cold face
    and a haughty.
And when your Highness talks of Cour-
    tenay—
Ay, true—a goodly one. I would his life
Were half as goodly *(aside).*
  Mary.   What is that you mutter?
  Gardiner. Oh, Madam, take it bluntly;
    marry Philip,
And be stepmother of a score of sons!
The prince is known in Spain, in Flanders,
    ha!
For Philip—
  Mary. You offend us; you may leave us.
You see thro' warping glasses.
  Gardiner.   If your Majesty—
  Mary. I have sworn upon the body and
    blood of Christ
I'll none but Philip.
  Gardiner. Hath your Grace so sworn?
  Mary. Ay, Simon Renard knows it.
  Gardiner.   News to me!
It then remains for your poor Gardiner,
So you still care to trust him somewhat
    less
Than Simon Renard, to compose the
    event
In some such form as least may harm your
    Grace.
  Mary. I'll have the scandal sounded to
    the mud.
I know it a scandal.
  Gardiner.   All my hope is now
It may be found a scandal.
  , Mary.   You offend us.
  Gardiner (aside). These princes are like
    children, must be physick'd,
The bitter in the sweet. I have lost mine
    office,
It may be, thro' mine honesty, like a fool.
                                        [*Exit.*

Enter USHER

  Mary. Who waits?
  Usher. The Ambassador from France,
    your Grace.
  Mary (sits down). Bid him come in.
    Good morning, Sir de Noailles.
                            [*Exit* USHER.
  Noailles (entering). A happy morning to
    your Majesty.
  Mary. And I should some time have a
    happy morning;
I have had none yet. What says the King
    your Master?
  Noailles. Madam, my master hears with
    much alarm,
That you may marry Philip, Prince of
    Spain—
Foreseeing, with whate'er unwillingness,
That if this Philip be the titular king
Of England, and at war with him, your
    Grace
And kingdom will be suck'd into the war,
Ay, tho' you long for peace; wherefore,
    my master,
If but to prove your Majesty's goodwill,
Would fain have some fresh treaty drawn
    bctwccn you.
  Mary. Why some fresh treaty? where-
    fore should I do it?
Sir, if we marry, we shall still maintain
All former treaties with his Majesty.
Our royal word for that! and your good
    master,
Pray God he do not be the first to break
    them,
Must be content with that; and so, fare-
    well.
  Noailles (going, returns). I would your
    answer had been other, Madam,
For I foresee dark days.
  Mary.   And so do I, sir;
Your master works against me in the dark.
I do believe he holp Northumberland
Against me.
  Noailles. Nay, pure phantasy, your
    Grace.
Why should he move against you?
  Mary.   Will you hear why?
Mary of Scotland,—for I have not own'd
My sister, and I will not,—after me

Is heir of England; and my royal father,
To make the crown of Scotland one with
     ours,
Had mark'd her for my brother Edward's
     bride;
Ay, but your king stole her a babe from
     Scotland
In order to betroth her to your Dauphin.
See then:
Mary of Scotland, married to your
     Dauphin,
Would make our England, France;
Mary of England, joining hands with
     Spain,
Would be too strong for France.
Yea, were there issue born to her, Spain
     and we,
One crown, might rule the world. There
     lies your fear.
That is your drift. You play at hide and
     seek.
Show me your faces!
     Noailles.   Madam, I am amazed:
French, I must needs wish all good things
     for France.
That must be pardon'd me; but I protest
Your Grace's policy hath a farther flight
Than mine into the future. We but seek
Some settled ground for peace to stand
     upon.
     Mary. Well, we will leave all this, sir, to
     our council.
Have you seen Philip ever?
     Noailles.   Only once.
     Mary. Is this like Philip?
     Noailles.   Ay, but nobler-looking.
     Mary. Hath he the large ability of the
     Emperor?
     Noailles. No, surely.
     Mary. I can make allowance for thee,
Thou speakest of the enemy of thy king.
     Noailles. Make no allowance for the
     naked truth.
He is every way a lesser man than Charles;
Stone-hard, ice-cold—no dash of daring
     in him.
     Mary. If cold, his life is pure.
     Noailles. Why (*smiling*), no, indeed.
     Mary. Sayst thou?
     Noailles. A very wanton life indeed
     (*smiling*).

Mary. Your audience is concluded, sir.
                    [*Exit* NOAILLES.
                You cannot
Learn a man's nature from his natural foe.

          Enter USHER

Who waits?
     Usher. The Ambassador of Spain, your
     Grace.   [*Exit.*

          Enter SIMON RENARD

Mary (*rising to meet him*). Thou art ever
     welcome, Simon Renard. Hast thou
Brought me the letter which thine Em-
     peror promised
Long since, a formal offer of the hand
Of Philip?
     Renard. Nay, your Grace, it hath not
     reach'd me.
I know not wherefore—some mischance
     of flood,
And broken bridge, or spavin'd horse, or
     wave
And wind at their old battle: he must have
     written.
     Mary. But Philip never writes me one
     poor word,
Which in his absence had been all my
     wealth.
Strange in a wooer!
     Renard.   Yet I know the Prince,
So your king-parliament suffer him to land,
Yearns to set foot upon your island shore.
     Mary. God change the pebble which his
     kingly foot
First presses into some more costly stone
Than ever blinded eye. I'll have one
     mark it
And bring it me. I'll have it burnish'd
     firelike;
I'll set it round with gold, with pearl, with
     diamond.
Let the great angel of the church come
     with him;
Stand on the deck and spread his wings
     for sail!
God lay the waves and strow the storms at
     sea,
And here at land among the people! O
     Renard,
I am much beset, I am almost in despair.
Paget is ours. Gardiner perchance is ours;

But for our heretic Parliament—
Renard.   O Madam,
You fly your thoughts like kites. My
     master, Charles,
Bad you go softly with your heretics here,
Until your throne had ceased to tremble.
     Then
Spit them like larks for aught I care.
     Besides,
When Henry broke the carcase of your
     church
To pieces, there were many wolves among
     you
Who dragg'd the scatter'd limbs into their
     den.
The Pope would have you make them
     render these;
So would your cousin, Cardinal Pole; ill
     counsel!
These let them keep at present; stir not yet
This matter of the Church lands. At his
     coming
Your star will rise.
     Mary.   My star! a baleful one.
I see but the black night, and hear the wolf.
What star?
     Renard. Your star will be your princely
     son,
Heir of this England and the Netherlands!
And if your wolf the while should howl for
     more,
We'll dust him from a bag of Spanish gold.
I do believe, I have dusted some already,
That, soon or late, your Parliament is ours.
     Mary. Why do they talk so foully of
     your Prince,
Renard?
     Renard. The lot of Princes. To sit high
Is to be lied about.
     Mary.   They call him cold,
Haughty, ay, worse.
     Renard. Why, doubtless, Philip shows
Some of the bearing of your blue blood—
     still
All within measure—nay, it well becomes
     him.
     Mary. Hath he the large ability of his
     father?
     Renard. Nay, some believe that he will
     go beyond him.
     Mary. Is this like him?

Renard. Ay, somewhat; but your Philip
Is the most princelike Prince beneath the
     sun.
This is a daub to Philip.
     Mary.   Of a pure life?
Renard. As an angel among angels. Yea,
     by Heaven,
The text—Your Highness knows it, 'Who-
     soever
Looketh after a woman,' would not graze
The Prince of Spain. You are happy in
     him there,
Chaste as your Grace!
     Mary.   I am happy in him there.
Renard. And would be altogether happy,
     Madam,
So that your sister were but look'd to
     closer.
You have sent her from the court, but then
     she goes,
I warrant, not to hear the nightingales,
But hatch you some new treason in the
     woods.
     Mary. We have our spies abroad to
     catch her tripping,
And then if caught, to the Tower.
     Renard.   The Tower! the block!
The word has turn'd your Highness pale;
     the thing
Was no such scarecrow in your father's
     time.
I have heard, the tongue yet quiver'd with
     the jest
When the head leapt—so common! I do
     think
To save your crown that it must come to
     this.
     Mary. No, Renard; it must never come
     to this.
     Renard. Not yet; but your old Traitors
     of the Tower—
Why, when you put Northumberland to
     death,
The sentence having past upon them all,
Spared you the Duke of Suffolk, Guildford
     Dudley,
Ev'n that young girl who dared to wear
     your crown?
     Mary. Dared? nay, not so; the child
     obey'd her father.
Spite of her tears her father forced it on her.

Renard. Good Madam, when the Roman
wish'd to reign,
He slew not him alone who wore the
purple,
But his assessor in the throne, perchance
A child more innocent than Lady Jane.
Mary. I am English Queen, not Roman
Emperor.
Renard. Yet too much mercy is a want
of mercy,
And wastes more life. Stamp out the fire,
or this
Will smoulder and re-flame, and burn the
throne
Where you should sit with Philip: he will
not come
Till she be gone.
Mary. Indeed, if that were true—
For Philip comes, one hand in mine, and one
Steadying the tremulous pillars of the
Church—
But no, no, no. Farewell. I am somewhat
faint
With our long talk. Tho' Queen, I am not
Queen
Of mine own heart, which every now and
then
Beats me half dead: yet stay, this golden
chain—
My father on a birthday gave it me,
And I have broken with my father—take
And wear it as memorial of a morning
Which found me full of foolish doubts, and
leaves me
As hopeful.
Renard (*aside*). Whew—the folly of all
follies
Is to be love-sick for a shadow. (*Aloud*)
Madam,
This chains me to your service, not with
gold,
But dearest links of love. Farewell, and
trust me,
Philip is yours.   [*Exit.*
Mary.   Mine—but not yet all mine.

Enter USHER

Usher. Your Council is in Session, please
your Majesty.
Mary. Sir, let them sit. I must have time
to breathe.

No, say I come. (*Exit* USHER.) I won by
boldness once.
The Emperor counsell'd me to fly to
Flanders.
I would not; but a hundred miles I rode,
Sent out my letters, call'd my friends
together,
Struck home and won.
And when the Council would not crown
me—thought
To bind me first by oaths I could not keep,
And keep with Christ and conscience—
was it boldness
Or weakness that won there? when I, their
Queen,
Cast myself down upon my knees before
them,
And those hard men brake into woman-
tears,
Ev'n Gardiner, all amazed, and in that
passion
Gave me my Crown.

Enter ALICE

         Girl; hast thou ever heard
Slanders against Prince Philip in our
Court?
Alice. What slanders? I, your Grace; no,
never.
Mary.   Nothing?
Alice. Never, your Grace.
Mary. See that you neither hear them
nor repeat!
Alice (*aside*). Good Lord! but I have
heard a thousand such.
Ay, and repeated them as often—mum!
Why comes that old fox-Fleming back
again?

Enter RENARD

Renard. Madam, I scarce had left your
Grace's presence
Before I chanced upon the messenger
Who brings that letter which we waited
for—
The formal offer of Prince Philip's hand.
It craves an instant answer, Ay or No.
Mary. An instant Ay or No! the Council
sits.
Give it me quick.

Alice (*stepping before her*). Your Highness is all trembling.

Mary. Make way.

[*Exit into the Council Chamber.*

Alice. O, Master Renard, Master Renard,
If you have falsely painted your fine Prince;
Praised, where you should have blamed
him, I pray God
No woman ever love you, Master Renard.
It breaks my heart to hear her moan at
night
As tho' the nightmare never left her bed.

Renard. My pretty maiden, tell me, did
you ever
Sigh for a beard?

Alice. That's not a pretty question.

Renard. Not prettily put? I mean, my
pretty maiden,
A pretty man for such a pretty maiden.

Alice. My Lord of Devon is a pretty
man.
I hate him. Well, but if I have, what
then?

Renard. Then, pretty maiden, you
should know that whether
A wind be warm or cold, it serves to fan
A kindled fire.

Alice. According to the song.

His friends would praise him, I believed 'em,
His foes would blame him, and I scorn'd 'em,
His friends—as Angels I received 'em,
His foes—the Devil had suborn'd 'em.

Renard. Peace, pretty maiden.
I hear them stirring in the Council
Chamber.
Lord Paget's 'Ay' is sure—who else? and
yet,
They are all too much at odds to close at
once
In one full-throated No! Her Highness
comes.

Enter MARY

Alice. How deathly pale!—a chair, your
Highness.

[*Bringing one to the* QUEEN.

Renard. Madam,
The Council?

Mary. Ay! My Philip is all mine.

[*Sinks into chair, half fainting.*

ACT II

SCENE I

Alington Castle

Sir Thomas Wyatt. I do not hear from
Carew or the Duke
Of Suffolk, and till then I should not move.
The Duke hath gone to Leicester; Carew
stirs
In Devon: that fine porcelain Courtenay,
Save that he fears he might be crack'd in
using,
(I have known a semi-madman in my
time
So fancy-ridd'n) should be in Devon too.

Enter WILLIAM

News abroad, William?

William. None so new, Sir Thomas, and
none so old, Sir Thomas. No new news
that Philip comes to wed Mary, no old
news that all men hate it. Old Sir Thomas
would have hated it. The bells are ringing
at Maidstone. Doesn't your worship hear?

Wyatt. Ay, for the Saints are come to
reign again.
Most like it is a Saint's-day. There's no
call
As yet for me; so in this pause, before
The mine be fired, it were a pious work
To string my father's sonnets, left about
Like loosely scatter'd jewels, in fair order,
And head them with a lamer rhyme of
mine,
To grace his memory.

William. Ay, why not, Sir Thomas? He
was a fine courtier, he; Queen Anne loved
him. All the women loved him. I loved
him, I was in Spain with him. I couldn't
eat in Spain, I couldn't sleep in Spain. I
hate Spain, Sir Thomas.

Wyatt. But thou could'st drink in Spain
if I remember.

William. Sir Thomas, we may grant the
wine. Old Sir Thomas always granted the
wine.

Wyatt. Hand me the casket with my
father's sonnets.

William. Ay—sonnets—a fine courtier
of the old Court, old Sir Thomas. [*Exit.*

Wyatt. Courtier of many courts, he
  loved the more
His own gray towers, plain life and letter'd
  peace,
To read and rhyme in solitary fields,
The lark above, the nightingale below,
And answer them in song. The sire begets
Not half his likeness in the son. I fail
Where he was fullest: yet—to write it
  down.   [*He writes.*

Re-enter WILLIAM

William. There *is* news, there *is* news,
and no call for sonnet-sorting now, nor for
sonnet-making either, but ten thousand
men on Penenden Heath all calling after
your worship, and your worship's name
heard into Maidstone market, and your
worship the first man in Kent and Christendom, for the Queen's down, and the
world's up, and your worship a-top of it.
Wyatt. Inverted Æsop—mountain out
  of mouse.
Say for ten thousand ten—and pothouse
  knaves,
Brain-dizzied with a draught of morning
  ale.

Enter ANTHONY KNYVETT

William. Here's Anthony Knyvett.
Knyvett.   Look you, Master Wyatt,
Tear up that woman's work there.
Wyatt.   No; not these,
Dumb children of my father, that will
  speak
When I and thou and all rebellions lie
Dead bodies without voice. Song flies you
  know
For ages.
Knyvett. Tut, your sonnet's a flying ant,
Wing'd for a moment.
Wyatt.   Well, for mine own work,
                        [*Tearing the paper.*
It lies there in six pieces at your feet;
For all that I can carry it in my head.
Knyvett. If you can carry your head
  upon your shoulders.
Wyatt. I fear you come to carry it off my
  shoulders,
And sonnet-making's safer.
Knyvett.   Why, good Lord,

Write you as many sonnets as you will.
Ay, but not now; what, have you eyes, ears,
  brains?
This Philip and the black-faced swarms of
  Spain,
The hardest, cruellest people in the world,
Come locusting upon us, eat us up,
Confiscate lands, goods, money—Wyatt,
  Wyatt,
Wake, or the stout old island will become
A rotten limb of Spain. They roar for you
On Penenden Heath, a thousand of them—
  more—
All arm'd, waiting a leader; there's no
  glory
Like his who saves his country: and you sit
Sing-songing here; but, if I'm any judge,
By God, you are as poor a poet, Wyatt,
As a good soldier.
Wyatt.   You as poor a critic
As an honest friend: you stroke me on one
  cheek,
Buffet the other. Come, you bluster,
  Anthony!
You know I know all this. I must not move
Until I hear from Carew and the Duke.
I fear the mine is fired before the time.
    Knyvett (*showing a paper*). But here's
  some Hebrew. Faith, I half forgot it.
Look; can you make it English? A strange
  youth
Suddenly thrust it on me, whisper'd,
  'Wyatt,'
And whisking round a corner, show'd his
  back
Before I read his face.
Wyatt. Ha! Courtenay's cipher.
                        [*Reads.*
'Sir Peter Carew fled to France: it is
thought the Duke will be taken. I am with
you still; but, for appearance sake, stay
with the Queen. Gardiner knows, but the
Council are all at odds, and the Queen
hath no force for resistance. Move, if you
move, at once.'

Is Peter Carew fled? Is the Duke taken?
Down scabbard, and out sword! and let
  Rebellion
Roar till throne rock, and crown fall. No;
  not that;

But we will teach Queen Mary how to reign.

Who are those that shout below there?

Knyvett.   Why, some fifty
That follow'd me from Penenden Heath in hope
To hear you speak.

Wyatt. Open the window, Knyvett;
The mine is fired, and I will speak to them.

Men of Kent; England of England; you that have kept your old customs upright, while all the rest of England bow'd theirs to the Norman, the cause that hath brought us together is not the cause of a county or a shire, but of this England, in whose crown our Kent is the fairest jewel. Philip shall not wed Mary; and ye have called me to be your leader. I know Spain. I have been there with my father; I have seen them in their own land; have marked the haughtiness of their nobles; the cruelty of their priests. If this man marry our Queen, however the Council and the Commons may fence round his power with restriction, he will be King, King of England, my masters; and the Queen, and the laws, and the people, his slaves. What? shall we have Spain on the throne and in the parliament; Spain in the pulpit and on the law-bench; Spain in all the great offices of state; Spain in our ships, in our forts, in our houses, in our beds?

Crowd. No! no! no Spain!

William. No Spain in our beds—that were worse than all. I have been there with old Sir Thomas, and the beds I know. I hate Spain.

A Peasant. But, Sir Thomas, must we levy war against the Queen's Grace?

Wyatt. No, my friend; war *for* the Queen's Grace—to save her from herself and Philip—war against Spain. And think not we shall be alone—thousands will flock to us. The Council, the Court itself, is on our side. The Lord Chancellor himself is on our side. The King of France is with us; the King of Denmark is with us; the world is with us—war against Spain! And if we move not now, yet it will be known that we have moved; and if Philip come to be

King, O, my God! the rope, the rack, the thumbscrew, the stake, the fire. If we move not now, Spain moves, bribes our nobles with her gold, and creeps, creeps snake-like about our legs till we cannot move at all; and ye know, my masters, that wherever Spain hath ruled she hath wither'd all beneath her. Look at the New World—a paradise made hell; the red man, that good helpless creature, starved, maim'd, flogg'd, flay'd, burn'd, boil'd, buried alive, worried by dogs; and here, nearer home, the Netherlands, Sicily, Naples, Lombardy. I say no more—only this, their lot is yours. Forward to London with me! forward to London! If ye love your liberties or your skins, forward to London!

Crowd. Forward to London! A Wyatt! a Wyatt!

Wyatt. But first to Rochester, to take the guns
From out the vessels lying in the river.
Then on.

A Peasant. Ay, but I fear we be too few, Sir Thomas.

Wyatt. Not many yet. The world as yet, my friend,
Is not half-waked; but every parish tower
Shall clang and clash alarum as we pass,
And pour along the land, and swoll'n and fed
With indraughts and side-currents, in full force
Roll upon London.

Crowd. A Wyatt! a Wyatt! Forward!

Knyvett. Wyatt, shall we proclaim Elizabeth?

Wyatt. I'll think upon it, Knyvett.

Knyvett.   Or Lady Jane?

Wyatt. No, poor soul; no.
Ah, gray old castle of Alington, green field
Beside the brimming Medway, it may chance
That I shall never look upon you more.

Knyvett. Come, now, you're sonnetting again.

Wyatt.   Not I.
I'll have my head set higher in the state;
Or—if the Lord God will it—on the stake.
[*Exeunt.*

SCENE II

Guildhall

SIR THOMAS WHITE (The Lord Mayor), LORD WILLIAM HOWARD, SIR RALPH BAGENHALL, ALDERMEN *and* CITIZENS.

White. I trust the Queen comes hither
with her guards.
Howard. Ay, all in arms.
    [*Several of the citizens move hastily
    out of the hall.*
            Why do they hurry out there?
White. My Lord, cut out the rotten
from your apple,
Your apple eats the better. Let them go.
They go like those old Pharisees in John
Convicted by their conscience, arrant
cowards,
Or tamperers with that treason out of Kent.
When will her Grace be here?
Howard.   In some few minutes.
She will address your guilds and com-
panies.
I have striven in vain to raise a man for her.
But help her in this exigency, make
Your city loyal, and be the mightiest man
This day in England.
White.   I am Thomas White.
Few things have fail'd to which I set my
will.
I do my most and best.
Howard.   You know that after
The Captain Brett, who went with your
train bands
To fight with Wyatt, had gone over to him
With all his men, the Queen in that distress
Sent Cornwallis and Hastings to the traitor,
Feigning to treat with him about her mar-
riage—
Know too what Wyatt said.
White.   He'd sooner be,
While this same marriage question was
being argued,
Trusted than trust—the scoundrel—and
demanded
Posession of her person and the Tower.
Howard. And four of her poor Council
too, my Lord,
As hostages.
White. I know it. What do and say
Your Council at this hour?
Howard.   I will trust you.
We fling ourselves on you, my Lord. The
Council,
The Parliament as well, are troubled
waters;
And yet like waters of the fen they know
not
Which way to flow. All hangs on her
address,
And upon you, Lord Mayor.
White.   How look'd the city
When now you past it? Quiet?
Howard.   Like our Council,
Your city is divided. As we past,
Some hail'd, some hiss'd us. There were
citizens
Stood each before his shut-up booth, and
look'd
As grim and grave as from a funeral.
And here a knot of ruffians all in rags,
With execrating execrable eyes,
Glared at the citizen. Here was a young
mother,
Her face on flame, her red hair all blown
back,
She shrilling 'Wyatt,' while the boy she
held
Mimick'd and piped her 'Wyatt,' as red as
she
In hair and cheek; and almost elbowing
her,
So close they stood, another, mute as death,
And white as her own milk; her babe in
arms
Had felt the faltering of his mother's heart,
And look'd as bloodless. Here a pious
Catholic,
Mumbling and mixing up in his scared
prayers
Heaven and earth's Maries; over his bow'd
shoulder
Scowl'd that world-hated and world-hating
beast,
A haggard Anabaptist. Many such groups.
The names of Wyatt, Elizabeth, Courtenay,
Nay the Queen's right to reign—'fore God,
the rogues—
Were freely buzzed among them. So I say
Your city is divided, and I fear
One scruple, this or that way, of success

Would turn it thither. Wherefore now the
    Queen
In this low pulse and palsy of the state,
Bad me to tell you that she counts on you
And on myself as her two hands; on you,
In your own city, as her right, my Lord,
For you are loyal.
    White.   Am I Thomas White?
One word before she comes. Elizabeth—
Her name is much abused among these
    traitors.
Where is she? She is loved by all of us.
I scarce have heart to mingle in this matter,
If she should be mishandled.
    Howard.   No; she shall not.
The Queen had written her word to come
    to court:
Methought I smelt out Renard in the letter,
And fearing for her, sent a secret missive,
Which told her to be sick. Happily or not,
It found her sick indeed.
    White.   God send her well;
Here comes her Royal Grace.

Enter GUARDS, MARY, *and* GARDINER. SIR
THOMAS WHITE *leads her to a raised seat
on the daïs.*

White. I, the Lord Mayor, and these our
    companies
And guilds of London, gathered here,
    beseech
Your Highness to accept our lowliest
    thanks
For your most princely presence; and we
    pray
That we, your true and loyal citizens,
From your own royal lips, at once may
    know
The wherefore of this coming, and so learn
Your royal will, and do it.—I, Lord Mayor
Of London, and our guilds and companies.
    Mary. In mine own person am I come
    to you,
To tell you what indeed ye see and know,
How traitorously these rebels out of Kent
Have made strong head against ourselves
    and you.
They would not have me wed the Prince
    of Spain;
That was their pretext—so they spake at
    first—

But we sent divers of our Council to them,
And by their answers to the question ask'd,
It doth appear this marriage is the least
Of all their quarrel.
They have betrayed the treason of their
    hearts:
Seek to possess our person, hold our
    Tower,
Place and displace our councillors, and use
Both us and them according as they will.
Now what I am ye know right well—your
    Queen;
To whom, when I was wedded to the
    realm
And the realm's laws (the spousal ring
    whereof,
Not ever to be laid aside, I wear
Upon this finger), ye did promise full
Allegiance and obedience to the death.
Ye know my father was the rightful heir
Of England, and his right came down to
    me,
Corroborate by your acts of Parliament:
And as ye were most loving unto him,
So doubtless will ye show yourselves to me.
Wherefore, ye will not brook that anyone
Should seize our person, occupy our state,
More specially a traitor so presumptuous
As this same Wyatt, who hath tamper'd
    with
A public ignorance, and, under colour
Of such a cause as hath no colour, seeks
To bend the laws to his own will, and yield
Full scope to persons rascal and forlorn,
To make free spoil and havock of your
    goods.
Now as your Prince, I say,
I, that was never mother, cannot tell
How mothers love their children; yet,
    methinks,
A prince as naturally may love his people
As these their children; and be sure your
    Queen
So loves you, and so loving, needs must
    deem
This love by you return'd as heartily;
And thro' this common knot and bond of
    love,
Doubt not they will be speedily over-
    thrown.
As to this marriage, ye shall understand

We made thereto no treaty of ourselves,
And set no foot theretoward unadvised
Of all our Privy Council; furthermore,
This marriage had the assent of those to
    whom
The king, my father, did commit his trust;
Who not alone esteem'd it honourable,
But for the wealth and glory of our realm,
And all our loving subjects, most expedient.
As to myself,
I am not so set on wedlock as to choose
But where I list, nor yet so amorous
That I must needs be husbanded; I thank
    God,
I have lived a virgin, and I noway doubt
But that with God's grace, I can live so
    still.
Yet if it might please God that I should
    leave
Some fruit of mine own body after me,
To be your king, ye would rejoice thereat,
And it would be your comfort, as I trust;
And truly, if I either thought or knew
This marriage should bring loss or danger
    to you,
My subjects, or impair in any way
This royal state of England, I would never
Consent thereto, nor marry while I live;
Moreover, if this marriage should not
    seem,
Before our own High Court of Parliament,
To be of rich advantage to our realm,
We will refrain, and not alone from this,
Likewise from any other, out of which
Looms the least chance of peril to our
    realm.
Wherefore be bold, and with your lawful
    Prince
Stand fast against our enemies and yours,
And fear them not. I fear them not. My
    Lord,
I leave Lord William Howard in your city,
To guard and keep you whole and safe
    from all
The spoil and sackage aim'd at by these
    rebels,
Who mouth and foam against the Prince
    of Spain.
Voices. Long live Queen Mary!
                    Down with Wyatt!
                    The Queen!

White. Three voices from our guilds and
    companies!
You are shy and proud like Englishmen,
    my masters,
And will not trust your voices. Under-
    stand:
Your lawful Prince hath come to cast
    herself
On loyal hearts and bosoms, hoped to fall
Into the wide-spread arms of fealty,
And finds you statues. Speak at once—
    and all!
For whom?
Our sovereign Lady by King Harry's will;
The Queen of England—or the Kentish
    Squire?
I know you loyal. Speak! in the name of
    God!
The Queen of England or the rabble of
    Kent?
The reeking dungfork master of the mace!
Your havings wasted by the scythe and
    spade—
Your right and charters hobnail'd into
    slush—
Your houses fired—your gutters bubbling
    blood——
Acclamation. No! No! The Queen! the
    Queen!
White.   Your Highness hears
This burst and bass of loyal harmony,
And how we each and all of us abhor
The venomous, bestial, devilish revolt
Of Thomas Wyatt. Hear us now make oath
To raise your Highness thirty thousand
    men,
And arm and strike as with one hand, and
    brush
This Wyatt from our shoulders, like a flea
That might have leapt upon us unawares.
Swear with me, noble fellow-citizens, all,
With all your trades, and guilds, and com-
    panies.
Citizens. We swear!
Mary. We thank your Lordship and
    your loyal city.
                    [*Exit* MARY *attended.*
White. I trust this day, thro' God, I have
    saved the crown.
First Alderman. Ay, so my Lord of Pem-
    broke in command

Of all her force be safe; but there are
    doubts.
Second Alderman. I hear that Gardiner,
    coming with the Queen,
And meeting Pembroke, bent to his saddle-
    bow,
As if to win the man by flattering him.
Is he so safe to fight upon her side?
First Alderman. If not, there's no man
    safe.
White.   Yes, Thomas White.
I am safe enough; no man need flatter me.
Second Alderman. Nay, no man need;
    but did you mark our Queen?
The colour freely play'd into her face,
And the half sight which makes her look
    so stern,
Seem'd thro' that dim dilated world of
    hers,
To read our faces; I have never seen her
So queenly or so goodly.
White.   Courage, sir,
That makes or man or woman look their
    goodliest.
Die like the torn fox dumb, but never
    whine
Like that poor heart, Northumberland, at
    the block.
Bagenhall. The man had children, and
    he whined for those.
Methinks most men are but poor-hearted,
    else
Should we so doat on courage, were it
    commoner?
The Queen stands up, and speaks for her
    own self;
And all men cry, She is queenly, she is
    goodly.
Yet she's no goodlier; tho' my Lord
    Mayor here,
By his own rule, he hath been so bold
    to-day,
Should look more goodly than the rest of
    us.
White. Goodly? I feel most goodly heart
    and hand,
And strong to throw ten Wyatts and all
    Kent.
Ha! ha! sir; but you jest; I love it: a jest
In time of danger shows the pulses even.
Be merry! yet, Sir Ralph, you look but sad.

I dare avouch you'd stand up for yourself,
Tho' all the world should bay like winter
    wolves.
Bagenhall. Who knows? the man is
    proven by the hour.
White. The man should make the hour,
    not this the man;
And Thomas White will prove this
    Thomas Wyatt,
And he will prove an Iden to this Cade,
And he will play the Walworth to this
    Wat;
Come, sirs, we prate; hence all—gather
    your men—
Myself must bustle. Wyatt comes to
    Southwark;
I'll have the drawbridge hewn into the
    Thames,
And see the citizens arm'd. Good day;
    good day.   [*Exit* WHITE.
Bagenhall. One of much outdoor bluster.
Howard.   For all that,
Most honest, brave, and skilful; and his
    wealth
A fountain of perennial alms—his fault
So thoroughly to believe in his own self.
Bagenhall. Yet thoroughly to believe in
    one's own self,
So one's own self be thorough, were to do
Great things, my Lord.
Howard.   It may be.
Bagenhall.   I have heard
One of your Council fleer and jeer at him.
Howard. The nursery-cocker'd child
    will jeer at aught
That may seem strange beyond his nursery.
The statesman that shall jeer and fleer at
    men,
Makes enemies for himself and for his
    king;
—And if he jeer not seeing the true man
Behind his folly, he is thrice the fool;
And if he see the man and still will jeer,
He is child and fool, and traitor to the
    State.
Who is he? let me shun him.
Bagenhall.   Nay, my Lord,
He is damn'd enough already.
Howard.   I must set
The guard at Ludgate. Fare you well, Sir
    Ralph.

Bagenhall. 'Who knows?' I am for England. But who knows,
That knows the Queen, the Spaniard, and the Pope,
Whether I be for Wyatt, or the Queen?

[*Exeunt.*

SCENE III

London Bridge

Enter SIR THOMAS WYATT *and* BRETT

Wyatt. Brett, when the Duke of Norfolk moved against us
Thou cried'st 'A Wyatt!' and flying to our side
Left his all bare, for which I love thee, Brett.
Have for thine asking aught that I can give,
For thro' thine help we are come to London Bridge;
But how to cross it balks me. I fear we cannot.
Brett. Nay, hardly, save by boat, swimming, or wings.
Wyatt. Last night I climb'd into the gate-house, Brett,
And scared the gray old porter and his wife.
And then I crept along the gloom and saw
They had hewn the drawbridge down into the river.
It roll'd as black as death; and that same tide
Which, coming with our coming, seem'd to smile
And sparkle like our fortune as thou saidest,
Ran sunless down, and moan'd against the piers.
But o'er the chasm I saw Lord William Howard
By torchlight, and his guard; four guns gaped at me,
Black, silent mouths: had Howard spied me there
And made them speak, as well he might have done,
Their voice had left me none to tell you this.
What shall we do?
Brett.   On somehow. To go back
Were to lose all.

Wyatt.   On over London Bridge
We cannot: stay we cannot; there is ordnance
On the White Tower and on the Devil's Tower,
And pointed full at Southwark; we must round
By Kingston Bridge.
Brett.   Ten miles about.
Wyatt.   Ev'n so.
But I have notice from our partisans
Within the city that they will stand by us
If Ludgate can be reach'd by dawn to-morrow.

Enter one of WYATT'S *men*

Man. Sir Thomas, I've found this paper; pray your worship read it; I know not my letters; the old priests taught me nothing.
Wyatt (reads). 'Whosoever will apprehend the traitor Thomas Wyatt shall have a hundred pounds for reward.'
Man. Is that it? That's a big lot of money.
Wyatt. Ay, ay, my friend; not read it? 'tis not written
Half plain enough. Give me a piece of paper!

[*Writes* 'THOMAS WYATT' *large.*
There, any man can read that.

[*Sticks it in his cap.*
Brett.   But that's foolhardy.
Wyatt. No! boldness, which will give my followers boldness.

Enter MAN *with a prisoner*

Man. We found him, your worship, a plundering o' Bishop Winchester's house; he says he's a poor gentleman.
Wyatt. Gentleman! a thief! Go hang him. Shall we make
Those that we come to serve our sharpest foes?
Brett. Sir Thomas—
Wyatt.   Hang him, I say.
Brett. Wyatt, but now you promised me a boon.
Wyatt. Ay, and I warrant this fine fellow's life.
Brett. Ev'n so; he was my neighbour once in Kent.

He's poor enough, has drunk and gambled
  out
All that he had, and gentleman he was.
We have been glad together; let him live.
  Wyatt. He has gambled for his life, and
    lost, he hangs.
No, no, my word's my word. Take thy
  poor gentleman!
Gamble thyself at once out of my sight,
Or I will dig thee with my dagger. Away!
Women and children!

Enter a CROWD *of* WOMEN *and* CHILDREN

  First Woman. O Sir Thomas, Sir
Thomas, pray you go away, Sir Thomas,
or you'll make the White Tower a black
'un for us this blessed day. He'll be the
death on us; and you'll set the Divil's
Tower a-spitting, and he'll smash all our
bits o' things worse than Philip o' Spain.
  Second Woman. Don't ye now go to think
that we be for Philip o' Spain.
  Third Woman. No, we know that ye be
come to kill the Queen, and we'll pray for
you all on our bended knees. But o' God's
mercy don't ye kill the Queen here, Sir
Thomas; look ye, here's little Dickon, and
little Robin, and little Jenny—though she's
but a side-cousin—and all on our knees,
we pray you to kill the Queen further off,
Sir Thomas.
  Wyatt. My friends, I have not come to
kill the Queen
Or here or there: I come to save you all,
And I'll go further off.
  Crowd. Thanks, Sir Thomas, we be
beholden to you, and we'll pray for you on
our bended knees till our lives' end.
  Wyatt. Be happy, I am your friend. To
Kingston, forward!   *[Exeunt.*

SCENE IV

*Room in the Gatehouse of
Westminster Palace*

MARY, ALICE, GARDINER, RENARD, LADIES

  Gardiner. Their cry is, Philip never shall
be king.
  Mary. Lord Pembroke in command of
all our force

Will front their cry and shatter them into
  dust.
  Alice. Was not Lord Pembroke with
    Northumberland?
O madam, if this Pembroke should be
  false?
  Mary. No, girl; most brave and loyal,
  brave and loyal.
His breaking with Northumberland broke
  Northumberland.
At the park gate he hovers with our guards.
These Kentish ploughmen cannot break
  the guards.

Enter MESSENGER

  Messenger. Wyatt, your Grace, hath
  broken thro' the guards
And gone to Ludgate.
  Gardiner.   Madam, I much fear
That all is lost; but we can save your Grace.
The river still is free. I do beseech you,
There yet is time, take boat and pass to
  Windsor.
  Mary. I pass to Windsor and I lose my
  crown.
  Gardiner. Pass, then, I pray your High-
  ness, to the Tower.
  Mary. I shall but be their prisoner in
  the Tower.
  Cries without. The traitor! treason!
  Pembroke!
  Ladies.   Treason! treason!
  Mary. Peace.
False to Northumberland, is he false to
  me?
Bear witness, Renard, that I live and die
The true and faithful bride of Philip—A
  sound
Of feet and voices thickening hither—
  blows—
Hark, there is battle at the palace gates,
And I will out upon the gallery.
  Ladies. No, no, your Grace; see there
  the arrows flying.
  Mary. I am Harry's daughter, Tudor,
  and not Fear.
    [Goes out on the gallery.
The guards are all driven in, skulk into
  corners
Like rabbits to their holes. A gracious
  guard

560

Truly; shame on them! they have shut the gates!

Enter SIR ROBERT SOUTHWELL

Southwell. The porter, please your Grace, hath shut the gates
On friend and foe. Your gentlemen-at-arms,
If this be not your Grace's order, cry
To have the gates set wide again, and they
With their good battleaxes will do you right
Against all traitors.
Mary. They are the flower of England; set the gates wide.

[*Exit* SOUTHWELL.

Enter COURTENAY

Courtenay. All lost, all lost, all yielded! A barge, a barge!
The Queen must to the Tower.
Mary. Whence come you, sir?
Courtenay. From Charing Cross; the rebels broke us there,
And I sped hither with what haste I might
To save my royal cousin.
Mary. Where is Pembroke?
Courtenay. I left him somewhere in the thick of it.
Mary. Left him and fled; and thou that would'st be King,
And hast nor heart nor honour. I myself
Will down into the battle and there bide
The upshot of my quarrel, or die with those
That are no cowards and no Courtenays.
Courtenay. I do not love your Grace should call me coward.

Enter another MESSENGER

Messenger. Over, your Grace, all crush'd; the brave Lord William
Thrust him from Ludgate, and the traitor flying
To Temple Bar, there by Sir Maurice Berkeley
Was taken prisoner.
Mary. To the Tower with *him!*

Messenger. 'Tis said he told Sir Maurice there was one
Cognisant of this, and party thereunto,
My Lord of Devon.
Mary. To the Tower with *him!*
Courtenay. O la, the Tower, the Tower, always the Tower,
I shall grow into it—I shall be the Tower.
Mary. Your Lordship may not have so long to wait.
Remove him!
Courtenay. La, to whistle out my life,
And carve my coat upon the walls again!

[*Exit* COURTENAY *guarded.*

Messenger. Also this Wyatt did confess the Princess
Cognisant thereof, and party thereunto.
Mary. What? whom—whom did you say?
Messenger. Elizabeth,
Your Royal sister.
Mary. To the Tower with *her!*
My foes are at my feet and I am Queen.

[GARDINER *and her* LADIES *kneel to her.*

Gardiner (rising). There let them lie, your footstool! (*Aside.*) Can I strike
Elizabeth?—not now and save the life
Of Devon: if I save him, he and his
Are bound to me—may strike hereafter.
(*Aloud.*) Madam,
What Wyatt said, or what they said he said,
Cries of the moment and the street—
Mary. He said it.
Gardiner. Your courts of justice will determine that.
Renard (advancing). I trust by this your Highness will allow
Some spice of wisdom in my telling you,
When last we talk'd, that Philip would not come
Till Guildford Dudley and the Duke of Suffolk,
And Lady Jane had left us.
Mary. They shall die.
Renard. And your so loving sister?
Mary. She shall die.
My foes are at my feet, and Philip King.

[*Exeunt.*

ACT III

SCENE I

The Conduit in Gracechurch

Painted with the Nine Worthies, among them King Henry VIII holding a book, on it inscribed 'Verbum Dei.'

Enter SIR RALPH BAGENHALL *and* SIR THOMAS STAFFORD

Bagenhall. A hundred here and hundreds hang'd in Kent.
The tigress had unsheath'd her nails at last,
And Renard and the Chancellor sharpen'd them.
In every London street a gibbet stood.
They are down to-day. Here by this house was one;
The traitor husband dangled at the door,
And when the traitor wife came out for bread
To still the petty treason therewithin,
Her cap would brush his heels.
Stafford.   It is Sir Ralph,
And muttering to himself as heretofore.
Sir, see you aught up yonder?
Bagenhall.   I miss something.
The tree that only bears dead fruit is gone.
Stafford. What tree, sir?
Bagenhall.   Well, the tree in Virgil, sir,
That bears not its own apples.
Stafford.   What! the gallows?
Bagenhall. Sir, this dead fruit was ripening overmuch,
And had to be removed lest living Spain
Should sicken at dead England.
Stafford.   Not so dead,
But that a shock may rouse her.
Bagenhall.   I believe
Sir Thomas Stafford?
Stafford.   I am ill disguised.
Bagenhall. Well, are you not in peril here?
Stafford. I think so.
I came to feel the pulse of England, whether
It beats hard at this marriage. Did you see it?

Bagenhall. Stafford, I am a sad man and a serious.
Far liefer had I in my country hall
Been reading some old book, with mine old hound
Couch'd at my hearth, and mine old flask of wine
Beside me, than have seen it: yet I saw it.
Stafford. Good, was it splendid?
Bagenhall. Ay, if Dukes, and Earls,
And Counts, and sixty Spanish cavaliers,
Some six or seven Bishops, diamonds, pearls,
That royal commonplace too, cloth of gold,
Could make it so.
Stafford. And what was Mary's dress?
Bagenhall. Good faith, I was too sorry for the woman
To mark the dress. She wore red shoes!
Stafford.   Red shoes!
Bagenhall. Scarlet, as if her feet were wash'd in blood,
As if she had waded in it.
Stafford.   Were your eyes
So bashful that you look'd no higher?
Bagenhall.   A diamond,
And Philip's gift, as proof of Philip's love,
Who hath not any for any,—tho' a true one,
Blazed false upon her heart.
Stafford.   But this proud Prince—
Bagenhall. Nay, he is King, you know, the King of Naples.
The father ceded Naples, that the son
Being a King, might wed a Queen—O he
Flamed in brocade—white satin his trunk-hose,
Inwrought with silver,—on his neck a collar,
Gold, thick with diamonds; hanging down from this
The Golden Fleece—and round his knee, misplaced,
Our English Garter, studded with great emeralds,
Rubies, I know not what. Have you had enough
Of all this gear?
Stafford. Ay, since you hate the telling it.
How look'd the Queen?
Bagenhall. No fairer for her jewels.

And I could see that as the new-made
   couple
Came from the Minster, moving side by
   side
Beneath one canopy, ever and anon
She cast on him a vassal smile of love,
Which Philip with a glance of some dis-
   taste,
Or so methought, return'd. I may be
   wrong, sir.
This marriage will not hold.
   Stafford.   I think with you.
The King of France will help to break it.
   Bagenhall.   France!
We once had half of France, and hurl'd
   our battles
Into the heart of Spain; but England now
Is but a ball chuck'd between France and
   Spain,
His in whose hand she drops; Harry of
   Bolingbroke
Had holpen Richard's tottering throne to
   stand,
Could Harry have foreseen that all our
   nobles
Would perish on the civil slaughter-field,
And leave the people naked to the crown,
And the crown naked to the people; the
   crown
Female, too! Sir, no woman's regimen
Can save us. We are fallen, and as I think,
Never to rise again.
   Stafford. You are too black-blooded.
I'd make a move myself to hinder that:
I know some lusty fellows there in France.
   Bagenhall. You would but make us
   weaker, Thomas Stafford.
Wyatt was a good soldier, yet he fail'd,
And strengthen'd Philip.
   Stafford.   Did not his last breath
Clear Courtenay and the Princess from the
   charge
Of being his co-rebels?
   Bagenhall.   Ay, but then
What such a one as Wyatt says is nothing:
We have no men among us. The new Lords
Are quieted with their sop of Abbeylands,
And ev'n before the Queen's face Gardiner
   buys them
With Philip's gold. All greed, no faith, no
   courage!

Why, ev'n the haughty prince, Northum-
   berland,
The leader of our Reformation, knelt
And blubber'd like a lad, and on the
   scaffold
Recanted, and resold himself to Rome.
   Stafford. I swear you do your country
   wrong, Sir Ralph.
I know a set of exiles over there,
Dare-devils, that would eat fire and spit
   it out
At Philip's beard: they pillage Spain
   already.
The French King winks at it. An hour will
   come
When they will sweep her from the seas.
   No men?
Did not Lord Suffolk die like a true man?
Is not Lord William Howard a true man?
Yea, you yourself, altho' you are black-
   blooded?
And I, by God, believe myself a man.
Ay, even in the church there is a man—
Cranmer.
Fly would he not, when all men bad him
   fly.
And what a letter he wrote against the
   Pope!
There's a brave man, if any.
   Bagenhall.   Ay; if it hold.
   Crowd (coming on). God save their
   Graces!
   Stafford.   Bagenhall, I see
The Tudor green and white. (*Trumpets.*)
   They are coming now.
And here's a crowd as thick as herring-
   shoals.
   Bagenhall. Be limpets to this pillar, or
   we are torn
Down the strong wave of brawlers.
   Crowd. God save their Graces!
     [*Procession of Trumpeters, Javelin-
     men, etc.; then Spanish and Flemish
     Nobles intermingled.*
   Stafford. Worth seeing, Bagenhall!
   These black dog-Dons
Garb themselves bravely. Who's the long-
   face there,
Looks very Spain of very Spain?
   Bagenhall.   The Duke
Of Alva, an iron soldier.

Stafford. And the Dutchman,
Now laughing at some jest?
Bagenhall. William of Orange,
William the Silent.
Stafford. Why do they call him so?
Bagenhall. He keeps, they say, some
secret that may cost
Philip his life.
Stafford. But then he looks so merry.
Bagenhall. I cannot tell you why they
call him so.
[*The* KING *and* QUEEN *pass, attended
by Peers of the Realm, Officers of
State, etc. Cannon shot off.*
Crowd. Philip and Mary, Philip and
Mary!
Long live the King and Queen, Philip and
Mary!
Stafford. They smile as if content with
one another.
Bagenhall. A smile abroad is oft a scowl
at home.
[KING *and* QUEEN *pass on. Procession.*
First Citizen. I thought this Philip had
been one of those black devils of Spain, but
he hath a yellow beard.
Second Citizen. Not red like Iscariot's.
First Citizen. Like a carrot's, as thou
say'st, and English carrot's better than
Spanish licorice; but I thought he was a
beast.
Third Citizen. Certain I had heard that
every Spaniard carries a tail like a devil
under his trunk-hose.
Tailor. Ay, but see what trunk-hoses!
Lord! they be fine; I never stitch'd none
such. They make amends for the tails.
Fourth Citizen. Tut! every Spanish
priest will tell you that all English heretics
have tails.
Fifth Citizen. Death and the Devil—if
he find I have one—
Fourth Citizen. Lo! thou hast call'd them
up! here they come—a pale horse for
Death and Gardiner for the Devil.

Enter GARDINER (*turning back from the
procession*)

Gardiner. Knave, wilt thou wear thy
cap before the Queen?

Man. My Lord, I stand so squeezed
among the crowd
I cannot lift my hands unto my head.
Gardiner. Knock off his cap there, some
of you about him!
See there be others that can use their
hands.
Thou art one of Wyatt's men?
Man. No, my Lord, no.
Gardiner. Thy name, thou knave?
Man. I am nobody, my Lord.
Gardiner (*shouting*). God's passion!
knave, thy name?
Man. I have ears to hear.
Gardiner. Ay, rascal, if I leave thee ears
to hear.
Find out his name and bring it me (*to
Attendant*).
Attendant. Ay, my Lord.
Gardiner. Knave, thou shalt lose thine
ears and find thy tongue,
And shalt be thankful if I leave thee that.
[*Coming before the Conduit.*
The conduit painted—the nine worthies
—ay!
But then what's here? King Harry with a
scroll.
Ha—Verbum Dei—verbum—word of
God!
God's passion! do you know the knave
that painted it?
Attendant. I do, my Lord.
Gardiner. Tell him to paint it out,
And put some fresh device in lieu of it—
A pair of gloves, a pair of gloves, sir; ha?
There is no heresy there.
Attendant. I will, my Lord;
The man shall paint a pair of gloves. I am
sure
(Knowing the man) he wrought it
ignorantly,
And not from any malice.
Gardiner. Word of God
In English! over this the brainless loons
That cannot spell Esaïas from St. Paul,
Make themselves drunk and mad, fly out
and flare
Into rebellions. I'll have their bibles burnt.
The bible is the priest's. Ay! fellow, what!
Stand staring at me! shout, you gaping
rogue!

564

Man. I have, my Lord, shouted till I am
   hoarse.

Gardiner. What hast thou shouted,
   knave?

Man.   Long live Queen Mary!

Gardiner. Knave, there be two. There
be both King and Queen,
Philip and Mary. Shout!

Man.   Nay, but, my Lord,
The Queen comes first, Mary and Philip.

Gardiner.   Shout, then,
Mary and Philip!

Man.   Mary and Philip!

Gardiner.   Now,
Thou hast shouted for thy pleasure, shout
   for mine!
Philip and Mary!

Man.   Must it be so, my Lord?

Gardiner. Ay, knave.

Man.   Philip and Mary!

Gardiner.   I distrust thee.
Thine is a half voice and a lean assent.
What is thy name?

Man.   Sanders.

Gardiner.   What else?

Man.   Zerubbabel.

Gardiner. Where dost thou live?

Man.   In Cornhill.

Gardiner.   Where, knave, where?

Man. Sign of the Talbot.

Gardiner. Come to me to-morrow.—
Rascal!—this land is like a hill of fire,
One crater opens when another shuts.
But so I get the laws against the heretic,
Spite of Lord Paget and Lord William
   Howard,
And others of our Parliament, revived,
I will show fire on my side—stake and
   fire—
Sharp work and short. The knaves are
   easily cow'd.
Follow their Majesties.
         [*Exit. The crowd following.*

Bagenhall.   As proud as Becket.

Stafford. You would not have him murder'd as Becket was?

Bagenhall. No—murder fathers murder:
   but I say
There is no man—there was one woman
   with us—
It was a sin to love her married, dead

I cannot choose but love her.

Stafford.   Lady Jane?

Crowd (going off). God save their Graces!

Stafford.   Did you see her die?

Bagenhall. No, no; her innocent blood
   had blinded me.
You call me too black-blooded—true
   enough
Her dark dead blood is in my heart with
   mine
If ever I cry out against the Pope
Her dark dead blood that ever moves with
   mine
Will stir the living tongue and make the
   cry.

Stafford. Yet doubtless you can tell me
   how she died?

Bagenhall. Seventeen—and knew eight
   languages—in music
Peerless—her needle perfect, and her
   learning
Beyond the churchmen; yet so meek, so
   modest,
So wife-like humble to the trivial boy
Mismatch'd with her for policy! I have
   heard
She would not take a last farewell of him,
She fear'd it might unman him for his end.
She could not be unmann'd—no, nor out-
   woman'd—
Seventeen—a rose of grace!
Girl never breathed to rival such a rose;
Rose never blew that equall'd such a bud.

Stafford. Pray you go on.

Bagenhall. She came upon the scaffold,
And said she was condemn'd to die for
   treason;
She had but follow'd the device of those
Her nearest kin: she thought they knew
   the laws.
But for herself, she knew but little law,
And nothing of the titles to the crown;
She had no desire for that, and wrung her
   hands,
And trusted God would save her thro' the
   blood
Of Jesus Christ alone.

Stafford.   Pray you go on.

Bagenhall. Then knelt and said the
   Miserere Mei—
But all in English, mark you; rose again,

And, when the headsman pray'd to be
    forgiven,
Said 'You will give me my true crown at
    last,
But do it quickly;' then all wept but she,
Who changed not colour when she saw the
    block,
But ask'd him, childlike: 'Will you take it
    off
Before I lay me down?' 'No, madam,' he
    said,
Gasping; and when her innocent eyes were
    bound,
She, with her poor blind hands feeling—
    'where is it?
Where is it?'—You must fancy that which
    follow'd,
If you have heart to do it!
    Crowd (*in the distance*). God save their
      Graces!
    Stafford. Their Graces, our disgraces!
      God confound them!
Why, she's grown bloodier! when I last
    was here,
This was against her conscience—would
    be murder!
    Bagenhall. The 'Thou shalt do no mur-
      der,' which God's hand
Wrote on her conscience, Mary rubb'd
    out pale—
She could not make it white—and over
    that,
Traced in the blackest text of Hell—'Thou
    shalt!'
And sign'd it—Mary!
    Stafford. Philip and the Pope
Must have sign'd too. I hear this Legate's
    coming
To bring us absolution from the Pope.
The Lords and Commons will bow down
    before him—
You are of the house? what will you do,
    Sir Ralph?
    Bagenhall. And why should I be bolder
    than the rest,
Or honester than all?
    Stafford.   But, sir, if I—
And oversea they say this state of yours
Hath no more mortice than a tower of
    cards;
And that a puff would do it—then if I

And others made that move I touch'd
    upon,
Back'd by the power of France, and land-
    ing here,
Came with a sudden splendour, shout, and
    show,
And dazzled men and deafen'd by some
    bright
Loud venture, and the people so unquiet—
And I the race of murder'd Buckingham—
Not for myself, but for the kingdom—Sir,
I trust that you would fight along with us.
    Bagenhall. No; you would fling your
    lives into the gulf.
    Stafford. But if this Philip, as he's like
    to do,
Left Mary a wife-widow here alone,
Set up a viceroy, sent his myriads hither
To seize upon the forts and fleet, and
    make us
A Spanish province; would you not fight
    then?
    Bagenhall. I think I should fight then.
    Stafford. I am sure of it.
Hist! there's the face coming on here of
    one
Who knows me. I must leave you. Fare
    you well,
You'll hear of me again.
    Bagenhall.   Upon the scaffold.
                         [*Exeunt*.

SCENE II

Room in Whitehall Palace

MARY. *Enter* PHILIP *and* CARDINAL POLE

    Pole. Ave Maria, gratia plena, Benedicta
    tu in mulieribus.
    Mary. Loyal and royal cousin, humblest
    thanks.
Had you a pleasant voyage up the river?
    Pole. We had your royal barge, and that
    same chair,
Or rather throne of purple, on the deck.
Our silver cross sparkled before the prow,
The ripples twinkled at their diamond-
    dance,
The boats that follow'd, were as glowing-
    gay
As regal gardens; and your flocks of swans,

As fair and white as angels; and your
    shores
Wore in mine eyes the green of Paradise.
My foreign friends, who dream'd us
    blanketed
In ever-closing fog, were much amazed
To find as fair a sun as might have flash'd
Upon their lake of Garda, fire the Thames;
Our voyage by sea was all but miracle;
And here the river flowing from the sea,
Not toward it (for they thought not of our
    tides),
Seem'd as a happy miracle to make glide—
In quiet—home your banish'd country-
    man.
Mary. We heard that you were sick in
    Flanders, cousin.
Pole. A dizziness.
Mary.   And how came you
    round again?
Pole. The scarlet thread of Rahab saved
    her life;
And mine, a little letting of the blood.
Mary. Well? now?
Pole.   Ay, cousin, as the
    heathen giant
Had but to touch the ground, his force
    return'd—
Thus, after twenty years of banishment,
Feeling my native land beneath my foot,
I said thereto: 'Ah, native land of mine,
Thou art much beholden to this foot of
    mine,
That hastes with full commission from the
    Pope
To absolve thee from thy guilt of heresy.
Thou hast disgraced me and attainted me,
And mark'd me ev'n as Cain, and I return
As Peter, but to bless thee: make me well.'
Methinks the good land heard me, for
    to-day
My heart beats twenty, when I see you,
    cousin.
Ah, gentle cousin, since your Herod's
    death,
How oft hath Peter knock'd at Mary's gate!
And Mary would have risen and let him in,
But, Mary, there were those within the
    house
Who would not have it.
    Mary.   True, good cousin Pole;

And there were also those without the
    house
Who would not have it.
    Pole.   I believe so, cousin.
State-policy and church-policy are con-
    joint,
But Janus-faces looking diverse ways.
I fear the Emperor much misvalued me.
But all is well; 'twas ev'n the will of God,
Who, waiting till the time had ripen'd,
    now,
Makes me his mouth of holy greeting.
    'Hail,
Daughter of God, and saver of the faith.
Sit benedictus fructus ventris tui!'
    Mary. Ah, heaven!
    Pole.   Unwell, your Grace?
    Mary.   No, cousin, happy—
Happy to see you; never yet so happy
Since I was crown'd.
    Pole.   Sweet cousin, you forget
That long low minster where you gave
    your hand
To this great Catholic King.
    Philip.   Well said, Lord Legate.
    Mary. Nay, not well said; I thought of
    you, my liege,
Ev'n as I spoke.
    Philip.   Ay, Madam; my Lord Paget
Waits to present our Council to the Legate.
Sit down here, all; Madam, between us
    you.
    Pole. Lo, now you are enclosed with
    boards of cedar,
Our little sister of the Song of Songs!
You are doubly fenced and shielded sitting
    here
Between the two most high-set thrones on
    earth,
The Emperor's highness happily symboll'd
    by
The King your husband, the Pope's
    Holiness
By mine own self.
    Mary.   True, cousin, I am happy.
When will you that we summon both our
    houses
To take this absolution from your lips,
And be regather'd to the Papal fold?
    Pole. In Britain's calendar the brightest
    day

Beheld our rough forefathers break their
   Gods,
And clasp the faith in Christ; but after that
Might not St. Andrew's be her happiest
   day?
Mary. Then these shall meet upon St.
   Andrew's day.

Enter PAGET, *who presents the Council.*
   Dumb show

Pole. I am an old man wearied with my
   journey,
Ev'n with my joy. Permit me to withdraw.
To Lambeth?
   Philip.   Ay, Lambeth has ousted
Cranmer.
It was not meet the heretic swine should
   live
In Lambeth.
   Mary.   There or anywhere, or at all.
   Philip. We have had it swept and
   garnish'd after him.
Pole. Not for the seven devils to enter
   in?
Philip. No, for we trust they parted in
   the swine.
Pole. True, and I am the Angel of the
   Pope.
Farewell, your Graces.
   Philip.   Nay, not here—to me;
I will go with you to the waterside.
Pole. Not be my Charon to the counter
   side?
Philip. No, my Lord Legate, the Lord
   Chancellor goes.
Pole. And unto no dead world; but
   Lambeth palace,
Henceforth a centre of the living faith.
   [*Exeunt* PHILIP, POLE, PAGET, *etc.*

Manet MARY

Mary. He hath awaked! he hath awaked!
He stirs within the darkness!
Oh, Philip, husband! now thy love to mine
Will cling more close, and those bleak
   manners thaw,
That make me shamed and tongue-tied in
   my love.
The second Prince of Peace—
The great unborn defender of the Faith,
Who will avenge me of mine enemies—

He comes, and my star rises.
The stormy Wyatts and Northumberlands,
The proud ambitions of Elizabeth,
And all her fieriest partisans—are pale
Before my star!
The light of this new learning wanes and
   dies:
The ghosts of Luther and Zuinglius fade
Into the deathless hell which is their doom
Before my star!
His sceptre shall go forth from Ind to Ind!
His sword shall hew the heretic peoples
   down!
His faith shall clothe the world that will
   be his,
Like universal air and sunshine! Open,
Ye everlasting gates! The King is here!—
My star, my son!

Enter PHILIP, DUKE OF ALVA, *etc.*

                  Oh, Philip, come with me;
Good news have I to tell you, news to
   make
Both of us happy—ay, the Kingdom too.
Nay come with me—one moment!
   Philip (*to* ALVA).   More than that:
There was one here of late—William the
   Silent
They call him—he is free enough in talk,
But tells me nothing. You will be, we trust,
Sometime the viceroy of those provinces—
He must deserve his surname better.
   Alva.   Ay, sir;
Inherit the Great Silence.
   Philip.   True; the provinces
Are hard to rule and must be hardly ruled;
Most fruitful, yet, indeed, an empty rind,
All hollow'd out with stinging heresies;
And for their heresies, Alva, they will fight;
You must break them or they break you.
   Alva (*proudly*).   The first.
   Philip. Good!
Well, Madam, this new happiness of mine?
                              [*Exeunt.*

Enter THREE PAGES

First Page. News, mates! a miracle, a
   miracle! news!
The bells must ring; Te Deums must be
   sung;

568

The Queen hath felt the motion of her
    babe!
Second Page. Ay; but see here!
First Page.   See what?
Second Page.   This paper, Dickon.
I found it fluttering at the palace gates:—
'The Queen of England is delivered of a
    dead dog!'
Third Page. These are the things that
    madden her. Fie upon it!
First Page. Ay; but I hear she hath a
    dropsy, lad,
Or a high-dropsy, as the doctors call it.
Third Page. Fie on her dropsy, so she
    have a dropsy!
I know that she was ever sweet to me.
First Page. For thou and thine are
    Roman to the core.
Third Page. So thou and thine must be.
    Take heed!
First Page.   Not I,
And whether this flash of news be false or
    true,
So the wine run, and there be revelry,
Content am I. Let all the steeples clash,
Till the sun dance, as upon Easter Day.
                                    [*Exeunt.*

SCENE III

Great Hall in Whitehall

*At the far end a daïs. On this three chairs,
two under one canopy for* MARY *and*
PHILIP, *another on the right of these for*
POLE. *Under the daïs on* POLE'S *side,
ranged along the wall, sit all the Spiritual
Peers, and along the wall opposite, all the
Temporal. The Commons on cross benches
in front, a line of approach to the daïs
between them. In the foreground,* SIR
RALPH BAGENHALL *and other* MEMBERS
OF THE COMMONS.

First Member. St. Andrew's day; sit
    close, sit close, we are friends.
Is reconciled the word? the Pope again?
It must be thus; and yet, cocksbody! how
    strange
That Gardiner, once so one with all of us
Against this foreign marriage, should have
    yielded

So utterly!—strange! but stranger still
    that he,
So fierce against the Headship of the Pope,
Should play the second actor in this pageant
That brings him in; such a cameleon he!
Second Member. This Gardiner turn'd
    his coat in Henry's time;
The serpent that hath slough'd will slough
    again.
Third Member. Tut, then we all are
    serpents.
Second Member. Speak for yourself.
Third Member. Ay, and for Gardiner!
    being English citizen,
How should he bear a bridegroom out of
    Spain?
The Queen would have him! being Eng-
    lish churchman
How should he bear the headship of the
    Pope?
The Queen would have it! Statesmen that
    are wise
Shape a necessity, as a sculptor clay,
To their own model.
Second Member. Statesmen that are wise
Take truth herself for model. What say
    you?   [*To* SIR RALPH BAGENHALL.
Bagenhall. We talk and talk.
First Member. Ay, and what use to talk?
Philip's no sudden alien—the Queen's
    husband,
He's here, and king, or will be—yet cocks-
    body!
So hated here! I watch'd a hive of late;
My seven-years' friend was with me, my
    young boy;
Out crept a wasp, with half the swarm
    behind.
'Philip!' says he. I had to cuff the rogue
For infant treason.
Third Member. But they say that bees,
If any creeping life invade their hive
Too gross to be thrust out, will build him
    round,
And bind him in from harming of their
    combs.
And Philip by these articles is bound
From stirring hand or foot to wrong the
    realm.
Second Member. By bonds of beeswax,
    like your creeping thing;

But your wise bees had stung him first to
    death.
Third Member. Hush, hush!
You wrong the Chancellor: the clauses
    added
To that same treaty which the emperor
    sent us
Were mainly Gardiner's: that no foreigner
Hold office in the household, fleet, forts,
    army;
That if the Queen should die without a
    child,
The bond between the kingdoms be dis-
    solved;
That Philip should not mix us any way
With his French wars—
    Second Member. Ay, ay, but what
      security,
Good sir, for this, if Philip——
    Third Member.   Peace—the Queen,
Philip, and Pole.   [*All rise, and stand.*

Enter MARY, PHILIP, *and* POLE

[GARDINER *conducts them to the three
chairs of state.* PHILIP *sits on the*
QUEEN'S *left,* POLE *on her right.*
Gardiner. Our short-lived sun, before
    his winter plunge,
Laughs at the last red leaf, and Andrew's
    Day.
    Mary. Should not this day be held in
      after years
More solemn than of old?
    Philip.   Madam, my wish
Echoes your Majesty's.
    Pole.   It shall be so.
    Gardiner. Mine echoes both your
    Graces'; (*aside*) but the Pope—
Can we not have the Catholic church as
    well
Without as with the Italian? if we cannot,
Why then the Pope.
        My lords of the upper house,
And ye, my masters, of the lower house,
Do ye stand fast by that which ye resolved?
    Voices. We do.
    Gardiner. And be you all one mind to
      supplicate
The Legate here for pardon, and acknow-
    ledge
The primacy of the Pope?

    Voices.   We are all one mind.
    Gardiner. Then must I play the vassal
    to this Pole.   [*Aside.*
    [*He draws a paper from under his
    robes and presents it to the* KING *and*
    QUEEN, *who look through it and return
    it to him; then ascends a tribune, and
    reads.*
We, the Lords Spiritual and Temporal,
And Commons here in Parliament as-
    sembled,
Presenting the whole body of this realm
Of England, and dominions of the same,
Do make most humble suit unto your
    Majesties,
In our own name and that of all the state,
That by your gracious means and inter-
    cession
Our supplication be exhibited
To the Lord Cardinal Pole, sent here as
    Legate
From our most Holy Father Julius, Pope,
And from the Apostolic see of Rome;
And do declare our penitence and grief
For our long schism and disobedience,
Either in making laws and ordinances
Against the Holy Father's primacy,
Or else by doing or by speaking aught
Which might impugn or prejudice the
    same;
By this our supplication promising,
As well for our own selves as all the realm,
That now we be and ever shall be quick,
Under and with your Majesties' authorities,
To do to the utmost all that in us lies
Towards the abrogation and repeal
Of all such laws and ordinances made;
Whereon we humbly pray your Majesties,
As persons undefiled with our offence,
So to set forth this humble suit of ours
That we the rather by your intercession,
May from the Apostolic see obtain,
Thro' this most reverend Father, absolu-
    tion,
And full release from danger of all censures
Of Holy Church that we be fall'n into,
So that we may, as children penitent,
Be once again received into the bosom
And unity of Universal Church;
And that this noble realm thro' after years
May in this unity and obedience

Unto the holy see and reigning Pope
Serve God and both your Majesties.
Voices.   Amen.   [All sit.
[He again presents the petition to the
KING and QUEEN, who hand it
reverentially to POLE.
Pole (sitting). This is the loveliest day
          that ever smiled
On England. All her breath should,
          incenselike,
Rise to the heavens in grateful praise of
          Him
Who now recalls her to His ancient fold.
Lo! once again God to this realm hath
          given
A token of His more especial Grace;
For as this people were the first of all
The islands call'd into the dawning church
Out of the dead, deep night of heathendom,
So now are these the first whom God hath
          given
Grace to repent and sorrow for their
          schism;
And if your penitence be not mockery,
Oh how the blessed angels who rejoice
Over one saved do triumph at this hour
In the reborn salvation of a land
So noble.   [A pause.
               For ourselves we do protest
That our commission is to heal, not harm;
We come not to condemn, but reconcile;
We come not to compel, but call again;
We come not to destroy, but edify;
Nor yet to question things already done;
These are forgiven—matters of the past—
And range with jetsam and with offal
          thrown
Into the blind sea of forgetfulness.
                              [A pause.
Ye have reversed the attainder laid on us
By him who sack'd the house of God; and
          we,
Amplier than any field on our poor earth
Can render thanks in fruit for being sown,
Do here and now repay you sixty-fold,
A hundred, yea, a thousand thousand-fold,
With heaven for earth.
[Rising and stretching forth his hands.
All kneel but SIR RALPH BAGENHALL,
who rises and remains standing.
     The Lord who hath redeem'd us

With His own blood, and wash'd us from
          our sins,
To purchase for Himself a stainless bride;
He, whom the Father hath appointed Head
Of all his church, He by His mercy absolve
          you!   [A pause.
And we by that authority Apostolic
Given unto us, his Legate, by the Pope,
Our Lord and Holy Father, Julius,
God's Vicar and Vicegerent upon earth,
Do here absolve you and deliver you
And every one of you, and all the realm
And its dominions from all heresy,
All schism, and from all and every censure,
Judgment, and pain accruing thereupon;
And also we restore you to the bosom
And unity of Universal Church.
                    [Turning to GARDINER.
Our letters of commission will declare this
          plainlier.
     [QUEEN heard sobbing. Cries of Amen!
Amen! Some of the MEMBERS em-
brace one another. All but SIR RALPH
BAGENHALL pass out into the neigh-
bouring chapel, whence is heard the
Te Deum.
Bagenhall. We strove against the papacy
          from the first,
In William's time, in our first Edward's
          time,
And in my master Henry's time; but now,
The unity of Universal Church,
Mary would have it; and this Gardiner
          follows;
The unity of Universal Hell,
Philip would have it; and this Gardiner
          follows!
A Parliament of imitative apes!
Sheep at the gap which Gardiner takes,
          who not
Believes the Pope, nor any of them
          believe—
These spaniel-Spaniard English of the
          time,
Who rub their fawning noses in the dust,
For that is Philip's gold-dust, and adore
This Vicar of their Vicar. Would I had been
Born Spaniard! I had held my head up
          then.
I am ashamed that I am Bagenhall,
English.

Enter OFFICER

Officer. Sir Ralph Bagenhall!

Bagenhall.   What of that?

Officer. You were the one sole man in
either house

Who stood upright when both the houses
fell.

Bagenhall. The houses fell!

Officer.   I mean the houses knelt

Before the Legate.

Bagenhall.   Do not scrimp your
phrase,

But stretch it wider; say when England fell.

Officer. I say you were the one sole man
who stood.

Bagenhall. I am the one sole man in
either house,

Perchance in England, loves her like a son.

Officer. Well, you one man, because you
stood upright,

Her Grace the Queen commands you to
the Tower.

Bagenhall. As traitor, or as heretic, or
for what?

Officer. If any man in any way would be

The one man, he shall be so to his cost.

Bagenhall. What! will she have my head?

Officer.   A round fine likelier.

Your pardon.   [*Calling to Attendant.*

By the river to the Tower.   [*Exeunt.*

SCENE IV

Whitehall. A Room in the Palace

MARY, GARDINER, POLE, PAGET,
BONNER, *etc.*

Mary. The King and I, my Lords, now
that all traitors

Against our royal state have lost the heads

Wherewith they plotted in their treasonous
malice,

Have talk'd together, and are well agreed

That those old statutes touching Lollardism

To bring the heretic to the stake, should be

No longer a dead letter, but requicken'd.

One of the Council. Why, what hath
fluster'd Gardiner? how he rubs

His forelock!

Paget. I have changed a word with him

In coming, and may change a word again.

Gardiner. Madam, your Highness is our
sun, the King

And you together our two suns in one;

And so the beams of both may shine upon
us,

The faith that seem'd to droop will feel
your light,

Lift head, and flourish; yet not light alone,

There must be heat—there must be heat
enough

To scorch and wither heresy to the root.

For what saith Christ? 'Compel them to
come in.'

And what saith Paul? 'I would they were
cut off

That trouble you.' Let the dead letter live!

Trace it in fire, that all the louts to whom

Their A B C is darkness, clowns and grooms

May read it! so you quash rebellion too,

For heretic and traitor are all one:

Two vipers of one breed—an amphisbæna,

Each end a sting: Let the dead letter burn!

Paget. Yet there be some disloyal
Catholics,

And many heretics loyal; heretic throats

Cried no God-bless-her to the Lady Jane,

But shouted in Queen Mary. So there be

Some traitor-heretic, there is axe and cord.

To take the lives of others that are loyal,

And by the churchman's pitiless doom of
fire,

Were but a thankless policy in the crown,

Ay, and against itself; for there are many.

Mary. If we could burn out heresy, my
Lord Paget,

We reck not tho' we lost this crown of
England—

Ay! tho' it were ten Englands!

Gardiner.   Right, your Grace.

Paget, you are all for this poor life of ours,

And care but little for the life to be.

Paget. I have some time, for curiousness,
my Lord,

Watch'd children playing at *their* life to be,

And cruel at it, killing helpless flies;

Such is our time—all times for aught I
know.

Gardiner. We kill the heretics that sting
the soul—

They, with right reason, flies that prick the
flesh.

Paget. They had not reach'd right reason; little children!
They kill'd but for their pleasure and the power
They felt in killing.
Gardiner.   A spice of Satan, ha!
Why, good! what then? granted!—we are fallen creatures;
Look to your Bible, Paget! we are fallen.
Paget. I am but of the laity, my Lord Bishop,
And may not read your Bible, yet I found
One day, a wholesome scripture, 'Little children,
Love one another.'
Gardiner.   Did you find a scripture,
'I come not to bring peace but a sword'?
The sword
Is in her Grace's hand to smite with. Paget,
You stand up here to fight for heresy,
You are more than guess'd at as a heretic,
And on the steep-up track of the true faith
Your lapses are far seen.
Paget.   The faultless Gardiner!
Mary. You brawl beyond the question; speak, Lord Legate!
Pole. Indeed, I cannot follow with your Grace:
Rather would say—the shepherd doth not kill
The sheep that wander from his flock, but sends
His careful dog to bring them to the fold.
Look to the Netherlands, wherein have been
Such holocausts of heresy! to what end?
For yet the faith is not established there.
Gardiner. The end's not come.
Pole.   No—nor this way will come,
Seeing there lie two ways to every end,
A better and a worse—the worse is here
To persecute, because to persecute
Makes a faith hated, and is furthermore
No perfect witness of a perfect faith
In him who persecutes: when men are tost
On tides of strange opinion, and not sure
Of their own selves, they are wroth with their own selves,
And thence with others; then who lights the faggot?

Not the full faith, no, but the lurking doubt.
Old Rome, that first made martyrs in the Church,
Trembled for her own gods, for these were trembling—
But when did our Rome tremble?
Paget.   Did she not
In Henry's time and Edward's?
Pole.   What, my Lord!
The Church on Peter's rock? never! I have seen
A pine in Italy that cast its shadow
Athwart a cataract; firm stood the pine—
The cataract shook the shadow. To my mind,
The cataract typed the headlong plunge and fall
Of heresy to the pit: the pine was Rome.
You see, my Lords,
It was the shadow of the Church that trembled;
Your church was but the shadow of a church,
Wanting the Papal mitre.
Gardiner (muttering). Here be tropes.
Pole. And tropes are good to clothe a naked truth,
And make it look more seemly.
Gardiner.   Tropes again!
Pole. You are hard to please. Then without tropes, my Lord,
An overmuch severeness, I repeat,
When faith is wavering makes the waverer pass
Into more settled hatred of the doctrines
Of those who rule, which hatred by and by
Involves the ruler (thus there springs to light
That Centaur of a monstrous Commonweal,
The traitor-heretic) then tho' some may quail,
Yet others are that dare the stake and fire,
And their strong torment bravely borne, begets
An admiration and an indignation,
And hot desire to imitate; so the plague
Of schism spreads; were there but three or four
Of these misleaders, yet I would not say

Burn! and we cannot burn whole towns;
    they are many,
As my Lord Paget says.
    Gardiner.   Yet my Lord Cardinal—
Pole. I am your Legate; please you let
    me finish.
Methinks that under our Queen's regimen
We might go softlier than with crimson
    rowel
And streaming lash. When Herod-Henry
    first
Began to batter at your English Church,
This was the cause, and hence the judg-
    ment on her.
She seethed with such adulteries, and the
    lives
Of many among your churchmen were so
    foul
That heaven wept and earth blush'd. I
    would advise
That we should thoroughly cleanse the
    Church within
Before these bitter statutes be requicken'd.
So after that when she once more is seen
White as the light, the spotless bride of
    Christ,
Like Christ himself on Tabor, possibly
The Lutheran may be won to her again;
Till when, my Lords, I counsel tolerance.
    Gardiner. What, if a mad dog bit your
        hand, my Lord,
Would you not chop the bitten finger
    off,
Lest your whole body should madden with
    the poison?
I would not, were I Queen, tolerate the
    heretic,
No, not an hour. The ruler of a land
Is bounden by his power and place to see
His people be not poison'd. Tolerate
    them!
Why? do they tolerate you? Nay, many of
    them
Would burn—have burnt each other; call
    they not
The one true faith, a loathsome idol-
    worship?
Beware, Lord Legate, of a heavier crime
Than heresy is itself; beware, I say,
Lest men accuse you of indifference
To all faiths, all religion; for you know

Right well that you yourself have been
    supposed
Tainted with Lutheranism in Italy.
    Pole (angered). But you, my Lord,
        beyond all supposition,
In clear and open day were congruent
With that vile Cranmer in the accursed lie
Of good Queen Catharine's divorce—the
    spring
Of all those evils that have flow'd upon us;
For you yourself have truckled to the
    tyrant,
And done your best to bastardise our
    Queen,
For which God's righteous judgment fell
    upon you
In your five years of imprisonment, my
    Lord,
Under young Edward. Who so bolster'd up
The gross King's headship of the Church,
    or more
Denied the Holy Father!
    Gardiner.   Ha! what! eh?
But you, my Lord, a polish'd gentleman,
A bookman, flying from the heat and tussle,
You lived among your vines and oranges,
In your soft Italy yonder! You were sent
    for,
You were appeal'd to, but you still pre-
    ferr'd
Your learned leisure. As for what I did
I suffer'd and repented. You, Lord Legate
And Cardinal-Deacon, have not now to
    learn
That ev'n St. Peter in his time of fear
Denied his Master, ay, and thrice, my
    Lord.
    Pole. But not for five-and-twenty years,
        my Lord.
    Gardiner. Ha! good! it seems then I was
        summon'd hither
But to be mock'd and baited. Speak, friend
    Bonner,
And tell this learned Legate he lacks zeal.
The Church's evil is not as the King's,
Cannot be heal'd by stroking. The mad
    bite
Must have the cautery—tell him—and at
    once.
What would'st thou do hadst thou his
    power, thou

That layest so long in heretic bonds with
  me;
Would'st thou not burn and blast them
  root and branch?
  Bonner.   Ay, after you, my Lord.
  Gardiner. Nay, God's passion, before
  me! speak!
  Bonner. I am on fire until I see them
  flame.
  Gardiner. Ay, the psalm-singing
  weavers, cobblers, scum—
But this most noble prince Plantagenet,
Our good Queen's cousin—dallying over
  seas
Even when his brother's, nay, his noble
  mother's,
Head fell—
  Pole.   Peace, madman!
Thou stirrest up a grief thou canst not
  fathom.
Thou Christian Bishop, thou Lord Chan-
  cellor
Of England! no more rein upon thine
  anger
Than any child! Thou mak'st me much
  ashamed
That I was for a moment wroth at thee.
  Mary. I come for counsel and ye give
  me feuds,
Like dogs that set to watch their master's
  gate,
Fall, when the thief is ev'n within the
  walls,
To worrying one another. My Lord Chan-
  cellor,
You have an old trick of offending us;
And but that you are art and part with us
In purging heresy, well we might, for
  this
Your violence and much roughness to the
  Legate,
Have shut you from our counsels. Cousin
  Pole,
You are fresh from brighter lands. Retire
  with me.
His Highness and myself (so you allow us)
Will let you learn in peace and privacy
What power this cooler sun of England
  hath
In breeding godless vermin. And pray
  Heaven

That you may see according to our sight.
Come, cousin.
        [*Exeunt* QUEEN *and* POLE, *etc.*
  Gardiner. Pole has the Plantagenet face,
But not the force made them our mightiest
  kings—
Fine eyes—but melancholy, irresolute—
A fine beard, Bonner, a very full fine beard.
But a weak mouth, an indeterminate—ha?
  Bonner. Well, a weak mouth, perchance.
  Gardiner.   And not like thine
To gorge a heretic whole, roasted or raw.
  Bonner. I'd do my best, my Lord; but
  yet the Legate
Is here as Pope and Master of the Church,
And if he go not with you—
  Gardiner.   Tut, Master Bishop,
Our bashful Legate, saw'st not how he
  flush'd?
Touch him upon his old heretical talk,
He'll burn a diocese to prove his orthodoxy.
And let him call me truckler. In those
  times,
Thou knowest we had to dodge, or duck,
  or die;
I kept my head for use of Holy Church;
And see you, we shall have to dodge again,
And let the Pope trample our rights, and
  plunge
His foreign fist into our island Church
To plump the leaner pouch of Italy.
For a time, for a time.
Why? that these statutes may be put in
  force,
And that his fan may thoroughly purge his
  floor.
  Bonner. So then you hold the Pope—
  Gardiner.   I hold the Pope!
What do I hold him? what do I hold the
  Pope?
Come, come, the morsel stuck—this Car-
  dinal's fault—
I have gulpt it down. I am wholly for the
  Pope,
Utterly and altogether for the Pope,
The Eternal Peter of the changeless chair,
Crown'd slave of slaves, and mitred king
  of kings,
God upon earth! what more? what would
  you have?
Hence, let's be gone.

Enter USHER

Usher. Well that you be not gone,
My Lord. The Queen, most wroth at first
    with you,
Is now content to grant you full forgive-
    ness,
So that you crave full pardon of the Legate.
I am sent to fetch you.
    Gardiner. Doth Pole yield, sir, ha!
Did you hear 'em? were you by?
    Usher.   I cannot tell you,
His bearing is so courtly-delicate;
And yet methinks he falters: their two
    Graces
Do so dear-cousin and royal-cousin him,
So press on him the duty which as Legate
He owes himself, and with such royal
    smiles—
    Gardiner. Smiles that burn men. Bonner,
    it will be carried.
He falters, ha? 'fore God, we change and
    change;
Men now are bow'd and old, the doctors
    tell you,
At three-score years; then if we change at
    all
We needs must do it quickly; it is an age
Of brief life, and brief purpose, and brief
    patience,
As I have shown to-day. I am sorry for it
If Pole be like to turn. Our old friend
    Cranmer,
Your more especial love, hath turn'd so
    often,
He knows not where he stands, which, if
    this pass,
We two shall have to teach him; let 'em
    look to it,
Cranmer and Hooper, Ridley and Latimer,
Rogers and Ferrar, for their time is come,
Their hour is hard at hand, their 'dies
    Iræ,'
Their 'dies Illa,' which will test their sect.
I feel it but a duty—you will find in it
Pleasure as well as duty, worthy Bonner,—
To test their sect. Sir, I attend the Queen
To crave most humble pardon—of her
    most
Royal, Infallible, Papal Legate-cousin.
                    [*Exeunt.*

SCENE V

Woodstock

ELIZABETH, LADY IN WAITING

Elizabeth. So they have sent poor
    Courtenay over sea.
Lady. And banish'd us to Woodstock,
    and the fields.
The colours of our Queen are green and
    white,
These fields are only green, they make me
    gape.
Elizabeth. There's whitethorn, girl.
Lady.   Ay, for an hour in May.
But court is always May, buds out in
    masques,
Breaks into feather'd merriments, and
    flowers
In silken pageants. Why do they keep us
    here?
Why still suspect your Grace?
    Elizabeth.   Hard upon both.
[*Writes on the window with a diamond.*

    Much suspected, of me
    Nothing proven can be.
        Quoth Elizabeth, prisoner.

Lady. What hath your Highness written?
Elizabeth.   A true rhyme.
Lady. Cut with a diamond; so to last
    like truth.
Elizabeth. Ay, if truth last.
Lady. But truth, they say, will out,
So it must last. It is not like a word,
That comes and goes in uttering.
Elizabeth.   Truth, a word!
The very Truth and very Word are one.
But truth of story, which I glanced at, girl,
Is like a word that comes from olden days,
And passes thro' the peoples: every tongue
Alters it passing, till it spells and speaks
Quite other than at first.
    Lady.   I do not follow.
Elizabeth. How many names in the long
    sweep of time
That so foreshortens greatness, may but
    hang
On the chance mention of some fool that
    once
Brake bread with us, perhaps: and my poor
    chronicle

Is but of glass. Sir Henry Bedingfield
May split it for a spite.
 Lady.   God grant it last,
And witness to your Grace's innocence,
Till doomsday melt it.
 Elizabeth. Or a second fire,
Like that which lately crackled underfoot
And in this very chamber, fuse the glass,
And char us back again into the dust
We spring from. Never peacock against
  rain
Scream'd as you did for water.
 Lady.   And I got it.
I woke Sir Henry—and he's true to you—
I read his honest horror in his eyes.
 Elizabeth. Or true to you?
 Lady. Sir Henry Bedingfield!
I will have no man true to me, your Grace,
But one that pares his nails; to me? the
  clown!
 Elizabeth. Out, girl! you wrong a noble
  gentleman.
 Lady. For, like his cloak, his manners
  want the nap
And gloss of court; but of this fire he says,
Nay swears, it was no wicked wilfulness,
Only a natural chance.
 Elizabeth. A chance—perchance
One of those wicked wilfuls that men make,
Nor shame to call it nature. Nay, I know
They hunt my blood. Save for my daily
  range
Among the pleasant fields of Holy Writ
I might despair. But there hath some one
  come;
The house is all in movement. Hence, and
  see.   [*Exit* LADY.

Milkmaid (singing without)

Shame upon you, Robin,
 Shame upon you now!
Kiss me would you? with my hands
 Milking the cow?
 Daisies grow again,
 Kingcups blow again,
And you came and kiss'd me milking the cow.

Robin came behind me,
 Kiss'd me well I vow;
Cuff him could I? with my hands
 Milking the cow?
 Swallows fly again,
 Cuckoos cry again,
And you came and kiss'd me milking the cow.

Come, Robin, Robin,
 Come and kiss me now;
Help it can I? with my hands
 Milking the cow?
 Ringdoves coo again,
 All things woo again.
Come behind and kiss me milking the cow!

 Elizabeth. Right honest and red-cheek'd;
  Robin was violent,
And she was crafty—a sweet violence,
And a sweet craft. I would I were a milk-
  maid,
To sing, love, marry, churn, brew, bake,
  and die,
Then have my simple headstone by the
  church,
And all things lived and ended honestly.
I could not if I would. I am Harry's
  daughter:
Gardiner would have my head. They are
  not sweet,
The violence and the craft that do divide
The world of nature; what is weak must
  lie;
The lion needs but roar to guard his young;
The lapwing lies, says 'here' when they
  are there.
Threaten the child; 'I'll scourge you if
  you did it:'
What weapon hath the child, save his soft
  tongue,
To say 'I did not?' and my rod's the block.
I never lay my head upon the pillow
But that I think, 'Wilt thou lie there
  tomorrow?'
How oft the falling axe, that never fell,
Hath shock'd me back into the daylight
  truth
That it may fall to-day! Those damp,
  black, dead
Nights in the Tower; dead—with the fear
  of death
Too dead ev'n for a death-watch! Toll of
  a bell,
Stroke of a clock, the scurrying of a rat
Affrighted me, and then delighted me,
For there was life—And there was life in
  death—
The little murder'd princes, in a pale light,
Rose hand in hand, and whisper'd, 'come
  away!

The civil wars are gone for evermore:
Thou last of all the Tudors, come away!
With us is peace!' The last? It was a
    dream;
I must not dream, not wink, but watch.
    She has gone,
Maid Marian to her Robin—by and by
Both happy! a fox may filch a hen by night,
And make a morning outcry in the yard;
But there's no Renard here to 'catch her
    tripping.'
Catch me who can; yet, sometimes I have
    wish'd
That I were caught, and kill'd away at
    once
Out of the flutter. The gray rogue,
    Gardiner,
Went on his knees, and pray'd me to
    confess
In Wyatt's business, and to cast myself
Upon the good Queen's mercy; ay, when,
    my Lord?
God save the Queen! My jailor—

Enter SIR HENRY BEDINGFIELD

Bedingfield.   One, whose bolts,
That jail you from free life, bar you from
    death.
There haunt some Papist ruffians here-
    about
Would murder you.
    Elizabeth. I thank you heartily, sir,
But I am royal, tho' your prisoner,
And God hath blest or cursed me with a
    nose—
Your boots are from the horses.
    Bedingfield.   Ay, my Lady.
When next there comes a missive from the
    Queen
It shall be all my study for one hour
To rose and lavender my horsiness,
Before I dare to glance upon your Grace.
    Elizabeth. A missive from the Queen:
    last time she wrote,
I had like to have lost my life: it takes my
    breath:
O God, sir, do you look upon your boots,
Are you so small a man? Help me: what
    think you,
Is it life or death?
    Bedingfield. I thought not on my boots;

The devil take all boots were ever made
Since man went barefoot. See, I lay it here,
For I will come no nearer to your Grace;
                    [*Laying down the letter.*
And, whether it brings you bitter news or
    sweet,
And God hath given your Grace a nose,
    or not,
I'll help you, if I may.
    Elizabeth.   Your pardon, then;
It is the heat and narrowness of the cage
That makes the captive testy; with free
    wing
The world were all one Araby. Leave me
    now,
Will you, companion to myself, sir?
    Bedingfield.   Will I?
With most exceeding willingness, I will;
You know I never come till I be call'd.
                              [*Exit.*
    Elizabeth. It lies there folded: is there
    venom in it?
A snake—and if I touch it, it may sting.
Come, come, the worst!
Best wisdom is to know the worst at once.
                              [*Reads:*

'It is the King's wish, that you should
wed Prince Philibert of Savoy. You are to
come to Court on the instant; and think
of this in your coming.
                    'MARY THE QUEEN.'

Think! I have many thoughts;
I think there may be birdlime here for me;
I think they fain would have me from the
    realm;
I think the Queen may never bear a child;
I think that I may be some time the
    Queen,
Then, Queen indeed: no foreign prince or
    priest
Should fill my throne, myself upon the
    steps.
I think I will not marry anyone,
Specially not this landless Philibert
Of Savoy; but, if Philip menace me,
I think that I will play with Philibert,—
As once the Holy Father did with mine,
Before my father married my good
    mother,—
For fear of Spain.

Enter LADY

Lady. O Lord! your Grace, your Grace,
I feel so happy: it seems that we shall fly
These bald, blank fields, and dance into
    the sun
That shines on princes.
Elizabeth.   Yet, a moment since,
I wish'd myself the milkmaid singing here,
To kiss and cuff among the birds and
    flowers—
A right rough life and healthful.
Lady.   But the wench
Hath her own troubles; she is weeping
    now;
For the wrong Robin took her at her word.
Then the cow kick'd, and all her milk was
    spilt.
Your Highness such a milkmaid?
Elizabeth.   I had kept
My Robins and my cows in sweeter order
Had I been such.
Lady (*slyly*). And had your Grace a
    Robin?
Elizabeth. Come, come, you are chill
    here; you want the sun
That shines at court; make ready for the
    journey.
Pray God, we 'scape the sunstroke. Ready
    at once.   [*Exeunt.*

SCENE VI

London. A Room in the Palace

LORD PETRE *and* LORD WILLIAM HOWARD

Petre. You cannot see the Queen. Renard
    denied her,
Ev'n now to me.
Howard.   Their Flemish go-between
And all-in-all. I came to thank her Majesty
For freeing my friend Bagenhall from the
    Tower;
A grace to me! Mercy, that herb-of-grace,
Flowers now but seldom.
Petre.   Only now perhaps.
Because the Queen hath been three days
    in tears
For Philip's going—like the wild hedge-
    rose
Of a soft winter, possible, not probable,

However you have prov'n it.
Howard.   I must see her.

Enter RENARD

Renard. My Lords, you cannot see her
    Majesty.
Howard. Why then the King! for I
    would have him bring it
Home to the leisure wisdom of his Queen,
Before he go, that since these statutes past,
Gardiner out-Gardiners Gardiner in his
    heat,
Bonner cannot out-Bonner his own self—
Beast!—but they play with fire as chil-
    dren do,
And burn the house. I know that these are
    breeding
A fierce resolve and fixt heart-hate in men
Against the King, the Queen, the Holy
    Father,
The faith itself. Can I not see him?
Renard.   Not now.
And in all this, my Lord, her Majesty
Is flint of flint, you may strike fire from
    her,
Not hope to melt her. I will give your
    message.
              [*Exeunt* PETRE *and* HOWARD.

Enter PHILIP (*musing*)

Philip. She will not have Prince Philibert
    of Savoy,
I talk'd with her in vain—says she will live
And die true maid—a goodly creature too.
Would *she* had been the Queen! yet she
    must have him;
She troubles England: that she breathes
    in England
Is life and lungs to every rebel birth
That passes out of embryo.
                    Simon Renard!—
This Howard, whom they fear, what was
    he saying?
Renard. What your imperial father said,
    my liege,
To deal with heresy gentlier. Gardiner
    burns,
And Bonner burns; and it would seem
    this people
Care more for our brief life in their wet
    land,

Than yours in happier Spain. I told my Lord
He should not vex her Highness; she would say
These are the means God works with, that His church
May flourish.
    Philip.   Ay, sir, but in statesmanship
To strike too soon is oft to miss the blow.
Thou knowest I bad my chaplain, Castro, preach
Against these burnings.
    Renard.   And the Emperor
Approved you, and when last he wrote, declared
His comfort in your Grace that you were bland
And affable to men of all estates,
In hope to charm them from their hate of Spain.
    Philip. In hope to crush all heresy under Spain.
But, Renard, I am sicker staying here
Than any sea could make me passing hence,
Tho' I be ever deadly sick at sea.
So sick am I with biding for this child.
Is it the fashion in this clime for women
To go twelve months in bearing of a child?
The nurses yawn'd, the cradle gaped, they led
Processions, chanted litanies, clash'd their bells,
Shot off their lying cannon, and her priests
Have preach'd, the fools, of this fair prince to come;
Till, by St. James, I find myself the fool.
Why do you lift your eyebrow at me thus?
    Renard. I never saw your Highness moved till now.
    Philip. So weary am I of this wet land of theirs,
And every soul of man that breathes therein.
    Renard. My liege, we must not drop the mask before
The masquerade is over—
    Philip.   —Have I dropt it?
I have but shown a loathing face to you,
Who knew it from the first.

Enter MARY

    Mary (aside).   With Renard. Still
Parleying with Renard, all the day with Renard,
And scarce a greeting all the day for me—
And goes to-morrow.   [*Exit* MARY.
    Philip (to RENARD, *who advances to him).*
Well, sir, is there more?
    Renard (who has perceived the QUEEN).
May Simon Renard speak a single word?
    Philip. Ay.
    Renard. And be forgiven for it?
    Philip.   Simon Renard
Knows me too well to speak a single word
That could not be forgiven.
    Renard.   Well, my liege,
Your Grace hath a most chaste and loving wife.
    Philip. Why not? The Queen of Philip should be chaste.
    Renard. Ay, but, my Lord, you know what Virgil sings,
Woman is various and most mutable.
    Philip. She play the harlot! never.
    Renard.   No, sire, no,
Not dream'd of by the rabidest gospeller.
There was a paper thrown into the palace,
'The King hath wearied of his barren bride.'
She came upon it, read it, and then rent it,
With all the rage of one who hates a truth
He cannot but allow. Sire, I would have you—
What should I say, I cannot pick my words—
Be somewhat less—majestic to your Queen.
    Philip. Am I to change my manners, Simon Renard,
Because these islanders are brutal beasts?
Or would you have me turn a sonneteer,
And warble those brief-sighted eyes of hers?
    Renard. Brief-sighted tho' they be, I have seen them, sire,
When you perchance were trifling royally
With some fair dame of court, suddenly fill
With such fierce fire—had it been fire indeed
It would have burnt both speakers.

Philip. Ay, and then?
Renard. Sire, might it not be policy in some matter
Of small importance now and then to cede
A point to her demand?
Philip. Well, I am going.
Renard. For should her love when you are gone, my liege,
Witness these papers, there will not be wanting
Those that will urge her injury—should her love—
And I have known such women more than one—
Veer to the counterpoint, and jealousy
Hath in it an alchemic force to fuse
Almost into one metal love and hate,—
And she impress her wrongs upon her Council,
And these again upon her Parliament—
We are not loved here, and would be then perhaps
Not so well holpen in our wars with France,
As else we might be—here she comes.

Enter MARY

Mary. O Philip!
Nay, must you go indeed?
Philip. Madam, I must.
Mary. The parting of a husband and a wife
Is like the cleaving of a heart; one half
Will flutter here, one there.
Philip. You say true, Madam.
Mary. The Holy Virgin will not have me yet
Lose the sweet hope that I may bear a prince.
If such a prince were born and you not here!
Philip. I should be here if such a prince were born.
Mary. But must you go?
Philip. Madam, you know my father,
Retiring into cloistral solitude
To yield the remnant of his years to heaven,
Will shift the yoke and weight of all the world
From off his neck to mine. We meet at Brussels.

But since mine absence will not be for long,
Your Majesty shall go to Dover with me,
And wait my coming back.
Mary. To Dover? no
I am too feeble. I will go to Greenwich,
So you will have me with you; and there watch
All that is gracious in the breath of heaven
Draw with your sails from our poor land, and pass
And leave me, Philip, with my prayers for you.
Philip. And doubtless I shall profit by your prayers.
Mary. Methinks that would you tarry one day more
(The news was sudden) I could mould myself
To bear your going better; will you do it?
Philip. Madam, a day may sink or save a realm.
Mary. A day may save a heart from breaking too.
Philip. Well, Simon Renard, shall we stop a day?
Renard. Your Grace's business will not suffer, sire,
For one day more, so far as I can tell.
Philip. Then one day more to please her Majesty.
Mary. The sunshine sweeps across my life again.
O if I knew you felt this parting, Philip,
As I do!
Philip. By St. James I do protest,
Upon the faith and honour of a Spaniard,
I am vastly grieved to leave your Majesty.
Simon, is supper ready?
Renard. Ay, my liege,
I saw the covers laying.
Philip. Let us have it. [*Exeunt.*

ACT IV

SCENE I

A Room in the Palace

MARY, CARDINAL POLE

Mary. What have you there?
Pole. So please your Majesty,
A long petition from the foreign exiles

To spare the life of Cranmer. Bishop
    Thirlby,
And my Lord Paget and Lord William
    Howard,
Crave, in the same cause, hearing of your
    Grace.
Hath he not written himself—infatuated—
To sue you for his life?
    Mary.   His life? Oh, no;
Not sued for that—he knows it were in
    vain.
But so much of the anti-papal leaven
Works in him yet, he hath pray'd me not
    to sully
Mine own prerogative, and degrade the
    realm
By seeking justice at a stranger's hand
Against my natural subject. King and
    Queen,
To whom he owes his loyalty after God,
Shall these accuse him to a foreign prince?
Death would not grieve him more. I can-
    not be
True to this realm of England and the
    Pope
Together, says the heretic.
    Pole.   And there errs;
As he hath ever err'd thro' vanity.
A secular kingdom is but as the body
Lacking a soul; and in itself a beast.
The Holy Father in a secular kingdom
Is as the soul descending out of heaven
Into a body generate.
    Mary.   Write to him, then.
    Pole. I will.
    Mary.   And sharply, Pole.
    Pole. Here come the Cranmerites!

Enter THIRLBY, LORD PAGET, LORD
        WILLIAM HOWARD

Howard. Health to your Grace! Good
    morrow, my Lord Cardinal;
We make our humble prayer unto your
    Grace
That Cranmer may withdraw to foreign
    parts,
Or into private life within the realm.
In several bills and declarations, Madam,
He hath recanted all his heresies.
    Paget. Ay, ay; if Bonner have not forged
    the bills.   [*Aside.*

Mary. Did not More die, and Fisher?
    he must burn.
Howard. He hath recanted, Madam.
Mary.   The better for him.
He burns in Purgatory, not in Hell.
Howard. Ay, ay, your Grace; but it was
    never seen
That any one recanting thus at full,
As Cranmer hath, came to the fire on
    earth.
Mary. It will be seen now, then.
Thirlby.   O Madam, Madam!
I thus implore you, low upon my knees,
To reach the hand of mercy to my friend.
I have err'd with him; with him I have
    recanted.
What human reason is there why my friend
Should meet with lesser mercy than
    myself?
Mary. My Lord of Ely, this. After a riot
We hang the leaders, let their following go.
Cranmer is head and father of these
    heresies,
New learning as they call it; yea, may God
Forget me at most need when I forget
Her foul divorce—my sainted mother—
    No!—
Howard. Ay, ay, but mighty doctors
    doubted there.
The Pope himself waver'd; and more than
    one
Row'd in that galley—Gardiner to wit,
Whom truly I deny not to have been
Your faithful friend and trusty councillor.
Hath not you Highness ever read his book,
His tractate upon True Obedience,
Writ by himself and Bonner?
Mary.   I will take
Such order with all bad, heretical books
That none shall hold them in his house
    and live,
Henceforward. No, my Lord.
    Howard.   Then never read it.
The truth is here. Your father was a man
Of such colossal kinghood, yet so cour-
    teous,
Except when wroth, you scarce could meet
    his eye
And hold your own; and were he wroth
    indeed,
You held it less, or not at all. I say,

Your father had a will that beat men
    down;
Your father had a brain that beat men
    down—
    Pole. Not me, my Lord.
    Howard. No, for you were not here;
You sit upon this fallen Cranmer's throne;
And it would more become you, my Lord
    Legate,
To join a voice, so potent with her High-
    ness,
To ours in plea for Cranmer than to stand
On naked self-assertion.
    Mary.   All your voices
Are waves on flint. The heretic must burn.
    Howard. Yet once he saved your
    Majesty's own life;
Stood out against the King in your behalf,
At his own peril.
    Mary.   I know not if he did;
And if he did I care not, my Lord Howard.
My life is not so happy, no such boon,
That I should spare to take a heretic
    priest's,
Who saved it or not saved. Why do you
    vex me?
    Paget. Yet to save Cranmer were to serve
    the Church,
Your Majesty's I mean; he is effaced,
Self-blotted out; so wounded in his
    honour,
He can but creep down into some dark
    hole
Like a hurt beast, and hide himself and
    die;
But if you burn him,—well, your Highness
    knows
The saying, 'Martyr's blood—seed of the
    Church.'
    Mary. Of the true Church; but his is
    none, nor will be.
You are too politic for me, my Lord Paget.
And if he have to live so loath'd a life,
It were more merciful to burn him now.
    Thirlby. O yet relent. O, Madam, if you
    knew him
As I do, ever gentle, and so gracious,
With all his learning—
    Mary.   Yet a heretic still.
His learning makes his burning the more
    just.

    Thirlby. So worshipt of all those that
    came across him;
The stranger at his hearth, and all his
    house—
    Mary. His children and his concubine,
    belike.
    Thirlby. To do him any wrong was to
    beget
A kindness from him, for his heart was
    rich,
Of such fine mould, that if you sow'd
    therein
The seed of Hate, it blossom'd Charity.
    Pole. 'After his kind it costs him
    nothing,' there's
An old world English adage to the point.
These are but natural graces, my good
    Bishop,
Which in the Catholic garden are as
    flowers,
But on the heretic dunghill only weeds.
    Howard. Such weeds make dunghills
    gracious.
    Mary.   Enough, my Lords.
It is God's will, the Holy Father's will,
And Philip's will, and mine, that he should
    burn.
He is pronounced anathema.
    Howard.   Farewell, Madam,
God grant you ampler mercy at your call
Than you have shown to Cranmer.
                     [*Exeunt* LORDS.
    Pole.   After this,
Your Grace will hardly care to overlook
This same petition of the foreign exiles
For Cranmer's life.
    Mary.   Make out the writ to-night.
                         [*Exeunt.*

SCENE II

Oxford. Cranmer in Prison

    Cranmer. Last night, I dream'd the
    faggots were alight,
And that myself was fasten'd to the stake,
And found it all a visionary flame,
Cool as the light in old decaying wood;
And then King Harry look'd from out a
    cloud,
And bad me have good courage; and I
    heard

An angel cry 'There is more joy in
    Heaven,'—
And after that, the trumpet of the dead.
                    [*Trumpets without.*
Why, there are trumpets blowing now:
    what is it?

Enter FATHER COLE

  Cole. Cranmer, I come to question you
    again;
Have you remain'd in the true Catholic
    faith
I left you in?
  Cranmer. In the true Catholic faith,
By Heaven's grace, I am more and more
    confirm'd.
Why are the trumpets blowing, Father
    Cole?
  Cole. Cranmer, it is decided by the
    Council
That you to-day should read your recanta-
    tion
Before the people in St. Mary's Church.
And there be many heretics in the town,
Who loathe you for your late return to
    Rome,
And might assail you passing through the
    street,
And tear you piecemeal: so you have a
    guard.
  Cranmer. Or seek to rescue me. I thank
    the Council.
  Cole. Do you lack any money?
  Cranmer.   Nay, why should I?
The prison fare is good enough for me.
  Cole. Ay, but to give the poor.
  Cranmer.   Hand it me, then!
I thank you.
  Cole.   For a little space, farewell;
Until I see you in St. Mary's Church.
                    [*Exit* COLE.
  Cranmer. It is against all precedent to
    burn
One who recants; they mean to pardon me.
To give the poor—they give the poor who
    die.
Well, burn me or not burn me I am fixt;
It is but a communion, not a mass:
A holy supper, not a sacrifice;
No man can make his Maker—Villa
    Garcia.

Enter VILLA GARCIA

  Villa Garcia. Pray you write out this
    paper for me. Cranmer.
  Cranmer. Have I not writ enough to
    satisfy you?
  Villa Garcia. It is the last.
  Cranmer.   Give it me, then.
                    [*He writes.*
  Villa Garcia.   Now sign.
  Cranmer. I have sign'd enough, and I
    will sign no more.
  Villa Garcia. It is no more than what
    you have sign'd already,
The public form thereof.
  Cranmer.   It may be so;
I sign it with my presence, if I read it.
  Villa Garcia. But this is idle of you.
    Well, sir, well,
You are to beg the people to pray for you;
Exhort them to a pure and virtuous life;
Declare the Queen's right to the throne;
    confess
Your faith before all hearers; and retract
That Eucharistic doctrine in your book.
Will you not sign it now?
  Cranmer.   No, Villa Garcia,
I sign no more. Will they have mercy on
    me?
  Villa Garcia. Have you good hopes of
    mercy! So, farewell.   [*Exit.*
  Cranmer. Good hopes, not theirs, have
    I that I am fixt,
Fixt beyond fall; however, in strange
    hours,
After the long brain-dazing colloquies,
And thousand-times recurring argument
Of those two friars ever in my prison,
When left alone in my despondency,
Without a friend, a book, my faith would
    seem
Dead or half-drown'd, or else swam heavily
Against the huge corruptions of the
    Church,
Monsters of mistradition, old enough
To scare me into dreaming, 'what am I,
Cranmer, against whole ages?' was it so,
Or am I slandering my most inward friend,
To veil the fault of my most outward foe—
The soft and tremulous coward in the
    flesh?

O higher, holier, earlier, purer church,
I have found thee and not leave thee any
    more.
It is but a communion, not a mass—
No sacrifice, but a life-giving feast!
(*Writes.*) So, so; this will I say—thus will
    I pray.   [*Puts up the paper.*

Enter BONNER

    Bonner. Good day, old friend; what, you
        look somewhat worn;
And yet it is a day to test your health
Ev'n at the best: I scarce have spoken
    with you
Since when?—your degradation. At your
    trial
Never stood up a bolder man than you;
You would not cap the pope's commis-
    sioner—
Your learning, and your stoutness, and
    your heresy,
Dumbfounded half of us. So, after that,
We had to dis-archbishop and unlord,
And make you simple Cranmer once again.
The common barber clipt your hair, and I
Scraped from your finger-points the holy
    oil;
And worse than all, you had to kneel to
    me;
Which was not pleasant for you, Master
    Cranmer.
Now you, that would not recognise the
    Pope,
And you, that would not own the Real
    Presence,
Have found a real presence in the stake,
Which frights you back into the ancient
    faith;
And so you have recanted to the Pope.
How are the mighty fallen, Master Cran-
    mer!
    Cranmer. You have been more fierce
        against the Pope than I;
But why fling back the stone he strikes me
    with?   [*Aside.*
O Bonner, if I ever did you kindness—
Power hath been given you to try faith by
    fire—
Pray you, remembering how yourself have
    changed,
Be somewhat pitiful, after I have gone,

To the poor flock—to women and to
    children—
That when I was archbishop held with me.
    Bonner. Ay—gentle as they call you—
        live or die!
Pitiful to this pitiful heresy?
I must obey the Queen and Council, man.
Win thro' this day with honour to your-
    self,
And I'll say something for you—so—
    good-bye.   [*Exit.*
    Cranmer. This hard coarse man of old
        hath crouch'd to me
Till I myself was half ashamed for him.

Enter THIRLBY

Weep not, good Thirlby.
    Thirlby.   Oh, my Lord, my Lord!
My heart is no such block as Bonner's is:
Who would not weep?
    Cranmer. Why do you so my-lord me,
Who am disgraced?
    Thirlby. On earth; but saved in heaven
By your recanting.
    Cranmer.   Will they burn me,
        Thirlby?
    Thirlby. Alas, they will; these burnings
        will not help
The purpose of the faith; but my poor
    voice
Against them is a whisper to the roar
Of a spring-tide.
    Cranmer.   And they will surely
        burn me?
    Thirlby. Ay; and besides, will have you
        in the church
Repeat your recantation in the ears
Of all men, to the saving of their souls,
Before your execution. May God help you
Thro' that hard hour!
    Cranmer. And may God bless you,
        Thirlby!
Well, they shall hear my recantation there.
                        [*Exit* Thirlby.
Disgraced, dishonour'd!—not by them,
    indeed,
By mine own self—by mine own hand!
O thin-skin'd hand and jutting veins,
    'twas you
That sign'd the burning of poor Joan of
    Kent;

585

But then she was a witch. You have written much,
But you were never raised to plead for Frith,
Whose dogmas I have reach'd: he was deliver'd
To the secular arm to burn; and there was Lambert;
Who can foresee himself? truly these burnings,
As Thirlby says, are profitless to the burners,
And help the other side. You shall burn too,
Burn first when I am burnt.
Fire—inch by inch to die in agony! Latimer
Had a brief end—not Ridley. Hooper burn'd
Three-quarters of an hour. Will my faggots
Be wet as his were? It is a day of rain.
I will not muse upon it.
My fancy takes the burner's part, and makes
The fire seem even crueller than it is.
No, I not doubt that God will give me strength,
Albeit I have denied him.

Enter SOTO *and* VILLA GARCIA

Villa Garcia.   We are ready
To take you to St. Mary's, Master Cranmer.
Cranmer. And I: lead on; ye loose me
from my bonds.   [*Exeunt.*

Scene III

St. Mary's Church

COLE *in the Pulpit*, LORD WILLIAMS OF THAME *presiding.* LORD WILLIAM HOWARD, LORD PAGET, *and others.* CRANMER *enters between* SOTO *and* VILLA GARCIA, *and the whole Choir strike up* 'Nunc Dimittis.' CRANMER *is set upon a Scaffold before the people.*

Cole. Behold him—
                [*A pause: people in the foreground.*
People. Oh, unhappy sight!
First Protestant. See how the tears run down his fatherly face.

Second Protestant. James, didst thou ever see a carrion crow
Stand watching a sick beast before he dies?
First Protestant. Him perch'd up there?
I wish some thunderbolt
Would make this Cole a cinder, pulpit and all.
Cole. Behold him, brethren: he hath cause to weep!—
So have we all: weep with him if ye will,
Yet——
It is expedient for one to die,
Yea, for the people, lest the people die.
Yet wherefore should he die that hath return'd
To the one Catholic Universal Church,
Repentant of his errors?
Protestant murmurs. Ay, tell us that.
Cole. Those of the wrong side will despise the man,
Deeming him one that thro' the fear of death
Gave up his cause, except he seal his faith
In sight of all with flaming martyrdom.
Cranmer. Ay.
Cole. Ye hear him, and albeit there may seem
According to the canons pardon due
To him that so repents, yet are there causes
Wherefore our Queen and Council at this time
Adjudge him to the death. He hath been a traitor,
A shaker and confounder of the realm;
And when the King's divorce was sued at Rome,
He here, this heretic metropolitan,
As if he had been the Holy Father, sat
And judged it. Did I call him heretic?
A huge heresiarch! never was it known
That any man so writing, preaching so,
So poisoning the Church, so long continuing,
Hath found his pardon; therefore he must die,
For warning and example.
                        Other reasons
There be for this man's ending, which our Queen
And Council at this present deem it not
Expedient to be known.

Protestant murmurs.   I warrant you.
    Cole. Take therefore, all, example by
       this man,
For if our Holy Queen not pardon him,
Much less shall others in like cause escape,
That all of you, the highest as the lowest,
May learn there is no power against the
       Lord.
There stands a man, once of so high degree,
Chief prelate of our Church, archbishop,
       first
In Council, second person in the realm,
Friend for so long time of a mighty King;
And now ye see downfallen and debased
From councillor to caitiff—fallen so low,
The leprous flutterings of the byway, scum
And offal of the city would not change
Estates with him; in brief, so miserable.
There is no hope of better left for him,
No place for worse.
           Yet, Cranmer, be thou glad.
This is the work of God. He is glorified
In thy conversion: lo! thou art reclaim'd;
He brings thee home: nor fear but that
       to-day
Thou shalt receive the penitent thief's
       award,
And be with Christ the Lord in Paradise.
Remember how God made the fierce fire
       seem
To those three children like a pleasant dew.
Remember, too,
The triumph of St. Andrew on his cross,
The patience of St. Lawrence in the fire.
Thus, if thou call on God and all the saints,
God will beat down the fury of the flame,
Or give thee saintly strength to undergo.
And for thy soul shall masses here be sung
By every priest in Oxford. Pray for him.
    Cranmer. Ay, one and all, dear brothers,
       pray with me;
Pray with one breath, one heart, one soul
       for me.
    Cole. And now, lest anyone among you
       doubt
The man's conversion and remorse of
       heart,
Yourselves shall hear him speak. Speak,
       Master Cranmer,
Fulfil your promise made me, and pro-
       claim

Your true undoubted faith, that all may
       hear.
    Cranmer. And that I will. O God, Father
       of Heaven!
O Son of God, Redeemer of the world!
O Holy Ghost! proceeding from them
       both,
Three persons and one God, have mercy
       on me,
Most miserable sinner, wretched man.
I have offended against heaven and earth
More grievously than any tongue can tell.
Then whither should I flee for any help?
I am ashamed to lift my eyes to heaven,
And I can find no refuge upon earth.
Shall I despair then?—God forbid! O God,
For thou art merciful, refusing none
That come to Thee for succour, unto Thee,
Therefore, I come; humble myself to Thee;
Saying, O Lord God, although my sins be
       great,
For thy great mercy have mercy! O God
       the Son,
Not for slight faults alone, when thou
       becamest
Man in the Flesh, was the great mystery
       wrought;
O God the Father, not for little sins
Didst thou yield up thy Son to human
       death;
But for the greatest sin that can be sinn'd,
Yea, even such as mine, incalculable,
Unpardonable,—sin against the light,
The truth of God, which I had proven and
       known.
Thy mercy must be greater than all sin.
Forgive me, Father, for no merit of mine,
But that Thy name by man be glorified,
And Thy most blessed Son's, who died
       for man.
    Good people, every man at time of death
Would fain set forth some saying that may
       live
After his death and better humankind;
For death gives life's last word a power to
       live,
And, like the stone-cut epitaph, remain
After the vanish'd voice, and speak to men.
God grant me grace to glorify my God!
And first I say it is a grievous case,
Many so dote upon this bubble world,

Whose colours in a moment break and fly,
They care for nothing else. What saith
St. John:—
'Love of this world is hatred against God.'
Again, I pray you all that, next to God,
You do unmurmuringly and willingly
Obey your King and Queen, and not for
dread
Of these alone, but from the fear of Him
Whose ministers they be to govern you.
Thirdly, I pray you all to live together
Like brethren; yet what hatred Christian
men
Bear to each other, seeming not as brethren,
But mortal foes! But do you good to all
As much as in you lieth. Hurt no man more
Than you would harm your loving natural
brother
Of the same roof, same breast. If any do,
Albeit he think himself at home with God,
Of this be sure, he is whole worlds away.
   Protestant murmurs. What sort of
brothers then be those that lust
To burn each other?
   Williams. Peace among you, there!
   Cranmer. Fourthly, to those that own
exceeding wealth,
Remember that sore saying spoken once
By Him that was the truth, 'How hard
it is
For the rich man to enter into Heaven;'
Let all rich men remember that hard word.
I have not time for more: if ever, now
Let them flow forth in charity, seeing now
The poor so many, and all food so dear.
Long have I lain in prison, yet have heard
Of all their wretchedness. Give to the poor,
Ye give to God. He is with us in the poor.
   And now, and forasmuch as I have come
To the last end of life, and thereupon
Hangs all my past, and all my life to be,
Either to live with Christ in Heaven with
joy,
Or to be still in pain with devils in hell;
And, seeing in a moment,
            [Pointing upwards.
Heaven or else hell ready to swallow me,
            [Pointing downwards.
I shall declare to you my very faith
Without all colour.
   Cole. Hear him, my good brethren.

   Cranmer. I do believe in God, Father
of all;
In every article of the Catholic faith,
And every syllable taught us by our Lord,
His prophets, and apostles, in the Testa-
ments,
Both Old and New.
   Cole. Be plainer, Master Cranmer.
   Cranmer. And now I come to the great
cause that weighs
Upon my conscience more than anything
Or said or done in all my life by me;
For there be writings I have set abroad
Against the truth I knew within my heart,
Written for fear of death, to save my life,
If that might be; the papers by my hand
Sign'd since my degradation—by this hand
        [Holding out his right hand.
Written and sign'd—I here renounce them
all;
And, since my hand offended, having
written
Against my heart, my hand shall first be
burnt,
So I may come to the fire.
               [Dead silence.
   Protestant murmurs.
   First Protestant. I knew it would be so.
   Second Protestant. Our prayers are
heard!
   Third Protestant. God bless him!
   Catholic murmurs. Out upon him! out
upon him!
Liar! dissembler! traitor! to the fire!
   Williams (raising his voice). You know
that you recanted all you said
Touching the sacrament in that same book
You wrote against my Lord of Winchester;
Dissemble not; play the plain Christian
man.
   Cranmer. Alas, my Lord,
I have been a man loved plainness all my
life;
I *did* dissemble, but the hour has come
For utter truth and plainness; wherefore,
I say,
I hold by all I wrote within that book.
Moreover,
As for the Pope I count him Antichrist,
With all his devil's doctrines; and refuse,
Reject him, and abhor him. I have said.

[*Cries on all sides,* 'Pull him down!
Away with him!'
Cole. Ay, stop the heretic's mouth! Hale
him away!
Williams. Harm him not, harm him not!
have him to the fire!

[CRANMER *goes out between Two
Friars, smiling; hands are reached to
him from the crowd.* LORD WILLIAM
HOWARD *and* LORD PAGET *are left
alone in the church.*

Paget. The nave and aisles all empty as
a fool's jest!
No, here's Lord William Howard. What,
my Lord,
You have not gone to see the burning?
Howard.   Fie!
To stand at ease, and stare as at a show,
And watch a good man burn. Never again.
I saw the deaths of Latimer and Ridley.
Moreover, tho' a Catholic, I would not,
For the pure honour of our common nature,
Hear what I might—another recantation
Of Cranmer at the stake.
Paget.   You'd not hear that.
He pass'd out smiling, and he walk'd
upright;
His eye was like a soldier's, whom the
general
He looks to and he leans on as his God,
Hath rated for some backwardness and
bidd'n him
Charge one against a thousand, and the
man
Hurls his soil'd life against the pikes and
dies.
Howard. Yet that he might not after all
those papers
Of recantation yield again, who knows?
Paget. Papers of recantation! Think you
then
That Cranmer read all papers that he
sign'd?
Or sign'd all those they tell us that he
sign'd?
Nay, I trow not: and you shall see, my
Lord,
That howsoever hero-like the man
Dies in the fire, this Bonner or another
Will in some lying fashion misreport
His ending to the glory of their church.

And you saw Latimer and Ridley die?
Latimer was eighty, was he not? his best
Of life was over then.
Howard.   His eighty years
Look'd somewhat crooked on him in his
frieze;
But after they had stript him to his shroud,
He stood upright, a lad of twenty-one,
And gather'd with his hands the starting
flame,
And wash'd his hands and all his face
therein,
Until the powder suddenly blew him dead.
Ridley was longer burning; but he died
As manfully and boldly, and, 'fore God,
I know them heretics, but right English
ones.
If ever, as heaven grant, we clash with
Spain,
Our Ridley-soldiers and our Latimer-
sailors
Will teach her something.
Paget.   Your mild Legate Pole
Will tell you that the devil helpt them
thro' it.
            [*A murmur of the Crowd in the
            distance.*
Hark, how those Roman wolfdogs howl
and bay him!
Howard. Might it not be the other side
rejoicing
In his brave end?
Paget.   They are too crush'd, too
broken,
They can but weep in silence.
Howard.   Ay, ay, Paget,
They have brought it in large measure on
themselves.
Have I not heard them mock the blessed
Host
In songs so lewd, the beast might roar his
claim
To being in God's image, more than they?
Have I not seen the gamekeeper, the
groom,
Gardener, and huntsman, in the parson's
place,
The parson from his own spire swung out
dead,
And Ignorance crying in the streets, and
all men

Regarding her? I say they have drawn the
    fire
On their own heads: yet, Paget, I do hold
The Catholic, if he have the greater right,
Hath been the crueller.
Paget.   Action and re-action,
The miserable see-saw of our child-world,
Make us despise it at odd hours, my Lord.
Heaven help that this re-action not re-act
Yet fiercelier under Queen Elizabeth,
So that she come to rule us.
Howard.   The world's mad.
Paget. My Lord, the world is like a
    drunken man,
Who cannot move straight to his end—but
    reels
Now to the right, then as far to the left,
Push'd by the crowd beside—and under-
    foot
An earthquake; for since Henry for a
    doubt—
Which a young lust had clapt upon the
    back,
Crying, 'Forward!'—set our old church
    rocking, men
Have hardly known what to believe, or
    whether
They should believe in anything; the
    currents
So shift and change, they see not how they
    are borne,
Nor whither. I conclude the King a beast;
Verily a lion if you will—the world
A most obedient beast and fool—myself
Half beast and fool as appertaining to it;
Altho' your Lordship hath as little of each
Cleaving to your original Adam-clay,
As may be consonant with mortality.
    Howard. We talk and Cranmer suffers.
The kindliest man I ever knew; see, see,
I speak of him in the past. Unhappy land!
Hard-natured Queen, half-Spanish in her-
    self,
And grafted on the hard-grain'd stock of
    Spain—
Her life, since Philip left her, and she lost
Her fierce desire of bearing him a child,
Hath, like a brief and bitter winter's day,
Gone narrowing down and darkening to a
    close.
There will be more conspiracies, I fear.

Paget. Ay, ay, beware of France.
Howard.   O Paget, Paget!
I have seen heretics of the poorer sort,
Expectant of the rack from day to day,
To whom the fire were welcome, lying
    chain'd
In breathless dungeons over steaming
    sewers,
Fed with rank bread that crawl'd upon the
    tongue,
And putrid water, every drop a worm,
Until they died of rotted limbs; and then
Cast on the dunghill naked, and become
Hideously alive again from head to heel,
Made even the carrion-nosing mongrel
    vomit
With hate and horror.
Paget.   Nay, you sicken *me*
To hear you.
Howard. Fancy-sick; these things are
    done,
Done right against the promise of this
    Queen
Twice given.
Paget.   No faith with heretics, my
    Lord!
Hist! there be two old gossips—gospellers,
I take it; stand behind the pillar here;
I warrant you they talk about the burning.

Enter TWO OLD WOMEN. JOAN, *and after*
    her TIB

Joan. Why, it be Tib!
    Tib. I cum behind tha, gall, and couldn't
make tha hear. Eh, the wind and the wet!
What a day, what a day! nigh upo' judgement daay loike. Pwoaps be pretty things,
Joan, but they wunt set i' the Lord's cheer
o' that daay.
    Joan. I must set down myself, Tib; it be
a var waay vor my owld legs up vro' Islip.
Eh, my rheumatizy be that bad howiver be
I to win to the burnin'.
    Tib. I should saay 'twur ower by now.
I'd ha' been here avore, but Dumble wur
blow'd wi' the wind, and Dumble's the
best milcher in Islip.
    Joan. Our Daisy's as good 'z her.
    Tib. Noa, Joan.
    Joan. Our Daisy's butter's as good 'z
hern.

Tib. Noa, Joan.

Joan. Our Daisy's cheeses be better.

Tib. Noa, Joan.

Joan. Eh, then ha' thy waay wi' me, Tib; ez thou hast wi' thy owld man.

Tib. Ay, Joan, and my owld man wur up and awaay betimes wi' dree hard eggs for a good pleace at the burnin'; and barrin' the wet, Hodge 'ud ha' been a-harrowin' o' white peasen i' the outfield—and barrin' the wind, Dumble wur blow'd wi' the wind, so 'z we was forced to stick her, but we fetched her round at last. Thank the Lord therevore. Dumble's the best milcher in Islip.

Joan. Thou's thy way wi' man and beast, Tib. I wonder at tha', it beats me! Eh, but I do know ez Pwoaps and vires be bad things; tell 'ee now, I heerd summat as summun towld summun o' owld Bishop Gardiner's end; there wur an owld lord a-cum to dine wi' un, and a wur so owld a couldn't bide vor his dinner, but a had to bide howsomiver, vor 'I wunt dine,' says my Lord Bishop, says he, 'not till I hears ez Latimer and Ridley be a-vire;' and so they bided on and on till vour o' the clock, till his man cum in post vro' here, and tells un ez the vire has tuk holt. 'Now,' says the Bishop, says he, 'we'll gwo to dinner;' and the owld lord fell to 's meat wi' a will, God bless un! but Gardiner wur struck down like by the hand o' God avore a could taste a mossel, and a set un all a-vire, so 'z the tongue on un cum a-lolluping out 'o 'is mouth as black as a rat. Thank the Lord, therevore.

Paget. The fools!

Tib. Ay, Joan; and Queen Mary gwoes on a-burnin' and a-burnin', to get her baaby born; but all her burnins' 'ill never burn out the hypocrisy that makes the water in her. There's nought but the vire of God's hell ez can burn out that.

Joan. Thank the Lord, therevore.

Paget. The fools!

Tib. A-burnin', and a-burnin', and a-makin' o' volk madder and madder; but tek thou my word vor't, Joan,—and I bean't wrong not twice i' ten year—the burnin' o' the owld archbishop 'll burn the

Pwoap out o' this 'ere land vor iver and iver.

Howard. Out of the church, you brace of cursed crones,
Or I will have you duck'd! (*Women hurry out.*) Said I not right?
For how should reverend prelate or throned prince
Brook for an hour such brute malignity?
Ah, what an acrid wine has Luther brew'd,

Paget. Pooh, pooh, my Lord! poor garrulous country-wives.
Buy you their cheeses, and they'll side with you;
You cannot judge the liquor from the lees.

Howard. I think that in some sort we may. But see,

Enter PETERS

Peters, my gentleman, an honest Catholic,
Who follow'd with the crowd to Cranmer's fire.
One that would neither misreport nor lie,
Not to gain paradise: no, nor if the Pope,
Charged him to do it—he is white as death.
Peters, how pale you look! you bring the smoke
Of Cranmer's burning with you.

Peters.   Twice or thrice
The smoke of Cranmer's burning wrapt me round.

Howard. Peters, you know me Catholic, but English.
Did he die bravely? Tell me that, or leave
All else untold.

Peters.   My Lord, he died most bravely.

Howard. Then tell me all.

Paget.   Ay, Master Peters, tell us.

Peters. You saw him how he past among the crowd;
And ever as he walk'd the Spanish friars
Still plied him with entreaty and reproach:
But Cranmer, as the helmsman at the helm
Steers, ever looking to the happy haven
Where he shall rest at night, moved to his death;
And I could see that many silent hands
Came from the crowd and met his own; and thus,

When we had come where Ridley burnt
    with Latimer,
He, with a cheerful smile, as one whose
    mind
Is all made up, in haste put off the rags
They had mock'd his misery with, and all
    in white,
His long white beard, which he had never
    shaven
Since Henry's death, down-sweeping to
    the chain,
Wherewith they bound him to the stake,
    he stood
More like an ancient father of the Church,
Than heretic of these times; and still the
    friars
Plied him, but Cranmer only shook his
    head,
Or answer'd them in smiling negatives;
Whereat Lord Williams gave a sudden
    cry:—
'Make short! make short!' and so they lit
    the wood.
Then Cranmer lifted his left hand to
    heaven,
And thrust his right into the bitter flame;
And crying, in his deep voice, more than
    once,
'This hath offended—this unworthy hand!'
So held it till it all was burn'd, before
The flame had reach'd his body; I stood
    near—
Mark'd him—he never uttered moan of
    pain:
He never stirr'd or writhed, but, like a
    statue,
Unmoving in the greatness of the flame,
Gave up the ghost; and so past martyr-
    like—
Martyr I may not call him—past—but
    whither?
    Paget. To purgatory, man, to purgatory.
    Peters. Nay, but, my Lord, he denied
    purgatory.
    Paget. Why then to heaven, and God ha'
    mercy on him.
    Howard. Paget, despite his fearful
    heresies,
I loved the man, and needs must moan
    for him;
O Cranmer!

Paget. But your moan is useless now:
Come out, my Lord, it is a world of fools.
                        [*Exeunt.*

ACT V

Scene I

London. Hall in the Palace

QUEEN, SIR NICHOLAS HEATH

    Heath. Madam,
I do assure you, that it must be look'd to:
Calais is but ill-garrison'd, in Guisnes
Are scarce two hundred men, and the
    French fleet
Rule in the narrow seas. It must be
    look'd to,
If war should fall between yourself and
    France;
Or you will lose your Calais.
    Mary.   It shall be look'd to;
I wish you a good morning, good Sir
    Nicholas:
Here is the King.   [*Exit* HEATH.

Enter PHILIP

    Philip.   Sir Nicholas tells you true,
And you must look to Calais when I go.
    Mary. Go? must you go, indeed—
    again—so soon?
Why, nature's licensed vagabond, the
    swallow,
That might live always in the sun's warm
    heart,
Stays longer here in our poor north than
    you:—
Knows where he nested—ever comes
    again.
    Philip. And, Madam, so shall I.
    Mary.   O, will you? will you?
I am faint with fear that you will come no
    more.
    Philip. Ay, ay; but many voices call me
    hence.
    Mary. Voices—I hear unhappy rumours
    —nay,
I say not, I believe. What voices call you
Dearer than mine that should be dearest
    to you?
Alas, my Lord! what voices and how
    many?

Philip. The voices of Castille and Aragon,
Granada, Naples, Sicily, and Milan,—
The voices of Franche-Comté, and the Netherlands,
The voices of Peru and Mexico,
Tunis, and Oran, and the Philippines,
And all the fair spice-islands of the East.
Mary (admiringly). You are the mightiest monarch upon earth,
I but a little Queen: and, so indeed,
Need you the more.
Philip.   A little Queen! but when
I came to wed your majesty, Lord Howard,
Sending an insolent shot that dash'd the seas
Upon us, made us lower our kingly flag
To yours of England.
Mary.   Howard is all English!
There is no king, not were he ten times king,
Ten times our husband, but must lower his flag
To that of England in the seas of England.
Philip. Is that your answer?
Mary.   Being Queen of England,
I have none other.
Philip.   So.
Mary.   But wherefore not
Helm the huge vessel of your state, my liege,
Here by the side of her who loves you most?
Philip. No, Madam, no! a candle in the sun
Is all but smoke—a star beside the moon
Is all but lost; your people will not crown me—
Your people are as cheerless as your clime;
Hate me and mine: witness the brawls, the gibbets.
Here swings a Spaniard—there an Englishman;
The peoples are unlike as their complexion;
Yet will I be your swallow and return—
But now I cannot bide.
Mary.   Not to help *me?*
They hate *me* also for my love to you,
My Philip; and these judgments on the land—

Harvestless autumns, horrible agues, plague—
Philip. The blood and sweat of heretics at the stake
Is God's best dew upon the barren field.
Burn more!
Mary. I will, I will; and you will stay?
Philip. Have I not said? Madam, I came to sue
Your Council and yourself to declare war.
Mary. Sir, there are many English in your ranks
To help your battle.
Philip.   So far, good. I say
I came to sue your Council and yourself
To declare war against the King of France.
Mary. Not to see me?
Philip.   Ay, Madam, to see you.
Unalterably and pesteringly fond! [*Aside.*
But, soon or late you must have war with France;
King Henry warms your traitors at his hearth.
Carew is there, and Thomas Stafford there.
Courtenay, belike—
Mary.   A fool and featherhead!
Philip. Ay, but they use his name. In brief, this Henry
Stirs up your land against you to the intent
That you may lose your English heritage.
And then, your Scottish namesake marrying
The Dauphin, he would weld France, England, Scotland,
Into one sword to hack at Spain and me.
Mary. And yet the Pope is now colleagued with France;
You make your wars upon him down in Italy:—
Philip, can that be well?
Philip.   Content you, Madam;
You must abide my judgment, and my father's,
Who deems it a most just and holy war.
The Pope would cast the Spaniard out of Naples:
He calls us worse than Jews, Moors, Saracens.
The Pope has pushed his horns beyond his mitre—
Beyond his province. Now,

Duke Alva will but touch him on the horns,
And he withdraws; and of his holy head—
For Alva is true son of the true church—
No hair is harm'd. Will you not help me
  here?
  Mary. Alas! the Council will not hear of
  war.
They say your wars are not the wars of
  England.
They will not lay more taxes on a land
So hunger-nipt and wretched; and you
  know
The crown is poor. We have given the
  church-lands back:
The nobles would not; nay, they clapt
  their hands
Upon their swords when ask'd; and there-
  fore God
Is hard upon the people. What's to be
  done?
Sir, I will move them in your cause again,
And we will raise us loans and subsidies
Among the merchants; and Sir Thomas
  Gresham
Will aid us. There is Antwerp and the
  Jews.
  Philip. Madam, my thanks.
  Mary.   And you will stay your
  going?
  Philip. And further to discourage and
  lay lame
The plots of France, altho' you love her
  not,
You must proclaim Elizabeth your heir.
She stands between you and the Queen of
  Scots.
  Mary. The Queen of Scots at least is
  Catholic.
  Philip. Ay, Madam, Catholic; but I will
  not have
The King of France the King of England
  too.
  Mary. But she's a heretic, and, when I
  am gone,
Brings the new learning back.
  Philip.   It must be done.
You must proclaim Elizabeth your heir.
  Mary. Then it is done; but you will stay
  your going
Somewhat beyond your settled purpose?
  Philip.   No!

  Mary. What, not one day?
  Philip.   You beat upon the rock.
  Mary. And I am broken there.
  Philip.   Is this a place
To wail in, Madam? what! a public hall.
Go in, I pray you.
  Mary.   Do not seem so changed.
Say go; but only say it lovingly.
  Philip. You do mistake. I am not one to
  change.
I never loved you more.
  Mary.   Sire, I obey you.
Come quickly.
  Philip. Ay.   [*Exit* MARY.

Enter COUNT DE FERIA

  Feria (aside). The Queen in tears!
  Philip.   Feria!
Hast thou not mark'd—come closer to
  mine ear—
How doubly aged this Queen of ours hath
  grown
Since she lost hope of bearing us a child?
  Feria. Sire, if your Grace hath mark'd it,
  so have I.
  Philip. Hast thou not likewise mark'd
  Elizabeth,
How fair and royal—like a Queen, indeed?
  Feria. Allow me the same answer as
  before—
That if your Grace hath mark'd her, so
  have I.
  Philip. Good, now; methinks my Queen
  is like enough
To leave me by and by.
  Feria.   To leave you, sire?
  Philip. I mean not like to live. Eliza-
  beth—
To Philibert of Savoy, as you know,
We meant to wed her; but I am not sure
She will not serve me better—so my Queen
Would leave me—as—my wife.
  Feria.   Sire, even so.
  Philip. She will not have Prince Phili-
  bert of Savoy.
  Feria. No, sire.
  Philip.   I have to pray you, some
  odd time,
To sound the Princess carelessly on this;
Not as from me, but as your phantasy;
And tell me how she takes it.

Feria. Sire, I will.

Philip. I am not certain but that Philibert
Shall be the man; and I shall urge his
suit
Upon the Queen, because I am not certain:
You understand, Feria.

Feria. Sire, I do.

Philip. And if you be not secret in this
matter,
You understand me there, too?

Feria. Sire, I do.

Philip. You must be sweet and supple,
like a Frenchman.
She is none of those who loathe the honeycomb. [*Exit* FERIA.

Enter RENARD

Renard. My liege, I bring you goodly
tidings.

Philip. Well?

Renard. There *will* be war with France,
at last, my liege;
Sir Thomas Stafford, a bull-headed ass,
Sailing from France, with thirty English-
men,
Hath taken Scarboro' Castle, north of
York;
Proclaims himself protector, and affirms
The Queen has forfeited her right to
reign
By marriage with an alien—other things
As idle; a weak Wyatt! Little doubt
This buzz will soon be silenced; but the
Council
(I have talk'd with some already) are for
war.
This is the fifth conspiracy hatch'd in
France;
They show their teeth upon it; and your
Grace,
So you will take advice of mine, should
stay
Yet for awhile, to shape and guide the
event.

Philip. Good! Renard, I will stay then.

Renard. Also, sire,
Might I not say—to please your wife, the
Queen?

Philip. Ay, Renard, if you care to put
it so. [*Exeunt.*

SCENE II

A Room in the Palace

MARY, *sitting: a rose in her hand.* LADY
CLARENCE. ALICE *in the background.*

Mary. Look! I have play'd with this
poor rose so long
I have broken off the head.

Lady Clarence. Your Grace hath been
More merciful to many a rebel head
That should have fallen, and may rise
again.

Mary. There were not many hang'd for
Wyatt's rising.

Lady Clarence. Nay, not two hundred.

Mary. I could weep for them
And her, and mine own self and all the
world.

Lady Clarence. For her? for whom, your
Grace?

Enter USHER

Usher. The Cardinal.

Enter CARDINAL POLE. (MARY *rises.*)

Mary. Reginald Pole, what news hath
plagued thy heart?
What makes thy favour like the bloodless
head
Fall'n on the block, and held up by the
hair?
Philip?—

Pole. No, Philip is as warm in life
As ever.

Mary. Ay, and then as cold as ever.
Is Calais taken?

Pole. Cousin, there hath chanced
A sharper harm to England and to Rome,
Than Calais taken. Julius the Third
Was ever just, and mild, and father-like;
But this new Pope Caraffa, Paul the Fourth,
Not only reft me of that legateship
Which Julius gave me, and the legateship
Annex'd to Canterbury—nay, but worse—
And yet I must obey the Holy Father,
And so must you, good cousin;—worse
than all,
A passing bell toll'd in a dying ear—
He hath cited me to Rome, for heresy,
Before his Inquisition.

Mary.   I knew it, cousin,
But held from you all papers sent by Rome,
That you might rest among us, till the
   Pope,
To compass which I wrote myself to Rome,
Reversed his doom, and that you might
   not seem
To disobey his Holiness.
   Pole.   He hates Philip;
He is all Italian, and he hates the Spaniard;
He cannot dream that *I* advised the war;
He strikes thro' me at Philip and yourself.
Nay, but I know it of old, he hates me too;
So brands me in the stare of Christendom
A heretic!
Now, even now, when bow'd before my
   time,
The house half-ruin'd ere the lease be out;
When I should guide the Church in peace
   at home,
After my twenty years of banishment,
And all my lifelong labour to uphold
The primacy—a heretic. Long ago,
When I was ruler in the patrimony,
I was too lenient to the Lutheran,
And I and learned friends among ourselves
Would freely canvass certain Lutheranisms.
What then, he knew I was no Lutheran.
A heretic!
He drew this shaft against me to the head,
When it was thought I might be chosen
   Pope,
But then withdrew it. In full consistory,
When I was made Archbishop, he ap-
   proved me.
And how should he have sent me Legate
   hither,
Deeming me heretic? and what heresy
   since?
But he was evermore mine enemy,
And hates the Spaniard—fiery-choleric,
A drinker of black, strong, volcanic wines,
That ever make him fierier. I, a heretic?
Your Highness knows that in pursuing
   heresy
I have gone beyond your late Lord Chan-
   cellor,—
He cried Enough! enough! before his
   death.—
Gone beyond him and mine own natural
   man

(It was God's cause); so far they call me
   now,
The scourge and butcher of their English
   church.
   Mary. Have courage, your reward is
   Heaven itself.
   Pole. They groan amen; they swarm into
   the fire
Like flies—for what? no dogma. They
   know nothing;
They burn for nothing.
   Mary.   You have done your best.
   Pole. Have done my best, and as a faith-
   ful son,
That all day long hath wrought his father's
   work,
When back he comes at evening hath the
   door
Shut on him by the father whom he loved,
His early follies cast into his teeth,
And the poor son turn'd out into the street
To sleep, to die—I shall die of it, cousin.
   Mary. I pray you be not so disconsolate;
I still will do mine utmost with the Pope.
Poor cousin!
Have not I been the fast friend of your life
Since mine began, and it was thought we
   two
Might make one flesh, and cleave unto
   each other
As man and wife?
   Pole.   Ah, cousin, I remember
How I would dandle you upon my knee
At lisping-age. I watch'd you dancing once
With your huge father; he look'd the
   Great Harry,
You but his cockboat; prettily you did it,
And innocently. No—we were not made
One flesh in happiness, no happiness here;
But now we are made one flesh in misery;
Our bridesmaids are not lovely—Dis-
appointment,
Ingratitude, Injustice, Evil-tongue,
Labour-in-vain.
   Mary.   Surely, not all in vain.
Peace, cousin, peace! I am sad at heart
   myself.
   Pole. Our altar is a mound of dead men's
   clay,
Dug from the grave that yawns for us
   beyond;

And there is one Death stands behind the Groom,
And there is one Death stands behind the Bride—
Mary. Have you been looking at the 'Dance of Death'?
Pole. No; but these libellous papers which I found
Strewn in your palace. Look you here— the Pope
Pointing at me with 'Pole, the heretic,
Thou hast burnt others, do thou burn thyself,
Or I will burn thee;' and this other; see!—
'We pray continually for the death
Of our accursed Queen and Cardinal Pole.'
This last—I dare not read it her. [*Aside.*
Mary.   Away!
Why do you bring me these?
I thought you knew me better. I never read,
I tear them; they come back upon my dreams.
The hands that write them should be burnt clean off
As Cranmer's, and the fiends that utter them
Tongue-torn with pincers, lash'd to death, or lie
Famishing in black cells, while famish'd rats
Eat them alive. Why do they bring me these?
Do you mean to drive me mad?
Pole.   I had forgotten
How these poor libels trouble you. Your pardon,
Sweet cousin, and farewell! 'O bubble world,
Whose colours in a moment break and fly!'
Why, who said that? I know not—true enough!

[*Puts up the papers, all but the last, which falls. Exit* POLE.

Alice. If Cranmer's spirit were a mocking one,
And heard these two, there might be sport
for him.   [*Aside.*
Mary. Clarence, they hate me; even while I speak
There lurks a silent dagger, listening

In some dark closet, some long gallery, drawn,
And panting for my blood as I go by.
Lady Clarence. Nay, Madam, there be loyal papers too,
And I have often found them.
Mary.   Find me one!
Lady Clarence. Ay, Madam; but Sir Nicholas Heath, the Chancellor,
Would see your Highness.
Mary.   Wherefore should I see him?
Lady Clarence. Well, Madam, he may bring you news from Philip.
Mary. So, Clarence.
Lady Clarence.   Let me first put up your hair;
It tumbles all abroad.
Mary.   And the gray dawn
Of an old age that never will be mine
Is all the clearer seen. No, no; what matters?
Forlorn I am, and let me look forlorn.

Enter SIR NICHOLAS HEATH

Heath. I bring your Majesty such grievous news
I grieve to bring it. Madam, Calais is taken.
Mary. What traitor spoke? Here, let my cousin Pole
Seize him and burn him for a Lutheran.
Heath. Her Highness is unwell. I will retire.
Lady Clarence. Madam, your Chancellor, Sir Nicholas Heath.
Mary. Sir Nicholas! I am stunn'd— Nicholas Heath?
Methought some traitor smote me on the head.
What said you, my good Lord, that our brave English
Had sallied out from Calais and driven back
The Frenchmen from their trenches?
Heath.   Alas! no.
That gateway to the mainland over which
Our flag hath floated for two hundred years
Is France again.
Mary.   So; but it is not lost—
Not yet. Send out: let England as of old
Rise lionlike, strike hard and deep into

597

The prey they are rending from her—ay, and rend
The renders too. Send out, send out, and make
Musters in all the counties; gather all
From sixteen years to sixty; collect the fleet;
Let every craft that carries sail and gun
Steer toward Calais. Guisnes is not taken yet?
Heath. Guisnes is not taken yet.
Mary. There yet is hope.
Heath. Ah, Madam, but your people are so cold;
I do much fear that England will not care.
Methinks there is no manhood left among us.
Mary. Send out; I am too weak to stir abroad:
Tell my mind to the Council—to the Parliament:
Proclaim it to the winds. Thou art cold thyself
To babble of their coldness. O would I were
My father for an hour! Away now—Quick!
[*Exit* HEATH.
I hoped I had served God with all my might!
It seems I have not. Ah! much heresy
Shelter'd in Calais. Saints, I have rebuilt
Your shrines, set up your broken images;
Be comfortable to me. Suffer not
That my brief reign in England be defamed
Thro' all her angry chronicles hereafter
By loss of Calais. Grant me Calais. Philip,
We have made war upon the Holy Father
All for your sake: what good could come of that?
Lady Clarence. No, Madam, not against the Holy Father;
You did but help King Philip's war with France,
Your troops were never down in Italy.
Mary. I am a byword. Heretic and rebel
Point at me and make merry. Philip gone!
And Calais gone! Time that I were gone too!
Lady Clarence. Nay, if the fetid gutter had a voice

And cried I was not clean, what should I care?
Or you, for heretic cries? And I believe,
Spite of your melancholy Sir Nicho.as,
Your England is as loyal as myself.
Mary (seeing the paper dropt by POLE).
There! there! another paper! Said you not
Many of these were loyal? Shall I try
If this be one of such?
Lady Clarence. Let it be, let it be.
God pardon me! I have never yet found one. [*Aside.*
Mary (reads). 'Your people hate you as your husband hates you.'
Clarence, Clarence, what have I done? what sin
Beyond all grace, all pardon? Mother of God,
Thou knowest never woman meant so well,
And fared so ill in this disastrous world.
My people hate me and desire my death.
Lady Clarence. No, Madam, no.
Mary. My husband hates me, and desires my death.
Lady Clarence. No, Madam; these are libels.
Mary. I hate myself, and I desire my death.
Lady Clarence. Long live your Majesty! Shall Alice sing you
One of her pleasant songs? Alice, my child,
Bring us your lute (ALICE *goes*). They say the gloom of Saul
Was lighten'd by young David's harp.
Mary. Too young!
And never knew a Philip.

Re-enter ALICE

Give *me* the lute.
He hates me!

(*She sings*)

Hapless doom of woman happy in betrothing!
Beauty passes like a breath and love is lost in loathing:
Low, my lute; speak low, my lute, but say the world is nothing—
Low, lute, low!

Love will hover round the flowers when they
    first awaken;
Love will fly the fallen leaf, and not be over-
    taken;
Low, my lute! oh low, my lute! we fade and are
    forsaken—
                    Low, dear lute, low!

Take it away! not low enough for me!
Alice. Your Grace hath a low voice.
Mary.   How dare you say it?
Even for that he hates me. A low voice
Lost in a wilderness where none can hear!
A voice of shipwreck on a shoreless sea!
A low voice from the dust and from the
    grave
    (*Sitting on the ground*). There, am I low
    enough now?
Alice. Good Lord! how grim and ghastly
    looks her Grace,
With both her knees drawn upward to her
    chin.
There was an old-world tomb beside my
    father's,
And this was open'd, and the dead were
    found
Sitting, and in this fashion; she looks a
    corpse.

          Enter LADY MAGDALEN DACRES

Lady Magdalen. Madam, the Count de
    Feria waits without,
In hopes to see your Highness.
    Lady Clarence (*pointing to* MARY). Wait
    he must—
Her trance again. She neither sees nor hears,
And may not speak for hours.
Lady Magdalen.   Unhappiest
Of Queens and wives and women!
    Alice (*in the foreground with* LADY MAG-
    DALEN).   And all along
Of Philip.
Lady Magdalen. Not so loud! Our
    Clarence there
Sees ever such an aureole round the Queen,
It gilds the greatest wronger of her peace,
Who stands the nearest to her.
    Alice.   Ay, this Philip;
I used to love the Queen with all my
    heart—
God help me, but methinks I love her less
For such a dotage upon such a man.
I would I were as tall and strong as you.

Lady Magdalen. I seem half-shamed at
    times to be so tall.
Alice. You are the stateliest deer in all
    the herd—
Beyond his aim—but I am small and
    scandalous,
And love to hear bad tales of Philip.
Lady Magdalen.   Why?
I never heard him utter worse of you
Than that you were low-statured.
Alice.   Does he think
Low stature is low nature, or all women
Low as his own?
Lady Magdalen. There you strike in the
    nail.
This coarseness is a want of phantasy.
It is the low man thinks the woman low;
Sin is too dull to see beyond himself.
Alice. Ah, Magdalen, sin is bold as well
    as dull.
How dared he?
Lady Magdalen. Stupid soldiers oft are
    bold.
Poor lads, they see not what the general
    sees,
A risk of utter ruin. I am *not*
Beyond his aim, or was not.
Alice.   Who? Not you?
Tell, tell me; save my credit with myself.
Lady Magdalen. I never breathed it to a
    bird in the eaves,
Would not for all the stars and maiden
    moon
Our drooping Queen should know! In
    Hampton Court
My window look'd upon the corridor;
And I was robing;—this poor throat of
    mine,
Barer than I should wish a man to see it,—
When he we speak of drove the window
    back,
And, like a thief, push'd in his royal hand;
But by God's providence a good stout staff
Lay near me; and you know me strong of
    arm;
I do believe I lamed his Majesty's
For a day or two, tho', give the Devil his
    due,
I never found he bore me any spite.
    Alice. I would she could have wedded
    that poor youth,

My Lord of Devon—light enough, God
knows,
And mixt with Wyatt's rising—and the boy
Not out of him—but neither cold, coarse,
cruel,
And more than all—no Spaniard.
Lady Clarence.   Not so loud.
Lord Devon, girls! what are you whisper-
ing here?
Alice. Probing an old state-secret—how
it chanced
That this young Earl was sent on foreign
travel,
Not lost his head.
Lady Clarence. There was no proof
against him.
Alice. Nay, Madam; did not Gardiner
intercept
A letter which the Count de Noailles wrote
To that dead traitor Wyatt, with full proof
Of Courtenay's treason? What became of
that?
Lady Clarence. Some say that Gardiner,
out of love for him,
Burnt it, and some relate that it was lost
When Wyatt sack'd the Chancellor's house
in Southwark.
Let dead things rest.
Alice.   Ay, and with him who died
Alone in Italy.
Lady Clarence. Much changed, I hear,
Had put off levity and put graveness on.
The foreign courts report him in his
manner
Noble as his young person and old shield.
It might be so—but all is over now;
He caught a chill in the lagoons of Venice,
And died in Padua.
Mary (looking up suddenly). Died in the
true faith?
Lady Clarence. Ay, Madam, happily.
Mary.   Happier he than I.
Lady Magdalen. It seems her Highness
hath awaken'd. Think you
That I might dare to tell her that the
Count—
Mary. I will see no man hence for ever-
more,
Saving my confessor and my cousin Pole.
Lady Magdalen. It is the Count de
Feria, my dear lady.

Mary.   What Count?
Lady Magdalen. The Count de Feria,
from his Majesty
King Philip.
Mary. Philip! quick! loop up my hair!
Throw cushions on that seat, and make it
throne-like.
Arrange my dress—the gorgeous Indian
shawl
That Philip brought me in our happy
days!—
That covers all. So—am I somewhat
Queenlike,
Bride of the mightiest sovereign upon
earth?
Lady Clarence. Ay, so your Grace would
bide a moment yet.
Mary. No, no, he brings a letter. I may
die
Before I read it. Let me see him at once.

Enter COUNT DE FERIA *(kneels)*

Feria. I trust your Grace is well. *(Aside)*
How her hand burns!
Mary. I am not well, but it will better
me,
Sir Count, to read the letter which you
bring.
Feria. Madam, I bring no letter.
Mary.   How! no letter?
Feria. His Highness is so vex'd with
strange affairs—
Mary. That his own wife is no affair of
his.
Feria. Nay, Madam, nay! he sends his
veriest love,
And says, he will come quickly.
Mary.   Doth he, indeed?
You, sir, do *you* remember what *you* said
When last you came to England?
Feria.   Madam, I brought
My King's congratulations; it was hoped
Your Highness was once more in happy
state
To give him an heir male.
Mary.   Sir, you said more;
You said he would come quickly. I had
horses
On all the road from Dover, day and night;
On all the road from Harwich, night and
day;

But the child came not, and the husband came not;
And yet he will come quickly. . . . Thou hast learnt
Thy lesson, and I mine. There is no need
For Philip so to shame himself again. Return,
And tell him that I know he comes no more.
Tell him at last I know his love is dead,
And that I am in state to bring forth death—
Thou art commission'd to Elizabeth,
And not to me!
 Feria. Mere compliments and wishes.
But shall I take some message from your Grace?
 Mary. Tell her to come and close my dying eyes,
And wear my crown, and dance upon my grave. •
 Feria. Then I may say your Grace will see your sister?
Your Grace is too low-spirited. Air and sunshine.
I would we had you, Madam, in our warm Spain.
You droop in your dim London.
 Mary.   Have him away!
I sicken of his readiness.
 Lady Clarence. My Lord Count,
Her Highness is too ill for colloquy.
 Feria (kneels, and kisses her hand). I wish her Highness better. (*Aside*) How her hand burns!   [*Exeunt.*

SCENE III

A House near London

ELIZABETH, STEWARD OF THE
HOUSEHOLD, ATTENDANTS

 Elizabeth. There's half an angel wrong'd in your account;
Methinks I am all angel, that I bear it
Without more ruffling. Cast it o'er again.
 Steward. I were whole devil if I wrong'd you Madam. [*Exit* STEWARD.
 Attendant. The Count de Feria, from the King of Spain.
 Elizabeth. Ah!—let him enter. Nay, you need not go: [*To her* LADIES.

Remain within the chamber, but apart.
We'll have no private conference. Welcome to England!

Enter FERIA

 Feria. Fair island star!
 Elizabeth.   I shine! What else, Sir Count?
 Feria. As far as France, and into Philip's heart.
My King would know if you be fairly served,
And lodged, and treated.
 Elizabeth. You see the lodging, sir,
I am well-served, and am in everything
Most loyal and most grateful to the Queen.
 Feria. You should be grateful to my master, too.
He spoke of this; and unto him you owe
That Mary hath acknowledged you her heir.
 Elizabeth. No, not to her nor him; but to the people,
Who know my right, and love me, as I love
The people! whom God aid!
 Feria.   You will be Queen,
And, were I Philip—
 Elizabeth. Wherefore pause you—what?
 Feria. Nay, but I speak from mine own self, not him;
Your royal sister cannot last; your hand
Will be much coveted! What a delicate one!
Our Spanish ladies have none such—and there,
Were you in Spain, this fine fair gossamer gold—
Like sun-gilt breathings on a frosty dawn—
That hovers round your shoulder—
 Elizabeth.   Is it so fine?
Troth, some have said so.
 Feria. —would be deemed a miracle.
 Elizabeth. Your Philip hath gold hair and golden beard;
There must be ladies many with hair like mine.
 Feria. Some few of Gothic blood have golden hair,
But none like yours.

Elizabeth. I am happy you approve it.

Feria. But as to Philip and your Grace—
consider,—
If such a one as you should match with
Spain,
What hinders but that Spain and England
join'd,
Should make the mightiest empire earth
has known.
Spain would be England on her seas, and
England
Mistress of the Indies.

   Elizabeth.   It may chance, that
England
Will be the Mistress of the Indies yet,
Without the help of Spain.

   Feria.   Impossible;
Except you put Spain down.
Wide of the mark ev'n for a madman's
dream.

   Elizabeth. Perhaps; but we have seamen.
Count de Feria,
I take it that the King hath spoken to you;
But is Don Carlos such a goodly match?

   Feria. Don Carlos, Madam, is but
twelve years old.

   Elizabeth. Ay, tell the King that I will
muse upon it;
He is my good friend, and I would keep
him so;
But—he would have me Catholic of Rome,
And that I scarce can be; and, sir, till now
My sister's marriage, and my father's
marriages,
Make me full fain to live and die a maid.
But I am much beholden to your King.
Have you aught else to tell me?

   Feria.   Nothing, Madam,
Save that methought I gather'd from the
Queen
That she would see your Grace before she
—died.

   Elizabeth. God's death! and wherefore
spake you not before?
We dally with our lazy moments here,
And hers are number'd. Horses there,
without!
I am much beholden to the King, your
master.
Why did you keep me prating? Horses,
there!   *[Exit* ELIZABETH, *etc.*

Feria. So from a clear sky falls the
thunderbolt!
Don Carlos? Madam, if you marry Philip,
Then I and he will snaffle your 'God's
death,'
And break your paces in, and make you
tame;
God's death, forsooth—you do not know
King Philip.   *[Exit.*

SCENE IV

London. Before the Palace

A light burning within. VOICES *of the night
passing*

   First. Is not yon light in the Queen's
chamber?

   Second.   Ay,
They say she's dying.

   First.   So is Cardinal Pole.
May the great angels join their wings, and
make
Down for their heads to heaven!

   Second.   Amen. Come on.
                     [Exeunt.

TWO OTHERS

   First. There's the Queen's light. I hear
she cannot live.

   Second. God curse her and her Legate!
Gardiner burns
Already; but to pay them full in kind,
The hottest hold in all the devil's den
Were but a sort of winter; sir, in Guernsey,
I watch'd a woman burn; and in her agony
The mother came upon her—a child was
born—
And, sir, they hurl'd it back into the fire,
That, being but baptized in fire, the babe
Might be in fire for ever. Ah, good neigh-
bour,
There should be something fierier than fire
To yield them their deserts.

   First.   Amen to all
Your wish, and further.

   A Third Voice. Deserts! Amen to what?
Whose deserts? Yours? You have a gold
ring on your finger, and soft raiment about
your body; and is not the woman up
yonder sleeping after all she has done, in
peace and quietness, on a soft bed, in a

602

closed room, with light, fire, physic, tendance; and I have seen the true men of Christ lying famine-dead by scores, and under no ceiling but the cloud that wept on them, not for them.

First. Friend, tho' so late, it is not safe to preach.
You had best go home. What are you?

Third. What am I? One who cries continually with sweat and tears to the Lord God that it would please Him out of His infinite love to break down all kingship and queenship, all priesthood and prelacy; to cancel and abolish all bonds of human allegiance, all the magistracy, all the nobles, and all the wealthy; and to send us again, according to His promise, the one King, the Christ, and all things in common, as in the day of the first church, when Christ Jesus was King.

First. If ever I heard a madman,—let's away!
Why, you long-winded—— Sir, you go beyond me.
I pride myself on being moderate.
Good night! Go home. Besides, you curse so loud,
The watch will hear you. Get you home at once.   [*Exeunt.*

Scene V

London. A Room in the Palace

A Gallery on one side. The moonlight streaming through a range of windows on the wall opposite. MARY, LADY CLARENCE, LADY MAGDALEN DACRES, ALICE. QUEEN *pacing the Gallery. A writing-table in front.* QUEEN *comes to the table and writes and goes again, pacing the Gallery.*

Lady Clarence. Mine eyes are dim: what hath she written? read.
Alice. 'I am dying, Philip; come to me.'
Lady Magdalen. There—up and down, poor lady, up and down.
Alice. And how her shadow crosses one by one
The moonlight casements pattern'd on the wall,
Following her like her sorrow. She turns again.

[QUEEN *sits and writes, and goes again.*
Lady Clarence. What hath she written now?
Alice. Nothing; but 'come, come, come,' and all awry,
And blotted by her tears. This cannot last.
          [QUEEN *returns.*
Mary. I whistle to the bird has broken cage,
And all in vain.   [*Sitting down.*
Calais gone—Guisnes gone, too—and Philip gone!
Lady Clarence. Dear Madam, Philip is but at the wars;
I cannot doubt but that he comes again;
And he is with you in a measure still.
I never look'd upon so fair a likeness
As your great King in armour there, his hand
Upon his helmet.
          [*Pointing to the portrait of* PHILIP *on the wall.*
Mary.   Doth he not look noble?
I had heard of him in battle over seas,
And I would have my warrior all in arms.
He said it was not courtly to stand helmeted
Before the Queen. He had his gracious moment,
Altho' you'll not believe me. How he smiles
As if he loved me yet!
Lady Clarence.   And so he does.
Mary. He never loved me—nay, he could not love me.
It was his father's policy against France.
I am eleven years older than he,
Poor boy!   [*Weeps.*
Alice. That was a lusty boy of twenty-seven;   [*Aside.*
Poor enough in God's grace!
Mary.   —And all in vain!
The Queen of Scots is married to the Dauphin,
And Charles, the lord of this low world, is gone;
And all his wars and wisdoms past away;
And in a moment I shall follow him.
Lady Clarence. Nay, dearest Lady, see your good physician.
Mary. Drugs—but he knows they cannot help me—says
That rest is all—tells me I must not think—

That I must rest—I shall rest by and by.
Catch the wild cat, cage him, and when he springs
And maims himself against the bars, say 'rest':
Why, you must kill him if you would have him rest—
Dead or alive you cannot make him happy.
  Lady Clarence. Your Majesty has lived so pure a life,
And done such mighty things by Holy Church,
I trust that God will make you happy yet.
  Mary. What is the strange thing happiness? Sit down here:
Tell me thine happiest hour.
  Lady Clarence.   I will, if that
May make your Grace forget yourself a little.
There runs a shallow brook across our field
For twenty miles, where the black crow flies five,
And doth so bound and babble all the way
As if itself were happy. It was May-time,
And I was walking with the man I loved.
I loved him, but I thought I was not loved.
And both were silent, letting the wild brook
Speak for us—till he stoop'd and gather'd one
From out a bed of thick forget-me-nots,
Look'd hard and sweet at me, and gave it me.
I took it, tho' I did not know I took it,
And put it in my bosom, and all at once
I felt his arms about me, and his lips——
  Mary. O God! I have been too slack, too slack;
There are Hot Gospellers even among our guards—
Nobles we dared not touch. We have but burnt
The heretic priest, workmen, and women and children.
Wet, famine, ague, fever, storm, wreck, wrath,—
We have so play'd the coward; but by God's grace,
We'll follow Philip's leading, and set up
The Holy Office here—garner the wheat,

And burn the tares with unquenchable fire!
Burn!—
Fie, what a savour! tell the cooks to close
The doors of all the offices below.
Latimer!
Sir, we are private with our women here—
Ever a rough, blunt, and uncourtly fellow—
Thou light a torch that never will go out!
'Tis out—mine flames. Women, the Holy Father
Has ta'en the legateship from our cousin Pole—
Was that well done? and poor Pole pines of it,
As I do, to the death. I am but a woman,
I have no power.—Ah, weak and meek old man,
Seven-fold dishonour'd even in the sight
Of thine own sectaries—No, no. No pardon!—
Why that was false: there is the right hand still
Beckons me hence.
Sir, you were burnt for heresy, not for treason,
Remember that! 'twas I and Bonner did it,
And Pole; we are three to one—Have you found mercy there,
Grant it me here: and see, he smiles and goes,
Gentle as in life.
  Alice. Madam, who goes? King Philip?
  Mary. No, Philip comes and goes, but never goes.
Women, when I am dead,
Open my heart, and there you will find written
Two names, Philip and Calais; open his,—
So that he have one,—
You will find Philip only, policy, policy,—
Ay, worse than that—not one hour true to me!
Foul maggots crawling in a fester'd vice!
Adulterous to the very heart of Hell.
Hast thou a knife?
  Alice.   Ay, Madam, but o' God's mercy—
  Mary. Fool, think'st thou I would peril mine own soul

By slaughter of the body? I could not, girl,
Not this way—callous with a constant
    stripe,
Unwoundable. The knife!
    Alice.   Take heed, take heed!
The blade is keen as death.
    Mary.   This Philip shall not
Stare in upon me in my haggardness;
Old, miserable, diseased,
Incapable of children. Come thou down.
    [*Cuts out the picture and throws it down.*
Lie there. (*Wails*) O God, I have kill'd my
    Philip!
    Alice.   No,
Madam, you have but cut the canvas out;
We can replace it.
    Mary.   All is well then; rest—
I will to rest; he said, I must have rest.
    [*Cries of* 'Elizabeth' *in the street.*
A cry! What's that? Elizabeth? revolt?
A new Northumberland, another Wyatt?
I'll fight it on the threshold of the grave.
    Lady Clarence. Madam, your royal sister
    comes to see you.
    Mary. I will not see her.
Who knows if Boleyn's daughter be my
    sister?
I will see none except the priest. Your arm.
                [*To* LADY CLARENCE.
O Saint of Aragon, with that sweet worn
    smile
Among thy patient wrinkles—Help me
    hence.   [*Exeunt.*

    The PRIEST *passes. Enter* ELIZABETH *and*
              SIR WILLIAM CECIL

    Elizabeth. Good counsel yours—
           No one in waiting? still,
As if the chamberlain were Death himself!
The room she sleeps in—is not this the
    way?
No, that way there are voices. Am I too
    late?
Cecil ... God guide me lest I lose the way.
                [*Exit* ELIZABETH.
    Cecil. Many points weather'd, many
    perilous ones,
At last a harbour opens; but therein
Sunk rocks—they need fine steering—
    much it is
To be nor mad, nor bigot—have a mind—

Nor let Priests' talk, or dream of worlds
    to be,
Miscolour things about her—sudden
    touches
For him, or him—sunk rocks; no pas-
    sionate faith—
But—if let be—balance and compromise;
Brave, wary, sane to the heart of her—a
    Tudor
School'd by the shadow of death—a
    Boleyn, too,
Glancing across the Tudor—not so well.

           Enter ALICE

How is the good Queen now?
    Alice.   Away from Philip.
Back in her childhood—prattling to her
    mother
Of her betrothal to the Emperor Charles,
And childlike-jealous of him again—and
    once
She thank'd her father sweetly for his book
Against that godless German. Ah, those
    days
Were happy. It was never merry world
In England, since the Bible came among
    us.
    Cecil. And who says that?
    Alice. It is a saying among the Catholics.
    Cecil. It never will be merry world in
    England,
Till all men have their Bible, rich and poor.
    Alice. The Queen is dying, or you dare
    not say it.

          Enter ELIZABETH

    Elizabeth. The Queen is dead.
    Cecil. Then here she stands! my homage.
    Elizabeth. She knew me, and acknow-
    ledged me her heir,
Pray'd me to pay her debts, and keep the
    Faith;
Then claspt the cross, and pass'd away in
    peace.
I left her lying still and beautiful,
More beautiful than in life. Why would
    you vex yourself,
Poor sister? Sir, I swear I have no heart
To be your Queen. To reign is restless
    fence,

Tierce, quart, and trickery. Peace is with
  the dead.
Her life was winter, for her spring was
  nipt:
And she loved much: pray God she be
  forgiven.
  Cecil. Peace with the dead, who never
    were at peace!
Yet she loved one so much—I needs must
  say—
That never English monarch dying left
England so little.
  Elizabeth.   But with Cecil's aid

And others, if our person be secured
From traitor stabs—we will make England
  great.

Enter PAGET, *and other* LORDS OF THE
COUNCIL, SIR RALPH BAGENHALL, *etc.*

  Lords. God save Elizabeth, the Queen
    of England!
  Bagenhall. God save the Crown! the
    Papacy is no more.
  Paget (aside). Are we so sure of that?
  Acclamation. God save the Queen!

HAROLD

A DRAMA

TO HIS EXCELLENCY
THE RIGHT HON. LORD LYTTON
Viceroy and Governor-General of India

MY DEAR LORD LYTTON,—After old-world records—such as the Bayeux tapestry and the Roman de Rou,—Edward Freeman's History of the Norman Conquest, and your father's Historical Romance treating of the same times, have been mainly helpful to me in writing this Drama. Your father dedicated his 'Harold' to my father's brother; allow me to dedicate my 'Harold' to yourself.   A. TENNYSON.

SHOW-DAY AT BATTLE ABBEY, 1876

A GARDEN here—May breath and bloom of spring—
The cuckoo yonder from an English elm
Crying 'with my false egg I overwhelm
The native nest:' and fancy hears the ring
Of harness, and that deathful arrow sing,
And Saxon battleaxe clang on Norman helm.
Here rose the dragon-banner of our realm:
Here fought, here fell, our Norman-slander'd king.
O Garden blossoming out of English blood!
O strange hate-healer Time! We stroll and stare
Where might made right eight hundred years ago;
Might, right? ay good, so all things make for good—
But he and he, if soul be soul, are where
Each stands full face with all he did below.

DRAMATIS PERSONÆ

KING EDWARD THE CONFESSOR.
STIGAND, *created Archbishop of Canterbury by the Antipope Benedict.*
ALDRED, *Archbishop of York.*   THE NORMAN BISHOP OF LONDON.
HAROLD, *Earl of Wessex, afterwards King of England* ⎫
TOSTIG, *Earl of Northumbria*   ⎬ *Sons of*
GURTH, *Earl of East Anglia*   ⎪ *Godwin.*
LEOFWIN, *Earl of Kent and Essex*   ⎪
WULFNOTH   ⎭
COUNT WILLIAM OF NORMANDY.   WILLIAM RUFUS.
WILLIAM MALET, *a Norman Noble.*[1]
EDWIN, *Earl of Mercia*   ⎱ *Sons of Alfgar of*
MORCAR, *Earl of Northumbria after Tostig* ⎰   *Mercia.*
GAMEL, *a Northumbrian Thane.*   GUY, *Count of Ponthieu.*
ROLF, *a Ponthieu Fisherman.*   HUGH MARGOT, *a Norman Monk.*
OSGOD *and* ATHELRIC, *Canons from Waltham.*
THE QUEEN, *Edward the Confessor's Wife, Daughter of Godwin.*
ALDWYTH, *Daughter of Alfgar and Widow of Griffyth, King of Wales.*
EDITH, *Ward of King Edward.*

Courtiers, Earls and Thanes, Men-at-Arms, Canons of Waltham, Fishermen, etc.

[1] . . . quidam partim Normannus et Anglus
Compater Heraldi. (*Guy of Amiens,* 587.)

ACT I

SCENE I

London. The King's Palace

(*A comet seen through the open window*)

ALDWYTH, GAMEL, COURTIERS *talking together*

First Courtier. Lo! there once more—this is the seventh night!
Yon grimly-glaring, treble-brandish'd scourge
Of England!
Second Courtier. Horrible!
First Courtier. Look you, there's a star
That dances in it as mad with agony!
Third Courtier. Ay, like a spirit in Hell who skips and flies
To right and left, and cannot scape the flame.
Second Courtier. Steam'd upward from the undescendible
Abysm.
First Courtier. Or floated downward from the throne
Of God Almighty.
Aldwyth.   Gamel, son of Orm,
What thinkest thou this means?
Gamel.   War, my dear lady!
Aldwyth. Doth this affright thee?
Gamel.   Mightily, my dear lady!
Aldwyth. Stand by me then, and look upon my face,
Not on the comet.

(*Enter* MORCAR)
                    Brother! why so pale?
Morcar. It glares in heaven, it flares upon the Thames,
The people are as thick as bees below,
They hum like bees,—they cannot speak—for awe;
Look to the skies, then to the river, strike
Their hearts, and hold their babies up to it.
I think that they would Molochize them too,
To have the heavens clear.
Aldwyth.   They fright not me.

(*Enter* LEOFWIN, *after him* GURTH)
Ask thou Lord Leofwin what he thinks of this!

Morcar. Lord Leofwin, dost thou believe, that these
Three rods of blood-red fire up yonder mean
The doom of England and the wrath of Heaven?
Bishop of London (*passing*). Did ye not cast with bestial violence
Our holy Norman bishops down from all
Their thrones in England? I alone remain.
Why should not Heaven be wroth?
Leofwin.   With us, or thee?
Bishop of London. Did ye not outlaw your archbishop Robert,
Robert of Jumiéges—well-nigh murder him too?
Is there no reason for the wrath of Heaven?
Leofwin. Why then the wrath of Heaven hath three tails,
The devil only one.
                    [*Exit* BISHOP OF LONDON.

(*Enter* ARCHBISHOP STIGAND)
                    Ask *our* Archbishop.
Stigand should know the purposes of Heaven.
Stigand. Not I. I cannot read the face of heaven;
Perhaps our vines will grow the better for it.
Leofwin (*laughing*). He can but read the king's face on his coins.
Stigand. Ay, ay, young lord, *there* the king's face is power.
Gurth. O father, mock not at a public fear,
But tell us, is this pendent hell in heaven
A harm to England?
Stigand.   Ask it of King Edward!
And he may tell thee, *I* am a harm to England.
Old uncanonical Stigand—ask of *me*
Who had my pallium from an Antipope!
Not he the man—for in our windy world
What's up is faith, what's down is heresy.
Our friends, the Normans, holp to shake his chair.
I have a Norman fever on me, son,
And cannot answer sanely . . . What it means?
Ask our broad Earl.
                    [*Pointing to* HAROLD, *who enters.*

Harold (*seeing* GAMEL). Hail, Gamel, son
of Orm!
Albeit no rolling stone, my good friend
Gamel,
Thou hast rounded since we met. Thy life
at home
Is easier than mine here. Look! am I not
Work-wan, flesh-fallen?
    Gamel.   Art thou sick, good Earl?
    Harold. Sick as an autumn swallow for
a voyage,
Sick for an idle week of hawk and hound
Beyond the seas—a change! When camest
thou hither?
    Gamel. To-day, good Earl.
    Harold. Is the North quiet, Gamel?
    Gamel. Nay, there be murmurs, for thy
brother breaks us
With over-taxing—quiet, ay, as yet—
Nothing as yet.
    Harold. Stand by him, mine old friend,
Thou art a great voice in Northumberland!
Advise him: speak him sweetly, he will
hear thee.
He is passionate but honest. Stand thou
by him!
More talk of this to-morrow, if yon weird
sign
Not blast us in our dreams.—Well, father
Stigand—
    [*To* STIGAND, *who advances to him.*
    Stigand (*pointing to the comet*). War
there, my son? is that the doom of
England?
    Harold. Why not the doom of all the
world as well?
For all the world sees it as well as Eng-
land.
These meteors came and went before our
day,
Not harming any: it threatens us no more
Than French or Norman. War? the worst
that follows
Things that seem jerk'd out of the common
rut
Of Nature is the hot religious fool,
Who, seeing war in heaven, for heaven's
credit
Makes it on earth: but look, where Edward
draws
A faint foot hither, leaning upon Tostig.

He hath learnt to love our Tostig much
of late.
    Leofwin. And *he* hath learnt, despite the
tiger in him,
To sleek and supple himself to the king's
hand.
    Gurth. I trust the kingly touch that cures
the evil
May serve to charm the tiger out of him.
    Leofwin. He hath as much of cat as tiger
in him.
Our Tostig loves the hand and not the man.
    Harold. Nay! Better die than lie!

Enter KING, QUEEN, *and* TOSTIG

    Edward.   In heaven signs!
Signs upon earth! signs everywhere! your
Priests
Gross, worldly, simoniacal, unlearn'd!
They scarce can read their Psalter; and
your churches
Uncouth, unhandsome, while in Norman-
land
God speaks thro' abler voices, as He dwells
In statelier shrines. I say not this, as being
Half Norman-blooded, nor as some have
held,
Because I love the Norman better—no,
But dreading God's revenge upon this realm
For narrowness and coldness: and I say it
For the last time perchance, before I go
To find the sweet refreshment of the
Saints.
I have lived a life of utter purity:
I have builded the great church of Holy
Peter:
I have wrought miracles—to God the
glory—
And miracles will in my name be wrought
Hereafter.—I have fought the fight and
go—
I see the flashing of the gates of pearl—
And it is well with me, tho' some of you
Have scorn'd me—ay—but after I am gone
Woe, woe, to England! I have had a vision;
The seven sleepers in the cave at Ephesus
Have turn'd from right to left.
    Harold.   My most dear Master,
What matters? let them turn from left to
right
And sleep again.

Tostig.   Too hardy with thy king!
A life of prayer and fasting well may see
Deeper into the mysteries of heaven
Than thou, good brother.
    Aldwyth (aside).   Sees he into thine,
That thou wouldst have his promise for
    the crown?
    Edward. Tostig says true; my son, thou
    art too hard,
Not stagger'd by this ominous earth and
    heaven:
But heaven and earth are threads of the
    same loom,
Play into one another, and weave the web
That may confound thee yet.
    Harold.   Nay, I trust not,
For I have served thee long and honestly.
    Edward. I know it, son; I am not thank-
    less: thou
Hast broken all my foes, lighten'd for me
The weight of this poor crown, and left me
    time
And peace for prayer to gain a better one.
Twelve years of service! England loves
    thee for it.
Thou art the man to rule her!
    Aldwyth (aside).   So, not Tostig!
    Harold. And after those twelve years a
    boon, my king,
Respite, a holiday: thyself wast wont
To love the chase: thy leave to set my feet
On board, and hunt and hawk beyond the
    seas!
    Edward. What with this flaming horror
    overhead?
    Harold. Well, when it passes then.
    Edward.   Ay if it pass.
Go not to Normandy—go not to Nor-
    mandy.
    Harold. And wherefore not, my king, to
    Normandy?
Is not my brother Wulfnoth hostage there
For my dead father's loyalty to thee?
I pray thee, let me hence and bring him
    home.
    Edward. Not thee, my son: some other
    messenger.
    Harold. And why not me, my lord, to
    Normandy?
Is not the Norman Count thy friend and
    mine?

Edward. I pray thee, do not go to Nor-
    mandy.
    Harold. Because my father drove the
    Normans out
Of England?—That was many a summer
    gone—
Forgotten and forgiven by them and thee.
    Edward. Harold, I will not yield thee
    leave to go.
    Harold. Why then to Flanders. I will
    hawk and hunt
In Flanders.
    Edward. Be there not fair woods and
    fields
In England? Wilful, wilful. Go—the
    Saints
Pilot and prosper all thy wandering out
And homeward. Tostig, I am faint again.
Son Harold, I will in and pray for thee.
        [*Exit, leaning on* TOSTIG, *and fol-
            lowed by* STIGAND, MORCAR, *and*
            COURTIERS.
    Harold. What lies upon the mind of our
    good king
That he should harp this way on Nor-
    mandy?
    Queen. Brother, the king is wiser than
    he seems;
And Tostig knows it; Tostig loves the king.
    Harold. And love should know; and—
    be the king so wise,—
Then Tostig too were wiser than he seems.
I love the man but not his phantasies.

(*Re-enter* TOSTIG)

Well, brother,
When didst thou hear from thy Northum-
    bria?
    Tostig. When did I hear aught but this
    'When' from thee?
Leave me alone, brother, with my North-
    umbria:
She is *my* mistress, let *me* look to her!
The King hath made me Earl; make me
    not fool!
Nor make the King a fool, who made me
    Earl!
    Harold. No, Tostig—lest I make myself
    a fool
Who made the King who made thee, make
    thee Earl.

610

Tostig. Why chafe me then? Thou knowest I soon go wild.

Gurth. Come, come! as yet thou art not gone so wild

But thou canst hear the best and wisest of us.

Harold. So says old Gurth, not I: yet hear! thine earldom,

Tostig, hath been a kingdom. Their old crown

Is yet a force among them, a sun set

But leaving light enough for Alfgar's house

To strike thee down by—nay, this ghastly glare

May heat their fancies.

Tostig.   My most worthy brother,

Thou art the quietest man in all the world—

Ay, ay and wise in peace and great in war—

Pray God the people choose thee for their king!

But all the powers of the house of Godwin

Are not enframed in thee.

Harold.   Thank the Saints, no!

But thou hast drain'd them shallow by thy tolls,

And thou art ever here about the King:

Thine absence well may seem a want of care.

Cling to their love; for, now the sons of Godwin

Sit topmost in the field of England, envy,

Like the rough bear beneath the tree, good brother,

Waits till the man let go.

Tostig.   Good counsel truly!

I heard from my Northumbria yesterday.

Harold. How goes it then with thy Northumbria? Well?

Tostig. And wouldst thou that it went aught else than well?

Harold. I would it went as well as with mine earldom,

Leofwin's and Gurth's.

Tostig.   Ye govern milder men.

Gurth. We have made them milder by just government.

Tostig. Ay, ever give yourselves your own good word.

Leofwin. An honest gift, by all the Saints, if giver

And taker be but honest! but they bribe

Each other, and so often, an honest world

Will not believe them.

Harold.   I may tell thee, Tostig,

I heard from thy Northumberland to-day.

Tostig. From spies of thine to spy my nakedness

In my poor North!

Harold.   There is a movement there,

A blind one—nothing yet.

Tostig.   Crush it at once

With all the power I have!—I must—I will!—

Crush it half-born! Fool still? or wisdom there,

My wise head-shaking Harold?

Harold.   Make not thou

The nothing something. Wisdom when in power

And wisest, should not frown as Power, but smile

As kindness, watching all, till the true *must*

Shall make her strike as Power: but when to strike—

O Tostig, O dear brother—If they prance,

Rein in, not lash them, lest they rear and run

And break both neck and axle.

Tostig.   Good again!

Good counsel tho' scarce needed. Pour not water

In the full vessel running out at top

To swamp the house.

Leofwin.   Nor thou be a wild thing

Out of the waste, to turn and bite the hand

Would help thee from the trap.

Tostig.   Thou playest in tune.

Leofwin. To the deaf adder thee, that wilt not dance

However wisely charm'd.

Tostig.   No more, no more!

Gurth. I likewise cry 'no more.' Unwholesome talk

For Godwin's house! Leofwin, thou hast a tongue!

Tostig, thou look'st as thou wouldst spring upon him.

St. Olaf, not while I am by! Come, come,

Join hands, let brethren dwell in unity;

Let kith and kin stand close as our shield-wall,

Who breaks us then? I say, thou hast a
   tongue,
And Tostig is not stout enough to bear it.
Vex him not, Leofwin.
   Tostig.   No, I am not vext,—
Altho' ye seek to vex me, one and all.
I have to make report of my good earldom
To the good king who gave it—not to
   you—
Not any of you.—I am not vext at all.
   Harold. The king? the king is ever at
   his prayers;
In all that handles matter of the state
I am the king.
   Tostig.   That shalt thou never be
If I can thwart thee.
   Harold.   Brother, brother!
   Tostig.   Away!
               [*Exit* TOSTIG.
   Queen. Spite of this grisly star ye three
   must gall
Poor Tostig.
   Leofwin.   Tostig, sister, galls himself;
He cannot smell a rose but pricks his nose
Against the thorn, and rails against the
   rose.
   Queen. I am the only rose of all the stock
That never thorn'd him; Edward loves
   him, so
Ye hate him. Harold always hated him.
Why—how they fought when boys—and,
   Holy Mary!
How Harold used to beat him!
   Harold.   Why, boys will fight.
Leofwin would often fight me, and I beat
   him.
Even old Gurth would fight. I had much
   ado
To hold mine own against old Gurth. Old
   Gurth,
We fought like great states for grave cause;
   but Tostig—
On a sudden—at a something—for a
   nothing—
The boy would fist me hard, and when we
   fought
I conquer'd, and he loved me none the less,
Till thou wouldst get him all apart, and
   tell him
That where he was but worsted, he was
   wrong'd.

Ah! thou hast taught the king to spoil
   him too;
Now the spoilt child sways both. Take
   heed, take heed;
Thou art the Queen; ye are boy and girl
   no more:
Side not with Tostig in any violence,
Lest thou be sideways guilty of the
   violence.
   Queen. Come fall not foul on me. I leave
   thee, brother.
   Harold. Nay, my good sister—
       [*Exeunt* QUEEN, HAROLD, GURTH, *and*
       LEOFWIN.
   Aldwyth.   Gamel, son of Orm,
What thinkest thou this means?
            [*Pointing to the comet.*
   Gamel.   War, my dear lady,
War, waste, plague, famine, all maligni-
   ties.
   Aldwyth. It means the fall of Tostig
   from his earldom.
   Gamel. That were too small a matter for
   a comet!
   Aldwyth. It means the lifting of the
   house of Alfgar.
   Gamel. Too small! a comet would not
   show for that!
   Aldwyth. Not small for thee, if thou
   canst compass it.
   Gamel. Thy love?
   Aldwyth.   As much as I can give
   thee, man;
This Tostig is, or like to be, a tyrant;
Stir up thy people: oust him!
   Gamel.   And thy love?
   Aldwyth. As much as thou canst bear.
   Gamel.   I can bear all,
And not be giddy.
   Aldwyth. No more now: to-morrow.

SCENE II

*In the Garden. The King's House near
London. Sunset*

   Edith. Mad for thy mate, passionate
   nightingale . . .
I love thee for it—ay, but stay a moment;
He can but stay a moment: he is going.
I fain would hear him coming! . . . near
   me . . . near,

Somewhere—To draw him nearer with a
  charm
Like thine to thine.

        (*Singing*)

Love is come with a song and a smile,
Welcome Love with a smile and a song:
Love can stay but a little while.
Why cannot he stay? They call him away:
Ye do him wrong, ye do him wrong;
Love will stay for a whole life long.

        Enter HAROLD

Harold. The nightingales in Havering-
  in-the-Bower
Sang out their loves so loud, that Edward's
  prayers
Were deafen'd and he pray'd them dumb,
  and thus
I dumb thee too, my wingless nightingale!
                [*Kissing her.*
Edith. Thou art my music! Would their
  wings were mine
To follow thee to Flanders! Must thou go?
Harold. Not must, but will. It is but for
  one moon.
Edith. Leaving so many foes in Edward's
  hall
To league against thy weal. The Lady
  Aldwyth
Was here to-day, and when she touch'd on
  thee,
She stammer'd in her hate; I am sure she
  hates thee,
Pants for thy blood.
Harold.   Well, I have given her
  cause—
I fear no woman.
Edith.   Hate not one who felt
Some pity for thy hater! I am sure
Her morning wanted sunlight, she so
  praised
The convent and lone life—within the
  pale—
Beyond the passion. Nay—she held with
  Edward,
At least methought she held with holy
  Edward,
That marriage was half sin.
Harold.   A lesson worth
Finger and thumb—thus (*snaps his fingers*).
                And my answer to it—

See here—an interwoven H and E!
Take thou this ring; I will demand his
  ward
From Edward when I come again. Ay,
  would she?
She to shut up my blossom in the dark!
Thou art *my* nun, thy cloister in mine
  arms.
Edith (*taking the ring*). Yea, but Earl
  Tostig—
Harold.   That's a truer fear!
For if the North take fire, I should be back;
I shall be, soon enough.
Edith.   Ay, but last night
An evil dream that ever came and went—
Harold. A gnat that vext thy pillow!
  Had I been by,
I would have spoil'd his horn. My girl,
  what was it?
Edith. Oh! that thou wert not going!
For so methought it was our marriage-
  morn,
And while we stood together, a dead man
Rose from behind the altar, tore away
My marriage ring, and rent my bridal veil;
And then I turn'd, and saw the church all
  fill'd
With dead men upright from their graves,
  and all
The dead men made at thee to murder
  thee,
But thou didst back thyself against a pillar,
And strike among them with thy battle-
  axe—
There, what a dream!
Harold.   Well, well—a dream
  —no more!
Edith. Did not Heaven speak to men in
  dreams of old?
Harold. Ay—well—of old. I tell thee
  what, my child;
Thou hast misread this merry dream of
  thine,
Taken the rifted pillars of the wood
For smooth stone columns of the sanc-
  tuary,
The shadows of a hundred fat dead deer
For dead men's ghosts. True, that the
  battle-axe
Was out of place; it should have been the
  bow.—

Come, thou shalt dream no more such
    dreams; I swear it,
By mine own eyes—and these two sap-
    phires—these
Twin rubies, that are amulets against all
The kisses of all kind of womankind
In Flanders, till the sea shall roll me back
To tumble at thy feet.
    Edith.   That would but shame me,
Rather than make me vain. The sea may
    roll
Sand, shingle, shore-weed, not the living
    rock
Which guards the land.
    Harold.   Except it be a soft one,
And undereaten to the fall. Mine amulet...
This last ... upon thine eyelids, to shut in
A happier dream. Sleep, sleep, and thou
    shalt see
My grayhounds fleeting like a beam of
    light,
And hear my peregrine and her bells in
    heaven;
And other bells on earth, which yet are
    heaven's;
Guess what they be.
    Edith.   He cannot guess who knows.
Farewell, my king.
    Harold. Not yet, but then—my queen.
                         [*Exeunt.*

    Enter ALDWYTH *from the thicket*

Aldwyth. The kiss that charms thine
    eyelids into sleep,
Will hold mine waking. Hate him? I could
    love him
More, tenfold, than this fearful child can
    do;
Griffyth I hated: why not hate the foe
Of England? Griffyth when I saw him
    flee,
Chased deer-like up his mountains, all the
    blood
That should have only pulsed for Griffyth,
    beat
For his pursuer. I love him or think I love
    him.
If he were King of England, I his queen,
I might be sure of it. Nay, I do love him.—
She must be cloister'd somehow, lest the
    king

Should yield his ward to Harold's will.
    What harm?
She hath but blood enough to live, not
    love.—
When Harold goes and Tostig, shall I play
The craftier Tostig with him? fawn upon
    him?
Chime in with all? 'O thou more saint
    than king!'
And that were true enough. 'O blessed
    relics!'
'O Holy Peter!' If he found me thus,
Harold might hate me; he is broad and
    honest,
Breathing an easy gladness . . . not like
    Aldwyth . . .
For which I strangely love him. Should
    not England
Love Aldwyth, if she stay the feuds that
    part
The sons of Godwin from the sons of
    Alfgar
By such a marrying? Courage, noble
    Aldwyth!
Let all thy people bless thee!
                  Our wild Tostig,
Edward hath made him Earl: he would be
    king:—
The dog that snapt the shadow, dropt the
    bone.—
I trust he may do well, this Gamel, whom
I play upon, that he may play the note
Whereat the dog shall howl and run, and
    Harold
Hear the king's music, all alone with him,
Pronounced his heir of England.
I see the goal and half the way to it.—
Peace-lover is our Harold for the sake
Of England's wholeness—so—to shake
    the North
With earthquake and disruption—some
    division—
Then fling mine own fair person in the gap
A sacrifice to Harold, a peace-offering,
A scape-goat marriage—all the sins of both
The houses on mine head—then a fair life
And bless the Queen of England.
    Morcar (coming from the thicket). Art
    thou assured
By this, that Harold loves but Edith?
    Aldwyth.   Morcar!

Why creep'st thou like a timorous beast of
    prey
Out of the bush by night?
    Morcar.   I follow'd thee.
    Aldwyth. Follow my lead, and I will
    make thee earl.
    Morcar. What lead then?
    Aldwyth.   Thou shalt flash it secretly
Among the good Northumbrian folk,
    that I—
That Harold loves me—yea, and presently
That I and Harold are betroth'd—and
    last—
Perchance that Harold wrongs me; tho' I
    would not
That it should come to that.
    Morcar.   I will both flash
And thunder for thee.
    Aldwyth.   I said 'secretly;'
It is the flash that murders, the poor
    thunder
Never harm'd head.
    Morcar. But thunder may bring down
That which the flash hath stricken.
    Aldwyth.   Down with Tostig!
That first of all.—And when doth Harold go?
    Morcar. To-morrow—first to Bosham,
    then to Flanders.
    Aldwyth. Not to come back till Tostig
    shall have shown
And redden'd with his people's blood the
    teeth
That shall be broken by us—yea, and thou
Chair'd in his place. Good-night, and
    dream thyself
Their chosen Earl.   [*Exit* ALDWYTH.
    Morcar.   Earl first, and after that
Who knows I may not dream myself their
    king!

ACT II

SCENE I

Seashore. Ponthieu. Night

HAROLD *and his* MEN, *wrecked*

    Harold. Friends, in that last inhospitable
    plunge
Our boat hath burst her ribs; but ours are
    whole;
I have but bark'd my hands.

    Attendant.   I dug mine into
My old fast friend the shore, and clinging
    thus
Felt the remorseless outdraught of the
    deep
Haul like a great strong fellow at my legs,
And then I rose and ran. The blast that
    came
So suddenly hath fallen as suddenly—
Put thou the comet and this blast to-
    gether—
    Harold. Put thou thyself and mother-
    wit together.
Be not a fool!

(*Enter* FISHERMEN *with torches,* HAROLD
    going up to one of them, ROLF)

                Wicked sea-will-o'-the-wisp!
Wolf of the shore! dog, with thy lying
    lights
Thou hast betray'd us on these rocks of
    thine!
    Rolf. Ay, but thou liest as loud as the
black herring-pond behind thee. We be
fishermen; I came to see after my nets.
    Harold. To drag us into them. Fisher-
men? devils!
Who, while ye fish for men with your false
    fires,
Let the great Devil fish for your own souls.
    Rolf. Nay then, we be liker the blessed
Apostles; *they* were fishers of men, Father
Jean says.
    Harold. I had liefer that the fish had
    swallowed me,
Like Jonah, than have known there were
    such devils.
What's to be done?
                [*To his* MEN—*goes apart with them.*
    Fisherman. Rolf, what fish did swallow
    Jonah?
    Rolf. A whale!
    Fisherman. Then a whale to a whelk we
have swallowed the King of England. I
saw him over there. Look thee, Rolf, when
I was down in the fever, *she* was down with
the hunger, and thou didst stand by her
and give her thy crabs, and set her up
again, till now, by the patient Saints, she's
as crabb'd as ever.

Rolf. And I'll give her my crabs again, when thou art down again.

Fisherman. I thank thee, Rolf. Run thou to Count Guy; he is hard at hand. Tell him what hath crept into our creel, and he will fee thee as freely as he will wrench this outlander's ransom out of him—and why not? for what right had he to get himself wrecked on another man's land?

Rolf. Thou art the human-heartedest, Christian-charitiest of all crab-catchers. Share and share alike!   [*Exit.*

Harold (to FISHERMAN). Fellow, dost thou catch crabs?

Fisherman. As few as I may in a wind, and less than I would in a calm. Ay!

Harold. I have a mind that thou shalt catch no more.

Fisherman. How?

Harold. I have a mind to brain thee with mine axe.

Fisherman. Ay, do, do, and our great Count-crab will make his nippers meet in thine heart; he'll sweat it out of thee, he'll sweat it out of thee. Look, he's here! He'll speak for himself! Hold thine own, if thou canst!

Enter GUY, COUNT OF PONTHIEU

Harold. Guy, Count of Ponthieu?

Guy.   Harold, Earl of Wessex!

Harold. Thy villains with their lying lights have wreck'd us!

Guy. Art thou not Earl of Wessex?

Harold.   In mine earldom
A man may hang gold bracelets on a bush,
And leave them for a year, and coming back
Find them again.

Guy.   Thou art a mighty man
In thine own earldom!

Harold.   Were such murderous liars
In Wessex—if I caught them, they should hang
Cliff-gibbeted for sea-marks; our sea-mew
Winging their only wail!

Guy.   Ay, but my men
Hold that the shipwreckt are accursed of God;—
What hinders me to hold with mine own men?

Harold. The Christian manhood of the man who reigns!

Guy. Ay, rave thy worst, but in our oubliettes
Thou shalt or rot or ransom. Hale him hence!   [*To one of his* ATTENDANTS.
Fly thou to William; tell him we have Harold.

SCENE II

Bayeux. Palace

COUNT WILLIAM *and* WILLIAM MALET

William. We hold our Saxon woodcock in the springe,
But he begins to flutter. As I think
He was thine host in England when I went
To visit Edward.

Malet.   Yea, and there, my lord,
To make allowance for their rougher fashions,
I found him all a noble host should be.

William. Thou art his friend: thou know'st my claim on England
Thro' Edward's promise: we have him in the toils.
And it were well, if thou shouldst let him feel,
How dense a fold of danger nets him round,
So that he bristle himself against my will.

Malet. What would I do, my lord, if I were you?

William. What wouldst thou do?

Malet.   My lord, he is thy guest.

William. Nay, by the splendour of God, no guest of mine.
He came not to see me, had past me by
To hunt and hawk elsewhere, save for the fate
Which hunted *him* when that un-Saxon blast,
And bolts of thunder moulded in high heaven
To serve the Norman purpose, drave and crack'd
His boat on Ponthieu beach; where our friend Guy
Had wrung his ransom from him by the rack,

616

But that I stept between and purchased
him,
Translating his captivity from Guy
To mine own hearth at Bayeux, where he
sits
My ransom'd prisoner.

Malet.   Well, if not with gold,
With golden deeds and iron strokes that
brought
Thy war with Brittany to a goodlier close
Than else had been, he paid his ransom
back.

William. So that henceforth they are not
like to league
With Harold against *me*.

Malet.   A marvel, how
He from the liquid sands of Coesnon
Haled thy shore-swallow'd, armour'd Nor-
mans up
To fight for thee again!

William.   Perchance against
Their saver, save thou save him from himself.

Malet. But I should let him home again,
my lord.

William. Simple! let fly the bird within
the hand,
To catch the bird again within the bush!
No.
Smooth thou my way, before he clash
with me;
I want his voice in England for the crown,
I want thy voice with him to bring him
round;
And being brave he must be subtly cow'd,
And being truthful wrought upon to swear
Vows that he dare not break. England our
own
Thro' Harold's help, he shall be my dear
friend
As well as thine, and thou thyself shalt have
Large lordship there of lands and territory.

Malet. I knew thy purpose; he and
Wulfnoth never
Have met, except in public; shall they
meet
In private? I have often talk'd with
Wulfnoth,
And stuff'd the boy with fears that these
may act
On Harold when they meet.

William.   Then let them meet!

Malet. I can but love this noble, honest
Harold.

William. Love him! why not? thine is a
loving office,
I have commission'd thee to save the man:
Help the good ship, showing the sunken
rock,
Or he is wreckt for ever.

Enter WILLIAM RUFUS

William Rufus.   Father.

William.   Well, boy.

William Rufus. They have taken away
the toy thou gavest me,
The Norman knight.

William.   Why, boy?

William Rufus.   Because I broke
The horse's leg—it was mine own to
break;
I like to have my toys, and break them too.

William. Well, thou shalt have another
Norman knight!

William Rufus. And may I break his
legs?

William. Yea,—get thee gone!

William Rufus. I'll tell them I have had
my way with thee.   [*Exit.*

Malet. I never knew thee check thy will
for ought
Save for the prattling of thy little ones.

William. Who shall be kings of England.
I am heir
Of England by the promise of her king.

Malet. But there the great Assembly
choose their king,
The choice of England is the voice of
England.

William. I will be king of England by the
laws,
The choice, and voice of England.

Malet.   Can that be?

William. The voice of any people is the
sword
That guards them, or the sword that beats
them down.
Here comes the would-be what I will be
. . . kinglike . . .
Tho' scarce at ease; for, save our meshes
break,
More kinglike he than like to prove a king.

(*Enter* HAROLD, *musing, with his eyes on the
ground*)

He sees me not—and yet he dreams of me.
Earl, wilt thou fly my falcons this fair day?
They are of the best, strong-wing'd against
the wind.
 Harold (*looking up suddenly, having
 caught but the last word*). Which way
 does it blow?
 William. Blowing for England, ha?
Not yet. Thou hast not learnt thy quarters
here.
The winds so cross and jostle among these
towers.
 Harold. Count of the Normans, thou
 hast ransom'd us,
Maintain'd, and entertain'd us royally!
 William. And thou for us hast fought as
 loyally,
Which binds us friendship-fast for ever!
 Harold.   Good!
But lest we turn the scale of courtesy
By too much pressure on it, I would fain,
Since thou hast promised Wulfnoth home
with us,
Be home again with Wulfnoth.
 William.   Stay—as yet
Thou hast but seen how Norman hands
can strike,
But walk'd our Norman field, scarce
touch'd or tasted
The splendours of our Court.
 Harold.   I am in no mood:
I should be as the shadow of a cloud
Crossing your light.
 William.   Nay, rest a week or two,
And we will fill thee full of Norman sun,
And send thee back among thine island mists
With laughter.
 Harold.   Count, I thank thee, but
 had rather
Breathe the free wind from off our Saxon
downs,
Tho' charged with all the wet of all the
west.
 William. Why if thou wilt, so let it be—
thou shalt.
That were a graceless hospitality
To chain the free guest to the banquet-
board;

To-morrow we will ride with thee to
Harfleur,
And see thee shipt, and pray in thy behalf
For happier homeward winds than that
which crack'd
Thy bark at Ponthieu,—yet to us, in faith,
A happy one—whereby we came to know
Thy valour and thy value, noble earl.
Ay, and perchance a happy one for thee,
Provided—I will go with thee to-morrow—
Nay—but there be conditions, easy ones,
So thou, fair friend, will take them easily.

Enter PAGE

 Page. My lord, there is a post from over
 seas
With news for thee.   [*Exit* PAGE.
 William.   Come, Malet, let us hear!
    [*Exeunt* COUNT WILLIAM *and* MALET.
 Harold. Conditions? What conditions?
 pay him back
His ransom? 'easy'—that were easy—
nay—
No money-lover he! What said the King?
'I pray you do not go to Normandy.'
And fate hath blown me hither, bound
me too
With bitter obligation to the Count—
Have I not fought it out? What did he
mean?
There lodged a gleaming grimness in his
eyes,
Gave his shorn smile the lie. The walls
oppress me,
And yon huge keep that hinders half the
heaven.
Free air! free field!
    [*Moves to go out. A* MAN-AT-ARMS
    follows him.
 Harold (*to the* MAN-AT-ARMS). I need
 thee not. Why dost thou follow me?
 Man-at-arms. I have the count's com-
 mands to follow thee.
 Harold. What then? Am I in danger in
 this court?
 Man-at-arms. I cannot tell. I have the
 Count's commands.
 Harold. Stand out of earshot then, and
 keep me still
In eyeshot.

Man-at-arms.   Yea, lord Harold.
                              [*Withdraws.*
Harold.   And arm'd men
Ever keep watch beside my chamber door,
And if I walk within the lonely wood,
There is an arm'd man ever glides behind!

(*Enter* MALET)

Why am I follow'd, haunted, harass'd,
    watch'd?
See yonder!
              [*Pointing to the* MAN-AT-ARMS.
Malet.   'Tis the good Count's care
    for thee!
The Normans love thee not, nor thou the
    Normans,
Or—so they deem.
Harold.   But wherefore is the wind,
Which way soever the vane-arrow swing,
Not ever fair for England? Why but now
He said (thou heardst him) that I must not
    hence
Save on conditions.
Malet.   So in truth he said.
Harold. Malet, thy mother was an Eng-
lishwoman;
There somewhere beats an English pulse
    in thee!
Malet. Well—for my mother's sake I
    love your England,
But for my father I love Normandy.
Harold. Speak for thy mother's sake,
    and tell me true.
Malet. Then for my mother's sake and
    England's sake
That suffers in the daily want of thee,
Obey the Count's conditions, my good
    friend.
Harold. How, Malet, if they be not
    honourable!
Malet. Seem to obey them.
Harold.   Better die than lie!
Malet. Choose therefore whether thou
    wilt have thy conscience
White as a maiden's hand, or whether
    England
Be shatter'd into fragments.
Harold.   News from England?
Malet. Morcar and Edwin have stirr'd
    up the Thanes

Against thy brother Tostig's governance;
And all the North of Humber is one storm.
Harold. I should be there, Malet, I
    should be there!
Malet. And Tostig in his own hall on
    suspicion
Hath massacred the Thane that was his
    guest,
Gamel, the son of Orm: and there be more
As villainously slain.
Harold.   The wolf! the beast!
Ill news for guests, ha, Malet! More?
    What more?
What do they say? did Edward know of this?
Malet. They say, his wife was knowing
    and abetting.
Harold. They say, his wife!—To marry
    and have no husband
Makes the wife fool. My God, I should be
    there.
I'll hack my way to the sea.
Malet.   Thou canst not, Harold;
Our Duke is all between thee and the sea,
Our Duke is all about thee like a God;
All passes block'd. Obey him, speak him
    fair,
For he is only debonair to those
That follow where he leads, but stark as
    death
To those that cross him.—Look thou, here
    is Wulfnoth!
I leave thee to thy talk with him alone;
How wan, poor lad! how sick and sad for
    home!   [*Exit* MALET.
Harold (*muttering*). Go not to Normandy
    —go not to Normandy!

(*Enter* WULFNOTH)

Poor brother! still a hostage!
Wulfnoth.   Yea, and I
Shall see the dewy kiss of dawn no more
Make blush the maiden-white of our tall
    cliffs,
Nor mark the sea-bird rouse himself and
    hover
Above the windy ripple, and fill the sky
With free sea-laughter—never—save in-
    deed
Thou canst make yield this iron-mooded
    Duke
To let me go.

Harold. Why, brother, so he will;
But on conditions. Canst thou guess at
them?
Wulfnoth. Draw nearer,—I was in the
corridor,
I saw him coming with his brother Odo
The Bayeux bishop, and I hid myself.
Harold. They did thee wrong who made
thee hostage; thou
Wast ever fearful.
Wulfnoth. And he spoke—I heard
him—
'This Harold is not of the royal blood,
Can have no right to the crown,' and Odo
said,
'Thine is the right, for thine the might; he
is here,
And yonder is thy keep.'
Harold. No, Wulfnoth, no.
Wulfnoth. And William laugh'd and
swore that might was right,
Far as he knew in this poor world of ours—
'Marry, the Saints must go along with us,
And, brother, we will find a way,' said he—
Yea, yea, he would be king of England.
Harold. Never!
Wulfnoth. Yea, but thou must not this
way answer *him.*
Harold. Is it not better still to speak the
truth?
Wulfnoth. Not here, or thou wilt never
hence nor I:
For in the racing toward this golden goal
He turns not right or left, but tramples flat
Whatever thwarts him; hast thou never
heard
His savagery at Alençon,—the town
Hung out raw hides along their walls, and
cried
'Work for the tanner.'
Harold. That had anger'd *me*
Had I been William.
Wulfnoth. Nay, but he had prisoners,
He tore their eyes out, sliced their hands
away,
And flung them streaming o'er the battle-
ments
Upon the heads of those who walk'd
within—
O speak him fair, Harold, for thine own
sake.

Harold. Your Welshman says, 'The
Truth against the World,'
Much more the truth against myself.
Wulfnoth. Thyself?
But for my sake, oh brother! oh! for my
sake!
Harold. Poor Wulfnoth! do they not
entreat thee well?
Wulfnoth. I see the blackness of my
dungeon loom
Across their lamps of revel, and beyond
The merriest murmurs of their banquet
clank
The shackles that will bind me to the wall.
Harold. Too fearful still!
Wulfnoth. Oh no, no—speak
him fair!
Call it to temporize; and not to lie;
Harold, I do not counsel thee to lie.
The man that hath to foil a murderous aim
May, surely, play with words.
Harold. Words are the man.
Not ev'n for thy sake, brother, would I lie.
Wulfnoth. Then for thine Edith?
Harold. There thou prick'st me
deep.
Wulfnoth. And for our Mother England?
Harold. Deeper still.
Wulfnoth. And deeper still the deep-
down oubliette,
Down thirty feet below the smiling day—
In blackness—dogs' food thrown upon thy
head.
And over thee the suns arise and set,
And the lark sings, the sweet stars come
and go,
And men are at their markets, in their
fields,
And woo their loves and have forgotten
thee;
And thou art upright in thy living grave,
Where there is barely room to shift thy
side,
And all thine England hath forgotten thee;
And he our lazy-pious Norman King,
With all his Normans round him once again,
Counts his old beads, and hath forgotten
thee.
Harold. Thou art of my blood, and so
methinks, my boy,
Thy fears infect me beyond reason. Peace!

Wulfnoth. And then our fiery Tostig,
while thy hands
Are palsied here, if his Northumbrians
rise
And hurl him from them,—I have heard
the Normans
Count upon this confusion—may he not
make
A league with William, so to bring him
back?
Harold. That lies within the shadow of
the chance.
Wulfnoth. And like a river in flood thro'
a burst dam
Descends the ruthless Norman—our good
King
Kneels mumbling some old bone—our
helpless folk
Are wash'd away, wailing, in their own
blood—
Harold. Wailing! not warring? Boy,
thou hast forgotten
That thou art English.
Wulfnoth. Then our modest women—
I know the Norman license—thine own
Edith—
Harold. No more! I will not hear thee—
William comes.
Wulfnoth. I dare not well be seen in talk
with thee.
Make thou not mention that I spake with
thee.
    [*Moves away to the back of the stage.*

Enter WILLIAM, MALET, *and* OFFICER

Officer. We have the man that rail'd
against thy birth.
William. Tear out his tongue.
Officer.   He shall not rail again.
He said that he should see confusion fall
On thee and on thine house.
William.   Tear out his eyes,
And plunge him into prison.
Officer.   It shall be done.
    [*Exit* OFFICER.
William. Look not amazed, fair earl!
Better leave undone
Than do by halves—tongueless and eye-
less, prison'd—
Harold. Better methinks have slain the
man at once!

William. We have respect for man's
immortal soul,
We seldom take man's life, except in war;
It frights the traitor more to maim and
blind.
Harold. In mine own land I should have
scorn'd the man,
Or lash'd his rascal back, and let him go.
William. And let him go? To slander
thee again!
Yet in thine own land in thy father's day
They blinded my young kinsman, Alfred
—ay,
Some said it was thy father's deed.
Harold.   They lied.
William. But thou and he—whom at thy
word, for thou
Art known a speaker of the truth, I free
From this foul charge—
Harold.   Nay, nay, he freed himself
By oath and compurgation from the charge.
The king, the lords, the people clear'd him
of it.
William. But thou and he drove our
good Normans out
From England, and this rankles in us yet.
Archbishop Robert hardly scaped with life.
Harold. Archbishop Robert! Robert the
Archbishop!
Robert of Jumiéges, he that—
Malet.   Quiet! quiet!
Harold. Count! if there sat within the
Norman chair
A ruler all for England—one who fill'd
All offices, all bishopricks with English—
We could not move from Dover to the
Humber
Saving thro' Norman bishopricks—I say
Ye would applaud that Norman who
should drive
The stranger to the fiends!
William.   Why, that is reason!
Warrior thou art, and mighty wise withal!
Ay, ay, but many among our Norman lords
Hate thee for this, and press upon me—
saying
God and the sea have given thee to our
hands—
To plunge thee into life-long prison
here:—
Yet I hold out against them, as I may,

Yea—would hold out, yea, tho' they should
  revolt—
For thou hast done the battle in my cause;
I am thy fastest friend in Normandy.
  Harold. I am doubly bound to thee . . .
  if this be so.
  William. And I would bind thee more,
  and would myself
Be bounden to thee more.
  Harold.   Then let me hence
With Wulfnoth to King Edward.
  William.   So we will.
We hear he hath not long to live.
  Harold.   It may be.
  William. Why then the heir of England,
  who is he?
  Harold. The Atheling is nearest to the
  throne.
  William. But sickly, slight, half-witted
  and a child,
Will England have him king?
  Harold.   It may be, no.
  William. And hath King Edward not
  pronounced his heir?
  Harold. Not that I know.
  William.   When he was here in
  Normandy,
He loved us and we him, because we found
  him
A Norman of the Normans.
  Harold.   So did we.
  William. A gentle, gracious, pure and
  saintly man!
And grateful to the hand that shielded
  him,
He promised that if ever he were king
In England, he would give his kingly voice
To me as his successor. Knowest thou
  this?
  Harold. I learn it now.
  William.   Thou knowest I am his
  cousin,
And that my wife descends from Alfred?
  Harold.   Ay.
  William. Who hath a better claim then
  to the crown
So that ye will not crown the Atheling?
  Harold. None that I know . . . if that but
  hung upon
King Edward's will.
  William.   Wilt *thou* uphold my claim?

Malet (*aside to* HAROLD). Be careful of
  thine answer, my good friend.
Wulfnoth (*aside to* HAROLD). Oh! Harold,
  for my sake and for thine own!
  Harold. Ay . . . if the king have not
  revoked his promise.
  William. But hath he done it then?
  Harold.   Not that I know.
  William. Good, good, and thou wilt help
  me to the crown?
  Harold. Ay . . . if the Witan will consent
  to this.
  William. Thou art the mightiest voice in
  England, man,
Thy voice will lead the Witan—shall I
  have it?
Wulfnoth (*aside to* HAROLD). Oh! Harold,
  if thou love thine Edith, ay.
  Harold. Ay, if—
Malet (*aside to* HAROLD). Thine 'ifs' will
  sear thine eyes out—ay.
  William. I ask thee, wilt thou help me
  to the crown?
And I will make thee my great Earl of
  Earls,
Foremost in England and in Normandy;
Thou shalt be verily king—all but the
  name—
For I shall most sojourn in Normandy;
And thou be my vice-king in England.
  Speak.
Wulfnoth (*aside to* HAROLD). Ay, brother
  —for the sake of England—ay.
  Harold. My lord—
Malet (*aside to* HAROLD). Take heed now
  Harold. Ay.
  William.   I am content,
For thou art truthful, and thy word thy
  bond.
To-morrow will we ride with thee to
  Harfleur.   [*Exit* WILLIAM.
Malet. Harold, I am thy friend, one life
  with thee,
And even as I should bless thee saving
  mine,
I thank thee now for having saved thyself.
                       [*Exit* MALET.
  Harold. For having lost myself to save
  myself,
Said 'ay' when I meant 'no,' lied like
  a lad

That dreads the pendent scourge, said 'ay'
    for 'no'!
Ay! No!—he hath not bound me by an
    oath—
Is 'ay' an oath? is 'ay' strong as an oath?
Or is it the same sin to break my word
As break mine oath? He call'd my word
    my bond!
He is a liar who knows I am a liar,
And makes believe that he believes my
    word—
The crime be on his head—not bounden
    —no.
    [*Suddenly doors are flung open, dis-*
    covering in an inner hall COUNT
    WILLIAM *in his state robes, seated*
    upon his throne, between two Bishops,
    ODO OF BAYEUX *being one: in the*
    centre of the hall an ark covered with
    cloth of gold; and on either side of it
    the Norman barons.

Enter a JAILOR *before* WILLIAM'S *throne.*

William (*to* JAILOR). Knave, hast thou
    let thy prisoner scape?
Jailor.   Sir Count,
He had but one foot, he must have hopt
    away,
Yea, some familiar spirit must have help'd
    him.
William. Woe knave to thy familiar and
    to thee!
Give me thy keys.   [*They fall clashing.*
Nay let them lie. Stand there and wait my
    will.   [*The* JAILOR *stands aside.*
William (*to* HAROLD). Hast thou such
    trustless jailors in thy North?
Harold. We have few prisoners in mine
    earldom there,
So less chance for false keepers.
William.   We have heard
Of thy just, mild, and equal governance;
Honour to thee! thou art perfect in all
    honour!
Thy naked word thy bond! confirm it now
Before our gather'd Norman baronage,
For they will not believe thee—as I believe.
    [*Descends from his throne and stands*
    by the ark.
Let all men here bear witness of our bond!
    [*Beckons to* HAROLD, *who advances.*

Enter MALET *behind him.*

Lay thou thy hand upon this golden pall!
Behold the jewel of St. Pancratius
Woven into the gold. Swear thou on this!
Harold. What should I swear? Why
    should I swear on this?
William (*savagely*). Swear thou to help
    me to the crown of England.
Malet (*whispering* HAROLD). My friend,
    thou hast gone too far to palter now.
Wulfnoth (*whispering* HAROLD). Swear
    thou to-day, to-morrow is thine own.
Harold. I swear to help thee to the
    crown of England . . .
According as King Edward promises.
William. Thou must swear absolutely,
    noble Earl.
Malet (*whispering*). Delay is death to
    thee, ruin to England.
Wulfnoth (*whispering*). Swear, dearest
    brother, I beseech thee, swear!
Harold (*putting his hand on the jewel*).
    I swear to help thee to the crown of
    England.
William. Thanks, truthful Earl; I did
    not doubt thy word,
But that my barons might believe thy
    word,
And that the Holy Saints of Normandy
When thou art home in England, with
    thine own,
Might strengthen thee in keeping of thy
    word,
I made thee swear.—Show him by whom
    he hath sworn.
    [*The two* Bishops *advance, and raise*
    the cloth of gold. The bodies and bones
    of Saints are seen lying in the ark.
The holy bones of all the Canonised
From all the holiest shrines in Normandy!
Harold. Horrible! [*They let the cloth fall*
    again.
William. Ay, for thou hast sworn an
    oath
Which, if not kept, would make the hard
    earth rive
To the very Devil's horns, the bright sky
    cleave
To the very feet of God, and send her
    hosts

Of injured Saints to scatter sparks of
plague
Thro' all your cities, blast your infants,
dash
The torch of war among your standing corn,
Dabble your hearts with your own blood.
—Enough!
Thou wilt not break it! I, the Count—the
King—
Thy friend—am grateful for thine honest
oath,
Not coming fiercely like a conqueror, now,
But softly as a bridegroom to his own.
For I shall rule according to your laws,
And make your ever-jarring Earldoms
move
To music and in order—Angle, Jute,
Dane, Saxon, Norman, help to build a
throne
Out-towering hers of France . . . The
wind is fair
For England now . . . To-night we will be
merry.
To-morrow will I ride with thee to
Harfleur.
    [*Exeunt* WILLIAM *and all the Norman
    barons, etc.*
  Harold. To-night we will be merry—
and to-morrow—
Juggler and bastard—bastard—he hates
that most—
William the tanner's bastard! Would he
heard me!
O God, that I were in some wide, waste
field
With nothing but my battle-axe and him
To spatter his brains! Why let earth rive,
gulf in
These cursed Normans—yea and mine
own self.
Cleave heaven, and send thy saints that I
may say
Ev'n to their faces, 'If ye side with William
Ye are not noble.' How their pointed
fingers
Glared at me! Am I Harold, Harold, son
Of our great Godwin? Lo! I touch mine
arms,
My limbs—they are not mine—they are a
liar's—
I mean to be a liar—I am not bound—

Stigand shall give me absolution for it—
Did the chest move? did it move? I am
utter craven!
O Wulfnoth, Wulfnoth, brother, thou hast
betray'd me!
Wulfnoth. Forgive me, brother, I will
live here and die.

Enter PAGE

Page. My lord! the Duke awaits thee at
the banquet.
Harold. Where they eat dead men's flesh,
and drink their blood.
Page. My lord—
Harold. I know your Norman cookery
is so spiced,
It masks all this.
Page.   My lord! thou art white
as death.
Harold. With looking on the dead. Am
I so white?
Thy Duke will seem the darker. Hence, I
follow.   [*Exeunt.*

ACT III

SCENE I

The King's Palace. London

KING EDWARD *dying on a couch, and by him
standing the* QUEEN, HAROLD, ARCHBISHOP
STIGAND, GURTH, LEOFWIN, ARCHBISHOP
ALDRED, ALDWYTH, *and* EDITH.

Stigand. Sleeping or dying there? If this
be death,
Then our great Council wait to crown thee
King—
Come hither, I have a power;
                  [*To* HAROLD.
They call me near, for I am close to thee
And England—I, old shrivell'd Stigand, I,
Dry as an old wood-fungus on a dead tree,
I have a power!
See here this little key about my neck!
There lies a treasure buried down in Ely:
If e'er the Norman grow too hard for thee,
Ask me for this at thy most need, son
Harold,
At thy most need—not sooner.
  Harold.   So I will.

Stigand. Red gold—a hundred purses—
yea, and more!
If thou canst make a wholesome use of
these
To chink against the Norman, I do believe
My old crook'd spine would bud out two
young wings
To fly to heaven straight with.
    Harold.   Thank thee, father!
Thou art English, Edward too is English
now,
He hath clean repented of his Normanism.
    Stigand. Ay, as the libertine repents who
cannot
Make done undone, when thro' his dying
sense
Shrills 'lost thro' thee.' They have built
their castles here;
Our priories are Norman; the Norman
adder
Hath bitten us; we are poison'd: our dear
England
Is demi-Norman. He!—
    [*Pointing to* KING EDWARD, *sleeping.*
    Harold.   I would I were
As holy and as passionless as he!
That I might rest as calmly! Look at him—
The rosy face, and long down-silvering
beard,
The brows unwrinkled as a summer
mere.—
    Stigand. A summer mere with sudden
wreckful gusts
From a side-gorge. Passionless? How he
flamed
When Tostig's anger'd earldom flung
him, nay,
He fain had calcined all Northumbria
To one black ash, but that thy patriot
passion
Siding with our great Council against
Tostig,
Out-passion'd his! Holy? ay, ay, forsooth,
A conscience for his own soul, not his
realm;
A twilight conscience lighted thro' a chink;
Thine by the sun; nay, by some sun to be,
When all the world hath learnt to speak
the truth,
And lying were self-murder by that state
Which was the exception.

Harold.   That sun may God speed!
Stigand. Come, Harold, shake the cloud
off!
Harold. Can I, father?
Our Tostig parted cursing me and Eng-
land;
Our sister hates us for his banishment;
He hath gone to kindle Norway against
England,
And Wulfnoth is alone in Normandy.
For when I rode with William down to
Harfleur,
'Wulfnoth is sick,' he said; 'he cannot
follow;'
Then with that friendly-fiendly smile of his
'We have learnt to love him, let him a little
longer
Remain a hostage for the loyalty
Of Godwin's house.' As far as touches
Wulfnoth
I that so prized plain word and naked truth
Have sinn'd against it—all in vain.
    Leofwin.   Good brother,
By all the truths that ever priest hath
preach'd,
Of all the lies that ever men have lied,
Thine is the pardonablest.
    Harold.   May be so!
I think it so, I think I am a fool
To think it can be otherwise than so.
    Stigand. Tut, tut, I have absolved thee:
dost thou scorn me,
Because I had my Canterbury pallium,
From one whom they dispoped?
    Harold.   No, Stigand, no!
    Stigand. Is naked truth actable in true
life?
I have heard a saying of thy father Godwin,
That, were a man of state nakedly true,
Men would but take him for the craftier
liar.
    Leofwin. Be men less delicate than the
Devil himself?
I thought that naked Truth would shame
the Devil
The Devil is so modest.
    Gurth.   He never said it!
    Leofwin. Be thou not stupid-honest,
brother Gurth!
    Harold. Better to be a liar's dog, and
hold

My master honest, than believe that lying
And ruling men are fatal twins that cannot
Move one without the other. Edward
wakes!—
Dazed—he hath seen a vision.
Edward.   The green tree!
Then a great Angel past along the highest
Crying 'the doom of England,' and at once
He stood beside me, in his grasp a sword
Of lightnings, wherewithal he cleft the tree
From off the bearing trunk, and hurl'd it
from him
Three fields away, and then he dash'd and
drench'd,
He dyed, he soak'd the trunk with human
blood,
And brought the sunder'd tree again, and
set it
Straight on the trunk, that thus baptized
in blood
Grew ever high and higher, beyond my
seeing,
And shot out sidelong boughs across the
deep
That dropt themselves, and rooted in far
isles
Beyond my seeing: and the great Angel
rose
And past again along the highest crying
'The doom of England!'—Tostig, raise
my head!   [*Falls back senseless.*
Harold (*raising him*). Let Harold serve
for Tostig!
Queen.   Harold served
Tostig so ill, he cannot serve for Tostig!
Ay, raise his head, for thou hast laid it low!
The sickness of our saintly king, for whom
My prayers go up as fast as my tears fall,
I well believe, hath mainly drawn itself
From lack of Tostig—thou hast banish'd
him.
Harold. Nay—but the council, and the
king himself,
Queen. Thou hatest him, hatest him.
Harold (*coldly*).   Ay—Stigand,
unriddle
This vision, canst thou?
Stigand.   Dotage!
Edward (*starting up*).   It is finish'd!
I have built the Lord a house—the Lord
hath dwelt

In darkness. I have built the Lord a
house—
Palms, flowers, pomegranates, golden
cherubim
With twenty-cubit wings from wall to
wall—
I have built the Lord a house—sing,
Asaph! clash
The cymbal, Heman! blow the trumpet,
priest!
Fall, cloud, and fill the house—lo! my two
pillars,
Jachin and Boaz!—
          [*Seeing* HAROLD *and* GURTH.
Harold, Gurth,—where am I?
Stigand. It lies beside thee, king, upon
thy bed.
Edward. Sign, sign at once—take, sign
it, Stigand, Aldred!
Sign it, my good son Harold, Gurth, and
Leofwin,
Sign it, my queen!
All.   We have sign'd it.
Edward.   It is finish'd!
The kingliest Abbey in all Christian lands,
The lordliest, loftiest minster ever built
To Holy Peter in our English isle!
Let me be buried there, and all our kings,
And all our just and wise and holy men
That shall be born hereafter. It is finish'd!
Hast thou had absolution for thine oath?
          [*To* HAROLD.
Harold. Stigand hath given me absolu-
tion for it.
Edward. Stigand is not canonical enough
To save thee from the wrath of Norman
Saints.
Stigand. Norman enough! Be there no
Saints of England
To help us from their brethren yonder?
Edward.   Prelate,
The Saints are one, but those of Norman-
land
Are mightier than our own. Ask it of
Aldred.   [*To* HAROLD.
Aldred. It shall be granted him, my
king; for he
Who vows a vow to strangle his own
mother
Is guiltier keeping this, than breaking it.

Edward. O friends, I shall not overlive the day.

Stigand. Why then the throne is empty. Who inherits?

For tho' we be not bound by the king's voice
In making of a king, yet the king's voice
Is much toward his making. Who inherits?
Edgar the Atheling?

Edward.   No, no, but Harold.
I love him: he hath served me: none but he
Can rule all England. Yet the curse is on him
For swearing falsely by those blessed bones;
He did not mean to keep his vow.

Harold.   Not mean
To make our England Norman.

Edward.   There spake Godwin,
Who hated all the Normans; but their Saints
Have heard thee, Harold.

Edith.   Oh! my lord, my king!
He knew not whom he sware by.

Edward.   Yea, I know
He knew not, but those heavenly ears have heard,
Their curse is on him; wilt thou bring another,
Edith, upon his head?

Edith.   No, no, not I.

Edward. Why then, thou must not wed him.

Harold.   Wherefore, wherefore?

Edward. O son, when thou didst tell me of thine oath,
I sorrow'd for my random promise given
To yon fox-lion. I did not dream then
I should be king.—My son, the Saints are virgins;
They love the white rose of virginity,
The cold, white lily blowing in her cell:
I have been myself a virgin; and I sware
To consecrate my virgin here to heaven—
The silent, cloister'd, solitary life,
A life of life-long prayer against the curse
That lies on thee and England.

Harold.   No, no, no.

Edward. Treble denial of the tongue of flesh,
Like Peter's when he fell, and thou wilt have
To wail for it like Peter. O my son!

Are all oaths to be broken then, all promises
Made in our agony for help from heaven?
Son, there is one who loves thee: and a wife,
What matters who, so she be serviceable
In all obedience, as mine own hath been:
God bless thee, wedded daughter.

                    [*Laying his hand on the* QUEEN'S *head.*
Queen.   Bless thou too
That brother whom I love beyond the rest,
My banish'd Tostig.

Edward.   All the sweet Saints bless him!
Spare and forbear him, Harold, if he comes!
And let him pass unscathed; he loves me, Harold!
Be kindly to the Normans left among us,
Who follow'd me for love! and dear son, swear
When thou art king, to see my solemn vow
Accomplish'd.

Harold.   Nay, dear lord, for I have sworn
Not to swear falsely twice.

Edward.   Thou wilt not swear?

Harold. I cannot.

Edward.   Then on thee remains the curse,
Harold, if thou embrace her: and on thee,
Edith, if thou abide it,—

                    [*The* KING *swoons*; EDITH *falls and kneels by the couch.*
Stigand.   He hath swoon'd!
Death? . . . no, as yet a breath.

Harold.   Look up! look up!
Edith!

Aldred. Confuse her not; she hath begun
Her life-long prayer for thee.

Aldwyth.   O noble Harold,
I would thou couldst have sworn.

Harold.   For thine own pleasure?

Aldwyth. No, but to please our dying king, and those
Who make thy good their own—all England, Earl.

Aldred. I would thou couldst have sworn.
      Our holy king
Hath given his virgin lamb to Holy Church
To save thee from the curse.

Harold.   Alas! poor man,
His promise brought it on me.

627

Aldred.   O good son!
That knowledge made him all the care-
    fuller
To find a means whereby the curse might
    glance
From thee and England.
    Harold.   Father, we so loved—
Aldred. The more the love, the mightier
    is the prayer;
The more the love, the more acceptable
The sacrifice of both your loves to heaven.
No sacrifice to heaven, no help from
    heaven;
That runs thro' all the faith of all the
    world.
And sacrifice there must be, for the king
Is holy, and hath talk'd with God, and
    seen
A shadowing horror; there are signs in
    heaven.
    Harold. Your comet came and went.
    Aldred.   And signs on earth!
Knowest thou Senlac hill?
    Harold.   I know all Sussex;
A good entrenchment for a perilous hour!
Aldred. Pray God that come not sud-
    denly! There is one
Who passing by that hill three nights ago—
He shook so that he scarce could out
    with it—
Heard, heard—
    Harold.   The wind in his hair?
    Aldred.   A ghostly horn
Blowing continually, and faint battle-
    hymns,
And cries, and clashes, and the groans of
    men;
And dreadful shadows strove upon the
    hill,
And dreadful lights crept up from out the
    marsh—
Corpse-candles gliding over nameless
    graves—
    Harold. At Senlac?
    Aldred.   Senlac.
    Edward (waking).   Senlac! Sanguelac,
The Lake of Blood!
    Stigand.   This lightning before death
Plays on the word,—and Normanizes too!
    Harold. Hush, father, hush!
    Edward.   Thou uncanonical fool,

Wilt *thou* play with the thunder? North
    and South
Thunder together, showers of blood are
    blown
Before a never ending blast, and hiss
Against the blaze they cannot quench—a
    lake,
A sea of blood—we are drown'd in blood—
    for God
Has fill'd the quiver, and Death has drawn
    the bow—
Sanguelac! Sanguelac! the arrow! the
    arrow!   [*Dies.*
Stigand. It is the arrow of death in his
    own heart—
And our great Council wait to crown thee
    King.

Scene II

*In the Garden. The King's House
near London*

    Edith. Crown'd, crown'd and lost,
    crown'd King—and lost to me!

(*Singing*)

Two young lovers in winter weather,
    None to guide them,
Walk'd at night on the misty heather;
Night, as black as a raven's feather;
Both were lost and found together,
    None beside them.

That is the burthen of it—lost and found
Together in the cruel river Swale
A hundred years ago; and there's another,

    Lost, lost, the light of day,

To which the lover answers lovingly

    'I am beside thee.'
Lost, lost, we have lost the way.
    'Love, I will guide thee.'
Whither, O whither? into the river,
Where we two may be lost together,
And lost for ever? 'Oh! never, oh!
    never,
Tho' we be lost and be found
    together.'

Some think they loved within the pale
    forbidden

By Holy Church: but who shall say? the
   truth
Was lost in that fierce North, where *they*
   were lost,
Where all good things are lost, where
   Tostig lost
The good hearts of his people. It is Harold!

(*Enter* HAROLD)

Harold the King!
   Harold.   Call me not King, but
   Harold.
   Edith. Nay, thou art King!
   Harold.   Thine, thine, or King
   or churl!
My girl, thou hast been weeping: turn not
   thou
Thy face away, but rather let me be
King of the moment to thee, and com-
   mand
That kiss my due when subject, which will
   make
My kingship kinglier to me than to reign
King of the world without it.
   Edith.   Ask me not,
Lest I should yield it, and the second
   curse
Descend upon thine head, and thou be only
King of the moment over England.
   Harold.   Edith,
Tho' somewhat less a king to my true self
Than ere they crown'd me one, for I have
   lost
Somewhat of upright stature thro' mine
   oath,
Yet thee I would not lose, and sell not thou
Our living passion for a dead man's dream;
Stigand believed he knew not what he
   spake.
Oh God! I cannot help it, but at times
They seem to me too narrow, all the faiths
Of this grown world of ours, whose baby
   eye
Saw them sufficient. Fool and wise, I fear
This curse, and scorn it. But a little light!—
And on it falls the shadow of the priest;
Heaven yield us more! for better, Woden,
   all
Our cancell'd warrior-gods, our grim
   Walhalla,
Eternal war, than that the Saints at peace

The Holiest of our Holiest one should be
This William's fellow-tricksters;—better
   die
Than credit this, for death is death, or else
Lifts us beyond the lie. Kiss me—thou art
   not
A holy sister yet, my girl, to fear
There might be more than brother in my
   kiss,
And more than sister in thine own.
   Edith.   I dare not.
   Harold. Scared by the church—'Love
   for a whole life long'
When was that sung?
   Edith.   Here to the nightingales.
   Harold. Their anthems of no church,
   how sweet they are!
Nor kingly priest, nor priestly king to cross
Their billings ere they nest.
   Edith.   They are but of spring,
They fly the winter change—not so with
   us—
No wings to come and go.
   Harold.   But wing'd souls flying
Beyond all change and in the eternal
   distance
To settle on the Truth.
   Edith.   They are not so true,
They change their mates.
   Harold. Do they? I did not know it.
   Edith. They say thou art to wed the
   Lady Aldwyth.
   Harold. They say, they say.
   Edith.   If this be politic,
And well for thee and England—and for
   her—
Care not for me who love thee.
   Gurth (*calling*).   Harold, Harold!
   Harold. The voice of Gurth! (*Enter*
   GURTH.) Good even, my good brother!
   Gurth. Good even, gentle Edith.
   Edith.   Good even, Gurth.
   Gurth. Ill news hath come! Our hapless
   brother, Tostig—
He, and the giant King of Norway, Harold
Hardrada—Scotland, Ireland, Iceland,
   Orkney,
Are landed North of Humber, and in a
   field
So packt with carnage that the dykes and
   brooks

Were bridged and damm'd with dead, have
    overthrown
Morcar and Edwin.
 Harold.   Well then, we must
fight.
How blows the wind?
 Gurth.   Against St. Valery
And William.
 Harold. Well then, we will to the
North.
 Gurth. Ay, but worse news: this William
sent to Rome,
Swearing thou swarest falsely by his
    Saints:
The Pope and that Archdeacon Hildebrand
His master, heard him, and have sent him
    back
A holy gonfanon, and a blessed hair
Of Peter, and all France, all Burgundy,
Poitou, all Christendom is raised against
    thee;
He hath cursed thee, and all those who
    fight for thee,
And given thy realm of England to the
    bastard.
 Harold. Ha! ha!
 Edith. Oh! laugh not! . . . Strange and
ghastly in the gloom
And shadowing of this double thundercloud
That lours on England—laughter!
 Harold.   No, not strange!
This was old human laughter in old Rome
Before a Pope was born, when that which
    reign'd
Call'd itself God.—A kindly rendering
Of 'Render unto Cæsar.' . . . . . The Good
    Shepherd!
Take this, and render that.
 Gurth.   They have taken York.
 Harold. The Lord was God and came as
man—the Pope
Is man and comes as God.—York taken?
 Gurth.   Yea,
Tostig hath taken York!
 Harold. To York then. Edith,
Hadst thou been braver, I had better
    braved
All—but I love thee and thou me—and
    that
Remains beyond all chances and all
    churches,

And that thou knowest.
 Edith. Ay, but take back thy ring.
It burns my hand—a curse to thee and me.
I dare not wear it.
 [*Proffers* HAROLD *the ring, which he takes.*
 Harold. But I dare. God with thee!
  [*Exeunt* HAROLD *and* GURTH.
 Edith. The King hath cursed him, if he
marry me;
The King hath cursed him, marry me
or no!
God help me! I know nothing—can but
    pray
For Harold—pray, pray, pray—no help
    but prayer,
A breath that fleets beyond this iron world,
And touches Him that made it.

ACT IV

Scene I

In Northumbria

ARCHBISHOP ALDRED, MORCAR, EDWIN, *and*
 Forces. *Enter* HAROLD. *The standard of
 the golden Dragon of Wessex preceding
 him.*

 Harold. What! are thy people sullen
from defeat?
Our Wessex dragon flies beyond the
    Humber,
No voice to greet it.
 Edwin.   Let not our great king
Believe us sullen—only shamed to the
    quick
Before the king—as having been so bruised
By Harold, king of Norway; but our help
Is Harold, king of England. Pardon us,
    thou!
Our silence is our reverence for the king!
 Harold. Earl of the Mercians! if the
truth be gall,
Cram me not thou with honey, when our
    good hive
Needs every sting to save it.
 Voices. Aldwyth! Aldwyth!
 Harold. Why cry thy people on thy
sister's name?
 Morcar. She hath won upon our people
thro' her beauty,
And pleasantness among them.

Voices.   Aldwyth, Aldwyth!
Harold. They shout as they would have
    her for a queen.
Morcar. She hath followed with our
    host, and suffer'd all.
Harold. What would ye, men?
Voice.   Our old Northumbrian
    crown,
And kings of our own choosing.
Harold.   Your old crown
Were little help without our Saxon carles
Against Hardrada.
Voice.   Little! we are Danes,
Who conquer'd what we walk on, our own
    field.
Harold. They have been plotting here!
                            [*Aside.*
Voice.   He calls us little!
Harold. The kingdoms of this world
    began with little,
A hill, a fort, a city—that reach'd a hand
Down to the field beneath it, 'Be thou
    mine,'
Then to the next, 'Thou also!' If the
    field
Cried out 'I am mine own;' another hill
Or fort, or city, took it, and the first
Fell, and the next became an Empire.
Voice.   Yet
Thou art but a West Saxon: *we* are Danes!
Harold. My mother is a Dane, and I am
    English;
There is a pleasant fable in old books,
Ye take a stick, and break it; bind a score
All in one faggot, snap it over knee,
Ye cannot.
Voice.   Hear King Harold! he says
    true!
Harold. Would ye be Norsemen?
Voices.   No!
Harold.   Or Norman?
Voices.   No!
Harold. Snap not the faggot-band then.
Voice.   That is true!
Voice. Ay, but thou art not kingly, only
    grandson
To Wulfnoth, a poor cow-herd.
Harold.   This old Wulfnoth
Would take me on his knees and tell me
    tales
Of Alfred and of Athelstan the Great

Who drove you Danes; and yet he held
    that Dane,
Jute, Angle, Saxon, were or should be all
One England, for this cow-herd, like my
    father,
Who shook the Norman scoundrels off the
    throne,
Had in him kingly thoughts—a king of
    men,
Not made but born, like the great king
    of all,
A light among the oxen.
Voice.   That is true!
Voice. Ay, and I love him now, for mine
    own father
Was great, and cobbled.
Voice.   Thou art Tostig's brother,
Who wastes the land.
Harold.   This brother comes to save
Your land from waste; I saved it once
    before,
For when your people banish'd Tostig
    hence,
And Edward would have sent a host
    against you,
Then I, who loved my brother, bad the
    king
Who doted on him, sanction your decree
Of Tostig's banishment, and choice of
    Morcar,
To help the realm from scattering.
Voice.   King! thy brother,
If one may dare to speak the truth, was
    wrong'd.
Wild was he, born so: but the plots against
    him
Had madden'd tamer men.
Morcar.   Thou art one of those
Who brake into Lord Tostig's treasure-
    house
And slew two hundred of his following,
And now, when Tostig hath come back
    with power,
Are frighted back to Tostig.
Old Thane.   Ugh! Plots and feuds!
This is my ninetieth birthday. Can ye not
Be brethren? Godwin still at feud with
    Alfgar,
And Alfgar hates King Harold. Plots and
    feuds!
This is my ninetieth birthday!

Harold.   Old man, Harold
Hates nothing; not *his* fault, if our two
    houses
Be less than brothers.
    Voices.   Aldwyth, Harold, Aldwyth!
Harold. Again! Morcar! Edwin! What
    do they mean?
Edwin. So the good king would deign to
    lend an ear
Not overscornful, we might chance—per-
    chance—
To guess their meaning.
    Morcar. Thine own meaning, Harold,
To make all England one, to close all feuds,
Mixing our bloods, that thence a king may
    rise
Half-Godwin and half-Alfgar, one to rule
All England beyond question, beyond
    quarrel.
    Harold. Who sow'd this fancy here
    among the people?
    Morcar. Who knows what sows itself
    among the people?
A goodly flower at times.
    Harold.   The Queen of Wales?
Why, Morcar, it is all but duty in her
To hate me; I have heard she hates me.
    Morcar.   No!
For I can swear to that, but cannot swear
That these will follow thee against the
    Norsemen,
If thou deny them this.
    Harold.   Morcar and Edwin,
When will ye cease to plot against my
    house?
    Edwin. The king can scarcely dream
    that we, who know
His prowess in the mountains of the West,
Should care to plot against him in the
    North.
    Morcar. Who dares arraign us, king, of
    such a plot?
    Harold. Ye heard one witness even now.
    Morcar.   The craven!
There is a faction risen again for Tostig,
Since Tostig came with Norway—fright
    not love.
    Harold. Morcar and Edwin, will ye, if
    I yield,
Follow against the Norseman?
    Morcar.   Surely, surely!

Harold. Morcar and Edwin, will ye
    upon oath,
Help us against the Norman?
    Morcar.   With good will;
Yea, take the Sacrament upon it, king.
    Harold. Where is thy sister?
    Morcar.   Somewhere hard at hand.
Call and she comes.
    [*One goes out, then enter* ALDWYTH.
    Harold. I doubt not but thou knowest
Why thou art summon'd.
    Aldwyth.   Why?—I stay with these,
Lest thy fierce Tostig spy me out alone,
And flay me all alive.
    Harold.   Canst thou love one
Who did discrown thine husband, unqueen
    thee?
Didst thou not love thine husband?
    Aldwyth.   Oh! my lord,
The nimble, wild, red, wiry, savage king—
That was, my lord, a match of policy.
    Harold.   Was it?
I knew him brave: he loved his land: he
    fain
Had made her great: his finger on her harp
(I heard him more than once) had in it
    Wales,
Her floods, her woods, her hills: had I
    been his,
I had been all Welsh.
    Aldwyth. Oh, ay—all Welsh—and yet
I saw thee drive him up his hills—and
    women
Cling to the conquer'd, if they love, the
    more;
If not, they cannot hate the conqueror.
We never—oh! good Morcar, speak for us,
His conqueror conquer'd Aldwyth.
    Harold.   Goodly news!
    Morcar. Doubt it not thou! Since
    Griffyth's head was sent
To Edward, she hath said it.
    Harold.   I had rather
She would have loved her husband.
    Aldwyth, Aldwyth,
Canst thou love me, thou knowing where
    I love?
    Aldwyth. I can, my lord, for mine own
    sake, for thine,
For England, for thy poor white dove, who
    flutters

Between thee and the porch, but then
　would find
Her nest within the cloister, and be still.
　Harold. Canst thou love one, who cannot
　　love again?
　Aldwyth. Full hope have I that love will
　　answer love.
　Harold. Then in the name of the great
　　God, so be it!
Come, Aldred, join our hands before the
　hosts,
That all may see.
　　　[ALDRED *joins the hands of* HAROLD
　　　and ALDWYTH *and blesses them.*
　Voices.　　Harold, Harold and Aldwyth!
　Harold. Set forth our golden Dragon,
　　let him flap
The wings that beat down Wales!
Advance our Standard of the Warrior,
Dark among gems and gold; and thou,
　brave banner,
Blaze like a night of fatal stars on those
Who read their doom and die.
Where lie the Norsemen? on the Der-
　went? ay
At Stamford-bridge.
Morcar, collect thy men; Edwin, my
　friend—
Thou lingerest.—Gurth,—
Last night King Edward came to me in
　dreams—
The rosy face and long down-silvering
　beard—
He told me I should conquer:—
I am no woman to put faith in dreams.

　　　　　(*To his army*)
Last night King Edward came to me in
　dreams,
And told me we should conquer.
　Voices.　　　　　Forward! Forward!
Harold and Holy Cross!
　Aldwyth.　　　　　The day is won!

SCENE II

*A Plain. Before the Battle of
Stamford-Bridge*

　HAROLD *and his* Guard

Harold. Who is it comes this way?
Tostig? (*Enter* TOSTIG *with a small
force.*) O brother,

What art thou doing here?
　Tostig.　　　　　I am foraging
For Norway's army.
　Harold.　　I could take and slay thee.
Thou art in arms against us.
　Tostig.　　　　　Take and slay me,
For Edward loved me.
　Harold.　　Edward bad me spare thee.
　Tostig. I hate King Edward, for he
　　join'd with thee
To drive me outlaw'd. Take and slay me,
　I say,
Or I shall count thee fool.
　Harold.　　　　Take thee, or free thee,
Free thee or slay thee, Norway will have
　war;
No man would strike with Tostig, save for
　Norway.
Thou art nothing in thine England, save
　for Norway,
Who loves not thee but war. What dost
　thou here,
Trampling thy mother's bosom into blood?
　Tostig. She hath wean'd me from it with
　　such bitterness.
I come for mine own Earldom, my
　Northumbria;
Thou hast given it to the enemy of our
　house.
　Harold. Northumbria threw thee off,
　　she will not have thee,
Thou hast misused her: and, O crowning
　crime!
Hast murder'd thine own guest, the son
　of Orm,
Gamel, at thine own hearth.
　Tostig.　　　　　The slow, fat fool!
He drawl'd and prated so, I smote him
　suddenly,
I knew not what I did. He held with
　Morcar.—
I hate myself for all things that I do.
　Harold. And Morcar holds with us.
　　Come back with him.
Know what thou dost; and we may find
　for thee,
So thou be chasten'd by thy banishment,
Some easier earldom.
　Tostig.　　　　What for Norway then?
He looks for land among us, he and
　his.

Harold. Seven feet of English land, or
something more,
Seeing he is a giant.
Tostig.   That is noble!
That sounds of Godwin.
Harold.   Come thou back, and be
Once more a son of Godwin.
Tostig (turns away). O brother, brother,
O Harold—
Harold (laying his hand on TOSTIG'S
shoulder). Nay then, come thou back
to us!
Tostig (after a pause turning to him).
Never shall any man say that I, that
Tostig
Conjured the mightier Harold from his
North
To do the battle for me here in England,
Then left him for the meaner! thee!—
Thou hast no passion for the House of
Godwin—
Thou hast but cared to make thyself a
king—
Thou hast sold me for a cry.—
Thou gavest thy voice against me in the
Council—
I hate thee, and despise thee, and defy thee.
Farewell for ever!   [*Exit.*
Harold.   On to Stamford-bridge!

Scene III

After the Battle of Stamford-Bridge.
Banquet

HAROLD *and* ALDWYTH. GURTH, LEOFWIN,
MORCAR, EDWIN, *and other* Earls *and*
Thanes.

Voices. Hail! Harold! Aldwyth! hail,
bridegroom and bride!
Aldwyth (talking with HAROLD). Answer
them thou!
Is this our marriage-banquet? Would the
wines
Of wedding had been dash'd into the cups
Of victory, and our marriage and thy glory
Been drunk together! these poor hands
but sew,
Spin, broider—would that they were man's
to have held
The battle-axe by thee!

Harold.   There *was* a moment
When being forced aloof from all my
guard,
And striking at Hardrada and his madmen
I had wish'd for any weapon.
Aldwyth.   Why art thou sad?
Harold. I have lost the boy who play'd
at ball with me,
With whom I fought another fight than this
Of Stamford-bridge.
Aldwyth.   Ay! ay! thy victories
Over our own poor Wales, when at thy side
He conquer'd with thee.
Harold.   No—the childish fist
That cannot strike again.
Aldwyth.   Thou art too kindly.
Why didst thou let so many Norsemen
hence?
Thy fierce forekings had clench'd their
pirate hides
To the bleak church doors, like kites upon
a barn.
Harold. Is there so great a need to tell
thee why?
Aldwyth. Yea, am I not thy wife?
Voices.   Hail, Harold, Aldwyth!
Bridegroom and bride!
Aldwyth. Answer them! [*To* HAROLD.
Harold (to all).   Earls and Thanes!
Full thanks for your fair greeting of my
bride!
Earls, Thanes, and all our countrymen!
the day,
Our day beside the Derwent will not shine
Less than a star among the goldenest hours
Of Alfred, or of Edward his great son,
Or Athelstan, or English Ironside
Who fought with Knut, or Knut who
coming Dane
Died English. Every man about his king
Fought like a king; the king like his own
man,
No better; one for all, and all for one,
One soul! and therefore have we shatter'd
back
The hugest wave from Norseland ever yet
Surged on us, and our battle-axes broken
The Raven's wing, and dumb'd his carrion
croak
From the gray sea for ever. Many are
gone—

Drink to the dead who died for us, the living
Who fought and would have died, but happier lived,
If happier be to live; they both have life
In the large mouth of England, till *her* voice
Die with the world. Hail—hail!
 Morcar. May all invaders perish like Hardrada!
All traitors fail like Tostig!
 [*All drink but* HAROLD.
 Aldwyth. Thy cup's full!
 Harold. I saw the hand of Tostig cover it.
Our dear, dead, traitor-brother, Tostig, him
Reverently we buried. Friends, had I been here,
Without too large self-lauding I must hold
The sequel had been other than his league
With Norway, and this battle. Peace be with him!
He was not of the worst. If there be those
At banquet in this hall, and hearing me—
For there be those I fear who prick'd the lion
To make him spring, that sight of Danish blood
Might serve an end not English—peace with them
Likewise, if *they* can be at peace with what
God gave us to divide us from the wolf!
 Aldwyth (*aside to* HAROLD). Make not our Morcar sullen: it is not wise.
 Harold. Hail to the living who fought, the dead who fell!
 Voices. Hail, hail!
 First Thane. How ran that answer which King Harold gave
To his dead namesake, when he ask'd for England?
 Leofwin. 'Seven feet of English earth, or something more,
Seeing he is a giant!'
 First Thane. Then for the bastard
Six feet and nothing more!
 Leofwin. Ay, but belike
Thou hast not learnt his measure.
 First Thane. By St. Edmund
I over-measure him. Sound sleep to the man

Here by dead Norway without dream or dawn!
 Second Thane. What is he bragging still that he will come
To thrust our Harold's throne from under him?
My nurse would tell me of a molehill crying
To a mountain 'Stand aside and room for me!'
 First Thane. Let him come! let him come. Here's to him, sink or swim!
 [*Drinks.*
 Second Thane. God sink him!
 First Thane. Cannot hands which had the strength
To shove that stranded iceberg off our shores,
And send the shatter'd North again to sea,
Scuttle his cockle-shell? What's Brunanburg
To Stamford-bridge? a war-crash, and so hard,
So loud, that by St. Dunstan, old St. Thor—
By God—we thought him dead—but our old Thor
Heard his own thunder again, and woke and came
Among us again, and mark'd the sons of those
Who made this Britain England, break the North:

Mark'd how the war-axe swang,
Heard how the war-horn sang,
Mark'd how the spear-head sprang,
Heard how the shield-wall rang,
Iron on iron clang,
Anvil on hammer bang—

 Second Thane. Hammer on anvil, hammer on anvil. Old dog,
Thou art drunk, old dog!
 First Thane. Too drunk to fight with thee!
 Second Thane. Fight thou with thine own double, not with me,
Keep that for Norman William!
 First Thane. Down with William!
 Third Thane. The washerwoman's brat!

Fourth Thane. The tanner's bastard!
Fifth Thane. The Falaise byblow!

[*Enter a* THANE, *from Pevensey,
spatter'd with mud.*

Harold.   Ay, but what late guest,
As haggard as a fast of forty days,
And caked and plaster'd with a hundred
mires,
Hath stumbled on our cups?
Thane from Pevensey. My lord the King!
William the Norman, for the wind had
changed—
Harold. I felt it in the middle of that
fierce fight
At Stamford-bridge. William hath landed,
ha?
Thane from Pevensey. Landed at Peven-
sey—I am from Pevensey—
Hath wasted all the land at Pevensey—
Hath harried mine own cattle—God con-
found him!
I have ridden night and day from Peven-
sey—
A thousand ships—a hundred thousand
men—
Thousands of horses, like as many lions
Neighing and roaring as they leapt to
land—
Harold. How oft in coming hast thou
broken bread?
Thane from Pevensey. Some thrice, or so.
Harold.   Bring not thy hollowness
On our full feast. Famine is fear, were it
but
Of being starved. Sit down, sit down, and
eat,
And, when again red-blooded, speak again;
(*Aside.*) The men that guarded England
to the South
Were scatter'd to the harvest. . . . No
power mine
To hold their force together. . . . Many are
fallen
At Stamford-bridge . . . the people stupid-
sure
Sleep like their swine . . . in South and
North at once
I could not be.
(*Aloud.*) Gurth, Leofwin, Morcar,
Edwin!

(*Pointing to the revellers.*) The curse of
England! these are drown'd in wassail,
And cannot see the world but thro' their
wines!
Leave them! and thee too, Aldwyth, must
I leave—
Harsh is the news! hard is our honeymoon!
Thy pardon. (*Turning round to his
attendants.*) Break the banquet up . . .
And thou, my carrier-pigeon òf black news,
Cram thy crop full, but come when thou
art call'd.   [*Exit* HAROLD.

ACT V

SCENE I

*A Tent on a Mound, from which can be seen
the Field of Senlac*

HAROLD, *sitting; by him standing* HUGH
MARGOT *the* Monk, GURTH, LEOFWIN

Harold. Refer my cause, my crown to
Rome! . . . The wolf
Mudded the brook and predetermined all.
Monk,
Thou hast said thy say, and had my con-
stant 'No'
For all but instant battle. I hear no more.
Margot. Hear me again—for the last
time. Arise,
Scatter thy people home, descend the hill,
Lay hands of full allegiance in thy Lord's
And crave his mercy, for the Holy Father
Hath given this realm of England to the
Norman.
Harold. Then for the last time, monk,
I ask again
When had the Lateran and the Holy Father
To do with England's choice of her own
king?
Margot. Earl, the first Christian Cæsar
drew to the East
To leave the Pope dominion in the West.
He gave him all the kingdoms of the West.
Harold. So!—did he?—Earl—I have a
mind to play
The William with thine eyesight and thy
tongue.
Earl—ay—thou art but a messenger of
William.

I am weary—go: make me not wroth with thee!

Margot. Mock-king, I am the messenger of God,

His Norman Daniel! Mene, Mene, Tekel! Is thy wrath Hell, that I should spare to cry,

Yon heaven is wroth with *thee*? Hear me again!

Our Saints have moved the Church that moves the world,

And all the Heavens and very God: they heard—

They know King Edward's promise and thine—thine.

Harold. Should they not know free England crowns herself?

Not know that he nor I had power to promise?

Not know that Edward cancell'd his own promise?

And for *my* part therein—Back to that juggler,   [*Rising.*

Tell him the Saints are nobler than he dreams,

Tell him that God is nobler than the Saints,

And tell him we stand arm'd on Senlac Hill,

And bide the doom of God.

Margot.   Hear it thro' me.

The realm for which thou art forsworn is cursed,

The babe enwomb'd and at the breast is cursed,

The corpse thou whelmest with thine earth is cursed,

The soul who fighteth on thy side is cursed,

The seed thou sowest in thy field is cursed,

The steer wherewith thou plowest thy field is cursed,

The fowl that fleeth o'er thy field is cursed,

And thou, usurper, liar—

Harold.   Out, beast monk!

[*Lifting his hand to strike him.*
GURTH *stops the blow.*

I ever hated monks.

Margot.   I am but a voice

Among you: murder, martyr me if ye will—

Harold.   Thanks, Gurth! The simple, silent, selfless man

Is worth a world of tonguesters. (*To* MARGOT.) Get thee gone!

He means the thing he says. See him out safe!

Leofwin. He hath blown himself as red as fire with curses.

An honest fool! Follow me, honest fool,

But if thou blurt thy curse among our folk,

I know not—I may give that egg-bald head

The tap that silences.

Harold.   See him out safe.

[*Exeunt* LEOFWIN *and* MARGOT.

Gurth. Thou hast lost thine even temper, brother Harold!

Harold. Gurth, when I past by Waltham, my foundation

For men who serve the neighbour, not themselves,

I cast me down prone, praying; and, when I rose,

They told me that the Holy Rood had lean'd

And bow'd above me; whether that which held it

Had weaken'd, and the Rood itself were bound

To that necessity which binds us down;

Whether it bow'd at all but in their fancy;

Or if it bow'd, whether it symbol'd ruin

Or glory, who shall tell? but they were sad,

And somewhat sadden'd me.

Gurth.   Yet if a fear,

Or shadow of a fear, lest the strange Saints

By whom thou swarest, should have power to balk

Thy puissance in this fight with him, who made

And heard thee swear—brother—*I* have not sworn?

If the king fall, may not the kingdom fall?

But if I fall, I fall, and thou art king;

And, if I win, I win, and thou art king;

Draw thou to London, there make strength to breast

Whatever chance, but leave this day to me.

Leofwin (*entering*). And waste the land about thee as thou goest,

And be thy hand as winter on the field,

To leave the foe no forage.

Harold.   Noble Gurth!
Best son of Godwin! If I fall, I fall—
The doom of God! How should the people
    fight
When the king flies? And, Leofwin, art
    thou mad?
How should the King of England waste
    the fields
Of England, his own people?—No glance
    yet
Of the Northumbrian helmet on the heath?
    Leofwin. No, but a shoal of wives upon
    the heath,
And someone saw thy willy-nilly nun
Vying a tress against our golden fern.
    Harold. Vying a tear with our cold dews,
    a sigh
With these low-moaning heavens. Let her
    be fetch'd.
We have parted from our wife without
    reproach,
Tho' we have pierced thro' all her prac-
    tices;
And that is well.
    Leofwin.   I saw her even now:
She hath not left us.
    Harold.   Nought of Morcar then?
    Gurth. Nor seen, nor heard; thine,
    William's or his own
As wind blows, or tide flows: belike he
    watches,
If this war-storm in one of its rough rolls
Wash up that old crown of Northumber-
    land.
    Harold. I married her for Morcar—a sin
    against
The truth of love. Evil for good, it seems,
Is oft as childless of the good as evil
For evil.
    Leofwin. Good for good hath borne at
    times
A bastard false as William.
    Harold.   Ay, if Wisdom
Pair'd not with Good. But I am somewhat
    worn,
A snatch of sleep were like the peace of
    God.
Gurth, Leofwin, go once more about the
    hill—
What did the dead man call it—Sanguelac,
The lake of blood?

    Leofwin. A lake that dips in William
As well as Harold.
    Harold.   Like enough. I have seen
The trenches dug, the palisades uprear'd
And wattled thick with ash and willow-
    wands;
Yea, wrought at them myself. Go round
    once more;
See all be sound and whole. No Norman
    horse
Can shatter England, standing shield by
    shield;
Tell that again to all.
    Gurth.   I will, good brother.
    Harold. Our guardsman hath but toil'd
    his hand and foot,
I hand, foot, heart and head. Some wine!
    (*One pours wine into a goblet which he
    hands to* HAROLD.)
                                   Too much!
What? we must use our battle-axe to-day.
Our guardsmen have slept well, since we
    came in?
    Leofwin. Ay, slept and snored. Your
    second-sighted man
That scared the dying conscience of the
    king,
Misheard their snores for groans. They
    are up again
And chanting that old song of Brunanburg
Where England conquer'd.
    Harold.   That is well. The Norman,
What is he doing?
    Leofwin.   Praying for Normandy;
Our scouts have heard the tinkle of their
    bells.
    Harold. And our old songs are prayers
    for England too!
But by all Saints—
    Leofwin.   Barring the Norman!
    Harold.   Nay,
Were the great trumpet blowing dooms-
    day dawn,
I needs must rest. Call when the Norman
    moves—   [*Exeunt all, but* HAROLD.
No horse—thousands of horses—our
    shield wall—
Wall—break it not—break not—break—
                                   [*Sleeps.*
    Vision of Edward. Son Harold, I thy
    king, who came before

638

To tell thee thou shouldst win at Stamford-
  bridge,
Come yet once more, from where I am at
  peace,
Because I loved thee in my mortal day,
To tell thee thou shalt die on Senlac hill—
Sanguelac!
    Vision of Wulfnoth. O brother, from my
    ghastly oubliette
I send my voice across the narrow seas—
No more, no more, dear brother, never-
  more—
Sanguelac!
    Vision of Tostig. O brother, most un-
    brotherlike to me,
Thou gavest thy voice against me in my
  life,
I give my voice against thee from the
  grave—
Sanguelac!
    Vision of Norman Saints. O hapless
    Harold! King but for an hour!
Thou swarest falsely by our blessed bone,
We give our voice against thee out of
  heaven!
Sanguelac! Sanguelac! The arrow! the
  arrow!
    Harold (*starting up, battle-axe in hand*).
                      Away!
My battle-axe against your voices. Peace!
The king's last word—'the arrow!' I shall
  die—
I die for England then, who lived for
  England—
What nobler? men must die.
I cannot fall into a falser world—
I have done no man wrong. Tostig, poor
  brother,
Art *thou* so anger'd?
Fain had I kept thine earldom in thy hands
Save for thy wild and violent will that
  wrench'd
All hearts of freemen from thee. I could do
No other than this way advise the king
Against the race of Godwin. Is it possible
That mortal men should bear their earthly
  heats
Into yon bloodless world, and threaten us
  thence
Unschool'd of Death? Thus then thou art
  revenged—

I left our England naked to the South
To meet thee in the North. The Norse-
  man's raid
Hath helpt the Norman, and the race of
  Godwin
Hath ruin'd Godwin. No—our waking
  thoughts
Suffer a stormless shipwreck in the pools
Of sullen slumber, and arise again
Disjointed: only dreams—where mine own
  self
Takes part against myself! Why? for a spark
Of self-disdain born in me when I sware
Falsely to him, the falser Norman, over
His gilded ark of mummy-saints, by whom
I knew not that I sware,—not for myself—
For England—yet not wholly—

           (*Enter* EDITH)
                    Edith, Edith,
Get thou into thy cloister as the king
Will'd it: be safe: the perjury-mongering
  Count
Hath made too good an use of Holy
  Church
To break her close! There the great God
  of truth
Fill all thine hours with peace!—A lying
  devil
Hath haunted me—mine oath—my wife—
  I fain
Had made my marriage not a lie; I could
  not:
Thou art my bride! and thou in after years
Praying perchance for this poor soul of
  mine
In cold, white cells beneath an icy moon—
This memory to thee!—and this to Eng-
  land,
My legacy of war against the Pope
From child to child, from Pope to Pope,
  from age to age,
Till the sea wash her level with her shores,
Or till the Pope be Christ's.

      Enter ALDWYTH

    Aldwyth (*to* EDITH). Away from him!
    Edith. I will . . . I have not spoken to the
    king
One word; and one I must. Farewell!
                      [*Going.*

Harold.   Not yet.
Stay.
Edith. To what use?
Harold. The king commands thee,
woman!

(*To* ALDWYTH)

Have thy two brethren sent their forces in?
Aldwyth. Nay, I fear not.
Harold. Then there's no force in thee!
Thou didst possess thyself of Edward's ear
To part me from the woman that I loved!
Thou didst arouse the fierce Northum-
brians!
Thou hast been false to England and to
me!—
As . . . in some sort . . . I have been false
to thee.
Leave me. No more—Pardon on both
sides—Go!
Aldwyth. Alas, my lord, I loved thee.
Harold (*bitterly*).   With a love
Passing thy love for Griffyth! wherefore
now
Obey my first and last commandment. Go!
Aldwyth. O Harold! husband! Shall we
meet again?
Harold. After the battle—after the
battle. Go.
Aldwyth. I go. (*Aside.*) That I could stab
her standing there!
                    [*Exit* ALDWYTH.
Edith. Alas, my lord, she loved thee.
Harold.   Never! never!
Edith. I saw it in her eyes!
Harold.   I see it in thine.
And not on thee—nor England—fall God's
doom!
Edith. On *thee*? on me. And thou art
England! Alfred
Was England. Ethelred was nothing. Eng-
land
Is but her king, and thou art Harold!
Harold.   Edith,
The sign in heaven—the sudden blast at
sea—
My fatal oath—the dead Saints—the dark
dreams—
The Pope's Anathema—the Holy Rood
That bow'd to me at Waltham—Edith, if
I, the last English King of England—

Edith.   No,
First of a line that coming from the people,
And chosen by the people—
Harold.   And fighting for
And dying for the people—
Edith.   Living! living!
Harold. Yea so, good cheer! thou art
Harold, I am Edith!
Look not thus wan!
Edith.   What matters how I look?
Have we not broken Wales and Norse-
land? slain,
Whose life was all one battle, incarnate
war,
Their giant-king, a mightier man-in-arms
Than William.
Harold. Ay, my girl, no tricks in him—
No bastard he! when all was lost, he yell'd,
And bit his shield, and dash'd it on the
ground,
And swaying his two-handed sword about
him,
Two deaths at every swing, ran in upon
us
And died so, and I loved him as I hate
This liar who made me liar. If Hate can
kill,
And Loathing wield a Saxon battle-axe—
Edith. Waste not thy might before the
battle!
Harold. No,
And thou must hence. Stigand will see
thee safe,
And so—Farewell.
                [*He is going, but turns back.*
The ring thou darest not wear,
I have had it fashion'd, see, to meet my
hand.
            [HAROLD *shows the ring which is on
his finger.*
Farewell!
            [*He is going, but turns back again.*
I am dead as Death this day to ought of
earth's
Save William's death or mine.
Edith.   Thy death!—to-day!
Is it not thy birthday?
Harold.   Ay, that happy day!
A birthday welcome! happy days and
many!
One—this!   [*They embrace.*

Look, I will bear thy blessing into the
   battle
And front the doom of God.
Norman cries (heard in the distance).
   Ha Rou! Ha Rou!

Enter GURTH

Gurth. The Norman moves!
Harold.   Harold and Holy Cross!
   [*Exeunt* HAROLD *and* GURTH.

Enter STIGAND

Stigand. Our Church in arms—the lamb
   the lion—not
Spear into pruning-hook—the counter
   way—
Cowl, helm; and crozier, battle-axe. Abbot
   Alfwig,
Leofric, and all the monks of Peterboro'
Strike for the king; but I, old wretch, old
   Stigand,
With hands too limp to brandish iron—
   and yet
I have a power—would Harold ask me
   for it—
I have a power.
Edith.   What power, holy father?
Stigand. Power now from Harold to
   command thee hence
And see thee safe from Senlac.
Edith.   I remain!
Stigand. Yea, so will I, daughter, until
   I find
Which way the battle balance. I can see it
From where we stand: and, live or die,
   I would
I were among them!

Canons from Waltham (singing without)

    Salva patriam
    Sancte Pater,
    Salva Fili,
    Salva Spiritus,
    Salva patriam,
    Sancta Mater.[1]

Edith. Are those the blessed angels
   quiring, father?

[1] The *a* throughout these Latin hymns
should be sounded broad, as in 'father'.

Stigand. No, daughter, but the canons
   out of Waltham,
The king's foundation, that have follow'd
   him.
Edith. O God of battles, make their wall
   of shields
Firm as thy cliffs, strengthen their pali-
   sades!
What is that whirring sound?
Stigand.   The Norman arrow!
Edith. Look out upon the battle—is he
   safe?
Stigand. The king of England stands
   between his banners.
He glitters on the crowning of the hill.
God save King Harold!
Edith.   —chosen by his people
And fighting for his people!
Stigand.   There is one
Come as Goliath came of yore—he flings
His brand in air and catches it again,
He is chanting some old warsong.
Edith.   And no David
To meet him?
Stigand. Ay, there springs a Saxon on
   him,
Falls—and another falls.
Edith.   Have mercy on us!
Stigand. Lo! our good Gurth hath
   smitten him to the death.
Edith. So perish all the enemies of
   Harold!
Canons (singing).
    Hostis in Angliam
    Ruit prædator,
    Illorum, Domine,
    Scutum scindatur!
    Hostis per Angliae
    Plagas bacchatur;
    Casa crematur,
    Pastor fugatur
    Grex trucidatur—

Stigand. Illos trucida, Domine.
Edith.   Ay, good father.
Canons (singing).
    Illorum scelera
    Pœna sequatur!

English cries.   Harold and Holy
   Cross! Out! out!

Stigand.   Our javelins
Answer their arrows. All the Norman foot
Are storming up the hill. The range of
    knights
Sit, each a statue on his horse, and wait.
English cries. Harold and God Almighty!
Norman cries.   Ha Rou! Ha Rou!

Canons (singing).
        Eques cum pedite
        Præpediatur!
        Illorum in lacrymas
        Cruor fundatur!
        Pereant, pereant,
        Anglia precatur.

Stigand. Look, daughter, look.
Edith.   Nay, father, look for *me!*
Stigand. Our axes lighten with a single
    flash
About the summit of the hill, and heads
And arms are sliver'd off and splinter'd
    by
Their lightning—and they fly—the Nor-
    man flies.
    Edith. Stigand, O father, have we won
    the day?
Stigand. No, daughter, no—they fall
    behind the horse—
Their horse are thronging to the barri-
    cades;
I see the gonfanon of Holy Peter
Floating above their helmets—ha! he is
    down!
    Edith. He down! Who down?
Stigand. The Norman Count is down.
    Edith. So perish all the enemies of
    England!
Stigand. No, no, he hath risen again—
    he bares his face—
Shouts something—he points onward—
    all their horse
Swallow the hill locust-like, swarming
    up.
    Edith. O God of battles, make his battle-
    axe keen
As thine own sharp-dividing justice, heavy
As thine own bolts that fall on crimeful
    heads
Charged with the weight of heaven where-
    from they fall!

Canons (singing).
        Jacta tonitrua
        Deus bellator!
        Surgas e tenebris,
        Sis vindicator!
        Fulmina, fulmina
        Deus vastator!

Edith. O God of battles, they are three
    to one,
Make thou one man as three to roll them
    down!

Canons (singing).
        Equus cum equite
        Dejiciatur!
        Acies, Acies
        Prona sternatur!
        Illorum lanceas
        Frange Creator!

Stigand. Yea, yea, for how their lances
    snap and shiver
Against the shifting blaze of Harold's axe!
War-woodman of old Woden, how he fells
The mortal copse of faces! There! And
    there!
The horse and horseman cannot meet the
    shield,
The blow that brains the horseman cleaves
    the horse,
The horse and horseman roll along the hill,
They fly once more, they fly, the Norman
    flies!

        Equus cum equite
        Præcipitatur.

Edith. O God, the God of truth hath
    heard my cry.
Follow them, follow them, drive them to
    the sea!

        Illorum scelera
        Pœna sequatur!

Stigand. Truth! no; a lie; a trick, a
    Norman trick!
They turn on the pursuer, horse against
    foot,
They murder all that follow.
    Edith.   Have mercy on us!
Stigand. Hot-headed fools—to burst the
    wall of shields!

They have broken the commandment of
   the king!

Edith.   *His* oath was broken—O holy
   Norman Saints,
Ye that are now of heaven, and see beyond
Your Norman shrines, pardon it, pardon it,
That he forsware himself for all he loved,
Me, me and all! Look out upon the battle!
Stigand. They thunder again upon the
   barricades.
My sight is eagle, but the strife so thick—
This is the hottest of it: hold, ash! hold,
   willow!

English cries. Out, out!
Norman cries.   Ha Rou!
Stigand. Ha! Gurth hath leapt upon
   him
And slain him: he hath fallen.
Edith.   And I am heard.
Glory to God in the Highest! fallen, fallen!
Stigand. No, no, his horse—he mounts
   another—wields
His war-club, dashes it on Gurth, and
   Gurth,
Our noble Gurth, is down!
Edith.   Have mercy on us!
Stigand. And Leofwin is down!
Edith.   Have mercy on us!
O Thou that knowest, let not my strong
   prayer
Be weaken'd in thy sight, because I love
The husband of another!
Norman cries.   Ha Rou! Ha Rou!
Edith.   I do not hear our English
   war-cry.
Stigand. No.
Edith. Look out upon the battle—is he
   safe?
Stigand. He stands between the banners
   with the dead
So piled about him he can hardly move.
Edith (takes up the war-cry). Out! out!
Norman cries. Ha Rou!
Edith (cries out). Harold and Holy Cross!
Norman cries. Ha Rou! Ha Rou!
Edith. What is that whirring sound?
Stigand. The Norman sends his arrows
   up to Heaven,
They fall on those within the palisade!
Edith. Look out upon the hill—is
   Harold there?

Stigand.   Sanguelac—Sanguelac—the
   arrow—the arrow!—away!

SCENE II

Field of the Dead. Night

ALDWYTH *and* EDITH

Aldwyth. O Edith, art thou here? O
   Harold, Harold—
Our Harold—we shall never see him more.
Edith. For there was more than sister in
   my kiss,
And so the saints were wroth. I cannot love
   them,
For they are Norman saints—and yet I
   should—
They are so much holier than their harlot's
   son
With whom they play'd their game against
   the king!
Aldwyth. The king is slain, the kingdom
   overthrown!
Edith. No matter!
Aldwyth. How no matter, Harold
   slain?—
I cannot find his body. O help me thou!
O Edith, if I ever wrought against thee,
Forgive me thou, and help me here!
Edith.   No matter!
Aldwyth. Not help me, nor forgive me?
Edith. So thou saidest.
Aldwyth. I say it now, forgive me!
Edith.   Cross me not!
I am seeking one who wedded me in
   secret.
Whisper! God's angels only know it. Ha!
What art *thou* doing here among the dead?
They are stripping the dead bodies naked
   yonder,
And thou art come to rob them of their
   rings!
Aldwyth. O Edith, Edith, I have lost
   both crown
And husband.
Edith.   So have I.
Aldwyth.   I tell thee, girl,
I am seeking my dead Harold.
Edith.   And I mine!
The Holy Father strangled him with a
   hair
Of Peter, and his brother Tostig helpt;

643

The wicked sister clapt her hands and
   laugh'd;
Then all the dead fell on him.
   Aldwyth.   Edith, Edith—
   Edith. What was he like, this husband?
   like to thee?
Call not for help from me. I knew him not.
He lies not here: not close beside the
   standard.
Here fell the truest, manliest hearts of
   England.
Go further hence and find him.
   Aldwyth.   She is crazed!
   Edith. That doth not matter either.
   Lower the light.
He must be here.
        [*Enter two* Canons, OSGOD *and*
        ATHELRIC, *with torches. They turn
        over the dead bodies and examine
        them as they pass.*
Osgod. I think that this is Thurkill.
Athelric. More likely Godric.
Osgod.   I am sure this body
Is Alfwig, the king's uncle.
   Athelric.   So it is!
No, no—brave Gurth, one gash from brow
   to knee!
Osgod. And here is Leofwin.
   Edith.   And here is *He!*
   Aldwyth. Harold? Oh no—nay, if it
   were—my God,
They have so maim'd and murder'd all his
   face
There is no man can swear to him.
   Edith.   But one woman!
Look you, we never mean to part again.
I have found him, I am happy.
Was there not someone ask'd me for
   forgiveness?
I yield it freely, being the true wife
Of this dead King, who never bore re-
   venge.

        Enter COUNT WILLIAM *and* WILLIAM
        MALET

William. Who be these women? And
   what body is this?
Edith. Harold, thy better!
William.   Ay, and what art thou?
Edith. His wife!
Malet. Not true, my girl, here is the

Queen!   [*Pointing out* ALDWYTH.
William (*to* ALDWYTH). Wast thou his
   Queen?
Aldwyth. I was the Queen of Wales.
William. Why then of England. Madam,
   fear us not.
(*To* MALET.) Knowest thou this other?
   Malet.   When I visited England,
Some held she was his wife in secret—
   some—
Well—some believed she was his para-
   mour.
Edith. Norman, thou liest! liars all of
   you,
Your Saints and all! *I* am his wife! and
   she—
For look, our marriage ring!
        [*She draws it off the finger of* HAROLD.
              I lost it somehow—
I lost it, playing with it when I was wild.
That bred the doubt! but I am wiser
   now . . .
I am too wise . . . Will none among you all
Bear me true witness—only for this once—
That I have found it here again?
                    [*She puts it on.*
                         And thou,
Thy wife am I for ever and evermore.
        [*Falls on the body and dies.*
William. Death!—and enough of death
   for this one day,
The day of St. Calixtus, and the day,
My day when I was born.
   Malet.   And this dead king's
Who, king or not, hath kinglike fought and
   fallen,
His birthday, too. It seems but yestereven
I held it with him in his English halls,
His day, with all his rooftree ringing
   'Harold,'
Before he fell into the snare of Guy;
When all men counted Harold would be
   king,
And Harold was most happy.
   William.   Thou art half English.
Take them away!
Malet, I vow to build a church to God
Here on the hill of battle; let our high altar
Stand where their standard fell . . . where
   these two lie.
Take them away, I do not love to see them.

Pluck the dead woman off the dead man,
    Malet!
    Malet. Faster than ivy. Must I hack her
    arms off?
How shall I part them?
    William. Leave them. Let them be!
Bury him and his paramour together.
He that was false in oath to me, it seems
Was false to his own wife. We will not
    give him
A Christian burial: yet he was a warrior,
And wise, yea truthful, till that blighted vow
Which God avenged to-day.
Wrap them together in a purple cloak
And lay them both upon the waste sea-
    shore
At Hastings, there to guard the land for
    which
He did forswear himself—a warrior—ay,
And but that Holy Peter fought for us,
And that the false Northumbrian held aloof,
And save for that chance arrow which the
    Saints
Sharpen'd and sent against him—who can
    tell?—
Three horses had I slain beneath me: twice
I thought that all was lost. Since I knew
    battle,

And that was from my boyhood, never
    yet—
No, by the splendour of God—have I
    fought men
Like Harold and his brethren, and his
    guard
Of English. Every man about his king
Fell where he stood. They loved him: and,
    pray God
My Normans may but move as true with
    me
To the door of death. Of one self-stock at
    first,
Make them again one people—Norman,
    English;
And English, Norman; we should have a
    hand
To grasp the world with, and a foot to
    stamp it . . .
Flat. Praise the Saints. It is over. No more
    blood!
I am king of England, so they thwart me
    not,
And I will rule according to their laws.
    (*To* ALDWYTH.) Madam, we will entreat
    thee with all honour.
    Aldwyth. My punishment is more than
    I can bear.

BECKET

TO THE LORD CHANCELLOR

THE RIGHT HONOURABLE EARL OF SELBORNE

MY DEAR SELBORNE—To you, the honoured Chancellor of our own day, I dedicate this dramatic memorial of your great predecessor;—which, altho' not intended in its present form to meet the exigencies of our modern theatre, has nevertheless—for so you have assured me—won your approbation.—Ever yours,   TENNYSON.

DRAMATIS PERSONÆ

HENRY II (*son of the Earl of Anjou*).
THOMAS BECKET, *Chancellor of England, afterwards Archbishop of Canterbury.*
GILBERT FOLIOT, *Bishop of London.*
ROGER, *Archbishop of York.*
   Bishop of Hereford.
HILARY, *Bishop of Chichester.*
JOCELYN, *Bishop of Salisbury.*
JOHN OF SALISBURY } *friends of Becket.*
HERBERT OF BOSHAM }
WALTER MAP, *reputed author of 'Golias,' Latin poems against the priesthood.*
KING LOUIS OF FRANCE.
GEOFFREY, *son of Rosamund and Henry.*
GRIM, *a monk of Cambridge.*
SIR REGINALD FITZURSE }
SIR RICHARD DE BRITO   } *the four knights of the King's household, enemies of Becket.*
SIR WILLIAM DE TRACY   }
SIR HUGH DE MORVILLE   }
DE BROC OF SALTWOOD CASTLE.
LORD LEICESTER.
PHILIP DE ELEEMOSYNA.
TWO KNIGHT TEMPLARS.
JOHN OF OXFORD (*called the Swearer*).
ELEANOR OF AQUITAINE, *Queen of England* (*divorced from Louis of France*).
ROSAMUND DE CLIFFORD.
MARGERY.

Knights, Monks, Beggars, etc.

PROLOGUE

*A Castle in Normandy. Interior of the Hall.
Roofs of a City seen thro' Windows*

HENRY *and* BECKET *at chess*

Henry. So then our good Archbishop
      Theobald
Lies dying.
   Becket. I am grieved to know as much.
   Henry. But we must have a mightier
      man than he
For his successor.
   Becket.   Have you thought of one?
   Henry. A cleric lately poison'd his own
      mother,

And being brought before the courts of the
      Church,
They but degraded him. I hope they whipt
      him.
I would have hang'd him.
   Becket.   It is your move.
   Henry.   Well—there. [*Moves.*
The Church in the pell-mell of Stephen's
      time
Hath climb'd the throne and almost
      clutch'd the crown;
But by the royal customs of our realm
The Church should hold her baronies
      of me,
Like other lords amenable to law.

646

I'll have them written down and made the law.

Becket. My liege, I move my bishop.

Henry. And if I live,
No man without my leave shall excommunicate
My tenants or my household.

Becket. Look to your king.

Henry. No man without my leave shall cross the seas
To set the Pope against me—I pray your pardon.

Becket. Well—will you move?

Henry. There. [*Moves.*

Becket. Check—you move so wildly.

Henry. There then! [*Moves.*

Becket. Why—there then, for you see my bishop
Hath brought your king to a standstill. You are beaten.

Henry (*kicks over the board*). Why, there then—down go bishop and king together.
I loathe being beaten; had I fixt my fancy
Upon the game I should have beaten thee,
But that was vagabond.

Becket. Where, my liege? With Phryne,
Or Lais, or thy Rosamund, or another?

Henry. My Rosamund is no Lais, Thomas Becket;
And yet she plagues me too—no fault in her—
But that I fear the Queen would have her life.

Becket. Put her away, put her away, my liege!
Put her away into a nunnery!
Safe enough there from her to whom thou art bound
By Holy Church. And wherefore should she seek
The life of Rosamund de Clifford more
Than that of other paramours of thine?

Henry. How dost thou know I am not wedded to her?

Becket. How should I know?

Henry. That is my secret, Thomas.

Becket. State secrets should be patent to the statesman
Who serves and loves his king, and whom the king
Loves not as statesman, but true lover and friend.

Henry. Come, come, thou art but deacon, not yet bishop,
No, nor archbishop, nor my confessor yet.
I would to God thou wert, for I should find
An easy father confessor in thee.

Becket. St. Denis, that thou shouldst not. I should beat
Thy kingship as my bishop hath beaten it.

Henry. Hell take thy bishop then, and my kingship too!
Come, come, I love thee and I know thee, I know thee,
A doter on white pheasant-flesh at feasts,
A sauce-deviser for thy days of fish,
A dish-designer, and most amorous
Of good old red sound liberal Gascon wine:
Will not thy body rebel, man, if thou flatter it?

Becket. That palate is insane which cannot tell
A good dish from a bad, new wine from old.

Henry. Well, who loves wine loves woman.

Becket. So I do.

Men are God's trees, and women are God's flowers;
And when the Gascon wine mounts to my head,
The trees are all the statelier, and the flowers
Are all the fairer.

Henry. And thy thoughts, thy fancies?

Becket. Good dogs, my liege, well train'd, and easily call'd
Off from the game.

Henry. Save for some once or twice,
When they ran down the game and worried it.

Becket. No, my liege, no!—not once—in God's name, no!

Henry. Nay, then, I take thee at thy word—believe thee
The veriest Galahad of old Arthur's hall.
And so this Rosamund, my true heart-wife,
Not Eleanor—she whom I love indeed

As a woman should be loved—Why dost
    thou smile
So dolorously?
    Becket.   My good liege, if a man
Wastes himself among women, how should
    he love
A woman, as a woman should be loved?
    Henry. How shouldst thou know that
        never hast loved one?
Come, I would give her to thy care in
    England
When I am out in Normandy or Anjou.
    Becket. My lord, I am your subject, not
        your——
    Henry.   Pander.
God's eyes! I know all that—not my
    purveyor
Of pleasures, but to save a life—her life;
Ay, and the soul of Eleanor from hellfire.
I have built a secret bower in England,
    Thomas,
A nest in a bush.
    Becket.   And where, my liege?
    Henry (*whispers*).   Thine ear.
    Becket. That's lone enough.
    Henry (*laying paper on table*). This chart
        here mark'd 'Her Bower,'
Take, keep it, friend. See, first, a circling
    wood,
A hundred pathways running everyway,
And then a brook, a bridge; and after that
This labyrinthine brickwork maze in maze,
And then another wood, and in the midst
A garden and my Rosamund. Look, this
    line—
The rest you see is colour'd green—but this
Draws thro' the chart to her.
    Becket.   This blood-red line?
    Henry. Ay! blood, perchance, except
        thou see to her.
    Becket. And where is she? There in her
        English nest?
    Henry. Would God she were—no, here
        within the city.
We take her from her secret bower in
    Anjou
And pass her to her secret bower in Eng-
    land.
She is ignorant of all but that I love her.
    Becket. My liege, I pray thee let me
        hence: a widow

And orphan child, whom one of thy wild
    barons——
    Henry. Ay, ay, but swear to see to her
        in England.
    Becket. Well, well, I swear, but not to
        please myself.
    Henry. Whatever come between us?
    Becket.   What should come
Between us, Henry?
    Henry. Nay—I know not, Thomas.
    Becket. What need then? Well—what-
        ever come between us.   [*Going.*
    Henry. A moment! thou didst help me
        to my throne
In Theobald's time, and after by thy
    wisdom
Hast kept it firm from shaking; but now I,
For my realm's sake, myself must be the
    wizard
To raise that tempest which will set it
    trembling
Only to base it deeper. I, true son
Of Holy Church—no croucher to the
    Gregories
That tread the kings their children under-
    heel—
Must curb her; and the Holy Father,
    while
This Barbarossa butts him from his chair,
Will need my help—be facile to my hands.
Now is my time. Yet—lest there should be
    flashes
And fulminations from the side of Rome,
An interdict on England—I will have
My young son Henry crown'd the King
    of England,
That so the Papal bolt may pass by Eng-
    land,
As seeming his, not mine, and fall abroad.
I'll have it done—and now.
    Becket.   Surely too young
Even for this shadow of a crown; and tho'
I love him heartily, I can spy already
A strain of hard and headstrong in him.
    Say,
The Queen should play his kingship
    against thine!
    Henry. I will not think so, Thomas.
        Who shall crown him?
Canterbury is dying.
    Becket.   The next Canterbury.

Henry. And who shall he be, my friend Thomas? Who?

Becket. Name him; the Holy Father will confirm him.

Henry (lays his hand on BECKET'S *shoulder).* Here!

Becket.   Mock me not. I am not even a monk.
Thy jest—no more. Why—look—is this a sleeve
For an archbishop?

Henry.   But the arm within
Is Becket's, who hath beaten down my foes.

Becket. A soldier's, not a spiritual arm.

Henry. I lack a spiritual soldier, Thomas—
A man of this world and the next to boot.

Becket. There's Gilbert Foliot.

Henry.   He! too thin, too thin.
Thou art the man to fill out the Church robe;
Your Foliot fasts and fawns too much for me.

Becket. Roger of York.

Henry.   Roger is Roger of York.
King, Church, and State to him but foils wherein
To set that precious jewel, Roger of York.
No.

Becket. Henry of Winchester?

Henry.   Him who crown'd Stephen—
King Stephen's brother! No; too royal for me.
And I'll have no more Anselms.

Becket.   Sire, the business
Of thy whole kingdom waits me: let me go.

Henry. Answer me first.

Becket.   Then for thy barren jest
Take thou mine answer in bare common-place—
Nolo episcopari.

Henry.   Ay, but *Nolo*
Archiepiscopari, my good friend,
Is quite another matter.

Becket.   A more awful one.
Make *me* archbishop! Why, my liege, I know
Some three or four poor priests a thousand times
Fitter for this grand function. *Me* archbishop!

God's favour and king's favour might so clash
That thou and I—— That were a jest indeed!

Henry. Thou angerest me, man: I do not jest.

Enter ELEANOR *and* SIR REGINALD FITZURSE

Eleanor (singing). Over! the sweet summer closes,
The reign of the roses is done——

Henry (to BECKET, *who is going).* Thou shalt not go. I have not ended with thee.

Eleanor (seeing chart on table). This chart with the red line! her bower! whose bower?

Henry. The chart is not mine, but Becket's: take it, Thomas.

Eleanor. Becket! O—ay—and these chessmen on the floor—the king's crown broken! Becket hath beaten thee again—and thou hast kicked down the board. I know thee of old.

Henry. True enough, my mind was set upon other matters.

Eleanor. What matters? State matters? love matters?

Henry. My love for thee, and thine for me.

Eleanor. Over! the sweet summer closes,
The reign of the roses is done;
Over and gone with the roses,
And over and gone with the sun.

Here; but our sun in Aquitaine lasts longer. I would I were in Aquitaine again —your north chills me.

Over! the sweet summer closes,
And never a flower at the close;
Over and gone with the roses,
And winter again and the snows.

That was not the way I ended it first—but unsymmetrically, preposterously, illogically, out of passion, without art—like a song of the people. Will you have it? The last Parthian shaft of a forlorn Cupid at the King's left breast, and all left-handedness and under-handedness.

And never a flower at the close,
Over and gone with the roses,
Not over and gone with the rose.

True, one rose will outblossom the rest,
one rose in a bower. I speak after my
fancies, for I am a Troubadour, you know,
and won the violet at Toulouse; but my
voice is harsh here, not in tune, a nightingale out of season; for marriage, rose or no
rose, has killed the golden violet.

Becket. Madam, you do ill to scorn
wedded love.

Eleanor. So I do. Louis of France loved
me, and I dreamed that I loved Louis of
France: and I loved Henry of England,
and Henry of England dreamed that he
loved me; but the marriage-garland withers
even with the putting on, the bright link
rusts with the breath of the first after-
marriage kiss, the harvest moon is the
ripening of the harvest, and the honeymoon
is the gall of love; he dies of his honeymoon. I could pity this poor world myself
that it is no better ordered.

Henry. Dead is he, my Queen? What,
altogether? Let me swear nay to that by
this cross on my neck. God's eyes! what a
lovely cross! what jewels!

Eleanor. Doth it please you? Take it and
wear it on that hard heart of yours—there.
                    [*Gives it to him.*

Henry (*puts it on*). On this left breast
before so hard a heart,
To hide the scar left by thy Parthian dart.

Eleanor. Has my simple song set you
jingling? Nay, if I took and translated that
hard heart into our Provençal facilities, I
could so play about it with the rhyme—

Henry. That the heart were lost in the
rhyme and the matter in the metre. May
we not pray you, Madam, to spare us the
hardness of your facility?

Eleanor. The wells of Castaly are not
wasted upon the desert. We did but jest.

Henry. There's no jest on the brows of
Herbert there. What is it, Herbert?

Enter HERBERT OF BOSHAM

Herbert. My liege, the good Archbishop
is no more.

Henry. Peace to his soul!

Herbert. I left him with peace on his
face—that sweet other-world smile, which
will be reflected in the spiritual body
among the angels. But he longed much to
see your Grace and the Chancellor ere he
past, and his last words were a commenda-
tion of Thomas Becket to your Grace as
his successor in the archbishoprick.

Henry. Ha, Becket! thou rememberest
our talk!

Becket. My heart is full of tears—I have
no answer.

Henry. Well, well, old men must die, or
the world would grow mouldy, would only
breed the past again. Come to me to-
morrow. Thou hast but to hold out thy
hand. Meanwhile the revenues are mine.
A-hawking, a-hawking! If I sit, I grow fat.
                    [*Leaps over the table, and exit.*

Becket. He did prefer me to the chan-
cellorship,
Believing I should ever aid the Church—
But have I done it? He commends me now
From out his grave to this archbishoprick.

Herbert. A dead man's dying wish should
be of weight.

Becket. His should. Come with me. Let
me learn at full
The manner of his death, and all he said.
                    [*Exeunt* HERBERT *and* BECKET.

Eleanor. Fitzurse, that chart with the
red line—thou sawest it—her bower.

Fitzurse. Rosamund's?

Eleanor. Ay—there lies the secret of her
whereabouts, and the King gave it to his
Chancellor.

Fitzurse. To this son of a London merchant—how your Grace must hate him.

Eleanor. Hate him? as brave a soldier as
Henry and a goodlier man: but thou—dost
thou love this Chancellor, that thou hast
sworn a voluntary allegiance to him?

Fitzurse. Not for my love toward him,
but because he had the love of the King.
How should a baron love a beggar on
horseback, with the retinue of three kings
behind him, outroyalling royalty? Besides,
he holp the King to break down our castles,
for the which I hate him.

Eleanor. For the which I honour him.

Statesman not Churchman he. A great and sound policy that: I could embrace him for it: you could not see the King for the kinglings.

Fitzurse. Ay, but he speaks to a noble as tho' he were a churl, and to a churl as if he were a noble.

Eleanor. Pride of the plebeian!

Fitzurse. And this plebeian like to be Archbishop!

Eleanor. True, and I have an inherited loathing of these black sheep of the Papacy. Archbishop? I can see further into a man than our hot-headed Henry, and if there ever come feud between Church and Crown, and I do not then charm this secret out of our loyal Thomas, I am not Eleanor.

Fitzurse. Last night I followed a woman in the city here. Her face was veiled, but the back methought was Rosamund—his paramour, thy rival. I can feel for thee.

Eleanor. Thou feel for me!—paramour —rival! King Louis had no paramours, and I loved him none the more. Henry had many, and I loved him none the less—now neither more nor less—not at all; the cup's empty. I would she were but his paramour, for men tire of their fancies; but I fear this one fancy hath taken root, and borne blossom too, and she, whom the King loves indeed, is a power in the State. Rival!—ay, and when the King passes, there may come a crash and embroilment as in Stephen's time; and her children—canst thou not— that secret matter which would heat the King against thee (*whispers him and he starts*). Nay, that is safe with me as with thyself: but canst thou not—thou art drowned in debt—thou shalt have our love, our silence, and our gold—canst thou not —if thou light upon her—free me from her?

Fitzurse. Well, Madam, I have loved her in my time.

Eleanor. No, my bear, thou hast not. My Courts of Love would have held thee guiltless of love—the fine attractions and repulses, the delicacies, the subtleties.

Fitzurse. Madam, I loved according to the main purpose and intent of nature.

Eleanor. I warrant thee! thou wouldst hug thy Cupid till his ribs cracked— enough of this. Follow me this Rosamund day and night, whithersoever she goes; track her, if thou canst, even into the King's lodging, that I may (*clenches her fist*)—may at least have my cry against him and her,—and thou in thy way shouldst be jealous of the King, for thou in thy way didst once, what shall I call it, affect her thine own self.

Fitzurse. Ay, but the young colt winced and whinnied and flung up her heels; and then the King came honeying about her, and this Becket, her father's friend, like enough staved us from her.

Eleanor. Us!

Fitzurse. Yea, by the Blessed Virgin! There were more than I buzzing round the blossom—De Tracy—even that flint De Brito.

Eleanor. Carry her off among you; run in upon her and devour her, one and all of you; make her as hateful to herself and to the King, as she is to me.

Fitzurse. I and all would be glad to wreak our spite on the rosefaced minion of the King, and bring her to the level of the dust, so that the King——

Eleanor. Let her eat it like the serpent, and be driven out of her paradise.

ACT I

Scene I

Becket's House in London

Chamber barely furnished. BECKET *unrobing.* HERBERT OF BOSHAM *and* SERVANT

Servant. Shall I not help your lordship to your rest?

Becket. Friend, am I so much better than thyself
That thou shouldst help me? Thou art wearied out
With this day's work, get thee to thine own bed.
Leave me with Herbert, friend.

[*Exit* SERVANT.

Help me off, Herbert, with this—and this.

Herbert. Was not the people's blessing as we past
Heart-comfort and a balsam to thy blood?
Becket. The people know their Church a tower of strength,
A bulwark against Throne and Baronage.
Too heavy for me, this; off with it, Herbert!
Herbert. Is it so much heavier than thy Chancellor's robe?
Becket. No; but the Chancellor's and the Archbishop's
Together more than mortal man can bear.
Herbert. Not heavier than thine armour at Thoulouse?
Becket. O Herbert, Herbert, in my chancellorship
I more than once have gone against the Church.
Herbert. To please the King?
Becket.   Ay, and the King of kings,
Or justice; for it seem'd to me but just
The Church should pay her scutage like the lords.
But hast thou heard this cry of Gilbert Foliot
That I am not the man to be your Primate,
For Henry could not work a miracle—
Make an Archbishop of a soldier?
Herbert.   Ay,
For Gilbert Foliot held himself the man.
Becket. Am I the man? My mother, ere she bore me,
Dream'd that twelve stars fell glittering out of heaven
Into her bosom.
Herbert.   Ay, the fire, the light,
The spirit of the twelve Apostles enter'd
Into thy making.
Becket.   And when I was a child,
The Virgin, in a vision of my sleep,
Gave me the golden keys of Paradise. Dream,
Or prophecy, that?
Herbert.   Well, dream and prophecy both.
Becket. And when I was of Theobald's household, once—
The good old man would sometimes have his jest—
He took his mitre off, and set it on me,

And said, 'My young Archbishop—thou wouldst make
A stately Archbishop!' Jest or prophecy there?
Herbert. Both, Thomas, both.
Becket.   Am I the man? That rang
Within my head last night, and when I slept
Methought I stood in Canterbury Minster,
And spake to the Lord God, and said, 'O Lord,
I have been a lover of wines, and delicate meats,
And secular splendours, and a favourer
Of players, and a courtier, and a feeder
Of dogs and hawks, and apes, and lions, and lynxes.
Am *I* the man?' And the Lord answer'd me,
'Thou art the man, and all the more the man.'
And then I asked again, 'O Lord my God,
Henry the King hath been my friend, my brother,
And mine uplifter in this world, and chosen me
For this thy great archbishoprick, believing
That I should go against the Church with him,
And I shall go against him with the Church,
And I have said no word of this to him:
Am *I* the man?' And the Lord answer'd me,
'Thou art the man, and all the more the man.'
And thereupon, methought, He drew toward me,
And smote me down upon the Minster floor.
I fell.
Herbert. God make not thee, but thy foes, fall.
Becket. I fell. Why fall? Why did He smite me? What?
Shall I fall off—to please the King once more?
Not fight—tho' somehow traitor to the King—
My truest and mine utmost for the Church?

Herbert. Thou canst not fall that way.
  Let traitor be;
For how have fought thine utmost for the
  Church,
Save from the throne of thine archbishop-
  rick?
And how been made Archbishop hadst
  thou told him,
'I mean to fight mine utmost for the
  Church,
Against the King'?
  Becket. But dost thou think the King
Forced mine election?
  Herbert. I do think the King
Was potent in the election, and why not?
Why should not Heaven have so inspired
  the King?
Be comforted. Thou art the man—be thou
A mightier Anselm.
  Becket. I do believe thee, then. I am the
  man.
And yet I seem appall'd—on such a
  sudden
At such an eagle-height I stand and see
The rift that runs between me and the
  King.
I served our Theobald well when I was
  with him;
I served King Henry well as Chancellor;
I am his no more, and I must serve the
  Church.
This Canterbury is only less than Rome,
And all my doubts I fling from me like
  dust,
Winnow and scatter all scruples to the
  wind,
And all the puissance of the warrior,
And all the wisdom of the Chancellor,
And all the heap'd experiences of life,
I cast upon the side of Canterbury—
Our holy mother Canterbury, who sits
With tatter'd robes. Laics and barons,
  thro'
The random gifts of careless kings, have
  graspt
Her livings, her advowsons, granges,
  farms,
And goodly acres—we will make her
  whole;
Not one rood lost. And for these Royal
  customs,

These ancient Royal customs—they *are*
  Royal,
Not of the Church—and let them be
  anathema,
And all that speak for them anathema.
  Herbert. Thomas, thou art moved too
  much.
  Becket. O Herbert, here
I gash myself asunder from the King,
Tho' leaving each, a wound; mine own, a
  grief
To show the scar for ever—his, a hate
Not ever to be heal'd.

Enter ROSAMUND DE CLIFFORD, *flying from*
SIR REGINALD FITZURSE. *Drops her veil*

  Becket. Rosamund de Clifford!
  Rosamund. Save me, father, hide me—
they follow me—and I must not be known.
  Becket. Pass in with Herbert there.
      [*Exeunt* ROSAMUND *and* HERBERT *by*
      side door.

Enter FITZURSE

  Fitzurse. The Archbishop!
  Becket. Ay! what wouldst thou,
  Reginald?
  Fitzurse. Why—why, my lord, I fol-
  low'd—follow'd one——
  Becket. And then what follows? Let me
  follow thee.
  Fitzurse. It much imports me I should
  know her name.
  Becket. What her?
  Fitzurse. The woman that I follow'd
  hither.
  Becket. Perhaps it may import her all as
  much
Not to be known.
  Fitzurse. And what care I for that?
Come, come, my lord Archbishop; I saw
  that door
Close even now upon the woman.
  Becket. Well?
  Fitzurse (*making for the door*). Nay, let
  me pass, my lord, for I must know.
  Becket. Back, man!
  Fitzurse. Then tell me who
  and what she is.
  Becket. Art thou so sure thou followedst
  anything?

Go home, and sleep thy wine off, for thine
    eyes
Glare stupid-wild with wine.
    Fitzurse (making to the door). I must and
        will.
I care not for thy new archbishoprick.
    Becket. Back, man, I tell thee! What!
Shall I forget my new archbishoprick
And smite thee with my crozier on the
    skull?
'Fore God, I am a mightier man than thou.
    Fitzurse. It well befits thy new arch-
        bishoprick
To take the vagabond woman of the street
Into thine arms!
    Becket.   O drunken ribaldry!
Out, beast, out, bear!
    Fitzurse.   I shall remember this.
    Becket. Do, and begone!
                              [*Exit* FITZURSE.
    [*Going to the door, sees* DE TRACY.
            Tracy, what dost thou here?
    De Tracy. My lord, I follow'd Reginald
        Fitzurse.
    Becket. Follow him out!
    De Tracy.   I shall remember this
Discourtesy.   [*Exit.*
    Becket. Do. These be those baron-brutes
That havock'd all the land in Stephen's
    day.
Rosamund de Clifford.

        Re-enter ROSAMUND *and* HERBERT
    Rosamund.   Here am I.
    Becket.   Why here?
We gave thee to the charge of John of
    Salisbury,
To pass thee to thy secret bower to-
    morrow.
Wast thou not told to keep thyself from
    sight?
    Rosamund. Poor bird of passage! so I
        was; but, father,
They say that you are wise in winged
    things,
And know the ways of Nature. Bar the
    bird
From following the fled summer—a chink
    —he's out,
Gone! And there stole into the city a
    breath

Full of the meadows, and it minded me
Of the sweet woods of Clifford, and the
    walks
Where I could move at pleasure, and I
    thought
Lo! I must out or die.
    Becket.   Or out *and* die.
And what hast thou to do with this
    Fitzurse?
    Rosamund. Nothing. He sued my hand.
        I shook at him.
He found me once alone. Nay—nay—I
    cannot
Tell you: my father drove him and his
    friends,
De Tracy and De Brito, from our castle.
I was but fourteen and an April then.
I heard him swear revenge.
    Becket.   Why will you court it
By self-exposure? flutter out at night?
Make it so hard to save a moth from the
    fire?
    Rosamund. I have saved many of 'em.
        You catch 'em, so,
Softly, and fling them out to the free air.
They burn themselves *within*-door.
    Becket.   Our good John
Must speed you to your bower at once.
    The child
Is there already.
    Rosamund.   Yes—the child—the
        child—
O rare, a whole long day of open field.
    Becket. Ay, but you go disguised.
    Rosamund.   O rare again!
We'll baffle them, I warrant. What shall
    it be?
I'll go as a nun.
    Becket.   No.
    Rosamund.   What, not good enough
Even to play at nun?
    Becket.   Dan John with a nun,
That Map, and these new railers at the
    Church
May plaister his clean name with scurrilous
    rhymes!
No!
Go like a monk, cowling and clouding up
That fatal star, thy Beauty, from the squint
Of lust and glare of malice. Good night!
    good night!

Rosamund. Father, I am so tender to all
    hardness!
Nay, father, first thy blessing.
Becket.   Wedded?
Rosamund.   Father!
Becket. Well, well! I ask no more.
    Heaven bless thee! hence!
Rosamund. O, holy father, when thou
    seest him next,
Commend me to thy friend.
Becket.   What friend?
Rosamund.   The King.
Becket. Herbert, take out a score of
    armed men
To guard this bird of passage to her cage;
And watch Fitzurse, and if he follow thee,
Make him thy prisoner. I am Chancellor
    yet.
       [*Exeunt* HERBERT *and* ROSAMUND.
Poor soul! poor soul!
My friend, the King! . . . O thou Great
    Seal of England,
Given me by my dear friend the King of
    England—
We long have wrought together, thou
    and I—
Now must I send thee as a common friend
To tell the King, my friend, I am against
    him.
We are friends no more: he will say that,
    not I.
The worldly bond between us is dissolved,
Not yet the love: can I be under him
As Chancellor? as Archbishop over him?
Go therefore like a friend slighted by one
That hath climb'd up to nobler company.
Not slighted—all but moan'd for: thou
    must go.
I have not dishonour'd thee—I trust I
    have not;
Not mangled justice. May the hand that
    next
Inherits thee be but as true to thee
As mine hath been! O, my dear friend, the
    King!
O brother!—I may come to martyrdom.
I am martyr in myself already.—Herbert!
   Herbert (*re-entering*). My lord, the town
    is quiet, and the moon
Divides the whole long street with light
    and shade.

No footfall—no Fitzurse. We have seen
    her home.
Becket. The hog hath tumbled himself
    into some corner,
Some ditch, to snore away his drunken-
    ness
Into the sober headache,—Nature's moral
Against excess. Let the Great Seal be sent
Back to the King to-morrow.
Herbert.   Must that be?
The King may rend the bearer limb from
    limb.
Think on it again.
Becket.   Against the moral excess
No physical ache, but failure it may be
Of all we aim'd at. John of Salisbury
Hath often laid a cold hand on my heats,
And Herbert hath rebuked me even now.
I will be wise and wary, not the soldier
As Foliot swears it.—John, and out of
    breath!

      Enter JOHN OF SALISBURY

John of Salisbury. Thomas, thou wast
    not happy taking charge
Of this wild Rosamund to please the King,
Nor am I happy having charge of her—
The included Danaë has escaped again
Her tower, and her Acrisius—where to
    seek?
I have been about the city.
Becket.   Thou wilt find her
Back in her lodging. Go with her—at
    once—
To-night—my men will guard you to the
    gates.
Be sweet to her, she has many enemies.
Send the Great Seal by daybreak. Both,
    good night!

SCENE II

Street in Northampton leading to the Castle

ELEANOR'S RETAINERS *and* BECKET'S
RETAINERS *fighting. Enter* ELEANOR *and*
BECKET *from opposite streets.*

Eleanor. Peace, fools!
Becket.   Peace, friends! what idle
    brawl is this?
Retainer of Becket. They said—her
    Grace's people—thou wast found—

Liars! I shame to quote 'em—caught, my lord,
With a wanton in thy lodging—Hell requite 'em!
Retainer of Eleanor. My liege, the Lord Fitzurse reported this
In passing to the Castle even now.
Retainer of Becket. And then they mock'd us and we fell upon 'em,
For we would live and die for thee, my lord,
However kings and queens may frown on thee.
Becket to his Retainers. Go, go—no more of this!
Eleanor to her Retainers. Away!—
(*Exeunt* RETAINERS) Fitzurse——
Becket. Nay, let him be.
Eleanor.   No, no, my Lord Archbishop,
'Tis known you are midwinter to all women,
But often in your chancellorship you served
The follies of the King.
Becket.   No, not these follies!
Eleanor. My lord, Fitzurse beheld her in your lodging.
Becket. Whom?
Eleanor.   Well—you know—the minion, Rosamund.
Becket. He had good eyes!
Eleanor.   Then hidden in the street
He watch'd her pass with John of Salisbury
And heard her cry 'Where is this bower of mine?'
Becket. Good ears too!
Eleanor. You are going to the Castle,
Will you subscribe the customs?
Becket.   I leave that,
Knowing how much you reverence Holy Church,
My liege, to your conjecture.
Eleanor.   I and mine—
And many a baron holds along with me—
Are not so much at feud with Holy Church
But we might take your side against the customs—
So that you grant me one slight favour.
Becket.   What?
Eleanor. A sight of that same chart which Henry gave you

With the red line—'her bower.'
Becket.   And to that end?
Eleanor. That Church must scorn herself whose fearful Priest
Sits winking at the license of a king,
Altho' we grant when kings are dangerous
The Church must play into the hands of kings;
Look! I would move this wanton from his sight
And take the Church's danger on myself.
Becket. For which she should be duly grateful.
Eleanor.   True!
Tho' she that binds the bond, herself should see
That kings are faithful to their marriage vow.
Becket. Ay, Madam, and queens also.
Eleanor.   And queens also!
What is your drift?
Becket.   My drift is to the Castle,
Where I shall meet the Barons and my King.   [*Exit.*

DE BROC, DE TRACY, DE BRITO,
DE MORVILLE (*passing*)

Eleanor. To the Castle?
De Broc.   Ay!
Eleanor. Stir up the King, the Lords!
Set all on fire against him!
De Brito.   Ay, good Madam!
                                [*Exeunt.*
Eleanor. Fool! I will make thee hateful to thy King.
Churl! I will have thee frighted into France,
And I shall live to trample on thy grave.

SCENE III

The Hall in Northampton Castle

On one side of the stage the doors of an inner Council-chamber, half-open. At the bottom, the great doors of the Hall. ROGER ARCHBISHOP OF YORK, FOLIOT BISHOP OF LONDON, HILARY OF CHICHESTER, BISHOP OF HEREFORD, RICHARD DE HASTINGS (*Grand Prior of Templars*), PHILIP DE ELEEMOSYNA (*the Pope's Almoner*), *and others.* DE BROC, FITZURSE, DE BRITO, DE

MORVILLE, DE TRACY, *and other* BARONS
assembled—a table before them. JOHN OF
OXFORD, *President of the Council.*

Enter BECKET *and* HERBERT OF BOSHAM

Becket. Where is the King?
Roger of York.   Gone hawking on
the Nene,
His heart so gall'd with thine ingratitude,
He will not see thy face till thou hast
sign'd
These ancient laws and customs of the
realm.
Thy sending back the Great Seal madden'd
him,
He all but pluck'd the bearer's eyes away.
Take heed, lest he destroy thee utterly.
     Becket. Then shalt thou step into my
place and sign.
     Roger of York. Didst thou not promise
Henry to obey
These ancient laws and customs of the
realm?
     Becket. Saving the honour of my order
—ay.
Customs, traditions,—clouds that come
and go;
The customs of the Church are Peter's
rock.
     Roger of York. Saving thine order! But
King Henry sware
That, saving his King's kingship, he would
grant thee
The crown itself. Saving thine order,
Thomas,
Is black and white at once, and comes to
nought.
O bolster'd up with stubbornness and
pride,
Wilt thou destroy the Church in fighting
for it,
And bring us all to shame?
     Becket.   Roger of York,
When I and thou were youths in Theo-
bald's house,
Twice did thy malice and thy calumnies
Exile me from the face of Theobald.
Now I am Canterbury and thou art York.
     Roger of York. And is not York the peer
of Canterbury?
Did not Great Gregory bid St. Austin here

Found two archbishopricks, London and
York?
     Becket. What came of that? The first
archbishop fled,
And York lay barren for a hundred years.
Why, by this rule, Foliot may claim the
pall
For London too.
     Foliot.   And with good reason too,
For London had a temple and a priest
When Canterbury hardly bore a name.
     Becket. The pagan temple of a pagan
Rome!
The heathen priesthood of a heathen creed!
Thou goest beyond thyself in petulancy!
Who made thee London? Who, but
Canterbury?
     John of Oxford. Peace, peace, my lords!
these customs are no longer
As Canterbury calls them, wandering
clouds,
But by the King's command are written
down,
And by the King's command I, John of
Oxford,
The President of this Council, read them.
     Becket.   Read!
     John of Oxford (*reads*). 'All causes of
advowsons and presentations, whether be-
tween laymen or clerics, shall be tried in
the King's court.'
     Becket. But that I cannot sign: for that
would drag
The cleric before the civil judgment-seat,
And on a matter wholly spiritual.
     John of Oxford. 'If any cleric be accused
of felony, the Church shall not protect
him; but he shall answer to the summons
of the King's court to be tried therein.'
     Becket. And that I cannot sign.
Is not the Church the visible Lord on
earth?
Shall hands that do create the Lord be
bound
Behind the back like laymen-criminals?
The Lord be judged again by Pilate? No!
     John of Oxford. 'When a bishoprick falls
vacant, the King, till another be appointed,
shall receive the revenues thereof.'
     Becket. And that I cannot sign. Is the
King's treasury

A fit place for the monies of the Church,
That be the patrimony of the poor?

John of Oxford. 'And when the vacancy
is to be filled up, the King shall summon
the chapter of that church to court, and the
election shall be made in the Chapel Royal,
with the consent of our lord the King, and
by the advice of his Government.'

Becket. And that I cannot sign: for that
would make
Our island-Church a schism from Christendom,
And weight down all free choice beneath
the throne.

Foliot. And was thine own election so
canonical,
Good father?

Becket. If it were not, Gilbert Foliot,
I mean to cross the sea to France, and lay
My crozier in the Holy Father's hands,
And bid him re-create me, Gilbert Foliot.

Foliot. Nay; by another of these customs
thou
Wilt not be suffer'd so to cross the seas
Without the license of our lord the King.

Becket. That, too, I cannot sign.

DE BROC, DE BRITO, DE TRACY, FITZURSE,
DE MORVILLE, *start up—a clash of swords.*
            Sign and obey!

Becket. My lords, is this a combat or a
council?
Are ye my masters, or my lord the King?
Ye make this clashing for no love o' the
customs
Or constitutions, or whate'er ye call them,
But that there be among you those that
hold
Lands reft from Canterbury.

De Broc.   And mean to keep them,
In spite of thee!

Lords (*shouting*). Sign, and obey the
crown!

Becket. The crown? Shall I do less for
Canterbury
Than Henry for the crown? King Stephen
gave
Many of the crown lands to those that
helpt him;
So did Matilda, the King's mother. Mark,
When Henry came into his own again,

Then he took back not only Stephen's gifts,
But his own mother's, lest the crown
should be
Shorn of ancestral splendour. This did
Henry.
Shall I do less for mine own Canterbury?
And thou, De Broc, that holdest Saltwood
Castle——

De Broc. And mean to hold it, or——

Becket.   To have my life.

De Broc. The King is quick to anger; if
thou anger him,
We wait but the King's word to strike thee
dead.

Becket. Strike, and I die the death of
martyrdom;
Strike, and ye set these customs by my
death
Ringing their own death-knell thro' all the
realm.

Herbert. And I can tell you, lords, ye are
all as like
To lodge a fear in Thomas Becket's heart
As find a hare's form in a lion's cave.

John of Oxford. Ay, sheathe your swords,
ye will displease the King.

De Broc. Why down then thou! but an
he come to Saltwood,
By God's death, thou shalt stick him like
a calf!   [*Sheathing his sword.*

Hilary. O my good lord, I do entreat
thee—sign.
Save the King's honour here before his
barons.
He hath sworn that thou shouldst sign, and
now but shuns
The semblance of defeat; I have heard
him say
He means no more; so if thou sign, my
lord,
That were but as the shadow of an assent.

Becket. 'Twould seem too like the substance, if I sign'd.

Philip de Eleemosyna. My lord, thine ear!
I have the ear of the Pope.
As thou hast honour for the Pope our
master,
Have pity on him, sorely prest upon
By the fierce Emperor and his Antipope.
Thou knowest he was forced to fly to
France;

He pray'd me to pray thee to pacify
Thy King; for if thou go against thy King,
Then must he likewise go against thy King,
And then thy King might join the Anti-
    pope,
And that would shake the Papacy as it
    stands.
Besides, thy King swore to our cardinals
He meant no harm nor damage to the
    Church.
Smoothe thou his pride—thy signing is
    but form;
Nay, and should harm come of it, it is the
    Pope
Will be to blame—not thou. Over and
    over
He told me thou shouldst pacify the King,
Lest there be battle between Heaven and
    Earth,
And Earth should get the better—for the
    time.
Cannot the Pope absolve thee if thou sign?
    Becket. Have I the orders of the Holy
    Father?
    Philip de Eleemosyna. Orders, my lord—
    why, no; for what am I?
The secret whisper of the Holy Father.
Thou, that hast been a statesman, couldst
    thou always
Blurt thy free mind to the air?
    Becket. If Rome be feeble, then should
    I be firm.
    Philip. Take it not that way—balk not
    the Pope's will.
When he hath shaken off the Emperor,
He heads the Church against the King
    with thee.
    Richard de Hastings (kneeling). Becket,
    I am the oldest of the Templars;
I knew thy father; he would be mine age
Had he lived now; think of me as thy
    father!
Behold thy father kneeling to thee, Becket.
Submit; I promise thee on my salvation
That thou wilt hear no more o' the
    customs.
    Becket.   What!
Hath Henry told thee? hast thou talk'd
    with him?
    Another Templar (kneeling). Father, I
    am the youngest of the Templars,

Look on me as I were thy bodily son,
For, like a son, I lift my hands to thee.
    Philip. Wilt thou hold out for ever,
    Thomas Becket?
Dost thou not hear?
    Becket (signs). Why—there then—there
    —I sign,
And swear to obey the customs.
    Foliot.   Is it thy will,
My lord Archbishop, that we too should
    sign?
    Becket. O ay, by that canonical obedience
Thou still hast owed thy father, Gilbert
    Foliot.
    Foliot. Loyally and with good faith, my
    lord Archbishop?
    Becket. O ay, with all that loyalty and
    good faith
Thou still hast shown thy primate, Gilbert
    Foliot.
    [BECKET *draws apart with* HERBERT.
Herbert, Herbert, have I betray'd the
    Church?
I'll have the paper back—blot out my
    name.
    Herbert. Too late, my lord: you see they
    are signing there.
    Becket. False to myself—it is the will of
    God
To break me, prove me nothing of myself!
This Almoner hath tasted Henry's gold.
The cardinals have finger'd Henry's gold.
And Rome is venal ev'n to rottenness.
I see it, I see it.
I am no soldier, as he said—at least
No leader. Herbert, till I hear from the
    Pope
I will suspend myself from all my functions.
If fast and prayer, the lacerating
    scourge——
    Foliot (from the table). My lord Arch-
    bishop, thou hast yet to seal.
    Becket. First, Foliot, let me see what I
    have sign'd.   [*Goes to the table.*
What, this! and this!—what! new and old
    together!
Seal? If a seraph shouted from the sun,
And bad me seal against the rights of the
    Church,
I would anathematise him. I will not seal.
    [*Exit with* HERBERT.

Enter KING HENRY

Henry. Where's Thomas? hath he
   sign'd? show me the papers!
Sign'd and not seal'd! How's that?
John of Oxford. He would not seal.
And when he sign'd, his face was stormy-
   red—
Shame, wrath, I know not what. He sat
   down there
And dropt it in his hands, and then a
   paleness,
Like the wan twilight after sunset, crept
Up even to the tonsure, and he groan'd,
'False to myself! It is the will of God!'
Henry. God's will be what it will, the
   man shall seal,
Or I will seal his doom. My burgher's
   son—
Nay, if I cannot break him as the prelate,
I'll crush him as the subject. Send for him
   back.   [*Sits on his throne.*
Barons and bishops of our realm of Eng-
   land,
After the nineteen winters of King
   Stephen—
A reign which was no reign, when none
   could sit
By his own hearth in peace; when murder
   common
As nature's death, like Egypt's plague, had
   fill'd
All things with blood; when every door-
   way blush'd,
Dash'd red with that unhallow'd passover;
When every baron ground his blade in
   blood;
The household dough was kneaded up
   with blood;
The millwheel turn'd in blood; the whole-
   some plow
Lay rusting in the furrow's yellow weeds,
Till famine dwarft the race—I came, your
   King!
Nor dwelt alone, like a soft lord of the
   East,
In mine own hall, and sucking thro' fools'
   ears
The flatteries of corruption—went abroad
Thro' all my counties, spied my people's
   ways;

Yea, heard the churl against the baron—
   yea,
And did him justice; sat in mine own
   courts
Judging my judges, that had found a King
Who ranged confusions, made the twilight
   day,
And struck a shape from out the vague,
   and law
From madness. And the event—our
   fallows till'd,
Much corn, repeopled towns, a realm again.
So far my course, albeit not glassy-smooth,
Had prosper'd in the main, but suddenly
Jarr'd on this rock. A cleric violated
The daughter of his host, and murder'd
   him.
Bishops—York, London, Chichester,
   Westminster—
Ye haled this tonsured devil into your
   courts;
But since your canon will not let you take
Life for a life, ye but degraded him
Where I had hang'd him. What doth hard
   murder care
For degradation? and that made me muse,
Being bounden by my coronation oath
To do men justice. Look to it, your own
   selves!
Say that a cleric murder'd an archbishop,
What could ye do? Degrade, imprison
   him—
Not death for death.
   John of Oxford. But I, my liege, could
      swear,
To death for death.
   Henry.   And, looking thro' my reign,
I found a hundred ghastly murders done
By men, the scum and offal of the Church;
Then, glancing thro' the story of this
   realm,
I came on certain wholesome usages,
Lost in desuetude, of my grandsire's day,
Good royal customs—had them written
   fair
For John of Oxford here to read to you.
   John of Oxford. And I can easily swear
      to these as being
The King's will and God's will and justice;
   yet
I could but read a part to-day, because——

Fitzurse. Because my lord of Canter-
bury——
De Tracy. Ay,
This lord of Canterbury——
De Brito.   As is his wont
Too much of late whene'er your royal
rights
Are mooted in our councils——
Fitzurse.   —made an uproar.
Henry. And Becket had my bosom on
all this;
If ever man by bonds of gratefulness—
I raised him from the puddle of the gutter,
I made him porcelain from the clay of the
city—
Thought that I knew him, err'd thro' love
of him,
Hoped, were he chosen archbishop, Church
and Crown,
Two sisters gliding in an equal dance,
Two rivers gently flowing side by side—
But no!
The bird that moults sings the same song
again,
The snake that sloughs comes out a snake
again.
Snake—ay, but he that lookt a fangless
one,
Issues a venomous adder.
For he, when having dofft the Chancellor's
robe—
Flung the Great Seal of England in my
face—
Claim'd some of our crown lands for
Canterbury—
My comrade, boon companion, my co-
reveller,
The master of his master, the King's
king.—
God's eyes! I had meant to make him all
but king.
Chancellor-Archbishop, he might well
have sway'd
All England under Henry, the young King,
When I was hence. What did the traitor
say?
False to himself, but ten-fold false to me!
The will of God—why, then it is my will—
Is he coming?
Messenger (entering). With a crowd of
worshippers,

And holds his cross before him thro' the
crowd,
As one that puts himself in sanctuary.
Henry. His cross!
Roger of York. His cross! I'll front him,
cross to cross.
[*Exit* ROGER OF YORK.
Henry. His cross! it is the traitor that
imputes
Treachery to his King!
It is not safe for me to look upon him.
Away—with me!
[*Goes in with his* BARONS *to the
Council-Chamber, the door of which
is left open.*

Enter BECKET, *holding his cross of silver
before him. The* BISHOPS *come round him.*

Hereford. The King will not abide thee
with thy cross.
Permit me, my good lord, to bear it for
thee,
Being thy chaplain.
Becket.   No: it must protect me.
Herbert. As once he bore the standard
of the Angles,
So now he bears the standard of the angels.
Foliot. I am the Dean of the province:
let me bear it.
Make not thy King a traitorous murderer.
Becket. Did not your barons draw their
swords against me?

Enter ROGER OF YORK, *with his cross,
advancing to* BECKET

Becket. Wherefore dost thou presume
to bear thy cross,
Against the solemn ordinance from Rome,
Out of thy province?
Roger of York. Why dost thou presume,
Arm'd with thy cross, to come before the
King?
If Canterbury brings his cross to court,
Let York bear his to mate with Canter-
bury.
Foliot (seizing hold of BECKET'S *cross).*
Nay, nay, my lord, thou must not
brave the King.
Nay, let me have it. I will have it!
Becket.   Away!
[*Flinging him off.*

Foliot. He fasts, they say, this mitred
    Hercules!
He fast! is that an arm of fast? My lord,
Hadst thou not sign'd, I had gone along
    with thee;
But thou the shepherd hast betray'd the
    sheep,
And thou art perjured, and thou wilt not
    seal.
As Chancellor thou wast against the
    Church,
Now as Archbishop goest against the King;
For, like a fool, thou knowst no middle
    way.
Ay, ay! but art thou stronger than the
    King?
    Becket. Strong—not in mine own self,
    but Heaven; true
To either function, holding it; and thou
Fast, scourge thyself, and mortify thy flesh,
Not spirit—thou remainest Gilbert Foliot,
A worldly follower of the worldly strong.
I, bearing this great ensign, make it clear
Under what Prince I fight.
    Foliot.   My lord of York,
Let us go in to the Council, where our
    bishops
And our great lords will sit in judgment
    on him.
    Becket. Sons sit in judgment on their
    father!—then
The spire of Holy Church may prick the
    graves—
Her crypt among the stars. Sign? seal?
    I promised
The King to obey these customs, not yet
    written,
Saving mine order; true too, that when
    written
I sign'd them—being a fool, as Foliot call'd
    me.
I hold not by my signing. Get ye hence,
Tell what I say to the King.
    [*Exeunt* HEREFORD, FOLIOT, *and other*
    BISHOPS.
Roger of York.   The Church will
    hate thee.   [*Exit.*
    Becket. Serve my best friend and make
    him my worst foe;
Fight for the Church, and set the Church
    against me!

Herbert. To be honest is to set all knaves
    against thee.
Ah! Thomas, excommunicate them all!
Hereford (re-entering). I cannot brook
    the turmoil thou hast raised.
I would, my lord Thomas of Canterbury,
Thou wert plain Thomas and not Canter-
    bury,
Or that thou wouldst deliver Canterbury
To our King's hands again, and be at
    peace.
Hilary (re-entering). For hath not thine
    ambition set the Church
This day between the hammer and the
    anvil—
Fealty to the King, obedience to thyself?
Herbert. What say the bishops?
Hilary. Some have pleaded for him,
But the King rages—most are with the
    King;
And some are reeds, that one time sway to
    the current,
And to the wind another. But we hold
Thou art forsworn; and no forsworn Arch-
    bishop
Shall helm the Church. We therefore place
    ourselves
Under the shield and safeguard of the
    Pope,
And cite thee to appear before the Pope,
And answer thine accusers. . . . Art thou
    deaf?
Becket. I hear you.   [*Clash of arms.*
Hilary. Dost thou hear those others?
Becket.   Ay!
Roger of York (re-entering). The King's
    'God's eyes!' come now so thick and
    fast,
We fear that he may reave thee of thine
    own.
Come on, come on! it is not fit for us
To see the proud Archbishop mutilated.
Say that he blind thee and tear out thy
    tongue.
    Becket. So be it. He begins at top
    with me:
They crucified St. Peter downward.
Roger of York.   Nay,
But for their sake who stagger betwixt
    thine
Appeal, and Henry's anger, yield.

Becket.   Hence, Satan!
    [*Exit* ROGER OF YORK.
Fitzurse (*re-entering*). My lord, the King
    demands three hundred marks,
Due from his castles of Berkhamstead and
    Eye
When thou thereof wast warden.
Becket.   Tell the King
I spent thrice that in fortifying his castles.
De Tracy (*re-entering*). My lord, the
    King demands seven hundred marks,
Lent at the siege of Thoulouse by the King.
Becket. I led seven hundred knights and
    fought his wars.
De Brito (*re-entering*). My lord, the King
    demands five hundred marks,
Advanced thee at his instance by the Jews,
For which the King was bound security.
Becket. I thought it was a gift; I thought
    it was a gift.

    Enter LORD LEICESTER (*followed by*
      BARONS *and* BISHOPS)

Leicester. My lord, I come unwillingly.
The King Demands a strict account of all
    those revenues
From all the vacant sees and abbacies,
Which came into thy hands when Chan-
    cellor.
Becket. How much might that amount
    to, my lord Leicester?
Leicester. Some thirty—forty thousand
    silver marks.
Becket. Are these your customs? O my
    good lord Leicester,
The King and I were brothers. All I had
I lavish'd for the glory of the King;
I shone from him, for him, his glory, his
Reflection: now the glory of the Church
Hath swallow'd up the glory of the King;
I am his no more, but hers. Grant me one
    day
To ponder these demands.
Leicester.   Hear first thy sentence!
The King and all his lords——
Becket.   Son, first hear *me!*
Leicester. Nay, nay, canst thou, that
    holdest thine estates
In fee and barony of the King, decline
The judgment of the King?
Becket.   The King! I hold

Nothing in fee and barony of the King.
Whatever the Church owns—she holds
    it in
Free and perpetual alms, unsubject to
One earthly sceptre.
Leicester. Nay, but hear thy judgment.
The King and all his barons——
Becket.   Judgment! Barons!
Who but the bridegroom dares to judge
    the bride.
Or he the bridegroom may appoint? Not
    he
That is not of the house, but from the
    street
Stain'd with the mire thereof.
           I had been so true
To Henry and mine office that the King
Would throne me in the great Archbishop-
    rick:
And I, that knew mine own infirmity,
For the King's pleasure rather than God's
    cause
Took it upon me—err'd thro' love of him.
Now therefore God from me withdraws
    Himself,
And the King too.
        What! forty thousand marks!
Why thou, the King, the Pope, the Saints,
    the world,
Know that when made Archbishop I was
    freed,
Before the Prince and chief Justiciary,
From every bond and debt and obligation
Incurr'd as Chancellor.
            Hear me, son.
               As gold
Outvalues dross, light darkness, Abel Cain,
The soul the body, and the Church the
    Throne,
I charge thee, upon pain of mine anathema,
That thou obey, not me, but God in me,
Rather than Henry. I refuse to stand
By the King's censure, make my cry to the
    Pope,
By whom I will be judged; refer myself,
The King, these customs, all the Church,
    to him,
And under his authority—I depart.
                [*Going.*
    [LEICESTER *looks at him doubtingly.*
Am I a prisoner?

Leicester.   By St. Lazarus, no!
I am confounded by thee. Go in peace.
   De Broc. In peace now—but after. Take
   that for earnest.
      [*Flings a bone at him from the rushes.*
De Brito, Fitzurse, De Tracy, and others
(*flinging wisps of rushes*). Ay, go in peace,
caitiff, caitiff! And that too, perjured pre-
late—and that, turncoat shaveling! There,
there! there! traitor, traitor, traitor!
   Becket. Mannerless wolves!
                     [*Turning and facing them.*
Herbert. Enough, my lord, enough!
Becket. Barons of England and of Nor-
mandy,
When what ye shake at doth but seem to
   fly,
True test of coward, ye follow with a yell.
But I that threw the mightiest knight of
   France,
Sir Engelram de Trie,——
   Herbert.   Enough, my lord.
Becket. More than enough. I play the
   fool again.

Enter HERALD

Herald. The King commands you, upon
   pain of death,
That none should wrong or injure your
   Archbishop.
Foliot. Deal gently with the young man
   Absalom.
      [*Great doors of the Hall at the back
      open, and discover a crowd. They
      shout:*
Blessed is he that cometh in the name of
   the Lord!

Scene IV

Refectory of the Monastery at Northampton.
A banquet on the Tables

Enter BECKET. BECKET'S RETAINERS

1st Retainer. Do thou speak first.
2nd Retainer. Nay, thou! Nay, thou!
Hast not thou drawn the short straw?
1st Retainer. My lord Archbishop, wilt
thou permit us——
Becket. To speak without stammering
and like a free man? Ay.

1st Retainer. My lord, permit us then to
leave thy service.
Becket. When?
1st Retainer. Now.
Becket. To-night?
1st Retainer. To-night, my lord.
Becket. And why?
1st Retainer. My lord, we leave thee not
without tears.
Becket. Tears? Why not stay with me
then?
1st Retainer. My lord, we cannot yield
thee an answer altogether to thy satisfac-
tion.
Becket. I warrant you, or your own
either. Shall I find you one? The King
hath frowned upon me.
1st Retainer. That is not altogether our
answer, my lord.
Becket. No; yet all but all. Go, go! Ye
have eaten of my dish and drunken of my
cup for a dozen years.
1st Retainer. And so we have. We mean
thee no wrong. Wilt thou not say, 'God
bless you,' ere we go?
Becket. God bless you all! God redden
your pale blood! But mine is human-red;
and when ye shall hear it is poured out
upon earth, and see it mounting to Heaven,
my God bless you, that seems sweet to you
now, will blast and blind you like a curse.
1st Retainer. We hope not, my lord. Our
humblest thanks for your blessing. Farewell!   [*Exeunt RETAINERS.*
Becket. Farewell, friends! farewell, swallows! I wrong the bird; she leaves only the
nest she built, they leave the builder. Why?
Am I to be murdered to-night?
                     [*Knocking at the door.*
Attendant. Here is a missive left at the
gate by one from the castle.
Becket. Cornwall's hand or Leicester's:
they write marvellously alike.   [*Reading.*
   'Fly at once to France, to King Louis
of France: there be those about our King
who would have thy blood.'

Was not my lord of Leicester bidden to
to our supper?
Attendant. Ay, my lord, and divers other
earls and barons. But the hour is past, and

our brother, Master Cook, he makes moan
that all be a-getting cold.

Becket. And I make my moan along with
him. Cold after warm, winter after summer,
and the golden leaves, these earls and
barons, that clung to me, frosted off me by
the first cold frown of the King. Cold, but
look how the table steams, like a heathen
altar; nay, like the altar at Jerusalem. Shall
God's good gifts be wasted? None of them
here! Call in the poor from the streets, and
let them feast.

Herbert. That is the parable of our
blessed Lord.

Becket. And why should not the parable
of our blessed Lord be acted again? Call
in the poor! The Church is ever at variance
with the kings, and ever at one with the
poor. I marked a group of lazars in the
marketplace—half-rag, half-sore—beggars,
poor rogues (Heaven bless 'em) who never
saw nor dreamed of such a banquet. I will
amaze them. Call them in, I say. They shall
henceforward be my earls and barons—
our lords and masters in Christ Jesus.

[*Exit* HERBERT.

If the King hold his purpose, I am
myself a beggar. Forty thousand marks!
forty thousand devils—and these craven
bishops!

A POOR MAN (*entering*) *with his dog*

My lord Archbishop, may I come in
with my poor friend, my dog? The King's
verdurer caught him a-hunting in the
forest, and cut off his paws. The dog
followed his calling, my lord. I ha' carried
him ever so many miles in my arms, and
he licks my face and moans and cries out
against the King.

Becket. Better thy dog than thee. The
King's courts would use thee worse than
thy dog—they are too bloody. Were the
Church king, it would be otherwise. Poor
beast! set him down. I will bind up his
wounds with my napkin. Give him a bone,
give him a bone! Who misuses a dog would
misuse a child—they cannot speak for
themselves. Past help! his paws are past
help. God help him!

Enter the BEGGARS (*and seat themselves at
the Tables*). BECKET *and* HERBERT *wait
upon them.*

1*st Beggar.* Swine, sheep, ox—here's a
French supper. When thieves fall out,
honest men——

2*nd Beggar.* Is the Archbishop a thief
who gives thee thy supper?

1*st Beggar.* Well, then, how does it go?
When honest men fall out, thieves—no, it
can't be that.

2*nd Beggar.* Who stole the widow's one
sitting hen o' Sunday, when she was at mass?

1*st Beggar.* Come, come! thou hadst thy
share on her. Sitting hen! Our Lord
Becket's our great sitting-hen cock, and
we shouldn't ha' been sitting here if the
barons and bishops hadn't been a-sitting
on the Archbishop.

Becket. Ay, the princes sat in judgment
against me, and the Lord hath prepared
your table—*Sederunt principes, ederunt
pauperes.*

A Voice. Becket, beware of the knife!

Becket. Who spoke?

3*rd Beggar.* Nobody, my lord. What's
that, my lord?

Becket. Venison.

3*rd Beggar.* Venison?

Becket. Buck; deer, as you call it.

3*rd Beggar.* King's meat! By the Lord,
won't we pray for your lordship!

Becket. And, my children, your prayers
will do more for me in the day of peril that
dawns darkly and drearily over the house
of God—yea, and in the day of judgment
also, than the swords of the craven syco-
phants would have done had they remained
true to me whose bread they have partaken.
I must leave you to your banquet. Feed,
feast, and be merry. Herbert, for the sake
of the Church itself, if not for my own, I
must fly to France to-night. Come with me.

[*Exit with* HERBERT.

3*rd Beggar.* Here—all of you—my lord's
health (*they drink*). Well—if that isn't
goodly wine——

1*st Beggar.* Then there isn't a goodly
wench to serve him with it: they were
fighting for her to-day in the street.

3rd Beggar. Peace!

1st Beggar. The black sheep baaed to the
miller's ewe-lamb,
The miller's away for to-night.
Black sheep, quoth she, too black a sin
for me.
And what said the black sheep, my
masters?
We can make a black sin white.

3rd Beggar. Peace!

1st Beggar. 'Ewe lamb, ewe lamb, I am
here by the dam.'
But the miller came home that night,
And so dusted his back with the meal in
his sack,
That he made the black sheep white.

3rd Beggar. Be we not of the family? be
we not a-supping with the head of the
family? be we not in my lord's own
refractory? Out from among us; thou art
our black sheep.

Enter the four KNIGHTS

Fitzurse. Sheep, said he? And sheep
without the shepherd, too. Where is my
lord Archbishop? Thou the lustiest and
lousiest of this Cain's brotherhood, answer.

3rd Beggar. With Cain's answer, my
lord. Am I his keeper? Thou shouldst call
him Cain, not me.

Fitzurse. So I do, for he would murder
his brother the State.

3rd Beggar (*rising and advancing*). No,
my lord; but because the Lord hath set
his mark upon him that no man should
murder him.

Fitzurse. Where is he? where is he?

3rd Beggar. With Cain belike, in the
land of Nod, or in the land of France for
aught I know.

Fitzurse. France! Ha! De Morville,
Tracy, Brito—fled is he? Cross swords all
of you! swear to follow him! Remember
the Queen!

[*The four* KNIGHTS *cross their swords.*

De Brito. They mock us; he is here.

[*All the* BEGGARS *rise and advance
upon them.*

Fitzurse. Come, you filthy knaves, let us
pass.

3rd Beggar. Nay, my lord, let *us* pass.

We be a-going home after our supper in
all humbleness, my lord; for the Archbishop loves humbleness, my lord; and
though we be fifty to four, we daren't fight
you with our crutches, my lord. There now,
if thou hast not laid hands upon me! and
my fellows know that I am all one scale
like a fish. I pray God I haven't given thee
my leprosy, my lord.

[FITZURSE *shrinks from him and
another presses upon* DE BRITO.

De Brito. Away, dog!

4th Beggar. And I was bit by a mad dog
o' Friday, an' I be half dog already by this
token, that tho' I can drink wine I cannot
bide water, my lord; and I want to bite,
I want to bite, and they do say the very
breath catches.

De Brito. Insolent clown. Shall I smite
him with the edge of the sword?

De Morville. No, nor with the flat of it
either. Smite the shepherd and the sheep
are scattered. Smite the sheep and the
shepherd will excommunicate thee.

De Brito. Yet my fingers itch to beat him
into nothing.

5th Beggar. So do mine, my lord. I was
born with it, and sulphur won't bring it
out o' me. But for all that the Archbishop
washed my feet o' Tuesday. He likes it,
my lord.

6th Beggar. And see here, my lord, this
rag fro' the gangrene i' my leg. It's humbling—it smells o' human natur'. Wilt thou
smell it, my lord? for the Archbishop likes
the smell on it, my lord; for I be his lord
and master i' Christ, my lord.

De Morville. Faugh! we shall all be
poisoned. Let us go.

[*They draw back,* BEGGARS *following.*

7th Beggar. My lord, I ha' three sisters
a-dying at home o' the sweating sickness.
They be dead while I be a-supping.

8th Beggar. And I ha' nine darters i' the
spital that be dead ten times o'er i' one day
wi' the putrid fever; and I bring the taint
on it along wi' me, for the Archbishop likes
it, my lord.

[*Pressing upon the* KNIGHTS *till they
disappear thro' the door.*

3rd Beggar. Crutches, and itches, and

leprosies, and ulcers, and gangrenes, and running sores, praise ye the Lord, for to-night ye have saved our Archbishop!

1st Beggar. I'll go back again. I hain't half done yet.

Herbert of Bosham (entering). My friends, the Archbishop bids you goodnight. He hath retired to rest, and being in great jeopardy of his life, he hath made his bed between the altars, from whence he sends me to bid you this night pray for him who hath fed you in the wilderness.

3rd Beggar. So we will—so we will, I warrant thee. Becket shall be king, and the Holy Father shall be king, and the world shall live by the King's venison and the bread o' the Lord, and there shall be no more poor for ever. Hurrah! Vive le Roy! That's the English of it.

ACT II

Scene I

Rosamund's Bower

A Garden of Flowers. In the midst a bank of wild-flowers with a bench before it

Voices heard singing among the trees

Duet

1. Is it the wind of the dawn that I hear
   in the pine overhead?
2. No; but the voice of the deep as it
   hollows the cliffs of the land.
1. Is there a voice coming up with the
   voice of the deep from the strand,
   One coming up with a song in the flush
   of the glimmering red?
2. Love that is born of the deep coming
   up with the sun from the sea.
1. Love that can shape or can shatter a
   life till the life shall have fled?
2. Nay, let us welcome him, Love that
   can lift up a life from the dead.
1. Keep him away from the lone little isle.
   Let us be, let us be.
2. Nay, let him make it his own, let him
   reign in it—he, it is he,
   Love that is born of the deep coming
   up with the sun from the sea.

Enter HENRY *and* ROSAMUND

Rosamund. Be friends with him again—
I do beseech thee.

Henry. With Becket? I have but one
hour with thee—
Sceptre and crozier clashing, and the mitre
Grappling the crown—and when I flee
from this
For a gasp of freer air, a breathing-while
To rest upon thy bosom and forget him—
Why thou, my bird, thou pipest Becket,
Becket—
Yea, thou my golden dream of Love's own
bower,
Must be the nightmare breaking on my
peace
With 'Becket.'

Rosamund. O my life's life, not to smile
Is all but death to me. My sun, no cloud!
Let there not be one frown in this one
hour.
Out of the many thine, let this be mine!
Look rather thou all-royal as when first
I met thee.

Henry. Where was that?

Rosamund.   Forgetting that
Forgets me too.

Henry.   Nay, I remember it well.
There on the moors.

Rosamund.   And in a narrow path.
A plover flew before thee. Then I saw
Thy high black steed among the flaming
furze,
Like sudden night in the main glare of day.
And from that height something was said
to me
I knew not what.

Henry.   I ask'd the way.

Rosamund.   I think so.
So I lost mine.

Henry. Thou wast too shamed to answer.

Rosamund. Too scared—so young!

Henry.   The rosebud of my rose!—
Well, well, no more of *him*—I have sent his
folk,
His kin, all his belongings, overseas;
Age, orphans, and babe-breasting mothers
—all
By hundreds to him—there to beg, starve,
die—

667

So that the fool King Louis feed them not.
The man shall feel that I can strike him
    yet.
Rosamund. Babes, orphans, mothers! is
    that royal, Sire?
Henry. And I have been as royal with
    the Church.
He shelter'd in the Abbey of Pontigny.
There wore his time studying the canon
    law
To work it against me. But since he cursed
My friends at Veselay, I have let them
    know,
That if they keep him longer as their guest,
I scatter all their cowls to all the hells.
Rosamund. And is that altogether royal?
Henry.   Traitress!
Rosamund. A faithful traitress to thy
    royal fame.
Henry. Fame! what care I for fame?
    Spite, ignorance, envy,
Yea, honesty too, paint her what way they
    will.
Fame of to-day is infamy to-morrow;
Infamy of to-day is fame to-morrow;
And round and round again. What
    matters? Royal—
I mean to leave the royalty of my crown
Unlessen'd to mine heirs.
Rosamund.   Still—thy fame too:
I say that should be royal.
Henry.   And I say,
I care not for thy saying.
Rosamund.   And I say,
I care not for *thy* saying. A greater King
Than thou art, Love, who cares not for
    the word,
Makes 'care not'—care. There have I
    spoken true?
Henry. Care dwell with me for ever,
    when I cease
To care for thee as ever!
Rosamund.   No need! no need! ...
There is a bench. Come, wilt thou sit?
    ... My bank
Of wild-flowers [*he sits*]. At thy feet!
                    [*She sits at his feet.*
Henry.   I bad them clear
A royal pleasaunce for thee, in the wood,
Not leave these countryfolk at court.
Rosamund.   I brought them

In from the wood, and set them here. I
    love them
More than the garden flowers, that seem
    at most
Sweet guests, or foreign cousins, not half
    speaking
The language of the land. I love *them* too,
Yes. But, my liege, I am sure, of all the
    roses—
Shame fall on those who gave it a dog's
    name—
This wild one (*picking a briar-rose*)—nay,
    I shall not prick myself—
Is sweetest. Do but smell!
Henry.   Thou rose of the world!
Thou rose of all the roses!   [*Muttering.*
I am not worthy of her—this beast-body
That God has plunged my soul in—I, that
    taking
The Fiend's advantage of a throne, so long
Have wander'd among women,—a foul
    stream
Thro' fever-breeding levels,—at her side,
Among these happy dales, run clearer,
    drop
The mud I carried, like yon brook, and
    glass
The faithful face of heaven—
    [*Looking at her, and unconsciously aloud,*
                        —thine! thine!
Rosamund.   I know it.
Henry (*muttering*). Not hers. We have
    but one bond, her hate of Becket.
Rosamund (*half hearing*). Nay! nay! what
    art thou muttering? *I* hate Becket?
Henry (*muttering*). A sane and natural
    loathing for a soul
Purer, and truer and nobler than herself;
And mine a bitterer illegitimate hate,
A bastard hate born of a former love.
Rosamund. My fault to name him! O let
    the hand of one
To whom thy voice is all her music, stay it
But for a breath.
            [*Puts her hand before his lips.*
                Speak only of thy love.
Why there—like some loud beggar at thy
    gate—
The happy boldness of this hand hath
    won it
Love's alms, thy kiss (*looking at her hand*)

—Sacred! I'll kiss it too.
                    [*Kissing it.*
There! wherefore dost thou so peruse it?
Nay,
There may be crosses in my line of life.
Henry. Not half *her* hand—no hand to
    mate with *her*,
If it should come to that.
Rosamund.   With her? with whom?
Henry. Life on the hand is naked gipsy-
stuff;
Life on the face, the brows—clear inno-
    cence!
Vein'd marble—not a furrow yet—and
    hers   [*Muttering.*
Crost and recrost, a venomous spider's
web——
  Rosamund (springing up). Out of the
    cloud, my Sun—out of the eclipse
Narrowing my golden hour!
Henry.   O Rosamund,
I would be true—would tell thee all—and
    something
I had to say—I love thee none the less—
Which will so vex thee.
Rosamund.   Something against *me*?
Henry. No, no, against myself.
Rosamund.   I will not hear it.
Come, come, mine hour! I bargain for
    mine hour.
I'll call thee little Geoffrey.
Henry.   Call him!
Rosamund.   Geoffrey!

          Enter GEOFFREY

Henry. How the boy grows!
Rosamund. Ay, and his brows are thine;
The mouth is only Clifford, my dear father.
Geoffrey. My liege, what hast thou
    brought me?
Henry.   Venal imp!
What say'st thou to the Chancellorship of
England?
Geoffrey. O yes, my liege.
Henry.   'O yes, my liege!' He
    speaks
As if it were a cake of gingerbread.
  Dost thou know, my boy, what it is to
be Chancellor of England?
Geoffrey. Something good or thou
wouldst not give it me.

Henry. It is, my boy, to side with the
King when Chancellor, and then to be
made Archbishop and go against the King
who made him, and turn the world upside
down.
Geoffrey. I won't have it then. Nay, but
give it me, and I promise thee not to turn
the world upside down.
Henry (giving him a ball). Here is a ball,
my boy, thy world, to turn anyway and
play with as thou wilt—which is more than
I can do with mine. Go try it, play.
                    [*Exit* GEOFFREY.
A pretty lusty boy.
Rosamund.   So like to thee;
Like to be liker.
Henry.   Not in my chin, I hope!
That threatens double.
Rosamund.   Thou art manlike
    perfect.
Henry. Ay, ay, no doubt; and were I
    humpt behind,
Thou'dst say as much—the goodly way of
    women
Who love, for which I love them. May
    God grant
No ill befall or him or thee when I
Am gone.
Rosamund.   Is *he* thy enemy?
Henry.   He? who? ay!
Rosamund. Thine enemy knows the
    secret of my bower.
Henry. And I could tear him asunder
    with wild horses
Before he would betray it. Nay—no fear!
More like is he to excommunicate me.
Rosamund. And I would creep, crawl
    over knife-edge flint
Barefoot, a hundred leagues, to stay his hand
Before he flash'd the bolt.
Henry.   And when he flash'd it
Shrink from me, like a daughter of the
    Church.
Rosamund. Ay, but he will not.
Henry.   Ay! but if he did?
Rosamund. O then! O then! I almost
    fear to say
That my poor heretic heart would excom-
    municate
His excommunication, clinging to thee
Closer than ever.

Henry (*raising* ROSAMUND *and kissing her*).
  My brave-hearted Rose!
Hath he ever been to see thee?
Rosamund.   Here? not he.
And it is so lonely here—no confessor.
Henry. Thou shalt confess all thy sweet
  sins to me.
Rosamund. Besides, we came away in
  such a heat,
I brought not ev'n my crucifix.
Henry.   Take this.
  [*Giving her the Crucifix which
  ELEANOR gave him.*
Rosamund. O beautiful! May I have it as
  mine, till mine
Be mine again?
Henry (*throwing it round her neck*).
  Thine—as I am—till death!
Rosamund. Death? no! I'll have it with
  me in my shroud,
And wake with it, and show it to all the
  Saints.
Henry. Nay—I must go; but when thou
  layest thy lip
To this, remembering One who died for
  thee,
Remember also one who lives for thee
Out there in France; for I must hence to
  brave
The Pope, King Louis, and this turbulent
  priest.
Rosamund (*kneeling*). O by thy love for
  me, all mine for thee,
Fling not thy soul into the flames of hell:
I kneel to thee—be friends with him again.
Henry. Look, look! if little Geoffrey
  have not tost
His ball into the brook! makes after it too
To find it. Why, the child will drown
  himself.
Rosamund. Geoffrey! Geoffrey!
                              [*Exeunt.*

SCENE II

Montmirail

'*The Meeting of the Kings.*' JOHN OF OXFORD
and HENRY. *Crowd in the distance*

John of Oxford. You have not crown'd
  young Henry yet, my liege?

Henry. Crown'd! by God's eyes, we will
  not have him crown'd.
I spoke of late to the boy, he answer'd
  me,
As if he wore the crown already—No,
We will not have him crown'd.
'Tis true what Becket told me, that the
  mother
Would make him play his kingship against
  mine.
John of Oxford. Not have him crown'd?
Henry.   Not now—not yet! and
  Becket—
Becket should crown him were he crown'd
  at all:
But, since we would be lord of our own
  manor,
This Canterbury, like a wounded deer,
Has fled our presence and our feeding-
  grounds.
John of Oxford. Cannot a smooth tongue
  lick him whole again
To serve your will?
Henry.   He hates my will, not me.
John of Oxford. There's York, my liege.
Henry. But England scarce would hold
Young Henry king, if only crown'd by
  York,
And that would stilt up York to twice
  himself.
There is a movement yonder in the
  crowd—
See if our pious—what shall I call him,
  John?—
Husband-in-law, our smooth-shorn suze-
  rain,
Be yet within the field.
John of Oxford.   I will.   [*Exit.*
Henry.   Ay! Ay!
Mince and go back! his politic Holiness
Hath all but climb'd the Roman perch
  again,
And we shall hear him presently with clapt
  wing
Crow over Barbarossa—at last tongue-free
To blast my realms with excommunication
And interdict. I must patch up a peace—
A piece in this long-tugged-at, threadbare-
  worn
Quarrel of Crown and Church—to rend
  again.

His Holiness cannot steer straight thro'
   shoals,
Nor I. The citizen's heir hath conquer'd
   me
For the moment. So we make our peace
   with him.

Enter LOUIS

Brother of France, what shall be done with
   Becket?
   Louis. The holy Thomas! Brother, you
   have traffick'd
Between the Emperor and the Pope,
   between
The Pope and Antipope—a perilous game
For men to play with God.
   Henry.   Ay, ay, good brother,
They call you the Monk-King.
   Louis.   Who calls me? she
That was my wife, now yours? You have
   her Duchy,
The point you aim'd at, and pray God she
   prove
True wife to you. You have had the better
   of us
In secular matters.
   Henry.   Come, confess, good brother,
You did your best or worst to keep her
   Duchy.
Only the golden Leopard printed in it
Such hold-fast claws that you perforce
   again
Shrank into France. Tut, tut! did we con-
   vene
This conference but to babble of our
   wives?
They are plagues enough in-door.
   Louis.   We fought in the East,
And felt the sun of Antioch scald our
   mail,
And push'd our lances into Saracen hearts.
We never hounded on the State at home
To spoil the Church.
   Henry. How should you see this rightly?
   Louis. Well, well, no more! I am proud
   of my 'Monk-King,'
Whoever named me; and, brother, Holy
   Church
May rock, but will not wreck, nor our
   Archbishop
Stagger on the slope decks for any rough sea

Blown by the breath of kings. We do for-
   give you
For aught you wrought against us.
             [HENRY *holds up his hand.*
                Nay, I pray you,
Do not defend yourself. You will do much
To rake out all old dying heats, if you,
At my requesting, will but look into
The wrongs you did him, and restore his
   kin,
Reseat him on his throne of Canterbury,
Be, both, the friends you were.
   Henry.   The friends we were!
Co-mates we were, and had our sport
   together,
Co-kings we were, and made the laws
   together.
The world had never seen the like before.
You are too cold to know the fashion of it.
Well, well, we will be gentle with him,
   gracious—
Most gracious.

Enter BECKET, *after him,* JOHN OF OXFORD,
   ROGER OF YORK, GILBERT FOLIOT, DE
   BROC, FITZURSE, *etc.*

               Only that the rift he made
May close between us, here I am wholly
   king,
The word should come from him.
   Becket (*kneeling*). Then, my dear liege,
I here deliver all this controversy
Into your royal hands.
   Henry.   Ah, Thomas, Thomas
Thou art thyself again, Thomas again.
   Becket (*rising*). Saving God's honour!
   Henry.   Out upon thee, man!
Saving the Devil's honour, his yes and no.
Knights, bishops, earls, this London
   spawn—by Mahound,
I had sooner have been born a Mussul-
   man—
Less clashing with their priests—
I am half-way down the slope—will no
   man stay me?
I dash myself to pieces—I stay myself—
Puff—it is gone. You, Master Becket, you
That owe to me your power over me—
Nay, nay—
Brother of France, you have taken,
   cherish'd him

Who thief-like fled from his own church
  by night,
No man pursuing. I would have had him
  back.
Take heed he do not turn and rend you
  too:
For whatsoever may displease him—that
Is clean against God's honour—a shift, a
  trick
Whereby to challenge, face me out of all
My regal rights. Yet, yet—that none may
  dream
I go against God's honour—ay, or himself
In any reason, choose
A hundred of the wisest heads from Eng-
  land,
A hundred, too, from Normandy and
  Anjou:
Let these decide on what was customary
In olden days, and all the Church of
  France
Decide on their decision, I am content.
More, what the mightiest and the holiest
Of all his predecessors may have done
Ev'n to the least and meanest of my own,
Let him do the same to me—I am con-
  tent.
    Louis. Ay, ay! the King humbles himself
  enough.
    Becket. (*Aside.*) Words! he will wriggle
out of them like an eel
When the time serves. (*Aloud.*) My lieges
  and my lords,
The thanks of Holy Church are due to
  those
That went before us for their work, which
  we
Inheriting reap an easier harvest. Yet——
    Louis. My lord, will you be greater than
  the Saints,
More than St. Peter? whom——what is it
  you doubt?
Behold your peace at hand.
    Becket.   I say that those
Who went before us did not wholly clear
The deadly growths of earth, which Hell's
  own heat
So dwelt on that they rose and darken'd
  Heaven.
Yet they did much. Would God they had
  torn up all

By the hard root, which shoots again; our
  trial
Had so been less; but, seeing they were
  men
Defective or excessive, must we follow
All that they overdid or underdid?
Nay, if they were defective as St. Peter
Denying Christ, who yet defied the tyrant,
We hold by his defiance, not his defect.
O good son Louis, do not counsel me,
No, to suppress God's honour for the sake
Of any king that breathes. No, God forbid!
    Henry. No! God forbid! and turn me
  Mussulman!
No God but one, and Mahound is his
  prophet.
But for your Christian, look you, you shall
  have
None other God but me—me, Thomas,
  son
Of Gilbert Becket, London merchant. Out!
I hear no more.   [*Exit.*
    Louis. Our brother's anger puts him,
Poor man, beside himself—not wise. My
  lord,
We have claspt your cause, believing that
  our brother
Had wrong'd you; but this day he proffer'd
  peace.
You will have war; and tho' we grant the
  Church
King over this world's kings, yet, my good
  lord,
We that are kings are something in this
  world,
And so we pray you, draw yourself from
  under
The wings of France. We shelter you no
  more.   [*Exit.*
    John of Oxford. I am glad that France
hath scouted him at last:
I told the Pope what manner of man he
  was.   [*Exit.*
    Roger of York. Yea, since he flouts the
  will of either realm,
Let either cast him away like a dead dog!
        [*Exit.*
    Foliot. Yea, let a stranger spoil his
  heritage,
And let another take his bishoprick!
        [*Exit.*

De Broc. Our castle, my lord, belongs to Canterbury.
I pray you come and take it.   [*Exit.*
Fitzurse. When you will.   [*Exit.*
Becket. Cursed be John of Oxford, Roger of York,
And Gilbert Foliot! cursed those De Brocs
That hold our Saltwood Castle from our see!
Cursed Fitzurse, and all the rest of them
That sow this hate between my lord and me!
Voices from the Crowd. Blessed be the Lord Archbishop, who hath withstood two Kings to their faces for the honour of God.
Becket. Out of the mouths of babes and sucklings, praise!
I thank you, sons; when kings but hold by crowns,
The crowd that hungers for a crown in Heaven
Is my true king.
Herbert.   Thy true King bad thee be
A fisher of men; thou hast them in thy net.
Becket. I am too like the King here; both of us
Too headlong for our office. Better have been
A fisherman at Bosham, my good Herbert,
Thy birthplace—the sea-creek—the petty rill
That falls into it—the green field—the gray church—
The simple lobster-basket, and the mesh—
The more or less of daily labour done—
The pretty gaping bills in the home-nest
Piping for bread—the daily want supplied—
The daily pleasure to supply it.
Herbert.   Ah, Thomas,
You had not borne it, no, not for a day.
Becket. Well, maybe, no,
Herbert.   But bear with Walter Map,
For here he comes to comment on the time.

Enter WALTER MAP

Walter Map. Pity, my lord, that you have quenched the warmth of France toward you, tho' His Holiness, after much

smouldering and smoking, be kindled again upon your quarter.
Becket. Ay, if he do not end in smoke again.
Walter Map. My lord, the fire, when first kindled, said to the smoke, 'Go up, my son, straight to Heaven.' And the smoke said, 'I go;' but anon the North-east took and turned him South-west, then the South-west turned him North-east, and so of the other winds; but it was in him to go up straight if the time had been quieter. Your lordship affects the un-wavering perpendicular; but His Holiness, pushed one way by the Empire and another by England, if he move at all, Heaven stay him, is fain to diagonalise.
Herbert. Diagonalise! thou art a word-monger.
Our Thomas never will diagonalise.
Thou art a jester and a verse-maker.
Diagonalise!
Walter Map. Is the world any the worse for my verses if the Latin rhymes be rolled out from a full mouth? or any harm done to the people if my jest be in defence of the Truth?
Becket. Ay, if the jest be so done that the people
Delight to wallow in the grossness of it,
Till Truth herself be shamed of her defender.
Non defensoribus istis, Walter Map.
Walter Map. Is that my case? so if the city be sick, and I cannot call the kennel sweet, your lordship would suspend me from verse-writing, as you suspended yourself after sub-writing to the customs.
Becket. I pray God pardon mine infirmity.
Walter Map. Nay, my lord, take heart; for tho' you suspended yourself, the Pope let you down again; and tho' you suspend Foliot or another, the Pope will not leave them in suspense, for the Pope himself is always in suspense, like Mahound's coffin hung between heaven and earth—always in suspense, like the scales, till the weight of Germany or the gold of England brings one of them down to the dust—always in suspense, like the tail of the horologe—to

and fro—tick-tack—we make the time, we
keep the time, ay, and we serve the time;
for I have heard say that if you boxed the
Pope's ears with a purse, you might stagger
him, but he would pocket the purse. No
saying of mine—Jocelyn of Salisbury. But
the King hath bought half the College of
Redhats. He warmed to you to-day, and
you have chilled him again. Yet you both
love God. Agree with him quickly again,
even for the sake of the Church. My one
grain of good counsel which you will not
swallow. I hate a split between old friendships as I hate the dirty gap in the face of
a Cistercian monk, that will swallow anything. Farewell.   [*Exit.*
    Becket. Map scoffs at Rome. I all but
        hold with Map.
Save for myself no Rome were left in
    England,
All had been his. Why should this Rome,
    this Rome,
Still choose Barabbas rather than the
    Christ,
Absolve the left-hand thief and damn the
    right?
Take fees of tyranny, wink at sacrilege,
Which even Peter had not dared? condemn
The blameless exile?—
    Herbert.   Thee, thou holy Thomas!
I would that thou hadst been the Holy
    Father.
    Becket. I would have done my most to
        keep Rome holy,
I would have made Rome know she still is
    Rome—
Who stands aghast at her eternal self
And shakes at mortal kings—her vacillation,
Avarice, craft—O God, how many an
    innocent
Has left his bones upon the way to Rome
Unwept, uncared for. Yea—on mine own
    self
The King had had no power except for
    Rome.
'Tis not the King who is guilty of mine
    exile,
But Rome, Rome, Rome!
    Herbert.   My lord, I see this Louis
Returning, ah! to drive thee from his
    realm.

    Becket. He said as much before. Thou
        art no prophet,
Nor yet a prophet's son.
    Herbert.   Whatever he say,
Deny not thou God's honour for a king.
The King looks troubled.

    Re-enter KING LOUIS

    Louis.   My dear lord Archbishop,
I learn but now that those poor Poitevins,
That in thy cause were stirr'd against King
    Henry,
Have been, despite his kingly promise
    given
To our own self of pardon, evilly used
And put to pain. I have lost all trust in him.
The Church alone hath eyes—and now
    I see
That I was blind—suffer the phrase—
    surrendering
God's honour to the pleasure of a man.
Forgive me and absolve me, holy father.
                                [*Kneels.*
    Becket. Son, I absolve thee in the name
        of God.
    Louis (*rising*). Return to Sens, where we
        will care for you.
The wine and wealth of all our France are
    yours;
Rest in our realm, and be at peace with all.
                                [*Exeunt.*
    Voices from the Crowd. Long live the
good King Louis! God bless the great
Archbishop!

    Re-enter HENRY *and* JOHN OF OXFORD

    Henry (*looking after* KING LOUIS *and*
BECKET). Ay, there they go—both
    backs are turn'd to me—
Why then I strike into my former path
For England, crown young Henry there,
    and make
Our waning Eleanor all but love me!
                                        John,
Thou hast served me heretofore with
    Rome—and well.
They call thee John the Swearer.
    John of Oxford.   For this reason,
That, being ever duteous to the King,
I evermore have sworn upon his side,
And ever mean to do it.

Henry (*claps him on the shoulder*).
　　　　　Honest John!
To Rome again! the storm begins again.
Spare not thy tongue! be lavish with our
　coins,
Threaten our junction with the Emperor
　—flatter
And fright the Pope—bribe all the Car-
　dinals—leave
Lateran and Vatican in one dust of gold—
Swear and unswear, state and misstate thy
　best!
I go to have young Henry crown'd by
　York.

ACT III

SCENE I

The Bower

HENRY *and* ROSAMUND

Henry. All that you say is just. I cannot
　answer it
Till better times, when I shall put
　away——
Rosamund. What will you put away?
Henry. 　　　　That which you ask me
Till better times. Let it content you now
There is no woman that I love so well.
Rosamund. No woman but should be
　content with that—
Henry. And one fair child to fondle!
Rosamund. 　　　　O yes, the child
We waited for so long—heaven's gift at
　last—
And how you doated on him then! To-day
I almost fear'd your kiss was colder—yes—
But then the child *is* such a child. What
　chance
That he should ever spread into the man
Here in our silence? I have done my best.
I am not learn'd.
Henry. 　　　I am the King, his father,
And I will look to it. Is our secret ours?
Have you had any alarm? no stranger?
Rosamund. 　　　　　　　No.
The warder of the bower hath given him-
　self
Of late to wine. I sometimes think he sleeps
When he should watch; and yet what fear?
　the people

Believe the wood enchanted. No one comes,
Nor foe nor friend; his fond excess of wine
Springs from the loneliness of my poor
　bower,
Which weighs even on me.
Henry. 　　　Yet these tree-towers,
Their long bird-echoing minster-aisles,—
　the voice
Of the perpetual brook, these golden
　slopes
Of Solomon-shaming flowers—that was
　your saying,
All pleased you so at first.
Rosamund. 　　　Not now so much.
My Anjou bower was scarce as beautiful.
But you were oftener there. I have none
　but you.
The brook's voice is not yours, and no
　flower, not
The sun himself, should he be changed to
　one,
Could shine away the darkness of that gap
Left by the lack of love.
Henry. 　　　The lack of love!
Rosamund. Of one we love. Nay, I would
　not be bold,
Yet hoped ere this you might——
　　　　　[*Looks earnestly at him.*
Henry. 　　　Anything further?
Rosamund. Only my best bower-maiden
　died of late,
And that old priest whom John of Salis-
　bury trusted
Hath sent another.
Henry. 　　　Secret?
Rosamund. 　　　　I but ask'd her
One question, and she primm'd her mouth
　and put
Her hands together—thus—and said, God
　help her,
That she was sworn to silence.
Henry. 　　　What did you ask her?
Rosamund. Some daily something-
　nothing.
Henry. 　　Secret, then?
Rosamund. I do not love her. Must you
　go, my liege,
So suddenly?
Henry. 　　I came to England suddenly,
And on a great occasion sure to wake
As great a wrath in Becket——

Rosamund.   Always Becket!
He always comes between us.
Henry.   —And to meet it
I needs must leave as suddenly. It is
raining,
Put on your hood and see me to the
bounds.   [*Exeunt.*

Margery (*singing behind scene*)
    Babble in bower
        Under the rose!
    Bee mustn't buzz,
        Whoop—but he knows.

    Kiss me, little one,
        Nobody near!
    Grasshopper, grasshopper,
        Whoop—you can hear.

    Kiss in the bower,
        Tit on the tree!
    Bird mustn't tell,
        Whoop—he can see.

Enter MARGERY

I ha' been but a week here and I ha'
seen what I ha' seen, for to be sure it's no
more than a week since our old Father
Philip that has confessed our mother for
twenty years, and she was hard put to it,
and to speak truth, nigh at the end of our
last crust, and that mouldy, and she cried
out on him to put me forth in the world
and to make me a woman of the world, and
to win my own bread, whereupon he asked
our mother if I could keep a quiet tongue
i' my head, and not speak till I was spoke
to, and I answered for myself that I never
spoke more than was needed, and he told
me he would advance me to the service of
a great lady, and took me ever so far away,
and gave me a great pat o' the cheek for a
pretty wench, and said it was a pity to
blindfold such eyes as mine, and such to be
sure they be, but he blinded 'em for all
that, and so brought me no-hows as I may
say, and the more shame to him after his
promise, into a garden and not into the
world, and bad me whatever I saw not to
speak one word, an' it 'ud be well for me
in the end, for there were great ones who
would look after me, and to be sure I ha'

seen great ones to-day—and then not to
speak one word, for that's the rule o'
the garden, tho' to be sure if I had been
Eve i' the garden I shouldn't ha' minded
the apple, for what's an apple, you know,
save to a child, and I'm no child, but more
a woman o' the world than my lady here,
and I ha' seen what I ha' seen—tho' to be
sure if I hadn't minded it we should all on
us ha' had to go, bless the Saints, wi' bare
backs, but the backs 'ud ha' countenanced
one another, and belike it 'ud ha' been
always summer, and anyhow I am as well-
shaped as my lady here, and I ha' seen
what I ha' seen, and what's the good of my
talking to myself, for here comes my lady
(*enter* ROSAMUND), and, my lady, tho' I
shouldn't speak one word, I wish you joy
o' the King's brother.
Rosamund. What is it you mean?
Margery. I mean your goodman, your
husband, my lady, for I saw your ladyship
a-parting wi' him even now i' the coppice,
when I was a-getting o' bluebells for your
ladyship's nose to smell on—and I ha' seen
the King once at Oxford, and he's as like
the King as fingernail to fingernail, and I
thought at first it was the King, only you
know the King's married, for King
Louis——
Rosamund. Married!
Margery. Years and years, my lady, for
her husband, King Louis——
Rosamund. Hush!
Margery. —And I thought if it were the
King's brother he had a better bride than
the King, for the people do say that his is
bad beyond all reckoning, and——
Rosamund. The people lie.
Margery. Very like, my lady, but most
on 'em know an honest woman and a lady
when they see her, and besides they say,
she makes songs, and that's against her,
for I never knew an honest woman that
could make songs, tho' to be sure our
mother 'ill sing me old songs by the hour,
but then, God help her, she had 'em from
her mother, and her mother from her
mother back and back for ever so long, but
none on 'em ever made songs, and they
were all honest.

Rosamund. Go, you shall tell me of her
some other time.

Margery. There's none so much to tell
on her, my lady, only she kept the seventh
commandment better than some I know
on, or I couldn't look your ladyship i' the
face, and she brew'd the best ale in all
Glo'ster, that is to say in her time when
she had the 'Crown.'

Rosamund. The crown! who?

Margery. Mother.

Rosamund. I mean her whom you call—
fancy—my husband's brother's wife.

Margery. Oh, Queen Eleanor. Yes, my
lady; and tho' I be sworn not to speak a
word, I can tell you all about her, if——

Rosamund. No word now. I am faint and
sleepy. Leave me. Nay—go. What! will
you anger me?   [*Exit* MARGERY.
He charged me not to question any of those
About me. Have I? no! she question'd *me.*
Did she not slander *him?* Should she stay
here?
May she not tempt me, being at my side,
To question *her?* Nay, can I send her
hence
Without his kingly leave? I am in the dark.
I have lived, poor bird, from cage to cage,
and known
Nothing but him—happy to know no
more,
So that he loved me—and he loves me—
yes,
And bound me by his love to secrecy
Till his own time.
           Eleanor, Eleanor, have I
Not heard ill things of her in France? Oh,
she's
The Queen of France. I see it—some con-
fusion,
Some strange mistake. I did not hear
aright,
Myself confused with parting from the
King.

Margery (*behind scene*). Bee mustn't buzz,
     Whoop—but he knows.

Rosamund. Yet her—what her? he hinted
of some her—
When he was here before—
Something that would displease me. Hath
he stray'd

From love's clear path into the common
     bush.
And, being scratch'd, returns to his true
     rose,
Who hath not thorn enough to prick him
     for it,
Ev'n with a word?

Margery (*behind scene*). Bird mustn't tell,
     Whoop—he can see.

Rosamund. I would not hear him. Nay—
there's more—he frown'd
'No mate for her, if it should come to
     that'—
To that—to what?

Margery (*behind scene*). Whoop—but he
     knows.
     Whoop—but he knows.

Rosamund. O God! some dreadful truth
is breaking on me—
Some dreadful thing is coming on me.
           [*Enter* GEOFFREY.
           Geoffrey!

Geoffrey. What are you crying for, when
the sun shines?

Rosamund. Hath not thy father left us
to ourselves?

Geoffrey. Ay, but he's taken the rain
with him. I hear Margery: I'll go play
with her.   [*Exit* GEOFFREY.

Rosamund. Rainbow, stay,
     Gleam upon gloom,
     Bright as my dream,
     Rainbow, stay!
     But it passes away,
     Gloom upon gleam,
     Dark as my doom—
     O rainbow stay.

SCENE II

Outside the Woods near Rosamund's Bower

ELEANOR. FITZURSE

Eleanor. Up from the salt lips of the
land we two
Have track'd the King to this dark inland
     wood;
And somewhere hereabouts he vanish'd.
     Here
His turtle builds; his exit is our adit:
Watch! he will out again, and presently,

Seeing he must to Westminster and crown
Young Henry there to-morrow.
    Fitzurse.   We have watch'd
So long in vain, he hath pass'd out again,
And on the other side.
              [*A great horn winded.*
              Hark! Madam!
    Eleanor.   Ay,
How ghostly sounds that horn in the black
    wood!
              [*A countryman flying.*
Whither away, man? what are you flying
    from?
    Countryman. The witch! the witch! she
sits naked by a great heap of gold in the
middle of the wood, and when the horn
sounds she comes out as a wolf. Get you
hence! a man passed in there to-day: I
holla'd to him, but he didn't hear me:
he'll never out again, the witch has got
him. I daren't stay—I daren't stay!
    Eleanor. Kind of the witch to give thee
    warning tho'.   [*Man flies.*
Is not this wood-witch of the rustic's
    fear
Our woodland Circe that hath witch'd the
    King?
         [*Horn sounded. Another flying.*
    Fitzurse. Again! stay, fool, and tell me
why thou fliest.
    Countryman. Fly thou too. The King
keeps his forest head of game here, and
when that horn sounds, a score of wolfdogs are let loose that will tear thee piecemeal. Linger not till the third horn. Fly!
              [*Exit.*
    Eleanor. This is the likelier tale. We
    have hit the place.
Now let the King's fine game look to itself.
              [*Horn.*
    Fitzurse. Again!—
And far on in the dark heart of the
    wood
I hear the yelping of the hounds of
    hell.
    Eleanor. I have my dagger here to still
    their throats.
    Fitzurse. Nay, Madam, not to-night—
    the night is falling.
What can be done to-night?
    Eleanor.   Well—well—away.

*Traitor's Meadow at Fréteval. Pavilions and
Tents of the English and French Baronage*
    BECKET *and* HERBERT OF BOSHAM

    Becket. See here!
    Herbert.   What's here?
    Becket.   A notice from the priest,
To whom our John of Salisbury committed
The secret of the bower, that our wolf-
    Queen
Is prowling round the fold. I should be
    back
In England ev'n for this.
    Herbert.   These are by-things
In the great cause.
    Becket.   The by-things of the Lord
Are the wrong'd innocences that will cry
From all the hidden by-ways of the world
In the great day against the wronger. I
    know
Thy meaning. Perish she, I, all, before
The Church should suffer wrong!
    Herbert.   Do you see, my lord,
There is the King talking with Walter
    Map?
    Becket. He hath the Pope's last letters,
    and they threaten
The immediate thunder-blast of interdict:
Yet he can scarce be touching upon those,
Or scarce would smile that fashion.
    Herbert.   Winter sunshine!
Beware of opening out thy bosom to it,
Lest thou, myself, and all thy flock should
    catch
An after ague-fit of trembling. Look!
He bows, he bares his head, he is coming
    hither.
Still with a smile.

    Enter KING HENRY *and* WALTER MAP

    Henry. We have had so many hours
    together, Thomas,
So many happy hours alone together,
That I would speak with you once more
    alone.
    Becket. My liege, your will and happi-
    ness are mine.
          [*Exeunt* KING *and* BECKET.
    Herbert. The same smile still.
    Walter Map. Do you see that great black

cloud that hath come over the sun and cast us all into shadow?

Herbert. And feel it too.

Walter Map. And see you yon sidebeam that is forced from under it, and sets the church-tower over there all a-hell-fire as it were?

Herbert. Ay.

Walter Map. It is this black, bell-silencing, anti-marrying, burial-hindering interdict, that hath squeezed out this side-smile upon Canterbury, whereof may come conflagration. Were I Thomas, I wouldn't trust it. Sudden change is a house on sand; and tho' I count Henry honest enough, yet when fear creeps in at the front, honesty steals out at the back, and the King at last is fairly scared by this cloud—this inter-dict. I have been more for the King than the Church in this matter—yea, even for the sake of the Church: for, truly, as the case stood, you had safelier have slain an archbishop than a she-goat: but our recoverer and upholder of customs hath in this crowning of young Henry by York and London so violated the immemorial usage of the Church, that, like the grave-digger's child I have heard of, trying to ring the bell, he hath half-hanged himself in the rope of the Church, or rather pulled all the Church with the Holy Father astride of it down upon his own head.

Herbert. Were you there?

Walter Map. In the church rope?—no. I was at the crowning, for I have pleasure in the pleasure of crowds, and to read the faces of men at a great show.

Herbert. And how did Roger of York comport himself?

Walter Map. As magnificently and archi-episcopally as our Thomas would have done: only there was a dare-devil in his eye—I should say a dare-Becket. He thought less of two kings than of one Roger the king of the occasion. Foliot is the holier man, perhaps the better. Once or twice there ran a twitch across his face as who should say what's to follow? but Salisbury was a calf cowed by Mother Church, and every now and then glancing about him like a thief at night when he

hears a door open in the house and thinks 'the master.'

Herbert. And the father-king?

Walter Map. The father's eye was so tender it would have called a goose off the green, and once he strove to hide his face, like the Greek king when his daughter was sacrificed, but he thought better of it: it was but the sacrifice of a kingdom to his son, a smaller matter; but as to the young crownling himself, he looked so malapert in the eyes, that had I fathered him I had given him more of the rod than the sceptre. Then followed the thunder of the captains and the shouting, and so we came on to the banquet, from whence there puffed out such an incense of unctuosity into the nostrils of our Gods of Church and State, that Lucullus or Apicius might have sniffed it in their Hades of heathenism, so that the smell of their own roast had not come across it——

Herbert. Map, tho' you make your butt too big, you overshoot it.

Walter Map. —For as to the fish, they de-miracled the miraculous draught, and might have sunk a navy——

Herbert. There again, Goliasing and Goliathising!

Walter Map. —And as for the flesh at table, a whole Peter's sheet, with all man-ner of game, and four-footed things, and fowls—

Herbert. And all manner of creeping things too?

Walter Map. —Well, there were Abbots —but they did not bring their women; and so we were dull enough at first, but in the end we flourished out into a merriment; for the old King would act servitor and hand a dish to his son; whereupon my Lord of York—his fine-cut face bowing and beaming with all that courtesy which hath less loyalty in it than the backward scrape of the clown's heel—'great honour,' says he, 'from the King's self to the King's son.' Did you hear the young King's quip?

Herbert. No, what was it?

Walter Map. Glancing at the days when his father was only Earl of Anjou, he answered:—'Should not an earl's son wait

on a king's son?' And when the cold
corners of the King's mouth began to
thaw, there was a great motion of laughter
among us, part real, part child-like, to be
freed from the dulness—part royal, for
King and kingling both laughed, and so
we could not but laugh, as by a royal
necessity—part childlike again—when we
felt we had laughed too long and could not
stay ourselves—many midriff-shaken even
to tears, as springs gush out after earthquakes—but from those, as I said before,
there may come a conflagration—tho', to
keep the figure moist and make it hold
water, I should say rather, the lacrymation
of a lamentation; but look if Thomas have
not flung himself at the King's feet. They
have made it up again—for the moment.
Herbert. Thanks to the blessed Magdalen, whose day it is.

Re-enter HENRY *and* BECKET. (*During their
conference the* BARONS *and* BISHOPS *of
FRANCE and ENGLAND come in at back
of stage.*)
Becket. Ay, King! for in thy kingdom,
    as thou knowest,
The spouse of the Great King, thy King,
    hath fallen—
The daughter of Zion lies beside the way—
The priests of Baal tread her underfoot—
The golden ornaments are stolen from
    her——
Henry. Have I not promised to restore
    her, Thomas,
And send thee back again to Canterbury?
Becket. Send back again those exiles of
    my kin
Who wander famine-wasted thro' the
    world.
Henry. Have I not promised, man, to
    send them back?
Becket. Yet one thing more. Thou hast
    broken thro' the pales
Of privilege, crowning thy young son by
    York,
London and Salisbury—not Canterbury.
Henry. York crown'd the Conqueror—
    not Canterbury.
Becket. There was no Canterbury in
    William's time.

Henry. But Hereford, you know, crown'd
    the first Henry.
Becket. But Anselm crown'd this Henry
    o'er again.
Henry. And thou shalt crown my Henry
    o'er again.
Becket. And is it then with thy goodwill
    that I
Proceed against thine evil councillors,
And hurl the dread ban of the Church on
    those
Who made the second mitre play the first,
And acted me?
Henry. Well, well, then—have thy way!
It may be they were evil councillors.
What more, my lord Archbishop? What
    more, Thomas?
I make thee full amends. Say all thy say,
But blaze not out before the Frenchmen
    here.
Becket. More? Nothing, so thy promise
    be thy deed.
Henry (*holding out his hand*). Give me
    thy hand. My Lords of France and
    England,
My friend of Canterbury and myself
Are now once more at perfect amity.
Unkingly should I be, and most un-
    knightly,
Not striving still, however much in vain,
To rival him in Christian charity.
Herbert. All praise to Heaven, and sweet
    St. Magdalen!
Henry. And so farewell until we meet
    in England.
Becket. I fear, my liege, we may not
    meet in England.
Henry. How, do you make me a traitor?
Becket.   No, indeed!
That be far from thee.
Henry.   Come, stay with us, then,
Before you part for England.
Becket.   I am bound
For that one hour to stay with good King
    Louis,
Who helpt me when none else.
Herbert.   He said thy life
Was not one hour's worth in England
    save
King Henry gave thee first the kiss of
    peace.

Henry. He said so? Louis, did he? look
you, Herbert,
When I was in mine anger with King
Louis,
I sware I would not give the kiss of peace,
Not on French ground, nor any ground
but English,
Where his cathedral stands. Mine old
friend, Thomas,
I would there were that perfect trust
between us,
That health of heart, once ours, ere Pope
or King
Had come between us! Even now—who
knows?—
I might deliver all things to thy hand—
If . . . but I say no more . . . farewell, my
lord.
Becket. Farewell, my liege!
   [*Exit* HENRY, *then the* BARONS *and*
BISHOPS.
Walter Map. There again! when the full
fruit of the royal promise might have dropt
into thy mouth hadst thou but opened it
to thank him.
Becket. He fenced his royal promise
with an *if.*
Walter Map. And is the King's *if* too
high a stile for your lordship to overstep
and come at all things in the next field?
Becket. Ay, if this *if* be like the Devil's '*if*
Thou wilt fall down and worship me.'
Herbert.   Oh, Thomas,
I could fall down and worship thee, my
Thomas,
For thou hast trodden this wine-press alone.
Becket. Nay, of the people there are
many with me.
Walter Map. I am not altogether with
you, my lord, tho' I am none of those that
would raise a storm between you, lest ye
should draw together like two ships in a
calm. You wrong the King: he meant what
he said to-day. Who shall vouch for his
to-morrows? One word further. Doth not
the *fewness* of anything make the fulness
of it in estimation? Is not virtue prized
mainly for its rarity and great baseness
loathed as an exception: for were all, my
lord, as noble as yourself, who would look
up to you? and were all as base as—who

shall I say—Fitzurse and his following—
who would look down upon them? My
lord, you have put so many of the King's
household out of communion, that they
begin to smile at it.
Becket. At their peril, at their peril——
Walter Map. —For tho' the drop may
hollow out the dead stone, doth not the
living skin thicken against perpetual whip-
pings? This is the second grain of good
counsel I ever proffered thee, and so cannot
suffer by the rule of frequency. Have I sown
it in salt? I trust not, for before God I
promise you the King hath many more
wolves than he can tame in his woods of
England, and if it suit their purpose to
howl for the King, and you still move
against him, you may have no less than to
die for it; but God and his free wind grant
your lordship a happy home-return and
the King's kiss of peace in Kent. Farewell!
I must follow the King.   [*Exit.*
Herbert. Ay, and I warrant the customs.
    Did the King
Speak of the customs?
Becket.   No!—To die for it—
I live to die for it, I die to live for it.
The State will die, the Church can never
die.
The King's not like to die for that which
dies;
But I must die for that which never dies.
It will be so—my visions in the Lord:
It must be so, my friend! the wolves of
England
Must murder her one shepherd, that the
sheep
May feed in peace. False figure, Map
would say.
Earth's falses are heaven's truths. And
when my voice
Is martyr'd mute, and this man disappears,
That perfect trust may come again between
us,
And there, there, there, not here I shall
rejoice
To find my stray sheep back within the
fold.
The crowd are scattering, let us move
away!
And thence to England.   [*Exeunt.*

ACT IV

SCENE I

The Outskirts of the Bower

Geoffrey (coming out of the wood). Light again! light again! Margery? no, that's a finer thing there. How it glitters!

Eleanor (entering). Come to me, little one. How camest thou hither?

Geoffrey. On my legs.

Eleanor. And mighty pretty legs too. Thou art the prettiest child I ever saw. Wilt thou love me?

Geoffrey. No; I only love mother.

Eleanor. Ay; and who is thy mother?

Geoffrey. They call her—— But she lives secret, you see.

Eleanor. Why?

Geoffrey. Don't know why.

Eleanor. Ay, but some one comes to see her now and then. Who is he?

Geoffrey. Can't tell.

Eleanor. What does she call him?

Geoffrey. My liege.

Eleanor. Pretty one, how camest thou?

Geoffrey. There was a bit of yellow silk here and there, and it looked pretty like a glowworm, and I thought if I followed it I should find the fairies.

Eleanor. I am the fairy, pretty one, a good fairy to thy mother. Take me to her.

Geoffrey. There are good fairies and bad fairies, and sometimes she cries, and can't sleep sound o' night because of the bad fairies.

Eleanor. She shall cry no more; she shall sleep sound enough if thou wilt take me to her. I am her good fairy.

Geoffrey. But you don't look like a good fairy. Mother does. You are not pretty, like mother.

Eleanor. We can't all of us be as pretty as thou art—*(aside)* little bastard. Come, here is a golden chain I will give thee if thou wilt lead me to thy mother.

Geoffrey. No—no gold. Mother says gold spoils all. Love is the only gold.

Eleanor. I love thy mother, my pretty boy. Show me where thou camest out of the wood.

Geoffrey. By this tree; but I don't know if I can find the way back again.

Eleanor. Where's the warder?

Geoffrey. Very bad. Somebody struck him.

Eleanor. Ay? who was that?

Geoffrey. Can't tell. But I heard say he had had a stroke, or you'd have heard his horn before now. Come along, then? we shall see the silk here and there, and I want my supper.   [*Exeunt.*

SCENE II

Rosamund's Bower

Rosamund. The boy so late; pray God, he be not lost.
I sent this Margery, and she comes not back;
I sent another, and she comes not back.
I go myself—so many alleys, crossings,
Paths, avenues—nay, if I lost him, now
The folds have fallen from the mystery,
And left all naked, I were lost indeed.

Enter GEOFFREY *and* ELEANOR

Geoffrey, the pain thou hast put me to!
                              [*Seeing* ELEANOR.
                              Ha, you!
How came you hither?

Eleanor.   Your own child brought me hither!

Geoffrey. You said you couldn't trust Margery, and I watched her and followed her into the woods, and I lost her and went on and on till I found the light and the lady, and she says she can make you sleep o' nights.

Rosamund. How dared you? Know you not this bower is secret,
Of and belonging to the King of England,
More sacred than his forests for the chase?
Nay, nay, Heaven help you; get you hence in haste
Lest worse befall you.

Eleanor.   Child, I am mine own self
Of and belonging to the King. The King
Hath divers ofs and ons, ofs and belong-ings,
Almost as many as your true Mussulman—

Belongings, paramours, whom it pleases
   him
To call his wives; but so it chances, child,
That I am his main paramour, his sultana.
But since the fondest pair of doves will jar,
Ev'n in a cage of gold, we had words of late,
And thereupon he call'd my children
   bastards.
Do you believe that you are married to
   him?
  Rosamund. I *should* believe it.
  Eleanor.   You must not believe it,
Because I have a wholesome medicine here
Puts that belief asleep. Your answer,
   beauty!
Do you believe that you are married to
   him?
  Rosamund. Geoffrey, my boy, I saw the
ball you lost in the fork of the great willow
over the brook. Go. See that you do not
fall in. Go.
  Geoffrey. And leave you alone with the
good· fairy. She calls you beauty, but I
don't like her looks. Well, you bid me go,
and I'll have my ball anyhow. Shall I find
you asleep when I come back?
  Rosamund. Go.   [*Exit* GEOFFREY.
  Eleanor. He is easily found again. *Do*
you believe it?
I pray you then to take my sleeping-
   draught;
But if you should not care to take it—see!
               [*Draws a dagger.*
What! have I scared the red rose from
   your face
Into your heart? But this will find it there,
And dig it from the root for ever.
  Rosamund.   Help! help!
  Eleanor. They say that walls have ears;
   but these, it seems,
Have none! and I have none—to pity thee.
  Rosamund. I do beseech you—my child
   is so young,
So backward too; I cannot leave him yet.
I am not so happy I could not die myself,
But the child is so young. You have
   children—his;
And mine is the King's child; so, if you
   love him—
Nay, if you love him, there is great wrong
   done

Somehow; but if you do not—there are
   those
Who say you do not love him—let me go
With my young boy, and I will hide my
   face,
Blacken and gipsyfy it; none shall know
   me;
The King shall never hear of me again,
But I will beg my bread along the world
With my young boy, and God will be our
   guide.
I never meant you harm in any way.
See, I can say no more.
  Eleanor. Will you not say you are not
   married to him?
  Rosamund. Ay, Madam, I can *say* it, if
   you will.
  Eleanor. Then is thy pretty boy a
   bastard?
  Rosamund.   No.
  Eleanor. And thou thyself a proven
   wanton?
  Rosamund.   No.
I am none such. I never loved but one.
I have heard of such that range from love
   to love,
Like the wild beast—if you can call it love.
I have heard of such—yea, even among
   those
Who sit on thrones—I never saw any such,
Never knew any such, and howsoever
You do misname me, match'd with any
   such,
I am snow to mud.
  Eleanor.   The more the pity then
That thy true home—the heavens—cry
   out for thee
Who art too pure for earth.

        Enter FITZURSE

  Fitzurse.   Give her to me.
  Eleanor. The Judas-lover of our passion-
   play
Hath track'd us hither.
  Fitzurse.   Well, why not? I follow'd
You and the child: he babbled all the way.
Give her to me to make my honeymoon.
  Eleanor. Ay, as the bears love honey.
   Could you keep her
Indungeon'd from one whisper of the
   wind,

Dark even from a side glance of the moon,
And oublietted in the centre—No!
I follow out my hate and thy revenge.
   Fitzurse. You bad me take revenge
     another way—
To bring her to the dust. . . . Come with
   me, love,
And I will love thee. . . . Madam, let her
   live.
I have a far-off burrow where the King
Would miss her and for ever.
   Eleanor.   How sayst thou,
   sweetheart?
Wilt thou go with him? he will marry thee.
   Rosamund. Give me the poison; set me
   free of him!
             [ELEANOR *offers the vial.*
No, no! I will not have it.
   Eleanor.   Then this other,
The wiser choice, because my sleeping-
   draught
May bloat thy beauty out of shape, and
   make
Thy body loathsome even to thy child;
While this but leaves thee with a broken
   heart,
A doll-face blanch'd and bloodless, over
   which
If pretty Geoffrey do not break his own,
It must be broken for him.
   Rosamund.   O I see now
Your purpose is to fright me—a trouba-
   dour
You play with words. You had never used
   so many,
Not if you meant it, I am sure. The
   child . . .
No . . . mercy! No! (*Kneels.*)
   Eleanor.   Play! . . . that
   bosom never
Heaved under the King's hand with such
   true passion
As at this loveless knife that stirs the riot,
Which it will quench in blood! Slave, if he
   love thee,
Thy life is worth the wrestle for it: arise,
And dash thyself against me that I may
   slay thee!
The worm! shall I let her go? But ha!
   what's here?
By very God, the cross I gave the King!

His village darling in some lewd caress
Has wheedled it off the King's neck to her
   own.
By thy leave, beauty. Ay, the same! I
   warrant
Thou hast sworn on this my cross a hun-
   dred times
Never to leave him—and that merits death,
False oath on holy cross—for thou must
   leave him
To-day, but not quite yet. My good
   Fitzurse,
The running down the chase is kindlier
   sport
Ev'n than the death. Who knows but that
   thy lover
May plead so pitifully, that I may spare
   thee?
Come hither, man; stand there. (*To* ROSA-
   MUND) Take thy one chance;
Catch at the last straw. Kneel to thy lord
   Fitzurse;
Crouch even because thou hatest him;
   fawn upon him
For thy life and thy son's.
   Rosamund (*rising*). I am a Clifford,
My son a Clifford and Plantagenet.
I am to die then, tho' there stand beside
   thee
One who might grapple with thy dagger,
   if he
Had aught of man, or thou of woman; or I
Would bow to such a baseness as would
   make me
Most worthy of it: both of us will die,
And I will fly with my sweet boy to heaven,
And shriek to all the saints among the
   stars:
'Eleanor of Aquitaine, Eleanor of Eng-
   land!
Murder'd by that adulteress Eleanor,
Whose doings are a horror to the east,
A hissing in the west!' Have we not heard
Raymond of Poitou, thine own uncle—nay,
Geoffrey Plantagenet, thine own husband's
   father—
Nay, ev'n the accursed heathen Salad-
   deen——
Strike!
I challenge thee to meet me before God.
Answer me there.

Eleanor (*raising the dagger*). This in thy
    bosom, fool,
And after in thy bastard's!

Enter BECKET *from behind. Catches hold of
        her arm*
Becket.   Murderess!
    [*The dagger falls; they stare at one
    another. After a pause.*
Eleanor. My lord, we know you proud
    of your fine hand,
But having now admired it long enough,
We find that it is mightier than it seems—
At least mine own is frailer: you are
    laming it.
    Becket. And lamed and maim'd to dis-
    location, better
Than raised to take a life which Henry
    bad me
Guard from the stroke that dooms thee
    after death
To wail in deathless flame.
    Eleanor.   Nor you, nor I
Have now to learn, my lord, that our good
    Henry
Says many a thing in sudden heats, which
    he
Gainsays by next sunrising—often ready
To tear himself for having said as much.
My lord, Fitzurse——
    Becket. He too! what dost thou here?
Dares the bear slouch into the lion's den?
One downward plunge of his paw would
    rend away
Eyesight and manhood, life itself, from
    thee.
Go, lest I blast thee with anathema,
And make thee a world's horror.
    Fitzurse.   My lord, I shall
Remember this.
    Becket.   I *do* remember thee;
Lest I remember thee to the lion, go.
                    [*Exit* FITZURSE.
Take up your dagger; put it in the sheath.
    Eleanor. Might not your courtesy stoop
    to hand it me?
But crowns must bow when mitres sit so
    high.
Well—well—too costly to be left or lost.
                    [*Picks up the dagger.*
I had it from an Arab soldan, who,

When I was there in Antioch, marvell'd at
Our unfamiliar beauties of the west;
But wonder'd more at my much constancy
To the monk-king, Louis, our former
    burthen,
From whom, as being too kin, you know,
    my lord,
God's grace and Holy Church deliver'd us.
I think, time given, I could have talk'd him
His ten wives into one. Look at the hilt.
What excellent workmanship. In our poor
    west
We cannot do it so well.
    Becket.   We can do worse.
Madam, I saw your dagger at her throat;
I heard your savage cry.
    Eleanor.   Well acted, was it?
A comedy meant to seem a tragedy—
A feint, a farce. My honest lord, you are
    known
Thro' all the courts of Christendom as one
That mars a cause with over-violence.
You have wrong'd Fitzurse. I speak not of
    myself.
We thought to scare this minion of the
    King
Back from her churchless commerce with
    the King
To the fond arms of her first love, Fitzurse,
Who swore to marry her. You have spoilt
    the farce.
My savage cry? Why, she—she—when I
    strove
To work against her license for her good,
Bark'd out at me such monstrous charges,
    that
The King himself, for love of his own
    sons,
If hearing, would have spurn'd her; where-
    upon
I menaced her with this, as when we
    threaten
A yelper with a stick. Nay, I deny not
That I was somewhat anger'd. Do you
    hear me?
Believe or no, I care not. You have lost
The ear of the King. I have it. . . . My lord
    Paramount,
Our great High-priest, will not your
    Holiness

Vouchsafe a gracious answer to your
   Queen?
  Becket. Rosamund hath not answer'd
   you one word;
Madam, I will not answer you one word.
Daughter, the world hath trick'd thee.
   Leave it, daughter;
Come thou with me to Godstow nunnery,
And live what may be left thee of a life
Saved as by miracle alone with Him
Who gave it.

Re-enter GEOFFREY

  Geoffrey. Mother, you told me a great
   fib: it wasn't in the willow.
  Becket. Follow us, my son, and we will
   find it for thee—
Or something manlier.

    [*Exeunt* BECKET, ROSAMUND, *and*
    GEOFFREY.
  Eleanor. The world hath trick'd her—
   that's the King; if so,
There was the farce, the feint—not mine.
   And yet
I am all but sure my dagger was a feint
Till the worm turn'd—not life shot up in
   blood,
But death drawn in;—(*looking at the vial*)
   this was no feint then? no.
But can I swear to that, had she but given
Plain answer to plain query? nay, me-
   thinks
Had she but bow'd herself to meet the
   wave
Of humiliation, worship whom she
   loathed,
I should have let her be, scorn'd her too
   much
To harm her. Henry—Becket tells him
   this—
To take my life might lose him Aquitaine.
Too politic for that. Imprison me?
No, for it came to nothing—only a feint.
Did she not tell me I was playing on her?
I'll swear to mine own self it was a feint.
Why should I swear, Eleanor, who am, or
   was,
A sovereign power? The King plucks out
   their eyes
Who anger him, and shall not I, the
   Queen,

Tear out her heart—kill, kill with knife or
   venom
One of his slanderous harlots? 'None of
   such?'
I love her none the more. Tut, the chance
   gone,
She lives—but not for him; one point is
   gain'd.
O I, that thro' the Pope divorced King
   Louis,
Scorning his monkery,—I that wedded
   Henry,
Honouring his manhood—will he not
   mock at me
The jealous fool balk'd of her will—with
   him?
But he and he must never meet again.
Reginald Fitzurse!

Re-enter FITZURSE

  Fitzurse.   Here, Madam, at your
   pleasure.
  Eleanor. My pleasure is to have a man
   about me.
Why did you slink away so like a cur?
  Fitzurse. Madam, I am as much man as
   the King.
Madam, I fear Church-censures like your
   King.
  Eleanor. He grovels to the Church when
   he's black-blooded,
But kinglike fought the proud archbishop,
   —kinglike
Defied the Pope, and, like his kingly sires,
The Normans, striving still to break or
   bind
The spiritual giant with our island laws
And customs, made me for the moment
   proud
Ev'n of that stale Church-bond which
   link'd me with him
To bear him kingly sons. I am not so sure
But that I love him still. Thou as much
   man!
No more of that; we will to France and be
Beforehand with the King, and brew from
   out
This Godstow-Becket intermeddling such
A strong hate-philtre as may madden him
   —madden
Against his priest beyond all hellebore.

ACT V

SCENE I

Castle in Normandy. King's Chamber

HENRY, ROGER OF YORK, FOLIOT,
JOCELYN OF SALISBURY

Roger of York. Nay, nay, my liege,
He rides abroad with armed followers,
Hath broken all his promises to thyself,
Cursed and anathematised us right and
left,
Stirr'd up a party there against your son—
Henry. Roger of York, you always hated
him,
Even when you both were boys at Theo-
bald's.
Roger of York. I always hated boundless
arrogance.
In mine own cause I strove against him
there,
And in thy cause I strive against him now.
Henry. I cannot think he moves against
my son,
Knowing right well with what a tender-
ness
He loved my son.
Roger of York. Before you made him
king.
But Becket ever moves against a king.
The Church is all—the crime to be a king.
We trust your Royal Grace, lord of more
land
Than any crown in Europe, will not yield
To lay your neck beneath your citizen's
heel.
Henry. Not to a Gregory of my throning!
No.
Foliot. My royal liege, in aiming at your
love,
It may be sometimes I have overshot
My duties to our Holy Mother Church,
Tho' all the world allows I fall no inch
Behind this Becket, rather go beyond
In scourgings, macerations, mortifyings,
Fasts, disciplines that clear the spiritual
eye,
And break the soul from earth. Let all
that be.
I boast not: but you know thro' all this
quarrel

I still have cleaved to the crown, in hope
the crown
Would cleave to me that but obey'd the
crown,
Crowning your son; for which our loyal
service,
And since we likewise swore to obey the
customs,
York and myself, and our good Salisbury
here,
Are push'd from out communion of the
Church.
Jocelyn of Salisbury. Becket hath trodden
on us like worms, my liege;
Trodden one half dead; one half, but half-
alive,
Cries to the King.
Henry (*aside*). Take care o' thyself, O
King.
Jocelyn of Salisbury. Being so crush'd
and so humiliated
We scarcely dare to bless the food we eat
Because of Becket.
Henry.   What would ye have me do?
Roger of York. Summon your barons;
take their counsel: yet
I know—could swear—as long as Becket
breathes,
Your Grace will never have one quiet hour.
Henry. What? . . . Ay . . . but pray you
do not work upon me.
I see your drift . . . it may be so . . . and yet
You know me easily anger'd. Will you
hence?
He shall absolve you . . . you shall have
redress.
I have a dizzying headache. Let me rest.
I'll call you by and by.
          [*Exeunt* ROGER OF YORK, FOLIOT, *and*
                    JOCELYN OF SALISBURY.
Would he were dead! I have lost all love
for him.
If God would take him in some sudden way—
Would he were dead.   [*Lies down.*
Page (*entering*). My liege, the Queen of
England.
Henry. God's eyes!   [*Starting up.*

Enter ELEANOR

Eleanor.   Of England? Say of
Aquitaine.

I am no Queen of England. I had dream'd
I was the bride of England, and a queen.
  Henry. And,—while you dream'd you
    were the bride of England,—
Stirring her baby-king against me? ha!
  Eleanor. The brideless Becket is thy
    king and mine:
I will go live and die in Aquitaine.
  Henry. Except I clap thee into prison
    here,
Lest thou shouldst play the wanton there
    again.
Ha, you of Aquitaine! O you of Aquitaine!
You were but Aquitaine to Louis—no
    wife;
You are only Aquitaine to me—no wife.
  Eleanor. And why, my lord, should I be
    wife to one
That only wedded me for Aquitaine?
Yet this no wife—her six and thirty sail
Of Provence blew you to your English
    throne;
And this no wife has born you four brave
    sons,
And one of them at least is like to prove
Bigger in our small world than thou art.
  Henry.   Ay—
Richard, if he be mine—I hope him mine.
But thou art like enough to make him
    thine.
  Eleanor. Becket is like enough to make
    all his.
  Henry. Methought I had recover'd of
    the Becket,
That all was planed and bevell'd smooth
    again,
Save from some hateful cantrip of thine
    own.
  Eleanor. I will go live and die in
    Aquitaine.
I dream'd I was the consort of a king,
Not one whose back his priest has broken.
  Henry.   What!
Is the end come? You, will you crown my
    foe
My victor in mid-battle? I will be
Sole master of my house. The end is mine.
What game, what juggle, what devilry are
    you playing?
Why do you thrust this Becket on me
    again?

  Eleanor. Why? for I am true wife, and
    have my fears
Lest Becket thrust you even from your
    throne.
Do you know this cross, my liege?
  Henry (turning his head). Away! Not I.
  Eleanor. Not ev'n the central diamond,
    worth, I think,
Half of the Antioch whence I had it.
  Henry.   That?
  Eleanor. I gave it you, and you your
    paramour;
She sends it back, as being dead to earth,
So dead henceforth to you.
  Henry. Dead! you have murder'd her,
Found out her secret bower and murder'd
    her.
  Eleanor. Your Becket knew the secret of
    your bower.
  Henry (calling out). Ho there! thy rest
    of life is hopeless prison.
  Eleanor. And what would my own
    Aquitaine say to that?
First, free thy captive from her hopeless
    prison.
  Henry. O devil, can I free her from the
    grave?
  Eleanor. You are too tragic: both of us
    are players
In such a comedy as our court of Provence
Had laugh'd at. That's a delicate Latin lay
Of Walter Map: the lady holds the cleric
Lovelier than any soldier, his poor tonsure
A crown of Empire. Will you have it
    again?
(Offering the cross. He dashes it down.)
St. Cupid, that is too irreverent.
Then mine once more. (Puts it on.)
                      Your cleric hath your lady.
Nay, what uncomely faces, could he see
    you!
Foam at the mouth because King Thomas,
    lord
Not only of your vassals but amours,
Thro' chastest honour of the Decalogue
Hath used the full authority of his Church
To put her into Godstow nunnery.
  Henry. To put her into Godstow nun-
    nery!
He dared not—liar! yet, yet I remember—
I do remember.

He bad me put her into a nunnery—
Into Godstow, into Hellstow, Devilstow!
The Church! the Church!
God's eyes! would the Church were down
    in hell!   [*Exit.*
Eleanor. Aha!

Enter the four KNIGHTS

Fitzurse. What made the King cry out so
    furiously?
Eleanor. Our Becket, who will not
    absolve the Bishops.
I think ye four have cause to love this
    Becket.
Fitzurse. I hate him for his insolence
    to all.
De Tracy. And I for all his insolence to
    thee.
De Brito. I hate him for I hate him is
    my reason,
And yet I hate him for a hypocrite.
De Morville. I do not love him, for he
    did his best
To break the barons, and now braves the
    King.
Eleanor. Strike, then, at once, the King
    would have him—See!

Re-enter HENRY

Henry. No man to love me, honour me,
    obey me!
Sluggards and fools!
The slave that eat my bread has kick'd his
    King!
The dog I cramm'd with dainties worried
    me!
The fellow that on a lame jade came to
    court,
A ragged cloak for saddle—he, he, he,
To shake my throne, to push into my
    chamber—
My bed, where ev'n the slave is private—
    he—
I'll have her out again, he shall absolve
The bishops—they but did my will—not
    you—
Sluggards and fools, why do you stand and
    stare?
You are no King's men—you—you—you
    are Becket's men.

Down with King Henry! up with the
    Archbishop!
Will no man free me from this pestilent
    priest?   [*Exit.*
    [*The* KNIGHTS *draw their swords.*
Eleanor. Are ye king's men? I am king's
    woman, I.
The Knights. King's men! King's men!

SCENE II

A Room in Canterbury Monastery

BECKET *and* JOHN OF SALISBURY

Becket. York said so?
John of Salisbury. Yes: a man may take
    good counsel
Ev'n from his foe.
Becket.   York will say anything.
What is he saying now? gone to the King
And taken our anathema with him. York!
Can the King de-anathematise this York?
John of Salisbury. Thomas, I would thou
    hadst return'd to England,
Like some wise prince of this world from
    his wars,
With more of olive-branch and amnesty
For foes at home—thou hast raised the
    world against thee.
Becket. Why, John, my kingdom is not
    of this world.
John of Salisbury. If it were more of this
    world it might be
More of the next. A policy of wise pardon
Wins here as well as there. To bless thine
    enemies——
Becket. Ay, mine, not Heaven's.
John of Salisbury.   And may
    there not be something
Of this world's leaven in thee too, when
    crying
On Holy Church to thunder out her rights
And thine own wrong so pitilessly? Ah,
    Thomas,
The lightnings that we think are only
    Heaven's
Flash sometimes out of earth against the
    heavens.
The soldier, when he lets his whole self go
Lost in the common good, the common
    wrong,

Strikes truest ev'n for his own self. I crave
Thy pardon—I have still thy leave to
    speak.
Thou hast waged God's war against the
    King; and yet
We are self-uncertain creatures, and we
    may,
Yea, even when we know not, mix our
    spites
And private hates with our defence of
    Heaven.

Enter EDWARD GRIM

Becket. Thou art but yesterday from
    Cambridge, Grim;
What say ye there of Becket?
    Grim.   *I* believe him
The bravest in our roll of Primates down
From Austin—there are some—for there
    are men
Of canker'd judgment everywhere——
    Becket.   Who hold
With York, with York against me.
    Grim.   Well, my lord,
A stranger monk desires access to you.
    Becket. York against Canterbury, York
        against God!
I am open to him.   [*Exit* GRIM.

Enter ROSAMUND *as a Monk*

Rosamund.   Can I speak with you
Alone, my father?
    Becket.   Come you to confess?
Rosamund. Not now.
    Becket.   Then speak; this
        is my other self,
Who like my conscience never lets me be.
Rosamund (*throwing back the cowl*). I
    know him; our good John of Salis-
    bury.
    Becket. Breaking already from thy novi-
        ciate
To plunge into this bitter world again—
These wells of Marah. I am grieved, my
    daughter.
I thought that I had made a peace for thee.
    Rosamund. Small peace was mine in my
        noviciate, father,
Thro' all closed doors a dreadful whisper
    crept

That thou wouldst excommunicate the
    King.
I could not eat, sleep, pray: I had with me
The monk's disguise thou gavest me for
    my bower:
I think our Abbess knew it and allow'd it.
I fled, and found thy name a charm to
    get me
Food, roof, and rest. I met a robber once,
I told him I was bound to see the Arch-
    bishop;
'Pass on,' he said, and in thy name I pass'd
From house to house. In one a son stone-
    blind
Sat by his mother's hearth: he had gone
    too far
Into the King's own woods; and the poor
    mother,
Soon as she learnt I was a friend of thine,
Cried out against the cruelty of the King.
I said it was the King's courts, not the
    King;
But she would not believe me, and she
    wish'd
The Church were king: she had seen the
    Archbishop once,
So mild, so kind. The people love thee,
    father.
    Becket. Alas! when I was Chancellor to
        the King,
I fear I was as cruel as the King.
    Rosamund. Cruel? Oh, no—it is the law,
        not he;
The customs of the realm.
    Becket.   The customs! customs!
    Rosamund. My lord, you have not ex-
        communicated him?
Oh, if you have, absolve him!
    Becket.   Daughter, daughter,
Deal not with things you know not.
    Rosamund.   I know *him*.
Then you have done it, and I call *you* cruel.
    John of Salisbury. No, daughter, you
        mistake our good Archbishop;
For once in France the King had been so
    harsh,
He thought to excommunicate him—
    Thomas,
You could not—old affection master'd you,
You falter'd into tears.
    Rosamund.   God bless him for it.

Becket. Nay, make me not a woman, John of Salisbury,
Nor make me traitor to my holy office.
Did not a man's voice ring along the aisle,
'The King is sick and almost unto death.'
How could I excommunicate him then?
Rosamund. And wilt thou excommunicate him now?
Becket. Daughter, my time is short, I shall not do it.
And were it longer—well—I should not do it.
Rosamund. Thanks in this life, and in the life to come.
Becket. Get thee back to thy nunnery with all haste;
Let this be thy last trespass. But one question—
How fares thy pretty boy, the little Geoffrey?
No fever, cough, croup, sickness?
Rosamund.   No, but saved
From all that by our solitude. The plagues
That smite the city spare the solitudes.
Becket. God save him from all sickness of the soul!
Thee too, thy solitude among thy nuns,
May that save thee! Doth he remember me?
Rosamund. I warrant him.
Becket. He is marvellously like thee.
Rosamund. Liker the King.
Becket.   No, daughter.
Rosamund.   Ay, but wait
Till his nose rises; he will be very king.
Becket. Ev'n so: but think not of the King: farewell!
Rosamund. My lord, the city is full of armed men.
Becket. Ev'n so: farewell!
Rosamund. I will but pass to vespers,
And breathe one prayer for my liege-lord the King,
His child and mine own soul, and so return.
Becket. Pray for me too: much need of prayer have I.
                    [ROSAMUND *kneels and goes.*
Dan John, how much we lose, we celibates,
Lacking the love of woman and of child.
John of Salisbury. More gain than loss; for of your wives you shall

Find one a slut whose fairest linen seems
Foul as her dust-cloth, if she used it—one
So charged with tongue, that every thread of thought
Is broken ere it joins—a shrew to boot,
Whose evil song far on into the night
Thrills to the topmost tile—no hope but death;
One slow, fat, white, a burthen of the hearth;
And one that being thwarted ever swoons
And weeps herself into the place of power;
And one an *uxor pauperis Ibyci.*
So rare the household honeymaking bee,
Man's help! but we, we have the Blessed Virgin
For worship, and our Mother Church for bride;
And all the souls we saved and father'd here
Will greet us as our babes in Paradise.
What noise was that? she told us of arm'd men
Here in the city. Will you not withdraw?
Becket. I once was out with Henry in the days
When Henry loved me, and we came upon
A wild-fowl sitting on her nest, so still
I reach'd my hand and touch'd; she did not stir;
The snow had frozen round her, and she sat
Stone-dead upon a heap of ice-cold eggs.
Look! how this love, this mother, runs thro' all
The world God made—even the beast—the bird!
John of Salisbury. Ay, still a lover of the beast and bird?
But these arm'd men—will you not hide yourself?
Perchance the fierce De Brocs from Saltwood Castle,
To assail our Holy Mother lest she brood
Too long o'er this hard egg, the world, and send
Her whole heart's heat into it, till it break
Into young angels. Pray you, hide yourself.
Becket. There was a little fair-hair'd Norman maid
Lived in my mother's house: if Rosamund is

The world's rose, as her name imports her
  —she
Was the world's lily.
  John of Salisbury. Ay, and what of her?
  Becket. She died of leprosy.
  John of Salisbury.   I know not why
You call these old things back again, my
  lord.
  Becket. The drowning man, they say,
  remembers all
The chances of his life, just ere he dies.
  John of Salisbury. Ay—but these arm'd
men—will *you* drown *yourself?*
He loses half the meed of martyrdom
Who will be martyr when he might escape.
  Becket. What day of the week? Tuesday?
  John of Salisbury.   Tuesday, my lord.
  Becket. On a Tuesday was I born, and
  on a Tuesday
Baptized; and on a Tuesday did I fly
Forth from Northampton; on a Tuesday
  pass'd
From England into bitter banishment;
On a Tuesday at Pontigny came to me
The ghostly warning of my martyrdom;
On a Tuesday from mine exile I return'd,
And on a Tuesday——
        [TRACY *enters, then* FITZURSE, DE
        BRITO, *and* DE MORVILLE. MONKS
        following.
        —on a Tuesday—— Tracy!
(*A long silence broken by* FITZURSE *saying,*
contemptuously),
        God help thee!
  John of Salisbury (*aside*). How the good
  Archbishop reddens!
He never yet could brook the note of
  scorn.
  Fitzurse. My lord, we bring a message
  from the King
Beyond the water; will you have it alone,
Or with these listeners near you?
  Becket.   As you will.
  Fitzurse. Nay, as *you* will.
  Becket.   Nay, as *you* will.
  John of Salisbury.   Why then
Better perhaps to speak with them apart.
Let us withdraw.
        [*All go out except the four* KNIGHTS
        and BECKET.
  Fitzurse. We are all alone with him.

Shall I not smite him with his own cross-
  staff?
  De Morville. No, look! the door is open:
  let him be.
  Fitzurse. The King condemns your ex-
  communicating——
  Becket. This is no secret, but a public
  matter.
In here again!
        [JOHN OF SALISBURY *and* MONKS *return.*
        Now, sirs, the King's commands!
  Fitzurse. The King beyond the water,
  thro' our voices.
Commands you to be dutiful and leal
To your young King on this side of the
  water,
Not scorn him for the foibles of his youth.
What! you would make his coronation void
By cursing those who crown'd him. Out
  upon you!
  Becket. Reginald, all men know I loved
  the Prince.
His father gave him to my care, and I
Became his second father: he had his faults,
For which I would have laid mine own life
  down
To help him from them, since indeed I
  loved him,
And love him next after my lord his father.
Rather than dim the splendour of his
  crown
I fain would treble and quadruple it
With revenues, realms, and golden pro-
  vinces
So that were done in equity.
  Fitzurse.   You have broken
Your bond of peace, your treaty with the
  King—
Wakening such brawls and loud distur-
  bances
In England, that he calls you oversea
To answer for it in his Norman courts.
  Becket. Prate not of bonds, for never, oh,
  never again
Shall the waste voice of the bond-breaking
  sea
Divide me from the mother church of
  England,
My Canterbury. Loud disturbances!
Oh, ay—the bells rang out even to
  deafening,

Organ and pipe, and dulcimer, chants and
   hymns
In all the churches, trumpets in the
   halls,
Sobs, laughter, cries: they spread their
   raiment down
Before me—would have made my path-
   way flowers,
Save that it was mid-winter in the street,
But full mid-summer in those honest
   hearts.
   Fitzurse. The King commands you to
   absolve the bishops
Whom you have excommunicated.
   Becket.   I?
Not I, the Pope. Ask *him* for absolution.
   Fitzurse. But you advised the Pope.
   Becket.   And so I did.
They have but to submit.
   The four Knights. The King commands
   you.
We are all King's men.
   Becket.   King's men at least
   should know
That their own King closed with me last
   July
That I should pass the censures of the
   Church
On those that crown'd young Henry in this
   realm,
And trampled on the rights of Canter-
   bury.
   Fitzurse. What! dare you charge the
   King with treachery?
He sanction thee to excommunicate
The prelates whom he chose to crown his
   son!
   Becket. I spake no word of treachery,
   Reginald.
But for the truth of this I make appeal
To all the archbishops, bishops, prelates,
   barons,
Monks, knights, five hundred, that were
   there and heard.
Nay, you yourself were there: you heard
   yourself.
   Fitzurse. I was not there.
   Becket.   I saw you there.
   Fitzurse.   I was not.
   Becket. You were. I never forget any-
   thing.

   Fitzurse. He makes the King a traitor,
   me a liar.
How long shall we forbear him?
   John of Salisbury (*drawing* BECKET *aside*).
                   O my good lord,
Speak with them privately on this here-
   after.
You see they have been revelling, and I
   fear
Are braced and brazen'd up with Christ-
   mas wines
For any murderous brawl.
   Becket.   And yet they prate
Of mine, my brawls, when those, that name
   themselves
Of the King's part, have broken down our
   barns,
Wasted our diocese, outraged our tenants,
Lifted our produce, driven our clerics
   out—
Why they, your friends, those ruffians, the
   De Brocs,
They stood on Dover beach to murder me,
They slew my stags in mine own manor
   here,
Mutilated, poor brute, my sumpter-mule,
Plunder'd the vessel full of Gascon wine,
The old King's present, carried off the
   casks,
Kill'd half the crew, dungeon'd the other
   half
In Pevensey Castle——
   De Morville.   Why not rather then,
If this be so, complain to your young King,
Not punish of your own authority?
   Becket. Mine enemies barr'd all access
   to the boy.
They knew he loved me.
Hugh, Hugh, how proudly you exalt your
   head!
Nay, when they seek to overturn our rights,
I ask no leave of king, or mortal man,
To set them straight again. Alone I do it.
Give to the King the things that are the
   King's,
And those of God to God.
   Fitzurse.   Threats! threats!
   ye hear him.
What! will he excommunicate all the
   world?
      [*The* KNIGHTS *come round* BECKET.

De Tracy. He shall not.

De Brito.   Well, as yet—
I should be grateful—
He hath not excommunicated *me*.

Becket. Because thou wast *born* excommunicate.
I never spied in thee one gleam of grace.

De Brito. Your Christian's Christian
charity!

Becket.   By St. Denis——

De Brito. Ay, by St. Denis, now will he
flame out,
And lose his head as old St. Denis did.

Becket. Ye think to scare me from my
loyalty
To God and to the Holy Father. No!
Tho' all the swords in England flash'd
above me
Ready to fall at Henry's word or yours—
Tho' all the loud-lung'd trumpets upon
earth
Blared from the heights of all the thrones
of her kings,
Blowing the world against me, I would
stand
Clothed with the full authority of Rome,
Mail'd in the perfect panoply of faith,
First of the foremost of their files, who die
For God, to people heaven in the great
day
When God makes up his jewels. Once I
fled—
Never again, and you—I marvel at you—
Ye know what is between us. Ye have
sworn
Yourselves my men when I was Chan-
cellor—
My vassals—and yet threaten your Arch-
bishop
In his own house.

Knights.   Nothing can be between us
That goes against our fealty to the King.

Fitzurse. And in his name we charge you
that ye keep
This traitor from escaping.

Becket.   Rest you easy,
For I am easy to keep. I shall not fly.
Here, here, here will you find me.

De Morville.   Know you not
You have spoken to the peril of your life?

Becket. As I shall speak again.

Fitzurse, De Tracy, and De Brito. To
arms!
                    [*They rush out,* DE MORVILLE *lingers.*

Becket.   De Morville,
I had thought so well of you; and even now
You seem the least assassin of the four.
Oh, do not damn yourself for company!
Is it too late for me to save your soul?
I pray you for one moment stay and speak.

De Morville. Becket, it *is* too late.   [*Exit.*

Becket.   Is it too late?
Too late on earth may be too soon in hell.

Knights (*in the distance*). Close the great
gate—ho, there—upon the town.

Becket's Retainers. Shut the hall-doors.
                    [*A pause.*

Becket. You hear them, brother John;
Why do you stand so silent, brother John?

John of Salisbury. For I was musing on
an ancient saw,
Suaviter in modo, fortiter in re,
Is strength less strong when hand-in-hand
with grace?
Gratior in pulchro corpore virtus. Thomas,
Why should you heat yourself for such as
these?

Becket. Methought I answer'd moder-
ately enough.

John of Salisbury. As one that blows the
coal to cool the fire.
My lord, I marvel why you never lean
On any man's advising but your own.

Becket. Is it so, Dan John? well, what
should I have done?

John of Salisbury. You should have taken
counsel with your friends
Before these bandits brake into your
presence.
They seek—you make—occasion for your
death.

Becket. My counsel is already taken,
John.
I am prepared to die.

John of Salisbury. We are sinners all,
The best of all not all-prepared to die.

Becket. God's will be done!

John of Salisbury.   Ay, well.
God's will be done!

Grim (*re-entering*). My lord, the knights
are arming in the garden
Beneath the sycamore.

Becket.   Good! let them arm.
Grim. And one of the De Brocs is with
    them, Robert,
The apostate monk that was with Randulf
here.
He knows the twists and turnings of the
place.
Becket. No fear!
Grim.   No fear, my lord.
    [*Crashes on the hall-doors. The*
    MONKS *flee.*
Becket (*rising*). Our dovecote flown!
I cannot tell why monks should all be
cowards.
John of Salisbury. Take refuge in your
    own cathedral, Thomas.
Becket. Do they not fight the Great
    Fiend day by day?
Valour and holy life should go together.
Why should all monks be cowards?
John of Salisbury.   Are they so?
I say, take refuge in your own cathedral.
Becket. Ay, but I told them I would wait
    them here.
Grim. May they not say you dared not
    show yourself
In your old place? and vespers are begin-
    ning.
    [*Bell rings for vespers till end of scene.*
You should attend the office, give them
    heart.
They fear you slain: they dread they know
    not what.
Becket. Ay, monks, not men.
Grim.   I am a monk, my lord.
Perhaps, my lord, you wrong us.
Some would stand by you to the death.
Becket.   Your pardon.
John of Salisbury. He said, 'Attend the
    office.'
Becket.   Attend the office?
Why then—The Cross!—who bears my
    Cross before me?
Methought they would have brain'd me
    with it, John.   [GRIM *takes it.*
Grim. I! Would that I could bear thy
    cross indeed!
Becket. The Mitre!
John of Salisbury. Will you wear it?—
    there!
    [BECKET *puts on the mitre.*

Becket.   The Pall!
I go to meet my King!
                    [*Puts on the pall.*
Grim.   To meet the King?
    [*Crashes on the doors as they go out.*
John of Salisbury. Why do you move
    with such a stateliness?
Can you not hear them yonder like a storm,
Battering the doors, and breaking thro' the
    walls?
Becket. Why do the heathen rage? My
    two good friends,
What matters murder'd here, or murder'd
    there?
And yet my dream foretold my martyrdom
In mine own church. It is God's will.
Go on.
Nay, drag me not. We must not seem to fly.

SCENE III

North Transept of Canterbury Cathedral

*On the right hand a flight of steps leading
    to the Choir, another flight on the left,
    leading to the North Aisle. Winter after-
    noon slowly darkening. Low thunder now
    and then of an approaching storm.* MONKS
    heard chanting the service. ROSAMUND
    kneeling.

Rosamund. O blessed saint, O glorious
    Benedict,—
These arm'd men in the city, these fierce
    faces—
Thy holy follower founded Canterbury—
Save that dear head which now is Canter-
    bury,
Save him, he saved my life, he saved my
    child,
Save him, his blood would darken
    Henry's name;
Save him till all as saintly as thyself
He miss the searching flame of purgatory,
And pass at once perfect to Paradise.
    [*Noise of steps and voices in the cloisters.*
Hark! Is it they? Coming! He is not here—
Not yet, thank heaven. O save him!
                [*Goes up steps leading to choir.*
Becket (*entering, forced along by John of
    Salisbury and Grim*). No, I tell you!
I cannot bear a hand upon my person,

Why do you force me thus against my
   will?
Grim. My lord, we force you from your
   enemies.
Becket. As you would force a king from
   being crown'd.
John of Salisbury. We must not force the
   crown of martyrdom.
      [*Service stops.* MONKS *come down
      from the stairs that lead to the choir.*
Monks. Here is the great Archbishop!
   He lives! he lives!
Die with him, and be glorified together.
Becket. Together? . . . get you back! go
   on with the office.
Monks. Come, then, with us to vespers.
Becket.   How can I come
When you so block the entry? Back, I say!
Go on with the office. Shall not Heaven be
   served
Tho' earth's last earthquake clash'd the
   minster-bells,
And the great deeps were broken up again,
And hiss'd against the sun?
                  [*Noise in the cloisters.*
Monks.   The murderers, hark!
Let us hide! let us hide!
Becket. What do these people fear?
Monks. Those arm'd men in the cloister.
Becket.   Be not such cravens!
I will go out and meet them.
Grim and others.   Shut the doors!
We will not have him slain before our
   face.
      [*They close the doors of the transept.
      Knocking.*
Fly, fly, my lord, before they burst the
   doors!   [*Knocking.*
Becket. Why, these are our own monks
   who follow'd us!
And will you bolt them out, and have *them*
   slain?
Undo the doors: the church is not a castle:
Knock, and it shall be open'd. Are you
   deaf?
What, have I lost authority among you?
Stand by, make way!
      [*Opens the doors. Enter* MONKS *from
      cloister.*
            Come in, my friends, come in!
Nay, faster, faster!

Monks.   Oh, my lord Archbishop,
A score of knights all arm'd with swords
   and axes—
To the choir, to the choir!
      [MONKS *divide, part flying by the
      stairs on the right, part by those on
      the left. The rush of these last bears*
      BECKET *along with them some way up
      the steps, where he is left standing
      alone.*
Becket. Shall I too pass to the choir,
And die upon the Patriarchal throne
Of all my predecessors?
John of Salisbury.   No, to the crypt!
Twenty steps down. Stumble not in the
   darkness,
Lest they should seize thee.
Grim.   To the crypt? no—no,
To the chapel of St. Blaise beneath the
   roof!
John of Salisbury (*pointing upward and
   downward*). That way, or this! Save
   thyself either way.
Becket. Oh, no, not either way, nor any
   way
Save by that way which leads thro' night
   to light.
Not twenty steps, but one.
And fear not I should stumble in the
   darkness,
Not tho' it be their hour, the power of
   darkness,
But my hour too, the power of light in
   darkness!
I am not in the darkness but the light,
Seen by the Church in Heaven, the Church
   on earth—
The power of life in death to make her free!
      [*Enter the four* KNIGHTS. JOHN OF
      SALISBURY *flies to the altar of St.
      Benedict.*
Fitzurse. Here, here, King's men!
      [*Catches hold of the last flying* MONK.
            Where is the traitor Becket?
Monk. I am not he! I am not he, my lord.
I am not he indeed!
Fitzurse.   Hence to the fiend!
                        [*Pushes him away.*
Where is this treble traitor to the King?
De Tracy. Where is the Archbishop,
   Thomas Becket?

Becket.   Here.
No traitor to the King, but Priest of God,
Primate of England.
          [*Descending into the transept.*
                    I am he ye seek.
What would ye have of me?
Fitzurse.   Your life.
De Tracy.   Your life.
De Morville. Save that you will absolve
the bishops.
Becket.   Never,—
Except they make submission to the
Church.
You had my answer to that cry before.
De Morville. Why, then you are a dead
man; flee!
Becket.   I will not.
I am readier to be slain, than thou to
slay.
Hugh, I know well thou hast but half a
heart
To bathe this sacred pavement with my
blood.
God pardon thee and these, but God's full
curse
Shatter you all to pieces if ye harm
One of my flock!
Fitzurse.   Was not the great gate
shut?
They are thronging in to vespers—half the
town.
We shall be overwhelm'd. Seize him and
carry him!
Come with us—nay—thou art our prisoner
—come!
De Morville. Ay, make him prisoner, do
not harm the man.
          [FITZURSE *lays hold of the* ARCH-
          BISHOP'S *pall.*
Becket. Touch me not!
De Brito.   How the good
priest gods himself!
He is not yet ascended to the Father.
Fitzurse. I will not only touch, but drag
thee hence.
Becket. Thou art my man, thou art my
vassal. Away!
          [*Flings him off till he reels, almost to*
          falling.
De Tracy (*lays hold of the pall*). Come;
as he said, thou art our prisoner.

Becket.   Down!
          [*Throws him headlong.*
Fitzurse (*advances with drawn sword*).
I told thee that I should remember
thee!
Becket. Profligate pander!
Fitzurse.   Do you hear that?
strike, strike.
          [*Strikes off the* ARCHBISHOP'S *mitre,*
          and wounds him in the forehead.
Becket (*covers his eyes with his hand*). I do
commend my cause to God, the
Virgin,
St. Denis of France and St. Alphege of
England,
And all the tutelar Saints of Canterbury.
          [GRIM *wraps his arms about the*
          ARCHBISHOP.
Spare this defence, dear brother.
          [TRACY *has arisen, and approaches,*
          hesitatingly, with his sword raised.
Fitzurse.   Strike him, Tracy!
Rosamund (*rushing down steps from the*
choir). No, No, No, No!
Fitzurse.   This wanton here. De
Morville,
Hold her away.
De Morville. I hold her.
Rosamund (*held back by* DE MORVILLE,
and stretching out her arms).
                    Mercy, mercy,
As you would hope for mercy.
Fitzurse.   Strike, I say.
Grim. O God, O noble knights, O
sacrilege!
Strike our Archbishop in his own cathe-
dral!
The Pope, the King, will curse you—the
whole world
Abhor you; ye will die the death of
dogs!
Nay. nay, good Tracy.   [*Lifts his arm.*
Fitzurse.   Answer not, but
strike.
De Tracy. There is my answer then.
          [*Sword falls on* GRIM'S *arm, and*
          glances from it, wounding BECKET.
Grim.   Mine arm is sever'd.
I can no more—fight out the good fight—
die
Conqueror.

[*Staggers into the chapel of St. Benedict.*

Becket (*falling on his knees*). At the right hand of Power—

Power and great glory—for thy Church, O Lord—

Into Thy hands, O Lord—into Thy hands!—— [*Sinks prone.*

De Brito. This last to rid thee of a world of brawls! (*Kills him.*)

The traitor's dead, and will arise no more.

Fitzurse. Nay, have we still'd him?

What! the great Archbishop!

Does he breathe? No?

De Tracy. No, Reginald, he is dead.
  [*Storm bursts.*[1]

De Morville. Will the earth gape and swallow us?

De Brito. The deed's done—

Away!

[DE BRITO, DE TRACY, FITZURSE, *rush out, crying 'King's men!'* DE MORVILLE *follows slowly. Flashes of lightning thro' the Cathedral.* ROSAMUND *seen kneeling by the body of* BECKET.

[1] *A tremendous thunderstorm actually broke over the Cathedral as the murderers were leaving it.*

THE CUP

A TRAGEDY

DRAMATIS PERSONÆ

GALATIANS

SYNORIX, *an ex-Tetrarch.*
SINNATUS, *a Tetrarch.*
Attendant.
Boy.

Maid.
PHŒBE.
CAMMA, *wife of Sinnatus, afterwards
Priestess in the Temple of Artemis.*

ROMANS

ANTONIUS, *a Roman General.*
PUBLIUS.

Nobleman.
Messenger.

ACT I

SCENE I

Distant View of a City of Galatia

*As the curtain rises, Priestesses are heard
singing in the Temple. Boy discovered on
a pathway among Rocks, picking grapes.
A party of Roman Soldiers, guarding a
prisoner in chains, come down the pathway
and exeunt.*

Enter SYNORIX (*looking round*). *Singing
ceases*

Synorix. Pine, beech and plane, oak,
  walnut, apricot,
Vine, cypress, poplar, myrtle, bowering-in
The city where she dwells. She past me
  here
Three years ago when I was flying from
My Tetrarchy to Rome. I almost touch'd
  her—
A maiden slowly moving on to music
Among her maidens to this Temple—O
  Gods!
She is my fate—else wherefore has my fate
Brought me again to her own city?—
  married
Since—married Sinnatus, the Tetrarch
  here—
But if he be conspirator, Rome will chain,
Or slay him. I may trust to gain her then
When I shall have my tetrarchy restored
By Rome, our mistress, grateful that I
  show'd her

The weakness and the dissonance of our
  clans,
And how to crush them easily. Wretched
  race!
And once I wish'd to scourge them to the
  bones.
But in this narrow breathing-time of life
Is vengeance for its own sake worth the
  while,
If once our ends are gain'd? and now this
  cup—
I never felt such passion for a woman.
  [*Brings out a cup and scroll from
    under his cloak.*
What have I written to her?
  [*Reading the scroll.*
'To the admired Camma, wife of Sinnatus, the Tetrarch, one who years ago,
himself an adorer of our great goddess,
Artemis, beheld you afar off worshipping
in her Temple, and loved you for it, sends
you this cup rescued from the burning of
one of her shrines in a city thro' which he
past with the Roman army: it is the cup
we use in our marriages. Receive it from
one who cannot at present write himself
other than

'A GALATIAN SERVING BY FORCE IN
  THE ROMAN LEGION.'
  [*Turns and looks up to Boy.*
Boy, dost thou know the house of Sinna-
tus?

Boy. These grapes are for the house of
  Sinnatus—
Close to the Temple.

Synorix.   Yonder?

Boy.   Yes.

Synorix (aside).   That I
With all my range of women should yet
    shun
To meet her face to face at once! My boy,

    [Boy comes down rocks to him.

Take thou this letter and this cup to
    Camma,
The wife of Sinnatus.

Boy.   Going or gone to-day
To hunt with Sinnatus.

Synorix.   That matters not.
Take thou this cup and leave it at her doors.

    [Gives the cup and scroll to the Boy.

Boy. I will, my lord.

    [Takes his basket of grapes and exit.

Enter ANTONIUS

Antonius (meeting the Boy as he goes out).
    Why, whither runs the boy?
Is that the cup you rescued from the fire?

Synorix. I send it to the wife of Sinnatus,
One half besotted in religious rites.
You come here with your soldiers to
    enforce
The long-withholden tribute: you suspect
This Sinnatus of playing patriotism,
Which in your sense is treason. You have
    yet
No proof against him: now this pious cup
Is passport to their house, and open arms
To him who gave it; and once there I
    warrant
I worm thro' all their windings.

Antonius.   If you prosper,
Our Senate, wearied of their tetrarchies,
Their quarrels with themselves, their
    spites at Rome,
Is like enough to cancel them, and throne
One king above them all, who shall be true
To the Roman: and from what I heard in
    Rome,
This tributary crown may fall to you.

Synorix. The king, the crown! their talk
    in Rome? is it so?

    [ANTONIUS nods.

Well—I shall serve Galatia taking it,
And save her from herself, and be to Rome
More faithful than a Roman.

    [Turns and sees CAMMA *coming.*

                Stand aside,
Stand aside; here she comes!

    [Watching CAMMA *as she enters with
    her Maid.*

Camma (to Maid). Where is he, girl?

Maid.   You know the waterfall
That in the summer keeps the mountain
    side,
But after rain o'erleaps a jutting rock
And shoots three hundred feet.

Camma.   The stag is there?

Maid. Seen in the thicket at the bottom
    there
But yester-even.

Camma.   Good then, we will climb
The mountain opposite and watch the
    chase.

    [They descend the rocks and exeunt.

Synorix (watching her). (Aside.) The bust
    of Juno and the brows and eyes
Of Venus; face and form unmatchable!

Antonius. Why do you look at her so
    lingeringly?

Synorix. To see if years have changed
    her.

Antonius (sarcastically). Love her, do
    you?

Synorix. I envied Sinnatus when he
    married her.

Antonius. She knows it? Ha!

Synorix. She—no, nor ev'n my face.

Antonius. Nor Sinnatus either?

Synorix.   No, nor Sinnatus.

Antonius. Hot-blooded! I have heard
    them say in Rome,
That your own people cast you from their
    bounds,
For some unprincely violence to a woman,
As Rome did Tarquin.

Synorix.   Well, if this were so
I here return like Tarquin—for a crown.

Antonius. And may be foil'd like Tar-
    quin, if you follow
Not the dry light of Rome's straight-going
    policy,
But the fool-fire of love or lust, which well
May make you lose yourself, may even
    drown you
In the good regard of Rome.

Synorix.   Tut—fear me not;

I ever had my victories among women.
I am most true to Rome.
    Antonius (*aside*).   I hate the man!
What filthy tools our Senate works with!
    Still
I must obey them. (*Aloud*.) Fare you well.
                 [*Going*.
    Synorix.   Farewell!
    Antonius (*stopping*). A moment! If you
    track this Sinnatus
In any treason, I give you here an order
             [*Produces a paper*.
To seize upon him. Let me sign it. (*Signs
    it*.) There
'Antonius leader of the Roman Legion.'
    [*Hands the paper to* SYNORIX. *Goes
    up pathway and exit*.
    Synorix. Woman again!—but I am wiser
    now.
No rushing on the game—the net,—the
    net.
    [*Shouts of* 'Sinnatus! Sinnatus!'
                 [*Then horn*.
Looking off stage.] He comes, a rough,
    bluff, simple-looking fellow.
If we may judge the kernel by the husk,
Not one to keep a woman's fealty when
Assailed by Craft and Love. I'll join with
    him:
I may reap something from him—come
    upon *her*
Again, perhaps, to-day—*her*. Who are with
    him?
I see no face that knows me. Shall I risk it?
I am a Roman now, they dare not touch me.
I will.
    Enter SINNATUS, HUNTSMEN *and hounds*
        Fair Sir, a happy day to you!
You reck but little of the Roman here,
While you can take your pastime in the
    woods.
    Sinnatus. Ay, ay, why not? What would
    you with me, man?
    Synorix. I am a life-long lover of the
    chase,
And tho' a stranger fain would be allow'd
To join the hunt.
    Sinnatus.   Your name?
    Synorix.   Strato, my name.
    Sinnatus. No Roman name?
    Synorix.   A Greek, my lord; you know

That we Galatians are both Greek and
    Gaul.
    [*Shouts and horns in the distance*.
    Sinnatus. Hillo, the stag! (*To* SYNORIX.)
What, you are all unfurnish'd?
Give him a bow and arrows—follow—
    follow.
    [*Exit, followed by* HUNTSMEN.
    Synorix. Slowly but surely—till I see
    my way.
It is the one step in the dark beyond
Our expectation, that amazes us.
        [*Distant shouts and horns*.
Hillo! Hillo!
    [*Exit* SYNORIX. *Shouts and horns*.

SCENE II

A Room in the Tetrarch's House

*Frescoed figures on the walls. Evening.
Moonlight outside. A couch with cushions
on it. A small table with a flagon of wine,
cups, plate of grapes, etc., also the cup of
Scene I. A chair with drapery on it.*

    CAMMA *enters, and opens curtains of
    window*

    Camma. No Sinnatus yet—and there
    the rising moon.
    [*Takes up a cithern and sits on
    couch. Plays and sings*.
Moon on the field and the foam,
    Moon on the waste and the wold,
Moon bring him home, bring him home
    Safe from the dark and the cold,
Home, sweet moon, bring him home,
    Home with the flock to the fold—
Safe from the wolf——
    (*Listening*.) Is he coming? I thought I
    heard
A footstep. No not yet. They say that
    Rome
Sprang from a wolf. I fear my dear lord
    mixt
With some conspiracy against the wolf.
This mountain shepherd never dream'd of
    Rome.
(*Sings*.) Safe from the wolf to the fold——
And that great break of precipice that runs
Thro' all the wood, where twenty years
    ago

Huntsman, and hound, and deer were all
  neck-broken!
Nay, here he comes.

Enter SINNATUS *followed by* SYNORIX

Sinnatus (*angrily*). I tell thee, my good
  fellow,
My arrow struck the stag.
Synorix.   But was it so?
Nay, you were further off: besides the
  wind
Went with *my* arrow.
Sinnatus.   I am sure *I* struck him.
Synorix. And I am just as sure, my lord,
  I struck him.
(*Aside.*) And I may strike your game when
  you are gone.
Camma. Come, come, we will not
  quarrel about the stag.
I have had a weary day in watching you.
Yours must have been a wearier. Sit and
  eat,
And take a hunter's vengeance on the
  meats.
Sinnatus. No, no—we have eaten—we
  are heated. Wine!
Camma. Who is our guest?
Sinnatus.   Strato he calls himself.
  [CAMMA *offers wine to* SYNORIX, *while*
  SINNATUS *helps himself.*
Sinnatus. I pledge you, Strato.
                                        [*Drinks.*
Synorix.   And I you, my lord.
                                        [*Drinks.*
Sinnatus (*seeing the cup sent to* CAMMA).
  What's here?
Camma.   A strange gift sent to me
  to-day.
A sacred cup saved from a blazing shrine
Of our great Goddess, in some city where
Antonius past. I had believed that Rome
Made war upon the peoples not the Gods.
Synorix. Most like the city rose against
  Antonius,
Whereon he fired it, and the sacred shrine
By chance was burnt along with it.
Sinnatus.   Had you then
No message with the cup?
Camma.   Why, yes, see here.
                          [*Gives him the scroll.*
Sinnatus (*reads*). 'To the admired

Camma,—beheld you afar off—loved you
—sends you this cup—the cup we use in
our marriages—cannot at present write
himself other than

'A GALATIAN SERVING BY FORCE IN THE
              ROMAN LEGION.'

Serving by force! Were there no boughs to
  hang on,
Rivers to drown in? Serve by force? No
  force
Could make me serve by force.
Synorix.   How then, my lord?
The Roman is encamped without your
  city—
The force of Rome a thousand-fold our
  own.
Must all Galatia hang or drown herself?
And you a Prince and Tetrarch in this
  province—
Sinnatus. Province!
Synorix.   Well, well, they call
  it so in Rome.
Sinnatus (*angrily*). Province!
Synorix. A noble anger! but Antonius
To-morrow will demand your tribute—
  you,
Can you make war? Have you alliances?
Bithynia, Pontus, Paphlagonia?
We have had our leagues of old with
  Eastern kings.
There is my hand—if such a league there
  be.
What will you do?
Sinnatus.   Not set myself abroach
And run my mind out to a random guest
Who join'd me in the hunt. You saw my
  hounds
True to the scent; and we have two-legg'd
  dogs
Among us who can smell a true occasion,
And when to bark and how.
Synorix.   My good Lord Sinnatus,
I once was at the hunting of a lion.
Roused by the clamour of the chase he
  woke,
Came to the front of the wood—his
  monarch mane
Bristled about his quick ears—he stood
  there
Staring upon the hunter. A score of dogs
Gnaw'd at his ankles: at the last he felt

The trouble of his feet, put forth one paw,
Slew four, and knew it not, and so remain'd
Staring upon the hunter: and this Rome
Will crush you if you wrestle with her;
    then
Save for some slight report in her own
    Senate
Scarce know what she has done.
    (*Aside.*) Would I could move him,
Provoke him any way! (*Aloud.*) The Lady
    Camma,
Wise I am sure as she is beautiful,
Will close with me that to submit at once
Is better than a wholly-hopeless war,
Our gallant citizens murder'd all in vain,
Son, husband, brother gash'd to death in
    vain,
And the small state more cruelly trampled
    on
Than had she never moved.
    Camma.   Sir, I had once
A boy who died a babe; but were he living
And grown to man and Sinnatus will'd
    it, I
Would set him in the front rank of the fight
With scarce a pang. (*Rises.*) Sir, if a state
    submit
At once, she may be blotted out at once
And swallow'd in the conqueror's chronicle.
Whereas in wars of freedom and defence
The glory and grief of battle won or lost
Solders a race together—yea—tho' they
    fail,
The names of those who fought and fell
    are like
A bank'd-up fire that flashes out again
From century to century, and at last
May lead them on to victory—I hope so—
Like phantoms of the Gods.
    Sinnatus.   Well spoken, wife.
    Synorix (*bowing*). Madam, so well I
    yield.
    Sinnatus.   I should not wonder
If Synorix, who has dwelt three years in
    Rome
And wrought his worst against his native
    land,
Returns with this Antonius.
    Synorix.   What is Synorix?
    Sinnatus. Galatian, and not know? This
    Synorix

Was Tetrarch here, and tyrant also—did
Dishonour to our wives.
    Synorix.   Perhaps you judge him
With feeble charity: being as you tell me
Tetrarch, there might be willing wives
    enough
To feel dishonour, honour.
    Camma.   Do not say so.
I know of no such wives in all Galatia.
There may be courtesans for aught I know
Whose life is one dishonour.

Enter ATTENDANT

    Attendant (*aside*). My lord, the men!
    Sinnatus (*aside*). Our anti-Roman fac-
    tion?
    Attendant (*aside*).   Ay, my lord.
    Synorix (*overhearing*). (*Aside.*) I have
    enough—their anti-Roman faction.
    Sinnatus (*aloud*). Some friends of mine
    would speak with me without.
You, Strato, make good cheer till I return.
                      [*Exit.*
    Synorix. I have much to say, no time to
    say it in.
First, lady, know myself am that Galatian
Who sent the cup.
    Camma.   I thank you from my heart.
    Synorix. Then that I serve with Rome
    to serve Galatia.
That is my secret: keep it, or you sell me
To torment and to death. [*Coming closer.*
              For your ear only—
I love you—for your love to the great
    Goddess.
The Romans sent me here a spy upon you,
To draw you and your husband to your
    doom.
I'd sooner die than do it.
[*Takes out paper given him by* ANTONIUS.
            This paper sign'd
Antonius—will you take it, read it? there!
    Camma. (*Reads.*) 'You are to seize on
    Sinnatus,—if——'
    Synorix. (*Snatches paper.*) No more.
What follows is for no wife's eyes. O
    Camma,
Rome has a glimpse of this conspiracy;
Rome never yet hath spar'd conspirator.
Horrible! flaying, scourging, crucify-
    ing——

703

Camma. I am tender enough. Why do
you practise on me?

Synorix. Why should I practise on you?
How you wrong me!
I am sure of being every way malign'd.
And if you should betray me to your
husband——

Camma. Will *you* betray him by this
order?

Synorix.   See,
I tear it all to pieces, never dream'd
Of acting on it.   [*Tears the paper.*

Camma. I owe you thanks for ever.

Synorix. Hath Sinnatus never told you
of this plot?

Camma. What plot?

Synorix.   A child's sand-
castle on the beach
For the next wave—all seen,—all calcu-
lated,
All known by Rome. No chance for
Sinnatus.

Camma. Why said you not as much to
my brave Sinnatus?

Synorix. Brave—ay—too brave, too over-
confident,
Too like to ruin himself, and you, and
me!
Who else, with this black thunderbolt of
Rome
Above him, would have chased the stag
to-day
In the full face of all the Roman camp?
A miracle that they let him home again,
Not caught, maim'd, blinded him.

          [CAMMA *shudders.*
(*Aside.*) I have made her tremble.
(*Aloud.*) I know they mean to torture him
to death.
I dare not tell him how I came to know it;
I durst not trust him with—my serving
Rome
To serve Galatia: you heard him on the
letter.
Not say as much? I all but said as much.
I am sure I told him that his plot was folly.
I say it to you—you are wiser—Rome
knows all,
But you know not the savagery of Rome.

Camma. O—have you power with
Rome? use it for him!

Synorix. Alas! I have no such power
with Rome. All that
Lies with Antonius.

          [*As if struck by a sudden thought.
Comes over to her.*

                        He will pass to-morrow
In the gray dawn before the Temple doors.
You have beauty,—O great beauty,—and
Antonius,
So gracious toward women, never yet
Flung back a woman's prayer. Plead to him,
I am sure you will prevail.

Camma.   Still—I should tell
My husband.

Synorix. Will he let you plead for him.
To a Roman?

Camma.   I fear not.

Synorix.   Then do not tell him.
Or tell him, if you will, when you return,
When you have charm'd our general into
mercy,
And all is safe again. O dearest lady,

          [*Murmurs of* 'Synorix! Synorix!'
heard outside.
Think,—torture,—death,—and come.

Camma.   I will, I will.
And I will not betray you.

Synorix (*aside*). (*As* SINNATUS *enters.*)
                        Stand apart.

Enter SINNATUS *and* ATTENDANT

Sinnatus. Thou art that Synorix! One
whom thou hast wrong'd
Without there, knew thee with Antonius.
They howl for thee, to rend thee head from
limb.

Synorix. I am much malign'd. I thought
to serve Galatia.

Sinnatus. Serve thyself first, villain!
They shall not harm
My guest within my house. There! (*points
to door*) there! this door
Opens upon the forest! Out, begone!
Henceforth I am thy mortal enemy.

Synorix. However I thank thee (*draws
his sword*); thou hast saved my life.
          [*Exit.*

Sinnatus. (*To* ATTENDANT.) Return and
tell them Synorix is not here.
          [*Exit* ATTENDANT.
What did that villain Synorix say to you?

Camma. Is *he—that*—Synorix?

Sinnatus.   Wherefore should you doubt it?

One of the men there knew him.

Camma.   Only one,

And he perhaps mistaken in the face.

Sinnatus. Come, come, could he deny it? What did he say?

Camma. What *should* he say?

Sinnatus.   What *should* he say, my wife!

He should say this, that being Tetrarch once

His own true people cast him from their doors

Like a base coin.

Camma.   Not kindly to them?

Sinnatus.   Kindly?

O the most kindly Prince in all the world!

Would clap his honest citizens on the back,

Bandy their own rude jests with them, be curious

About the welfare of their babes, their wives,

O ay—their wives—their wives. What should he say?

He should say nothing to my wife if I

Were by to throttle him! He steep'd himself

In all the lust of Rome. How should *you* guess

What manner of beast it is?

Camma.   Yet he seem'd kindly,

And said he loathed the cruelties that Rome

Wrought on her vassals.

Sinnatus.   Did he, *honest* man?

Camma. And you, that seldom brook the stranger here,

Have let him hunt the stag with you to-day.

Sinnatus. I warrant you now, he said *he* struck the stag.

Camma. Why no, he never touch'd upon the stag.

Sinnatus. Why so I said, *my* arrow. Well to sleep.   [*Goes to close door.*

Camma. Nay, close not yet the door upon a night

That looks half day.

Sinnatus. True, and my friends may spy him

And slay him as he runs.

Camma.   He is gone already.

Oh look,—yon grove upon the mountain, —white

In the sweet moon as with a lovelier snow!

But what a blotch of blackness underneath!

Sinnatus, you remember—yea, you must,

That there three years ago—the vast vine-bowers

Ran to the summit of the trees, and dropt

Their streamers earthward, which a breeze of May

Took ever and anon, and open'd out

The purple zone of hill and heaven; there

You told your love; and like the swaying vines—

Yea,—with our eyes,—our hearts, our prophet hopes

Let in the happy distance, and that all

But cloudless heaven which we have found together

In our three married years! You kiss'd me there

For the first time. Sinnatus, kiss me now.

Sinnatus. First kiss. (*Kisses her.*) There then. You talk almost as if it

Might be the last.

Camma.   Will you not eat a little?

Sinnatus. No, no, we found a goatherd's hut and shared

His fruits and milk. Liar! You will believe

Now that he never struck the stag—a brave one

Which you shall see to-morrow.

Camma.   I rise to-morrow

In the gray dawn, and take this holy cup

To lodge it in the shrine of Artemis.

Sinnatus. Good!

Camma.   If I be not back in half an hour,

Come after me.

Sinnatus. What! is there danger?

Camma.   Nay,

None that I know: 'tis but a step from here

To the Temple.

Sinnatus. All my brain is full of sleep.

Wake me before you go, I'll after you—

After *me* now!   [*Closes door and exit.*

Camma (*drawing curtains*). Your shadow.

Synorix—

His face was not malignant, and he said

That men malign'd him. Shall I go? Shall
    I go?
Death, torture—
'He never yet flung back a woman's
    prayer'—
I go, but I will have my dagger with me.
                         [*Exit.*

SCENE III

Same as Scene I. Dawn

Music and Singing in the Temple

Enter SYNORIX *watchfully, after him*
    PUBLIUS *and* SOLDIERS

Synorix. Publius!
Publius.   Here!
Synorix.   Do you remem-
ber what I told you?
  Publius. When you cry 'Rome, Rome,'
    to seize
On whomsoever may be talking with you,
Or man, or woman, as traitors unto Rome.
  Synorix. Right. Back again. How many
    of you are there?
  Publius. Some half a score.
             [*Exeunt* SOLDIERS *and* PUBLIUS.
  Synorix.   I have my guard
    about me.
I need not fear the crowd that hunted me
Across the woods, last night. I hardly
    gain'd
The camp at midnight. Will she come
    to me
Now that she knows me Synorix? Not if
    Sinnatus
Has told her all the truth about me. Well,
I cannot help the mould that I was cast in.
I fling all that upon my fate, my star.
I know that I am genial, I would be
Happy, and make all others happy so
They did not thwart me. Nay, she will not
    come.
Yet if she be a true and loving wife
She may, perchance, to save this husband.
    Ay!
See, see, my white bird stepping toward
    the snare.
Why now I count it all but miracle,
That this brave heart of mine should shake
    me so,

As helplessly as some unbearded boy's
When first he meets his maiden in a bower.
          [*Enter* CAMMA (*with cup*).
The lark first takes the sunlight on his
    wing,
But you, twin sister of the morning star,
Forelead the sun.
  Camma.   Where is Antonius?
  Synorix. Not here as yet. You are too
    early for him.
          [*She crosses towards Temple.*
  Synorix. Nay, whither go you now?
  Camma.   To lodge this cup
Within the holy shrine of Artemis,
And so return.
  Synorix.   To find Antonius here.
      [*She goes into the Temple, he looks
      after her.*
The loveliest life that ever drew the light
From heaven to brood upon her, and
    enrich
Earth with her shadow! I trust she *will*
    return.
These Romans dare not violate the Temple.
No, I must lure my game into the camp.
A woman I could live and die for. What!
Die for a woman, what new faith is this?
I am not mad, not sick, not old enough
To doat on one alone. Yes, mad for her,
Camma the stately, Camma the great-
    hearted,
So mad, I fear some strange and evil
    chance
Coming upon me, for by the Gods I seem
Strange to myself.

Re-enter CAMMA

  Camma.   Where is Antonius?
  Synorix. Where? As I said before, you
    are still too early.
  Camma. Too early to be here alone with
    thee;
For whether men malign thy name, or no,
It bears an evil savour among women.
Where is Antonius? (*Loud.*)
  Synorix.   Madam, as you know
The camp is half a league without the city;
If you will walk with me we needs must
    meet
Antonius coming, or at least shall find him
There in the camp.

Camma. No, not one step with thee.
Where is Antonius? (*Louder.*)
Synorix (*advancing towards her*).
                    Then for your own sake,
Lady, I say it with all gentleness,
And for the sake of Sinnatus your husband,
I must compel you.
    Camma (*drawing her dagger*). Stay!—too
near is death.
    Synorix (*disarming her*). Is it not easy to
disarm a woman?
Enter SINNATUS (*seizes him from behind by
            the throat*)
    Synorix (*throttled and scarce audible*).
Rome! Rome!
    Sinnatus.   Adulterous dog!
    Synorix (*stabbing him with* CAMMA'S
dagger). What! will you have it?
    [CAMMA *utters a cry and runs to*
        SINNATUS.
    Sinnatus (*falls backward*). I have it in
my heart—to the Temple—fly—
For *my* sake—or they seize on thee.
Remember!
Away—farewell!   [*Dies.*
    Camma (*runs up the steps into the Temple,
looking back*). Farewell!
    Synorix (*seeing her escape*). The women
of the Temple drag her in.
Publius! Publius! No,
Antonius would not suffer me to break
Into the sanctuary. She hath escaped.
        [*Looking down at* SINNATUS.
'Adulterous dog!' that red-faced rage at me!
Then with one quick short stab—eternal
peace.
So end all passions. Then what use in
passions?
To warm the cold bounds of our dying life
And, lest we freeze in mortal apathy,
Employ us, heat us, quicken us, help us,
    keep us
From seeing all too near that urn, those
    ashes
Which all must be. Well used, they serve
us well.
I heard a saying in Egypt, that ambition
Is like the sea wave, which the more you
    drink,
The more you thirst—yea—drink too
    much, as men

Have done on rafts of wreck—it drives
    you mad.
I will be no such wreck, am no such
    gamester
As, having won the stake, would dare the
    chance
Of double, or losing all. The Roman
    Senate,
For I have always play'd into their hands,
Means me the crown. And Camma for my
    bride—
The people love her—if I win her love,
They too will cleave to me, as one with her.
There then I rest, Rome's tributary king.
        [*Looking down on* SINNATUS.
Why did I strike him?—having proof
    enough
Against the man, I surely should have left
That stroke to Rome. He saved my life too.
Did he?
It seem'd so. I have play'd the sudden fool.
And that sets her against me—for the
    moment.
Camma—well, well, I never found the
    woman
I could not force or wheedle to my will.
She will be glad at last to wear my crown.
And I will make Galatia prosperous too,
And we will chirp among our vines, and
    smile
At bygone things till that (*pointing to*
    SINNATUS) eternal peace.
Rome! Rome!
        [*Enter* PUBLIUS *and* SOLDIERS.
Twice I cried Rome. Why came ye not
    before?
    Publius. Why come we now? Whom
shall we seize upon?
    Synorix (*pointing to the body of* SINNATUS).
The body of that dead traitor Sinnatus.
Bear him away.
    Music and Singing in Temple.

ACT II

SCENE

Interior of the Temple of Artemis

*Small gold gates on platform in front of the
veil before the colossal statue of the Goddess, and in the centre of the Temple a*

tripod altar, on which is a lighted lamp.
Lamps (lighted) suspended between each
pillar. Tripods, vases, garlands of flowers,
etc., about stage. Altar at back close to
Goddess, with two cups. Solemn music.
Priestesses decorating the Temple.

(*The Chorus of* PRIESTESSES *sing as*
they enter.)

Artemis, Artemis, hear us, O Mother, hear
    us, and bless us!
Artemis, thou that art life to the wind, to
    the wave, to the glebe, to the fire!
Hear thy people who praise thee! O help
    us from all that oppress us!
Hear thy priestesses hymn thy glory! O
    yield them all their desire!
  Priestess. Phœbe, that man from Synorix,
    who has been
So oft to see the Priestess, waits once more
Before the Temple.
  Phœbe.   We will let her know.
  [*Signs to one of the Priestesses, who*
    goes out.
Since Camma fled from Synorix to our
    Temple,
And for her beauty, stateliness, and power,
Was chosen Priestess here, have you not
    mark'd
Her eyes were ever on the marble floor?
To-day they are fixt and bright—they look
    straight out.
Hath she made up her mind to marry him?
  Priestess. To marry him who stabb'd her
    Sinnatus.
You will not easily make me credit that.
  Phœbe. Ask her.

Enter CAMMA *as Priestess (in front of the*
curtains)

  Priestess. You will not marry Synorix?
  Camma. My girl, I am the bride of
    Death, and only
Marry the dead.
  Priestess.   Not Synorix then?
  Camma.   My girl,
At times this oracle of great Artemis
Has no more power than other oracles
To speak directly.
  Phœbe.   Will you speak to him,

The messenger from Synorix who waits
Before the Temple?
  Camma.   Why not? Let him enter.
  [*Comes forward on to step by tripod.*

Enter a MESSENGER

  Messenger (*kneels*). Greeting and health
    from Synorix! More than once
You have refused his hand. When last I
    saw you,
You all but yielded. He entreats you now
For your last answer. When he struck at
    Sinnatus—
As I have many a time declared to you—
He knew not at the moment who had
    fasten'd
About his throat—he begs you to forget it
As scarce his act:—a random stroke: all
    else
Was love for you: he prays you to believe
    him.
  Camma. I pray him to believe—that I
    believe him.
  Messenger. Why that is well. You mean
    to marry him?
  Camma. I mean to marry him—if that
    be well.
  Messenger. This very day the Romans
    crown him king
For all his faithful services to Rome.
He wills you then this day to marry him,
And so be throned together in the sight
Of all the people, that the world may know
You twain are reconciled, and no more
    feuds
Disturb our peaceful vassalage to Rome.
  Camma. To-day? Too sudden. I will
    brood upon it.
When do they crown him?
  Messenger.   Even now.
  Camma.   And where?
  Messenger. Here by your temple.
  Camma.   Come once more to me
Before the crowning,—I will answer you.
    [*Exit* MESSENGER.
  Phœbe. Great Artemis! O Camma, can
    it be well,
Or good, or wise, that you should clasp a
    hand
Red with the sacred blood of Sinnatus?

Camma. Good! mine own dagger driven
    by Synorix found
All good in the true heart of Sinnatus,
And quench'd it there for ever. Wise!
Life yields to death and wisdom bows to
    Fate,
Is wisest, doing so. Did not this man
Speak well? We cannot fight imperial
    Rome,
But he and I are both Galatian-born,
And tributary sovereigns, he and I
Might teach this Rome—from knowledge
    of our people—
Where to lay on her tribute—heavily here
And lightly there. Might I not live for
    that,
And drown all poor self-passion in the
    sense
Of public good?
    Phœbe.   I am sure you will not
    marry him.
    Camma. Are you so sure? I pray you
        wait and see.
            [*Shouts (from the distance*),
                'Synorix! Synorix!'
    Camma. Synorix, Synorix! So they cried
        Sinnatus
Not so long since—they sicken me. The
    One
Who shifts his policy suffers something,
    must
Accuse himself, excuse himself; the Many
Will feel no shame to give themselves the
    lie.
    Phœbe. Most like it was the Roman
        soldier shouted.
    Camma. Their shield-borne patriot of
        the morning star
Hang'd at mid-day, their traitor of the
    dawn
The clamour'd darling of their afternoon!
And that same head they would have
    play'd at ball with
And kick'd it featureless—they now would
    crown.   [*Flourish of trumpets.*

Enter a Galatian NOBLEMAN *with crown on
        a cushion*

Noble (*kneels*). Greeting and health from
    Synorix. He sends you
This diadem of the first Galatian Queen,

That you may feed your fancy on the
    glory of it,
And join your life this day with his, and
    wear it
Beside him on his throne. He waits your
    answer.
    Camma. Tell him there is one shadow
        among the shadows,
One ghost of all the ghosts—as yet so new,
So strange among them—such an alien
    there,
So much of husband in it still—that if
The shout of Synorix and Camma sitting
Upon one throne, should reach it, *it* would
    rise
He! . . . HE, with that red star between the
    ribs,
And my knife there—and blast the king
    and me,
And blanch the crowd with horror. I dare
    not, sir!
Throne him—and then the marriage—ay
    and tell him
That I accept the diadem of Galatia—
                    [*All are amazed.*
Yea, that ye saw me crown myself withal.
                    [*Puts on the crown.*
I wait him his crown'd queen.
    Noble. So will I tell him.   [*Exit.*

*Music. Two Priestesses go up the steps before
    the shrine, draw the curtains on either side
    (discovering the Goddess), then open the
    gates and remain on steps, one on either
    side, and kneel. A priestess goes off and
    returns with a veil of marriage, then assists
    Phœbe to veil Camma. At the same time
    Priestesses enter and stand on either side
    of the Temple. Camma and all the
    Priestesses kneel, raise their hands to the
    Goddess, and bow down.*

        [*Shouts, 'Synorix! Synorix!' All rise.*

Camma. Fling wide the doors and let
    the new-made children
Of our imperial mother see the show.
        [*Sunlight pours through the doors.*
I have no heart to do it. (*To* PHŒBE).
    Look for me!
            [*Crouches.* PHŒBE *looks out.*
            [*Shouts, 'Synorix! Synorix!'*

Phœbe. He climbs the throne. Hot blood, ambition, pride
So bloat and redden his face—O would it were
His third last apoplexy! O bestial!
O how unlike our goodly Sinnatus.
Camma (on the ground). You wrong him surely; far as the face goes
A goodlier-looking man than Sinnatus.
Phœbe (aside). How dare she say it? I could hate her for it
But that she is distracted.
                    [*A flourish of trumpets.*
Camma.   Is he crown'd?
Phœbe. Ay, there they crown him.
            [*Crowd without shout,* 'Synorix! Synorix!'
            [*A Priestess brings a box of spices to* CAMMA, *who throws them on the altar-flame.*
Camma. Rouse the dead altar-flame, fling in the spices,
Nard, Cinnamon, amomum, benzoin.
Let all the air reel into a mist of odour,
As in the midmost heart of Paradise.
Lay down the Lydian carpets for the king.
The king should pace on purple to his bride,
And music there to greet my lord the king.
                    [*Music.*
(*To* PHŒBE). Dost thou remember when I wedded Sinnatus?
Ay, thou wast there—whether from maiden fears
Or reverential love for him I loved,
Or some strange second-sight, the marriage cup
Wherefrom we make libation to the Goddess
So shook within my hand, that the red wine
Ran down the marble and lookt like blood, like blood.
Phœbe. I do remember your first-marriage fears.
Camma. I have no fears at this my second marriage.
See here—I stretch my hand out—hold it there.
How steady it is!
Phœbe. Steady enough to stab him!

Camma. O hush! O peace! This violence ill becomes
The silence of our Temple. Gentleness,
Low words best chime with this solemnity.

Enter a procession of Priestesses and Children bearing garlands and golden goblets, and strewing flowers.

Enter SYNORIX (*as King, with gold laurel-wreath crown and purple robes*), *followed by* ANTONIUS, PUBLIUS, *Noblemen, Guards, and the Populace.*
Camma. Hail, King!
Synorix.   Hail, Queen!
The wheel of Fate has roll'd me to the top.
I would that happiness were gold, that I
Might cast my largess of it to the crowd!
I would that every man made feast to-day
Beneath the shadow of our pines and planes!
For all my truer life begins to-day.
The past is like a travell'd land now sunk
Below the horizon—like a barren shore
That grew salt weeds, but now all drown'd in love
And glittering at full tide—the bounteous bays
And havens filling with a blissful sea.
Nor speak I now too mightily, being King
And happy! happiest, Lady, in my power
To make you happy.
Camma.   Yes, sir.
Synorix.   Our Antonius,
Our faithful friend of Rome, tho' Rome may set
A free foot where she will, yet of his courtesy
Entreats he may be present at our marriage.
Camma. Let him come—a legion with him, if he will.
(*To* ANTONIUS.) Welcome, my lord Antonius, to our Temple.
(*To* SYNORIX.) You on this side the altar.
(*To* ANTONIUS.) You on that.
Call first upon the Goddess, Synorix.
            [*All face the Goddess. Priestesses, Children, Populace, and Guards kneel —the others remain standing.*
Synorix. O Thou, that dost inspire the germ with life,

The child, a thread within the house of birth,
And give him limbs, then air, and send him forth
The glory of his father—Thou whose breath
Is balmy wind to robe our hills with grass,
And kindle all our vales with myrtle-blossom,
And roll the golden oceans of our grain,
And sway the long grape-bunches of our vines,
And fill all hearts with fatness and the lust
Of plenty—make me happy in my marriage!

    Chorus (chanting). Artemis, Artemis, hear him, Ionian Artemis!

    Camma. O Thou that slayest the babe within the womb
Or in the being born, or after slayest him
As boy or man, great Goddess, whose storm-voice
Unsockets the strong oak, and rears his root
Beyond his head, and strows our fruits, and lays
Our golden grain, and runs to sea and makes it
Foam over all the fleeted wealth of kings
And peoples, hear.
Whose arrow is the plague—whose quick flash splits
The mid-sea mast, and rifts the tower to the rock,
And hurls the victor's column down with him
That crowns it, hear.
Who causest the safe earth to shudder and gape,
And gulf and flatten in her closing chasm
Domed cities, hear.
Whose lava-torrents blast and blacken a province
To a cinder, hear.
Whose winter-cataracts find a realm and leave it
A waste of rock and ruin, hear. I call thee
To make my marriage prosper to my wish!

    Chorus. Artemis, Artemis, hear her, Ephesian Artemis!

    Camma. Artemis, Artemis, hear me, Galatian Artemis!
I call on our own Goddess in our own Temple.

    Chorus. Artemis, Artemis, hear her, Galatian Artemis!

              [Thunder. All rise.

    Synorix (aside). Thunder! Ay, ay, the storm was drawing hither
Across the hills when I was being crown'd.
I wonder if I look as pale as she?

    Camma. Art thou—still bent—on marrying?

    Synorix.   Surely—yet
These are strange words to speak to Artemis.

    Camma. Words are not always what they seem, my King.
I will be faithful to thee till thou die.

    Synorix. I thank thee, Camma,—I thank thee.

    Camma (turning to ANTONIUS*).* Antonius,
Much graced are we that our Queen Rome in you
Deigns to look in upon our barbarisms.

    [Turns, goes up steps to altar before the Goddess. Takes a cup from off the altar. Holds it towards ANTONIUS.
ANTONIUS *goes up to the foot of the steps opposite to* SYNORIX.

You see this cup, my lord.

              [Gives it to him.

    Antonius.   Most curious!
The many-breasted mother Artemis
Emboss'd upon it.

    Camma.   It is old, I know not
How many hundred years. Give it me again.
It is the cup belonging our own Temple.

    [Puts it back on altar, and takes up the cup of Act I. Showing it to ANTONIUS.

Here is another sacred to the Goddess,
The gift of Synorix; and the Goddess, being
For this most grateful, wills, thro' me her Priestess,
In honour of his gift and of our marriage,
That Synorix should drink from his own cup.

    Synorix. I thank thee, Camma,—I thank thee.

Camma.   For—my lord—
It is our ancient custom in Galatia
That ere two souls be knit for life and death,
They two should drink together from one
    cup,
In symbol of their married unity,
Making libation to the Goddess. Bring me
The costly wines we use in marriages.
    [*They bring in a large jar of wine.*
    CAMMA *pours wine into cup.*
(*To* SYNORIX.) See here, I fill it. (*To*
    ANTONIUS.) Will you drink, my lord?
Antonius. I? Why should I? I am not to
    be married.
Camma. But that might bring a Roman
    blessing on us.
Antonius (*refusing cup*). Thy pardon,
    Priestess!
Camma.   Thou art in the right.
This blessing is for Synorix and for me.
See first I make libation to the Goddess,
    [*Makes libation.*
And now I drink.
    [*Drinks and fills the cup again.*
    Thy turn, Galatian King.
Drink and drink deep—our marriage will
    be fruitful.
Drink and drink deep, and thou wilt make
    me happy.
    [SYNORIX *goes up to her. She hands
    him the cup. He drinks.*
Synorix. There, Camma! I have almost
    drain'd the cup—
A few drops left.
Camma.   Libation to the Goddess.
    [*He throws the remaining drops on
    the altar and gives* CAMMA *the cup.*
Camma (*placing the cup on the altar*).
Why then the Goddess hears.
    [*Comes down and forward to tripod.*
    ANTONIUS *follows.*   Antonius,
Where wast thou on that morning when I
    came
To plead to thee for Sinnatus's life,
Beside this temple half a year ago?
Antonius. I never heard of this request
    of thine.
Synorix (*coming forward hastily to foot of
    tripod steps*). I sought him and I could
    not find him. Pray you,
Go on with the marriage rites.

Camma.   Antonius——
'Camma!' who spake?
Antonius.   Not I.
Phœbe.   Nor any here.
Camma. I am all but sure that some one
    spake. Antonius,
If you had found him plotting against
    Rome,
Would you have tortured Sinnatus to
    death?
Antonius. No thought was mine of tor-
    ture or of death,
But had I found him plotting, I had
    counsell'd him
To rest from vain resistance. Rome is fated
To rule the world. Then, if he had not
    listen'd,
I might have sent him prisoner to Rome.
Synorix. Why do you palter with the
    ceremony?
Go on with the marriage rites.
Camma.   They are finish'd.
Synorix.   How!
Camma. Thou hast drunk deep enough
    to make me happy.
Dost thou not feel the love I bear to thee
Glow thro' thy veins?
Synorix.   The love I bear to thee
Glows thro' my veins since first I look'd
    on thee.
But wherefore slur the perfect ceremony?
The sovereign of Galatia weds his Queen.
Let all be done to the fullest in the sight
Of all the Gods.
           Nay, rather than so clip
The flowery robe of Hymen, we would add
Some golden fringe of gorgeousness beyond
Old use, to make the day memorial, when
Synorix, first King, Camma, first Queen
    o' the Realm,
Drew here the richest lot from Fate, to live
And die together.
        This pain—what is it?—again?
I had a touch of this last year—in—Rome.
Yes, yes. (*To* ANTONIUS.) Your arm—a
    moment—It will pass.
I reel beneath the weight of utter joy—
This all too happy day, crown—queen at
    once.   [*Staggers.*
O all ye Gods—Jupiter!—Jupiter!
    [*Falls backward.*

Camma. Dost thou cry out upon the Gods of Rome?
Thou art Galatian-born. Our Artemis
Has vanquish'd their Diana.
Synorix (on the ground). I am poison'd.
She—close the Temple door. Let her not fly.
Camma (leaning on tripod). Have I not drunk of the same cup with thee?
Synorix. Ay, by the Gods of Rome and all the world,
She too—she too—the bride! the Queen! and I—
Monstrous! I that loved her.
Camma.   I loved *him.*
Synorix. O murderous mad-woman! I pray you lift me
And make me walk awhile. I have heard these poisons
May be walk'd down.
        [ANTONIUS *and* PUBLIUS *raise him up.*
                My feet are tons of lead,
They will break in the earth—I am sinking —hold me—
Let me alone.
        [*They leave him; he sinks down on ground.*
                Too late—thought myself wise—
A woman's dupe. Antonius, tell the Senate
I have been most true to Rome—would have been true
To *her*—if—if——   [*Falls as if dead.*
Camma (coming and leaning over him).
        So falls the throne of an hour.
Synorix (half rising). Throne? is it thou? the Fates are throned, not we—
Not guilty of ourselves—thy doom and mine—
Thou—coming my way too—Camma—good-night.   [*Dies.*
Camma (upheld by weeping Priestesses).
Thy way? poor worm, crawl down thine own black hole

To the lowest Hell. Antonius, is *he* there?
I meant thee to have follow'd—better thus.
Nay, if my people must be thralls of Rome,
He is gentle, tho' a Roman.
        [*Sinks back into the arms of the Priestesses.*
Antonius.   Thou art one
With thine own people, and though a Roman I
Forgive thee, Camma.
        Camma (raising herself). 'CAMMA!'— why there again
I am most sure that some one call'd. O women,
Ye will have Roman masters. I am glad
I shall not see it. Did not some old Greek
Say death was the chief good? He had my fate for it,
Poison'd. (*Sinks back again.*) Have I the crown on? I will go
To meet him, crown'd! crown'd victor of my will—
On my last voyage—but the wind has fail'd—
Growing dark too—but light enough to row.
Row to the blessed Isles! the blessed Isles!—
Sinnatus!
Why comes he not to meet me? It is the crown
Offends him—and my hands are too sleepy
To lift it off.   [PHŒBE *takes the crown off.*
Who touch'd me then? I thank you.
        [*Rises, with outspread arms.*
There—league on league of ever-shining shore
Beneath an ever-rising sun—I see him—
'Camma, Camma!' Sinnatus, Sinnatus!
                                [*Dies.*

THE FALCON

DRAMATIS PERSONÆ

THE COUNT FEDERIGO DEGLI ALBERIGHI.
FILIPPO, *Count's foster-brother.*
THE LADY GIOVANNA.
ELISABETTA, *the Count's nurse.*

SCENE

*An Italian Cottage. Castle and Mountains
seen through Window*

ELISABETTA *discovered seated on stool in
window darning. The Count with Falcon
on his hand comes down through the door
at back. A withered wreath on the wall.*

Elisabetta. So, my lord, the Lady
Giovanna, who hath been away so long,
came back last night with her son to the
castle.

Count. Hear that, my bird! Art thou not
jealous of her?
My princess of the cloud, my plumed
  purveyor,
My far-eyed queen of the winds—thou
  that canst soar
Beyond the morning lark, and howsoe'er
Thy quarry wind and wheel, swoop down
  upon him
Eagle-like, lightning-like—strike, make his
  feathers
Glance in mid heaven.
                    [*Crosses to chair.*
              I would thou hadst a mate!
Thy breed will die with thee, and mine
  with me:
I am as lone and loveless as thyself.
                              [*Sits in chair.*
Giovanna here! Ay, ruffle thyself—*be*
  jealous!
Thou should'st be jealous of her. Tho' I
  bred thee
The full-train'd marvel of all falconry,
And love thee and thou me, yet if Giovanna
Be here again—No, no! Buss me, my bird!
The stately widow has no heart for me.
Thou art the last friend left me upon
  earth—

No, no again to that.   [*Rises and turns.*
                    My good old nurse,
I had forgotten thou wast sitting there.
  Elisabetta. Ay, and forgotten thy foster-
    brother too.
  Count. Bird-babble for my falcon! Let
    it pass.
What art thou doing there?
  Elisabetta.   Darning, your lordship.
We cannot flaunt it in new feathers now:
Nay, if we *will* buy diamond necklaces
To please our lady, we must darn, my lord.
This old thing here (*points to necklace round
  her neck*),
  they are but blue beads—my Piero,
God rest his honest soul, he bought 'em
  for me,
Ay, but he knew I meant to marry him.
How couldst thou do it, my son? How
  couldst thou do it?
  Count. She saw it at a dance, upon a neck
Less lovely than her own, and long'd for
  it.
  Elisabetta. She told thee as much?
  Count.   No, no—a friend of hers.
  Elisabetta. Shame on her that she took
    it at thy hands,
She rich enough to have bought it for
  herself!
  Count. She would have robb'd me then
    of a great pleasure.
  Elisabetta. But hath she yet return'd thy
    love?
  Count.   Not yet!
  Elisabetta. She would return thy neck-
    lace then.
  Count.   Ay, if
She knew the giver; but I bound the seller
To silence, and I left it privily
At Florence, in her palace.
  Elisabetta.   And sold thine own

714

To buy it for her. She not know? She knows
There's none such other——
Count. Madman anywhere
Speak freely, tho' to call a madman mad
Will hardly help to make him sane again.

Enter FILIPPO

Filippo. Ah, the women, the women! Ah, Monna Giovanna, you here again! you that have the face of an angel and the heart of a—that's too positive! You that have a score of lovers and have not a heart for any of them—that's positive-negative: you that have *not* the head of a toad, and *not* a heart like the jewel in it—that's too negative; you that have a cheek like a peach and a heart like the stone in it—that's positive again—that's better!

Elisabetta. Sh—sh—Filippo!

Filippo (turns half round). Here has our master been a-glorifying and a-velveting and a-silking himself, and a-peacocking and a-spreading to catch her eye for a dozen year, till he hasn't an eye left in his own tail to flourish among the peahens, and all along o' you, Monna Giovanna, all along o' you!

Elisabetta. Sh—sh—Filippo! Can't you hear that you are saying behind his back what you see you are saying afore his face?

Count. Let him—he never spares me to my face!

Filippo. No, my lord, I never spare your lordship to your lordship's face, nor behind your lordship's back, nor to right, nor to left, nor to round about and back to your lordship's face again, for I'm honest, your lordship.

Count. Come, come, Filippo, what is there in the larder?

[ELISABETTA *crosses to fireplace and puts on wood.*

Filippo. Shelves and hooks, shelves and hooks, and when I see the shelves I am like to hang myself on the hooks.

Count. No bread?

Filippo. Half a breakfast for a rat!

Count. Milk?

Filippo. Three laps for a cat!

Count. Cheese?

Filippo. A supper for twelve mites.

Count. Eggs?

Filippo. One, but addled.

Count. No bird?

Filippo. Half a tit and a hern's bill.

Count. Let be thy jokes and thy jerks, man! Anything or nothing?

Filippo. Well, my lord, if all-but-nothing be anything, and one plate of dried prunes be all-but-nothing, then there is anything in your lordship's larder at your lordship's service, if your lordship care to call for it.

Count. Good mother, happy was the prodigal son,
For he return'd to the rich father; I
But add my poverty to thine. And all
Thro' following of my fancy. Pray thee make
Thy slender meal out of those scraps and shreds
Filippo spoke of. As for him and me,
There sprouts a salad in the garden still.
(*To the Falcon.*) Why didst thou miss thy quarry yester-even?
To-day, my beauty, thou must dash us down
Our dinner from the skies. Away, Filippo!
[*Exit, followed by* FILIPPO.

Elisabetta. I knew it would come to this. She has beggared him. I always knew it would come to this! (*Goes up to table as if to resume darning, and looks out of window.*) Why, as I live, there is Monna Giovanna coming down the hill from the castle. Stops and stares at our cottage. Ay, ay! stare at it: it's all you have left us. Shame on you! *She* beautiful: sleek as a miller's mouse! Meal enough, meat enough, well fed; but beautiful—bah! Nay, see, why she turns down the path through our little vineyard, and I sneezed three times this morning. Coming to visit my lord, for the first time in her life too! Why, bless the saints! I'll be bound to confess her love to him at last. I forgive her, I forgive her! I knew it would come to this—I always knew it must come to this! (*Going up to door during latter part of speech and opens it.*) Come in, Madonna, come in. (*Retires to front of table and curtseys as the* LADY GIOVANNA *enters, then moves chair towards the hearth.*) Nay, let me place this chair for your ladyship.

[LADY GIOVANNA *moves slowly down stage, then crosses to chair, looking about her, bows as she sees the Madonna over fireplace, then sits in chair.*

Lady Giovanna. Can I speak with the Count?

Elisabetta. Ay, my lady, but won't you speak with the old woman first, and tell her all about it and make her happy? for I've been on my knees every day for these half-dozen years in hope that the saints would send us this blessed morning; and he always took you so kindly, he always took the world so kindly. When he was a little one, and I put the bitters on my breast to wean him, he made a wry mouth at it, but he took it so kindly, and your ladyship has given him bitters enough in this world, and he never made a wry mouth at you, he always took you so kindly—which is more than I did, my lady, more than I did —and he so handsome—and bless your sweet face, you look as beautiful this morning as the very Madonna her own self— and better late than never—but come when they will—then or now—it's all for the best, come when they will—they are made by the blessed saints—these marriages.

[*Raises her hands.*

Lady Giovanna. Marriages? I shall never marry again!

Elisabetta (*rises and turns*). Shame on her then!

Lady Giovanna. Where is the Count?

Elisabetta. Just gone To fly his falcon.

Lady Giovanna. Call him back and say I come to breakfast with him.

Elisabetta. Holy mother! To breakfast! Oh sweet saints! one plate of prunes!

Well, Madam, I will give your message to him. [*Exit.*

Lady Giovanna. His falcon, and I come to ask for his falcon,
The pleasure of his eyes—boast of his hand—

Pride of his heart—the solace of his hours—
His one companion here—nay, I have heard
That, thro' his late magnificence of living
And this last costly gift to mine own self,
[*Shows diamond necklace.*
He hath become so beggar'd, that his falcon
Ev'n wins his dinner for him in the field.
That must be talk, not truth, but truth or talk,
How can I ask for his falcon?
[*Rises and moves as she speaks.*
O my sick boy!
My daily fading Florio, it is thou
Hath set me this hard task, for when I say
What can I do—what can I get for thee?
He answers, 'Get the Count to give me his falcon,
And that will make me well.' Yet if I ask,
He loves me, and he knows I know he loves me!
Will he not pray me to return his love—
To marry him?—(*pause*)—I can never marry him.
His grandsire struck my grandsire in a brawl
At Florence, and my grandsire stabb'd him there.
The feud between our houses is the bar
I cannot cross; I dare not brave my brother,
Break with my kin. My brother hates him, scorns
The noblest-natured man alive, and I—
Who have that reverence for him that I scarce
Dare beg him to receive his diamonds back—
How can I, dare I, ask him for his falcon?
[*Puts diamonds in her casket.*

Re-enter COUNT *and* FILIPPO. COUNT *turns to* FILIPPO

Count. Do what I said; I cannot do it myself.

Filippo. Why then, my lord, we are pauper'd out and out.

Count. Do what I said!
[*Advances and bows low.*
Welcome to this poor cottage, my dear lady.

Lady Giovanna. And welcome turns a cottage to a palace.

Count. 'Tis long since we have met!

Lady Giovanna. To make amends I come this day to break my fast with you.

Count. I am much honour'd—yes—
[*Turns to* FILIPPO.
Do what I told thee. Must I do it myself?

Filippo. I will, I will. (*Sighs.*) Poor fellow!
[*Exit.*

Count. Lady, you bring your light into my cottage
Who never deign'd to shine into my palace.
My palace wanting you was but a cottage;
My cottage, while you grace it, is a palace.

Lady Giovanna. In cottage or in palace, being still
Beyond your fortunes, you are still the king
Of courtesy and liberality.

Count. I trust I still maintain my courtesy;
My liberality perforce is dead
Thro' lack of means of giving.

Lady Giovanna. Yet I come
To ask a gift. [*Moves toward him a little.*

Count. It will be hard, I fear,
To find one shock upon the field when all
The harvest has been carried.

Lady Giovanna. But my boy—
(*Aside.*) No, no! not yet—I cannot!

Count. Ay, how is he,
That bright inheritor of your eyes—your boy?

Lady Giovanna. Alas, my Lord Federigo, he hath fallen
Into a sickness, and it troubles me.

Count. Sick! is it so? why, when he came last year
To see me hawking, he was well enough:
And then I taught him all our hawking-phrases.

Lady Giovanna. Oh yes, and once you let him fly your falcon.

Count. How charm'd he was! what wonder?—A gallant boy,
A noble bird, each perfect of the breed.

Lady Giovanna (*sinks in chair*). What do you rate her at?

Count. My bird? a hundred

Gold pieces once were offer'd by the Duke.
I had no heart to part with her for money.

Lady Giovanna. No, not for money.
[COUNT *turns away and sighs.*
Wherefore do you sigh?

Count. I have lost a friend of late.

Lady Giovanna. I could sigh with you
For fear of losing more than friend, a son;
And if he leave me—all the rest of life—
That wither'd wreath were of more worth to me. [*Looking at wreath on wall.*

Count. That wither'd wreath is of more worth to me
Than all the blossom, all the leaf of this
New-wakening year.
[*Goes and takes down wreath.*

Lady Giovanna. And yet I never saw
The land so rich in blossom as this year.

Count (*holding wreath toward her*). Was not the year when this was gather'd richer?

Lady Giovanna. How long ago was that?

Count. Alas, ten summers!
A lady that was beautiful as day
Sat by me at a rustic festival
With other beauties on a mountain meadow,
And she was the most beautiful of all;
Then but fifteen, and still as beautiful.
The mountain flowers grew thickly round about.
I made a wreath with some of these; I ask'd
A ribbon from her hair to bind it with;
I whisper'd, Let me crown you Queen of Beauty,
And softly placed the chaplet on her head.
A colour, which has colour'd all my life,
Flush'd in her face; then I was call'd away;
And presently all rose, and so departed.
Ah! she had thrown my chaplet on the grass,
And there I found it.
[*Lets his hands fall, holding wreath despondingly.*

Lady Giovanna (*after pause*). How long since do you say?

Count. That was the very year before you married.

Lady Giovanna. When I was married you were at the wars.

Count. Had she not thrown my chaplet on the grass,
It may be I had never seen the wars.
[*Replaces wreath whence he had taken it.*
Lady Giovanna. Ah, but, my lord, there ran a rumour then
That you were kill'd in battle. I can tell you
True tears that year were shed for you in Florence.
Count. It might have been as well for me. Unhappily
I was but wounded by the enemy there
And then imprison'd.
Lady Giovanna. Happily, however, I see
you quite recover'd of your wound.
Count. No, no, not quite, Madonna, not yet, not yet.

Re-enter FILIPPO

Filippo. My lord, a word with you.
Count.   Pray, pardon me!
[LADY GIOVANNA *crosses, and passes behind chair and takes down wreath; then goes to chair by table.*
Count (*to* FILIPPO). What is it, Filippo?
Filippo.   Spoons, your lordship.
Count.   Spoons!
Filippo. Yes, my lord, for wasn't my lady born with a golden spoon in her ladyship's mouth, and we haven't never so much as a silver one for the golden lips of her ladyship.
Count. Have we not half a score of silver spoons?
Filippo. Half o' one, my lord!
Count. How half of one?
Filippo. I trod upon him even now, my lord, in my hurry, and broke him.
Count. And the other nine?
Filippo. Sold! but shall I not mount with your lordship's leave to her ladyship's castle, in your lordship's and her ladyship's name, and confer with her ladyship's seneschal, and so descend again with some of her ladyship's own appurtenances?
Count. Why—no, man. Only see your cloth be clean.   [*Exit* FILIPPO.
Lady Giovanna. Ay, ay, this faded ribbon was the mode
In Florence ten years back. What 's here? a scroll

Pinned to the wreath.
          My lord, you have said so much
Of this poor wreath that I was bold enough
To take it down, if but to guess what flowers
Had made it; and I find a written scroll
That seems to run in rhymings. Might I read?
Count. Ay, if you will.
Lady Giovanna. It should be if you can.
(*Reads.*) 'Dead mountain.' Nay, for who could trace a hand
So wild and staggering?
Count. This was penn'd, Madonna,
Close to the grating on a winter morn
In the perpetual twilight of a prison,
When he that made it, having his right hand
Lamed in the battle, wrote it with his left.
Lady Giovanna. O heavens! the very letters seem to shake
With cold, with pain perhaps, poor prisoner! Well,
Tell me the words—or better—for I see
There goes a musical score along with them,
Repeat them to their music.
Count.   You can touch
No chord in me that would not answer you
In music.
Lady Giovanna. That is musically said.
          [COUNT *takes guitar.* LADY GIOVANNA *sits listening with wreath in her hand, and quietly removes scroll and places it on table at the end of the song.*
Count (*sings, playing guitar*). 'Dead mountain flowers, dead mountain-meadow flowers,
Dearer than when you made your mountain gay,
Sweeter than any violet of to-day,
Richer than all the wide world-wealth of May,
To me, tho' all your bloom has died away,
You bloom again, dead mountain-meadow flowers.'

Enter ELISABETTA *with cloth*

Elisabetta. A word with you, my lord!
Count (*singing*). 'O mountain flowers!'
Elisabetta. A word, my lord! (*Louder*).

Count (sings). 'Dead flowers!'
Elisabetta. A word, my lord!
(*Louder*).
Count. I pray you pardon me again!
[LADY GIOVANNA *looking at wreath.*
Count (to ELISABETTA). What is it?
Elisabetta. My lord, we have but one
piece of earthenware to serve the salad in
to my lady, and that cracked!
Count. Why then, that flower'd bowl my
ancestor
Fetch'd from the farthest east—we never
use it
For fear of breakage—but this day has
brought
A great occasion. You can take it, nurse!
Elisabetta. I did take it, my lord, but
what with my lady's coming that had so
flurried me, and what with the fear of
breaking it, I did break it, my lord: it is
broken!
Count. My one thing left of value in the
world!
No matter! see your cloth be white as
snow!
Elisabetta (pointing thro' window).
White? I warrant thee, my son, as the
snow yonder on the very tip-top o' the
mountain.
Count. And yet to speak white truth, my
good old mother,
I have seen it like the snow on the
moraine.
Elisabetta. How can your lordship say
so? There my lord! [*Lays cloth.*
O my dear son, be not unkind to me.
And one word more. [*Going—returns.*
Count (touching guitar). Good! let it be
but one.
Elisabetta. Hath she return'd thy love?
Count. Not yet!
Elisabetta. And will she?
Count (looking at LADY GIOVANNA). I
scarce believe it!
Elisabetta. Shame upon her then!
[*Exit.*
Count (sings). 'Dead mountain
flowers'——
Ah well, my nurse has broken
The thread of my dead flowers, as she has
broken

My china bowl. My memory is as dead.
[*Goes and replaces guitar.*
Strange that the words at home with me
so long
Should fly like bosom friends when needed
most.
So by your leave if you would hear the
rest,
The writing.
*Lady Giovanna (holding wreath toward
him).* There! my lord, you are a poet,
And can you not imagine that the wreath,
Set, as you say, so lightly on her head,
Fell with her motion as she rose, and she,
A girl, a child, then but fifteen, however
Flutter'd or flatter'd by your notice of her,
Was yet too bashful to return for it?
Count. Was it so indeed? was it so? was
it so?
[*Leans forward to take wreath, and
touches* LADY GIOVANNA'S *hand, which
she withdraws hastily; he places
wreath on corner of chair.*
Lady Giovanna (with dignity). I did not
say, my lord, that it was so;
I said you might imagine it was so.

Enter FILIPPO *with bowl of salad, which he
places on table*

Filippo. Here's a fine salad for my lady,
for tho' we have been a soldier, and ridden
by his lordship's side, and seen the red of
the battle-field, yet are we now drill-
sergeant to his lordship's lettuces, and
profess to be great in green things and in
garden-stuff.
Lady Giovanna. I thank thee, good
Filippo. [*Exit* FILIPPO.

Enter ELISABETTA *with bird on a dish which
she places on table*

Elisabetta (close to table). Here's a fine
fowl for my lady; I had scant time to do
him in. I hope he be not underdone, for
we be undone in the doing of him.
Lady Giovanna. I thank you, my good
nurse.
Filippo (re-entering with plate of prunes).
And here are fine fruits for my lady—
prunes, my lady, from the tree that my
lord himself planted here in the blossom

of his boyhood—and so I, Filippo, being, with your ladyship's pardon, and as your ladyship knows, his lordship's own foster-brother, would commend them to your ladyship's most peculiar appreciation.
[*Puts plate on table.*

Elisabetta. Filippo!

Lady Giovanna (COUNT *leads her to table*). Will you not eat with me, my lord?

Count. I cannot, Not a morsel, not one morsel. I have broken My fast already. I will pledge you. Wine! Filippo, wine!
[*Sits near table;* FILIPPO *brings flask, fills the* COUNT'S *goblet, then* LADY GIOVANNA'S; ELISABETTA *stands at the back of* LADY GIOVANNA'S *chair.*

Count. It is but thin and cold, Not like the vintage blowing round your castle. We lie too deep down in the shadow here. Your ladyship lives higher in the sun.
[*They pledge each other and drink.*

Lady Giovanna. If I might send you down a flask or two Of that same vintage? There is iron in it. It has been much commended as a medicine. I give it my sick son, and if you be Not quite recover'd of your wound, the wine Might help you. None has ever told me yet The story of your battle and your wound.

Filippo (*coming forward*). I can tell you, my lady, I can tell you.

Elisabetta. Filippo! will you take the word out of your master's own mouth?

Filippo. Was it there to take? Put it there, my lord.

Count. Giovanna, my dear lady, in this same battle We had been beaten—they were ten to one. The trumpets of the fight had echo'd down, I and Filippo here had done our best, And, having passed unwounded from the field, Were seated sadly at a fountain side, Our horses grazing by us, when a troop, Laden with booty and with a flag of ours Ta'en in the fight——

Filippo. Ay, but we fought for it back, And kill'd——

Elisabetta. Filippo!

Count. A troop of horse——

Filippo. Five hundred!

Count. Say fifty!

Filippo. And we kill'd 'em by the score!

Elisabetta. Filippo!

Filippo. Well, well, well! I bite my tongue.

Count. We may have left their fifty less by five.
However, staying not to count how many, But anger'd at their flaunting of our flag, We mounted, and we dash'd into the heart of 'em.
I wore the lady's chaplet round my neck; It served me for a blessed rosary. I am sure that more than one brave fellow owed His death to the charm in it.

Elisabetta. Hear that, my lady!

Count. I cannot tell how long we strove before Our horses fell beneath us; down we went Crush'd, hack'd at, trampled underfoot. The night, As some cold-manner'd friend may strangely do us The truest service, had a touch of frost That help'd to check the flowing of the blood. My last sight ere I swoon'd was one sweet face Crown'd with the wreath. *That* seem'd to come and go. They left us there for dead!

Elisabetta. Hear that, my lady!

Filippo. Ay, and I left two fingers there for dead. See, my lady! (*Showing his hand.*)

Lady Giovanna. I see, Filippo!

Filippo. And I have small hope of the gentleman gout in my great toe.

Lady Giovanna. And why, Filippo?
[*Smiling absently.*

Filippo. I left him there for dead too!

Elisabetta. She smiles at him—how hard the woman is!
My lady, if your ladyship were not Too proud to look upon the garland, you Would find it stain'd——

Count (rising).　　　Silence, Elisabetta!

Elisabetta. Stain'd with the blood of the
best heart that ever
Beat for one woman.

　　　　　　　　[Points to wreath on chair.

Lady Giovanna (rising slowly). I can eat
no more!

Count. You have but trifled with our
homely salad,
But dallied with a single lettuce-leaf;
Not eaten anything.

Lady Giovanna. Nay, nay, I cannot.
You know, my lord, I told you I was
troubled.
My one child Florio lying still so sick,
I bound myself, and by a solemn vow,
That I would touch no flesh till he were
well
Here, or else well in Heaven, where all is
well.

　　　　　　　[ELISABETTA *clears table of bird and
salad:* FILIPPO *snatches up the plate
of prunes and holds them to* LADY
GIOVANNA.

Filippo. But the prunes, my lady, from
the tree that his lordship——

Lady Giovanna. Not now, Filippo. My
lord Federigo,
Can I not speak with you once more
alone?

Count. You hear, Filippo? My good
fellow, go!

Filippo. But the prunes that your lordship——

Elisabetta. Filippo!

Count. Ay, prune our company of thine
own and go!

Elisabetta. Filippo!

Filippo (turning). Well, well! the women!
　　　　　　　　　　　　　　　　　[Exit.

Count. And thou too leave us, my dear
nurse, alone.

Elisabetta (folding up cloth and going).
And me too! Ay, the dear nurse will leave
you alone; but, for all that, she that has
eaten the yolk is scarce like to swallow the
shell.

　　　　　[*Turns and curtseys stiffly to* LADY
GIOVANNA, *then exit.* LADY GIOVANNA
*takes out diamond necklace from
casket.*

Lady Giovanna. I have anger'd your
good nurse; these old-world servants
Are all but flesh and blood with those they
serve.
My lord, I have a present to return you,
And afterwards a boon to crave of you.

Count. No, my most honour'd and long-
worshipt lady,
Poor Federigo degli Alberighi
Takes nothing in return from you except
Return of his affection—can deny
Nothing to you that you require of him.

Lady Giovanna. Then I require you to
take back your diamonds—

　　　　　　　　　　[Offering necklace.

I doubt not they are yours. No other heart
Of such magnificence in courtesy
Beats—out of heaven. They seem'd too
rich a prize
To trust with any messenger. I came
In person to return them.

　　　　　　　　　　[COUNT *draws back.*
　　　　　　　　　　　　If the phrase
'Return' displease you, we will say—
exchange them
For your—for your——

*Count (takes a step toward her and then
back).* For mine—and what of mine?

Lady Giovanna. Well, shall we say this
wreath and your sweet rhymes?

Count. But have you ever worn my
diamonds?

Lady Giovanna.　　　　　　　　　No!
For that would seem accepting of your
love.
I cannot brave my brother—but be sure
That I shall never marry again, my lord!

Count. Sure?

Lady Giovanna. Yes!

Count. Is this your brother's order?

Lady Giovanna.　　　　　　　　　No!
For he would marry me to the richest man
In Florence; but I think you know the
saying—
'Better a man without riches, than riches
without a man.'

Count. A noble saying—and acted on
would yield
A nobler breed of men and women. Lady,
I find you a shrewd bargainer. The wreath
That once you wore outvalues twentyfold

721

The diamonds that you never deign'd to
wear.
But lay them there for a moment!
[*Points to table.* LADY GIOVANNA
places necklace on table.
And be you
Gracious enough to let me know the boon
By granting which, if aught be mine to
grant,
I should be made more happy than I hoped
Ever to be again.
Lady Giovanna. Then keep your wreath,
But you will find me a shrewd bargainer
still.
I cannot keep your diamonds, for the gift
I ask for, to *my* mind and at this present
Outvalues all the jewels upon earth.
  Count. It should be love that thus out-
values all.
You speak like love, and yet you love me
not.
I have nothing in this world but love for
you.
  Lady Giovanna. Love? it *is* love, love
for my dying boy,
Moves me to ask it of you.
  Count.   What? my time?
Is it my time? Well, I can give my time
To him that is a part of you, your son.
Shall I return to the castle with you?
Shall I
Sit by him, read to him, tell him my tales,
Sing him my songs? You know that I can
touch
The ghittern to some purpose.
  Lady Giovanna.   No, not that!
I thank you heartily for that—and you,
I doubt not from your nobleness of nature,
Will pardon me for asking what I ask.
  Count. Giovanna, dear Giovanna, I that
once
The wildest of the random youth of
Florence
Before I saw you—all my nobleness
Of nature, as you deign to call it, draws
From you, and from my constancy to you.
No more, but speak.
  Lady Giovanna. I will. You know sick
people,
More specially sick children, have strange
fancies,

Strange longings; and to thwart them in
their mood
May work them grievous harm at times,
may even
Hasten their end. I would you had a son!
It might be easier then for you to make
Allowance for a mother—her—who comes
To rob you of your one delight on earth.
How often has my sick boy yearn'd for
this!
I have put him off as often; but to-day
I dared not—so much weaker, so much
worse
For last day's journey. I was weeping for
him;
He gave me his hand: 'I should be well
again
If the good Count would give me——'
  Count.   Give me.
  Lady Giovanna.   His falcon.
  Count (starts back). My falcon!
  Lady Giovanna.   Yes, your falcon,
Federigo!
  Count. Alas, I cannot!
  Lady Giovanna. Cannot? Even so!
I fear'd as much. O this unhappy world!
How shall I break it to him? how shall I
tell him?
The boy may die: more blessed were the
rags
Of some pale beggar-woman seeking alms
For her sick son, if he were like to live,
Than all my childless wealth, if mine
must die.
I was to blame—the love you said you
bore me—
My lord, we thank you for your entertain-
ment.   [*With a stately curtsey.*
And so return—Heaven help him!—to our
son.   [*Turns.*
  Count (rushes forward). Stay, stay, I am
most unlucky, most unhappy.
You never had look'd in on me before,
And when you came and dipt your
sovereign head
Thro' these low doors, you ask'd to eat
with me.
I had but emptiness to set before you,
No not a draught of milk, no not an egg,
Nothing but my brave bird, my noble
falcon,

THE FALCON

My comrade of the house, and of the field.
She had to die for it—she died for you.
Perhaps I thought with those of old, the nobler
The victim was, the more acceptable
Might be the sacrifice. I fear you scarce
Will thank me for your entertainment now.

    Lady Giovanna (returning). I bear with him no longer.

    Count.   No, Madonna!
And he will have to bear with it as he may.

    Lady Giovanna. I break with him for ever!

    Count.   Yes, Giovanna,
But he will keep his love to you for ever!

    Lady Giovanna. You? you? not you!
My brother! my hard brother!
O Federigo, Federigo, I love you!
Spite of ten thousand brothers, Federigo.
               [Falls at his feet.

    Count (impetuously). Why then the dying of my noble bird
Hath served me better than her living—
then   *[Takes diamonds from table.*
These diamonds are both yours and mine
—have won

Their value again—beyond all markets—there
I lay them for the first time round your neck.   *[Lays necklace round her neck.*
And then this chaplet—No more feuds, but peace,
Peace and conciliation! I will make
Your brother love me. See, I tear away
The leaves were darken'd by the battle—
      [Pulls leaves off and throws them down.
             —crown you
Again with the same crown my Queen of Beauty.   *[Places wreath on her head.*
Rise—I could almost think that the dead garland
Will break once more into the living blossom.
Nay, nay, I pray you rise.
      [Raises her with both hands.
          We two together
Will help to heal your son—your son and mine—
We shall do it—we shall do it.
              [Embraces her.
The purpose of my being is accomplish'd,
And I am happy!

    Lady Giovanna. And I too, Federigo.

THE PROMISE OF MAY

'A surface man of theories, true to none'

DRAMATIS PERSONÆ

FARMER DOBSON.
MR. PHILIP EDGAR (*afterwards* MR. HAROLD).
FARMER STEER (DORA *and* EVA'S *Father*).
MR. WILSON (*a Schoolmaster*).

HIGGINS
JAMES
DAN SMITH } *Farm Labourers.*
JACKSON
ALLEN

DORA STEER.
EVA STEER.

SALLY ALLEN } *Farm Servants.*
MILLY

Farm Servants, Labourers, etc.

ACT I

SCENE

Before Farmhouse

Farming Men and Women. Farming Men carrying forms, etc., Women carrying baskets of knives and forks, etc.

1st *Farming Man.* Be thou a-gawin' to the long barn?

2nd *Farming Man.* Ay, to be sewer! Be thou?

1st *Farming Man.* Why, o' coorse, fur it be the owd man's birthdaäy. He be heighty this very daäy, and 'e telled all on us to be i' the long barn by one o'clock, fur he'll gie us a big dinner, and haäfe th' parish 'll be theer, an' Miss Dora, an' Miss Eva, an' all!

2nd *Farming Man.* Miss Dora be coomed back, then?

1st *Farming Man.* Ay, haäfe an hour ago. She be in theer now. (*Pointing to house.*) Owd Steer wur afeärd she wouldn't be back i' time to keep his birthdaäy, and he wur in a tew about it all the murnin'; and he sent me wi' the gig to Littlechester to fetch 'er; and 'er an' the owd man they fell a kissin' o' one another like two sweet'arts i' the poorch as soon as he clapt eyes of 'er.

2nd *Farming Man.* Foälks says he likes Miss Eva the best.

1st *Farming Man.* Naäy, I knaws nowt o' what foälks says, an' I caäres nowt neither. Foälks doesn't hallus knaw thessens; but sewer I be, they be two o' the purtiest gels ye can see of a summer murnin'.

2nd *Farming Man.* Beänt Miss Eva gone off a bit of 'er good looks o' laäte?

1st *Farming Man.* Noä, not a bit.

2nd *Farming Man.* Why coöm awaäy, then, to the long barn. [*Exeunt.*

DORA *looks out of window. Enter* DOBSON.

Dora (*singing*)

The town lay still in the low sun-light,
The hen cluckt late by the white farm gate,
The maid to her dairy came in from the
   cow,
The stock-dove coo'd at the fall of night,
The blossom had open'd on every bough;
   O joy for the promise of May, of May,
   O joy for the promise of May.

(*Nodding at* DOBSON.) I'm coming down, Mr. Dobson. I haven't seen Eva yet. Is she anywhere in the garden?

Dobson. Noä, Miss. I ha'n't seed 'er neither.

Dora (*enters singing*)

But a red fire woke in the heart of the
   town,
And a fox from the glen ran away with the
   hen,

And a cat to the cream, and a rat to the
   cheese;
And the stock-dove coo'd, till a kite dropt
   down,
And a salt wind burnt the blossoming trees;
   O grief for the promise of May, of May,
   O grief for the promise of May.

I don't know why I sing that song; I don't
love it.

Dobson. Blessings on your pretty voice,
Miss Dora. Wheer did they larn ye that?

Dora. In Cumberland, Mr. Dobson.

Dobson. An' how did ye leäve the owd
uncle i' Coomberland?

Dora. Getting better, Mr. Dobson. But
he'll never be the same man again.

Dobson. An' how d'ye find the owd man
'ere?

Dora. As well as ever. I came back to
keep his birthday.

Dobson. Well, I be coomed to keep his
birthdaäy an' all. The owd man be heighty
to-daäy, beänt he?

Dora. Yes, Mr. Dobson. And the day's
bright like a friend, but the wind east like
an enemy. Help me to move this bench for
him into the sun. (*They move bench.*) No,
not that way—here, under the apple tree.
Thank you. Look how full of rosy blossom
it is.   [*Pointing to apple tree.*

Dobson. Theer be redder blossoms nor
them, Miss Dora.

Dora. Where do they blow, Mr. Dobson?

Dobson. Under your eyes, Miss Dora.

Dora. Do they?

Dobson. And your eyes be as blue as——

Dora. What, Mr. Dobson? A butcher's
frock?

Dobson. Noä, Miss Dora; as blue as——

Dora. Bluebell, harebell, speedwell,
bluebottle, succory, forget-me-not?

Dobson. Noä, Miss Dora; as blue as——

Dora. The sky? or the sea on a blue day?

Dobson. Naäy then. I meän'd they be as
blue as violets.

Dora. Are they?

Dobson. Theer ye goäs ageän, Miss, niver
believing owt I says to ye—hallus a-fobbing
ma off, tho' ye knaws I love ye. I warrants
ye'll think moor o' this young Squire Edgar

as ha' coomed among us—the Lord knaws
how—ye'll think more on 'is little finger
than hall my hand at the haltar.

Dora. Perhaps, Master Dobson. I can't
tell, for I have never seen him. But my
sister wrote that he was mighty pleasant,
and had no pride in him.

Dobson. He'll be arter you now, Miss
Dora.

Dora. Will he? How can I tell?

Dobson. He's been arter Miss Eva,
haän't he?

Dora. Not that I know.

Dobson. Didn't I spy 'em a-sitting i' the
woodbine harbour togither?

Dora. What of that? Eva told me that he
was taking her likeness. He's an artist.

Dobson. What's a hartist? I doänt believe
he's iver a 'eart under his waistcoat. And
I tells ye what, Miss Dora: he's no respect
for the Queen, or the parson, or the justice
o' peace, or owt. I ha' heärd 'im a-gawin'
on 'ud make your 'air—God bless it!—
stan' on end. And wuss nor that. When
theer wur a meeting o' farmers at Littlechester t'other daäy, and they was all a-cry-
ing out at the bad times, he cooms up, and
he calls out among our oän men, 'The land
belongs to the people!'

Dora. And what did *you* say to that?

Dobson. Well, I says, s'pose my pig's the
land, and you says it belongs to the parish,
and theer be a thousand i' the parish,
taäkin' in the women and childer; and
s'pose I kills my pig, and gi'es it among
'em, why there wudn't be a dinner for
nawbody, and I should ha' lost the pig.

Dora. And what did he say to that?

Dobson. Nowt—what could he saäy? But
I taäkes 'im fur a bad lot and a burn fool,
and I haätes the very sight on him.

Dora (*looking at* DOBSON). Master Dobson, you are a comely man to look at.

Dobson. I thank you for that, Miss Dora,
onyhow.

Dora. Ay, but you turn right ugly when
you're in an ill temper; and I promise you
that if you forget yourself in your be-
haviour to this gentleman, my father's
friend, I will never change word with you
again.

Enter FARMING MAN *from barn*

Farming Man. Miss, the farming men 'ull hev their dinner i' the long barn, and the master 'ud be straänge an' pleased if you'd step in fust, and see that all be right and reg'lar fur 'em afoor he coöm. [*Exit.*

Dora. I go. Master Dobson, did you hear what I said?

Dobson. Yeas, yeas! I'll not meddle wi' 'im if he doänt meddle wi' meä. (*Exit* DORA.) Coomly, says she. I niver thowt o' mysen i' that waäy; but if she'd taäke to ma i' that waäy, or ony waäy, I'd slaäve out my life fur 'er. 'Coomly to look at,' says she—but she said it spiteful-like. To look at—yeas, 'coomly'; and she mayn't be so fur out theer. But if that be nowt to she, then it be nowt to me. (*Looking off stage.*) Schoolmaster! Why if Steer han't haxed schoolmaster to dinner, thaw 'e knaws I was hallus ageän heving schoolmaster i' the parish! fur him as be handy wi' a book bean't but haäfe a hand at a pitchfork.

Enter WILSON

Well, Wilson. I seed that one cow o' thine i' the pinfold ageän as I wur a-coomin' 'ere.

Wilson. Very likely, Mr. Dobson. She *will* break fence. I can't keep her in order.

Dobson. An' if tha can't keep thy one cow i' horder, how can tha keep all thy scholars i' horder? But let that goä by. What dost a knaw o' this Mr. Hedgar as be a-lodgin' wi' ye? I coom'd upon 'im t'other daäy lookin' at the coontry, then a-scrattin upon a bit o' paäper, then a-lookin' agean; and I taäked 'im fur soom sort of a land-surveyor—but a beänt.

Wilson. He's a Somersetshire man, and a very civil-spoken gentleman.

Dobson. Gentleman! What be he a-doing here ten mile an' moor fro' a raäil? We laäys out o' the waäy fur gentlefoälk alto-gither—leästwaäys they niver cooms 'ere but fur the trout i' our beck, fur they be knaw'd as far as Littlechester. But 'e doänt fish neither.

Wilson. Well, it's no sin in a gentleman not to fish.

Dobson. Noä, but I haätes 'im.

Wilson. Better step out of his road, then, for he's walking to us, and with a book in his hand.

Dobson. An' I haätes booöks an' all, fur they puts foälk off the owd waäys.

Enter EDGAR, *reading—not seeing* DOBSON *and* WILSON

Edgar. This author, with his charm of simple style
And close dialectic, all but proving man
An automatic series of sensations,
Has often numb'd me into apathy
Against the unpleasant jolts of this rough road
That breaks off short into the abysses—made me
A Quietist taking all things easily.

Dobson. (*Aside.*) There mun be summut wrong theer, Wilson, fur I doänt understan' it.

Wilson. (*Aside.*) Nor I either, Mr. Dobson.

Dobson (*scornfully*). An' thou doänt understan' it neither—and thou schoolmaster an' all.

Edgar. What can a man, then, live for but sensations,
Pleasant ones? men of old would undergo
Unpleasant for the sake of pleasant ones
Hereafter, like the Moslem beauties waiting
To clasp their lovers by the golden gates.
For me, whose cheerless Houris after death
Are Night and Silence, pleasant ones—the while—
If possible, here! to crop the flower and pass.

Dobson. Well, I never 'eärd the likes o' that afoor.

Wilson. (*Aside.*) But I have, Mr. Dobson. It's the old Scripture text, 'Let us eat and drink, for to-morrow we die.' I'm sorry for it, for, tho' he never comes to church, I thought better of him.

Edgar. 'What are we,' says the blind old man in Lear?
'As flies to the Gods; they kill us for their sport.'

Dobson. (*Aside.*) Then the owd man i'
Lear should be shaämed of hissen, but
noän o' the parishes goäs by that naäme
'ereabouts.

Edgar. The Gods! but they, the shadows
of ourselves,
Have past for ever. It is Nature kills,
And not for *her* sport either. She knows
nothing.
Man only knows, the worse for him! for
why
Cannot *he* take his pastime like the
flies?
And if my pleasure breed another's pain,
Well—is not that the course of Nature
too,
From the dim dawn of Being—her main
law
Whereby she grows in beauty—that her
flies
Must massacre each other? this poor
Nature!

Dobson. Natur! Natur! Well, it be i' *my*
natur to knock 'im o' the 'eäd now; but I
weänt.

Edgar. A Quietist taking all things easily
—why—
Have I been dipping into this again
To steel myself against the leaving her?
                [*Closes book, seeing* WILSON.
Good day!

Wilson. Good day, sir.
                [DOBSON *looks hard at* EDGAR.
Edgar (*to* DOBSON). Have I the pleasure,
friend, of knowing you?

Dobson. Dobson.

Edgar. Good day, then, Dobson.
                                [*Exit.*
Dobson. 'Good daäy then, Dobson!'
Civil-spoken i'deed! Why, Wilson, tha
'eärd 'im thysen—the feller couldn't find
a Mister in his mouth fur me, as farms
five hoonderd haäcre.

Wilson. You never find one for me, Mr.
Dobson.

Dobson. Noä, fur thou be nobbut schoolmaster; but I taäkes 'im for a Lunnun
swindler, and a burn fool.

Wilson. He can hardly be both, and he
pays me regular every Saturday.

Dobson. Yeas; but I haätes 'im.

Enter STEER, FARM MEN *and* WOMEN

Steer (*goes and sits under apple tree*).
Hev' ony o' ye seen Eva?

Dobson. Noä, Mr. Steer.

Steer. Well, I reckons they'll hev' a fine
cider-crop to-year if the blossom 'owds.
Good murnin', neighbours, and the saäme
to you, my men. I taäkes it kindly of all o'
you that you be coomed—what's the news-
paäper word, Wilson?—celebrate—to celebrate my birthdaäy i' this fashion. Niver
man 'ed better friends, and I will saäy niver
master 'ed better men: fur thaw I may ha'
fallen out wi' ye sometimes, the fault,
mebbe, wur as much mine as yours; and,
thaw I says it mysen, niver men 'ed a better
master—and I knaws what men be, and
what masters be, fur I wur nobbut a
laäbourer, and now I be a landlord—burn
a plowman, and now, as far as money goäs,
I be a gentleman, thaw I beänt naw
scholard, fur I 'ednt naw time to maäke
mysen a scholard while I wur maäkin'
mysen a gentleman, but I ha taäen good
care to turn out boäth my darters right
down fine laädies.

Dobson. An' soä they be.

1st Farming Man. Soä they be! soä
they be!

2nd Farming Man. The Lord bless boath
on 'em!

3rd Farming Man. An' the saäme to you,
Master.

4th Farming Man. And long life to boath
on 'em. An' the saäme to you, Master
Steer, likewise.

Steer. Thank ye!

Enter EVA

Wheer 'asta been?

Eva (*timidly*). Many happy returns of
the day, father.

Steer. They can't be many, my dear,
but I 'oäpes they'll be 'appy.

Dobson. Why, tha looks haäle anew to
last to a hoonderd.

Steer. An' why shouldn't I last to a
hoonderd? Haäle! why shouldn't I be
haäle? fur thaw I be heighty this very daäy,
I niver 'es sa much as one pin's prick of

727

paäin; an' I can taäke my glass along wi'
the youngest, fur I niver touched a drop
of owt till my oän wedding-daäy, an' then
I wur turned huppads o' sixty. Why
shouldn't I be haäle? I ha' plowed the
ten-aäcre—it be mine now—afoor ony o'
ye wur burn—ye all knaws the ten-aäcre—
I mun ha' plowed it moor nor a hoonderd
times; hallus hup at sunrise, and I'd drive
the plow straäit as a line right i' the faäce
o' the sun, then back ageän, a-follering my
oän shadder—then hup ageän i' the faäce
o' the sun. Eh! how the sun 'ud shine, and
the larks 'ud sing i' them daäys, and the
smell o' the mou'd an' all. Eh! if I could
ha' gone on wi' the plowin' nobbut the
smell o' the mou'd 'ud ha' maäde ma live
as long as Jerusalem.

Eva. Methusaleh, father.

Steer. Ay, lass, but when thou be as owd
as me thou'll put one word fur another as
I does.

Dobson. But, Steer, thaw thou be haäle
anew I seed tha a-limpin' up just now wi'
the roomatics i' the knee.

Steer. Roomatics! Noä; I laäme't my
knee last night running arter a thief. Beänt
there house-breäkers down i' Littlechester,
Dobson—doänt ye hear of ony?

Dobson. Ay, that there be. Immanuel
Goldsmiths was broke into o' Monday
night, and ower a hoonderd pounds worth
o' rings stolen.

Steer. So I thowt, and I heärd the winder
—that's the winder at the end o' the passage, that goäs by thy chaumber. (*Turning
to* EVA.) Why, lass, what maäkes tha sa red?
Did 'e git into thy chaumber?

Eva. Father!

Steer. Well, I runned arter thief i' the
dark, and fell ageän coalscuttle and my
kneeä gev waäy or I'd ha' cotched 'im, but
afoor I coomed up he got thruff the winder
ageän.

Eva. Got thro' the window again?

Steer. Ay, but he left the mark of 'is foot
i' the flower-bed; now theer be noän o' my
men, thinks I to mysen, 'ud ha' done it
'cep' it were Dan Smith, fur I cotched 'im
once a-steälin' coäls an' I sent fur 'im, an'
I measured his foot wi' the mark i' the bed,

but it wouldn't fit—seeäms to me the mark
wur maäde by a Lunnun boot. (*Looks at*
EVA.) Why, now, what maäkes tha sa white?

Eva. Fright, father!

Steer. Maäke thysen eäsy. I'll hev the
winder naäiled up, and put Towser
under it.

Eva (*clasping her hands*). No, no, father!
Towser'll tear him all to pieces.

Steer. Let him keep awaäy, then; but
coom, coom! let's be gawin. They ha'
broached a barrel of aäle i' the long barn,
and the fiddler be theer, and the lads and
lasses 'ull hev a dance.

Eva. (*Aside.*) Dance! small heart have I
to dance. I should seem to be dancing upon
a grave.

Steer. Wheer be Mr. Edgar? about the
premises?

Dobson. Hallus about the premises!

Steer. So much the better, so much the
better. I likes 'im, and Eva likes 'im. Eva
can do owt wi' 'im; look for 'im, Eva, and
bring 'im to the barn. He 'ant naw pride
in 'im, and we'll git 'im to speechify for us
arter dinner.

Eva. Yes, father!   [*Exit.*

Steer. Coom along then, all the rest o'
ye! Churchwarden be a coomin, thaw me
and 'im we niver 'grees about the tithe;
and Parson mebbe, thaw he niver mended
that gap i' the glebe fence as I telled 'im;
and Blacksmith, thaw he niver shoes a
herse to my likings; and Baäker, thaw I
sticks to hoäm-maäde—but all on 'em welcome, all on 'em welcome; and I've hed
the long barn cleared out of all the
machines, and the sacks, and the taäters,
and the mangles, and theer'll be room
anew for all o' ye. Foller me.

All. Yeas, yeas! Three cheers for Mr.
Steer!

[*All exeunt except* DOBSON *into barn.*

Enter EDGAR

Dobson (*who is going, turns*). Squire!—if
so be you be a squire.

Edgar. Dobbins, I think.

Dobson. Dobbins, you thinks; and I
thinks ye weärs a Lunnun boot.

Edgar. Well?

Dobson. And I thinks I'd like to taäke the measure o' your foot.

Edgar. Ay, if you'd like to measure your own length upon the grass.

Dobson. Coom, coom, that's a good un. Why, I could throw four o' ye; but I promised one of the Misses I wouldn't meddle wi' ye, and I weänt.

[*Exit into barn.*

Edgar. Jealous of me with Eva! Is it so?
Well, tho' I grudge the pretty jewel, that I
Have worn, to such a clod, yet that might
   be
The best way out of it, if the child could
   keep
Her counsel. I am sure I wish her happy.
But I must free myself from this entangle-
   ment.
I have all my life before me—so has she—
Give her a month or two, and her affections
Will flower toward the light in some new
   face.
Still I am half-afraid to meet her now.
She will urge marriage on me. I hate tears.
Marriage is but an old tradition. I hate
Traditions, ever since my narrow father,
After my frolic with his tenant's girl,
Made younger elder son, violated the
   whole
Tradition of our land, and left his heir,
Born, happily, with some sense of art, to
   live
By brush and pencil. By and by, when
   Thought
Comes down among the crowd, and man
   perceives that
The lost gleam of an after-life but leaves
   him
A beast of prey in the dark, why then the
   crowd
May wreak my wrongs upon my wrongers.
   Marriage!
That fine, fat, hook-nosed uncle of mine,
   old Harold,
Who leaves me all his land at Littlechester,
He, too, would oust me from his will, if I
Made such a marriage. And marriage in
   itself—
The storm is hard at hand will sweep away
Thrones, churches, ranks, traditions, cus-
   toms, marriage

One of the feeblest! Then the man, the
   woman,
Following their best affinities, will each
Bid their old bond farewell with smiles,
   not tears;
Good wishes, not reproaches; with no fear
Of the world's gossiping clamour, and no
   need
Of veiling their desires.
                Conventionalism,
Who shrieks by day at what she does by
   night,
Would call this vice; but one time's vice
   may be
The virtue of another; and Vice and Virtue
Are but two masks of self; and what here-
   after
Shall mark out Vice from Virtue in the gulf
Of never-dawning darkness?

Enter EVA

                     My sweet Eva,
Where have you lain in ambush all the
   morning?
They say your sister, Dora, has return'd,
And that should make you happy, if you
   love her!
But you look troubled.

Eva.   Oh, I love her so,
I was afraid of her, and I hid myself.
We never kept a secret from each other;
She would have seen at once into my
   trouble,
And ask'd me what I could not answer.
   Oh, Philip,
Father heard you last night. Our savage
   mastiff,
That all but kill'd the beggar, will be
   placed
Beneath the window, Philip.

Edgar.   Savage, is he?
What matters? Come, give me your hand
   and kiss me
This beautiful May-morning.

Eva.   The most beautiful
May we have had for many years!

Edgar.   And here
Is the most beautiful morning of this May.
Nay, you must smile upon me! There—
   you make
The May and morning still more beautiful,

You, the most beautiful blossom of the May.

Eva. Dear Philip, all the world is beautiful
If we were happy, and could chime in with it.

Edgar. True; for the senses, love, are for the world;
That for the senses.

Eva.   Yes.

Edgar.   And when the man,
The child of evolution, flings aside
His swaddling-bands, the morals of the tribe,
He, following his own instincts as his God,
Will enter on the larger golden age;
No pleasure then taboo'd: for when the tide
Of full democracy has overwhelm'd
This Old world, from that flood will rise the New,
Like the Love-goddess, with no bridal veil,
Ring, trinket of the Church, but naked Nature
In all her loveliness.

Eva.   What are you saying?

Edgar. That, if we did not strain to make ourselves
Better and higher than Nature, we might be
As happy as the bees there at their honey
In these sweet blossoms.

Eva.   Yes; how sweet they smell!

Edgar. There! let me break some off for you.   [*Breaking branch off.*

Eva.   My thanks.
But, look, how wasteful of the blossom you are!
One, two, three, four, five, six—you have robb'd poor father
Of ten good apples. Oh, I forgot to tell you
He wishes you to dine along with us,
And speak for him after—you that are so clever!

Edgar. I grieve I cannot; but, indeed——

Eva.   What is it?

Edgar. Well, business. I must leave you, love, to-day.

Eva. Leave me, to-day! And when will you return?

Edgar. I cannot tell precisely; but——

Eva.   But what?

Edgar. I trust, my dear, we shall be always friends.

Eva. After all that has gone between us —friends!
What, only friends?   [*Drops branch.*

Edgar.   All that has gone between us
Should surely make us friends.

Eva.   But keep us lovers.

Edgar. Child, do you love me now?

Eva.   Yes, now and ever.

Edgar. Then you should wish us both to love for ever.
But, if you *will* bind love to one for ever,
Altho' at first he take his bonds for flowers,
As years go on, he feels them press upon him,
Begins to flutter in them, and at last
Breaks thro' them, and so flies away for ever;
While, had you left him free use of his wings,
Who knows that he had ever dream'd of flying?

Eva. But all that sounds so wicked and so strange;
'Till death us part'—those are the only words,
The true ones—nay, and those not true enough,
For they that love do not believe that death
Will part them. Why do you jest with me, and try
To fright me? Tho' you are a gentleman,
I but a farmer's daughter——

Edgar.   Tut! you talk
Old feudalism. When the great Democracy
Makes a new world——

Eva.   And if you be not jesting,
Neither the old world, nor the new, nor father,
Sister, nor you, shall ever see me more.

Edgar (*moved*). Then—(*aside*) Shall I
say it?—(*aloud*) fly with me to-day.

Eva. No! Philip, Philip, if you do not marry me,
I shall go mad for utter shame and die.

Edgar. Then, if we needs must be conventional,

When shall your parish-parson bawl our
    banns
Before your gaping clowns?
    Eva.   Not in our church—
I think I scarce could hold my head up
    there.
Is there no other way?
    Edgar.   Yes, if you cared
To fee an over-opulent superstition,
Then they would grant you what they call
    a licence
To marry. Do you wish it?
    Eva.   *Do* I wish it?
    Edgar. In London.
    Eva.   You will write to me?
    Edgar.   I will.
    Eva. And I will fly to you thro' the
    night, the storm—
Yes, tho' the fire should run along the
    ground,
As once it did in Egypt. Oh, you see,
I was just out of school, I had no mother—
My sister far away—and you, a gentleman,
Told me to trust you: yes, in everything—
That was the only *true* love; and I
    trusted—
Oh, yes, indeed, I would have died for you.
How could you—Oh, how could you?—
    nay, how could I?
But now you will set all right again, and I
Shall not be made the laughter of the
    village,
And poor old father not die miserable.
    Dora (*singing in the distance*).
O joy for the promise of May, of May,
O joy for the promise of May.
    Edgar. Speak not so loudly; that must
    be your sister.
You never told her, then, of what has past
Between us.
    Eva.   Never!
    Edgar.   Do not till I bid you.
    Eva. No, Philip, no.   [*Turns away.*
    Edgar (*moved*). How gracefully there she
    stands
Weeping—the little Niobe! What! we prize
The statue or the picture all the more
When we have made them ours! Is she less
    loveable,
Less lovely, being wholly mine? To stay—
Follow my art among these quiet fields,

Live with these honest folk——
                And play the fool!
No! she that gave herself to me so easily
Will yield herself as easily to another.
    Eva. Did you speak, Philip?
    Edgar.   Nothing more, farewell.
                    [*They embrace.*
Dora (*coming nearer*).
O grief for the promise of May, of May,
O grief for the promise of May.
    Edgar (*still embracing her*). Keep up your
    heart until we meet again.
    Eva. If that should break before we meet
    again?
    Edgar. Break! nay, but call for Philip
    when you will,
And he returns.
    Eva. Heaven hears you, Philip Edgar!
    Edgar (*moved*). And *he* would hear you
    even from the grave.
Heaven curse him if he come not at your
    call!   [*Exit.*

    Enter DORA

    Dora. Well, Eva!
    Eva. Oh, Dora, Dora, how long you have
been away from home! Oh, how often I
have wished for you! It seemed to me that
we were parted for ever.
    Dora. For ever, you foolish child!
What's come over you? We parted like the
brook yonder about the alder island, to
come together again in a moment and to
go on together again, till one of us be
married. But where is this Mr. Edgar
whom you praised so in your first letters?
You haven't even mentioned him in your
last?
    Eva. He has gone to London.
    Dora. Ay, child; and you look thin and
pale. Is it for his absence? Have you
fancied yourself in love with him? That's
all nonsense, you know, such a baby as you
are. But you shall tell me all about it.
    Eva. Not now—presently. Yes, I have
been in trouble, but I am happy—I think,
quite happy now.
    Dora (*taking* EVA'S *hand*). Come, then,
and make them happy in the long barn, for
father is in his glory, and there is a piece of
beef like a house-side, and a plum-pudding

as big as the round haystack. But see they
are coming out for the dance already.
Well, my child, let us join them.

Enter all from barn laughing. EVA *sits
reluctantly under apple tree.* STEER *enters
smoking, sits by* EVA.

Dance

ACT II

*Five years have elapsed between
Acts I and II*

SCENE

*A Meadow. On one side a Pathway going
over a rustic Bridge. At back the Farmhouse among trees. In the distance a
Church Spire.*

DOBSON *and* DORA

Dobson. So the owd uncle i' Coomberland be deäd, Miss Dora, beänt he?
Dora. Yes, Mr. Dobson, I've been
attending on his deathbed and his burial.
Dobson. It be five year sin' ye went afoor
to him, and it seems to me nobbut t'other
day. Hesn't he left ye nowt?
Dora. No, Mr. Dobson.
Dobson. But he were mighty fond o' ye,
warn't he?
Dora. Fonder of poor Eva—like every-
body else.
Dobson (*handing* DORA *basket of roses*).
Not like me, Miss Dora; and I ha' browt
these roses to ye—I forgits what they calls
'em, but I hallus gi'ed soom on 'em to Miss
Eva at this time o' year. Will ya taäke 'em?
fur Miss Eva, she set the bush by my dairy
winder afoor she went to school at Littlechester—so I allus browt soom on 'em to
her; and now she be gone, will ye taäke
'em, Miss Dora?
Dora. I thank you. They tell me that
yesterday you mentioned her name too
suddenly before my father. See that you
do not do so again!
Dobson. Noä; I knaws a deäl better now.
I seed how the owd man wur vext.
Dora. I take them, then, for Eva's sake.
[*Takes basket, places some in her dress.*
Dobson. Eva's saäke. Yeas. Poor gel, poor

gel! I can't abeär to think on 'er now, fur
I'd ha' done owt fur 'er mysen; an' ony o'
Steer's men, an' ony o' my men 'ud ha'
done owt fur 'er, an' all the parish 'ud ha'
done owt fur 'er, fur we was all on us
proud on 'er, an' them theer be soom of
her oän roses, an' she wur as sweet as ony
on 'em—the Lord bless 'er—'er oän sen;
an' weänt ye taäke 'em now, Miss Dora,
fur 'er saäke an' fur my saäke an' all?
Dora. Do you want them back again?
Dobson. Noä, noä! Keep 'em. But I hed
a word to saäy to ye.
Dora. Why, Farmer, you should be in
the hayfield looking after your men; you
couldn't have more splendid weather.
Dobson. I be a going theer; but I thowt
I'd bring tha them roses fust. The weather's
well anew, but the glass be a bit shaäky.
S'iver we've led moäst on it.
Dora. Ay! but you must not be too
sudden with it either, as you were last
year, when you put it in green, and your
stack caught fire.
Dobson. I were insured, Miss, an' I lost
nowt by it. But I weänt be too sudden wi'
it; and I feel sewer, Miss Dora, that I ha'
been noän too sudden wi' you, fur I ha'
sarved for ye well nigh as long as the man
sarved for 'is sweet'art i' Scriptur'. Weänt
ye gi'e me a kind answer at last?
Dora. I have no thought of marriage, my
friend. We have been in such grief these
five years, not only on my sister's account,
but the ill success of the farm, and the
debts, and my father's breaking down, and
his blindness. How could I think of leaving
him?
Dobson. Eh, but I be well to do; and if
ye would nobbut hev me, I would taäke
the owd blind man to hev my oän fireside. You
should hev him allus wi' ye.
Dora. You are generous, but it cannot
be. I cannot love you; nay, I think I never
can be brought to love any man. It seems
to me that I hate men, ever since my sister
left us. Oh, see here. (*Pulls out a letter.*)
I wear it next my heart. Poor sister, I had
it five years ago. 'Dearest Dora,—I have
lost myself, and am lost for ever to you and
my poor father. I thought Mr. Edgar the

best of men, and he has proved himself the worst. Seek not for me, or you may find me at the bottom of the river.—EVA.'

Dobson. Be that my fault?

Dora. No; but how should I, with this grief still at my heart, take to the milking of your cows, the fatting of your calves, the making of your butter, and the managing of your poultry?

Dobson. Naäy, but I hev an owd woman as 'ud see to all that; and you should sit i' your oän parlour quite like a laädy, ye should!

Dora. It cannot be.

Dobson. And plaäy the pianner, if ye liked, all daäy long, like a laädy, ye should an' all.

Dora. It cannot be.

Dobson. And I would loove tha moor nor ony gentleman 'ud loove tha.

Dora. No, no; it cannot be.

Dobson. And p'raps ye hears 'at I soomtimes taäkes a drop too much; but that be all along o' you, Miss, because ye weänt hev me; but, if ye would, I could put all that o' one side eäsy anew.

Dora. Cannot you understand plain words, Mr. Dobson? I tell you, it cannot be.

Dobson. Eh, lass! Thy feyther eddicated his darters to marry gentlefoälk, and see what's coomed on it.

Dora. That is enough, Farmer Dobson. You have shown me that, though fortune had born *you* into the estate of a gentleman, you would still have been Farmer Dobson. You had better attend to your hayfield. Good afternoon.   [*Exit.*

Dobson. 'Farmer Dobson!' Well, I be Farmer Dobson; but I thinks Farmer Dobson's dog 'ud ha' knaw'd better nor to cast her sister's misfortin inter 'er teeth arter she'd been a-reädin' me the letter wi' 'er voice a-shaäkin', and the drop in 'er eye. Theer she goäs! Shall I foller 'er and ax 'er to maäke it up? Noä, not yet. Let 'er cool upon it; I likes 'er all the better fur taäkin' me down, like a laädy, as she be. Farmer Dobson! I be Farmer Dobson, sewer anew; but if iver I cooms upo' Gentleman Hedgar ageän, and doänt laäy my cartwhip athurt

'is shou'ders, why then I beänt Farmer Dobson, but summun else—blaäme't if I beänt!

Enter HAYMAKERS *with a load of hay*

The last on it, eh?

1st Haymaker. Yeas.

Dobson. Hoäm wi' it, then.
       [*Exit surlily.*

1st Haymaker. Well, it be the last loäd hoäm.

2nd Haymaker. Yeas, an' owd Dobson should be glad on it. What maäkes 'im allus sa glum?

Sally Allen. Glum! he be wuss nor glum. He coom'd up to me yisterdaäy i' the haäyfield, when meä and my sweet'art was a workin' along o' one side wi' one another, and he sent 'im awaäy to t'other end o' the field; and when I axed 'im why, he telled me 'at sweet'arts niver worked well together; and I telled '*im* 'at sweet'arts allus worked best togither; and then he called me a rude naäme, and I can't abide 'im.

James. Why, lass, doänt tha knaw he be sweet upo' Dora Steer, and she weänt sa much as look at 'im? And wheniver 'e sees two sweet'arts togither like thou and me, Sally, he be fit to bust hissen wi' spites and jalousies.

Sally. Let 'im bust hissen, then, for owt *I* cares.

1st Haymaker. Well but, as I said afoor, it be the last loäd hoäm; do thou and thy sweet'art sing us hoäm to supper—'The Last Loäd Hoäm.'

All. Ay! 'The Last Loäd Hoäm.'

Song

What did ye do, and what did ye saäy,
Wi' the wild white rose, an' the woodbine
    sa gaäy,
An' the midders all mow'd, an' the sky sa
    blue—
What did ye saäy, and what did ye do,
When ye thowt there were nawbody
    watchin' o' you,
And you an' your Sally was forkin' the
    haäy,
    At the end of the daäy,
    For the last loäd hoäm?

What did we do, and what did we saäy,
Wi, the briar sa green, an' the willer sa
  graäy,
An' the midders all mow'd, an' the sky sa
  blue—
Do ye think I be gawin' to tell it to you,
What we mowt saäy, and what we mowt do,
When me an' my Sally was forkin' the
  haäy,
  At the end of the daäy,
  For the last loäd hoäm?

But what did ye saäy, and what did ye do,
Wi' the butterflies out, and the swallers at
  plaäy,
An' the midders all mow'd, an' the sky sa
  blue?
Why, coom then, owd feller, I'll tell it to
  you;
For me an' my Sally we sweär'd to be true,
To be true to each other, let 'appen what
  maäy,
  Till the end of the daäy
  And the last loäd hoäm.

All. Well sung!
James. Fanny be the naäme i' the song,
but I swopt it fur *she.* [*Pointing to* SALLY.
Sally. Let ma aloän afoor foälk, wilt tha?
1*st Haymaker.* Ye shall sing that ageän
to-night, fur owd Dobson 'll gi'e us a bit
o' supper.
Sally. I weänt goä to owd Dobson; he
wur rude to me i' tha haäyfield, and he'll be
rude to me ageän to-night. Owd Steer's
gotten all his grass down and wants a hand,
and I'll goä to him.
1*st Haymaker.* Owd Steer gi'es nubbut
cowd tea to '*is* men, and owd Dobson gi'es
beer.
Sally. But I'd like owd Steer's cowd tea
better nor Dobson's beer. Good-bye.
                        [*Going.*
James. Gi'e us a buss fust, lass.
Sally. I tell'd tha to let ma aloän!
James. Why, wasn't thou and me a-bus-
sin' o' one another t'other side o' the
haäycock, when owd Dobson coom'd upo'
us? I can't let tha aloän if I would, Sally.
                 [*Offering to kiss her.*
Sally. Git along wi' ye, do!   [*Exit.*
    [*All laugh; exeunt singing.*

'To be true to each other, let 'appen what
  maäy,
  Till the end o' the daäy
  An' the last loäd hoäm.'

Enter HAROLD

Harold. Not Harold! 'Philip Edgar,
  Philip Edgar!'
Her phantom call'd me by the name she
  loved.
I told her I should hear her from the grave.
Ay! yonder is her casement. I remember
Her bright face beaming starlike down
  upon me
Thro' that rich cloud of blossom. Since I
  left her
Here weeping, I have ranged the world,
  and sat
Thro' every sensual course of that full
  feast
That leaves but emptiness.

             Song

'To be true to each other, let 'appen what
  maäy,
  To the end o' the daäy
  An' the last loäd hoäm.'

Harold. Poor Eva! O my God, if man be
  only
A willy-nilly current of sensations—
Reaction needs must follow revel—yet—
Why feel remorse, he, knowing that he
  must have
Moved in the iron grooves of Destiny?
Remorse then is a part of Destiny,
Nature a liar, making us feel guilty
Of her own faults.
         My grandfather—of him
They say, that women—
          O this mortal house,
Which we are born into, is haunted by
The ghosts of the dead passions of dead
  men;
And these take flesh again with our own
  flesh,
And bring us to confusion.
            He was only
A poor philosopher who call'd the mind
Of children a blank page, a *tabula rasa.*
There, there, is written in invisible inks

'Lust, Prodigality, Covetousness, Craft,
Cowardice, Murder'—and the heat and
    fire
Of life will bring them out, and black
    enough,
So the child grow to manhood: better
    death
With our first wail than life—

Song (further off)
'Till the end o' the daäy
An' the last loäd hoäm,
    Loäd hoäm.'

This bridge again!   (*Steps on the bridge.*)
    How often have I stood
With Eva here! The brook among its
    flowers!
Forget-me-not, meadowsweet, willow-
    herb.
I had some smattering of science then,
Taught her the learned names, anatomized
The flowers for her—and now I only wish
This pool were deep enough, that I might
    plunge
And lose myself for ever.

Enter DAN SMITH (*singing*)
Gee oop! whoä! Gee oop! whoä!
Scizzars an' Pumpy was good uns to goä
    Thruf slush an' squad
    When roäds was bad,
But hallus ud stop at the Vine-an'-the-
    Hop,
Fur boäth on 'em knawed as well as
    mysen
That beer be as good fur 'erses as men.
Gee oop! whoä! Gee oop! whoä!
Scizzars an' Pumpy was good uns to goä.

The beer's gotten oop into my 'eäd.
S'iver I mun git along back to the farm,
fur she tell'd ma to taäke the cart to Littlechester.

Enter DORA
Half an hour late! why are you loitering
here? Away with you at once.
    [*Exit* DAN SMITH.
(*Seeing* HAROLD *on bridge*)
    Some madman, is it,
Gesticulating there upon the bridge?
I am half afraid to pass.

Harold.   Sometimes I wonder,
When man has surely learnt at last that all
His old-world faith, the blossom of his
    youth,
Has faded, falling fruitless—whether then
All of us, all at once, may not be seized
With some fierce passion, not so much for
    Death
As against Life! all, all, into the dark—
No more!—and science now could drug
    and balm us
Back into nescience with as little pain
As it is to fall asleep.
    This beggarly life,
This poor, flat, hedged-in field—no
    distance—this
Hollow Pandora-box,
With all the pleasures flown, not even Hope
Left at the bottom!
    Superstitious fool,
What brought me here? To see her grave?
    her ghost?
Her ghost is everyway about me here.
Dora (*coming forward*). Allow me, sir, to
    pass you.
Harold.   Eva!
Dora.   Eva!
Harold. What are you? Where do you
    come from?
Dora.   From the farm
Here, close at hand.
Harold.   Are you—you are—that
    Dora,
The sister. I have heard of you. The like-
    ness
Is very striking.
Dora.   You knew Eva, then?
Harold. Yes—I was thinking of her
    when—O yes,
Many years back, and never since have met
Her equal for pure innocence of nature,
And loveliness of feature.
Dora.   No, nor I.
Harold. Except, indeed, I have found it
    once again
In your own self.
Dora.   You flatter me. Dear Eva
Was always thought the prettier.
Harold.   And *her* charm
Of voice is also yours; and I was brooding
Upon a great unhappiness when you spoke.

Dora. Indeed, you seem'd in trouble, sir.
Harold.   And you
Seem my good angel who may help me
  from it.
Dora (*aside*). How worn he looks, poor
  man! who is it, I wonder.
How can I help him? (*Aloud.*) Might I ask
  your name?
Harold. Harold.
Dora. I never heard her mention you.
Harold. I met her first at a farm in
  Cumberland—
Her uncle's.
  Dora. She was there six years ago.
  Harold. And if she never mention'd me,
  perhaps
The painful circumstances which I heard—
I will not vex you by repeating them—
Only last week at Littlechester, drove me
From out her memory. She has dis-
  appear'd,
They told me, from the farm—and darker
  news.
  Dora. She has disappear'd, poor darling,
  from the world—
Left but one dreadful line to say, that we
Should find her in the river; and we
  dragg'd
The Littlechester river all in vain:
Have sorrow'd for her all these years in
  vain.
And my poor father, utterly broken down
By losing her—she was his favourite
  child—
Has let his farm, all his affairs, I fear,
But for the slender help that I can give,
Fall into ruin. Ah! that villain, Edgar,
If he should ever show his face among us,
Our men and boys would hoot him, stone
  him, hunt him
With pitchforks off the farm, for all of
  them
Loved her, and she was worthy of all love.
  Harold. They say, we should forgive our
  enemies.
  Dora. Ay, if the wretch were dead I
  might forgive him;
We know not whether he be dead or living.
  Harold. What Edgar?
  Dora.   Philip Edgar of Toft Hall
In Somerset. Perhaps you know him?

Harold.   Slightly.
(*Aside.*) Ay, for how slightly have I known
  myself.
  Dora. This Edgar, then, is living?
  Harold.   Living? well—
One Philip Edgar of Toft Hall in Somer-
  set
Is lately dead.
  Dora. Dead!—is there more than one?
  Harold. Nay—now—not one, (*aside*) for
  I am Philip Harold.
  Dora. That one, is he then—dead!
  Harold. (*Aside.*)   My father's death,
Let her believe it mine; this, for the
  moment,
Will leave me a free field.
  Dora.   Dead! and this world
Is brighter for his absence as that other
Is darker for his presence.
  Harold.   Is not this
To speak too pitilessly of the dead?
  Dora. My five-years' anger cannot die at
  once,
Not all at once with death and him. I
  trust
I shall forgive him—by-and-by—not now.
O sir, you seem to have a heart; if you
Had seen us that wild morning when we
  found
Her bed unslept in, storm and shower
  lashing
Her casement, her poor spaniel wailing
  for her,
That desolate letter, blotted with her tears,
Which told us we should never see her
  more—
Our old nurse crying as if for her own
  child,
My father stricken with his first paralysis,
And then with blindness—had you been
  one of us
And seen all this, then you would know it
  is not
So easy to forgive—even the dead.
  Harold. But sure am I that of your
  gentleness
You will forgive him. She, you mourn for,
  seem'd
A miracle of gentleness—would not blur
A moth's wing by the touching; would not
  crush

The fly that drew her blood; and, were she
    living,
Would not—if penitent—have denied him
    her
Forgiveness. And perhaps the man himself,
When hearing of that piteous death, has
    suffer'd
More than we know. But wherefore waste
    your heart
In looking on a chill and changeless Past?
Iron will fuse, and marble melt; the Past
Remains the Past. But you are young, and
    —pardon me—
As lovely as your sister. Who can tell
What golden hours, with what full hands,
    may be
Waiting you in the distance? Might I call
Upon your father—I have seen the world—
And cheer his blindness with a traveller's
    tales?
Dora. Call if you will, and when you
    will. I cannot
Well answer for my father; but if you
Can tell me anything of our sweet Eva
When in her brighter girlhood, I at least
Will bid you welcome, and will listen to
    you.
Now I must go.
    Harold. But give me first your hand:
I do not dare, like an old friend, to shake it.
I kiss it as a prelude to that privilege
When you shall know me better.
    Dora.   (*Aside.*) How beautiful
His manners are, and how unlike the
    farmer's!
You are staying here?
    Harold.   Yes, at the wayside inn
Close by that alder-island in your brook,
'The Angler's Home.'
    Dora.   Are *you* one?
    Harold.   No, but I
Take some delight in sketching, and the
    country
Has many charms, altho' the inhabitants
Seem semi-barbarous.
    Dora.   I am glad it pleases you;
Yet I, born here, not only love the country,
But its inhabitants too; and you, I doubt
    not,
Would take to them as kindly, if you cared
To live some time among them.

Harold.   If I did,
Then one at least of its inhabitants
Might have more charm for me than all the
    country.
Dora. That one, then, should be grateful
    for your preference.
Harold. I cannot tell, tho' standing in
    her presence.
(*Aside.*) She colours!
    Dora.   Sir!
    Harold.   Be not afraid of me,
For these are no conventional flourishes.
I do most earnestly assure you that
Your likeness——
        [*Shouts and cries without.*
Dora. What was that? my poor blind
    father—

Enter FARMING MAN

Farming Man. Miss Dora, Dan Smith's
cart hes runned ower a laädy i' the holler
laäne, and they ha' ta'en the body up inter
your chaumber, and they be all a-callin'
for ye.
    Dora. The body!—Heavens! I come!
    Harold.   But you are trembling.
Allow me to go with you to the farm.
        [*Exeunt.*

Enter DOBSON

Dobson. What feller wur it as 'a been
a-talkin' fur haäfe an hour wi' my Dora?
(*Looking after him.*) Seeäms I ommost
knaws the back on 'im—drest like a gentleman, too. Damn all gentlemen, says I! I
should ha' thowt they'd hed anew o' gentlefoälk, as I telled 'er to-daäy when she fell
foul upo' me.
    Minds ma o' summun. I could sweär to
that; but that be all one, fur I haätes 'im
afoor I knaws what 'e be. Theer! he turns
round. Philip Hedgar o' Soomerset! Philip
Hedgar o' Soomerset!—Noä—yeas—thaw
the feller's gone and maäde such a litter of
his faäce.
    Eh lad, if it be thou, I'll Philip tha!
a-plaäyin' the saäme gaäme wi' my Dora—
I'll Soomerset tha.
    I'd like to drag 'im thruff the hersepond,
and she to be a-lookin' at it. I'd like to
leather 'im black and blue, and she to be

a-laughin' at it. I'd like to fell 'im as deäd as a bullock! (*Clenching his fist.*) But what 'ud she saäy to that? She telled me once not to meddle wi' 'im, and now she be fallen out wi' ma, and I can't coom at 'er.

It mun be *him*. Noä! Fur she'd niver 'a been talkin' haäfe an hour wi' the divil 'at killed her oän sister, or she beänt Dora Steer.

Yeas! Fur she niver knawed 'is faäce when 'e wur 'ere afoor; but I'll maäke 'er knaw! I'll maäke 'er knaw!

Enter HAROLD

Naäy, but I mun git out on 'is waäy now, or I shall be the death on 'im. [*Exit.*

Harold. How the clown glared at me! that Dobbins, is it, With whom I used to jar? but can he trace me Thro' five years' absence, and my change of name, The tan of southern summers and the beard? I may as well avoid him.
Ladylike!
Lilylike in her stateliness and sweetness! How came she by it?—a daughter of the fields, This Dora! She gave her hand, unask'd, at the farm-gate; I almost think she half return'd the pressure Of mine. What, I that held the orange blossom Dark as the yew? but may not those, who march Before their age, turn back at times, and make Courtesy to custom? and now the stronger motive, Misnamed free-will—the crowd would call it conscience—Moves me—to what? I am dreaming; for the past Look'd thro' the present, Eva's eyes thro' hers—A spell upon me! Surely I loved Eva More than I knew! or is it but the past That brightens in retiring? Oh, last night, Tired, pacing my new lands at Little-chester, I dozed upon the bridge, and the black river Flow'd thro' my dreams—if dreams they were. She rose From the foul flood and pointed toward the farm, And her cry rang to me across the years, 'I call you, Philip Edgar, Philip Edgar! Come, you will set all right again, and father Will not die miserable.' I could make his age A comfort to him—so be more at peace With mine own self. Some of my former friends Would find my logic faulty; let them. Colour Flows thro' my life again, and I have lighted On a new pleasure. Anyhow we must Move in the line of least resistance when The stronger motive rules.
But she hates Edgar. May not this Dobbins, or some other, spy Edgar in Harold? Well then, I must make her Love Harold first, and then she will forgive Edgar for Harold's sake. She said herself She would forgive him, by-and-by, not now—For her own sake *then*, if not for mine—not now—But by-and-by.

Enter DOBSON *behind*

Dobson. By-and-by—eh, lad, dosta knaw this paäper? Ye dropt it upo' the road. 'Philip Edgar, Esq.' Ay, you be a pretty squire. I ha' fun' ye out, I hev. Eh, lad, dosta knaw what tha meäns wi' by-and-by? Fur if ye be goin' to sarve our Dora as ye sarved our Eva—then, by-and-by, if she weänt listen to me when I be a-tryin' to saäve 'er—if she weänt—look to thysen, for, by the Lord, I'd think na moor o' maäkin' an end o' tha nor a carrion craw—noä—thaw they hanged ma at 'Size fur it.

Harold. Dobbins, I think!

Dobson. I beänt Dobbins.

Harold. Nor am I Edgar, my good fellow.

Dobson. Tha lies! What hasta been saäyin' to *my* Dora?

Harold. I have been telling her of the death of one Philip Edgar of Toft Hall, Somerset.

Dobson. Tha lies!

Harold (*pulling out a newspaper*). Well, my man, it seems that you can read. Look there—under the deaths.

Dobson. 'O' the 17th, Philip Edgar, o' Toft Hall, Soomerset.' How coom thou to be sa like 'im, then?

Harold. Naturally enough; for I am closely related to the dead man's family.

Dobson. An' ow coom thou by the letter to 'im?

Harold. Naturally again; for as I used to transact all his business for him, I had to look over his letters. Now then, see these (*takes out letters*). Half a score of them, all directed to me—Harold.

Dobson. 'Arold! 'Arold! 'Arold, so they be.

Harold. My name is Harold! Good day, Dobbins! [*Exit.*

Dobson. 'Arold! The feller's cleän daäzed, an' maäzed, an' maäted, an' muddled ma. Deäd! It mun be true, fur it wur i' print as black as owt. Naäy, but 'Good daäy, Dobbins.' Why, that wur the very twang on 'im. Eh, lad, but whether thou be Hedgar, or Hedgar's business man, thou hesn't naw business 'ere wi' *my* Dora, as I knaws on, an' whether thou calls thysen Hedgar or Harold, if thou stick to she I'll stick to thee—stick to tha like a weasel to a rabbit, I will. Ay! and I'd like to shoot tha like a rabbit an' all. 'Good daäy, Dobbins.' Dang tha!

ACT III

Scene

A Room in Steer's House. Door leading into Bedroom at the back

Dora (*ringing a handbell*). Milly!

Enter MILLY

Milly. The little 'ymn? Yeäs, Miss; but I wur so ta'en up wi' leädin' the owd man about all the blessed murnin' 'at I ha' nobbut larned mysen haäfe on it.

'O man, forgive thy mortal foe,
Nor ever strike him blow for blow;
For all the souls on earth that live
To be forgiven must forgive.
Forgive him seventy times and seven;
For all the blessed souls in Heaven
Are both forgivers and forgiven.'

But I'll git the book ageän, and larn mysen the rest, and saäy it to ye afoor dark; ye ringed fur that, Miss, didn't ye?

Dora. No, Milly; but if the farming men be come for their wages, to send them up to me.

Milly. Yeäs, Miss.   [*Exit.*

Dora (*sitting at desk counting money*). Enough at any rate for the present. (*Enter* FARMING MEN.) Good afternoon, my friends. I am sorry Mr. Steer still continues too unwell to attend to you, but the schoolmaster looked to the paying you your wages when I was away, didn't he?

Men. Yeäs; and thanks to ye.

Dora. Some of our workmen have left us, but he sent me an alphabetical list of those that remain, so, Allen, I may as well begin with you.

Allen (*with his hand to his ear*). Halfabitical! Taäke one o' the young 'uns fust, Miss, fur I be a bit deaf, and I wur hallus scaäred by a big word; leästwaäys, I should be wi' a lawyer.

Dora. I spoke of your names, Allen, as they are arranged here (*shows book*)—according to their first letters.

Allen. Letters! Yeas, I sees now. Them be what they larns the childer' at school, but I were burn afoor schoolin-time.

Dora. But, Allen, tho' you can't read, you could whitewash that cottage of yours where your grandson had the fever.

Allen. I'll hev it done o' Monday.

Dora. Else if the fever spread, the parish will have to thank you for it.

Allen. Meä? why, it be the Lord's doin', noän o' mine; d'ye think *I'd* gi'e 'em the fever? But I thanks ye all the saäme, Miss. (*Takes money.*)

Dora (*calling out names*). Higgins, Jackson,

Luscombe, Nokes, Oldham, Skipworth!
(*All take money*.) Did you find that you
worked at all the worse upon the cold
tea than you would have done upon the
beer?

Higgins. Noä, Miss; we worked naw
wuss upo' the cowd tea; but we'd ha'
worked better upo' the beer.

Dora. Come, come, you worked well
enough, and I am much obliged to all of
you. There's for you, and you, and you.
Count the money and see if it's all right.

Men. All right, Miss; and thank ye
kindly.

[*Exeunt* LUSCOMBE, NOKES, OLDHAM,
SKIPWORTH.

Dora. Dan Smith, my father and I forgave you stealing our coals.

[DAN SMITH *advances to* DORA.

Dan Smith (*bellowing*). Whoy, O lor,
Miss! that wur sa long back, and the walls
sa thin, and the winders brokken, and the
weather sa cowd, and my missus a-gittin'
ower 'er lyin'-in.

Dora. Didn't I say that we had forgiven
you? But, Dan Smith, they tell me that
you—and you have six children—spent all
your last Saturday's wages at the ale-
house; that you were stupid drunk all
Sunday, and so ill in consequence all Monday, that you did not come into the hayfield. Why should I pay you your full
wages?

Dan Smith. I be ready to taäke the
pledge.

Dora. And as ready to break it again.
Besides it was you that were driving the
cart—and I fear you were tipsy then, too
—when you lamed the lady in the hollow
lane.

Dan Smith (*bellowing*). O lor, Miss! noä,
noä, noä! Ye sees the holler laäne be hallus
sa dark i' the arternoon, and wheere the
big eshtree cuts athurt it, it gi'es a turn like,
and 'ow should I see to laäme the laädy,
and meä coomin' along pretty sharp an' all?

Dora. Well, there are your wages; the
next time you waste them at a pot-house
you get no more from me. (*Exit* DAN
SMITH.) Sally Allen, you worked for Mr.
Dobson, didn't you?

Sally (*advancing*). Yeäs, Miss; but he
wur so rough wi' ma, I couldn't abide 'im.

Dora. Why should he be rough with
you? You are as good as a man in the hayfield. What's become of your brother?

Sally. 'Listed for a soädger, Miss, i' the
Queen's Real Hard Tillery.

Dora. And your sweetheart—when are
you and he to be married?

Sally. At Michaelmas, Miss, please God.

Dora. You are an honest pair. I will
come to your wedding.

Sally. An' I thanks ye fur that, Miss,
moor nor fur the waäge.

(*Going—returns.*) 'A cotched ma about
the waäist, Miss, when 'e wur 'ere afoor,
an' axed ma to be 'is little sweetart, an soä
I knaw'd 'im when I seed 'im ageän an I
telled feyther on 'im.

Dora. What is all this, Allen?

Allen. Why, Miss Dora, meä and my
maätes, us three, we wants to hev three
words wi' ye.

Higgins. That be 'im, and meä, Miss.

Jackson. An' meä, Miss.

Allen. An' we weänt mention naw
naämes, we'd a lief talk o' the Divil afoor
ye as 'im, fur they says the master goäs
cleän off his 'eäd when he 'eärs the naäme
on 'im; but us three, arter Sally'd telled us
on 'im, we fun' 'im out a-walkin' i' West
Field wi' a white 'at, nine o'clock, upo'
Tuesday murnin', and all on us, wi' your
leave, we wants to leather 'im.

Dora. Who?

Allen. Him as did the mischief here, five
year' sin'.

Dora. Mr. Edgar?

Allen. Theer, Miss! You ha' naämed
'im—not me.

Dora. He's dead, man—dead; gone to
his account—dead and buried.

Allen. I beänt sa sewer o' that, fur Sally
knaw'd 'im; Now then?

Dora. Yes; it was in the Somersetshire
papers.

Allen. Then yon mun be his brother, an'
we'll leather 'im.

Dora. I never heard that he had a
brother. Some foolish mistake of Sally's;
but what! would you beat a man for his

brother's fault? That were a wild justice indeed. Let bygones be bygones. Go home! Good-night! (*All exeunt.*) I have once more paid them all. The work of the farm will go on still, but for how long? We are almost at the bottom of the well: little more to be drawn from it—and what then? Encumbered as we are, who would lend us anything? We shall have to sell all the land, which Father, for a whole life, has been getting together, again, and that, I am sure, would be the death of him. What am I to do? Farmer Dobson, were I to marry him, has promised to keep our heads above water; and the man has doubtless a good heart, and a true and lasting love for me: yet—though I can be sorry for him—as the good Sally says, 'I can't abide him'—almost brutal, and matched with my Harold is like a hedge thistle by a garden rose. But then, he, too—will he ever be of one faith with his wife? which is my dream of a true marriage. Can I fancy him kneeling with me, and uttering the same prayer; standing up side by side with me, and singing the same hymn? I fear not. Have I done wisely, then, in accepting him? But may not a girl's love-dream have too much romance in it to be realised all at once, or altogether, or anywhere but in Heaven? And yet I had once a vision of a pure and perfect marriage, where the man and the woman, only differing as the stronger and the weaker, should walk hand in hand together down this valley of tears, as they call it so truly, to the grave at the bottom, and lie down there together in the darkness which would seem but for a moment, to be wakened again together by the light of the resurrection, and no more partings for ever and for ever. (*Walks up and down. She sings.*)

'O happy lark, that warblest high
  Above thy lowly nest,
O brook, that brawlest merrily by
  Thro' fields that once were blest,
O tower spiring to the sky,
  O graves in daisies drest,
O Love and Life, how weary am I,
  And how I long for rest.'

There, there, I am a fool! Tears! I have sometimes been moved to tears by a chapter of fine writing in a novel; but what have I to do with tears now? All depends on me —Father, this poor girl, the farm, everything; and they both love me—I am all in all to both; and he loves me too, I am quite sure of that. Courage, courage! and all will go well. (*Goes to bedroom door; opens it.*) How dark your room is! Let me bring you in here where there is still full daylight. (*Brings* EVA *forward.*) Why, you look better.

Eva. And I feel so much better, that I trust I may be able by-and-by to help you in the business of the farm; but I must not be known yet. Has anyone found me out, Dora?

Dora. Oh, no; you kept your veil too close for that when they carried you in; since then, no one has seen you but myself.

Eva. Yes—this Milly.

Dora. Poor blind Father's little guide, Milly, who came to us three years after you were gone, how should she know you? But now that you have been brought to us as it were from the grave, dearest Eva, and have been here so long, will you not speak with Father to-day?

Eva. Do you think that I may? No, not yet. I am not equal to it yet.

Dora. Why? Do you still suffer from your fall in the hollow lane?

Eva. Bruised; but no bones broken.

Dora. I have always told Father that the huge old ashtree there would cause an accident some day; but he would never cut it down, because one of the Steers had planted it there in former times.

Eva. If it had killed one of the Steers there the other day, it might have been better for her, for him, and for you.

Dora. Come, come, keep a good heart! Better for me! That's good. How better for me?

Eva. You tell me you have a lover. Will he not fly from you if he learn the story of my shame and that I am still living?

Dora. No; I am sure that when we are married he will be willing that you and Father should live with us; for, indeed, he tells me that he met you once in the old times, and was much taken with you, my dear.

Eva. Taken with me; who was he? Have you told him I am here?

Dora. No; do you wish it?

Eva. See, Dora; you yourself are ashamed of me (*weeps*), and I do not wonder at it.

Dora. But I should wonder at myself if it were so. Have we not been all in all to one another from the time when we first peeped into the bird's nest, waded in the brook, ran after the butterflies, and prattled to each other that we would marry fine gentlemen, and played at being fine ladies?

Eva. That last was my Father's fault, poor man. And this lover of yours—this Mr. Harold—is a gentleman?

Dora. That he is, from head to foot. I do believe I lost my heart to him the very first time we met, and I love him so much—

Eva. Poor Dora!

Dora. That I dare not tell him how much I love him.

Eva. Better not. Has he offered you marriage, this gentleman?

Dora. Could I love him else?

Eva. And are you quite sure that after marriage this gentleman will not be shamed of his poor farmer's daughter among the ladies in his drawing-room?

Dora. Shamed of me in a drawing-room! Wasn't Miss Vavasour our schoolmistress at Littlechester, a lady born? Were not our fellow-pupils all ladies? Wasn't dear mother herself at least by one side a lady? Can't I speak like a lady; pen a letter like a lady; talk a little French like a lady; play a little like a lady? Can't a girl when she loves her husband, and he her, make herself anything he wishes her to be? Shamed of me in a drawing-room, indeed! See here! 'I hope your Lordship is quite recovered of your gout?' (*Curtsies.*) 'Will your Ladyship ride to cover to-day?' (*Curtsies.*) I can recommend our Voltigeur.' 'I am sorry that we could not attend your Grace's party on the 10th!' (*Curtsies.*) There, I am glad my nonsense has made you smile!

Eva. I have heard that 'your Lordship,' and 'your Ladyship,' and 'your Grace' are all growing old-fashioned!

Dora. But the love of sister for sister can never be old-fashioned. I have been unwilling to trouble you with questions, but you seem somewhat better to-day. We found a letter in your bedroom torn into bits. I couldn't make it out. What was it?

Eva. From him! from him! He said we had been most happy together, and he trusted that some time we should meet again, for he had not forgotten his promise to come when I called him. But that was a mockery, you know, for he gave me no address, and there was no word of marriage; and, O Dora, he signed himself 'Yours gratefully'—fancy, Dora, 'gratefully'! 'Yours gratefully'!

Dora. Infamous wretch! (*Aside.*) Shall I tell her he is dead? No; she is still too feeble.

Eva. Hark! Dora, some one is coming. I cannot and I will not see anybody.

Dora. It is only Milly.

Enter MILLY, *with basket of roses*

Dora. Well, Milly, why do you come in so roughly? The sick lady here might have been asleep.

Milly. Pleäse, Miss, Mr. Dobson telled me to saäy he's browt some of Miss Eva's roses for the sick iaädy to smell on.

Dora. Take them, dear. Say that the sick lady thanks him! Is he here?

Milly. Yeäs, Miss; and he wants to speak to ye partic'lar.

Dora. Tell him I cannot leave the sick lady just yet.

Milly. Yeäs, Miss; but he says he wants to tell ye summut very partic'lar.

Dora. Not to-day. What are you staying for?

Milly. Why, Miss, I be afeard I shall set him a-sweäring like onythink.

Dora. And what harm will that do you, so that you do not copy his bad manners? Go, child. (*Exit* MILLY.) But, Eva, why did you write 'Seek me at the bottom of the river'?

Eva. Why? because I meant it!—that dreadful night! that lonely walk to Littlechester, the rain beating in my face all the way, dead midnight when I came upon the bridge; the river, black, slimy, swirling under me in the lamplight, by the rotten wharfs—but I was so mad, that I mounted upon the parapet——

Dora. You make me shudder!

Eva. To fling myself over, when I heard a voice, 'Girl, what are you doing there?' It was a Sister of Mercy, come from the death-bed of a pauper, who had died in his misery blessing God, and the Sister took me to her house, and bit by bit—for she promised secrecy—I told her all.

Dora. And what then?

Eva. She would have persuaded me to come back here, but I couldn't. Then she got me a place as nursery governess, and when the children grew too old for me, and I asked her once more to help me, once more she said, 'Go home;' but I hadn't the heart or face to do it. And then—what would Father say? I sank so low that I went into service—the drudge of a lodging-house—and when the mistress died, and I appealed to the Sister again, her answer— I think I have it about me—yes, there it is!

Dora (reads). 'My dear Child,—I can do no more for you. I have done wrong in keeping your secret; your Father must be now in extreme old age. Go back to him and ask his forgiveness before he dies.— SISTER AGATHA.' Sister Agatha is right. Don't you long for Father's forgiveness!

Eva. I would almost die to have it!

Dora. And he may die before he gives it; may drop off any day, any hour. You must see him at once. (*Rings bell. Enter* MILLY.) Milly, my dear, how did you leave Mr. Steer?

Milly. He's been a-moänin' and a-groänin' in 'is sleep, but I thinks he be wakkenin' oop.

Dora. Tell him that I and the lady here wish to see him. You see she is lamed, and cannot go down to him.

Milly. Yeäs, Miss, I will.

[*Exit* MILLY.

Dora. I ought to prepare you. You must not expect to find our Father as he was five years ago. He is much altered; but I

trust that your return—for you know, my dear, you were always his favourite—will give him, as they say, a new lease of life.

Eva (clinging to DORA). Oh, Dora, Dora!

Enter STEER *led by* MILLY

Steer. Hes the cow cawved?

Dora. No, Father.

Steer. Be the colt deäd?

Dora. No, Father.

Steer. He wur sa bellows'd out wi' the wind this murnin', 'at I tell'd 'em to gallop 'im. Be he deäd?

Dora. Not that I know.

Steer. What hasta sent fur me, then, fur?

Dora (taking STEER'S *arm*). Well, Father, I have a surprise for you.

Steer. I ha niver been surprised but once i' my life, and I went blind upon it.

Dora. Eva has come home.

Steer. Hoäm? fro' the bottom o' the river?

Dora. No, Father, that was a mistake. She's here again.

Steer. The Steers was all gentlefoälks i' the owd times, an' I worked early an' laäte to maäke 'em all gentlefoälks ageän. The land belonged to the Steers i' the owd times, an' it belongs to the Steers ageän: I bowt it back ageän; but I couldn't buy my darter back ageän when she lost hersen, could I? I eddicated boäth on 'em to marry gentlemen, an' one on 'em went an' lost hersen i' the river.

Dora. No, Father, she's here.

Steer. Here! she moänt coom here. What would her mother saäy? If it be her ghoäst, we mun abide it. We can't keep a ghoäst out.

Eva (falling at his feet). O forgive me! forgive me!

Steer. Who said that? Taäke me awaäy, little gell. It be one o' my bad daäys.

[*Exit* STEER *led by* MILLY.

Dora (smoothing EVA'S *forehead*). Be not so cast down, my sweet Eva. You heard him say it was one of his bad days. He will be sure to know you to-morrow.

Eva. It is almost the last of my bad days, I think. I am very faint. I must lie down. Give me your arm. Lead me back again.

[DORA *takes* EVA *into inner room.*

Enter MILLY

Milly. Miss Dora! Miss Dora!

Dora (returning and leaving the bedroom door ajar). Quiet! quiet! What is it?

Milly. Mr. 'Arold, Miss.

Dora. Below?

Milly. Yeäs, Miss. He be saäyin' a word to the owd man, but he'll coom up if ye lets 'im.

Dora. Tell him, then, that I'm waiting for him.

Milly. Yeäs, Miss.

[*Exit.* DORA *sits pensively and waits.*

Enter HAROLD

Harold. You are pale, my Dora! but the ruddiest cheek
That ever charm'd the plowman of your wolds
Might wish its rose a lily, could it look
But half as lovely. I was speaking with
Your father, asking his consent—you wish'd me—
That we should marry: he would answer nothing,
I could make nothing of him; but, my flower,
You look so weary and so worn! What is it
Has put you out of heart?

Dora.   It puts me in heart
Again to see you; but indeed the state
Of my poor father puts me out of heart.
Is yours yet living?

Harold. No—I told you.

Dora.   When?

Harold. Confusion!—Ah well, well! the state we all
Must come to in our spring-and-winter world
If we live long enough! and poor Steer looks
The very type of Age in a picture, bow'd
To the earth he came from, to the grave he goes to,
Beneath the burthen of years.

Dora.   More like the picture
Of Christian in my 'Pilgrim's Progress' here,
Bow'd to the dust beneath the burthen of sin.

Harold. Sin! What sin?

Dora.   Not his own.

Harold.   That nursery-tale
Still read, then?

Dora. Yes; our carters and our shepherds
Still find a comfort there.

Harold.   Carters and shepherds!

Dora. Scorn! I hate scorn. A soul with no religion—
My mother used to say that such a one
Was without rudder, anchor, compass—might be
Blown everyway with every gust and wreck
On any rock; and tho' you are good and gentle,
Yet if thro' any want—

Harold.   Of this religion?

Child, read a little history, you will find
The common brotherhood of man has been
Wrong'd by the cruelties of his religions
More than could ever have happen'd thro' the want
Of any or all of them.

Dora.   —But, O dear friend,
If thro' the want of any—I mean the true one—
And pardon me for saying it—you should ever
Be tempted into doing what might seem
Not altogether worthy of you, I think
That I should break my heart, for you have taught me
To love you.

Harold. What is this? some one been stirring
Against me? he, your rustic amourist,
The polish'd Damon of your pastoral here,
This Dobson of your idyll?

Dora.   No, Sir, no!
Did you not tell me he was crazed with jealousy,
Had threaten'd ev'n your life, and would say anything?
Did *I* not promise not to listen to him,
Nor ev'n to see the man?

Harold.   Good; then what is it
That makes you talk so dolefully?

Dora.   I told you—
My father. Well, indeed, a friend just now,

One that has been much wrong'd, whose
   griefs are mine,
Was warning me that if a gentleman
Should wed a farmer's daughter, he would
   be
Sooner or later shamed of her among
The ladies, born his equals.
   Harold.   More fool he!
What I that have been call'd a Socialist,
A Communist, a Nihilist—what you
   will!——
   Dora. What are all these?
   Harold.   Utopian idiotcies.
They did not last three Junes. Such ram-
   pant weeds
Strangle each other, die, and make the soil
For Cæsars, Cromwells, and Napoleons
To root their power in. I have freed myself
From all such dreams, and some will say
   because
I have inherited my Uncle. Let them.
But—shamed of you, my Empress! I
   should prize
The pearl of Beauty, even if I found it
Dark with the soot of slums.
   Dora.   But I can tell you,
We Steers are of old blood, tho' we be
   fallen.
See there our shield. (*Pointing to arms on
   mantelpiece.*)
           For I have heard the Steers
Had land in Saxon times; and your own
   name
Of Harold sounds so English and so old
I am sure you must be proud of it.
   Harold.   Not I!
As yet I scarcely feel it mine. I took it
For some three thousand acres. I have
   land now
And wealth, and lay both at your feet.
   Dora.   And *what* was
Your name before?
   Harold. Come, come, my girl, enough
Of this strange talk. I love you and you me.
True, I have held opinions, hold some still,
Which you would scarce approve of: for
   all that,
I am a man not prone to jealousies,
Caprices, humours, moods; but very ready
To make allowances, and mighty slow
To feel offences. Nay, I do believe

I could forgive—well, almost anything—
And that more freely than your formal
   priest,
Because I know more fully than *he* can
What poor earthworms are all and each
   of us,
Here crawling in this boundless Nature.
   Dora,
If marriage ever brought a woman happi-
   ness
I doubt not I can make you happy.
   Dora.   You make me
Happy already.
   Harold.   And I never said
As much before to any woman living.
   Dora. No?
   Harold. No! by this true kiss, *you* are
   the first
I ever have loved truly.
            [*They kiss each other.*
   Eva (*with a wild cry*). Philip Edgar!
   Harold. The phantom cry! *You*—did
   you hear a cry?
   Dora. She must be crying out 'Edgar' in
   her sleep.
   Harold. Who must be crying out 'Edgar'
   in her sleep?
   Dora. Your pardon for a minute. She
   must be waked.
   Harold. Who must be waked?
   Dora. I am not deaf: you fright me.
What ails you?
   Harold.   Speak.
   Dora.   You know her, Eva.
   Harold.   Eva!
   [EVA *opens the door and stands in the
   entry.*
She!
   Eva. Make her happy, then, and I for-
   give you.   [*Falls dead.*
   Dora. Happy! What? Edgar? Is it so?
   Can it be?
They told me so. Yes, yes! I see it all now.
O she has fainted. Sister, Eva, sister!
He is yours again—he will love *you* again;
I give him back to you again. Look up!
One word, or do but smile! Sweet, do you
   hear me?
         [*Puts her hand on* EVA'S *heart.*
There, there—the heart, O God!—the
   poor young heart

Broken at last—all still—and nothing left
To live for.   [*Falls on body of her sister.*
Harold. Living . . . dead . . . She said
'all still.
Nothing to live for.'
                She—she knows me—now . . .
                (*A pause.*)
She knew me from the first, she juggled
    with me,
She hid this sister, told me she was dead—
I have wasted pity on her—not dead now—
No! acting, playing on me, both of them.
They drag the river for her! no, not they!
Playing on me—not dead now—a swoon—
    a scene—
Yet—how she made her wail as for the
    dead!

Enter MILLY

Milly. Pleäse, Mister 'Arold.
Harold (*roughly*).   Well?
Milly. The owd man's coom'd ageän to
    'issen, an' wants
To hev a word wi' ye about the marriage.
Harold. The what?
Milly.   The marriage.
Harold.   The marriage?
Milly.   Yeäs, the marriage.
Granny says marriages be maäde 'i 'eaven.
Harold. She lies! They are made in Hell.
Child, can't you see?
Tell them to fly for a doctor.
Milly.   O law—yeäs, Sir!
I'll run fur 'im mysen.   [*Exit.*
Harold.   All silent there,
Yes, deathlike! Dead? I dare not look: if
    dead,
Were it best to steal away, to spare myself,
And her too, pain, pain, pain?
                My curse on all
This world of mud, on all its idiot gleams
Of pleasure, all the foul fatalities
That blast our natural passions into pains!

Enter DOBSON

Dobson. You, Master Hedgar, Harold, or
    whativer
They calls ye, for I warrants that ye goäs
By haäfe a scoor o' naämes—out o' the
    chaumber.
                [*Dragging him past the body.*

Harold. Not that way, man! Curse on
    your brutal strength!
I cannot pass that way.
Dobson.   Out o' the chaumber!
I'll mash tha into nowt.
Harold.   The mere wild-beast!
Dobson. Out o' the chaumber, dang tha!
Harold.   Lout, churl, clown!
    [*While they are shouting and strug-
        gling* DORA *rises and comes between
        them.*
Dora (*to* DOBSON). Peace, let him be: it
    is the chamber of Death!
Sir, you are tenfold more a gentleman,
A hundred times more worth a woman's
    love,
Than this, this—but I waste no words
    upon him:
His wickedness is like my wretchedness—
Beyond all language.
                (*To* HAROLD.)
                You—you see her there!
Only fifteen when first you came on her,
And then the sweetest flower of all the
    wolds,
So lovely in the promise of her May,
So winsome in her grace and gaiety,
So loved by all the village people here,
So happy in herself and in her home——
Dobson (*agitated*). Theer, theer! ha'
    done. I can't abeär to see her. [*Exit.*
Dora. A child, and all as trustful as a
    child!
Five years of shame and suffering broke
    the heart
That only beat for you; and he, the father,
Thro' that dishonour which you brought
    upon us,
Has lost his health, his eyesight, even his
    mind.
Harold (*covering his face*). Enough!
Dora. It seem'd so; only there was left
A second daughter, and to her you came
Veiling one sin to act another.
Harold.   No!
You wrong me there! hear, hear me! I
    wish'd, if you-   [*Pauses.*
Dora. If I——
Harold.   Could love me, could be
    brought to love me
As I loved you——

746

Dora.   What then?
Harold.   I wish'd, I hoped
To make, to make——
Dora. What did you hope to make?
Harold. 'Twere best to make an end of
my lost life.
O Dora, Dora!
Dora.   *What* did you hope to make?
Harold. Make, make! I cannot find the
word—forgive it—
Amends.
Dora.   For what? to whom?
Harold.   To him, to you!
          [*Falling at her feet.*
Dora. To *him!* to *me!*
     No, not with all your wealth,
Your land, your life! Out in the fiercest
storm

That ever made earth tremble—he, nor I—
The shelter of *your* roof—not for one
moment—
Nothing from *you!*
Sunk in the deepest pit of pauperism,
Push'd from all doors as if we bore the
plague,
Smitten with fever in the open field,
Laid famine-stricken at the gates of
Death—
Nothing from you!
          But she there—her last word
Forgave—and I forgive you. If you
ever
Forgive yourself, you are even lower and
baser
Than even I can well believe you. Go!
          [*He lies at her feet. Curtain falls.*

THE FORESTERS

ROBIN HOOD AND MAID MARIAN

DRAMATIS PERSONÆ

ROBIN HOOD, *Earl of Huntingdon.*
KING RICHARD, *Cœur de Lion.*
PRINCE JOHN.
LITTLE JOHN, ⎫
WILL SCARLET, ⎪
FRIAR TUCK, ⎬ *Followers of Robin Hood.*
MUCH, ⎪
A JUSTICIARY. ⎭
SHERIFF OF NOTTINGHAM.
ABBOT OF ST. MARY'S.
SIR RICHARD LEA.
WALTER LEA, *son of Sir Richard Lea.*
MAID MARIAN, *daughter of Sir Richard Lea.*
KATE, *attendant on Marian.*
OLD WOMAN.

Retainers, Messengers, Merry Men, Mercenaries, Friars, Beggars, Sailors,
Peasants (men and women), etc.

ACT I

SCENE I. *THE BOND*
SCENES II, III. *THE OUTLAWRY*

SCENE I

The Garden before Sir Richard Lea's Castle

Kate (gathering flowers). These roses for my Lady Marian; these lilies to lighten Sir Richard's black room, where he sits and eats his heart for want of money to pay the Abbot.   [*Sings.*

The warrior Earl of Allendale,
   He loved the Lady Anne;
The lady loved the master well,
   The maid she loved the man.

All in the castle garden,
   Or ever the day began,
The lady gave a rose to the Earl,
   The maid a rose to the man.

'I go to fight in Scotland
   With many a savage clan;'
The lady gave her hand to the Earl,
   The maid her hand to the man.

'Farewell, farewell, my warrior Earl!'
   And ever a tear down ran.
She gave a weeping kiss to the Earl,
   And the maid a kiss to the man.

Enter four ragged RETAINERS

First Retainer. You do well, Mistress Kate, to sing and to gather roses. You be fed with tit-bits, you, and we be dogs that have only the bones, till we be only bones our own selves.

Kate. I am fed with tit-bits no more than you are, but I keep a good heart and make the most of it, and, truth to say, Sir Richard and my Lady Marian fare wellnigh as sparely as their people.

Second Retainer. And look at our suits, out at knee, out at elbow. We be more like scarecrows in a field than decent serving men; and then, I pray you, look at Robin Earl of Huntingdon's men.

First Retainer. She hath looked well at one of 'em, Little John.

Third Retainer. Ay, how fine they be in their liveries, and each of 'em as full of meat as an egg, and as sleek and as round-about as a mellow codlin.

Fourth Retainer. But I be worse off than any of you, for I be lean by nature, and if you cram me crop-full I be little better than Famine in the picture, but if you starve me I be Gaffer Death himself. I would like to show you, Mistress Kate,

748

how bare and spare I be on the rib: I be lanker than an old horse turned out to die on the common.

Kate. Spare me thy spare ribs, I pray thee; but now I ask you all, did none of you love young Walter Lea?

First Retainer. Ay, if he had not gone to fight the king's battles, we should have better battels at home.

Kate. Right as an Oxford scholar, but the boy was taken prisoner by the Moors.

First Retainer. Ay.

Kate. And Sir Richard was told he might be ransomed for two thousand marks in gold.

First Retainer. Ay.

Kate. Then he borrowed the monies from the Abbot of York, the Sheriff's brother. And if they be not paid back at the end of the year, the land goes to the Abbot.

First Retainer. No news of young Walter?

Kate. None, nor of the gold, nor the man who took out the gold: but now ye know why we live so stintedly, and why ye have so few grains to peck at. Sir Richard must scrape and scrape till he get to the land again. Come, come, why do ye loiter here? Carry fresh rushes into the dining-hall, for those that are there, they be so greasy, and smell so vilely that my Lady Marian holds her nose when she steps across it.

Fourth Retainer. Why there, now! that very word 'greasy' hath a kind of unction in it, a smack of relish about it. The rats have gnawed 'em already. I pray Heaven we may not have to take to the rushes.

[*Exeunt.*

Kate. Poor fellows!

The lady gave her hand to the Earl,
The maid her hand to the man.

Enter LITTLE JOHN

Little John. My master, Robin the Earl, is always a-telling us that every man, for the sake of the great blessed Mother in heaven, and for the love of his own little mother on earth, should handle all woman-kind gently, and hold them in all honour, and speak small to 'em, and not scare 'em, but go about to come at their love with all manner of homages, and observances, and circumbendibuses.

Kate. The lady gave a rose to the Earl,
The maid a rose to the man.

Little John (seeing her). O the sacred little thing! What a shape! what lovely arms! A rose to the man! Ay, the man had given her a rose and she gave him another.

Kate. Shall I keep one little rose for Little John? No.

Little John. There, there! You see I was right. She hath a tenderness toward me, but is too shy to show it. It is in her, in the woman, and the man must bring it out of her.

Kate. She gave a weeping kiss to the Earl,
The maid a kiss to the man.

Little John. Did she? But there I am sure the ballad is at fault. It should have told us how the man first kissed the maid. She doesn't see me. Shall I be bold? shall I touch her? shall I give her the first kiss? O sweet Kate, my first love, the first kiss, the first kiss!

Kate (turns and kisses him). Why lookest thou so amazed?

Little John. I cannot tell; but I came to give thee the first kiss, and thou hast given it me.

Kate. But if a man and a maid care for one another, does it matter so much if the maid give the first kiss?

Little John. I cannot tell, but I had sooner have given thee the first kiss. I was dreaming of it all the way hither.

Kate. Dream of it, then, all the way back, for now I will have none of it.

Little John. Nay, now thou hast given me the man's kiss, let me give thee the maid's.

Kate. If thou draw one inch nearer, I will give thee a buffet on the face.

Little John. Wilt thou not give me rather the little rose for Little John?

Kate (throws it down and tramples on it). There!

[KATE, *seeing* MARIAN, *exit hurriedly.*

Enter MARIAN (*singing*)

Love flew in at the window
As Wealth walk'd in at the door.
'You have come for you saw Wealth coming,'
  said I.
But he flutter'd his wings with a sweet little cry,
I'll cleave to you rich or poor.

Wealth dropt out of the window,
Poverty crept thro' the door.
'Well now you would fain follow Wealth,'
  said I,
But he flutter'd his wings as he gave me the lie,
I cling to you all the more.

Little John. Thanks, my lady—inasmuch as I am a true believer in true love myself, and your Ladyship hath sung the old proverb out of fashion.

Marian. Ay but thou hast ruffled my woman, Little John. She hath the fire in her face and the dew in her eyes. I believed thee to be too solemn and formal to be a ruffler. Out upon thee!

Little John. I am no ruffler, my lady; but I pray you, my lady, if a man and a maid love one another, may the maid give the first kiss?

Marian. It will be all the more gracious of her if she do.

Little John. I cannot tell. Manners be so corrupt, and these are the days of Prince John. [*Exit.*

Enter SIR RICHARD LEA (*reading a bond*)

Sir Richard. Marian!

Marian. Father!

Sir Richard. Who parted from thee even now?

Marian. That strange starched stiff creature, Little John, the Earl's man. He would grapple with a lion like the King, and is flustered by a girl's kiss.

Sir Richard. There never was an Earl so true a friend of the people as Lord Robin of Huntingdon.

Marian. A gallant Earl. I love him as I hate John.

Sir Richard. I fear me he hath wasted his revenues in the service of our good king Richard against the party of John, as I have done, as I have done: and where is Richard?

Marian. Cleave to him, father! he will come home at last.

Sir Richard. I trust he will, but if he do not I and thou are but beggars.

Marian. We will be beggar'd then and be true to the King.

Sir Richard. Thou speakest like a fool or a woman. Canst thou endure to be a beggar whose whole life hath been folded like a blossom in the sheath, like a careless sleeper in the down; who never hast felt a want, to whom all things, up to this present, have come as freely as heaven's air and mother's milk?

Marian. Tut, father! I am none of your delicate Norman maidens who can only broider and mayhap ride a-hawking with the help of the men. I can bake and I can brew, and by all the saints I can shoot almost as closely with the bow as the great Earl himself. I have played at the foils too with Kate: but is not to-day his birthday?

Sir Richard. Dost thou love him indeed, that thou keepest a record of his birthdays? Thou knowest that the Sheriff of Nottingham loves thee.

Marian. The Sheriff dare to love me? me who worship Robin the great Earl of Huntingdon? I love him as a damsel of his day might have loved Harold the Saxon or Hereward the Wake. They both fought against the tyranny of the kings, the Normans. But then your Sheriff, your little man, if he dare to fight at all, would fight for his rents, his leases, his houses, his monies, his oxen, his dinners, himself. Now your great man, your Robin, all England's Robin, fights not for himself but for the people of England. This John—this Norman tyranny—the stream is bearing us all down, and our little Sheriff will ever swim with the stream! but our great man, our Robin, against it. And how often in old histories have the great men striven against the stream, and how often in the long sweep of years to come must the great man strive against it again to save his country, and the liberties of his people! God bless our well-beloved Robin, Earl of Huntingdon.

Sir Richard. Ay, ay. He wore thy colours once at a tourney. I am old and forget. Was Prince John there?

Marian. The Sheriff of Nottingham was there—not John.

Sir Richard. Beware of John and the Sheriff of Nottingham. They hunt in couples, and when they look at a maid they blast her.

Marian. Then the maid is not high-hearted enough.

Sir Richard. There—there—be not a fool again. Their aim is ever at that which flies highest—but O girl, girl, I am almost in despair. Those two thousand marks lent me by the Abbot for the ransom of my son Walter—I believed this Abbot of the party of King Richard, and he hath sold himself to that beast John—they must be paid in a year and a month, or I lose the land. There is one that should be grateful to me overseas, a Count in Brittany—he lives near Quimper. I saved his life once in battle. He has monies. I will go to him. I saved him. I will try him. I am all but sure of him. I will go to him.

Marian. And I will follow thee, and God help us both.

Sir Richard. Child, thou shouldst marry one who will pay the mortgage. This Robin, this Earl of Huntingdon—he is a friend of Richard—I know not, but he may save the land, he may save the land.

Marian (showing a cross hung round her neck). Father, you see this cross?

Sir Richard. Ay the King, thy godfather, gave it thee when a baby.

Marian. And he said that whenever I married he would give me away, and on this cross I have sworn [*kisses it*] that till I myself pass away, there is no other man that shall give me away.

Sir Richard. Lo there—thou art fool again—I am all as loyal as thyself, but what a vow! what a vow!

Re-enter LITTLE JOHN

Little John. My Lady Marian, your woman so flustered me that I forgot my message from the Earl. To-day he hath accomplished his thirtieth birthday, and he prays your ladyship and your ladyship's father to be present at his banquet to-night.

Marian. Say, we will come.

Little John. And I pray you, my lady, to stand between me and your woman, Kate.

Marian. I will speak with her.

Little John. I thank you, my lady, and I wish you and your ladyship's father a most exceedingly good morning.   [*Exit.*

Sir Richard. Thou hast answered for me, but I know not if I will let thee go.

Marian. I mean to go.

Sir Richard. Not if I barred thee up in thy chamber, like a bird in a cage.

Marian. Then I would drop from the casement, like a spider.

Sir Pichard. But I would hoist the draw-bridge, like thy master.

Marian. And I would swim the moat, like an otter.

Sir Richard. But I would set my men-at-arms to oppose thee, like the Lord of the Castle.

Marian. And I would break through them all, like the King of England.

Sir Richard. Well, thou shalt go, but O the land! the land! my great great great grandfather, my great great grandfather, my great grandfather, my grandfather and my own father—they were born and bred on it—it was their mother—they have trodden it for half a thousand years, and whenever I set my own foot on it I say to it, Thou art mine, and it answers, I am thine to the very heart of the earth—but now I have lost my gold, I have lost my son, and I shall lose my land also. Down to the devil with this bond that beggars me!

[*Flings down the bond.*

Marian. Take it again, dear father, be not wroth at the dumb parchment. Sufficient for the day, dear father! let us be merry to-night at the banquet.

SCENE II

A hall in the house of Robin Hood the Earl of Huntingdon. Doors open into a banqueting-hall where he is at feast with his Friends

DRINKING SONG

Long live Richard,
  Robin and Richard!
Long live Richard!
  Down with John!

Drink to the Lion-heart
Every one!
Pledge the Plantagenet,
Him that is gone.
Who knows whither?
God's good Angel
Help him back hither,
And down with John!
Long live Robin,
Robin and Richard!
Long live Robin,
And down with John!

Enter PRINCE JOHN *disguised as a monk and the* SHERIFF OF NOTTINGHAM. *Cries of 'Down with John,' 'Long live King Richard,' 'Down with John.'*

Prince John. Down with John! ha. Shall I be known? is my disguise perfect?

Sheriff. Perfect—who should know you for Prince John, so that you keep the cowl down and speak not?

[*Shouts from the banquet-room.*
Prince John. Thou and I will still these revelries presently.

[*Shouts,* 'Long live King Richard!'
I come here to see this daughter of Sir Richard of the Lea and if her beauties answer their report. If so—

Sheriff. If so—

[*Shouts,* 'Down with John!'
Prince John. You hear!

Sheriff. Yes, my lord, fear not. I will answer for you.

Enter LITTLE JOHN, SCARLET, MUCH, *etc., from the banquet singing a snatch of the Drinking Song.*

Little John. I am a silent man myself, and all the more wonder at our Earl. What a wealth of words—O Lord, I will live and die for King Richard—not so much for the cause as for the Earl. O Lord, I am easily led by words, but I think the Earl hath right. Scarlet, hath not the Earl right? What makes thee so down in the mouth?

Scarlet. I doubt not, I doubt not, and though I be down in the mouth, I will swear by the head of the Earl.

Little John. Thou Much, miller's son, hath not the Earl right?

Much. More water goes by the mill than the miller wots of, and more goes to make

right than I know of, but for all that I will swear the Earl hath right. But they are coming hither for the dance—

Enter FRIAR TUCK

be they not, Friar Tuck? Thou art the Earl's confessor and shouldst know.

Tuck. Ay, ay, and but that I am a man of weight, and the weight of the church to boot on my shoulders, I would dance too. Fa, la, la, fa, la, la [*Capering.*

Much. But doth not the weight of the flesh at odd times overbalance the weight of the church, ha friar?

Tuck. Homo sum. I love my dinner—but I can fast, I can fast; and as to other frailties of the flesh—out upon thee! Homo sum, sed virgo sum, I am a virgin, my masters, I am a virgin.

Much. And a virgin, my masters, three yards about the waist is like to remain a virgin, for who could embrace such an armful of joy?

Tuck. Knave, there is a lot of wild fellows in Sherwood Forest who hold by King Richard. If ever I meet thee there, I will break thy sconce with my quarterstaff.

Enter from the banqueting-hall SIR RICHARD LEA, ROBIN HOOD, *etc.*

Robin. My guests and friends, Sir Richard, all of you
Who deign to honour this my thirtieth year,
And some of you were prophets that I might be
Now that the sun our King is gone, the light
Of these dark hours; but this new moon, I fear,
Is darkness. Nay, this may be the last time
When I shall hold my birthday in this hall:
I may be outlaw'd, I have heard a rumour.

All. God forbid!

Robin. Nay, but we have no news of Richard yet,
And ye did wrong in crying 'Down with John;'
For be he dead, then John may be our King.

752

All. God forbid!

Robin. Ay God forbid,
But if it be so we must bear with John.
The man is able enough—no lack of wit,
And apt at arms and shrewd in policy.
Courteous enough too when he wills; and
yet
I hate him for his want of chivalry.
He that can pluck the flower of maiden-
hood
From off the stalk and trample it in the
mire,
And boast that he hath trampled it. I hate
him,
I hate the man. I may not hate the King
For aught I know,
So that our Barons bring his baseness under.
I think they will be mightier than the king.
                              [*Dance music.*

(MARIAN *enters with other damsels*)

Robin. The high Heaven guard thee from
his wantonness,
Who art the fairest flower of maidenhood
That ever blossom'd on this English isle.

Marian. Cloud not thy birthday with
one fear for me.
My lord, myself and my good father pray
Thy thirtieth summer may be thirty-fold
As happy as any of those that went before.

Robin. My Lady Marian you can make
it so
If you will deign to tread a measure with
me.

Marian. Full willingly, my lord.
                              [*They dance.*

Robin (after dance). My Lady, will you
answer me a question?

Marian. Any that you may ask.

Robin. A question that every true man
asks of a woman once in his life.

Marian. I will not answer it, my lord,
till King Richard come home again.

Prince John (to SHERIFF*).* How she looks
up at him, how she holds her face!
Now if she kiss him, I will have his head.

Sheriff. Peace, my lord; the Earl and
Sir Richard come this way.

Robin. Must you have these monies
before the year and the month end?

Sir Richard. Or I forfeit my land to the

Abbot. I must pass overseas to one that I
trust will help me.

Robin. Leaving your fair Marian alone
here.

Sir Richard. Ay, for she hath somewhat
of the lioness in her, and there be men-at-
arms to guard her.

        [ROBIN, SIR RICHARD, *and* MARIAN
          pass on.

Prince John (to SHERIFF*).* Why that will
be our opportunity
When I and thou will rob the nest of her.

Sheriff. Good Prince, art thou in need
of any gold?

Prince John. Gold? why? not now.

Sheriff. I would give thee any gold
So that myself alone might rob the nest.

Prince John. Well, well then, thou shalt
rob the nest alone.

Sheriff. Swear to me by that relic on thy
neck.

Prince John. I swear then by this relic on
my neck—
No, no, I will not swear by this; I keep it
For holy vows made to the blessed Saints
Not pleasures, women's matters.
Dost thou mistrust me? Am I not thy
friend?
Beware, man, lest thou lose thy faith in me.
I love thee much; and as I *am* thy friend,
I promise thee to make this Marian thine.
Go now and ask the maid to dance with
thee,
And learn from her if she do love this Earl.

Sheriff (advancing toward MARIAN *and*
ROBIN*).* Pretty mistress!

Robin. What art thou, man? Sheriff of
Nottingham?

Sheriff. Ay, my lord. I and my friend,
this monk, were here belated, and seeing
the hospitable lights in your castle, and
knowing the fame of your hospitality, we
ventured in uninvited.

Robin. You are welcome, though I fear
you be of those who hold more by John
than Richard.

Sheriff. True, for through John I had
my sheriffship. I am John's till Richard
come back again, and then I am Richard's.
Pretty mistress, will you dance?
                              [*They dance.*

Robin (*talking to* PRINCE JOHN). What
monk of what convent art thou? Why
wearest thou thy cowl to hide thy face?

[PRINCE JOHN *shakes his head.*

Is he deaf, or dumb, or daft, or drunk
belike?

[PRINCE JOHN *shakes his head.*

Why comest thou like a death's head at my
feast?

[PRINCE JOHN *points to the* SHERIFF,
who is dancing with MARIAN.

Is he thy mouthpiece, thine interpreter?

[PRINCE JOHN *nods.*

Sheriff (*to* MARIAN *as they pass*). Beware
of John!

Marian. I hate him.

Sheriff.   Would you cast
An eye of favour on me, I would pay
My brother all his debt and save the
land.

Marian. I cannot answer thee till
Richard come.

Sheriff. And when he comes?

Marian. Well, you must wait till then.

Little John (*dancing with* KATE). Is it
made up? Will you kiss me?

Kate. You shall give me the first kiss.

Little John. There (*kisses her*). Now then.

Kate. You shall wait for mine till Sir
Richard has paid the Abbot.

[*They pass on.*
[*The* SHERIFF *leaves* MARIAN *with her
father and comes towards* ROBIN.

Robin (*to* SHERIFF, PRINCE JOHN *standing
by*). Sheriff, thy friend, this monk, is but a
statue.

Sheriff. Pardon him, my lord: he is a
holy Palmer, bounden by a vow not to
show his face, nor to speak word to anyone,
till he join King Richard in the Holy
Land.

Robin. Going to the Holy Land to
Richard! Give me thy hand and tell
him—— Why, what a cold grasp is thine—
as if thou didst repent thy courtesy even in
the doing it. That is no true man's hand.
I hate hidden faces.

Sheriff. Pardon him again, I pray you;
but the twilight of the coming day already
glimmers in the east. We thank you, and
farewell.

Robin. Farewell, farewell. I hate hidden
faces.

[*Exeunt* PRINCE JOHN *and* SHERIFF.

Sir Richard (*coming forward with* MAID
MARIAN). How close the Sheriff peer'd
into thine eyes!
What did he say to thee?

Marian.   Bade me beware
Of John: what maid but would beware of
John?

Sir Richard. What else?

Marian.   I care not what he said.

Sir Richard.   What else?

Marian. That if I cast an eye of favour
on him,
Himself would pay this mortgage to his
brother,
And save the land.

Sir Richard. Did he say so, the Sheriff?

Robin. I fear this Abbot is a heart of flint,
Hard as the stones of his abbey.
O good Sir Richard,
I am sorry my exchequer runs so low
I cannot help you in this exigency;
For though my men and I flash out at times
Of festival like burnish'd summer-flies,
We make but one hour's buzz, are only like
The rainbow of a momentary sun.
I am mortgaged as thyself.

Sir Richard. Ay! I warrant thee—thou
canst not be sorrier than I am. Come away,
daughter.

Robin. Farewell, Sir Richard; farewell,
sweet Marian.

Marian. Till better times.

Robin. But if the better times should
never come?

Marian. Then I shall be no worse.

Robin. And if the worst time come?

Marian. Why then I will be better than
the time.

Robin. This ring my mother gave me: it
was her own
Betrothal ring. She pray'd me when I loved
A maid with all my heart to pass it down
A finger of that hand which should be mine
Thereafter. Will you have it? Will you
wear it?

Marian. Ay, noble Earl, and never part
with it.

Sir Richard Lea (coming up). Not till she clean forget thee, noble Earl.

Marian. Forget *him*—never—by this Holy Cross
Which good King Richard gave me when a child—
Never!
Not while the swallow skims along the ground,
And while the lark flies up and touches heaven!
Not while the smoke floats from the cottage roof,
And the white cloud is roll'd along the sky!
Not while the rivulet babbles by the door,
And the great breaker beats upon the beach!
Never—
Till Nature, high and low, and great and small
Forgets herself, and all her loves and hates
Sink again into chaos.

Sir Richard Lea. Away! away!
                    [*Exeunt to music.*

SCENE III

Same as Scene II

ROBIN *and his men*

Robin. All gone!—my ring—I am happy
—should be happy.
She took my ring. I trust she loves me—yet
I heard this Sheriff tell her he would pay
The mortgage if she favour'd him. I fear
Not her, the father's power upon her.
                    Friends, (*to his men*)
I am only merry for an hour or two
Upon a birthday: if this life of ours
Be a good glad thing, why should we make us merry
Because a year of it is gone? but Hope
Smiles from the threshold of the year to come
Whispering 'it will be happier,' and old faces
Press round us, and warm hands close with warm hands,
And thro' the blood the wine leaps to the brain

Like April sap to the topmost tree, that shoots
New buds to heaven, whereon the throstle rock'd
Sings a new song to the new year—and you
Strike up a song, my friends, and then to bed.

Little John. What will you have, my lord?

Robin.   'To sleep! to sleep!'

Little John. There is a touch of sadness in it, my lord,
But ill befitting such a festal day

Robin. I have a touch of sadness in myself.
Sing.

SONG

To sleep! to sleep! The long bright day is done,
And darkness rises from the fallen sun.
To sleep! to sleep!
Whate'er thy joys, they vanish with the day;
Whate'er thy griefs, in sleep they fade away.
To sleep! to sleep!
Sleep, mournful heart, and let the past be past!
Sleep, happy soul! all life will sleep at last
To sleep! to sleep!

                    [*A trumpet blown at the gates.*
Robin. Who breaks the stillness of the morning thus?

Little John (going out and returning).
It is a royal messenger, my lord:
I trust he brings news of the King's coming.

Enter a PURSUIVANT *who reads*

O yes, O yes, O yes! In the name of the Regent. Thou, Robin Hood Earl of Huntingdon, art attained and hast lost thine earldom of Huntingdon. Moreover thou art dispossessed of all thy lands, goods, and chattels; and by virtue of this writ, whereas Robin Hood Earl of Huntingdon by force and arms hath trespassed against the king in divers manners, therefore by the judgment of the officers of the said lord king, according to the law and custom of the kingdom of England Robin Hood Earl of Huntingdon is outlawed and banished.

Robin. I have shelter'd some that broke
the forest laws.

This is irregular and the work of John.
['Irregular,   irregular! (*tumult*)
Down with him, tear his coat from
his back!']

Messenger. Ho there! ho there, the
Sheriff's men without!

Robin. Nay, let them be, man, let them
be. We yield.

How should we cope with John? The
London folkmote

Has made him all but king, and he hath
seized

On half the royal castles. Let him alone!
(*to his men*)

A worthy messenger! how should he
help it?

Shall *we* too work injustice? what, thou
shakest!

Here, here—a cup of wine—drink and
begone!   [*Exit* MESSENGER.

We will away in four-and-twenty hours,
But shall we leave our England?

   Tuck.   Robin, Earl—

Robin. Let be the Earl. Henceforth I am
no more

Than plain man to plain man.

   Tuck.   Well, then, plain man,

There be good fellows there in merry
Sherwood

That hold by Richard, tho' they kill his
deer.

Robin. In Sherwood Forest. I have heard
of them.

Have they no leader?

   Tuck.   Each man for his own.

Be thou their leader and they will all of
them

Swarm to thy voice like bees to the brass
pan.

Robin. They hold by Richard—the wild
wood! to cast

All threadbare household habit, mix with
all

The lusty life of wood and under-
wood,

Hawk, buzzard, jay, the mavis and the
merle,

The tawny squirrel vaulting thro' the
boughs,

The deer, the highback'd polecat, the wild
boar,

The burrowing badger—By St. Nicholas

I have a sudden passion for the wild
wood—

We should be free as air in the wild
wood—

What say you? shall we go? Your hands,
your hands! [*Gives his hand to each.*

You, Scarlet, you are always moody
here.

Scarlet. 'Tis for no lack of love to you,
my lord,

But lack of happiness in a blatant wife.

She broke my head on Tuesday with a
dish.

I would have thwack'd the woman, but I
did not,

Because thou sayest such fine things of
women,

But I shall have to thwack her if I stay.

Robin. Would it be better for thee in the
wood?

Scarlet. Ay, so she did not follow me to
the wood.

Robin. Then, Scarlet, thou at least wilt
go with me.

Thou, Much, the miller's son, I knew thy
father:

He was a manly man, as thou art, Much,

And gray before his time as thou art,
Much.

Much. It is the trick of the family, my
lord.

There was a song he made to the turning
wheel—

Robin. 'Turn! turn!' but I forget it.

Much.   I can sing it.

Robin. Not now, good Much! And thou,
dear Little John,

Who hast that worship for me which
Heaven knows

I ill deserve—you love me, all of you,

But I am outlaw'd, and if caught, I
die.

Your hands again. All thanks for all your
service;

But if you follow me, you may die with
me.

All. We will live and die with thee, we
will live and die with thee.

ACT II

THE FLIGHT OF MARIAN

SCENE I

A broad forest glade, woodman's hut at one side with half-door. Foresters are looking to their bows and arrows, or polishing their swords

FORESTERS *sing (as they disperse to their work)*

There is no land like England
    Where'er the light of day be;
There are no hearts like English hearts
    Such hearts of oak as they be.
There is no land like England
    Where'er the light of day be;
There are no men like Englishmen
    So tall and bold as they be.

(*Full chorus.*) And these will strike for England
            And man and maid be free
            To foil and spoil the tyrant
            Beneath the greenwood tree.

There is no land like England
    Where'er the light of day be;
There are no wives like English wives
    So fair and chaste as they be.
There is no land like England
    Where'er the light of day be;
There are no maids like English maids
    So beautiful as they be.

(*Full chorus.*) And these shall wed with freemen,
            And all their sons be free,
            To sing the songs of England
            Beneath the greenwood tree.

Robin (*alone*). My lonely hour!
The king of day hath stept from off his throne,
Flung by the golden mantle of the cloud,
And sets, a naked fire. The King of England
Perchance this day may sink as gloriously,
Red with his own and enemy's blood—but no!
We hear he is in prison. It is my birthday.
I have reign'd one year in the wild wood.
    My mother,
For whose sake, and the blessed Queen of Heaven,
I reverence all women, bad me, dying,
Whene'er this day should come about, to carve
One lone hour from it, so to meditate

Upon my greater nearness to the birthday
Of the after-life, when all the sheeted dead
Are shaken from their stillness in the grave
By the last trumpet.
                Am I worse or better?
I am outlaw'd. I am none the worse for that.
I held for Richard, and I hated John.
I am a thief, ay, and a king of thieves.
Ay! but we rob the robber, wrong the wronger,
And what we wring from them we give the poor.
I am none the worse for that, and all the better
For this free forest-life, for while I sat
Among my thralls in my baronial hall
The groining hid the heavens; but since I breathed,
A houseless head beneath the sun and stars,
The soul of the woods hath stricken thro' my blood,
The love of freedom, the desire of God,
The hope of larger life hereafter, more
Tenfold than under roof.
                         [*Horn blown.*
                True, were I taken
They would prick out my sight. A price is set
On this poor head; but I believe there lives
No man who truly loves and truly rules
His following, but can keep his followers true.
I am one with mine. Traitors are rarely bred
Save under traitor kings. Our vice-king John,
True king of vice—true play on words—our John
By his Norman arrogance and dissoluteness,
Hath made *me* king of all the discontent
Of England up thro' all the forest land
North to the Tyne: being outlaw'd in a land
Where law lies dead, we make ourselves the law.
Why break you thus upon my lonely hour?

Enter LITTLE JOHN *and* KATE

Little John. I found this white doe
    wandering thro' the wood,

757

Not thine, but mine. I have shot her thro'
   the heart.
   Kate. He lies, my lord. I have shot *him*
   thro' the heart.
   Robin. My God, thou art the very
   woman who waits
On my dear Marian. Tell me, tell me of
   her.
Thou comest a very angel out of heaven.
Where is she? and how fares she?
   Kate.   O my good lord,
I am but an angel by reflected light.
Your heaven is vacant of your angel.
   John—
Shame on him!—
Stole on her, she was walking in the garden,
And after some slight speech about the
   Sheriff
He caught her round the waist, whereon
   she struck him,
And fled into the castle. She and Sir
   Richard
Have past away, I know not where; and I
Was left alone, and knowing as I did
That I had shot him thro' the heart, I
   came
To eat him up and make an end of him.
   Little John. In kisses?
   Kate. You, how dare you mention
   kisses?
But I am weary pacing thro' the wood.
Show me some cave or cabin where I may
   rest.
   Robin. Go with him. I will talk with thee
   anon.
          [*Exeunt* LITTLE JOHN *and* KATE.
She struck him, my brave Marian, struck
   the Prince,
The serpent that had crept into the garden
And coil'd himself about her sacred waist.
I think I should have stricken him to the
   death.
He never will forgive her.
                  O the Sheriff
Would pay this cursed mortgage to his
   brother
If Marian would marry him; and the son
Is most like dead—if so the land may come
To Marian, and they rate the land five-fold
The worth of the mortgage, and who
   marries her

Marries the land. Most honourable Sheriff!
(*Passionately*) Gone, and it may be gone
   for evermore!
O would that I could see her for a moment
Glide like a light across these woodland
   ways!
Tho' in one moment she should glance
   away,
I should be happier for it all the year.
O would she moved beside me like my
   shadow!
O would she stood before me as my queen,
To make this Sherwood Eden o'er again,
And these rough oaks the palms of
   Paradise!
Ah! but who be those three yonder with
   bows?—not of my band—the Sheriff, and
by heaven, Prince John himself and one of
those mercenaries that suck the blood of
England. My people are all scattered I
know not where. Have they come for me?
Here is the witch's hut. The fool-people
call her a witch—a good witch to me! I will
shelter here.
          [*Knocks at the door of the hut.*

          OLD WOMAN *comes out*

   Old Woman (*kisses his hand*). Ah dear
Robin! ah noble captain, friend of the
poor!
   Robin. I am chased by my foes. I have
forgotten my horn that calls my men
together. Disguise me—thy gown and thy
coif.
   Old Woman. Come in, come in; I would
give my life for thee, for when the Sheriff
had taken all our goods for the King without paying, our horse and our little
cart——
   Robin. Quick, good mother, quick!
   Old Woman. Ay, ay, gown, coif, and
petticoat, and the old woman's blessing
with them to the last fringe. [*They go in.*

   Enter PRINCE JOHN, SHERIFF OF
   NOTTINGHAM, *and* MERCENARY

   Prince John. Did we not hear the two
   would pass this way?
They must have past. Here is a woodman's
   hut.

Mercenary. Take heed, take heed! in Nottingham they say
There bides a foul witch somewhere hereabout.
Sheriff. Not in this hut I take it.
Prince John.   Why not here?
Sheriff. I saw a man go in, my lord.
Prince John.   Not two?
Sheriff. No, my lord, one.
Prince John. Make for the cottage then!

Interior of the hut

ROBIN *disguised as old woman*

Prince John (without). Knock again! knock again!
Robin (to OLD WOMAN). Get thee into the closet there, and make a ghostly wail ever and anon to scare 'em.
Old Woman. I will, I will, good Robin.
                              [*Goes into closet.*
Prince John (without). Open, open, or I will drive the door from the door-post.
Robin (opens door). Come in, come in.
Prince John. Why did ye keep us at the door so long?
Robin (curtseying). I was afear'd it was the ghost, your worship.
Prince John. Ghost! did one in white pass?
Robin (curtseying). No, your worship.
Prince John. Did two knights pass?
Robin (curtseying). No, your worship.
Sheriff. I fear me we have lost our labour, then.
Prince John. Except this old hag have been bribed to lie.
Robin. We old hags should be bribed to speak truth, for, God help us, we lie by nature.
Prince John. There was a man just now that enter'd here?
Robin. There is but one old woman in the hut.
                              [OLD WOMAN *yells.*
Robin. I crave your worship's pardon. There is yet another old woman. She was murdered here a hundred year ago, and whenever a murder is to be done again she yells out i' this way—so they say, your worship.

Mercenary. Now, if I hadn't a sprig o' wickentree sewn into my dress, I should run.
Prince John. Tut! tut! the scream of some wild woodland thing.
How came we to be parted from our men?
We shouted, and *they* shouted, as I thought,
But shout and echo play'd into each other
So hollowly we knew not which was which.
Robin. The wood is full of echoes, owls, elfs, ouphes, oafs, ghosts o' the mist, willso'-the-wisp; only they that be bred in it can find their way a-nights in it.
Prince John. I am footsore and famish'd therewithal.
Is there aught there?
                              [*Pointing to cupboard.*
Robin. Naught for the likes o' you.
Prince John. Speak straight out, crookback.
Robin. Sour milk and black bread.
Prince John. Well, set them forth. I could eat anything.
        [*He sets out a table with black bread.*
This is mere marble. Old hag, how should thy one tooth drill thro' this?
Robin. Nay, by St. Gemini, I ha' two; and since the Sheriff left me naught but an empty belly, they can meet upon anything thro' a millstone. You gentles that live upo' manchet-bread and marchpane, what should you know o' the food o' the poor? Look you here, before you can eat it you must hack it with a hatchet, break it all to pieces, as you break the poor, as you would hack at Robin Hood if you could light upon him (*hacks it and flings two pieces*). There's for you, and there's for you—and the old woman's welcome.
Prince John. The old wretch is mad, and her bread is beyond me: and the milk—faugh! Hast thou anything to sweeten this?
Robin. Here's a pot o' wild honey from an old oak, saving your sweet reverences.
Sheriff. Thou hast a cow then, hast thou?
Robin. Ay, for when the Sheriff took my little horse for the King without paying for it——

759

Sheriff. How hadst thou then the means to buy a cow?

Robin. Eh, I would ha' given my whole body to the King had *he* asked for it, like the woman at Acre when the Turk shot her as she was helping to build the mound against the city. I ha' served the King living, says she, and let me serve him dead, says she; let me go to make the mound: bury me in the mound, says the woman.

Sheriff. Ay, but the cow?

Robin. She was given me.

Sheriff. By whom?

Robin. By a thief.

Sheriff. Who, woman, who?

Robin (*sings*).

> He was a forester good;
> He was the cock o' the walk;
> He was the king o' the wood.

Your worship may find another rhyme if you care to drag your brains for such a minnow.

Sheriff. That cow was mine. I have lost a cow from my meadow. Robin Hood was it? I thought as much. He will come to the gibbet at last.   [OLD WOMAN *yells.*

Mercenary. O sweet sir, talk not of cows. You anger the spirit.

Prince John. Anger the scritch-owl.

Mercenary. But, my lord, the scritch-owl bodes death, my lord.

Robin. I beseech you all to speak lower. Robin may be hard by wi' three-score of his men. He often looks in here by the moonshine. Beware of Robin.
                    [OLD WOMAN *yells.*

Mercenary. Ay, do you hear? There may be murder done.

Sheriff. Have you not finished, my lord?

Robin. Thou hast crost him in love, and I have heard him swear he will be even wi' thee.   [OLD WOMAN *yells.*

Mercenary. Now is my heart so down in my heels that if I stay, I can't run.

Sheriff. Shall we not go?

Robin. And, old hag tho' I be, I can spell the hand. Give me thine. Ay, ay, the line o' life is marked enow; but look, there is a cross line o' sudden death. I pray thee go,

go, for tho' thou wouldst bar me fro' the milk o' my cow, I wouldn't have thy blood on my hearth.

Prince John. Why do you listen, man, to the old fool?

Sheriff. I will give thee a silver penny if thou wilt show us the way back to Nottingham.

Robin (*with a very low curtsey*). All the sweet saints bless your worship for your alms to the old woman! but make haste then, and be silent in the wood. Follow me.
                    [*Takes his bow.*

(*They come out of the hut and close the door carefully*)

Outside hut

Robin. Softly! softly! there may be a thief in every bush.

Prince John. How should this old lamester guide us? Where is thy goodman?

Robin. The saints were so kind to both on us that he was dead before he was born.

Prince John. Half-witted and a witch to boot! Mislead us, and I will have thy life! and what doest thou with that who art more bow-bent than the very bow thou carriest?

Robin. I keep it to kill nightingales.

Prince John. Nightingales!

Robin. You see, they are so fond o' their own voices that I cannot sleep o' nights by cause on 'em.

Prince John. True soul of the Saxon churl for whom song has no charm.

Robin. Then I roast 'em, for I have nought else to live on (*whines*). O your honour, I pray you too to give me an alms. (*To* PRINCE JOHN.)

Sheriff. This is no bow to hit nightingales; this is a true woodman's bow of the best yew-wood to slay the deer. Look, my lord, there goes one in the moonlight. Shoot!

Prince John (*shoots*). Missed! There goes another. Shoot, Sheriff!

Sheriff (*shoots*). Missed!

Robin. And here comes another. Why, an old woman can shoot closer than you two.

Prince John. Shoot then, and if thou miss I will fasten thee to thine own doorpost and make thine old carcase a target for us three.

Robin (raises himself upright, shoots, and hits). Hit! Did I not tell you an old woman could shoot better?

Prince John. Thou standest straight. Thou speakest manlike. Thou art no old woman—thou art disguised—thou art one of the thieves.

[*Makes a clutch at the gown, which comes in pieces and falls, showing* ROBIN *in his forester's dress.*

Sheriff. It is the very captain of the thieves!

Prince John. We have him at last; we have him at advantage. Strike, Sheriff! Strike, mercenary!

[*They draw swords and attack him; he defends himself with his.*

Enter LITTLE JOHN

Little John. I have lodged my pretty Katekin in her bower.

How now? Clashing of swords—three upon one, and that one our Robin! Rogues, have you no manhood?

[*Draws and defends* ROBIN.

Enter SIR RICHARD LEA (*draws his sword*)

Sir Richard Lea. Old as I am, I will not brook to see

Three upon two.

[MAID MARIAN *in the armour of a Redcross Knight follows, half unsheathing her sword and half-seen.*

Back! back! I charge thee, back! Is this a game for thee to play at? Away.

[*She retires to the fringe of the copse. He fights on* ROBIN'S *side. The other three are beaten off and exeunt.*

Enter FRIAR TUCK

Friar Tuck. I am too late then with my quarterstaff!

Robin. Quick, friar, follow them:

See whether there be more of 'em in the wood.

Friar Tuck. On the gallop, on the gallop,

Robin, like a deer from a dog, or a colt from a gad-fly, or a stump-tailed ox in May-time, or the cow that jumped over the moon.   [*Exit.*

Robin. Nay, nay, but softly, lest they spy thee, friar!

[*To* SIR RICHARD LEA *who reels.*

Take thou mine arm. Who art thou, gallant knight?

Sir Richard. Robin, I am Sir Richard of the Lea.

Who be those three that I have fought withal?

Robin. Prince John, the Sheriff, and a mercenary.

Sir Richard. Prince John again. We are flying from this John.

The Sheriff—I am grieved it was the Sheriff;

For, Robin, he must be my son-in-law.

Thou art an outlaw, and couldst never pay

The mortgage on my land. Thou wilt not see

My Marian more. So—so—I have presumed

Beyond my strength. Give me a draught of wine.

[MARIAN *comes forward*

This is my son but late escaped from prison,

For whom I ran into my debt to the Abbot,

Two thousand marks in gold. I have paid him half.

That other thousand—shall I ever pay it? A draught of wine.

Robin.   Our cellar is hard by.

Take him, good Little John, and give him wine.

[*Exit* SIR RICHARD *leaning on* LITTLE JOHN.

A brave old fellow but he angers me.

[*To* MAID MARIAN *who is following her father.*

Young Walter, nay, I pray thee, stay a moment.

Marian. A moment for some matter of no moment!

Well—take and use your moment, while you may.

Robin. Thou art her brother, and her voice is thine,

761

Her face is thine, and if thou be as gentle
Give me some news of my sweet Marian.
Where is she?

Marian. Thy sweet Marian? I believe
She came with me into the forest here.

    Robin. She follow'd thee into the forest
here?

    Marian. Nay—that, my friend, I am
sure I did not say.

    Robin. Thou blowest hot and cold.
Where is she then?

    Marian. Is she not here with thee?

    Robin.   Would God she were!

    Marian. If not with thee I know not
where she is.
She may have lighted on your fairies here,
And now be skipping in their fairy-rings,
And capering hand in hand with Oberon.

    Robin.   Peace!

    Marian. Or learning witchcraft of your
woodland witch,
And how to charm and waste the hearts of
men.

    Robin. That is not brother-like.

    Marian (pointing to the sky). Or there
perchance
Up yonder with the man i' the moon.

    Robin.   No more!

    Marian. Or haply fallen a victim to the
wolf.

    Robin. Tut! be there wolves in Sher-
wood?

    Marian. The wolf, John!

    Robin. Curse him! but thou art mocking
me. Thou art
Her brother—I forgive thee. Come be thou
My brother too. She loves me.

    Marian.   Doth she so?

    Robin. Do you doubt me when I say
she loves me, man?

    Marian. No, but my father will not lose
his land,
Rather than that would wed her with the
Sheriff.

    Robin. Thou hold'st with him?

    Marian.   Yes, in some sort I do.
He is old and almost mad to keep the land.

    Robin. Thou hold'st with him?

    Marian.   I tell thee, in some sort.

    Robin (angrily). Sort! sort! what sort?
what sort of man art thou

For land, not love? Thou wilt inherit the
land,
And so wouldst sell thy sister to the
Sheriff,
O thou unworthy brother of my dear
Marian!
And now, I do bethink me, thou wast by
And never drewest sword to help the old
man
When he was fighting.

    Marian.   There were three to three.

    Robin. Thou shouldst have ta'en his
place, and fought for him.

    Marian. He did it so well there was no
call for me.

    Robin. My God!
That such a brother—*she* marry the
Sheriff!
Come now, I fain would have a bout with
thee.
It is but pastime—nay, I will not harm
thee.
Draw!

    Marian. Earl, I would fight with any
man but thee.

    Robin. Ay, ay, because I have a name
for prowess.

    Marian. It is not that.

    Robin. That! I believe thou fell'st into
the hands
Of these same Moors thro' nature's base-
ness, criedst
'I yield' almost before the thing was ask'd,
And thro' thy lack of manhood hast
betray'd
Thy father to the losing of his land.
Come, boy! 'tis but to see if thou canst
fence.
Draw!   [*Draws.*

    Marian.   No, Sir Earl, I will not
fight to-day.

    Robin. To-morrow then?

    Marian.   Well, I will fight
to-morrow.

    Robin. Give me thy glove upon it.

    *Marian (pulls off her glove and gives it to
him).*   There!

    Robin.   O God!
What sparkles in the moonlight on thy
hand?   [*Takes her hand.*
In that great heat to wed her to the Sheriff

Thou hast robb'd my girl of her betrothal
ring.
Marian. No, no!
Robin.   What! do I not know
mine own ring?
Marian. I keep it for her.
Robin.   Nay, she swore it never
Should leave her finger. Give it me, by
heaven,
Or I will force it from thee.
Marian.   O Robin, Robin!
Robin. O my dear Marian,
Is it thou? is it thou? I fall before thee,
clasp
Thy knees. I am ashamed. Thou shalt not
marry
The Sheriff, but abide with me who love
thee.
    [*She moves from him, the moonlight
    falls upon her.*
O look! before the shadow of these dark
oaks
Thou seem'st a saintly splendour out from
heaven,
Clothed with the mystic silver of her
moon.
Speak but one word not only of forgiveness,
But to show thou art mortal.
Marian.   Mortal enough,
If love for thee be mortal. Lovers hold
True love immortal. Robin, tho' I love
thee,
We cannot come together in this world.
Not mortal! after death, if after death——
Robin (*springing up*). Life, life. I know
not death. Why do you vex me
With raven-croaks of death and after
death?
Marian. And I and he are passing over-
seas:
He has a friend there will advance the
monies,
So now the forest lawns are all as bright
As ways to heaven, I pray thee give us
guides
To lead us thro' the windings of the wood.
Robin. Must it be so? If it were so,
myself
Would guide you thro' the forest to the sea.
But go not yet, stay with us, and when thy
brother——

Marian. Robin, I ever held that saying
false
That Love is blind, but thou hast proven
it true.
Why—even your woodland squirrel sees
the nut
Behind the shell, and thee however mask'd
I should have known. But thou—to dream
that he
My brother, my dear Walter—now, per-
haps,
Fetter'd and lash'd, a galley-slave, or
closed
For ever in a Moorish tower, or wreckt
And dead beneath the midland ocean, he
As gentle as he's brave—that such as he
Would wrest from me the precious ring I
promised
Never to part with—No, not he, nor any.
I would have battled for it to the death.
    [*In her excitement she draws her sword.*
See, thou hast wrong'd my brother and
myself.
Robin (*kneeling*). See then, I kneel once
more to be forgiven.

Enter SCARLET, MUCH, *several of the*
FORESTERS, *rushing on*

Scarlet. Look! look! he kneels! he has
anger'd the foul witch,
Who melts a waxen image by the fire,
And drains the heart and marrow from a
man.
Much. Our Robin beaten, pleading for
his life!
Seize on the knight! wrench his sword
from him!
    [*They all rush on* MARIAN.
Robin (*springing up and waving his hand*).
                              Back!
Back all of you! this is Maid Marian
Flying from John—disguised.
Men.   Maid Marian? she?
Scarlet. Captain, we saw thee cowering
to a knight
And thought thou wert bewitch'd.
Marian.   You dared to dream
That our great Earl, the bravest English
heart
Since Hereward the Wake, would cower
to any

763

Of mortal build. Weak natures that impute
Themselves to their unlikes, and their own
  want
Of manhood to their leader! he would
  break,
Far as he might, the power of John—but
  you—
What rightful cause could grow to such a
  heat
As burns a wrong to ashes, if the followers
Of him, who heads the movement, held
  him craven?
Robin—I know not, can I trust myself
With your brave band? in some of these
  may lodge
That baseness which for fear or monies,
  might
Betray me to the wild Prince.
   Robin.   No, love, no!
Not any of these, I swear.
   Men.   No, no, we swear.

SCENE II

Another Glade in the Forest

ROBIN *and* MARIAN *passing*

Enter FORESTER

Forester. Knight, your good father had
  his draught of wine
And then he swoon'd away. He had been
  hurt,
And bled beneath his armour. Now he
  cries
'The land! the land!' Come to him.
   Marian.   O my poor father!
   Robin. Stay with us in this wood, till he
  recover.
We know all balms and simples of the field
To help a wound. Stay with us here, sweet
  love,
Maid Marian, till thou wed what man thou
  wilt.
All here will prize thee, honour, worship
  thee,
Crown thee with flowers; and he will soon
  be well:
All will be well.
   Marian.   O lead me to my father!
   [*As they are going out enter* LITTLE
JOHN *and* KATE *who falls on the neck
of* MARIAN.

   Kate. No, no, false knight, thou canst
  not hide thyself
From her who loves thee.
   Little John.   What!
By all the devils in and out of Hell!
Wilt thou embrace thy sweetheart 'fore
  my face?
Quick with thy sword! the yeoman braves
  the knight.
There! (*strikes her with the flat of his sword*).
   Marian (*laying about her*). Are the men
  all mad? there then, and there!
   Kate. O hold thy hand! this is our
  Marian.
   Little John. What! with this skill of
  fence! let go mine arm.
   Robin. Down with thy sword! She is my
  queen and thine,
The mistress of the band.
   Marian (*sheathing her sword*). A maiden
  now
Were ill-bested in these dark days of John,
Except she could defend her innocence.
O lead me to my father!
         [*Exeunt* ROBIN *and* MARIAN.
   Little John.   Speak to me,
I am like a boy now going to be whipt;
I know I have done amiss, have been a fool.
Speak to me, Kate, and say you pardon me!
   Kate. I never will speak word to thee
  again.
What? to mistrust the girl you say you love
Is to mistrust your own love for your girl!
How should you love if you mistrust your
  love?
   Little John. O Kate, true love and
  jealousy are twins,
And love is joyful, innocent, beautiful,
And jealousy is wither'd, sour and ugly:
Yet are they twins and always go together.
   Kate. Well, well, until they cease to go
  together,
I am but a stone and a dead stock to thee.
   Little John. I thought I saw thee clasp
  and kiss a man
And it was but a woman. Pardon me.
   Kate. Ay, for I much disdain thee, but
  if ever
Thou see me clasp and kiss a man indeed,
I will again be thine, and not till then.
                [*Exit.*

Little John. I have been a fool and I have
 lost my Kate.   [*Exit.*

Re-enter ROBIN

Robin. He dozes. I have left her watching
 him.
She will not marry till her father yield.
The old man dotes.
Nay—and she will not marry till Richard
 come,
And that's at latter Lammas—never per-
 haps.
Besides, tho' Friar Tuck might make us
 one,
An outlaw's bride may not be wife in law.
I am weary.   [*Lying down on a bank.*
What's here? a dead bat in the fairy ring—
Yes, I remember, Scarlet hacking down
A hollow ash, a bat flew out at him
In the clear noon, and hook'd him by the
 hair,
And he was scared and slew it. My men
 say
The fairies haunt this glade;—if one could
 catch
A glimpse of them and of their fairy
 Queen
Have our loud pastimes driven them all
 away?
I never saw them: yet I could believe
There came some evil fairy at my birth
And cursed me, as the last heir of my race:
'This boy will never wed the maid he loves,
Nor leave a child behind him' (*yawns*).
 Weary—weary
As tho' a spell were on me (*he dreams*).
    [*The whole stage lights up, and fairies
    are seen swinging on boughs and nest-
    ling in hollow trunks.*

TITANIA *on a hill,* FAIRIES *on either
side of her, the moon above the hill.*

First Fairy.
Evil fairy! do you hear?
So he said who lieth here.

Second Fairy.
We be fairies of the wood,
We be neither bad nor good.

First Fairy.
Back and side and hip and rib,
Nip, nip him for his fib.

Titania.
Nip him not, but let him snore.
We must flit for evermore.

First Fairy.
Tit, my queen, must it be so?
Wherefore, wherefore should we go

Titania.
I Titania bid you flit,
And you dare to call me Tit.

First Fairy.
Tit, for love and brevity,
Not for love of levity.

Titania.
Pertest of our flickering mob,
Wouldst thou call my Oberon Ob?

First Fairy.
Nay, an please your Elfin Grace,
Never Ob before his face.

Titania.
Fairy realm is breaking down
When the fairy slights the crown.

First Fairy.
No, by wisp and glowworm, no.
Only wherefore should we go?

Titania.
We must fly from Robin Hood
And this new queen of the wood.

First Fairy.
True, she is a goodly thing.
Jealousy, jealousy of the king.

Titania.
Nay, for Oberon fled away
Twenty thousand leagues to-day.

Chorus.
Look, there comes a deputation
From our finikin fairy nation.

Enter several FAIRIES

Third Fairy.

Crush'd my bat whereon I flew!
Found him dead and drench'd in dew,
                              Queen.

Fourth Fairy.

Quash'd my frog that used to quack
When I vaulted on his back,
                              Queen.

Fifth Fairy.

Kill'd the sward where'er they sat,
                              Queen.

Sixth Fairy.

Lusty bracken beaten flat,
                              Queen.

Seventh Fairy.

Honest daisy deadly bruised,
                              Queen.

Eighth Fairy.

Modest maiden lily abused,
                              Queen.

Ninth Fairy.

Beetle's jewel armour crack'd,
                              Queen.

Tenth Fairy.

Reed I rock'd upon broken-back'd,
                              Queen.

Fairies (in chorus).

We be scared with song and shout.
Arrows whistle all about.
All our games be put to rout.
All our rings be trampled out.
Lead us thou to some deep glen,
Far from solid foot of men,
Never to return again,
                              Queen.

Titania (to FIRST FAIRY).

Elf, with spiteful heart and eye,
Talk of jealousy? You see why
We must leave the wood and fly.

(*To all the* FAIRIES, *who sing at intervals
with* TITANIA)

Up with you, out of the forest and over the
    hills and away,
And over this Robin Hood's bay!
Up thro' the light of the seas by the moon's
    long-silvering ray!
To a land where the fay,
Not an eye to survey,
In the night, in the day,
Can have frolic and play.
Up with you, all of you, out of it! hear and
    obey.
Man, lying here alone,
Moody creature,
Of a nature
Stronger, sadder than my own,
Were I human, were I human,
I could love you like a woman.
Man, man,
You shall wed your Marian.
She is true, and you are true,
And you love her and she loves you;
Both be happy, and adieu for ever and for
    evermore—adieu.
Robin (half waking). Shall I be happy?
    Happy vision, stay.

Titania.

Up with you, all of you, off with you, out
    of it, over the wood and away!

Note.—In the stage copy of my play I have
had this Fairy Scene transferred to the end of
the Third Act, for the sake of modern dramatic
effect.

ACT III

THE CROWNING OF MARIAN

SCENE

Heart of the Forest

MARIAN *and* KATE (*in Foresters' green*)

Kate. What makes you seem so cold to
    Robin, lady?
Marian. What makes thee think I seem
    so cold to Robin?
Kate. You never whisper close as lovers
    do,
Nor care to leap into each other's arms.

Marian. There is a fence I cannot over-
leap,
My father's will.
Kate. Then you will wed the Sheriff?
Marian. When heaven falls, I may light
on such a lark!
But who art thou to catechize me—thou
That hast not made it up with Little John!
Kate. I wait till Little John makes up
to *me.*
Marian. Why, my good Robin fancied
me a man,
And drew his sword upon me, and Little
John
Fancied he saw thee clasp and kiss a man.
Kate. Well, if *he* fancied that *I* fancy a
man
Other than *him,* he is *not* the man for me.
Marian. And that would quite *un*man
him, heart and soul.
For both are thine.   (*Looking up.*)
          But listen—overhead—
Fluting, and piping and luting 'Love, love,
love'—
Those sweet tree-Cupids half-way up in
heaven,
The birds—would I were one of 'em! O
good Kate—
If my man-Robin were but a bird-Robin,
How happily would we lilt among the
leaves
'Love, love, love, love'—what merry mad-
ness—listen!
And let them warm thy heart to Little
John.
Look where he comes!
Kate.   I will not meet him yet,
I'll watch him from behind the trees, but
call
Kate when you will, for I am close at hand.

KATE *stands aside and enter* ROBIN, *and after
him at a little distance* LITTLE JOHN,
MUCH, *the Miller's son, and* SCARLET *with
an oaken chaplet, and other* FORESTERS.

Little John. My lord—Robin—I crave
pardon—you always seem to me my lord
—I Little John, he Much the miller's son,
and he Scarlet, honouring all womankind,
and more especially my lady Marian, do
here, in the name of all our woodmen,

present her with this oaken chaplet as
Queen of the wood, I Little John, he,
young Scarlet, and he, old Much, and all
the rest of us.
Much. And I, old Much, say as much,
for being every inch a man I honour every
inch of a woman.
Robin. Friend Scarlet, art thou less a
man than Much?
Why art thou mute? Dost thou not honour
woman?
Scarlet. Robin, I do, but I have a bad
wife.
Robin. Then let her pass as an exception,
Scarlet.
Scarlet. So I would, Robin, if any man
would accept her.
Marian (*puts on the chaplet*). Had I a
bulrush now in this right hand
For sceptre, I were like a queen indeed.
Comrades, I thank you for your loyalty,
And take and wear this symbol of your
love;
And were my kindly father sound again,
Could live as happy as the larks in heaven,
And join your feasts and all your forest
games
As far as maiden might. Farewell, good
fellows!
[*Exeunt several* FORESTERS, *the others
withdraw to the back.*
Robin. Sit here by me, where the most
beaten track
Runs thro' the forest, hundreds of huge
oaks,
Gnarl'd—older than the thrones of Europe
—look,
What breadth, height, strength—torrents
of eddying bark!
Some hollow-hearted from exceeding age—
That never be thy lot or mine!—and some
Pillaring a leaf-sky on their monstrous
boles,
Sound at the core as we are. Fifty leagues
Of woodland hear and know my horn, that
scares
The Baron at the torture of his churls,
The pillage of his vassals.
          O maiden-wife,
The oppression of our people moves me so,
That when I think of it hotly, Love himself

Seems but a ghost, but when thou feel'st
with me
The ghost returns to Marian, clothes itself
In maiden flesh and blood, and looks at
once
Maid Marian, and that maiden freedom
which
Would never brook the tyrant. Live thou
maiden!
Thou art more my wife so feeling, than if
my wife
And siding with these proud priests, and
these Barons,
Devils, that make this blessed England hell.
Marian. Earl——
Robin. Nay, no Earl am I. I am English
yeoman.
Marian. Then *I* am yeo-woman. O the
clumsy word!
Robin. Take thou this light kiss for thy
clumsy word.
Kiss me again.
Marian. Robin, I will not kiss thee,
For that belongs to marriage; but I hold
thee
The husband of my heart, the noblest
light
That ever flash'd across my life, and I
Embrace thee with the kisses of the soul.
Robin. I thank thee.
Marian.   Scarlet told me—is it
true?—
That John last week return'd to Notting-
ham,
And all the foolish world is pressing thither.
Robin. Sit here, my queen, and judge
the world with me.
Doubtless, like judges of another bench,
However wise, we must at times have
wrought
Some great injustice, yet, far as we knew,
We never robb'd one friend of the true
King.
We robb'd the traitors that are leagued
with John;
We robb'd the lawyer who went against
the law;
We spared the craftsman, chapman, all
that live
By their own hands, the labourer, the poor
priest;

We spoil'd the prior, friar, abbot, monk,
For playing upside down with Holy Writ.
'Sell all thou hast and give it to the poor;'
Take all they have and give it to thyself!
Then after we have eased them of their
coins
It is our forest custom they should revel
Along with Robin.
Marian. And if a woman pass——
Robin. Dear, in these days of Norman
license, when
Our English maidens are their prey, if
ever
A Norman damsel fell into our hands,
In this dark wood when all was in our
power
We never wrong'd a woman.
Marian.   Noble Robin.
Little John (coming forward). Here come
three beggars.

Enter the three BEGGARS

Little John. Toll!
First Beggar. Eh! we be beggars, we
come to ask o' you. We ha' nothing.
Second Beggar. Rags, nothing but our
rags.
Third Beggar. I have but one penny in
pouch, and so you would make it two I
should be grateful.
Marian. Beggars, you are sturdy rogues
that should be set to work. You are those
that tramp the country, filch the linen from
the hawthorn, poison the house-dog, and
scare lonely maidens at the farmstead.
Search them, Little John.
Little John. These two have forty gold
marks between them, Robin.
Robin. Cast them into our treasury, the
beggars' mites. Part shall go to the alms-
houses at Nottingham, part to the shrine
of our Lady. Search this other.
Little John. He hath, as he said, but one
penny.
Robin. Leave it with him and add a gold
mark thereto. He hath spoken truth in a
world of lies.
Third Beggar. I thank you, my lord.
Little John. A fine, a fine! he hath called
plain Robin a lord. How much for a
beggar?

Robin. Take his penny and leave him his gold mark.

Little John. Sit there, knaves, till the captain call for you.

   [*They pass behind the trunk of an oak on the right.*

Marian. Art thou not hard upon them, my good Robin?

Robin. They might be harder upon thee, if met in a black lane at midnight: the throat might gape before the tongue could cry who?

Little John. Here comes a citizen, and I think his wife.

Enter CITIZEN *and* WIFE

Citizen. That business which we have in Nottingham——

Little John. Halt!

Citizen. O dear wife, we have fallen into the hands
Of Robin Hood.

Marian. And Robin Hood hath sworn—
Shame on thee, Little John, thou hast forgotten—
That by the blessed Mother no man, so
His own true wife came with him, should be stay'd
From passing onward. Fare you well, fair lady!   [*Bowing to her.*

Robin. And may your business thrive in Nottingham!

Citizen. I thank you, noble sir, the very blossom
Of bandits. Curtsey to him, wife, and thank him.

Wife. I thank you, noble sir, and will pray for you
That *you* may thrive, but in some kindlier trade.

Citizen. Away, away, wife, wilt thou anger him?

   [*Exeunt* CITIZEN *and his* WIFE.

Little John. Here come three friars.

Robin. Marian, thou and thy woman (*looking round*),
Why, where is Kate?

Marian (*calling*). Kate!

Kate. Here!

Robin. Thou and thy woman are a match

for three friars. Take thou my bow and arrow and compel them to pay toll.

Marian. Toll!

Enter three FRIARS

First Friar (*advancing*). Behold a pretty Dian of the wood,
Prettier than that same widow which you wot of.
Ha, brother. Toll, my dear? the toll of love.

Marian (*drawing bow*). Back! how much money hast thou in thy purse?

First Friar. Thou art playing with us. How should poor friars have money?

Marian. How much? how much? Speak, or the arrow flies.

First Friar. How much? well, now I bethink me, I have one mark in gold which a pious son of the Church gave me this morning on my setting forth.

Marian (*bending bow at the second*). And thou?

Second Friar. Well, as he said, one mark in gold.

Marian (*bending bow at the third*). And thou?

Third Friar. One mark in gold.

Marian. Search them, Kate, and see if they have spoken truth.

Kate. They are all mark'd men. They have told but a tenth of the truth: they have each ten marks in gold.

Marian. Leave them each what they say is theirs, and take the twenty-seven marks to the captain's treasury. Sit there till you be called for.

First Friar. We have fall'n into the hands of Robin Hood.

   [MARIAN *and* KATE *return to* ROBIN.
   The FRIARS *pass behind an oak on the left.*

Robin. Honour to thee, brave Marian, and thy Kate.
I know them arrant knaves in Nottingham.
One half of this shall go to those they have wrong'd,
One half shall pass into our treasury.
Where lies that cask of wine whereof we plunder'd
The Norman prelate?

Little John. In that oak, where twelve
Can stand upright, nor touch each other.
Robin. Good!
Roll it in here. These friars, thieves, and
liars,
Shall drink the health of our new wood-
land Queen.
And they shall pledge thee, Marian, loud
enough
To fright the wild hawk passing overhead,
The mouldwarp underfoot.
Marian. They pledge me, Robin?
The silent blessing of one honest man
Is heard in heaven—the wassail yells of
thief
And rogue and liar echo down in Hell,
And wake the Devil, and I may sicken
by 'em.
Well, well, be it so, thou strongest thief
of all,
For thou hast stolen my will, and made it
thine.

FRIAR TUCK, LITTLE JOHN, MUCH,
and SCARLET *roll in cask*

Friar Tuck. I marvel is it sack or Mal-
voisie?
Robin. Do me the service to tap it, and
thou wilt know.
Friar Tuck. I would tap myself in thy
service, Robin.
Robin. And thou wouldst run more wine
than blood.
Friar Tuck. And both at thy service,
Robin.
Robin. I believe thee, thou art a good
fellow, though a friar.
    [*They pour the wine into cups.*
Friar Tuck. Fill to the brim. Our Robin,
King o' the woods,
Wherever the horn sound, and the buck
bound,
Robin, the people's friend, the King o' the
woods!   [*They drink.*
Robin. To the brim and over till the
green earth drink
Her health along with us in this rich
draught,
And answer it in flowers. The Queen o'
the woods,

Wherever the buck bound, and the horn
sound,
Maid Marian, Queen o' the woods!
    [*They drink.*
        Here, you three rogues,
    [*To the* BEGGARS. *They come out.*
You caught a lonely woodman of our band,
And bruised him almost to the death, and
took
His monies.
Third Beggar. Captain, nay, it wasn't me.
Robin. You ought to dangle up there
among the crows.
Drink to the health of our new Queen o'
the woods,
Or else be bound and beaten.
First Beggar.   Sir, sir—well,
We drink the health of thy new Queen o'
the woods.
Robin. Louder! louder! Maid Marian,
Queen o' the woods!
Beggars (*shouting*). Maid Marian, Queen
o' the woods: Queen o' the woods!

First and Second Beggars (*aside*). The
black fiend grip her!
        [*They drink.*
Robin (*to the* FRIARS). And you three holy
men,   [*They come out.*
You worshippers of the Virgin, one of you
Shamed a too trustful widow whom you
heard
In her confession; and another—worse!—
An innocent maid. Drink to the Queen o'
the woods,
Or else be bound and beaten.
First Friar.   Robin Hood,
These be the lies the people tell of us,
Because we seek to curb their viciousness.
However—to this maid, this Queen o' the
woods.
Robin. Louder, louder, ye knaves. Maid
Marian!
Queen o' the woods!
Friars (*shouting*).   Maid Marian,
Queen o' the woods.
First Friar (*aside*). Maid?
Second Friar (*aside*). Paramour!
Third Friar (*aside*). Hell take her!
        [*They drink.*
Friar Tuck. Robin, will you not hear one

of these beggars' catches? They can do it.
I have heard 'em in the market at Mansfield.

Little John. No, my lord, hear ours—
Robin—I crave pardon, I always think of
you as my lord, but I may still say my
lady; and, my lady, Kate and I have fallen
out again, and I pray you to come between
us again, for, my lady, we have made a song
in your honour, so your ladyship care to
listen.

Robin. Sing, and by St. Mary these
beggars and these friars shall join you.
Play the air, Little John.

Little John. Air and word, my lady, are
maid and man. Join them and they are a
true marriage; and so, I pray you, my
lady, come between me and my Kate and
make us one again. Scarlet, begin.

[*Playing the air on his viol.*

Scarlet.

By all the deer that spring
Thro' wood and lawn and ling,
     When all the leaves are green;
By arrow and gray goosewing,
When horn and echo ring,
We care so much for a King;
     We care not much for a Queen—
     For a Queen, for a Queen o' the woods.

Marian. Do you call that in my honour?
Scarlet. Bitters before dinner, my lady,
to give you a relish. The first part—made
before you came among us—they put it
upon me because I have a bad wife. I love
you all the same. Proceed.

[*All the rest sing.*

By all the leaves of spring,
And all the birds that sing
     When all the leaves are green
By arrow and by bowstring,
We care so much for a King
     That we would die for a Queen—
     For a Queen, for a Queen o' the woods.

Enter FORESTER

Forester. Black news, black news from
Nottingham! I grieve
I am the Raven who croaks it. My lord
John,
In wrath because you drove him from the
forest,
Is coming with a swarm of mercenaries

To break our band and scatter us to the
winds.
Marian. O Robin, Robin! See that men
be set
Along the glades and passes of the wood
To warn us of his coming! then each man
That owns a wife or daughter, let him
bury her
Even in the bowels of the earth to 'scape
The glance of John——
Robin. You hear your Queen, obey!

ACT IV

THE CONCLUSION

SCENE

*A forest bower, cavern in background.
Sunrise*

Marian (rising to meet ROBIN). Robin,
the sweet light of a mother's eye,
That beam of dawn upon the opening
flower,
Has never glanced upon me when a child.
He was my father, mother, both in one.
The love that children owe to both I give
To him alone.
          (ROBIN *offers to caress her*)
Marian. Quiet, good Robin, quiet!
You lovers are such clumsy summer-flies
For ever buzzing at your lady's face.
Robin. Bees rather, flying to the flower
for honey.

Marian (sings)

The bee buzz'd up in the heat.
'I am faint for your honey, my sweet.'
The flower said 'Take it, my dear,
For now is the spring of the year.
     So come, come!'
          'Hum!'
And the bee buzz'd down from the heat.

And the bee buzz'd up in the cold
When the flower was wither'd and old.
'Have you still any honey, my dear?'
She said 'It's the fall of the year,
     But come, come!'
          'Hum!'
And the bee buzz'd off in the cold.

Robin. Out on thy song!
Marian. Did I not sing it in tune?

Robin. No, sweetheart! out of tune with
Love and me.

Marian. And yet in tune with Nature
and the bees.

Robin. Out on it, I say, as out of tune
and time!

Marian. Till thou thyself shalt come to
sing it—in time.

Robin (*taking a tress of her hair in his
hand*). Time! if his backward-working
alchemy

Should change this gold to silver, why, the
silver

Were dear as gold, the wrinkle as the dimple.

Thy bee should buzz about the Court of
John.

No ribald John is Love, no wanton Prince,

The ruler of an hour, but lawful King,

Whose writ will run thro' all the range of
life.

Out upon all hard-hearted maidenhood!

Marian. And out upon all simple
batchelors!

Ah, well! thou seest the land has come
between us,

And my sick father here has come between
us

And this rich Sheriff too has come between
us;

So, is it not all over now between us?

Gone, like a deer that hath escaped thine
arrow!

Robin. What deer when I have mark'd
him ever yet

Escaped mine arrow? over is it? wilt thou

Give me thy hand on that?

Marian.   Take it.

Robin (*kisses her hand*). The Sheriff!

This ring cries out against thee. Say it
again,

And by this ring the lips that never
breathed

Love's falsehood to true maid will seal
Love's truth

On those sweet lips that dare to dally
with it.

Marian. Quiet, quiet! or I will to my
father.

Robin. So, then, thy father will not grace
our feast

With his white beard to-day.

Marian.   Being so sick
How should he, Robin?

Robin.   Then that bond he hath
Of the Abbot—wilt thou ask him for it?

Marian.   Why?

Robin. I have sent to the Abbot and
justiciary

To bring their counter-bond into the
forest.

Marian. But will they come?

Robin. If not I have let them know

Their lives unsafe in any of these our
woods,

And in the winter I will fire their farms.

But I have sworn by our Lady if they come

I will not tear the bond, but see fair play

Betwixt them and Sir Richard—promised
too,

So that they deal with us like honest men,

They shall be handled with all courteous-
ness.

Marian. What wilt thou do with the
bond then?

Robin.   Wait and see.

What wilt thou do with the Sheriff?

Marian.   Wait and see.

I bring the bond.   [*Exit* MARIAN.

Enter LITTLE JOHN, FRIAR TUCK, *and* MUCH,
and FORESTERS *and* PEASANTS *laughing and
talking.*

Robin. Have ye glanced down thro' all
the forest ways

And mark'd if those two knaves from York
be coming?

Little John. Not yet, but here comes one
of bigger mould.

              [*Enter* KING RICHARD.

Art thou a knight?

King Richard. I am.

Robin.   And walkest here

Unarmour'd? all these walks are Robin
Hood's

And sometimes perilous.

King Richard. Good! but having lived

For twenty days and nights in mail, at last

I crawl'd like a sick crab from my old
shell,

That I might breathe for a moment free of
shield

And cuirass in this forest where I dream'd

That all was peace—not even a Robin
Hood—
(*Aside*) What if these knaves should know
me for their King?
Robin. Art thou for Richard, or allied to
John?
King Richard. I *am* allied to John.
Robin.   The worse for thee.
King Richard. Art thou that banish'd
lord of Huntingdon,
The chief of these outlaws who break the
law?
Robin. I am the yeoman, plain Robin
Hood, and being out of the law how should
we break the law? if we broke into it again
we should break the law, and then we were
no longer outlaws.
King Richard. But, Earl, if thou be
he——
Friar Tuck. Fine him! fine him! he hath
called plain Robin an earl. How much is
it, Robin, for a knight?
Robin. A mark.
King Richard (*gives it*). There.
Robin. Thou payest easily, like a good
fellow,
But being o' John's side we must have thy
gold.
King Richard. But I am more for
Richard than for John.
Robin. What, what, a truckler! a word-
eating coward!
Nay, search him then. How much hast
thou about thee?
King Richard. I had one mark.
Robin. What more.
King Richard.   No more, I think.
But how then if I will not bide to be
search'd?
Robin. We are four to one.
King Richard. And I might deal with
four.
Robin. Good, good, I love thee for that!
but if I wind
This forest-horn of mine I can bring down
Fourscore tall fellows on thee.
King Richard.   Search me then.
I should be hard beset with thy fourscore.
Little John (*searching* KING RICHARD).
Robin, he hath no more. He hath
spoken truth.

Robin. I am glad of it. Give him back
his gold again.
King Richard. But I had liefer than this
gold again—
Not having broken fast the livelong day—
Something to eat.
Robin. And thou shalt have it, man.
Our feast is yonder, spread beneath an oak,
Venison, and wild boar, hare, geese,
besides
Hedge-pigs, a savoury viand, so thou be
Squeamish at eating the King's venison.
King Richard. Nay, Robin, I am like
thyself in that
I look on the King's venison as my own.
Friar Tuck. Ay, ay, Robin, but let him
know our forest laws: he that pays not for
his dinner must fight for it. In the sweat
of thy brow, says Holy Writ, shalt thou eat
bread, but in the sweat of thy brow and
thy breast, and thine arms, and thy legs,
and thy heart, and thy liver, and in the fear
of thy life shalt thou eat the King's venison
—ay, and so thou fight at quarterstaff for
thy dinner with our Robin, that will give
thee a new zest for it, though thou wert
like a bottle full up to the cork, or as
hollow as a kex, or the shambles-oak, or a
weasel-sucked egg, or the head of a fool,
or the heart of Prince John, or any other
symbol of vacuity.

[*They bring out the quarterstaffs, and
the* FORESTERS *and* PEASANTS *crowd
round to see the games, and applaud
at intervals.*

King Richard. Great woodland king, I
know not quarterstaff.
Little John. A fine! a fine! He hath called
plain Robin a king.
Robin. A shadow, a poetical fiction—did
ye not call me king in your song?—a mere
figure. Let it go by.
Friar Tuck. No figure, no fiction, Robin.
What, is not man a hunting animal? And
look you now, if we kill a stag, our dogs
have their paws cut off, and the hunters, if
caught, are blinded, or worse than blinded.
Is that to be a king? If the king and the law
work injustice, is not he that goes against
the king and the law the true king in the
sight of the King of kings? Thou art the

king of the forest, and I would thou wert
the king of the land.

King Richard. This friar is of much
boldness, noble captain.

Robin. He hath got it from the bottle,
noble knight.

Friar Tuck. Boldness out of the bottle!
I defy thee.
Boldness is in the blood, Truth in the
bottle.
She lay so long at the bottom of her well
In the cold water that she lost her voice,
And so she glided up into the heart
O' the bottle, the warm wine, and found it
again.
In vino veritas. Shall I undertake
The knight at quarterstaff, or thou?

Robin. Peace, magpie!
Give him the quarterstaff. Nay, but thy-
self
Shalt play a bout with me, that he may see
The fashion of it.

    [*Plays with* FRIAR TUCK *at quarterstaff.*

King Richard. Well, then, let me try.

             [*They play.*
I yield, I yield. I know no quarterstaff.

Robin. Then thou shalt play the game of
buffets with us.

King Richard. What's that?

Robin. I stand up here, thou there. I give
thee
A buffet, and thou me. The Holy Virgin
Stand by the strongest. I am over-
breathed,
Friar, by my two bouts at quarterstaff.
Take him and try him, friar.

Friar Tuck. There!   [*Strikes.*

King Richard (*strikes*). There!

            [FRIAR *falls.*

Friar Tuck.   There!
Thou hast roll'd over the Church militant
Like a tod of wool from wagon into ware-
house.
Nay, I defy thee still. Try me an hour
hence.
I am misty with my thimbleful of ale.

Robin. Thou seest, Sir Knight, our friar
is so holy
That he's a miracle-monger, and can make
Five quarts pass into a thimble. Up good
Much.

Friar Tuck. And show thyself more of a
man than me.

Much. Well, no man yet has ever bowl'd
me down.

Scarlet. Ay, for old Much is every inch
a man.

Robin. We should be all the more
beholden to him.

Much. Much and more! much and more!
I am the oldest of thy men, and thou and
thy youngsters are always muching and
moreing me.

Robin. Because thou art always so much
more of a man than my youngsters, old
Much.

Much. Well, we Muches be old.

Robin. Old as the hills.

Much. Old as the mill. We had it i' the
Red King's time, and so I *may* be more of
a man than to be bowled over like a ninepin.
There!   [*Strikes.*

King Richard. There!   [MUCH *falls.*

Robin. 'Much would have more,' says
the proverb; but Much hath had more
than enough. Give me thy hand, Much; I
love thee (*lifts him up*). At him, Scarlet!

Scarlet. I cannot cope with him: my
wrist is strain'd.

King Richard. Try, thyself, valorous
Robin!

Robin. I am mortally afear'd o' thee,
thou big man,
But seeing valour is one against all odds,
There!

King Richard. There!

    [ROBIN *falls back, and is caught in
    the arms of* LITTLE JOHN.

Robin. Good, now I love thee mightily,
thou tall fellow.
Break thine alliance with this faithless
John,
And live with us and the birds in the green
wood.

King Richard. I cannot break it, Robin,
if I wish'd.
Still I am more for Richard than for
John.

Little John. Look, Robin, at the far end
of the glade
I see two figures crawling up the hill.

    [*Distant sound of trumpets.*

Robin. The Abbot of York and his justiciary.

King Richard (aside). They know me. I must not as yet be known.

Friends, your free sports have swallow'd my free hour.

Farewell at once, for I must hence upon The King's affair.

Robin. Not taste his venison first?

Friar Tuck. Hast thou not fought for it, and earn'd it? Stay,

Dine with my brethren here, and on thine own.

King Richard. And which be they?

Friar Tuck. Geese, man! for how canst thou be thus allied

With John, and serve King Richard save thou be

A traitor or a goose? but stay with Robin;

For Robin is no scatterbrains like Richard,

Robin's a wise man, Richard a wiseacre,

Robin's an outlaw, but he helps the poor.

While Richard hath outlaw'd himself, and helps

Nor rich, nor poor. Richard's the king of courtesy,

For if he did me the good grace to kick me

I could but sneak and smile and call it courtesy,

For he's a king.

And that is only courtesy *by* courtesy—

But Robin is a thief of courtesy

Whom they that suffer by him call the blossom

Of bandits. There—to be a thief of courtesy—

There is a trade of genius, there's glory!

Again, this Richard sacks and wastes a town

With random pillage, but our Robin takes

From whom he knows are hypocrites and liars.

Again this Richard risks his life for a straw,

So lies in prison—while our Robin's life

Hangs by a thread, but he is a free man.

Richard, again, is king over a realm

He hardly knows, and Robin king of Sherwood,

And loves and dotes on every dingle of it.

Again this Richard is the lion of Cyprus,

Robin, the lion of Sherwood—may this mouth

Never suck grape again, if our true Robin

Be not the nobler lion of the twain.

King Richard. Gramercy for thy preachment! if the land

Were ruleable by tongue, thou shouldst be king.

And yet thou know'st how little of thy king!

What was this realm of England, all the crowns

Of all this world, to Richard when he flung

His life, heart, soul into those holy wars

That sought to free the tomb-place of the King

Of all the world? thou, that art churchman too

In a fashion, and shouldst feel with him. Farewell!

I left mine horse and armour with a Squire,

And I must see to 'em.

Robin. When wilt thou return?

King Richard. Return, I? when? when Richard will return.

Robin. No sooner? when will that be? canst thou tell?

But I have ta'en a sudden fancy to thee.

Accept this horn! if e'er thou be assail'd

In any of our forests, blow upon it

Three mots, this fashion—listen! *(blows)*

Canst thou do it!

[KING RICHARD *blows*.

Blown like a true son of the woods. Farewell! [*Exit* KING RICHARD.

Enter ABBOT *and* JUSTICIARY.

Friar Tuck. Church and Law, halt and pay toll!

Justiciary. Rogue, we have thy captain's safe-conduct; though he be the chief of rogues, he hath never broken his word.

Abbot. There is our bond.

[*Gives it to* ROBIN.

Robin. I thank thee.

Justiciary. Ay, but where, Where is this old Sir Richard of the Lea? Thou told'st us we should meet him in the forest,

Where he would pay us down his thousand marks.

Robin. Give him another month, and he will pay it.

Justiciary. We cannot give a month.

Robin.   Why then a week.

Justiciary. No, not an hour: the debt is due to-day.

Abbot. Where is this laggard Richard of the Lea?

Robin. He hath been hurt, was growing whole again,

Only this morning in his agony

Lest he should fail to pay these thousand marks

He is stricken with a slight paralysis.

Have you no pity? must you see the man?

Justiciary. Ay, ay, what else? how else can this be settled?

Robin. Go men, and fetch him hither on the litter.

[SIR RICHARD LEA *is brought in.* MARIAN *comes with him.*

Marian. Here is my father's bond.

[*Gives it to* ROBIN HOOD.

Robin.   I thank thee, dear.

Justiciary. Sir Richard, it was agreed when you borrowed these monies from the Abbot that if they were not repaid within a limited time your land should be forfeit.

Sir Richard. The land! the land.

Marian. You see he is past himself. What would you more?

Abbot.   What more? one thousand marks,

Or else the land.

You hide this damsel in your forest here,

[*Pointing to* MARIAN.

You hope to hold and keep her for yourself,

You heed not how you soil her maiden fame,

You scheme against her father's weal and hers,

For so this maid would wed our brother, he

Would pay us all the debt at once, and thus

This old Sir Richard might redeem his land.

He is all for love, he cares not for the land.

Sir Richard. The land, the land!

Robin (*giving two bags to the* ABBOT).

Here be one thousand marks

Out of our treasury to redeem the land.

[*Pointing to each of the bags.*

Half here, half there.

[*Plaudits from his band.*

Justiciary. Ay, ay, but there is use, four hundred marks.

Robin (*giving a bag to* JUSTICIARY).

There then, four hundred marks.

[*Plaudits.*

Justiciary.   What did I say?

Nay, my tongue tript—five hundred marks for use.

Robin (*giving another bag to him*). A hundred more? There then, a hundred more.   [*Plaudits.*

Justiciary. Ay, ay, but you see the bond and the letter of the law. It is stated there that these monies should be paid in to the Abbot at York, at the end of the month at noon, and they are delivered here in the wild wood an hour after noon.

Marian. The letter—O how often justice drowns

Between the law and letter of the law!

O God, I would the letter of the law

Were some strong fellow here in the wild wood,

That thou mightst beat him down at quarterstaff!

Have you no pity?

Justiciary. You run down your game,

We ours. What pity have you for your game?

Robin. We needs must live. Our bowmen are so true

They strike the deer at once to death—he falls

And knows no more.

Marian. Pity, pity!—There was a man of ours

Up in the north, a goodly fellow too,

He met a stag there on so narrow a ledge—

A precipice above, and one below—

There was no room to advance or to retire.

The man lay down—the delicate-footed creature

Came stepping o'er him, so as not to harm him—

The hunter's passion flash'd into the man,

He drove his knife into the heart of the deer,

The deer fell dead to the bottom, and the man
Fell with him, and was crippled ever after.
I fear I had small pity for that man.—
You have the monies and the use of them.
What would you more?

Justiciary. What? must we dance attendance all the day?

Robin. Dance! ay, by all the saints and all the devils ye shall dance. When the Church and the law have forgotten God's music, they shall dance to the music of the wild wood. Let the birds sing, and do you dance to their song. What, you will not? Strike up our music, Little John. (*He plays.*) They will not! Prick 'em in the calves with the arrow-points—prick 'em in the calves.

Abbot. Rogue, I am full of gout. I cannot dance.

Robin. And Sir Richard cannot redeem his land. Sweat out your gout, friend, for by my life, you shall dance till he can. Prick him in the calves!

Justiciary. Rogue, I have a swollen vein in my right leg, and if thou prick me there I shall die.

Robin. Prick him where thou wilt, so that he dance.

Abbot. Rogue, we come not alone.

Justiciary. Not the right.

Abbot. We told the Prince and the Sheriff of our coming.

Justiciary. Take the left leg for the love of God.

Abbot. They follow us.

Justiciary. You will all of you hang.

Robin. Let us hang, so thou dance meanwhile; or by that same love of God we will hang *thee*, prince or no prince, sheriff or no sheriff.

Justiciary. Take care, take care! I dance —I will dance—I dance.

[ABBOT *and* JUSTICIARY *dance to music, each holding a bag in each hand.*

Enter SCARLET

Scarlet. The Sheriff! the Sheriff, follow'd by Prince John
And all his mercenaries! We sighted 'em

Only this moment. By St. Nicholas
They must have sprung like Ghosts from underground,
Or, like the Devils they are, straight up from Hell.

Robin. Crouch all into the bush!

[*The* FORESTERS *and* PEASANTS *hide behind the bushes.*

Marian.   Take up the litter!

Sir Richard. Move me no more! I am sick and faint with pain!

Marian. But, Sir, the Sheriff——

Sir Richard. Let me be, I say!
The Sheriff will be welcome! let me be!

Marian. Give me my bow and arrows.
I remain
Beside my Father's litter.

Robin.   And fear not thou!
Each of us has an arrow on the cord;
We all keep watch.

Enter SHERIFF OF NOTTINGHAM

Sheriff. Marian!

Marian. Speak not. I wait upon a dying father.

Sheriff. The debt hath not been paid.
She will be mine.
What are you capering for? By old St. Vitus
Have you gone mad? Has it been paid?

Abbot (*dancing*).   O yes.

Sheriff. Have I lost her then?

Justiciary (*dancing*). Lost her? O no, we took
Advantage of the letter—O Lord, the vein!
Not paid at York—the wood—prick me no more!

Sheriff. What pricks thee save it be thy conscience, man?

Justiciary. By my halidome I felt him at my leg still. Where be they gone to?

Sheriff. Thou art alone in the silence of the forest
Save for this maiden and thy brother Abbot,
And this old crazeling in the litter there.

Enter on one side FRIAR TUCK *from the bush, and on the other* PRINCE JOHN *and his* SPEARMEN, *with banners and trumpets, etc.*

Justiciary (*examining his leg*). They have missed the vein.

Abbot. And we shall keep the land.
Sheriff. Sweet Marian, by the letter of
the law
It seems thy father's land is forfeited.
Sir Richard. No! let me out of the litter.
He shall wed thee:
The land shall still be mine. Child, thou
shalt wed him,
Or thine old father will go mad—he will,
He will—he feels it in his head.
Marian. O peace!
Father, I cannot marry till Richard comes.
Sir Richard. And then the Sheriff!
Marian. Ay, the Sheriff, father,
Would buy me for a thousand marks in
gold—
Sell me again perchance for twice as much.
A woman's heart is but a little thing,
Much lighter than a thousand marks in
gold;
But pity for a father, it may be,
Is weightier than a thousand marks in gold.
I cannot love the Sheriff.
Sir Richard. But thou wilt wed him?
Marian. Ay, save King Richard, when
he comes, forbid me.
Sweet heavens, I could wish that all the
land
Were plunged beneath the waters of the
sea,
Tho' all the world should go about in
boats.
Friar Tuck. Why, so should all the love-
sick be sea-sick.
Marian. Better than heart-sick, friar.
Prince John (*to* SHERIFF). See you not
They are jesting at us yonder, mocking us?
Carry her off, and let the old man die.
                    [*Advancing to* MARIAN.
Come, girl, thou shalt along with us on the
instant.
Friar Tuck (*brandishing his staff*). Then
on the instant I will break thy head.
Sheriff. Back, thou fool-friar! Knowest
thou not the Prince?
Friar Tuck (*muttering*). He may be
prince; he is not gentleman.
Prince John. Look! I will take the rope
from off thy waist
And twist it round thy neck and hang
thee by it.

Seize him and truss him up, and carry
her off.
            [FRIAR TUCK *slips into the bush.*
Marian (*drawing the bow*). No nearer to
me! back! My hand is firm,
Mine eye most true to one hair's-breadth
of aim.
You, Prince, our king to come—you that
dishonour
The daughters and the wives of your own
faction—
Who hunger for the body, not the soul—
This gallant Prince would have me of his
—what?
Household? or shall I call it by that new
term
Brought from the sacred East, his harem?
Never,
Tho' you should queen me over all the
realms
Held by King Richard, could I stoop so
low
As mate with one that holds no love is pure,
No friendship sacred, values neither man
Nor woman save as tools—God help the
mark—
To his own unprincely ends. And you, you,
Sheriff,   [*Turning to the* SHERIFF.
Who thought to buy your marrying me
with gold.
Marriage is of the soul, not of the body.
Win me you cannot, murder me you may,
And all I love, Robin, and all his men,
For I am one with him and his; but while
I breathe Heaven's air, and Heaven looks
down on me,
And smiles at my best meanings, I remain
Mistress of mine own self and mine own
soul.
[*Retreating, with bow drawn, to the bush.*
Robin!
Robin. I am here, my arrow on the cord.
He dies who dares to touch thee.
Prince John. Advance, advance!
What, daunted by a garrulous, arrogant
girl!
Seize her and carry her off into my castle.
Sheriff. Thy castle!
Prince John. Said I not, I loved thee,
man?
Risk not the love I bear thee for a girl.

Sheriff. Thy castle!

Prince John. See thou thwart me not, thou fool!

When Richard comes he is soft enough to pardon

His brother; but all those that held with him,

Except I plead for them, will hang as high

As Haman.

Sheriff. She is mine. I have thy promise.

Prince John. O ay, she shall be thine— first mine, then thine.

For she shall spend her honeymoon with me.

Sheriff. Woe to that land shall own thee for her king!

Prince John. Advance, advance!

[*They advance shouting. The* KING *in armour reappears from the wood.*

King Richard. What shouts are these · that ring along the wood?

Friar Tuck (coming forward). Hail, knight, and help us. Here is one would clutch

Our pretty Marian for his paramour,

This other, willy-nilly, for his bride.

King Richard. Damsel, is this the truth?

Marian.   Ay, noble knight.

Friar Tuck. Ay, and she will not marry till Richard come.

King Richard (raising his vizor). I am here, and I am he.

Prince John (lowering his, and whispering to his men). It is not he—his face— tho' very like—

No, no! we have certain news he died in prison.

Make at him, all of you, a traitor coming

In Richard's name—it is not he—not he.

[*The men stand amazed.*

Friar Tuck (going back to the bush). Robin, shall we not move?

Robin.   It is the King

Who bears all down. Let him alone awhile.

He loves the chivalry of his single arm.

Wait till he blow the horn.

Friar Tuck (coming back). If thou be king,

Be not a fool! Why blowest thou not the horn?

King Richard. I that have turn'd their Moslem crescent pale—

I blow the horn against this rascal rout!

[FRIAR TUCK *plucks the horn from him and blows.* RICHARD *dashes alone against the* SHERIFF *and* JOHN'S *men, and is almost borne down, when* ROBIN *and his men rush in and rescue him.*

King Richard (to ROBIN HOOD*).* Thou hast saved my head at the peril of thine own.

Prince John. A horse! a horse! I must away at once;

I cannot meet his eyes. I go to Nottingham.

Sheriff, thou wilt find me at Nottingham.

[*Exit.*

Sheriff. If anywhere, I shall find thee in hell.

What! go to slay his brother, and make *me*

The monkey that should roast his chest- nuts for him!

King Richard. I fear to ask who left us even now.

Robin. I grieve to say it was thy father's son.

Shall I not after him and bring him back?

King Richard. No, let him be. Sheriff of Nottingham,   [SHERIFF *kneels.*

I have been away from England all these years,

Heading the holy war against the Moslem,

While thou and others in our kingless realms

Were fighting underhand unholy wars

Against your lawful king.

Sheriff.   My liege, Prince John—

King Richard. Say thou no word against my brother John.

Sheriff. Why then, my liege, I have no word to say.

King Richard (to ROBIN*).* My good friend Robin, Earl of Huntingdon,

For Earl thou art again, hast thou no fetters

For those of thine own band who would betray thee?

Robin. I have; but these were never worn as yet.

I never found one traitor in my band.

King Richard. Thou art happier than thy king. Put him in chains.

[*They fetter the* SHERIFF.

Robin. Look o'er these bonds, my liege.
[*Shows the* KING *the bonds. They talk together.*
King Richard. You, my lord Abbot, you Justiciary,
[*The* ABBOT *and* JUSTICIARY *kneel.*
I made you Abbot, you Justiciary:
You both are utter traitors to your king.
Justiciary. O my good liege, we did believe you dead.
Robin. Was justice dead because the King was dead?
Sir Richard paid his monies to the Abbot.
You crost him with a quibble of your law.
King Richard. But on the faith and honour of a king
The land is his again.
Sir Richard.   The land! the land!
I am crazed no longer, so I have the land.
[*Comes out of the litter and kneels.*
God save the King!
King Richard (raising SIR RICHARD). I thank thee, good Sir Richard.
Maid Marian.
Marian.   Yes, King Richard.
King Richard.   Thou wouldst marry
This Sheriff when King Richard came again
Except—
Marian. The King forbad it. True, my liege.
King Richard. How if the King command it?
Marian.   Then, my liege,
If you would marry me with a traitor sheriff,
I fear I might prove traitor with the sheriff.
King Richard. But if the King forbid thy marrying
With Robin, our good Earl of Huntingdon.
Marian. Then will I live for ever in the wild wood.
Robin (coming forward). And I with thee.
King Richard. On nuts and acorns, ha!
Or the King's deer? Earl, thou when we were hence
Hast broken all our Norman forest laws,
And scruplest not to flaunt it to our face
That thou wilt break our forest laws again
When we are here. Thou art overbold.

Robin.   My king,
I am but the echo of the lips of love.
King Richard. Thou hast risk'd thy life for mine: bind these two men.
[*They take the bags from the* ABBOT *and* JUSTICIARY, *and proceed to fetter them.*
Justiciary. But will the King, then, judge us all unheard?
I can defend my cause against the traitors
Who fain would make me traitor. If the King
Condemn us without trial, men will call him
An Eastern tyrant, not an English king.
Abbot. Besides, my liege, these men are outlaws, thieves,
They break thy forest laws—nay, by the rood
They have done far worse—they plunder—yea, ev'n bishops,
Yea, ev'n archbishops—if thou side with these,
Beware, O King, the vengeance of the Church.
Friar Tuck (brandishing his staff). I pray you, my liege, let me execute the vengeance
of the Church upon them. I have a stout crabstick here, which longs to break itself
across their backs.
Robin. Keep silence, bully friar, before the King.
Friar Tuck. If a cat may look at a king, may not a friar speak to one?
King Richard. I have had a year of prison-silence, Robin,
And heed him not—the vengeance of the Church!
Thou shalt pronounce the blessing of the Church
On those two here, Robin and Marian.
Marian. He is but hedge-priest, Sir King.
King Richard. And thou their Queen.
Our rebel Abbot then shall join your hands,
Or lose all hope of pardon from us—yet
Not now, not now—with after-dinner grace.
Nay, by the dragon of St. George, we shall
Do some injustice, if you hold us here
Longer from our own venison. Where is it?
I scent it in the green leaves of the wood.

Marian. First, king, a boon!

King Richard. Why surely ye are pardon'd,

Even this brawler of harsh truths—I trust
Half truths, good friar: ye shall with us to
   court.

Then, if ye cannot breathe but woodland
   air,

Thou Robin shalt be ranger of this forest,
And have thy fees, and break the law no
   more.

Marian. It is not that, my lord.

King Richard. Then what, my lady?

Marian. This is the gala-day of thy
   return.

I pray thee, for the moment strike the
   bonds

From these three men, and let them dine
   with us,

And lie with us among the flowers, and
   drink—

Ay, whether it be gall or honey to 'em—
The king's good health in ale and Mal-
   voisie.

King Richard. By Mahound I could dine
   with Beelzebub!

So now which way to the dinner?

Marian.   Past the bank

Of foxglove, then to left by that one yew.
You see the darkness thro' the lighter leaf.
But look, who comes?

Enter SAILOR

Sailor. We heard Sir Richard Lea was
   here with Robin.

O good Sir Richard, I am like the man
In Holy Writ, who brought his talent back;
For tho' we touch'd at many pirate ports,
We ever fail'd to light upon thy son.
Here is thy gold again. I am sorry for it.

Sir Richard. The gold—my son—my
   gold, my son, the land—

Here Abbot, Sheriff—no—no, Robin
   Hood.

Robin. Sir Richard, let that wait till we
   have dined.

Are all our guests here?

King Richard. No—there's yet one
   other:

I will not dine without him. Come from
   out   [*Enter* WALTER LEA.

That oak-tree! This young warrior broke
   his prison

And join'd my banner in the Holy Land,
And cleft the Moslem turban at my side.
My masters, welcome gallant Walter Lea.
Kiss him, Sir Richard—kiss him, my
   sweet Marian.

Marian. O Walter, Walter, is it thou
   indeed

Whose ransom was our ruin, whose return
Builds up our house again? I fear I
   dream.

Here—give me one sharp pinch upon the
   cheek

That I may feel thou art no phantom—yet
Thou art tann'd almost beyond my knowing, brother.   [*They embrace.*

Walter Lea. But thou art fair as ever, my
   sweet sister.

Sir Richard. Art thou my son?

Walter Lea.   I am, good father, I am.

Sir Richard. I had despair'd of thee—
   that sent me crazed.

Thou art worth thy weight in all those
   marks of gold,

Yea, and the weight of the very land itself,
Down to the inmost centre.

Robin.   Walter Lea,

Give me that hand which fought for
   Richard there.

Embrace me, Marian, and thou, good Kate,
           [*To* KATE *entering.*

Kiss and congratulate me, my good Kate.
           [*She kisses him.*

Little John. Lo now! low now!

I have seen thee clasp and kiss a man
   indeed,

For our brave Robin is a man indeed.
Then by thine own account thou shouldst
   be mine.

Kate. Well then, who kisses first?

Little John.   Kiss both together.
           [*They kiss each other.*

Robin. Then all is well. In this full tide
   of love,

Wave heralds wave: thy match shall follow
   mine (*to* LITTLE JOHN).

Would there were more—a hundred lovers
   more

To celebrate this advent of our King!
Our forest games are ended, our free life,

And we must hence to the King's court. I trust
We shall return to the wood. Meanwhile, farewell
Old friends, old patriarch oaks. A thousand winters
Will strip you bare as death, a thousand summers
Robe you life-green again. *You* seem, as it were,
Immortal, and we mortal. How few Junes
Will heat our pulses quicker! How few frosts
Will chill the hearts that beat for Robin Hood!
    Marian. And yet I think these oaks at dawn and even,
Or in the balmy breathings of the night,
Will whisper evermore of Robin Hood.
We leave but happy memories to the forest.
We dealt in the wild justice of the woods.
All those poor serfs whom we have served will bless us,
All those pale mouths which we have fed will praise us—
All widows we have holpen pray for us,
Our Lady's blessed shrines throughout the land

Be all the richer for us. You, good friar,
You Much, you Scarlet, you dear Little John,
Your names will cling like ivy to the wood.
And here perhaps a hundred years away
Some hunter in day-dreams or half asleep
Will hear our arrows whizzing overhead,
And catch the winding of a phantom horn.
    Robin. And surely these old oaks will murmur thee
Marian along with Robin. I am most happy—
Art thou not mine?—and happy that our King
Is here again, never I trust to roam
So far again, but dwell among his own.
Strike up a stave, my masters, all is well.

SONG WHILE THEY DANCE
A COUNTRY DANCE

Now the King is home again, and nevermore to
    roam again,
Now the King is home again, the King will have
    his own again,
Home again, home again, and each will have
    his own again,
All the birds in merry Sherwood sing and sing
    him home again.

DEMETER

AND OTHER POEMS

TO THE MARQUIS OF DUFFERIN AND AVA

I

At times our Britain cannot rest,
   At times her steps are swift and rash;
   She moving, at her girdle clash
The golden keys of East and West.

II

Not swift or rash, when late she lent
   The sceptres of her West, her East,
   To one, that ruling has increased
Her greatness and her self-content.

III

Your rule has made the people love
   Their ruler. Your viceregal days
   Have added fulness to the phrase
Of 'Gauntlet in the velvet glove.'

IV

But since your name will grow with Time,
   Not all, as honouring your fair fame
   Of Statesman, have I made the name
A golden portal to my rhyme:

V

But more, that you and yours may know
   From me and mine, how dear a debt
   We owed you, and are owing yet
To you and yours, and still would owe.

VI

For he—your India was his Fate,
   And drew him over sea to you—
   He fain had ranged her thro' and thro',
To serve her myriads and the State,—

VII

A soul that, watch'd from earliest youth,
   And on thro' many a brightening year,
   Had never swerved for craft or fear,
By one side-path, from simple truth;

VIII

Who might have chased and claspt Renown
   And caught her chaplet here—and there
   In haunts of jungle-poison'd air
The flame of life went wavering down;

IX

But ere he left your fatal shore,
   And lay on that funereal boat,
   Dying, 'Unspeakable' he wrote
'Their kindness,' and he wrote no more;

X

And sacred is the latest word;
   And now the Was, the Might-have-
      been,
   And those lone rites I have not seen,
And one drear sound I have not heard,

XI

Are dreams that scarce will let me be,
   Not there to bid my boy farewell,
   When That within the coffin fell,
Fell—and flash'd into the Red Sea,

XII

Beneath a hard Arabian moon
   And alien stars. To question, why
   The sons before the fathers die,
Not mine! and I may meet him soon;

XIII

But while my life's late eve endures,
   Nor settles into hueless gray,
   My memories of his briefer day
Will mix with love for you and yours.

ON THE JUBILEE OF QUEEN VICTORIA

I

Fifty times the rose has flower'd and
   faded,
Fifty times the golden harvest fallen,
Since our Queen assumed the globe, the
   sceptre.

II

She beloved for a kindliness
Rare in Fable or History,
Queen, and Empress of India,
Crown'd so long with a diadem
Never worn by a worthier,
Now with prosperous auguries
Comes at last to the bounteous
Crowning year of her Jubilee.

III

Nothing of the lawless, of the Despot,
Nothing of the vulgar, or vainglorious,
All is gracious, gentle, great and Queenly.

IV

You then joyfully, all of you,
Set the mountain aflame to-night,
Shoot your stars to the firmament,
Deck your houses, illuminate
All your towns for a festival,
And in each let a multitude
Loyal, each, to the heart of it,
One full voice of allegiance,
Hail the fair Ceremonial
Of this year of her Jubilee.

V

Queen, as true to womanhood as Queen-
hood,
Glorying in the glories of her people,
Sorrowing with the sorrows of the lowest!

VI

You, that wanton in affluence,
Spare not now to be bountiful,
Call you poor to regale with you,
All the lowly, the destitute,
Make their neighbourhood health-fuller,
Give your gold to the Hospital,
Let the weary be comforted,
Let the needy be banqueted,
Let the maim'd in his heart rejoice
At this glad Ceremonial,
And this year of her Jubilee.

VII

Henry's fifty years are all in shadow,
Gray with distance Edward's fifty sum-
mers,
Ev'n her Grandsire's fifty half forgotten.

VIII

You, the Patriot Architect,
You that shape for Eternity,
Raise a stately memorial,
Make it regally gorgeous,
Some Imperial Institute,
Rich in symbol, in ornament,
Which may speak to the centuries,
All the centuries after us,
Of this great Ceremonial,
And this year of her Jubilee.

IX

Fifty years of ever-broadening Commerce!
Fifty years of ever-brightening Science!
Fifty years of ever-widening Empire!

X

You, the Mighty, the Fortunate,
You, the Lord-territorial,
You, the Lord-manufacturer,
You, the hardy, laborious,
Patient children of Albion,
You, Canadian, Indian,
Australasian, African,
All your hearts be in harmony,
All your voices in unison,
Singing 'Hail to the glorious
Golden year of her Jubilee!'

XI

Are there thunders moaning in the
distance?
Are there spectres moving in the darkness?
Trust the Hand of Light will lead her
people,
Till the thunders pass, the spectres vanish,
And the Light is Victor, and the darkness
Dawns into the Jubilee of the Ages.

TO PROFESSOR JEBB

WITH THE FOLLOWING POEM

FAIR things are slow to fade away,
Bear witness you, that yesterday[1]
  From out the Ghost of Pindar in you
Roll'd an Olympian; and they say[2]

[1] In Bologna.
[2] They say, for the fact is doubtful.

That here the torpid mummy wheat
Of Egypt bore a grain as sweet
  As that which gilds the glebe of England,
Sunn'd with a summer of milder heat.

So may this legend for awhile,
If greeted by your classic smile,
  Tho' dead in its Trinacrian Enna,
Blossom again on a colder isle.

DEMETER AND PERSEPHONE

(IN ENNA)

FAINT as a climate-changing bird that flies
All night across the darkness, and at dawn
Falls on the threshold of her native land,
And can no more, thou camest, O my child,
Led upward by the God of ghosts and
    dreams,
Who laid thee at Eleusis, dazed and dumb
With passing thro' at once from state to
    state,
Until I brought thee hither, that the day,
When here thy hands let fall the gather'd
    flower,
Might break thro' clouded memories once
    again
On thy lost self. A sudden nightingale
Saw thee, and flash'd into a frolic of song
And welcome; and a gleam as of the moon,
When first she peers along the tremulous
    deep,
Fled wavering o'er thy face, and chased
    away
That shadow of a likeness to the king
Of shadows, thy dark mate. Persephone!
Queen of the dead no more—my child!
    Thine eyes
Again were human-godlike, and the Sun
Burst from a swimming fleece of winter
    gray,
And robed thee in his day from head to
    feet—
'Mother!' and I was folded in thine arms.

  Child, those imperial, disimpassion'd
    eyes
Awed even me at first, thy mother—eyes
That oft had seen the serpent-wanded
    power
Draw downward into Hades with his drift

Of flickering spectres, lighted from below
By the red race of fiery Phlegethon;
But when before have Gods or men beheld
The Life that had descended re-arise,
And lighted from above him by the Sun?
So mighty was the mother's childless cry,
A cry that rang thro' Hades, Earth, and
    Heaven!

  So in this pleasant vale we stand again,
The field of Enna, now once more ablaze
With flowers that brighten as thy footstep
    falls,
All flowers—but for one black blur of earth
Left by that closing chasm, thro' which
    the car
Of dark Aïdoneus rising rapt thee hence.
And here, my child, tho' folded in thine
    arms,
I feel the deathless heart of motherhood
Within me shudder, lest the naked glebe
Should yawn once more into the gulf, and
    thence
The shrilly whinnyings of the team of Hell,
Ascending, pierce the glad and songful air,
And all at once their arch'd necks, mid-
    night-maned,
Jet upward thro' the mid-day blossom. No!
For, see, thy foot has touch'd it; all the
    space
Of blank earth-baldness clothes itself
    afresh,
And breaks into the crocus-purple hour
That saw thee vanish.

            Child, when thou wert gone,
I envied human wives, and nested birds,
Yea, the cubb'd lioness; went in search of
    thee
Thro' many a palace, many a cot, and gave
Thy breast to ailing infants in the night,
And set the mother waking in amaze
To find her sick one whole; and forth again
Among the wail of midnight winds, and
    cried,
'Where is my loved one? Wherefore do ye
    wail?'
And out from all the night an answer
    shrill'd,
'We know not, and we know not why we
    wail.'

I climb'd on all the cliffs of all the seas,
And ask'd the waves that moan about the
    world
'Where? do ye make your moaning for my
    child?'
And round from all the world the voices
    came
'We know not, and we know not why we
    moan.'
'Where'? and I stared from every eagle-
    peak,
I thridded the black heart of all the woods,
I peer'd thro' tomb and cave, and in the
    storms
Of Autumn swept across the city, and
    heard
The murmur of their temples chanting me,
Me, me, the desolate Mother! 'Where'?—
    and turn'd,
And fled by many a waste, forlorn of man,
And grieved for man thro' all my grief for
    thee,—
The jungle rooted in his shatter'd hearth,
The serpent coil'd about his broken shaft,
The scorpion crawling over naked skulls;—
I saw the tiger in the ruin'd fane
Spring from his fallen God, but trace of
    thee
I saw not; and far on, and, following out
A league of labyrinthine darkness, came
On three gray heads beneath a gleaming
    rift.
'Where'? and I heard one voice from all
    the three
'We know not, for we spin the lives of men,
And not of Gods, and know not why we
    spin!
There is a Fate beyond us.' Nothing knew.

Last as the likeness of a dying man,
Without his knowledge, from him flits to
    warn
A far-off friendship that he comes no more,
So he, the God of dreams, who heard my
    cry,
Drew from thyself the likeness of thyself
Without thy knowledge, and thy shadow
    past
Before me, crying 'The Bright one in the
    highest
Is brother of the Dark one in the lowest,

And Bright and Dark have sworn that I,
    the child
Of thee, the great Earth-Mother, thee, the
    Power
That lifts her buried life from gloom to
    bloom,
Should be for ever and for evermore
The Bride of Darkness.'

                    So the Shadow wail'd.
Then I, Earth-Goddess, cursed the Gods
    of Heaven.
I would not mingle with their feasts; to me
Their nectar smack'd of hemlock on the
    lips,
Their rich ambrosia tasted aconite.
The man, that only lives and loves an
    hour,
Seem'd nobler than their hard Eternities.
My quick tears kill'd the flower, my ravings
    hush'd
The bird, and lost in utter grief I fail'd
To send my life thro' olive-yard and vine
And golden grain, my gift to helpless man.
Rain-rotten died the wheat, the barley-
    spears
Were hollow-husk'd, the leaf fell, and the
    sun,
Pale at my grief, drew down before his
    time
Sickening, and Ætna kept her winter snow.

    Then He, the brother of this Darkness,
    He
Who still is highest, glancing from his
    height
On earth a fruitless fallow, when he miss'd
The wonted steam of sacrifice, the praise
And prayer of men, decreed that thou
    should'st dwell
For nine white moons of each whole year
    with me,
Three dark ones in the shadow with thy
    King.

    Once more the reaper in the gleam of
    dawn
Will see me by the landmark far away,
Blessing his field, or seated in the dusk
Of even, by the lonely threshing-floor,
Rejoicing in the harvest and the grange.

Yet I, Earth-Goddess, am but ill-content
With them, who still are highest. Those
    gray heads,
What meant they by their 'Fate beyond
    the Fates'
But younger kindlier Gods to bear us
    down,
As we bore down the Gods before us? Gods,
To quench, not hurl the thunderbolt, to
    stay,
Not spread the plague, the famine; Gods
    indeed,
To send the noon into the night and break
The sunless halls of Hades into Heaven?
Till thy dark lord accept and love the
    Sun,
And all the Shadow die into the Light,
When thou shalt dwell the whole bright
    year with me,
And souls of men, who grew beyond their
    race,
And made themselves as Gods against the
    fear
Of Death and Hell; and thou that hast
    from men,
As Queen of Death, that worship which is
    Fear,
Henceforth, as having risen from out the
    dead,
Shalt ever send thy life along with mine
From buried grain thro' springing blade,
    and bless
Their garner'd Autumn also, reap with me,
Earth-mother, in the harvest hymns of
    Earth
The worship which is Love, and see no
    more
The Stone, the Wheel, the dimly-glimmer-
    ing lawns
Of that Elysium, all the hateful fires
Of torment, and the shadowy warrior glide
Along the silent field of Asphodel.

OWD ROÄ[1]

NAÄY, noä mander[2] o' use to be callin' 'im
    Roä, Roä, Roä,
Fur the dog's stoän-deäf, an' e's blind, 'e
    can naither stan' nor goä.

----

[1] Old Rover.   [2] Manner.

But I meäns fur to maäke 'is owd aäge as
    'appy as iver I can,
Fur I owäs owd Roäver moor nor I iver
    owäd mottal man.

Thou's rode of 'is back when a babby,
    afoor thou was gotten too owd,
Fur 'e'd fetch an' carry like owt, 'e was
    allus as good as gowd.

Eh, but 'e'd fight wi' a will *when* 'e fowt;
    'e could howd[1] 'is oan,
An' Roä was the dog as knaw'd when an'
    wheere to bury his boane.

An' 'e kep his heäd hoop like a king, an'
    'e'd niver not down wi' 'is taäil,
Fur 'e'd niver done nowt to be shaämed
    on, when we was i' Howlaby Daäle.

An' 'e served me sa well when 'e lived,
    that, Dick, when 'e cooms to be deäd,
I thinks as I'd like fur to hev soom soort
    of a sarvice reäd.

Fur 'e's moor good sense na the Parliament
    man 'at stans fur us 'ere,
An' I'd voät fur 'im, my oän sen, if 'e could
    but stan fur the Shere.

'Faäithful an' True'—them words be 'i
    Scriptur—an' Faäithful an' True
Ull be fun[2] upo' four short legs ten times
    fur one upo' two.

An' maäybe they'll walk upo' two but I
    knaws they runs upo' four,[3]—
Bedtime, Dicky! but waäit till tha 'eärs it
    be strikin' the hour.

Fur I wants to tell tha o' Roä when we
    lived i' Howlaby Daäle,
Ten year sin—Naäy—naäy! tha mun nob-
    but hev' one glass of aäle.

Straänge an' owd-farran'd[4] the 'ouse, an'
    belt[5] long afoor my daäy
Wi' haäfe o' the chimleys a-twizzen'd[6] an'
    twined like a band o' haäy.

----

[1] Hold.   [2] Found.
[3] 'Ou' as in 'house'.
[4] 'Owd-farran'd,' old-fashioned.
[5] Built.   [6] 'Twizzen'd,' twisted.

The fellers as maäkes them picturs, 'ud
coom at the fall o' the year,
An' sattle their ends upo stools to pictur
the door-poorch theere,

An' the Heagle 'as hed two heäds stannin'
theere o' the brokken stick;[1]
An' they niver 'ed seed sich ivin'[2] as graw'd
hall ower the brick;

An' theere i' the 'ouse one night—but it's
down, an' all on it now
Goan into mangles an' tonups,[3] an, raäved
slick thruf by the plow—

Theere, when the 'ouse wur a house, one
night I wur sittin' aloän,
Wi' Roäver athurt my feeät, an' sleeäpin
still as a stoän,

Of a Christmas Eäve, an' as cowd as this,
an' the midders[4] as white,
An' the fences all on 'em bolster'd oop wi'
the windle[5] that night;

An' the cat wur a-sleeäpin alongside
Roäver, but I wur awaäke,
An' smoäkin' an' thinkin' o' things—
Doänt maäke thysen sick wi' the
caäke.

Fur the men ater supper 'ed sung their
songs an' 'ed 'ed their beer,
An' 'ed goän their waäys; ther was nobbut
three, an' noän on 'em theere.

They was all on 'em fear'd o' the Ghoäst
an' dussn't not sleeäp i' the 'ouse,
But Dicky, the Ghoäst moästlins[6] was
nobbut a rat or a mouse.

An' I looökt out wonst[7] at the night, an'
the daäle was all of a thaw,
Fur I seed the beck coomin' down like a
long black snaäke i' the snaw,

An' I heärd greät heäps o' the snaw slushin'
down fro' the bank to the beck,
An' then as I stood i' the doorwaäy, I
feeäld a drip o' my neck.

[1] On a staff *ragulé*.
[2] Ivy.   [3] Mangolds and turnips.
[4] Meadows.   [5] Drifted snow.
[6] 'Moästlins,' for the most part, generally.
[7] Once.

Saw I turn'd in ageän, an' I thowt o' the
good owd times 'at was goan,
An' the munney they maäde by the war,
an' the times 'at was coomin' on;

Fur I thowt if the Staäte was a gawin' to
let in furriners' wheät,
Howiver was British farmers to stan' ageän
o' their feeät.

Howiver was I fur to find my rent an' to
paäy my men?
An' all along o' the feller[1] as turn'd 'is back
of hissen.

Thou slep i' the chaumber above us, we
couldn't ha' 'eärd tha call,
Sa Moother 'ed tell'd ma to bring tha
down, an' thy craädle an' all;

Fur the gell o' the farm 'at slep wi' tha
then 'ed gotten wer leäve,
Fur to goä that night to 'er foälk by cause
o' the Christmas Eäve;

But I cleän forgot tha, my lad, when
Moother 'ed gotten to bed,
An' I slep i' my chair hup-on-end, an' the
Freeä Traäde runn'd i' my 'ead,

Till I dreäm'd 'at Squire walkt in, an' I
says to him 'Squire, ya're laäte,'
Then I seed at 'is faäce wur as red as the
Yule-block theer i' the graäte.

An' 'e says 'can ya paäy me the rent
to-night?' an' I says to 'im 'Noä,'
An' 'e cotch'd howd hard o' my hairm,[2]
'Then hout to-night tha shall goä.'

'Tha'll niver,' says I, 'be a-turnin ma hout
upo' Christmas Eäve'?
Then I waäked an' I fun it was Roäver
a-tuggin' an' teärin' my slieäve.

An' I thowt as 'e'd goän cleän-wud,[3] fur I
noäwaäys knaw'd 'is intent;
An' I says 'Git awaäy, ya beäst,' an' I
fetcht 'im a kick an' 'e went.

Then 'e tummled up stairs, fur I 'eärd 'im,
as if 'e'd 'a brokken 'is neck,
An' I'd cleär forgot, little Dicky, thy
chaumber door wouldn't sneck;[4]

[1] Peel.   [2] Arm.   [3] Mad.   [4] Latch.

An' I slep' i' my chair ageän wi' my hairm
    hingin' down to the floor,
An' I thowt it was Roäver a-tuggin' an'
    teärin' me wuss nor afoor,

An' I thowt 'at I kick'd 'im ageän, but I
    kick'd thy Moother istead.
'What arta snorin' theere fur? the house
    is afire,' she said.

Thy Moother 'ed beän a-naggin' about the
    gell o' the farm,
She offens 'ud spy summut wrong when
    there warn't not a mossel o' harm;

An' she didn't not solidly meän I wur
    gawin' that waäy to the bad,
Fur the gell[1] was as howry a trollope as
    iver traäpes'd i' the squad.

But Moother was free of 'er tongue, as I
    offens 'ev tell'd 'er mysen,
Sa I kep i' my chair, fur I thowt she was
    nobbut a-rilin' ma then.

An' I says 'I'd be good to tha, Bess, if tha'd
    onywaäys let ma be good,'
But she skelpt ma haäfe ower i' the chair,
    an' screeäd like a Howl gone wud[2]—

'Ya mun run fur the lether.[3] Git oop, if
    ya're onywaäys good for owt.'
And I says 'If I beänt noäwaäys—not
    nowadaäys—good fur nowt—

Yit I beänt sich a Nowt[4] of all Nowts as
    'ull hallus do as 'e's bid.'
'But the stairs is afire,' she said; then I
    seed 'er a-cryin', I did.

An' she beäld 'Ya mun saäve little Dick,
    an' be sharp about it an' all,'
Sa I runs to the yard fur a lether, an' sets
    'im ageän the wall,

An' I claums an' I mashes the winder hin,
    when I gits to the top,
But the heät druv hout i' my heyes till I
    feäld mysen ready to drop.

    [1] The girl was as dirty a slut as ever trudged in the mud, but there is a sense of slatternliness in 'traäpes'd' which is not expressed in 'trudged'.
    [2] She half overturned me and shrieked like an owl gone mad.   [3] Ladder.
    [4] A thoroughly insignificant or worthless person.

Thy Moother was howdin' the lether, an'
    tellin' me not to be skeärd,
An' I wasn't afeärd, or I thinks leästwaäys
    as I wasn't afeärd;

But I couldn't see fur the smoäke wheere
    thou was a-liggin, my lad,
An' Roäver was theere i' the chaumber
    a-yowlin' an' yaupin' like mad;

An' thou was a-beälin' likewise, an' a-
    squeälin', as if tha was bit,
An' it wasn't a bite but a burn, fur the
    merk's[1] o' thy shou'der yit;

Then I call'd out Roä, Roä, Roä, thaw I
    didn't haäfe think as'e'd 'ear,
But 'e coom'd thruf the fire wi' my bairn i'
    'is mouth to the winder theere!

He coom'd like a Hangel o' marcy as soon
    as 'e 'eärd 'is naäme,
Or like tother Hangel i' Scriptur 'at sum-
    mun seed i' the flaäme,

When summun 'ed hax'd fur a son, an' 'e
    promised a son to she,
An' Roä was as good as the Hangel i'
    saävin' a son fur me.

Sa I browt tha down, an' I says 'I mun
    gaw up ageän fur Roä.'
'Gaw up ageän fur the varmint?' I tell'd
    'er 'Yeäs I mun goä.'

An' I claumb'd up ageän to the winder,
    an' clemm'd[2] owd Roä by the 'eäd,
An' 'is 'air coom'd off i' my 'ands an' I
    taäked 'im at fust fur deäd;

Fur 'e smell'd like a herse a-singein', an'
    seeäm'd as blind as a poop,
An' haäfe on 'im bare as a bublin'.[3] I
    couldn't wakken 'im oop,

But I browt 'im down, an' we got to the
    barn, fur the barn wouldn't burn
Wi' the wind blawin' hard tother waäy, an'
    the wind wasn't like to turn.

An' *I* kep a-callin' o' Roä till 'e waggled 'is
    taäil fur a bit,
But the cocks kep a-crawin' an' crawin' all
    night, an' I 'ears 'em yit;

    [1] Mark.   [2] Clutched.
    [3] 'Bubbling,' a young unfledged bird.

An' the dogs was a-yowlin' all round, and
  thou was a-squeälin' thysen,
An' Moother was naggin' an' groänin' an'
  moänin' an' naggin' ageän;

An' I 'eärd the bricks an' the baulks[1]
  rummle down when the roof gev waäy,
Fur the fire was a-raägin' an' raävin' an'
  roarin' like judgment daäy.

Warm enew theere sewer-ly, but the barn
  was as cowd as owt,
An' we cuddled and huddled togither, an'
  happt[2] wersens oop as we mowt.

An' I browt Roä round, but Moother 'ed
  beän sa soäk'd wi' the thaw
'At she cotch'd 'er death o' cowd that
  night, poor soul, i' the straw.

Haäfe o' the parish runn'd oop when the
  rigtree[3] was tummlin' in—
Too laäte—but it's all ower now—hall
  hower—an' ten year sin;

Too laäte, tha mun git tha to bed, but I'll
  coom an' I'll squench the light,
Fur we moänt 'ev naw moor fires—and soa
  little Dick, good-night.

VASTNESS

I

Many a hearth upon our dark globe sighs
  after many a vanish'd face,
Many a planet by many a sun may roll with
  the dust of a vanish'd race.

II

Raving politics, never at rest—as this poor
  earth's pale history runs,—
What is it all but a trouble of ants in the
  gleam of a million million of suns?

III

Lies upon this side, lies upon that side,
  truthless violence mourn'd by the
  Wise,
Thousands of voices drowning his own in
  a popular torrent of lies upon lies;

[1] Beams.   [2] Wrapt ourselves.
[3] The beam that runs along the roof of the
house just beneath the ridge.

IV

Stately purposes, valour in battle, glorious
  annals of army and fleet,
Death for the right cause, death for the
  wrong cause, trumpets of victory,
  groans of defeat;

V

Innocence seethed in her mother's milk,
  and Charity setting the martyr aflame;
Thraldom who walks with the banner of
  Freedom, and recks not to ruin a
  realm in her name.

VI

Faith at her zenith, or all but lost in the
  gloom of doubts that darken the
  schools;
Craft with a bunch of all-heal in her hand,
  follow'd up by her vassal legion of
  fools;

VII

Trade flying over a thousand seas with her
  spice and her vintage, her silk and her
  corn;
Desolate offing, sailorless harbours, famishing populace, wharves forlorn;

VIII

Star of the morning, Hope in the sunrise;
  gloom of the evening, Life at a close;
Pleasure who flaunts on her wide down-
  way with her flying robe and her
  poison'd rose;

IX

Pain, that has crawl'd from the corpse of
  Pleasure, a worm which writhes all
  day, and at night
Stirs up again in the heart of the sleeper,
  and stings him back to the curse of the
  light;

X

Wealth with his wines and his wedded
  harlots; honest Poverty, bare to the
  bone;
Opulent Avarice, lean as Poverty; Flattery
  gilding the rift in a throne;

XI

Fame blowing out from her golden trumpet
    a jubilant challenge to Time and to
    Fate;
Slander, her shadow, sowing the nettle on
    all the laurel'd graves of the Great;

XII

Love for the maiden, crown'd with mar-
    riage, no regrets for aught that has
    been,
Household happiness, gracious children,
    debtless competence, golden mean;

XIII

National hatreds of whole generations, and
    pigmy spites of the village spire;
Vows that will last to the last death-ruckle,
    and vows that are snapt in a moment
    of fire;

XIV

He that has lived for the lust of the minute,
    and died in the doing it, flesh without
    mind;
He that has nail'd all flesh to the Cross, till
    Self died out in the love of his kind;

XV

Spring and Summer and Autumn and
    Winter, and all these old revolutions
    of earth;
All new-old revolutions of Empire—
    change of the tide—what is all of it
    worth?

XVI

What the philosophies, all the sciences,
    poesy, varying voices of prayer?
All that is noblest, all that is basest, all that
    is filthy with all that is fair?

XVII

What is it all, if we all of us end but in
    being our own corpse-coffins at last,
Swallow'd in Vastness, lost in Silence,
    drown'd in the deeps of a meaningless
    Past?

XVIII

What but a murmur of gnats in the gloom,
    or a moment's anger of bees in their
    hive?—

      *   *   *   *

Peace, let it be! for I loved him, and love
    him for ever: the dead are not dead
    but alive.

𝔇𝔢𝔡𝔦𝔠𝔞𝔱𝔢𝔡 𝔱𝔬 𝔱𝔥𝔢 𝔥𝔬𝔫. 𝔍. �...

Dedicated to the Hon. J. Russell
Lowell

THE RING

MIRIAM AND HER FATHER

Miriam (*singing*)

MELLOW moon of heaven,
    Bright in blue,
Moon of married hearts,
    Hear me, you!

Twelve times in the year
    Bring me bliss,
Globing Honey Moons
    Bright as this.

Moon, you fade at times
    From the night,
Young again you grow
    Out of sight.

Silver crescent-curve,
    Coming soon,
Globe again, and make
    Honey Moon.

Shall not *my* love last,
    Moon, with you,
For ten thousand years
    Old and new?

Father. And who was he with such love-
    drunken eyes
They made a thousand honey moons of
    one?
Miriam. The prophet of his own, my
    Hubert—his
The words, and mine the setting. 'Air and
    Words,'
Said Hubert, when I sang the song, 'are
    bride
And bridegroom.' Does it please you?

791

Father.   Mainly, child,
Because I hear your Mother's voice in
    yours.
She——, why, you shiver tho' the wind is
    west
With all the warmth of summer.
Miriam.   Well, I felt
On a sudden I know not what, a breath
    that past
With all the cold of winter.
    Father (muttering to himself). Even so.
The Ghost in Man, the Ghost that once
    was Man,
But cannot wholly free itself from Man,
Are calling to each other thro' a dawn
Stranger than earth has ever seen; the veil
Is rending, and the Voices of the day
Are heard across the Voices of the dark.
No sudden heaven, nor sudden hell, for
    man,
But thro' the Will of One who knows and
    rules—
And utter knowledge is but utter love—
Æonian Evolution, swift or slow,
Thro' all the Spheres—an ever opening
    height,
An ever lessening earth—and she perhaps,
My Miriam, breaks her latest earthly link
With me to-day.
    Miriam. You speak so low, what is it?
Your 'Miriam breaks'—is making a new
    link
Breaking an old one?
    Father.   No, for we, my child,
Have been till now each other's all-in-all.
    Miriam. And you the lifelong guardian
    of the child.
    Father. I, and one other whom you have
    not known.
    Miriam. And who? what other?
    Father.   Whither are you bound?
For Naples which we only left in May?
    Miriam. No! father, Spain, but Hubert
    brings me home
With April and the swallow. Wish me joy!
    Father. What need to wish when Hubert
    weds in you
The heart of Love, and you the soul of
    Truth
In Hubert?
    Miriam. Tho' you used to call me once

The lonely maiden-Princess of the wood,
Who meant to sleep her hundred summers
    out
Before a kiss should wake her.
    Father.   Ay, but now
Your fairy Prince has found you, take this
    ring.
    Miriam. 'Io t'amo'—and these diamonds
    —beautiful!
'From Walter,' and for me from you then?
    Father.   Well,
One way for Miriam.
    Miriam.   Miriam am I not?
    Father. This ring bequeath'd you by
    your mother, child,
Was to be given you—such her dying
    wish—
Given on the morning when you came of
    age
Or on the day you married. Both the days
Now close in one. The ring is doubly
    yours.
Why do you look so gravely at the tower?
    Miriam. I never saw it yet so all ablaze
With creepers crimsoning to the pinnacles,
As if perpetual sunset linger'd there,
And all ablaze too in the lake below!
And how the birds that circle round the
    tower
Are cheeping to each other of their flight
To summer lands!
    Father. And that has made you grave?
Fly—care not. Birds and brides must leave
    the nest.
Child, I am happier in your happiness
Than in mine own.
    Miriam.   It is not that!
    Father.   What else?
    Miriam. That chamber in the tower.
    Father.   What chamber, child?
Your nurse is here?
    Miriam. My Mother's nurse and mine.
She comes to dress me in my bridal veil.
    Father. What did she say?
    Miriam.   She said, that you and I
Had been abroad for my poor health so
    long
She fear'd I had forgotten her, and I
    ask'd
About my Mother, and she said, 'Thy hair
Is golden like thy Mother's, not so fine.'

Father. What then? what more?

Miriam.   She said—perhaps indeed
She wander'd, having wander'd now so far
Beyond the common date of death—that
    you,
When I was smaller than the statuette
Of my dear Mother on your bracket here—
You took me to that chamber in the tower,
The topmost—a chest there, by which you
    knelt—
And there were books and dresses—left to
    me,
A ring too which you kiss'd, and I, she
    said,
I babbled, Mother, Mother—as I used
To prattle to her picture—stretch'd my
    hands
As if I saw her; then a woman came
And caught me from my nurse. I hear
    her yet—
A sound of anger like a distant storm.

Father. Garrulous old crone.

Miriam.   Poor nurse!

Father.   I bad her keep,
Like a seal'd book, all mention of the
    ring,
For I myself would tell you all to-day.

Miriam. 'She too might speak to-day,'
    she mumbled. Still,
I scarce have learnt the title of your book,
But you will turn the pages.

Father.   Ay, to-day!
I brought you to that chamber on your
    third
September birthday with your nurse, and
    felt
An icy breath play on me, while I stoopt
To take and kiss the ring.

Miriam.   This very ring
Io t'amo?

Father.   Yes, for some wild hope
    was mine
That, in the misery of my married life,
Miriam your Mother might appear to me.
She came to you, not me. The storm, you
    hear
Far-off, is Muriel—your stepmother's
    voice.

Miriam. Vext, that you thought my
    Mother came to me?
Or at my crying 'Mother?' or to find

My Mother's diamonds hidden from her
    there,
Like worldly beauties in the Cell, not
    shown
To dazzle all that see them?

Father.   Wait a while.
Your Mother and step-mother—Miriam
    Erne
And Muriel Erne—the two were cousins—
    lived
With Muriel's mother on the down, that
    sees
A thousand squares of corn and meadow,
    far
As the gray deep, a landscape which your
    eyes
Have many a time ranged over when a
    babe.

Miriam. I climb'd the hill with Hubert
    yesterday,
And from the thousand squares, one silent
    voice
Came on the wind, and seem'd to say
    'Again.'
We saw far off an old forsaken house,
Then home, and past the ruin'd mill.

Father.   And there
I found these cousins often by the brook,
For Miriam sketch'd and Muriel threw
    the fly;
The girls of equal age, but one was fair,
And one was dark, and both were beautiful.
No voice for either spoke within my heart
Then, for the surface eye, that only doats
On outward beauty, glancing from the one
To the other, knew not that which pleased
    it most,
The raven ringlet or the gold; but both
Were dowerless, and myself, I used to
    walk
This Terrace—morbid, melancholy; mine
And yet not mine the hall, the farm, the
    field;
For all that ample woodland whisper'd
    'debt,'
The brook that feeds this lakelet murmur'd
    'debt,'
And in yon arching avenue of old elms,
Tho' mine, not mine, I heard the sober
    rook
And carrion crow cry 'Mortgage.'

Miriam.   Father's fault
Visited on the children!
Father.   Ay, but then
A kinsman, dying, summon'd me to
Rome—
He left me wealth—and while I journey'd
hence,
And saw the world fly by me like a dream,
And while I communed with my truest
self,
I woke to all of truest in myself,
Till, in the gleam of those mid-summer
dawns,
The form of Muriel faded, and the face
Of Miriam grew upon me, till I knew;
And past and future mix'd in Heaven and
made
The rosy twilight of a perfect day.
     Miriam. So glad? no tear for him, who
left you wealth,
Your kinsman?
     Father. I had seen the man but once;
He loved my name not me; and then I
pass'd
Home, and thro' Venice, where a jeweller,
So far gone down, or so far up in life,
That he was nearing his own hundred,
sold
This ring to me, then laugh'd 'the ring is
weird.'
And weird and worn and wizard-like was
he.
'Why weird?' I ask'd him; and he said
'The souls
Of two repentant Lovers guard the ring;'
Then with a ribald twinkle in his bleak
eyes—
'And if you give the ring to any maid,
They still remember what it cost them
here,
And bind the maid to love you by the ring;
And if the ring were stolen from the maid,
The theft were death or madness to the
thief,
So sacred those Ghost Lovers hold the
gift.'
And then he told their legend:
                         'Long ago
Two lovers parted by a scurrilous tale
Had quarrell'd, till the man repenting sent
This ring "Io t'amo" to his best beloved,

And sent it on her birthday. She in wrath
Return'd it on her birthday, and that day
His death-day, when, half-frenzied by the
ring,
He wildly fought a rival suitor, him
The causer of that scandal, fought and fell;
And she that came to part them all too late,
And found a corpse and silence, drew the
ring
From his dead finger, wore it till her death,
Shrined him within the temple of her
heart,
Made every moment of her after life
A virgin victim to his memory,
And dying rose, and rear'd her arms, and
cried
"I see him, Io t'amo, Io t'amo."'
     Miriam. Legend or true? so tender
should be true!
Did *he* believe it? did you ask him?
     Father.   Ay!
But that half skeleton, like a barren ghost
From out the fleshless world of spirits,
laugh'd:
A hollow laughter!
     Miriam.   Vile, so near the ghost
Himself, to laugh at love in death! But
you?
     Father. Well, as the bygone lover thro'
this ring
Had sent his cry for her forgiveness, I
Would call thro' this 'Io t'amo' to the
heart
Of Miriam; then I bad the man engrave
'From Walter' on the ring, and send it—
wrote
Name, surname, all as clear as noon, but
he—
Some younger hand must have engraven
the ring—
His fingers were so stiffen'd by the frost
Of seven and ninety winters, that he
scrawl'd
A 'Miriam' that might seem a 'Muriel';
And Muriel claim'd and open'd what I
meant
For Miriam, took the ring, and flaunted it
Before that other whom I loved and love.
     A mountain stay'd me here, a minster
there,
A galleried palace, or a battlefield,

Where stood the sheaf of Peace: but—
  coming home—
And on your Mother's birthday—all but
  yours—
A week betwixt—and when the tower as
  now
Was all ablaze with crimson to the roof,
And all ablaze too plunging in the lake
Head-foremost—who were those that
  stood between
The tower and that rich phantom of the
  tower?
Muriel and Miriam, each in white, and like
May-blossoms in mid autumn—was it
  they?
A light shot upward on them from the lake.
What sparkled there? whose hand was
  that? they stood
So close together. I am not keen of sight,
But coming nearer—Muriel had the ring—
'O Miriam! have you given your ring to
  her?
O Miriam!' Miriam redden'd, Muriel
  clench'd
The hand that wore it, till I cried again:
'O Miriam, if you love me take the ring!'
She glanced at me, at Muriel, and was
  mute.
'Nay, if you cannot love me, let it be.'
Then—Muriel standing ever statue-like—
She turn'd, and in her soft imperial way
And saying gently: 'Muriel, by your leave,'
Unclosed the hand, and from it drew the
  ring,
And gave it me, who pass'd it down her
  own,
'Io t'amo, all is well then.' Muriel fled.
Miriam. Poor Muriel!
Father.   Ay, poor Muriel
  when you hear
What follows! Miriam loved me from the
  first,
Not thro' the ring; but on her marriage-
  morn
This birthday, death-day, and betrothal
  ring,
Laid on her table overnight, was gone;
And after hours of search and doubt and
  threats,
And hubbub, Muriel enter'd with it,
  'See!—

Found in a chink of that old moulder'd
  floor!'
My Miriam nodded with a pitying smile,
As who should say 'that those who lose
  can find.'
Then I and she were married for a year,
One year without a storm, or even a cloud;
And you my Miriam born within the year;
And she my Miriam dead within the year.
  I sat beside her dying, and she gaspt:
'The books, the miniature, the lace are
  hers,
My ring too when she comes of age, or
  when
She marries; you—you loved me, kept
  your word.
You love me still "Io t'amo."—Muriel—
  no—
She cannot love; she loves her own hard
  self,
Her firm will, her fix'd purpose. Promise
  me,
Miriam not Muriel—she shall have the
  ring.'
And there the light of other life, which
  lives
Beyond our burial and our buried eyes,
Gleam'd for a moment in her own on earth.
I swore the vow, then with my latest kiss
Upon them, closed her eyes, which would
  not close,
But kept their watch upon the ring and you.
Your birthday was her death-day.
Miriam.   O poor Mother!
And you, poor desolate Father, and poor
  me,
The little senseless, worthless, wordless
  babe,
Saved when your life was wreck'd!
Father.   Desolate? yes!
Desolate as that sailor, whom the storm
Had parted from his comrade in the boat,
And dash'd half dead on barren sands,
  was I.
Nay, you were my one solace; only—you
Were always ailing. Muriel's mother sent,
And sure am I, by Muriel, one day came
And saw you, shook her head, and patted
  yours,
And smiled, and making with a kindly
  pinch

Each poor pale cheek a momentary rose—
'*That* should be fix'd,' she said; 'your
    pretty bud,
So blighted here, would flower into full
    health
Among our heath and bracken. Let her
    come!
And we will feed her with our mountain
    air,
And send her home to you rejoicing.' No—
We could not part. And once, when you
    my girl
Rode on my shoulder home—the tiny fist
Had graspt a daisy from your Mother's
    grave—
By the lych-gate was Muriel. 'Ay,' she
    said,
'Among the tombs in this damp vale of
    yours!
You scorn my Mother's warning, but the
    child
Is paler than before. We often walk
In open sun, and see beneath our feet
The mist of autumn gather from your lake,
And shroud the tower; and once we only
    saw
Your gilded vane, a light above the mist'—
(Our old bright bird that still is veering
    there
Above his four gold letters) 'and the light,'
She said, 'was like that light'—and there
    she paused,
And long; till I believing that the girl's
Lean fancy, groping for it, could not find
One likeness, laugh'd a little and found
    her two—
'A warrior's crest above the cloud of
    war'—
'A fiery phœnix rising from the smoke,
The pyre he burnt in.'—'Nay,' she said,
    'the light
That glimmers on the marsh and on the
    grave.'
And spoke no more, but turn'd and pass'd
    away.
    Miriam, I am not surely one of those
Caught by the flower that closes on the fly,
But after ten slow weeks her fix'd intent,
In aiming at an all but hopeless mark
To strike it, struck; I took, I left you there;
I came, I went, was happier day by day;

For Muriel nursed you with a mother's
    care;
Till on that clear and heather-scented
    height
The rounder cheek had brighten'd into
    bloom.
She always came to meet me carrying you,
And all her talk was of the babe she loved;
So, following her old pastime of the brook,
She threw the fly for me; but oftener left
That angling to the mother. 'Muriel's
    health
Had weaken'd, nursing little Miriam.
    Strange!
She used to shun the wailing babe, and
    doats
On this of yours.' But when the matron
    saw
That hinted love was only wasted bait,
Not risen to, she was bolder. 'Ever since
You sent the fatal ring'—I told her 'sent
To Miriam,' 'Doubtless—ay, but ever
    since
In all the world my dear one sees but
    you—
In your sweet babe she finds but you—she
    makes
Her heart a mirror that reflects but you.'
And then the tear fell, the voice broke.
    Her heart!
I gazed into the mirror, as a man
Who sees his face in water, and a stone,
That glances from the bottom of the pool,
Strike upward thro' the shadow; yet at
    last,
Gratitude—loneliness—desire to keep
So skilled a nurse about you always—nay!
Some half remorseful kind of pity too—
Well! well, you know I married Muriel
    Erne.
    'I take thee Muriel for my wedded
    wife'—
I had forgotten it was your birthday,
    child—
When all at once with some electric thrill
A cold air pass'd between us, and the
    hands
Fell from each other, and were join'd again.
    No second cloudless honeymoon was
    mine.
For by and by she sicken'd of the farce,

She dropt the gracious mask of mother-
hood,
She came no more to meet me, carrying
you,
Nor ever cared to set you on her knee,
Nor ever let you gambol in her sight,
Nor ever cheer'd you with a kindly smile,
Nor ever ceased to clamour for the ring;
Why had I sent the ring at first to her?
Why had I made her love me thro' the
ring,
And then had changed? so fickle are men
—the best!
Not she—but now my love was hers again,
The ring by right, she said, was hers again.
At times too shrilling in her angrier moods,
'That weak and watery nature love you?
No!
"*Io* t'amo, *Io* t'amo"!' flung herself
Against my heart, but often while her lips
Were warm upon my cheek, an icy breath,
As from the grating of a sepulchre,
Past over both. I told her of my vow,
No pliable idiot I to break my vow;
But still she made her outcry for the ring;
For one monotonous fancy madden'd her,
Till I myself was madden'd with her cry,
And even that 'Io t'amo,' those three sweet
Italian words, became a weariness.
    My people too were scared with eerie
sounds,
A footstep, a low throbbing in the walls,
A noise of falling weights that never fell,
Weird whispers, bells that rang without a
hand,
Door-handles turn'd when none was at the
door,
And bolted doors that open'd of them-
selves:
And one betwixt the dark and light had
seen
Her, bending by the cradle of her babe.
    Miriam. And I remember once that
being waked
By noises in the house—and no one near—
I cried for nurse, and felt a gentle hand
Fall on my forehead, and a sudden face
Look'd in upon me like a gleam and pass'd,
And I was quieted, and slept again.
Or is it some half memory of a dream?
    Father. Your fifth September birthday.

Miriam.   And the face,
The hand,—my Mother.
    Father.   Miriam, on that day
Two lovers parted by no scurrilous tale—
Mere want of gold—and still for twenty
years
Bound by the golden cord of their first
love—
Had ask'd us to their marriage, and to
share
Their marriage-banquet. Muriel, paler
then
Than ever you were in your cradle,
moan'd,
'I am fitter for my bed, or for my grave,
I cannot go, go you.' And then she rose,
She clung to me with such a hard embrace,
So lingeringly long, that half-amazed
I parted from her, and I went alone.
And when the bridegroom murmur'd, 'With
this ring,'
I felt for what I could not find, the key,
The guardian of her relics, of *her* ring.
I kept it as a sacred amulet
About me,—gone! and gone in that
embrace!
Then, hurrying home, I found her not in
house
Or garden—up the tower—an icy air
Fled by me.—There, the chest was open
—all
The sacred relics tost about the floor—
Among them Muriel lying on her face—
I raised her, call'd her 'Muriel, Muriel
wake!'
The fatal ring lay near her; the glazed eye
Glared at me as in horror. Dead! I took
And chafed the freezing hand. A red mark
ran
All round one finger pointed straight, the
rest
Were crumpled inwards. Dead!—and
maybe stung
With some remorse, had stolen, worn the
ring—
Then torn it from her finger, or as if—
For never had I seen her show remorse—
As if—
    Miriam. —those two Ghost lovers—
    Father.   Lovers yet—
    Miriam. Yes, yes!

Father. —but dead so long, gone up so
    far,
That now their ever-rising life has dwarf'd
Or lost the moment of their past on
    earth,
As we forget our wail at being born.
As if—
    Miriam.—a dearer ghost had—
    Father.   —wrench'd it away.
    Miriam. Had floated in with sad re-
    proachful eyes,
Till from her own hand she had torn the
    ring
In fright, and fallen dead. And I myself
Am half afraid to wear it.
    Father.   Well, no more!
No bridal music this! but fear not you!
You have the ring she guarded; that poor
    link
With earth is broken, and has left her
    free,
Except that, still drawn downward for an
    hour,
Her spirit hovering by the church, where
    she
Was married too, may linger, till she sees
Her maiden coming like a Queen, who
    leaves
Some colder province in the North to
    gain
Her capital city, where the loyal bells
Clash welcome—linger, till her own, the
    babe
She lean'd to from her Spiritual sphere,
Her lonely maiden-Princess, crown'd with
    flowers,
Has enter'd on the larger woman-world
Of wives and mothers.
            But the bridal veil—
Your nurse is waiting. Kiss me child
    and go.

FORLORN

I

'HE is fled—I wish him dead—
  He that wrought my ruin—
O the flattery and the craft
  Which were my undoing . . .
    In the night, in the night,
  When the storms are blowing.

II

'Who was witness of the crime?
  Who shall now reveal it?
He is fled, or he is dead,
  Marriage will conceal it . . .
    In the night, in the night,
  While the gloom is growing.'

III

Catherine, Catherine, in the night,
  What is this you're dreaming?
There is laughter down in Hell
  At your simple scheming . . .
    In the night, in the night,
  When the ghosts are fleeting.

IV

You to place a hand in his
  Like an honest woman's,
You that lie with wasted lungs
  Waiting for your summons . . .
    In the night, O the night!
  O the deathwatch beating!

V

There will come a witness soon
  Hard to be confuted,
All the world will hear a voice
  Scream you are polluted . . .
    In the night! O the night!
  When the owls are wailing!

VI

Shame and marriage, Shame and marriage,
  Fright and foul dissembling,
Bantering bridesman, reddening priest,
  Tower and altar trembling . . .
    In the night, O the night,
  When the mind is failing!

VII

Mother, dare you kill your child?
  How your hand is shaking!
Daughter of the seed of Cain,
  What is this you're taking? . . .
    In the night, O the night,
  While the house is sleeping.

VIII

Dreadful! has it come to this,
  O unhappy creature?
You that would not tread on a worm

For your gentle nature . . .
In the night, O the night,
O the night of weeping!

IX

Murder would not veil your sin,
Marriage will not hide it,
Earth and Hell will brand your name,
Wretch you must abide it . . .
In the night, O the night,
Long before the dawning.

X

Up, get up, and tell him all,
Tell him you were lying!
Do not die with a lie in your mouth,
You that know you're dying . . .
In the night, O the night,
While the grave is yawning.

XI

No—you will not die before,
Tho' you'll ne'er be stronger;
You will live till *that* is born,
Then a little longer . . .
In the night, O the night,
While the Fiend is prowling.

XII

Death and marriage, Death and marriage!
Funeral hearses rolling!
Black with bridal favours mixt!
Bridal bells with tolling! . . .
In the night, O the night,
When the wolves are howling.

XIII

Up, get up, the time is short,
Tell him now or never!
Tell him all before you die,
Lest you die for ever . . .
In the night, O the night,
Where there's no forgetting.

XIV

Up she got, and wrote him all,
All her tale of sadness,
Blister'd every word with tears,
And eased her heart of madness . . .
In the night, and nigh the dawn,
And while the moon was setting.

HAPPY
THE LEPER'S BRIDE

I

Why wail you, pretty plover? and what is
   it that you fear?
Is he sick your mate like mine? have you
   lost him, is he fled?
And there—the heron rises from his watch
   beside the mere,
And flies above the leper's hut, where
   lives the living-dead.

II

Come back, nor let me know it! would he
   live and die alone?
And has he now forgiven me yet, his
   over-jealous bride,
Who am, and was, and will be his, his own
   and only own,
To share his living death with him, die
   with him side by side?

III

Is that the leper's hut on the solitary moor,
   Where noble Ulric dwells forlorn, and
   wears the leper's weed?
The door is open. He! is he standing at the
   door,
My soldier of the Cross? it is he and he
   indeed!

IV

My roses—will he take them *now*—mine,
   his—from off the tree
We planted both together, happy in our
   marriage morn?
O God, I could blaspheme, for he fought
   Thy fight for Thee,
And Thou hast made him leper to com-
   pass him with scorn—

V

Hast spared the flesh of thousands, the
   coward and the base,
And set a crueller mark than Cain's on
   him, the good and brave!
He sees me, waves me from him. I will
   front him face to face.
You need not wave me from you. I
   would leap into your grave.

* * * * *

799

VI

My warrior of the Holy Cross and of the
  conquering sword,
  The roses that you cast aside—once
  more I bring you these.
No nearer? do you scorn me when you
  tell me, O my lord,
  You would not mar the beauty of your
  bride with your disease.

VII

You say your body is so foul—then here I
  stand apart,
  Who yearn to lay my loving head upon
  your leprous breast.
The leper plague may scale my skin but
  never taint my heart;
  Your body is not foul to me, and body
  is foul at best.

VIII

I loved you first when young and fair, but
  now I love you most;
  The fairest flesh at last is filth on which
  the worm will feast;
This poor rib-grated dungeon of the holy
  human ghost,
  This house with all its hateful needs no
  cleaner than the beast,

IX

This coarse diseaseful creature which in
  Eden was divine,
  This Satan-haunted ruin, this little city
  of sewers,
This wall of solid flesh that comes between
  your soul and mine,
  Will vanish and give place to the beauty
  that endures,

X

The beauty that endures on the Spiritual
  height,
  When we shall stand transfigured, like
  Christ on Hermon hill,
And moving each to music, soul in soul
  and light in light,
  Shall flash thro' one another in a moment
  as we will.

XI

Foul! foul! the word was yours not mine,
  I worship that right hand
  Which fell'd the foes before you as the
  woodman fells the wood,
And sway'd the sword that lighten'd back
  the sun of Holy land,
  And clove the Moslem crescent moon,
  and changed it into blood.

XII

And once I worshipt all too well this
  creature of decay,
  For Age will chink the face, and Death
  will freeze the supplest limbs—
Yet you in your mid manhood—O the
  grief when yesterday
  They bore the Cross before you to the
  chant of funeral hymns.

XIII

'Libera me, Domine!' you sang the Psalm,
  and when
  The Priest pronounced you dead, and
  flung the mould upon your feet,
A beauty came upon your face, not that of
  living men,
  But seen upon the silent brow when life
  has ceased to beat.

XIV

'Libera nos, Domine'—you knew not one
  was there
  Who saw you kneel beside your bier,
  and weeping scarce could see;
May I come a little nearer, I that heard,
  and changed the prayer
  And sang the married 'nos' for the
  solitary 'me.'

XV

My beauty marred by you? by you! so be
  it. All is well
  If I lose it and myself in the higher
  beauty, yours.
My beauty lured that falcon from his eyry
  on the fell,
  Who never caught one gleam of the
  beauty which endures—

XVI

The Count who sought to snap the bond
that link'd us life to life,
  Who whisper'd me 'your Ulric loves'—
  a little nearer still—
He hiss'd, 'Let us revenge ourselves, your
Ulric woos my wife'—
  A lie by which he thought he could
  subdue me to his will.

XVII

I knew that you were near me when I let
him kiss my brow;
  Did he touch me on the lips? I was
  jealous, anger'd, vain,
And I meant to make *you* jealous. Are you
jealous of me now?
  Your pardon, O my love, if I ever gave
  you pain.

XVIII

You never once accused me, but I wept
alone, and sigh'd
  In the winter of the Present for the
  summer of the Past;
That icy winter silence—how it froze you
from your bride,
  Tho' I made one barren effort to break
  it at the last.

XIX

I brought you, you remember, these roses,
when I knew
  You were parting for the war, and you
  took them tho' you frown'd;
You frown'd and yet you kiss'd them.
All at once the trumpet blew,
  And you spurr'd your fiery horse, and
  you hurl'd them to the ground.

XX

You parted for the Holy War without a
word to me,
  And clear myself unask'd—not I. My
  nature was too proud.
And him I saw but once again, and far
away was he,
  When I was praying in a storm—the
  crash was long and loud—

XXI

That God would ever slant His bolt from
falling on your head—
  Then I lifted up my eyes, he was coming
  down the fell—
I clapt my hands. The sudden fire from
Heaven had dash'd him dead,
  And sent him charr'd and blasted to the
  deathless fire of Hell.

XXII

See, I sinn'd but for a moment. I repented
and repent,
  And trust myself forgiven by the God
  to whom I kneel.
A little nearer? Yes. I shall hardly be
content
  Till I be leper like yourself, my love
  from head to heel.

XXIII

O foolish dreams, that you, that I, would
slight our marriage oath:
  I held you at that moment even dearer
  than before;
Now God has made you leper in His loving
care for both,
  That we might cling together never
  doubt each other more.

XXIV

The Priest, who join'd you to the dead,
has join'd our hands of old;
  If man and wife be but one flesh, let
  mine be leprous too,
As dead from all the human race as if
beneath the mould;
  If you be dead, then I am dead, who
  only live for you.

XXV

Would Earth tho' hid in cloud not be
follow'd by the Moon?
  The leech forsake the dying bed for
  terror of his life?
The shadow leave the Substance in the
brooding light of noon?
  Or if *I* had been the leper would you
  have left the wife?

XXVI

Not take them? Still you wave me off—
　poor roses—must I go—
I have worn them year by year—from
　the bush we both had set—
What? fling them to you?—well—that
　were hardly gracious. No!
Your plague but passes by the touch.
　A little nearer yet!

XXVII

There, there! he buried you, the Priest;
　the Priest is not to blame,
He joins us once again, to his either
　office true:
I thank him. I am happy, happy. Kiss me.
　In the name
Of the everlasting God, I will live and
　die with you.

[DEAN MILMAN has remarked that the protection and care afforded by the Church to this blighted race of lepers was among the most beautiful of its offices during the Middle Ages. The leprosy of the thirteenth and fourteenth centuries was supposed to be a legacy of the crusades, but was in all probability the offspring of meagre and unwholesome diet, miserable lodging and clothing, physical and moral degradation. The services of the Church in the seclusion of these unhappy sufferers were most affecting. The stern duty of looking to the public welfare is tempered with exquisite compassion for the victims of this loathsome disease. The ritual for the sequestration of the leprous differed little from the burial service. After the leper had been sprinkled with holy water, the priest conducted him into the church, the leper singing the psalm 'Libera me domine', and the crucifix and bearer going before. In the church a black cloth was stretched over two trestles in front of the altar, and the leper leaning at its side devoutly heard mass. The priest, taking up a little earth in his cloak, threw it on one of the leper's feet, and put him out of the church, if it did not rain too heavily; took him to his hut in the midst of the fields, and then uttered the prohibitions: 'I forbid you entering the church . . . or entering the company of others. I forbid you quitting your home without your leper's dress.' He concluded: 'Take this dress, and wear it in token of humility; take these gloves, take this clapper, as a sign that you are forbidden to speak to any one. You are not to be indignant at being thus separated from others, and as to your little wants, good people will provide for you, and God will not desert you.' Then in this old ritual

follow these sad words: 'When it shall come to pass that the leper shall pass out of this world, he shall be buried in his hut, and not in the churchyard.' At first there was a doubt whether wives should follow their husbands who had been leprous, or remain in the world and marry again. The Church decided that the marriage-tie was indissoluble, and so bestowed on these unhappy beings this immense source of consolation. With a love stronger than this living death, lepers were followed into banishment from the haunts of men by their faithful wives. Readers of Sir J. Stephen's *Essays on Ecclesiastical Biography* will recollect the description of the founder of the Franciscan order, how, controlling his involuntary disgust, St. Francis of Assisi washed the feet and dressed the sores of the lepers, once at least reverently applying his lips to their wounds.—BOUCHER-JAMES.]

This ceremony of *quasi*-burial varied considerably at different times and in different places. In some cases a grave was dug, and the leper's face was often covered during the service.

TO ULYSSES[1]

I

ULYSSES, much-experienced man,
　Whose eyes have known this globe of
　　ours,
　Her tribes of men, and trees, and flowers,
From Corrientes to Japan,

II

To you that bask below the Line,
　I soaking here in winter wet—
　The century's three strong eights have
　　met
To drag me down to seventy-nine

III

In summer if I reach my day—
　To you, yet young, who breathe the
　　balm
　Of summer-winters by the palm
And orange grove of Paraguay,

IV

I tolerant of the colder time,
　Who love the winter woods, to trace
　On paler heavens the branching grace
Of leafless elm, or naked lime,

[1] 'Ulysses,' the title of a number of essays by W. G. Palgrave. He died at Monte Video before seeing my poem.

V

And see my cedar green, and there
    My giant ilex keeping leaf
    When frost is keen and days are brief—
Or marvel how in English air

VI

My yucca, which no winter quells,
    Altho' the months have scarce begun,
    Has push'd toward our faintest sun
A spike of half-accomplish'd bells—

VII

Or watch the waving pine which here
    The warrior of Caprera set,[1]
    A name that earth will not forget
Till earth has roll'd her latest year—

VIII

I, once half-crazed for larger light
    On broader zones beyond the foam,
    But charming fancy now at home
Among the quarried downs of Wight,

IX

Not less would yield full thanks to you
    For your rich gift, your tale of lands
    I know not,[2] your Arabian sands;
Your cane, your palm, tree-fern, bamboo,

X

The wealth of tropic bower and brake;
    Your Oriental Eden-isles,[3]
    Where man, nor only Nature smiles;
Your wonder of the boiling lake;[4]

XI

Phra-Chai, the Shadow of the Best,[5]
    Phra-bat[6] the step; your Pontic coast;
    Crag-cloister;[7] Anatolian Ghost;[8]
Hong-Kong,[9] Karnac,[10] and all the rest.

[1] Garibaldi said to me, alluding to his barren island, 'I wish I had your trees.'
[2] The tale of Nejd.
[3] The Philippines.   [4] In Dominica.
[5] The Shadow of the Lord. Certain obscure markings on a rock in Siam, which express the image of Buddha to the Buddhist more or less distinctly according to his faith and his moral worth.
[6] The footstep of the Lord on another rock.
[7] The monastery of Sumelas.
[8] Anatolian Spectre stories.
[9] The Three Cities.
[10] Travels in Egypt.

XII

Thro' which I follow'd line by line
    Your leading hand, and came, my friend,
    To prize your various book, and send
A gift of slenderer value, mine.

TO MARY BOYLE

WITH THE FOLLOWING POEM

I

'SPRING-FLOWERS'! While you still delay to take
    Your leave of Town,
Our elmtree's ruddy-hearted blossom-flake
    Is fluttering down.

II

Be truer to your promise. There! I heard
    Our cuckoo call.
Be needle to the magnet of your word,
    Nor wait, till all

III

Our vernal bloom from every vale and plain
    And garden pass,
And all the gold from each laburnum chain
    Drop to the grass.

IV

Is memory with your Marian gone to rest,
    Dead with the dead?
For ere she left us, when we met, you prest
    My hand, and said

V

'I come with your spring-flowers.' You came not, friend;
    My birds would sing,
You heard not. Take then this spring-flower I send,
    This song of spring,

VI

Found yesterday—forgotten mine own rhyme
    By mine old self,
As I shall be forgotten by old Time,
    Laid on the shelf—

VII

A rhyme that flower'd betwixt the whitening sloe
    And kingcup blaze,
And more than half a hundred years ago,
    In rick-fire days,

VIII

When Dives loathed the times, and paced
his land
    In fear of worse,
And sanguine Lazarus felt a vacant hand
    Fill with *his* purse.

IX

For lowly minds were madden'd to the
height
    By tonguester tricks,
And once—I well remember that red night
    When thirty ricks,

X

All flaming, made an English homestead
Hell—
    These hands of mine
Have helpt to pass a bucket from the well
    Along the line,

XI

When this bare dome had not begun to
gleam
    Thro' youthful curls,
And you were then a lover's fairy dream,
    His girl of girls;

XII

And you, that now are lonely, and with
Grief
    Sit face to face,
Might find a flickering glimmer of relief
    In change of place.

XIII

What use to brood? this life of mingled
pains
    And joys to me,
Despite of every Faith and Creed, remains
    The Mystery.

XIV

Let golden youth bewail the friend, the
wife,
    For ever gone.

He dreams of that long walk thro' desert
life
    Without the one.

XV

The silver year should cease to mourn and
sigh—
    Not long to wait—
So close are we, dear Mary, you and I
    To that dim gate.

XVI

Take, read! and be the faults your Poet
makes
    Or many or few,
He rests content, if his young music wakes
    A wish in you

XVII

To change our dark Queen-city, all her
realm
    Of sound and smoke,
For his clear heaven, and these few lanes
of elm
    And whispering oak.

THE PROGRESS OF SPRING

I

THE groundflame of the crocus breaks the
mould,
    Fair Spring slides hither o'er the
    Southern sea,
Wavers on her thin stem the snowdrop
cold
    That trembles not to kisses of the bee:
Come, Spring, for now from all the drip
ping eaves
    The spear of ice has wept itself away,
And hour by hour unfolding woodbine
leaves
    O'er his uncertain shadow droops the
day.
She comes! The loosen'd rivulets run;
    The frost-bead melts upon her golden
hair;
Her mantle, slowly greening in the Sun,
    Now wraps her close, now arching leaves
her bare
    To breaths of balmier air;

II

Up leaps the lark, gone wild to welcome
        her,
    About her glance the tits, and shriek the
        jays,
Before her skims the jubilant woodpecker,
    The linnet's bosom blushes at her gaze,
While round her brows a woodland culver
        flits,
    Watching her large light eyes and
        gracious looks,
And in her open palm a halcyon sits
    Patient—the secret splendour of the
        brooks.
Come, Spring! She comes on waste and
        wood,
    On farm and field: but enter also here,
Diffuse thyself at will thro' all my blood,
    And, tho' thy violet sicken into sere,
        Lodge with me all the year!

III

Once more a downy drift against the
        brakes,
    Self-darken'd in the sky, descending
        slow!
But gladly see I thro' the wavering flakes
    Yon blanching apricot like snow in
        snow.
These will thine eyes not brook in forest-
        paths,
    On their perpetual pine, nor round the
        beech;
They fuse themselves to little spicy baths,
    Solved in the tender blushes of the
        peach;
They lose themselves and die
    On that new life that gems the hawthorn
        line;
Thy gay lent-lilies wave and put them by,
    And out once more in varnish'd glory
        shine
        Thy stars of celandine.

IV

She floats across the hamlet. Heaven lours,
    But in the tearful splendour of her
        smiles
I see the slowly-thickening chestnut
        towers
    Fill out the spaces by the barren tiles.

Now past her feet the swallow circling
        flies,
    A clamorous cuckoo stoops to meet her
        hand;
Her light makes rainbows in my closing
        eyes,
    I hear a charm of song thro' all the
        land.
Come, Spring! She comes, and Earth is
        glad
    To roll her North below thy deepening
        dome,
But ere thy maiden birk be wholly clad,
    And these low bushes dip their twigs in
        foam,
        Make all true hearths thy home.

V

Across my garden! and the thicket stirs,
    The fountain pulses high in sunnier jets,
The blackcap warbles, and the turtle
        purrs,
    The starling claps his tiny castanets.
Still round her forehead wheels the wood-
        land dove,
    And scatters on her throat the sparks of
        dew,
The kingcup fills her footprint, and above
    Broaden the glowing isles of vernal blue.
Hail ample presence of a Queen,
    Bountiful, beautiful, apparell'd gay,
Whose mantle, every shade of glancing
        green,
    Flies back in fragrant breezes to display
        A tunic white as May!

VI

She whispers, 'From the South I bring
        you balm,
    For on a tropic mountain was I born,
While some dark dweller by the coco-
        palm
    Watch'd my far meadow zoned with
        airy morn;
From under rose a muffled moan of floods;
    I sat beneath a solitude of snow;
There no one came, the turf was fresh, the
        woods
    Plunged gulf on gulf thro' all their vales
        below.

I saw beyond their silent tops
  The steaming marshes of the scarlet
    cranes,
The slant seas leaning on the mangrove
    copse,
And summer basking in the sultry plains
  About a land of canes;

VII

'Then from my vapour-girdle soaring
    forth
  I scaled the buoyant highway of the
    birds,
And drank the dews and drizzle of the
    North,
  That I might mix with men, and hear
    their words
On pathway'd plains; for—while my hand
    exults
  Within the bloodless heart of lowly
    flowers
To work old laws of Love to fresh results,
  Thro' manifold effect of simple powers—
I too would teach the man
  Beyond the darker hour to see the
    bright,
That his fresh life may close as it began,
  The still-fulfilling promise of a light
  Narrowing the bounds of night.'

VIII

So wed thee with my soul, that I may
    mark
  The coming year's great good and
    varied ills,
And new developments, whatever spark
  Be struck from out the clash of warring
    wills;
Or whether, since our nature cannot rest,
  The smoke of war's volcano burst again
From hoary deeps that belt the changeful
    West,
  Old Empires, dwellings of the kings of
    men;
Or should those fail, that hold the helm,
  While the long day of knowledge grows
    and warms,
And in the heart of this most ancient
    realm
  A hateful voice be utter'd, and alarms
  Sounding 'To arms! to arms!'

IX

A simpler, saner lesson might he learn
  Who reads thy gradual process, Holy
    Spring.
Thy leaves possess the season in their
    turn,
  And in their time thy warblers rise on
    wing.
How surely glidest thou from March to
    May,
  And changest, breathing it, the sullen
    wind,
Thy scope of operation, day by day,
  Larger and fuller, like the human mind!
Thy warmths from bud to bud
  Accomplish that blind model in the
    seed
And men have hopes, which race the rest-
    less blood,
  That after many changes may succeed
  Life, which is Life indeed.

MERLIN AND THE GLEAM

I

  O young Mariner,
  You from the haven
  Under the sea-cliff,
  You that are watching
  The gray Magician
  With eyes of wonder,
  I am Merlin,
  And I am dying,
  I am Merlin
  Who follow The Gleam.

II

  Mighty the Wizard
  Who found me at sunrise
  Sleeping, and woke me
  And learn'd me Magic!
  Great the Master,
  And sweet the Magic,
  When over the valley,
  In early summers,
  Over the mountain,
  On human faces,
  And all around me,
  Moving to melody,
  Floated The Gleam.

III

Once at the croak of a Raven who crost it,
A barbarous people,
Blind to the magic,
And deaf to the melody,
Snarl'd at and cursed me.
A demon vext me,
The light retreated,
The landskip darken'd,
The melody deaden'd,
The Master whisper'd
'Follow The Gleam.'

IV

Then to the melody,
Over a wilderness
Gliding, and glancing at
Elf of the woodland,
Gnome of the cavern,
Griffin and Giant,
And dancing of Fairies
In desolate hollows,
And wraiths of the mountain,
And rolling of dragons
By warble of water,
Or cataract music
Of falling torrents,
Flitted The Gleam.

V

Down from the mountain
And over the level,
And streaming and shining on
Silent river,
Silvery willow,
Pasture and plowland,
Innocent maidens,
Garrulous children,
Homestead and harvest,
Reaper and gleaner,
And rough-ruddy faces
Of lowly labour,
Slided The Gleam—

VI

Then, with a melody
Stronger and statelier,
Led me at length
To the city and palace
Of Arthur the king;

Touch'd at the golden
Cross of the churches,
Flash'd on the Tournament,
Flicker'd and bicker'd
From helmet to helmet,
And last on the forehead
Of Arthur the blameless
Rested The Gleam.

VII

Clouds and darkness
Closed upon Camelot;
Arthur had vanish'd
I knew not whither,
The king who loved me,
And cannot die;
For out of the darkness
Silent and slowly
The Gleam, that had waned to a wintry
    glimmer
On icy fallow
And faded forest,
Drew to the valley
Named of the shadow,
And slowly brightening
Out of the glimmer,
And slowly moving again to a melody
Yearningly tender,
Fell on the shadow,
No longer a shadow,
But clothed with The Gleam.

VIII

And broader and brighter
The Gleam flying onward,
Wed to the melody,
Sang thro' the world;
And slower and fainter,
Old and weary,
But eager to follow,
I saw, whenever
In passing it glanced upon
Hamlet or city,
That under the Crosses
The dead man's garden,
The mortal hillock,
Would break into blossom;
And so to the land's
Last limit I came——
And can no longer,
But die rejoicing,

For thro' the Magic
Of Him the Mighty,
Who taught me in childhood,
There on the border
Of boundless Ocean,
And all but in Heaven
Hovers The Gleam.

IX

Not of the sunlight,
Not of the moonlight,
Not of the starlight!
O young Mariner,
Down to the haven,
Call your companions,
Launch your vessel,
And crowd your canvas,
And, ere it vanishes
Over the margin,
After it, follow it,
Follow The Gleam.

ROMNEY'S REMORSE

'I read Hayley's Life of Romney the other day—Romney wanted but education and reading to make him a very fine painter; but his ideal was not high nor fixed. How touching is the close of his life! He married at nineteen, and because Sir Joshua and others had said that "marriage spoilt an artist" almost immediately left his wife in the North and scarce saw her till the end of his life; when old, nearly mad and quite desolate, he went back to her and she received him and nursed him till he died. This quiet act of hers is worth all Romney's pictures! even as a matter of Art, I am sure.' (*Letters and Literary Remains of Edward FitzGerald*, vol. i.)

'BEAT, little heart—I give you this and this'
    Who are you? What! the Lady Hamilton?
Good, I am never weary painting you.
To sit once more? Cassandra, Hebe, Joan,
Or spinning at your wheel beside the vine—
Bacchante, what you will; and if I fail
To conjure and concentrate into form
And colour all you are, the fault is less
In me than Art. What Artist ever yet
Could make pure light live on the canvas? Art!
Why should I so disrelish that short word?

Where am I? snow on all the hills! so hot,
So fever'd! never colt would more delight
To roll himself in meadow grass than I
To wallow in that winter of the hills.
    Nurse, were you hired? or came of your own will
To wait on one so broken, so forlorn?
Have I not met you somewhere long ago?
I am all but sure I have—in Kendal church—
O yes! I hired you for a season there,
And then we parted; but you look so kind
That you will not deny my sultry throat
One draught of icy water. There—you spill
The drops upon my forehead. Your hand shakes.
    I am ashamed. I am a trouble to you,
Could kneel for your forgiveness. Are they tears?
For me—they do me too much grace—for me?
O Mary, Mary!
                    Vexing you with words!
Words only, born of fever, or the fumes
Of that dark opiate dose you gave me,—words,
Wild babble. I have stumbled back again
Into the common day, the sounder self.
God stay me there, if only for your sake,
The truest, kindliest, noblest-hearted wife
That ever wore a Christian marriage-ring.
    My curse upon the Master's apothegm,
That wife and children drag an Artist down!
This seem'd my lodestar in the Heaven of Art,
And lured me from the household fire on earth.
    To you my days have been a life-long lie,
Grafted on half a truth; and tho' you say
'Take comfort you have won the Painter's fame,'
The best in me that sees the worst in me,
And groans to see it, finds no comfort there.
    What fame? I am not Raphaël, Titian —no
Nor even a Sir Joshua, some will cry.
Wrong there! The painter's fame? but mine, that grew

Blown into glittering by the popular
    breath,
May float awhile beneath the sun, may roll
The rainbow hues of heaven about it—
                      There!
The colour'd bubble bursts above the
    abyss
Of Darkness, utter Lethe.

                        Is it so?
Her sad eyes plead for my own fame with
    me
To make it dearer.

               Look, the sun has risen
To flame along another dreary day.
Your hand. How bright you keep your
    marriage-ring!
Raise me. I thank you.

              Has your opiate then
Bred this black mood? or am I conscious,
    more
Than other Masters, of the chasm between
Work and Ideal? Or does the gloom of Age
And suffering cloud the height I stand
    upon
Even from myself? stand? stood . . . no
    more.

                  And yet
The world would lose, if such a wife as you
Should vanish unrecorded. Might I crave
One favour? I am bankrupt of all claim
On your obedience, and my strongest wish
Falls flat before your least unwillingness.
Still would you—if it please you—sit to
    me?

    I dream'd last night of that clear summer
    noon,
When seated on a rock, and foot to foot
With your own shadow in the placid lake,
You claspt our infant daughter, heart to
    heart.
I had been among the hills, and brought
    you down
A length of staghorn-moss, and this you
    twined
About her cap. I see the picture yet,
Mother and child. A sound from far away,
No louder than a bee among the flowers,
A fall of water lull'd the noon asleep.

You still'd it for the moment with a song
Which often echo'd in me, while I stood
Before the great Madonna-masterpieces
Of ancient Art in Paris, or in Rome.
    Mary, my crayons! if I can, I will.
You should have been—I might have made
    you once,
Had I but known you as I know you now—
The true Alcestis of the time. Your song—
Sit, listen! I remember it, a proof
That I—even I—at times remember'd *you*.

    'Beat upon mine, little heart! beat, beat!
    Beat upon mine! you are mine, my
      sweet!
    All mine from your pretty blue eyes to
      your feet,
                    My sweet.'

Less profile! turn to me—three-quarter
    face.

    'Sleep, little blossom, my honey, my
      bliss!
    For I give you this, and I give you this!
    And I blind your pretty blue eyes with
      a kiss!
                    Sleep!'

Too early blinded by the kiss of death—

    'Father and Mother will watch you
      grow'—

You watch'd not I, she did not grow, she
    died.

    'Father and Mother will watch you grow,
    And gather the roses whenever they
      blow,
    And find the white heather wherever
      you go,
                    My sweet.'

Ah, my white heather only blooms in
    heaven
With Milton's amaranth. There, there,
    there! a child
Had shamed me at it—Down, you idle
    tools,
Stampt into dust—tremulous, all awry,
Blurr'd like a landskip in a ruffled pool,—
Not one stroke firm. This Art, that harlot-
    like
Seduced me from you, leaves me harlot-
    like,

Who love her still, and whimper, impotent
To win her back before I die—and then—
Then, in the loud world's bastard judg-
ment-day,
One truth will damn me with the mindless
mob,
Who feel no touch of my temptation, more
Than all the myriad lies, that blacken
round
The corpse of every man that gains a name;
'This model husband, this fine Artist'! Fool,
What matters? Six foot deep of burial
mould
Will dull their comments! Ay, but when
the shout
Of His descending peals from Heaven, and
throbs
Thro' earth, and all her graves, if *He*
should ask
'Why left you wife and children? for my
sake,
According to my word?' and I replied
'Nay, Lord, for *Art*,' why, that would
sound so mean
That all the dead, who wait the doom of
Hell
For bolder sins than mine, adulteries,
Wife-murders,—nay, the ruthless Mussul-
man
Who flings his bowstrung Harem in the
sea,
Would turn, and glare at me, and point
and jeer,
And gibber at the worm, who, living, made
The wife of wives a widow-bride, and lost
Salvation for a sketch.
                    I am wild again!
The coals of fire you heap upon my head
Have crazed me. Someone knocking there
without?
No! Will my Indian brother come? to find
Me or my coffin? Should I know the man?
This worn-out Reason dying in her house
May leave the windows blinded, and if so,
Bid him farewell for me, and tell him—
                                    Hope!
I hear a death-bed Angel whisper 'Hope.'
'The miserable have no medicine
But only Hope!' He said it . . . in the play.
His crime was of the senses; of the mind
Mine; worse, cold, calculated.

                                Tell my son—
O let me lean my head upon your breast,
'Beat little heart' on this fool brain of mine.
I once had friends—and many—none like
you.
I love you more than when we married.
Hope!
O yes, I hope, or fancy that, perhaps,
Human forgiveness touches heaven, and
thence—
For you forgive me, you are sure of that—
Reflected, sends a light on the forgiven.

PARNASSUS

Exegi monumentum . . .
Quod non . . .
Possit diruere . . .
                        . . . innumerabilis
Annorum series et fuga temporum.—HORACE.

I

WHAT be those crown'd forms high over
the sacred fountain?
Bards, that the mighty Muses have raised
to the heights of the mountain,
And over the flight of the Ages! O Goddesses, help me up thither!
Lightning may shrivel the laurel of Cæsar,
but mine would not wither.
Steep is the mountain, but you, you will
help me to overcome it,
And stand with my head in the zenith, and
roll my voice from the summit,
Sounding for ever and ever thro' Earth
and her listening nations,
And mixt with the great Sphere-music of
stars and of constellations.

II

What be those two shapes high over the
sacred fountain,
Taller than all the Muses, and huger than
all the mountain?
On those two known peaks they stand ever
spreading and heightening;
Poet, that evergreen laurel is blasted by
more than lightning!
Look, in their deep double shadow the
crown'd ones all disappearing!
Sing like a bird and be happy, nor hope
for a deathless hearing!

'Sounding for ever and ever?' pass on! the
  sight confuses—
These are Astronomy and Geology, terrible
  Muses!

III

If the lips were touch'd with fire from off
  a pure Pierian altar,
Tho' their music here be mortal need the
  singer greatly care?
Other songs for other worlds! the fire
  within him would not falter;
Let the golden Iliad vanish, Homer here
  is Homer there.

BY AN EVOLUTIONIST

THE Lord let the house of a brute to the
  soul of a man,
  And the man said 'Am I your debtor?'
And the Lord—'Not yet: but make it as
  clean as you can,
  And then I will let you a better.'

I

If my body come from brutes, my soul
  uncertain, or a fable,
  Why not bask amid the senses while the
    sun of morning shines,
I, the finer brute rejoicing in my hounds,
  and in my stable,
  Youth and Health, and birth and wealth,
    and choice of women and of wines?

II

What hast thou done for me, grim Old
  Age, save breaking my bones on the
  rack?
  Would I had past in the morning that
    looks so bright from afar!

OLD AGE

Done for thee? starved the wild beast that
  was linkt with thee eighty years back.
  Less weight now for the ladder-of-
    heaven that hangs on a star.

I

If my body come from brutes, tho' somewhat finer than their own,
  I am heir, and this my kingdom. Shall
    the royal voice be mute?

No, but if the rebel subject seek to drag
  me from the throne,
  Hold the sceptre, Human Soul, and rule
    thy Province of the brute.

II

I have climb'd to the snows of Age, and I
  gaze at a field in the Past,
  Where I sank with the body at times in
    the sloughs of a low desire,
But I hear no yelp of the beast, and the
  Man is quiet at last
  As he stands on the heights of his life
    with a glimpse of a height that is
    higher.

FAR—FAR—AWAY

(FOR MUSIC)

WHAT sight so lured him thro' the fields he
  knew
As where earth's green stole into heaven's
  own hue,
  Far—far—away?

What sound was dearest in his native
  dells?
The mellow lin-lan-lone of evening bells
  Far—far—away.

What vague world-whisper, mystic pain
  or joy,
Thro' those three words would haunt him
  when a boy,
  Far—far—away?

A whisper from his dawn of life? a breath
From some fair dawn beyond the doors of
  death
  Far—far—away?

Far, far, how far? from o'er the gates of
  Birth,
The faint horizons, all the bounds of earth,
  Far—far—away?

What charm in words, a charm no words
  could give?
O dying words, can Music make you live
  Far—far—away?

POLITICS

WE move, the wheel must always move,
  Nor always on the plain,
And if we move to such a goal
  As Wisdom hopes to gain,
Then you that drive, and know your Craft,
  Will firmly hold the rein,
Nor lend an ear to random cries,
  Or you may drive in vain,
For some cry 'Quick' and some cry 'Slow,'
  But, while the hills remain,
Up hill 'Too-slow' will need the whip,
  Down hill 'Too-quick,' the chain.

BEAUTIFUL CITY

BEAUTIFUL city, the centre and crater of
  European confusion,
O you with your passionate shriek for the
  rights of an equal humanity,
How often your Re-volution has proven
  but E-volution
Roll'd again back on itself in the tides of a
  civic insanity!

THE ROSES ON THE
TERRACE

ROSE, on this terrace fifty years ago,
  When I was in my June, you in your
    May,
Two words, '*My* Rose' set all your face
    aglow,
  And now that I am white, and you are
    gray,
That blush of fifty years ago, my dear,
  Blooms in the Past, but close to me
    to-day
As this red rose, which on our terrace here
  Glows in the blue of fifty miles away.

THE PLAY

ACT first, this Earth, a stage so gloom'd
  with woe
  You all but sicken at the shifting scenes.
And yet be patient. Our Playwright may
  show
  In some fifth Act what this wild Drama
    means.

ON ONE WHO AFFECTED
AN EFFEMINATE MANNER

WHILE man and woman still are incom-
  plete,
I prize that soul where man and woman
  meet,
Which types all Nature's male and female
  plan,
But, friend, man-woman is not woman-
  man.

TO ONE WHO RAN DOWN
THE ENGLISH

YOU make our faults too gross, and thence
  maintain
Our darker future. May your fears be vain!
At times the small black fly upon the pane
May seem the black ox of the distant plain.

THE SNOWDROP

MANY, many welcomes
February fair-maid,
Ever as of old time,
Solitary firstling,
Coming in the cold time,
Prophet of the gay time,
Prophet of the May time,
Prophet of the roses,
Many, many welcomes
February fair-maid!

THE THROSTLE

'SUMMER is coming, summer is coming,
  I know it, I know it, I know it.
Light again, leaf again, life again, love
  again,'
  Yes, my wild little Poet.

Sing the new year in under the blue,
  Last year you sang it as gladly.
'New, new, new, new'! Is it then *so* new
  That you should carol so madly?

'Love again, song again, nest again, young
  again,'
  Never a prophet so crazy!
And hardly a daisy as yet, little friend,
  See, there is hardly a daisy.

THE THROSTLE

'Here again, here, here, here, happy
    year'!
O warble unchidden, unbidden!
Summer is coming, is coming, my dear,
    And all the winters are hidden.

THE OAK

LIVE thy Life,
    Young and old,
Like yon oak,
Bright in spring,
    Living gold;

Summer-rich
    Then; and then
Autumn-changed,
Soberer-hued
    Gold again.

All his leaves
    Fall'n at length,
Look, he stands,
    Trunk and bough,
    Naked strength.

IN MEMORIAM

W. G. WARD

FAREWELL, whose living like I shall not
    find,
    Whose Faith and Work were bells of
    full accord,
My friend, the most unworldly of man-
    kind,
    Most generous of all Ultramontanes,
    Ward,
How subtle at tierce and quart of mind
    with mind,
    How loyal in the following of thy Lord!

THE DEATH OF ŒNONE

AND OTHER POEMS

JUNE BRACKEN AND HEATHER

TO E. T.

THERE on the top of the down,
The wild heather round me and over me
      June's high blue,
When I look'd at the bracken so bright
      and the heather so brown,
I thought to myself I would offer this
      book to you,
This, and my love together,
To you that are seventy-seven,
With a faith as clear as the heights of the
      June-blue heaven,
And a fancy as summer-new
As the green of the bracken amid the gloom
      of the heather.

TO THE MASTER OF BALLIOL

I

DEAR Master in our classic town,
You, loved by all the younger gown
      There at Balliol,
Lay your Plato for one minute down,

II

And read a Grecian tale re-told,
Which, cast in later Grecian mould,
      Quintus Calaber
Somewhat lazily handled of old;

III

And on this white midwinter day—
For have the far-off hymns of May,
      All her melodies,
All her harmonies echo'd away?—

IV

To-day, before you turn again
To thoughts that lift the soul of men,
      Hear my cataract's
Downward thunder in hollow and glen,

V

Till, led by dream and vague desire,
The woman, gliding toward the pyre,
      Find her warrior
Stark and dark in his funeral fire.

THE DEATH OF ŒNONE

ŒNONE sat within the cave from out
Whose ivy-matted mouth she used to gaze
Down at the Troad; but the goodly view
Was now one blank, and all the serpent
      vines
Which on the touch of heavenly feet had
      risen,
And gliding thro' the branches over-
      bower'd
The naked Three, were wither'd long ago,
And thro' the sunless winter morning-
      mist
In silence wept upon the flowerless earth.
   And while she stared at those dead cords
      that ran
Dark thro' the mist, and linking tree to
      tree,
But once were gayer than a dawning sky
With many a pendent bell and fragrant
      star,
Her Past became her Present, and she saw
Him, climbing toward her with the golden
      fruit,
Him, happy to be chosen Judge of Gods,
Her husband in the flush of youth and
      dawn,
Paris, himself as beauteous as a God.
   Anon from out the long ravine below,
She heard a wailing cry, that seem'd at
      first
Thin as the batlike shrillings of the Dead
When driven to Hades, but, in coming
      near,
Across the downward thunder of the brook
Sounded 'Œnone'; and on a sudden he,
Paris, no longer beauteous as a God,
Struck by a poison'd arrow in the fight,

Lame, crooked, reeling, livid, thro' the
   mist
Rose, like the wraith of his dead self, and
   moan'd
'Œnone, *my* Œnone, while we dwelt
Together in this valley—happy then—
Too happy had I died within thine arms,
Before the feud of Gods had marr'd our
   peace,
And sunder'd each from each. I am dying
   now
Pierced by a poison'd dart. Save me. Thou
   knowest,
Taught by some God, whatever herb or
   balm
May clear the blood from poison, and thy
   fame
Is blown thro' all the Troad, and to thee
The shepherd brings his adder-bitten
   lamb,
The wounded warrior climbs from Troy
   to thee.
My life and death are in thy hand. The
   Gods
Avenge on stony hearts a fruitless prayer
For pity. Let me owe my life to thee.
I wrought thee bitter wrong, but thou
   forgive,
Forget it. Man is but the slave of Fate.
Œnone, by thy love which once was mine,
Help, heal me. I am poison'd to the heart.'
'And I to mine' she said 'Adulterer,
Go back to thine adulteress and die!'
   He groan'd, he turn'd, and in the mist
   at once
Became a shadow, sank and disappear'd,
But, ere the mountain rolls into the plain,
Fell headlong dead; and of the shepherds
   one
Their oldest, and the same who first had
   found
Paris, a naked babe, among the woods
Of Ida, following lighted on him there,
And shouted, and the shepherds heard and
   came.
   One raised the Prince, one sleek'd the
   squalid hair,
One kiss'd his hand, another closed his
   eyes,
And then, remembering the gay playmate
   rear'd

Among them, and forgetful of the man,
Whose crime had half unpeopled Ilion,
   these
All that day long labour'd, hewing the
   pines,
And built their shepherd-prince a funeral
   pile;
And, while the star of eve was drawing
   light
From the dead sun, kindled the pyre, and
   all
Stood round it, hush'd, or calling on his
   name.
   But when the white fog vanish'd like a
   ghost
Before the day, and every topmost pine
Spired into bluest heaven, still in her
   cave,
Amazed, and ever seeming stared upon
By ghastlier than the Gorgon head, a
   face,—
His face deform'd by lurid blotch and
   blain—
There, like a creature frozen to the heart
Beyond all hope of warmth, Œnone sat
Not moving, till in front of that ravine
Which drowsed in gloom, self-darken'd
   from the west,
The sunset blazed along the wall of Troy.
   Then her head sank, she slept, and thro'
   her dream
A ghostly murmur floated, 'Come to me,
Œnone! I can wrong thee now no more,
Œnone, my Œnone,' and the dream
Wail'd in her, when she woke beneath the
   stars.
   What star could burn so low? not Ilion
   yet.
What light was there? She rose and slowly
   down,
By the long torrent's ever-deepen'd roar,
Paced, following, as in trance, the silent
   cry.
She waked a bird of prey that scream'd
   and past;
She roused a snake that hissing writhed
   away;
A panther sprang across her path, she
   heard
The shriek of some lost life among the
   pines,

But when she gain'd the broader vale, and
    saw
The ring of faces redden'd by the flames
Enfolding that dark body which had lain
Of old in her embrace, paused—and then
    ask'd
Falteringly, 'Who lies on yonder pyre?'
But every man was mute for reverence.
Then moving quickly forward till the heat
Smote on her brow, she lifted up a voice
Of shrill command, 'Who burns upon the
    pyre?'
Whereon their oldest and their boldest
    said,
'He, whom thou wouldst not heal!' and all
    at once
The morning light of happy marriage broke
Thro' all the clouded years of widowhood,
And muffling up her comely head, and
    crying
'Husband!' she leapt upon the funeral pile,
And mixt herself with *him* and past in fire.

ST. TELEMACHUS

HAD the fierce ashes of some fiery peak
Been hurl'd so high they ranged about the
    globe?
For day by day, thro' many a blood-red
    eve,
In that four-hundredth summer after
    Christ,
The wrathful sunset glared against a cross
Rear'd on the tumbled ruins of an old fane
No longer sacred to the Sun, and flamed
On one huge slope beyond, where in his
    cave
The man, whose pious hand had built the
    cross,
A man who never changed a word with
    men,
Fasted and pray'd, Telemachus the Saint.
  Eve after eve that haggard anchorite
Would haunt the desolated fane, and there
Gaze at the ruin, often mutter low
'Vicisti Galilæe'; louder again,
Spurning a shatter'd fragment of the God,
'Vicisti Galilæe!' but—when now
Bathed in that lurid crimson—ask'd 'Is
    earth
On fire to the West? or is the Demon-god

Wroth at his fall?' and heard an answer
    'Wake
Thou deedless dreamer, lazying out a life
Of self-suppression, not of selfless love.'
And once a flight of shadowy fighters crost
The disk, and once, he thought, a shape
    with wings
Came sweeping by him, and pointed to the
    West,
And at his ear he heard a whisper 'Rome'
And in his heart he cried 'The call of God!'
And call'd arose, and, slowly plunging
    down
Thro' that disastrous glory, set his face
By waste and field and town of alien tongue,
Following a hundred sunsets, and the
    sphere
Of westward-wheeling stars; and every
    dawn
Struck from him his own shadow on to
    Rome.
  Foot-sore, way-worn, at length he
    touch'd his goal,
The Christian city. All her splendour fail'd
To lure those eyes that only yearn'd to see,
Fleeting betwixt her column'd palace-
    walls,
The shape with wings. Anon there past a
    crowd
With shameless laughter, Pagan oath, and
    jest,
Hard Romans brawling of their monstrous
    games;
He, all but deaf thro' age and weariness,
And muttering to himself 'The call of
    God'
And borne along by that full stream of
    men,
Like some old wreck on some indrawing
    sea,
Gain'd their huge Colosseum. The caged
    beast
Yell'd, as he yell'd of yore for Christian
    blood.
Three slaves were trailing a dead lion away,
One, a dead man. He stumbled in, and sat
Blinded; but when the momentary gloom,
Made by the noonday blaze without, had
    left
His aged eyes, he raised them, and beheld
A blood-red awning waver overhead,

The dust send up a steam of human blood,
The gladiators moving toward their fight,
And eighty thousand Christian faces watch
Man murder man. A sudden strength from
   heaven,
As some great shock may wake a palsied
   limb,
Turn'd him again to boy, for up he sprang,
And glided lightly down the stairs, and o'er
The barrier that divided beast from man
Slipt, and ran on, and flung himself
   between
The gladiatorial swords, and call'd 'For-
   bear
In the great name of Him who died for
   men,
Christ Jesus!' For one moment afterward
A silence follow'd as of death, and then
A hiss as from a wilderness of snakes,
Then one deep roar as of a breaking sea,
And then a shower of stones that stoned
   him dead,
And then once more a silence as of death.
   His dream became a deed that woke the
      world,
For while the frantic rabble in half-amaze
Stared at him dead, thro' all the nobler
   hearts
In that vast Oval ran a shudder of shame.
The Baths, the Forum gabbled of his death,
And preachers linger'd o'er his dying
   words,
Which would not die, but echo'd on to
   reach
Honorius, till he heard them, and decreed
That Rome no more should wallow in this
   old lust
Of Paganism, and make her festal hour
Dark with the blood of man who murder'd
   man.

[For Honorius, who succeeded to the sove-
reignty over Europe, supprest the gladiatorial
combats practised of old in Rome, on occasion
of the following event. There was one Telemachus, embracing the ascetic mode of life,
who setting out from the East and arriving at
Rome for this very purpose, while that accursed
spectacle was being performed, entered himself
the circus, and descending into the arena,
attempted to hold back those who wielded
deadly weapons against each other. The spec-
tators of the murderous fray, possest with the
drunken glee of the demon who delights in such
bloodshed, stoned to death the preacher of
peace. The admirable Emperor learning this
put a stop to that evil exhibition.—Theodoret's
Ecclesiastical History.]

AKBAR'S DREAM

AN INSCRIPTION BY ABUL FAZL FOR A TEMPLE
   IN KASHMIR (Blochmann xxxii)

O GOD in every temple I see people that see
thee, and in every language I hear spoken,
people praise thee.
   Polytheism and Islám feel after thee.
   Each religion says, 'Thou art one, without
equal.'
   If it be a mosque people murmur the holy
prayer, and if it be a Christian Church, people
ring the bell from love to Thee.
   Sometimes I frequent the Christian cloister,
and sometimes the mosque.
   But it is thou whom I search from temple to
temple.
   Thy elect have no dealings with either heresy
or orthodoxy; for neither of them stands behind
the screen of thy truth.
   Heresy to the heretic, and religion to the
orthodox,
   But the dust of the rose-petal belongs to the
heart of the perfume seller.

AKBAR *and* ABUL FAZL *before the palace at
   Futehpur-Sikri at night*

'LIGHT of the nations' ask'd his Chronicler
Of Akbar 'what has darken'd thee to-
   night?'
Then, after one quick glance upon the
   stars,
And turning slowly toward him, Akbar
   said
'The shadow of a dream—an idle one
It may be. Still I raised my heart to heaven,
I pray'd against the dream. To pray, to
   do—
To pray, to do according to the prayer,
Are, both, to worship Alla, but the prayers,
That have no successor in deed, are faint
And pale in Alla's eyes, fair mothers they
Dying in childbirth of dead sons. I vow'd
Whate'er my dreams, I still would do the
   right
Thro' all the vast dominion which a sword,
That only conquers men to conquer peace,
Has won me. Alla be my guide!
                        But come,
My noble friend, my faithful counsellor,

Sit by my side. While thou art one with me,
I seem no longer like a lonely man
In the king's garden, gathering here and
  there
From each fair plant the blossom choicest-
  grown
To wreathe a crown not only for the king
But in due time for every Mussulmân,
Brahmin, and Buddhist, Christian, and
  Parsee,
Thro' all the warring world of Hindustan.
  Well spake thy brother in his hymn to
  heaven
"Thy glory baffles wisdom. All the tracks
Of science making toward Thy Perfectness
Are blinding desert sand; we scarce can
  spell
The Alif of Thine alphabet of Love."
  He knows Himself, men nor themselves
  nor Him,
For every splinter'd fraction of a sect
Will clamour "*I* am on the Perfect Way,
All else is to perdition."
                          Shall the rose
Cry to the lotus "No flower thou"? the
  palm
Call to the cypress "I alone am fair"?
The mango spurn the melon at his foot?
"Mine is the one fruit Alla made for man."
  Look how the living pulse of Alla beats
Thro' all His world. If every single star
Should shriek its claim "I only am in
  heaven"
Why that were such sphere-music as the
  Greek
Had hardly dream'd of. There is light
  in all,
And light, with more or less of shade, in all
Man-modes of worship; but our Ulama,
Who "sitting on green sofas contemplate
The torment of the damn'd" already, these
Are like wild brutes new-caged—the
  narrower
The cage, the more their fury. Me they
  front
With sullen brows. What wonder! I
  decreed
That even the dog was clean, that men
  may taste
Swine-flesh, drink wine; they know too
  that whene'er

In our free Hall, where each philosophy
And mood of faith may hold its own, they
  blurt
Their furious formalisms, I but hear
The clash of tides that meet in narrow
  seas,—
Not the Great Voice not the true Deep.
                              To drive
A people from their ancient fold of Faith,
And wall them up perforce in mine—
  unwise,
Unkinglike;—and the morning of my reign
Was redden'd by that cloud of shame
  when I . . .
  I hate the rancour of their castes and
  creeds,
I let men worship as they will, I reap
No revenue from the field of unbelief.
I cull from every faith and race the best
And bravest soul for counsellor and friend.
I loathe the very name of infidel.
I stagger at the Korân and the sword.
I shudder at the Christian and the stake;
Yet "Alla," says their sacred book, "is
  Love,"
And when the Goan Padre quoting Him,
Issa Ben Mariam, his own prophet, cried
"Love one another little ones" and "bless"
Whom? even "your persecutors"! there
  methought
The cloud was rifted by a purer gleam
Than glances from the sun of our Islâm.
  And thou rememberest what a fury
  shook
Those pillars of a moulder'd faith, when
  he,
That other, prophet of their fall, pro-
  claimed
His Master as "the Sun of Righteousness,"
Yea, Alla here on earth, who caught and
  held
His people by the bridle-rein of Truth.
  What art thou saying? "And was not
  Alla call'd
In old Irân the Sun of Love? and Love
The net of truth?"
                    A voice from old Irân!
Nay, but I know it—*his*, the hoary Sheik,
On whom the women shrieking "Atheist"
  flung
Filth from the roof, the mystic melodist

818

Who all but lost himself in Alla, him
Abû Saîd——
      ——a sun but dimly seen
Here, till the mortal morning mists of earth
Fade in the noon of heaven, when creed
    and race
Shall bear false witness, each of each, no
    more,
But find their limits by that larger light,
And overstep them, moving easily
Thro' after-ages in the love of Truth,
The truth of Love.
          The sun, the sun! they rail
At me the Zoroastrian. Let the Sun,
Who heats our earth to yield us grain and
    fruit,
And laughs upon thy field as well as mine,
And warms the blood of Shiah and Sunnee,
Symbol the Eternal! Yea and may not
    kings
Express Him also by their warmth of love
For all they rule—by equal law for all?
By deeds a light to men?
          But no such light
Glanced from our Presence on the face of
    one,
Who breaking in upon us yestermorn,
With all the Hells a-glare in either eye,
Yell'd "hast *thou* brought us down a new
    Korân
From heaven? art *thou* the Prophet? canst
    thou work
Miracles?" and the wild horse, anger,
    plunged
To fling me, and fail'd. Miracles! no, not I
Nor he, nor any. I can but lift the torch
Of Reason in the dusky cave of Life,
And gaze on this great miracle, the World,
Adoring That who made, and makes,
    and is,
And is not, what I gaze on—all else Form,
Ritual, varying with the tribes of men.
   Ay but, my friend, thou knowest I hold
    that forms
Are needful: only let the hand that rules,
With politic care, with utter gentleness,
Mould them for all his people.
          And what are forms?
Fair garments, plain or rich, and fitting
    close
Or flying looselier, warm'd but by the heart

Within them, moved but by the living
    limb,
And cast aside, when old, for newer,—
    Forms!
The Spiritual in Nature's market-place—
The silent Alphabet-of-heaven-in-man
Made vocal—banners blazoning a Power
That is not seen and rules from far away—
A silken cord let down from Paradise,
When fine Philosophies would fail, to draw
The crowd from wallowing in the mire of
    earth,
And all the more, when these behold their
    Lord,
Who shaped the forms, obey them, and
    himself
Here on this bank in *some* way live the life
Beyond the bridge, and serve that Infinite
Within us, as without, that All-in-all,
And over all, the never-changing One
And ever-changing Many, in praise of
    Whom
The Christian bell, the cry from off the
    mosque,
And vaguer voices of Polytheism
Make but one music, harmonising "Pray."
   There westward—under yon slow-fall-
    ing star,
The Christians own a Spiritual Head;
And following thy true counsel, by thine
    aid,
Myself am such in our Islâm, for no
Mirage of glory, but for power to fuse
My myriads into union under one;
To hunt the tiger of oppression out
From Office; and to spread the Divine
    Faith
Like calming oil on all their stormy creeds,
And fill the hollows between wave and
    wave;
To nurse my children on the milk of Truth,
And alchemise old hates into the gold
Of Love, and make it current; and beat
    back
The menacing poison of intolerant priests,
Those cobras ever setting up their hoods—
One Alla! one Kalifa!
          Still—at times
A doubt, a fear,—and yester afternoon
I dream'd,—thou knowest how deep a well
    of love

My heart is for my son, Saleem, mine
  heir,—
And yet so wild and wayward that my
  dream—
He glares askance at thee as one of those
Who mix the wines of heresy in the cup
Of counsel—so—I pray thee——
            Well, I dream'd
That stone by stone I rear'd a sacred fane,
A temple, neither Pagod, Mosque, nor
  Church,
But loftier, simpler, always open-door'd
To every breath from heaven, and Truth
  and Peace
And Love and Justice came and dwelt
  therein;
But while we stood rejoicing, I and thou,
I heard a mocking laugh "the new Korân!"
And on the sudden, and with a cry
  "Saleem"
Thou, thou—I saw thee fall before me, and
  then
Me too the black-wing'd Azrael overcame,
But Death had ears and eyes; I watch'd
  my son,
And those that follow'd, loosen, stone
  from stone,
All my fair work; and from the ruin arose
The shriek and curse of trampled millions,
  even
As in the time before; but while I groan'd,
From out the sunset pour'd an alien race,
Who fitted stone to stone again, and Truth,
Peace, Love and Justice came and dwelt
  therein,
Nor in the field without were seen or heard
Fires of Súttee, nor wail of baby-wife,
Or Indian widow; and in sleep I said
"All praise to Alla by whatever hands
My mission be accomplish'd!" but we hear
Music: our palace is awake, and morn
Has lifted the dark eyelash of the Night
From off the rosy cheek of waking Day.
Our hymn to the sun. They sing it. Let
  us go.'

HYMN

I

Once again thou flamest heavenward, once
  again we see thee rise.

Every morning is thy birthday gladdening
  human hearts and eyes.
Every morning here we greet it, bowing
  lowly down before thee,
Thee the Godlike, thee the changeless in
  thine ever-changing skies.

II

Shadow-maker, shadow-slayer, arrowing
  light from clime to clime,
Hear thy myriad laureates hail thee
  monarch in their woodland rhyme.
Warble bird, and open flower, and, men,
  below the dome of azure
Kneel adoring Him the Timeless in the
  flame that measures Time!

NOTES TO AKBAR'S DREAM

The great Mogul Emperor Akbar was born
October 14, 1542, and died 1605. At 13 he succeeded his father Humayun; at 18 he himself
assumed the sole charge of government. He
subdued and ruled over fifteen large provinces;
his empire included all India north of the
Vindhya Mountains—in the south of India he
was not so successful. His tolerance of religions
and his abhorrence of religious persecution put
our Tudors to shame. He invented a new eclec-
tic religion by which he hoped to unite all
creeds, castes and peoples: and his legisla-
tion was remarkable for vigour, justice and
humanity.

'Thy glory baffles wisdom.' The Emperor
quotes from a hymn to the Deity by Faizi,
brother of Abul Fazl, Akbar's chief friend and
minister, who wrote the *Ain i Akbari* (Annals
of Akbar). His influence on his age was
immense. It may be that he and his brother
Faizi led Akbar's mind away from Islám and
the Prophet—this charge is brought against
him by every Muhammadan writer; but Abul
Fazl also led his sovereign to a true appreciation
of his duties, and from the moment that he
entered Court, the problem of successfully
ruling over mixed races, which Islám in few
other countries had to solve, was carefully con-
sidered, and the policy of toleration was the
result (Blochmann xxix.).

Abul Fazl thus gives an account of himself
'The advice of my Father with difficulty kept
me back from acts of folly; my mind had no
rest and my heart felt itself drawn to the sages
of Mongolia or to the hermits on Lebanon. I
longed for interviews with the Llamás of Tibet
or with the padres of Portugal, and I would
gladly sit with the priests of the Parsis and the

learned of the Zendavesta. I was sick of the learned of my own land.'

He became the intimate friend and adviser of Akbar, and helped him in his tolerant system of government. Professor Blochmann writes 'Impressed with a favourable idea of the value of his Hindu subjects, he (Akbar) had resolved when pensively sitting in the evenings on the solitary stone at Futehpur-Sikri to rule with an even hand all men in his dominions; but as the extreme views of the learned and the lawyers continually urged him to persecute instead of to heal, he instituted discussions, because, believing himself to be in error, he thought it his duty as ruler to inquire.' 'These discussions took place every Thursday night in the Ibadat-khana a building at Futehpur-Sikri, erected for the purpose' (Malleson).

In these discussions Abul Fazl became a great power, and he induced the chief of the disputants to draw up a document defining the 'divine Faith' as it was called, and assigning to Akbar the rank of a Mujahid, or supreme khalifah, the vicegerent of the one true God.

Abul Fazl was finally murdered at the instigation of Akbar's son Salim, who in his Memoirs declares that it was Abul Fazl who had perverted his father's mind so that he denied the divine mission of Mahomet, and turned away his love from his son.

Faizi. When Akbar conquered the North-West Provinces of India, Faizi, then 20, began his life as a poet, and earned his living as a physician. He is reported to have been very generous and to have treated the poor for nothing. His fame reached Akbar's ears who commanded him to come to the camp at Chitor. Akbar was delighted with his varied knowledge and scholarship and made the poet teacher to his sons. Faizi at 33 was appointed Chief Poet (1588). He collected a fine library of 4300 MSS. and died at the age of 40 (1595) when Akbar incorporated his collection of rare books in the Imperial Library.

The warring world of Hindostan. Akbar's rapid conquests and the good government of his fifteen provinces with their complete military, civil and political systems make him conspicuous among the great kings of history.

The Goan Padre. Abul Fazl relates that 'one night the Ibadat-khana was brightened by the presence of Padre Rodolpho, who for intelligence and wisdom was unrivalled among Christian doctors. Several carping and bigoted men attacked him and this afforded an opportunity for the display of the calm judgment and justice of the assembly. These men brought forward the old received assertions, and did not attempt to arrive at truth by reasoning. Their statements were torn to pieces, and they were nearly put to shame, when they began to attack the contradictions of the Gospel, but they could not prove their assertions. With perfect calmness, and earnest conviction of the truth he replied to their arguments.

Abû Sa'îd. 'Love is the net of Truth, Love is the noose of God' is a quotation from the great Sufee poet Abû Sa'îd—born A.D. 968, died at the age of 83. He is a mystical poet, and some of his expressions have been compared to our George Herbert. Of Shaikh Abû Sa'îd it is recorded that he said, 'when my affairs had reacht a certain pitch I buried under the dust my books and opened a shop on my own account (*i.e.* began to teach with authority), and verily men represented me as that which I was not, until it came to this, that they went to the Qâdhî and testified against me of unbeliever-hood; and women got upon the roofs and cast unclean things upon me.' (*Vide* reprint from article in *National Review*, March 1891, by C. J. Pickering.)

Aziz. I am not aware that there is any record of such intrusion upon the king's privacy, but the expressions in the text occur in a letter sent by Akbar's foster-brother Aziz, who refused to come to court when summoned and threw up his government, and 'after writing an insolent and reproachful letter to Akbar in which he asked him if he had received a book from heaven, or if he could work miracles like Mahomet that he presumed to introduce a new religion, warned him that he was on the way to eternal perdition, and concluded with a prayer to God to bring him back into the path of salvation' (Elphinstone).

'The Koran, the Old and New Testament, and the Psalms of David are called *books* by way of excellence, and their followers "People of the Book" ' (Elphinstone).

Akbar according to Abdel Kadir had his son Murad instructed in the Gospel, and used to make him begin his lessons 'In the name of Christ' instead of in the usual way 'In the name of God.'

> *To drive*
> *A people from their ancient fold of Faith,* etc.

Malleson says 'This must have happened because Akbar states it, but of the forced conversions I have found no record. This must have taken place whilst he was still a minor, and whilst the chief authority was wielded by Bairam.'

'I reap no revenue from the field of unbelief'
The Hindus are fond of pilgrimages and Akbar removed a remunerative tax raised by his

predecessors on pilgrimages. He also abolished the fezza or capitation tax on those who differed from the Mahomedan faith. He discouraged all *excessive* prayers, fasts and pilgrimages.

Suttee. Akbar decreed that every widow who showed the least desire not to be burnt on her husband's funeral pyre, should be let go free and unharmed.

baby-wife. He forbad marriage before the age of puberty.

Indian widow. Akbar ordained that remarriage was lawful.

Music. 'About a watch before daybreak,' says Abul Fazl, the musicians played to the king in the palace. 'His Majesty had such a knowledge of the science of music as trained musicians do not possess.'

'The Divine Faith.' The Divine Faith slowly passed away under the immediate successors of Akbar. An idea of what the Divine Faith was may be gathered from the inscription at the head of the poem. The document referred to, Abul Fazl says 'brought about excellent results (1) the Court became a gathering place of the sages and learned of all creeds; the good doctrines of all religious systems were recognized, and their defects were not allowed to obscure their good features; (2) perfect toleration or peace with all was established; and (3) the perverse and evil-minded were covered with shame on seeing the disinterested motives of His Majesty, and these stood in the pillory of disgrace.' Dated September 1579—Ragab 987 (Blochmann xiv.).

THE BANDIT'S DEATH

TO SIR WALTER SCOTT[1]

O GREAT AND GALLANT SCOTT,
TRUE GENTLEMAN, HEART, BLOOD AND BONE,
I WOULD IT HAD BEEN MY LOT
TO HAVE SEEN THEE, AND HEARD THEE, AND
KNOWN.

SIR, do you see this dagger? nay, why do
 you start aside?
I was not going to stab you, tho' I *am* the
 Bandit's bride.

[1] I have adopted Sir Walter Scott's version of the following story as given in his last journal (Death of Il Bizarro)—but I have taken the liberty of making some slight alterations.

You have set a price on his head: I may
 claim it without a lie.
What have I here in the cloth? I will show
 it you by-and-by.

Sir, I was once a wife. I had one brief
 summer of bliss.
But the Bandit had woo'd me in vain, and
 he stabb'd my Piero with this.

And he dragg'd me up there to his cave in
 the mountain, and there one day
He had left his dagger behind him. I found
 it. I hid it away.

For he reek'd with the blood of Piero; his
 kisses were red with his crime,
And I cried to the Saints to avenge me.
 They heard, they bided their time.

In a while I bore him a son, and he loved
 to dandle the child,
And that was a link between us; but I—to
 be reconciled?—

No, by the Mother of God, tho' I think I
 hated him less,
And—well, if I sinn'd last night, I will find
 the Priest and confess.

Listen! we three were alone in the dell at
 the close of the day.
I was lilting a song to the babe, and it
 laugh'd like a dawn in May.

Then on a sudden we saw your soldiers
 crossing the ridge,
And he caught my little one from me: we
 dipt down under the bridge

By the great dead pine—you know it—and
 heard as we crouch'd below,
The clatter of arms, and voices, and men
 passing to and fro.

Black was the night when we crept away—
 not a star in the sky—
Hush'd as the heart of the grave, till the
 little one utter'd a cry.

I whisper'd 'give it to me,' but he would
 not answer me—then
He gript it so hard by the throat that the
 boy never cried again.

We return'd to his cave—the link was
broken—he sobb'd and he wept,
And cursed himself; then he yawn'd, for
the wretch *could* sleep, and he slept

Ay, till dawn stole into the cave, and a ray
red as blood
Glanced on the strangled face—I could
make Sleep Death, if I would—

Glared on at the murder'd son, and the
murderous father at rest, . . .
I drove the blade that had slain my husband thrice thro' his breast.

He was loved at least by his dog: it was
chain'd, but its horrible yell
'She has kill'd him, has kill'd him, has
kill'd him' rang out all down thro' the
dell,

Till I felt I could end myself too with the
dagger—so deafen'd and dazed—
Take it, and save me from it! I fled. I was
all but crazed

With the grief that gnaw'd at my heart, and
the weight that dragg'd at my hand;
But thanks to the Blessed Saints that I
came on none of his band;

And the band will be scatter'd now their
gallant captain is dead,
For I with this dagger of his—do you
doubt me? Here is his head!

THE CHURCH-WARDEN
AND THE CURATE

This is written in the dialect which was current in my youth at Spilsby and in the country
about it.

I

Eh? good daäy! good daäy! thaw it bean't
not mooch of a daäy,
Nasty, casselty[1] weather! an' mea haäfe
down wi' my haäy![2]

[1] 'Casselty,' casualty, chance weather.
[2] 'Haäfe down wi' my haäy,' while my grass
is only half-mown.

II

How be the farm gittin on? noäways.
Gittin on i'deeäd!
Why, tonups was haäfe on 'em fingers an'
toäs,[1] an' the mare brokken-kneeäd,
An' pigs didn't sell at fall,[2] an' wa lost wer
Haldeny cow,
An' it beäts ma to knaw wot she died on,
but wool's looking oop ony how.

III

An' soä they've maäde tha a parson, an'
thou'll git along, niver fear,
Fur I beän chuch-warden mysen i' the
parish fur fifteen year.
Well—sin ther beä chuch-wardens, ther
mun be parsons an' all,
An' if t'ōne stick alongside t'uther[3] the
chuch weänt happen a fall.

IV

Fur I wur a Baptis wonst, an' ageän the
toithe an' the raäte,
Till I fun[4] that it warn't not the gaäinist[5]
waäy to the narra Gaäte.
An' I can't abeär 'em, I can't, fur a lot on
'em coom'd ta-year[6]—
I wur down wi' the rheumatis then—to
my pond to wesh thessens theere—
Sa I sticks like the ivin[7] as long as I lives
to the owd chuch now,
Fur they wesh'd their sins i' *my* pond, an'
I doubts they poison'd the cow.

V

Ay, an' ya seed the Bishop. They says 'at
he coom'd fra nowt—
Burn i' traäde. Sa I warrants 'e niver said
haäfe wot 'e thowt,
But 'e creeäpt an' 'e crawl'd along, till 'e
feeäld 'e could howd 'is oän,
Then 'e married a greät Yerl's darter, an'
sits o' the Bishop's throän.

[1] 'Fingers and toes,' a disease in turnips.
[2] 'Fall,' autumn.
[3] 'If t'ōne stick alongside t'uther,' if the one
hold by the other. One is pronounced like
'own'. [4] 'Fun,' found.
[5] 'Gaäinist,' nearest.
[6] 'Ta-year,' this year.
[7] 'Ivin,' ivy.

VI

Now I'll gie tha a bit o' my mind an' tha
weant be taakin' offence,
Fur thou be a big scholard now wi' a
hoonderd haäcre o' sense—
But sich an obstropulous[1] lad—naay, naay
—fur I minds tha sa well,
Tha'd niver not hopple[2] thy tongue, an'
the tongue's sit afire o' Hell,
As I says to my missis to-daay, when she
hurl'd a plaäte at the cat
An' anoother ageän my noäse. Ya was niver
sa bad as that.

VII

But I minds when i' Howlaby beck won
daäy ya was ticklin' o' trout,
An' keeäper 'e seed ya an roon'd, an' 'e
beal'd[3] to ya 'Lad coom hout'
An' ya stood oop naäkt i' the beck, an' ya
tell'd 'im to knaw his awn plaäce
An' ya call'd 'im a clown, ya did, an' ya
thraw'd the fish i' 'is faäce,
An' 'e torn'd[4] as red as a stag-tuckey's[5]
wattles, but theer an' then
I coämb'd 'im down, fur I promised ya'd
niver not do it ageän.

VIII

An' I cotch'd tha wonst i' my garden,
when thou was a height-year-howd,[6]
An' I fun thy pockets as full o' my pippins
as iver they'd 'owd,[7]
An' thou was as peärky[8] as owt, an' tha
maäde me as mad as mad,
But I says to tha 'keeap 'em, an' welcome'
fur thou was the Parson's lad.

IX

An Parson 'e 'ears on it all, an' then taäkes
kindly to me,
An' then I wur chose Chuch-warden an'
coom'd to the top o' the tree,

Fur Quoloty's hall my friends, an' they
maäkes ma a help to the poor,
When I gits the plaäte fuller o'Soondays
nor ony chuch-warden afoor,
Fur if iver thy feyther 'ed riled me I kep'
mysen meeäk as a lamb,
An' saw by the Graäce o' the Lord, Mr.
Harry, I ham wot I ham.

X

But Parson 'e *will* speäk out, saw, now 'e
be sixty-seven,
He'll niver swap Owlby an' Scratby fur
owt but the Kingdom o' Heaven;
An' thou'll be 'is Curate 'ere, but, if iver
tha meäns to git 'igher,
Tha mun tackle the sins o' the Wo'ld,[1] an'
not the faults o' the Squire.
An' I reckons tha'll light of a livin' some-
wheers i' the Wowd[2] or the Fen,
If tha cottons down to thy betters, an'
keeäps thysen to thysen.
But niver not speäk plaain out, if tha wants
to git forrards a bit,
But creeäp along the hedge-bottoms, an'
thou'll be a Bishop yit.

XI

Naäy, but tha *mun* speäk hout to the
Baptises here i' the town,
Fur moäst on 'em talks ageän tithe, an' I'd
like tha to preäch 'em down,
Fur *they*'ve bin a-preächin' *mea* down,
they heve, an' I haätes 'em now,
Fur they leäved their nasty sins i' *my* pond,
an' it poison'd the cow.

CHARITY

I

WHAT am I doing, you say to me, 'wasting
the sweet summer hours'?
Haven't you eyes? I am dressing the grave
of a woman with flowers.

II

For a woman ruin'd the world, as God's
own scriptures tell,
And a man ruin'd mine, but a woman,
God bless her, kept me from Hell.

[1] 'Obstropulous', obstreperous—here the
Curate makes a sign of deprecation.
[2] 'Hopple' or 'hobble', to tie the legs of a
skittish cow when she is being milked.
[3] 'Beal'd', bellowed.
[4] In such words as 'torned' (turned),
'hurled', the *r* is hardly audible.
[5] 'Stag-tuckey', turkey-cock.
[6] 'Height-year-howd', eight-year-old.
[7] 'Owd', hold. [8] 'Peärky', pert.

[1] 'Wo'ld', the world. Short *o*.
[2] 'Wowd', wold.

CHARITY

III

Love me? O yes, no doubt—how long—
till you threw me aside!
Dresses and laces and jewels and never a
ring for the bride.

IV

All very well just now to be calling me
darling and sweet,
And after a while would it matter so much if
I came on the street?

V

You when I met you first—when *he*
brought you!—I turn'd away
And the hard blue eyes have it still, that
stare of a beast of prey.

VI

You were his friend—you—you—when he
promised to make me his bride,
And you knew that he meant to betray me
—you knew—you knew that he lied.

VII

He married an heiress, an orphan with
half a shire of estate,—
I sent him a desolate wail and a curse,
when I learn'd my fate.

VIII

For I used to play with the knife, creep
down to the river-shore,
Moan to myself 'one plunge—then quiet
for evermore.'

IX

Would the man have a touch of remorse
when he heard what an end was mine?
Or brag to his fellow rakes of his conquest
over their wine?

X

Money—my hire—*his* money—I sent him
back what he gave,—
Will you move a little that way? your
shadow falls on the grave.

XI

Two trains clash'd: then and there he was
crush'd in a moment and died,
But the new-wedded wife was unharm'd,
tho' sitting close at his side.

XII

She found my letter upon him, my wail
of reproach and scorn;
I had cursed the woman he married, and
him, and the day I was born.

XIII

They put him aside for ever, and after a
week—no more—
A stranger as welcome as Satan—a widow
came to my door:

XIV

So I turn'd my face to the wall, I was mad,
I was raving-wild,
I was close on that hour of dishonour, the
birth of a baseborn child.

XV

O you that can flatter your victims, and
juggle, and lie and cajole,
Man, can you even guess at the love of a
soul for a soul?

XVI

I had cursed her as woman and wife, and
in wife and woman I found
The tenderest Christ-like creature that
ever stept on the ground.

XVII

She watch'd me, she nursed me, she fed
me, she sat day and night by my bed,
Till the joyless birthday came of a boy
born happily dead.

XVIII

And her name? what was it? I ask'd her.
She said with a sudden glow
On her patient face 'My dear, I will tell
you before I go.'

XIX

And I when I learnt it at last, I shriek'd,
  I sprang from my seat,
I wept, and I kiss'd her hands, I flung
  myself down at her feet,

XX

And we pray'd together for *him*, for *him*
  who had given her the name.
She has left me enough to live on. I need
  no wages of shame.

XXI

She died of a fever caught when a nurse in
  a hospital ward.
She is high in the Heaven of Heavens, she
  is face to face with her Lord,

XXII

And He sees not her like anywhere in this
  pitiless world of ours!
I have told you my tale. Get you gone.
  I am dressing her grave with flowers.

KAPIOLANI

Kapiolani was a great chieftainess who lived
in the Sandwich Islands at the beginning of this
century. She won the cause of Christianity by
openly defying the priests of the terrible goddess
Peelè. In spite of their threats of vengeance she
ascended the volcano Mauna-Loa, then clam-
bered down over a bank of cinders 400 feet high
to the great lake of fire (nine miles round)—
Kilauëä—the home and haunt of the goddess,
and flung into the boiling lava the consecrated
berries which it was sacrilege for a woman to
handle.

I

WHEN from the terrors of Nature a people
  have fashion'd and worship a Spirit
  of Evil,
Blest be the Voice of the Teacher who calls
  to them
'Set yourselves free!'

II

Noble the Saxon who hurl'd at his Idol a
  valorous weapon in olden England!
Great and greater, and greatest of women,
  island heroine, Kapiolani

Clomb the mountain, and flung the berries,
  and dared the Goddess, and freed the
  people
Of Hawa-i-ee!

III

A people believing that Peelè the Goddess
  would wallow in fiery riot and revel
On Kilauëä,
Dance in a fountain of flame with her
  devils, or shake with her thunders and
  shatter her island,
Rolling her anger
Thro' blasted valley and flaring forest in
  blood-red cataracts down to the sea!

IV

Long as the lava-light
Glares from the lava-lake
Dazing the starlight,
Long as the silvery vapour in daylight
Over the mountain
Floats, will the glory of Kapiolani be
  mingled with either on Hawa-i-ee.

V

What said her Priesthood?
'Woe to this island if ever a woman should
  handle or gather the berries of Peelè!
Accursèd were she!
And woe to this island if ever a woman
  should climb to the dwelling of Peelè
  the Goddess!
Accursèd were she!'

VI

One from the Sunrise
Dawn'd on His people, and slowly before
  him
Vanish'd shadow-like
Gods and Goddesses,
None but the terrible Peelè remaining as
  Kapiolani ascended her mountain,
Baffled her priesthood,
Broke the Taboo,
Dipt to the crater,
Call'd on the Power adored by the Chris-
  tian, and crying 'I dare her, let Peelè
  avenge herself'!
Into the flame-billow dash'd the berries,
  and drove the demon from Hawa-i-ee.

THE DAWN

"You are but children."
Egyptian Priest to Solon

I

RED of the Dawn!
Screams of a babe in the red-hot palms of
a Moloch of Tyre,
Man with his brotherless dinner on man
in the tropical wood,
Priests in the name of the Lord passing
souls thro' fire to the fire,
Head-hunters and boats of Dahomey
that float upon human blood!

II

Red of the Dawn!
Godless fury of peoples, and Christless
frolic of kings,
And the bolt of war dashing down upon
cities and blazing farms,
For Babylon was a child new-born, and
Rome was a babe in arms,
And London and Paris and all the rest are
as yet but in leading-strings.

III

Dawn not Day,
While scandal is mouthing a bloodless
name at *her* cannibal feast,
And rake-ruin'd bodies and souls go
down in a common wreck,
And the press of a thousand cities is prized
for it smells of the beast,
Or easily violates virgin Truth for a coin
or a cheque.

IV

Dawn not Day!
Is it Shame, so few should have climb'd
from the dens in the level below,
Men, with a heart and a soul, no slaves
of a four-footed will?
But if twenty million of summers are
stored in the sunlight still,
We are far from the noon of man, there is
time for the race to grow.

V

Red of the Dawn!
Is it turning a fainter red? so be it, but
when shall we lay

The Ghost of the Brute that is walking
and haunting us yet, and be free?
In a hundred, a thousand winters? Ah,
what will *our* children be,
The men of a hundred thousand, a million
summers away?

THE MAKING OF MAN

WHERE is one that, born of woman, altogether can escape
From the lower world within him, moods
of tiger, or of ape?
Man as yet is being made, and ere the
crowning Age of ages,
Shall not æon after æon pass and touch
him into shape?

All about him shadow still, but, while the
races flower and fade,
Prophet-eyes may catch a glory slowly
gaining on the shade,
Till the peoples all are one, and all their
voices blend in choric
Hallelujah to the Maker 'It is finish'd.
Man is made.'

THE DREAMER

ON a midnight in midwinter when all but
the winds were dead,
'The meek shall inherit the earth' was a
Scripture that rang thro' his head,
Till he dream'd that a Voice of the Earth
went wailingly past him and said:

'I am losing the light of my Youth
And the Vision that led me of old,
And I clash with an iron Truth,
When I make for an Age of gold,
And I would that my race were run,
For teeming with liars, and madmen,
and knaves,
And wearied of Autocrats, Anarchs, and
Slaves,
And darken'd with doubts of a Faith
that saves,
And crimson with battles, and hollow
with graves,
To the wail of my winds, and the moan
of my waves
I whirl, and I follow the Sun.'

Was it only the wind of the Night shrilling
    out Desolation and wrong
Thro' a dream of the dark? Yet he thought
    that he answer'd her wail with a
    song—

Moaning your losses, O Earth,
    Heart-weary and overdone!
But all's well that ends well,
    Whirl, and follow the Sun!

He is racing from heaven to heaven
    And less will be lost than won,
For all's well that ends well,
    Whirl, and follow the Sun!

The Reign of the Meek upon earth,
    O weary one, has it begun?
But all's well that ends well,
    Whirl, and follow the Sun!

For moans will have grown sphere-
    music
Or ever your race be run!
And all's well that ends well,
    Whirl, and follow the Sun!

MECHANOPHILUS

(In the time of the first railways.)

Now first we stand and understand,
    And sunder false from true,
And handle boldly with the hand,
    And see and shape and do.

Dash back that ocean with a pier,
    Strow yonder mountain flat,
A railway there, a tunnel here,
    Mix me this Zone with that!

Bring me my horse—my horse? my wings
    That I may soar the sky,
For Thought into the outward springs,
    I find her with the eye.

O will she, moonlike, sway the main,
    And bring or chase the storm,
Who was a shadow in the brain,
    And is a living form?

Far as the Future vaults her skies,
    From this my vantage ground
To those still-working energies
    I spy nor term nor bound.

As we surpass our father's skill,
    Our sons will shame our own;
A thousand things are hidden still
    And not a hundred known.

And had some prophet spoken true
    Of all we shall achieve,
The wonders were so wildly new,
    That no man would believe.

Meanwhile, my brothers, work, and wield
    The forces of to-day,
And plow the Present like a field,
    And garner all you may!

You, what the cultured surface grows,
    Dispense with careful hands:
Deep under deep for ever goes,
    Heaven over heaven expands.

RIFLEMEN FORM!

THERE is a sound of thunder afar,
Storm in the South that darkens the day!
Storm of battle and thunder of war!
Well if it do not roll our way.
Storm, Storm, Riflemen form!
Ready, be ready against the storm!
Riflemen, Riflemen, Riflemen form!

Be not deaf to the sound that warns,
Be not gull'd by a despot's plea!
Are figs of thistles? or grapes of thorns?
How can a despot feel with the Free?
Form, Form, Riflemen Form!
Ready, be ready to meet the storm!
Riflemen, Riflemen, Riflemen form!

Let your reforms for a moment go!
Look to your butts, and take good aims!
Better a rotten borough or so
Than a rotten fleet and a city in flames!
Storm, Storm, Riflemen form!
Ready, be ready against the storm!
Riflemen, Riflemen, Riflemen form!

Form, be ready to do or die!
Form in Freedom's name and the Queen's!
True we have got—*such* a faithful ally

That only the Devil can tell what he means.
Form, Form, Riflemen Form!
Ready, be ready to meet the storm!
Riflemen, Riflemen, Riflemen form![1]

I count you kind, I hold you true;
But what may follow who can tell?
Give me a hand—and you—and you—
And deem me grateful, and farewell!

THE TOURNEY

RALPH would fight in Edith's sight,
 For Ralph was Edith's lover,
Ralph went down like a fire to the fight,
Struck to the left and struck to the right,
 Roll'd them over and over.
'Gallant Sir Ralph,' said the king.

Casques were crack'd and hauberks hack'd,
 Lances snapt in sunder,
Rang the stroke, and sprang the blood,
Knights were thwack'd and riven, and
 hew'd
 Like broad oaks with thunder.
'O what an arm,' said the king.

Edith bow'd her stately head,
 Saw them lie confounded,
Edith Montfort bow'd her head,
Crown'd her knight's, and flush'd as red
 As poppies when she crown'd it.
'Take her Sir Ralph,' said the king.

THE WANDERER

THE gleam of household sunshine ends,
And here no longer can I rest;
Farewell!—You will not speak, my friends,
Unfriendly of your parted guest.

O well for him that finds a friend,
Or makes a friend where'er he come,
And loves the world from end to end,
And wanders on from home to home!

O happy he, and fit to live,
On whom a happy home has power
To make him trust his life, and give
His fealty to the halcyon hour!

---

[1] I have been asked to republish this old poem, which was first published in *The Times*, May 9, 1859, before the Volunteer movement began.

POETS AND CRITICS

THIS thing, that thing is the rage,
Helter-skelter runs the age;
Minds on this round earth of ours
Vary like the leaves and flowers,
 Fashion'd after certain laws;
Sing thou low or loud or sweet,
All at all points thou canst not meet,
 Some will pass and some will pause.

What is true at last will tell:
Few at first will place thee well;
Some too low would have thee shine,
Some too high—no fault of thine—
 Hold thine own, and work thy will!
Year will graze the heel of year,
But seldom comes the poet here,
 And the Critic's rarer still.

A VOICE SPAKE OUT OF THE SKIES

A VOICE spake out of the skies
To a just man and a wise—
'The world and all within it
Will only last a minute!'
And a beggar began to cry
'Food, food or I die'!
Is it worth his while to eat,
Or mine to give him meat,
If the world and all within it
Were nothing the next minute?

DOUBT AND PRAYER

THO' Sin too oft, when smitten by Thy
 rod,
Rail at 'Blind Fate' with many a vain
 'Alas!'
From sin thro' sorrow into Thee we pass
By that same path our true forefathers
 trod;

And let not Reason fail me, nor the sod
Draw from my death Thy living flower
    and grass,
Before I learn that Love, which is, and was
My Father, and my Brother, and my God!
Steel me with patience! soften me with
    grief!
Let blow the trumpet strongly while I pray,
Till this embattled wall of unbelief
My prison, not my fortress, fall away!
Then, if Thou willest, let my day be brief,
So Thou wilt strike Thy glory thro' the
    day.

FAITH

I

DOUBT no longer that the Highest is the
    wisest and the best,
Let not all that saddens Nature blight thy
    hope or break thy rest,
    Quail not at the fiery mountain, at the
        shipwreck, or the rolling
Thunder, or the rending earthquake, or
    the famine, or the pest!

II

Neither mourn if human creeds be lower
    than the heart's desire!
Thro' the gates that bar the distance comes
    a gleam of what is higher.
    Wait till Death has flung them open,
        when the man will make the Maker
Dark no more with human hatreds in the
    glare of deathless fire!

THE SILENT VOICES

WHEN the dumb Hour, clothed in black,
Brings the Dreams about my bed,
Call me not so often back,
Silent Voices of the dead,
Toward the lowland ways behind me,
And the sunlight that is gone!
Call me rather, silent voices,
Forward to the starry track
Glimmering up the heights beyond me
On, and always on!

GOD AND THE UNIVERSE

I

WILL my tiny spark of being wholly vanish
    in your deeps and heights?
Must my day be dark by reason, O ye
    Heavens, of your boundless nights,
Rush of Suns, and roll of systems, and
    your fiery clash of meteorites?

II

'Spirit, nearing yon dark portal at the
    limit of thy human state,
Fear not thou the hidden purpose of that
    Power which alone is great,
Nor the myriad world, His shadow, nor
    the silent Opener of the Gate.'

THE DEATH OF THE DUKE OF CLARENCE AND AVONDALE

To the Mourners

THE bridal garland falls upon the bier,
The shadow of a crown, that o'er him
    hung,
Has vanish'd in the shadow cast by Death.
So princely, tender, truthful, reverent,
    pure—
Mourn! That a world-wide Empire mourns
    with you,
That all the Thrones are clouded by your
    loss,
Were slender solace. Yet be comforted;
For if this earth be ruled by Perfect Love,
Then, after his brief range of blameless
    days,
The toll of funeral in an Angel ear
Sounds happier than the merriest mar-
    riage-bell.
    The face of Death is toward the Sun of
    Life,
His shadow darkens earth: his truer name
Is 'Onward,' no discordance in the roll
And march of that Eternal Harmony
Whereto the worlds beat time, tho' faintly
    heard
Until the great Hereafter. Mourn in hope!

CROSSING THE BAR

SUNSET and evening star,
  And one clear call for me!
And may there be no moaning of the bar,
  When I put out to sea,

But such a tide as moving seems asleep,
  Too full for sound and foam,
When that which drew from out the
    boundless deep
  Turns again home.

Twilight and evening bell,
  And after that the dark!
And may there be no sadness of fare-
    well,
  When I embark;

For tho' from out our bourne of Time and
    Place
  The flood may bear me far,
I hope to see my Pilot face to face
  When I have crost the bar.

APPENDIX

OF POEMS NOT INCLUDED IN THE AUTHOR'S FINAL EDITION

TIMBUCTOO

[FIRST PUBLISHED IN 1829]

'Deep in that lion-haunted inland lies
A mystic city, goal of high emprise.'
Chapman

I STOOD upon the Mountain which o'er-
looks
The narrow seas, whose rapid interval
Parts Afric from green Europe, when the
Sun
Had fall'n below th' Atlantic, and above
The silent heavens were blench'd with
faëry light,
Uncertain whether faëry light or cloud,
Flowing Southward, and the chasms of
deep, deep blue
Slumber'd unfathomable, and the stars
Were flooded over with clear glory and
pale.
I gazed upon the sheeny coast beyond,
There where the Giant of old Time infix'd
The limits of his prowess, pillars high
Long time erased from Earth: even as the
Sea
When weary of wild inroad buildeth up
Huge mounds whereby to stay his yeasty
waves.
And much I mused on legends quaint and
old
Which whilom won the hearts of all on
Earth
Toward their brightness, ev'n as flame
draws air;
But had their being in the heart of man
As air is th' life of flame: and thou wert
then
A center'd glory-circled memory,
Divinest Atalantis, whom the waves
Have buried deep, and thou of later name,
Imperial Eldorado, roof'd with gold:
Shadows to which, despite all shocks of
Change,

All on-set of capricious Accident,
Men clung with yearning Hope which
would not die.
As when in some great City where the
walls
Shake, and the streets with ghastly faces
throng'd,
Do utter forth a subterranean voice,
Among the inner columns far retired
At midnight, in the lone Acropolis,
Before the awful Genius of the place
Kneels the pale Priestess in deep faith, the
while
Above her head the weak lamp dips and
winks
Unto the fearful summoning without:
Nathless she ever clasps the marble knees,
Bathes the cold hand with tears, and gazeth
on
Those eyes which wear no light but that
wherewith
Her phantasy informs them.

                              Where are ye,
Thrones of the Western wave, fair Islands
green?
Where are your moonlight halls, your
cedarn glooms,
The blossoming abysses of your hills?
Your flowering Capes, and your gold-
sanded bays
Blown round with happy airs of odorous
winds?
Where are the infinite ways, which, Seraph-
trod,
Wound thro' your great Elysian solitudes,
Whose lowest depths were, as with visible
love,
Fill'd with Divine effulgence, circumfused,
Flowing between the clear and polish'd
stems,
And ever circling round their emerald
cones
In coronals and glories, such as gird

The unfading foreheads of the Saints in
  Heaven?
For nothing visible, they say, had birth
In that blest ground, but it was play'd
  about
With its peculiar glory. Then I raised
My voice and cried, 'Wide Afric, doth thy
  Sun
Lighten, thy hills enfold a City as fair
As those which starr'd the night o' the
  elder World?
Or is the rumour of thy Timbuctoo
A dream as frail as those of ancient Time?'

A curve of whitening, flashing, ebbing
  light?
A rustling of white wings! the bright de-
  scent
Of a young Seraph! and he stood beside
  me
There on the ridge, and look'd into my face
With his unutterable, shining orbs.
So that with hasty motion I did veil
My vision with both hands, and saw before
  me
Such colour'd spots as dance athwart the
  eyes
Of those, that gaze upon the noonday Sun.
Girt with a zone of flashing gold beneath
His breast, and compass'd round about his
  brow
With triple arch of everchanging bows,
And circled with the glory of living light
And alternation of all hues, he stood.

'O child of man, why muse you here
  alone
Upon the Mountain, on the dreams of old
Which fill'd the earth with passing loveli-
  ness,
Which flung strange music on the howling
  winds,
And odours rapt from remote Paradise?
Thy sense is clogg'd with dull mortality;
Thy spirit fetter'd with the bond of clay:
Open thine eyes and see.'

I look'd, but not
Upon his face, for it was wonderful
With its exceeding brightness, and the
  light

Of the great Angel Mind which look'd
  from out
The starry glowing of his restless eyes.
I felt my soul grow mighty, and my spirit
With supernatural excitation bound
Within me, and my mental eye grew large
With such a vast circumference of thought,
That in my vanity I seem'd to stand
Upon the outward verge and bound alone
Of full beatitude. Each failing sense,
As with a momentary flash of light
Grew thrillingly distinct and keen. I saw
The smallest grain that dappled the dark
  Earth,
The indistinctest atom in deep air,
The Moon's white cities, and the opal
  width
Of her small glowing lakes, her silver
  heights
Unvisited with dew of vagrant cloud,
And the unsounded, undescended depth
Of her black hollows. The clear Galaxy
Shorn of its hoary lustre, wonderful,
Distinct and vivid with sharp points of
  light,
Blaze within blaze, an unimagin'd depth
And harmony of planet-girded suns
And moon-encircled planets, wheel in
  wheel,
Arch'd the wan sapphire. Nay—the hum
  of men,
Or other things talking in unknown
  tongues,
And notes of busy life in distant worlds
Beat like a far wave on my anxious ear.

A maze of piercing, trackless, thrilling
  thoughts,
Involving and embracing each with each,
Rapid as fire, inextricably link'd,
Expanding momently with every sight
And sound which struck the palpitating
  sense,
The issue of strong impulse, hurried
  through
The riv'n rapt brain; as when in some large
  lake
From pressure of descendant crags, which
  lapse
Disjointed, crumbling from their parent
  slope

At slender interval, the level calm
Is ridg'd with restless and increasing
    spheres
Which break upon each other, each th'
    effect
Of separate impulse, but more fleet and
    strong
Than its precursor, till the eye in vain
Amid the wild unrest of swimming shade
Dappled with hollow and alternate rise
Of interpenetrated arc, would scan
Definite round.

        I know not if I shape
These things with accurate similitude
From visible objects, for but dimly now,
Less vivid than a half-forgotten dream,
The memory of that mental excellence
Comes o'er me, and it may be I entwine
The indecision of my present mind
With its past clearness, yet it seems to me
As even then the torrent of quick thought
Absorbed me from the nature of itself
With its own fleetness. Where is he, that
    borne
Adown the sloping of an arrowy stream,
Could link his shallop to the fleeting edge,
And muse midway with philosophic calm
Upon the wondrous laws, which regulate
The fierceness of the bounding Element?

My thoughts which long had grovell'd
    in the slime
Of this dull world, like dusky worms which
    house
Beneath unshaken waters, but at once
Upon some Earth-awakening day of Spring
Do pass from gloom to glory, and aloft
Winnow the purple, bearing on both sides
Double display of star-lit wings, which
    burn,
Fan-like and fibred with intensest bloom;
Ev'n so my thoughts, erewhile so low, now
    felt
Unutterable buoyancy and strength
To bear them upward through the track-
    less fields
Of undefin'd existence far and free.

Then first within the South methought
    I saw
A wilderness of spires, and chrystal pile

Of rampart upon rampart, dome on dome,
Illimitable range of battlement
On battlement, and the Imperial height
Of Canopy o'ercanopied.

        Behind
In diamond light upsprung the dazzling
    peaks
Of Pyramids as far surpassing earth's
As heaven than earth is fairer. Each aloft
Upon his narrow'd eminence bore globes
Of wheeling Suns, or Stars, or semblances
Of either, showering circular abyss
Of radiance. But the glory of the place
Stood out a pillar'd front of burnish'd gold,
Interminably high, if gold it were
Or metal more etherial, and beneath
Two doors of blinding brilliance, where no
    gaze
Might rest, stood open, and the eye could
    scan,
Through length of porch and valve and
    boundless hall,
Part of a throne of fiery flame, wherefrom
The snowy skirting of a garment hung,
And glimpse of multitudes of multitudes
That minister'd around it—if I saw
These things distinctly, for my human
    brain
Stagger'd beneath the vision, and thick night
Came down upon my eyelids, and I fell.

With ministering hand he rais'd me up:
Then with a mournful and ineffable smile,
Which but to look on for a moment fill'd
My eyes with irresistible sweet tears,
In accents of majestic melody,
Like a swoln river's gushings in still night
Mingled with floating music, thus he
    spake:

'There is no mightier Spirit than I to
    sway
The heart of man: and teach him to attain
By shadowing forth the Unattainable;
And step by step to scale that mighty stair
Whose landing-place is wrapt about with
    clouds
Of glory, of Heaven.[1] With earliest light of
    Spring,

[1] 'Be ye perfect, even as your Father in
Heaven is perfect.'

And in the glow of sallow Summertide,
And in red Autumn when the winds are
  wild
With gambols, and when full-voiced
  Winter roofs
The headland with inviolate white snow,
I play about his heart a thousand ways,
Visit his eyes with visions, and his ears
With harmonies of wind and wave and
  wood,
—Of winds which tell of waters, and of
  waters
Betraying the close kisses of the wind—
And win him unto me: and few there be
So gross of heart who have not felt and
  known
A higher than they see: They with dim eyes
Behold me darkling. Lo! I have given thee
To understand my presence, and to feel
My fullness; I have fill'd thy lips with
  power.
I have rais'd thee nigher to the spheres of
  Heaven
Man's first, last home: and thou with
  ravish'd sense
Listenest the lordly music flowing from
Th' illimitable years. I am the Spirit,
The permeating life which courseth
  through
All th' intricate and labyrinthine veins
Of the great vine of Fable, which, out-
  spread
With growth of shadowing leaf and clusters
  rare,
Reacheth to every corner under Heaven,
Deep-rooted in the living soil of truth;
So that men's hopes and fears take refuge in
The fragrance of its complicated glooms,

And cool impleachèd twilights. Child of
  Man,
See'st thou yon river, whose translucent
  wave,
Forth issuing from the darkness, windeth
  through
The argent streets o' th' City, imaging
The soft inversion of her tremulous Domes,
Her gardens frequent with the stately
  Palm,
Her Pagods hung with music of sweet bells,
Her obelisks of rangèd Chrysolite,
Minarets and towers? Lo! how he passeth
  by,
And gulphs himself in sands, as not en-
  during
To carry through the world those waves,
  which bore
The reflex of my City in their depths.
Oh City! oh latest Throne! where I was
  rais'd
To be a mystery of loveliness
Unto all eyes, the time is well-nigh come
When I must render up this glorious home
To keen Discovery: soon yon brilliant
  towers
Shall darken with the waving of her wand;
Darken, and shrink and shiver into huts,
Black specks amid a waste of dreary sand,
Low-built, mud-wall'd, Barbarian settle-
  ments.
How chang'd from this fair City!'

                    Thus far the Spirit:
Then parted Heaven-ward on the wing:
  and I
Was left alone on Calpe, and the Moon
Had fallen from the night, and all was dark!

FROM 'POEMS, CHIEFLY LYRICAL'

[1830]

THE 'HOW' AND THE 'WHY'

?

I AM any man's suitor,
If any will be my tutor:
Some say this life is pleasant,
  Some think it speedeth fast:
In time there is no present,

In eternity no future,
  In eternity no past.
We laugh, we cry, we are born, we die,
Who will riddle me the *how* and the *why*?

The bulrush nods unto his brother,
The wheatears whisper to each other:
What is it they say? What do they there?

Why two and two make four? Why round
   is not square?
Why the rock stands still, and the light
   clouds fly?
Why the heavy oak groans, and the white
   willows sigh?
Why deep is not high, and high is not
   deep?
Whether we wake, or whether we sleep?
Whether we sleep, or whether we die?
How you are you? Why I am I?
Who will riddle me the *how* and the *why*?

The world is somewhat; it goes on some-
   how;
But what is the meaning of *then* and *now*?
 I feel there is something; but how and
   what?
I know there is somewhat; but what and
   why?
I cannot tell if that somewhat be I.

  The little bird pipeth—'why? why?'
In the summerwoods when the sun falls
   low
And the great bird sits on the opposite
   bough,
And stares in his face and shouts, 'how?
   how?'
And the black owl scuds down the mellow
   twilight,
And chaunts, 'how? how?' the whole of the
   night.

Why the life goes when the blood is spilt?
  What the life is? where the soul may lie?
Why a church is with a steeple built;
And a house with a chimneypot?
Who will riddle me the how and the what?
 Who will riddle me the what and the
   why?

THE BURIAL OF LOVE

His eyes in eclipse,
  Palecold his lips,
The light of his hopes unfed,
  Mute his tongue,
  His bow unstrung
With the tears he hath shed,
Backward drooping his graceful head,

Love is dead:
 His last arrow is sped;
He hath not another dart;
Go—carry him to his dark deathbed;
 Bury him in the cold cold heart—
Love is dead.

Oh, truest love! art thou forlorn,
  And unrevenged? thy pleasant wiles
  Forgotten, and thine innocent joy?
  Shall hollowhearted apathy,
The cruellest form of perfect scorn,
  With languor of most hateful smiles,
    For ever write,
    In the withered light
    Of the tearless eye,
  An epitaph that all may spy?
No! sooner she herself shall die.

For her the showers shall not fall,
  Nor the round sun shine that shineth to
    all;
   Her light shall into darkness change;
For her the green grass shall not spring,
  Nor the rivers flow, nor the sweet birds
    sing,
    Till Love have his full revenge.

TO ——

SAINTED Juliet! dearest name!
  If to love be life alone,
    Divinest Juliet,
  I love thee, and live; and yet
Love unreturned is like the fragrant
   flame
Folding the slaughter of the sacrifice
  Offered to gods upon an altarthrone;
My heart is lighted at thine eyes,
Changed into fire, and blown about with
   sighs.

SONG

I

I' THE glooming light
  Of middle night
  So cold and white,
Worn Sorrow sits by the moaning wave;
  Beside her are laid
  Her mattock and spade,

For she hath half delved her own deep
grave.
Alone she is there:
The white clouds drizzle: her hair falls
loose;
Her shoulders are bare;
Her tears are mixed with the beaded dews.

II

Death standeth by;
She will not die;
With glazèd eye
She looks at her grave: she cannot sleep;
Ever alone
She maketh her moan:
She cannot speak; she can only weep,
For she will not hope.
The thick snow falls on her flake by flake,
The dull wave mourns down the slope,
The world will not change, and her heart
will not break.

SONG

I

THE lintwhite and the throstlecock
Have voices sweet and clear;
All in the bloomèd May.
They from the blosmy brere
Call to the fleeting year,
If that he would them hear
And stay.
Alas! that one so beautiful
Should have so dull an ear.

II

Fair year, fair year, thy children call,
But thou art deaf as death;
All in the bloomèd May.
When thy light perisheth
That from thee issueth,
Our life evanisheth:
Oh! stay.
Alas! that lips so cruel-dumb
Should have so sweet a breath!

III

Fair year, with brows of royal love
Thou comest, as a king.
All in the bloomèd May.
Thy golden largess fling,

And longer hear us sing;
Though thou art fleet of wing,
Yet stay.
Alas! that eyes so full of light
Should be so wandering!

IV

Thy locks are all of sunny sheen
In rings of gold yronne,[1]
All in the bloomèd May.
We pri'thee pass not on;
If thou dost leave the sun,
Delight is with thee gone,
Oh! stay.
Thou art the fairest of thy feres,
We pri'thee pass not on.

SONG

I

EVERY day hath its night:
Every night its morn:
Thorough dark and bright
Wingèd hours are borne;
Ah! welaway!
Seasons flower and fade;
Golden calm and storm
Mingle day by day.
There is no bright form
Doth not cast a shade—
Ah! welaway!

II

When we laugh, and our mirth
Apes the happy vein,
We're so kin to earth,
Pleasaunce fathers pain—
Ah! welaway!
Madness laugheth loud:
Laughter bringeth tears:
Eyes are worn away
Till the end of fears
Cometh in the shroud,
Ah! welaway!

III

All is change, woe or weal;
Joy is Sorrow's brother;
Grief and gladness steal

[1] 'His crispè hair in ringis was yronne.'—
Chaucer, _Knight's Tale._

Symbols of each other;
   Ah! welaway!
Larks in heaven's cope
Sing: the culvers mourn
   All the livelong day.
Be not all forlorn:
Let us weep in hope—
   Ah! welaway!

HERO TO LEANDER

OH go not yet, my love,
   The night is dark and vast;
The white moon is hid in her heaven
      above,
   And the waves climb high and fast.
Oh! kiss me, kiss me, once again,
   Lest thy kiss should be the last.
Oh kiss me ere we part;
Grow closer to my heart.
My heart is warmer surely than the bosom
   of the main.

Oh joy! O bliss of blisses!
   My heart of hearts art thou.
Come bathe me with thy kisses,
   My eyelids and my brow.
Hark how the wild rain hisses,
   And the loud sea roars below.

Thy heart beats through thy rosy limbs,
   So gladly doth it stir;
Thine eye in drops of gladness swims.
I have bathed thee with the pleasant
      myrrh;
   Thy locks are dripping balm;
Thou shalt not wander hence to-night,
   I'll stay thee with my kisses.
To-night the roaring brine
Will rend thy golden tresses;
The ocean with the morrow light
Will be both blue and calm;
And the billow will embrace thee with a
   kiss as soft as mine.

No western odours wander
   On the black and moaning sea,
And when thou art dead, Leander,
   My soul must follow thee!
Oh go not yet, my love,
   Thy voice is sweet and low;

The deep salt wave breaks in above
   Those marble steps below.
The turretstairs are wet
   That lead into the sea.
Leander! go not yet.
The pleasant stars have set:
Oh! go not, go not yet,
   Or I will follow thee.

THE MYSTIC

ANGELS have talked with him, and showed
      him thrones:
Ye knew him not: he was not one of ye,
Ye scorned him with an undiscerning
      scorn:
Ye could not read the marvel in his eye,
The still serene abstraction: he hath felt
The vanities of after and before;
Albeit, his spirit and his secret heart
The stern experiences of converse lives,
The linkèd woes of many a fiery change
Had purified, and chastened, and made
      free.
Always there stood before him, night and
      day,
Of wayward varycoloured circumstance
The imperishable presences serene
Colossal, without form, or sense, or sound,
Dim shadows but unwaning presences
Fourfacèd to four corners of the sky:
And yet again, three shadows, fronting one,
One forward, one respectant, three but
      one;
And yet again, again and evermore,
For the two first were not, but only seemed,
One shadow in the midst of a great light,
One reflex from eternity on time,
One mighty countenance of perfect calm,
Awful with most invariable eyes.
For him the silent congregated hours,
Daughters of time, divinely tall, beneath
Severe and youthful brows, with shining
      eyes
Smiling a godlike smile (the innocent light
Of earliest youth pierced through and
      through with all
Keen knowledges of low-embowèd eld)
Upheld, and ever hold aloft the cloud
Which droops lowhung on either gate of
      life,

Both birth and death: he in the centre fixt,
Saw far on each side through the grated
    gates
Most pale and clear and lovely distances.
He often lying broad awake, and yet
Remaining from the body, and apart
In intellect and power and will, hath heard
Time flowing in the middle of the night,
And all things creeping to a day of doom.
How could ye know him? Ye were yet
    within
The narrower circle; he had wellnigh
    reached
The last, which with a region of white
    flame,
Pure without heat, into a larger air
Upburning, and an ether of black blue,
Investeth and ingirds all other lives.

THE GRASSHOPPER

I

Voice of the summerwind,
Joy of the summerplain,
Life of the summerhours,
Carol clearly, bound along.
No Tithon thou as poets feign
(Shame fall 'em they are deaf and blind)
But an insect lithe and strong,
Bowing the seeded summerflowers.
Prove their falsehood and thy quarrel,
    Vaulting on thine airy feet.
Clap thy shielded sides and carol,
    Carol clearly, chirrup sweet.
Thou art a mailèd warrior in youth and
    strength complete;
    Armed cap-a-pie,
    Full fair to see;
    Unknowing fear,
    Undreading loss,
A gallant cavalier,
Sans peur et sans reproche,
In sunlight and in shadow,
The Bayard of the meadow.

II

I would dwell with thee,
    Merry grasshopper,
Thou art so glad and free,
    And as light as air;
Thou hast no sorrow or tears,

Thou hast no compt of years,
No withered immortality,
But a short youth sunny and free.
Carol clearly, bound along,
    Soon thy joy is over,
A summer of loud song,
    And slumbers in the clover.
What hast thou to do with evil
In thine hour of love and revel,
    In thy heat of summerpride,
Pushing the thick roots aside
Of the singing flowerèd grasses,
That brush thee with their silken tresses?
What hast thou to do with evil,
Shotting, singing, ever springing
    In and out the emerald glooms,
Ever leaping, ever singing,
    Lighting on the golden blooms?

LOVE, PRIDE, AND FORGETFULNESS

Ere yet my heart was sweet Love's tomb,
Love laboured honey busily.
I was the hive, and Love the bee,
My heart the honeycomb.
One very dark and chilly night
Pride came beneath and held a light.

The cruel vapours went through all,
Sweet Love was withered in his cell;
Pride took Love's sweets, and by a spell
Did change them into gall;
And Memory though fed by Pride
Did wax so thin on gall,
Awhile she scarcely lived at all.
What marvel that she died?

CHORUS

IN AN UNPUBLISHED DRAMA, WRITTEN VERY EARLY

The varied earth, the moving heaven,
    The rapid waste of roving sea,
The fountainpregnant mountains riven
    To shapes of wildest anarchy,
By secret fire and midnight storms
    That wander round their windy cones,
The subtle life, the countless forms
    Of living things, the wondrous tones
Of man and beast are full of strange
Astonishment and boundless change.

The day, the diamonded night,
  The echo, feeble child of sound,
The heavy thunder's griding might,
  The herald lightning's starry bound,
The vocal spring of bursting bloom,
  The naked summer's glowing birth,
The troublous autumn's sallow gloom,
  The hoarhead winter paving earth
    With sheeny white, are full of strange
    Astonishment and boundless change.

Each sun which from the centre flings
  Grand music and redundant fire,
The burning belts, the mighty rings,
  The murmurous planets' rolling choir,
The globefilled arch that, cleaving air,
  Lost in its own effulgence sleeps,
The lawless comets as they glare,
  And thunder through the sapphire deeps
    In wayward strength, are full of strange
    Astonishment and boundless change.

LOST HOPE

You cast to ground the hope which once
    was mine:
  But did the while your harsh decree de-
    plore,
Embalming with sweet tears the vacant
    shrine,
  My heart, where Hope had been and was
    no more.

    So on an oaken sprout
    A goodly acorn grew;
  But winds from heaven shook the
    acorn out,
  And filled the cup with dew.

THE TEARS OF HEAVEN

Heaven weeps above the earth all night till
    morn,
In darkness weeps as all ashamed to weep,
Because the earth hath made her state for-
    lorn
With self-wrought evils of unnumbered
    years,
And doth the fruit of her dishonour reap.
And all the day heaven gathers back her
    tears
Into her own blue eyes so clear and deep,

And showering down the glory of lightsome
    day,
Smiles on the earth's worn brow to win her
    if she may.

LOVE AND SORROW

O maiden, fresher than the first green leaf
With which the fearful springtide flecks
    the lea,
Weep not, Almeida, that I said to thee
That thou hast half my heart, for bitter
    grief
Doth hold the other half in sovranty.
Thou art my heart's sun in love's crystal-
    line:
Yet on both sides at once thou canst not
    shine:
Thine is the bright side of my heart, and
    thine
My heart's day, but the shadow of my
    heart,
Issue of its own substance, my heart's
    night
Thou can'st not lighten even with *thy* light,
All powerful in beauty as thou art.
Almeida, if my heart were substanceless,
Then might thy rays pass through to the
    other side,
So swiftly, that they nowhere would abide,
But lose themselves in utter emptiness.
Half-light, half-shadow, let my spirit sleep;
They never learned to love who never
    knew to weep.

TO A LADY SLEEPING

O thou whose fringèd lids I gaze upon,
Through whose dim brain the wingèd
    dreams are borne,
Unroof the shrines of clearest vision,
In honour of the silverfleckèd morn:
Long hath the white wave of the virgin
    light
Driven back the billow of the dreamful
    dark.
Thou all unwittingly prolongest night,
Though long ago listening the poisèd lark,
With eyes dropt downward through the
    blue serene,
Over heaven's parapets the angels lean.

SONNET

COULD I outwear my present state of woe
With one brief winter, and indue i' the
    spring
Hues of fresh youth, and mightily outgrow
The wan dark coil of faded suffering—
Forth in the pride of beauty issuing
A sheeny snake, the light of vernal bowers,
Moving his crest to all sweet plots of flowers
And watered vallies where the young birds
    sing;
Could I thus hope my lost delight's renew-
    ing,
I straightly would command the tears to
    creep
From my charged lids; but inwardly I
    weep:
Some vital heat as yet my heart is wooing:
This to itself hath drawn the frozen rain
From my cold eyes and melted it again.

SONNET

THOUGH Night hath climbed her peak of
    highest noon,
And bitter blasts the screaming autumn
    whirl,
All night through archways of the bridgèd
    pearl,
And portals of pure silver walks the moon.
Walk on, my soul, nor crouch to agony,
Turn cloud to light, and bitterness to joy,
And dross to gold with glorious alchemy,
Basing thy throne above the world's annoy.
Reign thou above the storms of sorrow and
    ruth
That roar beneath; unshaken peace hath
    won thee:
So shalt thou pierce the woven glooms of
    truth;
So shall the blessing of the meek be on
    thee;
So in thine hour of dawn, the body's youth,
An honourable eld shall come upon thee.

SONNET

SHALL the hag Evil die with child of Good,
Or propagate again her loathèd kind,
Thronging the cells of the diseasèd mind,
Hateful with hanging cheeks, a withered
    brood,

Though hourly pastured on the salient
    blood?
Oh! that the wind which bloweth cold or
    heat
Would shatter and o'erbear the brazen beat
Of their broad vans, and in the solitude
Of middle space confound them, and blow
    back
Their wild cries down their cavernthroats,
    and slake
With points of blastborne hail their heated
    eyne!
So their wan limbs no more might come
    between
The moon and the moon's reflex in the
    night,
Nor blot with floating shades the solar light.

SONNET

THE pallid thunderstricken sigh for gain,
Down an ideal stream they ever float,
And sailing on Pactolus in a boat,
Drown soul and sense, while wistfully they
    strain
Weak eyes upon the glistering sands that
    robe
The understream. The wise, could he be-
    hold
Cathedralled caverns of thickribbèd gold
And branching silvers of the central globe,
Would marvel from so beautiful a sight
How scorn and ruin, pain and hate could
    flow:
But Hatred in a gold cave sits below;
Pleached with her hair, in mail of argent
    light
Shot into gold, a snake her forehead clips,
And skins the colour from her trembling
    lips.

LOVE

I

THOU, from the first, unborn, undying love,
Albeit we gaze not on thy glories near,
Before the face of God did'st breathe and
    move,
Though night and pain and ruin and death
    reign here.
Thou foldest, like a golden atmosphere,
The very throne of the eternal God:

Passing through thee the edicts of his fear
Are mellowed into music, borne abroad
By the loud winds, though they uprend the
    sea,
Even from its central deeps: thine empery
Is over all: thou wilt not brook eclipse;
Thou goest and returnest to His lips
Like lightning: thou dost ever brood above
The silence of all hearts, unutterable Love.

II

To know thee is all wisdom, and old age
Is but to know thee: dimly we behold thee
Athwart the veils of evil which infold thee.
We beat upon our aching hearts in rage;
We cry for thee; we deem the world thy
    tomb.
As dwellers in lone planets look upon
The mighty disk of their majestic sun,
Hollowed in awful chasms of wheeling
    gloom,
Making their day dim, so we gaze on thee.
Come, thou of many crowns, white-robèd
    love,
Oh! rend the veil in twain: all men adore
    thee;
Heaven crieth after thee; earth waiteth for
    thee:
Breathe on thy wingèd throne, and it shall
    move
In music and in light o'er land and sea.

III

And now—methinks I gaze upon thee now,
As on a serpent in his agonies
Awestricken Indians; what time laid low
And crushing the thick fragrant reeds he
    lies,
When the new year warmbreathèd on the
    earth,
Waiting to light him with her purple skies,
Calls to him by the fountain to uprise.
Already with the pangs of a new birth
Strain the hot spheres of his convulsèd
    eyes,
And in his writhings awful hues begin
To wander down his able-sheeny sides,
Like light on troubled waters: from within
Anon he rusheth forth with merry din,
And in him light and joy and strength
    abides;

And from his brows a crown of living light
Looks through the thickstemmed woods by
    day and night.

ENGLISH WARSONG

WHO fears to die? Who fears to die?
Is there any here who fears to die?
He shall find what he fears; and none shall
    grieve
    For the man who fears to die;
But the withering scorn of the many shall
    cleave
    To the man who fears to die.

Chorus.—Shout for England!
        Ho! for England!
        George for England!
        Merry England!
        England for ay!

The hollow at heart shall crouch forlorn,
He shall eat the bread of common scorn;
It shall be steeped in the salt, salt tear,
Shall be steeped in his own salt tear:
Far better, far better he never were born
Than to shame merry England here.

Chorus.—Shout for England! etc.

There standeth our ancient enemy;
Hark! he shouteth—the ancient enemy!
On the ridge of the hill his banners rise;
They stream like fire in the skies;
Hold up the Lion of England on high
Till it dazzle and blind his eyes.

Chorus.—Shout for England! etc.

Come along! we alone of the earth are
    free;
The child in our cradles is bolder than
    he;
For where is the heart and strength of
    slaves?
Oh! where is the strength of slaves?
He is weak! we are strong; he a slave, we
    are free;
Come along! we will dig their graves.

Chorus.—Shout for England! etc.

There standeth our ancient enemy;
Will he dare to battle with the free?

Spur along! spur amain! charge to the fight:
Charge! charge to the fight!
Hold up the Lion of England on high!
Shout for God and our right!

Chorus.—Shout for England! etc.

NATIONAL SONG

THERE is no land like England
Where'er the light of day be;
There are no hearts like English
hearts,
Such hearts of oak as they be.
There is no land like England
Where'er the light of day be;
There are no men like English-
men,
So tall and bold as they be.

Chorus.—For the French the pope may
shrive 'em.
For the devil a whit we heed 'em:
As for the French, God speed 'em
Unto their heart's desire,
And the merry devil drive 'em
Through the water and the fire.

Full Chorus.—Our glory is our freedom,
We lord it o'er the sea;
We are the sons of freedom,
We are free.

There is no land like England,
Where'er the light of day be;
There are no wives like English
wives,
So fair and chaste as they be.
There is no land like England,
Where'er the light of day be;
There are no maids like English
maids,
So beautiful as they be.

Chorus.—For the French, etc.

DUALISMS

Two bees within a chrystal flowerbell
rockèd
Hum a lovelay to the westwind at
noontide.
Both alike, they buzz together,
Both alike, they hum together

Through and through the flowered
heather.
Where in a creeping cove the wave un-
shockèd
Lays itself calm and wide,
Over a stream two birds of glancing
feather
Do woo each other, carolling to-
gether.
Both alike, they glide together.
Side by side;
Both alike, they sing together,
Arching blueglossèd necks beneath the
purple weather.

Two children lovelier than Love adown
the lea are singing,
As they gambol, lilygarlands ever
stringing:
Both in blosmwhite silk are frockèd:
Like, unlike, they roam together
Under a summervault of golden
weather;
Like, unlike, they sing together
Side by side,
MidMay's darling goldenlockèd,
Summer's tanling diamondeyed.

Οἱ ῥέοντες

I

ALL thoughts, all creeds, all dreams are
true,
All visions wild and strange;
Man is the measure of all truth
Unto himself. All truth is change:
All men do walk in sleep, and all
Have faith in that they dream:
For all things are as they seem to all,
And all things flow like a stream.

II

There is no rest, no calm, no pause,
Nor good nor ill, nor light nor shade,
Nor essence nor eternal laws:
For nothing is but all is made.
But if I dream that all these are,
They are to me for that I dream;
For all things are as they seem to all,
And all things flow like a stream.

Argal—this very opinion is only true
relatively to the flowing philosophers.

NO MORE

The Gem, 1831

OH sad *No More!* Oh sweet *No More!*
Oh strange *No More!*
By a mossed brookbank on a stone
I smelt a wildweed-flower alone;
There was a ringing in my ears,
And both my eyes gushed out with tears.
Surely all pleasant things had gone before,
Lowburied fathomdeep beneath with thee,
No More!

ANACREONTICS

The Gem, 1831

WITH roses muskybreathed,
And drooping daffodilly,
And silverleaved lily,
And ivy darkly-wreathed,
I wove a crown before her
For her I love so dearly,
A garland for Lenora.
With a silken cord I bound it.
Lenora, laughing clearly
A light and thrilling laughter,
About her forehead wound it,
And loved me ever after.

A FRAGMENT

The Gem, 1831

WHERE is the Giant of the Sun, which
stood
In the midnoon the glory of old Rhodes,
A perfect Idol with profulgent brows
Farsheening down the purple seas to those
Who sailed from Mizraim underneath the
star
Named of the dragon—and between whose
limbs
Of brassy vastness broadblown Argosies
Drave into haven? Yet endure unscathed
Of changeful cycles the great Pyramids
Broadbased amid the fleeting sands, and
sloped
Into the slumbrous summernoon; but
where,
Mysterious Egypt, are thine obelisks
Graven with gorgeous emblems undis-
cerned?

Thy placid Sphinxes brooding o'er the
Nile?
Thy shadowing Idols in the solitudes,
Awful Memnonian countenances calm
Looking athwart the burning flats, far off
Seen by the highnecked camel on the verge
Journeying southward? where thy monu-
ments
Piled by the strong and sunborn Anakim
Over their crowned brethren ON and OPH?
Thy Memnon when his peaceful lips are
kist
With earliest rays, that from his mother's
eyes
Flow over the Arabian bay, no more
Breathes low into the charmed ears of morn
Clear melody flattering the crisped Nile
By columned Thebes. Old Memphis hath
gone down:
The Pharaohs are no more: somewhere in
death
They sleep with staring eyes and gilded
lips,
Wrapped round with spiced cerements in
old grots
Rockhewn and sealed for ever.

SONNET

Englishman's Magazine, August 1831

CHECK every outflash, every ruder sally
    Of thought and speech; speak low, and
    give up wholly
    Thy spirit to mild-minded Melancholy;
    This is the place. Through yonder pop-
    lar alley,
Below, the blue-green river windeth slowly;
    But in the middle of the sombre valley,
    The crispèd waters whisper musically,
    And all the haunted place is dark and
    holy.
The nightingale, with long and low pre-
amble,
    Warbled from yonder knoll of solemn
    larches,   [arches
    And in and out the woodbine's flowery
    The summer midges wove their wanton
    gambol,
And all the white stemmed pinewood slept
above—
    When in this valley first I told my love.

SONNET

Yorkshire Literary Annual, 1832

THERE are three things which fill my heart
    with sighs,
And steep my soul in laughter (when I
    view
Fair maiden-forms moving like melodies)
Dimples, roselips, and eyes of any hue.
There are three things beneath the blessed
    skies
For which I live, black eyes and brown and
    blue:
I hold them all most dear, but oh! black
    eyes,
I live and die, and only die for you.
Of late such eyes looked at me—while I
    mused,
At sunset, underneath a shadowy plane,
In old Bayona nigh the southern sea—
From an half-open lattice looked at *me*.
I saw no more—only those eyes—confused
And dazzled to the heart with glorious pain.

SONNET

Friendship's Offering, 1832

ME my own Fate to lasting sorrow doom-
    eth:
Thy woes are birds of passage, transi-
    tory:
Thy spirit, circled with a living glory,
In summer still a summer joy resumeth.
Alone my hopeless melancholy gloometh,
    Like a lone cypress, through the twilight
    hoary,
From an old garden where no flower
    bloometh,
    One cypress on an inland promontory.
But yet my lonely spirit follows thine,
    As round the rolling earth night follows
    day:
But yet thy lights on my horizon shine
    Into my night, when thou art far away.
I am so dark, alas! and thou so bright,
When we two meet there's never perfect
    light.

FROM 'POEMS'

1833

SONNET

O BEAUTY, passing beauty! sweetest Sweet!
    How can'st thou let me waste my youth
    in sighs?
I only ask to sit beside thy feet.
    Thou knowest I dare not look into thine
    eyes.
Might I but kiss thy hand! I dare not
    fold
My arms about thee—scarcely dare to
    speak.
And nothing seems to me so wild and bold,
    As with one kiss to touch thy blessèd
    cheek.
Methinks if I should kiss thee, no control
    Within the thrilling brain could keep
    afloat
The subtle spirit. Even while I spoke,
The bare word KISS hath made my inner
    soul
    To tremble like a lutestring, ere the note
    Hath melted in the silence that it
    broke.

THE PALACE OF ART

When I first conceived the plan of the Palace
of Art, I intended to have introduced both
sculptures and paintings into it; but it is the
most difficult of all things to *devise* a statue in
verse. Judge whether I have succeeded in the
statues of Elijah and Olympias.

ONE was the Tishbite whom the raven fed,
    As when he stood on Carmel-steeps,
With one arm stretched out bare, and
    mocked and said,
    'Come cry aloud—he sleeps.'

Tall, eager, lean and strong, his cloak
    windborne
    Behind, his forehead heavenly-bright
From the clear marble pouring glorious
    scorn,
    Lit as with inner light.

One was Olympias: the floating snake
    Rolled round her ankles, round her waist
Knotted, and folded once about her neck,
    Her perfect lips to taste

Round by the shoulder moved: she seem-
ing blithe
Declined her head: on every side
The dragon's curves melted and mingled
with
The woman's youthful pride

Of rounded limbs.

If the Poem were not already too long, I
should have inserted in the text the following
stanzas, expressive of the joy wherewith the
soul contemplated the results of astronomical
experiment. In the centre of the four quad-
rangles rose an immense tower.

HITHER, when all the deep unsounded
skies
Shuddered with silent stars, she clomb,
And as with optic glasses her keen eyes
Pierced thro' the mystic dome,

Regions of lucid matter taking forms,
Brushes of fire, hazy gleams,
Clusters and beds of worlds, and bee-like
swarms
Of suns, and starry streams.

She saw the snowy poles of moonless Mars,
That marvellous round of milky light
Below Orion, and those double stars
Whereof the one more bright

Is circled by the other, &c.

THE HESPERIDES[1]

'Hesperus and his daughters three,
That sing about the golden tree.'
Comus

THE Northwind fall'n, in the newstarrèd
night
Zidonian Hanno, voyaging beyond
The hoary promontory of Soloë
Past Thymiaterion, in calmèd bays,
Between the southern and the western
Horn,
Heard neither warbling of the nightingale,
Nor melody o' the Lybian lotusflute
Blown seaward from the shore; but from a
slope

[1] Tennyson, in a conversation with his son,
regretted that he had done away with this poem
from among his 'Juvenilia' (*Life*, i. 61).

That ran bloombright into the Atlantic
blue,
Beneath a highland leaning down a weight
Of cliffs, and zoned below with cedarshade,
Came voices, like the voices in a dream,
Continuous, till he reached the outer sea.

SONG

I

THE golden apple, the golden apple, the
hallowed fruit,
Guard it well, guard it warily,
Singing airily,
Standing about the charmèd root.
Round about all is mute,
As the snowfield on the mountain-peaks,
As the sandfield at the mountain-foot.
Crocodiles in briny creeks
Sleep and stir not: all is mute.
If ye sing not, if ye make false measure,
We shall lose eternal pleasure,
Worth eternal want of rest.
Laugh not loudly: watch the treasure
Of the wisdom of the west.
In a corner wisdom whispers. Five and
three
(Let it not be preached abroad) make an
awful mystery.
For the blossom unto threefold music
bloweth;
Evermore it is born anew;
And the sap to threefold music floweth,
From the root
Drawn in the dark,
Up to the fruit,
Creeping under the fragrant bark,
Liquid gold, honeysweet, thro' and thro'.
Keen-eyed Sisters, singing airily,
Looking warily
Every way,
Guard the apple night and day,
Lest one from the East come and take it
away.

II

Father Hesper, Father Hesper, watch,
watch, ever and ay,
Looking under silver hair with a silver eye.
Father, twinkle not thy steadfast sight;

846

Kingdoms lapse, and climates change, and
   races die;
Honour comes with mystery;
Hoarded wisdom brings delight.
Number, tell them over and number
How many the mystic fruittree holds,
Lest the redcombed dragon slumber
Rolled together in purple folds.
Look to him, father, lest he wink, and the
   golden apple be stol'n away,
For his ancient heart is drunk with over-
   watchings night and day,
Round about the hallowed fruittree curled—
Sing away, sing aloud evermore in the
   wind, without stop,
Lest his scalèd eyelid drop,
For he is older than the world.
If he waken, we waken,
Rapidly levelling eager eyes.
If he sleep, we sleep,
Dropping the eyelid over the eyes.
If the golden apple be taken
The world will be overwise.
Five links, a golden chain, are we,
Hesper, the dragon, and sisters three,
Bound about the golden tree.

III

Father Hesper, Father Hesper, watch,
   watch, night and day,
Lest the old wound of the world be healèd,
The glory unsealèd,
The golden apple stol'n away,
And the ancient secret revealèd.
Look from west to east along:
Father, old Himala weakens, Caucasus is
   bold and strong.
Wandering waters unto wandering waters
   call;
Let them clash together, foam and fall.
Out of watchings, out of wiles,
Comes the bliss of secret smiles.
All things are not told to all.
Half-round the mantling night is drawn,
Purplefringèd with even and dawn.
Hesper hateth Phosphor, evening hateth
   morn.

IV

Every flower and every fruit the redolent
   breath

Of this warm seawind ripeneth,
Arching the billow in his sleep;
But the landwind wandereth,
Broken by the highland-steep,
Two streams upon the violet deep:
For the western sun and the western star,
And the low west wind, breathing afar,
The end of day and beginning of night
Make the apple holy and bright;
Holy and bright, round and full, bright and
   blest,
Mellowed in a land of rest;
Watch it warily day and night;
All good things are in the west.
Till midnoon the cool east light
Is shut out by the round of the tall hill-
   brow;
But when the fullfaced sunset yellowly
Stays on the flowering arch of the bough,
The luscious fruitage clustereth mellowly,
Goldenkernelled, goldencored,
Sunset-ripened above on the tree.
The world is wasted with fire and sword,
But the apple of gold hangs over the sea.
Five links, a golden chain, are we,
Hesper, the dragon, and sisters three,
Daughters three,
Bound about
All round about
The gnarlèd bole of the charmèd tree.
The golden apple, the golden apple, the
   hallowed fruit,
Guard it well, guard it warily,
Watch it warily,
Singing airily,
Standing about the charmèd root.

[NOTE TO *ROSALIND* (see p. 20)]

Perhaps the following lines may be allowed
to stand as a separate poem; originally they
made part of the text, where they were mani-
festly superfluous.

My Rosalind, my Rosalind,
Bold, subtle, careless Rosalind,
Is one of those who know no strife
Of inward woe or outward fear;
To whom the slope and stream of life,
The life before, the life behind,
In the ear, from far and near,
Chimeth musically clear.
My falconhearted Rosalind,

Fullsailed before a vigorous wind,
Is one of those, who cannot weep
For others' woes, but overleap
All the petty shocks and fears
That trouble life in early years,
With a flash of frolic scorn
And keen delight, that never falls
Away from freshness, self-upborne
With such gladness as, whenever
The freshflushing springtime calls
To the flooding waters cool,
Young fishes, on an April morn,
Up and down a rapid river,
Leap the little waterfalls
That sing into the pebbled pool.
My happy falcon, Rosalind,
Hath daring fancies of her own,
Fresh as the dawn before the day,
Fresh as the early seasmell blown
Through vineyards from an inland bay.
My Rosalind, my Rosalind,
Because no shadow on you falls
Think you hearts are tennisballs,
To play with, wanton Rosalind?

A DREAM OF FAIR WOMEN

[The four initial verses in 1833, subsequently omitted]

I

As when a man, that sails in a balloon,
    Downlooking sees the solid shining ground
Stream from beneath him in the broad blue noon,
    Tilth, hamlet, mead and mound:

II

And takes his flags and waves them to the mob,
    That shout below, all faces turned to where
Glows rubylike the far-up crimson globe,
    Filled with a finer air:

III

So, lifted high, the Poet at his will
    Lets the great world flit from him, seeing all,
Higher thro' secret splendours mounting still,
    Selfpoised, nor fears to fall,

IV

Hearing apart the echoes of his fame.
    While I spoke thus, the seedsman, memory,
Sowed my deepfurrowed thought with many a name,
    Whose glory will not die.

SONG

Who can say
Why Today
Tomorrow will be yesterday?
Who can tell
Why to smell
The violet, recalls the dewy prime
Of youth and buried time?
The cause is nowhere found in rhyme.

SONNET

WRITTEN ON HEARING OF THE OUT-
BREAK OF THE POLISH INSURRECTION

Blow ye the trumpet, gather from afar
The hosts to battle: be not bought and sold.
Arise, brave Poles, the boldest of the bold;
Break through your iron shackles—fling them far.
O for those days of Piast, ere the Czar
Grew to this strength among his deserts cold;
When even to Moscow's cupolas were rolled
The growing murmurs of the Polish war!
Now must your noble anger blaze out more
Than when from Sobieski, clan by clan,
The Moslem myriads fell, and fled before—
Than when Zamoysky smote the Tartar Khan;
Than earlier, when on the Baltic shore
Boleslas drove the Pomeranian.

O DARLING ROOM

I

O darling room, my heart's delight,
Dear room, the apple of my sight,
With thy two couches soft and white,
There is no room so exquisite,
No little room so warm and bright,
Wherein to read, wherein to write.

II

For I the Nonnenwerth have seen,
And Oberwinter's vineyards green,
Musical Lurlei; and between
The hills to Bingen have I been,
Bingen in Darmstadt, where the Rhene
Curves toward Mentz, a woody scene.

III

Yet never did there meet my sight,
In any town, to left or right,
A little room so exquisite,
With two such couches, soft and white;
Not any room so warm and bright,
Wherein to read, wherein to write.

TO CHRISTOPHER NORTH

You did late review my lays,
  Crusty Christopher;
You did mingle blame and praise,
  Rusty Christopher.
When I learnt from whom it came,
I forgave you all the blame,
  Musty Christopher;
I could *not* forgive the praise,
  Fusty Christopher.

STANZAS

[The last five of sixteen stanzas in *The Tribute*, 1837. The preceding stanzas, commencing 'Oh! that 'twere possible', were incorporated in 'Maud', see p. 282.]

But she tarries in her place,
And I paint the beauteous face
Of the maiden that I lost,
  In my inner eyes again;
Lest my heart be overborne
By the thing I hold in scorn,
  By a dull mechanic ghost
  And a juggle of the brain.

I can shadow forth my bride,
  As I knew her fair and kind,
As I woo'd her for my wife;
She is lovely by my side
In the silence of my life—
  'Tis a phantom of the mind.

'Tis a phantom fair and good
  I can call it to my side,
So to guard my life from ill,
  Tho' its ghastly sister glide;
And be moved around me still
  With the moving of the blood,
That is moved not of the will.

Let it pass the dreary brow,
  Let the dismal face go by;
Will it lead me to the grave?
  Then I lose it: it will fly:
Can it overlast the nerves?
  Can it overlive the eye?

But the other, like a star,
Thro' the channel windeth far
  Till it fade and fail and die;
To its archetype that waits,
Clad in light by golden gates—
Clad in light the Spirit waits
  To embrace me in the sky.

THE SKIPPING-ROPE

Poems, ed. i, 1842 to ed. 6, 1850

Sure never yet was Antelope
Could skip so lightly by.
Stand off, or else my skipping-rope
Will hit you in the eye.
How lightly whirls the skipping-rope!
How fairy-like you fly!
Go, get you gone, you muse and mope—
I hate that silly sigh.
Nay, dearest, teach me how to hope,
Or tell me how to die.
There, take it, take my skipping-rope,
And hang yourself thereby.

THE NEW TIMON, AND THE POETS

Punch, 28 Feb. 1846, signed 'Alcibiades'

We know him, out of Shakspeare's art,
  And those fine curses which he spoke;
The old Timon, with his noble heart,
  That, strongly loathing, greatly broke.

So died the Old: here comes the New.
  Regard him: a familiar face:
I *thought* we knew him: What, it's you,
  The padded man—that wears the stays—

Who kill'd the girls and thrill'd the boys,
  With dandy pathos when you wrote,
A Lion, you, that made a noise,
  And shook a mane en papillotes.

And once you tried the Muses too;
  You fail'd, Sir: therefore now you turn,
You fall on those who are to you,
  As Captain is to Subaltern.

But men of long-enduring hopes,
  And careless what this hour may bring,
Can pardon little would-be POPES
  And BRUMMELS, when they try to sting.

An artist, Sir, should rest in Art,
  And waive a little of his claim;
To have the deep Poetic heart
  Is more than all poetic fame.

But you, Sir, you are hard to please;
  You never look but half content:
Nor like a gentleman at ease,
  With moral breadth of temperament.

And what with spites and what with fears,
  You cannot let a body be:
It's always ringing in your ears,
  'They call this man as good as *me*.'

What profits now to understand
  The merits of a spotless shirt—
A dapper boot—a little hand—
  If half the little soul is dirt?

You talk of tinsel! why we see
  The old mark of rouge upon your cheeks.
You prate of Nature! you are he
  That spilt his life about the cliques.

A TIMON you! Nay, nay, for shame:
  It looks too arrogant a jest—
The fierce old man—to take *his* name,
  You bandbox. Off, and let him rest.

LINES

Manchester Athenaeum Album, 1850

HERE often, when a child, I lay reclined,
  I took delight in this locality.
Here stood the infant Ilion of the mind,
  And here the Grecian ships did seem to
    be.

And here again I come, and only find
  The drain-cut levels of the marshy lea,—
Grey sandbanks, and pale sunsets,—dreary
    wind,
  Dim shores, dense rains, and heavy-
    clouded sea!

STANZAS

Keepsake, 1851

WHAT time I wasted youthful hours,
One of the shining wingèd powers
Show'd me vast cliffs, with crowns of
    towers.

As towards that gracious light I bow'd,
They seem'd high palaces and proud,
Hid now and then with sliding cloud.

He said, 'The labour is not small;
Yet winds the pathway free to all:—
Take care thou dost not fear to fall!'

BRITONS, GUARD YOUR OWN

Examiner, 31 Jan. 1852

RISE, Britons, rise, if manhood be not dead;
The world's last tempest darkens over-
    head;
    The Pope has bless'd him;
    The Church caress'd him;
He triumphs: may be, we shall stand alone:
    Britons, guard your own.

His ruthless host is bought with plunder'd
    gold,
By lying priests the peasant's vote con-
    troll'd;
    All freedom vanish'd,
    The true men banish'd,
He triumphs; may be, we shall stand alone:
    Britons, guard your own.

Peace-lovers we—sweet Peace we all de-
    sire—
Peace-lovers we—but who can trust a
    liar?—
    Peace-lovers, haters
    Of shameless traitors,
We hate not France, but this man's heart
    of stone.
    Britons, guard your own.

We hate not France, but France has lost
      her voice,
This man is France, the man they call her
      choice.
      By tricks and spying,
      And craft and lying,
And murder, was her freedom overthrown.
      Britons, guard your own.

'Vive l'Empereur' may follow by and bye;
'God save the Queen' is here a truer cry,
      God save the nation,
      The toleration,
And the free speech that makes a Briton
      known.
      Britons, guard your own.

Rome's dearest daughter now is captive
      France,
The Jesuit laughs, and reckoning on his
      chance
      Would unrelenting
      Kill all dissenting,
Till we were left to fight for truth alone.
      Britons, guard your own.

Call home your ships across Biscayan tides,
To blow the battle from their oaken sides.
      Why waste they yonder
      Their idle thunder?
Why stay they there to guard a foreign
      throne?
      Seamen, guard your own.

We were the best of marksmen long ago,
We won old battles with our strength, the
      bow.
      Now practise, yeomen,
      Like those bowmen,
Till your balls fly as their true shafts have
      flown.
      Yeomen, guard your own.

His soldier-ridden Highness might incline
To shake Sardinia, Belgium, or the Rhine:
      Shall we stand idle,
      Nor seek to bridle
His vile aggressions till we stand alone?—
      Make their cause your own!

Should he land here, and for one hour pre-
      vail,

There must no man go back to bear the
      tale:
      No man to bear it,—
      Swear it! We swear it!
Although we fought the banded world
      alone,
      We swear to guard our own.

FOR THE PENNY-WISE

Fraser's Magazine, Feb. 1852

WE used to fight the French,
      And beat them, says the story;
But now the cry 'retrench'
      Has a little dock'd our glory.

We meant to beat the Kaffirs,
      We had the best intentions;
But the Kaffirs knock'd us over,
      With the last inventions.

Poor little people, we,
      And in the world belated!
Our musket, as it seems,
      Is superannuated.

Friends! the soldier still
      Is worthy of his calling,
But who are they that want
      A little over-hauling?

SUGGESTED BY READING AN
ARTICLE IN A NEWSPAPER

Examiner, 14 Feb. 1852

Sir,—I have read with much interest the
poems by MERLIN. The enclosed is longer than
either of those, and certainly not so good; yet
as I flatter myself that it has a smack of Merlin's
style in it, and as I feel that it expresses forcibly
enough some of the feelings of our time, perhaps you may be induced to admit it.
                                        TALIESSIN.

How much I love this writer's manly style!
      By such men led, our press had ever
            been
The public conscience of our noble isle,
      Severe and quick to feel a civic sin,
To raise the people and chastise the times
With such a heat as lives in great creative
      rhymes.

O you, the Press! what good from you
  might spring!
  What power is yours to blast a cause or
  bless!
I fear for you, as for some youthful king,
  Lest you go wrong from power in excess.
Take heed of your wide privileges! we,
The thinking men of England, loathe a
  tyranny.

A freeman is, I doubt not, freest here;
  The single voice may speak his mind
  aloud;
An honest isolation need not fear
  The court, the church, the Parliament,
  the crowd,
No, nor the Press! and look you well to
  that—
We must not dread in you the nameless
  Autocrat.

And you, dark Senate of the public pen,
  You may not, like yon tyrant, deal in
  spies.
Yours are the public acts of public men,
  But yours are not their household priva-
  cies.
I grant you one of the Great Powers on
  earth,
But be not you the blatant traitors of the
  hearth.

You hide the hand that writes: it must be
  so,
  For better so you fight for public ends;
But some you strike can scarce return the
  blow;
  You should be all the nobler, O my
  friends.
Be noble, you! nor work with faction's
  tools
To charm a lower sphere of fulminating
  fools.

But, knowing all your power to heat or
  cool,
  To soothe a civic wound or keep it raw,
Be loyal, if you wish for wholesome rule:
  Our ancient boast is this—we reverence
  law.
We still were loyal in our wildest fights,
Or, loyally disloyal, battled for our rights.

O Grief and Shame if while I preach of
  laws
  Whereby to guard our freedom from
  offence—
And trust an ancient manhood and the
  cause
  Of England and her health of common
  sense—
There hang within the heavens a dark disgrace,
Some vast Assyrian doom to burst upon
  our race.

I feel the thousand cankers of our state,
  I fain would shake their triple-folded
  ease,
The hogs, who can believe in nothing great,
  Sneering bedridden in the down of
  Peace,
Over their scrips and shares, their meats
  and wine,
With stony smirks at all things human and
  divine!

I honour much, I say, this man's appeal.
  We drag so deep in our commercial mire,
We move so far from greatness that I feel
  Exception to be character'd in fire.
Who looks for Godlike Greatness here shall
  see
The British Goddess, sleek Respectability.

Alas for her and all her small delights!
  She feels not how the social frame is
  rack'd.
She loves a little scandal which excites;
  A little feeling is a want of tact.
For her there lie in wait millions of foes,
And yet the 'Not too much' is all the rule
  she knows.

Poor soul! behold her: what decorous
  calm!—
  She, with her weekday worldliness suf-
  ficed,
Stands in her pew and hums her decent
  psalm,
  With decent dippings at the name of
  Christ!
And she has moved on that smooth way so
  long,
She hardly can believe that she shall suffer
  wrong.

Alas, our Church! alas, her growing ills,
  And those who tolerate not her tolerance,
But needs must sell the burthen of their
    wills
To that half-pagan harlot kept by France!
Free subjects of the kindliest of all thrones,
Headlong they plunge their doubts among
    old rags and bones.

Alas, church-writers, altercating tribes—
  The vessel of your church may sink in
    storms;
Christ cried, Woe, woe to Pharisees and
    scribes;
  Like them, you bicker less for truth than
    forms.
I sorrow when I read the things you write,
What unheroic pertness! what unchristian
    spite!

Alas, our youth, so clever yet so small,
  Thin dilettanti deep in nature's plan,
Who make the emphatic One, by whom is
    all,
  An essence less concentrated than a
    man!—
Better wild Mahmoud's war-cry once
    again!
O fools, we want a manlike God and God-
    like men.

Go, frightful omens. Yet once more I turn
  To you that mould men's thoughts, I
    call on you
To make opinion warlike, lest we learn
  A sharper lesson than we ever knew.
I hear a thunder though the skies are fair,
But shrill you, loud and long, the warning
    note—Prepare.

STANZAS ON THE MARRIAGE
OF THE PRINCESS ROYAL

Times, 26 Jan. 1858

GOD bless our Prince and Bride!
God keep their lands allied.
    God save the Queen!
Clothe them with righteousness,
Crown them with happiness,
Them with all blessings bless,
    God save the Queen!

Fair fall this hallow'd hour,
Farewell our England's flower,
    God save the Queen.
Farewell, fair rose of May!
Let both the peoples say,
God bless thy marriage day,
    God bless the Queen!

EPITAPH ON THE DUCHESS
OF KENT

Court Journal, 19 March 1864

'Her children rise up and call her blessed.'

LONG as the heart beats life within her
    breast,
  Thy child will bless thee, guardian,
    mother mild,
And far away thy memory will be blest,
  By children of the children of thy child.

THE RINGLET

Enoch Arden, etc., 1864

I

I

'YOUR ringlets, your ringlets,
  That look so golden-gay,
If you will give me one, but one,
  To kiss it night and day,
Then never chilling touch of Time
  Will turn it silver-grey;
And then shall I know it is all true gold
To flame and sparkle and stream as of old,
Till all the comets in heaven are cold,
  And all her stars decay.'
'Then take it, love, and put it by;
This cannot change, nor yet can I.'

II

'My ringlet, my ringlet,
  That art so golden-gay,
Now never chilling touch of Time
  Can turn thee silver-grey;
And a lad may wink, and a girl may hint,
  And a fool may say his say;
For my doubts and fears were all amiss,
And I swear henceforth by this and this,
That a doubt will only come for a kiss,
  And a fear to be kiss'd away.'
'Then kiss it, love, and put it by:
If this can change, why so can I.'

II

I

O Ringlet, O Ringlet,
  I kidd'd you night and day,
And Ringlet, O Ringlet,
  You still are golden-gay,
But Ringlet, O Ringlet,
  You should be silver-grey:
For what is this which now I'm told,
I that took you for true gold,
She that gave you 's bought and sold,
    Sold, sold.

II

O Ringlet, O Ringlet,
  She blush'd a rosy red,
When Ringlet, O Ringlet,
  She clipt you from her head,
And Ringlet, O Ringlet,
  She gave you me, and said,
'Come, kiss it, love, and put it by:
If this can change, why so can I.'
O fie, you golden nothing, fie,
    You golden lie.

III

O Ringlet, O Ringlet,
  I count you much to blame,
For Ringlet, O Ringlet,
  You put me much to shame,
So Ringlet, O Ringlet,
  I doom you to the flame.
For what is this which now I learn,
Has given all my faith a turn?
Burn, you glossy heretic, burn,
    Burn, burn.

SONG

Selections, 1865

LADY, let the rolling drums
Beat to battle where thy warrior stands:
Now thy face across his fancy comes,
And gives the battle to his hands.

Lady, let the trumpets blow,
Clasp thy little babes about thy knee:
Now their warrior father meets the foe,
And strikes him dead for thine and thee.

SONG

Selections, 1865

HOME they brought him slain with spears.
  They brought him home at even-fall:
All alone she sits and hears
  Echoes in his empty hall,
    Sounding on the morrow.

The Sun peep'd in from open field,
  The boy began to leap and prance,
  Rode upon his father's lance,
Beat upon his father's shield—
  'O hush, my joy, my sorrow.'

1865—1866

Good Words, March 1868

I STOOD on a tower in the wet
And New Year and Old Year met,
And winds were roaring and blowing;
And I said, 'O years, that meet in tears,
Have ye aught that is worth the knowing?
Science enough and exploring,
Wanderers coming and going,
Matter enough for deploring,
But aught that is worth the knowing?'
Seas at my feet were flowing,
Waves on the shingle pouring,
Old Year roaring and blowing,
And New Year blowing and roaring.

INDEX OF TITLES

INDEX OF FIRST LINES

859

INDEX OF FIRST LINES

INDEX OF FIRST LINES

INDEX OF FIRST LINES

INDEX OF FIRST LINES

867

INDEX OF FIRST LINES

PRINTED IN GREAT BRITAIN
AT THE UNIVERSITY PRESS, OXFORD
BY VIVIAN RIDLER
PRINTER TO THE UNIVERSITY